The Developing Person Through the Life Span

Christian Pierre, *On the Dock* **(front cover),** *Modern Madonna* **(back cover).** The luminous colors and figures in *On the Dock* and *Modern Madonna* reflect the hope and discovery apparent in all Christian Pierre's paintings—of adults, animals, plants, landscapes, and children. Christian Pierre has lived in several cultures, under many life circumstances, but she has said that she could never make herself paint anything depressing. Instead, by combining colors, shapes, and composition in ways that are simultaneously fantasy and reality, she opens new perspectives. Each of the trio above is wide-eyed and connected to us as well as to each other. This may be how we go through our lives, not only connected but rocking in time on a wooden pier that extends into our ocean. We need not fear the darkness, for here a bright moon illuminates the night, just as (on the back cover) a child turns on the computer. May this book also bring you light and knowledge.

The Developing Person Through the Life Span

Fifth Edition

KATHLEEN STASSEN BERGER

Bronx Community College

City University of New York

WORTH PUBLISHERS

The Developing Person Through the Life Span

Fifth Edition

Copyright © 2001, 1998, 1994, 1988, 1983 by Worth Publishers

Printed in the United States of America.

ISBN: 1-57259-429-2

Third printing, 2002

Publisher: Catherine Woods

Developmental Editor: Cecilia Gardner

Marketing Manager: Renée Ortbals

Design Director: Barbara Reingold

Designer: Mary McDonnell

Associate Managing Editor: Tracey Kuehn

Production Manager: Barbara Anne Seixas

Photo Research Coordinator: Jennifer MacMillan

Photo Editor: Inge King

Composition and separations: TSI Graphics, Inc.

Printing and binding: Von Hoffmann Press, Inc.

Acknowledgments begin on page IC-1, and constitute an extension
of the copyright page.

Library of Congress Cataloging-in-Publication Data

Berger, Kathleen Stassen.
    The developing person through the life span/Kathleen Stassen Berger; 5th ed.
        p. cm.
    Includes bibliographical references and indexes.
    1. Developmental psychology. I. Title.
BF713 .B463 2000
155–dc21

Worth Publishers

41 Madison Avenue

New York, NY 10010

www.worthpublishers.com

About the Author

Kathleen Stassen Berger received her undergraduate education at Stanford University and Radcliffe College, earned an M.A.T. from Harvard University and an M.S. and Ph.D. from Yeshiva University. Her broad experience as an educator includes directing a preschool, teaching philosophy and humanities at the United Nations International School, teaching child and adolescent development to graduate students at Fordham University, and teaching social psychology to inmates earning a paralegal degree at Sing Sing Prison.

For the past 27 years Berger has taught at Bronx Community College of the City University of New York. She is currently the elected chair of the Social Science Department. She has taught introduction to psychology, child and adolescent development, adulthood and aging, social psychology, abnormal psychology, and human motivation. Her students—who come from many ethnic, economic, and educational backgrounds, and who have a wide range of interests—consistently honor her with the highest teaching evaluations. She recently served as president of Community School Board Two in Manhattan.

Berger is also the author of *The Developing Person Through Childhood and Adolescence* and *The Developing Person Through Childhood*. Her three developmental texts are currently being used at nearly 700 colleges and universities worldwide. Her research interests include adolescent identity, sibling relationships, and employed mothers, and she has contributed articles on developmental topics to the *Wiley Encyclopedia of Psychology*. As the mother of four daughters, as well as wife, sister, and daughter of two parents in their 90s, she brings to her teaching and writing ample firsthand experience with human development.

Contents in Brief

Contents

CHAPTER 6   The First Two Years: Cognitive Development   159

CHAPTER 7   The First Two Years: Psychosocial Development   187

CHAPTER 8   The Play Years: Biosocial Development   219

PART V Adolescence 379

PART VIII **Late Adulthood**   613

Christian Pierre, *Modern Madonna* (back cover), acrylic on canvas (48" X 24"), private collection.

Preface

High standards and clear expectations are required for excellent education. But effective learning does not occur unless the instructor follows through with enthusiasm, humor, and intellectual honesty, as I know from my own teaching. I try to apply this philosophy to textbook writing as well.

The best developmental textbooks connect theory and practice with such power that students think deeply about the long-term implications of the research and concepts, and simultaneously master the specific facts and applied skills required of practiced professionals. There should be no gap between theory and practice; they need each other. This "best book" vision describes the high standards I hold; I hope these standards, as well as my enthusiasm for the field and my humor (especially about my own experiences), are apparent. If so, I thank my heroes and mentors. These include not only my own gifted professors who studied directly with Erikson, Piaget, and Skinner, but also researchers I admire from the cool distance of the printed page: Ainsworth, Baltes, Bem, the Coles, Garbarino, Gardner, the Gibsons, Lightfoot, Olweus, Plomin, Rutter, Schaie, Vygotsky, Whitbourne, Zigler—and many more (which explains why the bibliography is longer than any comparable book's).

I expect every student to learn and understand. Specific current issues—abortion, adoption, adult attachment, affordances, ageism, alcohol abuse, Alzheimer's disease, amniocentesis, anorexia, apprenticeship, assisted conception, asthma, attention deficit disorder, bilingual education, breast-feeding, birth abnormalities, bulimia, brain patterning, bullying, and many more—are defined and delineated fairly, raising questions that have no easy answers. More important, controversies are put into context: Genetic, cultural, historical, ethnic, and economic influences are never ignored.

NEW FEATURES

As for meeting expectations, this new edition has additional prompts to help students become scholars. Three new features are particularly designed to make learning interactive, which is the goal of the entire book.

Applications

Almost every topic leads to possible applications. Some of these are mentioned directly with a question or a comment in the text, others are left to the instructors and students to draw. However, several times in each chapter, **Especially for . . .** features addressed to parents, social

❷ Especially for Educators: Suppose a particular school has 30 children in the second grade. Five of them have special problems. One speaks very little and seems autistic, one is very talkative but cannot read, one is almost blind, and two have ADHD (one of them aggressive). What are the advantages and disadvantages of creating a special class for these five, rather than mainstreaming them in the regular class? (See answer page 321.)

Now a Toddler As this very young lady begins to walk, she demonstrates why such children are called toddlers: They move unsteadily from side to side as well as forward.

❷ Observational Quiz: *What emotions and fine motor skills usually accompany early walking, as shown here? (See answer page 143)*

workers, educators, researchers, or some other group appear in the margin, with a question that can be answered deductively from the implications of the next few paragraphs. To show you how this works, an Especially For, from Chapter 11's discussion of attention deficit hyperactivity disorder, is shown here.

Observational Quizzes

The second new interactive feature accompanies several photographs in each chapter. Since well-honed observational skills are essential for every student of human development, an **Observational Quiz** appears after the caption. An example, from Chapter 5's section on motor skills, is shown in the margin at left.

Web Companion Site

The third new feature is the Berger Web site (www.worthpublishers.com/bergerlifespan5e), an online educational setting for students and instructors, featuring:

- **PowerPoint Slides** use art from my texts and other print and video sources, organized around the developmental psychology table of contents. Slides feature outlined text and can be used directly or customized to suit specific needs.
- **Annotated Web Links** point the way to prominent development Web sites that correlate to the material in the textbook.
- **Simulations and Demonstrations** help students visualize biological processes or present behavior that elucidates key concepts in developmental psychology.
- **Interactive Flashcards** provide students with a reviewing tool for the most important new terms presented in each chapter.
- **Psychology in the News** keeps students up to date with the latest research and applications in developmental psychology.
- **Observational Quizzes** help students develop their observational skills.
- **Topical Table of Contents** organize the text for instuctors who prefer a topical approach.

TRIED AND TRUE FEATURES

Many characteristics of this text have been acclaimed since the first edition, and, of course, they continue.

- **Language that communicates the excitement and challenge of the field** I have carefully and thoroughly revised the text, using more bulleted lists and more—and more concretely worded—subheads. Sentences are shorter and less formal, although I still choose some vocabulary words and phrases that will challenge thought. I thank Cele Gardner for her careful and cheerful editing.
- **Up-to-date coverage** Here I thank my students, who always keep me current with their questions and concerns, not only in research but also in practice.
- **Topical organization within a chronological framework** The book's basic organization remains unchanged. The four chapters that begin the book focus on definitions, theories, genetics, and, finally, prenatal development as the first concrete example of risk analysis, cultural im-

pact, and the damage-repair cycle. The remaining seven parts corre-
spond to the seven major periods of life-span development: infancy,
early childhood, middle childhood, adolescence, early adulthood, middle adulthood, and late adulthood. Each part contains three chapters:
biosocial, cognitive, and psychosocial development.

   This topical organization within a chronological framework fosters
students' appreciation of the various aspects of development: Body, intellect, and personality develop through interaction rather than separately. As a visual aid, the page numbers are color-coded: Biosocial
chapters are turquoise, cognitive chapters are blue, and psychosocial
chapters are salmon.

- **Plentiful and relevant boxes**   In this edition, every chapter has one
  each of the four categories of boxes: Changing Policy, In Person,
  Research Report, and (new to this edition) A Life-Span View. The boxes
  are not spinoffs or add-ons; they are extensions of ideas explained in
  the text.

- **Enhanced multicultural coverage**   Frequent comparisons are made between the United States and other nations, between North America and
  other continents, and between ethnic groups within a geographical region—all to draw readers beyond their own experiences.

- **Pedagogical aids**   Each chapter ends with a chapter summary, a list of
  key terms (with page numbers indicating where the term is introduced
  and defined), and key questions for reviewing important concepts. A
  running glossary defines key terms in the margins next to the text
  where the terms are introduced. In addition, a glossary at the back of
  the book lists and defines all the key terms. The outline on the first
  page of each chapter and the major and minor subheads enable students to survey, question, and reflect as they study.

- **Photographs, tables, and graphs that are integral to the text**
  Sometimes such aspects of texts are mere glitter and flash to woo the
  novice without aiding education. From the very beginning, Worth
  Publishers has allowed authors to choose photos and graphs, write captions, and alter designs to better fit the words—not vice versa. As one
  result, students learn from reading captions, because material there
  supplements and extends the text. Similarly, tables illustrate important
  concepts and data.

CONTENT CHANGES FOR THE FIFTH EDITION

As always, the main work of a textbook is in the words. The basic message of those words has been retained, for there are certain facts—
stages and ages, dangers and diversities—that every student should
know. After all, human development is a science, and scientists build on
past discovery. However, life continues to unfold, so no page is exactly
what it was, and every chapter includes innovative organization and
content. Highlights of these new emphases and content appear below:

Chapter 1 (Introduction): There is now a nuanced exploration of the distinctions among ethnicity, race, and culture, with a research example of children's aggression after the 1992 Los Angeles riots. Some of the detailed
information about research methods has been moved to a new Appendix B.
Chapter 2 (Theories): The explanation of the distinction between the
"grand" theories (psychoanalytic, learning, cognitive) and "emergent"
theories makes clear the value of both comprehensive and innovative

thought. A completely new section on epigenetic systems theory shows how ethology, evolution, and genetics combine to form this groundbreaking theory.

Chapter 3 (Heredity and Environment): The power of genes *and* the power of context are explained with even greater precision.

Chapter 4 (Prenatal Development and Birth): New figures and charts highlight the increase in low-birthweight babies and in prenatal drug abuse—and controversial explanations for these trends.

Chapter 5 (The First 2 Years: Biosocial Development): Norms are described as the culturally influenced standards that they are, especially in an In Person box that describes my own children as they began to walk. A Research Report on otitis media emphasizes the importance of early experiences and the development of the brain.

Chapter 6 (The First 2 Years: Cognitive Development): The findings of all the key researchers—including the Gibsons, Piaget, Vygotsky, Rovee-Collier, Skinner, Chomsky, and Bloom—are now more firmly connected to show infant cognitive development as the perceptual, cultural, and social experience that it is.

Chapter 7 (The First 2 Years: Psychosocial Development): The longitudinal ramifications during adulthood of early secure and insecure attachments are explained, with alternative explanations of the research findings.

Chapter 8 (The Play Years: Biosocial Development): The connection between early experience and brain development is made. The discussion of maltreatment now includes kin care, permanency planning, and the reasons to distinguish between cases that require immediate legal intervention and those that need ongoing family support.

Chapter 9 (The Play Years: Cognitive Development): New cross-cultural and contextual material shows the impact of family composition and community values on a child's theory of mind. The latest research on the memory capabilities of preschool children and on bilingual education for immigrant children is cited.

Chapter 10 (The Play Years: Psychosocial Development): Emotional regulation as a critical development during the early years is described, including prosocial and antisocial attitudes and behavior. All five theories regarding gender roles are explored, with a new conclusion titled "Gender and Destiny."

Chapter 11 (The School Years: Biosocial Development): Four key ideas from the developmental psychopathology perspective—"abnormality is normal," "disability changes with time," "adulthood can be better or worse," and "diagnosis depends on social context" — are now explained, anchoring and structuring the entire special-needs section. The increase in obesity and asthma among school-age children is discussed.

Chapter 12 (The School Years: Cognitive Development): Actual transcripts from classrooms, new international data on math and science education, and new historical data on how North American children spend their time all enliven the discussion of cognition.

Chapter 13 (The School Years: Psychosocial Development): Functions of the family, as well as the effect of divorce on children, are the focus. The major discussion of bullying includes long-term consequences for victim and bully. Sexual harassment, social rejection, and possible law-breaking are considered as part of this issue, with practical ideas about how to stop bullying at school.

Chapter 14 (Adolescence: Biosocial Development): The discussion of sexual abuse of adolescents is updated. The discussion of drug use includes new material on the physical hazards of "gateway" drugs—alcohol, tobacco, and marijuana.

Chapter 15 (Adolescence: Cognitive Development): New cross-cultural findings are presented about the effect of part-time jobs on school performance. Data on fewer teen births, more condom use, and fewer abortions are presented, in part to explore the new methods of sex education. The idea that risk-taking is not only normative but also rational is presented.

Chapter 16 (Adolescence: Psychosocial Development): New discussions of homosexuality and suicide among teenagers are included. The myths of a generation gap and peer pressure are exploded (peers help adolescents explore identities, guide sexual interactions, and prevent parasuicide). The distinction between life-course persistent criminals and adolescent-limited delinquency is clarified to suggest effective crime prevention.

Chapter 17 (Early Adulthood: Biosocial Development): The discussion of fertility and alternate routes to conception is consolidated and expanded, with attention to the ethical and economic dilemmas posed.

Chapter 18 (Early Adulthood: Cognitive Development): An In Person box has been added on dialectical thinking as applied to cheating in college, with an account of my own experience with my students' ways of thinking about cheating.

Chapter 19 (Early Adulthood: Psychosocial Development): The discussion of family structures has been expanded, with an emphasis on the adults involved.

Chapter 20 (Middle Adulthood: Biosocial Development): A group of especially timely boxes is featured: In Person, "When You See Yourself in the Mirror," on women's reactions to the visible signs of middle age; Research Report, "Smoking and Health," with updated cross-cultural data on rates of smoking and disease; Changing Policy, "Beyond Black and White," on the cultural factors (especially low socioeconomic status) that have a greater impact on health than does race or ethnicity.

Chapter 21 (Middle Adulthood: Cognitive Development): The discussions of Robert Sternberg's three forms of intelligence and Gardner's eight intelligences have been expanded. Evidence for practical intelligence is clearly presented.

Chapter 22 (Middle Adulthood: Psychosocial Development): The Life-Span View box covers the "sandwich generation" of middle-aged adults who have young-adult children living at home as well as elderly parents to care for. Research is presented to counter the "midlife crisis" idea.

Chapter 23 (Late Adulthood: Biosocial Development): A new chapter opening draws readers in with questions from the Facts of Aging quiz (and answers incorporated into the chapter's text). New information is presented about the importance of diet and exercise in old age and about the implications of demographic trends toward lower birth and death rates in developed countries.

Chapter 24 (Late Adulthood: Cognitive Development): Recent findings about genes identified as factors in Alzheimer's disease and about memory in late adulthood are discussed, as is the close connection between the senses and the mind.

Chapter 25 (Late Adulthood: Psychosocial Development): The blessings and burdens of giving—and receiving—care among the frail elderly are considered.

Epilogue (Death and Dying): Coverage of the right-to-die issue is expanded with research from the Netherlands and Oregon. Cyberspace memorials are explained.

SUPPLEMENTS

As an instructor myself, I know the importance of good supplements. I have been known to decline to adopt a textbook because the company had a bad record on ancillaries and service. Fortunately, Worth has a well-deserved reputation for the quality of such materials—for both professors and students. With this book, you will find:

Observational Videos for Development over the Life Span

Bringing observational learning to the classroom, a new set of videos titled *The Journey Through the Life Span* allows students to observe dozens of people, from newborns to centenarians, of various ethnicities. The three-video set includes a segment for each chapter of the book and an hour of non-narrated observation modules. It is accompanied by an instructor's manual and a student guide to observation. These videos follow children and adults in natural settings—day care centers and schools, home and workplace. The series includes insights from some of the most noted experts in development, including Charles Nelson, Anne Petersen, and Barbara Rogoff, as well as teachers, nurses, and social workers who share their hands-on experience working with people across the life span.

The Scientific American Frontiers Video Collection

This valuable resource provides instructors with 17 video segments of approximately 15 minutes each, on topics ranging from language development to nature-nurture issues. The videos can be used to launch classroom lectures or to emphasize and clarify course material. The *Faculty Guide for Scientific American Frontiers Video Collection* by Richard O. Straub, University of Michigan, describes and relates each segment to specific topics in the text.

The Berger Web Site (www.worthpublishers.com)

See description on page xxiv.

Study Guide

The *Study Guide,* by Richard O. Straub, helps students evaluate their understanding and retain their learning longer. Each chapter includes a review of key concepts, guided study questions, and section reviews that encourage students' active participation in the learning process; two practice tests and a challenge test help them assess their mastery of the material.

Instructor's Resources

The *Instructor's Resources,* by Richard O. Straub, features a chapter-by-chapter preview and lecture guide, learning objectives, springboard topics for discussion and debate, handouts for student projects, and supplementary readings from journal articles. Course planning suggestions, ideas for term projects, and a guide to audiovisual and software materials are also included, as are new Internet assignments that help students find better research sources on the Web.

Printed Test Bank and Test Bank CD-ROM

Thoroughly revised by Karen Macrae, the test bank includes approximately 80 multiple-choice and 50 fill-in, true-false, and essay questions for each chapter—a total of more than 3,000 questions. Each question is keyed to the textbook by topic, page number, type (factual or conceptual), and level of difficulty. The disc includes both Windows and Macintosh versions of the test bank, downloadable in a format that lets the instructor add, edit, and resequence questions.

Online Testing

The test bank CD is also the access point for online testing. With Diploma, the instructor is able to create and administer exams on paper, over a network, or over the Internet. Questions may include graphics, movies, sound, or interactive activities, and the security features allow instructors to restrict tests to specific computers or time blocks. The package also includes a suite of grade book and question-analysis features.

Transparencies

A set of 125 full-color transparencies of key illustrations, charts, graphs, and tables from the textbook is available.

Image and Lecture Gallery

The Image and Lecture Gallery at www.worthpublishers.com/ILG provides access to electronic versions of lecture materials. Registered users can browse, search, and download illustrations from Worth titles plus pre-built PowerPoint presentation files for specific chapters, containing chapter art or chapter section headings in text form. Users can also create personal folders on a personalized home page for easy organization of the materials.

Thanks

I am grateful to the dozens of academic reviewers who have read this book in earlier editions, providing suggestions, criticisms, references, and encouragement. They have all made this a better book. I want to mention especially those who made suggestions for revision or reviewed draft chapters for this edition:

Gary L. Allen
University of South Carolina, Columbia

Jerry Bigner
Colorado State University

Leah Burgy
Lander University

Pamela Costa
Tacoma Community College

Susan J. Coubrough
Waikato Polytechnic, New Zealand

Dana H. Davidson
University of Hawaii, Manoa

Michelle Dunlap
Connecticut College

Krista D. Forrest
University of Nebraska, Kearney

Steven Funk
Northern Arizona University

Myra Heinrich
Mesa State College

Thomas Keenan
University of Canterbury, New Zealand

Veena Khandke
University of South Carolina, Spartanburg

Karen Macrae
University of South Carolina, Spartanburg

T. Darin Matthews
The Citadel

Sandra McDonald
Sierra College

Linda L. Morrison
The University of New England

Leslee K. Pollina
Southeast Missouri State University

David Powley
University of Mobile

Catherine Robertson
Grossmont College

Edythe Schwartz
California State University, Sacramento

Bonnie Seegmiller
Hunter College

Michael Sonntag
Lander University

Constance Toffle
West Virginia University

Kelly J. Welch
Kansas State University

In addition, I again want to thank those who reviewed the previous edition:

Marlene Adelman
Norwalk Community College

Kathy Brown
Southeastern Oklahoma State University

Mark A. Clement
Colby-Sawyer College

Donald R. Cusumano
St. Louis Community College

Sally Hill
Bakersfield College

Eric L. Johnson
Northwestern College

John A. Stefferud
Springfield Technical Community College

Don Stephenson
College of Southern Idaho

Mark A. Stewart
American River College

Trish Vandiver
University of St. Thomas

DEDICATION

Resentment rises in me whenever I read a husband's dedication of a book to his wife. Too often, the author expresses gratitude that he could be creative because his long-suffering spouse allowed him to work alone in the evening or did his typing or proofreading.

Therefore, I am chastened and surprised by my own decision to dedicate this book to my husband. He never proofread my work nor gave dinner parties without me. He did much more than that. He believed in me from the very start, agreeing to a lean year without my paycheck while I readied my first draft for a publisher's contract and listening appreciatively throughout the years as I expressed my fascination and frustration with my work.

"Do you think you and Daddy have a love made in heaven?" our daughter Sarah recently asked. Expecting an easy affirmation, she was taken aback by my "No." The truth is that our relationship has been made ever stronger by 33 years of marriage on earth. This man—brilliant, witty, passionate in his social values—is in the hospital now, and I am blindsided by my sudden feelings of appreciation, deep and wide. Love to you, Martin.

Kathleen Stassen Berger

New York City
May 2000

The Developing Person

Through the Life Span

PART I

The Beginnings

The study of human development has many beginnings, as you will see in the following four chapters. Chapter 1 introduces the scientific study of human development. From it, you will learn what the nature of developmental study is, what kinds of questions developmental scientists ask and try to answer, what the goals of their study are, and how they try to understand human development as it occurs within specific family, social, cultural, and historical contexts.

Chapter 2 introduces you to some of the major theories that guide the study of human development and to the research methods that developmental scientists use to gather data and test their ideas.

A different kind of beginning is described in Chapter 3, which traces the interaction of hereditary and environmental influences. Each human being grows and develops in accordance with chemical guidelines carried on the genes and chromosomes. Interacting with the environment, genes influence everything from the shape of your baby toe to the swiftness of your brain waves to basic aspects of your personality. Thus, understanding the fundamentals of gene—environment interaction is essential to an understanding of human development.

Finally, Chapter 4 details the beginning of human life, from the fusing of sperm and ovum to make one new cell to the birth of a new human being, a totally dependent individual who can nevertheless see, hear, and cry, and is ready to engage in social interaction.

Introduction

CHAPTER 1

You are about to begin a fascinating journey through the human life span. This chapter will serve as a kind of roadmap, outlining your route through this book and familiarizing you with the general terrain. More specifically, it will introduce you to the goals and values that define the scientific study of human development and will suggest the underlying assumptions, overarching themes, and practical applications of that science. But human development actually occurs not as a mass movement but individually—one person and one step at a time. So, to begin our journey, I would like to introduce you to one developing person, my brother's son David.

THE STUDY OF HUMAN DEVELOPMENT

David is a single college graduate in his early 30s, a chronological point that might make some people wonder when he will marry and settle down. But I think more about his past than his future, and I am astonished by his life today. Like most people, David has a family that has cared for him from the moment he was born; schools and teachers that brought out his best, and sometimes his worst; and a social life with peers and the community that gives him both joy and pain.

One detail of his college years may seem familiar to some of you. As a sophomore, criticized in front of the whole class, he reacted by skipping all his classes, soon flunking out, and spending more than a year at home doing odd jobs before returning to college. With great effort, David finally earned his B.A. degree, completing his senior year with a 3.7 average. As he expressed it, "College itself was one of my adversities, but I rebounded big time."

The truth is that college was the least of his adversities. David began life with so many handicaps that a normal life seemed impossible. His infancy, childhood, and adolescence were filled with harsh, often heartbreaking, obstacles.

Most of this book is about more typical development—the usual patterns of growth and change that everyone follows to some degree and that no one follows exactly. But David's story is woven throughout this chapter for two reasons:

- First, David's struggles and triumphs offer a poignant illustration of the underlying goal of the study of human development: to help each person develop throughout life as fully as possible.
- Second, David's example illuminates, with unusual vividness, the basic definitions and central questions that frame our study.

Just as suddenly entering an unfamiliar culture makes us more aware of our own daily routines, habits, and assumptions—which we usually don't notice precisely because they are so familiar—so, too, can David's story highlight the major factors that influence more typical human development. Let us begin, therefore, with the ideas that delineate our work and then return to David.

The Life-Span Perspective

scientific study of human development The science that seeks to understand how and why people change, and how and why they remain the same, as they grow older.

Briefly defined, *the **scientific study of human development** is the science that seeks to understand how and why people change, and how and why they remain the same, as they grow older.* In pursuing this goal, we examine whatever kinds of change we find—simple growth, radical transformation, improvement, and decline—and whatever elements stay the same, providing continuity from day to day, year to year, or generation to generation. We consider factors ranging from the elaborate genetic codes that lay the foundations for human development to the countless particular experiences that shape and refine development, from the impact of prenatal life to the influences of the family, school, peer groups, and community over the life span. We examine everything in light of ever-changing social and cultural contexts.

life-span perspective A view of human development that takes into account all phases of life, not just childhood or adulthood.

The science of human development not only includes all periods of life but also takes a **life-span perspective** on all phases of life, including childhood (Dixon & Lerner, 1999; Smith & Baltes, 1999). In fact, in the "reciprocal connection" between the study of childhood and adulthood (Baltes et al., 1998), the life-span perspective helps us see sources of *continuity* from the beginning of life to the end (such as with biological sex, family of origin, and perhaps personality) and *discontinuity* (such as with language skills in infancy, and with health habits in adulthood).

The life-span perspective actually envisions five distinct characteristics of development, each of which is illustrated throughout this text. Development is:

Hold on Tight Grasping begins as a reflex, but soon one human holding on to another becomes an emotional bond as well as a practical connection. Phrases such as "hand-in-hand," "hold my hand," "grab tight," and "don't let go" capture this tangible and metaphorical connection across the life span.

- Multidirectional: Change is not always linear. Gains and losses, compensations and deficits, predictable growth and unexpected transformations are part of the human experience.
- Multicontextual: Each human life must be understood as embedded in many contexts (further described in this chapter).
- Multicultural: To understand the universals and specifics of human development, many cultural settings—each with a distinct set of values, traditions, and tools for living—must be considered.
- Multidisciplinary: Many academic fields—especially psychology, biology, education, and sociology, but also neuroscience, economics, medicine, anthropology, history, and more—contribute data and insight to the science of development.
- Plastic: Every individual, and every trait within each individual, can be altered at any point in the life span.
  [Baltes et al., 1998; Smith & Baltes, 1999]

plasticity The capability of any human characteristic to be molded or reshaped by time and circumstance.

This last characteristic, **plasticity,** or the capability of change, is one of the most encouraging tenets of the life-span perspective. The term *plasticity* denotes two complementary aspects of development: human characteristics can be molded into different forms and shapes (as plastic can be), yet people (again like plastic) maintain a certain durability

biosocial domain The part of human development that includes physical growth and development as well as the family, community, and cultural factors that affect that growth and development.

cognitive domain The part of human development that includes all the mental processes through which the individual thinks, learns, and communicates, plus the institutions involved in learning and communicating.

psychosocial domain The part of human development that includes emotions, personality characteristics, and relationships with other people—family, friends, lovers, and strangers. This domain also includes the larger community and the culture.

Figure 1.1 The Three Domains. The division of human development into three domains makes it easier to study, but remember that very few factors belong exclusively to one domain or another. Development is not piecemeal but holistic: Each aspect of development is related to all three domains.

and substance from year to year. When it comes to a human life, nothing is ever chiseled in stone. People are always evolving, with the specific rates, degrees, aspects, and directions of their evolution being much more variable than scientists once thought.

We are always aware of the possible implications and applications of our study. Indeed,

> developmental science originated from the need to solve practical problems and . . . from pressures to improve the education, health, welfare, and legal status of children and their families. (Hetherington, 1998)

Because the study of human development is a science, it follows objective rules of evidence. Because it concerns human life and growth, it is also laden with personal implications and applications. It originated with children, but the same basic principles apply from the moment of conception to the last breath.

This interplay of the objective and the subjective, of change and continuity, of the individual and the universal, of young and old, and of past, present, and future makes developmental science a dynamic, interactive, and even transformative study. Of all the sciences, the study of human development is the least static, least predictable, and least narrow. It also may have the most noble goal: "explaining, assessing, and promoting change and development" (Renninger & Amsel, 1997). In other words, developmental scientists seek not only to understand and measure human change over the life span but also to use their knowledge to help all people develop their full human potential.

Three Domains

In an effort to organize this mutifaceted study, we often divide development into three major domains. The **biosocial domain** includes the brain and body, as well as changes in them and the social influences that direct them. The **cognitive domain** includes thought processes, perceptual abilities, and language mastery, as well as the educational institutions that encourage them. The **psychosocial domain** includes emotions, personality, and interpersonal relationships with family, friends, and the wider community. (See Figure 1.1.)

All three domains are important at every age. For instance, understanding an infant involves studying his or her health (biosocial), curiosity (cognitive), and temperament (psychosocial), as well as dozens of other aspects of development from all three domains. Similarly, understanding an adolescent requires studying

DOMAINS OF HUMAN DEVELOPMENT

Biosocial Development	Cognitive Development	Psychosocial Development
Includes all the growth and change that occur in a person's body, and the genetic, nutritional, and health factors that affect that growth and change. Motor skills—everything from grasping a rattle to driving a car—are also part of the biosocial domain. Social and cultural factors that affect these areas, such as duration of breast-feeding, education of children with special needs, and attitudes about ideal body shape, are also part of biosocial development.	Includes all the mental processes that are used to obtain knowledge or to become aware of the environment. Cognition encompasses perception, imagination, judgment, memory, and language—the processes people use to think, decide, and learn. Education, including the formal curriculum within schools, informal tutoring by family and friends, and the results of individual curiosity and creativity, is also part of this domain.	Includes development of emotions, temperament, and social skills. The influences of family, friends, the community, the culture, and the larger society are particularly central to the psychosocial domain. Thus cultural differences in the value accorded children, or in ideas about "appropriate" sex roles, or in what is regarded as the ideal family structure are considered part of this domain.

Every Domain, Every Moment Every aspect of human behavior reflects all three domains. Obviously, biosocial factors—such as hormones and body strength—are at work here, but so are cognitive and psychosocial ones. For instance, each student's mental concentration or lack of it is critical to karate success. So is the culture's message about who should learn the martial arts—a message that seems to have made this an all-male class.

the physical changes that mark the bodily transition from child to adult, the intellectual development that leads to efforts to think logically about such issues as sexual passion and future goals, and the emerging patterns of friendship and courtship that prepare the individual for the intimate relationships of adulthood.

In practical terms, given a particular developmental change, it is not always easy to decide which domain it belongs to. Where would you place fertility and infertility, or religious beliefs, or retirement from work? If you guessed biosocial, cognitive, and psychosocial, respectively, you are in accord with the placement of these topics in this text. But you also probably realized that there is always overlap. For instance, a person retires for biological and cognitive reasons as well as social ones.

Therefore, while the study of development is organized into domains and then segmented even further by age, the developmentalist is always aware that development is *holistic*. That means that each person grows as an integrated whole, although aspects of his or her development are studied separately by scientists in different academic disciplines.

CONTEXTS AND SYSTEMS

We often think of development as originating *within* the person—the result of such internal factors as genetic programming, physical maturation, cognitive growth, and personal inclination. However, development is also greatly influenced by forces *outside* the person, by the physical surroundings and social interactions that provide incentives, opportunities, and pathways for growth. Taken together, groups of these external forces form the *contexts*, or *systems* or *environments*, in which development occurs. Just as a naturalist studying a flower or a fish needs to ex-

Lonely or in Awe? Imagine yourself as the child on the left, spending much of your childhood following sheep near massive mountains, flowering meadows, running rivers. Would this childhood setting affect your skills, emotions, and attitudes as an adult? Research influenced by the ecological perspective has shown that it would. Depending on the values of the person describing them, the Indians shown here from the highlands of Peru are said to be more spiritual and poetic than most people or more fatalistic and passive. No one, however, sees their typical personality as just like that of residents of Chicago or Tokyo or Berlin.

❷ *Observational Quiz (answer on page 8): From the photo, what can you tell about the social relationships of the child in the left foreground?*

Figure 1.2 The Ecological Model.
According to developmental researcher Urie Bronfenbrenner, each person is significantly affected by interactions among a number of overlapping ecosystems. *Microsystems* are the systems that intimately and immediately shape human development. The primary microsystems for children include the family, peer group, classroom, neighborhood, and sometimes a church, temple, or mosque as well. Interactions among the microsystems, as when parents and teachers coordinate their efforts to educate the child, take place through the *mesosystem*. Surrounding the microsystems is the *exosystem,* which includes all the external networks, such as community structures and local educational, medical, employment, and communications systems, that influence the microsystems. And influencing all other systems is the *macrosystem,* which includes cultural values, political philosophies, economic patterns, and social conditions. Bronfenbrenner has recently added another system, the *chronosystem,* to emphasize the importance of historical time. Together, these systems are termed the context of human development.

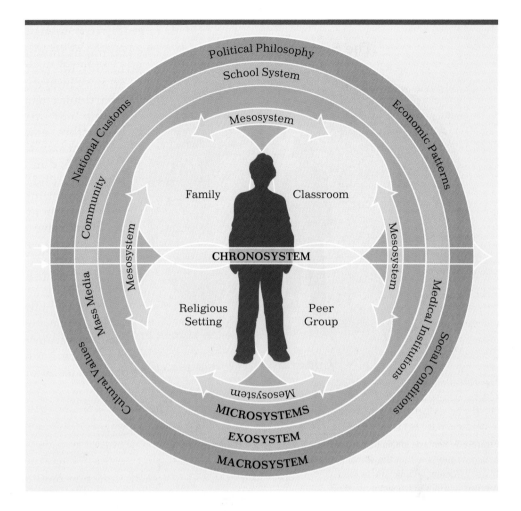

butterfly effect   The idea that a small action—such as the breeze caused by the flap of a butterfly's wings—may set off a series of powerful changes.

amine the organism's supporting ecosystems, developmentalists need to study the ecological systems, or contexts, in which each human being seeks to thrive.

This insight about the importance of developmental systems is integral to a life-span perspective. Developmental psychologist Urie Bronfenbrenner was one of the first to describe the various systems that surround each developing person (see Figure 1.2). The key concept is that the influences within and between these systems or contexts are multidirectional and interactive.

This idea is most clearly expressed in two theories from the natural sciences, *complexity theory* and *chaos theory*. These theories stress the unpredictability and dynamism of all natural systems. A temperature change in the Pacific Ocean, for example, can cause a blizzard in New England. Indeed, given the right conditions, the flap of a butterfly's wing on one continent can cause a hurricane on another—a phenomenon called the **butterfly effect.** This insight also applies to human thoughts and actions: A tiny change can have a profound effect not only on one person but also on another person far away. As one scientist puts it:

> There exists no one way to explain consciousness. Each individual self system reflects an infinite number of fractal microsystems and is interconnected at every level with other aspects of the biosphere. [Arden, 1998]

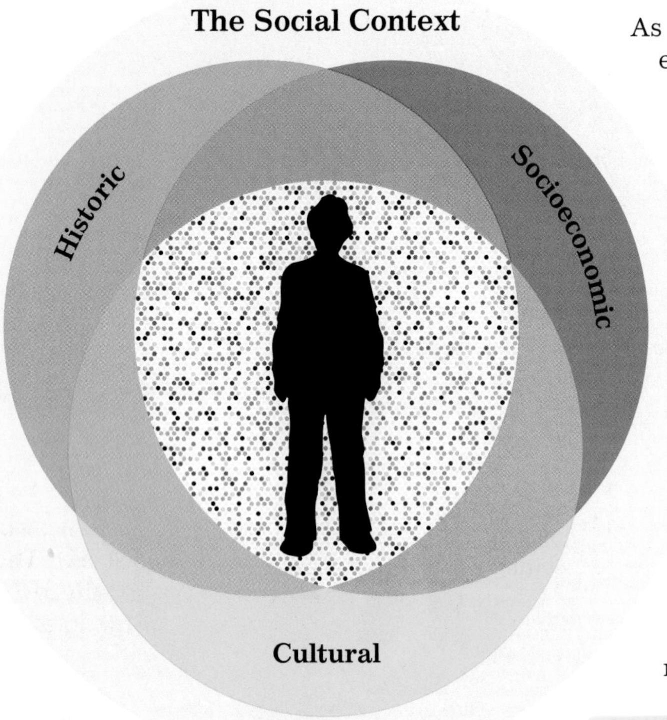

Overlapping Contexts

As you might imagine, neither in a single book nor in everyday life can anyone consider simultaneously all the contextual factors that might bear on any particular aspect of development. Throughout this text, we will examine a great many such factors, exploring the ways in which specific contexts tend to push development in one direction or another. They are all interactive and reciprocal, with a small change sometimes becoming the butterfly whose wingbeat produces a major shift, and a massive disaster sometimes not being strong enough to alter an individual's life course.

At the outset, however, we need to describe and define three contexts that can affect virtually every individual in every phase of development: the historical context, the socioeconomic context, and the cultural context. As Figure 1.3 suggests, these three contexts do not act in isolation.

The Social Context

Figure 1.3 Contexts Within Contexts. Three broad contexts within the social context—history, socioeconomic status, and culture—affect the development of children in many ways, sometimes distantly, sometimes directly, sometimes individually, sometimes in combination. Because these three contexts overlap, it is often impossible to determine whether a particular effect comes from cohort, social class, or ethnic heritage.

❷ *Observational Quiz (answer on page 10): Can you figure out the symbolism of the multicolored dots, or of the purple, green, and orange patches?*

cohort　A group of people who, because they were born within a few years of one another, experience many of the same historical and social conditions.

❶ *Answer to Observational Quiz (from page 6): She is not close enough to converse with anyone, no males are present in her immediate group, and each child in the photo is quite distant from the others—because of the need to keep each herd of sheep separate from the other herds. If this is typical of her life, her social circumstances discourage language learning, encourage gender roles, and make play with peers impossible.*

The Historical Context

All persons born within a few years of one another are said to be a **cohort,** a group of people whose shared age means that they travel through life together. The idea is that all the people in a particular cohort are subject to the same history—the same prevailing assumptions, important public events, technologies, and popular trends. How history affects the lives and thoughts of a specific person depends partly on how old the person was when he or she experienced a given historical event. People in a specific cohort tend to be affected in the same way; those in different cohorts are generally affected differently.

For example, are your attitudes about money, or marriage, or personal privacy the same as those of your parents or grandparents? They may value your college education considerably more (or considerably less) than you do. Such attitudes and values are affected by the economic and social environments that prevailed when one first reached adulthood—whether that was during the economically depressed 1930s, the affluent 1950s, or the financially unstable 1990s. In fact, for adults of all ages, events of their late adolescence and early adult years tend to be most significant and memorable (Rubin, 1999).

One more example of the effect of history: Contemporary adults who were teenagers in the 1960s may be politically and personally more independent and less passive than older or younger adults. One possible explanation is that the historical circumstances of their youth (the civil rights movement, the Vietnam war, the women's liberation movement) promoted independence and assertiveness. Another explanation is that certain inventions, including the birth control pill, the television, and the computer, changed the meaning of work and family. Still another explanation is that this cohort was the "baby boom"—the huge number of children born in the decade just after World War II—and

Changing Values To some extent, the experiences and values of late adolescence influence each cohort for a lifetime. Maturity does not usually change those values, but at least it can make each generation realize the limitations of its historical context.

"You'd better ask your grandparents about that, son—my generation is very uncomfortable talking about abstinence."

Figure 1.4 The Baby-Boom Population Bulge. Unlike earlier times, when each generation was slightly smaller than the one that followed, each cohort today has a unique position that was determined by the reproductive patterns of the preceding generation and by the medical advances that were developed during their own lifetime. As a result of these two factors, the baby boomers, born between 1947 and 1964, represent a huge bulge in the U.S. population. In another three decades, the leading edge of the baby-boom generation, largely intact, will begin moving into the upper age group.

their sheer numbers convinced them they could have their own way (Alwin, 1997). Cohort size, too, is part of the historical context. The age structure of the U.S. population has changed dramatically over the years, and the huge baby-boomer cohort has been a conspicuous feature of that shift (see Figure 1.4).

Values as a Social Construction.   As profound economic, political, and technological changes occur over the years, basic concepts about how things "should be" are influenced by how things *were* before such changes took place. Moreover, we often find that one or another of our most cherished assumptions about how things should be is not a fact of

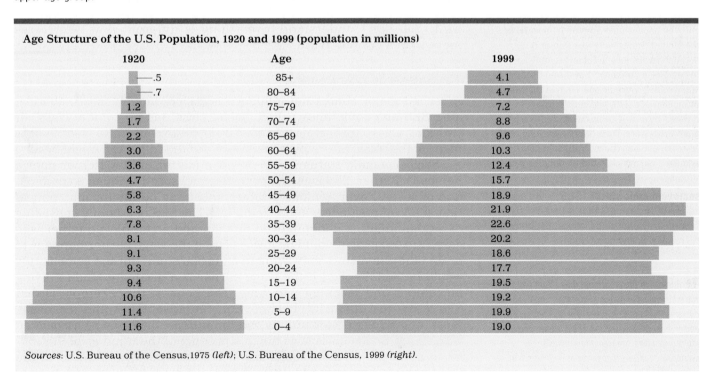

Age Structure of the U.S. Population, 1920 and 1999 (population in millions)

1920	Age	1999
.5	85+	4.1
.7	80–84	4.7
1.2	75–79	7.2
1.7	70–74	8.8
2.2	65–69	9.6
3.0	60–64	10.3
3.6	55–59	12.4
4.7	50–54	15.7
5.8	45–49	18.9
6.3	40–44	21.9
7.8	35–39	22.6
8.1	30–34	20.2
9.1	25–29	18.6
9.3	20–24	17.7
9.4	15–19	19.5
10.6	10–14	19.2
11.4	5–9	19.9
11.6	0–4	19.0

Sources: U.S. Bureau of the Census, 1975 *(left)*; U.S. Bureau of the Census, 1999 *(right)*.

social construction An idea about the way things are, or should be, that is built more on the shared perceptions of members of a society than on objective reality.

Why Not Put the Children to Work? The current view of childhood as a special period given over to formal education and play is fairly recent. As late as 1900, one out of every five children between the ages of 10 and 16 in the United States worked, often at dirty and dangerous jobs in factories, mills, and mines. These ''breaker'' boys, who usually started their work at age 10, had the task of picking out slate and rubble from crushed coal as it came down chutes from giant processors. Their hours were long; their environment was choked with coal dust; and their pay was less than a dollar a day.

socioeconomic status (SES) An indicator of social class that is based primarily on income, education, place of residence, and occupation.

❶ *Answer to Observational Quiz (from page 8):* *You may remember from art class that purple is a mixture of red and blue, green is of blue and yellow, and orange of yellow and red. The mixtures, and the multicolored dots, are meant to emphasize the overlapping contexts that surround each person at every stage.*

life but a **social construction**—an idea built more on the shared perceptions of a society than on objective reality. As changes occur, our basic ideas about things also tend to change. Right now, for example, we are in the midst of a change in our thinking about computers, and that change is occurring cohort by cohort. Older cohorts tend to consider computers as objects to be feared and mastered; middle cohorts see them as powerful tools; younger cohorts see them as no more remarkable than toothbrushes or bicycles. Each cohort is partially correct; each has its own social construction.

Even the most basic ideas about human development can change. For example, our very concept of childhood, as a precious and extended stage of life, is a social construction. In many historical contexts, children were nurtured only until they could care for themselves (at about age 7). Then they entered the adult world, working in the fields or at home and spending their leisure time engaged in the activities of grown-ups. Further, the social construction that children are born "little angels" would lead to quite different child rearing than would the once-common idea that adults have to "beat the devil out of them" in order to make them proper, God-fearing adults (Hwang et al., 1996; Straus, 1994).

The historical context of development is thus a continually changing one because "differences in year of birth expose people to . . . different priorities, constraints, and options" (Elder et al., 1995). For instance, if you were a high school student in the United States in the late 1970s, you are three times more likely to have been a fairly regular user of marijuana than you would be if you had reached age 18 in the United States in the early 1990s (Johnston et al., 1997). Drug habits change every few years with each adolescent generation, as further explained in Chapter 14. Likewise, each new generation defines its historical coming of age with distinctive clothes, hairstyles, slang, and values. Popular songs that once were considered risqué are now "golden oldies." A 15-year-old who rejects advice from a 30-year-old with "You don't understand; everything is different now" expresses more than a grain of truth.

The Socioeconomic Context

A second major contextual influence is **socioeconomic status,** abbreviated **SES** and sometimes called "social class" (as in "middle class" or "working class"). SES is part of the social context because it influences many of the social interactions and opportunities a person might have.

Socioeconomic status is *not* simply a matter of how rich or poor a person is. Rather, SES is most accurately measured through a combination of several overlapping variables, including family income, education, place of residence, and occupation. The SES of a family consisting of, say, an infant, a nonemployed mother, and an employed father who earns $10,000 a year would be lower-class if the wage earner happens to be an illiterate dishwasher living in an urban slum. But the same family would be middle-class if the wage earner is a graduate student living on campus and teaching part-time. The point of this example is that SES is not just financial: It entails *all* the advantages and disadvantages, and *all* the opportunities and limitations, that may be associated with status. Social class is as much a product of the mind as of the wallet, as much the result of social disparities as of personal income, as the Life-Span View on pages 12–13 further explains.

Cherish the Child Cultures vary tremendously in how much they value children. China's "one-child" policy urges every family to limit reproduction, which could be taken as a sign either that children are not as valuable as older people or that each child is destined to be precious.

❷ *Observational Quiz (answer on page 13):* *What three signs suggest that this community enjoys this boy?*

culture The set of shared values, assumptions, customs, and physical objects that are maintained by a group of people in a specific setting (a society) as a design for living daily life.

Closely Connected This Masai woman is often in close physical contact with her young children. Her sleeping daughter, covered in a decorative blanket, remains cradled in her arms rather than beside her, and her son is also nearby—indeed (do you see it?) in touch.

The Cultural Context

Culture is the third pervasive aspect of the social context. When social scientists use the term **culture,** they include hundreds of specific manifestations of a social group's *design for living*, developed over the years to provide a social structure for life together. Culture includes values, assumptions, and customs, as well as physical objects (clothing, dwellings, cuisine, technologies, works of art, and so on). The term "culture" is sometimes used rather loosely, as in "the culture of poverty," "the culture of children," or "the culture of America." However, whenever culture is considered as part of the social context, the emphasis is more on values, behaviors, and attitudes than on the specific foods, clothes, and objects of daily life.

Cultures: Poor and Rural, Rich and Urban. Culture guides human development in a multitude of interrelated ways. Here is one example: In many developing agricultural communities, children are an economic asset because they work the family's farm and, later, perpetuate the family unit by remaining on the land, having and raising their own children, and caring for the aged. Thus, every newborn benefits the entire family group. If that agricultural community is also poor, and dependent on subsistence farming, then nutrition and medical care are inadequate. As a result, infant mortality is high—a serious loss to the family unit. Therefore, infant care is designed to maximize survival and emphasize family cooperation. Typical features of infant care in poor rural communities include:

- intensive physical nurturance
- breast-feeding on demand
- immediate response to crying
- close body contact
- keeping the baby beside the mother at night
- constant care by siblings and other relatives

AGE AND POVERTY

In official government statistics, SES is usually measured solely by family income (adjusted for inflation and family size), perhaps because it is difficult to include measures of education and occupation. For example, in 1998 in the contiguous United States, a family of four with an annual income of $16,450 or less was considered to be at the bottom of the SES scale. Their income was below a dollar amount called the *poverty level,* which is calculated as the minimum amount needed to pay for basic necessities. (In Alaska and Hawaii, the poverty level is set somewhat higher.)

Looking only at family income is simplistic yet sometimes useful, especially when income falls below the poverty level. The reason is that inadequate family income both signals and creates a social context of limited opportunities and heightened pressures. These, in turn, make life much more difficult to manage than it is for families higher up on the socioeconomic ladder. For example, throughout the world infant mortality, child neglect, inadequate schools, and adolescent violence are all much more common among the poor than among the affluent (Huston et al., 1994; McLoyd, 1998).

Considerable debate among social scientists concerns whether low income alone creates such developmental problems. Alternatively, there may be a "culture of poverty," a set of social values and practices that tends to perpetuate low SES and its problems from generation to generation. If so, there may also be a "culture of privilege" that tends to create other problems as well as to maintain the social distance between the rich and the poor.

Another debate concerning SES is particularly significant when using a life-span perspective: Which generation deserves the greatest portion of public financial support? Five decades ago, the old were the poorest age group in the United States and in most other nations of the world. Now, as you can see from Figure 1.5, the youngest are poorest, with more than one in five children living in poverty. Some argue that this inequity is not only unfair but also foolish, because it creates problems in today's youth that will haunt society in years to come. Others contend that the older generations are more deserving of economic support and are more likely to spend it

wisely—often to help younger generations. Indeed, when researchers examine money transfers within families, they find that persons over age 65 are more likely to give than to receive (Crystal, 1996).

Although low income is a rough but useful indicator of poverty, and although poverty is a rough but useful signal for severe problems throughout the life span, we cannot simply say that lack of money creates overwhelming developmental difficulties. A better and more precise indicator is needed to differentiate between those low-SES individuals, families, and neighborhoods that are overcome by risks and those that seem relatively protected.

Supportive relationships within the family are one crucial variable that seems to benefit adults as well as children. For example, studies of children living in poverty find that some are "resilient: bouncing back from adversity, they become well-adjusted and successful, while others become angry, lonely, law-breaking, and failures" (Werner et al., 1992; see also Rutter et al., 1998). What seems to make the difference is nurturant, involved parents. One study of many factors found that, even if adults are poor, unmarried, and victims of childhood neglect and abuse, they can become good parents and that "competence and quality of parenting were the most sensitive predictors of resilient status" among the children (Wyman et al., 1999).

At the other end of the life span, African American women have the least income but also the least depression of any elderly group. The annual suicide rate over age 70 in the United States is only 1 per 100,000 black females compared to 6 for white females, 15 for black males, and 50 for white males (Kacher et al., 1995). Explanations center on the strength of ties to family and church among elderly African American women.

Neighborhoods have an impact as well, as you might expect from your understanding of ecosystems. A New Orleans study of 55 low-income block groups (each about 500 residents within 1/3 of a square mile) included some very poor neighborhoods where 95 percent of the households had an annual income below $15,000 and some not quite as poor neighborhoods, where only a third had annual incomes below $15,000 per household

All these measures protect the fragile infant from an early death while establishing the value of interdependence among family members (LeVine et al., 1994).

Middle-class parents in postindustrial nations need not be so fearful their baby will die, but they have other concerns. They believe their babies need cribs, strollers, diapers, high chairs, car seats, and toys—all quite expensive items. Even food, child care, and shelter are far more

(Cohen et al., 2000). (A household is defined as all the people living in one house, apartment, or trailer.) The researchers measured not only income, education, and employment but also signs of neighborhood deterioration, including abandoned cars, houses with broken windows or visible roof damage, graffiti on walls, uncollected garbage, schools in poor repair.

Then the researchers compared these neighborhood factors with the rate of gonorrhea, a sign of risky, uncommitted sexual behavior. The researchers found that the incidence of this sexually transmitted disease was more closely associated with neighborhood neglect than with any other variable, including low income, low education, single parenthood, and race (Cohen et al., 2000). In other words, when people work to keep a neighborhood decent, they experience fewer social problems than other poor people who are just a few blocks away. Similar results were found in Chicago by comparing signs of community caring and concern with rates of violent crime (Sampson et al., 1997).

No developmentalist doubts that poverty is a risk factor, or that many social problems would diminish if employment and wages rose. However, the data also show that poverty by itself is not always overwhelming; some people can find within themselves and their community other resources that protect individual growth despite financial stresses.

Figure 1.5 Children Are the Poorest. The American who sleeps hungry, in a crumbling house, in a crime-ridden community is more often a young child than an older adult. Is this fair? To those who study child development, it seems not, since children are the most vulnerable to the effects of deprivation. The question is, Who has an obligation to correct this imbalance—society as a whole or only the older family members of those children?

*The Life-Span View box in each chapter (always with a pale pink background) explores particular behaviors as they are both manifested at different periods of life and influenced by various generations.

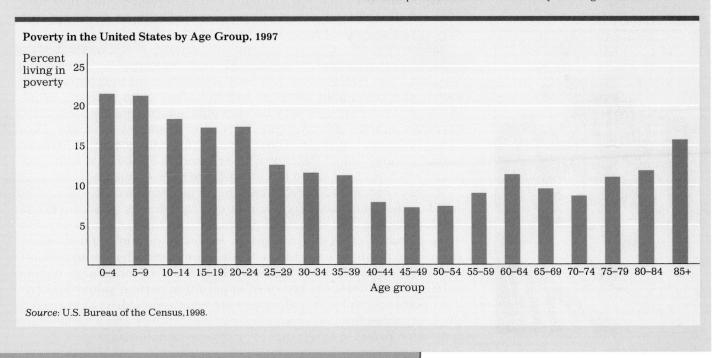

Poverty in the United States by Age Group, 1997

Source: U.S. Bureau of the Census, 1998.

❶ *Answer to Observational Quiz (from page 11):*
At least four adults are smiling at him; he is eating an apple that was brought to the market for sale; he is allowed to sit on the table with the food. If you noticed another sign—his new green sandals—give yourself bonus credit.

costly in an urban than a rural community, which is one reason most women in developed nations want just one or two children and most women in developing countries want three to five children (Tsui et al., 1997). The payoff for urban parents comes not when the child begins herding the sheep but when the young adult lands a prestigious job.

Therefore, hoping to ensure their children's future success in a technological and urbanized society, middle-class parents focus their

❷ Especially for Health Professionals: What do you think would be the biggest concern about their newborn for a family of recent immigrants from a developing country? For a family in which both native-born parents are well-paid professionals?

ethnic group   A collection of people who share certain background characteristics, such as national origin, religion, upbringing, and language, and who, as a result, tend to have similar beliefs, values, and cultural experiences.

race   A social construction that originated with biological differences among people whose ancestors came from various regions of the world and whose social status was considered inferior or superior. *Race* is a misleading term; social scientists prefer to use *ethnicity, national background,* or *culture* instead.

Give Your Baby the Best   Touching only himself, but watching one of the best mobiles that money can buy, this 3-month-old North American baby wears his soft-snapped, unisex, right-size stretch suit as he rests alone in his adjustable wooden crib. Most infants of the world do not have their own carriage, crib, or playpen. Ironically, many of their parents wonder why Westerners are so cruel as to put their babies behind bars.

child-rearing efforts on fostering cognitive growth and emotional independence. They typically provide intense cognitive and social stimulation. They talk to their babies more than touch them, put them to sleep by themselves in their own cribs in their own rooms, and often ignore their young children's whining, crying, and clinging so as not to "spoil" them.

Not surprisingly, such contrasting parental strategies produce children with quite different capacities, goals, and expectations, But, in every culture, the children become prepared to take their place in the social group and economic setting in which they have been raised (Coles, 1999; Harkness & Super, 1995).

Ethnicity and Culture.   An **ethnic group** is a collection of people who share certain attributes, such as ancestry, national origin, religion, and/or language. As a result, members of an ethnic group tend to recognize and identify with one another and have similar daily encounters with the social world. *Racial identity* can be considered an element of ethnicity. Indeed, sometimes outsiders assume that people of the same racial background are also from the same ethnic group. However, as social scientists emphatically point out, biological traits (such as hair or skin coloring, facial features, and body type) that distinguish one **race** from another are much less significant to development than are the attitudes and experiences that may arise from ethnic or racial consciousness, especially those resulting from minority or majority status (Templeton, 1998).

Ethnic identity, then, is not primarily genetic; it is a product of the social environment and the individual's consciousness. Two people may look like close relatives but may have quite different upbringings, heritages, and community settings and therefore quite different ethnic identities. Or two people may be very different in appearance but still share an ethnic identity. This is readily apparent in many Latin American ethnic groups. These groups include people of African, European, and Indian descent who are united by their common language and homeland as the key elements of their ethnicity.

Ethnicity is similar to culture in that it provides people with shared beliefs, values, and assumptions that can significantly affect their own development as well as how they raise their children. Indeed, sometimes ethnicity and culture overlap. However, people of many ethnic groups can all share one culture while maintaining their ethnic identities. Within multiethnic cultures, such as those of most large nations today, ethnic differences are most apparent in certain values and customs. Some examples of such values are whether children are raised in large, extended families or smaller, nuclear families and whether each generation defers to family elders or asserts its autonomy.

The Person Within the Systems

Since each individual develops within many contexts, it is obviously important to understand the special impact that each context has. But do not make the mistake of thinking that a person in a context or system is like a part of a complex machine. We cannot explain any individual's personality traits, abilities, or actions in terms of a single context. No one is exactly like the statistically "average" person of his or her cohort, socioeconomic status, or culture. This is because everyone is pulled in

Not the Usual Path If we were to consider only this woman's past history or the cultural values that her dyed hair and polished fingernails suggest, we would say that she belongs at home with her grandchildren and old-age pension. However, individual uniqueness can override contextual limitations—which explains why she is about to walk the Appalachian Trail from Maine to Georgia. If we use a life-span perspective, this is not a suprise, because she always enjoyed exercise and the outdoors, and covering the trail's entire 2,160-mile length was her lifelong ambition.

scientific method The principles and procedures used in the systematic pursuit of knowledge (formulating questions, testing hypotheses, and drawing conclusions), designed to reduce subjective reasoning, biased assumptions, and unfounded beliefs.

hypothesis A specific prediction that is stated in such a way that it can be tested and either proved or disproved.

replicate To repeat a previous scientific study, at a different time and place but with the same research design and procedures, in order to verify that study's conclusions.

subjects The people who are studied in a research project.

divergent directions by many contextual influences, whose power varies from individual to individual, age to age, situation to situation, and family to family.

Each of us differs in unexpected ways from any stereotypes or generalities that might seem pertinent, and our individual differences demand as much scientific respect and scrutiny as any of the commonalities that link us to a particular group. In fact, each of us is an active participant in every system that includes us. We contribute to the history of our cohort, help form our economic circumstances, and construct our own personal meanings from our cultural background (Rogoff, 1997; Valsiner, 1997). This power of the developing individual is well illustrated by David, whose story tells us of the many contexts that affected his development yet simultaneously reveals the uniqueness of each human being (see the In Person box on page 16).

DEVELOPMENTAL STUDY AS A SCIENCE

As David's case makes abundantly clear, the study of development requires taking into account the interplay of the biosocial, cognitive, and psychosocial domains, within a particular historical period, under the influence of familial, socioeconomic, cultural, and other contextual forces. Not surprisingly, assessing the relative impacts of all these factors is no simple matter. For help in proceeding through this complexity, developmentalists have adopted scientific methodology.

The **scientific method** is a general way to seek evidence—not biased or wishful thinking—to answer questions.

Steps in the Scientific Method

The scientific method, as it applies to developmental study, involves four basic steps, and sometimes a fifth:

1. *Formulate a research question.* On the basis of previous research or a particular theory or personal observation, pose a question about development.
2. *Develop a hypothesis.* Reformulate the question into a **hypothesis,** which is a specific prediction that can be tested.
3. *Test the hypothesis.* Design and conduct a research project that will provide evidence—in the form of data—about the truth or falsehood of the hypothesis.
4. *Draw conclusions.* Use the research data as evidence that supports or refutes the hypothesis. Describe any limitations of the research and any alternative explanations for the results.
5. *Make the findings available.* Publishing the results of the research is often the fifth step in the scientific method. In this step, you describe the procedure and results in sufficient detail so that other scientists can evaluate the conclusions. If they wish to, other scientists can **replicate** the research—that is, repeat it and verify the results—or extend it, using a different but related set of **subjects** (people who are studied) or procedures. Replication and extension are the means by which new scientific studies provide more definitive and comprehensive knowledge. Only after several studies have verified the findings of a particular research project is a conclusion considered confirmed, and thus accepted as "robust," or substantiated.

IN PERSON

DAVID'S STORY *

David's story begins in 1967, with an event that is straight out of the biosocial domain. In the spring of that year, in rural Kentucky, an epidemic of rubella (German measles) struck two particular victims—David's mother, who had a rash and a sore throat for a couple of days, and her 4-week-old embryo, who was damaged for life. David was born in November, with a life-threatening heart defect and thick cataracts covering both eyes. Other damage included minor malformations of the thumbs, feet, jaw, and teeth, as well as of the brain.

The historical context was crucial. Had David been conceived a decade later, widespread use of the rubella vaccine would probably have meant that his mother would not have contracted the disease. David would have been born unscathed. On the other hand, had he been born a few years earlier, he would have died. The microsurgery that saved his life was, in 1967, a recent medical miracle, as were all the support services that made life possible.

The Early Years: Heartbreaking Handicaps, Slow Progress

At that place and time, heart surgery in the first days after birth did save David's life. However, surgery 6 months later to open a channel around one of the cataracts failed, completely destroying that eye. It was not obvious then that David's successful heart surgery was a blessing.

David's physical handicaps produced cognitive and psychosocial handicaps—an example of one domain affecting the other two. Not only did his blindness make it impossible for him to learn by looking, but his parents overprotected him to the point that he spent almost all his early months in their arms or in his crib. An analysis of the family context would have revealed that David's impact on his family and their effect on him were harmful. Like many relatives of seriously impaired infants, David's parents felt guilt, anger, and despair. During the first months they were, at times, less responsive to David's cries than they had been to those of their older sons.

Fortunately, however, David's parents came from a socioeconomic context that encouraged them to seek outside help. (David's father is a college professor, and his mother is a nurse.) Fortunately, also, their community offered help. Their first step was to obtain advice from a teacher at the Kentucky

School for the Blind, who told them to stop blaming themselves and overprotecting David. If their son was going to learn about his world, he was going to have to explore it. For example, rather than confining David to a crib or playpen, they were to provide him with a large rug for a play area. Whenever he crawled off the rug, they were to say "No" and place him back in the middle of it. This would teach him to use his sense of touch to learn where he could explore safely without bumping into walls or furniture.

David's mother dedicated herself to a multitude of tasks that various specialists suggested, including exercising his twisted feet and cradling him frequently in her arms as she sang lullabies to provide extra tactile and auditory stimulation. His cries were more frequent and more grating than those of a normal infant, but his parents soon noticed that he quieted at his mother's touch and voice—an encouraging sign that he was capable of responding to human stimulation.

Instead of a destructive reciprocal process, a constructive one began. Soon, David's responsiveness mobilized the entire family. His father took over much of the housework and the care of David's two older brothers, ages 2 and 4, who began talking and playing with him. David's father sought a grant to study at Harvard, because the Perkins School for the Blind, in nearby Boston, had just begun an experimental program for blind toddlers. At Perkins, David's mother learned specific methods for developing physical and language skills in children with multiple disabilities, and she, in turn, taught the techniques to David's father and brothers. Every day the family spent hours rolling balls, doing puzzles, and singing with David.

Thus, a smooth collaboration between home and school helped young David develop, aided by the cultural affinity between the experts' attitudes and the family's values. In other words, contexts meshed neatly, with family systems connecting to cultural systems. The mesosystems worked well.

Nonetheless, progress was slow. It became painfully apparent that rubella had damaged much more than David's eyes and heart. At age 3, he could not yet talk, chew solid food, use the toilet, coordinate his fingers, or even walk normally. An IQ test showed him to be severely mentally retarded. Fortunately, although most children with rubella syndrome have hearing defects, David's hearing was normal.

At age 4, David said his first word, "Dada." Open-heart surgery corrected the last of his heart damage. His mother, with tears in her eyes, said, "I am so grateful that he is alive, and yet I know that soon I will be angry at him when he spits out his food." At age 5, an operation brought partial vision to David's remaining eye. Vision was far from perfect, but he could now recognize his family by sight as well as by sound. Soon after, when the family returned to rural Kentucky, further progress became obvious: He no longer needed diapers or baby food.

David's fifth birthday occurred in 1972. The social construction that children with severe disabilities are unteachable was being seriously challenged. Many schools were beginning to open their doors to children with special needs. David's parents found four schools that would accept him. In accordance with the family's emphasis on education, they enrolled him in all four. He attended two schools for children with cerebral palsy: One had morning classes, and the other—40 miles away—afternoon classes. (David ate lunch in the car with his mother on the daily trip.) On Fridays these schools were closed, so he attended a school for the mentally retarded. On Sundays he spent 2 hours in church school, which was his first experience with "mainstreaming"—the then new idea that children with special needs should be educated with normal children. Particularly in the church community, the cultural–ethnic background of Appalachia benefited David's development, for a strong commitment to accepting the disabled and helping neighbors in need is a value that Appalachian people hold dear.

Childhood and Adolescence: Heartening Progress

At age 7, David entered first grade in a public school, one of the first severely disabled children in the United States to be mainstreamed. Rubella continued to have an obvious impact on his biosocial, cognitive, and psychosocial development. His motor skills were poor (among other things, he had difficulty controlling a pencil); his efforts to learn to read were greatly hampered by the fact that he was legally blind even in his "good" eye; and his social skills were seriously deficient (he pinched people he didn't like, hugged girls too tightly, cried and laughed at inappropriate times).

During the next several years, development in the cognitive domain proceeded rapidly. By age 10, David had skipped a year of school and was a fifth-grader. He could read—with a magnifying glass—at the eleventh-grade level and was labeled "intellectually gifted" according to tests of verbal and math skills. Outside of school he began to learn a second language, play the violin, and sing in the choir. He proved to have extraordinary auditory acuity and memory, although holding the violin bow correctly was difficult.

David's greatest remaining problem was in the psychosocial domain. Schools generally ignored the need to cultivate the social skills of mainstreamed children. David was no exception. For instance, he was required to sit on the sidelines during most physical-education classes and to stay inside during most recess periods. Without a chance to experience the normal give-and-take of schoolyard play, David remained more childish than his years. His classmates were not helped to understand his problems; some teased him because he still looked and acted "different."

Because of David's problems with outsiders and classmates, for high school his parents decided to send him to the Kentucky School for the Blind. There, his biosocial, cognitive, and psychosocial development all advanced: David learned to wrestle and swim, studied algebra with large-print books, and made friends with people whose vision was worse than his. He mastered not only the regular curriculum but also specialized skills, such as how to travel independently in the city and how to cook and clean for himself. In his senior year he was accepted for admission by a large university in his home state. As you may remember from page 3, David calls his college experience an adversity. But when he finally graduated, he did so with a double major in Russian and German. He has since received a master's degree in German. His current status, and some reflections on his development, are noted at the end of this chapter.

*The In Person box in each chapter (always with a gold background) is designed to focus on one or two developing persons, with details and quotations illustrating the fact that the science of human development is directly and personally relevant.

Some Complications

In actual practice, scientific investigation is less straightforward than these five steps would suggest. The linkages between question, hypothesis, test, and conclusion are sometimes indirect, and the design and execution of research are influenced by (fallible) human judgment (Bauer, 1992; Howard, 1996). Human values tend to guide the choice of which topics to examine, which methods to use, and how to interpret the results. Minimizing the effects of such individual human values on research is always a challenge.

Further, there is always a question of whether researchers are aware of all the relevant **variables**—quantities that may differ, or vary, during an investigation. People vary in sex, age, education, ethnicity, economic status, nationality, values, jobs, family background, personality—the list could go on and on. Moreover, developmental researchers must deal with both *intrapersonal variation,* which is variation within one person from day to day, and *interpersonal variation,* which is variation between people or between groups of people. The two kinds of variation are not always easily distinguished.

Partly because of this complexity, certain controversies echo throughout the study of development, each time with different issues and questions—and often with different responses:

- *Nature/nurture.* How much and which aspects of development are affected by genes and how much by environment?
- *Continuity/discontinuity.* How much of human growth builds gradually on previous development, and how much transformation occurs suddenly?
- *Difference/deficit.* When a person develops differently from most other people, when is that difference considered diversity to be celebrated and when is it considered a problem to be corrected?

Each of these controversies is further explained and explored throughout this text. (See the Subject Index for specifics.)

Two other issues seem contentious to those unfamiliar with developmental study, though they are not issues for developmentalists:

- *Religion/science.* Do the tenets of religious faith and the methods of science necessarily conflict?
- *Individual/society:* Can we study the individual person without studying the family, the community, and the culture?

To both of these questions, the answer from scientists who study development is no. Religion and science are complementary, not conflicting (Gould, 1999), and individuals are inextricably involved with their social group (Cole, 1999).

RESEARCH METHODS

Between the questions developmental scientists ask and the answers they find lies their methodology—not only the steps of the scientific method but also the specific strategies used to gather and analyze data. These strategies are critical because "the ways that you attempt to clarify phenomena in large measure determine the worth of the solution" (Cairns & Cairns, 1994). In other words, *how* research is designed affects the *validity* (does it measure what it purports to measure?), *accuracy* (are the measurements correct?), *generalizability* (does it apply to other

variable   Any quantity, characteristic, or action that can differ between individuals, situations, or groups, or even within one individual from moment to moment.

❗ **Response for Health Professionals (from page 14):** As you can see from the text, the immigrant family's biggest concern might be about physical survival; the professional family's might be about intellectual achievement. In thinking about this, you can derive additional expectations: The immigrant parents would have more questions about nourishment, weight gain, illnesses, and crying; and the professional parents would have many questions about the possibility of mental retardation, finding good child care, language learning, and educational toys.

populations and situations?), and *usefulness* (can it solve real-life problems?) of the conclusions.

Some general strategies to make research valid, accurate, and useful are described in Appendix A, at the back of this book. Other strategies (e.g., statistical significance, correlation) will be described soon. Now we turn to specific methods of testing hypotheses: observations, experiments, surveys, and case studies.

Observation

scientific observation The unobtrusive watching and recording of subjects' behavior, either in the laboratory or in a natural setting.

An excellent method to test hypotheses regarding human development is **scientific observation**—that is, observing and recording, in a systematic and unbiased manner, what people do. Observations often occur in a naturalistic setting, such as at home, in a workplace, or on a public street. Typically, the observing scientist tries to be as unobtrusive as possible, so that the people being studied (the research subjects) act as they normally do.

Observation can also occur in a laboratory. In this setting, the scientists sometimes are not visibly present at all; they may sit behind one-way windows that allow them to peer, unnoticed, into the experimental room, or they may record data with a video camera placed on the wall. In the laboratory, scientists study topics ranging from the rate and duration of eye contact between infant and caregiver to the patterns of dominance and submission that emerge as an entire family discusses its vacation plans.

As you have already read, among the influences scientists particularly hope to understand are the effects of cultural backgrounds. Naturalistic observation is a good way to begin research on this topic, because when people of various ethnicities are all in the same setting, ethnic diversities may appear. For example, when Anglo American and Mexican American children in the same preschool classes are studied, the general finding of such research is that preschool children usually behave in similar ways no matter what their ancestry: They play together more than they play alone, and they rarely fight. A secondary finding from naturalistic observation is a slight trend toward ethnic differences (see the Research Report for details).

Do Not Disturb: Science in Progress Does any 6-month-old understand that cups go on saucers, that circles are not squares, and that mothers know the answers when a child does not? In this laboratory observation, one scientist elicits the answers while another videotapes the results for later analysis.

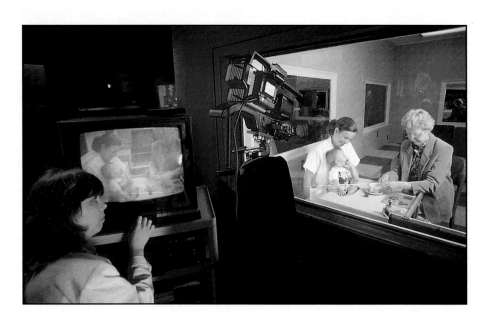

SOCIAL INVOLVEMENT OF 4-YEAR-OLDS

The value of scientific observation becomes clearer with an example. In one study, researchers examined 4-year-olds in various preschool settings in many cities and towns in the United States and Europe. They were concerned with the effect of the quality of child care, particularly on preschoolers' social and linguistic skills.

Generally, similar studies had found that day-care quality affects development but that the results depend not only on the quality of the care but also on the economic and cultural background of the children (Scarr, 1998). Therefore, before the team of researchers could replicate and extend earlier research, they had to test another specific hypothesis—that the children's ethnic background would affect the way they got along with other children. The researchers needed to prove or disprove this hypothesis and then, if necessary, take ethnic differences into account before they could draw conclusions about the impact of, say, Head Start versus private preschools. (Since many children in Head Start are members of racial or ethnic minorities, the researchers might need to distinguish between results attributable to ethnicity and results attributable to type of preschool.)

This research study is a continuing project that is investigating a number of issues in several nations using a variety of methods. We look here at one small part of it, which was focused on naturalistic observation of 96 European American and 96 Latino American children (Farver & Frosch, 1996).

The Research Procedure

Remember that naturalistic observation must be systematic, performed by a trained observer who is as unobtrusive as possible. In this study, the researchers spent "considerable time in the classrooms familiarizing themselves and playing with the children before the data collection began." Thus, the children were accustomed to the observers when they collected data during normal preschool activities. The data were recorded methodically: Each observer watched a single child for exactly 30 seconds and then immediately took 30

seconds to record what that child had done. Each observer collected data on one child for 10 minutes (ten 30-second observations interspersed with ten 30-second written descriptions) and then shifted to another child, according to a predetermined schedule, until each targeted child had been observed for eighty 30-second periods.

The social traits the scientists were looking for had been operationally defined—that is, described in a precise behavioral manner so that a trained observer could record whether that trait had been observed or not. Specifically, their observations were coded as to whether, during each half-minute, the child was

■ *solitary*, defined as unoccupied or engaged in an activity alone
■ *social*, defined as engaged in an activity with a partner or group of children
■ *aggressive*, defined as engaged in verbal aggression, such as name-calling, teasing, or quarreling, or engaged in physical aggression, such as pinching, hitting, pushing, poking, or grabbing another child

Since one hypothesis to be tested was the impact of ethnicity, other variables, such as age, SES, sex, type of program, and location, were held constant. To be specific, the children were all 4-year-olds from low-income families. Half the members of each group were boys and half were girls, and the children attended many types of programs (Head Start, private day care, public preschool) in several cities in the United States (Newark, Detroit, San José, and Los Angeles).

If you were one of the researchers connected with this project, would you expect that, in this situation, the children would be mainly social, solitary, or aggressive? Would you hypothesize ethnic differences? As you can see in Table 1.1, most of the time these 4-year-olds socialized well. In fact, the difference between the average amount of time spent in social and in solitary activity was significant. This finding is likely to be found in every similar preschool group. You can also see

A Limitation of Observation

Naturalistic observation is an excellent research method, but it has one major limitation: It does not indicate what causes the behavior we observe. If we observe that one mother spanks her children and another does not, or one employee works intensely and another slacks off, *why* do such differences appear? Some studies, including the one described in the Research Report, show that children of one ethnic background do not behave exactly like children of another background. Are such differences genetic, historical, economic, cultural? Even if there were dramatic differences between two ethnic groups, naturalistic observation

table **1.1**	**Time Spent in Social Behaviors**		
	Various Behaviors (percentage of time)		
Ethnic Group of Preschoolers	Social	Solitary	Aggressive
Latino Americans	70	28	2
European Americans	77	22	1
Average (both groups)	73.5	25	1.5

Source: Farver & Frosch, 1996.

Nonsignificant Ethnic Differences The important finding of this study is that 4-year-olds in preschools were pretty much alike, spending most of their time socializing and one-fourth of their time alone. There were some cultural influences, but these were very small compared to the impact of witnessing a riot—as the Changing Policy box explains on pages 24–25.

small ethnic differences in the rates of aggression. To interpret these findings, you need to understand something else about research: the concept of statistical significance.

Statistical Significance

Whenever researchers find a difference between two groups, they have to consider the possibility that the difference occurred purely by chance. For instance, if the researchers in this observational study looked only at five Anglo and five Latino children, the two most aggressive children, by chance, might both be of the same ethnicity. This would seriously distort the conclusions. Casual observers often judge a whole group on the basis of one or two memorable individuals, but scientists must avoid this mistake.

To determine whether or not the results of research are simply coincidence, researchers apply a test of **statistical significance**. The mathematical formula for computing significance includes many factors, including the sample size, the amount of variation within each group, and the difference between the averages of the two groups. Using the formula, the scientists calculate the *significance level,* a numerical indication of exactly how likely it is that the results reflect true differences, not random variation. (Note that the word "significance" here means

statistical significance A mathematical analysis, based on a formula, that indicates that the results of research are not likely to have occurred by chance.

something quite different from its usual sense; it refers to the validity of specific results, not to the scientific value of the study.) Generally, results are statistically significant if there is less than 1 possibility in 20 that they occurred by chance—that is, a significance level of 1/20, or .05. Some results are significant at the .01 level (only 1 possibility in 100 of occurring by chance) or the .001 level (1 possibility in 1,000). The ethnic differences in social behaviors just reported were *not* significant in the statistical sense of the term. No firm conclusions can be drawn without more research on a larger number of children, whose behavior will show if the particular results are just a fluke.

However, the study did suggest a trend toward ethnic differences in sociability. The Latino Americans were slightly more likely to be solitary than the European Americans and less likely to be social. Although the rates of aggression were very low, Anglo children were even less aggressive (1%) than Latino children (2%). These slight ethnic differences were apparent in children from several cities: The 64 children from Los Angeles (half Latino, half Anglo) acted very similarly to the 128 children from the other cities, an important detail discussed in the Changing Policy box on pages 24–25.

*Each chapter includes a Research Report (always with a blue background), in which the specifics of one or a few pertinent scientific studies are described in order to illustrate the process of research. Usually a chart or table of the results is included, as well as an explanation of some specific aspect of the scientific method, in this case, statistical significance.

allows us to conclude only that one variable (ethnic heritage in the Research Report) *correlates* with another variable (social play), *not* that one causes the other.

Correlation

A **correlation** is said to exist between two variables if one of them is likely—or less likely—to occur when the other variable occurs. For instance, there is a correlation between wealth and attending college: The richer your family, the more likely you are to go to college.

correlation A relation between two variables such that one is likely (or unlikely) to occur when the other occurs or one is likely to increase (or decrease) in value when the other increases (or decreases).

Fighting Over a Cat Naturalistic observation reveals that children are sometimes cruel to animals as well as to each other, but it does not explain why. Laboratory experiments, however, have shown that one factor is that children have observed cruelty and aggression in others. Chances are these children have seen someone else try to settle a dispute over a possession in a similar fashion.

❓ **Especially for Social Scientists:** There is a positive correlation between the number of storks living in certain towns of France and the birth rates of those towns. Does that prove that storks bring babies?

Accurate interpretation of correlations requires that two points be kept in mind. First, the fact that two variables are correlated does not mean that they occur together in every instance. Some wealthy people never finish high school, and many impoverished students go to college.

Second, correlation does not prove cause. Even when two variables are strongly (or highly) correlated, we should not, even must not, say that one variable causes the other. The correlation between education and wealth does not necessarily imply that having more money leads directly to more education. The reverse may occur: Well-educated people may become wealthier, in which case education leads to the wealth that makes education more possible for the descendants of wealthy people. Or there may be a third variable, perhaps intelligence or family values, that accounts for the level of both wealth and education. These possibilities are summed up in Table 1.2.

A correlation is *positive* if the occurrence of one variable makes it *more* likely that the other will occur. A correlation is *negative* if the occurrence of one makes it *less* likely that the other will occur. Because of the way correlation is calculated, the highest positive correlation is expressed as +1.0 and the greatest negative correlation as –1.0. Most actual correlations are neither so high nor so low: A correlation of 0.5 is impressive. Two variables that are not related at all have a correlation of zero, or .0, (exactly halfway between +1.0 and –1.0).

In the preschool study described in detail in the Research Report, we cannot tell what caused what. For example, did these children spend most of their time playing happily together because that is the nature of 4-year-olds? Or do good preschool programs provide many opportunities for social interaction and manage to keep aggression to a minimum? More to the point, what caused the trend in ethnic differences? It could be genes, family, or language. In fact, further study could reveal it to be random variation that would disappear instead of replicate. As the Research Report explains, tests of statistical significance indicate how likely it is that the results are the product of chance.

Given our recognition of the importance of social context, yet another hypothesis is that neighborhood is the crucial variable, with neighborhood differences as the cause of the ethnic differences. To answer questions about cause and effect, neither observation nor correlation is definitive. To demonstrate cause and effect, we need an experiment.

table **1.2**	**Possible Explanations for a Positive Correlation Between Wealth and Education**
Possible explanation:	More income produces more education.
Possible explanation:	More education produces more income.
Possible explanation:	Family values produce both income and education.
Conclusion:	Correlation indicates connection, but not causation.

The Experiment

experiment A research method in which the scientist deliberately causes changes in one variable (called the *independent variable*) and then observes and records the resulting changes in some other variable (called the *dependent variable*).

independent variable The variable that is added or changed in an experiment.

dependent variable The variable that might change as a result of changing or adding the independent variable in an experiment.

An **experiment** is an investigation designed to untangle cause from effect. In the social sciences, experimenters typically expose a group of people to a particular treatment or condition to see if their behavior changes as a result. In technical terms, experimenters manipulate an **independent variable** (the imposed treatment or special condition). They then note how that change affects the specific behavior they are studying, which is called the **dependent variable.** Thus the independent variable is the new, special treatment; the dependent variable is the response (which may or may not be affected by the independent variable). Finding out which independent variables affect which dependent variables, and how great that effect may be, is the purpose of an experiment. (See the Changing Policy box on page 24 for an example.)

By comparing changes in a dependent variable that occur after an independent (experimental) variable has been imposed, researchers are often able to uncover the link between cause and effect. This is the reason experiments are performed: because no other research method can so accurately pinpoint what leads to what.

But one question always remains: To what degree do the findings from an artificial experimental situation apply in the real world? A major problem with many experiments is that the controlled situation, with the scientist manipulating the independent variable, is different in important ways from normal, everyday life.

In addition, all experiments (except those with very young children) are hampered when the participants know they are research subjects. Subjects, especially older adults, may attempt to produce the results they believe the experimenter is looking for, or, especially if they are adolescents, they may try to undermine the study. Even if the subjects do not react in either of these ways, almost all experimental subjects are more nervous than they otherwise would be.

The last part of the preschool experiment described in the Changing Policy box avoided the pitfalls of being artificial because it was an "experiment in nature." By using young children, it also minimized the effect of subject awareness. However, another problem is that most experiments are of very limited duration, even though actual human development takes years to form, change, and transform.

All these limitations add layers of potential artificiality to experimental research. For that reason, an experiment is most valuable in developmental study when it is combined with other methods rather than relied on exclusively. Indeed, the results of the preschool study were strengthened by other research, published and unpublished, observational and experimental. This is what scientists do when a particular question becomes important to answer: They combine observations and experiments, in natural "field" conditions and in the controlled conditions of the laboratory. Usually the results of these various studies all lead to the same conclusions, and the scientific discovery process moves closer to finding the answer to the crucial question (Anderson et al., 1999). Further, the scientists in this preschool study themselves reexamined the same children 3 years later and found (in research not yet published) that the overall context of the neighborhood affected the children's ongoing temperament, attitudes, and behavior patterns—a conclusion found by other scientists as well (Garbarino & Kostelny, 1997; Rutter et al., 1998).

COMMUNITY VIOLENCE AND AGGRESSIVE CHILDREN

When we are looking at the specifics of the relationship between ethnic context and personality traits, neighborhood of residence might emerge as a particularly promising variable causing people to be shyer or more aggressive than they would be otherwise. Neighborhoods do vary markedly in level of violence, as measured by the number of homicides and serious personal-injury crimes that are reported. Might the level of violence in their community affect the level of aggression in young children?

Violence also correlates with the economic and ethnic makeup of neighborhoods: Poor minority neighborhoods have far more violence than middle-class majority neighborhoods. But low income and ethnic status are not the only relevant variables. At least among adults, when neighborhoods of similar ethnicity and poverty are compared, behavior seems affected by the stability and collective harmony of daily life in each particular community (Sampson & Loeb, 1997). But all this is merely correlation. Is there a direct effect on the personality and play patterns of 4-year-olds caused by the level of violence among adults in the community? Only an experiment can prove cause and effect.

Obviously, it would be unethical to increase the violence in a community in order to perform this experiment. It would be ethical to reduce violence, but neighborhoods rarely become less violent to the sudden, dramatic, and pervasive degree that would provide the contrast necessary for good research. Unexpectedly, in the case of the preschool study described in the Research Report, external forces provided the researchers with a dramatic increase in violence. That increase became an independent variable (Farver & Frosch, 1996).

Just as the researchers had completed the first part of their study, several Los Angeles police officers who had been videotaped beating an African American suspect, Rodney King, were acquitted by a jury. This variable (the verdict) dramatically affected another variable: the rate of violent crime. Los Angeles erupted in riots lasting several days. Normal life stopped, stores were burned and looted, innocent people were beaten. The streets echoed with gunfire while police patrolled overhead in helicopters.

During the same time period, normal life continued in the three other preschool cities. Fortuitously, the scientists in all the cities of the study were scheduled at that time to ask the children to tell make-believe stories about a set of toy figures:

> Children were taken individually to a familiar, private room where toys suggestive of imaginative play were placed on a large table. The toys included Smurf and Sesame Street characters, a car, four family figures, two horses, farm animals, and various sized Lego blocks. Children were told that they could play with the toys in any way they wished, but that they had to tell the experimenter what they were doing with the toys while they were playing. [Farver & Frosch, 1996]

Children whose home addresses correlated with police reports of areas with high incidence of shooting, burning, and looting told much more aggressive stories than the children from other neighborhoods and cities, no matter what the ethnicity of the children. For example, the riot-exposed children were twice as likely to include unfriendly characters in their stories and four times as likely to include aggressive characters. Ethnic differences were much smaller than the differences between the experimental, violence-exposed group, who were 64 Los Angeles children (half Latino and half Anglo), and the 128 children from other cities (again, half Latino and half Anglo). Further, the teachers in Los Angeles reported that their children were much more fearful, withdrawn, or aggressive in the daily play in school than they had been before the riots. This

Other Research Methods

Wherever possible, researchers try to verify and extend the results of scientific study. As you have read, they may do so by replicating previous research with the same methods but with other populations of subjects or by using different methods to investigate the same question. In addition to observation and experimentation, two of these methods are surveys and case studies.

The Survey

survey A research method in which information is collected from a large number of people, through written questionnaires or personal interviews.

In a scientific **survey,** information is collected from a number of people by personal interview, by written questionnaire, or by some other means. This is an easy, quick, and direct way to obtain data. Surveys are espe-

The L.A. Riots This drawing depicts 9-year-old Abdullah Abbar's memories of the spring of 1992 in his Los Angeles neighborhood: flames, bullets, looting, and death. Anyone who thinks children ignore the conditions of their neighborhood needs to look more closely.

was especially true of those children with the most intense exposure.

These results suggest an answer to the question we posed earlier: Four-year-olds *are* affected by violence in their communities. The experience of living in a riot-torn community made preschoolers more aggressive, as well as more fearful, in their thinking and their actions. This experimental finding provides some clues about the cause of the ethnic differences found in naturalistic observations. At least some of the difference in social play found among children from different ethnic groups is the consequence of living in their specific neighborhoods. This conclusion is confirmed by other re-

search on the relationship between neighborhood violence and children's temperament (Garbarino et al., 1992; Jenkins & Bell, 1997; Leavitt & Fox, 1993). It also confirms the effect of context on development. If a particular child or adult behaves in a destructive way, developmentalists may need to work on changing the context as well as the person.

*Each chapter includes a Changing Policy box (always with a green background), designed to report research that is pointed toward historical change—some aspect of human development that either has changed over the past years or may change in the future. Such boxes highlight the effect of past public policy and perhaps the possibility of future political, or cultural, changes.

❶ **Response for Social Scientists (from page 22):** A correlation between two variables may be caused by something other than those variables. Towns with many storks are probably quieter, more spacious, more rural, with more farms; such towns are usually less wealthy and more religious. All these variables might affect their birth rates.

cially useful when scientists want to learn about children, since an obvious way of doing so is to ask parents or teachers about the children. For example, in the preschool study we have discussed in the Research Report and Changing Policy boxes, the researchers asked the preschool teachers a series of questions about each child's social interactions. The teachers' responses confirmed the results of the naturalistic observation. Particularly significant (at the .001 level) were teachers' ratings of the children's hesitancy and shyness—traits that were more likely to be found in the Latino American children than the European American children.

Unfortunately, getting valid data through an interview or questionnaire is more difficult than it seems, because these methods are vulnerable to bias on the part of the researcher and the respondents. In addition, many people who are interviewed give answers that they think

table **1.3**	**Freedom of the Press**	

Do you agree that the United States should allow Communist reporters from other countries to send back the news as they see fit? (Percent answering yes.)

	Age of Respondents	
	18–54	55+
First group	55%	43%
Second group	81%	44%

Source: Knãuper, 1999.

the researcher expects, or that express opinion rather than fact, or that they think will make them seem wise or "good."

For example, in one survey adults in the United States were asked, "Do you think the United States should let Communist newspaper reporters from other countries come in here and send back the news as they see it?" About half answered yes, with younger adults slightly more likely to agree (see Table 1.3). Then the same question was asked of another, similar sample of adults. The second group of younger adults was much more likely than the first group to answer yes (81 percent, compared to 55 percent), while about the same proportion of older adults in the second group as in the first group agreed (44 percent, compared to 43 percent). Why the contrast? The second group were primed by being asked another question first: whether they believed a Communist country "should let American reporters come in and send back the news as they see it" (Knãuper, 1999).

Do these findings indicate that older adults are not only more conservative and less willing to consider fair play but also more willing to reveal these traits? Or is it that they have the wisdom of experience gained during the cold war, as well as the strength of their convictions? Or could it be that younger adults are more logical and consistent when reminded of their convictions? Further research would be needed to determine the correct interpretation of these survey results, but obviously the specific order of the survey questions sometimes makes a significant difference in the answers.

The Case Study

case study A research method that focuses on the life history, attitudes, behavior, and emotions of a single individual.

A **case study** is an intensive study of one individual. Typically, the case study is based on interviews with the subject regarding his or her background, current thinking, and actions; it may also utilize interviews of people who know the individual. Additional case-study material may be obtained through observation, experiments, and standardized tests, such as personality inventories and intelligence tests.

Case studies can provide a wealth of detail, which makes them rich in possible insights. Many developmentalists prefer case studies precisely for that reason: The complexity of a human life is easier to comprehend through the rich *qualitative*, or descriptive, information of a case study than through a study involving sheer numbers, even though statistical significance depends on such *quantitative*, or numerical, data.

However, the collection and interpretation of case-study information reflect the biases as well as the wisdom of the researcher. Even when a case study is carefully interpreted, the conclusions apply with certainty to only one person. Nevertheless, the case study has three important uses:

- to provide a provocative starting point for other research
- to understand a particular individual very well
- to illustrate general truths, as David's story does

Remember, however, that no confident conclusions about people in general can be drawn from a sample size of 1, or even 10 or 20, no matter how deep and detailed the study is.

Clearly, there are many ways to gather developmental data, and each method compensates for the weaknesses of the others. Researchers can observe people in naturalistic or laboratory settings, or they can experimentally elicit reactions under controlled conditions or take advantage of unusual natural experiments. They can survey hundreds or even thousands of people, or interview a smaller number of people in great depth, or study one life in detail. Because each method has weaknesses, none of them provide data with ample scope and precision to merit broad conclusions. But each brings researchers closer to the issues and answers. Together they can prove or disprove theories and hypotheses.

Figure 1.6 Patterns of Developmental Growth.
Many patterns of developmental growth have been discovered by careful research. Although linear (or near-linear) progress seems most common (people do get smarter as they get older, don't they?), scientists now find that almost no aspect of human change follows the linear pattern exactly.

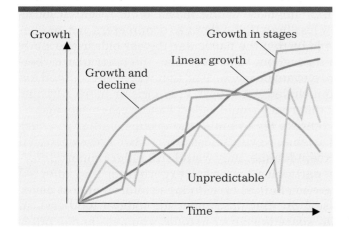

Studying Changes Over Time

Remember the definition on page 4: The science of human development seeks to understand how and why people change, and how and why they remain the same, as they grow older. Accordingly, for research to be truly developmental, it must be able to deal with things that change and continue *over time*.

Change is not always direct and linear; development might occur in fits and starts, zigzags, steps, or other ways as well (see Figure 1.6). Developmental scientists need to design their research so that it includes time, or age, as a factor. Usually they accomplish this with either of two basic research designs, cross-sectional and longitudinal.

Cross-Sectional Research

The more convenient, and thus more common, way to include age in a developmental study is by designing **cross-sectional research.** In a cross-sectional study, groups of people who differ in age but share other important characteristics (such as level of education, socioeconomic status, and ethnic background) are compared with regard to the variable under investigation. You just saw this in the discussion of the survey of attitudes about freedom of reporters. Younger adults were compared with older adults who were similar in other respects besides age, such as nationality and gender. Any differences on the dependent variable found between one age group and another are, presumably, the result of age-related developmental processes.

Cross-sectional design thus seems simple enough. However, it is very difficult to ensure that the various comparison groups are similar in every

cross-sectional research A research design in which groups of people, each group different from the others in age but similar to them in other important ways, are compared.

Compare These with Those The apparent similarity of these two groups in gender and ethnic composition makes them potential candidates for cross-sectional research. However, before we could be sure that any differences between the two groups are the result of age, we would have to be sure the groups are alike in other ways, such as socioeconomic background and religious upbringing.

background variable except age. Suppose a group of 10-year-olds are found to be taller by about 12 inches (30 centimeters) than a comparable group of 6-year-olds. It seems reasonable to conclude that during the 4 years between ages 6 and 10, children gain a foot in height. However, even such an obvious conclusion might be wrong. In fact, other research shows that most children grow less than that—about 25 centimeters, not 30—between those ages. It could be that the particular 10-year-olds in the study were better nourished throughout their lives than the particular 6-year-olds or had some other relevant characteristic that was not accounted for. Certainly, if one group included more boys than girls or more Africans than Asians, the height difference would reflect factors other than age.

Of course, good scientists try to make the groups similar in every relevant background variable. Nevertheless, even if two cross-sectional groups are identical except for age, they would still reflect cohort differences because of the particular historical experiences that affected each age group. Changes in medical care (today's children almost never get "childhood" diseases), in diet (less meat for today's toddlers), in housing conditions (play space is scarcer in today's homes), and in other historical factors might skew cross-sectional results, even for a biological variable such as height. If 20-year-olds want to know what their lives will be like when they are 80, they should not simply examine the lives of a group of 80-year-olds who are similar to them in such characteristics as genetics, socioeconomic status, ethnic background, and education. That is because by the year 2060, many other factors will have changed to affect how elderly people will be living at that time.

Longitudinal Research

longitudinal research A research design in which the same people are studied over a long time (which might range from months to decades) to measure both change and stability as they age.

To help discover if age, rather than some other background or historical variable, is really the reason for an apparent developmental change, researchers can study the *same individuals* over a long period of time. Because a **longitudinal research** design allows researchers to compare information about the same people at different ages, it eliminates the effects of background variables, even those that researchers are not aware of. If we know how tall a group of children are at 6 years old and at 10 years old, we can say definitively how much they grew, on average, during the 4 intervening years.

A Longitudinal Look at Kirsten Longitudinal research is ideal for discovering, as the definition of developmental study on page 2 states, "how and why people change, and how and why they remain the same, as they grow older." These photographs of Kirsten at 5 months, 18 months, 5 years, 8 years, and 12 years illustrate this well. In some ways, change is obvious—from baldness to chest-length hair, for instance. Similar changes can be seen for almost all children, although Kirsten's pattern was somewhat unusual since she didn't really start to grow a full head of hair until she was almost 3 years old. In other ways, continuity is clear: She is emotionally engaging at every age. This is most obvious when, as a toddler, she hid something forbidden from her parents, but it is apparent in the other snapshots as well.

Now, at age 13, it is not surprising that she is distinctive in predictable ways, such as her ballet, writing, social sensitivity, and cheerleading. She is also typical of her cohort in other ways—she likes boys, computers, and television—as cross-sectional research would show as well. Longitudinal research (and, in this case, even longitudinal photos) also helps spot the impact of unusual events, which are not typical of either that child or children in general.

❓ *Observational Quiz (answer on page 32): Kirsten's parents got divorced. Can you spot when?*

Longitudinal research is particularly useful in studying development over a long age span (Elder, 1998). It has yielded valuable and sometimes surprising findings on many topics, including the following:

- *Children's adjustment to divorce* (The negative effects linger, especially for school-age and older boys [Hetherington & Clingempeel, 1992].)
- *The role of fathers in child development* (Even 50 years ago, fathers were far more influential regarding their children's future happiness than the stereotype of the distant dad implies [Snarey, 1993].)
- *The consequences of an early delay in motor or language abilities* (Motor delays often disappear; language delays usually persist [Silva, 1996].)
- *The effects of enlisting in the military on juvenile delinquents* (Surprisingly positive achievement occurred [Sampson & Laub, 1996].)
- *The effects of menopause* (It may temporarily, but not longitudinally, increase depression, and even the temporary effects occur in only a minority of women [Avis, 1999].)

Repeated longitudinal research can uncover not only the degree of change but also the process of change. Do children learn to read suddenly, by "breaking the code," or gradually? The answer could not be found by simply comparing preliterate 4-year-olds and fluent 8-year-olds. However, following children month by month revealed the answer: Reading is usually a gradual process, although certain aspects can be grasped quite suddenly (Adams, et al., 1998).

Clearly, longitudinal research is "a design of choice from the developmental perspective" (Cairns & Cairns, 1994). You will see the results of many longitudinal studies throughout this book. Nevertheless, this design has some serious drawbacks. Over time, some subjects may withdraw, move far away, or die. These changes can skew the ultimate results because those who disappear may be different (perhaps more rebellious, perhaps of lower SES) from those who stay. In addition, some people who remain may change because of their involvement in the research study ("improving" over a series of tests, for example, only because they become increasingly familiar with the tests); this makes the results of the study less applicable to the average developing person, who is not in such a study.

Perhaps the biggest problem of all is that longitudinal investigations are very time-consuming and expensive. They involve far more commitment from scientists and funding agencies than does cross-sectional research.

Cross-Sequential Research

As you can see, both cross-sectional research and longitudinal research allow scientists to look at development over time, but each design has flaws. Because these two methods tend to make up for each other's disadvantages, scientists have devised various ways to use the two together (Hartman & George, 1999). The simplest is **cross-sequential research** (also referred to as *cohort-sequential* or *time-sequential* research) (Schaie, 1996). With this design, researchers first study several groups of people of different ages (a cross-sectional approach) and then follow those groups longitudinally.

Using cross-sequential design, we can compare findings for a group of, say, 50-year-olds with findings for the same individuals at age 30, as well as with findings for groups who were 50 a decade or two earlier and groups who are 30 years old now. Cross-sequential research thus allows scientists to disentangle differences related to chronological age from those related to historical period. This method has provided a wealth of surprising information on adult intelligence (see Chapter 21).

cross-sequential research   A research design that combines cross-sectional and longitudinal research. Groups of people of different ages are studied over time, to distinguish differences related to age from differences related to historical period. (Also called *cohort-sequential research* or *time-sequential research*.)

ETHICS AND SCIENCE

Every scientist must be concerned with the ethics of conducting and reporting research. At the most basic level, researchers who study humans must ensure that their subjects are not harmed by the research process and that subjects' participation is voluntary and confidential. In developmental studies, the need to protect the participants is especially acute when they are children. Accordingly, the Society for Research in Child Development (SRCD, 1996) lists the following ethical precautions:

- The investigator should use no research operation that may harm the child either physically or psychologically. . . .
- Before seeking consent or assent from the child, the investigator should inform the child of all features of the research that may affect his or her willingness to participate and should answer the child's questions in terms appropriate to the child's comprehension. [The child is free to] discontinue participation at any time.
- . . . Investigators working with infants should take special effort to explain the research procedures to the parents and be especially sensitive to any indicators of discomfort in the infant. . . .
- The investigators should keep in confidence all information obtained about research participants.

These same general principles—do no harm, secure informed consent, explain the procedures, and keep confidential all personal information about participants—are endorsed by researchers who study adults as well, indeed by scientists who study any aspect of human behavior. Worldwide, many governments and professional organizations require careful attention to the consent, confidentiality, and welfare of participants in research. In the United States, each college or university has an institutional review board (IRB) that examines all research plans before any study can begin (Fisher, 1999).

Such ethical guidelines—developed and enforced partly as a result of abuses of the past—deal with only part of the problem. For contemporary researchers, the thorniest issues arise not during but before and after the research. Every proposed study must be analyzed ahead of time to see if its benefits will outweigh its costs in time, money, and even momentary distress.

In human development, the possibility of distress varies with the subject's age and condition. A young child may become upset by a few minutes of separation from a caregiver; older children are more susceptible to loss of self-esteem and privacy; parents of adolescents may not want anyone to ask their offspring anything about sex, drugs, or discipline; older adults may be troubled by tests of intellectual ability. Often, the studies with the greatest potential social benefit involve the most vulnerable groups, such as children who have been maltreated or adults who have cancer. In fact, in research on drugs to combat AIDS, some groups (women, children, drug addicts) were excluded as subjects because of the possibility that the experimental drugs might do them some unexpected harm; as a result, ironically, the first treatments proven effective had never been tested on the people who might need them most (Kahn et al., 1998).

The Implications of Research

Once an investigation has been completed, additional ethical issues arise concerning the reporting of research findings. An obvious breach of scientific ethics is to "cook" the data, arranging the numbers so that a particular conclusion seems the only logical one. Sometimes this can be done unintentionally, which is one reason replication is so important. Deliberate deception regarding the data is cause for ostracism from the scientific community, dismissal from a teaching or research position, and, in some cases, criminal prosecution. Further, "in reporting results, . . . the investigator should be mindful of the social, political, and human implications of his [or her] research" (SRCD, 1996).

What does "mindful" of implications mean? An example makes it clear. A recent storm of controversy was evoked by a study of college students who had become sexually involved with adults before reaching the legal age of consent (Rind et al., 1998). The research correctly reported that the consequences depended on many factors, but some readers of the journal article took this to mean that the research implied that adult sexual involvement with minors was sometimes acceptable. The actual article was a *meta-analysis,* which is a compilation of data from many other sources, so no participants were directly involved. However, talk-show hosts and political candidates condemned the study—not because of its results, but because of their own misinterpretation of it. Such misinterpretation occurred for many reasons, but one reason was that the article's authors were not sufficiently mindful of the inferences that other people might draw.

❶ *Answer to Observational Quiz (from page 29):*
Kirsten's parents ended their marriage about when Kirsten was 8 (fourth picture). Signs of this disruption are that she is thoughtful, unsmiling, with arms held close.

In another research project, a group of college students who listened to Mozart before taking a cognitive test scored higher than another group who heard no music (Rausher et al., 1993; Rausher & Shaw, 1998). This "Mozart effect" was also misinterpreted; the governor of Georgia ordered that all newborns receive a free CD of Mozart music in order to improve their intelligence, and Florida passed a law requiring every infant day-care center in that state to play classical music in order to get state funding. The actual initial study was irrelevant to infants, and the results for college students could not be replicated in later research (Steele et al., 1999; Narais, 1999).

As these examples demonstrate, even when the scientific method is carefully used and proper safeguards for the participants are in place, ethics require a concern for the implications of the results. Conclusions must be honestly and carefully reported; hasty generalizations based on one study are often false.

Finally, every reader of this book should consider the most important ethical issue of all: Are scientists studying the issues that are crucial to human development? Do we know enough about infant growth that we can ensure that every human reaches full potential? Do we know enough about human sexual urges and actions to prevent sexually transmitted diseases, stop unwanted pregnancy, halt sexual abuse, and cure infertility? Do we know enough about stress, poverty, and prejudice to enable humans to be happier and less depressed? Do we know enough about learning throughout life to enable everyone to be as smart as they can be? The answer to all these questions is a loud *NO!* Sometimes such moral issues as informed consent and confidentiality distract us from the larger ethical concerns, thus depriving the very people who might benefit most.

David's Story Again

I wrestled with these very issues when I originally drafted David's story for an earlier edition of this book. I could see that his story would convey both the struggle and the hope of human development. But would publishing it hurt him in some way? I first asked my brother and sister-in-law. They said it might be okay, depending on what I wrote. I wrote the section, showed it to them, and they corrected it in minor ways.

Then I asked David, who was an adolescent at the time and was given to unexpected, contrary behavior. He took the draft of my manuscript to his room, read it with his magnifying glass, and told me, in a matter-of-fact voice, "It would be all right with me if you published it." Later I heard that he discussed with his parents some aspects of his infancy that they had never told him, including the extent of his many congenital disabilities.

❷ **Especially for Educators:** Although one case study is never enough to make a generalization, what does David's story suggest about testing severely handicapped preschoolers?

Over the years, David has become more and more interested in his story in this book. He has been a guest speaker at my college to answer students' questions about his life, he has attended my publisher's sales meetings, he has learned about editing from my editors, and he is eager to answer my questions to update each edition.

One basic lesson in the ethics of research is to look very closely at the responses of particular subjects, rather than impose preconceptions and assumptions about the effects of research. In David's case, I am grateful to report, year after year he has been proud to be included. But the ethical role of the scientist goes far beyond simply doing no harm. It

Three Brothers Studying the development of other people is fascinating in many ways, not the least of which is that no human is untouched by understanding the personal story of another. I have learned many things from David, shown in this recent family photo with his two older brothers, Bill (left) and Michael (right). One is the role of siblings: Bill and Michael protected their younger brother, but David also taught them, making them more nurturant than most young men in their community. I know this firsthand—these boys were the closest thing my daughters had to big brothers, and they tolerated teasing that some older cousins would have put a stop to.

entails being mindful of the "social, political, and human implications" of the research. My obligation is step 5 of the scientific method: to publish the results so that others can learn. Accordingly, here is the latest update of David's story.

Looking Forward

David's worst problems are now behind him. In the biosocial domain, doctors have helped improve the quality of his life: An artificial eye has replaced the blind one; a back brace has helped his posture; and surgery has corrected a misaligned jaw, improving his appearance and his speech. In the cognitive domain, the once severely "retarded" preschooler is beginning a career as a translator (an interesting choice for someone who had to listen very carefully to what people said because he could not read their facial expressions). And in the psychosocial domain, the formerly self-absorbed child is now an outgoing young man, eager for friendship. Although he still lives at home with his parents, he looks forward to "breaking away" soon.

This is not to suggest that David's life is all smooth sailing. In fact, every day presents its struggles, and David, like everyone else, has his moments of self-doubt and depression. As he once confided to me:

> I sometimes have extremely pejorative thoughts . . . dreams of vivid symbolism. In one, I am playing on a pinball machine that is all broken—glass besmirched, legs tilted and wobbly, the plunger knob loose. I have to really work at it to get a decent score.

Yet David never loses heart, at least not for long. He continues to "really work" on his life, no matter what, and bit by bit his "score" improves.

In looking at David's life thus far, we can see how domains and contexts interact to affect development, both positively and negatively. We can also see the importance of science and its application. For example, without research that demonstrated the crucial role of sensory stimulation in infant development, David's parents might not have been taught how to keep his young mind active. Without the efforts of hundreds of developmental scientists who proved that schools could teach even severely handicapped children, David might never have learned to read. He might have led a homebound and restricted life, as many children with his problems once did. Indeed, many children with David's initial level of disability have spent their entire lives in institutions that provide only custodial care and died before reaching age 30.

David's story does more than illustrate domains and contexts. His life illustrates a universal truth: None of us is simply a product of our past history and present setting. Each person is an individual who uniquely reacts to, and acts upon, the constellation of contexts that impinges on his or her development. And each person is buffeted, as David was, by all the genetic and contextual circumstances of life; but each person also exerts a butterfly effect, with some small event often becoming a turning point in the developmental path. The remaining chapters in this book describe when and how such crucial events occur.

SUMMARY

THE STUDY OF HUMAN DEVELOPMENT

1. The study of human development explores how and why people change, and how and why they remain the same, as they grow older. Development involves many academic and practical disciplines, especially biology, education, and psychology.

2. The life-span perspective views human development at every age as an ongoing process. This perspective emphasizes the multidirectional, multicontextual, multicultural, multidisciplinary, and plastic nature of development.

3. Development can be divided into three domains: the biosocial, the cognitive, and the psychosocial. While this division makes it easy to study the intricacies of development, researchers note that development in each domain is influenced by the other two, as body, mind, and emotion always affect one another.

CONTEXTS AND SYSTEMS

4. An ecological, or contextual, approach to development focuses on interactions between the individual and the various settings in which development occurs. Some of those settings involve the individual's physical surroundings—the layout of the neighborhood, the nature of the climate, and so on. Most settings, however, concern the people who create the social context for the individual's development.

5. Social contexts change over time, as changing historical events and conditions (the historical context) reshape the circumstances and perspectives surrounding development. There is quite a difference between being a child in an era when serious disease often meant death and being one when, except for accidents, almost every child is expected to reach old age.

6. Development is also strongly affected by a person's socioeconomic status, cultural values, and ethnicity. The influences of these social contexts often overlap, reinforcing and sometimes contradicting one another. Ultimately, however, each individual's path is unique, influenced but not determined by these contexts.

DEVELOPMENTAL STUDY AS A SCIENCE

7. The scientific method is used by developmental researchers. They first pose a research question; then they develop a hypoth-

esis, collect data, and finally test the hypothesis and draw conclusions based on the data.

8. Often, the final step of the scientific method is to publish the research in sufficient detail so that others can evaluate the conclusions and, if they choose to, replicate the research or extend the findings with research of their own. This is essential because conclusions based on a single study are often controversial and vulnerable to misinterpretation.

RESEARCH METHODS

9. One common method of gathering developmental research data is observation, which provides valid data but does not pinpoint cause and effect. The laboratory experiment indicates causes but is not necessarily applicable to daily life.

10. Surveys and case studies are also useful means of collecting data, but each is easily distorted unless the scientific method is carefully followed.

11. Developmental research is usually designed to detect change over time. A cross-sectional research design compares groups of people of different ages; a longitudinal design (which is preferable but more difficult to carry out) studies the same individuals over a long time period. Scientists combine both designs in cross-sequential research, which may provide more comprehensive findings.

ETHICS AND SCIENCE

12. The ethics of conducting and reporting research are a concern of every scientist. Before a study begins, its potential benefits must be weighed against its potential costs in time, money, and distress to participants. During a study, the researcher is ethically required to ensure that subjects are not harmed, that their participation is always voluntary, and that all information about them is kept confidential.

13. After a study has been completed, the researcher should take steps to ensure that the findings are honestly reported and are not subject to misinterpretation. This is not always done, partly because members of the public sometimes seize on a preliminary finding and exaggerate its significance.

14. No person is simply a product of his or her past history or present setting. Development is ongoing for each of us, which is one reason research in this area continually discovers new aspects of life-span growth.

⓵ **Response for Educators (from page 32):**
Tests, such as the IQ test that found David severely retarded, are a statement of the present, but not always predictive of the future. Effective teaching can have a decided impact, although it is unlikely teachers can ever erase the legacy of early neurological damage.

KEY TERMS

scientific study of human
  development (4)
life-span perspective (4)
plasticity (4)
biosocial domain (5)
cognitive domain (5)
psychosocial domain (5)
butterfly effect (7)
cohort (8)
social construction (10)
socioeconomic status
  (SES) (10)
culture (11)
ethnic group (14)
race (14)
scientific method (15)
hypothesis (15)

replicate (15)
subjects (15)
variable (18)
scientific observation (19)
statistical significance (21)
correlation (21)
experiment (23)
independent variable (23)
dependent variable (23)
survey (24)
case study (26)
cross-sectional research
  (27)
longitudinal research (28)
cross-sequential research
  (30)

KEY QUESTIONS

1. What is the main focus of the study of human development?

2. How does a life-span perspective apply to the study of childhood or adolescence?

3. Name and describe the three domains into which the study of human development is usually divided.

4. How might the historical context differ for someone born in 1900 as compared to 2000?

5. What are three socioeconomic factors that constitute SES, and how might each affect development?

6. What are the differences among culture, ethnicity, and race?

7 What are the advantages and complications of the scientific method?

8. What are the steps of the scientific method?

9. What are the advantages and disadvantages of observational research?

10. What are the advantages and disadvantages of experimental research?

11 Compare the uses of longitudinal research and cross-sectional research. How are the advantages of each method combined in cross-sequential research?

12. *In Your Experience* Is any one of the three domains of development more important in your own life than the other two? Why or why not?

Theories of Development

CHAPTER 2

As we saw in Chapter 1, the scientific effort to understand human development usually begins with questions. One of the most basic is: How do people develop into the persons they ultimately become?

- Do early experiences—of breast-feeding or bonding or abuse—linger into adulthood, even if they seem to be forgotten?
- How important are specific school experiences in human intelligence?
- Can a person develop moral values without being taught them?
- Do a person's chances of becoming a violent adult depend on whether she or he grows up in, say, Chile or Cambodia or Canada?
- If your parents or grandparents are depressed, schizophrenic, or alcoholic, will you develop the same conditions?

For every answer, more questions arise: Why or why not? When and how? And perhaps, most important of all, so what?

WHAT THEORIES DO

Each of the five questions listed above is answered by one of the five major theories described in this chapter. To frame various questions, and to begin to answer them, we need some way to determine which facts about development are relevant. Then we need to organize those facts to lead us to deeper understanding. In short, we need a theory.

A **developmental theory** is a systematic statement of principles and generalizations that provides a coherent framework for studying and explaining development. Such a theory is more than mere assumptions and facts; it connects facts and observations, putting the details of life into a meaningful whole. Theories are also quite practical, in three ways:

- Theories offer insight and guidance for everyday concerns by providing a broad and coherent view of human development.
- Theories form the basis for hypotheses that can be tested by research studies. Thus theories "provide a point of departure," "a conceptual connection" for individual scientists who study according to their own particular research interests (Renninger & Amsel, 1997).
- Theories are constantly modified by new research, and thus enable comprehensive communication of current knowledge in a way that makes sense (Meacham, 1997).

Learning Theory

The second grand theory arose in direct opposition to psychoanalytic theory. Early in the twentieth century, John B. Watson (1878–1958) argued that if psychology was to be a true science, psychologists should study only what they could see and measure. He directly opposed Freud's emphasis on the unconscious, especially on impulses and memories that patients might not recall until years later under psychoanalytic probing or might never remember except via dreams or other disguised manifestations. In Watson's words:

> Why don't we make what we can *observe* the real field of psychology? Let us limit ourselves to things that can be observed, and formulate laws concerned only with those things. . . . We can observe behavior—what the organism does or says. [Watson, 1930/1967]

According to Watson, anything can be learned. He said:

> Give me a dozen healthy infants, well-formed, and my own specified world to bring them up in and I'll guarantee to take any one at random and train him to become any type of specialist I might select—doctor, lawyer, artist, merchant, chief, and yes, even beggar-man and thief, regardless of his talents, penchants, tendencies, abilities, vocations, and race of his ancestors. [Watson, 1928]

Why No Kissing? A psychoanalytic theorist might see evidence of frustration of basic needs in this after-work gathering in Boston. Instead of intimacy (Erikson's stage 6) these young adults are forced by the social setting to be quite formal, with cultural symbols of sexuality (the men's ties, the women's high heels) rather than the actual thing. A learning theorist, by contrast, might point out that these adults are actually reinforced with alcohol, fresh fruit, and friendly conversation—since they have obviously learned to keep their distance and pair off appropriately, boy/girl, boy/girl, boy/girl, boy/girl.

learning theory A grand theory of development, built on behaviorism, that focuses on the sequences and processes by which behavior is learned.

stimulus An action or event that elicits a behavioral response.

response A behavior (either instinctual or learned) that is elicited by a certain stimulus.

conditioning Any learning process that occurs according to the laws of behaviorism or learning theory. This can be classical conditioning, in which one stimulus is associated with another, or operant conditioning, in which a response is gradually learned via reinforcement.

Other psychologists agreed, partly because they found it difficult to study the unconscious motives and drives identified in psychoanalytic theory. Actual behavior, by contrast, could be studied far more objectively and scientifically. Thus was developed the theory originally called *behaviorism.* Behaviorism gave rise to our second grand theory of development, **learning theory,** which focuses on the ways we learn specific behaviors—ways that can be described, analyzed, and predicted with far more scientific accuracy than the unconscious drives proposed by psychoanalysts (Horowitz, 1994).

Laws of Behavior

Learning theorists formulated laws of behavior that apply to every individual at every age, from newborn to octogenarian. These laws provide insights into how mature competencies are fashioned from simple actions and how environmental influences shape individual development. In the view of learning theorists, all development involves a process of learning and, therefore, does not occur in specific stages that are dependent only on age or maturation (Bijou & Baer, 1978).

The basic laws of learning theory explore the relationship between a **stimulus**—that is, an action or event—and a **response**—that is, the behavioral reaction with which the stimulus is associated. Some responses are automatic, such as reflexes. If someone suddenly waves a hand in your face, you blink; if a hungry dog smells food, it salivates. But most responses do not occur spontaneously; they are learned. Learning theorists emphasize that life is a continual learning process: New events and experiences evoke new behavior patterns, while old, unused, and unproductive responses tend to fade away.

Learning occurs through **conditioning,** a term for a learning process through which a particular response comes to be triggered by a particular stimulus (see Figure 2.1). There are two types of conditioning: classical and operant.

Learning occurs through:

- **Classical conditioning** Through association, neutral stimulus becomes conditioned stimulus.
- **Operant conditioning** Through reinforcement, weak or rare response becomes strong, frequent response.
- **Social learning** Through modeling, observed behaviors become copied behaviors.

Figure 2.1 **Three Types of Learning**

A Contemporary of Freud Ivan Pavlov was a physiologist who received the Nobel Prize in 1904 for his research on digestive processes. It was this line of study that led to his discovery of classical conditioning.

Answer to Observational Quiz (from page 41): *The signs suggest Asia, and the fact that overt rebellion is difficult in a small Asian town suggests a large city. If you guessed Tokyo, score one correct. A sharp observation of the T-shirt and an accurate memory of when Mohawk hairstyles were in fashion would give you another correct answer—probably 1992.*

Classical Conditioning. A century ago, Russian scientist Ivan Pavlov (1849–1936) began to study the link between stimulus and response. While doing research on salivation in dogs, Pavlov noted that his experimental dogs began to drool not only at the sight of food but also, eventually, at the sound of the approaching attendants who brought the food. This observation led him to perform his famous experiment in which he taught a dog to salivate at the sound of a bell. Pavlov began by ringing the bell just before presenting food to the dog. After a number of repetitions of this bell-then-food sequence, the dog began salivating at the bell's sound even when there was no food nearby.

This simple experiment in learning was one of the first scientific demonstrations of *classical conditioning* (also called *respondent conditioning*). In classical conditioning, an organism (any type of living creature) comes to associate a neutral stimulus with a meaningful one and then responds to the former stimulus as if it were the latter. In Pavlov's original experiment, the dog associated the sound of the bell (the neutral stimulus) with food (the meaningful stimulus) and responded to the sound as though it were the food itself. That response was a conditioned response, which meant learning had occurred.

Operant Conditioning. The most influential proponent of learning theory was B. F. Skinner (1904–1990), who agreed with Watson that psychology should focus on the scientific study of behavior. Skinner also agreed with Pavlov that classical conditioning explains some types of behavior. However, Skinner believed that another type of conditioning—*operant conditioning*—plays a much greater role in human behavior, especially in more complex learning. In operant conditioning, the organism learns that a particular behavior produces a particular consequence. If the consequence is useful or pleasurable, the organism will tend to repeat the behavior to achieve that response again. If the response is unpleasant, the organism will tend not to repeat the behavior. (Operant conditioning is also called *instrumental conditioning.*)

In operant conditioning, then, pleasurable consequences (such as rewards) might be used to train an animal. A simple example is training a dog to fetch newspapers by giving it a treat every time it performs the behavior. Or an action that the animal already sometimes performs can be operantly conditioned to occur more precisely or quickly. For example, early behaviorist experiments typically involved placing food at the end of a maze to condition rats to run the maze more efficiently.

Once a behavior has been conditioned (learned), animals (including humans) continue to perform it even if pleasurable consequences occur only occasionally. Almost all of a person's daily behavior, from

THEORIES OF MOTHER LOVE: FOOD VERSUS TOUCH

As the text explains, psychologists adhering to either the psychoanalytic or learning theories believed that the reason children loved their mothers was that the mothers satisfied basic hunger and sucking needs. In other words, they held that "the infant's attachment to the mother stemmed from internal drives which triggered activities connected with the libations of the mother's breast. This belief was the only one these two theoretical groups ever had in common," according to Harry Harlow as reported by his widow (Harlow, 1986).

Harlow, a psychologist who studied learning in infant monkeys, explained why his observations of monkeys in his laboratory caused him to question that belief:

> We had separated more than 60 of these animals from their mothers 6 to 12 hours after birth and suckled them on tiny bottles. The infant mortality rate was a fraction of what would have obtained had we let the monkey mothers raise their infants. Our bottle-fed babies were healthier and heavier than monkey-mother-reared infants. . . . During the course of our studies we noticed that the laboratory-raised babies showed strong attachment to the folded gauze diapers which were used to cover the hardware-cloth floors of their cages. (Harlow, 1986)

In fact, the infant monkeys seemed as emotionally attached to the diapers as to their bottles. This was contrary to the two prevailing theories. Psychoanalytic theory would say that the infant would love whatever satisfied its oral needs (the nipple), and learning theory would predict that the infant would become attached to whatever provided reinforcing food (the bottle). Accordingly, Harlow set out to make a "direct experimental analysis" of human attachment via his monkeys. Using monkeys to study emotional processes in humans may seem a stretch to some people, but not to Harlow, who had been trained as an experimental psychologist. He knew that it would be unethical to seperate human infants from their mothers, but he believed that "the basic processes relating to affection, including nursing, contact, clinging, and even visual and auditory exploration exhibit no fundamental differences in the two species" (Harlow, 1958).

Harlow provided infant monkeys with two "surrogate" (artificial) mothers, both the right size, with a face that included obvious eyes. One surrogate was made of bare wire, and the other was made of wire covered by soft terrycloth. He divided his monkeys into two groups: One was fed by a bottle periodically put through the chest of the cloth "mother"; the other was fed by a bottle put through the chest of the wire "mother." The hypothesis to be tested was that the cloth surrogate might be reinforcing, even for the monkeys that were fed by the wire mother. To collect his data, Harlow measured how much time each baby spent holding on to one or the other of the two surrogates. It was no surprise that the monkeys who had a cloth mother that provided milk clung to it and ignored the bare-wire, nonfeeding mother. However, beyond the few minutes needed to suck the milk, even the babies that fed from the wire mother had no interest in holding on to it, going to it only when hunger drove them to do so. No attachment, or love, for the nourishing wire mother could be observed, but the cloth mothers seemed to win the infant's affection (see Figure 2.2).

Clinging to "Mother" Even though it gave no milk, this "mother" was soft and warm enough that infant monkeys spent almost all their time holding on to it. Many infants, some children, and even some adults cling to a familiar stuffed animal when life becomes frightening. According to Harlow, the reasons are the same: All primates are comforted by something soft, warm, and familiar to touch.

socializing with others to earning a paycheck, can be understood as a result of operant conditioning. For instance, when a baby first gives a half smile in response to a full stomach, a mother might smile back. Soon the baby is conditioned by the mother's responsive smile to give a bigger smile, and the mother picks the baby up to reinforce the smile.

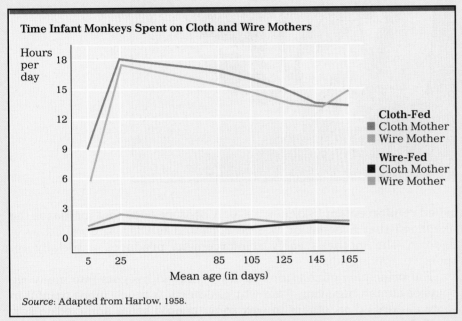

Time Infant Monkeys Spent on Cloth and Wire Mothers

Cloth-Fed
- Cloth Mother
- Wire Mother

Wire-Fed
- Cloth Mother
- Wire Mother

Source: Adapted from Harlow, 1958.

Figure 2.2 Softer Is Better. During the first three weeks of Harlow's experiment, the infant monkeys developed a strong preference for the cloth-covered "mothers." That preference lasted throughout the experiment, even among the monkeys who were fed by a wire-covered mother.

This reaction was so strong that Harlow then wondered if the cloth surrogate mothers might also reassure infant monkeys when frightening events occurred, just as a real mother does when a scared youngster runs to her. He set up another experiment, putting an unfamiliar mechanical toy into a cloth-reared infant monkey's cage. The monkey immediately sought comfort from its cloth mother, scrambling to cling to her with one hand and then timidly exploring the new object with the other.

Wire mothers provided no such reassurance. Monkeys who were exposed to the same stress without the cloth mother's presence showed obvious signs of fright—freezing, screaming, shivering, hiding, urinating. It seems, then, that mothering is not primarily about feeding, but about touching, comforting, and holding, which Harlow called "contact comfort" or "love" (Harlow, 1958).

Harlow's research is a classic example of the use of theories. Although it is noteworthy that his study disproved an aspect of both learning theory and psychoanalytic theory, that is not the most significant point. Remember, theories are meant to be useful, not necessarily true. (If they were known to be true in every aspect, they would be scientific laws, not theories.) In this example, because he knew what the psychoanalytic and learning theories said about attachment, the monkeys' interaction with the gauze diapers caught Harlow's attention. That led to closer observation, a hypothesis, a clever series of experiments, and some amazing results. For decades, perhaps centuries, no one had questioned the idea that feeding creates loyalty—until actual observations conflicted with both grand theories. This conflict prompted an alert scientist to ask new questions.

Both psychoanalytic and learning theory were revised and expanded as a result of Harlow's experiments and of other evidence. Freud's follower Erikson stressed psychosocial, not just psychosexual, development, and learning theory allowed for more varied social reinforcers. Advice to caregivers changed as well: Crying infants should be picked up and cuddled, even if they are not hungry. The result has been much more cradling and less crying in millions of human infants—all because a scientist compared a theoretical prediction with his own observations and performed ingenious experiments to test his hypothesis.

As time goes on, the baby becomes a smiling toddler, a cheerful child, an outgoing adolescent, and a friendly adult—all because of early operant conditioning and periodic reinforcing (see the Research Report).

In operant conditioning, the process of repeating a consequence to make it more likely that the behavior in question will recur is

Rats, Pigeons, and People B. F. Skinner is best known for his experiments with rats and pigeons, but he also applied his knowledge to human problems. For his daughter, he designed a glass-enclosed crib in which temperature, humidity, and perceptual stimulation could be controlled to make her time in the crib enjoyable and educational. He wrote about an ideal society based on principles of operant conditioning, where, for example, workers in less desirable jobs would earn greater rewards.

reinforcement   The process whereby a particular behavior is strengthened, making it more likely that the behavior will be repeated.

social learning   A theory that learning occurs through observation and imitation of other people.

modeling   Part of social learning theory; in particular, the process whereby a person tries to imitate the behavior of someone else. Modeling occurs with minor actions, such as how someone laughs or what shoes he or she wears, but it also occurs in powerful ways, as when a male child identifies with his father as a role model.

called **reinforcement** (Skinner, 1953). A consequence that increases the likelihood that a behavior will be repeated is therefore called a *reinforcer*. The mother's early reinforcement produces a socially responsive, smiling adult.

The principles of conditioning have yielded insights into many aspects of human behavior, from why childbirth is much more painful in some cultures than others to why some people seem addicted to sex, cigarettes, or money. Learning theory has also performed, like any good theory, as a source of hypotheses for scientific experiments—some of which have disproven aspects of both classical psychoanalytic theory and classical learning theory.

Learning to Read One of the more controversial implications of social learning is that a boy needs a father to teach him how to be a man. Children learn from many people, and no doubt fathers, their behaviors, and their relationships are powerful models for young children.

Social Learning

Originally, learning theorists sought to explain all behavior as arising directly from classical or operant conditioning. More recent learning theorists focus on less direct, though equally potent, forms of learning. They emphasize that humans can learn new behaviors merely by observing the behavior of others, without personally experiencing any conditioning. These theorists have developed an extension of learning theory called **social learning.**

An integral part of social learning is **modeling,** in which people observe behavior and then pattern their own after it. This is not simply a case of "monkey see, monkey do." People model only some actions of some individuals in some contexts.

Social Learning in Action Social learning validates the old maxim "Examples speak louder than words." If the moments here are typical for each child, the girl in the left photo is likely to grow up with a ready sense of the importance of this particular chore of infant care. Unfortunately, the boy on the right may become a cigarette smoker like his father—even if his father warns him of the dangers of this habit.

❷ *Observational Quiz (see answer page 49): Beyond what they are doing, what else shows that these children imitate their parents?*

cognitive theory A theory which holds that the way people think and understand the world shapes their perceptions, attitudes, and actions.

❷ **Especially for Parents:** Think of four specific suggestions for a parent who wants to teach a child to wash hands before every meal.

Would You Talk to This Man? Children loved talking to Jean Piaget, and he learned by listening carefully—especially to their incorrect explanations, which no one had paid much attention to before. All his life, Piaget was absorbed with studying the way children think. He called himself a "genetic epistemologist"—one who studies how children gain knowledge about the world as they grow up.

Generally, modeling is most likely to occur when the observer is uncertain or inexperienced and when the model is someone admirable, powerful, or similar to the observer (Bandura, 1986, 1997).

Social learning is also affected by self-understanding. The standards we set for ourselves and our confidence in our ability to meet them affect our willingness to learn from other people—whether they be parents, peers, mentors, or media stars. In this emphasis on both social understanding and self-understanding, social learning theory incorporates insights from the third grand theory we will examine.

Cognitive Theory

Cognitive theory focuses primarily on the structure and development of the individual's thought processes and understanding. Cognitive researchers try to determine how a person's thinking and the expectations that result from a particular understanding affect the development of attitudes, beliefs, and behavior. In other words, to understand people, don't delve into what they forgot from childhood (psychoanalytic theory) or what has happened to them (learning theory), but instead find out what they think.

Jean Piaget (1896–1980) was the major pioneer of cognitive theory. Although originally trained in the natural sciences, Piaget became interested in human thought processes when he was hired to field-test questions for a standard intelligence test for children. Piaget was supposed to find the age at which most children could answer each question correctly, but he found the children's wrong answers much more intriguing. He noted that children who were of the same age shared similar mistaken concepts, a fact suggesting a developmental sequence to intellectual growth.

● Response for Parents (from page 47):
(1) Make the behavior enjoyable—perhaps by making a game of it, going with the child to the sink, or using special soap. (2) Reward each occurrence—with a word of praise, a penny, a gold star, or whatever the particular child finds reinforcing. (3) Model appropriate behavior—the parent and other children should wash their hands, too. (4) Help the child understand—explain that dirty hands could make the child sick, or provide some other logical reason for washing.

cognitive equilibrium   A state of mental balance, in which a person's thoughts and assumptions about the world seem (at least to that person) not to clash with one another or with that person's experiences.

How children think is much more important and more revealing of mental ability, Piaget concluded, than what they know. Moreover, understanding how people think reveals how they interpret their experiences and thus explains how they construct their values and assumptions.

Periods of Cognitive Development

Piaget maintained that there are four major periods of cognitive development (see Table 2.2). These are age-related, and, as you will see in later chapters, each has features that permit certain types of knowing and understanding (Piaget, 1952, 1970).

How Cognitive Development Occurs

Underlying Piaget's theory is his basic view that cognitive development is a process that follows universal patterns. This process is guided, according to Piaget, by the human need for **cognitive equilibrium**—that is, a state of mental balance. What Piaget meant is that each person attempts to make sense of new experiences by reconciling them with his or her existing understanding. Cognitive equilibrium occurs when one's present understanding "fits" new experiences, whether this fitting involves a baby's discovery that new objects can be grasped in the same way as familiar objects or an adult's explanation of shifting world events as consonant with his or her political philosophy.

table **2.2**	**Piaget's Periods of Cognitive Development**		
Approximate Age	Period	Characteristics	Major Gains During the Period
Birth to 2 years	Sensorimotor	Infant uses senses and motor abilities to understand the world. There is no conceptual or reflective thought; an object is "known" in terms of what an infant can *do* to it.	The infant learns that an object still exists when it is out of sight *(object permanence)* and begins to think through mental actions as well as physical actions.
2–6 years	Preoperational	The child uses *symbolic thinking*, including language, to understand the world. Sometimes the child's thinking is *egocentric*, causing the child to understand the world from only one perspective, his or her own.	The imagination flourishes, and language becomes a significant means of self-expression and of influence from others. Children gradually begin to *decenter*, that is, become less egocentric, and to understand and coordinate multiple points of view.
7–11 years	Concrete operational	The child understands and applies logical operations, or principles, to help interpret experiences objectively and rationally rather than intuitively.	By applying logical abilities, children learn to understand the basic concepts of conservation, number, classification, and many other scientific ideas.
12 years through adulthood	Formal operational	The adolescent or adult is able to think about abstractions and hypothetical concepts.	Ethics, politics, and social and moral issues become more interesting and involving as the adolescent becomes able to take a broader and more theoretical approach to experience.

How to Think About Flowers A person's stage of cognitive growth influences how he or she thinks about everything, including flowers. To a baby, in the sensorimotor stage, flowers are "known" through pulling, smelling, and perhaps tasting. A slightly older child might be egocentric, wanting to pick and eat the vegetables now. At the adult's formal operational stage, flowers can be part of a larger, logical scheme—either to earn money or to cultivate beauty. Note, however, that thinking is an active process throughout the life span.

❶ *Answer to Observational Quiz (from page 47):* *Their clothes and hair.*

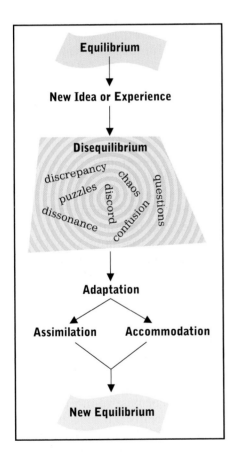

Figure 2.3 Challenge Me. Most of us, most of the time, prefer the comfort of our conventional conclusions. According to Piaget, however, when new ideas disturb our thinking, we have an opportunity to expand our cognition with a broader and deeper understanding.

Figure 2.3 diagrams how the need for cognitive equilibrium is fulfilled. When a new experience does not seem to fit existing understanding, the individual falls into a state of *cognitive disequilibrium*, an imbalance that initially produces confusion. Disequilibrium then leads to cognitive growth when the person modifies old concepts and constructs better ones to fit the new experience. In Piaget's terminology, cognitive adaptation occurs in two ways:

- reinterpreting new experiences so that they fit into, or *assimilate* with, the old ideas
- revamping old ideas so that they can *accommodate* the new

Assimilation is easier, since it does not require much adjustment; but accommodation is sometimes necessary, and it produces significant intellectual growth.

You may experience cognitive disequilibrium, for example, when a friend's argument reveals logical inconsistencies in your views, when your favorite chess strategy fails against a skilled opponent, or when your mother does or says something you never expected her to. In the last example, you might assimilate your mother's unusual statement by deciding that it was just something she heard and she didn't really mean. Growth occurs if, instead, you adjust your previous conception of your mother to accommodate a new, expanded, and more comprehensive view of who she is.

Not What He Expected Water spraying out of a pipe that he can hold in his hand—a surprising event that is likely to trigger first cognitive disequilibrium and then cognitive growth.

❷ *Observational Quiz (see answer page 54):* *This boy is 14 months old, in the sensorimotor period, and at an age when he loves to experiment. What is he likely to do next?*

❷ **Especially for Educators:** What might Piaget say of a classroom where all the children stay quietly at their desks?

Periods of disequilibrium are disquieting when we suspect that accepted ideas no longer hold true. But they are also exciting periods of mental growth, which is one reason why people of all ages seek challenging experiences. According to cognitive theory, babies poke, pull, and taste everything they get their hands on; preschool children ask thousands of questions; school-age children become avid readers and information collectors; adolescents try out a wide variety of roles and experiences; and adults continually increase their knowledge and expertise in areas that interest them—all because people at every age seek cognitive challenges.

Recognition of this active searching is the very essence of Piaget's theory of human cognitive development. Unlike psychoanalytic and learning theories, which depict children as buffeted and shaped by influences beyond their control, cognitive theory portrays a much more active person, who seeks ways to comprehend the world.

Evaluation of Grand Theories

All three of the theories we have just described deserve to be called "grand." They are insightful and provocative, stimulating not only to researchers in human development but also to historians, educators, novelists, and, particularly, therapists. Thousands of professionals still use techniques originated by Freud, Skinner, or Piaget. Further, each of these three theories has made significant contributions to developmental science.

Developmentalists owe a debt of gratitude both to Freud and to the neo-Freudians who extended and refined his concepts. Many psychoanalytic ideas are widely accepted today—for example, that unconscious motives affect our behavior and that the early years are a formative period of personality development.

The study of human development has also benefited from learning theory. The emphasis on the causes and consequences of observed behavior has led researchers to see that many behavior patterns that seem to be inborn, or to result from deeply rooted emotional problems, are actually learned. If they are learned, they can be "unlearned." This realization has encouraged scientists to find ways to eliminate particular problem behaviors, among them temper tantrums, phobias, and addictions, by analyzing and changing the stimulus–response patterns that sustain them. For researchers studying the human life span, learning theory emphasizes the variability and plasticity of adult development. Thus, for example, some nursing homes for the elderly have been redesigned to reinforce healthier activity because learning theory has alerted gerontologists to the destructive conditioning that poor design creates (as further discussed in Chapter 25).

Cognitive theory has revolutionized research by focusing attention on active mental processes, not inborn instincts or past reinforcements (Beilin, 1992). Studying thinking processes, especially the search for intellectual accommodation when disequilibrium occurs, provides new insight into human development. Hypotheses and concepts from cognitive theory are now much more often the topic of research than those from the other two grand theories (Robins et al., 1999).

However, the grand theories, as they attempted to explain the development of all humans everywhere, were probably too wide-ranging. The central idea that every person, in every culture, in every nation, passes through certain fixed stages (Freud, Erikson, Piaget), or can be conditioned according to the same laws of reinforcement (Watson, Pavlov,

No Theories Allowed These three elderly women are in a nursing home where research in human development has not yet been applied. Being confined to wheelchairs, unable to see or hear each other, means that they are cut off from the comforts of human contact (psychoanalytic), of tasty food (learning theory), and intellectual stimulation (cognitive theory). Although none of the grand theories are considered comprehensive in the twenty-first century, any one of them could suggest improvements in the situation depicted here.

The Founder of Sociocultural Theory Lev Vygotsky, now recognized as a seminal thinker whose ideas on the role of culture and history are revolutionizing education and the study of development, was a contemporary of Freud, Skinner, Pavlov, and Piaget. Vygotsky did not attain their eminence in his lifetime, partly because his work, conducted in Stalinist Russia, was largely inaccessible to the Western world and partly because he died prematurely, at age 38.

sociocultural theory A theory which holds that human development results from the dynamic interaction between developing persons and the surrounding culture, primarily as expressed by the parents and teachers who transmit it.

Skinner), does not square with the actual diversity of human beings worldwide. Careful observation of any living, breathing, growing person sooner or later evokes surprise and bewilderment, no matter what grand theory or basic assumptions the observer might hold.

In other words, all three grand theories seem much less comprehensive and inclusive now than they once did. This is apparent in the discussion of the central controversy of human development, the debate over the relative influence of nature and nurture on human development (see the Changing Policy box). As with almost any other basic issue of human development, the grand theories focus too much on the social context and seriously underestimate the role of biological and genetic influences. These limitations show that new theories are needed, and at least two are emerging to fill the gap (Green, 1997; Kessen, 1990; Overton, 1998).

EMERGENT THEORIES

Whereas the three grand theories originated almost a century ago as theories of psychology, the two emerging theories include observations, minitheories, and hypotheses from all the many sciences—in addition to psychology—that currently study human development. Sociocultural theory draws on research in education, sociology, and history; epigenetic theory is based on research from biology, genetics, ethology, and neuroscience. In part because of their scope and in part because of their recency, neither theory has become a comprehensive, coherent whole. However, as you will now see, both provide significant frameworks for the study of human development.

Sociocultural Theory

Although "sociocultural theory is still emerging and is not a single consolidated view," it stresses a new appreciation of the social context that developmentalists now recognize (Rogoff, 1998). **Sociocultural theory** seeks to explain the growth of individual knowledge, development, and competencies in terms of the guidance, support, and structure provided by the society. Social change over time results from the cumulative effect of individual choices. Note the bidirectional influence of culture and person: People are affected by society, but people also change society.

The central thesis of sociocultural theory is that human development is the result of dynamic interaction between developing persons and their surrounding culture. According to this theory, culture is not simply an external variable that impinges on the developing person; it is integral to development (Cole, 1996). As such, its effect cannot be under-

THE NATURE VERSUS NURTURE DEBATE

The very practical implications of the grand theories are highlighted by the central controversy of human development—the debate over the relative influence of heredity and environment in shaping personal traits and characteristics. This debate is often called the *nature–nurture controversy* (Dixon & Lerner, 1999).

Nature refers to the traits, capacities, and limitations that each person inherits genetically from his or her parents at the moment of conception. Body type, sex, and genetic diseases are obvious examples. Nature also includes a host of intellectual and personality characteristics that are powerfully influenced by genes (such as facility with numbers, attraction to novelty, sociability, and tendency to depression).

Nurture refers to all the environmental influences that come into play after conception, beginning with the mother's health during pregnancy and including all the individual's experiences in the outside world—in the family, the school, the community, and the culture at large.

The nature–nurture controversy has taken on many names, among them *heredity versus environment* and *maturation versus learning*. Under whatever name, the basic question remains: How much of any given characteristic, behavior, or pattern of development is the result of genes and how much is the result of experiences? Note that the question asks "How much?" not "Whether" or "Which ones?" All developmentalists agree that both nature and nurture interact to produce every specific trait; no characteristic develops as an exclusive response to either nature or nurture. Yet the specifics are hotly debated. Indeed, books that tilt toward one or the other side of this debate tend to capture public attention.

Three Best-Selling Arguments

Consider three controversial books about psychological development that became popular best-sellers in the 1990s. In one, *The Bell Curve: Intelligence and Class Structure in American Life* (1994), Richard Herrnstein and Charles Murray wrote: "Inequality of endowments, including intelligence, is a reality. Trying to pretend that inequality does not really exist is a disaster." By using the word "endowment," these authors imply that some people are naturally, genetically gifted with higher IQs than others. The book further asserts that group differences in intelligence are primarily racial and biological, not environmental, educational, or psychosocial, and thus are not likely to change. *The Bell Curve*'s thesis disputes each of the grand theories by emphasizing nature. Actually, the book overstates the point, because no contemporary scientist would "pretend" that inequality does not exist or deny that nature is always part of development. However, few developmentalists agree with the claim that nature is much more powerful than nurture, particularly as regards intelligence (Ceci & Williams, 1997; Huttenlocker et al., 1998).

In another popular book, *Emotional Intelligence* (1995), Daniel Goleman argues not only that a person's ability to understand emotions is more important to success in life than IQ is, but also that social forces, especially parents, are essential to fostering it. "There are very different emotional habits instilled by parents whose attunement means an infant's emotional needs are acknowledged and met . . . [and by] self-absorbed parents who ignore a child's distress [and] discipline capriciously by yelling and hitting." As you can see, this view is quite different from that of *The Bell Curve*, and thus is more in keeping with the grand theories. It stresses the parental role, as both Freud and Watson did, although each had his own perspective on why nurture was so important.

In a third popular book, *The Nurture Assumption* (1998), Judith Harris states, "Parents matter less than you think, and peers matter more." She argues that while psychologists have assumed that "nurture" means parenting, the peer group is really the primary influence on children. The importance of peers is actually well recognized by many psychologists, although psychoanalytic theory, in particular, holds that early mothering and fathering are much more influential than peer relationships.

Each of these books captured popular attention and scientific criticism for stressing one aspect of the nature–nurture relationship, typically a side that had not been showcased before. Controversy followed, partly because the nature–nurture debate is an important practical and political, as well as psychological, issue.

Nature and Nurture in Homosexuality

Now let us look at one specific issue that pivots on the nature–nurture debate, sexual orientation. Most psychiatrists stood simply by comparing the developmental patterns of different cultures (as did the "cross-cultural" research of the past) or by recognizing that such an effect exists.

Sociocultural theorists point to the many ways children learn from parents, teachers, and peers in their homes, schools, and neighbor-

and psychologists once assumed that adult homosexuality resulted from unusual patterns in the mother–father–child relationship, a belief strongly endorsed by psychoanalytic theory. Other psychologists asserted that a person learned to be homosexual through reinforcement and modeling. The cognitive perspective held that a person's concept of appropriate sexual interaction influenced his or her orientation—that the idea itself led to the action.

All these explanations from the three grand theories clearly emphasized nurture over nature. However, new research suggests that homosexuality is at least partly genetic (Bailey, 1998). For example, a man is more likely to be gay if his mother's brother or his own brother—especially his identical twin—is homosexual (Hamer et al., 1993; Pool, 1993; Whitam et al., 1993). Further evidence that nature has a strong impact on sexual orientation comes from studies of children raised by lesbian mothers. Most of these children are heterosexual, in similar proportions to children raised by heterosexual parents; this indicates that whatever they learned at home did not change their inborn orientation (Golombok & Tasker, 1996).

In fact, virtually no social scientist today believes that a warped mother–son relationship causes homosexuality (as psychoanalytic theory might hold) or that homosexuality is encouraged by society (learning theory) or that homosexuality is logically chosen after intellectual reflection (cognitive theory). Thus all three grand theories, at least in their simplest, all-inclusive versions, are inadequate for explaining sexual orientation.

Yet the evidence for a genetic influence on homosexuality is far from conclusive, however (Hamer, 1999; Rice et al., 1999). Culture may also play a role, as is evidenced by varying rates of homosexuality from nation to nation and from cohort to cohort (Bailey et al., 1993; Maddox, 1993).

The policy and human implications of the question are profound, which illustrates again why the nature–nurture debate is often controversial. If homosexuality is primarily the result of culture, those who are concerned about the future sexual orientation of the young should look to the influence of school curriculum, television programming, and laws about marriage, because these all reflect culture. In contrast, if the primary influences on a person's sexual orientation are genetic, different issues of public policy should be debated—and perhaps the debate itself is unnecessary.

Both of these positions may be too extreme for those who take "a developmental perspective." According to two psychologists:

> Those who dichotomize sexual orientation into pure biological or social causation fall into a dangerous quagmire. To deny any role for biology affirms an untenable scientific view of human development. Equally harsh and deterministic would be to deny the significance of the environment. (Savin-Williams & Diamond, 1997)

Policy and Practice

Theories about nature and nurture are implicit in many public policies. They are interwoven into controversies concerning such matters as the effects of alcohol exposure on fetal development, the impact of class size on school learning, the causes and consequences of teenage pregnancy, the laws governing divorce, and the relationships between grandparents and grandchildren. Political philosophy affects a person's tilt toward nature or nurture. To cite one example, "Individual differences in aggression can be accounted for by genetic or socialization differences, with politically conservative scientists tending to believe the former and more liberal scientists the latter" (Lewis, 1997).

On a more personal level, all prospective parents wonder just what influences their nurturing might have: Are they as significant as psychoanalytic and learning theories contend, or is the child's own thinking the determining factor, as cognitive theory might claim? Perhaps the emerging sociocultural or epigenetic systems theory (discussed in the text) can provide insight. No theory, however, can provide definitive answers to such questions, but theories do provide a framework for study and/or research on the impact of nature and nurture, of genes and sociey, that may yield the answers.

hoods. But they also look beyond that, to the ways in which instruction and learning are shaped by the beliefs and goals of the community. And they look even further, to the ways in which such learning continually affects all later development—of the individual at every age, of the family in every cohort, and of the ethnic group in every location.

❶ Answer to Observational Quiz (from page 50):
He will want to use all his senses and motor skills, so he might put the pipe to his mouth to taste it, rub it on his belly to feel the cold, shake it up and down to see and hear what happens, and—watch out—aim it at you to see your reaction.

❶ Response for Educators (from page 50):
That not much new learning is going on. According to Piaget, learning experiences need to include cognitive disequilibrium— challenging, surprising, or unexpected events that provoke questions, discussion, debate, and investigation.

guided participation A learning process in which an individual learns through social interaction with a "tutor" (a parent, a teacher, a more skilled peer) who offers assistance, structures opportunities, models strategies, and provides explicit instruction as needed.

Learning the Language In Bali, elegant ritualized body movement is a key element in many facets of religious life. Through guided participation, these young girls are acquiring their culture's language of ritualized dance—a language unknown in most cultures where the skills of in-line skating or video games are valued.

Guided Participation

A major pioneer of the sociocultural perspective was Lev Vygotsky (1896–1934), a psychologist from the former Soviet Union. As his writings and those of his student A. R. Luria have become widely available, they have attracted a large audience (Luria, 1976, 1979; Vygotsky, 1978, 1987). Many current researchers in developmental psychology take a sociocultural view that is deeply influenced by Vygotsky's ideas (Valsiner, 1998).

Vygotsky was particularly interested in the cognitive competencies that developed among the culturally diverse people of the then-new Soviet Union, including such skills as the proper use of tools in an agricultural community and the appropriate use of abstract words among people who had never been to school. In the sociocultural view, these competencies develop from interactions between novices and more skilled members of the society, acting as tutors or mentors, in a process called an "apprenticeship in thinking" (Rogoff, 1990, 1998).

The implicit goal of this apprenticeship is to provide the instruction and support that novices need in order to acquire the knowledge and capabilities that are valued by their culture. The best way to accomplish this goal is through **guided participation:** The tutor engages the learner in joint activities, offering not only instruction but also direct involvement in the learning process.

Note that this apprenticeship depends on social interaction, not on a student's discovering knowledge on his or her own or on a teacher's writing down what he or she knows. Neither student nor teacher is ever passive; one person learns from another, through the words and activities that they engage in *together* (Karpov & Haywood, 1998). This is one crucial difference between sociocultural theory and the grand theories of the past: Together, child and adult actively shape the knowledge in their culture, by participating in the learning process rather than receiving or transmitting existing knowledge; "cognitive development occurs in and emerges from social situations" (Gauvain, 1998). Adults learn from children as well as vice versa, and both adults and children learn as much from their peers as from older or younger individuals (see A Life-Span View).

Cultural Variations

Although the basic principles of sociocultural theory are universal, its major emphasis on culture has helped developmentalists recognize that the skills, challenges, and opportunities involved in human development vary, depending on the values and structures of the society in question. In order to understand the developmental process in a specific culture, researchers first study how values affect the individuals. Then they study how individuals shape the specific cultural context in a systematic way, with each component affecting the whole. For example, every adult knows things that he or she decides are not worth passing on, and every student is exposed to skills that he or she will resist learning. Unvalued, unneeded aspects of the culture are not transmitted, because either teacher or learner does not enter that zone—or neither does.

❓ **Especially for Health Professionals:** How might sociocultural theory guide a school nurse who discovers that a child is fed too many fried foods at home and has high cholesterol?

epigenetic systems theory A developmental theory that emphasizes the genetic origins of behavior but also stresses that genes, over time, are directly and systematically affected by many environmental forces.

The Epigenetic Perspective Although these parents may not realize it, their words echo the essence of epigenetic thought—that each human is born with genetic possibilities that must be nurtured in order to grow.

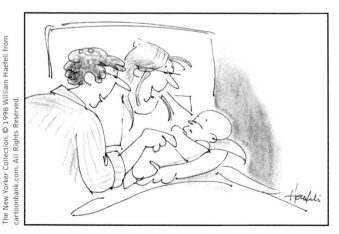

"Isn't she marvelous? Our own little bundle of untapped potential."

The importance of beliefs as a prerequisite for learning various skills was discovered by a team of researchers who were trying to assess the logical abilities of people in western Africa (Cole et al., 1971; Glick, 1968). At first the Africans seemed unable to arrange a set of items in abstract logical categories, rather than in practical clusters, even when they were explicitly told to do so. They responded that "a wise person" would always do as they did. However, their seeming ignorance disappeared when, "in total exasperation, the researchers finally said 'How would a fool do it?'" (Greenfield, 1997). Then they could, and did, achieve competence in the logical skills that American scientists hoped to measure.

In traditional societies, where decades come and go with little social change, most lessons learned in childhood are good for a lifetime. But in modern technological societies, especially those with strong multicultural influences, the tools, skills, customs, and values through which the culture functions are under continual pressure to change. In such societies, the older generations often find themselves having to learn from the innovations of a younger cohort. For everyone, development and change occur throughout life—an insight that becomes particularly important as we study the many decades of adulthood.

Sociocultural theorists have been criticized, however, for overlooking developmental processes that are not primarily social. Vygotsky's theory, in particular, has been viewed as neglecting the role of genes in guiding development, especially with regard to neurological maturation in mental processes (Wertsch, 1985; Wertsch & Tulviste, 1992). The final theory we will now discuss begins with the influence of genetics.

Epigenetic Systems Theory

Epigenetic systems theory emphasizes the interaction between genes and the environment, an interaction that is seen as dynamic and reciprocal (Dent-Read & Zukow-Goldring, 1997; Goldsmith et al., 1997). This is the newest developmental theory, but it builds on several established bodies of research. Many disciplines of the natural sciences, including evolution, genetics, and ethology, provided a foundation for this theory (see the In Person box on pages 60–61). Further, both Erikson and Piaget described aspects of their theories as "epigenetic."

Before and After the Genes

To understand what is involved in this theory, let us begin by examining the root word *genetic* and the prefix *epi*. The word *genetic* refers both to the genes that make each person (except monozygotic twins) unique and to the genes that humans have shared with all other humans for hundreds of thousands of years. Many of our basic "human" genes, about 98 percent of them, are also shared with other primates (Gibbons, 1998).

In emphasizing this genetic foundation, epigenetic systems theory stresses that we have powerful instincts and abilities that arise from our biological heritage. Even the timing and pace of certain developmental changes are genetically guided.

The fact that genes substantially affect every aspect of human behavior was at first unknown and then disputed

ZONE OF PROXIMAL DEVELOPMENT

According to sociocultural theory, how a person learns is the same at every age, whether a manual skill, a social custom, or a language is being learned. Cultural context, social customs, and guided participation are always part of the process. So is the concept of an active learning environment. Learning usually begins when a mentor senses that the learner is ready and therefore arranges social interactions that will push the learner's skills to new levels. To do so, the mentor draws the learner into the **zone of proximal development,** which is the range of skills that the learner can exercise with assistance but cannot perform independently (see Figure 2.4). Through sensitive assessment of the learner's abilities and capacity for growth, the teacher engages the learner's participation and gradually facilitates the learner's transition from assisted performance to independent performance.

To make this rather abstract-seeming process more concrete, let's take a simple example—a father teaching his 5-year-old daughter to ride a bicycle. He probably begins by helping his daughter to get the feel of the bicycle as he slowly rolls her along; he firmly supports her weight and holds her upright while telling her to keep her hands on the bars and her feet on the pedals, to push the right and left pedals in rhythm, and to look straight

zone of proximal development The range of skills, knowledge, and understanding that an individual cannot yet perform or comprehend on his or her own but could master with guidance; this is the arena where learning occurs.

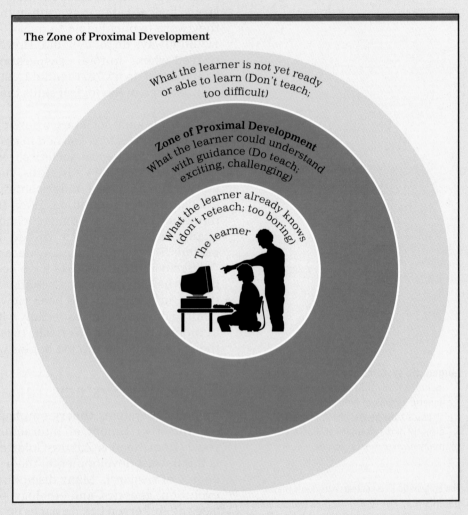

The Zone of Proximal Development

What the learner is not yet ready or able to learn (Don't teach; too difficult)

Zone of Proximal Development
What the learner could understand with guidance (Do teach; exciting, challenging)

What the learner already knows (don't reteach; too boring)

The learner

Figure 2.4 The Magic Middle. Somewhere between the boring and the impossible is the zone of proximal development, the place where interaction between teacher and learner results in knowledge never before grasped or skills not already mastered. The intellectual excitement of that zone is the origin of the joy that both instruction and study can bring.

for most of the twentieth century. (That explains why the earlier grand theories did not give heredity a substantial role in explaining human development.) Now research has shown that every psychological as well as every physical trait, from blood type to bashfulness, from metabolic rate to moodiness, from voice tone to vocational aptitude, is influenced by genes. Molecular genetics is beginning to explain exactly which

Learning to Ride Although they are usually not aware of it, children learn most of their skills because adults guide them carefully. What would happen if this father let go?

ahead. If she says she feels that she is going to fall, he reassures her—"I'm here, I won't let you get hurt"—and suggests that she lean forward a bit and relax her arms. As she becomes more comfortable and confident, he begins to roll her along more quickly, noting out loud that she is now able to keep her legs pumping in a steady rhythm. Within another lesson or two he is jogging beside her, holding on to just the handlebar, as he feels her control gradually go from dangerously wobbly to slightly shaky. Then comes the moment when he senses that, with a little more momentum, she could maintain her balance by herself. Accordingly, he urges her to pedal faster and slowly loosens his grip on the handlebar until, perhaps without her even realizing it, she is riding on her own.

Note that this is not instruction by rote. First, every parent realizes that some children need more assurance than others; from the start the instruction process is modified for the particular learner. Second, even knowing the child, a parent needs to listen and sense exactly whether more support or more freedom is needed at each moment, so the process is constantly modified. And third, such skills are almost impossible to transmit unless the teacher has mastered them: The father who does not know how to ride might intellectually understand the general principles, but he is best advised to let his bike-riding wife do the instructing.

Such excursions into and through the zone of proximal development are commonplace, not only in childhood but throughout life. Ideally, the learning process follows the same general pattern in all instances: The mentor, sensitively attuned to the learner's ever-shifting abilities and motivation, continually urges the learner on to new levels of competence, while the learner asks questions and shows signs of progress that guide and inspire the mentor.

genes interact with which factors to produce which traits (Plomin et al., 1997; Sherman & Waldman, 1999).

No longer ignored, the power of genes is now sometimes exaggerated. That is an error that epigenetic systems theory seeks to avoid—as is evident in the prefix *epi*, which means (among other things) "before," "after," "on," and "near." Thus *epigenetic* refers to all the factors that

ETHOLOGY OF INFANT CARE

The epigenetic systems approach focuses on both the "micro" interactions of genes at the individual level and the "macro" genetic systems that have developed within the species over time. In the latter respect, epigenetic theory builds on a well-established theory called *ethology* (Hinde, 1983). **Ethology** is the study of patterns of animal behavior, particularly as that behavior relates to evolutionary origins and species survival.

Typically, ethologists study such phenomena as the behaviors that trigger aggression, the particular rituals that precede mating, the means by which mammals or birds communicate that food or danger is nearby, and the behaviors involved in the care and raising of young. After collecting detailed data, ethologists attempt to determine how particular behavioral patterns evolved to contribute to the perpetuation of the species. Ethologists hold that to understand the typical actions of any species, including *Homo sapiens*, we must understand what role those behaviors have played in the species' evolutionary heritage and survival (Hinde, 1989; Schmitt et al., 1997).

Infant Instincts

The ethological perspective has particular relevance for infancy, not just that of rat pups, as discussed in the text, but that of human babies as well. Many of the instinctive behaviors of young infants and their caregivers tend to promote survival (Marvin, 1997).

Newborns are genetically programmed for social contact. To be specific, throughout the long evolution of our species, human babies have depended on those who feed, clothe, clean, and otherwise care for them. Consequently, infants come into the world already equipped with social predispositions and social skills that help ensure their nurturance and development. For example, they can distinguish the sounds and rhythms of speech, recognize the facial expressions of fear and pleasure, distinguish one person from another by smell, by touch, and by sound. They do all of this much more readily than they notice similar sensations from an inanimate source.

In addition, despite being so obviously immobile and helpless, human infants, are genetically programmed to display reflexes, including the grasping, clinging, crying, and grunting that summon adults or keep them nearby. In the be-

ethology The study of behavior as it is related to the evolution and survival of a species.

ginning, infants accept help from anyone—a good survival strategy in the centuries when women regularly died in childbirth. By the time they are able to crawl, however, infants have become emotionally attached to their specific caregivers, as well as fearful of unfamiliar situations. By the time infants are able to toddle away, their attachment and fear have triggered a new set of dependent behaviors. While moving away, they regularly glance in the caregiver's direction in order to confirm his or her presence (Lieberman, 1993).

Over the course of human history, infants who stayed near nurturing and protecting adults were more likely to survive. Hence, selective adaptation produced this broad repertoire of actions and emotions in the human genetic makeup to keep infants safe from harm.

Adult Impulses

Caregiving adults are similarly equipped. Logically, no reasonable adult would ever put up with the sleepless nights, dirty diapers, and frequent cries of a baby, with the rebellion of a teenager, or with all the tribulations of the years in between, simply to raise the child to the point where he or she leaves home but occasionally returns to request emotional or financial support. Fortunately, however, our genetic impulses are not logical. We are programmed to cherish and protect our children. As the mother of four, I have been surprised by the power of this programming many times. With my firstborn, I remember asking my pediatrician if she wasn't one of the most beautiful, perfect babies he had ever seen.

"Yes," he said, with a twinkle in his eyes, "and my patients are better looking than the patients of any other pediatrician in the city."

With my second newborn, the hospital offered to sell me a photo of her at 1 day old; I glanced at it and said no, because it didn't look at all like her—it was almost ugly. I was similarly enamored of my third and fourth. For the fourth, however, a new thought came to me: I am not only a woman who loves her children; I am a woman who loves her sleep. In the predawn hours, as I roused myself yet again to feed my baby, I asked myself how selective forgetting had allowed me, once again, to choose a disruptive addition to my life that was guaranteed to deprive me of my precious slumber. The answer, of course, is that some instincts are even stronger than the instinct for self-preservation.

Even if you are not a parent, you are irrational in the same way as I am. Imagine that you hear an infant crying. No matter where you are, no matter what you are doing, you are likely to feel distracted, sympathetic, and troubled. This reaction occurs because, universally, on some deep, primordial level, adults recognize the infant cry as a signal that a vulnerable, defenseless human is cold, hungry, or otherwise in danger. We are compelled to respond, at least by noticing and perhaps by helping. Surprisingly, even adults who have never cared for a baby become physiologically aroused, with focused attention and more rapid heartbeat, on hearing the sound of a baby's cry (Thompson & Frodi, 1984). Caregivers generally respond with greater urgency the more distressed the baby sounds (Corter & Fleming, 1995).

The emotions aroused by an infant cry are among the most powerful a parent feels, and the frustration at not being able to console a baby leads to even stronger feelings:

> I don't just hate it when my baby cries—I sometimes hate my crying baby. Often she cries for no reason I can understand: howls when I am washing her as if I put soap in her eyes and goes on as if I was just ignoring her even though I'm doing everything I can think of. . . . Sometimes I think I must be totally a hopeless, unfit mother; sometimes I think she's the crossest, worst-natured child in the world. It's probably both. [Quoted in Leach, 1997]

In fact, both parents and infants are reacting to deep urges that signal and respond, in a system that sometimes seems overwhelming in the early months but is much better than the opposite. If newborns never signaled their needs or parents were indifferent to their signals, the species would not survive.

In addition to responding to infants' cries, adults become emotionally and physiologically aroused by the sight of a baby's smile or by the sound of an infant's laughter or by the round-faced, chinless, hairless head or even the tiny feet of a newborn. (This truth leads advertisers to use images of babies to sell everything from toilet paper to political candidates.) Adults seem particularly mesmerized by their own children's simplest actions, doting on their every move, watching them sleep, listening to them breathe.

This is, beyond doubt, an example from epigenetic theory. Parental attention serves a survival function: It increases the likelihood that adults will notice when something is amiss with a child. Thus adults and infants are part of an epigenetic *system*, with interactive genetic actions and reactions that ensure survival of the next generation. Fortunately, these irrational responses include joy. According to the expert who reported on the self-described "totally . . . hopeless, unfit

mother" earlier, "The same baby who right now ruins all your evenings by crying may one day make all your mornings feel like Christmas" (Leach, 1997). My own four children now make me feel the same way.

Open Wide Caregivers and babies elicit responses in each other that ensure survival of the next generation. The caregiver's role in this vital interaction is obvious, but ethology has shown that infants starve if they themselves do not chirp, meow, whine, bleat, squeak, cry, or do whatever it is that they do to signal hunger, and then open their mouths wide when dinner comes. (Have you ever tried to feed a baby who refuses to "open"?)

❷ *Observational Quiz (see answer page 61): Infant feeding is universal among all species. However, at least three aspects of the bottom photo signify that the creatures there are human. What are these aspects?*

expression of our height genes has already occurred. Thus, on an individual level, the genes for height combine with influences from our early environment to yield our eventual height. On a species level, we humans are taller than our genetic cousins the chimpanzees, because greater height was adaptive for humans—and more so for our ancestors in central Africa than in northern Alaska (who survived better if they were relatively short and fat).

Research on genes finds that no genetic instruction—including instructions for basic traits such as physical structure and intellectual potential—is unaffected by environment (Barnett, 1998). Each person's genetic inheritance is so intertwined with experience that it is virtually impossible to isolate the specific effects of genes without considering the context; everything that seems to be genetic is actually epigenetic. The point in all these examples is that environmental factors make genetic influences stronger, weaker, or nonexistent over time, within individuals, within populations, and within the human race (see Figure 2.5) (Buss et al., 1998).

Systems that Support Development

Finally, this theory also emphasizes *systems*. The critical aspect of a system, as scientists use the term, is that change in one part of the system causes corresponding adjustments and changes in every other part. This is true for the biological systems that foster the development of an individual (e.g., the cardiovascular system), the systems that support an entire species (in an ecosystem), and the systems that govern all nature (Magnusson, 1996; Masterpasqua, 1997).

One example of how the environment causes a systemic change is the effect of human handling of rat pups. It has long been realized that rats become smarter if they are frequently held when they are young. Some scientists thought that the rats learned from their early human involvement. More recent research shows specifically how handling produces systemic change: Handling increases the mother's licking and grooming of her pup, which leads to decreased release of stress hormones, which leads to increased tolerance of potentially stressful conditions, which, in adulthood, leads to less brain degeneration than in unhandled rats (Sapolsky, 1997).

This example raises important questions for humans, of course, which the researcher wryly addressed:

> It is a rare parent of a newborn who does not feel panic built around the consequences that her or his actions now have. Developmental studies have indicated that the quality, quantity, and timing of infant stimulation can have long-lasting effects—and soon the anxious parent is convinced that one lullaby sung off-key ensures that a child will not only one day be a sociopath, but will also never use dental floss. If mothers of newborn rats harbor similar anxieties, a report by Liu and colleagues affirms their worries: The authors show that subtle stimulation in a rat's infancy has marked consequences that are probably life-long. (Sapolosky, 1997)

We will soon discuss the implications of such research for humans. We already know, however, that each individual is (among other things) an epigenetic system, continually adjusting to a never-ending flux of proteins, hormones, and electrical charges that occur in response to biochemical and physical forces inside and outside the body. Genes form the foundation of that system, but they never act alone (Goldsmith et al., 1997).

Figure 2.5 Always Human, but Ever Changing.
The genes inherited from our ancestors still echo throughout the centuries and affect every member of the human species today. However, the particulars are always influenced by ongoing experiences that can increase, decrease, or stop the expression of genes, a process that the epigenetic systems theory of development emphasizes.

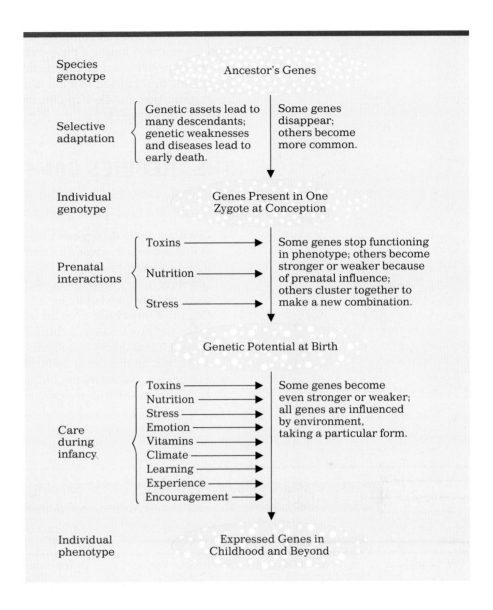

Each society and each species is also a system, gradually shaping its common genetic heritage in such a way as to adapt to the changing world. Humans depend on one another not only economically and politically but also for survival.

We should make it very clear that some predictions from epigenetic systems theory are not established certainties but remain parts of an emergent theory. As one psychologist reminds us:

> The attempt at integration [of genes, environment, and behavior] faces a daunting task—genes only make proteins, specifically enzymes, and the leap from the simple alphabet of molecular biology to the rich tapestry of human experience requires a combination of up-to-date scientific information in addition to some fast footwork. [Anderson, 1998]

How much of epigenetic systems theory is up-to-date information and how much is fancy footwork is still a matter of opinion, to be tested scientifically. Increasingly, epigenetic systems theory provides a framework to connect fast-breaking genetic discoveries and methodologies with intriguing speculations about exactly how genes and environments combine to propel development. Given the excitement of this field of study, a team of leading researchers warns that "it is difficult to strike the balance between enthusiasm and caution" (Plomin & Rutter, 1998). Recall our description of what a developmental theory does, on page 37: Epigenetic systems theory can frame the questions, but it does not yet provide the answers.

THE THEORIES COMPARED

Each of the theories presented in this chapter has contributed a great deal to the study of human development (see Table 2.3):

- *Psychoanalytic theory* has made us aware of the importance of early childhood experiences and of the impact of the "hidden dramas" that influence daily life.
- *Learning theory* has shown us the effect that the immediate environment can have on behavior.
- *Cognitive theory* has brought us to a greater understanding of how intellectual processes and thinking affect actions.
- *Sociocultural theory* has reminded us that development is embedded in a rich and multifaceted cultural context.
- *Epigenetic systems theory* emphasizes the inherited forces that affect each person—and all humankind—within particular contexts.

table **2.3**	**Five Perspectives on Human Development**			
Theory	Basic Focus	Fundamental Depiction of What People Do	Emphasis on Early Years?	Relative Emphasis: Nature and Nurture
Psychoanalytic	Psychosexual (Freud) or psychosocial (Erikson) stages	Battle unconscious impulses and overcome major crises	Yes (especially in Freudian theory)	More nature (biological, sexual impulses are very important, as are parent–child bonds and memories)
Learning	Conditioning through stimulus and response	Respond to stimuli, reinforcement, and models in the environment	No (conditioning and reconditioning are lifelong)	More nurture (direct environment influences produce various behaviors)
Cognitive	Thinking, remembering, analyzing	Seek to understand experiences, in the process forming concepts and cognitive strategies	No (new concepts and control processes are developed throughout life)	More nature (person's own mental activity and motivation are key)
Sociocultural	Social context, expressed through people, language, customs	Learn the tools, skills, and values of society through apprenticeships	Yes (family and school acculturation are critical)	More nurture (interaction of mentor and learner, within cultural context, is pivotal))
Epigenetic systems	Genes and their expression, in individuals and species	Express impulses, interests, and patterns inherited from ancestors and developed from childhood	Yes (early biochemical forces alter the manifestation of genes)	Nature begins the process; nurture affects it via hormones, enzymes, toxins, and selective adaptation

In order, these five theories present us with: the unconscious processes; the environment; the intellect; the culture; and the genes. No comprehensive view of development can ignore any one of these factors.

Each theory has been criticized. Psychoanalytic theory has been faulted for being too subjective; learning theory, for being too mechanistic; cognitive theory, for undervaluing genetic differences; sociocultural theory, for neglecting individuals; and epigenetic theory, for neglecting society.

Many developmentalists hope that "a new integration may be emerging in the form of a systems approach that will bring together biological, social, cognitive, and emotional theories into a more coherent framework" (Parke et al., 1994). Both sociocultural theory and epigenetic systems theory are moving in that direction, and both attempt to incorporate significant forces—cultural on the one hand and biochemical on the other—that traditional developmental science undervalued. However, both may stretch too far, losing the actual developing person amid diverse cultures or multifactorial genetic interactions. Further, sociocultural theory may overestimate the potential for human change throughout life in response to cultural and historical changes, while epigenetic systems theory may overestimate the impact of evolutionary adaptation or of early experiences.

eclectic perspective A perspective whose adherents choose what seem to be the best, or most useful, elements from the various theories, instead of adhering to only a single perspective.

Until a new grand theory is tested and established, most developmentalists will continue to take an **eclectic perspective.** That is, rather than adopt any one of these theories exclusively, they make selective use of many or all of them. When 45 leaders in the field were asked to identify their approach to developmental studies, "clear theoretical labels were hard to come by," with many describing themselves through some combination of terms, such as "cognitive social learning," "social interactive behaviorist," and even "social evolutionary cognitive behaviorism" (Horowitz, 1994). The state of research in development has been accurately characterized as "theoretical pluralism" because no single theory fully explains the behavior of humans as they go through life (Dixon & Lerner, 1999).

In later chapters, as you encounter elaborations and echoes of the five major theories and various minitheories, you will no doubt form your own opinion of the validity and usefulness of each. Probably you will also take an eclectic view—one that chooses the best from each theory to guide your exploration of development. You may even begin to devise a coherent, comprehensive, systematic approach of your own.

SUMMARY

WHAT THEORIES DO

1. A theory provides a framework of general principles that can be used to guide research and explain observations. Each developmental theory interprets human development from a somewhat different perspective.

2. All developmental theories attempt to provide a context for understanding how individual experiences and behavior change over time. Theories are practical in that they provide a framework for interpretation and research, as well as a coherent set of assumptions that aids inquiry.

GRAND THEORIES

3. Psychoanalytic theory emphasizes that human actions and thoughts originate from powerful impulses and conflicts that often are not part of our conscious awareness. Freud, the founder of psychoanalytic theory, explained how sexual urges arise during the oral, anal, phallic, and genital stages of development. Parents' reactions to conflicts associated with these urges have a lasting impact on the child's personality.

4. Erikson's version of psychoanalytic theory emphasizes psychosocial contexts, with individuals shaped by the interaction of personal characteristics and social forces. Erikson describes eight successive stages of psychosocial development, from infancy through old age, each of which involves a developmental crisis that must be resolved.

5. Behaviorists, or learning theorists, believe that the focus of psychologists' study should be behavior, which can be observed and measured. This theory seeks to discover the laws that govern the relationship between events and the reactions they produce—that is, between stimulus and response.

6. Learning theory emphasizes various forms of conditioning—a learning process by which particular stimuli become linked with particular responses. In classical conditioning, a neutral stimulus becomes associated with a meaningful stimulus. In operant conditioning, certain responses, called reinforcers, are used to make it more likely that certain behaviors will recur.

7. Social learning theory recognizes that much of human behavior is learned by observing the behavior of others. The basic process is modeling, in which we first observe a behavior and then repeat it. Generally, the person being observed is admirable in some way, or the behavior is one that the observer's self-understanding motivates him or her to imitate.

8. Cognitive theorists believe that a person's thought processes have an important effect on his or her understanding of the world, and thus on the person's development. Piaget proposed that an individual's thinking develops through four age-related periods. Sensorimotor intelligence develops in infancy, preoperational intelligence emerges during the preschool years, concrete operational intelligence comes into play during the school years, and formal operational intelligence begins in adolescence and continuing lifelong.

9. Piaget believed that cognitive development is an active and universal process. Curiosity is guided by the search for cognitive equilibrium, which is a person's ability to explain a new situation with existing understanding. When disequilibrium occurs, the person develops cognitively by modifying his or her understanding.

10. The nature–nurture controversy centers on how much influence heredity has on development, as compared to how much influence environment has. Every researcher agrees, however, that both factors influence human development.

EMERGENT THEORIES

11. Sociocultural theory explains human development in terms of the guidance, support, and structure provided by one's culture. For Vygotsky, learning occurs through the social interactions learners share with more knowledgeable members of the society.

12. Mentors guide learners through the zone of proximal development. Both learner and society develop as a result of the collaboration between mentor and learner. Societies and cultures change when individuals choose which knowledge to pass on.

13. Epigenetic systems theory begins by noting that genes are powerful and omnipresent, potentially affecting every aspect of development. This theory also stresses an ongoing interaction between the genes and environmental forces, which can range from prenatal toxins to lifelong stresses. This interaction can halt, modify, or strengthen the effects of the genes, both within the person and, over time, within the species.

14. Epigenetic systems theory also focuses on the systems, within the individual as well as the species, that support development. In one such system, infants are born with various drives and reflexes that help ensure their survival, while adults are normally also equipped with innate predispositions to nurture babies.

THE THEORIES COMPARED

15. Psychoanalytic, learning, cognitive, sociocultural, and epigenetic systems theories have each contributed to the understanding of human development. No one theory is broad enough to describe the full complexity and diversity of human experience.

16. Most developmentalists, well aware of the criticisms of these perspectives, take an eclectic perspective, selectively incorporating ideas and generating hypotheses from all of them. In addition, many find various minitheories, related to specific age groups or topics, useful for formulating research questions.

KEY TERMS

developmental theory (37)
grand theories (38)
minitheories (38)
emergent theories (38)
psychoanalytic theory (39)
learning theory (42)
stimulus (42)
response (42)
conditioning (42)
reinforcement (46)
social learning (46)
modeling (46)

cognitive theory (47)
cognitive equilibrium (48)
sociocultural theory (51)
guided participation (54)
epigenetic systems theory (55)
zone of proximal development (56)
ethology (58)
selective adaptation (60)
eclectic perspective (65)

KEY QUESTIONS

1. What functions does a good theory perform?

2. What is the major assumption of psychoanalytic theory?

3. What are the key differences between Freud and Erikson?

4. What is the major focus of learning theory?

5. How are stimulus and response related in classical conditioning? In operant conditioning?

6. According to Piaget, how do periods of disequilibrium lead to mental growth?

7. According to sociocultural theory, what is the relationship between the individual and the culture?

8. Describe guided participation, using an example.

9. According to epigenetic systems theorists, how can genetic instructions change?

10. What is the ethological view of behavior? How does it relate to epigenetic systems theory?

11. What are the main differences among the grand theories and between the two emergent theories discussed in this chapter?

12. *In Your Experience* Does the behavior of children at about age 4 or 5 years appear to be more the result of nature or nurture? Why?

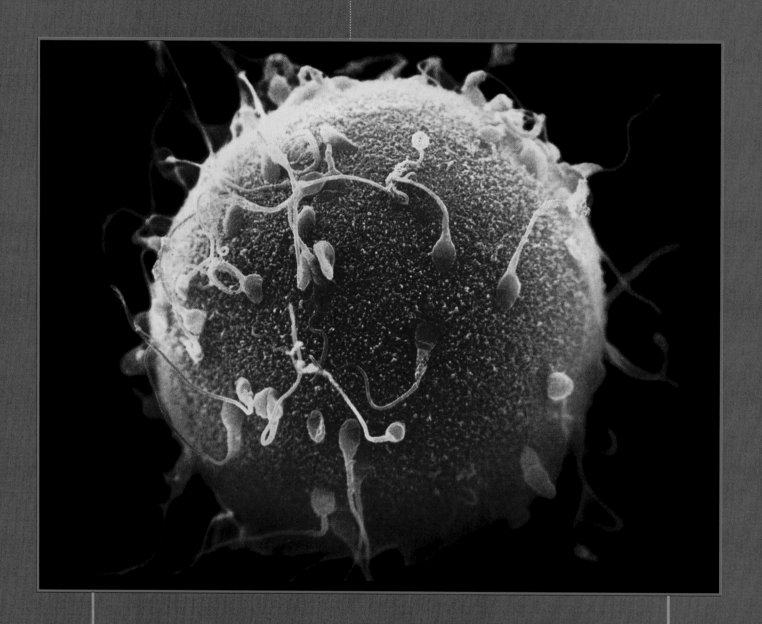

Heredity and Environment

CHAPTER 3

From the very beginning, individual development arises from the interaction of two prime forces: genetic instructions inherited at conception and environmental factors that allow those instructions to be expressed, shaped, deflected, or silenced. The term **environment,** as social scientists use it, includes every influence on an organism that is not genetic, from the effect on a fetus of the mother's nutrition and health to the social relationships and cultural values that impact on the elderly. All of a human being's experiences, from conception to death, are part of his or her environment. **Heredity** consists of the specific genetic material that an organism inherits from the parents. Of course, since heredity refers only to genetic traits, it does not include such things as inherited wealth or values or traditions.

The interaction between heredity and environment in each person is intimate, dynamic, and lifelong. This interaction is so varied and complex that accurate prediction is impossible. Yet understanding the interplay of genes and experiences provides valuable insight: How did we become who we are? What else can we become?

DEVELOPMENT BEGINS

Human development begins very simply, when a male reproductive cell, or *sperm* (plural: sperm), penetrates the membrane of a female reproductive cell, or *ovum* (plural: ova). Each human **gamete** (the name for any reproductive cell, whether it comes from a male or a female) contains more than a billion chemically coded genetic instructions. These instructions represent half of a rough blueprint for human development. At conception, when the sperm and ovum combine, the two blueprint halves form a complete set of instructions for creating a person.

From One Cell to Trillions

For the first hour or so after a sperm enters an ovum, the two cells maintain their separate identities, side by side, enclosed within the ovum's membrane. Suddenly they fuse, and a living cell called a **zygote** is formed: Two reproductive cells have literally become one.

Within hours, the zygote begins the first stages of growth through a process of *duplication* and *division*. First, the combined genetic material from both gametes duplicates itself, forming two complete sets of the genetic code. Then these two sets move toward opposite sides of the zygote,

environment All the nongenetic factors that can affect development—everything from the impact of the immediate cell environment on the genes themselves to the broader effects of nutrition, medical care, socioeconomic status, family dynamics, and the economic, political, and cultural contexts.

heredity The specific genetic material that an organism inherits from its parents.

gamete A reproductive cell; that is, a cell that can reproduce a new individual if it combines with a gamete from the other sex.

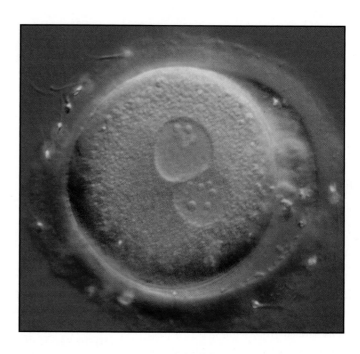

The Moment of Conception The ovum shown here is about to become a zygote. It has been penetrated by a single sperm, whose nucleus now lies next to the nucleus of the ovum. Shortly, the two nuclei will fuse, bringing together about 100,000 genes that will guide future development.

Figure 3.1 What One Human Cell Contains

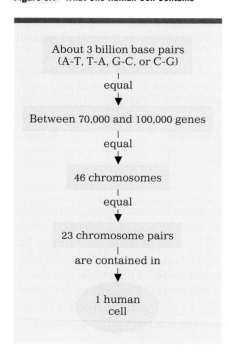

About 3 billion base pairs
(A-T, T-A, G-C, or C-G)

equal

Between 70,000 and 100,000 genes

equal

46 chromosomes

equal

23 chromosome pairs

are contained in

1 human
cell

zygote The single cell formed from the fusing of a sperm and an ovum.

gene The basic unit for the transmission of heredity instructions.

chromosome A carrier of genes; one of forty-six segments of DNA that together contain all human genes.

and the zygote divides neatly down the middle. Thus the one-celled zygote has become two cells, each containing a complete set of the original genetic code. These two cells duplicate and divide to become four; these four, in turn, duplicate and divide to become eight; and so on.

At about the eight-cell stage, a third process, *differentiation,* is added to duplication and division. Cells begin to specialize, taking different forms and reproducing at various rates, according to the functions they have been genetically programmed to perform in the developing organism. Before differentiation, any one of the cells could become a whole person; after differentiation, this is no longer true.

When you (or I, or any other person) were newborn, your body had about 10 trillion cells. By adulthood, the number of cells in your body had increased to between 300 trillion and 500 trillion. But no matter how many cells you may have, and no matter how much division, duplication, differentiation, and specialization has occurred, each body cell carries a copy of the complete genetic instructions inherited by the one-celled zygote that you were at the moment of conception. This explains why DNA testing of any body cell can identify "the real father" or "the guilty criminal" or "the long-lost twin" when the traditional methods of identification fail.

The Genetic Code

The basic unit of genetic instruction is the **gene.** A gene is a discrete segment of a **chromosome,** which is a molecule of *DNA (deoxyribonucleic acid).* Except for sperm and ova, every normal human cell has 23 pairs of chromosomes (46 chromosomes in all), which collectively carry between 70,000 and 100,000 distinct genes (see Figure 3.1).

The instructions on each gene are "written" in a chemical code made up of pairs of only four chemical *bases*—adenine, guanine, cytosine, and thymine, abbreviated A, G, C, and T, respectively. These chemical bases normally combine in only four pairings, A-T, T-A, G-C, and C-G, a fact that might seem to provide a very limited genetic vocabulary. In fact, there are approximately 3 billion base pairs in the DNA of every human and thousands of base pairs in every gene, which means there are many, many possible sequences.

genetic code The sequence of chemical compounds (called bases) that is held within DNA molecules and directs development, behavior, and form.

Human Genome Project An international effort to map the complete human genetic code.

The precise nature of a gene's instructions is determined by this **genetic code,** that is, the sequence in which base pairs appear along each segment of the DNA molecule. Numerous scientists are now engaged in the **Human Genome Project,** an international effort to map the complete genetic code. Originally scheduled to be completed by 2005 (see updates at www.nhgri.nih.gov/hgp), the Human Genome Project is progressing so rapidly that a "rough draft" was ready in 2000 (chromosome 22 was completed in December 1999). Once it is completed, we will know the usual sequence and location of all the human genes. Indeed, "the ultimate goal of the Human Genome Project is to understand how the genome builds, maintains, and operates an organism" (Durick, 1999). This goal is still years away. One complication is that some genes appear in several versions, called *alleles,* and most genes have several functions. Already, however, scientists have located more than half the genes, including 100 or more that often code for hereditary problems. Already it is known that the total number of human genes is probably less than the 100,000 previously estimated. And already we know the basics of what genes do—knowledge that was beyond even the most learned biologist 50 years ago (Barnett, 1998).

We now know that genes direct the synthesis of hundreds of different kinds of proteins, including enzymes, that serve as the body's building blocks and regulators. Following genetic instructions, certain cells become neurons (brain cells), others become the lens of the eye, others become the valves of the heart, and so on throughout the body. In short, "genes determine each organism's size, shape and structure—all the features that distinguish, say, humans from honeybees" (Pennisi & Roush, 1997).

The influence of genes doesn't stop there. Through some sort of on–off switching mechanism, genes control life itself, instructing cells to grow, to repair damage, to take in nourishment, to multiply, to atrophy, to die (Finch & Tanzi, 1997). Even certain kinds of cognitive development involve genes that switch on at particular ages, propelling maturation in specific areas of the brain (Plomin et al., 1997).

All this activity occurs in collaboration with other genes and with the environment. The gene that produces the legs of a butterfly, for example, is exactly the same gene that shapes the four legs of a cat, the many legs of a centipede, and the two legs of a person. The differences between your legs and those of other creatures are governed by additional genes that advise the leg gene as to the particular shape and number of legs to make (Pennisi & Roush, 1997).

Similarly, every mammal embryo is genetically commanded to make seven neck bones. Because of the influence of other genes, those seven bones in a whale's neck become flat, thin discs; those in a giraffe's neck become elongated; and those in a human's neck are in between—probably more than we would need if our bodies were perfectly designed to avoid neck injuries, but adequate as a template to accommodate mammalian diversity (Barnett, 1998).

Mapping the Karyotype A *karyotype* portrays a person's chromosomes. To create a karyotype, a cell is grown in a laboratory, magnified, and then usually photographed. The photo is cut into pieces and rearranged, matching the pairs of chromosomes, from pair 1, the largest pair *(top left)* to pair 23, here the XY of a normal male *(bottom right)*.

❓ *Observational Quiz (see answer page 73): Is this the karyotype of a normal human?*

Chromosomes

As we have noted, each normal human has 46 chromosomes, duplicated in every body cell except gametes. The chromosomes are arranged in 23 distinct pairs. One member of each pair is inherited from the mother, and the other one is inherited from the father. When the chromosomes match up, the genes also pair off, again with one from each parent (although, since many genes can have several alleles, a specific gene from one parent may not exactly match its mate from the other parent).

This very specific genetic and chromosomal pairing is encoded for life in every cell—with one important exception. When the human body makes sperm or ova, cell division occurs in such a way that each gamete receives only one member of each chromosome pair. This is why sperm and ova each have only 23 chromosomes: to ensure that when they combine, the new organism will have a total of 46 chromosomes. In other words, genetically, we are whatever we are: Every cell of your body, from the soles of your feet to the lining of your gut to the dancing neurons of your brain, contains the distinct code that makes you you, and every cell of my body contains the unique code that makes me me.

The one exception occurs if you and I reproduce. My gametes contain only half of my genes; your gametes contain only half of your genes. This means that our children would be neither yours nor mine but ours—half you, half me.

Sex Determination

Of the 23 pairs of human chromosomes, 22 are closely matched pairs, with the two chromosomes of each pair containing similar genes in almost identical positions and sequence. The **twenty-third pair,** which is the pair that determines the individual's sex (among other things), is a different case. In the female, the twenty-third pair of chromosomes is composed of two large X-shaped chromosomes. Accordingly, it is designated XX. In the male, the twenty-third pair is composed of one large X-shaped chromosome and one much smaller Y-shaped chromosome. It is designated XY.

Obviously, since a female's twenty-third chromosome pair is XX, every ovum that her body creates will contain either one X or the other—but always an X. And since a male's twenty-third pair is XY, half his sperm will contain an X chromosome and half will contain a Y. That Y chromosome (but not the X) contains a gene that directs a developing fetus to make male organs, so eventually a baby boy is born. Thus the critical factor in the determination of a zygote's sex is which sperm reaches the ovum first—a Y sperm, creating a male (XY), or an X sperm, creating a female (XX) (see Figure 3.2).

twenty-third pair The chromosome pair that, in humans, determines the zygote's (and hence the person's) sex, among other things.

Figure 3.2 Determining a Zygote's Sex. As you can see, any given couple can produce four possible combinations of sex chromosomes; two lead to female children, and two to male. In terms of the future person's sex, it does not matter at all which of the mother's Xs the zygote inherited. All that matters is whether the father's Y sperm or X sperm fertilized the ovum. However, for X-linked conditions it matters a great deal, since typically one, but not both, of the mother's Xs carries the trait.

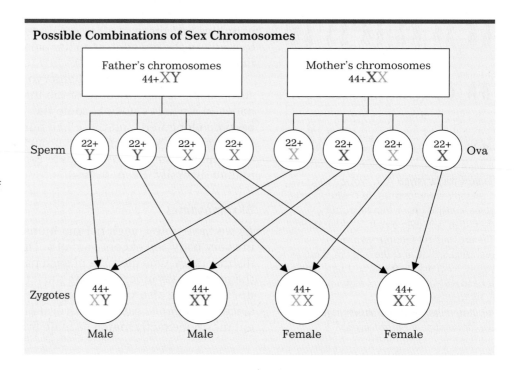

Possible Combinations of Sex Chromosomes

Father's chromosomes 44+XY

Mother's chromosomes 44+XX

Sperm: 22+Y, 22+Y, 22+X, 22+X   22+X, 22+X, 22+X, 22+X :Ova

Zygotes: 44+XY (Male), 44+XY (Male), 44+XX (Female), 44+XX (Female)

❶ *Answer to Observational Quiz (from page 71):* *No, there are 24 pairs here. This photo shows the two different possibilities for the twenty-third pair. (The normal female XX is just to the left of the normal male XY.)*

Continuity and Diversity

The vast majority of each person's genes are identical to those of every other human being, male or female, related or not (Plomin et al., 1997). As a result of the instructions carried by genes, each new member of the human race shares certain characteristics with everyone else, alive or dead or not yet born:

- Common physical structures (such as the pelvic alignment that allows us to walk upright)
- Common behavioral tendencies (such as the urge to communicate through language)
- Common reproductive potential (allowing any male and female to produce a new member of the species)

These species-specific characteristics, and thousands of others, have been fashioned throughout our long evolutionary history, promoting our survival by enabling humans to live successfully on Earth.

The remainder of each person's genes differ in various ways from those of other individuals. The diversity that these genes provide, over generations, is essential for human adaptation to new environments and needs. Thus the fact that each human differs genetically from others means that our species is able to survive as conditions and circumstances change.

Our diversity also benefits the entire community through specialization and cooperation. Because each of us inherits specific talents and abilities, each of us is better at some tasks or activities than at others. By specializing in those particular tasks, performing them for others as well as for ourselves, we can together achieve more than we could if each of us had to be his or her own priest, artist, carpenter, farmer, cook, doctor, teacher, and so on. We gain intellectually as well, by exchanging and combining ideas and perspectives. Both our commonalities and our diversities allow our survival as the human species.

The Mechanisms of Diversity

Given that each sperm or ovum from a particular parent contains only 23 chromosomes, how can every conception be genetically unique? The answer is that when the chromosome pairs divide during the formation of gametes, chance alone determines which one of each pair will wind up in one gamete and which in the other. A vast number of chromosome combinations are possible. According to the laws of probability, there are, in fact, 2^{23}—that is, about 8 million—possible combinations. In other words, approximately 8 million chromosomally different ova or sperm can be produced by a single individual.

In addition, just before a chromosome pair in a man's or woman's body divides to form sperm or ova, corresponding segments of the pair are sometimes broken off and exchanged, altering the genetic composition of both pair members. Through the new combinations it produces, this *crossing-over* of genes adds greatly to genetic diversity.

All things considered, then, a given mother and father can form more than 64 trillion genetically distinct offspring, all full brothers and sisters but each quite different from the others. Outsiders might see strong family resemblances in siblings (once a neighbor said my four children were "like four peas in a pod"). But every parent knows that each child is unlike the others. It is no exaggeration to say that every zygote is unique, with

TOO MANY BOYS?

Serious ethical questions arise in numerous aspects of genetic and chromosomal research. These questions are usually answered only by the individuals directly concerned about their own families, not by national policy or international agreements. Genetic engineering, human cloning, prenatal testing, and selective abortion are among such issues. Sex ratio is another.

Unless wars, epidemics, or other catastrophes occur, about an equal number of men and women reach young adulthood, the prime reproductive age. In earlier times, death in childbirth meant that more men than women survived to old age. Now heart attacks kill more middle-aged men, so the sex ratio favors women after age 50 (see Figure 3.3). In both circumstances, however, a balance occurs at about age 25, making it likely that most people will find a mate and become a parent. Should nations, or individuals, be allowed to change the natural sex ratio?

Some have tried. History finds numerous societies that allowed female infanticide (a practice so common that it had to be explictly forbidden in the Koran) or that allow husbands to divorce or even kill wives who produced only daughters (as did England's Henry VIII) or that advised pregnant women to eat certain foods, sleep on one side, or pray to the moon to make sure their baby was a boy or girl. Predictably, such methods failed half the time.

Now we know better:

- Sperm, not ova, determine a baby's sex.
- Each zygote is already XX or XY.
- Prenatal testing, even the sonogram, can predict whether an embryo or fetus is male or female, long before birth.

This knowledge has finally made sex selection feasible. For decades, women who carry genetic diseases that occur only in boys (such as hemophilia) have tested each pregnancy and allowed only their female fetuses to develop to

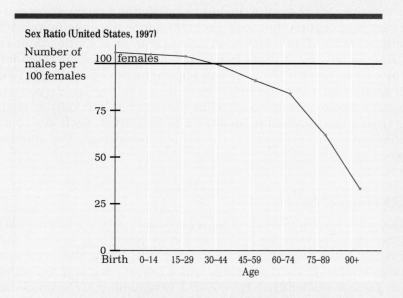

Sex Ratio (United States, 1997)

Number of males per 100 females

(graph: y-axis 100 females, 75, 50, 25, 0; x-axis Birth, 0–14, 15–29, 30–44, 45–59, 60–74, 75–89, 90+; Age)

Figure 3.3 Too Many Baby Boys? Worldwide, slightly more males than females are born each year. Given the slightly higher rate of death among males in childhood (and assuming no unequal, major killer, such as war), the result is a roughly equal number of men and women of reproductive age. In the past many women died in childbirth, whereas today heart attacks kill many more men than women—which is the main reason why the sex ratio now favors women after age 45. (Men are also somewhat more likely than women to die from other causes.) What would be the effect on marriage and divorce rates, on health costs, on crime statistics, and on population growth if couples chose to have either more boys or more girls?

the potential of becoming a genetically unique individual. No wonder it is sometimes said that the parents of one child believe in nurture but the parents of two or more children believe in nature (Wright, 1998).

Twins

Although every zygote is genetically unique, not every newborn is. In some pregnancies, the growing cluster of cells splits apart in the early stages of duplication and division, creating two or four identical, indepen-

term. Each year between 1990 and 1993, more than a million couples in China, where boys are favored and each couple is legally allowed to have only one child, aborted female fetuses. In reaction, China has outlawed abortion for the purpose of sex selection.

Couples wishing to have children of a certain sex but not wishing to abort now have another alternative. For decades, cattle breeders have successfully used sperm sorting and artificial insemination to produce only male or only female calves, depending on whether beef or milk is the desired product. Now a similar sperm-sorting technique is available experimentally for humans, with about a 95 percent success rate (Grifo et al., 1994).

Despite these advances, sex selection has not become widespread. Do we need a social policy to regulate this new technology? Before answering, consider the social consequences if half as many girls were born while every other element of society stayed the same:

In family life

- fewer single mothers, fewer widows, more never-married men
- weaker family ties between siblings, parents and children, grandparents and grandchildren (because women are the kinkeepers, as the chapter text notes)
- more children per woman, fewer children per man
- more children with learning disabilities and behavior problems

In economic life

- more engineers, architects, billionaires; fewer nurses, teachers, secretaries
- greater demand for fast food, fast cars, guns, prostitutes
- less demand for fashionable clothes, household furnishings, kitchen equipment

- more violent crime of all kinds, and thus a greater need for police, judges, prisons

In health care

- lower average life span, more accidental deaths, more suicides, more homicides
- less ongoing medical care (fewer specialists in gynecology, arthritis, gerontology)
- fewer people suffering from chronic depression
- more people suffering from chronic drug and alcohol abuse

In community life

- increased attendance at professional sports events; decreased attendance at libraries
- increased participation in sports teams; decreased participation in churches
- more wars; fewer day care centers
- more votes for conservative policies; fewer for liberal policies

These predictions probably make you protest that cultural practices, not biological sex, determines who participates in athletics or religion or politics. Your protest is valid for all sixteen of the items listed above. Neither genes nor chromosomes determine behavior; many nongenetic factors influence human actions. Nonetheless, modern sex-selection techniques make it possible for couples, doctors, or national policies to change the sex ratio, producing either many more boys (as China did for a few years) or many more girls (as may happen in European nations). If you had only one child, would you prefer a son or daughter? If everyone else felt the same way, what might be the consequences?

monozygotic twins Twins who have identical genes because they were formed from one zygote that split into two identical organisms very early in development.

dent clusters (Gall, 1996). These cell clusters become **monozygotic twins** (identical twins) or monozygotic quadruplets, so named because they originated from one *(mono)* zygote.

Since they originated from the same zygote, monozygotic multiple births share identical genetic instructions for physical appearance, psychological traits, vulnerability to diseases, and everything else. If conception occurs in a laboratory instead of inside a woman's body, it is technically possible to split a human organism at the two- or four- or even eight-cell stage. This would artificially create monozygotic twins or

Any Monozygotic Twins Here? Sometimes twins are obviously dizygotic, as when they are of different sexes or, like the girls on the right, differ notably in coloring, size, and perhaps visual acuity. However, sometimes dizygotic twins can look a lot alike, just as two siblings born a year or two apart can share many physical characteristics.

❓ *Observational Quiz (see answer page 78): What do the similarities and differences of the boys in the left-hand photo suggest about their zygosity?*

quadruplets or octuplets, which could be implanted in the uterus. At the moment, such cloning is considered unethical and illegal, and the incidence of monozygotic twins (about 1 in every 270 births) is holding steady for every ethnic group, in every nation, in mothers of every age.

Not all twins are monozygotic. **Dizygotic twins** (fraternal twins) begin life as two separate zygotes created by the fertilization of two ova at roughly the same time. Dizygotic conceptions may occur as frequently as one in every six pregnancies, but usually only one twin develops past the embryo stage. Dizygotic births occur naturally about once in every 60 births, with considerable variation in incidence among ethnic groups. (Women from Nigeria, for example, spontaneously produce dizygotic newborns about once in every 25 pregnancies; women from England, once in 100; and women from Japan, once in 700 [Gall, 1996].)

Age is also a factor, with women in their late 30s three times as likely to have dizygotic twins as women in their early 20s (Mange & Mange, 1999). Dizygotic twins share no more genes than do any other offspring of the same parents; that is, they share about 50 percent of the genes governing individual differences. They may not be the same sex or look like each other, or they may look a great deal alike, just as nontwin brothers and sisters sometimes do.

Other multiple births, such as triplets and quadruplets, can likewise be monozygotic, dizygotic, trizygotic, quadrazygotic, and so on (or even some combination of these). Over the past decade, the incidence of multiple births from separate zygotes has doubled in most medically advanced nations because of the increased use of fertility drugs and other methods of helping infertile couples have children.

Indeed, the rate of quadrazygotic births has increased by 2,000 percent (Gall, 1996). Generally, the more embryos that develop together in one uterus, the smaller, less mature, and more vulnerable each one is. This means that the increase in multiple births, which has produced many happy couples, has increased medical costs, infant mortality, and the incidence of children with special needs. For this reason, Finland limits to two the number of zygotes that can be implanted at one time. The limit is three in Norway and four in several other nations. The United States has no legal limit (see Chapter 17).

dizygotic twins Twins formed when two separate ova were fertilized by two separate sperm at roughly the same time. Such twins share about half their genes, like any other siblings.

Septuplets! Within weeks after seven healthy babies were born to Bobbi McCaughey in Des Moines, Iowa, two other women carrying septuplet pregnancies made international news. In England, a woman, like McCaughey, refused to undergo selective abortion (the aborting of some fetuses so that the rest could live); but this time the expected outcome occurred—all seven died. In Saudi Arabia, a woman gave birth to seven survivors. Her problem soon became one familiar to many new parents—not enough time and space. When this photo was taken, the hospital was threatening to call the police unless the parents took their 8-week-old septuplets home, but the mother refused—unless she got round-the-clock aides at public expense.

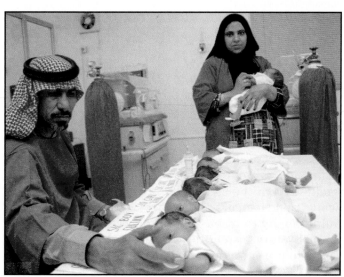

GENOTYPE TO PHENOTYPE

As we have seen, conception brings together, from both parents, genetic instructions concerning every human characteristic. Exactly how do these instructions influence the specific traits that a given offspring inherits? The answer is usually quite complex, because most traits are both **polygenic**—that is, affected by many genes—and **multifactorial**—that is, influenced by many factors, including factors in the environment.

To grasp the complexity of genetic influences, we must first distinguish between a person's genetic inheritance—his or her genetic *potential*—and the actual *expression* of that inheritance in the person's physiology, physical appearance, and behavioral tendencies. The sum total of all the genes a person inherits is the **genotype** (the genetic potential). The sum total of all the actual, expressed traits that result from the genes—including physical traits such as bushy eyebrows and nonphysical traits such as a hunger for excitement—is the person's **phenotype** (the genetic expression). As one scientist explains it, "Phenotype is the set of properties we can observe . . . . appearance and chemistry, size and shape, color and smell" (Tobin, 1999).

Clearly, we all have many genes in our genotypes that are not apparent in our phenotypes. In genetic terms, we are **carriers** of these unexpressed genes; that is, we "carry" them in our DNA and can pass them on to our sperm or ova and thus to our offspring. When a zygote inherits a gene that was only carried (not expressed) in one parent, the zygote will, at least, have that gene in the genotype. That gene may be expressed in the phenotype or may simply be carried again, with a chance of affecting the next generation.

Gene–Gene Interaction

Whether or not a genetic trait becomes expressed in the phenotype is determined by two levels of interaction:

- Interaction among the proteins synthesized according to the specific genes that affect the trait
- Ongoing interaction between the genotype and the environment

We will look first at interactions among the genes themselves.

Additive Genes

One common pattern of interaction among genes involves an **additive gene.** When genes interact additively, the phenotype reflects the contributions of all the genes that are involved. The many genes that affect height, hair curliness, and skin color, for instance, usually interact in an additive fashion.

Consider the simplified situation in which a tall man whose parents and grandparents were all very tall marries a short woman whose parents and grandparents were all very short. Let us assume that every one of his height genes is for tallness and that hers are all for shortness. The couple's children will inherit tall genes via the father's sperm and short genes via the mother's ova. Because the genes affecting height interact additively, the children will be of middling height (assuming that their nutrition and physical health are adequate). None of them will likely be as tall as their father or as short as their mother, because the contributions

polygenic traits Characteristics produced by the interaction of many genes (rather than by a single gene).

multifactorial traits Characteristics produced by the interaction of genetic and environmental (or other) influences (rather than by genetic influences alone).

genotype A person's entire genetic inheritance, including genes that are not expressed in the person.

phenotype All the genetic traits, including physical characteristics and behavioral tendencies, that are expressed in a person.

carrier A person who has a gene in his or her genotype that is not evident as part of the phenotype. Carriers can pass such a gene on to their offspring.

additive gene One of a number of genes affecting a specific trait, each of which makes an active contribution to that trait. Skin color and height are determined by additive genes.

Skin Color Is Inherited But ... Using "black," "white," "red," and "yellow" to denote human skin color is misleading, because humans actually have thousands of skin tones, each resulting from the combination of many genes, and none of them is one of these four colors. Depending on which half of each parent's skin-color genes children happen to inherit, each child can be paler, ruddier, lighter, darker, more sallow, more olive, or more freckled than either parent. This is particularly apparent in many African American families, like this one, whose ancestors came from at least three continents.

of all their genes for tallness and all their genes for shortness, somehow "averaged" together, will put them about halfway between the two.

In actuality, most people have both kinds of ancestors—relatively tall ones and relatively short ones—so we often see children who are notably taller or shorter than both their parents. How any additive trait turns out depends on all the contributions of whichever genes (half from each parent's varied genotype) a child happens to inherit. Every additive gene that is on a person's genotype has some impact on the phenotype.

Dominant and Recessive Genes

dominant gene The stronger of an interacting pair of genes.

recessive gene The weaker of an interacting pair of genes.

Less common are *nonadditive patterns,* in which the phenotype shows the influence of one gene much more than that of others. One kind of nonadditive pattern is the *dominant–recessive pattern,* which refers specifically to the interaction of gene pairs—one gene from the mother and one from the father, both influencing a particular trait. When a gene pair interacts according to this pattern, the phenotype reveals the influence of the more powerful gene, called the **dominant gene.** The other, weaker gene, the **recessive gene,** is not expressed in any obvious way. Sometimes the dominant gene completely controls the characteristic in question and the recessive gene is merely carried, with its influence not evident at all in the phenotype. In other instances, the outcome reflects *incomplete dominance,* with the phenotype influenced primarily, but not exclusively, by the dominant gene.

Hundreds of physical characteristics are determined according to the dominant–recessive pattern (with some epigenetic modification due to environmental factors and the influence of other genes). Blood types A and B are both dominant and O is recessive, leading to a complex relationship of genotype and phenotype in blood inheritance. (See Appendix A, page A-2.) Brown eyes are also said to be dominant over blue eyes, and many genetic diseases are recessive. However, with eye color and many diseases, some additive interactions are apparent.

X-Linked Genes

X-linked genes Genes that are on the X chromosome.

❶ Answer to Observational Quiz (from page 76):
They are almost certainly monozygotic. Their similarities include every obvious genetic trait—coloring, timing of tooth loss, thickness of lips, and shape of the ears and chin. Their differences include exactly the kinds that might be imposed by parents who have trouble distinguishing one child from the other—the color of their eyeglass frames and the length of their hair.

Some genes are called **X-linked** because they are located only on the X chromosome. If an X-linked gene is recessive—as are the genes for most forms of color-blindness, many allergies, several diseases, and some learning disabilities—the fact that it is on the X chromosome is critical. Recall that males have only one X chromosome. Thus, whatever recessive genes a male happens to inherit on his X chromosome cannot be counterbalanced or dominated by genes on his second X chromosome—there is no second X for a male, although there always is a second X for a female. So any recessive genes on his X chromosome will be expressed in his phenotype. This explains why some traits can be passed from mother to son (via the X) but not from father to son (since the Y does not carry the trait). (See Table 3.1.)

| table **3.1** | **The 23rd Pair and X-linked Color Blindness** |

X indicates an X chromosome with the X-linked gene for color blindness

	23rd Pair	Phenotype	Genotype	Next Generation
1.	XX	Normal woman	Not a carrier	No color blindness from mother.
2.	XY	Normal man	Normal X from mother	No color blindness from father.
3.	XX	Normal woman	Carrier from father	Half her children will inherit her X. The girls with her X will be carriers, the boys with her X will be color-blind.
4.	XX	Normal woman	Carrier from mother	Half her children will inherit her X. The girls with her X will be carriers, the boys with her X will be color-blind.
5.	XY	Color-blind man	Inherited from mother	All his daughters will have his X. None of his sons will have his X. All his children will have normal vision, unless their mother also had an X for color blindness.
6.	XX	Color-blind woman	Inherited from both parents	Every child will have one X from her. Therefore, every son will be color-blind. Daughters will be only carriers, unless they also inherit an X from the father, as their mother did.

Table 3.1 The phenotypes on lines 1 and 2 are normal because their genes are normal. Those on lines 3 and 4 are normal because the abnormal X-linked gene is recessive and the normal gene is dominant. Those on lines 5 and 6 are color-blind because they have only defective X-linked genes and no dominant, normal X.

genetic imprinting The tendency of certain genes to be expressed differently when they are inherited from the mother than when they are inherited from the father.

behavioral genetics The study of the effects of genes on behavior, including their effect on personality patterns, psychological disorders, and intellectual abilities.

More Complications

As complex as the preceding descriptions of gene interaction patterns may seem, they make gene–gene interaction appear much simpler than it actually is. That is because, to be able to discuss interaction at all, we are forced to treat genes as though they were discretely functioning "control devices." But, as we have noted, genes merely direct the synthesis of thousands of kinds of proteins, which then form the body's structures and direct its biochemical functions. The proteins of each body cell are continually affected by other proteins, enzymes, nutrients, and toxins that direct the cell's functioning (Masoro, 1999).

In regard to the dominant–recessive pattern, for example, a dominant gene might actually not "penetrate" the phenotype completely. Such incomplete penetrance may be caused by temperature, stress, or many other factors. Sometimes the split of a chromosome pair at or before conception is not precise, resulting in a person who is a *mosaic,* that is, who has a mixture of cells, some with a dominant gene, some without. A person could have one blue eye and one brown, or many other mosaicisms. And in the additive pattern, some genes contribute substantially more than others, either because they are naturally partially dominant or because their influence is amplified by the presence of certain other genes.

Moreover, certain genes behave differently depending on whether they are inherited from the mother or from the father. The full scope of, and the reason for, this parental **genetic imprinting,** or tagging, of certain genes has yet to be determined. We know that imprinting involves hundreds of genes but does not occur on every chromosome (Hurst, 1997). Some of the genes that influence height, insulin production, and several forms of mental retardation affect a child in different ways—even in opposite ways—depending on which parent they came from.

Such polygenic complexity is particularly apparent in **behavioral genetics,** which is the study of the genetic origins of psychological characteristics. These include personality traits such as sociability, assertiveness, moodiness, and fearfulness; psychological disorders such as schizophrenia, depression, and attention-deficit hyperactivity disorder; and cognitive traits such as memory for numbers, spatial perception, and fluency of expression. Mental retardation, for example, has been studied in great depth and detail. Virtually every type of inheritance pattern, including additive, dominant–recessive, X-linked, polygenic, multifactorial, and imprinting, is evident in at least one of the major types of mental retardation (Simonoff et al., 1996).

❷ Especially for Educators: Teaching genetic probabilities is sometimes hard. How could you illustrate the odds of dominant–recessive inheritance, if both parents are carriers, using a deck of ordinary playing cards?

The same is probably true for all aspects of personality and intellect. Every behavioral tendency is affected by many pairs of genes, some interacting in the dominant–recessive mode, some additive, and some creating new combinations of epigenetic functioning that are not yet catalogued or understood. And almost every behavior pattern can be caused by several different sets of genes (Yeung-Courchesne & Courchesne, 1997). One list of the "epigenetic rules" of behavioral genetics is particularly pertinent for a life-span perspective:

1. Large numbers of genes interact to produce a trait.
2. Environmental factors are important, affecting whether or not a trait is expressed and what form that expression takes.
3. Environment influences change during the life span. A trait that was quite plastic early in life can become difficult to alter once it is formed.
4. Despite rule #3, even adults retain developmental flexibility.
5. Despite all the rules above, the "butterfly effect" operates for behavioral genetics. For instance, a seemingly small factor such as birth order can affect genetic expression (Tobin, 1999).

Nature or Nurture?

In order to examine the complex interplay of heredity and the environment, researchers would like to distinguish the impacts of each of these two forces. This is difficult because, within any given trait, nature and nurture are intertwined at every moment. When the trait in question is an obvious physical one, the impact of genes on the phenotype seems fairly obvious. Family resemblances in facial features, coloring, or body shape can make it easy to say, "He has his mother's nose," meaning "That's hereditary."

But when a trait is a psychological one, especially a trait that changes over time, the fact that it runs in families could be explained by nurture just as easily as by nature. If children of highly intelligent parents excel in school, their school performance could, theoretically, be attributed entirely to their genetic inheritance, entirely to the family environment (which is likely to encourage reading, intellectual curiosity, and high academic standards), or to a combination of the two in any proportion. How, then, do scientists distinguish genetic from environmental influences on psychological characteristics?

Comparing Twins

One solution to this puzzle has been to study twins raised in the same families. As we have seen, monozygotic twins have all the same genes, whereas dizygotic twins, like any other two siblings from the same parents, share only half their genes. Thus, if monozygotic twins are found to be much more similar to each other on a particular trait than dizygotic twins are, it seems likely that genes play a significant role in the development of that trait. Conversely, if both kinds of twins are equally likely to express or not express a characteristic, family environment is probably the source of whatever similarities are found.

Such twin comparisons have revealed that many psychological traits are strongly influenced by genetics.

The Inheritance of the Throne Some people have much more to gain than others from the notion that genes are more influential than environment.

I don't know anything about the bell curve, but I say heredity is everything."

There is, however, one major problem with this approach: It assumes that twins growing up in a particular family share the same environment. In fact, however, twins in the same family sometimes have quite separate experiences—both in obvious ways, such as when one twin but not the other suffers a serious illness or learns from an extraordinary teacher, and in more subtle, ongoing ways, such as when parents punish one twin more harshly or when one twin defers to the other (Reiss, 1997). This means that twins may diverge on a particular trait not because they have different genes, but because they had different childhood experiences, even though both grew up in the same family surroundings.

Comparing Adoptees

An alternative approach to distinguishing the impact of genes from that of upbringing is to compare the traits of adopted children with the traits of both their biological and their adoptive parents. Traits that show a strong correlation between adoptees and their biological parents would seem to have a genetic basis; traits that show a strong correlation between children and their adoptive parents would suggest environmental influence. Blended stepfamilies, with children of various biological connections to one another (as full, half, or non-siblings) and to their parents, have also been studied.

Best of all, researchers can study identical twins who were separated at birth and adopted by different families. The results confirm that virtually every psychological characteristic and personal trait is genetically influenced. At the same time, these studies reinforce another, equally important conclusion: Virtually every psychological characteristic and personal trait is also affected, throughout the life span, by the person's environment (Bouchard, 1994, 1997).

Molecular Genetics

Neither twins nor adoptees can tell us exactly how genetic and environmental influences combine. Behavioral traits particularly are likely to be polygenic and multifactorial, with each impinging factor having so small and variable an influence that its effect is hard to detect. In fact, "genes that influence the susceptibility of complex traits . . . . do not act on their own, but interact with one or many genes and environmental factors. On their own, they explain only a small portion of the variance of the complex phenotype" (Sherman & Waldman, 1999).

How can "a small portion" be detected? Detailed analytic and statistical techniques developed in conjunction with the mapping of the genetic code in the Human Genome Project have been very helpful. This area of research involves **molecular genetics,** which includes the study of the chemical codes that constitute a particular molecule of DNA. Particularly promising is a locating technique called *quantitative trait loci (QTL)* (Plomin, 1995; Rowe & Jacobson, 1999). Instead of simply using the family connection (such as mother–child, or uncle–niece) as a measure of genetic closeness, researchers can now look directly at a pattern of genes two individuals share on a particular chromosome. If two people with the same genetic locus (location for a particular gene pattern) are also more similar in some aspect of their phenotypes than are people without that gene pattern at that location, researchers can conclude that the particular gene contributes something to that trait.

QTL has already found a gene that contributes to reading disability (Cardon et al., 1994) and one that contributes to high intelligence

molecular genetics The study of genetics at the molecular level, including the study of the chemical codes that constitute a particular molecule of DNA.

❶ Response for Educators (from page 80):
Dominant could be the black cards, and recessive the red. Divide the 52 cards into two half decks, each with 13 red cards and 13 black. One half deck represents a man's sperm, or his contribution to the genetic mix, and the other half deck represents a woman's ova, or her contribution. Shuffle each half deck, and then pick pairs of cards, one card coming from each deck. Odds are that in 6 pairs both cards will be black (not even a carrier of the recessive gene), in 14 pairs both cards will be mixed (hence, carriers), and in the remaining 6 pairs both cards will be red (the double recessive). Of course, reality doesn't always follow the odds—a lesson that can be taught if the pairs don't match what you expect.

(Chorney et al., 1998). As we learn more about the impact of various alleles of genes, it becomes increasingly important to realize that when we say something is "genetic," we do not mean that its genetic origins are substantial, fixed, or unalterable. We mean that it is part of a person's basic foundation, affecting many aspects of life while determining none. As one expert put it, "A gene is a framed canvas upon which the psychological environment paints the person" (Brown, 1999).

"Is that trait genetic?" someone might ask you.

"Of course," you reply. "Everything is genetic."

"No. I mean, is it *determined* by a gene?"

"Of course *not,*" you answer, "nothing ever is."

Frustrated as your questioner might be by your dismissive responses, you are completely correct in what you said. Every trait, action, and attitude of every living organism has a genetic component—without genes, no behavior could exist. Yet when one asks whether there can be purely genetic explanations for behavior,

> The simple answer to this question is "no." . . . Even when characterized in detail at the DNA level, genes do not, all by themselves, explain much. The genes have to be translated into phenotypes, and typically have to function in a specified environment. Furthermore, genes do not act in a solitary manner—they act in concert with other genes, often with many genes. [Schaffer, 1999]

Environmental Influences on Emotional Impairment

Environment, which social scientists use to mean everything nongenetic (from nutrition for the embryo to social support for the elderly), affects every human characteristic. Indeed, every emotion is partly genetic: the power and expression of emotions are universal human traits and are aspects of what makes each of us unique. Emotional expression is also partly environmental: one of the first lessons infants learn is how and when to express their feelings. This point is so important that we need to cite three examples for traits sometimes said to be "genetic," specifically shyness, mental disorders, and (in the Life-Span View box on page 84) alcoholism.

Painful Shyness

Being fearful of talking in public, of making new friends, of expressing emotions—in short, being shy—is a personality trait that psychologists refer to as *inhibition,* which can become a characteristic called *social phobia* (Beidel & Turner, 1998). Study after study has found that levels of inhibition are more similar in monozygotic twins than in dizygotic twins—a result which proves that genes affect this trait. Further evidence comes from studies that have found many linkages between inhibition and other genetic traits. Compared to other infants, babies who will later be shy show quicker *startle reactions* (when they are suddenly surprised by a loud noise, for instance), reacting with more motor activity and frightened crying. Then, as toddlers, they are less active overall but more fearful (as you would expect an inhibited child to be) (Calkins et al., 1996; Kagen, 1994).

However, inhibition is also affected by the social atmosphere. If parents are able to encourage their shy children without shaming or embarrassing them, the children might learn to relax in social settings and become less observably shy. Alternatively, if a shy child's parents are

Shyness Is Universal Inhibition is more common at some ages (late infancy and early adolescence) and in some gene pools (natives of northern Europe and East Asia) than others. But every community includes some individuals who are unmistakably shy, such as this toddler in Woleai, more than 3,000 miles west of Hawaii.

themselves very shy and socially isolated, but nonetheless blame their child for being fearful, the child might grow up much more socially timid than if the parents were outgoing—and be dramatically more inhibited than most other children.

The point here is not that genetically based tendencies disappear as life experiences accumulate. Shy people always feel a twinge of inhibition when entering a new school, for instance, or arriving at a party full of strangers—and these tendencies affect their life course. For example, on average, shy people marry later than nonshy people (Caspi et al., 1988; Kerr et al., 1996). But life experiences and cultural context do make a difference. A longitudinal study in the United States found that shyness slowed down young men's career advancement, but this was not found to be the case in similar longitudinal research in Sweden. The researchers speculated on one reason for the difference:

> Swedish culture values shy, reserved behavior . . . and support systems of various sorts made it possible for Swedish boys to enter universities and careers without being assertive. [Kerr et al., 1996]

The same conclusion applies to other psychological traits that have strong genetic influences, including intelligence, emotionality, activity level, aggression, and even religiosity (Plomin et al., 1997). In each case, various dimensions of environment can enhance, inhibit, or alter the phenotypic expression of a person's heredity.

Mental Disorders

Psychopathologies such as depression, antisocial behavior, phobias, and compulsions, as well as virtually every other neurotic or psychotic disorder, are also genetically based traits with strong environmental influence. For example, relatives of people with schizophrenia have a higher-than-normal risk of developing the illness themselves, with about 75 percent of the variation in schizophrenia traceable to genes (Rutter el al., 1999).

Most striking is the fact that if one monozygotic twin develops schizophrenia, about two-thirds of the time the other twin does, too. Viewed another way, however, the same statistic reveals the importance of the environment: One-third of monozygotic twins whose twin has schizophrenia are not themselves afflicted (Cannon et al., 1999). Moreover, many people diagnosed with schizophrenia have no close relatives with the illness, and most close relatives of schizophrenics do not themselves develop the disorder, even if that relative was their mother or father. Obviously, schizophrenia is multifactorial, with environmental elements—possibly a slow-acting virus, head injury, inadequate oxygen at birth, or other physical insult—playing a pivotal role (Cannon et al., 1999).

Using advanced genetic and epidemiological techniques, scientists are advancing in the treatment and prevention of schizophrenia. It is now known that one gene which predisposes for schizophrenia is on chromosome 6 (Sherman & Waldman, 1999). This gene does not act alone: Some people with the gene do not develop schizophrenia; some people without it, do. One predisposing factor is birth during late winter, probably because some virus more prevalent in winter can affect a vulnerable fetus (Mortensen et al., 1999).

A similar story is unfolding for Alzheimer's disease, which is definitely genetic in that people with a particular allele of a particular gene

THE GENOTYPE AND PHENOTYPE OF ALCOHOLISM

At various times, alcoholism was thought to be a moral weakness, a personality flaw, and a sign of psychopathology (Leonard & Blane, 2000). Alcoholics were once locked up in jails or in mental institutions. When that didn't stop the problem, entire nations banned alcohol, as the United States did during the Prohibition era, from 1919 to 1933. People who are not alcoholics have long wondered why some people just can't stop drinking to excess, and alcoholics have kept trying to stop after one or two drinks, like everyone else, and failing miserably.

Now we know better. The fact is that some people's inherited biochemistry makes them highly susceptible to alcohol addiction. Of course, anyone can abuse alcohol, but each person's genetic makeup creates an addictive pull that can be overpowering, or minuscule, or something in between.

Evidence for "alcoholic genes" is found in the fact that some ethnic groups (such as those from the British Isles and from northern Russia) have a much higher proportion of alcoholics than others. Biochemistry allows some people to "hold their liquor," drinking so much that they become alcoholics, and causes others, notably many East Asians, to sweat and become red-faced. This embarrassing response, particularly for women, is an incentive to avoid alcohol (McGue, 1995). Some people become sleepy, others nauseous, others aggressive, and others euphoric when alcohol hits their brains, and each person's reaction increases or decreases the eagerness to have another drink.

Alcoholism is not simply a biochemical reaction. It is psychological as well as physical. Not surprisingly, genes predispose a person to have certain personality traits that correlate with abusive addictions. Among these traits are a quick temper, a readiness to take risks, and a high level of anxiety. Thus alcoholism is polygenic, with almost every alcoholic inheriting a particular combination of biochemistry-affecting and temperament-affecting genes that push him or her toward abusive drinking. Originally this was more true for men than women, because women were typically discouraged by their cultures from drinking to excess. Now that women are more free to follow their genetic impulses, recent data show that for women also, the heritability of alcoholism is more than 50 percent (Heath et al., 1997).

The prevalence of alcoholism and the fact that it is partly genetic gives rise to another question: Since alcoholism is a destructive trait, why were genes for the disorder passed on from generation to generation in certain groups, when selective adaptation should have eliminated them? Part of the answer is that, in some regions, beer and wine were actually healthier for people than water—since the distillation process killed many of the destructive bacteria that thrived in drinking water. Thus, being able to drink alcohol in quantity was adaptive in most of Europe. East Asians had a different solution to the problem of bacteria: They boiled their water and drank it as tea. This explains why about half of all Asians lack the gene for an enzyme necessary to fully metabolize alcohol: Their ancestors didn't need it. Such a lack might have been life-threatening in a European, who had to drink beer or wine to avoid polluted water; it was not a problem for tea-drinking East Asians (Vallee, 1998).

As this example shows, even considering both the genes for temperament and the genes for physiological reactions, alcoholism is not solely genetic (McGue, 1999). Culture counts. If a person with a strong genetic tendency toward alcoholism spends a lifetime in an environment where alcohol is unavail-

(ApoE) almost always develop the disease and those with another allele of the same gene almost never do. However, some people with two copies of the destructive allele never develop the disease. Other genes, and environmental conditions, are undoubtedly the reason (Vickers et al., 2000). (This topic is discussed further in Chapter 24.)

In sum, it is quite clear that genes, the prenatal and postnatal biochemical environment, and the more distant social environment are all powerful influences on human development. Their complex interaction is involved in every aspect of development at every age and in every era. And in each person's life, the results of earlier genetic–environmental interactions guide further development. That said, we must also stress that the outcome is never predetermined, even at age 70 or 80. As one biologist explains:

able (in a devout Islamic family in Saudi Arabia, for example), the genotype will never be expressed in the phenotype. On the other hand, if the same person is allowed to drink frequently at an early age, the potential of the genes will be released. Further, if that person is raised in a culture that promotes alcohol consumption, with peer pressures that lead to alcohol abuse, he or she is likely to become an active alcoholic. Even for such unfortunates, wherever they live, social influences and personal choices can dramatically alter the eventual outcome. Some alcoholics die of the disease before they are 30; others spend decades alternating between abuse, controlled drinking, and abstinence; still others recognize the problem, get help, and are sober and productive throughout a long life.

In terms of the entire life span, a person is most likely to become an active alcoholic between ages 15 and 25, even though the genotype has been present since conception. However, it is possible for social influences to be sufficiently strong that a much older person who had been merely a problem drinker will succumb to alcoholism as a result of the combination of freedom and loneliness that retirement from work may bring.

Can public policy have any effect here? Apparently yes. In the United States between 1980 and 1990, alcohol consumption per capita was reduced by 10 percent. Moreover, in the 1990s, stricter enforcement of drunk-driving laws reduced the number of fatal accidents involving drunk drivers from 26 percent to 19 percent overall and from 24 percent to 13 percent among 16- to 20-year-olds (U.S. Bureau of the Census, 1998). Workplace employee-assistance programs and insurance policies that consider alcoholism as a treatable disease have also had an effect, but this seems to have diminished recently. Drinking and alcohol-related problems were at the same level or worse at the end of the 1990s as at the beginning (Greenfield et al., 2000; Midenik & Greenfield, 2000).

Obviously, not only genes but also laws, treatment, and cultural pressures influence alcoholism. Choices made by each person at every stage determine the final outcome (Bandura, 1999).

All Alcoholics? Probably not. These farm workers in Provence, France, pause for a meal—complete with bread, wine, glasses, and a tablecloth. Drinking alcohol with friends and food is not a sign of alcoholism; habitually drinking alone is. Of course, cultural pressure to drink creates problems, which is one reason France has a high rate of cirrhosis, but this might not be a pressure group: One of the two bottles is water.

At every stage of development, from moment to moment, the growing organism is interacting with a varying environment; and the form of each interaction depends on the outcome of earlier interactions. This process is indescribably complicated—which is why it is never described and rarely even acknowledged. The extreme of intricacy is reached in human development, for the conditions which we and our children experience are often the products of deliberate, sometimes intelligent, choice. [Barnett, 1998]

On a practical level, this means we must not ignore the genetic component in any given trait—whether it be something wonderful, such as a wacky sense of humor; something fearful, such as a violent temper; or something quite ordinary, such as the tendency to tire of the same routine. However, we must not forget that the environment affects every trait, in ways that change as maturational, cultural, and historical processes

PRENATAL PREDICTION

Over the past 30 years, researchers have refined dozens of prenatal tests. Many of these are now routine: blood tests reveal maternal diseases or drugs that might harm the fetus; urine analysis and blood-pressure readings indicate how the mother's system is coping with pregnancy. Many other tests are not routine. They are used selectively—especially when genetic or chromosomal damage is likely.

Pre-implantation Testing

If conception occurs *in vitro* ("in glass," or in a laboratory dish, with sperm being added to ova that have been surgically removed from the mother), one cell can be removed from each zygote at the four- or eight-cell stage and analyzed genetically. If a possible genetic defect is *not* found, the remaining developing cells can be inserted into the uterus. About 25 percent of the time, the cell mass implants, grows, and becomes a newborn without the chromosomal or genetic abnormality that the couple sought to avoid.

Pre-implantation testing is controversial and unusual, available only in specialized centers that screen for about twenty of the most commonly inherited conditions (Simpson et al., 1999). But some couples would not risk reproduction without the assurance of pre-implantation analysis. Experimenting on lower animals, researchers have added a gene or chromosome at the pre-implantation stage to replace a defective one—a measure not yet performed on human embryos.

Alphafetoprotein Assay

A sample of the mother's blood can be tested for the level of alphafetoprotein (AFP), an indicator of neural-tube defects, Down syndrome, or multiple embryos. About 10 percent of all pregnant women exhibit high or low AFP, but most of these are false alarms, caused by miscalculation of the age of the fetus or some other normal variation. Thus, the test itself is not risky, but unexpected AFP levels indicate that more tests are needed.

Ultrasound

A sonogram, or ultrasound image, uses high-frequency sound waves to produce a "picture" of the fetus. If done early in pregnancy, sonograms can reveal problems such as an abnormally small head or other body malformations, excess spinal fluid accumulating on the brain, and several diseases (for instance, of the kidney). In addition, sonograms are used to diagnose twins, to estimate fetal age, to determine the position of the placenta, and to reveal the rate of fetal growth. No known risks to mother or fetus result from sonograms, unlike the X-ray that it replaced.

Fetoscopy

In fetoscopy, a very narrow tube is inserted into the pregnant woman's abdomen, piercing the uterus. Then a fetoscope (a viewing instrument) is inserted into the tube, to allow the physician to observe the fetus and the inside of the placenta directly. Fetoscopy is most often performed when AFP or a sonogram have led the doctor to suspect a malformation (such as spina bifida). With a slightly different instrument, the fetoscope can sample blood from the placenta or the umbilicus or remove skin or liver tissue directly from the fetus to be analyzed for abnormalities. Fetoscopy can cause an unwanted abortion about once in 50 times.

---

unfold, with an impact that can be chosen or changed, depending on the people and society. Genes are always part of the tale, influential on every page, but they never determine the plot or the final paragraph.

INHERITED ABNORMALITIES

We now give particular attention to genetic and chromosomal abnormalities, for three reasons:

- Disruptions of normal development provide insight into the complexities of genetic interactions.
- Knowledge of the origins of genetic and chromosomal abnormalities suggests how to reduce or limit their harmful consequences.
- Misinformation and prejudice compound the problems of those affected by chromosomal and genetic abnormalities.

Amniocentesis

In amniocentesis, about half an ounce of the fluid inside the placenta is withdrawn through the mother's abdominal wall. The fluid contains sloughed-off fetal cells that can be cultured and analyzed to detect chromosomal abnormalities as well as many other genetic and prenatal problems. The amniotic fluid also reveals the sex of the fetus (useful knowledge if an X-linked disorder is likely). Amniocentesis has been the mainstay of prenatal diagnosis since 1973 (Evans et al., 1989). However, amniocentesis cannot be safely performed until midpregnancy (about 14 weeks), and many detected abnormalities have uncertain consequences. Both these facts make the women's decision about continuing the pregnancy very difficult. About once in 200 pregnancies, amniocentesis causes a spontaneous abortion.

Chorionic Villi Sampling

In chorionic villi sampling (CVS), a sample of the placental tissue that surrounds the fetus is obtained and analyzed. This test provides the same information as aminocentesis, but CVS can be performed as early as the sixth week of pregnancy (Carlson, 1994). This benefit comes at a price, however: Compared to amniocentesis, CVS is slightly less accurate and twice as likely to cause a spontaneous abortion.

Risks and Benefits

Medical decision making is an increasingly complex issue in the study of human development, not only in prenatal testing but throughout the life span. The ideal (not always attained) is to reserve testing for serious, well-understood conditions, for which diagnosis is quite accurate and treatment or prevention is available (Wingerson, 1998). Unfortunately, uncertain diagnosis, especially of unusual chromosomal abnormalities, means that many pregnant couples are faced with puzzling results (either positive or negative) or ambiguous findings. Doctors usually decide which tests should be done and when, and prospective parents are often unprepared to interpret the data. As a consequence, nations differ in when and to whom prenatal tests are offered, and couples with identical results sometimes make opposite decisions (Asch et al., 1996).

The risks of testing—including the stress on the parents, who experience uncertainty and fear mixed with their anticipation and joy, and the abortion of an embryo or fetus who might not have been defective after all—must be considered before the benefits can be realized (Serra-Pratt et al., 1998). The greatest harm of all may be to society as a whole. If couples at risk of bearing severely ill children are not told in advance what the options and consequences are, then nations or physicians are preventing individual choice and incurring the high cost of meeting the medical and educational needs of these children. Yet if prenatal testing becomes routine, then couples may come to expect to have genetically perfect children—not only healthy but also smart, athletic, and attractive—and children with special needs might be shunned as visible signs of their parents' mistakes and not accepted as fully human, with all the rights of any other citizen. Obviously, knowledge, even knowledge that might prevent serious birth defects, is never risk-free. Research needs to discover both risks and benefits, not only to fetus and mother, but also to families and societies.

Sophisticated prenatal tests are now available to diagnose such abnormalities and to enhance our understanding of these problems (see the Research Report).

Chromosomal Miscount

Sometimes when gametes are formed, the 46 chromosomes divide unevenly, producing a sperm or an ovum that does not have the normal complement of exactly 23 chromosomes. If such a gamete fuses with a normal gamete, the result is a zygote with more or fewer than 46 chromosomes. This is not unusual. An estimated half of all zygotes have an odd number of chromosomes. A recent count found 9,080 different chromosomal abnormalities; that is, part of or a whole chromosome is missing or misplaced (Borgaonkar, 1997). Most such zygotes do not even begin to develop, and most of the rest never come to term—usually

spontaneous abortion The naturally occurring termination of a pregnancy before the fetus is fully developed. (Also called *miscarriage.*)

syndrome A cluster of distinct characteristics that tend to occur together in a given disorder.

trisomy-21 (Down syndrome) A syndrome that includes such symptoms as a rounded head, thick tongue, unusual eyes, heart abnormalities, and mental retardation. It results when there is an extra chromosome at the site of the twenty-first pair.

because a **spontaneous abortion,** or *miscarriage,* occurs (Snijders & Nicolaides, 1996).

Once in about every 200 births, however, a baby is born with 45, 47, or, rarely, 48 or 49 chromosomes. In every case, the chromosomal abnormalities lead to a recognizable **syndrome**—a cluster of distinct characteristics that tend to occur together.

Down Syndrome

The most common of the extra-chromosome syndromes is **trisomy-21,** or **Down syndrome,** in which the individual has three chromosomes at site 21. Some 300 distinct characteristics can result from the presence of that extra chromosome, but no individual with Down syndrome is quite like another, either in the particular symptoms he or she has or in their severity. Despite this variability, almost all people with trisomy-21 have certain specific facial characteristics—a thick tongue, round face, slanted eyes—as well as distinctive hands, feet, and fingerprints. Many also have hearing problems, heart abnormalities, muscle weakness, and short stature.

Earning His Daily Bread This man with Down syndrome works in a cafeteria, and, by all reports, is a steady, conscientious employee.

❓ *Observational Quiz (see answer page 90): Visible are four signs of Down syndrome; not visible (and perhaps not present) are at least four other signs. Name all eight.*

In terms of neurological development, almost all individuals with Down syndrome experience mental slowness. Their eventual intellectual attainment varies: Some are severely retarded; others are average or even above average. Usually—but not always—those who are raised at home and given appropriate cognitive stimulation progress to the point of being able to read and write and care for themselves (and often much more), while those who are institutionalized tend to be, and to remain, much more retarded (Carr, 1995).

Many young children with trisomy-21 are unusually sweet-tempered; they are less likely to cry or complain than most other children. Temperament may be a liability, however. If a Down syndrome child is more passive and less motivated to learn than others, that characteristic produces a slower learning rate and a lower IQ as time goes on (Wishart, 1999).

By middle adulthood, individuals with Down syndrome "almost invariably" develop Alzheimer's disease, severely impairing their limited communication skills and making them much less compliant (Czech et al., 2000). They are also prone to a host of other problems more commonly found in older persons, including cataracts and certain forms of cancer. Consequently, their mortality rate begins to rise at about age 35, and their life expectancy is lower than that of other mentally retarded adults and much lower than that of average people (Strauss & Eyman, 1996).

Abnormalities at the Twenty-Third Location

Every newborn infant has at least one X chromosome in the twenty-third pair. About 1 in every 500 infants, however, either is missing a sex chromosome (thus the X stands alone) or has two or more other sex chromosomes in addition to the first X. These abnormalities usually impair cognitive and psychosocial development as well as sexual maturation. (Each particular syndrome has a specific set of effects.) In many

Not Too Old to Have a Baby The fact that older parents have a higher risk of conceiving an embryo with chromosomal abnormalities should not obscure another reality: With modern medical care and prenatal testing, pregnancies that occur when the parents are in their 40s can, and almost always do, result in healthy babies.

fragile-X syndrome A disorder in which part of the X chromosome is attached to the rest of it by a very slim string of molecules; it is caused by a genetic abnormality and often produces mental deficiency.

cases, treatment with hormone supplements can alleviate some of the physical problems, and special education may remedy some of the deficits related to psychological functioning.

The specific features of any syndrome vary considerably from one individual to another. In fact, in many cases, the presence of abnormal sex chromosomes goes undetected until a seemingly normal childhood is followed by an abnormally delayed puberty. This is particularly likely for a boy who has *Klinefelter syndrome,* XXY. Such a boy will be a little slow in elementary school, but it is usually not until puberty—when his penis does not grow and fat begins to accumulate around his breasts—that his parents wonder if something is seriously wrong.

The Fragile X. One of the most common syndromes associated with the sex chromosomes is **fragile-X syndrome,** which is actually genetic in origin. In some individuals, part of the X chromosome is attached to the rest of it by such a thin string of molecules that it seems about to break off (hence the name of the syndrome). This abnormality in the chromosome is caused by the mutation of a single gene. Unlike most other known mutations, the mutation involved in the fragile X intensifies as it is passed from one generation to the next.

Of the females who carry it, most are normal (perhaps because they also carry one normal X chromosome), but one-third show some mental deficiency. Among the males who inherit a fragile-X chromosome, about 20 percent are apparently completely normal, about 33 percent are somewhat retarded, and the rest are severely retarded. The last group is relatively large: The cognitive deficits caused by fragile-X syndrome represent the most common form of inherited mental retardation. In addition to cognitive problems, the fragile X is often associated with inadequate social skills and extreme shyness (Dykens et al., 1994; Hagerman, 1996).

The wide range of effects produced by this disorder is somewhat unusual. However, the more we learn about other abnormal genes, chromosomes, and syndromes, the more diversity we find in their effects.

Causes of Chromosomal Abnormalities

Chromosomal abnormalities are caused by many factors, some genetic and some environmental (such as the parents' exposure to excessive radiation). However, the variable that most often correlates with chromosomal abnormalities is maternal age. According to one detailed estimate, a 20-year-old woman has about 1 chance in 800 of carrying a fetus with Down syndrome; a 39-year-old woman has 1 chance in 67; and a 44-year-old woman has 1 chance in 16 (see Appendix A for the month-by-month, age-specific incidence).

Other chromosomal abnormalities are less common, but virtually all follow an age-related pattern (Snijders & Nicolaides, 1996). Since about half of all fetuses with these abnormalities are aborted spontaneously and some others are aborted by choice, the actual birth rate of infants with chromosomal abnormalities is lower than these statistics would suggest. Many doctors recommend prenatal testing for chromosomal abnormalities whenever a pregnant woman is 35 or older, although this step is controversial (see the In Person box on page 90).

GENETIC COUNSELING: DECISIONS AND VALUES

Until recently, after the birth of a child with a serious or even fatal genetic or chromosomal disorder, couples thought fate rather than genetics was to blame. They often had more children, who were likely to have the same problem or be carriers of it.

Today, many couples worry about their genes even before they marry. Almost every adult has a relative with a serious disease that may well be genetic. Genetic counseling can help relieve such worries, although it also requires careful decision making by the prospective parents.

In general, prenatal, preconceptual, or even prenuptial genetic counseling and testing are recommended for:

■ Individuals who have a parent, sibling, or child with a serious genetic condition
■ Couples who have a history of early spontaneous abortions, stillbirths, or infertility
■ Couples who are from the same ethnic group or subgroup—especially if the group is a small one and most particularly if the couple are close relatives
■ Women over age 34

When a couple begins counseling, the counselor constructs a family history, charting patterns of health and sickness over the generations, particularly with regard to early deaths and unexplained symptoms. The counselor then explains specific conditions based on age, ethnicity, and genetic history and discusses what the options will be if testing reveals high risk of serious conditions. This last step is crucial; as options increase, so do choices.

The couple then decides whether to proceed with genetic testing. Some may prefer not to know their specific risks if the only way to prevent the birth of a child with a serious genetic disorder is surgical sterilization or induced abortion—options some couples will not consider. Others want to know in any case, believing they will make the best decision only after learning all they can. At this point, the couple learns more about the reliability of the various tests, which are never 100 percent accurate. There is always a possibility of *false negatives* (the disorder is present, but the test does not indicate it) or *false positives* (the disorder is not present, but the test indicates it is).

There is an interesting paradox here. Genetic counselors, scientists, and the general public usually believe it best to proceed with testing because some information is better than none. However, high-risk individuals (who are most likely to hear bad news) do not necessarily agree, especially if the truth might jeopardize the marriage, health insurance coverage, or the chances of parenthood (Duster, 1999). If the genetic tests would reveal only the risk to the adult, not to a prospective child (such as tests for cancer), most high-risk adults say they would rather not know about their own fate.

As a result of testing, couples can know the approximate odds that their prospective child will have a serious genetic problem. In considering such odds, one must realize that *chance has no memory*, which means that the odds apply afresh to each child the couple might conceive. If both partners have the recessive gene for sickle-cell anemia, for instance, and the couple plans to have several children, then all of them, some of them, or none of them could have the disease. Probability laws tell us that one child in four will be afflicted, two in four will be carriers, and one in four will not even be a carrier. But gametes do not consult probability laws; nor do they remember the fate of earlier pregnancies before deciding which sperm and ovum should fuse.

Even when a couple has been tested and found to be at low risk, they may still have a child with genetic disease, either because of a spontaneous mutation or because certain tests are not yet accurate. Two additional complications are that most diseases vary in specific severity, so even if a fetus has the double recessive that causes sickle-cell anemia, for instance, it is not known how ill that child will be. Finally, knowledge sometimes brings shame instead of power. A mother of a child with a recessive disorder explains:

---

❶ *Answer to Observational Quiz (from page 88):* *Four visible signs: round head, short stature, large hands, slanted eye sockets. Not visible: mental retardation, heart abnormalities, muscle weakness, thick tongue.*

Harmful Genes

While relatively few people are born with abnormal chromosomes, everyone has at least 20 genes (usually additive or recessive) that could produce serious diseases or handicaps in the next generation. Most of the 7,000 *known* genetic disorders are dominant, since whenever a dominant gene is inherited, it is apparent in the person's phenotype. With a few exceptions, dominant disorders are not seriously disabling because people with disabling dominant disorders are unlikely to have

I feel responsible and his dad feels the same way. It's like we have done something. We have shamed ourselves real bad, but you just have to deal with it. Society puts people down about a whole lot of things . . . you know, they don't take kindly when you do something to a child. [quoted in Duster, 1999]

For many individuals and couples, discovering that they are carriers of destructive genes is a secret shame, undermining the ideals of romantic love and parental feelings (Duster, 1999). For many genetic counselors, too, explaining the results is a complex proposition in which the emotional tone of the discussion, the nature of the information given, and the odds presented make a decided difference. If the disorder is very serious, and if specific steps can be taken that will prevent an otherwise certain tragedy, most genetic counselors believe that being value-neutral is neither necessary nor desirable (Mahowald et al., 1998). Nonetheless, patient autonomy is a high priority in genetic counseling, and this can create thorny dilemmas. For example, what would you advise in the following four cases if you were the genetic counselor?

- A pregnant couple are both achondroplastic dwarfs, a genetic condition that affects appearance but not intellect. They want genetic analysis of their fetus, which they intend to abort if it would become a child of normal stature.
- A 40-year-old woman chooses to be tested and hears bad news: She has the BRCA1 gene, which gives her about an 80 percent chance of developing breast cancer before age 70, and perhaps ovarian or colon cancer as well. She refuses to believe the evidence and insists that no one tell her family, including her mother, her four sisters, and her three daughters. Several of them probably have the gene and may be in the early stages of cancer without knowing it.
- A 30-year-old mother of two daughters (no sons) learns that she is a carrier for hemophilia. She requests pre-

implantation analysis, demanding that only male embryos without her hemophilia-carrying X chromosome be implanted. This means that female zygotes, half of whom will not even be carriers, would be given no chance to develop.
- A couple has a child with cystic fibrosis. They want to know whether they both have the recessive gene or whether their child's condition was a spontaneous mutation (as is often the case). If the latter is true, they could have another child with very little risk of cystic fibrosis. During testing, the counselor learns that the wife has the gene but the husband does not—and also realizes that the husband is not the biological father of the child.

Similar dilemmas were posed in the December 17, 1994, issue of *Science News*. The responses from readers revealed an interesting age gap, with college students much less likely to follow the wishes of the hypothetical clients than older adults were.

More recently, a high school student with spina bifida—a congenital cleft in the vertebral column—asked via a forum on the World Wide Web whether births of spina bifida babies should be prevented (by detection through ultrasound, followed by abortion). He found that most people who knew only generalities voted for prevention of spina bifida births, whereas parents of children with disabilities were more likely to allow spina bifida pregnancies to proceed. The student himself said that he enjoyed his life most of the time, despite the fact that he had had eleven operations and always used a wheelchair (Wingerson, 1998).

These various situations make clear that genetic and fertility choices are very personal. In fact, many prospective parents find that the best sources of wisdom are other adults who have been in the same situation, have made the difficult decisions, (both for prevention and not) and are living with the consequences.

children and thus are unlikely to pass their genes on. One exception is *Huntington's chorea,* a central nervous system disease caused by a gene that remains inactive until adulthood, by which time a person could have had many children (as the original Mr. Huntington did).

Another dominant disorder that can be severe is *Tourette syndrome,* which is quite common but variable. About 30 percent of those who inherit the gene exhibit recurrent uncontrollable tics and explosive outbursts of verbal obscenities. The remaining 70 percent experience milder symptoms, such as an occasional twitch that is barely noticeable and a postponable impulse to speak inappropriately.

Recessive and multifactorial disorders are less likely to be recognized but actually claim many more victims, largely because such disorders can pass unchecked (and unnoticed) from carrier to carrier for generations. As a result, carrier status can easily become widespread in a population. Among the more commonly known recessive disorders are cystic fibrosis, thalassemia, and sickle-cell anemia, with as many as 1 in 12 North Americans being a carrier for one or another of the three. (See Table A.1 in the Appendix.) Most genetic research has been done in Europe and North America; undoubtedly, many other dominant and recessive conditions are prevalent in Asia, Africa, and South America that have not yet been named and described (Wright, 1998).

Genetic counseling (the process of testing a person to discover what genetic conditions are present on the genotype and then advising that person how likely the condition is to occur in the offspring's phenotype) is widely available in developed nations. Often, but not always, a couple can learn what their chances are of bearing a child with a specific genetic disease and can seek advice about what they can do to prevent such an outcome. In the United States, genetic counselors try to follow two ethical guidelines:

- The results are kept confidential, beyond the reach of insurance companies and out of public records.
- The final decision is made by the clients, not by the counselor, whose job is to provide facts and options, not to impose values and conclusions.

genetic counseling Consultation and testing that enables individuals to learn about their genetic heritage, including conditions that might affect future children.

Choosing to Have a Child

The awareness of chromosomal and genetic abnormalities is a mixed blessing, depending on the reactions of the parents, as the In Person box explains. However, we need to emphasize that genetic testing is a tool for individuals to use, not a final answer. To be specific, the results of genetic testing do not usually end a couple's hopes of becoming parents. Some couples may learn that only one partner carries a harmful recessive trait and therefore none of their children will have the disease. Others may learn that their odds of bearing a child with a serious illness are not much higher than those for any other couple.

Even if both partners are carriers of a serious condition or are at high risk in other ways, they still have many alternatives, as Figure 3.4 on page 93 indicates. Some may avoid pregnancy and, perhaps, plan adoption. Some might choose a reproductive alternative such as artificial insemination with donor sperm, in vitro fertilization with a donor ovum, or in vitro fertilization using the parents' own gametes but then testing the cell mass to determine the genetic situation before inserting it into the uterus. If testing during pregnancy shows serious problems, a couple can consider abortion or begin gathering information that will help them deal with the child-care problems that may lie ahead.

Some may decide to postpone pregnancy until promising treatments—either prenatal or postnatal—are further developed. Genetic engineering (altering of an organism's genetic instructions through the insertion of additional genes) is the most innovative of these, but it has not yet proved feasible on a large scale. Many other, more conventional, treatments have already made a dramatic difference for those with sickle-cell anemia, cystic fibrosis, and various other conditions (Wingerson, 1998).

Figure 3.4 At-Risk Decision Making. With the help of a genetic counselor, even couples who know they run a risk of having a baby with a genetic defect might decide to have a child. Although the process of making that decision is more complicated for them than it is for couples with no family genetic illness and no positive tests for harmful recessive genes, the outcome is usually a healthy baby. Genetic counselors provide facts and alternatives; couples make decisions.

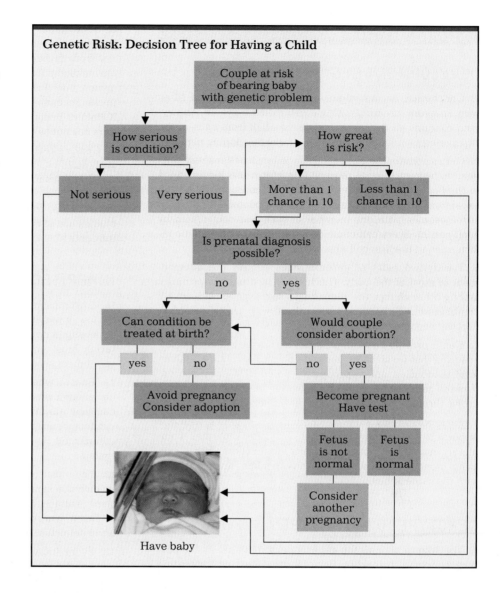

Genetic Risk: Decision Tree for Having a Child

Obviously, decisions about conception are not based simply on genetic analysis. Two couples with identical odds of conceiving zygotes with the same condition might make quite different choices—depending on their age, ethnicity, religion, finances, ethics, personal relationship, and the number and health status of any other children they may have. (This topic is discussed further in Chapter 17.) Counseling begins with objective facts but ends with a very personal decision.

This is as it must be, for a child with special needs is ultimately the primary responsibility of the parents. Doctors, neighbors, teachers, and political leaders may all have opinions, and certainly can offer help, but the mother and father are the ones who must pound on a child's chest to loosen mucus (cystic fibrosis), hold the body still for the injection (diabetes, hemophilia), and ignore the stares or comments of strangers (almost all disabilities). They are also the ones who kiss their children goodnight and watch them dream. Finally, they are the ones who hope that each child will become an adolescent, an adult, and, ultimately, a happy and healthy old man or old woman. The rest of this book describes that ongoing process, filled with problems and promise at every stage.

SUMMARY

DEVELOPMENT BEGINS

1. Conception occurs when a sperm penetrates and fuses with an ovum, creating a single cell called a zygote. The zygote contains all the genetic material—half from each of the two gametes—needed to create a unique developing person.

2. Genes contain the chemically coded instructions that cells need to become specialized and to perform specific functions in the body. Genes are arranged on chromosomes. With the exception of gametes, every human cell contains 23 pairs of chromosomes, with one member of each pair contributed by each parent. Every cell contains a duplicate of the genetic information in the first cell, the zygote.

3. Twenty-two pairs of chromosomes control the development of most of the body. The twenty-third pair determines, among other things, the individual's sex: zygotes with an XY combination will become males; those with an XX combination will become females.

4. Genes provide genetic continuity across the human species, ensuring that we all share common physical structures, behavioral tendencies, and reproductive potential. Genes also ensure the genetic diversity that allows our species to continue to evolve through adaptation and natural selection.

5. Each person has a unique combination of genes, with one important exception. Sometimes a zygote separates completely into two or more genetically identical organisms, creating monozygotic (identical) twins, triplets, and so on, all with the same genes.

GENOTYPE TO PHENOTYPE

6. The sum total of all the genes a person inherits is the person's genotype. The expression of those genes, in combination with the many influences of the environment, is the person's phenotype, or observable traits.

7. The various genes in the genotype interact in many ways to influence the phenotype. Most often, genes from both parents contribute to a trait in an additive fashion, both having an influence on the trait. Sometimes genes act in a nonadditive pattern. The dominant–recessive pattern is one such case: The phenotype reflects the influence of the dominant gene for the trait, while the recessive gene's effects are obscured.

8. Some genes are located only on the X chromosome. Traits controlled by such genes are passed from mother to son but not from father to son, because a male inherits his only X chromosome from his mother. Females inherit two X chromosomes, one from each parent. Thus, males are likely to express recessive traits, such as color blindness, that are X-linked. Females are likely to be carriers of X-linked disorders but not to express them.

9. Genes affect almost every human trait, including intellectual abilities, personality patterns, and mental illnesses. Similarly, from the moment of conception and throughout life, the environment influences genetic tendencies. Gene–environment interaction is thus ongoing and complex. Twin studies are often used to separate genetic and environmental influences.

INHERITED ABNORMALITIES

10. Chromosomal abnormalities occur when the zygote has too few or too many chromosomes or when a chromosome has a missing, a nonfunctioning, or an extra piece of genetic material. Most embryos with chromosomal abnormalities are spontaneously aborted early in pregnancy.

11. Babies who survive with chromosomal defects usually have extra or missing sex chromosomes. One of the most common abnormalities of the sex chromosomes is fragile-X syndrome, which actually has a genetic origin; it is often accompanied by some mental deficiency, particularly in males.

12. The most common chromosomal abnormality that does not involve the sex chromosomes occurs when an extra chromosome is attached to the twenty-first pair. This causes trisomy-21, or Down syndrome, a varying cluster of problems in physical and intellectual functioning.

13. Every individual carries some genes for genetic handicaps and diseases. However, most of the dominant disorders are not seriously disabling. Recessive disorders claim more victims and can be disabling or lethal, but they remain common because carriers are unaware that they can pass on a destructive gene—until their offspring express the disorder.

KEY TERMS

environment (69)
heredity (69)
gamete (69)
zygote (69)
gene (70)
chromosome (70)
genetic code (71)
Human Genome Project (71)
twenty-third pair (72)
monozygotic twins (75)
dizygotic twins (76)
polygenic traits (77)
multifactorial traits (77)
genotype (77)

phenotype (77)
carrier (77)
additive gene (77)
dominant gene (78)
recessive gene (78)
X-linked genes (78)
genetic imprinting (79)
behavioral genetics (79)
molecular genetics (81)
spontaneous abortion (88)
syndrome (88)
trisomy-21 (Down syndrome) (88)
fragile-X syndrome (89)
genetic counseling (92)

KEY QUESTIONS

1. How is genetic diversity among people ensured, and why is this diversity useful?

2. In what ways does genetics affect fertility and infertility?

3. What is the difference between phenotype and genotype?

4. What are the differences between the additive pattern of gene–gene interaction and the dominant–recessive pattern?

5. Why is the expression of a recessive X-linked gene affected by whether a male or a female inherits it?

6. What research strategies are used to separate genetic influences on psychological characteristics from environmental influences?

7. How can environment influence genetic psychological traits, such as shyness?

8. Which are more serious and which are more common: dominant genetic disorders or recessive genetic disorders?

9. What factors determine whether a couple is at risk for having a child with genetic abnormalities?

10. How can genetic counseling help parents who are at risk for having a child with genetic problems?

11. *In Your Experience* What would you do if you knew you were the carrier of a gene for a serious disease?

Prenatal Development and Birth

CHAPTER 4

As we saw in Chapter 1, every moment of development results from continuing interaction among all three domains, influenced by contexts of many kinds. This is as true in the first 9 months of life as it is in the 900 or so that follow.

Our primary focus in this chapter is on the astounding biological transformation from a single-cell zygote to a fully formed baby. You will see that this is a social, not just biological, event. The mother-to-be's health habits and activities, the community's laws and practices, and the culture's customs regarding birth itself are just some of the myriad contextual factors that make some newborns—those fortunate enough to be born to certain mothers in certain communities and cultures—much better prepared for a long and happy life than others.

FROM ZYGOTE TO NEWBORN

Human growth before birth is often divided into three main periods. The first 2 weeks of development are called the **germinal period**; from the third week through the eighth week is the **period of the embryo**; and from the ninth week until birth is the **period of the fetus**. (Alternative terms for these and other milestones of pregnancy are discussed in the table on the following page.)

Germinal: The First 14 Days

Within hours after conception, the one-cell zygote, traveling slowly down the Fallopian tube toward the uterus, begins the process of cell division and growth (see Figure 4.1 on page 98). The zygote first divides into two cells, which soon become four, then eight, then sixteen, and so on. As explained in Chapter 3, at least through the third doubling, each of these cells is identical. Any one of them could (and sometimes does) become a complete human being. If one cell is removed for pre-implantation testing, the remaining cells can develop into a normal person.

As you also saw in Chapter 3, at about the eight-cell stage the process of differentiation begins. The cells take on distinct characteristics and gravitate toward particular locations that foreshadow the types of cells they will become. One unmistakable sign of differentiation occurs about a week after conception, when the multiplying cells (now numbering more than 100) separate into two distinct masses. The outer

germinal period The first 2 weeks of development after conception; characterized by rapid cell division and the beginning of cell differentiation.

period of the embryo From approximately the third through the eighth week after conception, the period during which the rudimentary forms of all anatomical structures develop.

period of the fetus From the ninth week after conception until birth, the period during which the organs grow in size and complexity.

❓ **Especially for Fathers:** When does a man's nongenetic influence on his children begin?

Milestones of Pregnancy: A Note on Terminology and Dates

The terms used in popular and professional books to describe the timing of various significant events during pregnancy can be confusing. The following comments may help.

- ■ *Beginning of pregnancy:* In this text, pregnancy is considered to begin at conception. Conception is also regarded as the starting point of the baby's *gestational age.* However, the organism does not become an *embryo* until about 2 weeks later, and pregnancy does not affect the woman (and cannot be confirmed by blood or urine testing) until implantation occurs. Paradoxically, many obstetricians date the onset of pregnancy at about 14 days *before* conception, from the date on which the woman's last menstrual period (LMP) began.

- ■ *Trimesters:* Instead of using the terms *germinal period, embryonic period,* and *fetal period,* as is done in this text, some writers simply divide pregnancy into 3-month periods called *trimesters.* Months 1, 2, and 3 are called the *first trimester;* months 4, 5, and 6, the *second trimester;* and months 7, 8, and 9 the *third trimester.*

- ■ *Due date:* Although doctors assign a specific due date (based on the woman's LMP), only 5 percent of babies are born on their exact due date. Babies born between 3 weeks before their due date and up to 2 weeks after it are considered "on time." Babies born earlier than this are called *preterm;* babies born later are called *post-term.*

implantation Beginning about a week after conception, the burrowing of the organism into the lining of the uterus, where it can be nourished and protected during growth.

neural tube A fold of outer embryonic cells that appears about 3 weeks after conception and later develops into the central nervous system.

Figure 4.1 The Most Dangerous Journey. In the first 10 days after conception, the organism does not increase in size because it is not yet nourished by the mother. However, the number of cells increases rapidly as the organism prepares for implantation.

cells form a protective circle that will become the *placenta* (the organ that surrounds and protects the developing creature), and the inner cells form a nucleus that will become the embryo.

The first task of the outer cells is to achieve **implantation,** that is, to embed themselves in the nurturant environment of the uterus. This is accomplished as the cells nestle into the uterine lining, rupturing tiny blood vessels in order to obtain nourishment and to build a connective web of membranes and blood vessels linking the mother and the developing organism. It is this connective web that allows the organism to grow over the next 9 months or so.

Implantation is far from automatic, however. An estimated 58 percent of all natural conceptions and 75 percent of all in vitro conceptions fail to become properly implanted (Barbieri, 1999; Gilbert et al., 1987) (see Table 4.1). Most new life ends even before the embryo begins to form or the woman suspects she is pregnant.

Embryo: From the Third Through the Eighth Week

The start of the third week after conception initiates the *period of the embryo,* during which the formless mass of cells becomes a distinct being—one that is not yet recognizably human but is definitely living. First the developing organism begins differentiating into three layers, which eventually form key body systems. Then a perceptible sign of body formation appears, a fold in the outer layer of cells. At 22 days after conception this fold becomes the **neural tube,** which will later develop into the central nervous system, including the brain and spinal column (Larsen, 1998).

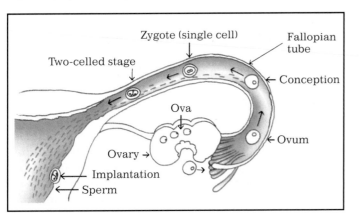

Zygote (single cell)

Fallopian tube

Two-celled stage

Conception

Ova

Ovum

Ovary

Implantation

Sperm

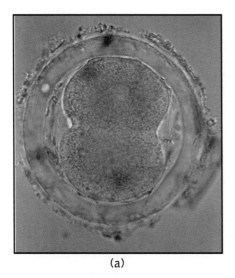

(a)

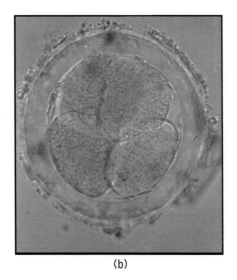

(b)

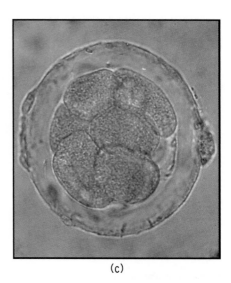

(c)

First Stages of the Germinal Period The original zygote as it divides into (a) two cells, (b) four cells, and (c) eight cells. Occasionally at this early stage, the cells separate completely, forming the beginning of monozygotic twins, quadruplets, or octuplets.

The head starts to take shape in the fourth week after conception. It begins as a featureless protrusion. Within days, eyes, ears, nose, and mouth start to form. Also in the fourth week, a blood vessel that will become the heart begins to pulsate, making the cardiovascular system the first to show any sign of activity. By the fifth week, buds that will become arms and legs appear, and a tail-like appendage extends from the spine. The upper arms and then forearms, palms, and webbed fingers appear about 5 weeks after conception. Legs, feet, and webbed toes, in that order, emerge a few days later, each having the beginning of a skeletal structure (Larsen, 1998).

At 8 weeks after conception, the embryo weighs about 1/30 ounce (1 gram) and is about 1 inch (2½ centimeters) long. The head has become more rounded than the narrow protrusion it was, and the features of the face have formed. The embryo has all the basic organs and body parts

table **4.1**	**The Vulnerability of Prenatal Development**

The Germinal Period

From the moment of conception until 14 days later. Fifty-eight percent of all developing organisms fail to grow or implant properly, and thus do not survive the germinal period. Most of these organisms were grossly abnormal.

The Period of the Embryo

From 14 days until 56 days after conception. During this time all the major external and internal body structures begin to form. About 20 percent of all embryos are aborted spontaneously, most often because of chromosomal abnormalities.

The Period of the Fetus

From the ninth week after conception until birth. About 5 percent of all fetuses are aborted spontaneously before viability at 22 weeks or are stillborn after 22 weeks.

Birth

Only 31 percent of all conceptions survive prenatal development to become living newborn babies.

Sources: Carlson, 1994; Gilbert et al., 1987; Moore & Persaud, 1998.

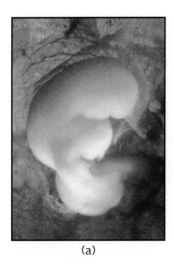
(a)

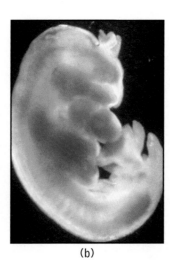
(b)

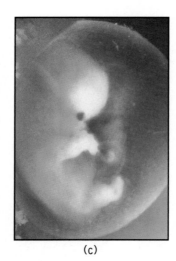
(c)

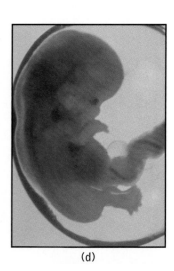
(d)

The Embryonic Period (a) At 4 weeks past conception, the embryo is only about ⅛ inch (3 millimeters) long, but already the head (top right) has taken shape. (b) At 5 weeks past conception, the embryo has grown to twice the size it was at 4 weeks. Its primitive heart, which has been pulsing for a week now, is visible, as is what appears to be a primitive tail, which will soon be enclosed by skin and protective tissue at the tip of the backbone (the coccyx).
(c) By 7 weeks, the organism is somewhat less than an inch (2½ centimeters) long. Eyes, nose, the digestive system, and even the first stage of toe formation can be seen.
(d) At 8 weeks, the 1-inch-long organism is clearly recognizable as a human fetus.

❶ **Response for Fathers (from page 98):**
Before conception, through his influence on the mother's attitudes and health.

(except sex organs) of a human being, including elbows and knees. The fingers and toes separate (at 52 and 54 days after conception, respectively), and the "tail" is no longer visible, having been incorporated into the lower spine at about 55 days.

Fetus: From the Ninth Week Until Birth

The organism is called a fetus from the ninth week after conception until it is born. That one name covers tremendous change, from a tiny, sexless creature smaller than the final joint of your thumb to a boy or girl who could nest comfortably in your arms. We will now describe some of the details of this transformation.

The Third Month

During the third month, the sex organs take discernible shape. The first stage of their development actually occurs at the sixth week, with the appearance of the *indifferent gonad,* a cluster of cells that can develop into male or female sex organs. Through the seventh week, males and females are virtually identical (Larsen, 1998). Then, if the embryo is male (XY), a gene on the Y chromosome sends a biochemical signal that initiates the development of male sexual organs. If the embryo is female (XX), no such signal is sent and the indifferent gonad develops female sex organs, first the vagina and uterus and then the external structures (Koopman et al., 1991).

Sex organs take several weeks to develop, but by the twelfth week after conception the external genital organs are fully formed. At the end of the third month, the fetus has all its body parts, weighs approximately 3 ounces (87 grams), and is about 3 inches (7.5 centimeters) long. You should be aware, though, that early prenatal growth is very rapid and that there is considerable variation from fetus to fetus, especially in body weight. The numbers given above—3 months, 3 ounces, 3 inches—have been rounded off for easy recollection. (For those on the metric system, "100 days, 100 millimeters, 100 grams" is similarly useful.) Actually, at 12 weeks after conception, the average fetus weighs about 1½ ounces (45 grams), while at 14 weeks the average weight is about 4 ounces (110 grams) (Moore & Persaud, 1998). So you can see that the 3-ounce (100-gram) point is just a moment in a period of rapid change.

By the end of the third month, the fetus can and does move almost every part of its body—kicking its legs, sucking its thumb, even squinting and frowning. It changes position easily within the **placenta,** which is now fully formed. The placenta is the organ composed of membranes and interwoven blood vessels that is connected to the umbilical cord to nourish the fetus.

The Middle Three Months: Preparing to Survive

In the fourth, fifth, and sixth months, the heartbeat becomes stronger and the digestive and excretory systems develop more fully. Fingernails, toenails, and buds for teeth form, and hair (including eyelashes) grows. Amazing as all that is, the most impressive growth is in the brain, which increases about six times in size and begins to react to stimuli. In fact, the entire central nervous system first becomes responsive and sentient during mid-pregnancy (see the In Person box).

These advances in brain functioning may be the critical factor in the fetus's attaining the **age of viability** (the age at which a preterm newborn can survive), because it is the brain that regulates basic body functions, such as breathing and sucking. Viability now begins at about 22 weeks after conception (Moore & Persaud, 1998). Babies born before 22 weeks' gestational age rarely survive more than a few days, because even the most sophisticated respirators and heart regulators cannot maintain life in a fetus whose brain has not yet begun to function.

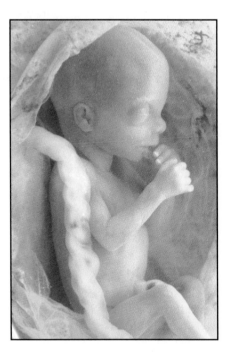

If such babies survive, they are nearly always severely brain-damaged. At 26 weeks, the survival rate improves to about 50 percent, with 14 percent of the survivors being severely mentally retarded and 12 percent having cerebral palsy (Lorenz et al., 1998).

At about 28 weeks after conception, brain maturation takes a "striking" leap forward (Carlson, 1994). At that time the brain-wave pattern shifts from a flat pattern to one with occasional bursts of activity, resembling the sleep–wake cycles of a newborn. Similarly, because of ongoing brain maturation, the heart rate becomes regulated by body movement (speeding up during activity, slowing during rest) between 28 and 32 weeks after conception (DiPietro et al., 1996). Movement patterns also become "increasingly sophisticated and integrated," with regular cycles of rest and activity beginning at about 25 to 28 weeks, as the brain matures (James et al., 1995). Largely because of this neurological awakening, the odds of survival are much better for a preterm infant who is at least 28 weeks old.

Weight is also crucial to viability. By 28 weeks, the typical fetus weighs about 3 pounds (1,300 grams), and its chances of survival have increased to more than 90 percent. The Nigerian American octuplets born at 28

placenta The organ that encases the embryo and connects its circulatory system with that of its mother. The placenta allows nourishment to flow to the embryo and wastes to flow away but maintains the separation of the two circulatory systems.

age of viability The age (about 22 weeks after conception) at which a fetus can survive outside the mother's uterus if specialized medical care is available.

The Fetus At the end of 4 months, this fetus, now 6 inches long, looks fully formed but out of proportion—the distance from the top of the skull to the neck is almost as large as that from the neck to the rump. For many more weeks, the fetus must depend on the translucent membranes of the placenta and umbilical cord (the long white object in the foreground) for survival.
❓ *Observational Quiz (see answer page 104): Can you see eyebrows, fingernails, and genitals?*

The fetus is no passive passenger in the womb, nor is the pregnant woman simply "carrying" the fetus. Development is interactive, even before birth (Kisilevsky & Low, 1998). Biologically, of course, fetal growth is closely linked to the mother-to-be's nutrition and physiology. This means not only that the fetus is affected by every aspect of her lifestyle but also that the expectant woman is affected by the development of the fetus—with nausea, increased urination, and digestive upsets being fairly routine, and perhaps gestational diabetes, high blood pressure, and even toxemia. The fetus reacts to the specifics of the woman's body, and the woman experiences each pregnancy differently because the idiosyncrasies of the fetus make her adjust to it (Haig, 1995).

Beyond this physiological interdependence, fetus and adult have a much more intellectual, brain-based interaction. Beginning at about 9 weeks, the fetus moves its body in response to shifts in the woman's body position, with imperceptible movements of tiny heels, fists, elbows, and buttocks. Soon the woman notices flutters, at first so faint she wonders if gas or imagination, instead of a developing fetus, is the cause. Then movements become easier to detect and more predictable, and she learns to expect a reaction when sitting, stretching, or, especially, changing position while lying down. As the due date approaches, a sudden fetal kick or somersault can turn delight into dismay over a sore rib or interrupted sleep.

Such momentary discomfort aside, fetal movements usually evoke feelings of wonder. Indeed, many parents-to-be, fathers as well as mothers, enjoy rubbing the woman's rippling belly. The fetus feels and responds to such stimulation, beginning what may become a lifelong pattern of communication by touch (Ronca & Alberts, 1995). Interestingly, a busy woman's daily rhythms of running, bending, and resting affect fetal movement schedules, and infants who are quite active were often unusually active in the womb (DiPietro et al., 1996). Thus both parties adjust to each other's particular movement habits before birth.

Toward the end of prenatal development, other fetal sensory systems begin to function. Again, interaction between fetus and mother-to-be is apparent. For example, how much amniotic fluid the fetus swallows depends partly on the taste of that fluid: Fetuses swallow sweetened fluid more rapidly than noxious fluid, and thus their lungs, digestion, and nutrition are intimately related to the particulars of their mother's diet (Carlson, 1994). Immediately after birth, the smell of amniotic fluid is more soothing than other smells or than no smell at all, again indicating sensory adaptation before birth (Porter et al., 1998). Further, at about the twenty-seventh week, the eyelids open, and the fetus perceives the reddish glow of sunlight or other bright illumination that diffuses through the woman's belly (Kitzinger, 1989).

The most remarkable fetal learning involves hearing. Most mothers-to-be are well aware that their fetus can hear, having felt the developing person quiet down when they sing a lullaby or startle with a kick when a door slams. But many people do not realize that newborns remember certain sounds heard before birth. The most obvious example is that infants typically stop crying when they are held with an ear close to the mother's heart, comforted by the familiar rhythm they have heard for months. Few mothers know this explicitly, but most instinctively cradle their infants on their left side rather than their heartless right.

Newborns also remember voices heard in the womb (Fifer & Moon, 1995). In a series of experiments, pregnant

weeks in December 1998 in Houston, Texas, would probably all have survived if they had each weighed at least 2 pounds. The one baby who died was also the smallest: Her birthweight was only 10.3 ounces (300 grams).

The Final Three Months: From Viability to Full Term

Attaining the age of viability simply means that life outside the womb is possible. Each day of the final 3 months of prenatal growth improves the odds, not only of survival but also of a healthy and happy first few months for baby and parents. A viable preterm infant born in the seventh month is a tiny creature requiring intensive hospital care, dependent on life-support systems for each gram of nourishment and for every shallow breath. By contrast, after 9 months or so (the "due date" is exactly

Sensory Stimulation An expectant father serenades his future child.

❷ Observational Quiz (see answer page 104): *Is this behavior weird, irrational, or other? What three senses are involved in this early family interaction?*

women read the same children's book aloud daily during the ninth month. Three days after birth, their infants listened to recordings of the same story, read either by the infant's own mother or by another baby's mother. Laboratory monitoring indicated that the newborns paid greater attention to the recordings of their own mother's voice. What's more, the newborns responded less when their mothers read an unfamiliar story than when they read the familiar one.

In other words, the newborns remembered both who talked to them before birth and what was said—or, to be accurate, they recognized the voice and the speech patterns. Not surprisingly, then, infants born to monolingual English or Spanish mothers, when listening to the taped speech of a stranger speaking English or Spanish, preferred to listen to their native language (Moon et al., 1993).

Such results suggest that fetuses prepare more than just their reflexes and organ systems for physiological functioning after birth; they also begin to accustom themselves to the particulars of the social world that they soon will join. Meanwhile, mothers begin to identify features of their future offspring: Almost all pregnant women, by the last 3 months, are talking to, patting, and dreaming about their long-awaited child.

266 days, or 38 weeks, after conception) the typical full-term infant is a vigorous person, ready to thrive at home on mother's milk—no expert help, oxygenated air, special food, or technical assistance required.

The critical difference between the fragile preterm baby and the robust full-term newborn is maturation of the respiratory and cardiovascular systems. This occurs in the last 3 months of prenatal life. During that period, the lungs begin to expand and contract, exercising the muscles that are involved in breathing by using the amniotic fluid surrounding the fetus as a substitute for air. The fetus takes in fluid through mouth and nose and then exhales it, much as a fish would. At the same time, the valves of the heart go through a final maturation that, at birth, enables the circulatory system to function independently.

table **4.2**	**Average Prenatal Weights***			
Period of Development	Weeks After Conception	Weight (Nonmetric)	Weight (Metric)	Notes
End of embryo period	8	1/30 oz	1 g	A birthweight below 2 lb (1,000 g) is considered extremely low birth-weight **(ELBW).**
End of first trimester	13	3 oz	100 g	
At viability (50–50 chance of survival)	24	22 oz	600 g	
End of second trimester	26–28	2–3 lb	1,000 – 1,300 g	Below 3½ lb (1,500 g) is very low birthweight **(VLBW).**
End of preterm period	35	5½ lb	2,500 g	Below 5½ lb (2,500 g) is low birthweight **(LBW).**
Full term	38	7½ lb	3,400 g	Between 5½ and 9 lb (2,500–4,500 g) is considered normal weight.

*To make them easier to remember, the weights are rounded off (which accounts for the inexact correspondence between metric and nonmetric measures). Actual weights vary. For instance, a normal full-term infant can weigh between 5½ and 9 pounds (2.5 and 4 kilograms); a viable infant, especially one of several born at 26 or more weeks, can weigh less than shown here.

In addition, the fetus usually gains more than 4.5 pounds (2,000 grams) of critical weight in the last 10 weeks, increasing, on average, to 7½ pounds (3,400 grams) at birth (see Table 4.2). This weight gain is primarily fat, which not only insulates the baby no longer surrounded by the mother, but also provides calories that will be burned while the mother's breast milk is being fully established.

In many ways, the relationship between mother and child begins during the final 3 months, for during this time the size and movements of the fetus make her very aware of it, and her sounds, smells, and behavior become part of fetal consciousness (as described in the In Person box).

RISK REDUCTION

The 9 months that transform a single-cell zygote into a viable human newborn are a time of miraculous growth but also of considerable vulnerability. Lest the future parents reading this book become needlessly frightened as we examine a number of potential prenatal hazards, keep two facts in mind:

■ Despite the complexity of prenatal development and the many dangers to the developing organism, the large majority of babies are born healthy and capable.

■ Most hazards can be avoided, or their effects reduced, through care taken by an expectant woman, her family, and the community.

Thus, prenatal development should be thought of not as a dangerous period to be feared, but as a natural process to be protected. The

❶ *Answer to Observational Quiz (from page 101):*
Yes, yes, and no. Genitals are formed, but they are not visible in this photo. That object growing from the lower belly is the umbilical cord.

❶ *Answer to Observational Quiz (from page 103):*
The auditory, tactile, and visual senses. The fetus can hear the father's flute, and both parents can see and feel the movement of the fetus. This scene may be weird in that it is unusual, but it is actually quite rational: Early communication is not only possible but also beneficial to mother, father, and offspring.

teratology The scientific study of birth defects caused by genetic or prenatal problems or by birth complications.

teratogens Agents and conditions, including viruses, drugs, chemicals, stressors, and malnutrition, that can impair prenatal development and lead to birth defects or even death.

behavioral teratogens Teratogens that tend to harm the prenatal brain, affecting the future child's intellectual and emotional functioning.

risk analysis The process of weighing the potential outcomes of a particular event, substance, or experience to determine the likelihood of harm. In teratology, the attempt to evaluate all the factors that can increase or decrease the likelihood that a particular teratogen will cause harm.

critical period In prenatal development, the time when a particular organ or other body part is most susceptible to teratogenic damage.

goal of **teratology,** the study of birth defects, is to increase the odds that every newborn will have a healthy start in life.

Scientists now understand a great deal about **teratogens,** the broad range of substances (such as drugs and pollutants) and conditions (such as severe malnutrition and extreme stress) that increase the risk of prenatal abnormalities. These abnormalities include physical problems that are obvious at birth and more subtle impairments, including learning disabilities, that first appear in elementary school. A specific teratogen may damage the body structures, the growth rate, the neurological networks, or all three. Teratogens that can harm the brain, and therefore make a child hyperactive, antisocial, retarded, and so on, are called **behavioral teratogens.** Although not causing problems as readily apparent as missing limbs or sightless eyes, behavioral teratogens can be far more damaging over the life of the person than physical defects.

Determining Risk

Teratology is a science of **risk analysis,** of weighing the factors that affect the likelihood that a particular teratogen will cause harm. Although all teratogens increase the risk of harm, none *always* cause damage. The ultimate impact depends on the complex interplay of many factors, both destructive and protective. This means that exposure to a particular teratogen might be of low risk for one embryo, causing no harm at all, and of high risk for another, almost certainly causing damage. Obviously, a goal of research and analysis is to pinpoint exactly what separates these two outcomes in order to improve the odds for all babies.

Timing of Exposure

One crucial factor is timing—when the developing organism is exposed to which teratogen. Some teratogens cause damage only during specific days or weeks early in pregnancy, when a particular part of the body is undergoing formation. Others can be harmful at any time, but the severity of the damage depends on when the exposure occurred.

The time of greatest susceptibility is called the **critical period.** As you can see in Figure 4.2 on page 106, each body structure has its own critical period: It begins for the ears, limbs, and eyes at about 4 weeks after conception, for the lips at about 5 weeks, and for the teeth and palate at about 7 weeks. The entire embryonic stage can be called a critical period for physical structure and form, with the specifics varying somewhat week by week (Moore & Persaud, 1998).

For conditions (such as severe malnutrition) and substances (such as heroin) that disrupt and destabilize the overall functioning of the woman's body, there are two critical periods. The first is at the very beginning of pregnancy, when stress during the germinal period can impede implantation. (The many factors that reduce fertility are described in Chapter 17.) The second is toward the end of pregnancy, when the fetus most needs to gain weight and when the cortex of the brain is developing, making the fetus particularly vulnerable to damage that can cause learning disabilities. Further, near the end of pregnancy, instability of the mother's body systems (for instance, if she has chills or the shakes) can loosen the placenta or cause hormonal changes, both of which can precipitate birth.

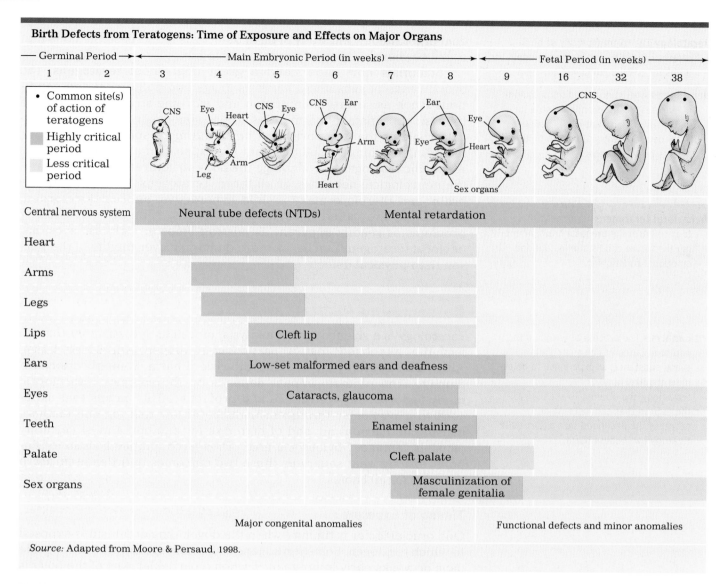

Birth Defects from Teratogens: Time of Exposure and Effects on Major Organs

Germinal Period → ← Main Embryonic Period (in weeks) → ← Fetal Period (in weeks) →

| 1 | 2 | 3 | 4 | 5 | 6 | 7 | 8 | 9 | 16 | 32 | 38 |

- Common site(s) of action of teratogens
- Highly critical period
- Less critical period

CNS / Eye / Heart / CNS / Eye / CNS / Ear / Arm / Leg / Ear / Eye / Heart / Sex organs / CNS

Central nervous system — Neural tube defects (NTDs)   Mental retardation

Heart

Arms

Legs

Lips — Cleft lip

Ears — Low-set malformed ears and deafness

Eyes — Cataracts, glaucoma

Teeth — Enamel staining

Palate — Cleft palate

Sex organs — Masculinization of female genitalia

Major congenital anomalies   Functional defects and minor anomalies

Source: Adapted from Moore & Persaud, 1998.

Figure 4.2 Critical Periods in Human Development. The most serious damage from teratogens is likely to occur in the first 8 weeks after conception (light shading). However, significant damage to many vital parts of the body, including the brain, eyes, and genitals, can occur during the last months of pregnancy as well (dark shading).

threshold effect The phenomenon in which a particular teratogen is relatively harmless in small doses but becomes harmful when exposure reaches a certain level (the threshold).

interaction effect The phenomenon in which a teratogen's potential for causing harm increases when it is combined with another teratogen or another risk factor.

Note, however, that for behavioral teratogens there is no safe period. The brain and nervous system can be harmed throughout prenatal development, a process that continues after birth (see Changing Policy box).

Amount of Exposure

A second important factor is the dose and/or frequency of exposure. Some teratogens have a **threshold effect;** that is, they are virtually harmless until exposure reaches a certain level, at which point they "cross the threshold" from being innocuous to being damaging. Indeed, a few substances, such as vitamin A, are actually beneficial in small amounts but fiercely teratogenic in large quantities (Kraft & Willhite, 1997). Vitamin A is an essential part of a good prenatal diet, so vitamin A from beta-carotene is a component of most multivitamins for pregnant women; but more than 10,000 units per day (not from beta-carotene) may be too much.

For most teratogens, experts are reluctant to specify a threshold below which the substance is safe. One reason is that many teratogens have an **interaction effect;** that is, one poison intensifies the effects of another.

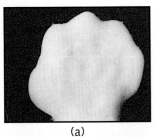

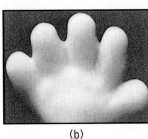

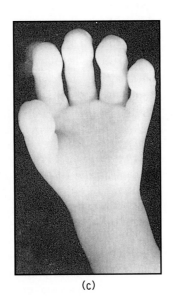

(a)

(b)

(c)

A Week for Fingers The impact of a potential teratogen partially depends on when the developing organism is exposed to it. This is because there is a critical period in the formation of every body part during which the part is especially vulnerable. Shown here are three stages in finger development that define the critical period: (a) notches appear in the hand at day 44; (b) fingers are separated and lengthened by day 50; (c) fingers are completely formed by day 55, and the critical period for hand development is over. Other parts of the body, including the eyes, heart, and central nervous system, take much longer to complete development, so the critical period during which they are vulnerable to teratogens lasts for months rather than days.

rubella A viral disease that, if contracted early during pregnancy, can harm the fetus, causing blindness, deafness, and damage to the central nervous system. (Sometimes called *German measles*.)

Genetic Vulnerability

A third factor that determines whether a specific teratogen will be harmful, and to what extent, is the developing organism's genes. When a woman carrying dizygotic twins drinks alcohol, for example, the twins' blood alcohol levels are exactly equal; yet one may be more severely affected than the other (Maier et al., 1996). This difference probably involves a gene affecting a specific enzyme (alcohol dehydrogenase) that is crucial to the breakdown of alcohol. Similar genetic susceptibilities are suspected in other birth disorders, including cleft palate and club foot (Hartl & Jones, 1999).

Genes are also implicated in the teratogenic effect of a deficiency of folic acid (a B-complex vitamin) in the mother-to-be's diet. Researchers have known for several years that folic-acid deficiency can produce neural-tube defects—either spina bifida, in which the spine does not close properly, or anencephaly, in which part of the brain does not form. Neural-tube defects occur more commonly in certain families and ethnic groups (specifically, Irish, English, and Egyptians) and not often in others (most Asian and African groups) (Perlow, 1999). That fact led to research that found the source: A defective gene produces an enzyme that prevents the normal utilization of folic acid (Mills et al., 1995).

In some cases, genetic vulnerability is related to the sex of the developing organism. Generally, male (XY) embryos and fetuses are at greater risk than female (XX), in that male fetuses are more often aborted spontaneously. In addition, newborn boys have more birth defects, and older boys have more learning disabilities and other problems caused by behavioral teratogens.

Specific Teratogens

Because of the many variables involved, risk analysis cannot precisely predict the results of teratogenic exposure in individual cases (Jacobson & Jacobson, 1996). However, decades of research have revealed the possible effects of some of the most common and damaging teratogens. More important, much has been learned about how individuals and society can reduce the risks.

Diseases

Many diseases, including most viruses and virtually all sexually transmitted diseases, can harm a fetus. Here we will focus on only two conditions, rubella and HIV, that also illustrate the potential for public health measures to prevent birth defects.

Rubella. One of the first teratogens to be recognized was **rubella** (sometimes called *German measles*). Rubella was long considered a harmless childhood disease. But 50 years ago doctors discovered that if a woman contracts rubella early in pregnancy, her embryo might suffer blindness,

PREVENTING DRUG DAMAGE

Despite the ambiguity of much of the longitudinal research on drug use, the evidence leads to a strong recommendation: Pregnant women should avoid drugs entirely. Nothing is risk-free. Unfortunately, many women in their prime reproductive years drink alcohol, smoke cigarettes, and/or use illicit drugs. Most continue their drug use in the first weeks before they realize that they are pregnant. If they then stop, it is already late, after the early formation of the embryo. To make matters worse, those who are addicts, alcoholics, or heavy users of multiple drugs are least likely to be able to stop their drug use on their own, least likely to recognize their condition in the first few weeks and obtain early medical care, and sometimes deliberately excluded from residential drug treatment programs.

General education helps, but it is not enough. For example, the danger of alcohol and tobacco use during pregnancy is well known. Yet a recent survey found that about one in six pregnant women in the United States smoked during the final three months of pregnancy, with those under age 25 twice as likely to smoke as those over age 35 (*MMWR*, September 24, 1999). Similarly, in a 1995 U.S. survey, 15 percent of pregnant women admitted drinking, at least a little, and 3.5 percent said that they had drunk a lot within the previous month—at least one drink per day or five or more drinks on one occasion, a level that is definitely risky. Moreover, 4 years earlier in a similar survey, only .9 percent had admitted drinking a lot. This suggests an alarming increase of 400 percent in the number of pregnant heavy drinkers between 1991 and 1995 (Ebrahim et al., 1998). Worse, the actual amount and prevalence of drinking are undoubtedly higher than these numbers indicate, because many alcoholics hide the extent of their drinking. A careful assessment in Seattle, Washington, of babies born in 1981 found that 3 in 1,000 had FAS and another 6 in 1,000 had less obvious brain damage (Sampson et al., 1997). The overall rate, about 1 in 100, shows that while not every drinker harms her fetus, far too many do.

What can be done, beyond general education? The research suggests five protective steps:

1. *Abstinence from all drugs even before pregnancy.* The best course is to avoid drugs altogether. This can make a dramatic difference, as is shown by data on babies born to women who have recently emigrated to the United States. For many reasons, including poverty and lack of medical care, such women are at high risk for prenatal and birth complications of every kind. However, their newborns weigh more, and are born with fewer defects, than those of native-born women of the same ethnicity (Singh & Yu, 1996; Zambrana et al., 1997). One reason is that immigrants are more often drug-free, not only because of cultural patterns but also because their husbands and parents discourage any substance use in pregnancy.

2. *Abstinence from all drugs after the first month.* The teratogenic effects of psychoactive drugs accumulate throughout pregnancy. Thus early prenatal care, with routine testing for drug use and effective treatment toward abstinence, would reduce fetal brain damage substantially. In fact, because the last 3 months of pregnancy are critical for brain development, a drug-free second half of pregnancy *may* be enough to prevent brain damage if drug use during the first half was moderate (Maier et al., 1996). Since alcohol and tobacco are at least as teratogenic as illegal drugs, they need to be tested for and targeted just as much as cocaine, heroin, marijuana, and the like.

3. *Moderation throughout pregnancy* (if abstinence from all drugs is impossible). The prenatal effects of psychoactive drugs are dose-related, interactive, and cumulative; therefore, each dose that is reduced, each drug that is eliminated, and each day that is drug-free represents a reduction in the damage that can be caused.

4. *Social support.* Maternal stress, psychological problems, loneliness, and poor housing correlate with prenatal complications as well as with drug use (Nordentoft et al., 1996; Shiono et al., 1997). In fact, the correlation between psycho-

deafness, heart abnormalities, and brain damage. (Some of these problems and their effects were apparent in David's story in Chapter 1.)

The seriousness of this teratogen became all too evident in a worldwide rubella epidemic in the mid-1960s. In the United States alone, 20,000 infants had obvious rubella-caused impairments, including hundreds who were born both deaf and blind (Franklin, 1984). Thousands more showed no immediate effects because damage was done only to

Drug Abuse Smoking and drinking are an essential part of daily life for millions of young women, many of whom find these habits impossible to give up when they become pregnant. If you met this woman at a party and you thought complete abstinence was too much to ask, temperance might be a reasonable suggestion. Taking a few puffs and a few sips, or using just one drug and not the other, might prevent damage to the fetus's developing body and brain.

active drugs and prenatal problems may be due, in part, to a hidden factor—psychological difficulties (Robert, 1996). If this is true, then befriending, encouraging, and assisting pregnant drug users may not only reduce their use of teratogens but also, even without directly affecting drug use, aid fetal development. (Of course, the assistance should not include any help in obtaining or using drugs.)

5. *Postnatal care.* Newborns with alcohol, cocaine, or even heroin in their systems sometimes become quite normal,

intelligent children if they receive optimal care (Mayes et al., 1992; Richardson & Day, 1994). Thus, another way to protect children is to ensure sensitive nurturance after birth (through parenting education, preventive medicine, home visits, early day care, and, if necessary, foster care). Note that social prejudices work against these children; for instance, the assumption that "crack babies" are destined to have serious learning problems might reduce educational outreach to children of crack-using mothers (Lyons & Rittner, 1998). The most recent research continues to suggest that cocaine alone does no more damage than alcohol alone and that environmental factors after birth (such as a highly stressed mother and multiple caregivers) are the primary cause of the so-called crack-baby syndrome (Alessandri et al., 1998; Brown et al., 1998).

One preventive measure that does *not* seem to help is prosecuting pregnant women who use drugs. Jailing such women does lead to enforced drug abstinence, and, ironically, imprisoned pregnant women have healthier babies than their peers outside the walls (Martin et al., 1997); but the threat of prosecution and imprisonment, in effect, keeps thousands of pregnant women away from prenatal care. This increases fetal damage that might have been prevented (Lyons & Rittner, 1998). When it comes to imprisoning drug addicts, the math is simple. If preventing drug abuse in one pregnant woman by keeping her in jail results in ongoing drug abuse in 99 other women who avoid all prenatal care, the harm far exceeds the benefit. If there were some way to get all 99 to reduce their drug use, however, the benefits might be substantial. How much harm is prevented by any measure short of total abstinence before pregnancy starts? The truth is that we do not know, and we cannot know for sure until all newborns who were exposed to drugs before birth are assured of excellent care in the first months and years of their lives (Byrd et al., 1999).

the brain, but behavioral or learning problems appeared years later (Enkin et al., 1989).

Since that epidemic, widespread immunization—either of preschool children (as in the United States) or of all adolescent girls who are not already immune (as in England)—has reduced the rubella threat. Consequently, only eight rubella-syndrome infants were born in the United States in 1999 (*MMWR,* January 7, 2000). Other teratogenic diseases (for example, chicken pox) likewise have been diminished by immunization and now rarely cause damage to fetuses.

Pediatric AIDS. No widespread immunization is yet available for the most devastating viral teratogen of all: **human immunodeficiency virus (HIV).** HIV gradually overwhelms the body's natural immune responses, leaving the individual vulnerable to a host of diseases and infections that together constitute **acquired immune deficiency syndrome (AIDS).**

About one in every four newborns whose mothers are HIV-positive has the deadly virus, which is acquired from the mother during pregnancy or birth. Within months or years, an infant with the virus always develops pediatric AIDS, partly because drugs that reverse the course of HIV have not even been tested on children (much less proven successful) and partly because the virus overwhelms a very young body faster than a fully grown one (Wilfert & McKinney, 1998).

The best way to prevent pediatric AIDS is to prevent adult AIDS. The second best way is to prevent pregnancy in HIV-positive women. Both strategies are complicated by the disease's long incubation period in adults—up to 10 years or more—during which people can transmit the virus without knowing that they are infected.

As a third prevention strategy, women with the HIV virus who take the drug AZT during pregnancy and at birth have far fewer HIV-positive newborns: 8 percent of births with AZT versus 26 percent without. Between 1992 and 1996, AZT, plus cesarean delivery, cut the number of HIV-positive newborns by 43 percent (Soto et al., 1999). Obviously, testing women for HIV when they give birth (as some U.S. states require) is testing at least 6 months too late. The National Institute of Medicine recommends that every woman get confidential prenatal care, including a routine HIV test, in the first 3 months of pregnancy (Soto et al., 1999). Even in developed nations, this does not necessarily occur. And in sub-Saharan Africa, where AIDS is epidemic, few pregnant women are tested and treated, and hundreds of thousands of children die of AIDS each year. Unless all women obtain early prenatal testing and good care, another million of the world's children will contract AIDS from their mothers every 3 years (Wilfert & McKinney, 1998).

Many other maternal conditions, including Rh-negative blood (a recessive genetic trait, not a disease), syphilis and other sexually transmitted diseases, and drug use, also need to be recognized months before birth in order to protect the fetus. In the United States in 1999, for example, 277 newborns had congenital syphilis; all these cases could have been prevented in early pregnancy (*MMWR,* January 7, 2000).

Medicines and Drugs

Many widely used *medicinal drugs*—drugs that remedy some real or potential problem in a person's body—are teratogenic in some cases. The list includes tetracycline,

human immunodeficiency virus (HIV) A virus that gradually overwhelms the body's immune responses, leaving the individual defenseless against a host of pathologies that eventually manifest themselves as AIDS.

acquired immune deficiency syndrome (AIDS) The diseases and infections, many of them fatal, that result from the degradation of the immune system by HIV.

❷ **Especially for Social Workers:** When is it most important to convince women to be tested for HIV—a month before pregnancy, a month after conception, or immediately after birth?

Fighting AIDS, One Child at a Time These children, all born to HIV-positive mothers, do not all have the deadly virus, but they suffer from the disease nonetheless. Although those who are HIV-negative will survive, their mothers are unable to care for them because they are dying, or already dead, of the disease. Nonetheless, these children are more fortunate than many others in their condition: They are residents of Hale House, founded by a grandmother in Harlem who opened her home and heart to children with AIDS.

table **4.3**	**Effects of Psychoactive Drugs on Prenatal Development**	
Drug	Usage	Effects
Alcohol	3 or more drinks daily, or binge drinking of 5 or more drinks on one occasion early in pregnancy	Causes *fetal alcohol syndrome (FAS)*. Symptoms include a small head, abnormal facial characteristics (wide spacing between the eyes, a flattened nose and a narrow upper lip, unusual eyelids, and missing skin indent between nose and upper lip), overall growth retardation, learning disabilities, and behavior problems (including poor concentration and impaired social skills).
	More than ½ oz. of absolute alcohol a day	Causes *fetal alcohol effects (FAE)*. FAE does not observably affect facial appearance or physical growth, but it affects brain functioning. The first sign is noisy, higher-frequency cries at birth. Later signs, on cognitive tests, include lower IQ (by about 5 points).
	Moderate drinking: less than 1 or 2 servings of beer or wine or 1 mixed drink, a few days per week	Probably has no negative effects on prenatal development, although this is controversial.
Tobacco	Maternal smoking early in pregnancy	Increases risk of abnormalities, including malformations of the limbs and the urinary tract.
	Maternal smoking late in pregnancy	Reduces birthweight and size. Babies born to habitual smokers weigh, on average, about 9 oz. (250 g) less than would otherwise be expected, and they are shorter, both at birth and in the years to come. They may have childhood problems, particularly with respiration, and, in adulthood, increased risk of becoming smokers themselves.
	Paternal smoking	Reduces birthweight by about 2 oz. (45 g) on average.
Marijuana	Heavy use	Affects the central nervous system, as evidenced by the tendency of affected newborns to emit a high-pitched cry that denotes brain damage.
	Light use	Has no proven long-term effects.
Heroin		Because of the physiological "highs" and "crashes" of the addiction (such as the reduction of oxygen, irregular heartbeat, and sweating and chills that occur during withdrawal), heroin causes slower fetal growth and premature labor. (See also *methadone*, below.)
Methadone	Later in pregnancy	Moderates the effects of heroin withdrawal during pregnancy but is as addictive as heroin. Heavily addicted newborns require regulated drug doses in the first days of life to prevent the pain and convulsions associated with sudden opiate withdrawal.
Cocaine		Causes overall growth retardation, problems with the placenta, and specific learning problems in the first months of life. Research on long-lasting effects is confounded by the effects of poverty and the ongoing addiction of the mother. The major concern is in language development (Lester et al., 1998).
Solvents	Especially early in pregnancy	Causes smaller heads, crossed eyes, and other abnormalities.

Overall sources: Larsen, 1998; Lyons & Rittner, 1998.

Alcohol (Manteuffel, 1996; Nugent el al., 1996; Streissguth, 1997); *tobacco* (Eskenazi et al., 1995; Kallen, 1997; Kandel et al., 1994; Li et al., 1996); *marijuana* (Lester & Dreher, 1989); *methadone* (Schneider & Hans, 1996); *cocaine* (including crack) (Hurt et al., 1996); *solvents* (glue, other inhalants) (Arnold, 1997).

anticoagulants, bromides, anticonvulsants, phenobarbital, retinoic acid (a common treatment for acne, as in Accutane), and most hormones. Other prescription drugs and nonprescription drugs (such as aspirin, antacids, and diet pills) may be teratogenic. Obviously, then, women who might become pregnant, or who are pregnant, should avoid any medication unless recommended by a doctor who is both well versed in teratology *and* aware of the possible pregnancy.

Prenatal damage caused by *psychoactive drugs* (Table 4.3)—that is, drugs that affect the psyche, which include beer and wine, liquor,

fetal alcohol syndrome (FAS) A cluster of birth defects, including abnormal facial characteristics, slow physical growth, and retarded mental development, that is caused by the mother's drinking excessive quantities of alcohol when pregnant.

Differences and Similarities The differences between these two children are obvious at a glance: One is an African American teenager, the other a Swedish toddler. One similarity is obvious, too: Both are girls. However, the most important similarity—fetal alcohol syndrome—is apparent only on closer observation.

❓ *Observational Quiz (see answer page 114):* *How many of the five visible facial characteristics of fetal alcohol syndrome can you see in both girls?*

low birthweight (LBW) A birthweight of less than 5½ pounds (2,500 grams).

cigarettes and smokeless tobacco, heroin and methadone, LSD, marijuana, cocaine in any form, inhalants, antidepressant pills, and many other substances—is far too common. All psychoactive drugs slow down fetal growth and increase the risk of premature labor. And all can affect the developing brain, producing both short-term and long-term deficits. For days or weeks after birth, infants who were prenatally addicted to any of these drugs sleep fitfully, startle easily, cry unhappily, suck voraciously, eat erratically, and show other signs of drug withdrawal.

As they develop, children who were exposed prenatally to psychoactive drugs may exhibit ongoing learning difficulties, impaired self-control, poor concentration, and overall irritability. Beyond these general effects, each drug varies in its specific effects; thus, tobacco causes low birthweight, while alcohol causes **fetal alcohol syndrome (FAS),** the leading teratogenic cause of mental retardation.

Little or no definitive longitudinal research on the dosage, timing, and particular effects of specific illegal drugs is available, because it is virtually impossible to locate a sizable representative sample of newly pregnant women who use one, and only one, illicit drug at a steady and measurable dose. The problem is that illicit drug users almost always use several legal as well as illegal drugs—not just their drug of choice.

Furthermore, when a mother-to-be is *addicted* to an illicit drug, the fetal hazards are compounded by her erratic sleeping and eating habits; her bouts of anxiety, stress, and depression; and her increased risk of accidents, violence, and sexual abuse. One study of more than 3,000 women found that, fortunately, most of those who used psychoactive drugs quit during pregnancy. The unfortunate exceptions were the 100 or so who were physically abused by their partners; they were more likely to continue drug abuse (Martin et al., 1996). Finally, severely addicted women are often malnourished and sick, unsupported by concerned family members, and without medical care. After the baby is born, all these problems typically surround the child for years, along with possible additional stresses from an absent or abusive father and living in a poor and dangerous neighborhood. So targeting prenatal use of a particular illegal drug as *the* cause of the child's learning problems is obviously unscientific.

LOW BIRTHWEIGHT

The final complication we will discuss here is **low birthweight (LBW),** defined by the World Health Organization as a weight of less than 5½ pounds (2,500 grams) at birth. LBW babies are further grouped into *very low birthweight (VLBW)* babies, weighing less than 3 pounds (1,500 grams), and *extremely low birthweight (ELBW)* babies, weighing less than about 2 pounds (1,000 grams). The rate of LBW varies enormously from nation to nation (see Figure 4.3); the U.S. 1998 rate of 7.5 percent was twice that of some other developed nations (see Figure 4.4).

Many factors can cause low birthweight, including malnutrition and poverty. As you will see, the worst problems occur when several factors combine.

Too Soon

Remember that the fetal body weight doubles in the last months of pregnancy, with a typical gain of almost 2 pounds (about 900 grams) occurring

Figure 4.3 Low Birthweight Around the World, 1990s. Poverty and policy interact to affect the rate of infants born weighing less than 5½ pounds (2,500 grams), as shown in a sample of 24 nations (among the 148 reported by the United Nations). Generally, the nations of Europe do best on this indicator of national health, and those of southern Asia do worst. However, income alone does not result in excellent medical and social care. For example, although the U.S. gross national product (at more than $7 trillion a year) is larger than that of any other nation, 33 nations do better than the United States on LBW, 20 nations are tied at 7 percent, and 95 nations do worse. Except for the last four nations shown here, none have more than 20 percent LBW, a worldwide improvement over the rate 20 years ago.

❶ Response for Social Workers (from page 110): Voluntary testing and then treatment can be useful at any time, since those who learn they are HIV-positive are more likely to get treatment, in order to reduce the likelihood of transmission, and to avoid pregnancy. If pregnancy does occur, diagnosis early in pregnancy is best, since abortion is one option and taking AZT is another—one that prevents many cases of pediatric AIDS.

preterm birth Birth that occurs 3 weeks or more before the full term of pregnancy has elapsed, that is, at 35 or fewer weeks past conception rather than at the full term of about 38 weeks.

❷ Especially for Women: If you have decided to become pregnant soon, you obviously cannot change your genes, your age, or your economic status. But you can do three things in the next month or two that can markedly reduce the chance of having a low-birthweight baby a year from now. What are they?

Figure 4.4 Not Improving. The rate of LBW infants is often taken to be a measure of a nation's overall health. In the United States, the rise and fall of this rate is related to many factors, among them the availability of good prenatal care, maternal use of drugs, and overall nutrition.

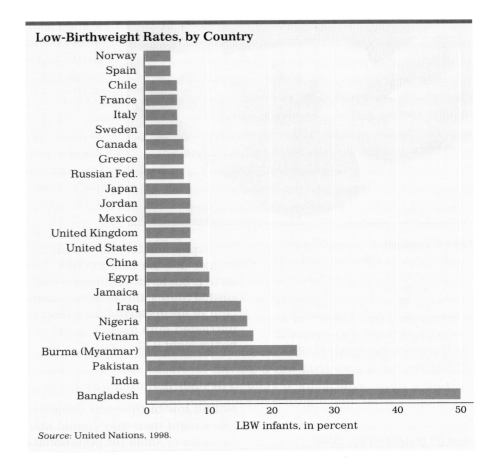

Low-Birthweight Rates, by Country

Source: United Nations, 1998.

in the final 3 weeks. Thus, a baby born **preterm,** defined as 3 or more weeks before the usual 38 weeks, is usually of low birthweight. Not always, however. Babies born even a month early may not be LBW if they were well nourished throughout prenatal development. They may weigh 6½ pounds (more than 3,000 grams), well above the 5½-pound (2,500-gram) cutoff. Most preterm infants, however, are too small as well as too early.

Why would pregnancy end prematurely? Sometimes factors specific to a particular pregnancy are to blame. A placenta may become detached from the uterine wall, or a uterus may be unable to accommodate further fetal growth. This last factor helps explain why small women and

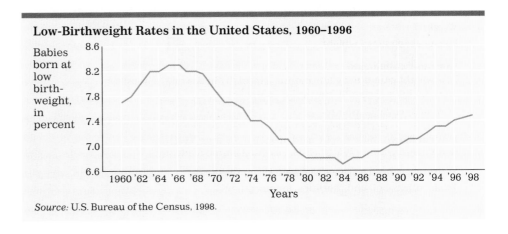

Low-Birthweight Rates in the United States, 1960–1996

Source: U.S. Bureau of the Census, 1998.

LOW-BIRTHWEIGHT RATES AND PROTECTIVE FACTORS

Overall, the United States VLBW and ELBW rates are rising even more rapidly than LBW. At the same time, the median birthweight has actually been increasing (from 7 pounds, 4 ounces in 1970 to 7 pounds, 8 ounces in 1997) and neonatal deaths have plummeted, from 15 to 5 per 1,000. Thus most newborns are healthier, but there are far more tiny newborns who survive for years than ever before. This raises a new choice among three desirable goals:

- Better care during pregnancy so that fewer LBW infants are born
- Better intensive care so that more tiny infants survive
- Better long-term family support so that children who were low-birthweight reach their full potential

All three are obviously important, but currently the most costly and intensive effort is devoted to the most dramatic goal: saving the lives of the tiniest babies. Fewer resources are given to prevention, and almost no public or private insurance provides adequate at-home care during the early years or specialized education until preschool age. Without such help, many parents are overwhelmed by the special needs of a very tiny baby, who typically is more demanding and less responsive than a full-term, full-size infant. Perhaps as a result, the rates of child abuse and neglect are elevated for children who were LBW, especially if they are disabled as well (Giardino et al., 1997). To make matters worse, LBW infants are more often raised in low-income homes, which increases the stress on the family and reduces the chance of the initial handicap's being overcome.

Taken as a whole, these statistics provide sobering evidence of the need for a life-span perspective on the LBW rate and on the entire question of how best to protect the developing fetus. Remember from the discussion in Chapter 1 that the life-span perspective stresses the entire social and cultural context and emphasizes long-term plasticity. Instead of looking at only one moment in a person's life—the moment when an infant is born underweight and with evidence of drug exposure or other developmental problems—it is essential to consider the mother's experiences before birth and the infant's experiences in the months after birth. The best medicine may be preventive medicine; the best treatment may include not highly specialized monitors, respirators, or microsurgery, but rather ongoing education, nutrition, and family support. In fact, adequate maternal nutrition, early prenatal care, and public health measures (maternal immunization, prevention of domestic violence, reduction of environmental pollution) can have a greater impact than acute medical care in ensuring the birth of healthy babies. Indeed, when we look at worldwide data, the best way to reduce the incidence of low birthweight seems to be educating and feeding girls, because women with better education and larger body size are far less likely than smaller, illiterate women to have LBW infants (Tsui et al., 1997).

❶ *Answer to Observational Quiz (from page 115):*
The woman is probably married (see the ring) and probably practices good hygiene (even her fingernails are very clean), and both correlate with healthier pregnancies. However, the four bottles of pills are troubling: Unless she has some special deficiency, one multivitamin with folic acid should be enough.

to eat sporadically and unhealthily, and because their own bodies are still developing, their diet is inadequate to support the growth of two.

Virtually all the many risk factors for low birthweight correlate with poverty (Hughes & Simpson, 1995). Compared with women of higher socioeconomic status, pregnant women at the bottom of the economic ladder are more likely to be ill, malnourished, teenaged, and stressed. If they are employed, their jobs often require long hours of physically stressful work, exactly the kind of work that correlates with preterm and SGA birth (Ceron-Mireles et al., 1996). They often receive late or inadequate prenatal care, breathe polluted air, live in overcrowded conditions, move from place to place, and ingest unhealthy substances, from psychoactive drugs to spoiled foods—all of which can have deleterious effects on the developing fetus (Shiono et al., 1997). Poverty is part of the explanation for differences between nations and, within the United States, for ethnic and historical differences (see Table 4.5). Within the broad racial categories used by the U.S. Bureau of the Census, the poorer groups (Appalachian whites, Filipino Asians, Puerto Rican Hispanics) are more likely to have underweight newborns than the wealthier groups.

table **4.5**	**Percent of Low-Birthweight Infants in U.S. by Census Category**				
	1985	1990	1993	1996	1998
White	5.6	5.7	6.0	6.3	6.5
Black	12.4	13.3	13.3	13.0	13.0
Hispanic	6.2	6.1	6.2	6.3	6.4
Native American	5.9	6.1	6.4	N.A.*	N.A.
Overall	6.8	7.0	7.2	7.4	7.5

*N.A.=not available.
Sources: U. S. Bureau of the Census, 1992, 1996, 1998, 1999.

Why? Some reasons for the increase in low-birthweight babies are known: more multiple births because of fertility drugs and better prenatal care, which means fewer stillbirths. However, this explains only part of the increase, especially since several other nations continue to decrease the number of infants born below 5½ pounds (2,500 grams).

Figure 4.6 A Normal, Uncomplicated Birth.
(a) The baby's position as the birth process begins. (b) The first stage of labor: The cervix dilates to allow passage of the baby's head. (c) Transition: The baby's head moves into the "birth canal," the vagina. (d) The second stage of labor: The baby's head moves through the opening of the vagina ("crowns") and (e) emerges completely. The head is turned, and the rest of the body emerges.

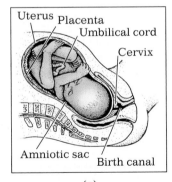

(a)

Of course, socioeconomic status is only a rough gauge, and other factors sometimes have more effect in some cases. This is apparent with another Hispanic group—Americans of Mexican descent. Their LBW rate is only 5.6 percent, much lower than the rates of other groups with similar levels of income and education (U.S. Bureau of the Census, 1996). Cultural values and paternal support are among the probable reasons for this relatively low rate (Singh & Yu, 1996; Zambrana et al., 1997). Other protective factors and trends in LBW rates are discussed in A Life-Span View.

THE NORMAL BIRTH

For a full-term fetus and a healthy mother, birth can be simple and quick. At some time during the last month of pregnancy, most fetuses change position for the final time, turning upside down so that the head is low in the mother's pelvic cavity. They are now in position to be born in the usual way, head first. (About 1 in 20 does not turn and is born "breech," that is, buttocks first.) The sequence of a normal birth is shown in Figure 4.6.

Then, at about the 266th day after conception, the fetal brain signals the release of certain hormones that pass into the mother's bloodstream. These hormones trigger her uterine muscles to contract and relax, starting the process that becomes actual labor. The baby is born, on average, after 6 hours of labor for first births and 3 hours for subsequent births (Nichols & Zwelling, 1997).

The Newborn's First Minutes

People who have never witnessed a birth might picture the newborn being held upside down and spanked by the attending doctor or midwife, to make the baby start crying and therefore breathing. Actually, newborns usually breathe and cry on their own as soon as they are born. In fact, they sometimes cry as their heads emerge from the birth canal, even before their shoulders—one by one—appear. As the first spontaneous cries occur, the newborn's circulatory system begins to function; soon the infant's color changes from a bluish tinge to pink, because oxygen circulates throughout the system. The eyes open wide; the tiny

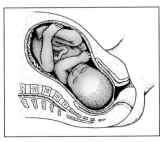

(b)

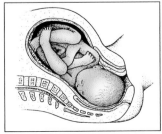

(c)

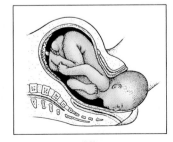

(d)

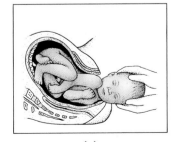

(e)

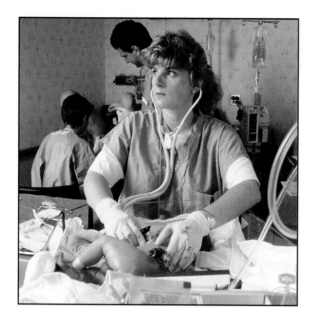

100 or More Heartbeats per Minute A minute after birth, this newborn is undergoing his first exam, the Apgar. From the newborn's ruddy color and obvious muscle tone, it looks as if he will pass with a score of 7 or higher.

Apgar scale A means of quickly assessing a newborn's body functioning. The baby's color, heart rate, reflexes, muscle tone, and respiratory effort are scored (from 0 to 2) 1 minute and 5 minutes after birth and compared with a standard for healthy babies (a perfect 10).

fingers grab anything they can; the even tinier toes stretch and retract. The newborn is instantly, zestfully, ready for life.

Checking for Problems

Nevertheless, there is much for those attending the birth to do. Any mucus that might be in the baby's throat is removed, especially if the first breaths seem shallow or strained. The umbilical cord is cut to detach the placenta, leaving the "belly button." The infant is wiped dry of fluid and blood, weighed, and wrapped to preserve body heat. If the birth is assisted by a trained health worker—as are 99 percent of the births in industrialized nations and about half of the births worldwide (Tsui et al., 1997)—the newborn is immediately checked for body functioning.

One common means of assessing the newborn's condition is a measure called the **Apgar scale** (see Table 4.6). From a brief examination, the examiner assigns a score of 0, 1, or 2 to the heart rate, breathing, muscle tone, color, and reflexes at 1 minute after birth and again at 5 minutes. A low score at 1 minute is a warning, but usually newborns quickly improve. If the 5-minute total score is 7 or better, there is no danger. If the 5-minute total score is below 7, the infant needs help establishing normal breathing. If the score is below 4, the baby is in critical condition and needs immediate medical attention to prevent respiratory distress and death. Few newborns score a perfect 10, but most readily adjust to life outside the womb.

The Parents' Reaction

Immediately after birth, the mother often cradles the newborn against her skin, perhaps offering the breast for the first time. Some infants are too dazed or drugged (from birth anesthesia) to react, but most begin sucking vigorously. They have flat noses and virtually no chins, so it is easy to latch on to the nipple.

Here is a warning for those who have never seen a newborn until their own is handed to them: Newborns look strange. Especially if they are born a bit early, their skin may be covered with a waxy white substance called *vernix;* if they are a bit late, their skin is often red and wrinkled. Whatever color their complexion will eventually take on, at birth their skin is usually lighter, is often uneven in color (with whitish, bluish, or reddish patches), and sometimes shows visible bruises and birthmarks. The body looks

table **4.6**	**Criteria and Scoring of the Apgar Scale**				
Score	Color	Heartbeat	Reflex Irritability	Muscle Tone	Respiratory Effort
0	Blue, pale	Absent	No response	Flaccid, limp	Absent
1	Body pink, extremities blue	Slow (below 100)	Grimace	Weak, inactive	Irregular, slow
2	Entirely pink	Rapid (over 100)	Coughing, sneezing, crying	Strong, active	Good, baby is crying

Source: Apgar, 1953.

Picture Perfect One-day-old James looks bruised, scraped, and squashed—a perfectly normal, beautiful newborn.

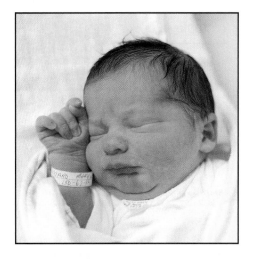

strange, too. Not only is the baby chinless and the hair merely fuzz, but the skull is sometimes misshapen, a result of the bones' pushing together to squeeze through the birth canal. A pulse is visible in the top of the head, where the skull has not yet fused. And the tiny legs and arms flail out, or tuck in, instead of extending quietly and straight.

All these characteristics are temporary. The Apgar score and the birthweight are the critical measures of early health—not the newborn's appearance. Every day that passes makes the newborn look more normal (advertisements involving "newborns" typically feature babies several weeks old) and behave more predictably. (The particulars of their early physical development are described in Chapter 5.)

Medical Attention

How closely any given birth approaches the foregoing description depends on many factors. Among them are the mother's preparation for birth (gained through prenatal classes, conversations with women friends and relatives, or personal experience), the physical and emotional support provided by birth attendants (both professional and familial), the position and size of the fetus, and the cultural context (Creasy, 1997). An additional and sometimes very important factor is medical intervention.

Almost every birth in every developed nation now occurs amid ongoing medical activity, typically including drugs to dull pain or speed contractions; sterile procedures that involve special gowns, gloves, and washing; and electronic monitoring of both the mother and the fetus. Often surgery is performed, typically an *episiotomy* (a minor incision of the tissue at the opening of the vagina to speed the last moments before birth) or, in about 22 percent of births in the United States, a **cesarean section** to remove the fetus from the uterus through the mother's abdomen.

cesarean section A means of childbirth in which the fetus is taken from the mother surgically, through an incision that extends from the mother's abdomen through the uterus.

Same Event, Thousands of Miles Apart Both these birth attendants—the obstetrician in New York City and the midwife in Rajasthan, India—are assessing the size, position, and heartbeat of a developing fetus. Which pregnancy is more likely to result in a healthy baby? If the birth is of high risk, the high-tech equipment on the left might be critical. However, if the pregnancy is a normal one, as most pregnancies are, the experience and empathy of the trained attendant are more important than the diagnostic tools used.

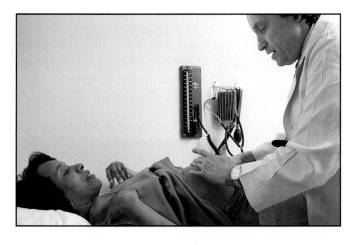

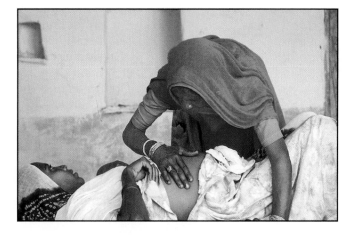

table **4.7**	**A Woman's Lifetime Risk of Dying in Childbirth, by Region, 1990s**
Region	Risk
Africa	1 in 16
Asia	1 in 65
Latin America and Caribbean	1 in 130
Most of Europe and North America	1 in 10,000
Northern Europe	1 in 10,000

Sources: Nowak, 1995; Tsui et al., 1997.

Worldwide, the actions of doctors, midwives, and nurses save millions of lives each year—the lives of mothers as well as of infants. Indeed, a lack of medical attention during childbirth is a major reason why motherhood is still hazardous in the least developed nations (see Table 4.7).

Medical attention makes delivery faster, easier, and safer. In many nations (including some of the most advanced), increasing numbers of trained midwives fill the gap between the busy, highly trained obstetrician, who specializes in serious complications, and the neighborhood "granny nurse," whose ministrations are most welcome in uncomplicated births but whose expertise is limited. In developed countries, licensed midwives not only deal with medical aspects but also understand the psychic impact of birth on the new mother. As one midwife stresses, "Let's not leave any woman holding her baby without having conveyed to her our complete respect and belief in her ability to think clearly, to make decisions, and to be a good parent" (Walton & Hamilton, 1998).

From several perspectives, there seems little to fault in a medicalized, technological approach to birth. Most women prefer to give birth in a hospital rather than at home, want pain relief instead of a drug-free birth, and prefer receiving medical attention to being left alone. In some nations, such as England, about half of all births occurred at home in 1970; now almost all women choose to give birth in a hospital. Indeed, the Netherlands is unique among developed nations in its high rate of home births: about 35 percent (Ferguson, 1997).

However, many specific aspects of hospital births, including the routine use of medication, intravenous fluids, electronic monitoring, and episiotomy, have been criticized as being more rooted in medical tradition than in medical necessity (Emory et al., 1996; Ferguson, 1997). Even worse, financial considerations or fear of lawsuits may affect medical decisions. For example, one careful study in the Midwest found that the rate of cesarean deliveries was 17 percent among women with private insurance, 14 percent for those with government insurance (i.e., Medicaid), and only 10 percent for those who had no insurance (Aron et al., 2000).

As a result of these criticisms, by the early 1990s only 41 percent of all U.S. hospital births occurred in delivery rooms with high-tech equipment, whereas 53 percent occurred in the *labor room*—typically a smaller, friendlier room where a woman stays, with her husband or other familiar person, from the time she enters the hospital until she and her baby are recovered from birth (Nichols & Zwelling, 1997). In this

Eight Hands, One Focus While the birth attendant checks the fetal heartbeat, the husband wipes the brow of the laboring woman and her mother looks on. This is a cultural switch: In earlier generations of home births, the mother was the main caregiver during labor, while the future father waited anxiously in another room.

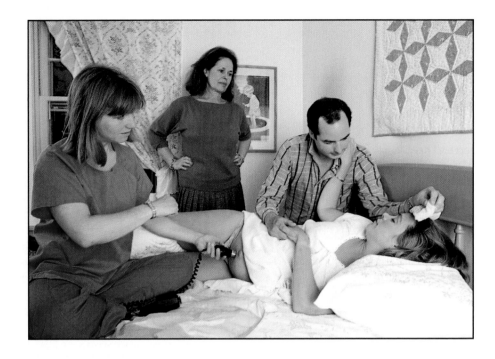

setting, doctors and nurses intervene when needed, but the woman has much more control. The facts that it is *her* room and that she is with *her* husband make it *her* birth—and that itself reduces anxiety, pain, and complications. Even if there are complications, they seem to cause less stress.

Another 5 percent of U.S. births occur in freestanding *birthing centers*, which are even more family-centered. As one women recounts:

> When we arrived at the Birthing Center to have the baby, we were told to go right to the room we had chosen ahead of time. There weren't any strong hospital odors, no people rushing around, no papers for Gary to fill out while I was wheeled off down a long hall without him. We just walked together to our room.
>
> There is always some amount of anxiety in starting labor; but the atmosphere at the Birthing Center was so relaxing that it had a calming effect on me. The thing that meant the most to my husband was his feeling that he belonged there. No one made him feel that he was in the way. (The comfortable recliner in our room helped, too.)
>
> I can remember how great it felt to be able to get up and shower to relieve my back labor and to take a walk out in the hall when I felt the need to walk. I wasn't confined to bed; I was in control.
>
> Several hours later, our third daughter was born. She never left us to go to the nursery with harsh lights and lots of other crying babies. She remained in our quiet room with us. We could hold her when she wanted to be held and feed her when she wanted to be fed. Gary and I both were there when the pediatrician checked her.
>
> Even though it was my most difficult labor and delivery, it was our happiest. (La Leche, 1997)

Bike Versus Baby? Often neglected in the medicalization of birth are the new baby's older siblings. Few are as sophisticated as this boy, making the connection between the cost of the new baby and his own material condition, but most miss the absent mother. If the mother is gone for several days because she is recovering from surgery or other complications, and if she comes home tired, depressed, distracted, or in pain, many siblings develop deep resentments against the innocent cause of it all.

Only 1 percent of U.S. births occur at home—about half of these by choice and attended by a midwife, and half due to unexpectedly rapid birth (Nichols & Zwelling, 1997).

"I suppose this puts my new bike on the back burner?"

BIRTH COMPLICATIONS

If a fetus is already at risk because of low weight, preterm birth, genetic abnormality, or teratogenic exposure, or because the mother is unusually young, old, small, or ill, birth complications are much more likely. The crucial concept to emphasize is that birth risks and complications are part of a continuum, beginning long before the first contractions and continuing in the months and years thereafter.

As an example, **cerebral palsy** (difficulties with movement control resulting from brain damage) was once thought to be solely caused by birth procedures such as excessive analgesia, slow breech birth, or misapplied forceps. (Forceps are sometimes used to pull the fetal head through the birth canal.) Now we realize, however, that cerebral palsy often results from genetic vulnerability, worsened by teratogens and a birthing process that includes **anoxia**—a temporary lack of oxygen that can cause brain damage. Anoxia is always risky—that's why nurses listen closely to the fetal heart rate during birth and why the newborn's color is one of the five criteria on the Apgar scale. However, how long a baby can experience anoxia without brain damage depends on genes, weight, drugs in the bloodstream, and a host of other factors.

Similarly, low-birthweight infants are at risk for many problems before, during, and immediately after birth, especially when they are very early or very small. These problems sometimes affect them throughout life, but here, too, the impact depends on many influences.

First, Intensive Care . . .

Vulnerable infants are typically placed in intensive-care nurseries where they are confined to enclosed *isolettes* (so that their environment can be monitored and controlled), hooked up to one or another medical machine, and surrounded by bright lights and noise. Although these measures are often medically warranted, they also deprive neonates of certain kinds of stimulation, such as the gentle rocking they would have experienced if they still were in the womb or the regular handling involved in feeding and bathing if they were at low risk. To overcome this deprivation, many hospitals provide high-risk infants with regular massage and soothing stimulation, which aid weight gain and increase overall alertness (Als, 1995).

Ideally, parents share in this early caregiving, in recognition of the fact that they, too, are deprived and stressed (Goldberg & Divitto, 1995). Not only must they cope with uncertainty about their baby's future, but they must also struggle with feelings of inadequacy and perhaps with sorrow, guilt, and anger. Such emotions are relieved somewhat if they can cradle and care for their vulnerable newborn. Anything that strengthens the family may forestall difficulties later on.

cerebral palsy A disorder that results from damage to the brain's motor centers, usually as a result of events during or before birth. People with cerebral palsy have difficulty with muscle control, which can affect speech or other body movements.

anoxia A lack of oxygen that, if prolonged, can cause brain damage or death.

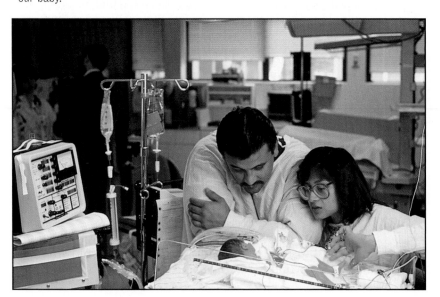

Getting to Know You If these new parents were kept at a distance, they might be troubled by the intravenous drips, the beeping monitor, and the protective plastic of the intensive-care nursery. Through the intimacy of closeness and touch, the LBW patient becomes, to the parents, simply "our baby."

...Then Home

For high-risk infants who survive, complications await, including unexpected minor medical problems and slow development. Preterm infants often are late to smile, to hold a bottle, and to communicate. As the months go by, short- and long-term cognitive difficulties may emerge. Cerebral palsy, first evident weeks after birth, affects 20 percent of those who weighed less than 35 ounces (1,000 grams) at birth, 15 percent of those who weighed between 2 and 3½ pounds (1,000 and 1,500 grams), and 7 percent of those who weighed between 3½ and 5½ pounds (1,500 and 2,500 grams) (Hack et al., 1995). High-risk infants who escape such obvious impairments are often more distractible, less obedient, and slower to talk (Jarel et al., 1998; Girouard et al., 1998).

Fortunately, long-term handicaps are not inevitable. Some newborns who had heart defects or other serious abnormalities, or were very small, can and do develop quite normally (Bigsby et al., 1996; Cherkes-Julkowski, 1998). Thus, parents of high-risk infants should not assume either that birth was the child's last major challenge or, conversely, that severe intellectual and medical problems will soon emerge.

Risks increase when the infant is very, very tiny—less than 3½ pounds (1,500 grams)—or when medical complications affect brain development for days or weeks, or when the infant is raised in a home already burdened by low socioeconomic status (Taylor et al., 1998). Preterm babies are always "more work and less fun," and their mothers rate them more difficult and less adaptable (Langkamp et al., 1998). But even when mothers are young and poor, intervention—including parent-support programs and intensive high-quality day care beginning at age 1—can result in substantial intellectual gains for the child and notable benefits for the mother–child relationship (Holloman & Scott, 1998; Ramey et al., 1992). Let us look, then, at that relationship.

THE BEGINNING OF BONDING

parent–newborn bond The strong feelings of attachment that arise between parents and their newborn infants.

Popular attention has been captured by the concept of the **parent–newborn bond,** an almost instant connection between parents and newborns as they touch each other in the first hours after birth. Over the past decades, hundreds of newspaper and magazine articles have waxed rhapsodic over the joy and the necessity of forming this special

Better to Hold Them This photo depicts what not to do. An instructor reading from a notebook, one mother whose newborn is absent, one uncomfortable-looking father, and five babies, blanketed and out of easy reach—all suggest that caregiving is an intellectual, detached experience. The truth is obvious when a new mother cradles her infant in privacy—babies go straight to your heart and soul before they go to your mind.

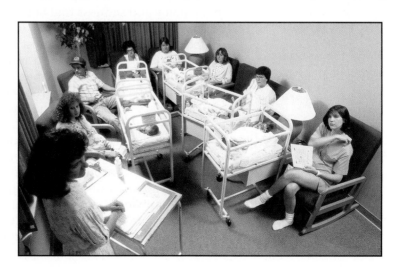

Expressions of Love Smell and touch are essential components for mother–infant bonding for many animals, including the nuzzling lions seen here. Fortunately, bonding between humans can occur in varied ways, with early contact not at all essential—although physical intimacy, from breast-feeding at infancy to hugs at adolescence, sustains close attachment between parent and child.

postpartum depression The profound feeling of sadness and inadequacy that sometimes is experienced by new mothers, leading to an inability to eat, sleep, or care normally for their newborns.

❓ Especially for Social Scientists: When is animal research used too quickly to support conclusions about people?

bond. Without immediate physical contact, according to some, the long-term love between parent and child will be diminished and the child will suffer. Many people have come to believe that bonding is a critically important "magical social glue." As one mother who was deprived of early contact said, "It made me feel like a rotten mother when I didn't get to bond with my first two children. Made me feel they were going to go out and rob a bank" (Eyer, 1992).

However, as the Research Report on page 125 makes clear, the popular concept that early touch leads to a close mother–newborn bond that lasts a lifetime is false—unsupported by the evidence and actually contrary to the research. That contradiction itself makes scientists ask, "Why was the notion of essential bonding so quickly accepted, when the research evidence was so sparse?"

Diane Eyer, a social scientist who has studied this topic, concluded that bonding is a *social construction,* an idea formed as a rallying cry against the medicalization, depersonalization, and patriarchy of the traditional hospital birth. Eyer argues that women and developmental experts were ready to believe that newborns and mothers need to be together from the start, so it took only a tiny nudge from scientific research for the mystique of early bonding to become generally accepted. She fears that this zealous acceptance came at a high price: the setting of a standard of instant affection and "active love right after birth . . . that many women find impossible to meet" (Eyer, 1992).

Depression and Love

Indeed, too rigidly applying the idea of bonding may be worse than not promoting it at all. If a medicated mother, exhausted from the birth process, is handed her infant for 10 minutes or so while the episiotomy is stitched, and then the baby is removed because "bonding" has supposedly occurred, she may well feel guilty for not experiencing the surge of love that the mystique prescribes. Or if an inexperienced mother, for any reason, does not hold her infant in the minutes after birth, all her fears about her own ability to be a good mother may overwhelm her.

One possible consequence is **postpartum depression,** the feeling of inadequacy and sadness that between 10 and 20 percent of women feel in the days and weeks after birth (called *baby blues* in the mild version, *postpartum psychosis* in the most severe form). There are many possible causes of this reaction. As you would probably expect from a developmental perspective, some of these causes predate the pregnancy (such as earlier bouts of major depression, financial stress, marital problems) and others are specific to the particular infant (health, feeding, or sleeping problems) (Beck & Tatano, 1998; Brown & Johnson, 1998). One cause is directly related to the first hours after birth: the mother's perception that she is incompetent to care for her infant (O'Hara, 1997). The attitudes and actions of the birth attendants can make a difference here. For mothers who are vulnerable to depression or for first-time low-income mothers, individual observation and discussion of their own newborn's reflexes and motor skills have a demonstrated impact on their mothering skills and attentiveness to their babies in the next weeks (Brazelton & Cramer, 1991; Hart et al., 1999; Wendland-Carro et al., 1999).

The best evidence for a parent–newborn bond comes from studies of a quite specific and powerful bond between mother and newborn in various species of mammals (Fleming & Corter, 1995). Many female animals, for instance, nourish and nurture their own young and ignore, reject, or mistreat the young of others. And many male animals kill newborns that seem abnormal or that do not seem to be theirs.

At least three factors have been identified as contributing to this mother–infant bond:

■ *Hormones* released during and after birth that trigger maternal behavior
■ The mother's *recognition* of her particular infant by its smell
■ The *timing* of the first physical contact between mother and newborn

The third of these factors can be remarkably precise: In some species, contact must occur within a critical period in order for bonding to take place. For example, if a baby goat is removed from its mother immediately after birth and returned a few hours later, the mother sometimes rejects it, kicking and butting it away no matter how pitifully it bleats or how persistently it tries to nurse. However, if a newborn goat remains with a mother who nuzzles and suckles it for the critical first 5 minutes and then is separated from her, the mother goat welcomes its return (Klopfer, 1971). Sheep and cows react in like fashion, with contact in the first hours after birth leading to the mother's strong urge to be with the infant. Other species display a less pronounced form, with touching in the "sensitive" period soon after birth helpful but not essential (Rosenblith, 1992).

It is not only the mother who searches for her missing newborn. Newborn animals are primed to seek out their mothers. Even baby rats have multiple pathways for bonding, including acute senses of smell and taste that enable them to identify their particular mother before birth and thus lead the blind newborns to nuzzle up to her. Newborn rats also signal severe distress with a high-pitched cry that is inaudible to humans but piercing to mother rats, who typically respond with signs of mother-rat love, licking and nuzzling. This mutual mother–newborn bond is crucial for metabolism, temperature regulation, heart rate, and cognition and hence allows the newborn rats to thrive (Hofer, 1995).

Does a corresponding sensitive time period exist for bonding in humans? Some early research (with a few dozen women) suggested that it does. In those studies, the benefits of both immediate contact in the moments after birth and extended contact during the first days of life were apparent over the entire first year. This was especially true for first-time mothers who were very young, poor, or otherwise stressed or whose preterm infants might have been deemed too frail, or too dependent on life support, to be touched. The mothers who had held their infants soon after birth were more attentive and attached to them 1 year later than were the mothers who had barely seen their infants in the early days (Grossman et al., 1981; Klaus & Kennell, 1976; Leifer et al., 1972).

This research is credited with ending several *postpartum* (after-birth) hospital practices that were once routine. These include whisking newborns away to the nursery, preventing mothers from holding their newborns for the first 24 hours, and barring parents even from setting foot in intensive-care units. All these practices were originally thought to protect mother and child from infection; all are now seen as unnecessary and perhaps cruel.

Today almost no one questions the wisdom of early contact between mother and child. It can provide a wondrous beginning to the parent–child relationship, as suggested by this mother's account:

> The second he came out, they put him on my skin and I reached down and I felt him and it was something about having that sticky stuff on my fingers . . . it was really important to feel that waxy stuff [vernix] and he was crying and I made soothing sounds to him. . . . And he started calming down and somehow that makes you feel—like he already knows you, he knows who you are—like animals or something, perhaps the smell of each other . . . it was marvelous to hold him and I just touched him for a really long time and then they took him over but something had already happened. Just instant love. [quoted in Davis-Floyd, 1992]

But is this early contact, as has been claimed, essential for formation of the mother–child bond? Absolutely not. Extensive later research found that immediate or extended early skin-to-skin togetherness made no measurable long-term differences in the mother–child relationship (Lamb, 1982; Myers, 1987). In retrospect, this makes sense. All human children need parental nurturance, through a steady stream of the infant's nighttime feeding, the toddler's temper, the preschooler's incessant questioning, the schoolchild's self-absorption, and the adolescent's rebellion—punctuated by illness, disappointment, and other unhappiness.

Devoted parents must sacrifice some of their own wishes and plans for at least 20 years. Surely, the relationship between parent and child could not hinge on a critical episode of bonding at birth—nature is not so foolhardy as to create one, and only one, pathway for survival.

● Response for Social Scientists (from page 124): When it supports a point of view that is popular but not yet substantiated by research data, as in the social construction about mother–infant bonding.

All in all, we must ensure that the mystique of bonding does not boomerang, undermining the very relationship it is supposed to protect. If the mystique of early bonding were taken too far, the experts might end up emphasizing the first few minutes and ignoring the day-to-day support and knowledge that beleaguered new mothers need. Fortunately, the evidence now confirms that immediate contact is neither necessary nor sufficient for bonding, as evidenced by the millions of very affectionate and dedicated biological, adoptive, or foster parents who never touched their children when they were newborns.

Does this mean that hospital routines can go back to the old ways, separating mother and newborn? Never. As one leading developmentalist states:

> I hope that the weakness of the findings for bonding will not be used as an excuse to keep mothers and their infants separated in the hospital. Although such separation may do no permanent harm for most mother–infant pairs, providing contact in a way that is acceptable to the mother surely does no harm and gives much pleasure to many. It is my belief that anything that may make the postpartum period more pleasurable surely is worthwhile. (Rosenblith, 1992)

In general, the mother's hormonal and physiological condition during the hours and days right after birth "is clearly a state of intense affect" (Corter & Fleming, 1995). In this emotional period, everything possible should be done to help the mother cherish her infant's touch, smell, and appearance. But care should be taken not to overwhelm the mother with a cultural ideal she cannot reach—lest the "bonding" between a crying, scrawny newborn and an exhausted mother lead to anger, rejection, and depression. Love between a parent and a child is affected by their ongoing interactions throughout infancy and childhood and beyond, as well as by the manifold social contexts in which their relationship flourishes. As the chapters that follow will reveal, the nature of the parent–infant relationship is critical for healthy development, but the specifics of its formation are not.

SUMMARY

FROM ZYGOTE TO NEWBORN

1. The first 2 weeks of prenatal growth are called the germinal period. During this period, the single-cell zygote develops into an organism of more than 100 cells, travels down the Fallopian tube, and implants itself in the uterine lining, where it continues to grow.

2. The period from the third through the eighth week after conception is called the period of the embryo. During this period the heart begins to beat and the eyes, ears, nose, and mouth begin to form.

3. At 8 weeks after conception, the future baby is only about 1 inch (2½ centimeters) long. Yet it already has the basic organs and features of a human baby, with the exception of the sex organs.

4. The fetal period extends from the ninth week until birth. By the twelfth week all the organs and body structures have formed. The fetus attains viability when the brain is sufficiently mature to regulate basic body functions, around the twenty-second week after conception.

5. The average fetus weighs approximately 3 pounds at the beginning of the last 3 months of pregnancy and 7½ pounds at birth. The additional weight, plus maturation of brain, lungs, and heart, ensures survival for more than 99 percent of all full-term babies.

RISK REDUCTION

6. Many teratogens can harm the embryo and fetus. Diseases, drugs, and pollutants can all cause birth defects. Some cause explicit physical impairment. Others, called behavioral teratogens, harm the brain and therefore impair the child's intellect and actions.

7. Teratogens are risky substance or conditions, not inevitable destroyers. Whether a particular teratogen will harm a particular embryo or fetus depends on the timing and amount of exposure and on the developing organism's genetic vulnerability.

8. To protect against prenatal complications, a woman can avoid or limit exposure to teratogens, maintain good nutrition, and seek early and competent prenatal care. Social support from family and the community is also important.

9. In developed countries, many serious teratogens, including rubella and some prescription drugs, now rarely reach a fetus. However, psychoactive drugs remain common hazards. How and when the community should intervene when a woman uses drugs or alcohol is a controversial topic.

10. Epidemic in developing nations, and ongoing in developed nations, is the HIV virus. If women know their HIV status before they become pregnant and take AZT during pregnancy, most cases of pediatric AIDS can be prevented.

LOW BIRTHWEIGHT

11. Low birthweight arises from a variety of causes, which often occur in combination. They include the mother's poor health or nutrition, smoking, drinking, drug use, and age. Many of these factors are associated with poverty.

12. Preterm or small-for-gestational-age babies are more likely than full-term babies to suffer from stress during the birth process and to experience medical difficulties, especially breathing problems, in the days after birth. Long-term cognitive difficulties may occur as well, depending on whether the newborn was of very low birthweight, had serious medical problems, or is raised in an impoverished home.

THE NORMAL BIRTH

13. Birth typically begins with contractions that push the fetus, head first, out from the uterus and then through the vagina. The Apgar scale, which rates the neonate's vital signs at 1 minute after birth and again at 5 minutes after birth, provides a quick evaluation of the infant's health.

14. Medical intervention in the birth process can speed contractions, dull pain, and save lives. However, many aspects of the medicalized birth have been faulted. Many contemporary birthing practices are aimed at finding a balance between these results.

BIRTH COMPLICATIONS

15. Birth complications, such as unusually long and stressful birth that includes anoxia (a lack of oxygen to the fetus), have many causes. Vulnerable newborns are placed in an intensive-care unit for monitoring and treatment. Long-term handicaps are not inevitable for such children, but careful nurturing is required once they are taken home by parents.

THE BEGINNING OF BONDING

16. Ideally, both parents spend time with their baby in the hours and days after birth. However, most developmentalists believe that early, skin-to-skin contact between mother and child is much less important for humans than for some animals. The human parent–infant bond develops continuously over a long period of time.

KEY TERMS

germinal period (97)
period of the embryo (97)
period of the fetus (97)
implantation (98)
neural tube (98)
placenta (101)
age of viability (101)
teratology (105)
teratogens (105)
behavioral teratogens (105)
risk analysis (105)
critical period (105)
threshold effect (106)
interaction effect (106)
rubella (107)
human immunodeficiency virus (HIV) (110)
acquired immune deficiency syndrome (AIDS) (110)
fetal alcohol syndrome (FAS) (112)
low birthweight (LBW) (112)
preterm birth (113)
small for gestational age (SGA) (114)
Apgar scale (118)
cesarean section (119)
cerebral palsy (122)
anoxia (122)
parent–newborn bond (123)
postpartum depression (124)

KEY QUESTIONS

1. What developments occur during the germinal period?

2. What major developments occur during the period of the embryo?

3. What major developments occur during the period of the fetus?

4. How and when does a fetus respond to the outside world?

5. What are the factors that make a fetus more likely to survive if born at 38 weeks rather than at 24?

6. What factors determine how likely a fetus is to be harmed by teratogens?

7. What public health measures can prevent many cases of rubella and pediatric AIDS?

8. What are some effects of drug abuse on the fetus?

9. What can be done to reduce the damage done by a pregnant woman's use of psychoactive drugs?

10. What are the causes and consequences of low birthweight?

11. What is the relationship among the newborn's appearance, the Apgar scale, and health?

12. What are the advantages and disadvantages of the intensive-care nursery?

13. How is the formation of the parent–infant bond different in animals and in humans?

14. *In Your Experience* How do the preparation for birth, the actual birth process, and the newborn's appearance affect parents' attitudes toward their baby?

PART II

The First Two Years:
Infants and Toddlers

Adults usually don't change much in a year or two. Sometimes their hair gets longer or grows thinner, or they gain or lose a few pounds, or they become a little wiser. But if you were to be reunited with friends not seen for several years, you would recognize them immediately.

If, in contrast, you were to care for a newborn 24 hours a day for the first month, and then did not see the baby until a year later, you probably would not recognize him or her. After all, would you recognize a best friend who had quadrupled in weight, grown 14 inches, and sprouted a new head of hair? Nor would you find the toddler's behavior familiar. A hungry newborn just cries; a hungry toddler says "more food" or climbs up on the kitchen counter to reach the cookies.

A year or two is not much time compared to the almost 80 years of the average life span. However, children in their first two years reach half their adult height, develop cognitive abilities that have surprised even researchers, and learn to express almost every emotion—not just joy and fear but also many others, including jealousy and shame. And two of the most important human abilities, talking and loving, are already apparent.

The next three chapters describe these radical and wonderful changes.

The First Two Years:
Biosocial Development

In the first 2 years of life, the forces of biosocial growth and development are very powerful. Proof of this is visible to any observer, as infants quickly outgrow one set of clothes after another, attempt new behaviors almost daily, and display a rapidly increasing mastery of emerging skills: Sit . . . stand . . . walk . . . run! Reach . . . touch . . . grab . . . throw! Point . . . poke . . . pinch! And each object becomes something to explore with every sense and limb.

Proof is also available from laboratory data on brain development. Small infant brains not only become larger overall but also show the increasing density and complexity that are vital to the maturing of physical and mental capacities.

All these changes are, of course, biologically rooted. But they are also facilitated by the social context, as parents and others nourish, protect, and encourage the infant's development. This is no easy job. Infants develop so quickly that, as one expert explains, "Parenting an infant is akin to trying to hit a moving target" (Bornstein, 1995). In this chapter we will look at both the physical development of the child's body and brain and the social environment—particularly as it involves health and nutrition—which can enhance or inhibit that development.

PHYSICAL GROWTH AND HEALTH

Monitoring growth and protecting health are critical from birth throughout the growing years. During most of childhood, annual visits to the doctor for preventive care are sufficient. In early infancy, by contrast, growth is so fast and vulnerability so great that medical checkups should occur monthly—not only to spot early signs of trouble but also to guide parents, who can be the first, and best, defense against illness and injury.

Size and Shape

Every medical checkup begins with weighing and measuring, for good reason. Except for prenatal development, infancy is the period of the most notable changes in size and proportion. Any slowdown is a cause for immediate concern.

Exactly how rapidly does normal growth occur? Recall that at birth the average North American weighs a little more than 7 pounds (3.2 kilograms) and measures about 20 inches (51 centimeters). This means that the typical newborn is lighter than a gallon of milk and about as long as the distance from a man's elbow to the tips of his fingers.

In the first days of life, most newborns lose between 5 and 10 percent of their birthweight because they eliminate more substances as body wastes than they take in as nourishment. Then they make up that loss and begin to gain, doubling their birthweight by the fourth month and tripling it by the end of the first year. Much of the weight increase in the early months of life is fat, which provides insulation for warmth and a store of nourishment. After 8 months or so, weight gain derives more from growth in bone, muscle, and body organs.

Infants get taller or, more accurately, longer as well. In each of the first 12 months they grow almost an inch (2.5 centimeters) in length. By age 1, the typical baby weighs about 22 pounds (10 kilograms) and measures almost 30 inches (75 centimeters) (Behrman, 1992).

Physical growth is slower in the second year, but it still is quite rapid. By 24 months most children weigh almost 30 pounds (13 kilograms) and measure between 32 and 36 inches (81 and 91 centimeters), with boys being slightly taller and heavier than girls. In other words, typical 2-year-olds have attained almost one-fifth of their adult weight and half their adult height (see Figures A-6 and A-7 in Appendix A for details).

As infants grow, their body proportions change. Most newborns seem top-heavy because their heads are about one-fourth of their total length, compared to one-fifth at 1 year and one-eighth in adulthood. Their legs, by contrast, represent only about a quarter of their total body length, whereas for adults, legs account for about half the total height. Thus, while every part of a child's body grows, some parts grow more than others. Those parts that grew most slowly in prenatal development now grow fastest. By adulthood, a person's feet, for example, will be about five times as long as they were at birth, whereas the head will have only doubled in length from crown to chin.

Every Child in the World Measles can be a deadly disease for undernourished children and infirm adults in developing nations. This boy's immunization will not only protect him but will also help to protect those in his village in northern India who are too young, too enfeebled, or too frightened to obtain their own shots.

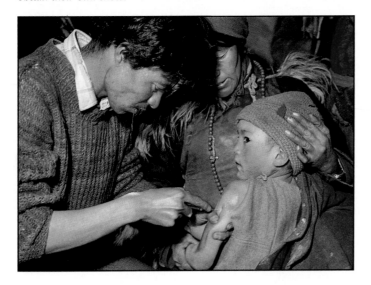

Preventive Medicine

Nowadays, the growth just outlined is taken for granted. However, a century ago in developed nations and a mere decade or two ago in less developed ones, not only growth but even survival was very much in doubt. About 35 percent of all newborns died before age 7 (Bogin, 1996).

Most of these infants were sick with measles, whooping cough, or some other obvious illness. But some of these babies died mysteriously and suddenly in their sleep, victims of *sudden infant death syndrome (SIDS),* also called "crib death" in the United States and "cot death" in Great Britain. Various causes were assigned—a mother "overlaying" her child and causing suffocation or such superstitions as a cat sucking out the baby's breath or a witch casting a spell—but now we know that the cause is an unsteady breathing reflex, usually between 2 and 4 months. Although absolute prevention has not yet been attained, epidemiology and cross-cultural research find that removing soft bedding, eliminating second-hand smoke, prolonging breast-feeding, and—most important—laying babies down to sleep on their backs, not stomachs, cut the rate of SIDS deaths by more than half (Willinger, 1998; Ottolini et al., 1999).

Historically, the cause of most other infant deaths was known: small-pox, whooping cough, polio, diphtheria, measles. Any of these or several other infectious diseases might suddenly and rapidly spread from child to child, putting them all at risk for stunted growth, serious complications, and death. This is no longer true, thanks to widespread immunization (see A Life-Span View on page 134).

BRAIN GROWTH AND DEVELOPMENT

No growth is more critical than the rapid growth of the brain, which has been called "by far the most complex structure in the known universe" (Thompson, 2000). Recall that the newborn's skull is disproportionately large. That's because it must be big enough to hold the brain, which at birth has already attained 25 percent of its adult weight. (The neonate's body weight, by comparison, is typically less than 5 percent of adult weight.)

The brain develops rapidly, not only during the prenatal period but also during infancy. By age 2, the brain is about 75 percent of its adult weight, while the 2-year-old's body weight is only about 20 percent of what it will eventually be. It is imperative that the brain grow and develop *ahead of* the rest of the body, for it is the brain that makes all other development possible (Shore, 1997).

Connections in the Brain

Weight provides only a crude index of brain development. More significant are changes that occur in the brain's communication systems and that greatly advance the brain's functioning. These communication systems consist primarily of nerve cells, called **neurons,** connected by intricate networks of nerve fibers called **axons** and **dendrites.** Each neuron has a single axon and numerous dendrites; the axon of one neuron meets the dendrites of other neurons at intersections called **synapses** (see Figure 5.2).

neuron A nerve cell of the central nervous system. Most neurons are in the brain.

axon The single nerve fiber that extends from a neuron and transmits impulses from that neuron to the dendrites of other neurons.

dendrites Nerve fibers that extend from a neuron and receive the impulses transmitted from other neurons via their axons.

synapse The point at which the axon of one neuron meets the dendrites of another neuron.

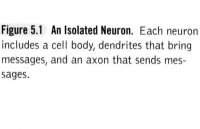

Figure 5.1 An Isolated Neuron. Each neuron includes a cell body, dendrites that bring messages, and an axon that sends messages.

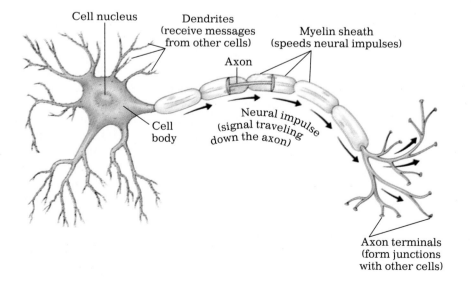

Cell nucleus

Dendrites (receive messages from other cells)

Myelin sheath (speeds neural impulses)

Axon

Neural impulse (signal traveling down the axon)

Cell body

Axon terminals (form junctions with other cells)

A LIFE SPAN VIEW

LONGER LIVES AND IMMUNIZATIONS

Today, deadly childhood epidemics are rare. An infant's chance of dying from infectious disease in North America, western Europe, Japan, or Australia is less than 1 in 500, down from 1 in 20 in the first half of the twentieth century. This dramatic reduction in early death, not the extension of life in old age, is the primary reason for the almost 20 years added to the average life span worldwide since 1950 (see Figure 5.1).

The single most important cause of the dramatic improvement in child survival is **immunization.** In fact, immunization is said to have had "a greater impact on human mortality reduction and population growth than any other public health intervention besides clean water" (Baker, 2000).

Immunization can occur in many ways: through injection (as when a person is vaccinated in the arm or leg), ingestion (as when a child eats a sugar cube soaked in oral vaccine), inhalation (as when a substance is breathed through the nostrils), or naturally, by actually catching the disease and surviving. The required timing and dosage of the immunization, as well as the incidence and success of immunization programs, vary from illness to illness, but in every case the goal is to stimulate the body's own immune system to defend against a particular disease. In the less developed nations, the rate of immunization against the deadliest childhood diseases improved from about 20 to 80 percent during the 1980s, reducing deaths from these diseases by three-fourths (UNICEF, 1990).

- Smallpox, the most lethal disease of all for children, has been eradicated worldwide. Consequently, immunization against smallpox is no longer necessary.
- Polio is a crippling disease that still affects many older adults with "post-polio syndrome," a gradual weakening of the muscles in middle and late adulthood because of a polio episode 50 years or

immunization A process that stimulates the body's own defensive (immune) system to defend against attack by a particular infectious disease.

so earlier. New cases of polio are very rare (there have been none in the past ten years in the United States) because no one can catch it or transmit it, and soon the polio vaccine, first developed in 1955, will also be unnecessary (Hull & Aylward, 1997).

- Measles (which can be fatal in the early months of life, when it causes dehydration) is disappearing, too. In the United States, only 100 cases of measles were reported in 1998, a marked contrast to the peak of 770,000 in 1958 and the lowest number since 1911, when disease statistics were first recorded (*MMWR*, December 31, 1999).

Worldwide, both the quality and the scope of immunization have improved every decade. Often, especially in the United States and in some developing nations, the first widespread trials of a vaccine are effective at reducing illness and death but also reveal some rare side effects that make the public wary. European nations, especially England, have tended to proceed more cautiously (Baker, 2000).

Now, more than 90 percent of all infants in the world are immunized against the childhood diseases of diphtheria, pertussis, tetanus, measles, polio, and mumps (UNICEF, 1995). In developed nations, many infants are immunized against hepatitis B, hemophilus influenza type B (HIB), rubella, and chicken pox as well. (See Appendix A, Figure A-5, for a recommended immunization schedule.) Some developed countries also routinely immunize children against tuberculosis, whereas others, including the United States, test children for exposure to TB and then follow up with further testing and treatment if needed.

Obviously, lack of complete immunization puts the child at risk; childhood illnesses are usually mild, but not always. In addition to the problems already mentioned, mumps can produce nerve deafness, and HIB is the leading cause of meningitis. Less obviously, lack of immunization jeopardizes the well-being of others: Infants too young to be immunized may die if they catch a disease from an older child; pregnant women who contract rubella may transmit the virus to their fetuses (as happened to David, described in Chapter 1), causing blind-

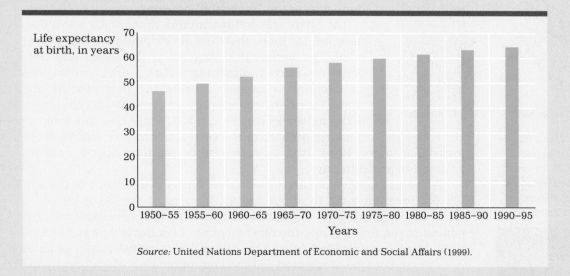

Life expectancy at birth, in years

Source: United Nations Department of Economic and Social Affairs (1999).

Figure 5.2 World Life Expectancy at Birth. The average life expectancy worldwide today is about 20 years longer than it was just 40 years ago. This is not primarily because older people are living longer (if a person reaches age 30, his or her life expectancy is now only about 5 years longer than it was 50 years ago), but because fewer infants and children die. A century ago almost every family mourned the death of a young child. Now, of all the children who reach age 1, fewer than 1 in 1,000 die before age 5.

ness, deafness, and brain damage; healthy adults who contract mumps or measles suffer much worse consequences than a child might; and those who are particularly vulnerable, such as the elderly, those who are HIV-positive, or cancer patients, can be killed by any number of "childhood" diseases.

Chicken pox, for instance, can be fatal. Before the chicken pox vaccine was approved in 1995, about 100 Americans, mostly adults, died of that disease each year. Now the rate is falling, but not fast enough, as you can see from the case of two preschool children who, unvaccinated, came down with chicken pox in early January 1997. Their 23-year-old mother caught it from them and died on February 2 (*MMWR*, May 16, 1997).

Individual tragedies such as this one highlight the need for large-scale immunization programs. It is not possible for every person, from newborn to

centenarian, to be immunized, and in some cases immunization would jeopardize an individual's health more than protect it. Fortunately, 100 percent immunization is not necessary. For most diseases, if 90 percent or more of all children under age 6 are immunized, a disease is unlikely to spread. Note that the young mother described earlier, because of her particular circumstances (perhaps poverty or language difficulties), had left her two children unprotected. Nevertheless, she would not have died if they had not gotten the disease from someone else, who got it from someone else, and so on. Thus, although only a few unimmunized children would become seriously ill if they contracted a childhood disease, every unimmunized child is a potential carrier of death to others in the community.

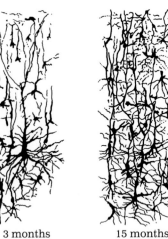

1 month   3 months   15 months

Figure 5.3 Brain Proliferation. Within the brain, nerve fibers increase in size and number over the first 2 years of life, greatly increasing the number of neuronal connections and enabling impressive advances in cognition and the control of actions.

Electric Excitement This infant's delight at his mother's facial expressions is visible, not just in his eyes and mouth but also in the neurons of his brain. Electrodes map his brain activation region by region and moment by moment. Every month of life up to age 2 shows increased electrical excitement.

neurotransmitter A brain chemical that carries information across the synaptic gap between one neuron and another.

cortex The outer layer of the brain, about an eighth of an inch thick. This area is involved in the voluntary, cognitive aspects of the mind.

transient exuberance The great increase in the number of neurons, dendrites, and synapses that occurs in an infant's brain over the first 2 years of life.

myelination The process in which axons are coated with myelin, a fatty substance that speeds communication between neurons.

To be more specific, a neuron communicates by sending an electrical impulse through its axon to the dendrites of other neurons. However, axon and dendrites do not actually touch at synapses. Instead, the electrical impulse triggers brain chemicals called **neurotransmitters** to carry information from the axon of the "sending" neuron, across the *synaptic gap*, to the dendrites of the "receiving" neurons.

At birth, the brain contains more than 100 billion neurons, far more than any developing person will ever need. The networks composed of the axons and dendrites are fairly rudimentary at first, with relatively few connections (synapses). During the first months and years, there are major spurts of growth and refinement in the networks (see Figure 5.3). These changes are particularly notable in the **cortex,** the brain's eighth-of-an-inch-thick outer layer (the so-called gray matter), which controls perception and thinking.

An estimated fivefold increase in the density of dendrites in the cortex occurs from birth to about age 2 (Diamond, 1990). As a result, in some cases, as many as 15,000 new connections may be established *per neuron* in the first 2 years; the total number of connections has been estimated at a quadrillion (a million billion). This proliferation enables neurons to become connected to (and communicate with) a greatly expanding variety of other neurons within the brain. The establishment of dendrites continues, less rapidly, throughout life (Thompson, 2000).

The phenomenal increase in neural connections over the first 2 years has been called **transient exuberance** (Nowakowski, 1987), a label that highlights two key aspects of early brain development. "Exuberance," of course, refers to the sheer magnitude of the growth in neural connections. "Transient" means transitory or temporary, referring to the fact that the rate of growth of neural connections slows down as the child grows older. More important, it also refers to the fact that unused connections shrink, atrophy, and then disappear, in a kind of pruning action that is particularly evident in the first years of life. As one review expresses it:

> The brain massively overproduces synapses early in life, only to be followed postnatally by selective elimination of these exuberant connections. Presumably, the purpose of overproducing synapses is to "prepare" the nervous system for experience by proliferation of connections. . . . If synapses are not confirmed or stabilized, they regress according to a developmental schedule or due to competition from confirmed synapses. [Nelson & Bloom, 1997]

Thus, many areas of the human brain have more neural connections at age 2 than at any later age. During infancy the human brain prepares to process every type of experience. Then, through the early years, neural pathways that are exercised become stronger and larger, developing more connections; those that are not used die. Together, proliferation and pruning enhance the efficiency of neural communication while simplifying the brain's overall organization (Huttenlocher, 1994).

The functioning of the brain's communication networks is also enhanced by a process called **myelination,** in which axons become coated with *myelin*, a fatty insulating substance that speeds the transmission of neural impulses. Myelination proceeds most rapidly from birth to age 4 and continues through adolescence. Myelination allows children to gain

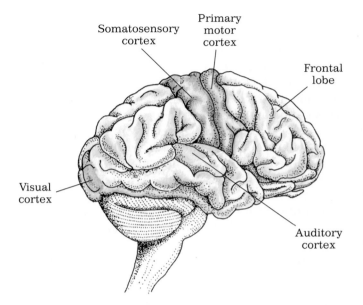

Somatosensory cortex

Primary motor cortex

Frontal lobe

Visual cortex

Auditory cortex

Figure 5.4 Brain Specialization. Areas of the brain are specialized for the reception and transmission of different types of information. Research has shown that both experience and maturation play important roles in brain development. For example, myelination of the nerve fibers leading from the visual cortex of the brain will not proceed normally unless the infant has had sufficient visual experience in a lighted environment.

increasing neurological control over their motor functions and sensory abilities, and this control facilitates their intellectual functioning.

Myelination is not essential for communication between neurons, but it is essential for fast and complex brain activity (Johnson, 1998). The speed made possible by myelin underlies most intellectual functions; it is no accident that we often praise individuals for being quick thinkers or for being able to hold many ideas in their heads at once, a theme as relevant in late adulthood (Chapter 24) as in early childhood.

Brain Growth and Brain Function

Different areas of the brain mature at different times and at different rates. For example, the frontal area of the cortex (located right behind the forehead; see Figure 5.4) assists in self-control and self-regulation. This area is immature in the newborn—with the result that a young infant cannot stifle a cry of pain or stay awake when drowsiness hits. As the neurons of the frontal area become more interconnected and their axons more myelinated during the first year, the baby becomes better able to regulate everything from reflexive responses to sleep-wake patterns (Johnson, 1997).

With continued development in the frontal area, cognitive skills requiring deliberation begin to emerge, along with a basic capacity for emotional self-control (Bell & Fox, 1992; Shore, 1997). As a result, by age 1 the child's emotions are already much more nuanced and predictable than at birth, responsive as much to the external world (such as a frightening stranger) as to internal states (such as hunger). The frontal lobe is the part of the brain that "shows the most prolonged period of postnatal development, of any region of the human brain," with increased density of dendrites throughout adolescence (Johnson, 1998).

We will see the results of these developments in more detail in later chapters. At the moment, the crucial fact to remember is that early brain growth is rapid and widespread. The specifics of which neurons become connected to which other neurons depend on genes, degree of maturation, and—of critical importance throughout life—the infant's experiences (Nelson & Bloom, 1997).

The Role of Experience in Brain Development

As suggested by our discussion of transient exuberance, at least a minimal amount of experience is essential for neural pathways to develop. This is true even for the full development of the brain structures that make seeing, hearing, touching, and other functions possible. A part of the cortex is dedicated to each such function (hence we speak of the visual cortex, the auditory cortex, and so on); and each such function depends partly on experience to develop. As one scholar explains:

> Experience can exert powerful effects on the growth of dendrites and the formation of synapses in the brain, particularly during early growth and development. Synapses, the points of functional connections among neurons, are much more plastic than was earlier thought to be the case. [Thompson, 2000]

The role of experience in the development of neural pathways is demonstrated clearly by experiments with animals that are temporarily prevented from using one sensory system or another in infancy. They can become permanently handicapped in that sensory system. For example, if kittens are blindfolded for the first several weeks of life, they never acquire normal vision, even though the anatomy of their eyes appears to be normal. This handicap develops because, without visual experience, the neural pathways that transmit signals from the eyes to the visual cortex of the brain will atrophy, or fail to develop. If only one eye is temporarily blinded and the other remains normal, the kitten will be able to see well with one eye but will never acquire **binocular vision,** the ability to focus two eyes together on a single object. Binocular vision plays a role in depth perception; thus a one-eyed adult cat seems to see normally until, unexpectedly, it falls while jumping onto a table or leaping from one chair to another.

binocular vision The ability to use both eyes together to focus on a single object.

What does this fine-tuning process imply for human development?

> Some have advocated providing extremely enriched environments, full of bells, whistles, moving objects and so on, for human infants. Actually there is no evidence at all that such "super rich" environments have any effect on the development of normally raised human infants. The normal environment provided by caring parents or other caregivers seems quite sufficient. On the other hand, tragic situations where human infants are left alone in cribs except for feeding and changing do result in substantially retarded development. [Thompson, 2000]

Some of the specifics, particularly what might happen if an infant were deprived cognitively or socially, have far-reaching implications (Schore, 1994; Serbin, 1997). An adult might be mentally retarded or emotionally stunted—perhaps never able to understand poetry or sustain a loving relationship—because of deprivation in the early years. But that is speculation. In fact, most scientists believe that deprivation must be quite severe to stunt normal brain development. One neuroscientist explains:

> Development really wants to happen. It takes very impoverished environments to interfere with development because the biological system has evolved so that the environment alone stimulates development. What does this mean? Don't raise your children in a closet, starve them, or hit them in the head with a frying pan. [Petersen, quoted in Hall, 1998]

For the moment, our understanding of brain maturation leads us to conclude that caressing a newborn, talking to a preverbal infant, and showing affection toward a small person too immature to love in return may be essential first steps toward developing that person's full human potential.

At the same time, the life-span perspective reminds us that loving and stimulating experiences should occur throughout life. The brain retains some plasticity—that is, some capacity for developing new pathways—as long as experiences continue (Bruer, 1999).

MOTOR SKILLS

We now come to the most visible and dramatic body changes of infancy, those that ultimately allow the child to "stand tall and walk proud." Thanks to their ongoing changes in size and proportion and their increasing brain maturation, infants markedly improve their motor skills, their abilities to move and control their bodies.

developmental biodynamics Maturation of the developing person's ability to move through, and with, the environment, by means of crawling, running, grasping, and throwing.

Researchers who have studied **developmental biodynamics,** as the maturation of movement skills is called, see a seemingly simple act like grabbing a toy as a remarkable achievement—one that evolves through a painstaking trial-and-error process that gradually assembles and fine-tunes the proper sequence of smooth motor actions (Goldfield, 1995; Thelen & Smith, 1994). Thus developmental biodynamics—whether it involves learning to take a step or learning to grasp small objects with the fingers—is not simply a matter of waiting for a maturational timetable to unfold. It also requires the infant's active efforts to master and coordinate the several components of each complex skill.

Because of the growing independence they afford the child, motor skills become a "catalyst for developmental change" (Thelen, 1987), as they open new possibilities for the child's discovery of the world. New vistas are seen, new dangers are within reach, and, fortunately for safety's sake, new fears develop. It is important to study the development of motor skills—including the usual sequence and timing of their emergence—and the various factors that might cause one child to develop certain skills "behind" or "ahead of" schedule.

reflexes Involuntary physical responses to stimuli.

breathing reflex A reflex that ensures an adequate supply of oxygen and the discharge of carbon dioxide by causing the individual to inhale and exhale.

Reflexes

Strictly speaking, the infant's first motor skills are not skills at all but **reflexes,** or involuntary responses to particular stimuli. Three sets of reflexes that are critical for survival and become stronger as the baby matures are:

- *Reflexes that maintain oxygen supply.* The **breathing reflex** begins in normal newborns even before the umbilical cord, with its supply of oxygen, is cut. Additional reflexes that maintain oxygen are reflexive *hiccups* and *sneezes,* as well as *thrashing* (moving the arms and legs about) to escape something that covers the face.
- *Reflexes that maintain constant body temperature.* When infants are cold, they *cry, shiver,* and *tuck in their legs* close to their bodies, thereby helping to keep themselves warm. When they are hot, they try to *push away* blankets and then stay still, as well as drink plain water if it's offered. To what extent these are reflexes is debatable, but they do seem universal to all infants.

Never Underestimate the Power of a Reflex

For developmentalists, newborn reflexes are mechanisms for survival, indicators of brain maturation, and vestiges of evolutionary history. For parents, they are mostly delightful and sometimes amazing. This is demonstrated by three star performers: a 2½-week-old infant eagerly stepping forward on legs too tiny to support her body; a 3-day-old infant, still wrinkled from being immersed in amniotic fluid, contentedly sucking his thumb; and a newborn grasping so tightly that his legs dangle in space.

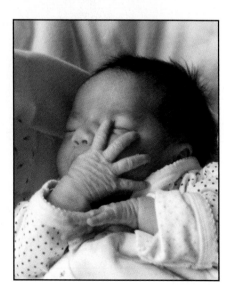

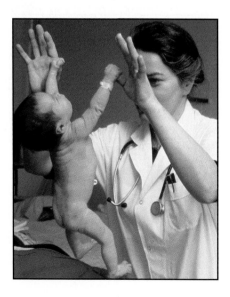

sucking reflex A reflex that causes newborns to suck anything that touches their lips.

rooting reflex A reflex that helps babies find a nipple by causing them to turn their heads toward anything that brushes against their cheeks and to attempt to suck on it.

■ *Reflexes that manage feeding.* The **sucking reflex,** which is crucial to their taking in nourishment, causes newborns to suck anything that touches their lips—fingers, toes, blankets, and rattles, as well as natural and artificial nipples of various textures and shapes. The **rooting reflex** causes babies to turn their mouths toward anything that brushes against their cheeks—a reflexive search for a nipple—and start to suck. Even if a mother does nothing but put a newborn within striking distance of the nipple, the neonate instinctively grasps and sucks with sufficient skill to feed (Koepke & Bigelow, 1997). *Swallowing* is another important reflex that aids feeding, as are *crying* when the stomach is empty and *spitting up* when too much has been swallowed too quickly.

Gross Motor Skills

gross motor skills Physical skills involving large body movements such as waving the arms, walking, and jumping.

Gross motor skills, which involve large body movements, emerge directly from reflexes. Newborns placed on their stomachs reflexively move their arms and legs as if they were swimming and attempt to lift their heads to look around. As they gain muscle strength, they start to wiggle, attempting to move forward by pushing their arms, shoulders, and upper bodies against the surface they are on. Although these initial efforts usually get them nowhere (or even move them backward), infants persist in these motions whenever they have the opportunity. Usually by the age of 5 months or so, they become able to use their arms, and then legs, to inch forward on their bellies.

By the age of 6 months, most infants have succeeded at this belly-crawl. A few months later, usually between 8 and 10 months after birth, most infants can lift their midsections and crawl (or *creep*) on "all fours," coordinating the movements of their hands and knees in a smooth, balanced manner (Adolph et al., 1998). Within the next couple of months, most infants also learn to climb up onto couches and chairs—as well as up onto ledges and windowsills, and down into other dangerous places, including pools and lakes.

Walking shows a similar progression: from reflexive, hesitant, adult-supported newborn stepping to a smooth, speedy, coordinated gait

(a)

(b)

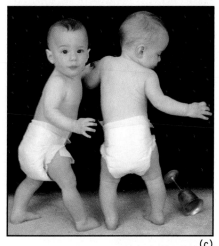

(c)

(d)

More Than Brothers Nicholas and Daniel are monozygotic (identical) twins, and consequently they reach various stages of motor skills virtually together. The abilities shown here are (a) lifting the head and shoulders at 4 months, (b) preparing to crawl at 6 months, (c) standing with one supporting hand at 8 months, and (d) walking at 12 months—right on time.

Onward and Upward Gross motor skills develop rapidly during the first two years, partly because infants and toddlers take advantage of every opportunity to use whatever abilities they have—crawling, creeping, climbing. For this reason, dangerous falls are most likely to occur between ages 1 and 3, so every caregiver needs to make sure that "onward and upward" doesn't become "down and out."

toddler A child, usually between the ages of 1 and 2, who has just begun to master the art of walking.

Now a Toddler As this very young lady begins to walk, she demonstrates why such children are called toddlers: They move unsteadily from side to side as well as forward.

❷ *Observational Quiz (see answer page 143):* *What emotions and fine motor skills usually accompany early walking, as shown here?*

fine motor skills Physical skills involving small body movements, especially with the hands and fingers, such as picking up a coin or drawing.

(Bertenthal & Clifton, 1998). On average, a child can walk while holding a hand at 9 months, can stand alone momentarily at 10 months, and can walk well, unassisted, at 12 months. In recognition of their accomplishment of walking, infants at this stage are given the additional name **toddler,** for the characteristic way they move their bodies, toddling from side to side. Since their heads and stomachs are relatively heavy and large, they spread out their short little legs for stability, which makes them seem bow-legged, flat-footed, and unbalanced.

Interestingly, once an infant can take steps, walking becomes the preferred mode of movement—except when speed is an issue; then many new walkers quickly drop to their hands and knees to crawl. Two-year-olds are proficient walkers and almost never crawl except when, with a mocking grin, they pretend to be babies. Within a short time, mastery of walking leads to mastery of running, and then watchful caregivers need to be ready to dash to the rescue if an attractive hazard catches a toddler's attention.

Fine Motor Skills

Fine motor skills, which are skills that involve small body movements (usually of the hands and fingers), are more difficult to master than gross motor skills because they require the precise coordination of complex muscle groups. These skills develop step-by-step, unlike some gross motor skills, such as standing up, which seem to emerge quite suddenly.

Successful Grabbing

The best example of an early fine motor skill is grabbing. Infants are born with a reflexive grasp, but they seem to have no control over it. During their first 2 months, babies excitedly stare and wave their arms at an object dangling within reach; by 3 months of age, they can usually touch it. But they cannot yet grab and hold on unless the object is placed in their hands, partly because their eye–hand coordination is so limited.

By 4 months of age they sometimes grab, but their timing is off: They close their hands too early or too late, and their grasp tends to be of short duration. Finally, by 6 months of age, with a concentrated stare and deliberation, most babies can reach for, grab at, and hold onto (usually successfully) almost any object that is of the right size. They can hold a bottle, shake a rattle, and yank a sister's braids. Moreover, they no longer need to see their hands in order to grab; they can grasp a moving object that is illuminated in an otherwise dark room (Robin et al., 1996), although when the lights are on, they use vision to help them carefully reach for objects (McCarty & Ashmead, 1999).

Exercise Equipment for the Hand All babies, including 8-month-old Edwin, reach and finger any object that challenges their hand skills. Paper is generally safe, so an old book or newspaper to tear, a roll of toilet paper to unravel, or a box of tissues to empty out one by one is much better than any of the glass, metal, or plastic objects that are equally attractive to the infant.

Fingering and Holding

Once grabbing is possible, infants explore everything within reach, mastering other fine motor skills while learning about the physical properties of their immediate world. Eleanor Gibson, a leading researcher in infant perception, describes the infant at 6 months of age as having "a wonderful eye–hand–mouth exploratory system." Several weeks before age 1 year, this system becomes sufficiently developed that the infant can "hold an object in one hand and finger it with the other, and turn it around while examining it. This is an ideal way to learn about the distinctive features of an object" and, bit by bit, about the tangible world (Gibson, 1988). (Some of the specifics of this learning are described in Chapter 6.)

Other developing hand skills contribute to the child's ability to explore. By the time they are 4 to 8 months of age, most infants can transfer objects from one hand to the other. By 8 or 9 months, they can adjust their reach in an effort to catch objects that are tossed toward them. And by 11 or 12 months, they can coordinate both hands to enclose an object that is too big for one hand alone (de Róiste & Bushnell, 1996).

Development of these fine motor skills is enhanced by the development of gross motor skills, and vice versa. The floor-bound creature who has learned how to sit steadily suddenly becomes more adept at reaching and manipulating objects (Rochat & Bullinger, 1994; Rochat & Goubet, 1995). Then, once the child is able to grab, he or she can hold onto chair legs, tabletops, and crib rails. This makes standing and even walking possible, strengthening leg muscles in the process. Once walking is possible, toddlers can poke, pick, pinch, and pull at hundreds of objects that were previously beyond their reach. They can even move out of sight or run away, if they choose. Now, more than ever, careful attention to "babyproofing" the home is needed, especially with regard to poisons and breakables.

Maturation and Patience Almost the only thing that might prevent a child from growing up as fast as possible is pressure to speed up the process.

"All right. Time to grow up."

Variations and Ethnic Differences in Timing

Although all healthy infants develop the same motor skills in the same sequence, the age at which these skills are acquired varies greatly from infant to infant. Table 5.1 shows the age at which half of all infants in the United States master each major motor skill and the age at which 90 percent master each skill.

norm A standard, or average, derived or developed for a specified group population. What is "normal" may not be what is ideal.

These averages, or **norms,** are based on a large representative sample of infants from a wide range of ethnic groups. Representative sampling is necessary because norms vary from group to group and place to place. For example, throughout infancy, African Americans are more advanced in motor skills than Americans of European ancestry (Rosser & Randolph, 1989). Internationally, the earliest walkers in the world seem to be in Uganda, where, if well nourished and healthy, the typical baby walks at 10 months. Some of the latest walkers are in France, where taking one's first unaided steps at 15 months is not unusual.

What factors account for this variation in the acquisition of motor skills? Of primary importance are inherited factors, such as how active, how physically mature, and how fat a particular child might be. The power of the genetic component is suggested by the fact that identical twins are far more likely to sit up, and to walk, on the same day than fraternal twins are. Moreover, there are striking individual differences in the strategies, effort, and concentration that infants apply to the mastering of motor actions. These differences, too, may be genetic, and they certainly affect the timing of motor-skill achievements (Thelen et al., 1993).

❶ Answer to Observational Quiz (from page 141):
Walking is thrilling to most toddlers, a source of pride and joy (see the infant's face)—and perhaps disobedience, if the seated woman is unwilling to follow along and so asks her to stop. Finger skills take a leap forward, too: Notice the dirt in the baby's right hand and the extended finger pointing on the left.

Patterns of infant care are also influential. For example, in many African cultures, infants are held next to an adult's body, usually in the upright position, virtually all day long; they are cradled and rocked as the adult works. Being able to continually feel the rhythm and changes of an adult's gait tends to stimulate the infant to practice movement. This may well give African babies an advantage in gross motor skills

table **5.1**	**Age Norms (in Months) for Motor Skills**	
Skill	When 50% of All Babies Master the Skill	When 90% of All Babies Master the Skill
Lifts head 90° when lying on stomach	2.2 months	3.2 months
Rolls over	2.8	4.7
Sits propped up (head steady)	2.9	4.2
Sits without support	5.5	7.8
Stands holding on	5.8	10.0
Walks holding on	9.2	12.7
Stands momentarily	9.8	13.0
Stands alone well	11.5	13.9
Walks well	12.1	14.3
Walks backward	14.3	21.5
Walks up steps (with help)	17.0	22.0
Kicks ball forward	20.0	24.0

Source: The Denver Developmental Screening Test (Frankenburg et al., 1981)

voice, and sweet and sour tastes—reveal much about their comprehension of the surrounding world.

Here, we will briefly consider the infant's sensory capacities. The fuller cognitive dimensions of infant perception will be examined in Chapter 6.

Vision

At birth, vision is the least developed of the senses, with distance vision particularly blurry. Newborns focus most readily on objects between 4 and 30 inches (10 and 75 centimeters) away. Their distance vision is about 20/400, which means a baby sees an object that is 20 feet (6.1 meters) away no better than an adult with 20/20 vision sees the same object at 400 feet (122 meters) away. Distance vision develops rapidly, however, reaching 20/40 by the age of 6 months and 20/20 by 12 months (Haith, 1990, 1993).

Increasing maturation of the visual cortex accounts for other improvements in infant visual abilities. When 1-month-olds look at an object, their gaze often wanders; their ability to *scan the object* (examine it completely, side to side and from top to bottom) and *attend to the critical areas* (peruse the most prominent features) is quite imperfect. When

What a Baby Sees Very young infants stare at objects within their reach and not much else for a very good reason—that's all they can see. Five stages of infant distance vision are here illustrated by artist Tony Young, working with Davida Teller, a noted researcher. Teller warns that these images (actually photos) may overestimate infant perception, because we see them "with the adult visual system, with all of the higher level perceptual capacities brought to bear." We see a middle-aged couple, perhaps in love. Since a 6-month-old, but not a 3-month-old, can see yellow, an older baby might be excited to see some amazing yellow flowers, hidden somewhat by two human shapes.

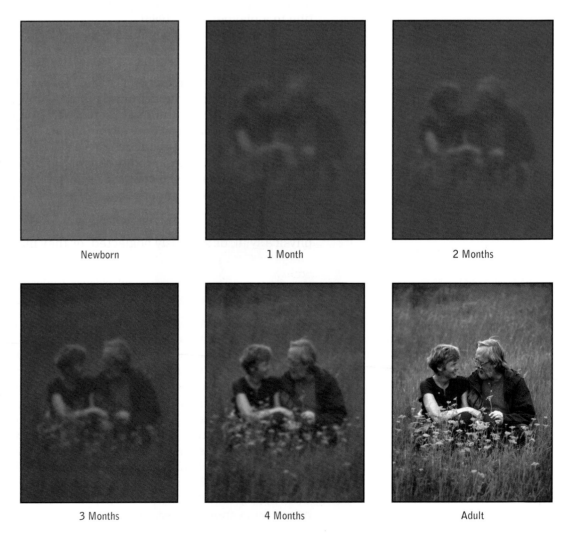

Newborn   1 Month   2 Months

3 Months   4 Months   Adult

Four People, All Staring Intently Scientists, aided by Donald Duck, monitor a 7-month-old girl's responses to visual stimuli. As various pictures flash on the screen, the infant's brain activity is recorded by means of the headband device she is wearing. From the recording, researchers can tell not only what she sees and how well she sees it but also which parts of her developing brain are processing visual stimuli.

looking at a face, for example, they stare at peripheral features, such as the hairline, and then stare off into space. By 3 months of age, scanning is more organized, more efficient, and centered on important aspects of a visual stimulus. Thus, when 3-month-olds look at a face, they look more closely at the eye and mouth regions, which contain the most information (Aslin, 1988; Braddick & Atkinson, 1988).

Binocular vision also develops in the early months, occurring quite suddenly at about 14 weeks, on average (Held, 1995). Binocular vision is required for depth perception (as you saw in our discussion of cats' eyes earlier in this chapter), so babies can see the edges of beds and such long before they can use vision to guide their crawling.

Color vision is probably absent at birth, but it rapidly becomes refined during the early months (Teller, 1997). One-month-old infants can distinguish among red, green, and white, but their ability to detect other colors is limited. By 3 to 4 months of age, infants can distinguish many more colors and can also differentiate them more acutely, perceiving aqua, for example, as a shade of blue rather than green (Bornstein & Lamb, 1992; Haith, 1990).

As a result of all these achievements, depth and motion perception improve dramatically. Evidence of this comes from infants' ability to *track* a moving object, that is, to visually follow its movement. Some instances of tracking are apparent in the first days of life—newborns are more interested in objects that move and lights that flicker than in static, dull displays—but newborns' ability to track and focus is very unstable (Teller, 1997).

In the months after birth, however, tracking improves week by week, with large, slow-moving, high-contrast objects being tracked more readily than small, fast-moving, low-contrast objects. By 2 months, an infants' eyes can smoothly follow a slow-moving object, and by 3 to 5 months the eyes dart ahead to track a fast-moving object (Richards & Holley, 1999). Tracking continues to improve—gradually—through infancy, and then through childhood and adolescence, to the point at which a skilled adult can track a baseball traveling 90 miles per hour or faster. The crack of the bat is evidence of fully developed tracking skill.

Hearing

Relative to vision, hearing at birth is already quite sensitive. Sudden noises startle newborns, making them cry; rhythmic sounds, such as a lullaby or a heartbeat, soothe them and put them to sleep. When they are awake, they turn their heads in an effort to locate the source of a noise, and they begin to connect sight and sound (Morrongiello et al., 1998). Young infants are particularly attentive to the sound of conversation. Indeed, as we saw in Chapter 4, newborns can distinguish their mothers' voices from the voices of other women soon after birth, because even in the womb they listen.

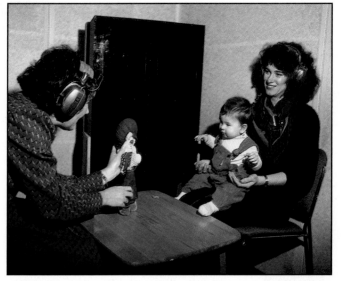 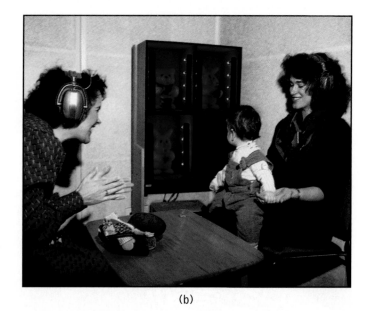

(a)　　　　　　　　　　　　　　　　　　　(b)

The Baby Can Hear The procedure pictured here tests an infant's ability to detect changes in speech sounds. While the child is focused on a toy held by the experimenter (a), a single speech sound is played repetitively through a loudspeaker. At random intervals the speech sound changes, and then toys on the infant's right become illuminated and begin to move (b). After this routine is repeated a number of times, the infant learns that a change in speech sounds signals a delightful sideshow. Then researchers can tell whether the infant discriminates between similar speech sounds by whether or not the child looks expectantly over to the toys after a particular sound.

❷ *Observational Quiz (see answer page 151): Can you guess why both the mother and the experimenters are wearing headphones but the baby is not?*

habituation The process of becoming so familiar with a particular stimulus that it no longer elicits the physiological responses it did when it was originally experienced.

❷ **Especially for Educators:** Suppose you are the director of a day-care center for infants. Should you do anything special to overcome the effects of otitis media? If so, what?

otitis media A middle-ear infection that can impair hearing temporarily and therefore can impede language development and socialization if it continues too long in the first years of life.

By the age of 1 month, infants can perceive differences between very similar speech sounds, as was first shown in an experiment that astonished scientists 30 years ago. The experiment was set up so that the subject babies activated a recording of the "bah" sound whenever they sucked on a nipple. Even 1-month-olds quickly appreciated that their sucking reflex produced the sound. At first they sucked diligently, but as they became **habituated** (or accustomed) to the "bah" sound, their rate of sucking decreased. At this point, the experimenters changed the sound from "bah" to "pah." Immediately the babies sucked more, indicating by this sign of interest that they perceived the difference (Eimas et al., 1971). Later research finds that very young infants may have some ability to discriminate between vowels (a much harder task) and to sense differences of emphasis in spoken two- and three-syllable words (Sansavini et al., 1997).

Young infants can also distinguish between speech sounds that are not used in their native languages—and that are indistinguishable to adult speakers of their native languages. For example, English-speaking adults cannot tell the difference between different "t" sounds that are used in Hindi speech, or between various glottal consonants used in some Native American dialects, but their infants are able to differentiate these sounds. Japanese adults have trouble hearing the distinction between the English "l" and "r," but Japanese babies know the difference; English-speaking adults have trouble with sounds in Thai and Czech, but their babies, who will soon speak English, can discriminate these "foreign" sounds (Jusczyk, 1995).

Early Hearing Loss

Since hearing is the most acute sense of the newborn, deafness usually becomes obvious to the parents and pediatrician in the first few months. About 1 in 1,000 newborns are profoundly deaf (Mason & Herrmann, 1998). In many cases, hearing aids or surgery can ameliorate the deafness. If not, the primary caregivers need to learn sign language, because the neurons and dendrites that apply to language develop rapidly, and once an infant learns a first language—even American Sign Language—a second language is easier to learn (Bruer, 1999).

Many normal babies have mild to moderate hearing losses for a period of weeks or months, a problem not apparent in early testing. Middle-ear infections, called **otitis media,** are common in infancy, with almost every child having at least one bout. Indeed, between birth and

CHRONIC OTITIS MEDIA

An intensive study on the effects of hearing loss (Vernon-Feagens & Manlove, 1996) included weekly medical checkups of infants who spent 30 hours or more per week in day care, beginning at 3 or 4 months of age. Researchers were surprised to find that almost half the children had chronic otitis media.

The 36 infants in this study were at "very low risk" for serious intellectual or cognitive problems. All were healthy, with no significant history of birth complications or medical problems. They lived in middle-class communities with middle-class parents—all high school–educated and native English-speaking, more than half of them college-educated with family incomes over $45,000 per year. Of these 36 babies, 33 had both parents living at home, and for 2 of the 3 infants who lived in single-parent homes, the missing parent was serving in the armed forces.

Further, the day-care centers in the study were well staffed and designed to be cognitively stimulating as well as medically sound. Thus, if any cognitive or health problems were found, they could not be blamed on the quality of these infants' home life or day care.

On the basis of careful weekly checks by a nurse and a doctor, infants were divided into two groups: those with chronic otitus media (findings of infection more than 20 percent of the time) and those who had the disease less frequently. Seventeen children were found to be in the chronic group; on average, they had otitis media for 5 months per year. The 19 less affected children averaged 1 month of otitis media per year.

The two groups were tested on several cognitive and social variables. No differences in language ability—either in expressing themselves or in understanding simple words—were found between them. However, the children with chronic otitis media were more likely to play alone and were less likely to talk with their peers, either positively or negatively (see Figure 5.5). Such findings suggest that ear problems, an experience in the physical domain, affect socialization, a behavior in the psychosocial domain.

This study suggests that chronic otitis media is widespread but not typically noticed, with the potential of causing developmental lags in the ability to learn, make friends, solve social problems, deflect aggression, and such. As the researchers noted:

> Children in day care must continually negotiate the noisy verbal environment with other children and adults in close proximity. Children with a hearing loss for even part of the time may learn to withdraw as much as possible from a verbal environment because it is more difficult for them than for other children. Over time this pattern of behavior may persist even when they are not experiencing otitis media and the accompanying hearing loss. [Vernon-Feagens & Manlove, 1996]

Note, however, that this study included only 36 children. The results provide a reason for concern, not for jumping to

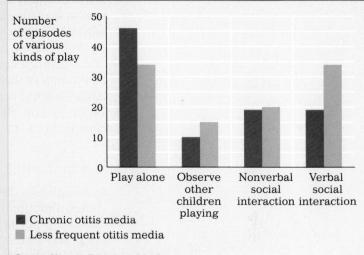

Chronic otitis media
Less frequent otitis media

Source: Vernon-Feagens & Manlove, 1996.

Figure 5.5 Social Behavior With and Without Ear Infections. Toddlers with a history of frequent ear infections are much more likely to play alone rather than talk and play with others. If this pattern persists, it may affect the development of social skills.

conclusions. A noted critic of the idea that the first years of life are pivotal for later development makes it clear that slow language development in infancy can be overcome during childhood. However, he also warns that "chronic middle ear infections . . . muffle normal speech sounds. This abnormal auditory experience . . . seems to result in language-learning-impaired children being unable to process rapidly changing auditory inputs, the kind of inputs that carry information about consonants and vowels in a language" (Bruer, 1999).

Research to date suggests that ear infections need prompt and repeated attention, and caregivers should do what they can to prevent them, such as ensuring frequent handwashing (among children and caregivers alike), preventing toddlers from sharing food with one another, and extending breast-feeding at least until the age of 1 year (since breast-fed babies get sick less often). Because infections spread quickly among infants and toddlers, a child's exposure to other children who might be sick should be minimized.

Precautions should be not only medical but also linguistic. Toddlers with possible hearing loss should hear language frequently and clearly, without the continual background noise of some day-care centers and even some homes.

There are two medical treatments for chronic otitis media—repeated antibiotics and placement of a tube in the inner ear to drain the fluid. Both are controversial, as each has negative side effects. Each is warranted in certain cases, but some research finds that the best treatment for chronic, but mild, cases is time, since maturation of the ear makes infection less likely.

age 3, one-third of all children have three or more episodes of otitis media—and these are only the diagnosed and recorded episodes (Behrman, 1992). Otitis media often begins with the sniffles and then leads not only to inflamed ears and temporary hearing reduction but also to acute pain—with crying that propels parents to the doctor for diagnosis and the antibiotics that can clear up the problem.

Sometimes, however, the original infection can develop into *chronic otitis media*, a condition in which the inner ear becomes filled with fluid. As a result of that condition, which may last for weeks or months, the infant's hearing is usually impaired in one or both ears (Werner & Ward, 1997). As the Research Report describes, caregivers should prevent chronic otitus media if they can.

Taste, Smell, and Touch

Although less developed than their hearing, neonates' sense of taste is clearly functioning. This was vividly shown in a demonstration with a dozen 2-hour-old infants who were each given tastes of sweet, sour, salty, and bitter water (Rosenstein & Oster, 1988). Careful analysis of their videotaped facial expressions revealed distinctive reactions to all the samples except the salty one, with the infants preferring sweet tastes. Indeed, the sense of taste may be particularly significant for the very young. One study found that sugar calmed 2-week-olds but had no effect on 4-week-olds—unless accompanied by eye contact (Zeifman et al., 1996).

Infants' sense of smell is even more acute, especially for odors that are particularly meaningful to them—like those associated with feeding (Porter et al., 1992). In a number of experiments, breast-fed infants a few days old were positioned in a crib between two gauze pads, one that had been worn by the infant's mother in her bra for several hours, the other similarly worn by another breast-feeding mother. In trial after trial, infants tended to turn their heads toward the mother's pad, preferring her smell to that of another woman (Schaal, 1986).

Together, taste and smell continue to develop during the early months, and they become quite acute by age 1. By late infancy, these senses are probably sharper than at any other time in the entire life span. Experts recommend giving infants a wide variety of foods, not because nutrition demands it but because taste preferences develop so rapidly that the introduction of new foods becomes more difficult with each passing year (Birch, 1990). Tastes and smells of early childhood probably are remembered for a lifetime: Many an adult will catch the scent of a flowering tree, burning leaves, or baking bread and suddenly identify it as a childhood smell. The brain records and collects the sensations of infancy, creating the template for a lifetime of later perceptions.

Finally, the sense of touch is remarkably acute during the first year (Bushnell & Boudreau, 1993). Even in the early months, long before their limited visual skills permit careful visual inspection, babies manipulate objects to examine them (and often transfer them to their mouths for exploration with their tongues, gums, cheeks, and lips, which are very sensitive to touch). By 6 months of age, infants distinguish objects on the basis of their temperature, size, hardness, and texture; somewhat later, they are able to differentiate objects by weight.

Sometimes the sense of motion is considered a sixth sense, and if this is the case, it is obviously strong at birth. Many a crying infant will

❶ **Response for Educators (from page 148):** You must do what you can, because even moderate hearing loss over a long period might impair language and social skills. Begin by doing what you can to prevent infections, particularly colds. You could mandate handwashing, eliminate food sharing, take the children outside as much as possible, and insist that sick babies stay home. Further, your language-learning and social-skill activities should be planned as if you had several hard-of-hearing children (because you probably do). For instance, play areas and settings should include relatively quiet and intimate areas, so that the child with a hearing loss is not disadvantaged, and soundproofing should minimize outside and inside background noises.

❓ **Especially for Parents:** Is it likely that your next newborn will be breast-fed for 2 years, as WHO recommends? Why or why not?

not hush unless carried, cradled, or cuddled in a parent's arms, a moving car, or a pushed carriage.

You may have noticed that our focus here has been primarily on the first 6 months or so. As time goes on, the role of cognition increases in significance. Accordingly, we discuss perception among older babies at length in Chapter 6, including the question of how early memories of perceptions are preserved.

NUTRITION

Good nutrition is the foundation for all development. As you saw, newborns usually double their birthweight in the first 4 months, a growth that requires feeding at least every 3 or 4 hours, day and night. The actual feeding "schedule" varies considerably from child to child and from culture to culture. Some experts in some regions advocate a rigid pattern of feeding every 4 hours immediately after birth, soon increasing to every 6 hours; others recommend feeding at first whimper, which can sometimes mean every half hour or so.

Preferred feeding schedules also vary from generation to generation. One developmental researcher writes:

> It is easy to forget how rapidly ideas about parenting have changed. I was brought up as a Truby King baby. Influenced by this New Zealand pediatrician, my father, also a physician, believed that babies should be fed on a strict 6-hour schedule. Whenever we visited my father after our first child was born, at 6 p.m. he would start to fidget in his chair and say, "Isn't it time he was nursed?" [Hinde, 1995]

This researcher was influenced by the attitudes of his own era, not his father's era, so his son was fed whenever the son cried, rarely at precisely 6 o'clock because, usually, he had been fed an hour or two before and hunger had not yet reappeared. Timing is not the critical factor in feeding, however. What matters is the overall quality and quantity of the infant's nutritional intake. Good quality and sufficient quantity are vital not only for physical growth and health but also for brain development and skill mastery.

The Ideal Diet

At first, infants are unable to eat or digest solid food, but their rooting, sucking, swallowing, and breathing reflexes are designed to ensure that they consume large quantities of liquid nourishment. In fact, when you consider how much eating you would have to do to double your own weight in 4 months, it becomes clear that the new infant must be a dedicated eating machine. The inevitable stomach upsets also become easy to understand.

What should that small human eat? Something easy to swallow and digest that provides everything essential for growth. Given these requirements, the ideal infant food is obvious: breast milk.

Breast milk is always sterile and at body temperature; it contains more iron, vitamin C, and vitamin A than cow's or goat's milk; it provides antibodies to protect against any disease that the mother is immunized against, either through vaccine or through having had the illness herself. The specific fats and sugars in breast milk make it more

A Day in the Park Breast-feeding in public has recently become more common in the United States. One reason is that mothers are more aware of the importance of nursing when the baby is hungry rather than adhering to a fixed feeding schedule. Another reason is that, in some parts of the country, pioneering women who have been arrested for indecent exposure because they breast-fed their infants in public have challenged the law and won.

digestible than any prepared baby formula, which means that breast-fed babies have fewer allergies and stomachaches than bottle-fed babies. And breast-feeding decreases the frequency of almost every other common infant ailment (Beaudry et al., 1995; Dewey et al., 1995; Isolauri et al., 1998). As a result, breast-fed babies require fewer doctor visits, medications, and hospital admissions (Ball & Wright, 1999).

Given all the benefits of breast milk, doctors worldwide recommend breast-feeding for almost all babies, unless the mother is an active drug user (including alcohol and tobacco), HIV-positive, or severely malnourished. More precisely, the World Health Organization (WHO) recommends that infants should be fed *exclusively* on breast milk at least for the first 4 to 6 months of life. At that point, other foods should be added—cereals and fruits particularly, because breast milk does not have adequate iron, vitamin D, or vitamin K—but breast-feeding should continue until age 2 or later (Lawrence, 1998; Wharton, 1996).

Nutritional Problems

Nutritional problems of every sort, including obesity and life-threatening vitamin deficiencies, can occur throughout the life span. Young adolescents undertake crazy fad diets, senior citizens try to subsist on toast and tea, and people of all ages eat too much fat, salt, and sugar. In the first 2 years, however, there is usually only one simple nutritional problem—not enough nourishing food. The consequences can be devastating to body, brain, and life itself.

Long-Term Consequences Many people hope that breast-fed babies will become smarter, healthier, and more loving adults. However, research finds no such guarantees. Hiring a worker on the basis of his infant experiences would be like using a laundry detergent because your grandmother once used that brand. There might be something to it, but the cleanliness of last week's wash (or how the worker did at his last job) is a better guide.

"I forgot to say I was breast-fed."

Severe Malnutrition

protein-calorie malnutrition A nutritional problem that results when a person does not consume enough nourishment to thrive.

marasmus A disease that afflicts young infants suffering from severe malnutrition. Growth stops, body tissues waste away, and death may eventually occur.

kwashiorkor A disease resulting from a protein deficiency in children. The symptoms include thinning hair and bloating of the legs, face, and abdomen.

In infancy, the most serious nourishment problem is **protein-calorie malnutrition,** which occurs when a child does not consume sufficient nourishment (of any kind) to thrive. Roughly 7 percent of the world's children are severely protein-calorie malnourished during their early years, with rates running above 50 percent in impoverished nations (including Peru, the Sudan, and the Philippines) (United Nations, 1994).

In the first year of life, severe protein-calorie malnutrition can cause **marasmus,** a condition in which growth stops, body tissues waste away, and the infant eventually dies. During toddlerhood, malnourished children are more likely to suffer **kwashiorkor,** a condition caused by a deficiency of protein in which the child's face, legs, and abdomen swell with water; this swelling sometimes makes the child appear well fed to anyone who doesn't know the real cause of the bloating. In children with kwashiorkor, the essential organs claim whatever nutrients are available, so other parts of the body become degraded. This includes the children's hair, which usually becomes thin, brittle, and colorless—a telltale sign of systemic malnutrition.

Kwashiorkor is usually not fatal in itself, but it makes the child vulnerable to death from almost any other disease, including measles, diarrhea, and even the flu. Kwashiorkor may result when a woman has babies too close together, which prevents her from breast-feeding each child exclusively for at least 2 years. One consequence of kwashiorkor is reduced organ size, which makes the person, even as an adult, have reduced caloric needs but also reduced energy (Henry, 1996).

Malnutrition: At a Glance, and with a Closer Look
New photos of children near death from starvation are published almost every year. The photo on the right, from the Sudan, is similar to photos from Chile, Somalia, Brazil, India, Biafra, Indonesia, and Ethiopia published in earlier editions of this text. The photo below is equally sad, but more subtle. It shows child victims of a continuing famine in North Korea.
❓ *Observational Quiz (see answer page 154): What signs of undernutrition can you see in the North Korean children? (Consider body size, clothes, hair, and behavior.)*

❶ **Response for Parents (from page 151):** The arguments for and against breast-feeding fall neatly into two camps, with the baby's well-being favoring breast-feeding and cultural customs opposing it. The physiological advantages are numerous; you can cite 10 or more listed in the text. The cultural arguments against breast-feeding are not listed, but you can read between the lines; they include inconvenience for the mother, jealousy of the father and siblings, disapproval by outsiders, and the difficulty of breast-feeding at the workplace.

❶ *Answer to Observational Quiz (from page 153): The most obvious signs of malnutrition are the large heads and skinny arms and legs on most of the children—the human body sacrifices overall fat and growth to protect the brain, if possible. Another sign is the clothes: Most children of this age have outgrown their baby clothes, but these children have actually lost weight because of the famine. Did you note the shaved heads on all but the two best-fed children? Here we can speculate that kwashiorkor made their hair so dull and sparse that shaving seemed best or that lice appeared and the parents had no energy or medicine to remove them. Finally, the children's behavior—docile, sad, immobile—may reflect their diminished energy. A child who is unusually quiet and "good" may actually be chronically hungry.*

More broadly, the primary cause of malnutrition in developing countries is early cessation of breast-feeding for any reason. In many countries, breast-feeding used to continue for at least 2 years, as WHO recommends. Now it is often stopped much earlier in favor of bottle-feeding, usually with powdered formulas, which too often are overdiluted with unsafe water. For older children, the primary cause of malnutrition is political leaders who do not care about, and mothers who do not know about, the consequences of undernourishment. Simply shipping surplus food from one nation to another does not solve the problem, as the Changing Policy box explains.

Even in wealthy nations, isolated cases of severe protein-calorie malnutrition during infancy do occur. Usually this happens because emotional and physical stress, or the devastating effects of drug addiction, are so overwhelming that the parents ignore the infant's feeding needs or prepare food improperly, *and* the larger community does not notice the resulting malnutrition. This is one reason New Zealand, among other countries, requires well-baby checkups for every registered birth, at home by visiting nurses as well as at a doctor's office. Such home visits yield multiple health benefits for babies, including longer-term breast-feeding and better nutrition (Moffitt, 1997). A similar experimental program in the United States also lengthened the average interval between pregnancies; it improved the health of both mother and child in many other ways as well (Olds et al., 1997).

Long-Term Effects

The consequences of infant nutritional problems extend far beyond the obvious threats to life and health, and even beyond the shorter stature of the adult who went hungry as a child. Because the brain is developing rapidly during the early years, an inadequate supply of nutrients can stunt intellectual growth for decades. Only in extreme cases does malnutrition directly starve brain development, but undernutrition can *indirectly* impair neurological networks.

The process is as follows: Undernourished infants and toddlers are less likely than normal infants to be interested in the sensory, intellectual, and social events that surround them, and their lack of interest limits their experiences. With only limited experience, their brains may not develop as many neural connections as they ordinarily might. In addition, an undernourished infant crawls and walks later, thus postponing experience and limiting perceptual growth. Further, parents of relatively docile, small, immobile (that is, undernourished) toddlers treat them as "good babies" and thus tend to give them fewer of the language and intellectual challenges they need (Lozoff et al., 1998; Pollitt et al., 1996). Finally, when they are hungry, such infants fuss impatiently—not the best stimulus for storytelling, singing, and other language-rich experiences.

For all these reasons, it should not be surprising that longitudinal research on children in Mexico, Kenya, Egypt, Jamaica, Indonesia, and Barbados, as well as in Europe and North America, reveals that children who are underfed in infancy tend to show impaired learning—especially in their ability to concentrate and in their language skills—throughout childhood and adolescence (Pollitt et al., 1996; Ricciuti, 1993; Wachs, 1995). However, the same research also shows that if a severely malnourished infant later receives good caregiving as a toddler and young child—with adequate food, balanced nutrients, cognitive stimulation, and caring social support—many of the deficits caused by the early hunger will disappear.

PREVENTING UNDERNUTRITION

Undernutrition is caused by a complex interaction of factors, with political and familial problems being of prime importance (Pollitt et al., 1996; Wright & Talbot, 1996). That importance is most obvious in those less developed nations where almost everyone is undernourished. Typically, socioeconomic policies in those nations do not reflect the importance of infant nutrition; political conflicts such as civil war make the problem worse; and parents may not even realize that their somewhat thin offspring are undernourished. Undernutrition becomes evident when the poor children are found to be notably shorter than wealthier children, or when families emigrate to well-nourished nations and teenagers born in the new country grow to tower over their immigrant grandparents. In Guatemala, civil war between 1979 and 1982 fostered a generation of undernourished children who are now stunted adults. Some families escaped by emigrating to Florida or California. Their children are significantly taller, heavier, and more muscular than children who were left behind (Bogin, 1995).

Because a variety of factors may be involved, programs that assume undernutrition to be solely a problem of poverty, and that seek to provide poor families with free food, are too narrowly focused (Brown & Sherman, 1995; Ricciuti, 1991). To be successful in staving off the harm of inadequate nutrition, social policy must deal with the entire context. This includes raising "nutritional consciousness" in every nation and, particularly in developing nations, making sure leaders realize that the intellectual potential of the next generation is jeopardized when small children are underfed.

In one program, free nutritional supplements were fed to children in impoverished rural communities of Guatemala. This resulted in better nutrition, which led to better performance, years later, on tests of reading, vocabulary, arithmetic, and general knowledge. The difference was particularly apparent for the poorest children who received extra food as infants and toddlers, but it was also evident for older, less impoverished children (Pollitt et al., 1993). However, close analysis of the data reveals that not all the children who could have benefited actually did—primarily because not all the mothers faithfully brought their children to be fed the supplements. Mothers who lived farther away did not usually make

the trek unless they themselves had some school education (Carmichael et al., 1994). Thus, this program makes the point again: To reduce the effects of undernutrition, at least two things must be done together:

- Provide supplements, nearby and nourishing, for all children.
- Improve maternal education so that every mother will participate.

Simply providing free food, without careful attention to the cultural and family contexts, might not help at all (McGuire & Bundy, 1996).

These basic facts are no less true in developed countries. As an example, one common nutritional deficiency in the United States is *milk anemia*—a deficiency of iron—so named because it arises from parents' giving their toddler a bottle of milk (which has no iron) before every nap and with every meal, inadvertently destroying the child's appetite for other foods that are iron-rich. A bottle of juice is equally harmful in this regard; so is a diet that consists mostly of rice and vegetables. One careful survey in Massachusetts found 15 percent of all 6- to 12-month-olds to be iron-deficient, with the rate among Hispanics about 50 percent higher and that among Asians about 300 percent higher than the rates among those of European or African ancestry (Sargent et al., 1996). Such deficiencies may become obvious only when the child's teeth show early signs of decay—a result of the continual presence of sugar on the gums, called "milk mouth." The permanent teeth, fortunately, replace the rotted baby teeth, but the effects of an early nutritional deficiency can remain throughout life.

Also fairly common in the early years is a deficiency of zinc, which is found in seafood, beef, poultry, and dairy products and is essential for normal growth. Many children who become stunted in their first years as a result of this deficiency will catch up if they are well fed later on, but only if they get enough zinc (Golden, 1996). Worldwide, in both developing and developed nations, public attention to good preventive care for every infant, and education for every mother, would produce a much healthier and more intelligent population in another decade or two.

This research echoes one of the themes of biosocial growth illustrated throughout this chapter: The remarkable unfolding of brain maturation, physical growth, and perceptual development is guided by a genetic plan but requires a supportive social environment to reach full inherited potential.

SUMMARY

PHYSICAL GROWTH AND HEALTH

1. In their first 2 years, most babies gain about 22 pounds (10 kilograms) and grow about 15 inches (38 centimeters), with growth particularly rapid in the first year. Proportions change: The head is relatively large at birth, and fat accumulates quickly at first and then more slowly after age 1.

2. Improved immunization programs have almost wiped out many of the diseases that once sickened almost every child and killed many.

BRAIN GROWTH AND DEVELOPMENT

3. At birth the brain contains more than 100 billion nerve cells, or neurons, but the networks of nerve fibers that interconnect them are relatively rudimentary. During the first few years of an infant's life, there are major spurts of growth in these networks, enabling the emergence of new capabilities, including self-regulation and certain cognitive skills.

4. Over the course of the early years, neural pathways in the brain that are used become strengthened and further developed, and those that are not used die.

MOTOR SKILLS

5. At first, the newborn's motor abilities consist only of reflexes — involuntary responses to stimuli. Some reflexes, such as breathing and sucking, are essential for survival.

6. Gross motor skills involve large movements, such as running and jumping; fine motor skills involve small, precise movements, such as picking up a penny. The development of both kinds of motor abilities during the first 2 years allows the infant new possibilities in discovering the world.

7. Although the sequence of motor-skill development is the same for all healthy infants, variations — for hereditary, developmental, and environmental reasons — are normal in the ages at which infants master specific skills. Unusual slowness, however, is a cause for concern, because it might be a symptom of a deeper problem.

SENSORY AND PERCEPTUAL CAPACITIES

8. Both sensation and perception are apparent at birth, and both become more developed with time. Newborns show evidence of all five senses, although their sensory abilities are limited.

9. At birth, vision is the least developed of the senses, but during the first months of life, distance and binocular vision, focusing skills, and color perception improve considerably. Tracking, the ability to follow a moving object with the eyes, develops rapidly.

10. Hearing is very sensitive, even at birth. Infants listen particularly to speech sounds, quickly distinguishing even those that are not used in their native languages. Hence, moderate hearing loss is a cause for concern.

NUTRITION

11. Physical growth, brain development, and the mastery of motor skills all depend on adequate nutrition. Doctors worldwide recommend breast milk as the ideal food for most babies.

12. Although breast-feeding on demand may be best throughout infancy, the crucial question is whether an infant gets sufficient food or is undernourished. Severe protein-calorie deficiency can cause two serious conditions: In the first year, marasmus results in a cessation of growth, the wasting away of body tissues, and eventual death; during toddlerhood, kwashiorkor results in bloating and degradation of various parts of the body, and long-term cognitive deficits may occur.

KEY TERMS

neuron (133)

axon (133)

dendrites (133)

synapse (133)

neurotransmitter (136)

cortex (136)

transient exuberance
  (136)

myelination (136)

binocular vision (138)

developmental
  biodynamics (139)

reflexes (139)

breathing reflex (139)

sucking reflex (140)

rooting reflex (140)

gross motor skills (140)

toddler (141)

fine motor skills (141)

norm (143)

sensation (145)

perception (145)

habituation (148)

otitis media (148)

protein-calorie
  malnutrition (153)

marasmus (153)

kwashiorkor (153)

KEY QUESTIONS

1. How do the weight, length, and proportions of the infant's body change during the first 2 years?

2. How does immunizing infants protect the entire community?

3. What specific changes occur in the brain's communication system during infancy?

4. How does experience affect the development of the brain's neural pathways?

5. Which reflexes are critical to an infant's survival?

6. What is the general sequence of the development of gross motor and fine motor skills?

7. What factors account for individual differences in the timing of motor achievements?

8. How do the sensory capabilities of a newborn infant change over the first year of life?

9. What kinds of sensory experiences do babies typically prefer in early infancy, and why?

10. What are the advantages of breast-feeding?

11. What are some of the consequences of serious, long-term malnutrition?

12. What are the major causes of undernutrition?

13. *In Your Experience* What are the factors that determine what, and when, a young infant is fed?

The First Two Years:
Cognitive Development

C H A P T E R 6

This chapter is about infant *cognition*, by which we mean thinking in a very broad sense. Cognition involves intelligence and learning, memory and language, facts and concepts, perception and assumptions. You might think that a chapter on cognition during the first 2 years of life would be quite short, but you can see that this is not the case. Why?

Imagine, for a moment, that you are a newborn. New and constantly changing images, sounds, smells, and physical sensations swirl around you, and you must make sense of them all, connecting smells with visual images, tastes with feelings. You need to develop perceptions of objects, people, and even the parts of your own body and to figure out which ones endure and which ones change, in what sequence, and how they relate to you. Then you need to put it all together: sensations, sequences, objects, people, significant characteristics, permanent and transient features, causes and effects. And this is just the beginning.

By the end of the first year—and often much sooner—you will have a concept of number, demonstrate simple problem-solving capacities, and have begun to talk. By the end of the second year, you can speak in short sentences, think before acting, and can pretend to be someone or something (a mother, an airplane) that you know you are not. No wonder, then, that this is a full-length chapter: There is much to describe about infant cognition.

PERCEPTION AND COGNITION

As you learned in Chapter 5, infants possess remarkably acute sensory abilities from their very first days. They also develop early preferences for what they experience, showing a hunger for novelty and stimulation. This fact—that infants become habituated to familiar things and attentive to new experiences—helps scientists discover what they sense and perceive. But how do infants understand their experiences? Our examination of this side of perception—which is closely related to cognitive growth—will reveal that infants are active and eager interpreters of the world.

The first major theorist to stress that infants are active learners and that early learning is based on sensory abilities was Jean Piaget, whose depiction of infants' *sensorimotor intelligence* was first described in Chapter 2 and is presented later in this chapter. We begin, however, with the work of Eleanor and James Gibson, a husband-and-wife team of researchers. Their understanding of the links between perception and cognition has inspired much of the current research on infants' cognitive growth (Gibson, 1969; Gibson, 1979).

The Gibsons' Affordances

Perception, remember, is the mental processing of information that arrives from sensory organs. The Gibsons' central insight regarding perception is that it is not an automatic phenomenon that everyone, everywhere, experiences in the same way. Rather, perception is, essentially, an active cognitive process in which each individual interacts selectively with a vast array of perceptual possibilities: "We don't simply see, we look" (Gibson, 1988).

In the Gibsons' view, "the environment *affords* opportunities"; that is, every event, object, or place affords, or offers, the potential to be perceived and interacted with in a variety of ways (Gibson, 1997). Each of those opportunities for perception and interaction is called an **affordance.** Which particular affordance (of the many available) an individual perceives and acts on depends on that person's:

affordance   Each of the various opportunities for perception, action, and interaction that an object or place offers to any individual.

- Past experiences
- Current developmental or maturational level
- Sensory awareness of the opportunities
- Immediate needs and motivation

As a simple example, a lemon may be perceived as something that affords smelling, tasting, touching, viewing, throwing, squeezing, and biting (among other things). Which affordance a particular person perceives and acts on depends on the four factors above: A lemon might elicit quite different perceptions from an artist about to paint a still life, a thirsty adult in need of a refreshing drink, and a teething baby wanting something to gnaw on. This example implies (correctly) that affordances require an ecological fit between the individual and his or her environment. Hence, affordances arise both from specific qualities of an object and from the way the individual subjectively perceives the object. As one psychologist explains:

A Hole Is to Dig As for any scientist, discovery and application are the motivating forces for infant activity. Clamshells have many uses, one for clams, one for hungry people, and another—shown here—for toddlers on the beach.

If I want to sit down in a sparsely furnished bus station, a floor or a stack of books or a not-too-hot radiator might afford sitting. None of these are chairs, and thus their affordance of "sit-ability" is in relationship to my perception. [Gauvain, 1990]

Affordances are not limited just to objects; they are also perceived in the physical characteristics of a setting and the living creatures in it (Reed, 1993). A toddler's idea of what affords running might be any unobstructed surface—a meadow, a long hallway in an apartment building, or an empty road. To an adult eye, the degree to which these places afford running may be restricted by such factors as a bull grazing in the meadow, neighbors in the hallway, or traffic patterns on the road.

Graspable? Suckable?

As you remember from Chapter 5, all the senses are active processors from birth. Infants learn what parts of the visual array best afford focusing, what sounds merit listening, and so on. In terms of actions controlled by the infant, the grasping and sucking reflexes are among the first to afford information.

Graspability—whether an object is the right size, shape, and texture for grasping and whether it is within reach—is an early affordance. This is vital information, since infants learn about their world by handling objects. Extensive research has shown that infants perceive graspability long before their manual dexterity enables them to actually grasp successfully. For instance, when 3-month-olds view objects, some graspable and some not, they move their arms excitedly in the direction of those that are of the right size and distance for grasping, but they merely follow ungraspable objects with their eyes (Bower, 1989). By 5 months, infants are able to grab objects successfully, usually taking longer to coordinate their hand movements than older babies and adults do. This shows that deliberate and thoughtful perception precedes the action that will soon become automatic (McCarty & Ashmead, 1999).

The fact that babies perceive graspability so early helps explain how they explore a face. Once they have some control over their arm and hand movements, they will grab at any face that comes within their reach. But their grabbing is not haphazard: They do not grab at the eyes or mouth (although they might poke at them), because they already perceive that these objects are embedded and thus do not afford grasping. A tug at the nose or ears is more likely, because these features do afford grasping. Even better are eyeglasses, earrings, and long mustaches—all of which are quickly yanked by most babies, who perceive at a glance the graspability these objects afford.

Similarly, from very early on, an infant begins to understand which objects afford *suckability,* which afford *noisemaking,* which afford *movability,* and which afford other interesting opportunities. An impressive feature of this understanding is the infant's ability to find similar affordances in dissimilar objects (rattles, flowers, and pacifiers do not look alike, but they are all graspable) and to distinguish different affordances in similar objects (among objects of the same color, size, and shape, furry ones are more likely to be patted and rubber ones more likely to be squeezed) (Palmer, 1989). Best of all are objects that afford both grasping and sucking, which explains why most infants can hold their own bottles before 6 months.

graspability The perception of whether or not an object is of the proper shape, size, texture, and distance to afford grasping or grabbing.

It's OK to Grasp Daddy's Nose Infants quickly learn what objects are of the right size and proximity for grasping. If the adults in their life allow it, graspability also affords sociability, an impulse that requires one to distinguish appropriate objects from inappropriate ones.

❷ Especially for Parents: At which age—4 months, 8 months, or 12 months—is an infant most likely to fall off a bed or a table if you put him or her there for a moment?

visual cliff An apparent (but not actual) drop between one surface and another. The illusion of the cliff is created by connecting a transparent glass surface to an opaque patterned one, with the floor below the glass the same pattern as the opaque surface.

Sudden Drops and Sloping Surfaces

The affordances that an infant perceives in common objects evolve as the infant gains experience with those objects. An example is provided by the **visual cliff,** a firm surface that seemingly (but not actually) ends with a sudden drop.

Researchers once thought that perception of a visual cliff was purely a matter of visual maturity: 8-month-olds could see the difference; younger babies, because of their inadequate depth perception, could not. "Proof" came when 6-month-olds could be enticed to wiggle forward over the supposed edge of the visual cliff, in contrast to 10-month-olds, who fearfully refused to budge, even when their mothers called them (Gibson & Walk, 1960).

Later research found, however, that this hypothesis was wrong. In fact, even 3-month-olds notice the difference between a solid surface

Depth Perception Like thousands of crawling babies before him, this infant refuses to crawl to his mother.

❓ *Observational Quiz (see answer page 164):* *What does he see when he looks down?*

Affordances for Locomotion (a) Like the other 14-month-olds in Karen Adolph's study, Lauren perceives that a gently sloping ramp affords walking and she confidently descends it. (b) When later confronted with a steep slope, Lauren, like the other experienced walkers in the study, perceives the affordance of falling; consequently, she descends the slope by sliding down it. (c) This is in marked contrast to the inexperienced 8½-month-olds, who, like Jack, try to descend every slope, no matter how steep, by crawling, and who sometimes end up in a nosedive.

and an apparent cliff, as evidenced by their speeding heart rates and wide-open eyes when they are placed over the "edge." But they do not realize that one affordance of the cliff is falling. That realization comes when they start crawling, and their memories of caregiver fear (and perhaps their own tumble off a bed) teach them what cliffs afford to crawling infants (Campos et al., 1978).

A more subtle example comes from research with a sloping ramp—which may afford ascent and descent but may also afford falling. The research showed that which affordances an infant perceives in the ramp depend in part on prior experience. In one experiment, Karen Adolph and her colleagues observed two groups of infants as they moved up and down ramps pitched at different inclines (Adolph & Gibson, 1993). One group consisted of 14-month-olds with plenty of walking experience; the other consisted of 8½-month-olds with crawling (but not walking) experience. The researchers expected that the older infants would respond more cautiously to the inclines since they could better perceive the affordance of falling because of their prior experience of walking—and falling—over various surfaces.

This time the researchers' hypothesis was correct. The 14-month-olds confidently walked down gentle slopes; but when the slopes were made steeper, they negotiated the descent by sliding down in a sitting position, often after much hesitation and much searching for the best position. By contrast, the 8½-month-olds, regardless of the steepness of the slope, tried to descend by crawling rather than sliding, often falling headlong (their mothers were nearby to catch them). Thus, although infants of both ages could perceive the ramp's affordance of descent, only the older infants (with prior walking experience) could perceive its affordance of falling. They responded more cautiously as a result. In longitudinal follow-up research, Adolph (1997) found that experience with

(a)

(b)

(c)

● Response for Parents (from page 161):
Don't do it! The 4-month-old cannot move much and can see depth, so you might think he or she is safe. But 4-month-olds have no understanding of the danger, so any wiggle might produce a fall. The 12-month-old has a firm grasp of depth and of the dangers of a headlong drop but might try to get down feet first. In the most danger of all is the 8-month-old, because at that age babies have only a beginning awareness of the dangers of depth but are quite able to move.

dynamic perception Perception that arises from the movement of objects and changes in their positions.

One Constant, Multisensual Perception From the angle of her arm and the bend of her hand, it appears that this infant recognizes the constancy of the furry mass, perceiving it as a single entity whether it is standing still, rolling in the sand, or walking along the beach.

walking made the infants less reckless and also more astute in their preliminary exploration (looking, swaying, touching, thinking) before they descended the slope.

The Gibsons' contextual view emphasizes, therefore, that early perceptual development involves a growing knowledge of affordances, acquired through infants' active interactions with the objects, events, and people around them. Each infant, in each social context, will learn somewhat different affordances than other infants learn.

Dynamic Perception

As in the preceding example of the affordances of a sloping ramp, movement plays a key role in infants' perception of the properties of objects and in the development of their perceptual and cognitive skills generally (Kellman & Banks, 1998). Babies prefer to look at things in motion, whether those things are a mobile rotating overhead, their own flexing fingers, or their favorite bobbing, talking, human face. Beginning in the first days of life, they attend to movement cues to discern not only the boundaries of objects but also their rigidity, wholeness, shape, and size. Infants soon form simple expectations of the path that a moving object will follow (Haith et al., 1993; Nelson & Horowitz, 1987).

The fact that infants have **dynamic perception**—that is, perception primed to focus on movement and change—works well in a world in which stimuli are constantly moving within their field of vision. Movement captures the baby's attention, highlights certain attributes of the moving object (such as its boundaries), and advances the infant's perception of the object, enabling him or her to learn about its other qualities. By 3 months, infants are able to connect the feel of an unseen object with its appearance a few moments later (Steri, 1987). By 6 months, they can listen to a voice speak and match it to the face on film of a talking person, ignoring the face of another person whose mouth movements do not match the speech sounds they are hearing (Kuhl & Meltzoff, 1988). With this task, as with all affordances, the motivation of the infant is part of the selective process. Seven-month-olds correctly match speech and face when facial movements convey that the person is happy, angry, or interested. However, they prefer not to look at a sad face, even when the voice matches it. They would much rather stare at the happy, mismatched face (Soken & Pick, 1999).

As babies scoot, crawl, creep, walk, and climb, they are able to perceive and explore many new and old objects from many different perspectives, thereby gaining important information about the world around them. Indeed, once infants are able to move from one place to another, the way their eyes scan the environment changes to adapt to their movement (Higgins et al., 1996).

Object Permanence

One of the most important cognitive accomplishments of infancy is the ability to understand that objects and people exist independently of one's perception of them even when they are moved out of sight. With

object permanence   The realization that objects (including people) still exist even when they cannot be seen, touched, or heard.

Where's Rosa? At 18 months, Rosa knows all about object permanence and hiding. Her only problem here is distinguishing between "self" and "other."

this understanding, referred to as **object permanence,** infants realize that when objects (such as a familiar toy, the family cat, or Mommy) cannot be seen or heard, they exist somewhere else in the world.

Although object permanence no doubt seems obvious to you, it is not obvious to very young infants; their early awareness of reality is strictly limited to what they can see, hear, and otherwise sense at any given moment. Consequently, the development of object permanence has been the subject of much developmental research.

One way to test for awareness of object permanence is to use dynamic perception—specifically, to assess whether an infant searches for a hidden object. In an experiment devised by Piaget, an adult shows an infant an interesting toy and then covers it up with a blanket or cloth. If the infant searches under the covering for the toy, he or she realizes the toy still exists even though the object cannot be seen at the moment.

Various forms of Piaget's basic experiment have been carried out in virtually every university, every city, and every nation of the world. The result: Infants do not search for hidden objects until about 8 months of age. Even then, their search abilities are limited. They cannot find an object that they see concealed in one hiding place and then moved to a second hiding place (until they are about 12 months old, they tend to look for the object in the first hiding place, not where they just saw it hidden). If 8-month-olds are made to wait even a few seconds between the time they see an object disappear and the time they are allowed to search, they seem to lose all interest in searching.

Thus a firm understanding of object permanence develops rather slowly, over the first 2 years of life. In fact, even 3-year-olds playing hide-and-seek sometimes become fearful that someone has really disappeared or sometimes hide themselves in very obvious places, both signs that object permanence is not entirely understood.

But does a 6-month-old's failure to search necessarily mean that the infant does not have any concept at all of object permanence? Is it possible that younger babies have some understanding of object permanence but that other factors—motivation, motor skills, or memory—involved in Piaget's classic test mask that understanding? The answer is yes, as the Research Report makes clear.

KEY ELEMENTS OF COGNITIVE GROWTH

From our discussion so far, it is clear that a considerable portion of infants' knowledge of the world is built upon their developing perceptual skills. These skills form the basic tools that infants use to structure the data they receive through their daily experiences. This enables them to build for themselves a coherent intellectual map to predict the territory they inhabit. Essential to this structuring are several key cognitive abilities. We will look at three of them: the abilities to develop categories, to remember, and to understand cause and effect.

Categories

From a very early age, infants coordinate and organize their perceptions into categories such as soft, hard, flat, round, rigid, and flexible. For the preverbal infant, of course, these categories do not have labels

❶ *Answer to Observational Quiz (from page 162):*
He sees a visual cliff. It has the same attractive pattern as the surface on which he rests, but he perceives a 1-meter drop (that's why he hesitates).

BAILLARGEON'S TEST OF OBJECT PERMANENCE

Renée Baillargeon and her colleagues conducted a series of experiments to see whether infants under 8 months of age realize that objects still exist when they cannot be seen. In one, Baillargeon (1987) placed 3½- and 4½-month-old infants directly in front of a large screen that was hinged along its base to the center of a tabletop. The screen was then repeatedly rotated back and forth through a 180-degree arc (see Figure 6.1) until, as habituation occurred, the infants began to look away. At that point, a box was placed directly in the path of the screen's backward descent. Then the screen was rotated again, rising until it reached its full vertical height, which concealed the box from view. Thereafter, two experimental conditions followed. In the first, named the "possible event," the screen continued to move until it was intercepted by the box and stopped, as one would expect. In the second, named the "impossible event," the screen moved through its entire 180-degree arc, as if no box were in the way. (In fact, although the babies didn't see it happen, the box had dropped through a trapdoor before the screen could hit it.)

(a) Habituation

(b) Placing the box

(c) Possible event

(d) Impossible event

Even 4½-month-old infants stared longer at the impossible event than at the possible event, as if they were curious and surprised. Their longer stares mean that the babies had three expectations (Baillargeon & DeVos, 1992):

- The box continued to exist behind the screen.
- The screen could not rotate through the space occupied by the box.
- The screen would stop short.

When the screen did not stop short (in the impossible event), the infants' reactions proved that they have some concept of object permanence, as well as dynamic perception, long before they uncover attractive toys at 8 months.

Many other procedures also prove that infants understand object permanence months before they demonstrate it on Piaget's hidden-object task (Baillargeon, 1995). In each case, young infants have looked significantly longer at "impossible events" in which objects appeared to move through other—hidden—solid objects. These experiments also reveal that infants expect hidden objects to retain their original size, rigidity, and location and even expect hidden objects to support other—visible—objects. All told, young infants have an impressive understanding of object permanence long before they can uncover a hidden toy.

This series of experiments proves something about adult concepts as well. Piaget's experiment proved to him that infants do not understand object permanence, because he failed to realize that the experiment's design itself kept babies from showing what they know. Piaget's mistake is not so unusual; anyone might notice a bit of ignorance in someone else and assume that it represents much more incompetence than it really does. The surprising part is that Piaget's basic finding was accepted by the scientific community for almost 50 years, from about 1940 to 1990—until finally some iconoclastic young researchers began to prove him wrong.

Figure 6.1 The Old Screen-and-Box Game. The basic steps of Renée Baillargeon's test of object permanence—a test that doesn't depend on the infant's searching abilities or motivation to search. (a) First the infant is habituated to the movement of a hinged screen that rotates through a 180-degree arc toward and (as shown) away from the infant. (b) Next, with the infant observing, a box is placed in the backward path of the screen. Then the infant witnesses two events: (c) the "possible event," in which the screen's movement through the arc is stopped by the box, and (d) the "impossible event," in which the screen completes its movement through the arc as though the box did not exist. Infants as young as 4½ months old stare longer at the impossible event, indicating they are aware that the box does exist even though they cannot see it behind the screen.

Peek-a-Boo Edwin's father ducks down behind the pillow and then reappears, time after time, to his son's delight.
❓ *Observational Quiz (see answer page 168):* How old is Edwin?

such as "soft" and "hard," yet they provide a useful and important way of organizing the world. For example, once an object is mentally placed into a category (say, "soft"), the infant has a ready set of expectations about what that object affords (perhaps "nice to touch" and "graspable") and can distinguish it from objects that belong to other categories.

Infants younger than 6 months can categorize objects on the basis of their shape, color, angularity, density, relative size, and, to the amazement of researchers, number (up to three objects) (Haith & Benson, 1998). Taken as a whole, the evidence suggests that young infants do not merely perceive the difference between shapes such as circles versus squares or relative sizes such as larger and smaller; they also apply organizing principles that enable them to develop a concept of what is, or is not, relevant for inclusion in each category.

Many researchers believe that a rudimentary understanding of certain categories in the natural world may be biologically based ("hard-wired" in the brain) but that experience with different objects and events is also essential for developing the innate ability to sort things into categories.

Experience becomes especially significant when we observe that as infants get older, they categorize with increasing complexity. For example, infants as young as 3 months old seem to understand "above" and "below." At least, after they see several depictions of a small diamond-shaped dot above a line, their longer stares suggest that they notice when the diamond switches to being below the line. However, the above–below distinction escapes them if the target object varies from trial to trial—from the diamond to, say, a tiny arrow, to the letter "E," a plus sign, and then a triangle. By the age of 6 months, though, the concepts of "above" and "below" are more firmly established. Then, varying the object does not distract babies from paying attention to an object below a line after seeing various objects above it (Quinn et al., 1996).

Other experiments have shown that by the end of the first year, babies can categorize and discriminate between photographs, all the same size, of:

- Animals, distinguishing them according to tail width or leg length (Younger, 1990, 1993)
- Birds (as a group different from other animals), by perceiving pictures of parakeets as being similar to pictures of hawks but distinct from those of horses (Roberts, 1988)
- Kitchen utensils, as a category different from other objects (Mandler & McDonough, 1998)
- Physical appearance of strangers, distinguishing men from women, children from adults, and beautiful people from less attractive ones (Rubenstein et al., 1999)
- At about a year, dogs as distinct from cats (Mandler & McDonough, 1998)

The categories that infants construct and use to recognize the subjects of photos, as in these examples, are quite simple; they have little of the complexity of the verbally labeled, and often highly ordered, categories that older children construct. Nevertheless, they form a foundation for later cognitive accomplishments, and they enable young infants to conceptualize their world in increasingly more meaningful ways.

Memory

Most adults cannot remember specific events from their very early years. (The experiences they think they recall are often ones that they were later told about by relatives or friends or that have been memorialized in family photographs, home movies, and the like.) Freud specifically described **infantile amnesia,** a hypothesis he thought was a fact—that no one could remember anything that happened before the age of 2 years or anything but very important events that occurred before the age of 5. Piaget likewise emphasized the absence of early memories and the pure fantasy of what we "recollect" from early childhood.

infantile amnesia The inability, hypothesized by Freud, to remember anything that happened before the age of 2 years or anything but very important events that occurred before the age of 5.

Freud and Piaget were not alone in their conclusion. The consensus, from both common sense and research, has been that infants' *long-term memory*—the ability to store information in memory and then retrieve it after days, months, and years—is very poor.

However, here again, researchers have recently revised their assessment. To be sure, in their first 6 months babies have great difficulty storing new memories. But they can show that they remember provided that (1) the situations used by researchers are similar to real life, (2) motivation is high, and (3) special measures aid memory retrieval.

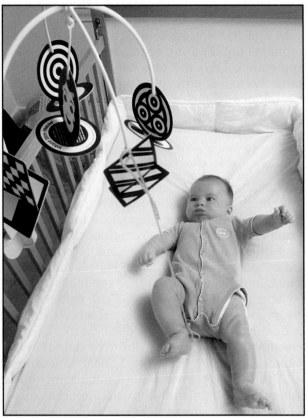

He Remembers! In this demonstration of Rovee-Collier's experiment, a young infant immediately remembers how to make the familiar mobile move. (Unfamiliar mobiles don't provoke the same reaction.) He kicks both legs and flails both arms, just as he learned to do so successfully several weeks ago.

❷ Observational Quiz (see answer page 170): *What four physiological signs of concentrated effort do you see?*

reminder session An experience that includes some aspect (a sight, a smell, a sound) of something to be remembered and thus serves to trigger the entire memory.

Memory Span and Reminder Sessions

A series of innovative experiments, notable in memory research, taught 3-month-olds to make a mobile move by kicking their legs (Rovee-Collier, 1987, 1990, 1999). The infants lay on their backs, in their own cribs, connected to a brightly colored mobile by means of a ribbon tied to one foot. Virtually all the infants began making some occasional kicks (as well as random arm movements and noise) and realized after a while that kicking made the mobile move. They then kicked more vigorously and often, sometimes laughing at their accomplishment. So far, this is no surprise—we know that such control of movement is highly reinforcing to infants. But would the infants remember this experience?

When some infants had the mobile-and-ribbon apparatus reinstalled in their cribs *1 week later,* most started to kick immediately—indicating that they did remember. But when other infants were retested 2 *weeks later,* they did not kick any more than they had before they were hooked up to the mobile. Apparently they forgot what they had learned.

However, a further experiment demonstrated a remarkable effect: The infants could remember after 2 weeks *if* they were given a brief reminder session prior to the retesting (Rovee-Collier & Hayne, 1987). A **reminder session** is any perceptual experience that might make a person recollect an idea or thing but that does not test the actual memory. In this particular reminder session, 2 weeks after the initial training the infants watched the mobile move but were not tied to the ribbon and were positioned so that they could not kick. The next day, when they were again connected to the mobile and positioned so that they could move their legs, they kicked as they had learned to do 2 weeks earlier. In effect, their faded memory had been reactivated by watching the mobile move on the previous day.

❓ **Especially for Social Workers:** Suppose you suspect that an infant, not yet talking, has been mistreated, but no bruises or other signs are present. Is there any way you can confirm your suspicions?

❶ *Answer to Observational Quiz (from page 166):* Look at his legs—he is trying to stand, a milestone normally attained at 10 months, but variable. Edwin could be as young as 7 months or as old as 1 year. The better clue is cognitive. Unless he is mentally retarded, object permanence in this manifestation begins at 8 months and is no longer so much fun at 12 months (unless the hiding is less obvious). In fact, Edwin is 10 months old.

deferred imitation   The ability to witness, remember, and later copy a particular behavior.

Further research shows that the specific conditions of the reminder session can make remembering either easier or harder. For example, a mobile in the same room is easier to remember than the identical mobile in a different room. It is even better if the same music is playing and the same smells are in the air (Rubin et al., 1998). A slight difference—for example, between a mobile with an obvious letter "Q" and one with an obvious letter "O"—can make remembering much less likely (Gerhardstein et al., 1998).

Carolyn Rovee-Collier, the lead researcher in this series of experiments, believes that natural reminder sessions are part of every infant's daily experience, because the same events and circumstances occur day after day. For example, parents regularly shake a rattle and then put it in the baby's hand. If one day they simply show the rattle, the infant might reach out to grab and shake it, remembering what the rattle does. Such events are common, and if adults are alert, they will notice that very young infants remember. They will also notice that infants do not remember much. Under the age of 6 months, they recall only for a limited period of time, only under specific conditions, and probably only events that include their own activities (Hayne, Rovee-Collier, & Gerhardstein, 1995).

Deferred Imitation

After they are 6 months old, infants become capable of retaining information for longer periods of time, and they can do so with less training and less reminding. Toward the end of the first year, a new memory ability is apparent: **deferred imitation,** the ability to remember and imitate behaviors that have been witnessed but never personally performed. For example, suppose a 9-month-old watches someone playing with a toy the baby has never seen before. The next day, if given the toy, the 9-month-old is likely to play with it in the same way as the person he or she observed had played. (Younger infants do not usually do this.)

Over the next few months, deferred imitation becomes more elaborate (Barr et al., 1996; Heimann & Meltzoff, 1996). Infants retain more details, including the sequence of events, and they can duplicate those details days later, prompted by only minimal clues associated with the experience—such as a sound or a part of the setting (Bauer & Mandler, 1992). A 1-year-old, for instance, might stare intently as an adult opens the refrigerator, takes out an egg carton, and cracks a few eggs into a bowl. The next day (perhaps when the adult has left the refrigerator open while answering the phone), the child might take out the egg carton and crack all the remaining eggs—in a bowl, if one happens to be visible and within reach, or, if not, in the sink or the garbage pail or even on the floor.

Play It Again, Sam This is probably deferred imitation if this toddler saw someone else playing the piano and now has a chance to try it.

Cause and Effect

Another major cognitive accomplishment is recognizing the causes of events and the effects they produce. Infants' ability to understand and even anticipate events (e.g., shoving one toy into another to send the

MEMORY OVER YEARS

What about memories that last not merely for days or weeks, but for years? We know that this accomplishment is possible in older children and adults, but researchers are amazed that it occurs in infancy as well.

In one study, conducted in a university laboratory, 6-month-olds were trained during a single 20-minute session to reach for a dangling Big Bird toy when it made a noise, first in normal lighting and then in the dark (Perris et al., 1990). Two years later, the same children were brought back to the lab and retested on this reaching task, as were 2½-year-olds—a control group—who had received no training. Prior to the retesting, the trained children were interviewed to see if they had any explicit memory of the laboratory setting or the training experience. They did not. Then, 30 minutes before testing, half of all the children who were to participate were randomly selected and given a 3-second exposure to the sound of the toy in the dark—intended as a possible reminder session for those in the trained group.

In the retesting that followed, the conditions of the original test were repeated: Each child sat in his or her mother's lap and was told the lights would go out. Then, in the dark, the experimenter dangled the noisemaking toy in front of the child. Compared with the untrained children, those who had been trained at 6 months were more likely to reach for and grab the toy—just as they had done long ago! In fact, among those who experienced the 3-second reminder session, the trained children reached for the toy almost four times as often as the untrained children. Moreover, their reaction to suddenly being in the dark was "an almost global emotional acceptance," in marked contrast to the discomfort and fussiness exhibited by many children from the control group (and, indeed, by most 2½-year-olds who suddenly find themselves in a dark, unfamiliar room!). Thus, not only the specific behaviors of a single training experience at age 6 months but also the emotional tone of that experience can remain in the memory of a young child for 2 full years.

Developmentalists now are reexamining many aspects of infant memory to discover exactly how it functions. So far, they have concluded that:

- Early in life, even under the best of conditions, long-term-memory storage and retrieval appear to be fragile and uncertain, facilitated by repetition, reminders, and active involvement of the infant.
- Improvement in memory ability seems tied to brain maturation and language development, with notable increases in memory capacity and duration occurring at about 8 months, again at around 18 months, and again at age 5.

More research in this area is now under way. Thus far, we have found one surprise: Early memories are "highly enduring, and become even more so after repeated encounters with reminders" (Rovee-Collier & Gerhardstein, 1997).

The awareness that infant memories exist has been one amazing outcome of a heightened interest in human memory over the life span. As you will read later in this book, researchers are likewise impressed by the potential of preschool children to remember unusual episodes, especially ones in which they were emotionally involved. At the same time, researchers are struck by the inaccuracy of memory in adults, even during the years when we think we remember best. For all people of all ages, memory is highly selective, sometimes false,and often self-serving; this may be more so the younger a person is (Loftus, 1997).

Moreover, just like the baby whose memory is aided by reminders, adults find their memories strengthened by reminders. The difference is that for children and adults, language provides significant assistance that babies do not receive (Schneider & Bjorklund, 1998). Reminders typically occur when we write or tell our memories to someone else; this gives our audience considerable power over what those memories will be. As one psychologist explains:

> Our recollections are often elicited by and formed with other people. When this is the case, the past is created through narrative rather than being translated into narrative. . . . Think back to some charged event in your own life—perhaps the first fight you had with your spouse. Now imagine telling that story to your mate, many years later at the celebration of your twenty-fifth wedding anniversary, telling it to your divorce lawyer, telling it to your children now that they are grown up, writing it in a humorous memoir of your now famous life, or telling it to your therapist. In each case the person you are telling it to, and the reasons you are telling it, will have a formative effect on the memory itself. [Engel, 1999]

At any age, the social aspects of memory are remarkable. Someone else's memories and interpretations of an event can merge with our own; a single dramatic moment can be forgotten if others react neutrally but can be seared in our minds if others echo or exaggerate our own reaction. Just as with a baby, direct involvement, repetition, personal action, and emotional excitement make a memory last longer. Which are you most likely to remember: what your instructor said in class last week, what you said in class, or the last time you argued with your best friend?

❷ Especially for Researchers: How could you assess implicit memory for a second language in adults who heard a language in infancy (perhaps from a grandmother) but who now say they have no knowledge (explicit memory) of it?

launching event   Something that seems to start, or trigger, a particular happening. Launching events are used to study understanding of cause-and-effect relationships.

❶ Answer to Observational Quiz (from page 167):
Look again at the baby's mouth. Even though only the right leg is doing the work, infants' immature cognitive capacity makes them use every body part when they concentrate. This infant clenches his fingers, focuses both eyes, spreads the toes of his left foot, and—can you see it?—thrusts out his tongue.

❶ Response for Social Workers (from page 168): Infants do remember what has happened to them, and they show it by emotional expressions (crying or pulling away when they see someone) or deferred imitation (slapping a doll, putting a stuffed animal in a dark closet). However, lack of such evidence is not proof that nothing occurred, and it is impossible to prove all the details based on an infant's actions.

second toy flying), as well as to act effectively in the world (e.g., kicking their legs to make a mobile move or lifting a blanket to find a concealed toy), hinges on the capacity to identify cause and effect.

Cause-and-effect understanding may be studied by observing whether a child intentionally repeats some action that has produced an interesting result. An infant may squeeze a rubber duck, producing a squeak. If the child, delighted by the noise, squeezes the duck again, he or she has connected squeeze and squeak. But this method of study requires that the infant possess certain motor skills. (Even deliberately squeezing a rubber duck demands strength and hand control that are beyond the youngest infants.) For this reason, to examine early awareness of cause and effect, researchers again turn to habituation—that is, getting the infants so used to a particular experience that they become bored, then providing another experience and testing whether they realize that the situation has changed.

One specific technique uses a **launching event,** in which one action produces, or seems to produce, another. In this technique, the infant sees an object, such as a square, move in one direction across a table until it bumps into another object, such as a circle. The square stops, and the circle immediately begins moving in the same direction. The square appears to push, or "launch," the circle into motion. By contrast, if the circle begins to move before the square bumps it, or a second or two after it is hit, most adults would conclude that the square was not the cause of the circle's movement.

Do young babies draw similar inferences? In some studies, infants were first habituated to the bump-and-move launching event as described above and were then shown variations of it (such as the circle moving before contact or after a delay). These studies revealed that infants under 6 months notice whether an object is moving along or not, but they do not seem to understand cause and effect; they don't seem surprised or even particularly interested when movement occurs without a bump or much after it. However, 10-month-olds can properly interpret the cause-and-effect nature of simple launching events like this, and they are surprised when the effect doesn't happen as it should (Cohen & Amsel, 1998; Cohen & Oakes, 1993; Leslie & Keeble, 1987).

The surprising competencies we have surveyed—dynamic perception, object permanence, number awareness, categorization, memory, expectation, delayed imitation, and cause-and-effect understanding—can all be considered indications of intelligence in infancy. Clearly, this kind of thinking is not the symbolic, language-based intelligence used by older children and adults. Nonetheless, research reflects astonishing abilities in very young beings, far beyond what most people assume possible and beyond what even the experts recently believed.

PIAGET'S SENSORIMOTOR INTELLIGENCE

So far, our account of infant cognitive development relies heavily on laboratory research. It may, therefore, seem to depict infants as unable to demonstrate any cognition except under very unusual conditions. Do not be misled. Such an image omits one of the most important characteristics of young babies: their *active intelligence*. This aspect of intelligence is central to Jean Piaget's theory of infants' cognitive development.

Active Intelligence

More than 70 years ago, starting with the study of his own three children, Piaget discovered that infants are indeed active learners. Piaget believed that humans of every age actively seek to comprehend their world and that their understanding of it reflects specific, age-related cognitive stages. This seeking, he said, begins at birth and accelerates rapidly in the early months of life. To Piaget, infants might lack words, concepts, and ideas, but they are nevertheless intelligent; their intelligence functions exclusively through the senses and motor skills. Consequently, Piaget called the intelligence of infants **sensorimotor intelligence** and the first period of cognitive development the *sensorimotor period* (as we saw in Chapter 2).

What did Piaget mean by saying that infants think exclusively with their senses and motor skills? As Flavell (1985) expresses it, the infant "exhibits a wholly practical, perceiving-and-doing, action-bound kind of intellectual functioning: he does not exhibit the more contemplative, reflective, symbol-manipulating kind we usually think of in connection with cognition." Piaget was actually incorrect in his belief that infants do not develop concepts—as we have seen, infants have a fairly rich set of conceptual categories and assumptions—and some of his other proposals have also been revised by recent findings. Nonetheless, his portrayal of the "practical, perceiving-and-doing" side of early intelligence remains valid.

sensorimotor intelligence Piaget's term for the intelligence of infants during the first (sensorimotor) period of cognitive development, when babies think by using the senses and motor skills.

Six Stages of Infant Cognition

According to Piaget, sensorimotor intelligence develops through six successive stages, each characterized by a somewhat different way of understanding the world. Taken together, they provide a vivid description of the ways in which infants demonstrate their growing cognitive abilities. We shall follow the arrangement in Table 6.1 as we briefly examine these stages. We shall also be highlighting the progression of infants' cognitive growth—from reflexes to deliberate responses to the beginning of symbolic understanding.

Stages One and Two: Reflexes and First Adaptations

Sensorimotor intelligence begins with newborns' *reflexes*, such as sucking and grasping, and with sensory responses that are so automatic they seem like reflexes, such as looking and listening. Through the repeated exercise of these reflexes over the first month, newborns gain important information about the world—information that allows them to

---

table **6.1**	**The Six Stages of Sensorimotor Intelligence**

For an overview of the stages of sensorimotor thought, it helps to group the six stages into pairs.

The first two stages involve the infant's responses to its own body (sometimes called *primary circular reactions*):

Stage One (birth to 1 month)	*Reflexes*—sucking, grasping, staring, listening.
Stage Two (1–4 months)	*The first acquired adaptations*—assimilation and coordination of reflexes—sucking a pacifier differently from a nipple; grabbing a bottle to suck it.

The next two stages involve the infant's responses to objects and people (sometimes called *secondary circular reactions*):

Stage Three (4–8 months)	*Making interesting sights last*—actively responding to people and objects.
Stage Four (8–12 months)	*New adaptation and anticipation*—becoming more planful, deliberate, and purposeful in responding to people and objects.

The last two stages are the most creative, first with action and then with ideas (sometimes called *tertiary circular reactions*):

Stage Five (12–18 months)	*New means through active experimentation*—experimentation and creativity in the actions of the "little scientist."
Stage Six (18–24 months)	*New means through mental combinations*—considering before doing provides the child with new ways of achieving a goal without resorting to trial-and-error experiments.

Stage Two Sucking everything is a mere reflex in the first month of life, but by 3 months Katie has already learned that some objects afford better sucking than others. Many infants her age have learned not to suck on people's faces, but with this mother, that adaptation is not necessary.

❶ **Response for Researchers (from page 170):**
You could not simply test them, because that would be explicit memory. You would need to try to teach them something, perhaps a poem, in the original language, to see how quickly they would learn it. To make it scientifically valid, you would need to teach the same poem to a control group who never knew that language and then compare learning time for the two groups.

begin stage two, the *adaptation* of their reflexes to the specifics of the environment.

Adaptation occurs in two complementary ways: by assimilation and by accommodation (as you learned in Chapter 2). *Assimilation* means taking new information into the mind by incorporating it into previously developed mental categories, or action patterns, or, in Piaget's terminology, "schemas." *Accommodation* means taking new information into the mind in such a way that the person readjusts, refines, or expands previous schemas.

Consider sucking, for example. Newborns suck anything that touches their lips—a reflex that shows assimilation. Then, at about the age of 1 month, according to Piaget, infants start to adapt their sucking to specific objects. Some items, such as the nipple of a bottle (for a breast-fed infant), require merely assimilation: Suck it reflexively and get nourishment. Others require more accommodation: Pacifiers need to be sucked without the suction, tongue-pushing, and swallowing, since they do not provide food.

By 3 months, infants have organized their world into objects to be sucked for nourishment (breasts or bottles), objects to be sucked for pleasure (fingers or pacifiers), and objects not to be sucked at all (fuzzy blankets and large balls). The particulars of the sucking reflex (intensity, suction, frequency, and such) have been accommodated to these various types of objects. For example, once infants learn that some objects satisfy hunger and others do not, they will suck contentedly on a pacifier when their stomachs are full but will usually spit one out when they are hungry, again adapting a reflex.

In other words, adaptation in the beginning weeks relies on reflexive assimilation—everything suckable is assimilated as a worthy object, unless other accommodation is required. After several months, however, patterns are established: If the baby is hungry, only familiar nourishment nipples will do, and all others are to be rejected. Similarly, most babies want something to suck for comfort; if a pacifier has not been offered, they begin sucking their thumbs, fingers, or knuckles (a choice that depends on the baby).

Obviously, parents need to decide in the first—reflexes—stage whether they want to feed the baby via breast or bottle and whether they will use a pacifier. By the age of 6 months, it is difficult to introduce a pacifier to a thumb-sucking baby or a bottle to an exclusively breast-fed baby, because babies of this age are already past the stage when they can "understand" it.

Stage Three: Making Interesting Experiences Last

During stage three (age 4 to 8 months), babies interact diligently with people and objects to produce exciting experiences. Realizing that rattles make noise, for example, they shake their arms and laugh whenever someone puts a rattle in their hand. Even the sight of something that normally delights an infant—a favorite toy, a favorite food, a smiling parent—can trigger an active attempt at interaction.

Vocalization of all sorts increases a great deal at this time, and not just in a chorus (as with younger infants—when one newborn in the nursery cries, they all tend to cry). Now that babies realize that other people can and will respond, they love to make a noise, listen for a response, and answer back. Interestingly, by the age of 3 or 4 months, babies are already unlikely to make sounds at the same moment that

Stage Three This 7½-month-old knows that a squeal of delight is one way to make the interesting experience of a tickle from Daddy last.

goal-directed behavior Purposeful action initiated by infants in anticipation of events that will fulfill their needs and wishes.

someone else is talking to them. They prefer to wait for silence, then vocalize, then wait for a response. This behavior pattern becomes more pronounced as time goes on, continuing throughout stages four and five until it peaks at age 18 months, when—just as they are about to add many words to their vocabulary—babies listen most intently (Elias & Broerse, 1996).

Overall, in the third stage infants become more aware of objects and other people; they recognize some of the specific characteristics of the things in their environment, and they develop ways to interact in order to continue whatever sensations they seek. One way in which infants show this new awareness is by repeating a specific action that has just elicited a pleasing response from some person or thing. As you saw earlier, a baby might accidentally squeeze a rubber duck, hear a squeak, and squeeze the duck again. If the squeak is repeated, the infant will probably laugh and give another squeeze, delighted to be able to control the toy's actions.

Stage Four: New Adaptation and Anticipation

In stage four (age 8 to 12 months), babies adapt in new, more deliberate ways. They anticipate events that will fulfill their needs and wishes, and they try to make such events occur. A 10-month-old girl who enjoys playing in the tub might see a bar of soap, crawl over to her mother with it as a signal to start her bath, and then remove all her clothes to make her wishes crystal clear—finally squealing with delight when she hears the bath water being turned on. Similarly, if a 10-month-old boy sees his mother putting on her coat to go out without him, he might begin tugging at it to stop her or he might drag over his jacket to signal that he wants to come along.

Both these examples reveal anticipation and, even more noteworthy, **goal-directed behavior**—that is, purposeful action. The baby's obvious goal-directedness at this age stems from the development of an enhanced awareness of cause and effect and memory for actions the baby completed during this phase (as you already saw in the discussion of cognitive growth) (Willatts, 1999). And that cognitive awareness coincides with the emergence of the motor skills needed to achieve the infant's goals.

Thus a stage-four baby might see something from across the room, be attracted to it, and crawl toward it, ignoring many interesting distractions along the way. Or the baby might grab a forbidden object—a box of matches, a thumbtack, a cigarette—and cry with rage when it is taken away. Because the baby is now goal-directed, the wailing continues even if the infant is offered a substitute that he or she normally finds fascinating.

As we noted earlier, Piaget thought that the concept of object permanence begins to emerge during stage four, because at this point—and usually not before—infants actively search for objects that are no longer in view. Researchers have since shown that the concept of object permanence actually begins to emerge much earlier. However, the *goal-directed* search for toys that have fallen from the baby's crib, rolled under a couch, or disappeared under a blanket does not begin to emerge until the age of about 8 months, just as Piaget indicated.

Stages Five and Six: Experimentation

Stage five (age 12 to 18 months) builds directly on the accomplishments of stage four, as infants' goal-directed and purposeful activities become more expansive and creative after the first birthday. Toddlerhood is a time of active exploration and experimentation, a time when babies "get into everything," as though trying to discover all the possibilities their world has to offer.

Because of the experimentation that characterizes this stage, Piaget referred to the stage-five toddler as the **little scientist** who "experiments in order to see." Having discovered some action or set of actions that is possible with a given object, stage-five infants seem to ask, "What else can I do with this? What happens if I take the nipple off the bottle, or turn over the trash basket, or pour water on the cat?" Their scientific method is one of trial and error, but their devotion to discovery sounds familiar to every adult researcher.

In the final stage of sensorimotor intelligence (age 18 to 24 months), toddlers begin to anticipate and solve simple problems by using **mental combinations,** a kind of intellectual experimentation that supersedes the active experimentation of stage five. They try out various actions mentally, before actually performing them, to test what consequences the actions might bring. Thus stage-six children can invent new ways to achieve a goal without resorting to physical trial-and-error experiments. Consider how Piaget's daughter Jacqueline solved a problem she encountered at the age of 20 months:

> Jacqueline arrives at a closed door with a blade of grass in each hand. She stretches out her right hand toward the knob but sees that she cannot turn it without letting go of the grass. She puts the grass on the floor, opens the door, picks up the grass again and enters. But when she wants to leave the room, things become complicated. She puts the grass on the floor and grasps the doorknob. But then she perceives that in pulling the door toward her she will simultaneously chase away the grass which she placed between the door and the threshold. She therefore picks it up in order to put it outside the door's zone of movement. [Piaget, 1952]

Being able to use mental combinations also makes it possible for the child to pretend. A toddler might lie down on the floor, pretend to go to sleep, and then jump up laughing. Or a child might sing to a doll before tucking it into bed. This is in marked contrast to the behavior of the younger infant, who might treat a doll like any other toy, throwing it, biting it, or banging it on the floor. Piaget believed that deferred imitation also begins at stage six, although (as you saw earlier) under proper conditions deferred imitation (and many other abilities of sensorimotor intelligence) can begin much earlier than Piaget's stages.

Nonetheless, Piaget was not completely wrong about deferred imitation—or anything else, for that matter. Deferred imitation comes to full flower at stage six, as children then act out entire sequences of actions that they have observed earlier. This is one of many reasons why adults need to mind their behavior when a toddler is present: Embarrassing actions might be revealed to other people a few days later.

little scientist   Piaget's term for the stage-five toddler (age 12 to 18 months), who actively experiments to learn about the properties of objects.

mental combinations   Sequences of actions developed intellectually, before they are actively performed. Mental combinations are a characteristic of the toddlers at Piaget's stage six of sensorimotor intelligence.

Intellectual Ability in Evidence Brandon has a goal firmly in mind and is wielding the tools to attain it—an achievement beyond most younger babies. At age 12 months he is about to enter a more elaborate stage of goal-directedness, one in which he might deliberately drop a few peas on the floor, or smash a few noodles on his head, or turn his plate upside down—all as "experiments in order to see."

LANGUAGE DEVELOPMENT

Mastering the sounds and meanings of one's first language is "doubtless the greatest intellectual feat any one of us is ever required to perform," according to one early developmental scholar (Bloomfield, 1933).

Children the world over follow the same sequence of early language development, although the timing of their accomplishments may vary considerably (see Table 6.2). Indeed, about 10 percent of 24-month-olds have a vocabulary of more than 550 words, but another 10 percent speak fewer than 100 words—more than a fivefold difference (Merriman, 1998). Researchers agree about both the variability and the sequence of language learning, so our discussion begins with those topics.

First Noises and Gestures

Infants are equipped to learn language even before birth, partly due to brain readiness and partly due to their auditory experiences during the final prenatal months (Aslin et al., 1998). Newborns prefer hearing speech over other sounds, prefer "baby talk" over normal speech, and, as you saw in Chapter 4, listen more readily to their own mothers' voices than to voices of other adults, even other mothers (Fifer & Moon, 1995). Moreover, as you also saw in Chapter 4, infants as young as 1 month can distinguish among many different speech sounds, including sounds that adults no longer can differentiate (Sansavini et al., 1997; Werker, 1989). To every young infant, the sound of the human voice—whether it comes from Mommy or Daddy, another child, or a stranger

table 6.2	The Development of Spoken Language: The First 2 Years
Age*	Means of Communication
Newborn	Reflexive communication—cries, movements, facial expressions.
2 months	A range of meaningful noises—cooing, fussing, crying, laughing.
3–6 months	New sounds, including squeals, growls, croons, trills, vowel sounds.
6–10 months	Babbling, including both consonant and vowel sounds repeated in syllables.
10–12 months	Comprehension of simple words; simple intonations; specific vocalizations that have meaning to those who know the infant well. Deaf babies express their first signs; hearing babies use specific gestures (e.g., pointing) to communicate.
13 months	First spoken words that are recognizably part of the native language.
13–18 months	Slow growth of vocabulary, up to about 50 words.
18 months	Vocabulary spurt—three or more words learned per day.
21 months	First two-word sentence.
24 months	Multiword sentences. Half the infant's utterances are two or more words long.

*The ages of accomplishment in this table reflect norms. Many healthy and intelligent children attain these steps in language development earlier or later than indicated here.
Sources: Bloom, 1993; Lenneberg, 1967.

speaking a language no one understands—evokes special interest and curiosity.

Very young babies do much more than listen. They are noisy creatures—crying, cooing, and making a variety of other sounds even in the first weeks of life. These noises gradually become more varied over the first months, and by the age of 4 months, most babies have verbal repertoires that include squeals, growls, gurgles, grunts, croons, and yells, as well as some speechlike sounds.

The first sounds are actually reflexes, uttered whether or not someone else is talking, but by 4 months they are more deliberate, uttered now as conversation, with the pauses that are proper to turn-taking. If caregivers have been attentive in the early weeks, a whimper now means "I'm awake and hungry," and the response "Oh, I'm coming" is usually sufficient to halt a demanding cry (perhaps meaning "Get me food now!").

Babbling

babbling   The extended repetition of certain syllables, such as "ba-ba-ba," that begins at about 6 or 7 months of age.

By 6 or 7 months of age, babies begin to repeat certain syllables ("ma-ma-ma," "da-da-da," "ba-ba-ba"), a phenomenon referred to as **babbling** because of the way it sounds. In some respects, babbling is universal—all babies do it, and the sounds they make are similar no matter what language their parents speak. However, over the next few months, babbling begins to vary and to incorporate more and more sounds from the native language, perhaps as infants imitate the sounds they hear (Boysson-Bardies et al., 1989; Masataka, 1992). Many cultures assign important meanings to some of these sounds, with "ma-ma-ma," "da-da-da," and "pa-pa-pa" usually taken to apply to significant people in the infant's life (Bloom, 1998). (See Table 6.3.)

Deaf babies begin to make babbling sounds several months later than hearing infants, and they make the sounds less frequently (Oller & Eilers, 1988). However, deaf infants may actually begin babbling manually at about the same time hearing infants begin babbling orally (Petitto & Marentette, 1991). Analysis of videotapes of deaf children whose parents communicate via sign language reveals that before their tenth month, these infants use about a dozen distinct hand gestures—most of which resemble basic elements of the American Sign Language used by their parents—in a rhythmic, repetitive manner analogous to oral babbling.

Too Young for Language? No. The early stages of language are communication through noise, gestures, and facial expressions—all very evident between this Kung grandmother and granddaughter.

Actually, both hearing and deaf babies communicate with gestures, such as lifting their hands to be picked up, at about 10 months of age. And both hearing and deaf babies do some spontaneous manual babbling as well as oral babbling. For obvious reasons, however, deaf infants reduce their oral babbling and increase their gesturing just when hearing babies do the opposite (Petitto & Marentette, 1991).

First Words and Sentences

Finally, at about 1 year of age, the average baby speaks a few words, not pronounced clearly or used precisely. Usually, caregivers hear and understand the first word before strangers do, which makes it hard for re-

table **6.3**	**First Sounds and First Words: Cross-Linguistic Similarities**	
	Baby's Word for:	
Language	Mother	Father
English	mama, mommy	dada, daddy
Spanish	mama	papa
French	maman, mama	papa
Italian	mamma	babbo, papa
Latvian	mama	tēte
Syrian Arabic	mama	baba
Bantu	ba-mama	taata
Swahili	mama	baba
Sanskrit	nana	tata
Hebrew	ema	abba
Korean	oma	apa

searchers to pinpoint exactly what a 12-month-old can say (Bloom, 1998). For example, at 13 months, Kyle knew "da," "ba," "tam," "opma," and "daes," which his parents knew to be "downstairs," "bottle," "tummy," "oatmeal," and "starfish" (yes, that's what "daes" meant) (Lewis et al., 1999).

Once the vocabulary reaches about 50 words, it begins to build more rapidly—in some children by 100 or more words per month (Fensen et al., 1994). Toddlers differ in how their vocabularies grow: Some children (called *referential*) primarily learn naming words (such as "dog," "cup," and "ball"), whereas others (called *expressive*) acquire mainly words that can be used in social interaction (such as "please," "want," and "stop") (Nelson, 1981). Such differences no doubt reflect individual personality and family emphases (Dixon & Shore, 1997). Culture also shapes early language acquisition. North American infants, for example, tend to be more referential than Japanese infants, partly because playing with toys and labeling objects are more central in North American families (Fernald & Morikawa, 1993).

At first, toddlers are quite imprecise in the way they connect the words they know to the people, objects, and events around them. One common inaccuracy is **underextension,** applying a word more narrowly than it usually is applied. The word "cat" may be used to name only the family cat, for example, and no other feline. Another inaccuracy is that a toddler might learn one name for something and then resist alternative names—insisting, for example, that the little fuzzy, yellow, winged thing the toddler calls a "bird" is not a "chick," as Grandpa keeps calling it (Shatz, 1994). This is called the *mutual exclusivity bias* (Merriman, 1998).

A bit later the opposite tendency appears, with words being applied beyond their meaning. This characteristic, known as **overextension,** or *overgeneralization,* might lead one child to call anything round "ball" and another to call every four-legged creature "doggie."

As their vocabularies expand, toddlers seem to "experiment in order to see" with words just as they do with objects. Little scientists

underextension   The use of a word to refer only to certain things, even though the word is generally applied more broadly by most people.

overextension   The application of a newly learned word to a variety of objects that may share a particular characteristic but are not in the general category described by that word. (Also called *overgeneralization.*)

become "little linguists." It is not unusual for 18-month-olds to walk down the street pointing to every animal, asking "Doggie?" or "Horsie?" or "Kitty?" or, again and again, "Wha' dat?"—perhaps to confirm their hypotheses about which words go with which animals.

As children learn their first words, they become adept at expressing intention, using intonation and gestures and a single word that expresses a complete thought; such a word is called a **holophrase.** "Doggie?" is a holophrase meaning "Is that a dog?" Of course, the same word can express different ideas, depending on the situation. When a toddler pushes at a closed door and says "bye-bye!" in a demanding tone, it is clear that the child wishes to go out. When a toddler, upon the arrival of the baby-sitter, holds on to Mommy's legs and plaintively says "bye-bye," it is equally clear that the child is pleading with Mommy not to leave.

Within about 6 months of speaking their first words, children begin to learn new words more rapidly. Soon after that spurt, they start to put words together. As a general rule, the first two-word sentence occurs at about 21 months of age, with some normal infants achieving this milestone at 15 months and others not reaching it until 24 months.

Combining words demands considerable linguistic understanding because word order affects the meaning of a sentence. However, even in their first sentences, toddlers demonstrate that they have figured out the basics. They declare "Baby cry" or ask "More juice" rather than the reverse. And, by the time they get to three-word sentences at age 2, they will say, properly, "Kitty jumping down," as Sarah does in the In Person box.

holophrase A single word that expresses a complete thought.

Cultural Values If his infancy is like that of most babies raised in the relatively taciturn Ottavado culture of Ecuador, this 2-month-old will hear significantly less conversation than infants from most other regions of the world. According to many learning theorists, a lack of reinforcement will result in a child who is much less verbal, and in most Western cultures that might be called educational neglect. However, each culture tends to encourage the qualities it most needs and values, and verbal fluency is not a priority in this community. In fact, people who talk too much are ostracized, and those who keep secrets are valued.

❷ **Especially for Educators:** How would you instruct caregivers to interact with infants to help language development proceed as well as possible?

Adults and Babies Teach Each Other

As we said, researchers agree as to what the early stages of language acquisition are, but they do not agree about why. Theories of language learning abound. Early researchers on language development tended to choose one of two positions. They focused either on the ways parents teach language to their infants or on the emergence of the infant's innate language abilities.

Two Theories: Nurture versus Nature

The focus on parents' teaching arose from B. F. Skinner's learning theory, which held that conditioning (learning) could explain verbal behavior just as well as it could explain other types of behavior (Skinner, 1957). According to this theory, for example, if a baby's babbling is reinforced with food and attention from the very first time it occurs, the baby will soon be calling "mama," "dada," or "baba" whenever the baby wants his or her mother, father, or bottle. Many learning theorists believe that the quantity and quality of parents' talking to their child affect the child's rate of language development, from the early words through complex sentences. Further, just as Pavlov's dogs learned to associate the sound of the bell with the smell of the meat (Chapter 2), learning theorists find that infants associate objects with names, thus learning their first words (Smith, 1995).

LISTEN TO YOUR OWN

It is easy to undervalue children's language learning, since it seems to occur quite effortlessly. But, as with sunrise and sunset, we should not take it for granted just because it happens often. Imagine yourself as a tourist in a foreign land, surrounded by natives chattering rapidly in a language quite different from your own. Without extensive experience in that language, you could not even tell where one word stops and another begins; or which nuances of tone and pronunciation are significant and which are merely variations in individual speech; or how the string of sounds works together to make statements or questions; or, most important, whether the content of the conversation should make you embarrassed, frightened, or delighted.

Lost as you might be, at least you would know that spoken sounds have specific meanings. The newborn, of course, does not know even this, yet typically by age 2 "children, bright and dull, pampered or neglected, exposed to Tlingit or to English" all learn language (Wanner & Gleitman, 1982).

Consider, for example, the words, grammar, and conversational skill of 24-month-old Sarah, who was determined to distract her silent mother from intently revising an earlier edition of this textbook:

"Uh, oh. Kitty jumping down."

"What drawing? Numbers?" [said as her words were being transcribed]

"Want it, paper."

"Wipe it, pencil."

"What time it is?" [said about her mother's watch]

These sentences show that Sarah had a varied vocabulary and a basic understanding of word order. For example, Sarah said "Kitty jumping down" (noun, verb, adverb) rather than "Down jumping kitty" or any of the four other, less conventional combinations of these three words. Sarah's speech also shows that she had much to learn, for she incorrectly used the pronoun "it" and its referent together ("it, paper," "it, pencil"), omitted personal pronouns, and used declarative rather than inquisitive word order in asking a question ("What time it is?").

But beyond demonstrating specifics of English vocabulary and grammar, Sarah's words show something even more critical. By the time she reached age 2, Sarah had learned the universal function of language—to express one's thoughts and wishes to another using accepted signals, codes, and cues. Despite my preoccupation and nonresponsiveness, Sarah produced seven successive sentences crafted to entice me into a dialogue. The final question—"What time it is?"—reveals considerable sophistication about the rules of polite conversation: Sarah must have noticed that almost any adult, even a stranger on the street, usually answers that particular question.

Sarah's impressive though imperfect language is quite similar to that of 2-year-olds in many families and cultures. Much of the research on early language over the past 30 years began with a researcher writing down the words of his or her own child and then testing various hypotheses by studying many other children. You can do the same with your own children, your relatives, or even strangers at the supermarket. Writing down exactly what a 24-month-old says and then noting the communication skill embedded in the simple words may astonish you—just as a sunrise might.

language acquisition device (LAD)
Chomsky's term for a brain structure or organization that he hypothesized was responsible for the innate human ability to acquire language, including the basic aspects of grammar.

The opposite focus, on innate language ability, came from the theories of Noam Chomsky (1968, 1980) and his followers, who believe that language is too complex to be mastered so early and so easily through conditioning. Chomsky noted that all young children worldwide master the rudiments of grammar and that all do so at approximately the same age. This, he said, implies that the human brain is uniquely equipped with some sort of structure or organization that facilitates language development. Somewhat boldly, Chomsky labeled this theoretical facilitator the **language acquisition device,** abbreviated **LAD.** The LAD enables children to quickly and efficiently derive rules of grammar from the

Lots of Communication Mother–toddler conversations that are rich with facial expressions, gestures, and the dramatic intonation of an occasional word are universal, as is illustrated by this winning pair in a Mexican market.

baby talk The special form of language that adults use when they talk to babies, with shorter, more emphatic sentences and higher, more melodious pitch. (Sometimes called *motherese.*)

❶ **Response for Educators (from page 178):** Encourage communication of all sorts—with facial expressions, gestures, and words. Talk should be responsive, simple, and repetitious. "Baby talk" is fine, as long as infants also hear some talk at a level slightly above their expressed ability.

speech they hear every day, regardless of whether their native language is English, Chinese, or Urdu. Other theorists have proposed other innate structures to facilitate other features of language learning (Pinker, 1994).

Social Interaction

Research in recent years has suggested that both Skinner's and Chomsky's theories have some validity but that both miss the mark (Bates & Carnevale, 1994; Bloom, 1991; Golinkoff & Hirsh-Pasek, 1990; Jusczyk, 1997). One reason is that both theories overlook the social context in which the actual language-learning process occurs, a social context framed by the adult's teaching sensitivity as well as the child's learning ability. Every infant makes expressive noises, but if caregivers are too intrusive (interrupting with a lesson, demanding responses) or too negligent (ignoring various preverbal noises), the infant will learn more slowly (Baumwell et al., 1997). The crucial factor seems to be catching the infant's mood and attention and responding with simple language as if the exchange were a conversation (Tomasello, 1996). Adults often use **baby talk,** with shorter words and sentences, higher and more varied pitch, repetitions, and longer pauses than they use in ordinary speech.

Infants are genetically primed to pick up language (Chomsky was right), and, on the whole, caregivers are surprisingly skilled at facilitating infants' language learning (Skinner was right). However, it is this *combination* of learner and teacher and context that achieves the language explosion we see in children (Messer, 1994; Moerk, 1996). This gives rise to a third theory, which emphasizes the social interaction, or sociocultural, approach. Within that theory, some emphasize the parent's side of the interaction. Jerome Bruner, for instance, emphasized that LAD could work only if something he called LASS (Language Acquisition Support System) was firmly in place (Bruner, 1983). Others emphasize that the child takes the lead, initiating most early conversa-

A Family in Nairobi This baby's intellectual development is well nourished.
❷ *Observational Quiz (see answer page 183): Can you spot four signs of this?*

tions, incorporating some words and rejecting others (most 1-year-olds use "no" often and "yes" never), and, in some cultures, learning to talk without any explicit adult encouragement (Bloom, 1998). What adults should do is also controversial, as the discussion of baby talk in the Changing Policy box explains.

Evidence for the interactive nature of early language is apparent to anyone who observes babies. Infants have a "deep biological need to interact emotionally with the people that love and care for them," and this pushes them to talk (Locke, 1993). The need of adults to communicate with infants is no less strong. Even strangers on the street feel compelled to smile and talk to a baby, as they never would to an unfamiliar adult. Language is essentially a social activity, not merely a cognitive one (Carpenter et al., 1998).

Once the child begins to talk, observations of exchanges between parent and child show the adult interpreting the child's imperfect speech and then responding by using short, repeated, clear sentences the child can understand and by placing special emphasis on important words. Naturalistic observation is the best way to study such interactions, for facial expression and intonation are as much a part of baby talk as the words that are spoken. However, recorded dialogues convey the flavor of these exchanges. One mother is putting her toddler son to bed:

Mother: And when you get up in the morning, you'll go for a walk.
Nigel: Tik.
Mother: And you'll see some sticks, yes.
Nigel: Hoo.
Mother: And some holes, yes.
Nigel: Da.
Mother: Yes, now it's getting dark.
Nigel: I wa. *(Repeats this 12 times.)*
Mother: What?
Nigel: I wa. *(Repeats this 6 times.)* Peaz.
Mother: What do you want in bed? Jamie? *(his doll)*
Nigel: No!
Mother: You want your eiderdown? *(his quilt)*
Nigel: *(Grins.)* Yeah!
Mother: Why didn't you say so? Your eiderdown.
Nigel: Ella. *(Repeats 2 times.)* [Halliday, 1979]

In most episodes of two-way baby talk, the toddler is an active participant, responding to the speaker and making his or her needs known. In this one, Nigel asked for his quilt a total of 18 times, persisting until his mother got the point. An analysis of toddlers' speech shows that, especially after the vocabulary spurt begins, early speech is almost never idle conversation. Babies seem intent on communicating their needs and desires, as well as commenting on their own actions.

BABY TALK OR NOT?

Typically, the type of speech adults use to talk with babies is a special form of language that developmentalists call *baby talk* or, sometimes, *motherese*. Baby talk differs from normal speech in a number of features that are consistent throughout all language communities (Ferguson, 1977). It is distinct in its pitch (higher than that of normal language), its intonation (more low-to-high fluctuations), its vocabulary (simpler and more concrete), and its sentence length (shorter). It also employs more questions, commands, and repetitions and fewer past tenses, pronouns, and complex sentences than adult talk does.

People of all ages, from preschoolers to elders, speak baby talk with infants, and almost everyone is fluent without ever having to be taught. Preverbal infants prefer listening to motherese over normal speech (Cooper, 1993; Fernald & McRoberts, 1996), even if the motherese is in a language the infants have never heard (Fernald, 1993). Indeed, 5-month-old deaf infants prefer to look at a film of an unfamiliar deaf mother signing to her baby (only the mother can be seen in the movie) than a film of the same mother signing the identical message to her adult friend (Masataka, 1996).

Part of the appeal, and the impact, of baby talk is thought to arise from its energy and exaggerated expressiveness. This idea is supported by research showing that the baby talk of depressed mothers is too flat in intonation and too slow in its conversational responses to hold babies' interest (Bettes, 1988; Kaplan et al., 1999).

Many parents have learned that singing captures their babies' attention; the melody, repetition, and rhythm all facilitate learning, just as baby talk does, and for the same reasons—because babies enjoy learning language and will take every opportunity to do so. No wonder mothers and fathers, even those with far-from-perfect singing voices, croon to their infants—usually more slowly and emotionally than they do when singing the same song in their infants' absence. They also sing more imaginatively, as is exemplified by one father's favorite song for his baby, "It's bath time in Canada" (Trehub et al., 1997).

The function of baby talk is clearly to facilitate language learning, for the sounds and words are those that infants attend to, and speak, most readily. Difficult sounds are avoided: consonants like "l" and "r" are regularly omitted, and hard-to-say words are given simple forms, often with a "-y" ending. Thus, "father" becomes "daddy," "stomach" becomes "tummy," and "rabbit" becomes "bunny," because if they didn't, infants and parents would have difficulty talking about them. Moreover, the intonations and special emphases of baby talk help infants make connections between

Adults have many ways to support infants in their acquisition of language. We have discussed four:

■ Holding prelinguistic "conversations" with the infant
■ Engaging in baby talk
■ Persistently naming objects and events that capture the child's attention
■ Expanding the child's sounds and words into meaningful communications

As you should recall from Chapter 2, Lev Vygotsky and his followers maintained that a child's intellectual competencies emerge through an "apprenticeship in thinking," in which skilled mentors instruct and guide the learner through shared activities that facilitate the development of skills. The four activities listed above are very much in keeping with this theory. In fact, in many ways, early language development provides an almost perfect example of how an important feature of intellectual

specific words and the objects or events to which they refer (Fernald & Mazzie, 1991). Imagine a man telling a baby girl, in a higher-than-normal voice, "Daddy's going to kiss your tum-tum-tummy," and then doing so with a loud, wet smooch. Wouldn't the baby remember who Daddy is, and where the tummy is, better than she would if the man said "Your father will now kiss your stomach"—especially if he said it in a low-voiced monotone?

Given that baby talk facilitates early language learning, why would it be controversial? The first reason is that, although everyone can do it, not everyone does. The study just mentioned of parents singing to their children found that fathers sing less than mothers; the lullaby is usually a woman's song (Trehub et al., 1997). Teenage and low-income mothers talk less to their infants than middle-class mothers do, and when they do communicate, it is less often with baby talk and more often with nonverbal emotions (Barratt & Roach, 1995; Blake, 1993; Hart & Risley, 1995). In some cultures and subcultures, adults do not talk to infants at all (Ochs, 1988; Shore, 1995).

The second reason is related to the first. If baby talk is not universal, might there be a good reason some adults prefer to say very little or to speak in a more formal code? The most verbal infants—first to speak, first to utter sentences, first to use abstract vocabulary—are raised by baby-talking parents who are highly educated, upper-middle-class Westerners. Much of the detailed research comes from scientists who study their own children carefully, as Piaget himself did. Could it be that the early verbal emphasis of this research in these families is simply one way to raise an infant? Is a child who is quiet, respectful, and unlikely to interrupt preferred within some cultures? This chapter's stress on the early development of cognition, especially language as parents read, sing, and talk with nonverbal babies, or as early childhood educators do what low-income parents do not do, may be culturally insensitive and even destructive of other forms of healthy, loving care (Bruer, 1999).

Personally, I am—like everyone else—a product of my culture; I baby talked to my children, was delighted when they talked back, and now am proud of their verbal skills. Certainly early language learners become better students in school and more successful in mainstream Western culture. One of my eldest children is a lawyer, the other a journalist—both verbal, critical, and argumentative professions. But it is worth asking whether another mother, in a different culture, seeking an alternate life for her young adult daughters, might never babble, use baby talk, or eagerly respond to every noise, gesture, "Wha' dat?" "Who is?" or "Why?"

❶ **Answer to Observational Quiz (from page 181):**
The delight on both parents' faces, the "breast is best" shirt, the variety of surrounding objects that stimulate exploration and conceptualization, and the language of gesture that obviously communicates to all three.

growth—mastery of a child's native tongue—is structured, guided, and nurtured under the sensitive tutelage of the adults in the child's world.

Of course, this does not mean that adults should "talk down" to children, using baby talk when children are capable of understanding more advanced language. Remember that Vygotsky emphasized teaching to the *potential* of the child. The 1-year-old needs "tummy," "kitty," and "bunny"; the 3-year-old can already understand "stomach," "cat," and "rabbit."

As you have seen repeatedly in this chapter on early cognition, infants are motivated to understand the world. Very young babies look, listen, and grab whatever they can, developing a knowledge of affordances and concepts as they do so. And the same motivation that makes toddlers resemble little scientists makes infants seek to understand the noises, gestures, words, and grammatical systems that describe the world in which they live, as well as to use words to engage in social relationships. Those relationships lead them to learn not only the perception and expression described in this chapter but also emotions and social understanding, as the next chapter explains.

SUMMARY

PERCEPTION AND COGNITION

1. Infants quickly begin to grasp the affordances of things, that is, the opportunities for interaction that objects, people, and circumstances offer. New affordances are discovered and old ones are expanded as an infant's experience and repertoire of skills and abilities increase.

2. Infants' perceptual skills are fostered by such early cognitive understanding as dynamic perception; that is, a focus on movement and change.

3. Young infants have a basic appreciation for the permanence of objects at the age of 5 months, even though they will not search for a hidden object until later in their first year, at about 8 or 9 months.

KEY ELEMENTS OF COGNITIVE GROWTH

4. Even infants younger than 6 months are quite skilled at categorization—the ability to mentally sort objects by their properties. With increasing experience, both the categories and the properties used for categorizing grow in complexity.

5. Early memory is fragile yet surprisingly capable. Infants easily forget, but their memory can be reactivated with reminder sessions to help them remember past events.

6. The ability to understand cause-and-effect relationships develops slowly in the first few months of life. Toward the end of the first year, this understanding leads to early problem-solving abilities.

PIAGET'S SENSORIMOTOR INTELLIGENCE

7. From birth to age 2, during what Piaget called the sensorimotor stage, infants use their senses and motor skills to understand their environment. They begin by using and then adapting their reflexes; soon they become aware of their own and others' actions and reactions, and this awareness guides their cognition. By the end of the first year, they can, and do, set simple goals and have the knowledge and ability to achieve them.

8. In the second year, toddlers find new ways to achieve their goals, first by actively experimenting with objects and actions and then, toward the end of the second year, by manipulating mental images of objects and behaviors. They can pretend; they can play; they can remember what they saw days before and then repeat it.

LANGUAGE DEVELOPMENT

9. Language skills begin to develop as babies communicate through noises and gestures and then practice babbling. Infants typically say a few words at the end of the first year and, thereafter, gradually add a few words to their vocabulary each month. At about 18 months, rapid vocabulary acquisition begins.

10. Children vary in how rapidly they learn vocabulary, as well as in the ways in which they use words. In the first 2 years, children's comprehension of simple words and gestures and their willingness and ability to communicate are more significant than the size of their vocabulary.

11. Language learning occurs so rapidly in part because infants are primed to listen to speech sounds (or, for deaf babies, to see linguistic gestures) and to try to repeat them. On their part, most caregivers are adept at early language teaching.

12. The specifics of infant language learning depend on infant temperament, caregiver sensitivity, and cultural guidelines, but universally human babies are predisposed to learn, and caregivers to teach, linguistic skills.

KEY TERMS

affordance (160)
graspability (161)
visual cliff (161)
dynamic perception (163)
object permanence (164)
infantile amnesia (167)
reminder session (167)
deferred imitation (168)
launching event (170)
sensorimotor intelligence (171)

goal-directed behavior (173)
little scientist (174)
mental combinations (174)
babbling (176)
underextension (177)
overextension (177)
holophrase (178)
language acquisition device (LAD) (179)
baby talk (180)

KEY QUESTIONS

1. What is an affordance, and how does an affordance depend on the individual and on the individual's environment?

2. Distinguish between dynamic perception and object permanence.

3. In what ways can infants coordinate their perceptions of the same object through different senses?

4. Give an example of the early growth of categorization skills.

5. How can a scientist show that infants have object permanence even before they are capable of searching for a hidden object?

6. How good is the long-term memory of young infants, and what specifics strengthen their memory?

7. Explain the link between an understanding of cause-and-effect relations and the beginning of problem-solving ability.

8. What emphasis did Piaget bring to the study of cognitive development in infancy?

9. Describe how changes in a baby's actions and behaviors over the first 2 years of life reveal the growth of sensorimotor intelligence.

10. What are the major milestones in the growth of language ability in infancy, and when, typically, are these milestones reached?

11. What are the major factors that promote language acquisition?

12. How does baby talk differ from adult speech, and why do the differences exist?

13. *In Your Experience* What is the most surprising cognitive ability that a toddler (one you know or know of) has exhibited, and, from what you know of the context, how was that ability acquired?

The First Two Years:
Psychosocial Development

CHAPTER 7

Psychosocial development, by definition, involves interaction between the *psyche* (from the Greek word meaning "soul," "spirit," "feelings") and the *social context* (family, community, culture). The second half of this compound word is easy to observe. Every infant obviously gets a great deal of social attention. As a result, the infant's social context has been examined and debated extensively over the years. But it has not been obvious how the baby's (internal) psyche should be studied. Consequently, scientists examining infant psychosocial development first studied social events—and mainly the actions of the mother. They believed that babies themselves brought little to the interaction.

However, developmentalists now realize that even newborns are innately predisposed to sociability—capable, in the very first month of life, of expressing their own spirited emotions and of responding to the moods, feelings, and actions of others. Thus, we begin this chapter with the infant's own contribution to psychosocial growth.

EARLY EMOTIONS

Examining infant emotional development reveals how young infants begin to perceive, understand, and respond to their surroundings. It also shows that infant emotions contribute to social interactions: a baby's cry, frown, grimace, and smile are significant signals. And, as you learned in our discussion of epigenetic systems theory in Chapter 2, caregivers react to such social signs with precisely the responses necessary to protect and nurture the youngest members of the human family.

The First Half Year

The first emotion we can discern in newborns is *distress,* most obviously signaled by cries of hunger or pain. In addition to such physical discomfort, a loud noise, a sudden loss of bodily support, or an object looming toward them can distress very young infants—and once again their cries are a call for help, alerting caregivers that protection, or at least reassurance, is needed.

Sadness, or at least a sensitivity to it, is also apparent early in infancy. In one experiment, mothers of infants between 1 and 3 months old were asked to look sad and appear downcast; their infants responded by looking away and fussing (Cohn & Tronick, 1983; Tronick et al., 1986).

Social Referencing Is it dangerous or joyous to ride in a bicycle basket through the streets of Osaka? Check with Mom to find out.

❓ **Especially for Fathers:** What are the implications of the current research on fathers' role in caregiving?

parents' expressions and gestures; then they actively share in mutual emotional experiences; finally, they are able to lead the process, using their own words and gestures to engage their parents' attention (Carpenter et al., 1995).

Social referencing is particularly noticeable at mealtime. As the menu expands because milk is no longer the primary food, infants look to caregivers for cues about new foods. This explains why caregivers the world over smack their lips, pretend to taste, and say "yum-yum" (or the equivalent) as they feed toddlers beets, liver, spinach, or whatever. They are trying to lead the infants to like whatever is offered. On their part, toddlers become quite astute at reading expressions, insisting on the table food that the adults *really* like.

Referring to Dad

An infant uses father for social reference as much as mother, if both are present. In fact, fathers tend to be more encouraging and mothers more protective, so when toddlers are about to explore, they wisely seek a man's opinion to spur their curiosity (Parke, 1995).

As researchers looked closely at mothers, fathers, and infants, they discovered a curious difference: Although fathers provide less basic care, they play more. In general, infants look to fathers for fun and to mothers for comfort. Compared to mothers' play, fathers' play is more noisy, emotional, boisterous, physical, and idiosyncratic (as fathers tend to make up active and exciting games on the spur of the moment) (Fagot, 1997; MacDonald & Parke, 1986).

For instance, even in the first months of a baby's life, fathers are more likely to move the baby's legs and arms in imitation of walking, kicking, or climbing, to zoom the baby through the air (playing "airplane"), or to tap and tickle the baby's stomach. Mothers are more likely to caress, murmur, or sing soothingly, to combine play with caretaking routines such as diapering and bathing, or to use standard sequences that involve only one part of the body, such as peek-a-boo and patty-cake. Not surprisingly, young infants typically laugh more, and cry more, when playing with Daddy.

In all probability, the more physical play of fathers helps the children master motor skills and develop muscle control (Pellegrini & Smith, 1998). In addition, play with father may contribute to the growth of social skills and emotional expressions. In one study, 18-month-olds met a stranger while either parent sat passively nearby. In the father's presence, the toddlers were more likely to smile and play with the new person than in the mother's presence, a difference especially apparent for the boys. The authors of the study speculated that the toddlers' past boisterous, idiosyncratic play with Dad made his presence a signal to be bold and playful (Kromelow et al., 1990).

Similar speculations have been raised about fathers' teasing, which requires the baby's social response to an unpredictable game—and thereby may increase not only excitement but also emotional regulation and social understanding (Pecheux & Labrell, 1994). Another study, this one of very low-birthweight infants in Japan, found that they were much

Up, Up, and Away! The more vigorous play typical of fathers is likely to help in the infant's mastery of motor skills and the development of muscle control.

self-awareness A person's sense of himself or herself as being distinct from other people.

more likely to develop normal social skills if their fathers were actively involved with them (Itoigawa et al., 1996). And in Israel, father–infant involvement led to an increase in exploratory play (Feldman et al., 1997).

The fact that fathers are good playmates does not mean they are limited to that role. If called on, fathers are quite capable of providing the necessary emotional and cognitive nurturing, speaking motherese like a native, and forming secure relationships both as secondary caregivers and as primary ones (Geiger, 1996; Lamb, 1997). Although every set of parents develop their own mother and father roles, one thing is clear: The father's complete absence is not good for infant development. For example, one study found that adolescent boys who did not know their own fathers were more likely to abuse drugs and be arrested. Indeed, in this group who themselves became fathers before age 20, 40 percent of them had had no contact with their fathers at all by age 2 (Fagot et al., 1998). Throughout today's changing world, mothers and fathers together are better able to meet all their infant's needs—biological, cognitive, and psychosocial—than is either parent alone.

Self-Awareness

A pivotal accomplishment of later infancy is the onset of **self-awareness,** a person's realization that he or she is a distinct individual whose body, mind, and actions are separate from those of other people. This emerging sense of "me" and "mine" fosters the growth of many self-conscious emotions—from pride and confidence to guilt, shame, and embarrassment. Simultaneously, self-awareness leads to new consciousness of others. That, in turn, fosters other-directed emotions, such as defiance and jealousy as well as empathy and affection.

The onset of self-awareness is strikingly evident when infants of various ages are compared. Very young infants have no sense of self; in fact, they do not even have an awareness of their bodies as theirs (Lewis, 1990). To them, for example, their hands are interesting objects that appear and disappear. In effect, 2-month-olds discover their hands each time they catch sight of them, become fascinated with the movements, and then lose interest as the hands slip out of view. Even 8-month-olds often don't seem to know where their bodies end and someone else's body begins. An 8- or 9-month-old might grab a toy that is in another child's hand and then react with surprise when the toy "resists." By 1 year, however, most infants are aware that another child is a distinct person, and they might show this awareness with a smile or a shove if the coveted toy is not immediately forthcoming.

The awareness of other people, emerging between 9 and 15 months, leads to an even more stunning discovery: the awareness of oneself. The period from 15 to 18 months "is noteworthy for the emergence of the Me-self, the sense of self as the object of one's knowledge" (Harter, 1998).

Who's in the Mirror

The emerging sense of self was demonstrated in a classic experiment (Lewis & Brooks, 1978). Babies looked in a mirror after a dot of rouge had been surreptitiously put on their noses. If the babies reacted to the mirror image by touching their own noses, they knew they were seeing their own faces. By trying this experiment with 96 babies between the ages of 9 and 24 months, the experimenters found a distinct, age-related developmental shift. None of the babies under 12 months reacted to the

A Beautiful Bonnet At 18 months, Austin recognizes himself, obviously delighted by his colander hat. Once self-recognition begins at about this age, many children spend hours admiring themselves with various hats, makeup, and other accessories. Almost every view of themselves is a joy; they are not yet worried about looking stupid or ugly.

mark as if it were on their own faces (they sometimes smiled at the baby in the mirror and touched the dot on the mirror baby). However, most of those between ages 15 and 24 months did react with self-awareness, perhaps by touching their own faces with an expression of curiosity and puzzlement.

The link between self-awareness and self-conscious emotions was shown in a later extension of the rouge-and-mirror experiment (Lewis et al., 1989). In this study, 15- to 24-month-olds who showed self-recognition in the mirror also looked *embarrassed* when they were effusively praised by an adult; that is, they smiled and looked away, covered their faces with their hands, and so on. Infants without self-recognition, in that they had not recognized that the rouge was on their own noses, were not embarrassed.

Pride and Shame

Developing self-awareness enables toddlers to be self-critical and to have emotional responses such as guilt (Emde et al., 1991). By age 2, for example, most children are aware of the basic do's and don'ts they should follow, and they sometimes show distress or anxiety when they have misbehaved—even when no adult is present. In one experimental demonstration of this behavior, 2-year-olds were "set up" to experience two mild mishaps: They were left alone in a playroom with (1) a doll whose leg was rigged to fall off when the doll was picked up and (2) a juice drink in a trick cup that dribbled when drunk from. Many of the children responded to their "accidents" with expressions of sadness or tension, along with efforts to repair the damage (Cole et al., 1992).

The link between self-awareness and emotions is evident at home as well as in the laboratory: Mothers report that toddlers' sense of *shame and guilt* appears for the first time only after self-awareness develops (Stipek et al., 1992). At that point, being angry over an injustice (such as another child's getting the first slice of pie) as well as being "sorry" for a misdeed become part of the child's developing moral sense (Zahn-Waxler et al., 1992).

Self-awareness also permits a child to react in an entirely new way to his or her misdeeds—with pride at going against another's wishes. Shortly before his second birthday, for example, a certain toddler named Ricky teased his mother by deliberately pouring a cup of juice onto a rug. Evidence that Ricky knew he was being naughty was in his reaction to his mother's scolding: He was unsurprised and unfazed by her angry words and was quite willing to help her clean up the mess. Only when his mother sent him to his room did he protest angrily, apparently not anticipating such punishment. Later that day he told his grandmother, "Juice on a floor." Her response was "Juice doesn't go on the floor," delivered somewhat sternly. "Yes, juice on a floor, juice on a floor," Ricky laughingly repeated several times, pretending to turn an imaginary cup upside down. As Ricky's grandmother, a noted psychologist, comments:

> The boy's pleasure at watching the juice spill and anger at being sent to his room are emotions that are typical at all periods of infancy, but his obvious pride at his ability to act counter to convention or his mother's wishes is possible only when self-awareness is firmly established. [Shatz, 1994]

⚠ Response for Fathers (from page 190): Fathers are much more capable than some women think, and paternal caregiving makes the infant happier and braver. This means that fathers should be active parents, even when work schedules, personal preferences, or maternal criticism pushes them in the other direction.

THE ORIGINS OF PERSONALITY

personality The emotions, behaviors, and attitudes that make an individual unique.

By **personality** we mean the multitude of emotions, behaviors, and attitudes that characterize each person, distinguishing one from another. We have just described the universal progression of infant emotions, from distress to anger to guilt or from pleasure to laughter to pride. Now we look at those aspects which differentiate persons, which make one infant's personality different from that of another baby of the same age. What evokes or creates the traits and social habits that become the patterns that form personality?

In the first half of the twentieth century, the prevailing view among psychologists was that personality is permanently molded by the actions of the parents—most especially the mother—in the early years of childhood. There were two major theoretical versions of how this comes about.

Learning Theory

From the perspective of traditional learning theory (discussed in Chapter 2), personality is molded as parents reinforce or punish their child's spontaneous behaviors. Behaviorists proposed, for example, that if parents smile and pick up their baby at every glimmer of an infant grin, the baby will become a child—and later an adult—with a sunny disposition. Similarly, if parents continually tease their infant by, say, removing the nipple as the baby is contentedly sucking or by playfully pulling at a favorite toy that a toddler is clutching, that child will develop a suspicious, possessive nature.

The strongest statement of this early view came from John Watson, the leading behaviorist of the time, who cautioned:

> Failure to bring up a happy child, a well-adjusted child—assuming bodily health—falls squarely upon the parents' shoulders. [By the time the child is 3] parents have already determined . . . whether . . . [the child] is to grow into a happy person, wholesome and good-natured, whether he is to be a whining, complaining, neurotic, an anger-driven, vindictive, over-bearing slave driver, or one whose every move in life is definitely controlled by fear. [Watson, 1928]

Later theorists in the behaviorist tradition incorporated social learning into personality formation; they found that infants observe and

"I get along fine with people my age and I get along fine with people your age—it's the ones in the middle who give me all kinds of problems."

Parents Are the Problem According to psychoanalytic theory, the inevitable conflicts between parents and young children create the need for personality quirks and defensive measures.

Tasty Toes Most of us (including the photographer) are amazed at this toes-in-mouth demonstration, but such is not the concern of the baby. Instead, at 6 months she is very interested in and not too comfortable with the stranger taking the photograph. Body awareness, including the realization that those toes are her own, will take months to appear, propelled not only by cognitive maturation but perhaps by the emergence of top and bottom teeth at about 1 year of age.

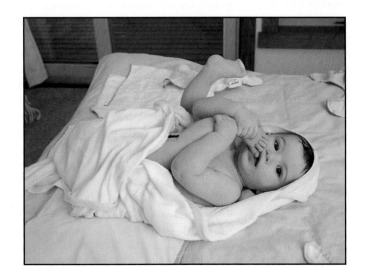

then imitate personality traits of their parents, even if they are not directly reinforced for doing so. A child might develop a quick temper, for instance, if a parent regularly displays anger and in return gets respect—or at least obedience—from other family members. Although not all personality traits are directly reinforced in babyhood, "the guiding belief of these social learning theorists was that personality is learned" (Miller, 1993).

Social referencing strengthens this learning by observation. Generally, if toddlers receive more signals of interest and encouragement than of fear and prohibition as they explore, they are likely to be more friendly, and less aggressive, than they would be if the opposite messages had been received (Calkins, 1994). If an infant or toddler sees few signals of any kind (as might happen if the primary caregiver is depressed, neglectful, or overtired), the child becomes relatively emotionless and passive (Field, 1995).

Psychoanalytic Theory

Beginning with a different set of assumptions about human nature, psychoanalytic theorists (also discussed in Chapter 2) similarly concluded that the individual's personality is first formed and then permanently fixed in early childhood. Sigmund Freud, who established the framework for this view, felt that the experiences of the first 4 years "play a decisive part in determining whether and at what point the individual shall fail to master the real problems of life" (Freud, 1918/1963). He thought that the mother was "unique, without parallel, established unalterably for a whole lifetime as the first and strongest love-object and as the prototype of all later love relations" (Freud, 1940/1964). Other psychoanalytic theorists agreed: Mother–child relationships in the first months and years are pivotal.

Oral and Anal Stages

As we noted in Chapter 2, Freud viewed human development in terms of psychosexual stages that occur at specific ages. According to Freud (1935), psychological development begins in the first year of life, with an **oral stage,** so named because the mouth is the young infant's prime source of gratification. In the second year, the infant's prime focus of gratification shifts to the anus—particularly the sensual pleasure taken in bowel movements and, eventually, the psychological pleasure in controlling them. Accordingly, Freud referred to this period as the **anal stage.**

The shift from oral to anal gratification is more than a simple change of body focus; it is a shift in the mode of interaction with the environment—from a passive, dependent mode to a more active, controlling mode in which the child has some power. In the anal stage, mothers strive to foster the toddler's self-control through potty training as well as in other ways. And the toddler has the self-awareness and self-control to resist. The situation is thus prime for a power struggle. More than one toddler has spent time sitting unhappily on the potty, with no outcome, only to get off, get diapered, and poop. The mother's subsequent exasperation is not just about the cleanup but also about the loss of her power to "train" the child.

Indeed, according to Freud, both oral and anal stages are fraught with potential conflicts that can have long-term consequences. If a

oral stage   Freud's term for the first stage of psychosexual development, in which the infant gains pleasure through sucking and biting.

anal stage   Freud's second stage of psychosexual development, in which the anus becomes the main source of bodily pleasure and control of defecation and toilet training are therefore important activities.

❓ **Especially for Mothers:** What are the implications of Freud's perspective that mothers are crucial?

More Than a Balanced Meal To psychoanalytic theorists, breast-feeding is important not just because it is a source of nourishment but also because the pleasurable, intimate contact it affords strengthens the infant's attachment to the mother and fosters a feeling of "basic trust" in the world.

❷ *Observational Quiz (see answer page 198): What is the infant receiving in this important process?*

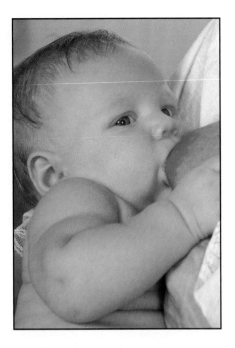

mother frustrates her infant's urge to suck—by, say, weaning the infant from the nipple too early or preventing the child from sucking on fingers or toes—the child may become distressed and anxious and eventually be an adult with an *oral fixation.* Such a person is stuck (fixated) at the oral stage and therefore eats, drinks, chews, bites, or talks excessively, in quest of mouthy pleasures that were denied in infancy.

Similarly, if toilet training is overly strict or if it occurs before the child is mature enough to participate (before age 18 to 24 months), interaction between parents and child may become locked into a conflict over the toddler's resistance or inability to comply. This conflict, too, may have important consequences for the child's future personality. The child becomes fixated and develops an *anal personality;* as an adult, he or she may seek control of self and others and demonstrate an unusual need for regularity in all aspects of life.

Freud's ideas have been extremely influential. In fact, the view that women should be "stay-at-home moms" for their small children is a direct outgrowth of Freud's personality theory—which is one reason both Freud and infant day care are such emotional controversies for many people (see the Changing Policy box on pages 196–197). However, research has failed to link specific oral- and anal-stage conflicts with later personality traits. Rather, the overall pattern of parental warmth and sensitivity, or coldness and domination, affects the child's emotional development much more than the particulars of either feeding or toilet training. This broader perspective is reflected in the theory of Erik Erikson.

Trust and Autonomy

trust versus mistrust Erikson's first stage of psychosocial development, in which the infant experiences the world either as secure and comfortable or as unpredictable and uncomfortable.

autonomy versus shame and doubt Erikson's second stage of psychosocial development, in which the toddler struggles for self-control but feels shame and doubt about his or her abilities if it is not achieved.

As you remember from Chapter 2, Erik Erikson believed that development proceeds through a series of developmental crises, or challenges, that occur throughout the life span. The first crisis of infancy, in Erikson's view, is **trust versus mistrust.** In this crisis, the infant learns whether the world is essentially a secure place, where basic needs will be readily satisfied, or the opposite, an unpredictable arena where needs are met only after much crying—and sometimes not even then. Erikson (1963) contended that babies begin to develop a sense of security when their mothers provide food and comfort with "consistency, continuity, and sameness of experience." When interaction with the mother inspires trust and security, the child (and later the adult) experiences confidence in engaging and exploring the world.

The next crisis, which occurs in toddlerhood, is **autonomy versus shame and doubt.** Toddlers want autonomy, or self-rule, over their own actions and bodies. If they fail in their effort to gain it, either because

INFANT DAY CARE

For many children today, day-care providers have become important caregivers. (By *day care* we mean nonmaternal care during the daytime hours, typically while the mother is working at a part-time or full-time job.) Until recently, developmentalists in the United States were engaged in a heated debate over the effects of day care, especially during the first year of infancy. The first to sound the alarm was Jay Belsky, who reported that infants who experience early and extended day care are 10 percent more likely than other infants to avoid and ignore their mothers in the Strange Situation, a laboratory measurement of the bond between caregivers and children. On that basis, he warned that more than 20 hours of nonmaternal care per week in the first year of life represents a "risk factor" for future child development.

Developmentalists on the opposing side rejected Belsky's analysis. First, they called attention to a number of weaknesses in the research, including a failure to take into account the parents' early relationship with the child at home. Second, they emphasized the infant's past experiences. If attachment is measured by the Strange Situation, day-care infants may seem to be insecure merely because they are less upset by separation from or reunion with their mothers. Finally, Belsky's critics asserted that if any attachment problems at all are associated with extended day care, the crucial variable is the *quality* of caregiving, not the fact of day care (Clarke-Stewart, 1989; Fox & Fein, 1990; Lamb & Sternberg, 1990; Thompson, 1997).

Nowadays most researchers, including Belsky, agree that when infant day care is "of high quality, there should be little reason to anticipate negative developmental outcomes" (Belsky, 1990). In fact, there is strong evidence that, for some children, high-quality day care is more beneficial to the development of cognitive and social skills than is exclusive home care (Aureli & Colecchia, 1996; National Institute of Child Health and Development, 1997; Roggman et al., 1994).

Trained caregivers in well-designed settings foster healthy development by means of toys, games, and social stimulation that few homes can surpass. When the mother is severely depressed, the home is conflict-filled, or the family is neglectful, day care not only is a lifesaver for the infant but also may help repair a family context that is destructive. Even without these special circumstances, high-quality day care offers something that no home provides—a wide assortment of potential playmates and friends.

Characteristics of High-Quality Day Care

What are the signs of high-quality day care that parents should look for? Researchers have identified four factors that seem essential:

- *Adequate attention to each infant.* This means a low caregiver-to-infant ratio and a small group of infants. The ideal situation might be two reliable caregivers for five infants.
- *Encouragement of sensorimotor exploration and language development.* Infants should be provided with a variety of easily manipulated toys and should have a great deal of language exposure through games, songs, and conversation.
- *Attention to health and safety.* Cleanliness routines (such as handwashing before meals), accident prevention (such as the absence of small objects that could be swallowed), and safe areas for exploration (such as a clean, soft-surfaced area for crawling and climbing) are all good signs.
- *Well-trained and professional caregivers.* Ideally, every caregiver should have a degree and certification in early-childhood education and should have worked in this field for several years. Turnover should be low, morale high, enthusiasm evident. Indeed, if the caregivers are knowledgeable and committed, the first three items on this list will follow automatically.

Who Should Pay for Day Care?

Beyond the specifics that a particular parent might seek in a day-care setting are broader public-policy issues. In some nations, including the United States, parents must find and finance infant care on their own. That typically results in a patchwork arrangement of baby-sitters, relatives, and neighbors—some excellent, some dangerous, many mediocre, and almost all untrained, underpaid, and unregulated. Few working mothers in the United States can find, much less afford, a small day-care setting with two college-educated caregivers for every group of five babies.

How bad is poor-quality care? The answer, of course, depends on exactly how inadequate the supervision is (Is it dangerous?); how unstimulating the cognitive setting is (Do the babies play?); and, if intellectual stimulation is sparse, how much time the infant spends there. A large-scale study of infant day care throughout the United States found that even mediocre care was generally harmless. Infants were likely to become insecurely attached only if

- their own mothers were insensitive
- day-care quality was poor
- day care was more than 20 hours per week

Even under these circumstances, girls were less likely to have problems than boys, and steady care was better than care from a patchwork of caregivers (National Institute of Child Health and Development, 1997).

Other large-scale research confirms that maternal employment during the first years of a child's life has very little, or no effect on the child's behavior or intellectual development from ages 3 to 10 (Harvey, 1999). Nevertheless, to judge some care as simply harmless is faint praise indeed, given the benefits than can occur when the best care is provided.

Developmentalists contend that any nation committed to the future of its youngest citizens must develop high-quality care, especially for the children of parents who are too young, too stressed, or too unaware to provide intellectual stimulation and responsive caregiving. As Sandra Scarr, past president of the Society for Research in Child Development, writes:

For children from middle- and upper-income families—especially stable, two-parent families in non-dangerous neighborhoods—day care merely supplements what parents can offer. For children from disturbed and seriously disadvantaged families—especially unstable, one-parent families who live in dangerous neighborhoods—good day care is the most powerful, positive intervention we now have. . . . Most low-income, working families cannot afford to buy decent child care, not to mention good quality care. Federally funded child care assistance is insufficient to meet even present needs, which will expand with welfare reform. Do we in the United States have the political will to provide quality care for poor children? [Scarr, 1996]

This final question will become more urgent as state and federal welfare reforms result in many more infants needing care outside the home. If such care is provided by unregulated baby-sitters, it is likely to impede child development; if it is provided by a relative, it is neutral; if it is provided by a licensed day-care center, it is beneficial (Yoshikawa, 1999). Since high-quality day care reduces the incidence of many major hazards—from accidental injury to academic failure—it is imperative that the answer to Scarr's question be a resounding *yes*.

Infant Day Care In Grenoble, France, infant day care is subsidized by the government. Consequently, many children are in day-care centers like this one.
? Observational Quiz (see answer page 202): *If you were grading this center on quality of care, what grade would you give it, and why?*

Just Looking or About to Pull? If the girl's explorations result in smashed dinnerware, will her parents react with anger, as though her goal were destruction, or with a firm but understanding caution, as though her goal were discovery? According to Erikson, how parents react to their children's efforts at autonomy can shape how young children resolve the psychosocial crisis of autonomy versus shame and doubt.

❶ Answer to Observational Quiz (from page 195): *Breast milk, of course, with nutrients, antibodies, and hormones, as explained in Chapter 5. But this baby may also be gaining an outgoing and generous personality, a confident and easygoing attitude toward humanity, and a lifelong affection for Mother.*

❶ Response for Mothers (from page 194): If mothers are crucial, they must devote themselves exclusively to infant care, keeping baby-sitters, day-care teachers, and even fathers at a distance. For better or worse, children will be strongly identified with their mothers, who can take pride in their accomplishments and blame for their failures. Fortunately for today's women, Freud's theories are unproven.

temperament The set of innate tendencies, or dispositions, that underlie and affect each person's interactions with people, situations, and events.

they are incapable or because their caregivers are too restrictive and forbidding, they feel ashamed of their actions and doubtful of their abilities. According to Erikson, the key to meeting this crisis and gaining a sense of autonomy is parental guidance and protection:

> Firmness must protect him [the toddler] against the potential anarchy of his as yet untrained sense of discrimination, his inability to hold on and let go with discretion. As his environment encourages him to "stand on his own feet," it must protect him against meaningless and arbitrary experiences of shame and of early doubt. [Erikson, 1963]

If parents accomplish this, the child will become increasingly self-confident when encountering new challenges.

Like Freud, Erikson believed that problems arising in early infancy can last a lifetime. He maintained that the adult who is suspicious and pessimistic or who always seems burdened by shame may have been an infant who did not develop sufficient trust or a toddler who did not achieve sufficient autonomy. However, Erikson also emphasized that experiences later in life can alter or transform the effects of early experiences and that early developmental crises can be revisited and resolved later in life.

Overall, then, traditional psychological theories maintained that personality is shaped primarily by early nurture, particularly the mother's caregiving. This view has serious challengers who say the basic elements of temperament emerge so early that caregiving influences cannot be credited or blamed for personality.

Epigenetic Systems Theory

Every individual is born with a distinct, genetically based set of psychological tendencies, or dispositions. These tendencies, which together are called **temperament,** affect and shape virtually every aspect of the person's developing personality. Temperament has been defined as

Twins They were born on the same day and now are experiencing a wading pool for the first time.

❷ *Observational Quiz (see answer page 203):* *Are these monozygotic or dizygotic twins?*

Which Sister Has a Personality Problem?
Culture always affects the expression of temperament. In Mongolia and many other Asian countries, females are expected to display shyness as a sign of respect to elders and strangers. Consequently, if the younger of these sisters is truly as shy as she seems, her parents are less likely to be distressed about her withdrawn behavior than the typical North American parent would be. On the other hand, they may consider the relative boldness of her older sister to be a serious problem.

"constitutionally based individual differences in emotional, motor, and attentional reactivity and self-regulation" (Rothbart & Bates, 1998). As an example of temperamental tendencies, we might note that one person is a *cautious* individual whereas another is a *risk taker*.

The distinction between temperament and personality is a matter of time and complexity. Temperament is composed of basic tendencies, apparent early in life, that are the foundation ("constitutionally based") for later personality differences. Thus, if risk taking is a temperamental tendency, the personality of an individual with that tendency might include a propensity to gamble, to speak bluntly, to seek physical challenges (like mountain climbing), to be sexually promiscuous, and/or to change jobs often. Probably each risk taker develops a distinct set of personality traits, all connected to his or her basic temperament but not dictated by it in every detail.

Temperament (and therefore personality) is epigenetic, not merely genetic: It begins in the multitude of genetic instructions that guide the development of the brain and then is affected by the prenatal environment, especially the nutrition and health of the mother, and probably by postnatal experiences as well. As the person develops, the social context and the individual's experiences continue to influence the nature and expression of temperament (see the Research Report on pages 200–201).

Current research confirms that infants are born with definite and distinct temperaments, and that these are genetic in origin and affect later personality. However, researchers also stress that early temperamental traits can change; there is much more stability, from year to year, in temperament after age 2 than before it (Lemery et al., 1999). Further, in adulthood, almost any basic trait may take either a benign or a destructive turn. The cautious person may be either stable and trustworthy or fearful and stagnant; the risk taker may be either innovative and brave or erratic and foolhardy.

DIMENSIONS OF TEMPERAMENT

Because temperament is fundamental in determining the kind of individuals we become and how we interact with others, many researchers have set out to describe and measure the various dimensions of temperament (Buss, 1991; Lemery et al., 1999; Rothbart & Bates, 1998). The most famous, most comprehensive, and longest ongoing study of children's temperament remains the classic New York Longitudinal Study (NYLS), begun over four decades ago (Thomas & Chess, 1977; Thomas et al., 1963). For this study parents of very young infants were interviewed repeatedly and extensively. The researchers detailed the various aspects of the infants' behavior, and they described the approach they used to reduce the possibility of parental bias:

> For example, if a mother said that her child did not like his first solid food, we asked her to describe his actual behavior. We were satisfied only when she gave a description such as, "When I put the food into his mouth he cried loudly, twisted his head away, and let it drool out."
>
> If we asked what a six-month-old baby did when his father came home in the evening, and his mother said, "He was happy to see him," we pressed for a detailed description: "As soon as he saw his father he smiled and reached out his arms." [Chess et al., 1965]

According to the researchers' initial findings, in the first days and months of life babies differ in nine characteristics:

- *Activity level.* Some babies are active. They kick a lot in the uterus before they are born, they move around a great deal in their bassinets, and, as toddlers, they are nearly always running. Other babies are much less active.
- *Rhythmicity.* Some babies have regular cycles of activity. They eat, sleep, and defecate on schedule almost from birth. Other babies are much less predictable.
- *Approach–withdrawal.* Some babies delight in everything new; others withdraw from every new situation. The first bath makes some babies react in wide-eyed wonder and others tense up and scream; the first playtime with another child makes some crawl toward their new playmate with excitement and makes others try to hide.
- *Adaptability.* Some babies adjust quickly to change. Others are unhappy at every disruption of their normal routine.
- *Intensity of reaction.* Some babies chortle when they laugh and howl when they cry. Others are much calmer, responding with a smile or a whimper.
- *Threshold of responsiveness.* Some babies seem to sense every sight, sound, and touch. For instance, they waken at a slight noise or turn away from a distant light. Others seem blissfully unaware, even of bright lights, loud street noises, or wet diapers.
- *Quality of mood.* Some babies seem constantly happy, smiling at almost everything. Others seem chronically unhappy; they are ready to protest at any moment.
- *Distractibility.* All babies fuss when they are hungry, but some will stop if someone gives them a pacifier or sings them a song. Others will keep fussing. Similarly, some babies can easily be distracted from a fascinating but dangerous object and diverted to a safer plaything. Others are more single-minded, refusing to be distracted.
- *Attention span.* Some babies play happily with one toy for a long time. Others quickly drop one activity for another.

The lead NYLS researchers, Alexander Thomas and Stella Chess (1977), believe that "temperamental individuality is well established by the time the infant is two to three months old." In terms of combinations of the above characteristics, most young infants can be described as being one of three types: About 40 percent are *easy,* about 15 percent are *slow to warm up,* and about 10 percent are *difficult.* (Difficult babies are irregular, intense, disturbed by every noise, unhappy, and hard to distract for very long—quite a handful, even for the experienced parent. Easy babies are the opposite of difficult, and slow-to-warm-up babies are distinguished by their initial unwillingness to approach, adapt, and be distracted. They do, however, adjust with time.)

Most parents can personally validate these categories, in that they readily describe their infants as good (meaning easy), shy (meaning slow to warm up), or difficult. But notice that about 35 percent of normal infants do not fit into any of these specific types. If your mother says you were a good baby, consider her assessment a compliment but remain skeptical: Your actual behavior may have been more ambiguous. You might ask her, just as the researchers did, to describe your "good" behavior by giving specific behavioral examples.

Researchers who study adult personality have also searched for the basic temperamental dimensions that underlie personality in humans everywhere (Digman, 1990; McDonald, 1995; McCrea et al., 1999). Through a series of statistical calculations they have found what are called the "Big Five" dimensions of temperament. The Big Five are discussed in detail in Chapter 22. They can be briefly characterized as follows:

- *Extroversion:* outgoing, assertive, and active
- *Agreeableness:* kind, helpful, and easygoing
- *Conscientiousness:* organized, deliberate, and conforming
- *Neuroticism:* anxious, moody, and self-punishing
- *Openness:* imaginative, curious, and artistic, welcoming new experiences

As you can see, these five tendencies are not identical to the nine characteristics of the NYLS, but there are many similarities. The Big Five are found in international studies of adult personality, as well as in descriptions of children's traits by parents from many nations (Kohnstamm et al., 1996; McCrae et al., 1999). This confirms that temperament is probably innate and that patterns that distinguish one infant, child, or adult from another transcend culture or child-rearing specifics. Other research finds that temperament is linked to biological and neurological patterns (in heartbeat, crying, activity, and such) that appear in the first months of life, so parents cannot be blamed or credited for all their infants' actions (Huffman et al., 1998; Rothbart & Bates, 1998).

The environment affects temperamental tendencies in several ways. One way is through the **goodness of fit,** or "match," between the child's temperamental pattern and the demands of his or her social context—mainly through parenting. When parents adapt their child-rearing expectations to their offspring's temperament, the result is a harmonious fit, with good outcomes for both child and family. This might involve setting up a spacious, childproof play area where an active, curious child can use up excess energy without risk, or it might require allowing extra time for a slow-to-warm-up child to adjust to new situations.

By contrast, when there is a poor match between the child's temperamental pattern and the caregiving expectations, parents and offspring experience greater conflict. Suppose an irregular infant, who is sometimes hungry 1 hour after a meal and sometimes 6 hours later, happens to be born to a busy mother who makes schedules and follows routines to cope with her own anxieties and insecurities. That's a volatile combination, leading to mutual resentment and conflict unless one or the other adjusts. Even as grown-ups, temperamentally irregular people who have learned to fight their mothers' rules might resist any attempt to become organized and predictable. Such people might undermine their own potential by procrastinating, arriving late for appointments, or losing things.

goodness of fit The degree to which a child's temperament matches the demands of his or her environment.

The importance of goodness of fit is illustrated by one of the original subjects of the NYLS:

Carl was one of our most extreme cases of difficult temperament from the first months of life through 5 years of age. However, he did not develop a behavior disorder, primarily due to optimal handling by his parents and stability of his environment. His father, who himself had an easy temperament, took delight in his son's "lusty" characteristics, recognized on his own Carl's tendencies to have intense negative reactions to the new, and had the patience to wait for eventual adaptability to occur. He was clear, without any orientation by us, that these characteristics were in no way due to his or his wife's influences. His wife tended to be anxious and self-accusatory over Carl's tempestuous course. However, her husband was supportive and reassuring and this enabled her to take an appropriately objective and patient approach to her son's development.

By [Carl's] middle childhood and early adolescent years, few new situations arose which provoked the difficult temperament responses. The family, school, and social environment was stable and Carl flourished and appeared to be temperamentally easy rather than difficult. . . .

When Carl went off to college, however, he was faced simultaneously with a host of new situations and demands—an unfamiliar locale, a different living arrangement, new academic subjects and expectations, and a totally new peer group. Within a few weeks his temperamentally difficult characteristics reappeared in full force. He felt negative about the school, his courses, the other students, couldn't motivate himself to study, and was constantly irritable. Carl knew something was wrong, and discussed the situation with his family and us and developed an appropriate strategy to cope with his problem. He limited the new demands by dropping several extracurricular activities, limited his social contact, and policed his studying. Gradually he adapted, his distress disappeared, and he was able to expand his activities and social contacts. . . . [In] the most recent follow-up at age 29 . . . his intensity remains but is now an asset rather than a liability. [Chess & Thomas, 1990]

This fortunate outcome is what researchers in temperament hope for us all: Awareness and appreciation of inborn personality tendencies can lead to fulfillment, not frustration.

● *Answer to Observational Quiz (from page 197):* *This clearly is not an F or an A. Perhaps a C, for average. Most signs indicate a fairly good setting, in that the infants all seem active, the caregivers are attentive, the toys are appropriate, children's artwork is displayed, and the setting seems clean. On the other hand, eight 1-year-olds may be a handful for two adults, and the toys and the activities seem scattered. Is there a curriculum or just individual play? Obviously a more accurate rating would require more than a snapshot, with attention given to peer interactions and to the relationship of each caregiver with each child.*

INTERACTION AGAIN

As our discussion of temperament in the Research Report makes clear, the traditional psychological view of the mother as the sole shaper of the child's personality was in error. A more inclusive view, involving the father, siblings, and other family members, still gives too little acknowledgment to inborn tendencies. Yet we also see that personality is not determined solely by the individual's temperamental tendencies. The *interaction* between caregiver and child—not just genetics and not just the mother—is crucial to all psychosocial growth. This interaction is affected by the personality of the parent, the temperament of the child, the surrounding culture, and the child's stage of development. Synergy between caregiver and infant is the spark that ignites development.

Becoming Social Partners

You saw earlier that even very young infants communicate emotionally, through sounds, movements, and facial expressions. And they are interested in social interaction virtually from birth: Voices and faces are among the first stimuli to capture a newborn's attention. But although tiny babies are social, they are not equal partners. New parents who eagerly anticipate joyous exchanges may be disappointed to discover that their newborn spends most of the day sleeping, awakening mainly to cry and suck and rarely responding to a caregiver. A fixed stare is typically the best that parents can expect from an attentive newborn; managing to soothe a crying infant is a major success.

Even this success eludes some parents. Certain colicky infants engage in prolonged, aversive bouts of crying—typically after the evening feeding and due to intestinal discomfort. Such crying makes parents feel helpless and angry, worried that they are failures or that their baby already hates them. The cry of such a baby is, in fact, a very unpleasant sound, as upsetting as the scratching nails on a blackboard might be (Zeskind & Barr, 1997). Even if they are not colicky, immature infants (under 3 months of age) often become upset for reasons that have little to do with the care they receive. Boys, for instance, tend to be fussier than girls, even though their parents try harder to comfort them (Weinberg et al., 1999). When babies are between 3 and 9 months old, their parents are much more influential. As a result, some fussy young infants become more placid and others more irritable as they mature (Scher & Mayseless, 1997).

Personality of Caregiver Both nature and nurture may be in evidence here, in that the mother's personality obviously affects the quality of interaction with her offspring. Adults typically use special social behaviors (a) with their young infants—leaning in close, opening their eyes and mouths wide in exaggerated expressions of surprise or delight, maintaining eye contact—because those behaviors elicit the baby's attention and pleasure. But such behaviors are subdued or absent when the adult is depressed or stressed (b), and this makes social interaction much less enjoyable for each partner.

(a)

(b)

synchrony Coordinated interaction between infant and parent (or other caregiver) in which each individual responds to and influences the other.

Synchrony

By the age of 2 to 3 months, changes occur that make parents rejoice: Their baby begins to respond to them in special ways. To be sure, any face elicits smiles, but the mother, the father, or another familiar caregiver now provokes widened grins, lilting cooing, and other reactions that signify special status in that infant's world. Many parents report that their own affection for their baby deepens at this time. In a sense the parents proceed from a newborn phase of caregiving, when the child seem to be a delicate guest requiring careful treatment, to a family phase in which the child becomes a social partner who reciprocates their love. Instead of merely gazing intently over the crib rails, trying to decipher what the baby's needs might be, caregivers begin to initiate focused episodes of face-to-face social play, eliciting unmistakable responses from the infant.

One of the goals of face-to-face play is to develop and maintain **synchrony,** coordinated interaction between infant and caregiver. Synchrony has been variously described by researchers as the meshing of a finely tuned machine (Snow, 1984), an emotional "attunement" of an improvised musical duet (Stern, 1985), and a smoothly flowing "waltz" that is mutually adaptive (Barnard & Martell, 1995). The critical factor is the split-second timing of the interaction, such that each responds to the other. Synchrony helps infants learn to express and read emotions (Bremner, 1988). Through synchrony they begin to develop some of the basic skills of social interaction, such as taking turns, that they will use throughout life.

These play episodes occur in almost any context—during a feeding, a diaper change, or a bath, for example. After a while, they can be initiated by either the adult or the infant: The caregiver might notice the baby's expression or vocalization and echo it (such as cooing when the baby coos), or the baby might notice the adult's wide-eyed beaming and break into a grin.

What really distinguishes episodes of synchrony from routine caregiving are the moment-by-moment actions and reactions of both partners. To complement the infant's animated but quite limited repertoire, as well as to elicit new or increased reactions, caregivers perform dozens of actions that seem to be reserved exclusively for babies. Typically, they may open their eyes and mouths wide in exaggerated expressions of mock delight or surprise; make rapid clucking noises or repeat one-syllable sounds ("ba-ba-ba-ba-ba," "di-di-di-di," "bo-bo-bo-bo");

Synchrony can be observed even in the early months of an infant's life. Adults tend to modify the timing and pace of their invitations to play in accordance with their babies' readiness to respond, and infants modify their social and emotional expressiveness (smiling, looking, cooing) to match their caregivers' overtures. But synchrony is not necessarily common or constant. In fact, true synchrony occurs less than one-third of the time in normal adult–infant play. Gradually, however, infants and caregivers learn how to socialize smoothly and how to remedy or repair social awkwardness and lapses—a process that is an invaluable life lesson (Biringen et al., 1997).

Generally, repair is not difficult. The signs of dyssynchrony are obvious—the baby's averted eyes, stiffening or abrupt shifting of the body, an unhappy noise—and the alert caregiver can quickly make adjustments, allowing the infant to recover and return to synchrony. Depending on their temperament and maturity, some infants take longer than others to recover. Because development of the central nervous system improves awareness and timing, 5-month-olds are able to lead the "dance" notably better than 3-month-olds (Lester et al., 1985). Gender differences are apparent by 6 months, with boys displaying more synchrony but also more distress. Mothers need to be more adept at relationship repair with sons than with daughters (Weinberg et al., 1999). Throughout the first year, the main choreographer of synchrony is the caregiver (Feldman et al., 1999).

There are two main impediments to the initiation and repair of synchrony:

- *Either* the caregiver ignores the infant's invitation to interact,
- *Or* the caregiver overstimulates a baby who wants to pause and rest (Isabella & Belsky, 1991).

If infants are repeatedly ignored, they do not try as much to respond. Offspring of depressed mothers, for example, are less likely than others to smile and vocalize, not only when interacting with their mothers but also when responding to a nondepressed adult (Field, 1995). At the other extreme, infants whose caregivers are intrusive and overstimulating are more obvious in their self-defense: they turn away or even "shut down" completely—perhaps crying inconsolably or going to sleep. Unfortunately, some caregivers miss all the cues, as Jenny's mother did in what follows:

> Whenever a moment of mutual gaze occurred, the mother went immediately into high-gear stimulating behaviors, producing a profusion of fully displayed, high-intensity, facial and vocal . . . social behavior. Jenny invariably broke gaze rapidly. Her mother never interpreted this temporary face and gaze aversion as a cue to lower her level of behavior, nor would she let Jenny self-control the level by gaining distance. Instead she would swing her head around following Jenny's to reestablish the full-face position. Jenny again turned away, pushing her face further into the pillow to try to break all visual contact. Again, instead of holding back, the mother continued to chase Jenny. . . . She also escalated the level of her stimulation more by adding touching and tickling to the unabated flow of vocal and facial behavior. . . . Jenny closed her eyes to avoid any mutual visual contact and only reopened them after [she had moved her head to the other side]. All of these behaviors on Jenny's part were performed with a sober face or at times a grimace. [Stern, 1977]

This example clearly shows the mother's insensitivity, but an infant's personality and predispositions also affect the ease of synchrony. In particular, infants who are oversensitive to stimulation have problems with an intrusive caregiver like Jenny's mother. Fortunately, even with such a mismatch, repair is achievable. Sometimes a helpful outsider can teach the caregiver how to read the baby's signals, and sometimes the baby and caregiver begin to adjust to each other spontaneously. Jenny, for example, eventually became more able to adjust to her mother's episodes of overstimulation. Then her mother, finding Jenny more responsive, no longer felt the need to bombard her with stimulation as she had earlier. With time, Jenny and her mother established a mutually rewarding relationship.

raise and lower the pitch of their voices; change the pace of their movements (gradually speeding up or slowing down); imitate the infant's actions; bring their faces close to the baby's and then pull back; tickle, pat, poke, lift, rock, stroke, and do many other simple things. (You may well recognize some of these behaviors as your own natural reaction to a baby—sometimes surprising yourself and amusing those around you!) Infants' responses complement the actions of adults: They may stare at

Not every difficult relationship finds repair on its own, however. One example involves a boy who was welcomed, but perhaps somewhat ignored, in infancy. Here is his father's description of Jacob's infancy:

We were convinced that we were set. We had surpassed our quota of 2.6 children and were ready to engage parental auto-pilot. I had just begun a prestigious job and was working 10–11 hours a day. The children would be fine. We hired a nanny to watch Jacob during the day.

As each of Jacob's early milestones passed we felt that we had taken another step toward our goal of having three normal children. We were on our way to the perfect American family. Yet, somewhere back in our minds we had some doubts. Jacob seemed different than the girls. He had some unusual attributes. There were times when we would be holding him and he would arch his back and scream so loud that it was painful for us.

Jacob was unable to relate to his parents (or to anyone else) for the first two years of his life, although his parents were not really aware of the problem. They already had two daughters, so they noticed that something was odd, but they told themselves "boys are different"; they blamed his inability to talk on a nanny who did not speak English well. His father continues:

Jacob had become increasingly isolated [by age 2]. I'm not a psychologist, but I believe that he just stopped trying. It was too hard, perhaps too scary. He couldn't figure out what was expected of him. The world had become too confusing, and so he withdrew from it. He would seek out the comfort of quiet, dark places and sit by himself. He would lose himself in the bright colorful images of cartoons and animated movies.

When Jacob was finally diagnosed with a "pervasive development disorder" at age 3, his despairing parents were advised to consider residential placement. Then, luckily, they found a psychologist who taught them about "floor time," 4 hours a day when the parents were supposed to get on their son's level and do anything to interact with the child, imitating him, acting as if they were part of the game, putting their faces and bodies in front of his, creating synchrony even though Jacob did nothing to initiate it. The father continues:

We rebuilt Jacob's connection to us and to the world—but on his terms. We were drilled to always follow his lead, to always build on his initiative. In a sense, we could only ask Jacob to join our world if we were willing to enter his. . . . He would drop rocks and we would catch them. He would want to put pennies in a bank and we would block the slot. He would want to run in a circle and we would get in his way. I remember a cold fall day when I was putting lime on our lawn. He dipped his hand in the powder and let it slip through his fingers. He loved the way it felt. I took the lawn spreader and ran to the other part of our yard. He ran after me. I let him have one dip and ran across the yard again. He dipped, I ran, he dipped, I ran. We did this until I could no longer move my arms.

Jacob's case is obviously extreme, but many infants and parents have difficulty establishing synchronistic interaction. From the perspective of early psychosocial development, nothing could be more important.

In Jacob's case it worked. He said his first word at age 3, and by age 5 [as his father notes], . . . he speaks for days at a time. He talks from the moment he wakes up to the moment he falls asleep, as if he is making up for lost time. He wants to know everything. "How does a live chicken become an eating chicken? Why are microbes so small? Why do policemen wear badges? Why are dinosaurs extinct? What is French? [A question I often ask myself.] Why do ghosts glow in the dark?" He is not satisfied with answers that do not ring true or that do not satisfy his standards of clarity. He will keep on asking until he gets it. Rebecca and I have become expert definition providers. Just last week, we were faced with the ultimate challenge: "Dad," he asked: "Is God real or not?" And then, just to make it a bit more challenging, he added: "How do miracles happen?"

❶ *Answer to Observational Quiz (from page 203):*
The positioning of the mouths and lips, the half-closed eyes, and the tilt of the heads of both father and son.

their partners or look away, vocalize, widen their eyes, smile, move their heads forward or back, or turn aside. (See the In Person box.)

Cross-Cultural Variation

It appears that episodes of face-to-face play are a universal feature of the early interaction between caregivers and infants. However, the frequency and duration of these episodes, as well as the goals of the adults who initiate them, differ in different cultures. Here are the results of three studies contrasting mother–infant play:

- North American mothers often direct their infants' attention to a nearby toy, object, or event, while Japanese mothers typically focus on establishing mutual intimacy by maintaining eye contact with their infants as well as kissing, hugging, and such (Bornstein et al., 1992).
- Whereas mothers in a New England city employed social overtures (such as tickling) that stimulated and excited their babies, mothers from the Gusii community in rural Kenya were more soothing and quieting in their initiatives (LeVine et al., 1994).
- Among three French-speaking cultures in Quebec, Canada—Vietnamese, Haitian, and native-born Quebeçois—mothers responded to their infants' active curiosity in different ways. The Vietnamese mothers tended to guide and restrict many of their infants' exploratory activities, limiting the infants' individual initiative. By contrast, the Haitian mothers encouraged their infants, particularly to interact socially with anyone nearby. The Quebeçois mothers were also encouraging, particularly with toys—including allowing their infants to mouth objects that the Vietnamese or Haitian mothers would have immediately taken away (Sabatier, 1994).

Mothers are not the only ones who engage infants in face-to-face play. Fathers are also active partners and, as you have seen, sometimes are better playmates than mothers. In many non-Western cultures, older siblings and other adults also assume an active role in infant care and participate in social play with babies (Tronick et al., 1992; Zukow-Goldring, 1995).

Attachment

The relationship between parent and child is lifelong, and even adult children and their parents can have episodes of quick-response interaction, with mutual glances and laughter. The term "synchrony" is, however, usually reserved for the first year, when preverbal play predominates. Another term, **attachment,** is used particularly to describe the relationship between parents and slightly older infants. Attachment, according to Mary Ainsworth (1973), "may be defined as an affectional tie that one person or animal forms between himself and another specific one—a tie that binds them together in space and endures over time."

Not surprisingly, when people are attached to each other, they try to be near one another and they interact with each other often. Thus children show attachment through **proximity-seeking behaviors**—such as approaching, following, and climbing onto the caregiver's lap—and through **contact-maintaining behaviors,** such as clinging, resisting being put down, and using social referencing once they are moving around on their own. Parents show their attachment by keeping a watchful eye, even when safety

attachment   An enduring emotional connection between people that produces a desire for continual contact as well as feelings of distress during separation.

proximity-seeking behaviors   Behaviors that are intended to place a person close to another person to whom he or she is attached.

contact-maintaining behaviors   Behaviors that are intended to keep a person near another person to whom he or she is attached.

A Demonstration of Attachment   The man on the right is John Bowlby, a British scholar who was the first to link Freud's theories of mother–infant connection with practical research on other animal species. After studying with Bowlby in London, a young American woman named Mary Ainsworth (at left) went to central Africa to observe attachment between mothers and infants. Her naturalistic observations led to an experimental measurement of attachment which she used in Baltimore and which has now been used in every region of the world. Note that although the photo shows these two colleagues in a formal academic context, attachment is evident in various "contact-maintaining behaviors."

does not require it, and by responding affectionately and sensitively to vocalizations, expressions, and gestures. Many parents enjoy tiptoeing to the crib to gaze at their sleeping infant, and many like to smooth the toddler's hair or pat a hand or a cheek—examples of proximity seeking and contact maintaining, respectively. Attachment not only deepens the parent–child relationship but, over our long evolutionary history, may also have contributed to human survival by keeping infants near their caregivers and keeping caregivers vigilant.

Measuring Attachment

Ainsworth found, as many other scientists have, that universal human characteristics are most easily noticed in a place where one's usual cultural blindness is removed. She therefore went to Central Africa to observe mothers and infants in a culture different from her own. She found that, while the specifics of mother–infant interaction were different from those in England or the United States (for example, there was more physical contact but no kissing), the bonds of affection were still visible in various proximity-seeking and contact-maintaining behaviors (Ainsworth, 1967). Ainsworth discovered that virtually all normal infants develop special attachments to the people who care for them and that some infants are more secure in their attachments than others—a fact later confirmed by hundreds of other researchers (Bretherton, 1992; Colin, 1996).

Secure attachment provides comfort and confidence, as evidenced first by the infant's attempts to be close to the caregiver and then, equally important, by the infant's readiness to explore. In such a relationship the caregiver acts as a *secure base for exploration* from which the child is willing to venture forth. The child might, for example, scramble down from the caregiver's lap to play with a toy but periodically look back, vocalize a few syllables, or return for a hug. This is a step beyond social referencing; it is reestablishing contact.

By contrast, **insecure attachment** is characterized by an infant's fear, anxiety, anger, or seeming indifference toward a caregiver. The insecurely attached child has much less confidence, perhaps being unwilling to let go of the caregiver's arms or perhaps playing aimlessly without trying to maintain contact with the caregiver.

Ainsworth developed a laboratory procedure, called the **Strange Situation,** to measure attachment. The now-classic Strange Situation is designed to evoke an infant's reactions to the caregiver (usually the mother) under somewhat stressful conditions. In a well-equipped playroom, the subject infant is closely observed in eight 3-minute-long episodes. In each segment, the infant is with the caregiver, with a stranger, with both, or alone. The first episode has caregiver and child together, and then every 3 minutes one or the other of two adults (stranger or caregiver) enters or leaves the playroom.

The infant's reactions indicate motivation to be near the caregiver (proximity and contact) and whether the caregiver's presence is a secure base (confidence to venture forth). The key observational aspects of the Strange Situation are:

- *Exploration of the toys.* A securely attached toddler plays happily when the caregiver is present.
- *Reaction to the caregiver's departure.* A securely attached toddler may or may not show some sign that the caregiver is missed—a loud cry, or perhaps only a pause and a woeful look.
- *Reaction to the caregiver's return.* A securely attached toddler exhibits

secure attachment A caregiver–infant relationship that provides comfort and confidence, as evidenced first by the infant's attempts to be close to the caregiver and then by the infant's readiness to explore.

insecure attachment A caregiver–infant relationship characterized by the child's overdependence on, or lack of interest in, the caregiver and by a lack of confidence on the part of the child.

Strange Situation An experimental condition devised by Mary Ainsworth to assess an infant's attachment to a caregiver. The infant's behavior is observed in an unfamiliar room while the caregiver (usually the mother) and a stranger move in and out of the room.

The Attachment Experiment In this episode of the Strange Situation, Brian shows every sign of secure attachment. *(a)* He explores the playroom happily when his mother is present; *(b)* he cries when she leaves; and *(c)* he is readily comforted when she returns.

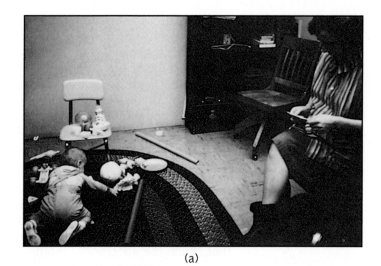

(a)

(b)

(c)

a welcoming response when the caregiver returns to the room after leaving—especially when this occurs for a second time.

Almost two-thirds of all normal infants tested in the Strange Situation demonstrate secure attachment. The mother's presence in the playroom is enough to give them courage to explore the room and investigate the toys; her departure may cause some distress (usually expressed through verbal protest and a pause in playing); and her return is a signal to reestablish positive social contact (with a smile or by climbing into the mother's arms) and then resume playing. This balanced reaction—concerned about the mother's departure but not overwhelmed by it—is called type-B attachment. The remaining one-third of infants show one of three types of insecure attachment, which are referred to as types A, C, and D: avoidant, resistant, and disorganized (see Table 7.1).

Attachment and Context

Ainsworth's Strange Situation has been used in thousands of studies, and her seminal concepts regarding attachment have been the basis for additional thousands of studies. From them we have learned that attachment is powerfully affected by the quality of care in early infancy, as well as by the caregiver's past experiences and the infant's tempera-

table 7.1	Patterns of Attachment in Infancy
Type of Attachment	**Characteristics of Infant**
Type B: Secure	Uses caregiver as a "secure base," explores freely when the caregiver is available, may or may not be distressed at separation but greets caregiver positively on reunion, seeks contact if distressed, settles down, returns to exploration. Includes 55 to 65% of infant population.
Type A: Insecure-avoidant	Appears minimally interested in caregiver, explores busily, shows minimal distress at separation, ignores or avoids caregiver on reunion. Includes 15 to 25% of infant population.
Type C: Insecure-resistant	Does minimal exploration, is preoccupied with caregiver, has difficulty settling down, both seeks and resists contact on reunion, may be angry or very passive. Includes 10 to 15% of infant population.
Type D: Insecure-disorganized (disoriented and ambivalent)	Exhibits disorganized and/or disoriented behavior in the caregiver's presence (e.g., approaches with head averted, engages in trancelike freezing, adopts anomalous postures). Infants placed in this category are also "forced" into the best fit of the preceding categories. Includes 10 to 20% of infant population.
Other (cannot classify)	Some children may not fit any of the four patterns. This is rare, except in combination with insecure-disorganized classification.

Source: Adapted from Goldberg et al., 1995.

ment (Ainsworth, 1993; Belsky & Cassidy, 1995; DeWolff & van Ijzendoorn, 1997; Thompson, 1998). Among the caregiving features that have been shown to increase the quality of attachment are:

- General sensitivity to the infant's needs
- Responsiveness to the infant's specific signals
- Infant–caregiver play that actively encourages the child's growth and development

Not surprisingly, greater synchrony in early interactions between a mother and a young infant tends to produce more secure attachment between mother and toddler.

Attachment is also influenced by the broader family context, including the extent and quality of the father's involvement in the child's care and the nature of the marital relationship, and by the overall social context (Belsky, 1996; Colin, 1996; van Ijzendoorn & DeWolff, 1997). Attachment can be affected by any change in family circumstances—such as a parent losing his or her job—that alters established patterns of family interaction. Partly for this reason, changes in attachment status are not uncommon during toddlerhood. Further, an infant can be attached to one caregiver but not another—to the father or grandmother but not the mother, for instance. Or the infant can be attached, quite securely, to two or three caregivers.

The Importance of Attachment

An infant's attachment pattern may be a preview of the child's social and personality development in the years to come. Securely attached infants tend to become children who interact with teachers in friendly and appropriate ways, who seek help when needed, and who are competent in a wide array of social and cognitive skills (Belsky & Cassidy, 1995; Fagot, 1997; Turner, 1993).

Does this mean that whether attachment is secure or insecure in infancy *determines* whether the child will grow up to be sociable or

❷ **Especially for Social Workers:** Suppose you are sent to investigate an accusation of maltreatment of a 1-year-old. What will you look for?

No One Cares This Romanian boy was born under the totalitarian Ceausescu regime, which prohibited abortion and all forms of birth control. Like thousands of other babies, he had been abandoned by both parents and put in an orphanage, where personal attention, any sort of attachment, and toys were absent. This photo was taken in 1990, shortly after the rest of the world became aware of these conditions and sent clothes and toys to the orphanages (which explains the doll's head). If he is still alive, this boy is now an adolescent, and he probably still shows many signs of his early deprivation.

aggressive, self-directed or dependent, curious or withdrawing? No. As measured by the Strange Situation, attachment is not the cause, but a sign, a symptom, and sometimes a predictor of the direction a child's development will take. Attachment often indicates the nature of the relationship between child and caregiver, and that usually continues through childhood (Crittenden, 1995). A sensitive caregiver who fosters secure attachment is likely to maintain this approach as the child matures, encouraging the development of sociability, curiosity, and independence. And, unfortunately, insensitive care that contributes to insecure attachment is also likely to be maintained, pushing the child toward caution, aggressiveness, or dependence.

Remember, however, that attachment relationships sometimes change. As we noted, shifts in family circumstances (a divorce, a new job, better day care, a new baby) often alter patterns of family interaction and, thus, of attachment. And, as attachment patterns change, so do their long-term effects. Thus, a child who is insecurely attached at age 1 might become securely attached by age 2, and this would considerably brighten any long-term predictions about personality. Conversely, disruptions in the family, such as divorce or abuse, can shake loose an early, secure attachment (Beckwith et al., 1999).

The idea that early relationships do not inevitably determine later social relationships is important; it provides a basis for helpful intervention. In one study with Spanish-speaking immigrant families in the United States, for example, three groups of 1-year-olds were compared: a securely attached group and two groups of insecurely attached infants. The mothers of one insecure group were visited weekly at home by an empathic bilingual and bicultural adviser. Within a year, these mothers and infants were relating to each other almost as well as the mothers and group of infants who were originally securely attached—and far better than the nontreatment infants and their mothers, as indicated by infant anger, maternal responsiveness, and similar measures (Lieberman et al., 1991).

Another study involved 100 Dutch infants who were at risk of insecure attachment because of their own difficult temperaments and their mothers' stressful low-income status. Half of them received three home visits designed to foster synchrony—advisers taught the mothers when and how to play with, feed, and soothe their babies. Four months later, in the Strange Situation, 72 percent of these infants qualified as securely attached, compared to only 32 percent of the remaining 50 infants, who had had no such home visits (Van den Boom, 1995). Happy outcomes like these tell us that although temperament and early stresses may provide a fragile foundation for later growth, that foundation can usually be strengthened (see the Research Report on pages 212–213).

Research also reminds us that although responsive parenting and frequent synchrony are likely to lead to secure attachment, it is not always the parents' fault when the attachment is insecure. For example, one study examined the four possible attachment relationships in families of four: mother, father, 1½-year-old, and 4½-year-old. Thus each family had four attachment relationships: mother–infant, mother–child, father–infant, father–child. In almost a third (30%) of the families, all four relationships were secure. None of the families completely lacked secure relationships. However, as Figure 7.1 shows, the percentages of infants and children who tended to be insecure with their parents were higher than the percentages of parents who were insecure with their children. Thus the child's temperament, even more than the parent's caregiving pattern, seems to affect the parent–child connection (Rosen & Burke, 1999).

A theme emerges from this and the other two chapters on early infancy. Tremendous growth—physical, cognitive, linguistic, emotional, and social—occurs in the first 2 years of life. That growth may be hampered, guided, or encouraged by both the immediate family and the cultural context. The theme is that impressive growth demands a nurturant context. To ask "Is maternal care, paternal care, or day care best for infants?" and "Who should pay for infant care?" and "How does infant temperament affect the quality of attachment relationships?" is to ask the wrong questions. Every infant should experience high-quality care, but many infants have only one good caregiver and some have none. Chapters 5, 6, and 7 describe many signs of excellent care, manifested by everything from early eye–hand coordination to responsive vocalization, as detailed by thousands of researchers. The right question for all of us, scientists and practitioners alike, is, How can we make sure that somehow, somewhere, somebody provides it?

Figure 7.1 How Attached? A study of the four possible attachment relationships within families of four found that the child's temperament had a stronger effect on the attachment relationship than did the parent's caregiving pattern. As the middle bar in each set of three bars reveals, infants and children were more likely to have an insecure attachment to their parents than parents were to have an insecure attachment to their children.

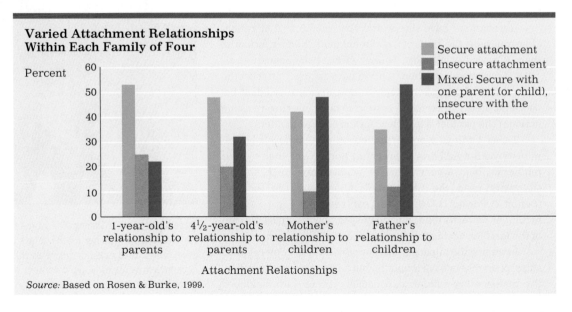

Source: Based on Rosen & Burke, 1999.

ATTACHMENT THROUGHOUT THE LIFE SPAN

Each of us has a long history of attachment experiences with our parents, best friends, and romantic partners. As you know from your own experience, every new relationship can inspire trust or anxiety, thereby influencing expectations about future attachments. Recently, researchers have begun to examine whether the security or insecurity of adults' past relationships affects attachment with the next generations.

Mary Main and her colleagues created the Adult Attachment Interview (AAI), an hour-long series of questions about childhood attachment experiences, perceptions of early trust and security, and current relationships with parents and adult partners (Main, 1995). On the basis of the responses, adults are classified into four categories:

- *Autonomous.* Autonomous adults value close relationships and regard them as influential. However, they are not overwhelmed by emotions concerning their childhood attachments; they can discuss them with some objectivity, including negative as well as positive aspects.
- *Dismissing.* Dismissing adults tend to devalue the importance and influence of their attachment relationships. Sometimes they idealize their early relationships with their parents without being able to provide specific examples to support their view.
- *Preoccupied.* Preoccupied adults are very involved with their childhood experiences. They are unable to discuss early attachment relationships objectively, and they often show considerable emotion when asked about their relationships with their parents.
- *Unresolved.* Unresolved adults have not yet reconciled their past attachments with their current ones. They are still trying to understand parental rejection, death, or other early experiences.

Researchers have discovered that mothers' AAI ratings closely parallel the kinds of attachment their children form with them (Crowell et al., 1996; Fonagy et al., 1995; Zeanah et al., 1993). Autonomous mothers tend to have securely attached infants; dismissing mothers tend to have insecure-avoidant babies; and preoccupied mothers tend to have insecure-resistant infants. (The parallel is less clear for unresolved mothers.)

These findings were extended by researchers who administered the AAI first to pregnant women and then to their mothers. About a year after the women gave birth, the researchers used the Strange Situation with the toddlers (Benoit & Parker, 1994). As you can see from Figure 7.2, attachment patterns tended to be passed down, with 64 percent of the families having the same status in all three generations.

In tracing the impact of early experiences on adult relationships, researchers have found that an adult's ability to be reflective makes a big difference, especially if their own childhood attachments were insecure and if current life is stressful. If adults realize that their parents may have intended one thing but had done another, they are much more likely to develop secure relationships with their own children. Indeed, one group of researchers found that, even under stressful conditions, highly reflective mothers had securely attached infants. By contrast, mothers who were unable to reflect on past experiences almost always had insecurely attached infants (one such woman said, "My mother loved all us children; I don't remember any more") (Fonagy et al., 1995). Why is this true? Another study has found that mothers who describe their own past attachment as autonomous also tend to express more joy in their infants and are more responsive because of it. Mothers who are dismissive of their past relationship tend to show anger toward their infants (Slade et al., 1999).

As you may remember from Chapters 1 and 2, scientists look for the connections between theory and observation and simultaneously develop alternative hypotheses for the research results that are found. The conclusion of this research—that early mother–child relationships have long-term effects that can be influenced by adult insights—tends to confirm the central tenets of psychoanalytic and cognitive theories: First, childhood experiences, even those of early infancy, affect adult attitudes and behavior, and, second, understanding those experiences (as might happen in cognitive therapy) can overcome some of the damage that may have occurred. However, such conclusions are controversial, especially for those who believe

Three Generations of Smiling The woman in the middle is the mother, watching happily as her mother plays with 1-year-old Jonathon. Not every adult child is as fortunate as this mother; some who had insecure attachments may avoid contact with their mothers throughout their lives or may resist becoming caregivers for their own children.

Three Generations of Attachment

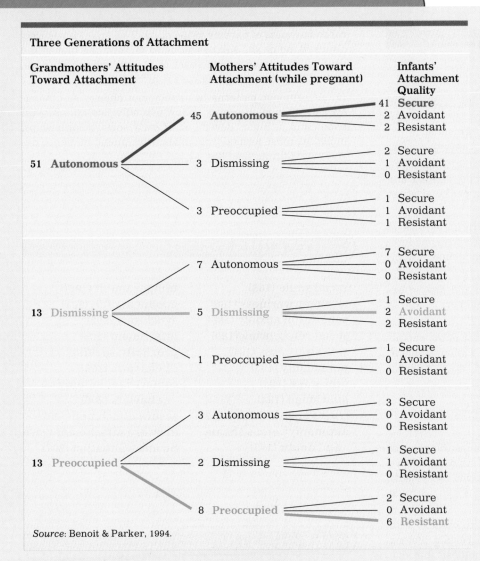

Grandmothers' Attitudes Toward Attachment — **Mothers' Attitudes Toward Attachment (while pregnant)** — **Infants' Attachment Quality**

51 Autonomous
- 45 **Autonomous**
  - 41 Secure
  - 2 Avoidant
  - 2 Resistant
- 3 Dismissing
  - 2 Secure
  - 1 Avoidant
  - 0 Resistant
- 3 Preoccupied
  - 1 Secure
  - 1 Avoidant
  - 1 Resistant

13 Dismissing
- 7 Autonomous
  - 7 Secure
  - 0 Avoidant
  - 0 Resistant
- 5 Dismissing
  - 1 Secure
  - 2 Avoidant
  - 2 Resistant
- 1 Preoccupied
  - 1 Secure
  - 0 Avoidant
  - 0 Resistant

13 Preoccupied
- 3 Autonomous
  - 3 Secure
  - 0 Avoidant
  - 0 Resistant
- 2 Dismissing
  - 1 Secure
  - 1 Avoidant
  - 0 Resistant
- 8 Preoccupied
  - 2 Secure
  - 0 Avoidant
  - 6 Resistant

Source: Benoit & Parker, 1994.

Figure 7.2 Attitudes and Attachment Using the Adult Attachment Interview, researchers rated the attachment attitudes of pregnant women and those of their mothers. The ratings comprised three categories: autonomous (valuing attachment objectively), dismissing (tending to devalue attachment), and preoccupied (emotional about attachment). More than a year later, blind observers (researchers who know nothing of the subjects' previous ratings) rated the attachment quality of the formerly pregnant women and their infants by using the Strange Situation. The results show that attachment attitudes tend to be transmitted intergenerationally (e.g., of the 51 autonomous grandmothers, 45 had autonomous daughters). Further, the attitudes of the mothers seem to be reflected in the quality of their infants' attachment (e.g., of the 55 autonomous mothers, 51 had securely attached infants).

that childhood experiences are less powerful than psychoanalytic theorists believed. Here are five alternative explanations:

- Adults who value attachment and can reflect objectively on their own experiences (i.e., autonomous adults) may be naturally more sensitive to their offspring and therefore inspire a secure attachment as a result. This explanation suggests that it is not past attachment experiences but, rather, current attitudes that are crucial.
- Inherited temperament may predispose individuals to reciprocate certain attachment patterns, so what seems like a generational legacy of learned mother–infant patterns is actually a genetic transmission.
- Parents' current attachment with their own children may affect their memories of first attachments. Thus the AAI is a snapshot of the present, disguised as a mirror of the past.
- Some cultural contexts may encourage attachments while others do not; so what appears to be a correlation within families actually reflects a cultural influence that each generation of a family experiences (Grossman, 1995).

- Finally, life experiences after infancy may have an impact (Bruer, 1999). One study began by rating the responsiveness of mothers of 86 low-birthweight infants. At age 18, children of responsive mothers were usually secure (52%) compared to children of unresponsive mothers (33%). More telling, even with mothers who were responsive in infancy, is that children who experienced life stresses (divorce, abuse, etc.) were rarely secure 18-year-olds (39%). This was in marked contrast to those children who had responsive mothers but who also had relatively stable childhoods (71%) (Beckwith et al., 1999).

Whatever the explanation for the connections that are found, it does seem useful for each of us to look back to our attachments with our early caregivers and understand how those attachments might influence our current actions and attitudes with partners, parents, and children. If Ainsworth is correct and attachment provides a secure base for exploration, our approach to learning and to intellectual inquiry may be the result of long-ago playfulness at our mothers' knees!

SUMMARY

EARLY EMOTIONS

1. From birth onward infants express distress, sadness, and contentment. Pleasure is expressed in a first social smile at about 6 weeks and the first laughter at about 4 months.

2. Fear also begins early, and stranger wariness and other clear signs of fear are evident at about 6 months, when cognitive advances allow differentiation between the familiar and the unexpected. Typically, fearful behavior peaks at about 14 months.

3. Anger builds in the first 2 years, particularly in response to frustration. All the emotions become more selective and individualized in their expression, and all are influenced by culture.

4. The social context teaches infants when and how to express their emotions. Social referencing—to fathers as well as mothers—begins at about 6 months.

5. Self-awareness develops in the second year of life and allows a new set of emotions, including pride, embarrassment, and jealousy. At this time the infant becomes less predictable and less compliant.

THE ORIGINS OF PERSONALITY

6. Learning theorists believe that personality is the product of early reinforcement and punishment that mold the infant's traits. Young children also observe their parents' personality traits and try to copy them, according to social learning theory.

7. Freud believed that an infant's early experiences with feeding and toilet training could establish certain lifelong personality traits. This is an influential hypothesis, but one that has not been proved by research. Psychoanalytic theory also emphasized the central role of the mother, the child's first and most enduring love object.

8. Erikson believed that an infant's early experiences, first in trusting that basic needs will be met and then in developing self-expression (autonomy), create personality traits. He also felt that a person can, later in life, resolve developmental crises that appear during these early stages.

9. Epigenetic systems theorists regard personality as an expression of temperament, which is a set of inborn tendencies that affect, and are affected by, each person's interactions with people, situations, and events.

INTERACTION AGAIN

10. The interaction between caregiver and child, or, more specifically, between the social context and the innate temperament of the young infant, is crucial to the shaping of personality. Ideally, in the early months this interaction becomes synchrony, a coordinated series of actions and reactions between infant and caregiver.

11. The attachment between caregiver and infant can be secure or insecure, depending on many factors, including the responsiveness of parents to the child. If an infant is securely attached, he or she will be willing to explore and play in the caregiver's presence, will react to the caregiver's absence, and will welcome the caregiver's return.

12. Attachment patterns in infancy can change as circumstances change. However, many psychologists believe that habits and attitudes developed in early social relationships, including those formed from infant attachment, influence development throughout life.

KEY TERMS

social smile (188)	temperament (198)
stranger wariness (188)	goodness of fit (201)
separation anxiety (188)	synchrony (203)
social referencing (189)	attachment (206)
self-awareness (191)	proximity-seeking
personality (193)	behaviors (206)
oral stage (194)	contact-maintaining
anal stage (194)	behaviors (206)
trust versus mistrust (195)	secure attachment (207)
autonomy versus shame	insecure attachment (207)
and doubt (195)	Strange Situation (207)

KEY QUESTIONS

1. What is the first notable emotion of a newborn, and how does that emotion benefit the newborn?

2. How do emotions develop (change) over the first 2 years of life?

3. What does an infant get from social referencing—both when the infant engages in it (at, say, 8 months of age and older) and later in life?

4. What are some consequences of the toddler's developing sense of self?

5. What are the similarities and differences between mother–infant and father–infant interactions?

6. In the classical view, who and what determine personality?

7. What is temperament, and how is it related to personality?

8. How does synchrony help in the development of the infant?

9. What are the four main types of attachment?

10. How does early attachment affect later psychosocial growth?

11. *In Your Experience* How do infants under age 2 react to you? What is it about your actions, the infant's age and cognitive development, and the parents' presence that affect these reactions?

BIOSOCIAL

Body, Brain, and Nervous System

Over the first 2 years, the body quadruples in weight and the brain triples in weight. Connections between brain cells grow into increasingly dense and complex neural networks of dendrites and axons. As neurons become coated with an insulating layer of myelin, they send messages faster and more efficiently. The infant's experiences are essential in "fine-tuning" the brain's ability to respond to stimulation.

Motor Abilities

Brain maturation allows the development of motor skills from reflexes to coordinated voluntary actions, including grasping and walking. At birth, the infant's senses of smell and hearing are quite acute; although vision at first is sharp only for objects that are about 10 inches away, visual acuity approaches 20/20 by age 1 year.

Health

The health of the infant depends on nutrition (ideally, breast milk), immunization, and parental practices. Survival rates are much higher today than they were even a few decades ago.

COGNITIVE

Perceptual Skills

The infant's senses are linked by both intermodal and cross-modal perception, allowing information to be transferred among senses. The infant is most interested in affordances, that is, what various experiences and events offer to the infant. Movement and personal sensory experiences contribute to the perception of affordances.

Cognitive Skills

The infant's active curiosity and inborn abilities interact with various experiences to develop early categories, such as object size, shape, texture, and even number, as well as an understanding of object permanence. Memory capacity, while fragile, grows during the first years. The infant progresses from knowing his or her world through immediate sensorimotor experiences to being able to "experiment" on that world through the use of mental images.

Language

Babies' cries are their first communication; they then progress through cooing and babbling. Interaction with adults through "baby talk" teaches them the surface structure of language. By age 1, an infant can usually speak a word or two, and by age 2 is talking in short sentences.

PSYCHOSOCIAL

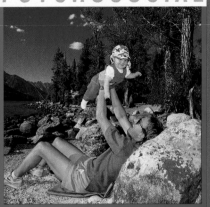

Emotions and Personality Development

Emotions change from quite basic reactions to complex, self-conscious responses. Infants become increasingly independent, a transition explained by Freud in terms of the oral and anal stages, by Erikson in terms of the crises of trust versus mistrust and autonomy versus shame and doubt. While these theories emphasize the parents' role, research finds that much of basic temperament—and therefore personality—is inborn and apparent lifelong.

Parent–Infant Interaction

Early on, parents and infants respond to each other by synchronizing their behavior in social play. Toward the end of the first year, secure attachment between child and parent sets the stage for the child's increasingly independent exploration of the world. The infant becomes an active participant in this social interaction, first in directly reacting to others and then in seeking out opinions through social referencing. By age 2, toddlers have definite personalities, the product of the interaction of nature and nurture.

PART III

The Play Years

The period from ages 2 to 6 is usually called early childhood, or the preschool period. Here we shall call it the "play years" as well, to underscore the importance of play during that time. Play occurs at every age, of course. But the years of early childhood are the most playful of all, for it is then that young children spend most of their waking hours at play, acquiring the skills, ideas, and values that are crucial for growing up. They chase each other and dare themselves to attempt new tasks, developing their bodies; they play with words and ideas, developing their minds; they invent games and dramatize fantasies, learning social skills and moral rules.

The playfulness of young children can cause them to be delightful or exasperating. To them growing up is a game, and their enthusiasm for it seems unlimited—whether they are quietly tracking a beetle through the grass or riotously turning their play area into a shambles. Their minds seem playful too, for the immaturity of their thinking enables them to explain that "a bald man has a barefoot head" or that "the sun shines so children can go outside to play."

If you expect them to sit quietly, think logically, or act realistically, you are bound to be disappointed. But if you enjoy playfulness, you might enjoy caring for, listening to, and even reading about children between 2 and 6 years old.

The Play Years:
Biosocial Development

CHAPTER 8

Between ages 2 and 6, significant biosocial development occurs on several fronts. The most obvious changes are in size and shape, as chubby toddlers seem to stretch up and become thinner as well as taller. Less obvious but more crucial changes occur in the brain and central nervous system. There, maturation turns the clumsy toddler into an accomplished and deft 6-year-old.

Together, these changes in body and brain allow children's exploration and mastery of their world to proceed by leaps and bounds, both literally and figuratively. That exploration typically occurs with joy and imagination, which is one reason this period is called "the play years." But playfulness is not the opposite of productivity; in these years the two coincide. Unfortunately, the combination of growth and play makes the preschool child vulnerable to many biosocial hazards, including accidental injury and, for some children, abuse.

We begin our examination of the play years by looking at the way the child's body proportions change.

SIZE AND SHAPE

During early childhood, children generally become slimmer as the lower body lengthens and some baby fat melts away. Gone are the protruding belly, round face, short limbs, and large head that characterize the toddler. By age 6, body proportions are similar to those of an adult, although muscles, curves, and stature are obviously quite different.

Steady increases in height and weight accompany these changes in proportions. Each year from ages 2 through 6, well-nourished children add almost 3 inches (about 7 centimeters) in height and gain about 4½ pounds (2 kilograms) in weight. By age 6, the average child in a developed nation weighs about 46 pounds (21 kilograms) and measures 46 inches (117 centimeters). These are averages; actual children vary a great deal, especially in weight (see Appendix A).

Several factors that influence growth are listed in Table 8.1. Of these, the three most influential are:

- Genetic background
- Health care
- Nutrition

POOR EATING HABITS

For all children, even in the richest families and nations, annual height and weight gains are much lower between ages 2 and 6 than they were during the first 2 years of life (Eveleth & Tanner, 1990). Growth gradually speeds up again, especially at puberty, until it slows once more at about age 16 (for girls) or 18 (for boys).

As a result, preschool children need fewer calories per pound of body weight than they did as infants—especially if they are modern sedentary children who spend most of their time indoors. Their appetites decrease markedly, a fact that causes many parents to fret, threaten, and cajole to get their children to eat more ("If you eat your dinner, you can have your cake"). However, reduced appetite is not a medical problem unless a child is unusually thin or is not gaining any weight at all.

Of course, the food consumed during the preschool years should be nutritious, but it often isn't. The most common diet deficiency in developed countries during early childhood is *iron-deficiency anemia,* and one of its main symptoms is chronic fatigue. Anemia, which stems from an insufficiency of quality meats, whole grains, eggs, and dark-green vegetables, is three times more common among low-income families than among others, because less expensive foods tend to contain less iron. Adding to this problem among families of every social class is the tendency to give young children candy, sugary drinks (soda, fruit-flavored punch, chocolate milk), sweetened cereals, and other sweets. Because these items spoil a small appetite very quickly, they can keep a child from consuming foods that contain essential vitamins and minerals.

Since some essential nutrients have not yet been identified, foods (usually high in sugar) that are advertised as containing a day's worth of added vitamins nonetheless lack crucial nourishment. Such advertisements are particularly misleading for parents of preschoolers, because the child who eats these foods ends up eating fewer healthy foods and thus is more likely to have a vitamin deficiency.

Too much sugar also is the main cause of early tooth decay, the most prevalent disease of young children in developed nations (Lewit & Kerrebrock, 1998). Many cultures promote children's eating of sweets, in the form of birthday cake, holiday candy, Halloween treats, and such. The details (e.g., chocolate Easter bunnies or Hanukkah gelt) depend on family ethnicity and religion, but the general trend is pervasive and hard to resist.

A related problem is that many children, like most adults, eat too few fruits and vegetables and consume too much fat. No more than 30 percent of daily calories should come from fat, but six out of seven preschoolers in the United States exceed that limit. Interestingly, one North American study found that children whose family income is either below the poverty level or three times above it are more likely to exceed the 30 percent fat limit, compared to those whose income lies between the two extremes (Thompson & Dennison, 1994).

Adding to the complications of feeding a 4-year-old well is the fact that many preschoolers are quite compulsive about daily routines, including meals. For example:

> Whereas parents may insist that the child eat his vegetables at dinner, the child may insist that the potatoes be placed only in a certain part of the plate and must not touch any other food; should the potatoes land outside of this area, the child may seem to experience a sense of near-contamination, setting off a tirade of fussiness for which many 2- and 3-year-olds are notorious. [Evans et al., 1997]

Most preschoolers' food preferences and rituals are far from nutritionally ideal. (One preschooler I know wanted to

The last factor—nutrition—is largely responsible for dramatic differences between children in developed and underdeveloped nations. In the Netherlands, average 4-year-olds are already taller than 6-year-olds in India, Nepal, or Bangladesh, where undernourishment stunts the growth of 65 percent of children (Eveleth & Tanner, 1991; United Nations, 1994). Similar height disparities occur when children living in Africa or South America are compared to children of the same African or Latino descent who grow up in Europe or North America. Genetically, such children are quite similar, but marked differences in food supply cause dramatic contrasts in height (see the Research Report).

eat only cream cheese sandwiches on white bread; another, only fast-food chicken nuggets.)

The preschool child's insistence on eating only certain foods, prepared and placed in a particular way, would be pathological in an adult but is normal for young children. About 1,500 parents answered questions about the desire of their 1- to 6-year-olds to have familiar routines and habits (Evans et al., 1997). More than 75 percent of the 2- to 4-year-olds

- preferred to have things done in a particular order or in a certain way
- had a strong preference for wearing (or not wearing) certain articles of clothing
- prepared for bedtime by engaging in a special activity or routine or by doing or saying things in a certain order or certain way
- had strong preferences for certain foods.

By age 6, this insistence on routine begins to fade. The items measuring demand that things be "just right" (e.g., "liked to eat food in a particular way") showed a marked decline after age 4 (see Figure 8.2).

Given both the power and the transience of this behavior in normal children, parents should probably be tolerant of most of its manifestations. Insistence on a particular bedtime routine or preferred pair of shoes or favorite cup can usually be accommodated until the child no longer wants the item. Malnutrition is another story; the best approach here is to offer ample healthy foods when the child is hungry.

Fortunately, many of the foods that parents think are essential are not the only ways to nourish a child. Milk can be replaced by cheese, meat by beans and rice, cereal by bread, spinach by other green vegetables. It is also fortunate that children are naturally active and hungry: If high-fat and high-

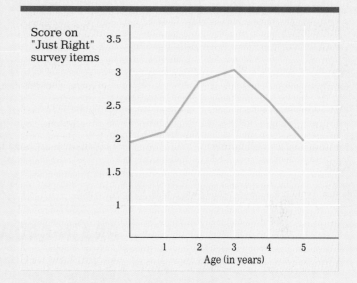

Figure 8.2 Young Children's Insistence on Routine. This chart shows the average scores of children (who are rated by their parents) on a survey indicating the child's desire to have certain things—including food selection and preparation—done "Just right." Such strong preferences for rigid routines tend to fade by age 6.

sugar foods are kept unavailable, a hungry child will settle for eating something nutritious. If that turns out to be a sandwich for breakfast, a bowl of oatmeal for dinner, or a lunch consisting of exactly 50 peas, 50 raisins, and five peanut butter crackers, parents are well advised to yield the victory in this particular battle.

When many ethnic groups live together in one developed nation (such as England, France, Canada, Australia, or the United States), children of African descent tend to be tallest, followed by Europeans, then Asians, and then Latinos. However, these are very broad generalities; many ethnic groups and individual families exhibit quite different inherited height patterns (Eveleth & Tanner, 1990). Even in developed nations, height is particularly variable among children of African descent, because various groups living in Africa over many centuries developed more genetic diversity than did people on any other continent.

table **8.1**	**Factors Affecting the Height of Preschoolers**	
Taller Than Average if		**Shorter Than Average if**
Well nourished		Malnourished
Rarely sick		Frequently or chronically sick
Of African or northern European ancestry		Of Asian ancestry
Mother is nonsmoker		Mother smoked during pregnancy
Of upper socioeconomic status		Of lower socioeconomic status
Live in urban area		Live in rural area
Live at sea level		Live high above sea level
Firstborn in a small family		Third- or later-born in a large family
Male		Female

Sources: Eveleth & Tanner, 1976; Lowrey, 1986; Meredith, 1978.

Cultural patterns also have an impact. Traditionally, on the Indian subcontinent and in many South Asian families today, males are more highly valued and, consequently, better fed when food is scarce. Consequently, girls are much smaller than boys. In contrast, if a particular North American family has ample food but requires that children be polite and quiet at meals if they are to be rewarded with an extra helping of dessert, it is more often the boys of the family who are skinny.

BRAIN GROWTH AND DEVELOPMENT

As you saw in Chapter 5, during infancy and early childhood the brain develops faster than any other part of the body. By age 2 the brain has already reached 75 percent of its eventual adult weight; by age 5 it has grown to 90 percent; and by age 7 it is full-grown. By comparison, the total body weight of the average 7-year-old is about one-third that of the average adult.

Part of the increase in brain weight is due to the continued proliferation of communication pathways (via the growth of dendrites and axons) among the brain's various specialized areas, in response to the child's specific experiences (Thompson, 2000). Another part of brain growth is due to ongoing **myelination**—the insulating process that speeds up the transmission of neural impulses. Finally, several areas of the brain undergo notable expansion—in particular those areas dedicated to control and coordination of the body, the emotions, and thinking processes.

As a result of all these changes, during the play years children not only react more quickly to stimuli but also become better at control-

myelination   The insulating process that speeds up the transmission of neural impulses.

Each to His Own Lifelong food preferences are formed during early childhood, which may be one reason why the two children on the right seem dubious about the contents of the pink lunchbox, broccoli and all. Nevertheless, each of these children appears to be a model of healthful eating.

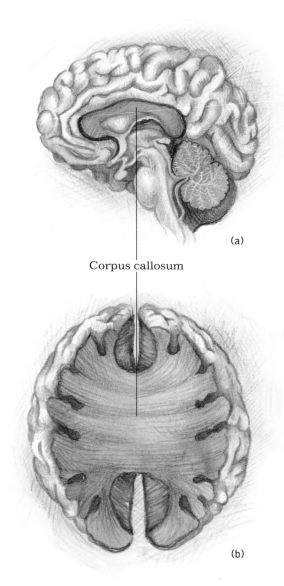

Corpus callosum

Figure 8.1 Connections. Two views of the corpus callosum, a band of nerve fibers (axons) that conveys information between the two hemispheres of the brain. When developed, this "connector" allows the person to coordinate functions that are performed mainly by one hemisphere or the other. (a) A view from between the hemispheres, looking toward the right side of the brain. (b) A view from above, with the gray matter not shown in order to expose the corpus callosum.

corpus callosum A network of nerves connecting the left and right hemispheres of the brain.

ling their reactions. For instance, compared to 2-year-olds, 5-year-olds are quicker to notice when another child begins playing with their favorite toy, but they are less likely to throw a stomping, screaming tantrum over the misappropriation. Instead, they might think of a better tactic, perhaps presenting another toy as a distraction, explaining the rules of ownership, or even offering to compromise, take turns, or share, which 2-year-olds almost never do unless guided or coerced by an adult.

Again owing to brain maturation, older preschool-age children are better at games that require quick thinking followed by deliberate action. To play Musical Chairs, Simon Says, Steal the Bacon, or Duck-Duck-Goose, the child must first think, then act. If older preschoolers let a 2-year-old join in any of these games, he or she is likely still thinking about what to do long after the moment to act has passed. Then, if the 2-year-old is, say, bumped from a game of Musical Chairs, his or her lack of emotional control might produce bawling, sulking, or knocking over furniture. A 5-year-old can sometimes (but not always) take minor disappointments in stride.

New Connections

At about age 5, children show important gains as a result of growth in the **corpus callosum,** a band of nerve fibers connecting the right and left hemispheres, or sides, of the brain (see Figure 8.1). The corpus callosum becomes notably thicker due to dendrite growth and myelination, developing "250–800 million fibers that do nothing other than keep the hemispheres coordinated in their processing" (Branch & Heller, 1998). As a result, communication between the two sides of the brain becomes more efficient, allowing children to coordinate functions that involve both sides of the brain and body. A simple example of such coordination is hopping on one foot while using both arms for balance, something few children under age 4 can do.

A more complex illustration of coordination of the right and left sides of the brain is the older child's increased ability to process information from several parts of the brain all at once and, simultaneously, connect and interweave sensory observations, emotions, thoughts, and reactions. Gradually, children learn to think before they leap, or, in a practical lesson taught to school-age children, to "cross at the green and not in between." Such ability to monitor their behavior and sensations is one reason older children are less likely to suffer serious injury than younger children.

Accidents and the Brain

In all but the most disease-ridden or war-torn countries of the world, accidents are by far the major cause of childhood death. (See the Changing Policy box.) In the United States, a child has about 1 chance in 600 of dying due to an accident before age 15—four times the risk of dying

INJURY CONTROL IS NO ACCIDENT

Although it is true that, everywhere and always, impoverished younger boys are more at risk of injury than older, wealthier girls, it is also true that the risk of serious injury could be much rarer for all children, everywhere and always. With forethought, many accidents can be avoided completely. Further, proper precautions reduce the seriousness of injury when accidents do occur.

Forethought

The first step in reducing childhood injury, many believe, is to approach the problem in terms of "injury control" instead of "accident prevention." The word "accident" misleadingly implies that no one was at fault, but most serious childhood injuries involve someone's lack of forethought. *Injury control* means taking precautions to prevent as many injuries as we can and to reduce the harm done by those that do occur.

Often, forethought involves little more than providing adequate adult supervision. But what is "adequate" for controlling injury? There are no absolutes and no guarantees: Sometimes children get hurt even when they are closely watched in their own homes; sometimes children play alone in dangerous places without incident; and sometimes children are overprotected to the point of losing their opportunity to develop the independence, judgment, and self-confidence they need.

Nonetheless, research finds some consensus. Pediatricians, child-protection workers, and most parents agree that a crawling baby cannot be safely left alone anywhere, even for a minute, and that children between the ages of 4 and 8 should never be left unsupervised in an area that contains an attractive danger, such as a pond, swimming pool, or other accessible body of water (Peterson et al., 1993). For older children, temperament, cognitive maturity, and past

(a)

(b)

(c)

Protective Settings In order for parents to safeguard their children from injury, they need first to be aware of safety hazards and then to take whatever action is necessary to prevent accidents. In two of these photos, the parents are to be commended: The parents of the child in (b) not only put a helmet on their skater but protected his knees, wrists, elbows, and hands as well. The mother in (c) probably has been securing her child in a safety seat from infancy. However, the boy in (a) may be in trouble. What is immediately below him? We hope it is a "safety surface" designed to prevent serious injury or an adult ready to catch him. Such forethought is essential for injury control.

history are important indicators of how long a particular child can safely go unsupervised in an area that poses any kind of risk.

Injury control also involves instituting safety measures *in advance* to reduce the need for vigilant supervision and to prevent serious injury if an accident does occur. For instance, compared to adults, children are more likely to drown, choke on a nonfood object, tumble from a bicycle, suffocate in a fire, and fall out a window. Advance precautions, such as teaching children to swim, removing swallowable objects from reach, requiring a helmet for bicycling, and installing smoke alarms and window guards, would prevent many deaths. The goal is not to change the nature of the child but to change the nature of the child's situation. Many laws have already accomplished some of this. For instance, in the United States an active, curious preschooler can never swallow a lethal dose of baby aspirin because the bottle doesn't contain enough pills to cause death.

Other Measures

Note that the responsibility for injury control does not fall on the parents alone. Not until accurate nationwide data became available did parents even realize the extent of the hazards associated with, for example, poisons in the medicine cabinet, cribs with widely spaced slats, playgrounds surfaced with concrete, balloons that can pop, and in-line skating without headgear and protective pads. Scientists need to identify hazards, and then journalists must publicize risks so that parents, community leaders, and legislators can take action. What action should they take?

General, broad-based television announcements and poster campaigns do not have a direct impact on children's risk taking. Such educational broadsides may, however, foster a safety-consciousness that reduces resistance to specific safety programs. Similarly, educational programs in schools and preschools can teach children to verbalize safety rules, but unless parents become involved, classroom education appears to have little effect on children's actual behavior (Garbarino, 1988; Rivara, 1993).

More effective than educational measures are safety laws that include penalties. Significant reductions in accidental death rates for children in the United States have been achieved by laws requiring:

- That childproof safety caps be used on medicine bottles (resulting in an 80 percent reduction in poisoning deaths of 1- to 4-year-olds)
- That children's sleepwear be flame-retardant (decreasing deaths from burning pajamas and nightgowns by 97 percent)
- That fencing be placed around swimming pools (reducing childhood drowning in Arizona and southern California by 51 percent)

- That car safety seats be used for children (bringing passenger deaths down by 70 percent for children under age 5 between 1980 and 1991)
- That helmets be worn by bicyclists (credited for reducing serious bicycle head injuries by 88 percent)

(National Center for Injury Prevention and Control, 1992, 1993; Rivara, 1994)

Largely as a result of laws like these, accidental deaths of 1- to 5-year-olds in the United States decreased by 50 percent between 1980 and 1986. It continues to decline, with the 1996 rate (14 per 100,000) about 25 percent less than the 1991 rate (U.S. Bureau of the Census, 1994, 1999). Downward trends are apparent in most other nations as well, although the specifics vary from nation to nation. The leading nation for injury control is Sweden. Over a 45-year period, annual childhood deaths in Sweden decreased to one-fifth of what they had been, from 450 to 88 (Bergman & Rivara, 1991).

Think, Think Again, Analyze, and Advocate

It is increasingly apparent that the child who escapes serious injury in childhood is not "just lucky" and that no accident is "just an accident." Every parent can practice injury control on a small scale. First, parents must *think prevention* and *protection*, locking away poisons, checking the smoke detector, always using a child safety seat, and so on. Then they must *analyze actual injuries*. Repeated scrapes on the knees, for instance, suggest that a better play surface or protective gear is called for—not because scraped knees themselves are a problem but because a brain concussion or broken limb may result if the next tumble occurs in slightly different circumstances.

On a broader scale, prevention and protection can become part of a community pattern, as adults teach each other about the hazards facing children. Then, together, the community can analyze and modify the conditions whenever a child is hurt, so that more children survive their early years with only tiny scars and no serious traumas.

This leads to the final step: *Advocate safety*. Children need to be protected until they are wise enough to protect themselves—a fact that places everyone, not only the parents, at fault when a serious childhood injury occurs. We all must work to ensure that research and practice keep every child safe.

Steps to Injury Control	
Step	**Example**
Think prevention	Lock up guns.
Think protection	Require safety helmets.
Analyze injuries	Consider scraped knees as a warning.
Advocate safety	Work for laws that prevent speeding near schools.

? **Especially for Parents:** What signs would indicate that your preschool child is at high risk of serious injury or accidental death?

from cancer, the second-leading cause of childhood death (U.S. Bureau of the Census, 1999). Roughly two-thirds of accidental deaths among preschool children involve nonvehicular causes, such as falling, drowning, choking, and poisoning. These kinds of accidents are particularly prevalent among preschool children.

Accidents do not occur randomly. Rather, some children, because of their sex, socioeconomic status, and neighborhood, are at much higher risk than others (Rivara, 1994). Boys, as a group, suffer more injuries and accidental deaths than girls—about one-third more between ages 1 and 5, twice as many between ages 5 and 14, and three times as many between 15 and 24. Sex differences are particularly salient when the neighborhood is filled with attractive hazards, as is the case in crowded cities and rural areas.

The strongest risk factor of all is socioeconomic status (SES). One detailed study of childhood deaths in North Carolina found that low-SES children were three times more likely to die accidentally than other children (Nelson, 1992). Overall, the impact of SES was most evident during infancy and the play years, when brain immaturity makes children least able to understand danger and coordinate their responses.

Indeed, because of their brain immaturity, preschool children of all SES groups dart into the street, swallow pieces of toys, climb onto the ledge of a window, or play carelessly with fire more often than school-age children. But such impulsiveness is particularly likely to injure low-SES preschool children because they live in homes where hazards are more prevalent. As a result, in the North Carolina study, 1- to 4-year-olds whose families were on welfare were found to be four times more likely to be fatally hit by a car, four times more likely to die by choking, and nine times more likely to burn to death, compared to children of less impoverished families (Nelson, 1992).

Another study of school-age children in Montreal found that the most powerful predictor of young pedestrians being hit by a car was SES, with the poorest children six times more likely to be injured than the richest. Age was also a factor: Even though younger children crossed fewer streets, they were more likely than older children to be hit by a car (Macpherson et al., 1998).

Obviously, young children need the protection of adults. **Injury control,** as the various measures to reduce harm are called, is everyone's responsibility (as we saw in the Changing Policy box).

injury control   The practice of limiting the extent of injuries by planning ahead, controlling the circumstances, preventing certain dangerous activities, and adding safety features to other activities.

Eyes, Brain, and Reading

Researchers have extensively studied visual pathways in the brain. They have discovered that the areas of the brain associated with the control of eye movements and visual focusing undergo measurable myelination and growth throughout the preschool years. As a result, 4-year-olds are much better at looking at—and recognizing—letters and other small shapes than are younger children. As 4-year-olds move their eyes across a printed page, they can usually track the small variations from word to word, in sequence; younger children's eyes dart around a page much more randomly (Aslin, 1987; Borsting, 1994).

This development of the visual pathways combines with improved communication between the left and right sides of the brain to enhance eye–hand coordination, enabling older preschoolers to draw people, button sweaters, and—most important for later reading—copy familiar letters and numbers. By age 5, eye–hand coordination becomes fairly well at-

❓ **Especially for Educators:** Suppose you are a preschool teacher of 3-year-olds and their parents want you to begin teaching the children to read and write. What would you do?

tuned to left–right distinctions; children then are first able to copy a diamond (which measures the ability to draw diagonals) and to write letters such as "b" and "d" facing in the proper direction (Borsting, 1994). Children who are left-handed might take longer to write a language such as English that is designed for right-handed individuals (as will be discussed in Chapter 11), but handedness seems largely inborn. As a result, educators no longer try to switch a preschooler who wants to write left-handed.

Brain growth is not necessarily linear, developing as a straight line that gradually rises. Sometimes it occurs in spurts and plateaus (Fischer, 1998). And neuroscientists are starting to draw connections between growth spurts in specific brain areas and forward leaps in cognitive ability. For example, the left hemisphere of a child's brain, where the primary language abilities are usually located, undergoes a growth spurt at around age 2, just when the language explosion occurs. The right hemisphere, where the primary area for recognition of visual shapes is usually located, undergoes a growth spurt between ages 4 and 5 (Thatcher, 1994)—as does the brain overall. Beginning at around age 5, expansion of the corpus callosum, development of the frontal lobe of the brain, and other qualitative (not just quantitative) changes in the brain allow most children to link spoken and written language, remembering what sounds go with what symbols (Janowsky & Carper, 1996).

It is for this reason that formal instruction in reading, writing, and arithmetic begins in earnest all around the world at about age 6. By that age, children's brains are usually mature enough to forge ahead on these basic literacy skills. One study looked at reading ability in school-age children who had sustained head injuries. Children whose brains had been damaged before age 6½ were much poorer readers than children who had sustained the same injury after they had learned basic reading skills (Barnes et al., 1999). The crucial factor was that the children who had been injured when they were older had already formed connections among the various parts of the brain, and thus the injury affected only one part of a complex skill. Without that maturation and learning, children had much more trouble compensating for the loss caused by the injury.

Of course, the social and intellectual preparation for literacy—reading picture books, memorizing rhymes, identifying signs such as EXIT in a theater and OFF on a computer, and writing one's name—begins years before, at home. But the sudden acceleration of reading skill must wait until brain maturation occurs (Bialystok, 1997). In the meantime, the parents' job is to read books out loud, point out signs, provide paper, pencils, and markers—but not to push or demand more from the child than he or she can do.

MASTERING MOTOR SKILLS

As their bodies grow slimmer, stronger, and less top-heavy, and as their brain maturation permits greater control and coordination of their extremities, children between 2 and 6 years move with greater speed and grace and become more capable of directing and refining their own activity.

Gross Motor Skills

Gross motor skills, involving large body movements such as running, climbing, jumping, and throwing, improve dramatically. Watch a group of children at play. You will see that 2-year-olds are quite clumsy, falling

More Curiosity Than Caution As they master their gross motor skills, children of every social group, in every setting, seem to obey a universal command: "If it can be climbed, climb it." That command is usually heard louder than any words of caution—one reason direct supervision is needed during the play years.

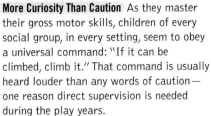

❶ **Response for Parents (from page 226):** In general, age, sex, and family income are the demographic indicators of injury vulnerability, with 2-year-old lower-income boys most at risk. However, these generalities are less useful when analyzing risk for a specific child. Even if your child is a 5-year-old girl in a middle-class family, if her particular history includes many bruises, scrapes, stitches, and so on, or if your neighborhood is filled with "attractive hazards" that have injured other children, it is wise to increase prevention and protection.

What Is She Accomplishing? The papier-mâché animals produced by this girl and her preschool classmates are more likely to be mushy and misshapen than artistic. However, the real product is development of eye–hand coordination. With intensive, dedicated practice, fine motor skills are mastered by the school years, when children's artwork is sometimes truly remarkable.

down frequently and sometimes bumping into stationary objects. But by age 5, many children are both skilled and graceful. Most North American 5-year-olds can ride a tricycle, climb a ladder, pump a swing, and throw, catch, and kick a ball. Some of them can even ice-skate, ski, whiz along on in-line skates, and ride a bicycle, activities that demand balance as well as coordination. Skills vary by culture, of course; in certain nations, some 5-year-olds swim in waves or climb cliffs that few adults in other nations would attempt. Underlying the development of such skills is a combination of the brain maturation we have just discussed and guided practice.

Generally, children learn basic motor skills by teaching themselves and learning from other children, rather than through adult instruction. According to sociocultural theory, this is no problem, because learning from peers is probably the ideal way for children to master skills needed for the future. As long as a child has the opportunity to play in an adequate space and has suitable playmates and play structures, gross motor skills develop as rapidly as maturation, body size, and innate ability allow. Unfortunately, neither opportunity nor play space can be taken for granted—especially in large cities.

Fine Motor Skills

Fine motor skills, involving small body movements (especially those of the hands and fingers), are much harder to master than gross motor skills. Such things as pour-

CHILDREN'S ART

(a)

Drawing is an important form of play. On the simplest level, "the child who first wields a marker is learning in many areas of his young life about tool use" (Gardner, 1980). Few children try to reproduce in their art exactly what they see. Instead, they realize the affordances provided by art materials, and use even their early mark-making to express their symbolic understanding (Pufall, 1997).

Drawing requires that the child think about what to draw, manipulate the pencil, crayon, or brush to execute the thought, and then view, and perhaps explain, the product. A developmental study of children's painting found that 3-year-olds usually just plunked their brushes into the paint, pulled them out dripping wet, and then pushed them across the paper without much forethought or skill. However, by age 5 most children took care to get just enough paint on their brushes, planned just where to put each stroke, and stood back from their work to examine the result (Allison, 1985). By doing so, 5-year-olds experience a sequence that not only provides practice with fine motor skills but also involves coordination of action and thought and, in the end, enhances their sense of accomplishment.

(b)

Children's artwork provides a testing ground for another important skill: self-correction. Older preschool children are eager to practice their skills, drawing essentially the same picture again and again, with the later versions usually having more details and better proportions.

Such mastery of drawing skills is related to overall intellectual growth. In general, as children become more skilled and detailed in their drawing, their level of cognitive development rises as well (Bensur & Eliot, 1993; Chappell & Steitz, 1993). There is no sure way of distinguishing correlation from causation here—of knowing how much the mastery of drawing skills *contributes* to cognitive advances and how much it is a *consequence* of them. But it is quite possible that a sketch pad and a box of crayons are no less an "educational toy" than traditional alphabet blocks or counting games.

(c)

Artists in Progress The maturation of fine motor skills is evident in this progression, from the two-handed overlapping vertical lines (circles and horizontals are more advanced) in (a) to the left-handed artistic control, combining imagination and representation, in (d). Steps along the way include (b) the imaginative use of color and design but no representation of reality and (c) the careful observation of conventions (five fingers on each hand, a triangle nose, a line of grass at the bottom) with little imagination. All four of these artists are mastering the skills appropriate for their ages, and all show the strong concentration signaling that intense brain activity accompanies motor skill advancement.

(d)

❶ Response for Educators (from page 227):
You might explain that the brain maturation required for reading and writing small print does not occur in most children until age 5 or so and that you don't want to create anxiety about skills that should be a joy. However, you might also explain that the curriculum of a good school for 3-year-olds includes extensive spoken language, reading from picture books, and other activities that prepare the children for learning to read and write when their brains are ready.

ing juice from a pitcher into a glass, cutting food with a knife and fork, and achieving anything more artful than a scribble with a pencil are difficult for young children, even with great concentration and effort. Preschoolers can spend hours trying to tie a bow with their shoelaces, often producing knot upon knot instead.

The chief reason many children experience difficulty with fine motor skills is simply that they have not yet developed the necessary muscular control, patience, and judgment—in part because the central nervous system is not yet sufficiently myelinated. For many, this deficit is compounded by short, stubby fingers. Unless caregivers keep these limitations in mind when selecting utensils, toys, and clothes, frustration and destruction can result: Preschool children may burst into tears when they cannot zip their pants, or may mash a puzzle piece into place when they are unable to position it correctly, or may tear up the paper when they cannot cut it with their blunt "safety" scissors.

Fortunately, such frustrations usually fade as a child's persistence at practicing fine motor skills gradually leads to mastery. Adults can certainly help by offering tools, time, and encouragement. One fine motor skill that seems particularly linked to later success in school is also one that is easy for parents and teachers to encourage—the skill of making meaningful marks on paper.

CHILD MALTREATMENT

Throughout this chapter and elsewhere in this text, we have assumed that parents naturally want to foster their children's development and protect them from every danger. Yet daily, it seems, reporters describe parents who harm their offspring. When the harm takes the form of horrific abuse or results in death, the story makes national news, as when the mother of a 6-year-old

Forgive Us The name is misspelled, and the flowers and gorilla arrived too late to help—testimony to the truth that "we were not there" until 6-year-old Elisa was killed by her mother. Sadly, whenever a child is severely maltreated, dozens of people—relatives, neighbors, teachers, social workers—notice that something is wrong but fail to act to prevent further abuse.

> confessed to killing Elisa by throwing her against a concrete wall. She confessed that she had made Elisa eat her own feces and that she had mopped the floor with her head . . . there was no part of the six-year-old's body that was not cut or bruised. Thirty circular marks that at first appeared to be cigarette burns turned out to be impressions left by the stone in someone's ring. [Van Biema, 1995]

We are shocked by the brutality and senselessness of cases like Elisa's and appalled at the pathological perpetrators, indifferent neighbors, and overworked professionals (in education, medicine, and especially child welfare) who share the blame. Yet sensational cases like Elisa's represent only a small portion of all maltreatment cases. And, as experts in child-maltreatment research point out, "journalism is an impatient enterprise and the tragic, bungled case will always be more newsworthy . . . than the small successes of family reunification or the incremental process of reform" (Larner et al., 1998).

Not only do sensational cases distract attention from other, far more typical and common, incidents, but the emotional reaction to the extremes dwarfs the lessons we need to learn. Such lessons begin with an understanding of what typical abuse is, and then lead to knowledge of its causes and consequences, and finally teach us what works to treat and, even better, prevent maltreatment of every sort. If we could only remember those lessons and apply them, all children would benefit.

Changing Definitions of Maltreatment

The irrational rage of Elisa's mother is rare; the ignorance of caregivers who do not understand how to love and guide a child is common. Some parents, for example, might not realize that children need to be patiently shown how to "do things right," such as the mother whose 3-year-old was having trouble carrying an umbrella:

> "Carry that umbrella right or I'll slap the [expletive] out of you," she screamed at him. "Carry it right, I said . . . " and then she slapped him in the face, knocking him off balance. [Dash, 1986]

Another example is the father who has set ideas of how children should behave and believes that his son should be "kept on his toes":

> So his dad teases him a lot . . . [and] plays games with him. If Jon wins, his dad makes fun of him for being an egghead; if he loses, he makes fun of him for being a dummy. It is the same with affection. Jon's dad will call him over for a hug; when Jon responds, his dad pushes him away, telling him not to be a sissy. . . . Jon is tense, sucks his thumb, and is tongue-tied (which his dad teases him about). [Garbarino et al., 1986]

Neither of the above-described incidents would have been recognized as maltreatment a few decades ago. Until about 1960, child maltreatment was thought of as obvious physical assault, assumed to result from a rare outburst of a mentally disturbed person who was typically not a member of the child's family. However, we now recognize that maltreatment is neither rare nor sudden, and that 80 percent of the time its perpetrators are not deranged and not strangers but the child's own parents (National Child Abuse and Neglect Data System, 2000; Wang & Daro, 1998).

With this recognition has come a broader definition: **Child maltreatment** includes all intentional harm to, or avoidable endangerment of, anyone under 18 years of age. Thus, child maltreatment includes both **abuse**—deliberate action that is harmful to a child's well-being—and **neglect**—failure to appropriately meet a child's basic needs. Abuse and neglect are further subdivided into more specific categories, with abuse including physical, emotional, and sexual abuse, and neglect including inattention to the child's emotional as well as physical needs. Neglect is twice as common, and at least as damaging, as abuse.

child maltreatment Any intentional harm or avoidable endangerment to anyone under age 18.

abuse Any action that is harmful (either physically or psychologically) to an individual's well-being. The severity of abuse depends on how much and how often it occurs and on the vulnerability of the victim.

neglect Any inaction that harms or endangers a person. Neglect can involve physical needs (food, warmth) or psychological needs (love, language).

Failure to Protect Self-centered parents neglect their children's basic needs in a pattern of maltreatment that may be even more harmful than abuse.

Reported and Substantiated Maltreatment

Obviously, historical and cultural norms influence our ideas about what constitutes child maltreatment: Behaviors that would be considered abusive in some eras or cultural settings may be regarded as legitimate and acceptable in other times and places.

However, no one can deny that in many nations, the rate of child maltreatment has been, and continues to be, alarmingly high. Since 1993, in the United States, the official number of *reported* cases has been about 3 million per year, and the number of *substantiated* cases has been about 1 million, a rate that represents roughly 1 child in every 70 (Wang & Daro, 1998). "Reported" cases are those about which the authorities have been informed, and "substantiated" cases are those which have been investigated and verified as maltreatment.

Consequences of Maltreatment In many nations of the world, abused and neglected children are not runaways but throwaways, pushed out onto the streets by their parents and communities.

❷ Observational Quiz (see answer page 235): *Can you guess where these boys are, and can you see two activities they use for comfort?*

The gap between the 3 million reported cases and the 1 million substantiated cases is attributable to three factors:

■ A particular case may be reported many times but will be tallied as only one substantiated case because it involves just one child, who is repeatedly abused.
■ Before a case is substantiated, investigators must find some proof—usually visible, unmistakable signs or credible witnesses (such as the other parent and the maltreated child).
■ The report may be mistaken or even deliberately misleading (especially when the child's feuding parents or other relatives are fighting over custody).

Standards of proof vary from state to state, with neither high nor low ratios of reported to substantiated maltreatment being necessarily better. As an example, the highest 1997 substantiation rate was in Kentucky (56 percent) and the lowest was in Kansas (10 percent), but the two states probably have similar rates of severe maltreatment, at least as indicated by the fact that the rate of maltreatment deaths (about 1 death for every 60,000 children) is the same in both states.

The Cultural and Community Context

Cultural diversity makes the problem substantiating reports even more complex. Before a particular practice can be considered abusive, customs and community standards must be taken into account (Hansen, 1998). One set of examples comes from the numerous customs that give children pain: Pierced ears, circumcisions, castor oil, forced feeding of hated foods, ceremonial facial scars, permed or tightly braided hair, encouragement of sports that bring exhaustion and bruises, forced sleep-

❷ Especially for Social Workers: Which would be most helpful in figuring out if a specific child is mistreated: the particular child-discipline practices used, signs of injury on the child's body, the relationship between the child and the parent, or the overall social and intellectual patterns of the child?

Figure 8.3 What Correlates with Maltreatment—Income, Sex, Age, Race? Rates of neglect skyrocket as family income falls, with the highest rates of neglect found among single mothers who have either four or more children or only one child. Abuse also correlates with income. Fathers are more likely than mothers to be perpetrators of abuse (as opposed to neglect). Interestingly, neither age nor race correlates with maltreatment.

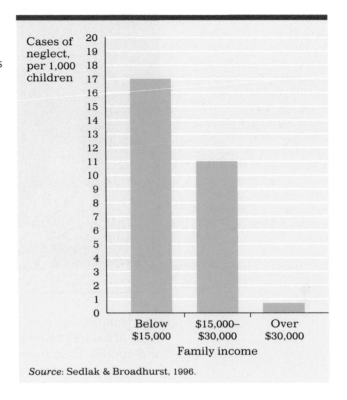

Source: Sedlak & Broadhurst, 1996.

ing alone despite tears of protest, harsh words designed to shame a child into proper behavior, and many other such examples are commonplace in some cultures and criticized in others.

In some neighborhoods, not letting children play outside for hours every day is considered maltreatment; in others, letting a child play outside unsupervised for even 10 minutes is considered neglectful. The Japanese say, "Before seven, among the gods" to advise parents that young children are pure and not to be punished; but that saying promotes "the Western view that Japanese adults are indulgent with their children . . . not playing their roles as socializing agents properly" (Chen, 1996).

Despite such variation, two aspects of the overall context seem universally conducive to maltreatment: poverty and social isolation. No matter how maltreatment is defined or counted, it occurs more frequently as family income falls (see Figure 8.3) (Drake & Zuravin, 1998; Pelton, 1994). This is particularly true for neglect and physical abuse, which fall most heavily on children under age 6 who live in families with an income below the poverty line, an unemployed father, and four or more children. In such families, children obviously add to the financial pressures and are likely to become victims because of it (Wolfner & Gelles, 1993). Such families are also likely to live in high-crime neighborhoods, a situation that adds to both the risk and the trauma of child abuse (Lynch & Cicchetti, 1998).

The second major risk factor that stems from the culture is social isolation. Every society has certain "family values"—beliefs that encourage parents to care for their children. The human species could not have survived if communities had not developed such values. One of these values is the belief that each family should decide how to raise its own children—a useful principle in nations with many ethnic and religious groups, such as the United States. However, this value can boomerang when children need

Watching the World Go By How can passersby ignore the impoverished families in front of them, knowing that poverty multiplies the incidence of maltreatment? One way is to blame the parents. Did you protect your conscience by asking why this couple had four children so close together, or whether the husband can get a job, or whether this mother got welfare payments for each child? Whatever the answers to the first two questions, we know that these children are sitting on the boardwalk of Atlantic City, New Jersey, a state that now subsidizes only the first two children per low-income mother.

intervention, because it encourages privacy and social isolation; thus, signs of maltreatment become "not my business," and abuse can continue and spread. Even in equally ethnically homogeneous low-income neighborhoods, there are markedly lower rates of abuse among families who are less socially isolated (Korbin et al., 1998).

Consequences of Maltreatment

The more we learn about child maltreatment, the more we see that its causes are many and its consequences extend far beyond any immediate injury or deprivation. Compared to well-cared-for children, chronically abused and neglected children tend to be underweight, slower to talk, less able to concentrate, and delayed in academic growth (Cicchetti et al., 1993; Eckenrode et al., 1993).

Deficits are even more apparent in social skills: Maltreated children tend to regard other children and adults as hostile and exploitative, and hence they are less friendly, more aggressive, and more isolated than other children. The longer their abuse continues, and the earlier it started, the worse their relationships with peers are (Bolger et al., 1998). As adolescents and adults, those who were severely maltreated in childhood (either physically or emotionally) often use drugs or alcohol to numb their emotions, choose unsupportive relationships, and then become victims or aggressors, sabotage their own careers, eat too much or too little, and generally engage in self-destructive behavior (Crittenden et al., 1994; Wolfe et al., 1998).

Those are some of the human costs. The financial costs of child maltreatment, both to the victim and to society, are difficult to measure. One estimate puts the average cost at $813 per investigation (whether the abuse charges are substantiated or not), $2,702 for providing in-home services such as homemaker assistance, and $21,902 annually per child for providing foster care (Courtney, 1998). When abuse results in admission to the intensive-care unit of a hospital, according to one report, the costs are much higher. While such admissions were only 1.4 percent of pediatric admissions, they were among the most expensive ($33,641 per case) and most often involved fatal injuries. When the total hospital costs were averaged, the cost per survivor was $109,333

❶ **Response for Social Workers (from page 232):** All these indicators are useful, and none by itself indicates abuse. However, the most important are probably the latter two: If the child seems afraid of or indifferent to the parent, or if the child does not play well with other children or communicate and explore as most preschoolers do, something is amiss. Your job is to find out if that "something" is in the family or if it is a serious inborn problem in the child.

MALTREATMENT FROM GENERATION TO GENERATION?

The human costs of maltreatment are paid not only by the victim and by persons who interact with the victim but perhaps by members of the next generation who will experience maltreatment as well. In assessing those costs over the years, we must neither minimize nor exaggerate. It is sadly true that virtually every child who experiences serious, ongoing maltreatment will bear some lifelong scars, including depression, fear of intimacy, difficulty controlling emotions, or low self-esteem. Yet it is also true that many adults who were victims of childhood abuse or neglect live normal, law-abiding lives—working, marrying, and raising healthy children.

Many people erroneously believe that the **intergenerational transmission** of maltreatment—that is, maltreated children becoming adults who abuse or neglect their own children—is automatic and unalterable. This assumption is not only false but destructive. As one review of research explains:

> Uncritical acceptance of the intergenerational hypothesis has caused undue anxiety in many victims of abuse, led to biased response by mental health workers, and influenced the outcome of court decisions, even in routine divorce child custody cases. In one such case . . . a judge refused a mother custody rights because it was discovered during the trial that the mother had been abused as a child. Despite the fact that much of the evidence supported the children's placement with their mother, the judge concluded that the mother was an unfit guardian, since everyone "knows" abused children become abusive parents. [Kaufman & Zigler, 1989]

intergenerational transmission The assumption that mistreated children grow up to become abusive or neglectful parents themselves. This is less common than is generally supposed.

Retrospective analyses, which ask maltreating parents to recall their own childhoods, invariably show high rates of intergenerational transmission; almost all adults who seriously mistreat their children remember having a painful, neglectful, and abusive childhood. But to determine the actual rate of intergenerational transmission, researchers must study the problem longitudinally, not retrospectively, because retrospective analyses omit victims who do not themselves become abusers (Buchanan, 1996). And there are many, many such people.

On the basis of longitudinal studies that begin before abused individuals become parents, experts estimate that between 30 and 40 percent of abused children actually become child abusers themselves. This rate is many times that of the general population, but it shows that more than half of all severely mistreated children do not become abusive or neglectful parents (Egeland, 1993; Kaufman & Zigler, 1993). Least likely to transmit abuse are those who have been loved and cared for by someone—perhaps by the other parent or a foster caregiver in childhood, by their spouses in adulthood, or even by a network of friends and relatives. In addition, adults who remember their maltreatment and understand its effects are much less likely to harm their own children than are adults who do not even recall or recognize that something was seriously wrong with the care they received.

These findings about intergenerational transmission should not be surprising, given what you learned about attachment in Chapter 7—specifically, that attachment status influences, but does not completely determine, later social relationships. An adult who was insecurely attached, but remembers and understands why, may form a secure relationship with his or her own children (Main, 1995). Conversely, parents who deny the abuse they suffered as children, especially if they think they might have deserved it, are likely to maltreat their offspring.

❶ *Answer to Observational Quiz (from page 232):* They're in Rio de Janeiro, Brazil. You might have guessed that they were somewhere in South America from the wide gap between rich and poor, the warm climate (the only shoes are sandals), and the contrasting facial features of the mannequin and the boys. The two comforting actions are less ambiguous and more universal: The boys buddy up (note the pairs who choose to sit right next to each other), and they sniff glue through soda cans (the cheapest high).

(Irazuzta et al., 1997). To all those costs must be added special education for learning disabilities, medical treatment for physical handicaps, institutionalization for emotional problems, and, in some cases, imprisonment for acts of misdirected anger. Prevention would obviously be a much more effective way to spend the same money.

Intervention Policies

As we finally grasp the broad spectrum and devastating consequences of child maltreatment, public policies aimed at intervention are intensifying. As you will see, such efforts are still clumsy and piecemeal.

Show Me What Happened Professionals like this social worker sometimes use dolls to elicit information about possible maltreatment or other events from children who are too young to provide accurate verbal descriptions of their experiences.

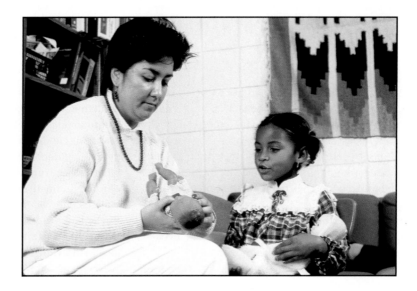

Figure 8.4 Reports of Child Maltreatment in the United States. The great increase in reports of maltreatment since 1975 is attributed primarily to increased awareness on the part of the public and mandated reporting for professionals. No expert believes that the actual rate of maltreatment tripled over two decades.

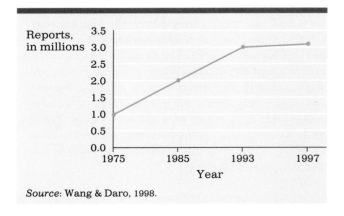

Source: Wang & Daro, 1998.

differential response The idea that child-maltreatment reports should be separated into those that require immediate investigation, possibly leading to foster care and legal prosecution, and those that require supportive measures to encourage better parental care.

Linking Reports to Action

In many countries worldwide, laws now require that any teacher, health professional, police officer, or social worker who becomes aware of possible maltreatment must report it. These laws have made a difference. Reporting has increased, and in the United States more than half of all reports of maltreatment come from professionals. With better awareness, many public and private organizations now tally reports of abuse and neglect, monitor treatment, and fund research (see Figure 8.4).

Some people wonder whether alerting the police or social workers might harm rather than help a maltreated child (Finkelhor, 1993). This is a particular concern if the professional fears that the parents will be arrested or deported (Geltman & Meyers, 1998). There are two reasons for concern. The first is that reporting does not create enough protection (Levine & Doueck, 1995). The second reason, related to the first, is that the sheer number of reports sometimes overwhelms the ability of public workers to investigate properly as well as to provide appropriate protection and treatment. In fact, not only in the United States but also in Australia, where reporting is mandated, many professionals have suspected maltreatment but decided not to report it because they did not believe the family would get the needed services (Van Haeringen et al., 1998).

One solution is to institute a policy of **differential response**, that is, deciding to respond either one way or another, depending on the particular situation. High-risk cases may require complete investigation, perhaps with removal of the child—which should be done quickly and legally. By contrast, low-risk cases may require only an offer of help (such as providing day care, income supplementation, or health care) that the family can accept or reject (Waldfogel, 1998).

The acceptance of such help in a low-risk case might prevent a later incident of serious neglect while freeing caseworkers' time for more difficult cases. It would not, however, protect a child from a high-risk fam-

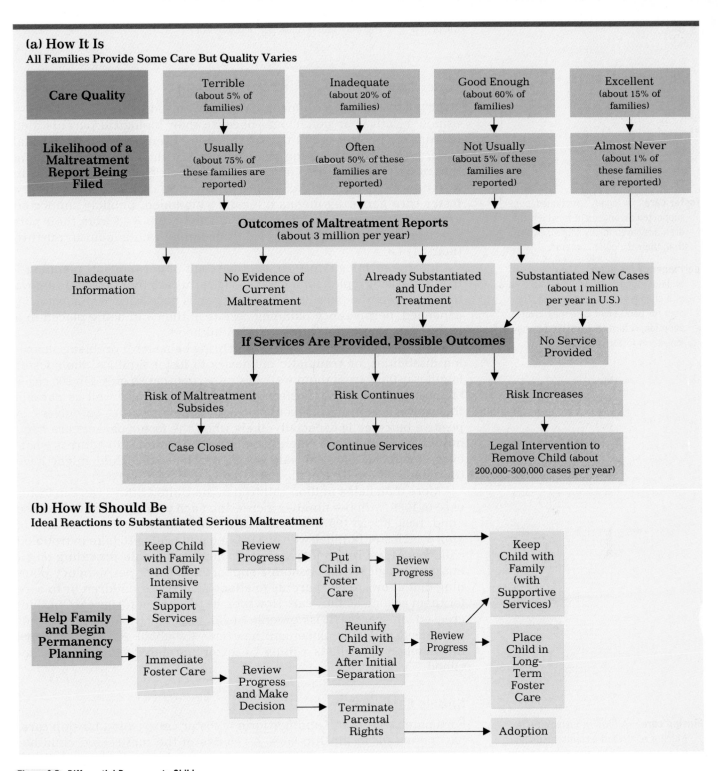

(a) How It Is
All Families Provide Some Care But Quality Varies

Care Quality	Terrible (about 5% of families)	Inadequate (about 20% of families)	Good Enough (about 60% of families)	Excellent (about 15% of families)
Likelihood of a Maltreatment Report Being Filed	Usually (about 75% of these families are reported)	Often (about 50% of these families are reported)	Not Usually (about 5% of these families are reported)	Almost Never (about 1% of these families are reported)

Outcomes of Maltreatment Reports
(about 3 million per year)

- Inadequate Information
- No Evidence of Current Maltreatment
- Already Substantiated and Under Treatment
- Substantiated New Cases (about 1 million per year in U.S.)

If Services Are Provided, Possible Outcomes

No Service Provided

- Risk of Maltreatment Subsides → Case Closed
- Risk Continues → Continue Services
- Risk Increases → Legal Intervention to Remove Child (about 200,000–300,000 cases per year)

(b) How It Should Be
Ideal Reactions to Substantiated Serious Maltreatment

Help Family and Begin Permanency Planning

- Keep Child with Family and Offer Intensive Family Support Services → Review Progress → Put Child in Foster Care → Review Progress → Keep Child with Family (with Supportive Services)
- Immediate Foster Care → Review Progress and Make Decision → Reunify Child with Family After Initial Separation → Review Progress → Place Child in Long-Term Foster Care
- Terminate Parental Rights → Adoption

Figure 8.5 Differential Response to Child Maltreatment. One goal of differential response is to move more effectively when a case is deemed serious. Immediate and intensive help is provided to the family, often with temporary removal of the child. Permanency planning begins immediately, so all options can be considered. Then the decision is made either to begin long-term, extensive support to the family or to place the child permanently in a foster or adoptive home. Ideally, progress review is frequent, and decisions serve the child.

ily that is already locked in a pattern of serious abuse. In situations of the latter type, a differential-response policy would give child-care workers both the mandate and the focused time to proceed with full legal force (not the superficial, hasty response necessitated by a caseload of hundreds per week). This would provide more effective protection and assistance to the child than would be possible if all reports had to be investigated with equal attention. As Figure 8.5(b) shows, in high-risk cases intensive services and repeated review should speed progress toward a safe setting for every child.

Foster Care

Over the years, many children have been raised by "foster parents"—usually relatives or neighbors—because their biological parents died or were too poor or too ill to care for them. Even today, such informal foster care is common. One study of severely alcoholic mothers found that more than one-third of them placed their children informally in foster care (Goldberg et al., 1996). However, in contemporary society, **foster care** generally means a legally sanctioned, publicly supported arrangement in which children are officially removed from their parents and entrusted to another adult or family who is paid to nurture them.

Ideally, such legal fostering is the result of **permanency planning**—that is, devising a plan for a child's long-term care that does not remove the child from the parents unless doing so is necessary. When fostering is needed, permanency planning results in the child being placed in a home where he or she can stay until adulthood.

Even though foster children often bring behavioral problems, learning disabilities, or traumatic memories to foster families, their foster families usually treat them well. Foster parents cause only 1 in 200 cases of substantiated abuse. Foster children often do quite well as parents themselves, eventually becoming good, nonmaltreating caregivers. A positive outcome is especially likely when the foster parents are committed to the child and when they have the resources to address whatever emotional, physical, and social problems the child might have (Barth et al., 1994; Klee et al., 1997; Reddy & Pfeiffer, 1997).

More than half a million children in the United States were in foster care in 1996, with the number increasing each year (Children's Defense Fund, 1999; Kools, 1997). It is not surprising, then, that there is a lack of approved foster families who are trained and willing to take in troubled children. Measures to increase their number include providing ongoing psychological and economic support and using permanency planning that allows foster parents to adopt their foster children or to care for them as long as they can. However, as the stay in foster care has decreased (on average, it is now only 2 to 3 years) and the numbers of children needing foster placement has risen (by about 200,000 per year), the number of families willing to foster unrelated children has declined.

Kinship Care

Fortunately, the use of another form of foster care, called **kinship care,** has increased. In kinship care, a relative of the maltreated child becomes the approved caregiver. It is estimated that 40 percent of all foster children in the United States are staying with relatives, who receive some financial support for doing what, traditionally, they might have done on their own.

Many experts have raised concerns about the quality of kinship care. The available kin are usually the grandparents who raised the abusive parents in the first place and who are older, poorer, less healthy, and less educated than traditional foster parents. Indeed, some states and cities have policies that make it very difficult for any kin to be officially sanctioned and reimbursed to care for their mistreated relatives. Other communities find that since many relatives could not afford to take in additional family members without financial support, subsidizing kinship care seems the best plan—especially since kin are more

foster care   A legally sanctioned, publicly supported arrangement in which children are cared for by someone other than their biological parents.

permanency planning   The process of finding a long-term solution to the care of a child who has been abused. The plan for permanent care may involve adoption, return to a restored family, or long-term foster care.

kinship care   A form of foster care in which a relative of a maltreated child takes over from the abusive or neglectful parents.

likely to allow the biological parents to see their children, hence making more likely their eventual reunion.

That there are diverse opinions about kinship care is indicated by comparing Baltimore, where 2 of every 3 foster-care children are with kin, to Norfolk, Virginia, 100 miles away, where only 2 of every 100 foster children are in kinship care (Curtis et al., 1995). The most recent research finds that children fare as well in kinship homes as in the homes of strangers and that kinship care is often better than conventional foster care if the kin receive the same screening, supervision, and support as other foster parents (Berrick, 1998).

Adoption and Other Outcomes

Adoption is the final option, ideal when families are inadequate and children are young. However, primarily because judges and parents are reluctant to release children for adoption, this ideal solution is actually the least likely to occur. For example, Elisa, whose death was described in the beginning of this section, had five siblings who witnessed her torture and death when they were 2, 3, 4, 9, and 10 years old. They entered the foster-care system, stayed in more than four foster homes, and 3 years later had still not been released for adoption (Swarns, 1998). The three youngest children were together in one foster family by 1998. They may be adopted once the courts have severed the parental rights of their mother, who has been convicted for Elisa's death and is now in prison. Elisa's two oldest siblings will probably never be adopted.

Sadly, the children who fare worst in foster care are children like these older two, who have witnessed and endured years of maltreatment in their biological family—and therefore are likely to hate themselves, distrust others, and feel so angry at life that they suffer no matter where they are raised. Permanency planning for them is difficult. Such children are often sent to group homes—which are better for children than living on the street but sometimes create new problems faster than they solve old ones. As one child says:

The Chosen Family Two of these three children are adopted, and adoption is probably the best solution for children whose birth parents are unable to care for them. The third child, the 6-week-old girl, is a foster child who could be returned to her mother—which might protect the legal rights of the original family but likely not the emotional needs of the child.

> My parents didn't want me. I lived in three foster homes. My foster parents didn't want me. Now, I live in a group home, and I'm a loner. Probably for what's happened to me in my life, I'll never fit in. [Kools, 1997]

Each state and each nation has its own mix of treatment options, and particular mixes can often do harm to the child. In fact, no nation has a good record of permanency planning. About one-third of all British children removed from their homes are placed in group homes, with sometimes abusive results (Buchanan, 1996). Thousands of mistreated children in Brazil, India, Romania, and many other nations simply leave home for

🛈 *Answer to Observational Quiz (from page 241):* None! The baby is obviously well-cared-for, with a hat to protect him from the sun, warm and colorful socks, and a chance to experience the fresh air and the view. If you thought this was neglect, you need to note from the sign that this shop is in Germany, where toddlers are often parked in carriages or strollers outside restaurants without injury, kidnapping, or any other distress. (A Danish mother did the same thing in New York City in 1997. She was arrested and jailed, and her baby was put in temporary foster care.)

Likewise, consider tertiary prevention of child maltreatment. Sometimes authorities wait too long before removing a child from a family, as with Elisa. Other times, the need for ongoing family support without removal is clear, but again only in retrospect. An example is the case of Lia, a preschooler in California whose parents were immigrants from Cambodia. The child had epilepsy and was given many medications, which the parents eventually discarded as worthless. Fearful that Lia would die of medical neglect and impatient with the parents' religious rituals that were supposed to cure the problem, a caseworker removed the child to foster care and then to the hospital. With medication but without the comfort of her parents, Lia had a massive seizure that left her brain-dead (Fadiman, 1997).

For both Lia and Elisa, good secondary prevention might have prevented the severe maltreatment that occurred, and better tertiary prevention might have prevented the death of brain or body. Best of all, of course, would have been primary prevention—education and community support that might have prevented the strain on the parents in the first place.

Although primary-prevention policies are understandably controversial, both theories and research in human development suggest that prevention programs should be broad enough to involve the entire social context. We know that poverty, youth, drug abuse, isolation, and ignorance tend to correlate with unwanted births, inadequate parenting, and then mistreated children. Measures to raise the lowest family incomes, discourage teenage pregnancies, treat addicts, encourage community involvement, and increase education may provide the most cost-effective prevention of all.

SUMMARY

SIZE AND SHAPE

1. During early childhood, children grow about 3 inches (7 centimeters) and gain about 4½ pounds (2 kilograms) a year. Normal variation in growth is caused primarily by genes, health care, and nutrition, with genes most important in developed nations but nutrition most important in developing nations worldwide. Generally, appetite decreases by age 5, especially for children who do not exercise much, and the decrease can lead to nutritional imbalance, parental concern, or both.

BRAIN GROWTH AND DEVELOPMENT

2. Brain maturation, including increased myelination and improved coordination between the two halves of the brain, brings important gains in children's physical abilities and emotional self-regulation. As they get older, preschool children develop quicker reactions to stimuli and are more able to control those reactions.

3. Brain maturation helps make older children less at risk for accidents than younger ones, even though younger ones are more closely supervised. Although boys and low-income children are more at risk, injury control can substantially reduce accidental deaths and serious harm.

4. Better control of eye movements and improved focusing are associated with brain maturation. Development of the visual pathways also enhances eye–hand coordination. These improvements enable children to begin mastery of basic literacy skills at around age 6.

MASTERING MOTOR SKILLS

5. Gross motor skills improve dramatically during early childhood, making it possible for the average 5-year-old to perform many physical activities with grace and skill. Safe play space, maturation, and guided practice help to move this process along.

6. Fine motor skills, such as holding a pencil or tying a shoelace, improve more gradually during early childhood, with guidance much more essential than with gross motor skills. Mastery of drawing skills develops steadily and is correlated with intellectual growth.

CHILD MALTREATMENT

7. Child maltreatment takes many forms, including physical, emotional, or sexual abuse and emotional or physical neglect. In the United States, about 3 million cases of child maltreatment are reported and 1 million are substantiated each year. Although certain cultural conditions and values—poverty and social isolation among them—are almost universally harmful, some practices that are considered abusive in one culture or in one time period are acceptable in others.

8. The consequences of child maltreatment are far-reaching; in general, it tends to impair the child's learning, self-esteem, social relationships, and emotional control. Some of its effects can scar the person for life. However, it is not inevitable that maltreated children become maltreating parents themselves.

9. Once maltreatment is reported, the response should depend on the particular situation. Intervention should support and restore families that can be helped and should provide permanent placement with foster parents, kin, or adoptive families for the minority of children whose family pattern of maltreatment proves to be unbreakable.

10. The most effective primary- and secondary-prevention strategies for maltreatment are those that enhance community support and address the material and emotional needs of troubled families. One specific measure is home-visitation programs that offer support and assistance to families at risk.

KEY TERMS

myelination (222)
corpus callosum (223)
injury control (226)
child maltreatment (231)
abuse (231)
neglect (231)
intergenerational
  transmission (235)

differential response (236)
foster care (238)
permanency planning
  (238)
kinship care (238)
primary prevention (240)
secondary prevention (240)
tertiary prevention (241)

KEY QUESTIONS

1. How do the size, shape, and proportions of the child's body change between ages 2 and 6?

2. What causes variations in height and weight during childhood in both developed and developing countries?

3. What effect does maturation of the corpus callosum have in older preschoolers?

4. In what ways do the gross and fine motor skills develop differently?

5. What measures are most effective in reducing the rate of injuries in children?

6. What are the similarities and differences between abuse and neglect?

7. What factors in the culture, the community, and the family increase the risk of child maltreatment?

8. What are the long-term consequences of childhood abuse and neglect?

9. What are the advantages and disadvantages of foster care, including kinship care?

10. Give an example of effective primary, secondary, and tertiary prevention of child abuse.

11. *In Your Experience* What child-rearing practice do you know that one culture or family considered necessary but that you considered maltreatment? Explain both viewpoints.

The Play Years:
Cognitive Development

CHAPTER 9

The cognitive development that begins even before birth continues through the play years. As you now know, developmentalists underestimated the thinking skills of infants—until new research strategies allowed them to probe more closely into infants' capacities for memory and thought. Recent research has also led to appreciation of cognitive abilities during early childhood, which include mathematics, language, and social understanding. Indeed, research on intellectual development before age 7 has inspired a completely new understanding of preschool education, once thought of as merely "day care" and now considered an important learning experience. One developmental psychologist explains:

> People often call this the "preschool period," but that's not only a mundane name for a magic time, it's also a misnomer. These three-ish and five-ish years are not a waiting time before school or even a time of preparation for school, but an age stage properly called "early childhood" that has a developmental agenda of its own. [Leach, 1997]

IN THEORY: HOW CHILDREN THINK

One of the delights of observing young children is listening to their fanciful and subjective understanding of their lives. They beguile us with their imaginative, even magical, thinking when they chatter away with an invisible playmate, or wonder where the sun sleeps, or confidently claim that they themselves sleep with their eyes open. At the same time, they startle us when they are confused by metaphors (as in "Mommy is tied up at the office" or "The car's engine just died") and when they are illogical about common occurrences (for instance, believing that the moon follows them when they walk at night). At 3 years old, they believe that wishes usually come true and that adults, children, and probably cats and dogs (but not babies) can make wishes if they so desire (Woolley et al., 1999). Clearly, their thinking is often dictated more by their own subjective views than by reality.

For many years, the magical and self-absorbed nature of young children's thinking dominated developmental conceptions of preschooler cognition, guided by Swiss developmentalist Jean Piaget, who called such thinking *egocentric*—literally, self-centered. He thought preschoolers were inevitably limited by their own perspective.

More recent research has highlighted another side of preschool thought. That side is suggested by the following episode between a

2-year-old child and his mother, who has been trying to hold his sweet tooth in check:

> *(Child sees chocolate cake on table.)*
> *Child:* Bibby on.
> *Mother:* You don't want your bibby on. You're not eating.
> *Child:* Chocolate cake. Chocolate cake.
> *Mother:* You're not having any more chocolate cake, either.
> *Child:* Why?
> *Mother: (No answer)*
> *Child: (Whines)* Tired.
> *Mother:* You tired? Ooh! *(Sympathetically)*
> *Child:* Chocolate cake.
> *Mother:* No chance.
> [adapted from Dunn et al., 1987]

The young child in this episode is definitely *not* being illogical or oblivious to the constraints of the real world. He is showing strategic skill in pursuing his goal—from asking for his bib (a noncontroversial request) to eliciting sympathy by feigning fatigue. He is, as Vygotsky would recognize, thinking beyond the bounds of egocentrism. Piaget and Vygotsky had divergent views of early childhood.

Piaget: Preoperational Thought

symbolic thinking   Thinking that involves the use of words, gestures, pictures, or actions to represent ideas, things, or behaviors.

According to Piaget, one striking difference between cognition during infancy and cognition during the preschool years is **symbolic thinking,** the use of symbols such as words or objects to signify other objects, behaviors, or experiences. The idea of a cat is not contained solely in the furry creature that an infant in the sensorimotor stage sees and touches; it is also what a preschooler signifies when sounding out the word "cat," or when pointing at a picture of a cat, or when crawling on the floor and saying "meow." Symbols free us from the narrow restrictions of our immediate senses and actions.

preoperational thought   Piaget's term for the cognition of children between the ages of about 2 and 6, implying that such children have not yet learned to use logical principles in their thinking.

As monumental as symbolic thought may be, however, Piaget chose to refer to cognitive development between the ages of about 2 and 6 as **preoperational thought.** In doing so, he was referring to what preschool children *cannot* do, rather than the symbolic thinking they can now use. And what they cannot yet do is think *operationally;* that is, they cannot develop a thought or an idea according to some set of logical principles.

Obstacles to Logical Operations

centration   The tendency to focus on one way of thinking and perceiving, without acknowledging any alternatives.

The observation that young children are not logical (or, to Piaget, that they are prelogical) does not mean that they are stupid or ignorant. Rather, it means their thinking reflects certain characteristics. One such prelogical characteristic is **centration,** a tendency to focus thought on one aspect of a situation to the exclusion of all others. We already saw centration in Chapter 6, with the underextension of first words. This continues. Young children may, for example, insist that lions and tigers are not cats because the children center on the house-pet aspect of the cats they know. Or they may insist that Father is a *daddy* and not a son or brother because children center on each family member exclusively in the role that person plays for them.

egocentrism The tendency to perceive events and interpret experiences exclusively from one's own, self-centered, perspective.

Four Aspects of Preoperational Thought

1. Centration
2. Appearance-based
3. Static reasoning
4. Irreversibility

conservation The concept that the total quantity, number, or amount of something is the same (preserved) no matter what the shape or configuration.

Demonstration of Conservation Professor Berger's daughter Sarah, here at age 5¾, demonstrates Piaget's conservation-of-liquids experiment. First, she examines both short glasses to be sure they contain the same amount of milk. Then, after the contents of one are poured into the tall glass and she is asked "Which has more?" she points to the tall glass, just as Piaget would have expected. Later she added, "It looks like it has more because it is taller," indicating that some direct instruction might change her mind.

A particular type of centration is ego-centration, better known as **egocentrism.** The egocentric child contemplates the world exclusively from his or her personal perspective. In the daddy example above, the fact that the man's relationship to the child is the only role the child sees is an example of egocentrism. This severely limits cognitive development until about age 7. As Piaget described it, preschoolers are not necessarily selfish; they would, for example, rush to comfort a tearful parent. But the comfort would come in a decidedly egocentric form, such as a teddy bear or a lollipop.

A second characteristic of preoperational thought is its focus on *appearance* to the exclusion of other attributes. A girl given a short haircut might worry that she has turned into a boy; a boy might refuse to wear a pink shirt because he is not a girl. Or upon meeting, say, a tall 4-year-old and a shorter 5-year-old, a child might explain that the 4-year-old is actually older because "bigger is old."

Further, preschoolers tend to be *static* in their reasoning, assuming the world is unchanging, always in the state in which they currently encounter it. If anything does change, it changes totally and suddenly. When she awakened on her fifth birthday, my daughter Rachel asked, "Am I 5 yet?" Told yes, she grinned, stretched out her arms, and said, "Look at my 5-year-old hands."

A closely related characteristic of preoperational thought is *irreversibility*. Preschoolers fail to recognize that reversing a process brings about the conditions that existed before the transformation began. A preschooler who cries because his mother put lettuce on his hamburger might not think to suggest removing the lettuce and might refuse to eat the hamburger even after the lettuce is removed.

Conservation and Logic

Piaget devised many experiments to test and illustrate the ways in which these four preoperational characteristics (centration, appearance-based, static reasoning, and irreversibility) limit young children's ability to reason logically. In several experiments, he studied children's understanding of **conservation,** the principle that the amount of a substance is unaffected by changes in its appearance. Piaget found that conservation,

taken for granted by older children and adults, is not at all obvious to preschoolers. Rather, preschoolers tend to focus exclusively on one facet of shape or placement and to use that as a measure of amount.

As one example, suppose some young children are shown two identical glasses containing the same amount of liquid. Then the liquid from one of the glasses is poured into a taller, narrower glass. If the children are asked whether one glass contains more liquid than the other, they will insist that the narrower glass, now with the higher liquid level, contains more. They make that mistake because they center on liquid height, noticing only the static appearance and ignoring the idea that they could reverse the process and re-create what they had seen a moment earlier.

Similarly, if an experimenter lines up, say, seven pairs of checkers in two rows of equal length and asks a 4-year-old whether both rows have the same number of checkers, the child will usually say yes. But suppose that, while the child watches, the experimenter elongates one of the rows by spacing its checkers farther apart. If the experimenter then asks again whether the rows have the same number of checkers, the child will most likely reply no. The child seems compelled by appearance to conclude that the row with the greater length contains the greater number of checkers. Other conservation tests, shown in Figure 9.1, produce similar results.

In such tests of conservation, Piaget believed, preschoolers center on appearances and ignore or discount the transformation—even though they watched as it occurred. They are not yet able to understand simple, logical transformations.

Figure 9.1 Conservation, Please. According to Piaget, until children grasp the concept of conservation at (he believed) about age 6 or 7, they cannot understand that the transformations shown here do not change the total amount of liquid, checkers, clay, and wood.

Tests of Various Types of Conservation

Type of conservation	Initial presentation	Transformation	Question	Preoperational child's answer
Liquid	Two equal glasses of liquid.	Pour one into a taller, narrower glass.	Which glass contains more?	The taller one.
Number	Two equal lines of checkers.	Increase spacing of checkers in one line.	Which line has more checkers?	The longer one.
Matter	Two equal balls of clay.	Squeeze one ball into a long, thin shape.	Which piece has more clay?	The long one.
Length	Two sticks of equal length.	Move one stick.	Which stick is longer?	The one that is farther to the right.

Vygotsky: Children as Apprentices

Every developmentalist, every preschool teacher, and every parent knows that young children strive to understand a world that fascinates and sometimes confuses them. They are active learners, as Piaget emphasized. Russian developmentalist Lev Vygotsky would certainly agree, as would every contemporary researcher (Brandtstadter, 1998).

But Vygotsky also emphasized another point: Children do not strive alone; their efforts are embedded in a social context. They notice things and they ask "Why?" with the assumption that others know why. They want to know how machines work, why weather changes, where the sky ends—and they expect answers.

Meanwhile, parents, as well as older children, preschool teachers, and many others, do more than just answer. They try to guide a young child's cognitive growth by:

- Presenting challenges for new learning
- Offering assistance with tasks that may be too difficult
- Providing instruction
- Encouraging the child's interest and motivation

guided participation The process by which a mentor facilitates the involvement of a learner in some educational activity.

In many ways, then, a young child is an *apprentice in thinking* whose intellectual growth is stimulated and directed by older and more skilled members of society. Children learn to think through their **guided participation** in social experiences and in explorations of their universe (Rogoff, 1990; Rogoff et al., 1993).

If this social (apprenticeship) aspect of cognitive development seems familiar, that's because it is given particular emphasis in the sociocultural perspective discussed in Chapter 2. Vygotsky's ideas have become the basis for much research that emphasizes the cultural foundations of growth and development. In contrast to many developmentalists (including Piaget) who regard cognitive growth as a process of individual discovery propelled by personal experience and biological maturation, Vygotsky believed that cognitive growth is driven by cultural processes (see the Research Report). More specifically, Vygotsky saw cognition not as a process of private discovery but as a social activity. Parents and other teachers motivate, channel, and construct children's learning.

Guided Participation Through shared social activity, adults in every culture guide the development of their children's cognition, values, and skills. Typically, the child's curiosity and interests, rather than the adult's planning for some future need, motivate the process. That seems to be the case as this Guatemalan girl eagerly tries to learn her mother's sewing skills.

How to Solve a Puzzle

To see how Vygotsky's approach works in practical terms, let's look at an example. Suppose a child tries to assemble a jigsaw puzzle, fails, and stops trying. Does that mean the task is beyond the child's ability? Not necessarily. The child may do better if he or she is given guidance that provides motivation to solve the puzzle, that focuses attention on the important steps, and that restructures the task to make its solution more attainable.

An adult or older child might begin such guidance by encouraging the child to look for a missing puzzle piece for a particular section ("Does it need to be a big piece or a little piece?" "Do you see any blue pieces with a line of red?"). Suppose the child finds some pieces of the right size, and then some blue pieces with a red line, but again seems

COMPARING PIAGET AND VYGOTSKY

As is evident in Table 9.1, the theories of Piaget and Vygotsky are similar in a number of ways. However, each perspective suggests limitations of the other. Both egocentrism (Piaget's idea) and scaffolding (Vygotsky's idea) may be criticized.

Eliciting Conservation

Piaget believed that preoperational children cannot grasp the idea of conservation (as well as other principles of concrete operational thought), no matter how carefully adults explain such thinking to them. But some later researchers wondered if perhaps the specific nature of Piaget's conservation experiments—including their formal or testlike features—might affect children's performance.

In a variety of experiments that include training, most preschool children are able to follow the examiner's guided instructions and then, apparently, grasp the idea of conservation. Several weeks after such training, many 4- and 5-year-olds (but almost no 3-year-olds) still understand the concept.

Indeed, older preschoolers not only grasp the type of conservation taught to them (such as for liquids) but also other types (such as for number or matter) (Field, 1987). As Vygotsky would have stressed, much depends on the child's past cultural experiences and on the specific context in which the child's cognitive capacity is measured. A responsive adult, who uses an interactive game to measure conservation or perspective taking or any other concrete-operational concept, can elicit such thinking years before age 6, when Piaget said it began.

This point highlights one criticism of Vygotsky's concept of scaffolding. Responsive adults are not always available, and children do not always want to learn whatever their parents want them to learn (Goodnow, 1993). Piaget would not have worried about this, because he believed that children can teach themselves. However, Vygotsky's emphasis on the social context might mean that some children never learn certain skills or are much slower to master whatever the dominant culture expects.

Piaget's insistence that preschoolers are egocentric, restricted to their own immediate perspective, seems mistaken. However, Vygotsky's supposition that children are willing apprentices, needing only to be encouraged to enter their zone of proximal development, may be mistaken as well.

Let us look carefully at one experiment designed to elicit perspective taking (Rall & Harris, 2000). Preschoolers were told two familiar stories, each with four simple episodes, using one of the verb pairs *come* and *go*, *take* and *bring*. For example:

> Little Red Riding Hood was sitting in her bedroom when her mother *went* [or came] and asked her to go to Grandmother's house.

Or:

> Cinderella was looking and looking in the kitchen for a pumpkin so that she could *bring* [or take] it to her fairy godmother.

Twenty-seven children, aged 3 to 5, were asked questions such as "Little Red Riding Hood was in her bedroom and what happened next?" The researchers listened to the answers very carefully, to see if the child changed the verb to reflect the protagonist's viewpoint. When the verb was inconsistent with the main character's location (as were the italicized verbs above), the children changed it three times more often than they repeated it. For example, they said the mother *came* in,

stymied. The tutor might then be more directive, selecting a piece to be tried next, or rotating a piece so that its proper location is more obvious, or actually putting a piece in place with a smile of satisfaction. Throughout, the teacher would praise momentary successes, maintain enthusiasm, and help the child recognize their joint progress toward the goal of finishing the puzzle.

The critical element in guided participation is that the mentor and child interact to accomplish the task, with the teacher sensitive and responsive to the precise needs of the child. Eventually, as the result of such mutuality, the child will be able to succeed independently.

In our example, once the child puts the puzzle together with the tutor's help, he or she might try it again soon—this time needing less assistance or perhaps none at all. The tutor gradually guides the child to do more on his or her own, encouraging each step toward indepen-

table **9.1**

Concepts from the Theories of Piaget and Vygotsky

Piaget	Vygotsky
Active Learning The child's own search for understanding, motivated by the child's inborn curiosity.	*Guided Participation* The adult or other mentor's aid in guiding the next step of learning, motivated by the learner's need for social interaction.
Egocentrism The preschooler's tendency to perceive everything from his or her own perspective and to be limited by that viewpoint.	*Apprenticeship in Thinking* The preschooler's tendency to look to others for insight and guidance, particularly in the cognitive realm.
Structure The mental assumptions and modalities (schema) the child creates to help him or her organize an understanding of the world. Structures are torn down and rebuilt when disequilibrium makes new structures necessary.	*Scaffold* The building blocks for learning put in place by a "teacher" (a more knowledgeable child or adult) or a culture. Learners use scaffolds and then discard them when they are no longer needed.
Symbolic Thought The ability to think using symbols, including language. This ability emerges spontaneously at about age 2 and continues lifelong.	*Proximal Development* The next step in cognition, the ideas and skills a child can grasp with assistance but not alone; influenced not only by the child's own abilities and interests but also by the social context.

Both theories emphasize that learning is not passive but is affected by the learner. The two theories share concepts and sometimes terminology; the differences are in emphasis.

or that Cinderella *took* the pumpkin instead of repeating what they had actually heard. However, when the verb in the sentence was consistent (as were the bracketed verbs above), almost all the children repeated exactly what they had heard. According to the researchers, this result proves that Piaget was in error: Specifically,

> The findings of the present study indicate that such perspective taking is not just an occasional capacity that is sometimes deployed to override a predominantly egocentric stance. The systematic tendency to misrecall inconsistent verbs indicates rather that children spontaneously and tenaciously maintain an alternative perspective. [Rall & Harris, 2000]

One question remains: What does it mean that the children clung to the heroine's perspective, rejecting the viewpoint of the mother, the fairy godmother, and even the verbal scaffolding provided by the experimenter? Could it be that neither Piaget's nor Vygotsky's theory is completely right?

dence. If puzzle solving is a valued skill in the culture, the adult might find a new puzzle for the child. Then, skills mastered with the first puzzle—such as locating pieces with the proper coloring or finding and connecting all the edge pieces first—will be transferred to the next puzzle. Eventually, these skills will generalize to all possible puzzles. In families that value and encourage puzzle solving, the children learn to perform and enjoy that activity, just as in other families children learn to play musical instruments, to bake bread, to catch balls, or whatever.

Such interactive apprenticeships are commonplace and continual. In every culture of the world, adults provide guidance and assistance to teach various skills. Soon, children who are given such guided practice learn to perform the skills on their own. Eventually, they become the tutors.

ZPD The best way to learn almost any practical or intellectual skill is with the help of a "mentor" who guides one's entry into the zone of proximal development, the area between what one can do alone and what one might do with help.

❷ *Observational Quiz (see answer page 256): In social apprenticeship, three elements—the teacher, the context, and the learner—each make a unique contribution. What evidence of such contributions can you see here?*

zone of proximal development (ZPD)
The skills or knowledge that are within the potential of the learner but are not yet mastered.

scaffold   To structure participation in learning encounters in order to foster a child's emerging capabilities. Scaffolds can be provided in many ways: by a mentor, by the objects or experiences of a culture, or by the child's past learning.

private speech   The dialogue that occurs when one talks to oneself, either silently or out loud, to form thoughts and analyze ideas.

social mediation   In regard to language, the use of speech as a tool to bridge the gap in understanding or knowledge between learner and tutor.

Language as Mediation One of the problems with cultural transmission of knowledge is that children are ready to learn whatever they are told—as myths about storks or cabbage patches, boogiemen or witches, will attest.

Scaffolding

Key to the success of apprenticeship is the tutor's sensitivity to the child's abilities and readiness to learn new skills. According to Vygotsky (1934/1986),

> The only good kind of instruction is that which marches ahead of development and leads it. It must be aimed not so much at the ripe as at the ripening functions. It remains necessary to determine the lowest threshold at which instruction may begin, since a certain ripeness of functions is required. But we must consider the upper threshold as well: instruction must be oriented toward the future, not the past.

As you saw in Chapter 2, Vygotsky believed that for each developing individual at each skill level, there is a **zone of proximal development (ZPD),** that is, a range of skills that the person can exercise with assistance but is not yet quite able to perform independently. How and when children master potential skills depends, in part, on the willingness of others to **scaffold,** or sensitively structure, participation in learning encounters. Most parents of preschoolers do this, at least to some extent (Conner et al., 1997; Rogoff et al., 1993).

Talking to Learn

Vygotsky believed that verbal interaction is a cognitive tool, essential to intellectual growth in two crucial ways. The first way is through **private speech,** the internal dialogue that occurs when people talk to themselves (Vygotsky, 1987). In adults, private speech is usually silent, but in children, especially preschoolers, it is likely to be uttered out loud. With time, children's loud self-talk becomes first soft-voiced and then inner, silent speech. During the play years, however, most children are not aware that they—or anyone else—can ever talk to themselves without talking out loud (Flavell et al., 1997).

Researchers studying private speech have found that preschoolers use it to help themselves think and learn—to review what they know, decide what to do, and explain events to themselves and, incidentally, to anyone else within earshot. Children who have learning difficulties tend to develop private speech more slowly and to use it less (Diaz, 1987). Training children to say things to themselves to focus their thoughts sometimes helps them learn—another sign that private speech aids the learning process.

The second way in which language advances thinking, according to Vygotsky, is as the *mediator of the social interaction* that, as you have seen, is vital to learning. Whether this **social mediation** function of speech occurs during explicit instruction or only during casual conver-

Calvin and Hobbes   by Bill Watterson

sation, whether it is intellectual interpretation or simply enthusiastic comment, language as a tool of verbal interaction refines and extends a person's skills. Language allows a person to enter and traverse the zone of proximal development, because words provide a bridge from the child's current understanding to what is almost understood.

IN FACT: WHAT CHILDREN THINK

As you have seen, developmentalists can—and do—debate how much a preschooler's cognitive accomplishments are the result of maturation and how much the result of culture. However, while this nature–nurture debate continues, there is no doubt that preschoolers demonstrate amazing competency in several areas, two of which—memory and theory of mind—we will now describe.

Memory

Preschoolers are notorious for having poor memory, even when compared with children only a few years older. Ask a school-age child "What did you do today?" and you may get a detailed accounting, complete with reflections about why people acted as they did and how their current behavior relates to their past actions. Ask that older child what happened in a television sitcom, and again you might hear a lengthy, blow-by-blow sequence, with more specifics than you ever wanted to know. Ask a preschooler the same questions, and you are likely to hear "I don't remember" or "I liked it" or a string of seemingly irrelevant details.

Even with skilled help from a patient mother who knows her child and understands the basics of early memory, preschool children's memory is far from fluent. This example is typical:

> *Mother:* Did you like the apartment at the beach?
> *Rachel:* Yeah, and I have fun in the, in the, water.
> *Mother:* You had fun in the water?
> *Rachel:* Yeah, I come to the ocean.
> *Mother:* You went to the ocean?
> *Rachel:* Yeah.
> *Mother:* Did you play in the ocean?
> *Rachel:* And my sandals off.
> *Mother:* You took your sandals off?
> *Rachel:* And my jamas off.
> *Mother:* And your jamas off. And what did you wear to the beach?
> *Rachel:* I wear hot cocoa shirt.
> *Mother:* Oh, your cocoa shirt, yeah. And your bathing suit.
> *Rachel:* Yeah, and my cocoa shirt.
> *Mother:* And did you go in the water?
> *Rachel: (No response)*
> *Mother:* Who went in the water with you?
> *Rachel:* Daddy and Mommy.
> *Mother:* Right. Did the big waves splash you?
> *Rachel:* Yeah.
> [Hudson, 1990]

The difficulty is not primarily that preschoolers have deficient memory circuits in their brains. Sometimes they remember particular events

❷ **Especially for Social Scientists:** For 50 years Piaget's conservation experiments were the standard that indicated the nature of preschool thought. Children almost always answered as predicted. Can you think of any reasons, other than lack of logic, why preschoolers would not demonstrate conservation?

WITNESS TO A CRIME

Until quite recently, most countries prohibited young children from testifying in court. It was assumed that children are egocentric, suggestible, likely to confuse fact and fiction, and therefore unable to "provide a truthful and accurate account" (as the witness's oath requires) of stressful events. It is also feared that adults might manipulate child witnesses. Who would do such a thing? The possibilities include parents in custody battles, or overzealous authorities handling alleged abuse in day-care centers (where abuse is actually far less common than in homes), or prosecutors hoping for some publicity, or drug addicts seeking sympathy.

However, sometimes a child is the only witness who can testify against an accused suspect. As the text discussion points out, young children often retain accurate memories of happy past events. If they could also recount stressful events truthfully, more of the guilty and fewer of the innocent would be convicted.

Of course, causing stress to children merely to test their memories of emotionally traumatic events, is unethical. Therefore, researchers use events that normally occur in every child's life, such as a medical inoculation or a dental exam, as the basis for experiments.

Recall of Stressful Experiences

In one series of such studies, children between the ages of 3 and 6 were videotaped during a medical examination that included a DPT inoculation administered by a nurse they had never seen before (Goodman et al., 1990). The children's reactions varied widely. Most looked frightened, but some were quite stoic and unfazed. Indeed, some claimed, "It didn't hurt." A few, at the other extreme, became nearly hysterical. They had to be physically restrained, often by two or three people, so that they could get the inoculation. They cried, screamed, yelled for help, tried to run out of the room, and sobbed afterward while complaining about the pain—they reacted as if they had been attacked.

Several days later, the children were asked to tell about the experience, then to answer specific questions about it, and finally to identify the nurse who had administered the shot from a lineup of photos. None of the children offered any false information during the free recall. Contrary to the hypothesis

that emotional arousal might scramble a child's memory, those who had shown the most distress during the exam were the ones who provided the most detailed, accurate accounts.

When asked specific questions, all the children were quite good witnesses. Notably, none of them answered yes to "Did she hit you?" "Did she kiss you?" "Did she put anything in your mouth?" and "Did she touch you anyplace other than your arm?" However, although the children were very clear about what had and had not been done to them, they were less sure about who did it. In the photo lineup, only half picked the right nurse's photograph, 41 percent picked other photos, and 9 percent said they couldn't remember.

To test the durability of these children's memories, they were interviewed again a year later. Their overall recall had diminished, but they reported virtually no significant false memories. Most of the children again failed the photo-identification task, with only 14 percent correctly identifying the nurse this time around. Many said they didn't remember, but 32 percent picked the wrong photo.

What about children who are even younger who were interviewed even later? In another study, children who had had a medical emergency (a broken bone, a swallowed poison) at age 1 or 2 were interviewed as long as 2 years after the event. Those who were preverbal at the time of the trauma remembered very little, but those who were at least 2 years old had vivid and accurate memories, even 2 years later. The reports were not completely accurate, however, with distortion of the social context (who and why) more likely than distortion of the actual emergency (Peterson & Rideout, 1998).

Effects of Misleading Questions

Can children's memories be deliberately distorted? In another series of experiments, the initial interview after a medical checkup included purposely misleading questions. Questions such as "She touched your bottom, didn't she?" and "How many times did she kiss you?" were asked, either in a friendly, encouraging manner or in an intimidatingly stern one.

Older children (ages 5 to 7) were rarely misled by such questions; they affirmed false occurrences less than 9 percent

or details very well, as Rachel remembered the "hot cocoa shirt." But they have not yet acquired the strategies they need for deliberately storing memories of events and later retrieving them. Preschoolers rarely try to retain an experience or a bit of information in memory, and they seldom know precisely how to recall some hard-to-retrieve bit of past experience (Kail, 1990). As a result, they sometimes appear strangely incapable of remembering what older children can recall with ease.

of the time, whether the questioning was friendly or stern. Of the 3- and 4-year-olds, 10 percent responded untruthfully to the friendly questions, and 23 percent were misled by the stern questions.

This actually happened in at least one notorious day-care abuse case, during which the following exchange took place:

> *Prosecutor:* Did she touch you with a spoon?
> *Child:* No
> *Prosecutor:* No? Okay. Did you like it when she touched you with the spoon?
> *Child:* No.
> *Prosecutor:* No? Why not?
> *Child:* I don't know.
> *Prosecutor:* You don't know?
> *Child:* No.
> *Prosecutor:* What did you say to Kelly when she touched you?
> *Child:* I don't like that.
> [quoted in Ceci & Bruck, 1998]

Some Conclusions

The research provides five useful guidelines.

- When children are required to give eyewitness testimony, they should be provided a structured sequence that enhances their ability to remember accurately.
- Children should be interviewed by a neutral professional who asks specific but not misleading questions in a friendly—not stern or shocked—manner.
- The interview of a child should occur only once, soon after the event, and be videotaped for later trial use.
- Although quite young children can provide accurate details concerning what happened, remembering who was involved may be more difficult.
- Children sometimes add false information to follow a script that makes sense to them, especially if a long delay occurs between the event and the account. (Cassel et al., 1996; Pipe et al., 1999; Schneider & Pressley, 1997)

Would You Believe Her? As the only eyewitness to the slaying of a playmate, 4-year-old Jennifer Royal was allowed to testify in open court. Her forthright answers, and the fact that she herself had been wounded, helped convict the accused gunman. While most developmentalists agree that, when questioned properly, children can provide reliable testimony about events they have experienced or witnessed, many advocate arranging a more sheltered way for young children to give testimony.

One of the most important findings is that adults also misremember important details, and adults can and do distort children's memories. Nobody always tells the truth. Indeed,

> The safest conclusion that can be reached at this point in time is that subjects of all ages will lie when the motives are right. Children may be no different from adults in this regard. Thus the argument that children are incapable of "lying" should be discounted, as should the insinuation that they are hopeless liars. . . . Children have tremendous strengths in recollecting their pasts, provided that the adults do not do anything to usurp their memories. [Ceci & Bruck, 1998]

❶ **Response for Social Scientists (from page 253):** We now know that preschoolers want to please adults, and if they think an adult expects a particular answer, they will try to give it. In playful situations, or after careful instruction, preschoolers sometimes do demonstrate conservation.

Rachel seemed to forget that she wore a bathing suit and played in the waves, surely the most important part of a trip to the beach.

Script Creation

This does not, however, tell the whole story about memory in young children. In some ways, young children are remarkably capable of storing

scripts   Skeletal outlines of the usual sequence of events during certain common, recurring experiences.

in their minds useful representations of past events that they can later retrieve. One way they do so is by retaining **scripts** of familiar, recurring experiences. A script is a familiar sequence of events.

Each script acts as a kind of self-made scaffold, or skeletal outline. By age 3, for example, children can tell you what happens in a restaurant (you order food, eat it, and then pay for it); at a birthday party (you arrive, give presents, play games, have cake and ice cream, and sing "Happy Birthday"); at bedtime (first a bath, then a story, and then lights out); and during other everyday events. Here is one 5-year-old's description of what happens during grocery shopping:

> Um, we get a cart, uh, and we look for some onions and plums and cookies and tomato sauce, onions, and all that kind of stuff, and when we're finished we go to the paying booth, and um, then we, um, then the lady puts all our food in a bag, then we put it in the cart, walk out to our car, put the bags in the trunk, then leave. [quoted in Nelson, 1986]

This is a typical script in two key respects. First, it has a beginning and an end. Second, it recognizes the causal flow of events—reflecting an awareness that some events (like putting food in the cart) must precede other events (like going to the "paying booth") (Bauer & Mandler, 1990; Ratner et al., 1990). Preschoolers use scripts not only when recounting familiar routines but also when, in pretend play, they enact everyday events such as eating dinner, shopping, and going to work.

The Script: Birthday Child Blows Out Candles
The fact that preschoolers have scripts for events such as birthdays is especially evident when someone "violates" the script. If this birthday boy's sister (on his right) had blown out the last candle rather than merely pointing at it, he might have exploded in angry tears.

Memories of Special Experiences

Under certain circumstances, however, children show surprising long-term memory. As you saw above, this is particularly so for experiences that happen so many times that a script is formed—especially when parents aid in the development of the script. Children also can remember distinctive experiences—including natural disasters, family changes, or traumatic events—that occur only once (Howe, 1997). (We saw this in the Changing Policy box.)

In one study, children who had visited Disney World at age 3 or 4 were interviewed in their homes, either 6 or 18 months later (Hamond & Fivush, 1991). When asked "Tell me about Disney World," the 3-year-olds were not very forthcoming, but when asked specific questions ("What rides did you go on? Which one did you like most? What did that feel like?"), their memories were accurate, detailed, and almost as good as those of children who had visited at age 4. This was especially true if they had seen photographs of their experiences. Photos may be nonverbal "reminder" events similar to the familiar mobiles used with 3-month-old infants, as described in Chapter 5.

This study is particularly helpful in explaining why preschoolers' memory abilities often appear inadequate. Sometimes they may be asked to remember experiences that had little meaning for them. At other times, seemingly vague memories may be the result of vague

❗ *Answer to Observational Quiz (from page 252): First, the teacher's work is most obvious. She is using both hands, and very watchful eyes, to guide the process. Without her, the nail would never be safely pounded, and the child might be hurt and frustrated. Second, note the table and the completed model right in front of them, which suggests a woodworking activity within an educational program—not something offered in most cultures to most students. Finally, the child provides something only he can—concentrated, dedicated effort. Evidence for that: his tongue.*

questioning. "What did you do today?" is an example of a question that is much too general. Preschool children do not necessarily tell everything they know, especially when the questioner does not know what to ask (MacDonald & Hayne, 1996). However, with specific questions, and especially with visual reminders of the event, their memories can be amazingly accurate (Priestly et al., 1999).

Theory of Mind

Human emotions, motives, thoughts, and intentions are among the most complicated and thought-provoking phenomena in a young person's world. Whether trying to understand a playmate's unexpected anger, or determine when a sibling will be generous or selfish, or avoid an aunt's too-wet kiss, or persuade a parent to purchase a toy, children want to understand. In other words, young children develop a **theory of mind,** an understanding of human mental processes.

Beginning to Understand Mental Processes

By age 3 or 4, some children have sufficiently advanced in theory of mind to be able to:

- Clearly distinguish between mental phenomena and the physical events to which they refer (for example, you can pet a dog that is in front of you but not one that is in your thoughts)
- Appreciate how mental phenomena (like beliefs, expectations, and desires) can arise from experiences in the real world
- Understand that mental phenomena are subjective (others cannot "see" what you are imagining)
- Recognize that people have differing opinions and preferences (someone might like a game that you dislike)
- Realize that beliefs and desires can form the basis for human action (Dad is driving the car fast because he doesn't want to be late for Grandma's dinner)
- Realize that emotion arises not only from physical events but also from goals and expectations (a 4-year-old might eat lunch by himself at day care to avoid his friends' envy of and request to share his dessert) (Flavell, 1999; Stein & Levine, 1989; Wellman & Gelman, 1992)

All six of these abilities signify something parents and psychologists did not appreciate until recently: Children commit as much effort to understanding their social surroundings as they do to understanding their physical world, and sometimes they succeed.

The growth of children's theory of mind during the play years has broad implications. As an older preschooler begins to grasp how people's thinking is affected by past experiences and by other people's opinions, he or she becomes far more capable of anticipating and influencing the thoughts, emotions, and intentions of others (Astington, 1993; Flavell et al., 1995). Not surprisingly, this conceptual growth quickly becomes enlisted for various practical purposes, such as persuasion ("If you buy me a TV for my room, Mom, then I won't always fight with Susie over what to watch!"), or sympathy (consoling a sad friend by reminding her of an upcoming birthday party), teasing, and pretending.

An important advance in theory of mind occurs sometime between the ages of 3 and 6, when children realize that mental phenomena may

❷ Especially for Parents: If you want to know the truth about something, what is the best way to ask a preschooler?

theory of mind   An understanding of human mental processes, that is, of one's own and others' emotions, perceptions, intentions, and thoughts.

Brotherly Love At age 2, Robert is not yet supposed to have much theory of mind. That means he is not yet supposed to know what his baby brother might think about having a rubber frog put on his head. If the same scenario occurred 2 years later, however, brother Peter might consider this a hostile act, and Robert would have enough theory of mind to anticipate his brother's reaction, as well as that of his parents. Indeed, the same advances that would allow him to imagine other people's reactions might also enable him to claim, in his most aggrieved voice, "I thought he would like it." Siblings learn not only how to read emotions but also how to try to fool each other and how to convince their parents that they are the innocent ones.

Meeting Barney A preschooler might be told that a person is actually inside this Barney costume but nonetheless believe that Barney himself is there. During the play years, the relationship between appearance and reality is a tenuous, tricky one.

❓ *Observational Quiz (see answer page 260): What would happen if the preschooler saw Barney take his costume off?*

⬤ **Response for Parents (from page 257):** Ask very specific questions, but not leading questions, in a nonthreatening manner— NOT "Did you break the plate?" but "Did you hear when the plate fell? Did you see it?" all expressed in a friendly, interested manner. Never punish a child for telling the truth or for being afraid to tell the truth.

not reflect reality. This idea leads to the concept that individuals can believe various things and, therefore, that people can be deliberately deceived or fooled—an idea beyond most younger preschoolers, even when they have themselves been deceived. Consider the following experiment involving a child who does not understand pretense.

An adult shows a 3-year-old a candy box and asks, "What is inside?" The child says, naturally, "Candy." But, in fact, the child has been tricked:

> *Adult:* Let's open it and look inside.
> *Child:* Oh . . . holy moly . . . pencils!
> *Adult:* Now I'm going to put them back and close it up again. (Does so) Now . . . when you first saw the box, before we opened it, what did you think was inside it?
> *Child:* Pencils.
> *Adult:* Nicky (friend of the child) hasn't seen inside this box. When Nicky comes in and sees it . . . when Nicky sees the box, what will he think is inside it?
> *Child:* Pencils.
> [adapted from Astington & Gopnik, 1988]

Like this child, most 3-year-olds have considerable difficulty realizing that a belief can be false or that subjective understanding can be wrong. Since false belief is not possible to them, when children learn that they have the wrong mental image, they not only correct the mistake but also believe that they have always held the correct view. They even think that others (like Nicky) will intuitively know what they now know is correct (that pencils are in the candy box). In other words, they fail to understand how someone would be fooled by appearance; their theory of mind is inadequate to explain this difference between a person's thinking and the actual case. By age 5, almost all children understand this.

Culture and Context as Influences on Theory of Mind

Recently, developmentalists have asked what, precisely, strengthens theory of mind at about age 4. Is it brain maturation alone, or does experience play a role? Consider one study, in which 68 children aged 2½ to 5½ were presented with four standard theory-of-mind situations, including a Band-Aid box that really contained pencils (similar to the candy-box experiment described above) (Jenkins & Astington, 1996). More than one-third of the children succeeded at all four tasks (for example, they understood that someone else might initially believe, as they did, that the Band-Aid box would contain Band-Aids); more than one-third failed on three or four tasks; and the remaining 26 percent were in between, succeeding at two or three tasks. Not surprisingly, age had a powerful effect: The 5-year-olds were most likely to succeed on all four tasks and the 3-year-olds most likely to fail every time. This result suggests that maturation is a powerful influence.

Interestingly, however, as a predictive variable, general language ability was as significant as maturation: The greater a child's verbal proficiency (at any age), the better he or she did. Other research also finds that language ability, particularly the ability to use the words "think" and "know," correlates with theory-of-mind development (Moore et al., 1990).

In the Jenkins & Astington (1996) study, when the effects of both age and language ability were accounted for, a third important factor emerged: having at least one brother or sister. Having a sibling particularly aided younger children whose language ability was not quite up to the norm for children of their age. The researchers suggest that the "familiarity and intimacy of the sibling relationship facilitates the learning process"—especially the understanding of false belief.

Before we conclude that brain maturation, with a little help from language and siblings, always produces theory of mind by age 5, consider one more study (Vinden, 1996). All the 4- to 8-year-olds in a certain Peruvian village were tested on a culturally appropriate version of the candy-box situation, in this case with a sugar bowl that contained tiny potatoes. Of course, the children at first thought the bowl contained sugar, as anyone from that village would. But surprisingly, even up to age 8, these children often answered questions about the bowl's contents incorrectly: They could not explain why someone would initially expect sugar to be in a sugar bowl and then be surprised to discover potatoes. They also had difficulty with other theory-of-mind experiments and questions that most North American 5-year-olds could answer.

Culture is probably the key difference between the Peruvian and the North American children. In the Peruvians' mountainous, isolated village, "there is no reason or time for elaborate deception . . . where subsistence farmers, working from dawn to dusk just to survive, . . . live mostly on the landscape of action, and not on the landscape of consciousness" (Vinden, 1996). Neither their language nor their culture describes false belief or "how people's thoughts might affect their actions." Thus, culture is a fourth crucial factor in the development of theory of mind (Lillard, 1999; Vinden, 1996).

LANGUAGE

As we noted in Chapter 6, humans normally begin talking at about 1 year, with new vocabulary and expressions added slowly at first. Toddlers typically master new spoken words relatively slowly, talking mostly in one-word sentences about immediate experiences. They do not yet think, or talk, symbolically. They tend to frustrate themselves, and even the most patient caregiver, as they seek to communicate.

During the preschool years, however, the pace and scope of language learning increase dramatically, and language becomes a pivotal part of cognition. We sometimes say that a *language explosion* occurs, with words and sentences bursting forth.

Vocabulary

In the preschool period, vocabulary increases exponentially. By age 6, the average child has a lexicon containing more than 10,000 words (Anglin, 1993). According to one source, "Children typically produce their first 30 words at a rate of three to five new words per month. The same children learn their next 30,000 words at a rate of 10 to 20 new words per day" (Jones et al., 1991).

How does this rapid learning happen? One explanation is that after a year or so of painstakingly learning one word at a time, the human mind develops an interconnected set of categories for vocabulary, a kind of grid or mental map on which to chart the meanings of various words. This speedy and not very precise process of acquiring vocabulary

A One-to-One Ratio of Teachers to Learners One of the key features of any good preschool program is the frequent opportunity it affords children to hear and express new vocabulary. Of course, adults should read to young children and engage them in conversation, but the best language teachers for children are sometimes other children.

fast mapping   Used by children to add words to their vocabulary, the process of hearing a word once or twice and then quickly defining it by categorizing it with other words.

by "charting" new words is called **fast mapping.** Children quickly learn new animal names, for instance, because they can be mapped in the brain close to old animal names. "Tiger" is easy if you already know "lion." Similarly, children learn new color names by connecting them with those they already know.

The process is called fast mapping because, rather than stopping to figure out an exact definition and waiting until a word has been understood in several contexts, the child simply hears a word once or twice and sticks it on a mental language map. (Something similar occurs when someone is asked, for instance, where Nepal is. Most people can locate it approximately ["near India"] in their mental map of the world, but few can locate it precisely, citing each border.)

Evidence for the underlying aptness of this mapping concept (specifically, that people spontaneously organize their language into categories) comes from adults who suffer a stroke or other brain damage. They sometimes lose or confuse whole categories of words. For instance, they may remember the names of fruits very well but forget the names of most vegetables. Or they may mix up words that are conceptually related but not synonymous: A tunnel may be called a bridge, or a skunk may be called a zebra.

Apparently, we all store words according to categories, although this organizational map does not usually become obvious until it is damaged. During the language explosion, children do the same thing; they categorize words with a speed that sometimes leads to notable and telling mistakes (Golinkoff et al., 1992; Wilkinson et al., 1996). On hearing a new word, a child uses clues from the immediate context to create a quick, partial understanding and then categorizes the word on the basis of that partial understanding. (See A Life-Span View.)

Young children's fast mapping is aided by the way adults label new things for them. A helpful parent might point at an animal the child is watching at the zoo and say, "See the *lion* resting by the water. It's a *lion!* A very big cat." In less than a minute, "lion" enters the child's vocabu-

❶ *Answer to Observational Quiz (from page 258):* She might be upset and think Barney had gone away, because her thinking is still static and irreversible, and current appearance is taken as reality. She might cry "Bring Barney back," but not know how to do it.

FAST MAPPING

Fast mapping has an obvious advantage, in that it fosters quick vocabulary acquisition. However, it also means that children *seem* to know words because they use them, when in fact their understanding is quite limited. One very simple common example is the word "big," a word even 2-year-olds use and seem to understand. In fact, however, young preschoolers often use "big" when they mean "tall" or "old" or "great" ("My love is so big!") and only gradually come to use "big" correctly (Sena & Smith, 1990).

A more amusing example involves a 3-year-old who told her father that her preschool group had visited a farm, where she saw some Dalmatian cows. Luckily her father (my student) remembered that, a week before, the girl had met her uncle's Dalmatian dog, so he understood his daughter's fast-mapping mistake.

When adults realize that children often do not fully comprehend the meanings of words they use, it becomes easier to understand—and forgive—the mistakes children make. I still vividly recall an incident that stemmed from fast mapping and that occurred when my youngest daughter, then 4, was furious at me.

Sarah had apparently fast-mapped several insulting words into her vocabulary. However, her fast mapping did not provide precise definitions or reflect nuances. In her anger, she called me first a "mean witch" and then a "brat." I smiled at her innocent imprecisions, knowing the first was garnered from fairy tales and the second from comments she got from her older sisters. Neither invective bothered me, as I don't believe in witches and my brother is the only person who can appropriately call me a brat.

But then Sarah let loose an X-rated epithet that sent me reeling. Struggling to contain my anger, I tried to convince myself that fast mapping had probably left her with no real idea of what she had just said. "That word is never to be used in this family!" I sputtered. My appreciation of the speed of fast mapping was deepened by her response: "Then how come Rachel [her sister] called me that this morning?"

On a broader level, Sarah's reflection of her family's values and interactions is similar to that found in many children and adults. We all tend to learn lessons most quickly from the significant people in our lives, especially lessons regarding emotions. From the social referencing described in Chapter 7 to the attitudes toward elder care described in Chapter 25, words and actions that indicate fear, delight, anger, or support are taken to heart and repeated long after the initial episode. What does this mean for parents? Watch your tongue; expect an echo.

lary. Zoos and children's first picture books do the same thing, organizing animals and objects into categories.

In addition, children make some basic assumptions that help them learn (Woodward & Markman, 1998). They assume, for example, that words refer to whole objects (rather than to their parts), that each object has only one label (underextension again), or that a word means more than it does (overextension). These assumptions usually lead to good provisional definitions, although they sometimes prove misleading—as is obvious when we hear a child say, "That's not an animal, it's a *dog*!" or "I have two sisters, big sister Susan and kitty-cat Fluffy."

The vocabulary-building process occurs so quickly that, by age 5, some children seem to be able to understand and use almost any term they hear. In fact, 5-year-olds *can* learn almost any word or phrase, as long as it is explained to them with specific examples and used in context. A preschool teacher, for example, asked the children what they did over the weekend. "I went to a protest," one said. Another child asked, "What is a protest?" The first child answered, "A lot of people get together, walk around, and yell." At age 5, my colleague's son Scott surprised his kindergarten teacher by stating that he was ambidextrous. When queried, he explained, "That means I can use my left or my right hand just the same."

Hi, Grandma This boy has been having telephone conversations with his grandmother since he was 1 year old. At first, he mostly listened and then cried when the phone was taken away. Now, almost 3 years old, he chatters away unstoppably, revealing an extensive grasp of vocabulary and grammar. However, he still doesn't necessarily provide all the details that would let his grandmother follow the conversation: He may sometimes refer to events she has no knowledge of and people she does not know or tell the ending of a story without a beginning.

In fact, preschoolers soak up language like a sponge. Most researchers regard early childhood as a crucial period for language learning.

The vocabulary acquisition that occurs between ages 2 and 6 is so impressive that we occasionally need to remind ourselves that young children cannot comprehend *every* word they hear. Abstract nouns, such as "justice" and "government," are difficult for them because there is no referent in their experience. Metaphors and analogies are also difficult, because the fast-mapping process is quite literal, allowing only one meaning per word. When a mother, exasperated by her son's frequent inability to find his belongings, told him that someday he would lose his head, he calmly replied, "I'll never lose my head. If I feel it coming off, I'll find it and pick it up." Another mother warned her child who was jumping on the bed:

> *Mother:* Stop. You'll hurt yourself.
> *Child:* No I won't. *(Still jumping)*
> *Mother:* You'll break the bed.
> *Child:* No I won't. *(Still jumping)*
> *Mother:* OK. You'll just have to live with the consequences.
> *Child: (Stops jumping).* I'm not going to live with the consequences. I don't even know them.
> [adapted from *The New York Times*, November 2, 1998]

Young children can most easily grasp nouns because nouns have objective meanings; they name things. Most verbs and adjectives are also relatively easy. One interesting exception is color names. Since colors are not precise—some blues are not the same as other blues, and azure, turquoise, and navy are all mapped into already ambiguous territory—children may have difficulty answering the question "What color is this?" (Sandhofer & Smith, 1999).

Children also have difficulty with words expressing comparisons, such as "tall" and "short," "near" and "far," "high" and "low," "deep" and "shallow," because they do not understand the *relative* nature of these words. Once preschoolers know which end of the swimming pool is the deep end, for instance, its depth becomes their definition of "deep." They might obey parental instructions to stay out of deep puddles by splashing through every puddle they see, insisting that none of those is "deep."

Words expressing relationships of place and time, such as "here," "there," "yesterday," and "tomorrow," are difficult as well. More than one pajama-clad child has awakened on Christmas morning and asked, "Is it tomorrow yet?"

Grammar

The *grammar* of a language includes the structures, techniques, and rules that are used to communicate meaning. Word order and word repetition, prefixes and suffixes, intonation and pronunciation—all are part of this element of language. Grammar is apparent in toddlers' two-word sentences, and even one-word thoughts are expressed differently depending on whether they are questions, statements, or commands.

By the time children are 3 years old, their grammar is quite impressive: English-speaking children not only place the subject before the verb but also put the verb before the object and the adjective before the noun. They say "I eat red apple" and not any of the 23 other possible combinations of those four words. They can form the plurals of nouns; the past, present, and future tenses of verbs; and the subjective, objective, and possessive forms of pronouns. They rearrange word order to create questions and can use auxiliary verbs ("I *can* do that"). They are well on their way to mastering the negative, having progressed past the simple "no" of the 2-year-old ("No sleepy" or "I no want it") to more complex negatives such as "I am not sleepy" or "I want no more."

Children's understanding of grammar is also facilitated by hearing conversations at home that are models of good grammar and by receiving helpful feedback about their language use (Tomasello, 1992). Reflecting this fact was a study that followed the language development of two groups of 2-year-olds (Hoff-Ginsberg, 1986). The mothers of one group frequently asked questions (such as "Where does the duck live?") and then repeated their child's answers, rephrased correctly (changing "Duck, water," for example, into "Yes, the duck lives on the water"). The mothers of the other group rarely used such strategies. After 6 months, the children who had received "lessons" in grammar as part of normal dialogue with their mothers advanced in their use of grammar compared to the children in the other group.

Cultural and social context profoundly influences the acquisition of both vocabulary and grammar: The child learns what he or she is exposed to. Thus, young Mandarin-speaking children have more verbs than nouns in their vocabulary, because their mothers are more likely to emphasize actions than objects (Tardif, 1996). Most North American children have difficulty with the passive voice; even at age 6 a child may think that "The dog was bitten by the boy" means the dog did the biting. For some time, experts assumed that a certain amount of brain maturation had to occur before children could understand the unusual word order (object, verb, subject). However, we now know that Inuit children in Alaska acquire the passive voice as early as age 2. From other evidence such as this, it seems that context, more than maturation, is the engine that drives grammar (Allen & Crago, 1996).

Young children learn their grammar lessons so well that they often tend to apply the rules of grammar even when they should not. This tendency, called **overregularization,** creates trouble when a child's language includes many exceptions to the rules. As an example, one of the first rules that English-speaking children apply is to add "s" to form the plural. Overregularization leads many preschoolers to talk about foots, tooths, sheeps, and mouses. They may even put the "s" on adjectives when the adjectives are acting as nouns, as in this dinner-table exchange between my 3-year-old and her father:

> *Sarah:* I want somes.
> *Father:* You want some what?
> *Sarah:* I want some mores.
> *Father:* Some more what?
> *Sarah:* I want some more chickens.

Once preschool children learn a rule, they can be surprisingly stubborn in applying it. One developmentalist reports the following conversation between herself and a 4-year-old:

> *She said:* "My teacher *holded* the baby rabbits and we *patted* them."
> *I asked:* "Did you say your teacher *held* the baby rabbits?"
> *She answered:* "Yes."
> *I then asked:* "What did you say she did?"
> *She answered again:* "She *holded* the baby rabbits and we *patted* them."
> "Did you say she *held* them tightly?" I asked.
> "No," she answered, "she *holded* them loosely." [Gleason, 1967]

overregularization   The tendency to make a language more logical and "regular" than it actually is, which leads to mistaken application of the rules of grammar.

No, Timmy, not "I sawed the chair." It's "I saw the chair" or "I have seen the chair."

Drawing by Glenn Bernhardt

Correct Grammar This mother has obviously become too accustomed to her son's over-regularization.

Although technically wrong, such overregularization is actually a sign of verbal sophistication; it shows that children are applying the rules. Indeed, as preschoolers become more conscious of grammatical usages, they exhibit increasingly sophisticated misapplications of them. A child who at age 2 correctly says she "broke" a glass may at age 4 say she "braked" one and then at age 5 say she "did broked" another. After children hear the correct form often enough, they spontaneously correct their own speech, so parents can probably best help a child's development of grammar by example rather than by explanation or criticism. In this case, for example, a parent might simply respond, "You mean you broke it?" While few children will immediately correct their grammar, continual exposure to good grammar speeds language mastery (Farrar, 1992).

During the preschool years, children comprehend more complex grammar, and more difficult vocabulary, than they produce. Thus, although it is a mistake to expect proper grammar, it is also an error to always mirror preschoolers' speech, "talking down" to their level. Surely some grammatical forms (the future subjunctive, the past perfect) are beyond preschoolers, but most other forms are potentially within their comprehension. The zone of proximal development is a useful concept here, suggesting that between the simple grammatical forms that are well understood and those that are as yet incomprehensible lies a zone of potential improvement. In that zone, social mediation facilitates language learning. Similarly, given children's ability to fast-map vocabulary, several new words should be used and explained every day.

PRESCHOOL EDUCATION

The most dramatic cohort change that has occurred in the life of the typical preschool child in the past 30 years is that he or she is now very likely to be "in school." Indeed, the word "preschool" once meant before school begins; now it often means a school for younger children, complete with curriculum, homework, and graduation. In the United States in 1970, only 30 percent of married mothers with children under age 6 were in the labor force, and only 20 percent of all 3- and 4-year-olds were in an organized program of some type (including day-care centers, which used to provide simply "care" but now provide education as well). In 1998, the figures were 66 percent of mothers working and 53 percent of 3- and 4-year-olds in a program (U.S. Bureau of the Census, 1999). Further, almost all 5-year-olds are in preschool now, often called kindergarten, usually all day (see Figure 9.2). In most other developed countries, the rate of preschool attendance for 3- and 4-year-olds is even higher than it is in the United States, because their governments sponsor education in early childhood.

Over the past 30 years, social scientists have shown that young children learn a great deal through formal as well as informal preschool education. This is apparent particularly in verbal skills and social understanding. The preschools that consistently provide the most extensive benefits are characterized by:

- A low teacher–child ratio
- Staff with training and credentials in early-childhood education
- Curriculum geared toward cognitive development
- Learning spaces organized for creative and constructive play

See the In Person box for an example of the benefits of preschool education.

❷ Especially for Teachers: In helping plan a new preschool with limited resources, you need to rank the four characteristics of preschools from most to least important. How would you do that?

Figure 9.2 Changing Times. As research increasingly finds that preschool education provides a foundation for later learning, more and more young children are in educational programs. Currently, almost half of all 3- and 4-year-olds are in school. That proportion is expected to increase even more in the twenty-first century.

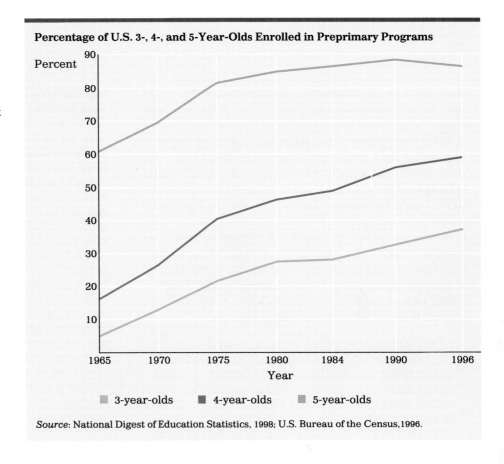

Percentage of U.S. 3-, 4-, and 5-Year-Olds Enrolled in Preprimary Programs

3-year-olds   4-year-olds   5-year-olds

Source: National Digest of Education Statistics, 1998; U.S. Bureau of the Census, 1996.

Cultural Differences

In every culture, preschool education not only includes but goes beyond cognitive preparation for later schooling (Mallory & New, 1994). As an example, Japanese culture places great emphasis on social consensus and conformity. Therefore, Japan's preschools provide training in the behavior and attitudes appropriate for group activity: Children are encouraged to show concern for others and to contribute cooperatively in group activities (Rohlen & LeTendre, 1996). These social attitudes and habits prepare young children for both the formal school system and later work settings (Peak, 1991). In China, similarly, learning how to be part of the group is combined with creativity in self-expression, both drawn from the culture's Confucian ethic of disciplined study.

In the United States, by contrast, preschools are often designed to foster self-confidence and self-reliance and to give children a good academic start through emphasis on language skills. Since most North American preschools are privately or parochially sponsored, they vary a great deal in rules, curriculum, and values.

Project Head Start

The first massive public effort to create quality preschools in the United States was in 1965, with Project Head Start, a federally funded program designed for low-income children who, at least in theory, needed a "head start" on their education.

PETER'S PRESCHOOL

Some adults, whose childhood ended long before the expansion of early-childhood education in the 1970s, may still equate "school" (and hence "preschool") with sitting at desks in rows, memorizing times tables, and practicing penmanship—skills beyond the zone of proximal development for even the brightest 4-year-old. For them, a "preschool" child is literally what the word says, a child before school age. If such adults were asked whether massive amounts of public money should underwrite schools for young children, where one goal is to encourage children's play (Jones & Reynolds, 1992), they might ask, "Why pay for play?" Perhaps the following account would convince them. It surely would give them a better idea of what preschool is like. It also illustrates how a preschool setting offers experiences, facilitates social interaction, and expands language as few families do, or even can.

The children were settling in for a videotaped movie and a little boy offered Peter the empty chair beside his own. . . . Peter's thumb went into his mouth. . . . Miss Murray put a stuffed teddy bear in Peter's lap and whispered, "You need to hold onto Mr. Bear and don't let him get away until the story is over. Help him listen too, by holding him in your lap with both hands." Peter held Mr. Bear in a death grip with both arms. The little boy who had offered Peter the chair asked if he could have an animal and Miss Murray pulled one out of the basket on the shelf. The movie was Jack and the Beanstalk, a favorite of many of the children. The two boys held their stuffed animals and echoed the giant's "Fee, fie, foe, fum" in their best and deepest "giant" voices.

The last activity of the day was a watermelon party. The class went out on the grass near the classroom door to begin the festivities. The teacher placed the watermelon in the middle of the circle of children and they all admired it and talked about how it grew. The teacher encouraged the children to touch it and allowed them to try and pick up the "Monster Melon."

Peter was fascinated. "Boy, this is real, real, big!" he exclaimed, trying to lift up one end of the melon. "I bet my Dad could pick it up though. He's real strong." He ran his hands along the sides and ends of the melon and then commented, "It's like a ball . . . but not really . . . just sorta like a ball."

The teacher made the first cut, lengthwise, and then she and Miss Murray (another teacher) each took a group of children to cut the two halves into smaller pieces. One at a time, the children were allowed to help cut their own slice of watermelon. The children were soon busy biting, chewing, spitting seeds, and enjoying the sloppy affair. But Peter stood immobile. He was holding his watermelon in front of him with the pink juice running down his arms. He looked forlorn and helpless, seeming not to know what to do with the slice of watermelon. It then dawned on Miss Murray that Peter may have never experienced watermelon before or perhaps he couldn't relate this cold slab of wetness to the neat chunks he may have been given at home.

She took Peter's index finger and poked it into the pink part of the melon and then into the firmer rind. She explained that the soft part was for eating, but there were small, hard bits called "seeds" all mixed up in it. She helped Peter find a seed and feel how hard and slippery it was. She then encouraged him to take a bite and asked him if his teeth or tongue had found any seeds yet. Perplexed, he nodded his head "yes," but he didn't know how to spit them out. They just slid down his chin. Miss Murray coaxed Peter to blow the seeds out, but he was only minimally successful. Even so, he managed to get a few seeds into the air instead of on his chin. From the look on Peter's face, it was safe to say that he did not especially enjoy this new experience. This was confirmed when Peter announced sheepishly, "I like my mom's watermelon better—hers doesn't have seeds."

The buckets of water available for cleanup were the source of as much fun as the watermelon itself. The splashing of water and giggling that accompanied it were much more to Peter's liking. In the midst of the fun, a taller version of Peter strode into view and said, "Hey there, Buddy . . . whatcha doin'?"

Peter turned and hugged his dad's knees. "Guess what, Dad? We had watermelon today, and guess what? Their watermelon has a lot of seeds. And guess what? I know how to spit now! I can show you how to spit. Wanna see me spit? I can show Mommy how to spit too. What d'ya think of that, huh?"

Peter's father smiled, patted his son on the back, and said, "Okay, Buddy, we'll go home and show Mommy how to spit. Find my pocket and let's go." Peter put his fingers in his dad's back pocket and followed him toward the gate. [Bishop, 1993]

The most obvious benefit of school as compared to home is friendship, as the two boys in the excerpt illustrate. Same-sex and same-age playmates are preferred by children, but this is difficult to arrange in most at-home settings. Likewise, the facilitated sharing (here, of the chair, the stuffed animal, and the giant voices) are common in preschool but virtually impossible at home. Varied experiences are also more likely to happen at preschool. Peter was probably not the only child who, for the first time that day, wielded a knife to slice a large fruit, spat out watermelon seeds, or tried to lift a "monster melon." Such new experiences teach words as well as motor skills—here, "spit," "slippery," "oval," and "monster" became better understood.

Social skills also develop as children share—here, the carrying and cutting, eating and spitting, washing and drying. In this instance, the preschool children learned an additional lesson: that disabilities need not prevent a person from taking part in normal activities. Did you guess? Peter is blind.

Happy Kindergartners These photos show happy kindergartners in teacher-directed exercise in two settings, southern California and Tokyo.

❷ *Observational Quiz (see answer page 268): If you were a stranger to both cultures, with no data other than what you see in the photos, what would you conclude about the values, habits, and attitudes adults hope to foster in these two groups of children?*

❶ **Response for Teachers (from page 264):** Obviously, the ranking of the four characteristics in a particular case depends on the specifics of the audience—the ages and background of the children, for example. However, experts generally find that a good, detailed, well-executed curriculum is the most important element and that the adult–child ratio is least important—provided that training, skill, curriculum, and space organization are reasonable.

Over the decades, various longitudinal studies of former Head Start students have found that they score higher on achievement tests and have more positive school report cards by age 10 than non–Head Start children from the same backgrounds and neighborhoods. By junior high school, they are significantly less likely to be placed in special classes for slow or disruptive children or to repeat a year of school. In adolescence, Head Start graduates have higher aspirations and a greater sense of achievement than their non–Head Start peers. And as they enter adulthood, Head Start graduates are more likely to be in college, are less likely to be in jail, and have fewer children (Haskins, 1989; Zigler, 1998).

Longitudinal research on similar programs, some also begun in the 1960s, yields similar findings. Ideally, preschool programs should begin earlier (at age 3 or even younger) and should provide more hours per day and more days per year (Ramey & Ramey, 1998). They should also continue to provide support during elementary school (Reynolds & Temple, 1998).

A new concern arises regarding children who not only are poor but also are immigrants to the United States. The fear, particularly among Spanish-speaking immigrants, is that preschool will interfere with their children's learning of their native language and culture. Fortunately, with high-quality subsidized preschools, this is not the case. Indeed, one cluster of bilingual preschools not only taught children to become proficient in English but also advanced their knowledge of Spanish; these preschoolers' knowledge of Spanish surpassed that of children who had stayed at home within the community (Winsler et al., 1999).

Do the same conclusions hold for children who are not poor? Yes, to a degree. Longitudinal research on more advantaged children in the United States and elsewhere finds that all children benefit from a quality preschool setting (Warash & Markstrom-Adams, 1995). There is one caution, however: Poor preschools (crowded, unsafe, focused on discipline rather than cognition) can be worse than an average home.

Considering all the research we've discussed about cognitive development between the ages of 2 and 6, you probably are not surprised at the benefits of a well-run preschool. Piaget described young children as

❶ *Answer to Observational Quiz (from page 267):* *The most obvious difference is the greater emphasis on individualism in California—no uniforms, diverse ethnicity, smaller group size. Evaluation of this contrast depends on the values of the beholder. In addition, three other differences might have caught your attention (you are an excellent observer if you saw all three): The Japanese head teacher is male (virtually never the case in a U.S. early-childhood classroom); the Japanese children are segregated by gender (indicated by hats as well as position), whereas the U.S. children are not; and the wall decorations are creative in the U.S. classroom and serious in the Tokyo classroom.*

being capable of symbolic thought. Vygotsky stressed that actual learning requires guided participation and opportunities to manipulate objects, use language, and interact with other children. When all goes well, children can learn everything from mathematics to grammar to social insight.

In the ongoing debate described near the beginning of this chapter, developmentalists are now tilting toward Vygotsky. The influence of culture and scaffolding on various cognitive abilities and the discovery of the benefits of quality preschool education are evidence for sociocultural theory. Few developmentalists are content to follow Piaget, merely letting time lead to cognitive development.

Past history, however, teaches that new research will find additional abilities in the minds of 2- to 6-year-olds and additional strategies to develop that potential. Although our view of young children has changed, it probably will change again. What will the new discoveries be? Some readers of this book will be among the scientists who find out.

SUMMARY

HOW YOUNG CHILDREN THINK

1. Preschoolers are active and eager thinkers, at times showing the effects of egocentrism, in which their cognitive development is limited by their own narrow perspective, and at times grasping the basic concepts of their world.

2. Piaget described preschoolers as able to think symbolically, a major advance over sensorimotor thought. However, this preoperational thought is, essentially, also prelogical. This is because preschoolers are distracted by appearances and irreversible in their thought processes. They center on one aspect of a situation to the exclusion of others, and they reason in a static rather than a dynamic fashion.

3. Vygotsky viewed cognitive development as an apprenticeship in which children acquire cognitive skills through guided participation in social experiences that stimulate intellectual growth. He and other sociocultural theorists contend that how well children master potential skills depends in great part on how willing and able other people and the culture are to scaffold participation in learning.

4. According to Vygotsky, there exists, for each child, a range of potential development, called the zone of proximal development, that foreshadows new cognitive accomplishments. Social guidance needs to move children forward through the zone, from what they can already do to what they are ready to learn to do next.

5. Also according to Vygotsky, language fosters cognitive growth as an intermediary between learner and tutor, facilitating the social interaction that teaches new skills. In addition, children use private speech to guide and direct their own actions.

6. Although preschoolers do not possess the well-established, systematic, logical reasoning skills of older children, they are

not as illogical as Piaget believed them to be. In particular, young children can understand the concept of conservation in certain situations. However, parents and the culture may not always be as helpful in teaching young children as sociocultural theory contends.

WHAT PRESCHOOLERS CAN DO

7. Young children are not skilled at deliberately storing or retrieving memories, but they can devise and use scripts, or outlines of familiar, recurring events. Children sometimes display surprising long-term-memory ability when adults use directive questions to help them focus their attention on specific aspects of meaningful past events.

8. Children develop elementary theories about mental processes—theirs and other people's. A preschooler's theory of mind reflects developing concepts about human mental phenomena and their relation to the real world, as well as the difference between the two. A strengthened theory of mind at about age 4 allows preschoolers to see that subjective understanding may not always accurately reflect reality.

LANGUAGE LEARNING

9. Language accomplishments during the play years include learning 10,000 words or more. Preschool children increase their vocabulary almost explosively. They seem to do so by quickly inferring an approximate meaning for each new word and mentally categorizing it with similar familiar words.

10. Preschoolers also show marked growth in their understanding of basic grammatical forms. Children of this age, however, often overregularize, or apply grammatical rules where they do not fit. Again, in the acquisition of language, parental guidance and support are invaluable.

PRESCHOOL EDUCATION

11. Over the past 30 years, insights from developmental psychology and changes in family composition and work patterns have resulted in great increases in early-childhood education throughout the world. Programs, whether called day care, preschool, or kindergarten, that emphasize cognitive development tend to benefit children. To a great extent, each nation's preschools reflect its cultural values.

12. Project Head Start was initiated to bring the skills of disadvantaged preschoolers up to the level of those of other students by the time they enter elementary school. Longitudinal studies have shown that Head Start provides long-lasting educational and social benefits.

13. The learning potential of all children during early childhood is remarkable. Organized education before age 6 helps develop the young mind, although the specifics depend on the values of the culture.

KEY TERMS

symbolic thinking (246)
preoperational thought
  (246)
centration (246)
egocentrism (247)
conservation (247)
guided participation (249)
zone of proximal
  development (ZPD) (252)

scaffold (252)
private speech (252)
social mediation (252)
scripts (256)
theory of mind (257)
fast mapping (260)
overregularization (263)

KEY QUESTIONS

1. In what ways does preoperational thought limit a child's ability to think logically?

2. What sets Vygotsky's ideas apart from those of Piaget?

3. Give a hypothetical illustration (not the one in the chapter) of how a parent can foster cognitive accomplishments in the zone of proximal development.

4. How do young children's scripts aid recall of specific past experiences, and how do they distort recollections?

5. How can caregivers aid in the development of memory during the preschool years?

6. What advice might you give to a police officer who is planning to interview a preschool child who witnessed a crime?

7. How do 2-year-olds differ from 6-year-olds in theory of mind?

8. What four factors influence whether a young child will understand a false belief?

9. How does the rapid acquisition of new words occur during the preschool years?

10. What limitations are to be expected in a young child's accurate use of words and grammar?

11. What social change and what research discovery combined to increase the numbers of children in preschool programs?

12. What findings indicate that preschool education programs such as Project Head Start succeed?

13. *In Your Experience* What misunderstanding did you have as a preschool child because of your limited theory of mind or because of your magical or egocentric perspective?

The Play Years:
Psychosocial Development

Picture a typical 2-year-old and a typical 6-year-old, and consider how emotionally and socially different they are. Chances are the 2-year-old still has many moments of clinging, of tantrums, and of stubbornness, vacillating between dependence and self-determination. Further, the 2-year-old cannot be left alone, even for a few moments, in any place where curiosity might lead to danger or destruction.

The 6-year-old, by contrast, has both the confidence and the competence to be relatively independent. A typical child at that age can be trusted to do many things alone and is proud to do them—perhaps fixing breakfast before school and even helping to feed and dress a younger sibling. This child shows affection toward family members without the obvious clinging, exasperating demands, or exaggerated self-assertion of the 2-year-old. The 6-year-old might say good-bye to Mom or Dad at the door of the first-grade classroom and then take care of business: following classroom routines, befriending certain classmates and ignoring others, respecting and learning from teachers. This chapter details how that 2-to-6 transformation occurs.

THE SELF AND THE SOCIAL WORLD

Self-concept, self-esteem, and self-understanding, as well as social attitudes, social skills, and social roles, are familiar topics for psychologists who study adults. Increasingly, the same topics intrigue researchers studying children, especially those looking at the early years (Eisenberg & Fabes, 1992; Sroufe, 1996; Tangney & Fischer, 1995; Harter, 1998). They find that, between ages 1 and 6, children progress from a dawning awareness that they are independent individuals to a firm understanding of who they are, what they like to do, and how their selfhood relates to their social environment.

Initiative versus Guilt

One crucial aspect of selfhood during the preschool years was described by Erik Erikson almost 50 years ago. Positive enthusiasm, effort, and self-evaluation characterize ages 3 to 6, according to Erikson's psychosocial theory (first discussed in Chapter 2). During the

initiative versus guilt   The third of Erikson's eight "crises" of psychosocial development, in which the preschool child eagerly begins new projects and activities—and feels guilt when his or her efforts result in failure or criticism.

developmental stage that Erikson calls **initiative versus guilt,** young children's self-esteem is largely defined by the skills and competencies that demonstrate their independence and initiative. Most preschoolers leap at almost any opportunity to show that "I can do it!" Spontaneous play becomes goal-directed; children not only want to do something (as in Piaget's sensorimotor intelligence or Erikson's autonomy stage), they want to begin and complete their own activities for a purpose (Lysynki, 1998).

According to Erikson, as the larger society motivates them to take on new activities, children develop their sense of themselves and others, feeling guilty when their efforts result in failure or criticism. Social awareness becomes evident.

Cooperation Six hands and one bowl of ingredients to mix—it could be a recipe for disaster. Here it seems just fine, because these Head Start children have learned to coordinate their efforts, in an advanced form of social play.

Self-Concept and Social Awareness

Just prior to the preschool years, parents typically find themselves dealing with a demanding, stubborn toddler whose primary negotiating skills seem to be whining and throwing tantrums. A parent's attempt to discuss matters with a 2-year-old might be met with a defiant command of "No talk!" But as children's theory of mind expands, giving them a better grasp of how other people think and feel, their ability to compromise—over what they will wear, what they will eat, when they will go to bed, and such—gradually evolves. From obstinate demands and defiance they shift to bargaining, explaining, and rationalizing (Crockenberg & Litman, 1990; Kuczynski & Kochanska, 1990).

One of the most important aspects of preschoolers' self-definition is that they feel older, stronger, and more skilled than younger children. The significance of this feeling, as well as their skill in negotiation, is shown in this episode of play involving three 4-year-old girls:

Beth: How about this. Pretend he married two of us and you were the sister. OK? You were the sister of us—OK? Of both of us, cause you were the littler one.
Celia: No, I don't want to be a little one.
Beth: No, you're both, you're big. Um, let's pretend.
Annie: But we were a little bigger.
Beth: You're 20.
Celia: Yeah.
Beth: And both of us are 21.
Celia: OK, so that means . . .
Annie: So, we're one month older than you.
[Furth, 1996]

The young ladies' chronological understanding clearly is immature, but their social skills are not. All three want to maintain their self-esteem as big girls without giving up their social interaction, and they have combined assertion and compromise to achieve that end.

For children of all ages, psychologists emphasize the importance of developing a positive self-concept. (In fact, too much self-criticism is one sign of psychosocial problems in a preschooler.) Normally, preschoolers have no such problem; typical 2- to 6-year-olds form quite

ONE BIG HAPPY By RICK DETORIE

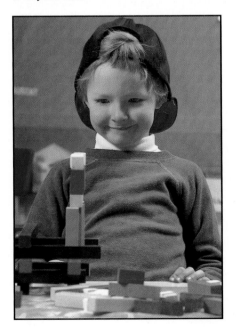

©1997 by Creators Syndicate, Inc.

Know-It-Alls Have Something to Learn Like many preschoolers, Ruthie thinks her art is worth money and she would love to be the rescuer of another child, an animal, or even a bird. In the real world, however, that self-concept will need some modification.

And It Was Good During the play years, pride in the final accomplishment generally overshadows any reasons for self-doubt or self-criticism—such as whether the skyscraper this child just built is recognizable to anyone else.

optimistic impressions of themselves. They regularly overestimate their own abilities, believing that they can win any race, skip perfectly, count accurately, and make up beautiful songs. They enjoy undertaking various tasks, and they expect all others—grandparents, playmates, stuffed animals—to be a patient audience for their showing off and to applaud when it is over. The next day, they might gather the identical audience for a repeat performance. Self-confidence is tied to competence, and competence demands repeated demonstration of mastery.

Such typically high self-esteem was demonstrated in a laboratory test in which 4- to 6-year-olds were given 2 minutes to solve an impossible puzzle. When they failed, they were asked to guess how many of two additional puzzles they could solve if they tried. Almost all the children, despite having just failed, answered "both." When the same children were asked to indicate how smart they were by awarding themselves one, two, three, four, or five stars (representing the range from "not smart at all" to "very smart"), more than 90 percent confidently chose five stars (Stipek et al., 1995).

In this study, confidence was affected by the style of school the child attended (those in nurturing, child-centered preschools were more likely to be proud of themselves and rate themselves highly than were those in more critical, work-centered preschools), but all the children were quite self-assured. Interestingly, the 6-year-olds were decidedly *more* competent (on other, skill-based tests) but slightly *less* confident of their abilities than the younger children.

As this example suggests, the fact that preschoolers evaluate themselves highly does not mean they are impervious to the judgments of others. Over early childhood, children become increasingly aware of, and concerned with, what others think. They begin to appraise their own behavior, using standards they have heard (Butler, 1998). (The special situation of the only child is discussed in the Changing Policy box.)

THE ONLY CHILD

Worldwide, the number of both lifelong and temporary only children is clearly rising. For example, in the United States, among all the families that included at least one child under age 18, the percentage with only one such child rose from 33 percent in 1970 to 41 percent in 1999. Spending at least several years with no brothers or sisters at home is now a common experience for young American children: In 1999, two-thirds of all children under age 6 were the only such child in their families (U.S. Bureau of the Census, 1999).

Some of these children are only temporary "onlies"; a younger child will soon be born. This experience may be difficult. It is called *dethronement*, implying that the older child is no longer treated royally.

Family composition in many nations of the world is shifting from many children to only one or two. Italian women once had large families, for instance; now the average Italian woman has only 1.2 children, which means that many families have only one. Similar low rates are found in several other European nations—Spain, Germany, and Portugal among them. The most dramatic shift has occurred in China, where the government enacted and enforces a strict "one-child policy" to combat overpopulation. In 1991, 95 percent of the student body of most primary schools in Beijing consisted of only children (Bakken, 1993). Even without government policies, the economics of modern life have markedly reduced family size. The largest average family sizes occur in Africa; but even there, fertility rates have declined from 6.3 children per woman of child-bearing age in 1985 to 5.4 children in 1998 (United Nations, 1999).

Is it actually difficult to be an only child? It used to be, and many people still believe that children are handicapped if they have no brothers or sisters, because their parents are too permissive. In China, among the older generations, there is widespread prejudice against only children, especially boys. They are stereotyped as lonely, spoiled, and overly dependent on their parents, as disrespectful "little emperors" and potential delinquents.

The truth, however, is usually otherwise: Only children typically gain more from increased parental attention than they lose from lack of siblings. Single-child status is particularly beneficial intellectually; only children are generally more verbal, more creative, and more likely to attend college than children who have one or more siblings. The contrast is most marked when one-child families are compared to families with four or more children. All the experiences known to develop the child's mind, such as "conversations" at age 1, reading books together at age 2, quality day care at ages 3 to 5, and homework help throughout the school years, are much harder for parents of several children to provide than for parents with only one child. Further, parenting styles at both extremes—very permissive or very authoritative—are particularly rare in a family that chooses to have only one child. No

And Baby Makes Three Chinese couples, like this one in Shanghai, typically marry late, live in cramped quarters, and have only one child, who benefits from paternal and maternal devotion.

wonder only children are smarter and more successful—a result found in China, in Europe, and in North America (Bakken, 1993; Blake, 1989; Yang et al., 1995).

The main disadvantage for only children might be in social skills, particularly in the development of cooperative play, theory of mind, negotiation strategies, and self-assertion, all of which are usually enhanced through sibling interaction (Falbo & Poston, 1993). However, preschool education and public day care tend to make up for some of the lack of sibling interaction. Most only children today develop social skills that are comparable to those of their peers and have a better sense of self-esteem than do those with many siblings, especially those who happened to be a middle- or last-born child.

Indeed, as policies (not only in China) and practices have been changing, only children have themselves been changing for the better. Fifty years ago, families who had just one child were those with fertility or relationship problems, and sometimes their children suffered because of the parents' stress. Now many adults choose to have only one child, not only for personal reasons but for financial ones as well. This is true for two-parent families, since most married mothers are in the labor force, but it is even more true for single parents. An additional child is too great a financial strain on most single parents. Consequently, the historical shift toward one-child families is even more marked in single-parent households. In 1970, only one-third of such parents had a single child; in 1998, half did (35 percent compared to 51 percent) (U.S. Bureau of the Census, 1971, 1999). Now "only" children benefit from their status, in terms of their self-confidence, language development, emotional attachment, and social understanding.

Children in the laboratory study described earlier admitted they were somewhat anxious about their performance at school—especially those children in the more demanding preschools, where they actually learned more but were frequently made aware of how they were doing (Stipek et al., 1995).

Children as young as 2 or 3 years of age begin to respond with disappointment or guilt when they fail at a task (perhaps knotting instead of tying their shoelaces) or when they cause some mishap (such as spilling a cup of juice), even when no adult is present. Many older preschoolers take this one step further, trying to make reparations and spontaneously confessing that they caused a problem. Sometimes they feel much more guilty at their inadequacies than is warranted (Cole et al., 1992; Lewis et al., 1992). When my daughter Sarah was 4, she asked me:

> "Can God see everything I do?"
> "Yes," I reassured her. But worry rather than relief crossed her face.
> "Oh no," she said. "Then God knows that I pick my nose."

Emotional Regulation

The most important emotional development during early childhood, however, is not the emergence of new emotions, such as pride and guilt, but the growing "ability to inhibit, enhance, maintain, and modulate emotional arousal to accomplish one's goals" (Eisenberg et al., 1997). Thus pride is tempered by guilt (and vice versa); joy by sadness; anger by fear; fear by rituals. All are regulated and controlled by the 3- or 4-year-old in ways unknown to the exuberant, expressive, and often-overwhelmed toddler.

This ability, called **emotional regulation,** is developed in response to society's expectations that preschoolers "manage frustration" and "modulate emotional expression" (Sroufe, 1996). And most preschoolers become quite successful at this difficult task. As one expert explains, preschoolers must:

> delay, defer, and accept substitutions without becoming aggressive or disorganized . . . cope well with high arousal, whether due to environmental challenge or fatigue. At the same time they are to be spontaneous and exuberant when circumstances permit. . . . Occasional breakdowns in emotional control, especially when taxed, fatigued, or ill, are an expected part of healthy emotional development. Still, progress is remarkable during this period. [Sroufe, 1996]

How does emotional regulation develop? Part of it is neurological (Schore, 1994). The ability to regulate one's emotions, to think before acting, is related to a specific part of the brain in the frontal cortex. This area is immature in toddlers but develops during the preschool years. If a child was damaged prenatally or stunted in infancy (by stress or poor nutrition), the child may be intellectually intact in most ways but unable to regulate his or her emotions (Casey, 1996; Diamond et al., 1997). Unfortunately, evidence from lower animals finds that extremely stressful experiences in infancy permanently alter brain structures; it is feared that the same applies to humans (Zahn-Waxler et al., 1996).

Learning and Emotional Regulation

Learning is also crucial to emotional regulation. During infancy, caregivers guide children in the "appropriate" expression of emotion. For example, parents teach their infant to keep fear at bay because the

emotional regulation The ability to direct or modify one's feelings, particularly feelings of fear, frustration, and anger. Because of brain maturation, emotional regulation becomes more possible during the preschool years.

❷ **Especially for Social Workers:** Suppose a 3-year-old is unable to control his or her emotions, crying and attacking, for example, when that is not the appropriate response. Should you blame the way the parents treat the child, take some sort of action, or expect that the child will grow out of it in a few years?

parents repeatedly respond to the infant's anxiety with reassurance. Then, in the "terrible twos," parents teach their children to moderate anger and other negative emotions (Kochanska et al., 1997).

The best teacher is example, so ideally the parents never lose their own tempers when the child erupts in protest and never express fear when a dog approaches, thunder roars, or a mouse scampers across the floor. The circuits of the child's developing brain respond to such experiences. Gradually, innate emotional triggers are connected to intellectual responses, allowing the 4-year-old girl to stand her ground when a circus clown approaches or the 4-year-old boy to restrain himself when another child bumps into him.

Learning can also work in the opposite direction. Many preschoolers develop fears. Some become so afraid of certain things that the fear could be called a **phobia**: an irrational and exaggerated fear that terrifies the person. Phobias are particularly likely if a child's parents are also somewhat phobic, because children by age 3 or 4 become quite astute at sensing their parents' feelings. Even when a worried parent says, "Let's pet the nice doggie," children will notice the hesitant hand, the fast breathing, or the sudden startle if the dog moves.

Nightmares also increase during the preschool years, because enhanced imagination is not yet held in check by emerging rationalization, especially when the child is half asleep. Parents can help their children by telling stories in which the child masters the feared experience. For example, if the dream is about being chased by tigers, the story can involve a hole the tigers fall into, a stick with which to frighten them away, Superman to stop them, wings to escape them, or a gift that turns them into surprised and grateful friends (Brett, 1988).

phobia An irrational fear that is strong enough to make a person try to avoid the feared object or experience.

Attachment and Emotional Regulation

The results of past caregiving are revealed when children react to another child's cry of pain. Children who have been well nurtured and have formed secure attachments regulate their own emotions and express empathy, comforting the hurting child, reassuring the frightened child, or getting help if need be. (Attachment is described in Chapter 7.)

Longitudinal research finds that those with insecure attachments respond abnormally to other children's distress. Some might do whatever

Just What He Should Do? This 3-year-old might like either to slap his baby brother or to lift him and hold him, but his emotional regulation yields an appropriate gesture and expression. He avoids both emotional extremes, being neither too worried and solicitous nor too angry and upset at the crying.

would precisely further distress the child (e.g., scaring a child with the very mask that had been frightening, taunting a crying child and calling him or her a "cry baby," or punching a child with a stomach ache in the stomach). . . . [Others] would often become upset themselves when another was distressed (e.g., holding their own lip and seeking a teacher's lap when another child had fallen). [Sroufe, 1996]

Another example of emotional regulation is appropriate expression of friendliness. Toddlers sometimes take shyness or sociability to an extreme, perhaps literally hiding behind a mother's skirt when a strange man offers ice cream, or exhibiting the opposite reaction, taking not only the ice cream but also the stranger's hand, asking to go home with him. Most preschoolers learn to moderate these extremes. However, children who failed to develop secure attachment in the first year of life are sometimes excessively friendly at age 4 or 5, seeking out strangers and sitting on their laps, for instance.

In one study, researchers examined a group of adopted Canadian children who had spent their first year or so in a Romanian orphanage and the next 3 years with their adoptive families. Most of the children still showed insecure attachments (Chisholm, 1998). Compared to Romanian orphans who had been adopted in the first 4 months of life and to a control group of Canadian-born, nonadopted, children who had never been institutionalized, more of those with a year of orphanage experience were characterized by strongly insecure attachment together with very poor emotional regulation.

According to their adoptive parents, 71 percent were "overly friendly," a characterization rare in the early-adopted Romanians or in the nonadopted children. Many of these children did form some kind of attachment, but "when the attachment process does go wrong in previously institutionalized children it may go very wrong. . . . On a practical level this may mean that parents need to be more than merely adequate parents to deal with children from orphanages" (Chisholm, 1998). Emotional regulation requires a balance between friendliness and fear that was hard for these children to attain.

According to Daniel Goleman (1998), the ability to modulate and direct emotions is crucial to *emotional intelligence*. This is learned during early childhood when the reflective, intellectual areas of the cortex gradually come to govern the rush of fear, anger, and other passions from the amygdala, an area deep within the brain. Infants need to become attached to their caregivers. When the caregivers use that relationship to teach how and when to express feelings, the children will become balanced and empathetic human beings, neither overwhelmed by nor unresponsive to their own emotions.

ANTISOCIAL AND PROSOCIAL BEHAVIOR

Some of the emotions that mature during the preschool years lead to **prosocial behavior,** actions that are voluntarily performed to help another person without obvious benefit to oneself (Eisenberg & Fabes, 1998). Expressing sympathy, offering to share, and including a shy child in a game or conversation are all examples of prosocial behavior. Such behavior is indicative of social competence and appears during the later play years, continues to develop during the school years, and is correlated with emotional regulation (Eisenberg et al., 1997).

Prosocial attitudes also correlate with the making of new friends. Throughout the period from age 2 to 5, violent temper tantrums, uncontrollable crying, and terrifying phobias diminish. The capacity for self-control—such as not opening a wrapped present immediately if asked to wait—becomes more evident (Kochanska et al., 2000). "Social skills and relationships are developing as networks widen to include peers as well as family members" (Zahn-Waxler et al., 1996).

Of more concern is **antisocial behavior**—deliberately hurtful or destructive actions. Antisocial behavior during childhood and adolescence is often predicted by a lack of emotional regulation during the preschool years (Eisenberg et al., 1997).

❗ Response for Social Workers (from page 275): A lack of emotional regulation is a potentially serious sign in a 3-year-old, since the child may become unhappy and uncontrollable later on, and there is a risk he or she will end up as a criminal. Often the problem began earlier, either in brain damage or in poor attachment relationships. At this point, blaming the parents is no help. However, emotional control is not beyond the child, who can still learn to regulate his or her emotions if the parents now provide the proper guidance and if a structured setting with other children—such as a good preschool with a skilled teacher—is available.

prosocial behavior   An action, such as sharing, cooperating, or sympathizing, that is performed to benefit other people without the expectation of reward for oneself.

antisocial behavior   An action, such as hitting, insulting, lying about, or taking from another person, that is intended to harm someone else.

Aggression

Prosocial and antisocial behavior take many forms. However, aggression is a form of antisocial behavior that is of particular concern; it begins with a negative self-concept and inadequate emotional regulation during the early preschool years, and it can become a serious social problem as time goes by (Coie & Dodge, 1998). As one group of researchers reports:

> Children with [emotional] control problems observed by home visitors at ages 3 and 4 years were seen by teachers as more hostile and hyperactive in the classroom at age 5 years. . . . Early onset aggression, in particular, is likely to become entrenched and linked to multiple problems late in development. [Zahn-Waxler et al., 1996]

In other words, a child who is angry and hurtful at age 3 is a child headed for trouble at ages 5, 10, or even (as discussed later in this book) at 15 or 25. Here we will look at the forms, causes, and consequences of aggression that are specific to children aged 2 to 6. The consequences are not always dire: Every normal preschool child sometimes hurts another child or an adult by unexpectedly and deliberately hitting, kicking, biting, pinching, hair pulling, name calling, arm twisting, or the like.

Normally, children are more aggressive at age 4 than age 2, because as children become more aware of themselves and their needs, they become more likely to defend their interests. In fact, the 4-year-old who internalizes every insult and never lashes out is at risk for serious anxiety and depression later on (Eisenberg et al., 1997). But even though the 4-year-olds are more aggressive, they are usually more controlled than the 2-year-olds; they do not lash out indiscriminately, but choose their issues and targets.

In looking at aggression, developmentalists distinguish between aggression that is quite normal and innocuous and aggression that is more unusual and ominous. Researchers recognize four forms of aggression:

Me First! An increase in aggression by about age 4 is typically accompanied by an increase in self-control. This struggle will not escalate to instrumental aggression if both children have learned some emotional regulation and if neither has been misguided by racism or by a false image of maleness.

- **Instrumental aggression** is used to obtain or retain a toy or other object.
- **Reactive aggression** involves angry retaliation for an intentional or accidental act.
- **Relational aggression** is designed to inflict psychic, not physical, pain.
- **Bullying aggression** consists of an unprovoked attack.

Instrumental aggression is common in the play years and is the form of aggression that is most likely to increase from age 2 to 6. Although it should be discouraged as a strategy, instrumental aggression involves objects more than people, is quite normal, and therefore is not of serious concern. However, *reactive aggression* is a special concern, because it can indicate a lack of emotional regulation.

Relational aggression can be even more hurtful than physical aggression. Preschoolers who are less prosocial and are less likely to have friends are more likely to be victims of relational aggression (Crick et al., 1999). *Bullying aggression* is most worrisome overall. (Bullies and victims are discussed in more detail in Chapter 13.)

instrumental aggression   Aggressive behavior whose purpose is to obtain or retain an object desired by another.

reactive aggression   Aggressive behavior that is an angry retaliation for some intentional or accidental act by another.

relational aggression   Aggressive behavior that takes the form of insults or social rejection.

bullying aggression   Aggressive behavior in the form of an unprovoked physical or verbal attack on another person.

How is it that children develop these attributes? To some extent, developmental processes are at work. It is typical for children to become more prosocial and less aggressive between ages 3 and 6. However, with some children, antisocial behavior does not decrease (Campbell, 1995). These children are of great concern, because their aggression may lead to worse problems later on. The reasons range from genetic and prenatal influences to those of school and society. Here we look at two influences that are particularly powerful during the preschool years: playing with peers and responding to parents.

Learning Social Skills Through Play

During childhood, play is the most productive and adaptive activity children can undertake. Indeed, the fact that play is variable, related to the culture and the gender as well as the age of the playmates, makes it an ideal forum for learning specific social skills (Sutton-Smith, 1997).

Compare the peer interactions of a 2-year-old and a 5-year-old. The younger child's social play consists mainly of simple games (such as bouncing and trying to catch a ball and becoming angry or upset if the other child does not cooperate). By contrast, the more sophisticated 5-year-old has learned how to gain entry to a play group, to manage conflict through the use of humor, and to select and keep friends and playmates.

Many of these new social skills are learned from play with peers, because only with agemates do children themselves assume responsibility for initiating and maintaining harmonious social interaction. Whether learning how to share crayons or sand toys, or how to include everybody in the construction of a spaceship, or how to respond to a friend's accusation that "it's not fair," children must deal with playmates who are not always understanding and self-sacrificing (as a mother might be). How does this learning of social play occur? With physical activity and with shared imagination.

Rough-and-Tumble Play

rough-and-tumble play Play such as wrestling, chasing, and hitting that mimics aggression but actually occurs purely in fun, with no intent to harm.

One beneficial form of social play is called **rough-and-tumble play.** The aptness of its name is made clear by the following example:

> Jimmy, a preschooler, stands observing three of his male classmates building a sand castle. After a few moments he climbs on a tricycle and, smiling, makes a beeline for the same area, ravaging the structure in a single sweep. The builders immediately take off in hot pursuit of the hit-and-run phantom, yelling menacing threats of "come back here, you." Soon the tricycle halts and they pounce on him. The four of them tumble in the grass amid shouts of glee, wrestling and punching until a teacher intervenes. The four wander off together toward the swings. [cited in Maccoby, 1980]

One distinguishing characteristic of rough-and-tumble play is its mimicry of aggression, but rough-and-tumble play is clearly prosocial, not antisocial. Unlike aggression, rough-and-tumble play is both fun and constructive; it teaches children how to enter a relationship, assert themselves, and respond to the actions of someone else while exercising gross motor skills, all without hurting the other person (Pellegrini & Smith,1998). Adults who are unsure whether they are observing a fight that should be broken up or a social activity that should continue

A Sign of Social Maturity For many young children, especially boys who know each other well, rough-and-tumble play brings the most pleasure. Many developmentalists believe that this kind of play teaches social skills—such as how to compete without destroying a friendship—that are hard to learn any other way.

sociodramatic play Pretend play in which children act out various roles and themes in stories of their own creation.

should look for a "play face." Children almost always smile, and often laugh, in rough-and-tumble play, whereas they frown and scowl in real fighting.

Rough-and-tumble play is universal. It has been observed in Japan, Kenya, and Mexico as well as in every income and ethnic group in North America, Europe, and Australia (Boulton & Smith, 1989). There are some cultural and situational differences, however. One of the most important is space and supervision: Children are much more likely to instigate rough-and-tumble play when they have room to run and chase and when adults are not directly nearby. This is one reason the ideal physical environment for children includes ample safe space for gross motor activities, with adults within earshot but not underfoot (Bradley, 1995).

In addition, rough-and-tumble play usually occurs among children who have had considerable social experience, often with each other. Not surprisingly, then, older preschoolers are more likely to engage in rough-and-tumble play than younger ones. In fact, the incidence of rough-and-tumble play increases with age, peaking at about age 8 to 10, and then decreasing (Pellegrini & Smith, 1998). Finally, boys are much more likely to engage in rough-and-tumble play than girls are. Indeed, preschool girls typically withdraw from boys' rough-and-tumble play (Fabes, 1994).

Sociodramatic Play

In the type of social play called **sociodramatic play,** children act out various roles and themes in stories they themselves have created. Typically, children create family dramas, scenarios involving sickness or death, or stories that include monsters and superheroes. From simple plots at age 2 (a mother–baby script that consists mainly of eating, sleeping, and waking) to elaborate ones by age 5 (such as a trip through the jungle confronting various challenging animals, people, and geological barriers), sociodramatic play provides a way for children to:

- Explore and rehearse the social roles they see being enacted around them
- Test their own ability to explain and convince others of their ideas
- Regulate their emotions through imagination
- Examine personal concerns in a nonthreatening manner

The beginnings of dramatic play can be seen in solitary or parallel play, when a toddler "feeds" or "cuddles" or "punishes" a doll or stuffed animal. However, dramatic play greatly increases in frequency and complexity between the ages of 2 and 6. As young children develop their theory of mind and their emotional regulation, they practice what they learn (Goncu, 1993; Harris & Kavanaugh, 1993; Lillard, 1993a, 1993b, 1994). They can, for instance, use sociodramatic play to try out various means of managing their emotions, as in a scary situation in the dark (in a tent made of blankets, quickly opened if the "dark" becomes too much), or providing nurturance to an injured playmate (who falls down

VIDEO AND REALITY

Children between the ages of 2 and 5 in the United States watch more television than any other age group (Neilsen, 1997) (see Table 10.1). Other research confirms that 2- to 4-year-olds spend about 3 hours per day watching TV and 5- to 6-year-olds spend about 2 hours, only about 15 minutes of which is educational TV (Huston et al., 1999). It's easy to understand why. Parents of preschoolers soon learn how good a baby-sitter the "idiot box" is; it can keep children relatively quiet and in place for hours at a time.

In the past 10 years, television has become even more attractive to younger children, as Barney and Teletubbies captured the attention of 1-year-olds and video games became increasingly mesmerizing for older children. Many developmentalists agree that watching any video screen has the following effects (Huston & Wright, 1998):

■ Takes time from active, interactive, and imaginative play
■ Sends faulty messages about nutrition
■ Provides sexist, racist, and ageist stereotypes
■ Undermines sympathy for emotional pain, because bold, quick actions are emphasized
■ Undercuts attributes, skills, and values that lead to prosocial activity

This last criticism has been the subject of most research. The conclusion is that the effect is interactive and cumulative: Children of any age who watch a lot of television are likely to be more aggressive than children who do not, and children who are already inclined to be aggressive are likely to watch a lot of violent programming (Huston et al., 1989; Singer et al., 1999). The good guys (Mighty Morphin Power Rangers, Teenage Mutant Ninja Turtles, Batman, and other "heroes") do as much hitting, shooting, and kicking as the bad guys, yet the consequences of *their* violence are made comic or are sanitized; they are never portrayed as bloody or evil. In cartoonland, demolition—whether of people or of things—is just plain fun. Supposedly "real-life" programs portray the pure police battling the thoroughly evil criminals, a message that is believed not only by children but also by many adults who accept violence as a necessary part of life (Jo & Berkowitz, 1994; Shanahan & Morgan, 1999). If anything, video games are worse—more violent, more sexist, more racist (Dietz, 1998).

Watching television or playing video games desensitizes viewers to violence in real life, making physical aggression seem normal. Moreover, prosocial emotions and emotional regulation are hard to portray on the screen, where quick dramatic action captures the eye much better than a thoughtful, self-reflective monologue. For all these reasons, children who watch substantial amounts of video violence are more likely than others to be bullies, more likely to retaliate physically for any perceived attack, more likely to be passive victims, and more likely to be onlookers rather than mediators when other children fight (Slaby & Eron, 1994). Similarly, adults tend to believe the distortions they see on TV—not literally, of course, but they are pushed in that direction (Shanahan & Morgan, 1999).

Obviously, not everyone who watches television becomes a bully or victim as a result. Humans, even at age 3, are not so mindless as to copy everything they see. However, summing up the evidence for the relationship between viewing violence and behaving aggressively, Leonard Eron, head of the American Psychological Association's Commission on Violence and Youth, observes, "The evidence is overwhelming and longitudinal. The strength of the relationship is the same as for cigarettes causing lung cancer" (quoted in Mortimer, 1994).

Most of the research in this area has focused on children, partly because they watch the most television. But not only are adults the ones who allow such heavy viewing; they are vulnerable themselves. Adults who watch the most television tend to be the most fearful, the most biased, and the most violent (Shanahan & Morgan, 1999). This may be a correlation, not a cause; no longitudinal research has been done with adults. We know that adults who feel most stressed also watch the most television—but, again, it is not clear what causes what (Anderson et al., 1996).

table **10.1**	**Television Watching, by Age and Sex**		
	Viewing Time per Week		
Age/Sex	November 1994	November 1995	November 1996
Children:			
Age 2 to 5 years	24 h 42 min	24 h 52 min	23 h 21 min
Age 6 to 11 years	21 h 30 min	21 h 40 min	19 h 59 min
Teenagers:			
Girls	20 h 20 min	19 h 59 min	18 h 19 min
Boys	21 h 59 min	20 h 38 min	19 h 59 min

Source: Neilsen Media Research, 1997.

Sociodramatic Play Just like the boys in the previous photograph, these girls are developing their social skills—in this case, as store owner and grocery shopper.

❓ Observational Quiz (see answer page 283): *Which specifics of the girls' fantasy play are similar to the real thing, and which are not?*

dead and needs to be miraculously revived), or exhibiting courage when the bad guys attack (with machine guns, bombs, or poison gas—but the defenders always prevail). In this sense, then, sociodramatic play is a testing ground for early psychological knowledge, always protecting the self-esteem of the players.

Interestingly, girls tend to engage in sociodramatic play more often than boys do, just as boys initiate more rough-and-tumble play. Both sexes learn important prosocial lessons in the process. The best place for children to learn and practice these social skills with peers is a high-quality preschool. Indeed, high-quality day-care or preschool programs not only benefit cognitive growth (as you saw in Chapter 9), they also advance psychosocial development. Children in well-run programs acquire a wide range of social skills and become more competent socially as a result of their frequent interactions with other children of the same age.

They also make many friends. Indeed, friendships are remarkably consistent during the play years. Young children choose regular playmates, usually of the same age and sex, and then their ongoing rough-and-tumble or sociodramatic play together becomes obviously different from play with casual acquaintances in its complexity, self-disclosure, and reciprocity (Hinde et al., 1985; Park et al., 1993).

Parenting Patterns

Many components, including genes, peers, gender, and culture, affect children's behavior. However, although it is no longer seen as the most powerful determinant of all, many developmentalists are convinced that parenting patterns are very influential (Collins et al., 2000; Patterson, 1998).

It is important neither to exaggerate nor to understate the role of parents—mistakes often made in the media or by scientists of earlier periods.

> Contemporary students of socialization largely agree that early researchers often overstated conclusions from correlational findings; relied excessively on singular, deterministic views of parental influence; and failed to attend to the potentially confounding effects of heredity. Contemporary researchers have taken steps to remedy many of these shortcomings. Unfortunately, the weakness of old studies still permeate presentations of socialization research in introductory textbooks and the mass media, partly because they appeal to preferences for simple generalizations. [Collins et al., 2000]

❓ Especially for Parents: Although it might be hard on the adults, wouldn't children be happier if their parents let them do almost anything they wanted, as long as they didn't do anything really dangerous?

The seminal work on parenting patterns began in the early 1960s, when Diana Baumrind set out to study 100 preschool children, all from California and almost all European American and middle-class (Baumrind, 1967, 1971). As a careful researcher, she used many measures

❶ *Answer to Observational Quiz (from page 281):* The particular hats, necklaces, and shoes are all quite different from those their mothers would likely wear to the store, and the stock, the money holder, and the grocery bag are quite different. However, the essence of shopping is here: Money is exchanged for goods, and both participants politely play their roles.

❶ **Response for Parents (from page 281):** No! Perhaps surprisingly, children are quite unhappy if their parents don't set limits and guidelines. Further, their lack of self-control gets them into trouble with peers and teachers.

authoritarian parenting   A style of child rearing in which standards for proper behavior are high, misconduct is strictly punished, and parent–child communication is low.

permissive parenting   A style of child rearing in which the parents rarely punish, guide, or control their children but are nurturant and communicate well with their children.

authoritative parenting   A style of child rearing in which the parents set limits and provide guidance but are willing to listen to the child's ideas and make compromises.

of behavior, several of them involving naturalistic observation. First, she observed the children in their preschool activities and, on the basis of their actions, rated their self-control, independence, self-confidence, and other attributes. She then interviewed both parents of each child and observed parent–child interaction in two settings, at home and in the laboratory, in search of possible relationships between the parents' behavior at home and the child's behavior at preschool.

Baumrind found that parents differed on four important dimensions:

- Their expressions of *warmth,* or nurturance, which ranged from very affectionate to quite cold
- Their strategies for *discipline,* which might involve explanation, persuasion, and/or punishment
- The quality of their *communication,* which ranged from extensive listening to demands for silence
- Their expectations for *maturity,* evident in how much responsibility and self-control they demanded

On the basis of these four dimensions, Baumrind found three basic styles:

1. **Authoritarian parenting.** The parents' word is law, not to be questioned. Misconduct brings strict punishment, usually physical, although authoritarian parents do not necessarily cross the line into physical abuse. Demands for maturity are high, and parent–child communication, especially about emotions, is low. Authoritarian parents seem aloof from their children, showing little affection or nurturance.
2. **Permissive parenting.** The parents make few demands on their children, hiding any impatience they feel. Discipline is lax because demands for maturity are low. Permissive parents are nurturant, accepting, and communicate well with their offspring. They view themselves as available to help their children but not as responsible for shaping how their children turn out.
3. **Authoritative parenting.** Authoritative parents are similar in some ways to authoritarian parents, in that they set limits and enforce rules. However, they also listen to their children's requests and questions and discuss feelings and problems. Family rule is more democratic than dictatorial. The parents demand maturity of their offspring, but they also are nurturant and understanding, forgiving (rather than punishing) a child when demands for maturity are not met.

The characteristics of these styles are summarized in Table 10.2.

table **10.2**	**Characteristics of Baumrind's Parenting Styles**				
		Characteristics			
			Communication		
Style	Warmth	Discipline	Parent to Child	Child to Parent	Expectations of Maturity
Authoritarian	Low	Strict, often physical	High	Low	High
Permissive	High	Rare	Low	High	Low
Authoritative	High	Moderate, with much talk	High	High	Moderate

ANY HARM IN SPANKING?

One research team (Strassberg et al., 1994) tracked 273 children aged 4 to 6 and their parents to study the relationship between punishment at home and aggression at school. The families were from a full range of socioeconomic and cultural backgrounds. For example, roughly one-third were single parents, about three-fourths were European American, and about one-fourth were African American.

Before their children entered kindergarten, the parents were asked how frequently they had spanked, hit, or beaten their children over the past year. If the parents asked the difference between spanking and hitting, *spanking* was defined as "an open hand or an object on the child's buttocks in a controlled manner," whereas *hitting* was "the impulsive or spontaneous use of a fist or closed hand (or object) to strike the child more strongly than one would while spanking." Beating, apparently, did not need to be defined. Of the 408 parents surveyed, 9 percent never used physical punishment, 72 percent spanked but did not use more violent punishment, and 19 percent hit and/or beat, as well as spanked, their preschool children.

Six months later, observers, blind to the children's punishment history, recorded their behavior in kindergarten, taking particular note of acts of aggression. For an accurate snapshot of behavior, the observation phase was divided into twelve 5-minute segments per child, occurring over several days. Within each segment, the observers recorded how many times each child engaged in instrumental, reactive, or bullying aggression. Every child was watched by two observers overall. The pairs of observers agreed 96 percent of the time about whether aggression had occurred and 90 percent of the time about what type of aggression it was. (This level of agreement is especially important in naturalistic observation that requires some subjective judgment. This study would have been

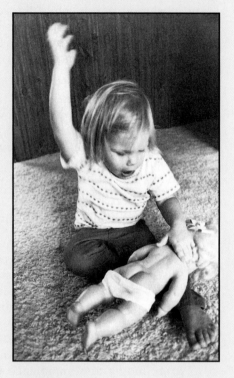

Angela at Play Research suggests that being spanked is a salient and memorable experience for young children, not because of the pain but because of the emotions. Children seek to do what they have learned; they know not only how to place their hands but also that an angry person is likely to do the hitting. The only part of the lesson they usually forget is what particular misdeed precipitated the punishment. Asked why she is spanking her doll, Angela will likely explain, "She was bad."

much less valid if, say, one observer was likely to see bullying where another saw reactive aggression.)

Analysis of the data (see Figure 10.1) revealed that family punishment affected the types of aggression differently:

- *Instrumental aggression* by the children seemed unrelated to the punishment they had experienced in the home. In other words, a kindergarten child was just as likely to fight over a toy whether he or she was spanked, hit, beaten, or not physically punished at all.
- *Reactive aggression* in the preschool was powerfully affected by spanking at home. Compared to children who were not spanked, children who were spanked were *more than twice as likely* to retaliate for any wrong, real or imagined, via reactive aggression. They angrily shoved, punched, and kicked at any provocation, rather than, say, moving away, asking for an explanation, telling the other child that that child had transgressed, or apologizing themselves.
- *Bullying aggression*, as expected, was clearly associated with being violently punished, particularly in the

Baumrind and others have continued this research, following the original 100 children as they grew and studying thousands of other children of various backgrounds and ages. Their basic conclusions are:

- *Authoritarian* parents raise children who are likely to be conscientious, obedient, and quiet; however, the children are not happy.

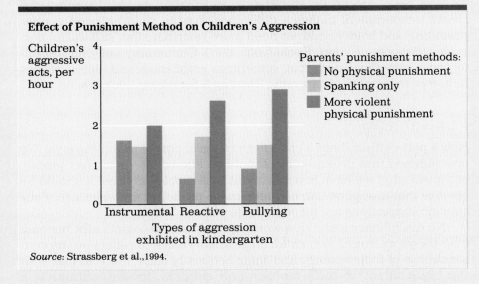

Effect of Punishment Method on Children's Aggression

Children's aggressive acts, per hour

Parents' punishment methods:
- No physical punishment
- Spanking only
- More violent physical punishment

Types of aggression exhibited in kindergarten

Source: Strassberg et al.,1994.

Figure 10.1 Punishment and Aggression. All the children, regardless of how their parents punished them, were about equally likely to exhibit instrumental aggression—fighting to get or retain something, such as a toy. The typical child did so once or twice an hour. By contrast, children who were severely punished by their parents were most often the bullies. The most interesting result involves reactive aggression—children's retaliation for intentional or accidental actions by another child. Children who were spanked were more than twice as likely as those who were not punished physically to consider such actions as hostile and requiring an aggressive response.

case of "a few extremely aggressive children," mostly boys who were frequently hit or beaten as well as spanked by both parents.

The researchers point out that while violent punishment (hitting or beating) seems to lead a child to be aggressive under all circumstances (to be a bully), spanking does not produce that blatant result. Rather, it seems to create a specific emotional-response pattern—a quick physical reaction to a perceived attack. Because the "anger accompanying the spanking is highly salient to the child," the child models "the emotional behavior pattern and not the form of aggression, per se" (Strassberg et al., 1994). Interestingly, frequency of spanking and which parent did the spanking (in the 29 percent of two-parent families in which one parent punished differently than the other) were not particularly influential, with one exception: Boys who were spanked by their fathers were more likely to react as if they had been hit as well as spanked; that is, they tended to become bullies.

However, spanking even a few times a year by only one of the parents was still likely to make the child higher in reactive aggression. Close analysis of all their data led the researchers to conclude that "in spite of parents' goals, spanking fails to promote prosocial development and, instead, is associated with higher rates of aggression toward peers" (Strassberg et al., 1994).

Although no single study proves a general point, the conclusions of this study have been not contradicted, but merely refined, by other research. For example, one prospective, longitudinal study of adolescent mothers found that those who controlled their children by yelling, grabbing, and spanking had children whose aggressive and disruptive behavior increased between the ages of 3 and 6. The correlation was more powerful for European American than African American mothers, perhaps because the latter scored high on measures of warmth and affection as well as control (Spieker et al., 1999). The conclusion seems to be that although physical punishment may be quick and effective at ages 2 or 3, it is likely to have negative repercussions later.

- *Permissive* parents raise children who are even less happy and who lack self-control.
- *Authoritative* parents raise children who are more likely to be successful, articulate, intelligent, happy with themselves, and generous with others.

Follow-up research has also found that, at least for middle-class families of European American ancestry, the initial advantages of the authoritative approach are likely to grow even stronger over time (Steinberg et al., 1994). Authoritative parents, for example, "are remarkably successful in protecting their adolescents from problem drug use and in generating competence" (Baumrind, 1991).

This basic conclusion still stands. However, it is also true that the child's temperament makes a difference. Fearful children need gentler parenting, and bolder children need more restrictive (but still warm) parenting (Bates et al., 1998; Kochanska, 1997). Community and cultural differences sometimes undercut, sometimes emphasize, and almost always influence the quality of parenting (Darling & Steinberg, 1997; Wachs, 1999).

Punishment

How a parent disciplines a child is an integral part of parenting style. No one suggests that preschoolers should be allowed to do as they please; but given what we have learned about preschool cognition, it should be obvious that discipline can be much more proactive than punitive. Four specific suggestions are listed in Table 10.3.

No disciplinary technique works quickly and automatically. Instead, over the years from 2 to 6, children gradually learn to reflect on the consequences of their actions, and their actions become more in line with the expectations of their families and cultures. Indeed, culture is a strong influence on actions and disciplinary techniques. Japanese mothers, for example, use reasoning, empathy, and expressions of disappointment as techniques to control their preschoolers' social behavior more than North American mothers do. By contrast, parents in the United States are more likely than Japanese parents to encourage emotional expressions of all sorts, including anger. Perhaps as a result, in a series of experimental situations designed to elicit distress and conflict, American 4- to 5-year-olds were more aggressive than their Japanese counterparts (Zahn-Waxler et al., 1996).

What about physical punishment? It is popular, and it seems to work. At least, most children stop doing whatever they are doing if they are spanked or even threatened with spanking. More than 90 percent of today's American adults were spanked when they were young, and most consider themselves none the worse for it. Indeed, most parents, not only

| table 10.3 | Relating Discipline to Developmental Characteristics of Preschool Children |

■ *Remember theory of mind.* Preschool children gradually understand things from other viewpoints. Hence involving empathy ("How would you feel if . . . ") will increase prosocial and decrease antisocial behavior.

■ *Remember emerging self-concept.* Preschool children are developing a sense of who they are and what they want, sometimes egocentrically. Hence adults should protect that emerging self: They should not force 3-year-olds to share their favorite toys, nor should they tell them, "Words will never hurt me."

■ *Remember language explosion and fast mapping.* Preschool children are eager to talk and think, but they are not always accurate in their verbal understanding. Hence a child who doesn't "listen" should not necessarily be punished, because a command might be misunderstood. However, conversation before and after an event helps the child learn.

■ *Remember that preschoolers are still illogical.* The connection between the misdeed and the punishment needs to be immediate and transparent. A child might learn nothing from waiting several hours to be spanked for breaking a dish but might learn a lot from having to pick up the pieces, mop the floor, and perhaps contribute some saved pennies toward a replacement.

Certainly Not Permissive It's hard to tell what kind of parenting is occurring here, but this is not permissive. Both authoritarian and authoritative parents might sometimes scold a child. The difference is that the authoritarian parent tolerates no back talk and is likely to use physical punishment in response to a display of disrespect. The authoritative parent, however, might listen to a child's response, paying close attention not only to the child's words but also to his or her gestures and body language.

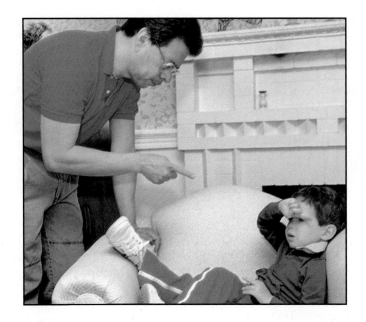

in North America but also throughout Asia, Africa, and South America, still believe that spanking is acceptable, legitimate, and necessary at times (Durrant, 1996; Levinson, 1989). They are especially likely to spank their children during the preschool years, when children are considered "old enough to know better" but not "old enough to listen to reason." Spanking is so common that parents of all types resort to it: permissive types in exasperation; authoritative types as a last resort, after extensive warning; and authoritarian types as a legitimate consequence of breaking a rule.

However, many developmentalists wonder if spanking has a boomerang effect—if children who are physically punished learn to be more aggressive. The answer is probably yes. Domestic violence of any type, from spanking a child to letting siblings "fight it out" to exposing children to mutual insults or hitting between the parents, makes children likely to be aggressive with peers and, later on, with their own families (Straus, 1994) (see the Research Report, pages 284–285).

BOY OR GIRL: SO WHAT?

sex differences Biological differences between males and females.

gender differences Cultural differences in the roles and behavior of the two sexes.

Male or female identity is an important feature of self-understanding during the play years, as well as a particular concern of many parents. Social scientists distinguish between **sex differences,** which are the biological differences between males and females, and **gender differences,** which are cultural differences in the roles and behaviors of the two sexes. Curiously, although true *sex* differences are far less apparent in childhood (when boys and girls are about the same size and shape) than in adulthood (when physical differences become more visible and anatomy becomes critical in sexual intercourse, pregnancy, and birth), *gender* differentiation seems more significant to children than to adults.

Developmental Progression of Gender Awareness

Even at age 2, gender-related preferences and play patterns are apparent. Children already know whether they are boys or girls, can identify adult strangers as mommies or daddies, and apply gender labels (Mrs.,

Two Sets of Cousins Same day, same trampo-line, and similar genes and culture, because these eight children are cousins. But sex or gender differences are quite apparent in the later preschool years. Of course, no one should read too much into a photograph. Nonetheless, this group, like any group of preschoolers, offers suggestive evidence of boy–girl differences—here including one specific aspect of their wearing apparel.

❷ Observational Quiz (see answer page 290): *What sex or gender differences can you see?*

Mr., lady, man) consistently. That simple cognitive awareness becomes, by age 3, a rudimentary understanding that male and female distinctions are lifelong (although some pretend, hope, or imagine otherwise). By age 4, children are convinced that certain toys (such as dolls and trucks) and certain roles (such as nurses and soldiers) are appropriate for one gender but not the other (Bauer et al., 1998; Fagot et al., 1992; Levy, 1994). When given a choice, children play with children of their own sex, a tendency apparent at age 2 and clear-cut by age 5 (Moller & Serbin, 1996). Partly because of their largely gender-segregated play patterns, victims of physical aggression in preschool are more often boys, while most victims of relational aggression are girls (Crick et al., 1999).

Of course, a child who follows same-sex play patterns does not necessarily understand biological sex differences. A leading researcher of gender identity, Sandra Bem, described the day her young son Jeremy

> naively decided to wear barrettes to nursery school. Several times that day, another little boy insisted that Jeremy must be a girl because "only girls wear barrettes." After repeatedly asserting that "wearing barrettes doesn't matter; being a boy means having a penis and testicles," Jeremy finally pulled down his pants as a way of making his point more convincingly. The boy was not impressed. He simply said, "Everybody has a penis; only girls wear barrettes." [Bem, 1989]

As in this example, even though children confuse gender and sex throughout the preschool years, a child's awareness of differences is soon associated with what is good, bad, or simply wrong (Fagot & Leinbach, 1993).

By age 6, children have well-formed ideas (and prejudices) and also know which sex is better (their own) and which sex is stupid (the other one) (Huston, 1993). Young children also insist on dressing in stereotypic ways: Shoes for preschoolers are often designed with such decorations as pink ribbons or blue footballs, and no child would dare wear the shoes meant for the other sex. Such dress codes become rigidly enforced by first grade, with some of the cruelest barbs of relational aggression used against children who dress oddly. When they reach school age, a few children still may have a good friend of the other sex, but they rarely play with that friend when other children are around (Kovacs et al., 1996). Awareness that a person's sex is a biological characteristic that is not changed by clothing or activities develops gradually, not becoming solid until age 8 or so (Szkrybalo & Ruble, 1999).

Preschoolers maintain their sex and gender stereotypes, despite the efforts of some adults to deemphasize gender distinctions. Consider the following examples, which were cited by Beal (1994).

Boys Will Be Boys Even in today's world, preschool boys and girls tend to engage in play that is gender-stereotyped, especially with a good friend of the same sex. While some gender barriers have fallen, they have related more to girls than to boys. These girls might sword fight, for example, but the boys would probably not play patty-cake, especially for the camera. The question, still not answered with certainty, is "Why?"

A mother who had struggled through medical school, in part so that she would be a strong role model for her daughter, was startled when the little girl told her that she must be a nurse because only men could be doctors. Another little girl said, "Mommy cleans the living room," even though she had seen only her father doing the vacuuming and dusting. When another girl was given a truck to play with, she said, "My Mommy would want me to play with this, but I don't want to." [Bussey & Bandura, 1992]

Why?

Theories of Gender-Role Development

Experts disagree about what proportion of observed gender differences is biological—perhaps a matter of hormones, of brain structure, or of body size and musculature—and what proportion is environmental—perhaps embedded in centuries of cultural history or in the immediate, explicit home training each child receives (Beal, 1994). One reason for their disagreement is that the topic is so vast, individual experiences so varied, and the research so various that clear conclusions are difficult to reach. To develop a framework for analyzing the conflicting evidence, we need a theory. Fortunately, we have five theories, first described in Chapter 2.

Psychoanalytic Theory

phallic stage The third stage of psychosexual development, occurring in early childhood, in which the penis becomes the focus of psychological concern as well as physiological pleasure.

Freud (1938) called the period from about age 3 to 6 the **phallic stage,** because he believed its center of focus is the *phallus,* which is an ancient word for penis. At about 3 or 4 years of age, said Freud, the process of maturation makes a boy aware of his male sexual organ. He begins to masturbate, to fear castration, and to develop sexual feelings toward his mother. These feelings make him jealous of his father—so jealous, according to Freud, that every son secretly wants to replace his dad. Freud called this the **Oedipus complex,** after Oedipus, son of a king in Greek mythology. Abandoned as an infant and raised in a distant kingdom, Oedipus later returned to his birthplace and, not realizing who they were, killed his own father and married his mother. When he discovered what he had done (after disaster struck the entire kingdom), he blinded himself in a spasm of guilt.

Oedipus complex In the phallic stage of psychosexual development, the sexual desire that boys have for their mothers and the related hostility they have toward their fathers.

Freud believed that this bizarre, ancient story still echoes through history because every boy feels horribly guilty for his incestuous and murderous emotions. He fears that his father will inflict terrible punishment

identification A defense mechanism that lets a person symbolically take on the role and attitudes of someone more powerful than himself or herself.

superego The part of the personality that is self-critical and judgmental and that internalizes the moral standards set by parents and society.

Electra complex In the phallic stage of psychosexual development, the female version of the Oedipus complex: Girls have sexual feelings for their fathers and accompanying hostility toward their mothers.

❶ Answer to Observational Quiz (from page 288): *The most obvious ones are in appearance. The girls have longer hair, and the colors and styles of their clothes are different. Did you notice the wearing-apparel difference—that the soles of all four boys' shoes are black, whereas the girls' are white or pink? Now let's get more speculative. The girl on the left, who may need to establish her alliance with the group since she is the only one in colors a boy might wear, is looking at and talking with her cousins—a very female thing to do. In addition, the girls' facial and body expressions suggest they are much more comfortable with this close contact. In fact, the two boys on the left seem about to relieve their tension with a bout of rough-and-tumble play.*

on him if his evil secret is ever discovered. Boys cope with their guilt and fear through **identification,** a defense mechanism that allows a person to ally himself or herself with another person. Since they cannot replace their fathers, young boys strive to become them, copying their fathers' masculine mannerisms, opinions, and actions.

Boys also develop, again in self-defense, a powerful conscience, called the **superego,** that is quick to judge and punish "the bad guys." According to Freud's theory, a young boy's fascination with superheroes, guns, karate chops, and the like comes directly from his patricidal urges. An adult man's obsession with crime and punishment might be a product of an imperfectly resolved phallic stage. In this perspective, homosexuality, either overt or latent, is also evidence of a poorly managed phallic stage, as is homophobia.

Freud offered two overlapping descriptions of the phallic stage in girls. One form, the **Electra complex** (also named after a figure in classical mythology), is similar to the Oedipus complex: The little girl wants to eliminate her mother and become intimate with her father. In the other version, the little girl becomes jealous of boys because they have penises, an emotion called *penis envy.* The girl blames her mother for this "incompleteness" and decides the next best thing to having a penis is to become sexually attractive so that someone with a penis—preferably her father—will love her (Freud, 1933/1965). Her *identification* is with women her father finds attractive; her superego strives to avoid his disapproval.

Thus, the origins and consequences of the phallic stage are basically the same for girls as they are for boys. Biological impulses within a family context first produce lust and anger and, then, guilt and fear. By the end of the preschool years these emotions have caused the development of a strict superego that mandates gender-appropriate behavior and harsh punishment for those who do not abide by the code. No wonder, then, that 5-year-olds seem obsessed by gender roles; this is their best defense against unconscious urges.

Other psychoanalytic theorists agree that male–female distinctions are important to the young child's psychic development, although, as you might imagine and as the In Person box makes clear, many disagree about the specifics.

Learning Theory

In contrast with psychoanalytic theorists, learning theorists believe that virtually all roles are learned and hence are the result of nurture, not nature. Therefore, to learning theorists, the gender distinctions that are so obvious by age 5 are evidence of years of ongoing reinforcement and punishment, rather than the product of any specific stage.

What evidence supports learning theory? Parents, peers, and teachers all reward "gender-appropriate" more than "gender-inappropriate" behavior (Etaugh & Liss, 1992; Fagot, 1995; Ruble & Martin, 1998). Parents praise their sons for not crying when hurt, for example, but caution their daughters about the hazards of rough play. Interestingly, males seem to be caught in the learned-gender curriculum more than females. Researchers have found that boys are criticized for being "sissies" more than girls are criticized for being "tomboys" and that fathers, more than mothers, expect their daughters to be feminine and their sons to be tough.

BERGER AND FREUD

As a woman, and as a mother of four daughters, I have always regarded Freud's theory of sexual development as ridiculous, not to mention antifemale. I am not alone. Psychologists generally agree that Freud's explanation of sexual and moral development is one of the weaker parts of his theory, reflecting the values of middle-class Victorian society at the end of the nineteenth century more than any universal developmental pattern. Many female psychoanalysts (e.g., Horney, 1967; Klein, 1957; Lerner, 1978) have been particularly critical of Freud's idea of penis envy. They believe that girls envy not the male sex organ but the higher status males are generally accorded. They also suggest that boys may experience "womb envy," wishing that they could have babies and suckle them. Virtually no contemporary psychologist or psychiatrist believes that homosexual urges are caused by problems during the phallic stage.

However, my own view of Freud's theory as utter nonsense has been modified somewhat by my four daughters. Our first "Electra episode" occurred in a conversation with my eldest, Bethany, when she was about 4 years old:

Bethany: When I grow up, I'm going to marry Daddy.
Mother: But Daddy's married to me.
Bethany: That's all right. When I grow up, you'll probably be dead.
Mother: (Determined to stick up for myself) Daddy's older than me, so when I'm dead, he'll probably be dead, too.
Bethany: That's OK. I'll marry him when he gets born again.

At this point, I couldn't think of a good reply, especially since I had no idea where she had gotten the concept of reincarnation. Bethany saw my face fall, and she took pity on me:

Bethany: Don't worry, Mommy. After you get born again, you can be our baby.

Our second episode was also in conversation, this time with my daughter Rachel, when she was about 5:

Rachel: When I get married, I'm going to marry Daddy.
Mother: Daddy's already married to me.
Rachel: (With the joy of having discovered a wonderful solution) Then we can have a double wedding!

Pillow Talk Elissa placed this artwork on my husband's pillow. My pillow, beside it, had a less colorful, less elaborate note—an afterthought. It read "Dear Mom, I love you too."

The third episode was considerably more graphic. It took the form of a "valentine" left on my husband's pillow by my daughter Elissa, who was about 8 years old at the time. It is reproduced here.

Finally, when Sarah turned 5, she also expressed the desire to marry my husband. When I told her she couldn't, because he was married to me, her response revealed one more reason why TV can be pernicious: "Oh yes, a man can have two wives. I saw it on television."

I am not the only feminist developmentalist to be taken aback by her own children's words. Nancy Datan (1986) wrote about the Oedipal conflict: "I have a son who was once five years old. From that day to this, I have never thought Freud mistaken." Obviously, these bits of "evidence" do not prove that Freud was correct. I still think he was wrong on many counts. But Freud's description of the phallic stage now seems less bizarre than it once appeared to be.

Social learning theorists remind us that children learn about behavior not only through reinforcement (such as a gift or a word of praise) but also by observation, especially of people seen as nurturing, powerful, and yet similar to themselves. Thus, mothers of small children still do most of the cooking, cleaning, and child care, while fathers "help out"

Modeling Much of gender-role learning happens without adult realization or intention. This father did not ask his son to pretend to fix his toy lawn mower, just as no mother asks her daughter to pretend to iron the clothes, set the table, or wear high heels. The impulse to copy obviously comes from the children—which is one of the reasons the lessons are learned so well, even when we would rather teach something else.

or, in about one-third of all households, are absent altogether (Barnett & Rivers, 1996; Hochschild, 1989).

Thus, gender-role conformity is still rewarded, punished, and modeled, especially for preschool children and especially for boys, according to research inspired by learning theory. This can explain why girls and women sometimes wear pants and aspire to male occupations but boys cannot wear skirts or aspire to female roles without experiencing massive disapproval, especially from other males. Note again that this gender prejudice is strongest during the preschool years. If a college man aspires to be a nurse or a preschool teacher, most of his classmates will respect his choice. If a 4-year-old boy wants the same thing, his peers will probably soon set him straight. As one professor reports:

> My son came home after 2 days of preschool to announce that he could not grow up to teach seminars (previously his lifelong ambition, because he knew from personal observation that everyone at seminars got to eat cookies) because only women could be teachers. [Fagot, 1995]

Cognitive Theory

In explaining gender identity and gender-role development, cognitive theorists focus on children's understanding—the way a child intellectually grasps a specific matter at hand. Preschool children, they point out, have many gender-related experiences but not much cognitive complexity. They tend to see the world in intellectually simple terms. They see male and female as complete opposites, on the basis of appearances at the moment, even when past evidence (such as the father whom they saw cleaning the living room) contradicts such a sexist assumption.

Remember that the basic tenet of cognitive theory is that a person's thinking determines how the world is perceived and how that perception is acted on. Preschoolers' thinking about gender follows preschoolers' cognitive patterns, which are static and egocentric. When personal experience is ambiguous or contradictory, preschoolers search for the "script" they have formed describing what the various gender roles should be. For example, when researchers gave children unfamiliar, gender-neutral toys, the children first tried to figure out if the toys were for boys or for girls and then decided whether they personally would like to play with the toys or not (Martin et al., 1995).

Sociocultural Theory

Proponents of the sociocultural perspective note that many traditional cultures emphasize gender distinctions, and these are quickly evidenced in the gender patterns adopted by children. In societies where adults have quite distinct gender roles, girls and boys attend sex-segregated schools beginning in kindergarten, and they virtually never play together (Beal, 1994). They are also taught different skills. For instance, in rural communities throughout the world, girls tend the chickens and the younger children, while boys tend the larger animals, such as sheep, pigs, and cattle (Whiting & Edwards, 1988). As a result, gender distinctions are clear and inflexible in the mind and behavior of both children and adults.

When immigrants from such traditional societies come to less segregated societies, they tend to maintain their gender values strenuously. For example, among Khmer refugees from Cambodia in the United States, the boys are urged to continue their education, and the girls are urged to become wives and mothers before graduating from high school so that they will be protected from the sexual permissiveness that the Khmer see as corrupting American daughters (Smith-Hefner, 1993). Similar gender distinctions can be found worldwide. Almost every study of preschool children finds that boys are encouraged by their culture to take on different roles than girls.

Socioculturalists point out that the particulars of gender education—such as which activities are promoted for which sex—vary by region, socioeconomic status, and historical period. But every society has values and attitudes regarding preferred behavior for men and women, and every culture teaches these to the young. Children could become less gender-conscious, but only if their entire culture were to become so.

This possibility of cultural change leads to another idea: androgyny. As a biological term, *androgyny* is defined as the presence of both male and female sexual characteristics in an organism. As developmentalists use the term, **androgyny** means a balance, within a person, of what are commonly regarded as male and female psychological characteristics. The idea is to break through the restrictiveness of cultural gender roles and to encourage the individual to define himself or herself primarily as a human being, rather than as male or female. To achieve androgyny, boys should be encouraged to be nurturant and girls to be assertive, so that with maturity and patience they will develop less restrictive and rule-bound gender patterns.

Sociocultural theory stresses, however, that androgyny (or any other gender concept) cannot be taught to children simply through

❷ **Especially for Teachers:** Suppose you want children to fulfill all their potential, and therefore you plan to structure your preschool to counter the gender training children might have had at home. For instance, you encourage the girls to engage in rough-and-tumble play and the boys to dress up, and you make sure each play group has children of both sexes. Is androgyny going to appear in your classroom?

androgyny   A balance, within an individual, of male and female gender characteristics such that the individual feels comfortable in breaking through gender stereotypes; thus, for example, an androgynous male will feel comfortable being nurturant as well as being assertive.

Nature or Nurture? At first glance, the boy–girl differences seen here seem entirely cultural. The boy must have seen a fireman, and the girl a fancy lady, if not in person then on television. However, epigenetic systems theory urges us to go deeper, to see if something innate is also portrayed in this photo.
❷ *Observational Quiz (see answer page 295): Can you see it?*

cognition or parental reinforcement. The only way children will be truly androgynous is if their entire culture promulgates the ideas and practices—something no culture has yet done. Why not? The reasons may lie far deeper than the political forces or social values of the moment, as our final theory suggests.

Epigenetic Systems Theory

Epigenetic systems theory contends that every aspect of human behavior, including gender attitudes and behavior roles, is the result of interaction between genes and early experience—not just for the individual but also for the species. The idea that many gender differences are genetically based is supported by recent research in neurobiology, which finds biological differences between male and female brains. In females, for example, the corpus callosum tends to be thicker, and overall brain maturation seems to occur more quickly than in males. This could account for the fact that girls tend to be slightly more advanced than boys in skills such as reading and writing, which demand simultaneous coordination of various areas of the brain (Dudek et al., 1994). In males, neural activity and dendrite formation in the right hemisphere tend to be more pronounced than in females. The right hemisphere is concerned with logic, spatial skills, and mathematical processes, so this could account for the typical superiority of boys in these areas, a superiority that eventually leads to more men than women among engineers, physicists, and pilots.

These brain differences are probably not the result of any single sex-linked gene. More likely, they appear because sex hormones produced by XX or XY chromosomes begin to circulate in the fetal stage, affecting the development of the brain. Those hormones continue to influence brain development through childhood (Gaulin, 1993; Hines, 1993). The social context may then enter the picture by affecting the brain in ways that program proper male and female behavior.

Of course, this programming is not inevitable. Remember: Although epigenetic systems theory stresses the biological and genetic origins of behavior, it also stresses that the manifestations of those origins are shaped, enhanced, or halted by environmental factors. Here is one example: Infant girls seem to be genetically inclined to talk earlier than boys. However, the language parts of an infant's brain do not develop fully unless someone talks to the infant. Suppose a boy is an only child, raised in a household with several adult women. He might be talked to, sung to, and read to quite often by his devoted caregivers. He will develop superior verbal ability in his brain, because of the interaction between his genetic potential (which might be slightly less than that of the typical girl) and his social environment (which is much richer than it is for most children of either sex). Environmental factors will have enhanced his genetic capabilities greatly.

Of course, this is not the usual scenario. In a typical family that includes one man, one woman, and two or more children of both sexes,

● Response for Teachers (from page 293):
The goal of androgyny may be a good one, and you can decrease the worst of sexism, but children have powerful reasons of their own to stick to male and female patterns. These may be biological, or they may be cultural, but they are not easy for one teacher to change. If you don't want to have a room full of frustrated children, and perhaps angry parents, you need to be selective when you cross the gender boundaries. For example, to get the boys to engage in sociodramatic play, you might stock the room with dress-up clothes that boys would like and encourage games that are best played with both sexes—playing a family that has a father and a big brother, for instance.

● *Answer to Observational Quiz (from page 294):* *Universally, boys and men seem more intrigued by moving gadgets and manipulated tools, and women seem attracted to frills, lace, and fuzzy shoes. Of course, many individuals are involved in activities dominated by the other sex: Women use machines to accomplish many things, and men wear expensive tuxedos and gold cufflinks to indicate status. But in both those examples, the behavior is a means to an end. In more usual cases, males tend to be fascinated with machines and women with wearing sheer fabrics—just for the fun of it.*

language stimulation will differ by sex. Since girls are more responsive to language and since mothers are usually more verbal than fathers, mother–daughter pairs will typically talk most and father–son pairs, least. This will likely turn the females' slight linguistic advantage in their brain circuitry into a notably higher level of language proficiency (Leaper et al., 1998).

Conclusion: Gender and Destiny

The first and last of our five theories emphasize the power of biology as regards gender development. A reader who is quick to form opinions might decide that the gender roles and stereotypes exhibited by preschoolers are unchangeable. This conclusion might be reinforced by the fact that gender awareness emerges very early, by age 2, or that play patterns and social interactions of young boys and girls differ. But the three middle theories all present persuasive evidence for the influence of family and culture in guiding and shaping the powerful gender patterns we see by age 5. Actually, even psychoanalytic theory and epigenetic systems theory acknowledge some learning in gender development as well. Boy–girl differences are partly innate, a matter of sex, but much is taught, a matter of gender.

Thus our five theories, collectively, have led to at least two conclusions and one critical question.

■ Gender differences are not simply cultural or learned: The biological foundation for gender differences is far more pervasive than the minor anatomical differences between boys and girls.
■ Biology is not destiny: Children are shaped by their experiences.

This raises the question: What gender patterns should children learn, ideally? Answers vary. In those cultures and families that encourage each child to develop his or her own inclinations, many children grow up to choose gender roles, express emotions, and develop talents that would be taboo—or even punished—in cultures that adhere to strict gender guidelines. In contrast, some societies and families encourage gender differences, widening whatever innate sex distinctions there may be. In these societies, adults fall naturally into two quite separate worlds, one designed for men and one for women.

To what extent would you want your children to follow gender roles, and to what extent would you want them to be androgynous? Is harm done to individuals' development by requiring them to adhere to social guidelines and thereby changing their natural orientation, so that they become either more or less gender-bound than they might naturally be?

If you agree that the theories we have examined have at least some merit, you must conclude that both nature and nurture influence gender behaviors. But the theories don't answer value questions. Perhaps that is why various cultures and individuals—and the theories themselves—come to such different conclusions about gender.

Of course, the same can be said about the proper expression of aggression, or the preferred parenting style, or the degree of emotional regulation that should be evident in a person. The research describes what is, and what can develop, during early childhood. It is up to you to decide what should be.

SUMMARY

THE SELF AND THE SOCIAL WORLD

1. Increasing self-understanding helps preschoolers increase their social understanding and become more skilled in their relationships with others. Confidence is quite high, since these children focus not on their failures but on their new successes, developed through their own initiative and the efforts of appreciative adults.

2. Learning to regulate emotions is one key aspect of emotional intelligence developed during the preschool years. Normally, children modulate their fear and anger, becoming quite sympathetic and outgoing (but not overly solicitous or excessively friendly) to others.

ANTISOCIAL AND PROSOCIAL BEHAVIOR

3. Prosocial behavior is correlated with emotional regulation and with making new friends. Antisocial behavior, particularly aggression, is of greater concern. Instrumental aggression is normal; other types—reactive, relational, and bullying aggression—may lead to serious problems later in life.

4. Children learn social skills primarily through interaction, especially in play. Although all children benefit from all kinds of play, boys are more likely to engage in rough-and-tumble play, and girls are more likely to become involved in sociodramatic play.

5. Parent–child interaction is complex. A child's culture always affects the outcome of parenting.

6. In general, authoritative parents, who are warm and loving but are willing to set and enforce reasonable limits, have children who are happy, self-confident, and capable. Highly authoritarian parents tend to raise unhappy and aggressive children, whereas children with very permissive parents are often even more unhappy and also lack self-control.

BOY OR GIRL: SO WHAT?

7. Developmentalists agree that children begin to adopt gender roles and display gender identity during early childhood, with consciousness of male–female differences apparent as early as age 2. However, psychologists disagree about why sex differences are so important during the preschool years. Boys and girls become quite distinct in their behavior and attitudes by age 5.

8. Each of the major theories has a somewhat different explanation for gender differences. Psychoanalytic theorists describe fears and fantasies that motivate children to adore their opposite-sex parent and then identify with their same-sex parent. Learning theorists emphasize reinforcement, punishment, and modeling, which are particularly strong for males. Cognitive theory begins by noting preschool children's simplified, stereotypic understanding overall.

9. Two emerging theories note the influence of the wider society, both currently and in earlier times. Sociocultural theory notes the pervasive influence of cultural patterns. Epigenetic systems theory points out the biological tendencies that are inherited through genetic transmission and explains how these tendencies may affect the child's brain patterns as well as other aspects of behavior.

10. These theories together suggest that biology and society (sex and gender) are both powerful influences on children. They do not, however, specify how parents and cultures should attempt to mold children. Although every child has innate tendencies, those tendencies can be strengthened, directed, or overcome by the child's upbringing.

KEY TERMS

initiative versus guilt (272)
emotional regulation (275)
phobia (276)
prosocial behavior (277)
antisocial behavior (277)
instrumental aggression (278)
reactive aggression (278)
relational aggression (278)
bullying aggression (278)
rough-and-tumble play (279)
sociodramatic play (280)
authoritarian parenting (283)
permissive parenting (283)
authoritative parenting (283)
sex differences (287)
gender differences (287)
phallic stage (289)
Oedipus complex (289)
identification (290)
superego (290)
Electra complex (290)
androgyny (293)

KEY QUESTIONS

1. How would you describe preschoolers' evaluations of themselves?

2. How do children learn emotional regulation?

3. What are the types of aggression, and which are most troubling?

4. What are the similarities between rough-and-tumble play and sociodramatic play?

5. What can children learn from peers that they are unlikely to learn from adults?

6. What behaviors in preschool children might be the result of an insecure early attachment?

7. How do the three classic parenting styles differ?

8. How does punishment of young children influence their behavior?

9. What evidence do you know of that indicates that preschool children are aware of sex differences?

10. Which theory of development seems to offer the best explanation of gender roles, and why?

11. *In Your Experience* Can you describe a parenting style that influenced the types of discipline used by the parents?

BIOSOCIAL

Brain and Nervous System

The brain continues to develop, attaining 90 percent of its adult weight by the time the child is 5 years old. Both the proliferation of neural pathways and myelination continue. Coordination between the two halves and the various areas of the brain increase, allowing the child to settle down and concentrate when necessary, and to use various parts of the body in harmony. Gross motor skills, such as running and jumping, improve dramatically. Fine motor skills, such as writing and drawing, develop more slowly.

Maltreatment

Child abuse and neglect, potential problems at every age, are particularly likely in homes with many children and few personal or community resources. During early childhood, home-visitation programs can be an effective preventive measure. Recognition of the problem has improved, but treatment is still uneven. Distinguishing the ongoing problems of a family that needs support, and the immediate danger for a child who needs to be removed and placed in foster care, is critical for long-term development.

COGNITIVE

Cognitive Skills

Many cognitive abilities, including some related to number, memory, and problem solving, become more mature, if the social context is supportive. Children begin to develop a theory of mind, in which they take into account the ideas and emotions of others. Social interaction, particularly in the form of guided participation, is of help in this cognitive advancement. At the same time, however, children's thinking can be quite illogical and egocentric.

Language

Language abilities develop rapidly; by the age of 6, the average child knows 10,000 words and demonstrates extensive grammatical knowledge. Children also learn to adjust their communication to their audience, and use language to help themselves learn. Preschool education helps children develop language and express themselves, as well as prepare them for later education and adult life.

PSYCHOSOCIAL

Emotions and Personality Development

Self-concept emerges, as does the ability to regulate emotions. Children boldly initiate new activities, especially if they are praised for their endeavors.

Play

Children engage in play that helps them master physical and intellectual skills and that teaches or enhances social roles. As their social and cognitive skills develop, children engage in ever more complex and imaginative types of play, sometimes by themselves but increasingly with others. Antisocial behavior is troubling, because it can lead to serious aggression and delinquency.

Parent–Child Interaction

Some parenting styles are more effective than others in encouraging the child to develop autonomy and self-control; those that are most responsive to the child, with much communication, seem to do best. Parenting styles are influenced by cultural and community standards, the parents' economic situation, upbringing, and personality, and the characteristics of the child.

Gender Roles

Increasingly, children develop stereotypic concepts of sex differences in appearance and gender differences in behavior. The precise roles of nature and nurture in this process are unclear, but both are obviously involved.

PART IV

The School Years

If someone asked you to pick the best years of the entire life span, you might choose the years from about 7 to 11 and defend your choice persuasively. Physical development is usually almost problem-free, making it easy to master dozens of new skills. With regard to cognitive development, most children are able to learn quickly and think logically, provided that the topic is not too abstract. Moreover, they are usually eager to learn, mastering new concepts, new vocabulary, and new skills with a combination of enthusiasm, perseverance, and curiosity that makes them a joy to teach. Indeed, we call these the "school years" because every culture worldwide takes advantage of the fact that these children are ready and eager to learn.

The child's moral reasoning and behavior have reached that state where right seems clearly distinguished from wrong, without the ambiguities and conflicts that complicate morality during adolescence.

Finally, the social world of middle childhood seems perfect, for most school-age children think their parents are helpful, their teachers fair, and their friends loyal. As you will see, however, not every child emerges from middle childhood unscathed.

The next three chapters celebrate the joys, and commemorate the occasional tragedies, of middle childhood.

The School Years:
Biosocial Development

CHAPTER 11

Compared with other periods of the life span, biosocial development between ages 7 and 11 is relatively uneventful. Most school-age children easily master new physical skills, from tree climbing to hammer pounding to in-line skating, without extensive adult instruction. Disease and death are rare, sex-related differences in physical development and ability are minimal, and sexual urges are quiescent. Almost nobody dies, gets pregnant, or even needs much adult assistance during these years. Certainly when growth in these years is compared with the rapid and dramatic growth that occurs during infancy and adolescence, middle childhood seems a period of smooth progress and tranquility.

For some children, however, the school years are particularly challenging, because their disabilities become more evident and disturbing. In this chapter, we will examine the body changes and variations that characterize middle childhood, the tests used to compare these children, and several biosocial difficulties that sometimes occur.

SIZE AND SHAPE

Children grow more slowly from age 7 to 11 than they did earlier or than they will later, in adolescence. Although the actual pounds or kilograms gained per year are more than those gained between ages 2 and 6, the rate of increase is slower. Each year, the typical well-nourished school-age child gains about 5 pounds (2¼ kilograms) and grows about 2½ inches (6 centimeters); by age 10, he or she weighs about 70 pounds (32 kilograms) and measures 54 inches (137 centimeters). (See Appendix A.)

Children generally seem to become slimmer as their height increases, their limbs lengthen, and their body proportions change. Muscles become stronger as well. Thus, the average 10-year-old, for instance, throws a ball twice as far as the average 6-year-old. Lung capacity expands, so with each passing year children can run faster and exercise longer.

Variations in Physique

In the poorer nations, most variation in children's height and weight is caused by differences in nutrition. Wealthier children are generally several inches taller than their impoverished classmates from the other side of town—whether the town is Nairobi, Rio de Janeiro, or New Delhi

All Healthy, All Different During the school years, variations in children's size and rate of physical maturation are the result of genetic inheritance and nutrition, as well as of chronological age.

❓ **Especially for Parents:** Suppose your 6-year-old is quite chubby and also quite happy. Should you upset the child by imposing a weight-loss diet?

(Eveleth & Tanner, 1991). In more affluent countries, heredity is the main source of variation, since most children get enough food during middle childhood to grow as tall as their genes allow.

Genes also affect body shape, but here family habits have obvious impact. Parents of children who are either too thin or too fat need to understand how they influence their children's weight. Professional help may be needed. Teachers, medical professionals, and other members of the community need to understand the serious consequences of being an underweight or overweight child.

Childhood Obesity

Children tend to be conformists. Every difference, from having freckles to wearing the wrong shoes, can become a source of embarrassment during the sensitive years from 7 to 17. However, overweight is the most common "real" problem, affecting emotional and physical well-being. The point at which a particular child is considered not just chubby but truly obese varies, depending partly on the child's body type, partly on the child's proportion of fat to muscle, and partly on the culture's standards. One measure is the **body mass index (BMI),** which is the weight in kilograms divided by the square of the height in meters (see the accompanying chart and Chapter 17, page 480). At age 6, obesity begins at about 19 BMI. At age 10, if the BMI is over 24, the child is probably obese (Rosner et al., 1998).

Experts believe that between 20 and 30 percent of American children are obese, a rate that has doubled since 1980 (Dietz, 1999). The causes are many, but since genes do not change much from one generation to the next, nurture, not nature, must be to blame. The various social causes and consequences of obesity are discussed further in the Research Report on page 304.

body mass index (BMI) A measure of obesity determined by dividing weight in kilograms by height squared in meters.

How to Calculate Body Mass Index

Many current studies of the relationship between body size and overall health focus on the ratio of body weight to height, referred to as the *body mass index,* or *BMI.* The formula for calculating body mass index is

$$BMI = w/h^2$$

w = weight in kilograms (pounds divided by 2.2)
h = height in meters (inches divided by 39.4)

Thus if a 12-year-old measures 1.47 meters (about 58 inches), his or her height squared is 2.16. BMI reaches 23 if that child weighs 50 kilograms (110 pounds) or more. For younger school-age children, obesity begins between 18 and 21 BMI, depending on the child's age; for adults, overweight begins at 25 BMI and obesity begins at about 28 BMI (new U.S. standard) or 30 BMI (world standard).

Obese children are especially prone to orthopedic and respiratory problems and are at risk for a number of other illnesses. In fact, "overnutrition in children is as important a risk factor as is malnutrition" (Eveleth & Tanner, 1991), with the risks eventually including heart disease, diabetes, and stroke.

Being overweight as a child is often a psychological problem as well. Indeed, compared to overweight adults who were normal-weight children, overweight adults who were obese as children tend to be more distressed and to have more psychophysiological problems (Mills & Adrianopoulos, 1993).

Variations in Health

In general, in developed nations, children age 7 to 11 are the healthiest humans of all—least likely to die or become seriously ill or injured (see Figure 11.1). Even accidents and serious abuse, which are the leading causes of mortality and morbidity during these years, occur less often than in the preschool or adolescent years. (These topics were first discussed in the chapters on the play years.)

However, for two reasons, differences in physique and health between one child and another become important. First, as we have said, children are more aware of each other's and their own physical imperfections during these years, so minor health problems can take on major importance. Second, the requirements of regular school attendance and steady performance, intended to enable every child to master the same

❓ **Especially for Health Professionals:** Since a predisposition for asthma is genetic, should medical advice be limited to controlling the severity of asthma rather than preventing it?

Figure 11.1 Death at an Early Age? Never! Schoolchildren are remarkably hardy, as measured in many ways. These charts show that death rates for 7- to 11-year-olds are lower than those for younger or older children, 15 times as low as their parents' rates, and 1,000 times lower than their grandparents' rates.

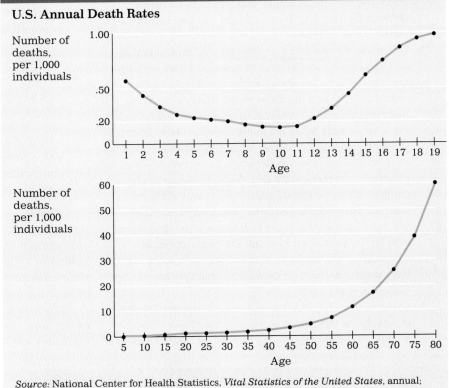

U.S. Annual Death Rates

Source: National Center for Health Statistics, *Vital Statistics of the United States,* annual; and unpublished data.

"Baby fat" is considered normal, "chubby" preschoolers are considered cute; but fat children are at a physical, psychological, and social disadvantage, and obese adults are at greater risk for almost every disease. Childhood obesity is a serious problem with many causes—all but one of which (heredity) is affected by the behavior of the adults in the child's life (Dietz, 1999).

- *Heredity.* Body type, including height, bone structure, and the amount and distribution of fat on the body, is inherited. So are individual differences in metabolic rate and activity level. Certain combinations of body type and metabolism result in excessive storage of fat on the body and higher-than-average BMI. Indeed, research on adopted children shows that heredity is at least as strong as family context in predisposing a person toward being overweight (Bray, 1989). However, changes in population genetics occur slowly, over generations, so the recent increase in obesity is not genetic.

- *Lack of exercise.* Inactive people burn fewer calories and are more likely to be overweight than active people, especially in infancy and childhood, when many children seem to be on the move all day. A child's activity level is influenced not only by heredity but also by a willingness to engage in strenuous play, the availability of safe play areas, the parents' example, and weight itself, which slows down precisely those children who need more exercise.

- *Television.* While watching television, children eat more and burn fewer calories than they would if they were actively playing. In fact, they burn fewer calories when watching television than they would if they were doing *nothing.* One study found that when children are "glued to the tube," they fall into a deeply relaxed state, akin to semiconsciousness, that lowers their metabolism below its normal at-rest rate—on average, 12 percent lower in children of normal weight and 16 percent lower in obese children (Klesges, 1993). Further, 60 percent of the commercials shown during Saturday morning cartoons on U.S. television are for food products—almost all of them with high fat and sugar content. The foods are usually shown being consumed by slim children who seem to be having a wonderful time because of what they are eating (Ogletree et al., 1990).

- *Cultural attitudes.* In some cultures, overeating is a sign of wealth and happiness, so parents urge their offspring to have a second helping. The implied message seems to

All in the Family Partly because of heredity and partly because of cultural and behavioral factors, overweight and obesity tend to run in families. This boy's chubbiness may be the result of eating behaviors learned from his parents.

be that a father's love is measured by how much food he can provide; a mother's love, by how well she can cook; and a child's love, by how much he or she can eat. This attitude is especially evident in families whose parents or grandparents grew up in places where starvation was a real possibility; the cultural values that once protected against death have now become a cause of disease.

- *Precipitating event.* For many children, obesity begins with a critical event or traumatic experience—a hospitalization, a move to a new neighborhood, a parental divorce or death. Generally, such an event or experience creates a sense of loss or diminished self-image, along with a corresponding need for an alternative source of gratification. When the new source of gratification is food, obesity can result (Neumann, 1983).

What is a parent to do? It is a mistake to use ultimatums ("You can't play until you eat your broccoli") or bribes ("Eat all your spinach and you can have dessert") or critiques ("You're getting fat"). Those strategies usually backfire, reinforcing the child's dislike of healthy foods, enhancing the attractiveness of sweets, or making the child crave the solace of food.

It is also a mistake to put children on a crash diet, because they become irritable and, ironically, fatter. Why? Centuries ago, humans developed an automatic, physiologi-

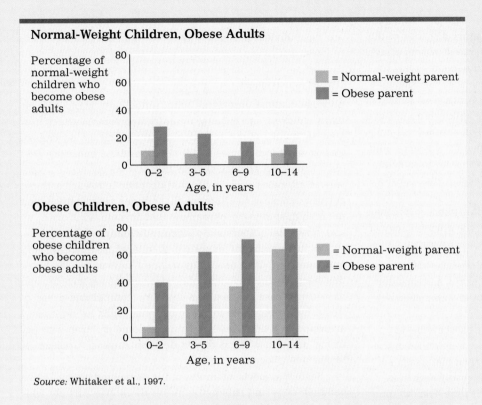

Normal-Weight Children, Obese Adults

Percentage of normal-weight children who become obese adults

= Normal-weight parent
= Obese parent

Age, in years

Obese Children, Obese Adults

Percentage of obese children who become obese adults

= Normal-weight parent
= Obese parent

Age, in years

Source: Whitaker et al., 1997.

Figure 11.2 A Reason to Slim Down. As you can see, a child's chance of becoming an obese adult is increased by having an obese parent. By middle childhood, however, the child's own obesity is a better predictor. Of normal-weight 10-year-olds, less than 15 percent become obese adults—whether or not their parents are obese. But of obese 10-year-olds, most remain obese as adults, with parental obesity making only a small difference (64 percent compared to 80 percent).

cal defense against starvation. Specifically, in periods of "famine," metabolism slows down to enable the body to maintain its weight with fewer calories. Thus, after rapid initial weight loss, additional pounds become more difficult to lose (Wing, 1992), and a few days of overeating quickly produces fat. This is one reason crash diets are inadvisable; they don't work. The other is that, in childhood, severe reduction of basic nourishment can hinder important brain and bone growth.

The best way to get obese children to slim down is to increase their physical activity (Dietz, 1995). However, since overweight children tend to move more slowly and awkwardly than other children, obese children are not often selected for teams, invited to join backyard games, or inclined to exercise on their own. Adults can encourage children to engage in exercise in which size is no disadvantage, such as walking to school, bicycling, and swimming. Parents can also exercise with their children to provide a good model, bolster the children's self-confidence, and make physical exercise more enjoyable. In fact, one of the strongest influences on

childhood weight is the parents' own exercise habits, whether a parent exercises alone or with the child (Ross et al., 1987).

Proper health habits can counter even the genetic tendency toward obesity. As Figure 11.2 indicates, among normal-weight children under age 3, the risk of becoming an obese adult is about 30 percent for those with an obese parent but only about 10 percent for those with normal-weight parents—strong evidence of heredity. However, by age 10, the child's own weight is much more critical than his or her genes (Whitaker et al., 1997). This seems to indicate that a child's biological inclination may be to overeat, but if the family can rechannel that urge until at least age 10, the child has a good chance of becoming a normal-weight adult. Given the culture, this is difficult to achieve, because few adults see chubbiness as a warning sign of serious disease that can be prevented. Given the burden on the overweight child, it is worth the work.

ASTHMA ON THE RISE

Asthma, defined as a "chronic inflammatory disorder of the airways," affects between 10 and 20 percent of school-age children. For almost half the children, it becomes less troubling by late adolescence (Clark & Rees, 1996). Simply waiting for the problem to recede with age is not a wise strategy, however. For one thing, some asthmatic children do not get better with time, and a few even die. For another, all children with asthma miss a significant amount of school, and study after study has shown that children who miss school for illness or any other reason between ages 6 and 10 fall behind.

The origin of asthma is genetic—but, like every other characteristic, not solely genetic. In fact, the epidemiology of asthma suggests that environmental factors are crucial.

- The rate of asthma has at least doubled since 1980 in virtually every developed nation in the world, a far greater increase than can be accounted for by any change in the gene pool.
- Asthma patients tend to be those least susceptible to other childhood diseases. Children who are onlies or the oldest in their families, who have not had many serious childhood infections, and who live relatively easy lives are also the children most likely to visit the hospital time after time with asthma attacks (Cookson & Moffatt, 1997; Matricardi et al., 2000).
- Asthma is at least 10 times more common in the urban areas of developed nations than in the rural areas of developing nations. It was rare in any nation 100 years

asthma A disorder characterized by chronic inflammation of the airways.

ago. Obviously, something contextual, not genetic, is the reason.

Causes and Triggers

Because asthma interferes with school attendance for so many children, and because an untreated asthma attack may lead to death, many researchers are studying its causes. Genes on chromosomes 2, 11, 12, 13, and 21; infections that once protected against asthma but now rarely occur; exposure to allergens early in life that predispose toward asthma; current exposure to allergens that trigger attacks (including pet hair, dust mites, cockroaches, and air pollution); exercise; and emotional outbursts are among the many causes.

Actually, current exposure to allergens, exercise, and emotional outbursts are really triggers, not causes. We know this because the heavily polluted areas of eastern Europe have fewer cases of asthma than the comparable areas of western Europe, some forms of exercise (such as swimming) are actually good for asthmatics, and some children with extreme emotional stress never develop asthma (Cookson & Moffat, 1997; Vogel, 1997).

Several aspects of modern life—carpeted floors, more bedding, dogs and cats living inside the house, airtight windows, less outdoor play for children, and urbanization, which crowds people together in buildings where cockroaches multiply—all increase the risk (Carpenter, 1999). The last of these may be the worst. Not all asthmatic children are sensitive to cockroach particles in dust, but those who are, and who are exposed to them, are more likely to wake up in the middle of the night, go to the hospital, and miss school than are asth-

---

❶ Response for Parents (from page 302):
Unless they slim down, chubby, happy 6-year-olds tend to become unhappy 10-year-olds and unhealthy adults, so you should not simply let nature take its course. However, imposing a diet is probably not the best solution. Better would be to change the entire family's eating habits and begin regular exercise for both you and your 6-year-old.

basic curriculum, mean that any impediment can become a notable educational handicap. Prevention of such problems should be a major concern of every educator: Every absence from school is a signal that help is needed now (see the Changing Policy box).

SKILL DEVELOPMENT

At least partly because children grow slowly during middle childhood, many become quite skilled at controlling their own bodies. This is in contrast to the sudden changes in body shape and size that occur during toddlerhood and puberty, which are typically accompanied by an obvi-

Already Too Late A nurse uses an inhaler to open a young asthma patient's airways. Such hospital care is tertiary prevention, which will avoid even more serious consequences; but it represents a failure of primary and secondary prevention.

matic children who are allergic, and exposed, to such other substances as pet hair or dust mites.

Medical and Ecological Treatments

Let us apply the lessons of prevention learned at the end of Chapter 8 to asthma. Medical measures now treat acute asthma fairly effectively, either controlling asthma before it gets past the nighttime coughing and occasional wheezing stage or relieving serious attacks when they occur (Vogel, 1997). This is *tertiary prevention*.

However, from a developmental point of view, the medical focus is too narrow and too late, because it ignores the overall ecological setting and the earliest symptoms. Asthma begins when a certain level of sensitivity is reached, so a parent who notices a young child coughing at night could determine whether this is an early warning. If so, it is already time to rid the house of animals, rugs, down comforters, and dust, as well as get the child to play outside more often. These *secondary prevention* measures may forestall or delay the increase in the level of sensitivity that makes a child vulnerable to a full-scale attack.

Primary prevention could begin even sooner than that, undertaken by the entire community before the first symptoms appear. Fresh air could circulate in schools and homes, pollution could be decreased, cockroaches could be eradicated, and safe outdoor play spaces could be maintained. These measures would make life and health better for every school-age child and would particularly protect children vulnerable to asthma.

Such a shift in practice will occur only if more people become aware of the consequences and the causes of asthma. It is a disabling, sometimes lethal, disease. Architects, city planners, parents, and political leaders share the responsibility for the increase in its prevalence and for taking steps to prevent serious harm.

ous clumsiness. School-age children can master almost any basic skill, as long as it doesn't require too much strength or split-second judgment of speed and distance.

Motor Skills

The maxim "Practice makes perfect" does not always hold true. Every motor skill involves several abilities, some requiring practice alone (for those, practice *does* lead to mastery), others requiring a certain body size, brain maturation, or inherited talent—as well as practice—to be perfected. For instance, **reaction time,** the length of time it takes a person to respond to a particular stimulus, is a component of several

reaction time The time it takes to respond to a particular stimulus.

athletic skills, but quick reactions require brain maturation that is attained only with adolescence. Hand–eye coordination, balance, and judgment of movement (including time, distance, and trajectory) are other key abilities that are still developing during the school years, and thus 12-year-olds are better than 9-year-olds who are better than 6-year-olds in all of these. Beginning at about age 20, reaction time slows down again, so that older adults (aged 60–81) are about as quick as 8-year-olds (Williams et al., 1999).

Gender Boys and girls are just about equal in their physical abilities during the school years, although boys tend to have greater upper-arm strength and girls to have greater overall flexibility. Consequently, boys have the advantage in sports such as baseball, whereas girls have the edge in sports such as gymnastics. However, for most physical activities during middle childhood, biological sex differences are minimal: Boys can do cartwheels, and girls can hit home runs. Usually they don't—not because they are unable to do so, but because the social setting discourages them from doing so.

Expertise in many areas, athletic prowess among them, depends primarily on three elements: motivation, guidance, and many hours of practice. These three are rarely equal for both sexes in any particular area.

Culture National policy also affects motor-skill development. For example, the average schoolchild in France or Switzerland gets 3 hours a week of physical education, compared to 1½ hours for a child in the United States and only 1 hour for a child in England or Ireland. During such classes, or during recess, boys tend to be much more active than girls (Armstrong & Welsman, 1997). Japan requires physical activity for all schoolchildren, boys and girls. Most Japanese schools are well equipped with gyms and fields, and 75 percent also have swimming pools.

Unfortunately, many sports that North American adults value (and often push their children into) demand precisely those skills that are hardest for children. Softball and baseball, for example, are

Mastery of Motor Skills The impressive gross motor skills of school-age children are well illustrated in these two photos: Many adults could neither climb a rope nor clap in quick rhythm. What is not clear from these photos is that whatever notable gender gaps there may be in motor ability usually arise from influences in the social context.

Boys are admired for taking risks, so they practice climbing, not just up ropes high above the gym floor but up trees, cliffs, and almost anything else that offers a challenge and a bit of danger. Girls are encouraged to be verbal and cooperative, so they develop more sedentary group games involving clapping, chanting, passing objects from hand to hand, and the like.

❓ *Observational Quiz (see answer page 310): What sex differences and similarities do you see, and how do you explain them?*

Soccer for 8-Year-Olds Many children around the world play soccer, with some nations much more involved than others.
❷ *Observational Quiz (see answer page 312): What nation is this?*

difficult, because throwing, catching, and batting all involve more distance judgment, better hand–eye coordination, and shorter reaction time than many elementary school children possess. Younger children are therefore apt to drop the ball even if it lands in their mitts, since they are slow to enclose the ball once it lands. They are similarly likely to strike out, because they swing too late to hit a pitched ball.

Genetics Hereditary differences also can be pivotal. Some children, no matter how hard they try, never can throw or kick a ball with as much strength and accuracy as others—a fact that parents, teachers, coaches, and teammates sometimes forget. Sports programs need to include everyone, talented or not. Whether the "program" is part of a school curriculum, or a children's sports league, or simply a group of neighborhood children playing together, it should provide fun and activity for all, boys and girls, fat and thin, gifted and clumsy (Armstrong & Welsman, 1997). Programs are counterproductive when they:

- Are too competitive (especially if less skilled children continually sit on the sidelines)
- Foster disparaging comparisons (as when skillful children laugh at another's clumsiness)
- Lack excitement (substantial time spent waiting, resting, or repeating the same routine)

The same is true for fine motor skills. Some children naturally write more neatly than others, and these are the children who are more likely to practice their penmanship, refining the curve of the "s" or the slant of the "t," for instance. Adults need to provide extra motivation and time for the children with less natural skill. This may be particularly true for left-handed children, for whom writing a right-handed language such as English runs against the natural direction of their

❶ **Response for Health Professionals (from page 303):** Since the rate of asthma is so much higher in modern cities than it was anywhere a few decades ago, genetics is not the only cause. Every parent of a young child should be counseled on the benefits of fresh air, lung-strengthening exercise, and dust- and cockroach-free homes. If a child comes from an allergic or asthmatic family, or has early episodes of night coughing or wheezing, preventive measures include ridding the home of down pillows, carpets, curtains, and cats.

Figure 11.3 Write It Right.

Left-handed children naturally draw from right to left and clockwise, a preference apparent in their early scribbles with crayons as well as their first attempts to write words. This natural inclination requires some readjustment not only when they need to read from left to right but even when they learn to form their letters, since most languages are biased against them (Hebrew is the only major language that is written from right to left, with books starting at the "back" and pages turned toward the "front"). Look at the alphabet in capital letters, as a left-handed and right-handed child would be inclined to draw them:

Right: A B C D E F G H I L K L M N O P Q R S T U V W X Y Z

Left: Z Y X W V U T S R Q P O N M L X L I H G F E D C B A

All children naturally draw the dominant line from top to bottom, but then right-handed children put the "add-ons" to the right and begin their curves counter-clockwise—which gets them into trouble only once, with the rarely used "J." Left-handed children's directional sense makes them write 12 letters wrong, until they work against nature to do it "right." Incidentally, why is right called *right*? Are some children *left* back or *left* out or *left* over?

❶ *Answer to Observational Quiz (from page 308):* *Differences are that boys are slightly advantaged in upper-arm strength, and girls in quick rhythmic reactions—assets that these children have developed into skills. As for similarities, the children are all enjoying the activity they are engaging in.*

❷ **Especially for Social Workers:** What would you do if a child who had an IQ of 65 was referred to you?

achievement tests   Tests designed to measure how much a person has learned in a specific subject area.

aptitude tests   Tests designed to measure potential, rather than actual, accomplishment.

IQ tests   Aptitude tests designed to measure a person's intelligence (which was originally defined as mental age divided by chronological age, times 100—hence, intelligence quotient, or IQ). (See below)
An example
Actual age of three children: 12, 12, 12
Mental ages of the three: 15, 12, 8
IQ of each of these three:
$15/12 = 1.25 \times 100 = 125$ (superior)
$12/12 = 1 \times 100 = 100$ (average)
$8/12 = .75 \times 100 = 75$ (slow learner)

hands and brains. (See Figure 11.3.) Patience at teaching, rather than forced hand-switching or competitive ranking, seems to be the best strategy.

A child's motor habits, especially in coordinating both sides of the body and performing complex tasks, benefit from repeated connections formed in the brain because the corpus callosum between the brain's hemispheres continues to mature during middle childhood (Banich, 1998). According to research on lower animals, brain development is further advanced through play, especially the active, erratic, rough-and-tumble frolicking that many children love (see Chapter 10). Indeed, one expert believes that such play particularly helps boys overcome their tendencies toward hyperactivity and learning disabilities, because it helps with regulation in the frontal lobes of the brain (Panksepp, 1998). Whether or not that is true, it is apparent that children's impulse toward active play should be guided, perhaps, but not repressed.

Intellectual Skills

Children's brains develop as rapidly as their bodies during the school years. As you might expect, then, intellectual skills are mastered through motivation, guidance, and practice in much the same way that motor skills are. Genetics, gender, and culture all play roles in a child's intellectual progress.

In infancy and early childhood, maturation of the brain is indicated by measures of motor abilities, such as reflexes at birth, walking by age 1, and holding a pencil and making a mark by age 6. During the school years, brain development is usually measured with aptitude tests that focus on language use, reasoning ability, and memory. These are all measures of **achievement,** defined as what the child has actually learned. The underlying idea, however, is that achievement can be separated from **aptitude,** or innate potential for learning.

During childhood, the most commonly used aptitude tests are *intelligence tests,* often called **IQ tests** (*IQ* being an abbreviation for "intelligence quotient"). Originally, a score on an IQ test was actually calculated as a quotient—the child's mental age (that is, the age at

Performance IQ This puzzle, part of a performance subtest on the Wechsler IQ test, seems simple until you try to do it. Actually the limbs are difficult to align correctly and time is of the essence, with a bonus for speed and failure after a minute and a half. However, this boy has at least one advantage over most African American boys who are tested. Especially during middle childhood, boys tend to do better when their examiner is of the same sex and race.

which most children attain the score that this particular child did) divided by the child's chronological age, times 100. The calculation currently used to determine IQ scores is more complex than the original formula and is designed to ensure that the score variation follows the bell curve (see Figure 11.4), but the underlying concept is the same.

Two highly regarded IQ tests are the *Stanford-Binet* and *Wechsler* intelligence scales. Both measure general knowledge, reasoning ability, mathematical skill, memory, vocabulary, and spatial perception (see Figure 11.5). Both tests are administered orally by a trained examiner to an individual. Many school systems also use paper-and-pencil aptitude tests, given to groups of students, but these are less accurate.

IQ tests are quite reliable in predicting school achievement (Neisser et al., 1996). When there is a mismatch between IQ score and achievement, something is amiss in the child, the home, or the school. A 2-year discrepancy between aptitude and achievement is the usual indicator of a learning disability.

Problems with IQ Tests

Using a single test score to designate a child's level of intelligence seems contrary to our knowledge that children develop at different rates, depending on their genes, family, school, and culture. Thus, IQ scores should be used with caution: They are only black-and-white snapshots of a rapidly moving, multicolored subject.

Further, it is impossible to measure potential without also measuring achievement. Scores on IQ tests reflect knowledge of vocabulary, understanding of basic math, and familiarity with cultural ideas and artifacts—all of which are learned, not innate. Performance on an IQ test also reflects the ability to pay attention

---

Questions Similar to Those on the WISC

Half of the items on the WISC are designed to measure five aspects of *verbal intelligence*:

- Knowledge ("How many thumbs do you have?")
- Reasoning ("How are an elephant and a whale alike?")
- Arithmetic ("If a train traveling at 32 miles per hour takes 3 days to get from one place to another, how fast must a train go to travel the same distance in half a day?")
- Vocabulary ("What is a stanza?")
- Memory ("Say these numbers backward: 8, 6, 3, 7, 1, 9.")

The other half includes various tasks that assess performance intelligence, such as putting together a puzzle, organizing pictures into a sequence that tells a story, and arranging colored blocks to match a specific design.

Figure 11.5 The Wechsler Intelligence Scale for Children.

Figure 11.4 In Theory, Most People Are Average. IQ scores between 85 and 115 are considered average, and almost 70 percent of the scores fall in that range. Note, however, that this is a norm-referenced test. In fact, actual IQ scores have risen in many nations; 100 is no longer exactly the midpoint. Further, in practice, scores below 50 are slightly more frequent than indicated by the normal curve shown here, because severe retardation is the result, not of the normal distribution, but of genetic and prenatal causes.

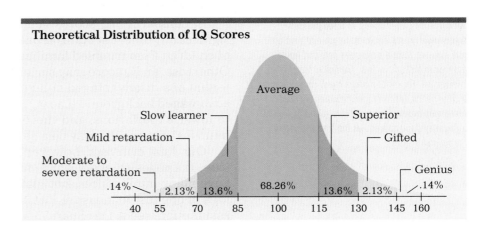

Theoretical Distribution of IQ Scores

Average

Slow learner · Superior

Mild retardation · Gifted

Moderate to severe retardation · Genius

.14% · 2.13% · 13.6% · 68.26% · 13.6% · 2.13% · .14%

40 55 70 85 100 115 130 145 160

MULTIPLE INTELLIGENCES

A number of researchers stress that there are many kinds of abilities and many ways to demonstrate potential. Robert Sternberg (1996) describes three distinct types of intelligence: *academic* (measured by IQ and achievement tests), *creative* (evidenced by imaginative endeavors), and *practical* (seen in everyday interactions). In the usual academic test setting, according to Sternberg, the highly creative or practical child not only might fail to shine but might also become stressed and distracted.

Similarly, Howard Gardner (1983) described seven (and, later, eight) distinct intelligences: linguistic, logical-mathematical, musical, spatial, body-kinesthetic, interpersonal (social-understanding), and intrapersonal (self-understanding). Gardner believes that every normal person has at least a basic aptitude for all seven, but each of us is stronger in some than in others. For example, a person may be an able writer because of strong linguistic intelligence but may get lost easily when driving a car because spatial intelligence is fairly weak. Another person may paint extraordinarily revealing portraits because his or her spatial, body-kinesthetic, and social-understanding intelligences are strong but may have difficulty talking about the creative process owing to weaker linguistic and self-understanding intelligences. If there are indeed many kinds of intelligence, the common assumption that children who are gifted in one area are gifted in all areas is likely to be false (Winner, 1996).

When aptitude tests measure only linguistic and logical-mathematical ability, scores do not reflect the actual potential or skills that children possess. Note that schools traditionally emphasize language and math, and this may explain why traditional IQ tests predict school success fairly accurately. However, such validation is circular. If intelligence is seen as the multifaceted jewel that Gardner believes it to be, schools will need to develop a broader curriculum so that every child can shine (Gardner, 1993).

Recently, Gardner added an eighth kind of intelligence, which he called *naturalistic*, the ability to understand the varieties of life in the natural world and to use that understanding (as in biology, zoology, or even farming) (Torff & Gardner, 1999). This eighth kind of intelligence was added because some people seem to have a gift for it, and some cultures (more often in Africa than in North America) seem to encourage it.

Indeed, it now seems that children and adults have a wide variety of talents, abilities, and learning styles, all related to

Gardner's Intelligences
- Linguistic
- Logical-Mathematical
- Musical
- Spatial
- Body-Kinesthetic
- Interpersonal (social-understanding)
- Intrapersonal (self-understanding)
- Naturalistic

❶ *Answer to Observational Quiz (from page 309):* Surprise – it's the United States. Soccer evokes life-and-death national passions in many nations, but not in the United States, so if you guessed Argentina or France, for instance, you had good reason. However, there are two clues here that would have led to the right answer. The first is the girls' involvement. For sports that are highly competitive in a given nation, teams of young children are usually segregated by sex. The second clue—hard to spot but a giveaway if you noticed—is the map of Texas on the children's jerseys.

and concentrate, to express thoughts verbally, and to ask questions if the instructions are unclear. In addition, a child's performance can be affected by emotional stress, illness, test-taking anxiety, and similar factors.

In comparing IQ scores—especially the scores of individuals from significantly different cultural backgrounds—or in evaluating the scores of children from troubled families, all these factors must be considered. Otherwise, an IQ score may seriously underestimate the intellectual potential of a disadvantaged child or overestimate that of a child from an advantaged background (Laosa, 1996). Especially when a low score leads to lower expectations, and therefore inferior education (as sometimes happens), the results may be a self-fulfilling prophecy (Rosenthal, 1996).

Our final criticism, however, is even more devastating, because if true, it applies to every child, from retarded to genius. Humans may have many intelligences, not just one, which would mean that the very idea of one test to measure intelligence is based on a false, and narrow, assumption (see A Life-Span View).

A Demonstration of High IQ? If North American intelligence tests truly reflected all the aspects of the mind, children would be considered mentally slow if they could not replicate the proper hand, arm, torso, and facial positions of a traditional dance, as this young Indonesian girl does brilliantly. She is obviously adept in body-kinesthetic and interpersonal intelligence. Given her culture, it would not be surprising if she were deficient in the logical-mathematical intelligence required to use the Internet effectively or to surpass an American peer's performance on a video game.

genes, personality, and culture. With "new theories of intelligence . . . researchers can begin to acquire deeper insight into how and why some children develop to the best of their potential while, sadly, others do not" (Ferrari & Sternberg, 1998).

The implications of multiple intelligences extend far beyond the school years. Adult intelligence tests—the SAT (Scholastic Aptitude Test), GRE (Graduate Record Exam), and WAIS (Wechsler Adult Intelligence Scale)—are based primarily on verbal and mathematical abilities, so adults who are gifted in areas other than these may seem to be deficient. A good business manager, teacher, or parent must have strong interpersonal intelligence—a quality that is not measured at all by adult intelligence tests. Similarly the star athlete, the gifted musician, or the street-savvy community leader may appear quite stupid by conventional measures. As you will see later in this book, many adult abilities are overlooked by IQ tests designed for schoolchildren. Keep this expanded perspective in mind when interpreting IQ scores of average, gifted, and disabled children.

CHILDREN WITH SPECIAL NEEDS

All parents watch with pride and satisfaction as their offspring become smarter, taller, and more skilled. For many parents, however, these feelings mingle with worry and uncertainty when their children manifest unexpected difficulties in one area of development or another. Although the origin of many problems is biological, the observable symptoms are often more psychological and cognitive than physical, and thus more apparent in the classroom or on the playground (when a child is compared to others the same age) than at home or in the pediatrician's office.

child with special needs A child for whom learning new skills and developing friendships are hampered by a psychological or physical disorder.

If the problem is sufficiently severe, this may be a **child with special needs,** defined as a child who requires particular accommodations (physical, intellectual, or social) in order to learn. For these children, the development of new skills, closer friendships, and more mature ways of thinking is impaired by psychological disorders and symptoms—including aggression, anxiety, autism, conduct disorder, depression, developmental delay, hyperactivity, learning disabilities, mutism, and mental slowness—or as a direct consequence of physical disabilities such as blindness, deafness, or paralysis.

Developmental Psychopathology

developmental psychopathology A field of psychology that applies the insights from studies of normal development to the study and treatment of childhood disorders.

In recent years, psychologists who study childhood disorders have joined with psychologists who study normal development to create the new field of **developmental psychopathology.** In developmental psychopathology, knowledge about normal development is applied to the study and treatment of psychological disorders.

Developmental psychopathology is practical as well as scholarly, because

> An ongoing goal of developmental psychopathology has been to become a science that not only bridges fields of study and aids in the discovery of important new truths about the processes underlying adaptation and maladaptation across the life span, but also to provide the best means of preventing and ameliorating maladaptive and pathological outcomes. [Cicchetti & Toth, 1998]

Research from this perspective has already provided four developmental lessons:

1. *Abnormality is normal.* The distinction between normal and abnormal can become quite blurred and even disappear. Most children sometimes act in ways that are decidedly unusual, and most children with serious disorders are, in many respects, quite normal. If we ignore this complexity, we may "seriously distort the variability of development" for all children (Fischer et al., 1997). Children with psychological disorders should be viewed as children first—with the many developmental needs that all children share—and only secondarily as children with special challenges.

2. *Disability changes over time.* The behaviors associated with almost any special problem change as the person grows older. A child who seems severely handicapped by a disability at one stage of development may seem much less handicapped at the next stage, or vice versa (Sigman & Rustein, 1998). Such changes are not simply due to the passage of time; they result from the interplay of developmental changes within the individual, treatment regimens, and forces in the ecological setting (Berkson, 1993; Eyberg et al., 1998).

3. *Adulthood can be better or worse.* Many children with seemingly serious disabilities, from blindness to mental retardation, become happy and productive adults once they find a vocational setting in which they can perform well. Conversely, any disability that makes a child unusually aggressive and socially inept becomes more serious during adolescence and adulthood, when physical maturity and social demands make self-control and social interaction particularly important (Davidson et al., 1994; Lahey & Loeber, 1994).

DSM-IV The fourth edition of the *Diagnostic and Statistical Manual of Mental Disorders,* developed by the American Psychiatric Association, which describes and distinguishes the symptoms of various emotional and behavioral disorders.

4. *Diagnosis depends on the social context.* The social context must be considered as part of the diagnosis. The official fourth edition of the diagnostic guide of the American Psychiatric Association, the ***Diagnostic and Statistical Manual of Mental Disorders,*** or **DSM-IV,** now recognizes that the "nuances of an individual's cultural frame of reference" need to be understood before any disorder can be diagnosed (American Psychiatric Association, 1994). Nonetheless, according to

many researchers, DSM-IV does not go far enough in this direction, because disorders may not reside "inside the skin of an individual" but "between the individual and the environment" (Jensen & Hoagwood, 1997).

Because the disorders that developmental psychopathologists study are too great in number to discuss here, we will focus on only three: autism, learning disabilities, and attention-deficit hyperactivity disorder. Each originates in the biosocial domain, and each is a typical example of many disorders. By applying our knowledge of these three, we can begin to understand the development of all children, no matter what special needs they might have.

Autism

autism   A disorder characterized by an inability or unwillingness to communicate with others, poor social skills, and diminished imagination.

One of the most severe disturbances of childhood is called **autism.** According to American physician Leo Kanner (1943), an autistic child has an "inability to relate in an ordinary way to people . . . an extreme aloneness that, whenever possible, disregards, ignores, shuts out anything that comes to the child from the outside." Kanner's choice of terminology was apt. "Auto-" means "self," and autistic individuals seem unusually restricted by their own perspective, by their need for predictable routines, and by their inability to learn normal speech or to form normal human relationships. This severe form of the disorder is quite rare; it occurs in about 1 of every 2,000 children, according to DSM-IV (American Psychiatric Association, 1994).

However, the first lesson from the developmental psychopathological perspective is to look for the similarities between people diagnosed as "abnormal" (in this case, as autistic) and people considered "normal." Many children have less severe autistic symptoms. They are sometimes diagnosed as *high-functioning autistic,* or as having **Asperger syndrome,** still self-absorbed but sometimes quite intelligent and verbal (Prior et al., 1998).

Asperger syndrome   A disorder in which a person masters verbal communication (sometimes very well) but has unusual difficulty with social perceptions and skills. (Also called *high-functioning autism.*)

When the entire spectrum of autistic disorders is taken into account, as many as 1 child in 100 shows autistic traits (Szatmari, 1992). Both the severe and the less severe instances of the disorder are at least twice as common in boys as in girls. Indeed, one careful study done in Sweden found the ratio was six to one. There is no doubt that autism is multifactorial and that genes are one of the factors. No matter what the causes are, boys are more likely to suffer the consequences than girls (Bailey et al., 1998; Rutter et al., 1997).

The Early Developmental Path of Autism

Autism is truly a *developmental* disorder (as "lesson" 2, above, emphasizes), because its manifestations change markedly with age. As babies, many autistic children seem quite normal and sometimes unusually "good" (that is, undemanding), although they are often hypersensitive to stimulation, and the way they roll over, sit up, crawl, and walk may be less coordinated than the norm (Teitelbaum et al., 1998). Soon, however, severe deficiencies appear in three areas:

- Communication ability
- Social skills
- Imaginative play

Deficiencies in the first two areas become apparent at age 1 or 2, as autistic children lack spoken language or normal responses to others. Without social awareness, they have "difficulties in understanding the

● Response for Social Workers (from page 310): You would realize that this low score is in the mentally retarded range and that the child might need special education in school and special help at home. But before you would act on your knowledge, you would find out if anything (illness, abuse, anxiety, language barriers) might have interfered with the child's best performance on the test. Even if none of these factors was evident, you would still have the child retested by a conscientious trained examiner with a background similar to the child's.

signs and signals" of human communication, and thus lose out on many opportunities to learn, despite their high IQs (Leekam et al., 2000). During the preschool years, many autistic children continue to be mute, not talking at all, while others engage exclusively in a type of speech called *echolalia,* in which they repeat, word for word, such things as advertising jingles or questions that are put to them. "Good morning, John" is echoed with "Good morning, John." Autistic preschoolers also avoid eye contact with others and prefer to be by themselves.

Also during the preschool years, the third deficit, in play, suddenly becomes obvious, because most normal children at this age are quite playful. Autistic preschoolers avoid spontaneous imaginative interaction with peers, such as the rough-and-tumble play and sociodramatic play described in Chapter 10. Instead, they engage in repetitive movements (such as spinning a top over and over) or compulsive play (assembling a puzzle in a particular order time after time). One autistic adult remembers her childhood in the following manner:

> When left alone, I would often space out and become hypnotized. I could sit for hours on the beach watching sand dribbling through my fingers. I'd study each individual grain of sand as it flowed between my fingers. Each grain was different, and I was like a scientist studying the grains under a microscope. As I scrutinized their shapes and contours, I went into a trance which cut me off from the sights and sounds around me.
>
> Rocking and spinning were other ways to shut out the world when I became overloaded with too much noise. Rocking made me feel calm. It was like taking an addictive drug. The more I did it, the more I wanted to do it. My mother and my teachers would stop me so I would get back in touch with the rest of the world. I also loved to spin, and I seldom got dizzy. When I stopped spinning, I enjoyed the sensation of watching the room spin. [Grandin, 1996]

This woman developed verbal skills beyond that of most autistic children, in part because of unusual support from the parents and teachers and, later, medication and therapy. However, even as a successful professional, she was still puzzled by the normal give-and-take of human emotions, describing herself as like an "anthropologist on Mars," bewildered by the customs she observed (Sacks, 1995).

Autism in Later Childhood and Beyond

Deficiencies in communication, social skills, and play remain pronounced from the preschool years on, but in childhood and adolescence the lack of social understanding often proves to be the most devastating because human relationships are the usual path toward learning and self-concept. Autistic children appear to lack a theory of mind—an awareness of the thoughts, feelings, and intentions of other people (Holroyd & Baron-Cohen, 1993; Ziatas et al., 1998). People seem of no greater interest than objects, because these children develop no theories about the internal processes that make people unique and provocative.

Unaffected by the opinions of others, autistic children also lack emotional regulation. Many seem cold, aloof, and uninvolved until something triggers an outburst of laughter or, worse, fury. Then other people are frustrated and bewildered, surprised by the unexpected explosion and unable to respond in a way that satisfies the child, because they do not know what triggered the behavior in the first place.

Hope for Autism The prime prerequisite in breaking through the language barrier in a nonverbal autistic child, such as this 4-year-old, is to get the child to pay attention to another person's speech. Note that this teacher is sitting in a low chair to facilitate eye contact and is getting the child to focus on her mouth movements—a matter of little interest to most children but intriguing to many autistic ones. Sadly, even such efforts were not enough: at age 13 this child was still mute.

As children with autism grow older, their symptoms vary widely. Most score in the mentally retarded range on intelligence tests, but a closer look at their intellectual performance shows isolated areas of remarkable skill (such as memory for numbers or for putting together puzzles). In general, their strongest cognitive skills are in abstract reasoning; their weakest, in social cognition (Scott & Baron-Cohen, 1996). For example, on a trip to the grocery store, a child might be able to calculate that each apple in a bag of a dozen costs exactly 10½ cents but might not understand why certain shoppers refuse to buy such a bargain.

Some autistic children never speak or have only minimal verbal ability, but many who are diagnosed as autistic at age 2 or 3 learn to express themselves in language by age 6. They may demonstrate exceptional academic skills during the school years, eventually becoming self-supporting adults, although less imaginative and communicative and more ritualistic and socially isolated than most people.

Occasionally, Asperger individuals may be quite successful (as lesson 3, that remarkable success or failure can occur in adulthood, suggests), especially in professions in which their attention to routine, concentration on detail, and relative indifference to sentiment are an asset (Schopler et al., 1999). One study of individuals with Asperger traits found a dentist, a financial lawyer, a military historian, and a university professor among them (Gillberg, 1991). Temple Grandin, quoted above remembering the flow of sand, is an international expert in the design of humane slaughtering facilities for animals. Her ability to analyze the process from the animal's perspective makes her able to reduce pain and panic for cows, sheep, and pigs (Grandin, 1995).

Learning Disabilities

Children vary a great deal in how quickly and how well they learn to read, to write, and to do arithmetic. Among those who have obvious difficulty, some seem slow in almost every aspect of intellectual development. Their thinking is like that of a much younger child—sometimes several years younger than their actual age. These children are considered to suffer **mental retardation,** that is, a notable delay in their overall cognitive development, with an IQ test score of 70 or below. Some of these children eventually catch up to normal levels, in which case they are said to have experienced a *pervasive developmental delay*.

Other children are slow learners only in certain areas. They show remarkable "scatter" in their abilities, and they are generally quite competent except in particular skills. Such a child is said to have a **learning disability,** that is, a failing in a specific cognitive skill that is not due to overall intellectual slowness, to a physical handicap such as hearing loss, to severely stressful living conditions, or to a lack of basic education (Silver, 1991). As you can see, the diagnosis of learning disability is based on *disparity* and *exclusion*. First, there must be a disparity, or surprising difference, between expected performance on a given skill (based on age and intelligence) and actual performance; second, all the obvious reasons (such as abuse, inadequate teachers, or biological disability) must be excluded, or ruled out. This again illustrates lesson 4, that the social context must be considered before the diagnosis is made.

The most commonly diagnosed learning disability is **dyslexia,** unusual difficulty with reading. Dyslexic children seem bright and happy

mental retardation Slow learning in all, or almost all, intellectual abilities. The degree of retardation is usually measured by an intelligence test. In young children, mental retardation is often called *pervasive developmental delay* to allow for the possibility that the child will catch up to normal, age-appropriate development.

learning disability Difficulty in mastering a specific cognitive skill that is *not* attributable to intellectual slowness, obvious impairment of the senses, lack of education, or family dysfunction.

dyslexia A specific learning disability involving unusual difficulty with reading.

The Joy of Books These third-graders are fortunate: They all seem to know how to read, and their classroom includes many books and this wonderful reading tent, where they can take off their shoes and relax with a book of their choice. Probably a teacher who provides such individualized opportunities for readers is also sensitive to the special needs of the dyslexic for intense, one-on-one training in specific skills.

dyscalcula A specific learning disability involving unusual difficulty with math.

Figure 11.6 Reading and Comprehension. In this study, three groups of children were compared, all reading at the third-grade level. The children in one group were dyslexic, and they were age 11, on average. The children in the other two groups were 8 years old, but half of them were normal readers and the other half had problems with reading comprehension. As you can see, the ability of the groups to pronounce a nonword (letters combined to make a possible word that does not mean anything, such as "wug" or "tedork") or to comprehend a passage read to them differed markedly. Each group would require a different pattern of reading instruction.

in the early years of school, volunteering answers to sometimes difficult questions, diligently completing their worksheets, sitting quietly and looking at their books in class. However, as time goes on, it becomes clear that they are reading only with great difficulty or not at all. They guess at even simple words (occasionally making surprising mistakes) and explain what they have just "read" by talking about the pictures. In fact, one of the signs of dyslexia is a child who is advanced in comprehension through the use of contextual clues and behind in ability to match letters to sounds (Nation & Snowling, 1998). (See Figure 11.6.)

Another fairly common learning disability is **dyscalcula,** difficulty with math. Dyscalcula usually becomes apparent somewhat later in childhood, at about age 8, when even simple number facts, such as 3 + 3 = 6, are memorized one day and forgotten the next. It soon becomes clear—especially with word problems—that the child is guessing at whether numbers should be added, subtracted, multiplied, or ignored to solve a problem, and that almost everything the child knows about arithmetic is a matter of rote memory rather than understanding.

Other specific academic subjects that may reveal a learning disability are spelling and handwriting. A child might read at the fifth-grade level but repeatedly make simple spelling mistakes ("kum accros the rode"), or a child might take three times as long as any other child to copy something from the chalkboard, and then produce only a large, illegible scrawl.

Because of various cutoff levels (how much disparity between actual and expected scores means a child is disabled?) and the fact that many children are not even tested,

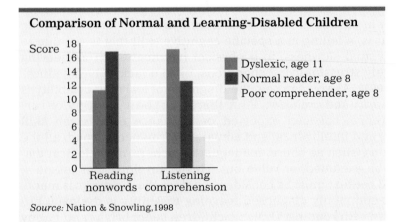

Comparison of Normal and Learning-Disabled Children

Score

☐ Dyslexic, age 11
■ Normal reader, age 8
☐ Poor comprehender, age 8

Reading nonwords   Listening comprehension

Source: Nation & Snowling, 1998

? Especially for Educators: Suppose a particular school has 30 children in the second grade. Five of them have special problems. One speaks very little and seems autistic, one is very talkative but cannot read, one is almost blind, and two are ADHD (one of them aggressive). What are the advantages and disadvantages of creating a special class for these five, rather than mainstreaming them in the regular class?

ADHD (attention-deficit hyperactivity disorder) A behavior problem characterized by excessive activity, an inability to concentrate, and impulsive, sometimes aggressive, behavior.

the percentage of children who are "learning-disabled" varies from place to place. For example, all the 6-year-olds in Bergen, Sweden, were given a battery of tests (Gjessing & Karlsen, 1989). Seven percent were rated dyslexic. This incidence is greater than that found by the usual method, which is counting only children whose learning problems are noticed in school and who are then tested and diagnosed as learning-disabled. Using that method, DSM-IV finds dyslexia at 4 percent and dyscalcula at 1 percent, and the prevalence of other learning disabilities is "difficult to establish" (American Psychiatric Association, 1994).

ADHD

One of the most puzzling and exasperating of childhood problems is **ADHD (attention-deficit hyperactivity disorder),** in which the child has great difficulty concentrating for more than a few moments at a time and, indeed, is almost constantly in motion. After sitting down to do homework, for instance, an ADHD child might repeatedly look up, ask irrelevant questions, think about playing outside, get up to get a drink of water, sit down, fidget, squirm, tap the table, jiggle his or her legs, and then get up again to get a snack or—if an adult says "no food"—insist that a trip to the bathroom is urgent. Often this need for distraction and diversion is accompanied by excitability and impulsivity.

The crucial factor in attention-deficit disorder seems to be neurological (Aman et al., 1998): a brain deficit that results in great difficulty in "paying attention." This deficit, which may be caused by genetic vulnerability, prenatal teratogens, or postnatal damage such as lead poisoning, makes it hard for the child to focus on any one thought or experience long enough to process it (Oosterlaan et al., 1998). In the classroom, the child might not have the concentration to read and remember a passage in a school textbook and might impulsively blurt out the wrong answer to a teacher's question.

Teachers notice such disruptive children, but often a formal diagnosis is never made. In one study, a checklist of DSM-IV symptoms was given to all teachers in every elementary school in one Tennessee county. Although fewer than 5 percent (the usual proportion) of the children had already been diagnosed as having ADHD, actually 16 percent of the children met the criteria for the disorder (Wolraich et al., 1998). In this study, as well as generally, about four boys are diagnosed with ADHD for every girl.

Normal or Not? It's impossible to judge just from this photo. In some children, actions like this may be an isolated instance of showing off or of outrageous mischief. In children with ADHD, they are commonplace. When such behavior is accompanied by aggression, the child may be at risk of developing a conduct disorder—possibly becoming the kind of stubborn, disobedient daredevil who is constantly in trouble at home, at school, and in the neighborhood.

Related Problems

Attention-deficit disorder can also occur without hyperactivity. Children with this form of the problem, sometimes called ADD, appear to be prone to anxiety and depression. More often, however, children with ADHD are also prone to aggression, likely to suddenly attack a playmate or an adult. Some researchers have proposed ADHDA—*attention-deficit hyperactivity disorder with aggression*—as a subtype of this problem. Children who exhibit aggression with ADHD appear to be at increased risk for developing oppositional and conduct disorders, as you will soon see (Dykman & Ackerman, 1993).

DSM-IV categorizes these forms of ADHD, as well as oppositional disorder (OD) and conduct disorder (CD), as distinct disabilities. One critical factor in all these disorders is the context (developmental psychopathology's lesson 4). For instance, DSM-IV states that in threatening, impoverished, high-crime, or war-ravaged situations, *conduct disorder behaviors* (aggression, destructiveness, and stealing) may be protective and that the clinician should "consider the social and economic context" before diagnosing such actions as pathological (American Psychiatric Association, 1994). More detail from DSM-IV is in Appendix A.

There may be a developmental sequence in problems with attention, activity, opposition, and aggression (Stormshak et al., 1998). The toddler who cannot pay attention may be especially unresponsive when parents demand that the child be quiet and stay put (something every parent of a 2-year-old has tried, with limited success). Further, an attention-deficit child soon learns that one way to increase mental concentration is to move around (just as some adults think better when walking than when standing still). Thus the child may begin as ADD but become ADHD by age 4 or 5.

Then, if others try to force quiet or to demand concentration from a child who is unable to comply, the child may become oppositional—that is, may refuse to comply with authority. If that opposition ("I won't do it") is met with aggression ("Do it or I'll spank you"), the child may become aggressive and create disruptions in the classroom once formal schooling begins. Aggression is especially likely to develop if the teacher demands that every child concentrate quietly at his or her desk (an impossible task for an ADHD child).

Such a developmental sequence, as well as contextual considerations, would explain why these conceptually distinct disorders often occur in the same child (Stormshak et al., 1998). They also help explain cultural differences in the frequency of these disorders. Children in Britain, for instance, are less likely to be diagnosed as having ADHD than are children in the United States, but they are more likely to be diagnosed with conduct disorder (Epstein et al., 1991; MacArdle et al., 1995).

In any case, parents and teachers need to do whatever they can to keep the disorder at the simplest level, ADD or ADHD, because once the child becomes oppositional and aggressive, it is much harder to prevent serious antisocial activities later on. A disproportionate number of ADHD children are eventually arrested for major felonies, a sad example of lesson 3, that adulthood can be worse rather than better (Patterson et al., 1989).

Help for Children with ADHD

Not surprisingly, children with ADHD are usually troublesome to adults and rejected by their peers. Medication, psychological therapy, and changes in the family and school environments can each help some children. Ideally, all three forms of treatment are at least considered.

For reasons not yet determined, certain drugs that stimulate adults have the reverse effect on many—but not all—children with attention-deficit problems, whether or not they are hyperactive and/or aggressive. Among these psychoactive drugs are amphetamines (e.g.,

Adderall) and methylphenidate (Ritalin). For many children, the results are remarkable; taking the drug allows them to sit still and concentrate for the first time. However, while the new ability to pay attention is a welcome relief to many teachers, parents, and children, it does not necessarily produce gains in intelligence scores or achievement (Solanto, 1998; Swanson et al., 1993).

Moreover, despite the remarkable results that psychoactive drugs provide for some children with ADHD, drug therapy is not a cure. The actual effects of any drug cannot be predicted merely by diagnosis: Some children are finally able to learn with medication, while others are not helped by it at all. If drugs are prescribed without proper diagnosis or follow-up, an overmedicated child can become too lethargic to participate in class or play with peers.

Unfortunately, children are more often misdiagnosed and under-diagnosed than properly diagnosed and treated for ADHD. For example, in one study of 9- to 17-year-olds in four diverse locations (San Juan, Puerto Rico; New Haven, Conn.; Atlanta, Ga.; and Westchester County, N.Y.), almost exactly 5 percent (66 children out of 1,285) met the DSM-IV criteria for ADHD. Slightly more than 1 percent (16 children) were receiving stimulant medication for ADHD—but only half of them met the criteria and the other half did not. In other words, if a child had ADHD, there was only one chance in eight that he or she was on medication for it. But for each child who was medicated for ADHD, there was a 50-50 chance that the disorder had been misdiagnosed (Jensen et al., 1999).

By the time an ADHD child has become a candidate for psychoactive drugs, the child's behavior has usually created problems that drugs alone cannot reverse. Children diagnosed with ADHD need help overcoming their confused perception of their social world and their low opinion of themselves, while the family members need help with their own management techniques and interaction. That help must come from the other two crucial components of ADHD treatment: individual and family psychological therapy, plus contextual changes within the home and school (Pelham et al., 1998).

Teacher behavior at either extreme—too rigid or too permissive—is most likely to exacerbate ADHD, because these children cannot follow strict guidelines exactly; nor can such children set their own limits when guidelines do not exist, as some children can. Thus some teachers unwittingly make the problem worse, creating the symptoms that qualify the child to be diagnosed as disruptive, oppositional, and aggressive. The treatment may be placement in a special class, a solution that creates problems of its own. (See the In Person box on pages 322–323.)

Conclusion

What happens if a problem is not diagnosed? This was the case for three-fourths of the ADHD children in the Tennessee study, probably half the learning-disabled children in the United States (if the prevalence found in the Swedish study is accurate), more than half of the high-functioning autistic children, and a large number of children who have other disorders. Adult heart disease, obesity, and asthma usually have roots in childhood but are not usually diagnosed soon enough for effective early intervention. Life-span developmental research finds that childhood problems rarely disappear but that their

❶ **Response for Educators (from page 319):** Ideally, your answer considers the benefits to the 5 children as well as the 25 and the challenge for the teachers involved. From the special children's perspective, being segregated and educated in such a disparate group would hurt their learning. Unless the aggressive child could be controlled, the others might learn only self-defense. For the regular teacher, however, it would be easier to teach 25 children who could all achieve at grade level. Simple mainstreaming is clearly unworkable: No one would learn much, and the teacher might quit. The unanswered question is whether the regular teacher and the 25 ordinary children could team up with the special teacher and the 5 children with disabilities so that they all could learn in one classroom. Inclusion, especially inclusion with integration, should be attempted.

WHERE TO PUT THE "SPECIAL" CHILDREN?

All types of special problems need to be recognized early, long before first grade if possible. Although some "developmentally delayed" children catch up on their own, most do not. For example, reading disabilities do not usually correct themselves, and ADHD children become more problematic, to themselves and others, as they grow older (Fergusson et al., 1996).

After a problem is recognized, what is the best educational setting in which to solve it? The first answer was segregated classes, in which all the special-needs children were taught together by a special-education teacher. However, this approach made the children feel as though a spotlight were being focused on their problem. Often they were right: All sorts of disabled children were being educated together—including those with overall retardation and delay—with no recognition of an individual child's strengths and abilities. Further, segregated classrooms impaired the development of normal social skills, as well as slowing advancement in areas in which a child was not disabled, a violation of all four lessons from the developmental psychopathology perspective (see page 314).

In response, **mainstreaming** emerged about 30 years ago. Mainstreaming is a way to organize students and teachers in which children with special educational needs are taught with children in the general (main) classroom. The regular teacher is asked to be particularly sensitive to the special children, perhaps using alternative methods to teach them or allowing extra time for them to complete assignments and tests.

Unfortunately, mainstreaming tended to become a "sink-or-swim" situation for special-needs students. Many teachers were untrained, unwilling, or simply unable to cope with the special needs of a few children—especially in a classroom of 30 or so students. As one teacher complained:

I do not have the training that you people [speech-language pathologists] have. However, I've been in the business for a long time, and I think I know when I see a child with a language problem. So I make all the referrals. Now I don't know what happens in the 1:1 session, or what kinds of tests you give the kids, but my speech person keeps sending these children back to me saying they don't have a language problem. Finally I just said to her, "Then you get in the classroom and see what is wrong." [quoted in Constable, 1987]

Some schools then set aside a **resource room,** where special-needs children would spend part of each day with a teacher trained and equipped to remedy whatever disability they might have. But pulling the child out of regular class once again undermined classroom social relationships and left the regular teacher unaccountable for the progress of the child. Further, scheduling resource-room time meant the child missed out on vital parts of the day, either play periods or academic-skill practice.

One recent approach is called **inclusion:** Children with disabilities are included in the regular class, as in mainstreaming, but the burden does not rest on the regular teacher; a specially trained teacher or paraprofessional assists with the included children, for all or part of the day. This solution may be the most expensive, and it necessitates adjustment on the part of classroom teachers, who are not used to working side by side with other teachers. Nonetheless, children who need both social interaction with their schoolmates and special remediation for their learning difficulties may be well served (Banerji & Dailey, 1995; Waldron & McLeskey, 1998). To take the idea of inclusion one logical step further, many teachers and parents now emphasize *integration,* the idea that each child within the classroom, learning-disabled

mainstreaming   An approach to educating children with special needs by putting them in the same "stream"—the general-education classroom— as all the other children, rather than segregating them.

resource room   A designated room, equipped with special material and staffed by a trained teacher, where children with special needs spend part of their school day getting help with basic skills.

inclusion   An approach to educating children with special needs whereby they are included in the regular classroom while also receiving special individualized instruction, typically from a teacher or paraprofessional trained in special education.

lifelong legacy depends on the specifics of the home and school contexts. These contexts affect a person's fortune, ability, or misfortune in finding a vocation, a partner, and a community who guide him or her.

Ideally, children with special needs are spotted and their teachers and parents provide the necessary educational and emotional support.

What Are These Children Learning? This deaf boy is fortunate—he is with his hearing peers and his teacher knows how to sign to him. Are the other children doing their work? One hopes, over the course of the year, they will learn more from the inclusion of the special child than they miss from the teacher's targeted attention.

or not, is a vital part of that social and educational group. Some experts suggest that almost every school-age child has some sort of special need and that therefore schools should develop an individualized education plan (IEP) for every student (Branson, 1998).

Unfortunately for children with special needs, none of these approaches may solve their academic or social problems (Siperstein et al., 1997). From a developmental perspective, this is not surprising: All manner of handicaps, from severe physical impairment to subtle learning disabilities, are real, longstanding, often brain-based problems. This makes them quite likely to be helped by the proper educational context but quite unlikely to disappear.

The key seems to be to help the child understand what the problem is and how he or she might be helped. This did not happen with Sally Osbourne:

> I was in the seventh grade when my teacher asked me to stand up and read. I stood up, but couldn't recognize even one word on the page. After what seemed an eternity, the teacher got angry and told me to go into another classroom where I was to write again and again, "I am stupid because I cannot read."
>
> I didn't say a word. But I couldn't do what the teacher wanted, because I couldn't spell. So I just sat and waited until a friend came in at the end of the day to collect the assignment. After she had spelled it out for me, I wrote it over and over again. Then I gave it to the teacher and went home.
>
> That was the end of it. The teacher never helped me with my reading or writing before or after that time. [Levine & Osbourne, 1989]

It did, however, happen with the late Ennës Cosby:

> The happiest day of my life occurred when I found out I was dyslexic. I believe that life is finding solutions, and the worst feeling to me is confusion. [Cosby, 1997]

If not, the children may still find ways to compensate for, overcome, or circumscribe their difficulties in the larger social context. On this all researchers agree. Development during the school years is a multifaceted combination of risks and assets, with the particular educational and familial contexts usually able to prevent serious problems from growing worse as development continues.

SUMMARY

SIZE AND SHAPE

1. Children grow more slowly during middle childhood than at any other time until the end of adolescence. Variation in size, shape, and rate of maturation is caused by genes, nutrition, family, and national policy.

2. Childhood obesity is caused by the interaction of genes, inactivity (including excessive TV viewing), family habits, and the child's own psychological stress. More exercise, rather than severe dieting, is the best solution.

3. Most school-age children are quite healthy. Asthma, however, which is aggravated by modern life (including more indoor pollutants and less outdoor play), is one impediment affecting children's school attendance and overall well-being.

SKILL DEVELOPMENT

4. School-age children can master almost any motor skill as long as it doesn't require adult strength, size, or judgment. Boys and girls are about equal in motor-skill potential, with differences between one child and another more a matter of genes, practice, culture, and maturation than of sex.

5. All children should be physically active, with specific activities geared to the gross motor skills that children of this age are physically prepared to master. Fine motor skills are as important to practice as gross motor skills are.

6. A growing interest in individual and international differences in intellectual achievement in the school years accounts for the increasingly widespread use of standardized achievement and aptitude tests, including intelligence tests, for school-age children. Achievement tests index how much a child has learned, whereas aptitude tests measure cognitive potential.

7. Although tests of cognitive development are useful, and often less biased than evaluation by teacher and parents, many factors other than inherent ability are reflected in performance on aptitude and achievement tests. Researchers such as Howard Gardner argue that there are many more kinds of intelligence and ways to assess achievement than traditional tests reflect.

CHILDREN WITH SPECIAL NEEDS

8. Developmental psychopathology applies research regarding normal development to an understanding of childhood psychological disorders, and vice versa. It emphasizes that special-needs youngsters are children first—with the developmental needs that all children share.

9. The developmental psychopathology perspective also stresses that the manifestations of any disorder change as the person grows older and that the social context has an impact on the diagnosis of a problem. Two contexts—family interactions and school structure—are pivotal in treatment and prognosis.

10. Autism is characterized by a lack of interest in other people, delays in language acquisition and communication, and extreme self-preoccupation.

11. Specific learning disabilities can impair any of several particular abilities, such as learning to read (dyslexia) or do math (dyscalcula), or an underlying ability, such as abstract reasoning or spatial organization. Learning disabilities have many causes, including genes, prenatal teratogens, and postnatal brain damage.

12. Children who have unusual difficulty with concentration are often unusually active as well and may be diagnosed as hyperactive or as having attention-deficit hyperactivity disorder (ADHD). It is important to treat this problem, both in school and at home, and often with drugs, to prevent low achievement, antisocial behavior, and outright aggression.

13. A developmental perspective suggests that all special-needs children can benefit from early diagnosis and appropriate schooling techniques. Targeted education, interaction with "normal" children, and adjustments at home can often remedy the problem sufficiently so that the child eventually becomes a normally functioning adult.

KEY TERMS

body mass index (BMI) (302)

asthma (306)

reaction time (307)

achievement tests (310)

aptitude tests (310)

IQ tests (310)

child with special needs (313)

developmental psychopathology (314)

DSM-IV (314)

autism (315)

Asperger syndrome (315)

mental retardation (317)

learning disability (317)

dyslexia (317)

dyscalcula (318)

ADHD (attention-deficit hyperactivity disorder) (319)

mainstreaming (322)

resource room (322)

inclusion (322)

KEY QUESTIONS

1. How do nutrition and heredity affect stature and physique in middle childhood?

2. What are the causes of obesity?

3. How is asthma sometimes caused by modern life?

4. What factors affect which specific motor skills a child masters during the school years?

5. What gender differences and similarities are apparent in motor skills between ages 7 and 11?

6. What does an IQ test measure?

7. What are some of the benefits and problems involved in the use of standardized achievement tests?

8. How does developmental psychopathology view children with psychological disorders relative to "normal" children?

9. What are the three major characteristics of autism?

10. What are the signs of at least two specific learning disabilities?

11. How might the symptoms of ADHD in a specific child change with age?

12. What are the arguments for and against the use of psychoactive drugs to control ADHD?

13. What are the advantages and disadvantages of inclusion for learning-disabled students?

14. *In Your Experience* What aspects of your physical appearance or behavior made you different from other children during the school years? What were the psychological and social consequences (both positive and negative) of your special situation?

The School Years:
Cognitive Development

CHAPTER 12

As you saw in Chapters 6 and 9, parents, teachers, and researchers have tended to underestimate the cognitive competency of the infant and young child. No such error occurs with middle childhood, ages 7 to 11. We are well aware of the cognitive skills of school-age children; we see them in action every day. Many 7- to 11-year-olds not only learn rapidly in school but can also outscore their elders on computer games, repeat the rapid-fire lyrics of a rap song, and recognize out-of-towners by the clothes they wear—accomplishments beyond some people twice their age, and beyond almost everyone six times their age.

To understand the development of cognition, we will first turn to the insights of current research, then to the overview provided by Piaget and by language learning, and finally to school itself—obviously a powerful influence that can channel, fortify, or hinder cognition during middle childhood.

REMEMBERING, KNOWING, AND PROCESSING

A 9- or 10-year-old child is a very different kind of thinker from, say, a 4- or 5-year-old preschooler. Not only do older children know more; they also use their minds much more effectively when they must solve a problem or remember a piece of information. By middle childhood, most children have acquired a sense of "the game of thinking," and they enjoy an intellectual challenge as much as an athletic one. They begin to realize that good thinking involves considering evidence, planning ahead, thinking logically, formulating alternative hypotheses, and being consistent; they try to incorporate these qualities into their own reasoning and use them to evaluate the thinking of others (Flavell et al., 1993).

Information Processing

One way to understand this advance in thinking is to consider each component of the intellectual process (Demetriou & Raftopoulos, 1999; Kuhn et al., 1995). **Information-processing theory** likens many aspects of human thinking to the way computers analyze and process data. Of course, no computer can match the mind's capacity for reflection, creativity, and intuition. However, information-processing theorists suggest that by focusing on the step-by-step mechanics of human thinking, we

information-processing theory   A theory of learning that focuses on the steps of thinking—such as sorting, categorizing, storing, and retrieving—that are similar to the functions of a computer.

sensory register   A memory system that functions for only a fraction of a second, retaining a fleeting impression of a stimulus on a particular sense organ.

working memory   The part of memory that handles current, conscious mental activity. (Also called *short-term memory*.)

long-term memory   The part of memory that stores information for days, months, or years.

control processes   That part of the information-processing system that regulates the analysis and flow of information, including memory and retrieval strategies, selective attention, and rules or strategies for problem solving.

can derive a more precise understanding of cognitive development (Anderson, 1993; Klahr, 1989, 1992; Klahr & MacWhinney, 1998; Siegler & Shipley, 1995). Like computers, humans must store large amounts of information, get access to that information when it is needed, and analyze situations in terms of the particular problem-solving strategies that are likely to yield correct solutions.

One example of how researchers portray the information-processing system is shown in Figure 12.1. The **sensory register** stores incoming stimulus information for a split second after it is received, to allow it to be processed. To use the terms used in Chapters 6 and 7, sensations are retained for a moment while the person selects some sensations to become perceptions. Most sensations that come into the sensory register are lost or discarded, but meaningful information is transferred to working memory for further analysis.

It is in **working memory** (sometimes called *short-term memory*) that your current, conscious mental activity occurs. Your working memory includes, at this moment, your understanding of this paragraph, any previous knowledge you recall that is related to it, and also, perhaps, distracting thoughts about your weekend plans or the interesting person who sat next to you in class today. Working memory is constantly replenished with new information, so thoughts and memories are usually not retained for very long. Some are discarded, while a few are transferred to long-term memory.

Long-term memory stores information for minutes, hours, days, months, or years. The capacity of long-term memory—how much information can be crammed into one brain—is virtually limitless. Together with the sensory register and working memory, long-term memory assists in organizing your reactions to stimuli. Crucial here is not merely *storage* (how much material has been deposited in long-term memory) but also *retrieval* (how readily the material can be brought to the conscious mind to be used). Certain information is more readily retrievable (you remember your birth date more easily than your phone number), but all the information in long-term memory is stored somehow, unless something (such as a stroke) destroys it.

Putting it all together are **control processes**, which regulate the analysis and flow of information within the system. When you want to

Figure 12.1 Information Processing. From stimulus to response, from input to output, much goes on in the human mind that makes thinking analogous to operating a computer. The solid arrows indicate the transfer of information, and the broken arrows indicate control processes that govern how and when the transfers occur. As with a computer, innate speed and capacity are important, but the crucial factor is the program. This is what is developed most in middle childhood.

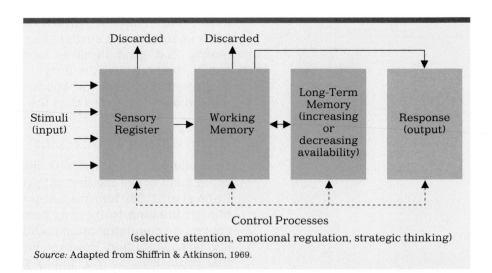

Source: Adapted from Shiffrin & Atkinson, 1969.

Concentration This girl's ability to ignore her classmates, and to push the right keys in proper sequence, is an impressive example of selective attention. Fortunately, the human brain becomes better at selective attention with maturation and experience, so this girl is not necessarily an extraordinary student.

selective attention The ability to concentrate on relevant information and ignore distractions.

concentrate on only one part of all the material in your sensory register, or summon a rule of thumb from long-term memory to working memory to solve a problem, control processes assume an executive role in the information-processing system, regulating the analysis and transfer of information.

Information-processing theorists believe that advances in the thinking of school-age children occur primarily because of basic changes in control processes—that is, in the way children process and analyze information. As you will see, these changes are directly related to improvements in various aspects of memory.

Improvements in Memory

A marked improvement in memory occurs between ages 7 and 11, particularly apparent in older children's ability to remember essential facts over a period of days or longer, with almost no forgetting (Brainerd & Reyna, 1995). Selective attention and metacognition are factors behind the improvement (Schneider & Pressley, 1997). A third factor, an increase in processing speed, is discussed in A Life-Span View on pages 330–331.

Selective Attention

If you were to observe children learning in a kindergarten classroom and a fifth-grade classroom, you would see many differences. Kindergartners are easily distracted, whether they are listening to a story or printing letters of the alphabet. While they are working, they chatter to each other, look around, fidget, call out to the teacher, and sometimes get up to visit friends or just wander around. Their curriculum is designed to be highly motivating, with plenty of changes of activity, because the teachers know the nature of their 5-year-old charges.

By contrast, fifth-graders might work independently at desks or in groups around a table, managing to read, write, discuss, and seek assistance without distracting, or being distracted by, other students. Or they might all quietly follow a demonstration at the chalkboard, raising their hands to be called on rather than shouting out. Their academic tasks are more difficult, of course, and take longer to complete, but their teachers rightly expect them to persist in the face of that challenge, because it is within their intellectual capacity to do so.

Selective attention, the ability to screen out distractions and concentrate on relevant information, is the critical difference between these two scenarios. Indeed, memory and thought depend on the ability to ignore most of the information that bombards the senses and to focus on details that will help in later recall—perhaps using an already-memorized address to remember a historical date—rather than allowing a conversation across the room to interfere with concentration. Focusing on what should be remembered and ignoring what should be forgotten are equally important components of selective attention (Cowan, 1997).

Improvements in Control Processes

The ability to control one's mental processes begins during the preschool years, as children show signs of emotional regulation—holding their anger instead of hitting their friends, distracting themselves

A LIFE-SPAN VIEW

PROCESSING SPEED

Information-processing concepts and analysis apply at every stage of life, from infancy through old age. As we will summarize in this box and describe in later chapters, the overall power of a person's intellectual ability depends in part on the balance among three factors: speed, automatization, and knowledge.

Older children are much quicker thinkers than younger children, young adults are faster than older adults, and this greater speed benefits memory and a host of other cognitive skills (Williams et al., 1999). Speed directly increases mental capacity, because faster thinking makes it possible to hold and process more thoughts in one's conscious mind (working memory) at once. A sixth-grader can listen to the dinner-table conversation of her parents, respond to the interruptions of her younger siblings, think about her weekend plans, and still remember to ask for her allowance. In school, increased processing capacity means that she can answer a teacher's question with several relevant ideas rather than just one and, at the same time, monitor her words for accuracy and note her classmates' reactions to her answer.

Speed of thinking continues to increase throughout adolescence. In adulthood, it gradually slows down. Why do thinking speed and capacity increase? Neurological maturation, especially the ongoing myelination of neural axons and the development of the frontal cortex, partly accounts for these changes (Dempster, 1993). But the advances seem more a matter of learning than maturation. Indeed, there is no evidence that the critical parts of the brain literally grow bigger during middle childhood. Instead, speed and capacity increase because as children learn to use the brain more efficiently, myelination increases and dendrites become more

dense (Schneider & Pressley, 1997). Neurological deterioration may affect the eventual slowdown, but, as Chapter 25 explains, the correlation between age and thinking speed is far from perfect.

Two other factors aid the more efficient use of the brain: automatization and an increase in knowledge. **Automatization** is the process in which familiar, well-practiced mental activities become routine and automatic. As people use their intellectual skills, many processes that at first required hard mental labor now become automatized. This increases processing speed, frees up capacity, allows more to be remembered, and thus advances thinking in every way (Schneider & Pressley, 1997).

Progress from initial effort to automatization often takes years. Many children lose cognitive skills over the summer because the halt in daily schooling erases earlier learning (Huttenlocher et al., 1998). Not until something is overlearned does it become automatic. Automatization continues throughout life. Adults who are learning to drive often require intense concentration but still make mistakes, even when they drive slowly where traffic is light. Over time and with practice, they can drive flawlessly while carrying on a conversation in rush-hour traffic—but only when the route is familiar (another instance of automatization).

The other thinking aid that takes years is an increase in knowledge. The more you know, the more you can learn.

automatization   The process by which familiar and well-rehearsed mental activities become routine and automatic.

---

metacognition   The ability to evaluate a cognitive task to determine how best to accomplish it, and then to monitor one's performance—"thinking about thinking."

instead of crying at the dentist, and so on. However, during the school years, control processes become markedly better, especially in regard to intellectual, not just emotional, efforts. Children become aware that the content of their thinking is partly under their conscious control (Flavell et al., 1995). They develop **metacognition,** which means "thinking about thinking," the ability to evaluate a cognitive task to determine how best to accomplish it, and then to monitor and adjust their performance on that task. Metacognition leads to the development of effective

table **12.1**	**Who Remembers Most After Reading a Passage About Soccer?**	
	Intelligence	
	High IQ	Low IQ
Expert soccer players	Most	Second most
Novice soccer players	Third most	Least

Experts Versus Novices That intelligent children who are experienced soccer players remember the most, or that their opposites remember the least, about a written passage concerning soccer is not surprising. What is surprising is the group that came in second: those children who were not very intelligent overall but who happened to know a lot about soccer. Given a passage they had never seen before, both their comprehension and memory were better than were those of smarter children with less knowledge about the subject.

Having an extensive **knowledge base,** a broad body of knowledge in a particular subject area, makes it easier to master new learning in that area.

One study compared fourth-graders of varied intelligence, some expert soccer players and some novices, on the ability to understand and remember a written passage about soccer (see Table 12.1). As expected, high-IQ children did somewhat better than low-IQ children—but this was true only for children at the same level of soccer expertise. When an expert soccer player with low intelligence was compared to a highly intelligent novice, the expert did better. A larger knowledge base was sufficient to overcome slower thinking overall (Schneider et al., 1996).

Further research emphasizes that the connections between bits of information improve as the knowledge base expands. As a person learns more about a particular topic, that person learns how the new knowledge relates to the previous knowledge. This explains why learning by rote is fragile, while learning by comprehension endures.

It also explains adult learning. Most of us do not seek out knowledge in fields we know nothing about. It is painful to study electrical engineering or water skiing or ancient Greek if we have no related knowledge and practice. At first we feel slow and stupid, convinced that we will never learn. With time, however, our knowledge base builds and some parts become automatic—so much so that it is hard for an expert in any field to empathize with the ignorance of the novice. There is a lesson here, to be applied whenever an adult becomes impatient with a child who says that reading is hard or decimals are impossible or chemistry makes no sense. The same patience we should use in teaching a child might be used on ourselves, especially when we resist learning something new because it is unfamiliar.

knowledge base A body of knowledge in a particular area that has been learned and on which additional learning can be based.

cognitive strategies—ways to think—which are practiced so often that they become automatic.

There are many indicators of school-age children's development of metacognition (Flavell et al., 1993; Schneider & Pressley, 1997; Siegler, 1991). As one example, preschoolers have difficulty judging whether a problem is easy or difficult, and thus they devote equal effort to both kinds of problems. In contrast, children in the school years know how to identify challenging tasks, and they devote greater effort to them—with

They've Read the Book Acting in a play based on *The Lion, the Witch and the Wardrobe* suggests that these children have metacognitive abilities beyond almost any preschooler. Indeed, the book itself requires a grasp of the boundary between reality (the wardrobe) and fantasy (the witch), which demands "thinking about thinking" in order to appreciate the allegory.

❷ *Observational Quiz (see answer page 334): Beyond the book, what are three examples of metacognition implied here? Specifically, how does the ability to memorize lines, play a part, and focus on the play illustrate metacognition?*

greater success. They know how to evaluate their learning progress, judging whether they have learned a set of spelling words or science principles, rather than simply asserting (as many younger children do) that they know it all. In short, older children approach cognitive tasks in a more strategic and analytic manner. Storage and retrieval strategies improve.

STAGES OF THINKING

The information-processing perspective tends to conceptualize cognitive development as occurring in small steps along many paths. By contrast, another perspective conceives intellectual development as occurring in stages, with sudden and widespread shifts taking place as certain ideas become understood. Jean Piaget is the most famous of such stage theorists, although others—notably Lawrence Kohlberg, with his theory of stages of moral development—agree.

Concrete Operational Thought

concrete operational thought In Piaget's theory, the third period of cognitive development, in which a child can reason logically about concrete events and problems but cannot yet reason about abstract ideas and possibilities.

5-to-7 shift A notable reorganization of the thinking process that occurs between ages 5 and 7, enabling the school-age child to reason and respond at a much more advanced level than the younger child.

In Piaget's view, the most important cognitive achievement of middle childhood is the attainment of **concrete operational thought**, whereby children can reason logically about the things and events they perceive. According to Piaget, at about age 5 many children begin to switch to concrete operational thought, the **5-to-7 shift** that occurs in every domain of thinking. Then, between ages 7 and 11 years, children understand logical principles, and they apply them in *concrete* situations, that is, situations that deal with visible, tangible, real things. They thereby become more systematic, objective, scientific—and educable—thinkers.

Here is an example of this change: Preschoolers tend to use intuition and subjective insights to understand the results of a science experiment ("Maybe the caterpillar just felt like becoming a butterfly!"), but school-

The Scientific Method During middle childhood, as Piaget described it, children become able to transcend their subjective and egocentric notions and objectively observe the world around them. This is an ideal age for budding scientists to undertake the steps of the scientific method. These girls not only have asked which food cats prefer but are gathering evidence before they reach their conclusion. Given the position of their pencils, they may even reach the ultimate step, "Publish the results."

age children seek explanations that are rational, consistent, and generalizable ("Does the caterpillar use the air temperature to know when it's time to begin a cocoon?"). Preschoolers ask "Why" but reject answers not to their liking; school-age children ask "Why" and then want to know more.

Similarly, out on the playground, first-graders may argue over the rules of a game by using increasingly loud and assertive protests ("Is!" "Is not!" "Is!" "Is not!"), whereas fifth-graders temper their arguments with reason and justification ("That *can't* be right, because if it was, we'd have to score points differently!"). In both academic and nonacademic contexts, school-age children's logical thinking is crucial to understanding, to acquiring knowledge, and to communicating clearly and persuasively with others.

Two Logical Principles

identity The logical principle that certain characteristics of an object remain the same when other characteristics are changed.

To understand the place of logic in concrete operational thought, we will consider two of the many logical structures that Piaget describes: identity and reversibility. **Identity** is the idea that certain characteristics of an object remain the same even when other characteristics change.

Learning By Doing This science teacher and student are demonstrating the effects of static electricity. Such demonstrations bring out the logical abilities of concrete operational children much better than do abstract descriptions in textbooks.

reversibility   The logical principle that something that has been changed can be returned to its original state by reversing the process of change.

❶ *Answer to Observational Quiz (from page 332):* (1) Memorizing extensive passages requires an understanding of advanced memory strategies that combine meaning with form. (2) Understanding how to play a part so that other actors and the audience respond well requires a sophisticated theory of mind. (3) Staying focused on the moment in the play despite distractions from the audience requires selective attention.

preconventional moral reasoning   Kohlberg's term for the first level (stages 1 and 2) of moral thinking, in which the individual reasons in terms of his or her own welfare.

conventional moral reasoning   Kohlberg's term for the second level (stages 3 and 4) of moral thinking, in which the individual considers social standards and laws to be the primary arbiters of moral values.

postconventional moral reasoning   Kohlberg's term for the third and highest level (stages 5 and 6) of moral thinking, in which the individual follows moral principles that may supersede the standards of society or the wishes of the individual.

Children who understand identity realize that superficial changes in an object's appearance do not alter its underlying substance or quantity. In conservation tests (see page 247), for example, identity tells us that pouring a liquid from one container into a different container does not change the amount of liquid present. "It's still the same milk," a 9-year-old might say; "you haven't changed that."

School-age children also come to understand that sometimes a thing that has been changed can be returned to its original state by reversing the process of change (**reversibility**). A school-age child might prove that the amount of liquid has not changed by pouring it back into the first container (reversibility).

Identity is relevant to mathematical understanding. Children need a firm grasp of identity to realize, for example, that the number 24 is always 24, whether it is obtained by adding 14 and 10, or adding 23 and 1, or adding 6 + 6 + 6 + 6. This logical principle also enhances scientific understanding, whether that means grasping the underlying oneness of the tadpole and the frog or seeing that frozen water is still H_2O.

Reversibility is also essential to a school-age child's understanding of math and science. For example, subtraction is the reverse of addition (if 5 + 9 = 14, then 14 − 9 = the original 5).

Logical principles also apply to everyday social encounters. Identity enables a school-age child to understand—as most preschoolers cannot—that his mother was once a child and that her baby picture is, in fact, a picture of his mother. School-age children are even able to imagine their parents growing old—and to promise, as one child did, always to be around to push their wheelchairs. Similarly, a school-age child might say, "Let's start over and be friends again, OK?" (reversibility).

Note that for Piaget, as well as for information-processing theorists, the distinguishing feature of school-age children is the ability to apply certain logical principles, or general strategies, or metacognitive insights to a variety of specific situations (see the Research Report). This may be true in moral decision making as well.

Stages of Moral Development

Building on Piaget's theories and research, Lawrence Kohlberg (1963, 1981) studied moral reasoning by presenting subjects with a set of ethical dilemmas. Responses to several scenarios allowed Kohlberg to describe how people reasoned about situations that demanded moral judgments. The most famous story involves the conflict between private property and human life as experienced by Heinz, a poor man whose wife is dying of cancer. A local pharmacist has developed the only cure, a drug sold for thousands of dollars—far more than Heinz can pay and 10 times what the drug costs to make:

> Heinz went to everyone he knew to borrow the money, but he could only get together about half of what it cost. He told the druggist that his wife was dying and asked him to sell it cheaper or let him pay later. But the druggist said "no." The husband got desperate and broke into the man's store to steal the drug for his wife. Should the husband have done that? Why? [Kohlberg, 1963]

In people's responses to such dilemmas, Kohlberg found three levels of moral reasoning—**preconventional, conventional,** and **postconventional**—with two stages at each level (see Table 12.2).

SELLING LEMONADE

The shift toward logical thinking during middle childhood was highlighted by researchers who asked a total of 138 children to predict how various circumstances would affect sales at a child's lemonade stand (Siegler & Thompson, 1998). Specifically, the researchers manipulated five variables:

■ Demand ("A lot of people were out of town")
■ Supply ("Both kids next door decided to run lemonade stands, too")
■ Motivation (the child running the stand "really wanted to earn a lot of money")
■ Morality (the child mistreated a sibling that morning)
■ Appearance (the child switched from red to green cups)

As you can see from Figure 12.2, even the prekindergartners had a pretty good understanding of the effect of demand: Fewer customers mean fewer sales. However, understanding the effect (or lack of effect) of changes in supply, motivation, morality, and cup color were hard for the youngest children but quite easy for the older children. The most dramatic increase in the use of logic to analyze those variables occurred between ages 5 and 7, just when Piaget said the shift to concrete operational thought occurs.

Note that to understand the effect of supply, one must understand that more lemonade stands mean fewer lemonade sales per stand—a complicated concept. To understand the effect of cup color, one must understand identity (it's still the same drink). To understand all the effects of motivation and morality, one must grasp the logical connection, or lack of it, between those variables and sales.

Answers to questions about cup color, motivation, and morality were considered correct either if the child said "no effect" or if the child thought of some plausible explanation. Most of the youngest children lost track of the issue and many gave irrelevant, wrong answers (e.g., "because people had electricity"). Even those young children (about 30 percent) who were considered correct usually said "no effect," an answer that, although technically right, could have been a lucky guess.

A further experiment confirmed that "no effect" was not much better than "I don't know." In this version girls were told, for example:

Terri really wanted to earn a lot of money, she wanted to earn a lot of money to buy toys, and because she wanted to earn a lot of money, she sold more cups of lemonade than she usually did.

Boys were told the same story, with masculine pronouns.

None of the 6-year-olds of either sex could provide a plausible explanation for this result. However, 30 percent of the 8-year-olds and 45 percent of the 10-year-olds not only gave an explanation but filled in the missing links, specifying something Terri did to increase sales. In follow-up analysis, the investigators noted that the older children who scored correct (as shown in Figure 12.2) were less likely to say merely "no effect" and were more likely to offer a plausible explanation. For example, in explaining how motivation could lead to an increase in sales, one child said, "He probably jumped out and said to every person he saw, 'Hey, would you like a nice cold cup of lemonade today?'" (Siegler & Thompson, 1998).

Figure 12.2 Understanding Supply and Demand. When children age 4 to 10 were asked to explain which factors might affect lemonade sales, and how that might happen, dramatic improvement occurred at about age 7.

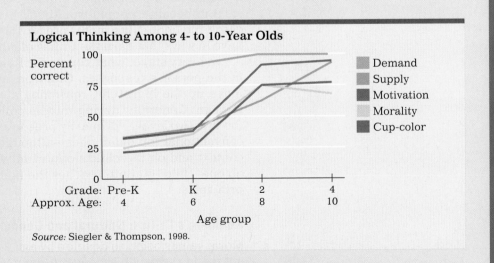

Logical Thinking Among 4- to 10-Year Olds

Source: Siegler & Thompson, 1998.

table **12.2**	**Kohlberg's Three Levels and Six Stages of Moral Reasoning**

Level I: Preconventional Moral Reasoning
Emphasis is placed on getting rewards and avoiding punishments; this is a self-centered level.

- *Stage One: Might makes right* (a punishment and obedience orientation). The most important value is obedience to authority, so as to avoid punishment while still advancing self-interest.
- *Stage Two: Look out for number one* (an instrumental and relativist orientation). Each person tries to take care of his or her own needs. The reason to be nice to other people is so that they will be nice to you.

Level II: Conventional Moral Reasoning
Emphasis is placed on social rules; this is a community-centered level.

- *Stage Three: "Good girl" and "nice boy."* Proper behavior is now behavior that pleases other people. Social approval is more important than any specific reward.
- *Stage Four: "Law and order."* Proper behavior means being a dutiful citizen and obeying the laws set down by society.

Level III: Postconventional Moral Reasoning
Emphasis is now on moral principles; this level is centered on ideals.

- *Stage Five: Social contract.* One should obey the rules of society because they exist for the benefit of all and are established by mutual agreement. If the rules become destructive, however, or if one party doesn't live up to the agreement, the contract is no longer binding.
- *Stage Six: Universal ethical principles.* General universal principles, and not individual situations or community practices, determine right and wrong. Ethical values (such as "Life is sacred") are established by individual reflection and may contradict the egocentric or legal values of earlier stages.

According to Kohlberg, *how* people reason, rather than what specific moral conclusions they reach, determines their stage of moral development. For example, reasoning that seeks social approval (stage 3) might produce opposite conclusions: Either Heinz should steal the drug (because people will blame him for not saving his wife) or he should not steal it (because people would call him a thief if he stole). But in both cases, the underlying moral precept is the same—that people should behave in ways that earn the praise of others, a stage-3 way of thinking.

In every stage, what counts for Kohlberg is the thinking that results in the person's responses. Children, adolescents, and adults gradually move up the hierarchy, reasoning at a more advanced stage as time goes on. Generally, during middle childhood, children's answers are at the first two levels—primarily preconventional for younger children and conventional for older ones—although much depends on the specific context and on the child's opportunity to discuss moral issues. Almost no one, child or adult, reaches the highest level of all, universal ethical principles.

Kohlberg's Critics: Cultural and Gender Differences

Moral values begin to develop by age 2 and continue to change throughout the life span. Childhood, however, is the time when moral values are taught, ethical principles are tested, and religious beliefs are laid down.

It also is a time when the various parts of the brain—emotional and intellectual—become better connected, enabling children to think through their instinctive reactions, setting moral values and then acting on them:

> It's a real passion for them. . . . In elementary school, maybe as never before or afterward, given favorable family and neighborhood circumstances, the child becomes an intensely moral creature, quite interested in figuring out the reasons of this world: how and why things work, but also, how and why he or she should behave in various situations. [Coles, 1997]

Given the fertile ground for moral thought during the school years, Kohlberg's moral-stages theory was welcomed by many developmentalists who sought to understand and measure moral thinking. Over the past two decades, however, this theory has met with substantial criticism. For example, some critics suggest that Kohlberg's dilemmas and hierarchy, with their "philosophical emphasis on justice and psychological emphasis on reasoning," are too narrow and restrictive (Walker et al., 1995).

Others believe that Kohlberg's level III (stages 5 and 6) reflects only liberal, Western intellectual values. In many non-Western nations and among many non-Western ethnic groups within Western cultures, the good of the family, the well-being of the community, or adherence to religious tradition takes moral precedence over all other considerations (Wainryb & Turiel, 1995). This makes it harder for non-Westerners to score at Kohlberg's postconventional level or even to move up the hierarchy as fast as others. For example, in a study of teenagers in the Netherlands, Moroccan and Turkish students were significantly behind Dutch and Surinamese adolescents in Kohlberg's dilemmas (De May et al., 1999).

Carol Gilligan (1982) has raised the most telling criticism. She contends that Kohlberg overlooks significant differences in the way males and females view moral dilemmas, in part because his original research used only boys as subjects. Gilligan explains that females develop a **morality of care** more than a **morality of justice**. The morality of care makes girls and women reluctant to judge right and wrong in absolute terms (justice) because they are socialized to be nurturant, compassionate, and nonjudgmental (caring).

As an example, Gilligan cites the responses of two bright 11-year-olds, Jake and Amy, to the Heinz story. Jake considered the dilemma "sort of like a math problem with humans," and he set up an equation that showed that life is more important than property. Amy, in contrast, seemed to sidestep the issue, arguing that Heinz "really shouldn't steal the drug—but his wife shouldn't die either." She tried to find an alternative solution (a bank loan, perhaps) and then explained that stealing wouldn't be right because Heinz "might have to go to jail, and then his wife might get sicker again, and he couldn't get more of the drug."

Amy's response may seem just as ethical as Jake's, but Kohlberg would score it lower. Gilligan argues that this is unfair, because what appears to be females' moral weakness—their hesitancy to take a definitive position based on abstract moral premises—is, in fact,

> inseparable from women's moral strength, an overriding concern with relationships and responsibilities. The reluctance to judge may itself be indicative of the care and concern that infuse the psychology of women's development. [Gilligan, 1982]

morality of care Moral thought and behavior based on comparison, nurturance, and concern for the well-being of other people. This morality is said to be more common among girls and women.

morality of justice Moral thought and behavior based on depersonalized standards of right and wrong, with judgments based on abstractions, not relationships. This morality is said to be more common among boys and men.

Prosocial Behavior: Two Versions School-age children, such as these Habitat for Humanity builders and this Girl Scout, are able to perform many useful prosocial tasks. Although prosocial acts are performed without expectation of rewards, they can result in a very important benefit: a sense of connection. The adults' role is to find suitable prosocial activities for school-age children—not always an easy task because children don't always feel comfortable "helping." These boys, for instance, might not enjoy wearing a uniform and chatting with the elderly, but they certainly take pride in pounding nails with their friends.

Many researchers have tested Gilligan's ideas with children, by looking for a morality of care or a morality of justice. Some have found that school-age children (both boys and girls) are more likely to seek justice, whereas more mature subjects tend to show caring (Walker, 1988). Others have found just the opposite (Garrod & Beal, 1993).

In one study, the moral dilemma presented was not Kohlberg's but a fable about a family of moles who invite a lonely and cold porcupine to share their underground home for the winter. He accepts, but then the moles realize that the porcupine's size and quills make them very uncomfortable. They politely ask him to leave, but he refuses. What to do? One 8-year-old was very caring:

> They should all go on an expedition for marshmallows and stick the marshmallows on the porcupine's quills and then the moles will really, really, really not get pricked. Then the porcupine would be happy because he could live in the moles' house that suited him just fine and the moles could have tasty tidbits as well as a warm home because of the porcupine's body heat . . . and all would be happy. [Garrod, 1993]

By contrast, law and order were evident in another response:

> The central problem, as I see it, is that the moles want the porcupine to leave and he's refusing. I think that they should kick him out. They were nice to let him in in the first place. And it's not their fault that he has quills. They have a right to be comfortable in their own home . . . they can do what they want in their cave. It's like if a homeless man moved into my home while my family was vacationing in Florida. We'd definitely call the police. [Garrod, 1993]

Both these respondents were boys. Thus, in this research (and in other research involving the actual responses and actions of school-age children) there is no clear gender distinction regarding the morality of justice or the morality of care. However, all the researchers agree that moral dilemmas are provocative issues for school-age children. These children have opinions, and they like to express them. Almost all researchers also agree that abstract reasoning about the justice of hypothetical situations is not the only, or necessarily the best, way to measure moral judgment (Emler, 1998). What children actually do when they personally care about an issue is crucial.

Especially for Parents: Many parents object to the clutter created by their children's passion for collecting, especially when the objects are of little material value. When adults feel like storing or discarding the assortment of shells, pencils, advertisements, stickers, gum wrappers, cards, or whatever, what should they remember?

Stages and Cultures

Some of Piaget's writings imply that children suddenly progress from one stage to the next in every cognitive area, in social activities as well as in schoolwork, in geography as well as in language arts. The very idea of "stage" implies a steplike progression.

However, the movement to a new level of thinking is much more erratic. A certain type of logic (say, reversibility) might be evident in one domain of a school-age child's thought—perhaps, math or biology—but not in another, such as social understanding or economics. Moreover, whether the shift to concrete operational thought is evident between ages 5 and 7 years or at some other time (even earlier, as you saw in Chapter 9) seems to depend on the specific child and the contexts in which the shift occurs. Education and practice are the forces behind many aspects of cognitive maturation (Alibali, 1999; Siegler, 1996).

In other words, cognitive development seems to be considerably more affected by sociocultural factors than Piaget's descriptions imply. In fact, because acquisition of a knowledge base and educational guidance are pivotal during the school years, the 5-to-7 shift itself may be the result of the first-grade curriculum rather than brain maturation. Is a similar contextual effect apparent in moral development?

Moral Thoughts and Deeds

As we have seen, during middle childhood children are passionately concerned with issues of right and wrong. Overall, these are the

> years of eager, lively searching on the part of children, whose parents and teachers are often hard put to keep up with them as they try to understand things, to figure them out, but also to weigh the rights and wrongs of this life. This is the time for growth of the moral imagination, fueled constantly by the willingness, the eagerness of children to put themselves in the shoes of others. [Coles, 1997]

The specifics, however, depend heavily on the values of the child's parents and society. If a family and culture are conscientious about providing children with guided participation in their set of values, with both adult and child undertaking moral actions, school-age children learn and, eventually, behave accordingly (Goodnow, 1997). As you saw in Chapter 10, prosocial behavior—acts of sharing, helping, and caring—is learned in much the same way that antisocial behavior is, from parents, schools, and peers (Eisenberg et al., 1996).

Few children *always* follow their parents' moral standards, their culture's conventions, or their own best moral thinking; yet moral thought has a decided influence on children's actions (Eisenberg, 1986; Rest, 1983). Increasingly, as they grow older, children try to figure out their own standards of what is the "right" thing to do, and they feel guilty and ashamed when they do "wrong," even if no one else knows (Harter, 1996).

For example, when children were asked whether they would break a law to help their siblings or peers, the answer was almost always yes. In general, school-age children considered loyalty to siblings or peers—especially to a close friend—a compelling reason to

Give Peace a Chance The setting is Israel; the sheep washers include Jews and Muslims. In all probability, these boys are aware that their cooperative efforts are in accord with moral values but are contrary to the social customs prevailing around them. The school years are a good time to teach children about other races and cultures, a lesson best learned through personal experience.

CHALLENGING THE ADULTS

As a mother of four, teaching moral thinking and behavior is very important to me. I have often said that I would rather have my children become loving and caring adults than become successful and rich—although I take great pride in their successes. It is not surprising, then, that they also pay attention to moral issues, sometimes taking actions that are not the ones I would choose.

For example, my daughter Sarah regularly gives her pocket money to homeless people and is quick to criticize me for rudely (her word) passing them by. The strength of her conviction was illustrated years ago when her fourth-grade class visited the local police precinct in New York City to hear an officer instruct them on street safety. Most of his talk was accepted without protest, until:

> *Officer:* Never take money out of your pocket while you are on the street—
>
> *(At this point, according to the mother who helped chaperone the school trip, Sarah raised her hand insistently, "the way children do who have to go to the bathroom right away.")*
>
> *Officer: (Interrupting his speech)* Yes?

> *Sarah:* But what if a homeless man wants money?
> *Officer:* Your parents give you money for lunch, not to give away.
> *Sarah:* But what if you decide you don't need lunch?
> *Officer:* You should not give money to beggars; you don't know how they will spend it.
> *Sarah:* But what if you decide he really really needs it?
> *Officer:* Don't give it. Adults are taking care of the homeless people who really need help.
> *Sarah: (Shaking her head)* Well, you aren't doing a very good job.

That incident made me proud, as the mother who telephoned me to report it knew it would.

Although I still disagree about the most moral response to street beggars, I appreciate at least one aspect of this incident. Sarah's active sense of morality bodes well. Children who engage in moral discussion and feel personally responsible for their ethical behavior tend to be more accomplished than others, socially as well as academically (Bandura et al., 1996). Active reflection is much more likely to lead to moral action than is merely accepting social conventions and laws.

❷ Especially for Social Scientists: Measuring all variables that constitute a good education is complex. Which research designs (from Chapter 1) would indicate whether a particular school provides a good education?

ignore community standards of proper action. Many children said they would cheat, lie, or steal to help a needy friend (Smetana et al., 1991; Turiel et al., 1991). Further, authority figures—parents, teachers, police officers, store owners—are not necessarily seen as right (see the In Person box).

In one study, school-age children from India and the United States were asked about the seriousness of various behaviors. Children from both cultures agreed that it was wrong to break a promise, destroy another's picture, or kick harmless animals, and they said that they themselves did not do these things. However, consistent with their cultural and religious beliefs, children from India believed that eating beef, addressing one's father by his first name, and cutting one's hair after a father's death were far worse violations than did American children. By contrast, American children believed that inflicting serious corporal punishment and eating dinner with one's hands were more serious offenses than did children in India (Schweder et al., 1990).

Because cultural and religious values shape moral perception, what is merely conventional may take on moral significance. Children behave in accordance with their moral beliefs, nurtured by family, school, and especially the peer group. As they grow older, their actions are seen as more ethical, and less self-interested, because they have the social experiences, the cultural awareness, and the cognitive capacity to generate more persuasive arguments—both in convincing themselves

● Response for Parents (from page 339): During the concrete operational period, children learn through active manipulation. Counting and classifying those collections, and comparing and trading them with each other, are fuel for the intellectual fire.

to do the right thing and in justifying their actions to others (Emler, 1998). They continue the patterns established as older children and adolescents when they are grown. Many middle-aged and older adults obey conventions they learned and internalized when young, finding it hard to adjust their moral behavior.

LEARNING AND SCHOOLING

The school-age child described thus far is eager to learn, able to focus attention, to remember interrelated facts, to master logical operations, and to use several linguistic codes. That description is universal: It holds for children age 7 to 11 the world over, and it evokes numerous adult efforts to train, teach, and educate.

Consequently, schooling of some sort during middle childhood is available in every nation. But the specifics—who receives instruction, in what subjects, and how—vary enormously. In the past, boys and wealthier children were much more likely to receive formal education than girls and poor children. Some of that inequality is still apparent today. In developing countries, more boys than girls attend elementary school (58 percent to 42 percent). In developed countries, less is generally demanded of girls and poor children, particularly in mathematics and science (UNESCO, 1997; U.S. Department of Education, 1997).

Teaching techniques also vary widely, from the *strict lecture method,* in which students are forbidden to talk, whisper, or even move during class, to *open education,* in which students are encouraged to interact and make use of all classroom resources—with the teacher serving as an adviser, guide, and friend more than as a subject-matter authority and disciplinarian. In general, school-age children who believe that their efforts will help them learn the skills they need are more motivated and involved in schoolwork, and hence learn more. Teachers who are seen as warm and encouraging are more likely to foster such engagement (Skinner et al., 1998). Two examples of such teachers and students are given in the Changing Policy box. A further discussion of some aspects of school and culture appears in Chapter 15.

Learning to Learn These two classes, in Somalia *(left)* and Japan *(right),* are different from each other in many ways. However, they both share several characteristics that are rare in most nations where this textbook is used.

INTERACTIVE TEACHING

Good teachers differ greatly in how they teach, what they teach, and what their educational goals are. Yet, worldwide, as classroom practice comes closer to developmental theory, teachers have become much more encouraging of children's efforts. Look for the similarities and differences in the two examples extracted below:

In a first grade classroom in central Tokyo, 6-year-old Shoji Itoh repeatedly jumped up from his seat during the reading lesson. Each time he shouted "baka yaro" (you're a jerk) at the teacher so loudly that it could be heard several classrooms away. Each time little Itoh yelled, Ms. Nakanishi went over to his seat, put her arm around him and pointed to the sentence currently being read out loud. The class read aloud, with intermittent outbursts from Itoh, for about 15 minutes. Then they began an activity called "collecting words." Up and down the rows, each of the 35 students named a favorite object in a picture projected on the front wall: Mrs. Nakanishi wrote each named object on the board.

When Itoh's turn came, he named "electric rice cooker." Ms. Nakanishi asked him to come to the front of the class, put her arm around him, and praised him extravagantly. "You are very smart . . . let's all clap for him. . . ." Itoh gave a theatrical bow to the class's applause and took his seat, beaming. [Lewis, 1996]

Halfway around the world, an American teacher uses some of the same techniques. It is the beginning of the school year, and there is a math problem to be solved. Specifically, "There are six runners on each team. There are two teams in the race. How many runners altogether?" The children have already worked in pairs to come up with the process for answering, called the "answer solution."

> *Teacher:* Jack, what answer solution did you come up with?
> *Jack:* Fourteen.
> *Teacher:* Fourteen. How did you get that answer?
> *Jack:* Because 6 plus 6 is 12. Two runners on two teams . . .

(Jack stops talking, puts his hands to the side of his face and looks down at the floor. Then he looks at the teacher and at his partner, Ann. He turns and faces the front of the room with his back to the teacher and mumbles inaudibly.)

> *Teacher:* Would you please say that again. I didn't quite get the whole thing. You had—say it again please.
> *Jack: (Softly, still facing the front of the room)* It's six runners on each team.
> *Teacher:* Right.
> *Jack: (Turns to look at the teacher)* I made a mistake. It's wrong. It should be twelve. *(He turns and faces the front of the room again.)*

(Jack's acute embarrassment . . . confounded the teacher's intention that the children should publicly express their thinking and, more generally, engage in mathematical practice characterized by conjecture, argument, and justification.)

---

❶ Response for Social Scientists (from page 340): There are many right answers as long as you realize that single impressions are likely to be simplistic and that context is critical. You would use several methods, including naturalistic observation, multifaceted testing, and some controlled experimentation in order to compare and evaluate the impact of several variables. A survey might not be appropriate, since cultural values, rather than objective analysis, affect students' opinions about the quality of their education. You certainly would want to study long-term results, ideally with a longitudinal study of outcomes.

Communication Skills

One of the most important skills for children to learn in school is communication—in speech, in writing, and in reading. Math and science are no less dependent on literacy than are social studies or the language arts. Fortunately, during middle childhood, children really enjoy words, as demonstrated in the poems they write, the secret languages they create, and the jokes they tell. Joke telling actually demands several skills not usually apparent in younger children: the ability to listen carefully; the ability to know what someone else will think is funny; and, hardest of all, the ability to remember the right way to tell a joke. Vocabulary is often key, with puns a mainstay of school-age humor. The intellectual flexibility required to understand a pun is the consequence of the brain maturation described in Chapter 8. A child who seems bright but is unable to grasp jokes that most peers find hilarious may be brain-damaged in some way.

Teacher: (Softly) Oh, okay. Is it okay to make a mistake?
Andrew: Yes.
Teacher: Is it okay to make a mistake, Jack?
Jack: Yeah.
Teacher: You bet it is. As long as you're in my class it is okay to make a mistake. Because I make them all the time, and we learn from our mistakes—a lot. Jack already figured out, "Ooops, I didn't have the right answer the first time" *(Jack turns and looks at the teacher and smiles),* but he kept working at it and he got it. [Cobb et al., 1993]

Educators have been criticized for swinging from harsh, dull, standards-based lessons to a warm, lax, nondirectional approach. These excerpts, different as they are, avoid both extremes. In both cases, the teacher saw something wrong and worked to correct it—getting one boy to conform to the group discipline and the other boy to find and correct an error. In both cases, the teacher used the other students as allies, rather than allowing antagonism. Finally, in both cases, the child's ego was protected, so, it is hoped, he will want to learn again.

The first example was cited by an American educator who observed many Japanese classrooms. He was struck by the cultural emphasis on cooperation—not only in this instance but overall.

Teachers explained that disruptive children needed to strengthen their bonds to other children. What I saw as issues of control and misbehavior, teachers talked about as issues of community; they transformed any questions about discipline into discussions of the teacher–child bond and the bonds among children. [Lewis, 1996]

It is easy to ask if these teachers were misguided. Is the Japanese teacher rewarding disruption instead of controlling it? Is the American teacher downplaying accurate computation by not only allowing the student's mistake but emphasizing that she makes mistakes as well?

In both cases, the proof is in the results—not just in the apparent success for these two boys but also in careful research that finds that this interactive approach works well. A similar approach is being taken in many math classes, as workbooks, rote learning, and pure memorization are being replaced by instruction that involves hands-on materials, cooperative problem solving, and active discussion.

This is the direction that developmentalists hope to see in the future. The specific styles and methods of education will vary, depending on teacher personality and cultural assumptions, but any developmental approach to education attempts to engage every student in the process (Renninger, 1998).

The child's usual delight with words makes middle childhood a good time for adults to work with children to expand their vocabularies. By some estimates, the rate of school-age vocabulary growth exceeds that of the preschool years; school-age children acquire as many as 20 words daily to achieve a vocabulary of nearly 40,000 words by the fifth grade (Anglin, 1993).

But this vocabulary increase does not qualify as an "explosion" (with the implication of sudden, scattershot eruption), as it did in earlier years. During middle childhood, children become more analytic and logical in their comprehension of vocabulary, which means that explicit instruction becomes useful.

Suppose a teacher asks a child to say the first thing that comes to mind on hearing, say, "apple." A preschooler is likely to respond with a word about perceptions or appearance ("red" or "round") or egocentric action ("eat" or "cook"). An older child, however, might respond to "apple" by referring to an appropriate category ("fruit" or "snack") or to other objects

PEANUTS

Drawing by Charles Schultz © 1980 by United Features Syndicate

Are Kids Goats? With a language as irregular as English, it should be no surprise that many children (as well as adults) sometimes generate grammatical errors by applying logic to their language constructions. By school age, at least they understand that the same word can mean several things. Only one meaning per word is allowed in early childhood, but by age 9, "kid" can mean "child," "baby goat," and "deceive," and "behooves" does not mean "bee-hooves."

that logically extend the apple context ("pie" or "tree"). Then suppose the older child is asked to deduce the meanings of new words that have "apple" as their root (such as "apple butter" and "applecart"). This ability to see logical word connections is a major reason vocabulary expands rapidly in middle childhood: in "applesauce," "applecart," "apple butter," "applewood," and "apple polisher," five separate words are connected to the word "apple" and are acquired through that connection.

The exact meaning of each word also becomes better understood. For example, most 4-year-olds consider something "forgotten" if it is an unfulfilled desire or if it was never known. ("I forgot the cheesecake" can mean "I did not get any cheesecake" or "I do not know what cheesecake is"). By age 8, however, most children use "forgot" to mean "failed to remember" (Hill et al., 1997). Part of this growth comes as a result of adult instruction, but children working cooperatively also help each other with language and logic, especially during the school years (Rogoff, 1998). As we will now see, however, some of the communication between children may not be what adults would wish.

Code-Switching

By elementary school, children become sensitive to variations in the speech and tone of others—realizing, for example, that a father's clipped speech is an indication of growing anger or that the whole range of linguistic conventions may be changed to suit particular audiences. The latter concept is apparent in this example:

> A brand-new black teacher is delivering her first reading lesson to a group of first-grade students in inner-city Philadelphia. She has almost memorized the entire basal-provided lesson dialogue [the introduction provided in the teacher's edition of the textbook] while practicing in front of a mirror the night before.
>
> "Good morning, boys and girls. Today we're going to read a story about where we live, in the city."
>
> A small brown hand rises.
>
> "Yes, Marti."
>
> Marti and this teacher are special friends, for she was a kindergartner in the classroom where her new teacher student-taught.
>
> "Teacher, how come you talkin' like a white person? You talkin' just like my momma talk when she get on the phone."
>
> I was that first-year teacher many years ago, and Marti was among the first to teach me the role of language diversity in the classroom. Marti let me know that children, even young children, are often aware of the different codes we all use in our everyday lives. They may not yet have learned how to produce those codes or what social purposes they serve, but children often have a remarkable ability to discern and identify different codes in different settings. [Delpit, 1995]

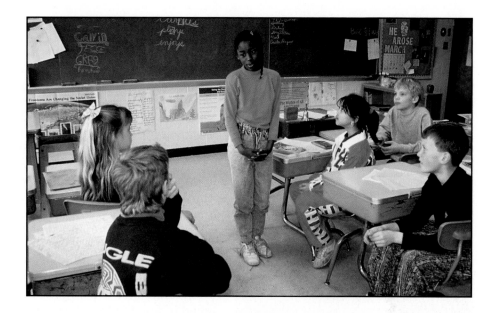

Recitation The formal code is appropriate in the classroom, as this girl demonstrates.
❷ *Observational Quiz (see answer page 347): What signs suggest that she is trying to avoid the informal code?*

code-switching A pragmatic communication skill that involves a person's switching from one form of language, such as dialect or slang, to another.

formal code A form of speech used by children in school and in other formal situations; characterized by extensive vocabulary, complex syntax, lengthy sentences, and conformity to other middle-class norms for correct language. (Sometimes called *elaborated code*.)

informal code A form of speech characterized by limited use of vocabulary and syntax; meaning is communicated by gestures, intonation, and shared understanding. (Sometimes called *restricted code*.)

In addition to recognizing codes, children can change from one form of speech to another, a process called **code-switching.** Children in middle childhood censor profanity when they talk to adults, use picturesque slang and drama on the playground, and even switch back and forth from one language to another. All these are changes in code.

Formal and Informal Communication

In a universal example of code-switching, almost every child shifts from formal communication in the classroom to informal communication with friends outside of school. In general, the **formal code**, sometimes called *elaborated code*, is characterized by extensive vocabulary, complex syntax, and lengthy sentences. By comparison, the **informal code**, sometimes called *restricted code*, uses fewer words, simpler syntax, and relies more on gestures and intonation to convey meaning.

The formal code is relatively *context-free*; that is, the meaning is clear regardless of the immediate context. The informal code tends to be *context-bound*; that is, the meaning relies on the shared understandings and experiences of speaker and listener, as well as on the immediate subject at hand. A dispirited student might tell a teacher, in formal code, "I'm depressed today because [a detailed excuse that the teacher is likely to accept], and I would rather not read out loud or write my book response," and later confide to a friend informally, "I'm down; school ——s" [the particular word depends on the specific local code].

Children of all backgrounds code-switch, changing pronunciation, grammar, and vocabulary depending on the context. Black English, southern dialect, patois, Valley talk, Cockney, mountain speech, Newyorican, pidgin, street language, broken English, and slang all refer to informal codes that are used not only by children but also by adults (especially when speaking with other adults who had similar childhood origins). However, even children who do not know a designated, regionalized informal code (such as the ones just mentioned) tend to speak to their friends informally, with less crisp enunciation and non-textbook grammar (Romaine, 1984; Yoon, 1992).

Secrets In many ways, the informal speech of 7- to 11-year-olds reflects their overall desire to distinguish themselves from adult culture.

❷ *Observational Quiz (see answer page 348): Beyond the whispered words, what three characteristics do you see here that run contrary to formal adult standards?*

total immersion   An approach to learning a second language in which the learner is placed in an environment where only the second language is spoken.

Formal language is sometimes called correct, proper, high, or standard (as in *Standard English* or *High German/Hoch Deutsch*). Such adjectives imply that the formal code is best, but actually both codes have their place. It is important to be able to speak in formal terms, partly because standard language is considered educated speech and its vocabulary is more precise. Indeed, the two pivotal skills learned during middle childhood—reading and writing—depend on understanding and employing formal language without the benefit of informal gestures, intonations, and immediate context.

At the same time, peer communication via informal code is vital—not only for social acceptance but also for more direct, emotional dialogue. While many adults rightly stress their children's mastery of proper language ("Say precisely what you mean in complete sentences, and no slang"), the code that is used with peers is also evidence of the child's ability (Goodwin, 1990). This same distinction can be made between children who speak the dominant language of a nation and those who have another mother tongue. Both languages are important, for different reasons, and educators need to find a way to foster fluent bilingualism—no easy task.

Second-Language Learners

Almost every nation has a sizable minority who speak a nonmajority language; for them, learning the majority language is a necessity. In fact, most of the estimated 6,000 languages of the world are never used in formal educational settings. Consequently, most of the world's children are educated in a language other than their mother tongue (Tucker, 1998). Even for those whose home language is also their school language, a second language is useful, even required, as multinational business, finance, and travel become more common. An added intellectual benefit is that learning another language enhances children's overall linguistic and cognitive development, especially if it occurs before puberty (Baker, 1993; Edwards, 1994; Romaine, 1995). How, and when, should children learn other languages?

The best time to *learn* a second language by listening and talking is during early childhood, although the best time to *teach* a second language seems to be during middle childhood. Because of their readiness to understand code-switching, their eagerness to communicate, their wish to be good students, their grasp of logic, and their ear for nuances of pronunciation, children aged 6 to 11 are at their prime for being taught a second language.

Strategies

The question of how to teach another language to nonnative speakers has been one of intense concern and emotion, but no educational approach has yet been recognized as best. Strategies include both extremes—from **total immersion,** in which the child's instruction occurs entirely in the second (majority) language, to *reverse immersion,* in which the child is taught in his or her first (native) language for several years, until the second language can be taught as a "foreign" language. Variations between these extremes include presenting some topics of instruction in one language and other topics in the other language, or presenting every topic in both languages, or conducting separate after-school classes in a "heritage language" to allow children to connect with their culture while learning all academic subjects in the dominant language.

In the United States, three approaches attempt to avoid the shock of complete immersion in the teaching of English:

English as a second language (ESL)
An approach to teaching English in which English is the only language of instruction for students who speak many other native languages.

■ **English as a second language,** or ESL, requires all non-English-speaking students to go through an intensive instructional period together, with the goal of mastering the basics of English in six months or so. In classes using ESL, the teacher does not speak the child's native language (indeed, the teacher may not even understand all the languages spoken by the students); but at least everyone has a common goal of helping every child master an alien tongue. A total of 43 percent of all public schools in the United States provided ESL classes in 1994, up from 34 percent in 1988 (Henke et al., 1996).

bilingual education An approach to teaching a second language that also advances knowledge in the first language. Instruction occurs, side by side, in two languages.

■ **Bilingual education** requires that the teacher instruct the children in school subjects using their native language as well as English. In the early years, children are greeted, instructed, and (when necessary) disciplined in two languages, in the hope that they will progress in both. Informal talk between one child and another is almost always in the native language, as is much of the teacher's informal conversation. In 1994, 18 percent of U.S. public schools provided bilingual education, down from 20 percent in 1988 (Henke et al., 1996). The "English-only" movement, particularly in the western United States, has further reduced bilingual classes.

bilingual-bicultural education An approach to teaching a second language that adds preservation of nonnative cultural symbols and strategies (such as in the way teaching occurs) to a bilingual program.

■ **Bilingual-bicultural education** recognizes that non-English-speaking children come to school with non-Anglo values, traditions, and perceptions that some think need to be preserved within the larger American culture. Implementation of the strategy may be as simple as celebrating special holidays (such as, for Mexican American children, Three Kings Day, Cinco de Mayo, and the Day of the Dead), or it may be as complex as instituting new classroom strategies (such as more or less cooperative learning, or special punishment tactics). Unlike ESL, bilingual-bicultural education preserves a child's native language and heritage. Practically as well as politically, bilingual-bicultural education requires a large concentration of children with the same linguistic and ethnic background and a large group of adults who value the native language. In the United States bilingual-bicultural programs during school usually involve Hispanic children, and bilingual-bicultural after-school programs more commonly serve Asian children.

Success and Failure

Which teaching strategy is best? In Canada, immersion has succeeded with more than 300,000 English-speaking children who were initially placed in French-only classrooms. These children showed no decline in English skills (learned at home) or in other academic achievement (Edwards, 1994; Lambert et al., 1993). Indeed, even when Canadian children whose native language is English are immersed in two other languages—French and Hebrew—from the first to the sixth grade, they do well on achievement tests in all three languages (Genesee, 1998). Note, however, that this was a six-year program.

By contrast, reverse immersion works best in Guatemala, where children learn the second language (Spanish) only after they have already been well taught in their native Mayan language (Tucker, 1998). In Belgium, biculturalism works with children of Italian ancestry if teachers who are native to Belgium and teachers who are native to Italy each teach the students for half a day (Byram, 1998). Thus, all three strategies can succeed—sometimes.

❶ *Answer to Observational Quiz (from page 345): Her clasped hands, touching feet, and serious expression suggest that she will not use the gestures, body movements, and humor that characterize the informal code. Note that her audience is equally serious, even stiff. On the playground, this same group would be much more active, relaxed, smiling, and informal.*

Figure 12.3   Que Pasa? Most dropouts are alienated from school years before they drop out, often because English is the language of instruction but they are not fluent in that language. As this graph shows, the white dropout rate is below 4 percent and the black rate has declined to 5 percent, but the rate among Latino students remains high, averaging 10 percent since 1972. (This is the somewhat misleading "event dropout" rate, which is the percentage of students who dropped out before graduation in the tenth, eleventh, or twelfth grade. That means the actual rate is about three times the figure given here.)

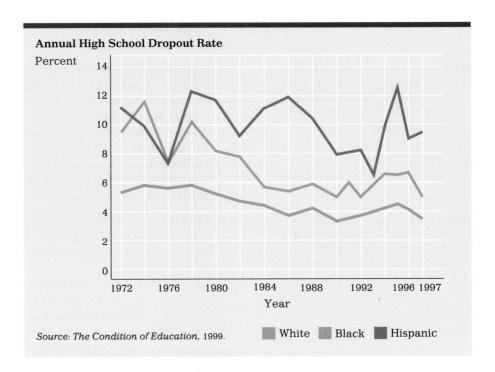

Annual High School Dropout Rate

Percent

Source: *The Condition of Education, 1999.*

White   Black   Hispanic

● *Answer to Observational Quiz (from page 346):* Actually, distinctions between child and adult culture are apparent in every part of this photo. Any three of the following would be correct: mismatched shoes, men's boxers, cotton "bracelet," overlarge shirts, missing sock on the right, braces on the left, and, finally, physical touching, from knees up to foreheads.

Immersion tends to fail if children are made to feel shy, stupid, or socially isolated because of their language difference. In such cases, this educational approach might more aptly be called *submersion,* because children are more likely to sink than swim (Edwards, 1994).

In the United States, many school systems use none of the three approaches described earlier. For most of the twentieth century, Native American children were sent to boarding schools to learn white ways. Many of them became sick, ran away, or became alienated from their families, victims of an attempt at cultural obliteration that only recently has been recognized (Coontz, 1998). Even today, many Spanish-speaking children who are instructed only in English become slow learners who repeat a grade or two until they are old enough to drop out of school (see Figure 12.3). Unfortunately, the main alternative—bilingual education—does not necessarily produce children who are so fluent in English that they can perform well in an English-only high school. In both cases, their poor performance is blamed on their deficit in English rather than on the teachers and educational programs that failed to take into account the special needs of such children (Romo & Fable, 1996).

The crucial difference between success and failure in second-language learning seems to rest with the attitudes of the parents, the teachers, and the larger community, who indicate to the child whether mastering a new language is really valued. As one review regarding the need for well-trained language teachers explained, "Whether policies are overtly articulated, covertly implied, or invisibly in the making, the central concern in multilingual education appears to be how much status and recognition within the educational system should be given to the languages of the minority group" (Nunan & Lam, 1998).

Another important factor is the age of the children. As children grow older and more self-conscious about making friends, it becomes

Friendly Immersion The poster is in English, because this Toronto teacher is explaining a sign in the city, but all the instruction occurs in French, even though none of these children are French-speaking natives. Their parents chose it not only because French immersion works successfully in Canada but also because such programs have a reputation for academic rigor, including high standards for conduct and achievement. Attitudes, not just instruction, facilitate learning a second language.

harder simply to put them in a classroom and expect them to learn. One boy recalled his early experiences in a Toronto classroom:

> I did not know what to do when the other students spoke to me because I did not understand them. I was forced to use signs with my hands to communicate with people, just as if I were deaf and dumb. I hated the students who spoke with me. . . . Sometimes there was a joke, and I had to laugh with the others even though I did not know what the joke was, because I was afraid of being laughed at. [quoted in Coelho, 1991]

This experience raises a basic question: What is the goal of second-language education? Almost all evaluations of such programs focus on one measure of success: proficiency in the new language. Other measures—school graduation, personal success, family disruption, cultural alienation—are often ignored. But can a program be called successful when it teaches one language at the expense of another?

Obviously, school-age children need to learn the language of their society, but they also need to develop their understanding of themselves and of others. Educational practices, including attitudes regarding children's native languages, can be instrumental in determining whether "the linguistic, cognitive, and sociocultural resources children bring to school" are used to achieve the larger goal—seeing that "the developing child becomes a fully functioning and valued member of the community" (Genesee, 1994). They should always work toward that goal.

To reach that goal, developmental research emphasizes four findings:

- Children learn a first and second spoken language best early in life, ideally under age 5, otherwise under age 11.
- Peers are the best teachers, with the encouragement and guidance of adults who understand the school-age child's eagerness to learn new structures, strategies, and vocabulary.
- Each combination of child, family, and culture is unique, and goals and attitudes vary tremendously. No single language-teaching approach is best for everyone, everywhere, but attitudes are an important gateway—or barrier—for language learning.
- Immigrant children are great learners—if given the opportunity.

The last fact was made clear in a research study that compared immigrant children with children of their own racial-ethnic group who were born in North America (Fuligni, 1997). (For example, Latin American immigrants were compared with children of Hispanic heritage, children from the Caribbean and Africa were compared with African Americans, European immigrants were compared with white, non-Hispanic Americans.)

By high school, the immigrant children had higher motivation and spent more time studying. They outperformed the native-born Americans of the same heritage in grade-point average, not only in math and science but also in English (although their English standardized test scores were lower). Two expected factors correlated with their success: socioeconomic status (SES) and whether or not the family spoke English at home. However, even when the family was poor and non-English-speaking, immigrant children were better students than nonimmigrants. Thus children born in Mexico or China did better in high school than their U.S.-born classmates whose parents or grandparents were born in those countries. The authors of this study concluded:

> The increased presence of the children from immigrant families in American schools has recently become a subject of great public concern. The results of this study suggest that the vast majority of these students who possess a working knowledge of English actually perform just as well as if not better than their counterparts from native-born families. These students possess an academic eagerness and initiative that would be welcomed by most teachers and schools. [Fuligni, 1997]

Thus speaking a language other than the majority language, or using a code other than the standard one, is not a cognitive problem during middle childhood, as long as the student has "a working knowledge of English." However, 7- to 10-year-olds do not master the intellectual or linguistic skills they need in isolation, spontaneously. They need to be taught, informally through positive cultural and familial attitudes and formally through school.

Schooling and Cultural Values

School-age children in the United States are in school more and outdoors less, studying more and playing less, than before (see Table 12.3). This shift results from the perception of parents, educators, and the general public that the superior performance of Asian children can be attributed to the fact that they spend more months of the year, more days of the week, more hours of the day, and even more minutes of each school hour actively engaged in academic work. Children in Japanese and Taiwanese schools do not have to wait for others to finish, or go on errands, or mindlessly copy materials, or repeat work they have already done as much as students in North America do (Stevenson & Stigler, 1992).

However, even the researchers who first made North Americans aware of the extra time spent on education in Asian nations are concerned about mindlessly extending the school day and adding homework:

> In East Asia meticulous care is given to the construction of homework assignments. It's a great contrast to the routine assignments given in the U.S. Here we don't recognize that changing a child's mind is as complex as open-heart surgery. [Harold Stevenson, quoted in Tovey, 1997]

A Trade-Off? When international comparisons revealed that children in the United States were not first in academic achievement, parents and schools demanded more homework, longer school years, and less television. The results include advances in math and reading and less time for play, especially for the youngest children.

table **12.3**	**A Week in the Life of an American Child: Time Spent on Activity, per Week**				
	6- to 8-Year-Olds		9- to 11-Year-Olds*		
Activity	1981	1997	1981	1997	Average Time Change (1981–1997)
School	24:20	33:54	26:15	33:50	8h 34 min more
Sports	3:00	4:38	3:09	5:14	1h 52 min more
Studying	0:44	2:03	2:49	3:37	1h 3 min more
Art	0:28	0:45	0:23	0:56	25 min more
Reading	0:49	1:14	1:05	1:16	18 min more
Being outdoors	0:36	0:32	1:58	0:47	37 min less
Playing	15:15	11:26	8:29	8:44	1h 47 min less
Watching TV	12:47	12:38	18:20	13:36	2h 27 min less

*The 1997 figures are for children age 9 to 12.
Source: Institute for Social Research, 1997.

Who Is the Smart One Here? Research on child street vendors in Brazil, such as this boy in São Paulo, reveals that few have attended school but that most have quite advanced arithmetic skills, allowing them to divide per-item cost, subtract to determine change, and even convert currency of another nation into the Brazilian equivalent—adjusted for inflation. Other research confirms that school-age children use their cognitive capacities to master whatever their culture values or requires, including the social skills needed, in this case, to convince tourists to buy lemons.

The debate about what specific skills to stress in elementary education is ongoing. School-age children, as the research shows, are able and eager to learn almost anything, but they cannot learn everything at once. Comparing nations, comparing schools, and comparing children can show which educational strategies and curricula succeed, and in what ways. Another set of criteria is needed to measure which approaches should be valued. For example, when the need "to ensure a competitive workforce . . . to fill the jobs of the future and compete in a global economy" led the United States to set the goal of being first worldwide in math and science by the year 2000, most Americans probably agreed that this was a desirable achievement (National Endowment Goals Panel, 1997). But as math and science become priorities, and scores continue to rise, what will happen in literacy and creativity, areas in which the United States has traditionally excelled? Already historians are bemoaning children's ignorance: Only 32 percent of fourth-graders can name even one of the original thirteen colonies (Hitchens, 1998). Music, art, and physical education programs have been cut back in almost every school.

We will close this chapter with an example that again stresses the strong intellectual capacity of the school-age child, if experience and motivation are in place. Young Brazilian street vendors—all in middle childhood, with little formal education—do very poorly when given standard problems presented the way achievement tests usually present them (such as 420 + 80). However, when given oral problems involving fruit purchases and making change for a customer ("I'll take two coconuts that cost one real [about 50 cents] apiece. Here's a 10-real [about $5] bill. What do I get back?"), they solved the problems far more quickly and successfully, often using unconventional but effective math strategies (Carraher et al., 1985, 1988). In other words, although they seemed to lack the cognitive strategies necessary to solve arithmetic problems, these children had developed sophisticated math abilities. In fact, the price of the fruit they sold had to be recalculated often, as wholesale prices varied with supply and as inflation changed the value of the currency. These unschooled children mastered that math very well: Their survival depended on it.

Further research in Brazil, on 4- to 14-year-olds in a broad range of living situations, confirms the special relationship of thinking and experience during middle childhood. The cognitive advantage of actually having dealt with money was greatest for children age 6 to 11. Younger children were less able to understand the arithmetic problems as presented to them, and older ones could do just as well whether or not they had personal experience (Guberman, 1996). This is exactly what we might have predicted on the basis of the research described in this chapter as well as on the theories of Piaget (remember, *concrete* operational thought) and Vygotsky (who emphasized the tools of culture that help children learn). The years of middle childhood are especially well suited for both teaching and learning.

SUMMARY

REMEMBERING, KNOWING, AND PROCESSING

1. The thinking processes of school-age children are quite different from those of younger children. An understanding of "the game of thinking" gives school-age children the ability to direct their thinking and to become more effective learners in formal settings such as a school classroom.

2. The information-processing approach looks specifically at how the person takes in, remembers, and processes new material. This approach, inspired by the computer, finds that working memory and control processes in particular advance in middle childhood.

3. A marked improvement occurs in children's ability to concentrate on the task at hand and ignore distractions. Cognitive improvement is also apparent in school-age children's increased capacity for, and speed of, thinking. In addition, the knowledge base increases with each year of school, making it easier for new information to be assimilated.

4. Some of the advances in school-age thinking are the result of brain maturation For the most part, however, accumulated experience, motivated practice, and explicit instruction aid children to develop metacognitive skills.

STAGES OF THINKING

5. According to Piaget, the 5-to-7 shift involves a switch to concrete operational thought. Between those ages, children become able to apply logical principles such as identity and reversibility to problems of conservation, mathematics, science, and social understanding.

6. While Piaget's theory captures some essential qualities of the development of 7- to 11-year-old children's reasoning, most developmentalists believe that older children are not as consistently logical or objective as his theory portrays. Further, sociocultural factors may have a considerable effect on cognitive development.

7. Lawrence Kohlberg described how people reason about ethical dilemmas. He identified three levels of moral reasoning: preconventional, conventional, and postconventional.

8. Kohlberg's moral-stages theory has been criticized on grounds of intellectual narrowness, Western bias, and emphasis on (in Carol Gilligan's terms) a male "morality of justice" over a female "morality of care."

9. Middle childhood is marked by a passionate concern with issues of right and wrong. The specific area of concern varies with the parents' moral standards, the culture's conventions, the peer group's consensus, and, increasingly, the child's own developing moral code.

LEARNING AND SCHOOLING

10. Language abilities continue to improve during middle childhood, partly because increased cognitive development makes it easier to acquire new vocabulary. Children successfully learn code-switching, the ability to change from one form of speech to another, depending on the context and audience.

11. International comparisons reflect substantial variation in what and how school systems teach their children. Universally, however, school-age children are eager and able to learn whatever their community considers important.

KEY TERMS

information-processing theory (327)

sensory register (328)

working memory (328)

long-term memory (328)

control processes (328)

selective attention (329)

automatization (330)

metacognition (330)

knowledge base (331)

concrete operational thought (332)

5-to-7 shift (332)

identity (333)

reversibility (334)

preconventional moral reasoning (334)

conventional moral reasoning (334)

postconventional moral reasoning (334)

morality of care (337)

morality of justice (337)

code-switching (345)

formal code (345)

informal code (345)

total immersion (346)

English as a second language (ESL) (347)

bilingual education (347)

bilingual-bicultural education (347)

KEY QUESTIONS

1. How does the information-processing approach analyze cognitive development?

2. What accounts for the better working memory of school-age children compared to that of younger children?

3. What factors account for the increase in cognitive processing speed and capacity during the school years?

4. How does an expanded knowledge base affect thinking and memorization?

5. How does metacognition enhance the thinking of school-age children?

6. Describe several of Piaget's logical operations, or principles, that enhance reasoning during middle childhood.

7. Identify and briefly describe Kohlberg's three levels and six stages of moral development.

8. How does vocabulary increase in middle childhood?

9. What are the chief characteristics of formal and informal language codes, and when is each type of code used?

10. What changes in teaching practices have resulted from the application of cognitive theory regarding middle childhood?

11. *In Your Experience* What was the best measure of your ability to think and learn in childhood: your parents' and teachers' opinions, your scores on tests, or the evaluation of your peers? Why?

The School Years:
Psychosocial Development

CHAPTER 13

At age 6 or so, children break free from the closely supervised and limited arena of the younger child. Usually with their parents' blessing, school-age children explore the wider world of neighborhood, community, and school. They experience new vulnerability, increasing competence, ongoing friendships, troubling rivalries, and deeper social understanding.

Although they are often unobserved by adults, their lives are still shaped by family structures and community values. Our goal in this chapter is to examine the interplay between expanding freedom and guiding forces. First we will look at emotional and moral growth, then at the peer and family influences that direct and propel that growth, and, finally, at the coping strategies and personal strengths that enable most children to move forward, ready for their adolescence.

AN EXPANDING SOCIAL WORLD

Throughout the world, school-age children are noticeably more independent, more responsible, and more capable than younger children. This increased competence is recognized by parents and schools, in research results, and in every developmental theory.

Theories of School-Age Development

Freud describes middle childhood as the period of *latency*, during which children's emotional drives are quieter, their psychosexual needs are repressed, and their unconscious conflicts are submerged. This makes latency "a time for acquiring cognitive skills and assimilating cultural values as children expand their world to include teachers, neighbors, peers, club leaders, and coaches" (Miller, 1993).

Erikson (1963) agrees with Freud that middle childhood is a quiet period emotionally, a period in which the child "becomes ready to apply himself to given skills and tasks." During Erikson's crisis of **industry versus inferiority,** children busily try to master whatever their culture values. On the basis of their degree of success, they judge themselves as either industrious or inferior or, in other words, competent or incompetent, productive or failing, winners or losers.

Developmentalists influenced by three of the other major theories—learning, cognitive, or sociocultural—are concerned with acquisition

355

Celebrating Spring No matter where they live, 7- to 11-year-olds seek to understand and develop whatever skills are valued by their culture. They do so in active, industrious ways, as described in cognitive, learning, sociocultural, psychoanalytic, and epigenetic systems theories. This universal truth is illustrated here, as four friends in Assam, northeastern India, usher in spring with a Bihu celebration. Soon they will be given sweets and tea, which is the sociocultural validation of their energy, independence, and skill.

industry versus inferiority The fourth of Erikson's eight crises of psychosocial development, in which school-age children attempt to master many skills and develop a sense of themselves as either industrious and competent or incompetent and inferior.

social cognition A person's awareness and understanding of human personality, motives, emotions, intentions, and interactions.

of new skills (learning theory), of self-understanding (cognitive), or of social awareness (sociocultural). The overview from these three theories is quite similar to that from psychoanalytic theory: School-age children meet the challenges of the outside world with an openness, insight, and confidence that few younger children possess.

The epigenetic systems perspective also acknowledges the new independence of school-age children, viewing it as the result of the need, within the species, for parents to focus on the younger children and for school-age children to reach out to their peers and to the adults in the wider community. Responding to genetic mechanisms, the maturing brain and body allow much greater intellectual focus (what we called *selective attention* in Chapter 12), rationality (concrete operational thought), physical hardiness (slowed growth and increased strength), and motor skill.

Thus all five major theories explain a reality that is universal: Cultures throughout history have selected about age 6 as the time for more independence and responsibility, from attending first grade to making one's First Communion, from doing significant chores at home to facing major challenges at school.

Understanding Others

The emotional development of school-age children depends on advances in **social cognition,** that is, in understanding the social world. At younger ages, in their simple theory of mind, children began to realize that other people are motivated by thoughts and emotions that differ from their own. But the preschoolers' early theorizing is prone to error, because their grasp of other viewpoints is quite limited and fragile.

In contrast, during the school years theory of mind evolves into a complex, multifaceted perspective. Cognitive advances allow children to understand that human behavior is not simply a response to specific thoughts or desires. Instead, they see behavior as actions that are influenced—simultaneously—by a variety of needs, emotions, relationships, and motives.

For example, a preschooler who was told to stop getting into fights with his friends said he couldn't help it because sometimes the fight "just crawled out of me." By contrast, school-age children know what leads to the fights—and what might follow if they choose to fight back. They judge where, when, why, and with whom to fight according to this new, deeper understanding.

The development of social understanding was demonstrated in a simple study in which 4- to 10-year-olds were shown pictures and asked how the mother might respond and why (Goldberg-Reitman, 1992). In one picture, for example, a child curses while playing with blocks. As you can see in the following typical responses, the 4-year-olds focused

❷ Especially for Parents: Suppose you are the parent of an 8-year-old, wondering if you should make your child come home immediately after school and socialize only with family members because you are worried that peer pressure might lead your child into trouble. What should you do?

only on the immediate behavior, whereas the older children recognized the implications and possible consequences:

> *4-year-old:* "The mother spanks her because she said a naughty word."
> *6-year-old:* "The mother says 'Don't say that again' because it's not nice to say a bad word."
> *10-year-old:* "The mother maybe hits her or something because she's trying to teach her . . . because if she grew up like that she'd get into a lot of trouble . . . she might get a bad reputation." [Goldberg-Reitman, 1992]

Similar research studies and everyday experience tell us that younger children are likely to focus solely on observable behavior—not on motives, feelings, or social consequences. They know when an adult might protect, nurture, scold, or teach a child, but not why. Older children add three more elements:

- They understand the motivation and origin of various behaviors.
- They can analyze the future impact of whatever action a person might take.
- They recognize personality traits and use them to predict a person's future reactions.

Read Their Expressions This girl seems hesitant to proceed, perhaps in anticipation of getting a cold shock. However, because of the expanded emotional understanding that is typical of school-age children, she probably realizes that if she stalls much longer, she is bound to get teased. This greater emotional understanding may also help her to control her anxiety long enough to take the plunge.

❷ Observational Quiz (see answer page 359): What gender differences do you see?

peer group A group of individuals of roughly the same age and social status who play, work, or learn together.

Overall, from ages 5 to 11, a "developmental sequence reflects children's growing understanding of the multiple or changing representations of emotional situations" (Terwogt & Styge, 1998).

As a result of their new social cognition, children can better manage their own emotions. They can mentally distract themselves to avoid becoming fidgety during a boring concert, for example, or can look attentive in class even when they are not paying attention. They can even mask or alter inborn tendencies. For example, a group of 7-year-olds looked at videotapes of themselves being shy at age 2. Most were distressed to see how timid they had once been, but only a few still acted shy. Many said they had learned to understand themselves and adjust their timidity. As one explained, "I was a total idiot then [but] I learned a lot of new stuff, so now I'm not as scared as I was when I was a baby . . . I've gotten older and I don't want to be embarrassed" (Fox et al., 1996). This new self-understanding is discussed further in the In Person box on page 358.

THE PEER GROUP

Perhaps the most influential system for developing the self-concept is the **peer group**—a group of individuals of roughly the same age and social status who play, work, or learn together. Increasing contact with peers leads to an increasing sense of self-competence (Feiring & Lewis, 1989; France & Levitt, 1998; Vandell & Hembree, 1994). Most developmental researchers consider getting along with peers to be a crucial social skill during middle childhood (although parents and teachers do not always agree) (Merrell & Gimpel, 1998). Indeed, some think peers are the deciding influence on children (Harris, 1998).

There is an important developmental progression here. Preschool children have friends and learn from playmates, of course, but they are

THE RISING TIDE OF SELF-DOUBT

School-age children begin to measure themselves in terms of a variety of competencies. They might, for example, realize they are weak at playing sports, okay at playing a musical instrument, and a whiz at playing Nintendo. Similarly, they might feel that they are basically good at making friends but that they have a quick temper that sometimes jeopardizes their friendships.

Increased self-understanding comes at a price. Self-criticism rises and self-esteem dips. Children evaluate themselves through social comparison, comparing their skills and achievements with those of others (Pomerantz et al., 1995). They accept and use the standards set by parents, teachers, and peers and then look at their own actual behavior (abandoning the imaginary, rosy self-evaluation of preschoolers) (Grolnick et al., 1997). This means that older children are more likely to feel personally at fault for their shortcomings and are less likely to blame luck or someone else. Further, as they compare themselves to others, "children become increasingly concerned about self-presentation" (Merrell & Gimpel, 1998), with other children becoming more important critics than parents or teachers.

The age changes are illustrated by these two self-descriptions:

Four-year-old. My name is Jason and I live in a big house with my mother and father and sister, Lisa. I have a kitty that's orange and a television in my own room. I know all of my A B C's, listen: A, B, C, D, E, F, G, H, J, L, K, O, M, P, Q, X, Z. I can run faster than anyone! I like pizza and I have a nice teacher. I can count up to 100, want to hear me? I love my dog, Skipper. I can climb to the top of the jungle gym, I'm not scared! Just happy. You can't be happy and scared, no way! I have brown hair and I go to preschool. I'm really strong. I can lift this chair, watch me! [Harter, 1996]

social comparison The tendency to assess one's abilities, achievements, social status, and the like by measuring them against those of others, especially those of one's peers.

What Is She Saying? An outsider, or even an elder of this tribe, might see all these girls as dressed magnificently, in appropriate style. But knowing schoolchildren, we can surmise that the girl on the left, with the red and yellow vest, may be criticizing the blue dress of the girl beside her. Almost every schoolgirl worries about her attire and sometimes tells her mother, in tears or anger, "I'm never wearing this again."

Eight-year-old. I'm in third grade this year, and pretty popular, at least with the girls. That's because I'm nice and helpful and can keep secrets. Most of the boys at school are pretty yukky. I don't feel that way about my little brother Jason, although he does get on my nerves. I love him but at the same time, he also does things that make me mad. But I control my temper, I'd be ashamed of myself if I didn't. At school, I'm feeling pretty smart in certain subjects: Language Arts and Social Studies. I got A's in these subjects on my last report card and was really proud of myself. But I'm feeling pretty dumb in Arithmetic and Science, particularly when I see how well the other kids are doing. Even though I'm not doing well in those subjects, I still like myself as a person, because Arithmetic and Science just aren't that important to me. How I look and how popular I am are more important. [Harter, 1996]

more egocentric and hence slower to use social comparison. At the other end of childhood, teenagers typically identify with the opinions of one group and reject those of another. In middle childhood, however, children tend to be concerned with the judgment of the entire group of classmates. They become more dependent on each other, not only for companionship but also for self-validation and advice. One reason is that peer relationships, unlike adult–child relationships, involve partners who must learn to negotiate, compromise, share, and defend themselves as equals (Hartup, 1996).

❶ Answer to Observational Quiz (from page 357): *All the girls look distressed, but the boys do not. The girls also seem more likely to cover their bodies, a recognition of their problems with social comparison, self-esteem, and gender norms that often accompany middle childhood. The boys may be unaffected by such problems or may have already learned to appear tough.*

Most parents are now employed outside the home, so after-school supervision is a problem sometimes solved by enrolling the children in organized programs. Children themselves, however, generally prefer the freedom to choose their own activities with their own friends (Belle, 1999). A study comparing parents' and children's perceptions of middle childhood found that most parents worried about strangers and illicit drug use and tended to watch their children closely. The children, however, were much more concerned about breakdowns in their peer relationships and about their parents' fights or alcohol and cigarette use. Thus, the peer group was feared by the parents but could have been, and sometimes was, very helpful to the children (Borland et al., 1998). Many developmentalists wonder if adults, by restricting their children's free play with peers, are depriving them of one of the most important joys, challenges, and opportunities of childhood.

The Society of Children

When school-age children play together, they develop patterns of interaction that are distinct from those of adult society and culture. Accordingly, some social scientists call the peer group the **society of children**, highlighting the fact that children create their own subculture, which is firmly in place by age 10 or so.

society of children The social culture of children, including the games, vocabulary, dress codes, and rules of behavior that characterize their interactions.

The society of children typically has special norms, vocabulary, rituals, and rules of behavior that flourish without the approval, or even the knowledge, of adults. Its slang words and nicknames are often ones adults would frown on (if they understood them), and its activities—such as hanging out at the mall, playing games in the playground, and having long, meandering phone conversations—do not invite adult participation (Opie, 1993; Zarbatany et al., 1990). Its dress codes become known to parents only when they try to get their son or daughter to wear something that violates those codes—as when a perfectly fine pair of hand-me-down jeans is something the child "would not be caught dead in" because, by the norms of the society of children, they are an unfashionable color, have the wrong label, are too loose or too tight.

Many of the norms and rules of the peer group implicitly encourage independence from adults, and some go even further, demanding distance from adult society. By age 10, if not before, children (especially boys) whose parents kiss them in public are pitied ("momma's boy"),

Children's Games One expression of the society of children is its play behavior, including the rules, rituals, and chants of hide-and-seek, kick the can, and, as shown here, jump-rope and stickball. Double-dutch skills and jumping rhymes, as well as rules for choosing teams and leaders, are passed down from slightly older children to younger ones, with each new cohort likely to put its own distinctive twist on both. Sex segregation is typical during the school years, with "No boys [girls] allowed" a common rule.

seek a compromise that maintains the friendship and are least likely to seek revenge (Rose & Asher, 1999).

Note that since most children develop social cognition from the normal give-and-take with peers, rejected children are excluded from the very learning situations they need most. As the years go by, their problems worsen, partly because their peers become more critical of social ineptness and partly because their own behavior becomes more self-defeating. They become victims, disliking themselves and being repeatedly vulnerable to children who are temporarily accepted, even encouraged, in their aggression.

Bullies

bullying Repeated efforts by a child or group of children to inflict harm on another child through physical, verbal, or social attacks.

Bully and Victim? Several signs indicate that this is not an incident of typical bullying: There is only a single aggressor; his victim is actively resisting; and both aggressor and victim seem close to the same size and strength. In advanced bullying, typically a much larger boy or group of children humiliates another child to the point that resistance is either obviously inadequate or completely absent.

Researchers define **bullying** as *repeated,* systematic efforts to inflict harm through physical attack (such as hitting, punching, pinching, or kicking), verbal attack (such as teasing, taunting, or name-calling), or social attack (such as deliberate social exclusion or public mocking). Implicit in this definition is an imbalance of power. Boys who are bullies are often above average in size, whereas girls who are bullies are often above average in verbal assertiveness. Bullies' victims tend to be less assertive and physically weaker (boys) and more shy (girls).

These gender differences are reflected in bullying tactics: Boys typically use force or the threat of force; girls often mock or ridicule their victims, making fun of their clothes, behavior, or appearance or revealing their most embarrassing secrets (Lagerspetz & Bjorkquist, 1994). In many cases, the strength differential is multiplied by the fact that the bullying is done by a group of children. In one ongoing study, at least 60 percent of bullying incidents involved group attacks (Olweus, 1992, 1993, 1994).

Bullying was once thought to be an unpleasant but normal part of child's play—not to be encouraged, of course, but of little consequence in the long run. However, developmental researchers who have looked closely at the society of children now realize that bullying is a serious problem, harming both the victim and the aggressor (Garrity & Baris, 1996).

The leading researcher in this area is Dan Olweus, who has studied bullying for 25 years. The cruelty, pain, and suffering that he has documented are typified by the details he provided for two cases:

Linda was systematically isolated by a small group of girls, who pressured the rest of the class, including Linda's only friend, to shun her. Then the ringleader of the group persuaded Linda to give a party and invite everyone. She did. Everyone accepted, but, following the ringleader's instructions, no one came. Linda was devastated, her self-confidence "completely destroyed."

Henry's experience was worse. Daily, his classmates called him "Worm," broke his pencils, spilled his books on the floor, and mocked him whenever he answered a teacher's questions. Finally, a few boys took him to the bathroom and made him lie, face down, in the urinal drain. After school that day he tried to kill himself. His parents found him unconscious, and only then learned about his torment.

Figure 13.1 Every Country Has Bullies. The rates of being bullied in the various grades as reported by Norwegian schoolchildren are typical of the rates in many other countries. This chart shows physical bullying only; relational bullying may increase with age. Although physical bullying is less common among older children, it is more devastating, because older children depend much more on peers for self-esteem.

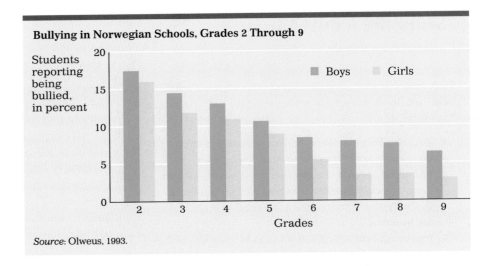

Bullying in Norwegian Schools, Grades 2 Through 9

Source: Olweus, 1993.

Bullying Around the World

Following the suicides of three victims of bullying in Norway, the government asked Olweus to determine the extent and severity of the problem. After concluding a confidential survey of nearly all of Norway's 90,000 school-age children, Olweus reported that bullying was widespread and serious (see Figure 13.1); that teachers and parents were "relatively unaware" of specific incidents; and that even when adults noticed, they rarely intervened. Of all the children Olweus surveyed, 9 percent were bullied "now and then"; 3 percent were victims once a week or more; and 7 percent admitted that they themselves sometimes deliberately hurt other children, verbally or physically.

As high as these numbers may seem, they are equaled and even exceeded in research done in other countries (Smith & Sharp, 1994). For instance, a British study of 8- and 9-year-olds found that 17 percent were victims of regular bullying and that 13 percent were bullies (Boulton & Underwood, 1992). A study of middle-class children in Florida found that 10 percent were "extremely victimized" (Perry et al., 1988). And a study of a multiethnic group of Los Angeles children of diverse SES found that 10 percent (three-quarters of them boys) were teased and picked on and another 17 percent (57 percent of them girls) were probably socially rejected (Graham & Juvonen, 1998). Finally, a study of American middle-school students found that only 20 percent engaged in no bullying at all (Bosworth et al., 1999).

Middle school is also the prime time for sexual harassment in childhood bullying. Fully one-third of all 9- to 15-year-old girls say they have experienced sexual teasing and touching sufficiently troubling that they wanted to avoid school (American Association of University Women Foundation, 1993). Among boys who are approaching puberty, almost every one who is perceived as homosexual by his peers is bullied, sometimes mercilessly (Savin-Williams, 1995).

A word about boys' and girls' problems is appropriate here. Both sexes are restricted by overly rigid sex roles, according to many psychologists (e.g., Garbarino, 1999; Pollack, 1999). Boys are expected to become tough and not to ask for help if they are victimized; girls are

? Especially for Educators: Imagine you are the principal of a school that is about to change from assigning children with special needs in a specialized class to including them in the regular classroom. In view of the lessons learned from a program to eliminate school bullying, what would you do to prepare for the change?

STOPPING A BULLY

Each bullying event requires at least two participants: the bully and the victim. Efforts to reeducate both participants have involved:

- *Teaching social problem-solving skills* (such as how to use humor or negotiation to reduce a conflict)
- *Changing negative assumptions* (such as the view of many rejected children that nothing can protect them, or the bully's assumption that accidental slights are deliberate threats)
- *Improving academic skills* (hoping to improve confidence and raise low self-esteem) (Crick & Grotpeter, 1996; Merrell & Gimpel, 1998; Ogilvy, 1994)

These approaches sometimes help individuals. However, because they target one child at a time, they are piecemeal, time-consuming, and late in the sequence—an example of tertiary rather than primary prevention. Further, they are up against habits that have been learned and reinforced and are resistant to change. After all, why should bullies learn new social skills when their current attitudes and actions bring them status and pleasure, often including a few friends and protection from being bullied themselves (Poulin & Boivin, 2000)? And "even if rejected children change their behavior, they still face a difficult time recovering accepted positions in the peer group," gaining friends who will support and defend them (Coie & Cillessen, 1993).

Not only do both bullies and victims have established behavior patterns, but they also share a firm cognitive assumption: Adults will not intervene. Robert Coles (1997) describes a 9-year-old boy who reported that one of his classmates, a girl, was cheating. The boy was then victimized, not only by the girl and her friends but more subtly by the teacher and the principal, who made excuses for the girl (her grandfather had died several months earlier). Coles believes the overall moral climate taught this boy what it teaches many children: that they can, and should, ignore the actions of bullies and the feelings and needs of victims of bullying.

The best solution begins with the recognition that bullies and their victims are both caught within a particular social dynamic (Pepler et al., 1999). Accordingly, intervention must change the social climate so that bully–victim cycles no longer spiral out of control. This intervention was attempted by a government-funded campaign for every school in Norway (Olweus, 1992, 1993, 1994).

First, the bullying problem was explained at community-wide meetings. All parents received pamphlets that described signs of victimization (such as a child's having bad dreams, no real friends, damaged clothes, torn books, or unexplained bruises). Videotapes were shown to all students to evoke sympathy for victims. Teachers were given special training on intervention.

The second phase was more direct. In every classroom, students discussed reasons to stop bullying, ways to mediate peer conflicts, and how to befriend lonely children. The last action is particularly crucial: Having at least one peer who loyally protects and defends you, "watching your back," not only prevents the escalation of bullying but reduces the emotional sting (Hodges et al., 1999). Teachers organized cooperative learning groups so that no child could be isolated and then bullied, and they halted each incident of name-calling or minor assault as soon as they noticed it, recognizing the undercurrent beneath the bully's excuses and the terror behind the victim's silence. Principals learned that schools where bullying was rare were characterized by adequate supervision in the lunchroom, bathroom, and playground, and they redeployed staff to keep watch.

If bullying occurred despite these preventive steps, counselors were ready to try a third set of measures, which included conducting intensive therapy with the bully and his or

expected not to be physically assertive, but they are given free rein to be verbally caustic. The costs of rigid sex roles are discussed in detail in Chapter 17, but it should be noted here that both bullies and victims suffer unnecessarily from misinterpretations of the idea that "boys will be boys" (Pollack, 1999).

Thus, bullying during middle childhood seems to be pervasive. It occurs in every nation, in small rural schools and in large urban ones, and is prevalent among well-to-do majority children as well as poor immigrant children. Contrary to popular belief, victims are no more likely to be fat or homely or to speak with an accent than nonvictims are. But they usually are rejected-withdrawn children, anxious and insecure, unable or unwilling to defend themselves, lonely, without friends who will take their side (Boulton, 1999).

Shake Hands or Yell "Uncle" Many schools, such as this one in Alaska, have trained peer mediators who intervene in disputes, hear both sides, take notes, and seek a resolution. Without such efforts, antagonists usually fight until one gives up, giving bullies free rein. Despite Alaska's high rate of alcohol abuse, the state's adolescent homicide rate is lower than the national average.

❓ *Observational Quiz (see answer page 367): Could this mediation program be one reason?*

her parents to restructure discipline; reassigning the bully to a different class, grade, or even school; and helping the victim strengthen social and academic skills. (Note that the bully and his or her family bore the major burden. If the victim were to change schools and the bully were to stay, the wrong child would be punished.)

Twenty months after this campaign began, Olweus resurveyed the children. He found that bullying had been reduced overall by more than 50 percent, with dramatic improvement for both boys and girls at every grade level (Olweus, 1992). These results are thrilling to developmentalists because they show that research can lead to an inexpensive, widespread intervention that effectively reduces a serious problem. This research and intervention program

provides a model approach to other problems that might be tackled in the future.

Olweus (1993) concludes:

It is no longer possible to avoid taking action about bullying problems at school using lack of awareness as an excuse . . . it all boils down to a matter of will and involvement on the part of adults.

Unfortunately, at the moment, only Norway has mounted a nationwide attack on bullying. Many other school systems, in many other nations, have not even acknowledged the harm caused by this problem, much less shown the "will and involvement" to stop it. A recent study in Ontario, Canada, that unobtrusively recorded playground bullying (verbal and physical) found that girls were as involved as boys, teachers intervened in only 4 percent of the situations, and other children stopped 12 percent of the incidents. As in other communities, the frequency of bullying varied markedly from school to school. The principal of the school with the highest rate of bullying told the researchers to leave because "there was no bullying at his school" (Pepler et al., 1999). Whether this was ignorance or indifference, the children in that school were suffering.

Children themselves are quite aware of bullying even when they do not experience it. One 8-year-old explains:

He sits across the aisle from me, and he doesn't give me any trouble, because I'm able to defend myself, and he knows it, but he's a bully, that's what he is, a real meanie. He tries to get his way by picking on kids who he's decided are weaker than him. They help him with his homework—they give him answers. They give him candy from their lunches. They take orders from him. He cheats—I see him. I think the teacher knows, but the kid's father is a lawyer, and my dad says the teacher is probably afraid—she's got to be careful, or he'll sue her. [Coles, 1997]

As in this example, children usually do not intervene to stop bullying unless a close friend is the victim or unless adults encourage intervention (see the Research Report).

The Consequences of Bullying

A key word in the definition of bullying is "repeated." Most children experience isolated attacks or social slights from other children and come through unscathed. But when a child endures such shameful experiences again and again—being forced to hand over lunch money, or to drink milk mixed with detergent, or to lick someone's boots, or to be the butt of insults and practical jokes, with everyone watching and no one ever coming to his or her defense—the effects can be deep and long-lasting. Bullied children are anxious, depressed, and underachieving during the months and years of their torment. Even years later, they still have damaged self-esteem as well as painful memories.

The picture is more ominous for bullies. Contrary to the public perception that bullies are actually insecure and lonely, at the peak of their bullying they usually have friends who abet, fear, and admire them. They seem brashly unapologetic about the pain they have inflicted "all in fun." Their parents do nothing to stop them. In fact, their parents often seem indifferent to what their children do outside the home but use "power-assertive" discipline on them at home, with physical punishment, verbal criticism, and displays of dominance meant to control and demean them (Olweus, 1993).

But the popularity and school success of bullies fade over the years, as their peers become increasingly critical. Bullies become more hostile, challenging everyone who tries to stop them, getting into trouble not only with peers but also with the police. In one longitudinal study, by age 24 two-thirds of boys who were bullies in the second grade had been convicted of at least one felony, and one-third of those who were bullies in the sixth through ninth grades had been convicted of three or more crimes, often violent ones, and had already done prison time (Olweus, 1993). This particular study came from Norway, but international research confirms that children who regularly victimize other children often become violent criminals later on (Junger-Tas et al., 1994; Loeber et al., 1998).

Like Father, Like Son If parents and grandparents use their greater physical power to punish and criticize their offspring, the children (especially the boys) are often hostile to everyone they know.

Jimmy, Sixth-Generation Pain in the Ass

COPING WITH PROBLEMS

As you have seen in these last three chapters, the expansion of a child's social world sometimes brings new and disturbing problems. The beginning of formal education forces learning disabilities to the surface, making them an obvious handicap. Speaking another language in school may hinder learning and provoke prejudice. The peer group may reject and attack. Living in a family that is angry, impoverished, or unstable is destructive.

These problems of middle childhood are often exacerbated by long-standing problems that harm children of every age, such as having a parent who is emotionally disturbed, drug addicted, or imprisoned, or growing up in a community that is crumbling, violent, and crime-filled. Because of a combination of problems, some children fail at school, fight with their friends, fear the future, or cry themselves to sleep. Indeed, every academic and psychiatric difficulty that school-age children suf-

Response for Educators (from page 363):
First you would inform everyone—parents, teachers, and children—of the need for the community to respond well to these children. Once the children were in place, you would make sure each teacher took steps to integrate them into the peer groups, for example, by pairing each one with a socially skilled buddy and using the special child's intellectual strengths (whatever each one might have) to benefit the group. If problems arise, you would get the guidance counselor, the parents, and other adults to help the children and the teachers find the best way to cope, perhaps adding another adult to help all the children (including the special child) and the teacher.

Answer to Observational Quiz (from page 365): *Yes. Children learn their conflict-resolution patterns in elementary school and then tend to use them in adolescence.*

fer can be traced, at least in part, to psychosocial stresses (DeFries et al., 1994; Luthar & Zigler, 1991; Sroufe, 1997).

The stresses and hassles of middle childhood are so common that almost every child experiences some of them. Fortunately, school-age children commonly develop coping measures as well. As a result, between ages 7 and 11, the overall frequency of psychological problems decreases while the number of evident competencies—at school, at home, and on the playground—increases (Achenbach et al., 1991). Two factors described in this chapter—the development of social cognition and an expanding social world—combine to protect school-age children against many of the stresses they encounter (Ackerman et al., 1999). According to some observers, many school-age children seem "stress-resistant," or even "resilient" and "invincible" (Conan et al., 1996; Garmezy, 1985; Werner & Smith, 1992). Let us look more closely at what it takes for children to rise above problems that might seem potentially devastating.

Family Support

Children need families, and all families provide support. While no developmental scientist doubts that peers are an important influence, they all stress not only that parents can be crucial but also that peers are often family members, the child's slightly older brother or sister or cousin. Worldwide, all societies share the belief that children are best raised in families, nurtured and guided by their parents and other relatives. Families differ greatly, however, in both structure and function.

Family function refers to how well the family nurtures its children to develop their full potential. Although the details obviously vary, a functional family nurtures school-age children in five essential ways:

- *Meets basic needs by providing food, clothes, and shelter.* In middle childhood, children are old enough to dress and wash themselves and put themselves to bed, but they cannot yet obtain the basic necessities of life without their families' help.
- *Encourages learning.* A critical task during middle childhood is to master academic skills. Families must get their children to school and then guide and motivate their education.
- *Develops self-esteem.* As they become more cognitively aware, children become more self-critical. Families need to make their children feel competent, loved, and appreciated.
- *Nurtures peer friendship.* Families can provide the time, space, opportunity, and skills needed to develop peer relationships.
- *Provides harmony and stability.* Children need to feel safe and secure at home, confident that family routines are protective and predictable.

Thus, a family that functions well provides material and cognitive resources, as well as emotional security, so that the children grow in body and mind. Of course, no family functions perfectly for every child. Conflict between the adults is harmful, whether or not the child is directly involved in it and whether or not it leads to divorce. Even relatively minor, nonphysical disagreements between parents can affect the children (Kitzmann, 2000).

Furthermore, families have various styles, and some children are more comfortable with, and develop better with, one style than another

Harmony and Stability A single parent can—and should—provide the nurturance children need. Some studies show that when a single father embraces the custodial role, the community is supportive, and the children are aged 6 or older, offspring, particularly boys, thrive under paternal care.

family structure The legal and genetic relationships between members of a particular family.

(Constantine, 1986, 1993). Especially when older children are adopted into families, matching the family style with the child's temperament may be crucial (Ward, 1997).

As an example, families with an *open* style value contributions from every family member, including children. This style tends to develop a child's confidence and self-esteem. But an open family might emphasize family cooperation and conversation so much that a defiant or demanding child, who needs structured guidance and carefully set limits, might founder. Or a family with a *closed* style (in which one parent, usually the father, sets strict guidelines, limits, and rules) might function well if scarce family resources need to be carefully shared or if the school and neighborhood are so chaotic that the parents must monitor the child's homework, peer group, and so on. But for some creative children, closed families may be stifling, and the result may be depression or rebellion—both of which are destructive to children.

There are many other ways to categorize family styles, as you know from reading Chapter 10. In a well-functioning family of any type, a mutual adjustment process between child and parents begins at birth; this enables the family to become flexible enough to serve the child well, while the child becomes used to the family style. Flexibility and mutual adjustment may very well be the keys to a proper balance between the family's nurturance and the child's need for independence (Maccoby, 1992). Obviously, the danger comes at either extreme—a family so open as to be disconnected, letting the child drift alone, or so closed that the family becomes enmeshed, entangling the child with family intimacy.

Family structure is defined as the legal and genetic relationship between adults and their children. Families come in many structures, including the multigeneration extended family of 20 members or more and the single parent/only child twosome. The choice of a particular

Happily Ever After Traditions, especially religious ones, help keep families together, as shown by this Christmas dinner with three generations in Florida. Note, however, that the only couple sitting together are the grandparents, who were married decades ago, when the nuclear family was strong. Their children and grandchildren are experiencing several variations of family structure.

structure depends on the individual adults and their culture, not on the children. For that reason, our main discussion of the variations in family structure appears in Chapter 19, on psychosocial development in adulthood. Here, we need to make just two points regarding the impact of family structure on children:

- Structure does not determine function or dysfunction. All five nurturing elements, especially the harmony and stability that school-age children particularly need, are affected by the family structure, but no structure has a monopoly on successful function. Children thrive in many circumstances.
- Harmony and stability are particularly appreciated by school-age children, because these elements help them cope with the stresses of daily life. For this reason, separation and divorce, even under the best of circumstances, always changes the lives of the children involved (see A Life-Span View on page 370).

Assessing Stress

The likelihood that divorce or some other problem will adversely affect a child depends on three factors:

- How many other stresses the child is already experiencing
- How much these stresses affect daily life
- How many protective buffers and coping patterns are in place

In general, a single chronic problem may create vulnerability in a child without causing obvious harm. However, if that vulnerability is added to other burdens—even mild ones that might be called "daily hassles" rather than "stressful events"—the child can suffer evident damage (Durlak, 1998; Shaw et al., 1994).

The pivotal question is, "How much does the stress affect the child's daily life?" For example, having an emotionally dysfunctional parent may affect a child very little if the other parent compensates for, and protects from, the parent's irrationality. Conversely, having such a parent may affect daily life if the child has to:

- Assume many of the responsibilities for his or her own daily care and school attendance
- Contend directly with an adult's confused, depressed, or irrational thinking
- Supervise and discipline younger siblings
- Keep friends away from the house

The situation may become overwhelming if additional major stress makes ordinary daily life impossible. Among such major stresses are poverty and high-risk living conditions. For example, if the dysfunctional parent is the only adult in the child's life, he or she may be unable to provide a steady place to live or a reliable supply of food and clothes. For school-age children especially, frequent changes of address are strongly correlated with low self-esteem, school failure, and parental neglect; poverty can be shameful, not simply a burden. The worst situation occurs when the child has *no* address—except, perhaps, that of a shelter for the homeless (see the Changing Policy box on page 371).

On the brighter side, we should note that even multiple stresses need not be devastating. In our example, living with a dysfunctional

DIVORCE AND CHILDREN

The disruption and discord of divorce usually harm the children for at least a year or two. Immediately before and after a divorce, most children show signs of emotional pain, such as depression or rebellion, and symptoms of stress, such as lower school achievement, poorer health, and fewer friends.

The effects of divorce depend somewhat on the child's age; children younger than 2 and older than 18 seem to cope better overall. But research finds that divorce is always disruptive in the short term on the adults directly involved, on their own parents, and on their children—even if the children are already living on their own. Divorce at the beginning (age 5 to 7) or end (age 10 to 12) of middle childhood may be hardest of all, because children need a stable home life at these times, when they themselves are experiencing new challenges.

As we have noted, harmony and stability are crucial to a well-functioning family. Both are jeopardized by divorce. For instance, the feeling of being abandoned by a trusted adult (parent, grandparent, baby-sitter)—even if that is not literally the case—is devastating to a child. Moving to a less desirable neighborhood and attending a different school can be particularly unsettling for children who are old enough to have best friends (Erwin, 1998).

Yet divorce does not have to be disastrous. An extensive study comparing children of divorce with similar children in both happy and unhappy marriages found that most parents in every family structure were adequate and, consequently, that most children seemed to develop well enough. However, if a mother who was the primary caregiver was financially stressed, emotionally depressed, or inadequate as a parent (all at least twice as common among divorced than among married mothers), then children were likely to suffer (Simons et al., 1996).

As you can surmise, divorce may not harm the children if the family income remains stable, if fights between the parents are few, and if caregiving by both parents is as good as or better than it was before the divorce (Amato & Rezac, 1994; King, 1994). In two-parent families, both parents are naturally involved in custody or caregiving duties, dividing up the tasks (e.g., who puts the children to bed, who takes them to the doctor, who decides about schools or vacation destinations) and sharing the responsibility. No such flexibility is available to separated or divorced parents. Usually one parent (often the mother) is granted primary custody, the other parent is granted visitation rights, and both feel their needs and contributions are mocked, ignored, and undervalued.

In theory, the best plan is *joint custody,* in which the divorced parents share legal and financial custody and work out physical custody, deciding where, when, and with whom the child will live. In practice, however, joint custody is difficult, especially when the parents disagree. Thus, the custody solution that at first appears best for the children may actually be the worst (Mason, 1999). It is also the pattern most likely to change over time, usually in the direction of mothers getting sole custody of daughters who had previously been shared (Cloutier & Jacques, 1997).

When only one parent has primary custody, which parent should that be? In the nineteenth century, the answer was almost always the father (because he had the resources); in the twentieth century, the answer was almost always the mother (because she had the nurturing instincts); today the answer is, "It depends" (Downey et al., 1998).

In some ways custodial fathers have an advantage over custodial mothers: Typically they have more income, more authority over their sons, and greater willingness to accept caregiving help from relatives of the other sex, including the children's mother. This last point is particularly important, since ideally children maintain close ties with both parents. Children in their fathers' custody see their mothers more often than vice versa (Hetherington et al., 1998). However, fathers with primary custody are still the exception, so such men may be unusually skilled or dedicated. Certainly most single parents are women, and many do an excellent job of child rearing.

A crucial factor always is economic support. Indeed, some developmentalists believe that the stresses of poverty, especially because they often lead parents to feel overwhelmed and angry, are the most devastating of all. Divorce usually means an economic loss for the children, even if the father pays child support. The loss is likely to be more severe if the father pays no support, if the father pays or withholds support according to the mother's behavior, or if the father remarries and has a child with his new wife (Manning & Smock, 2000).

Individual differences and personal relationships are so complex that any gender guidelines regarding custody need to be applied gingerly, if at all. Probably the most important point to emerge from the study of human development is that everyone changes throughout life. Accordingly, no custody pattern can be singled out as the best one for all children or all adults at every age (Hetherington & Stanley-Hagen, 1999; Simons, 1996).

POOR AND HOMELESS

Poverty itself is a risk factor for children's development, because it triggers a cascade of stresses that affect children: Their parents' stress about money leads to ineffective caregiving; overcrowded schools in low-income areas give children little competence; violent neighborhoods make friendship difficult (Duncan & Brooks-Gunn, 1997). Every problem of poverty, however, is magnified if a child is homeless. Unfortunately, children are the segment of the homeless population that is increasing most rapidly in the United States and in many other nations as well.

Most children who are literally without a roof over their heads are adolescents, either runaways whose parents have abused them or throwaways whose parents have disowned them. Homeless children under age 12 usually live with their families in shelters. Although these children have, for the moment, the assurance of a bed and meals, they are troubled in many ways. As one report explains:

> By the time they arrive in a shelter, children may have experienced many chronic adversities and traumatic events. More immediately, children may have gone hungry and lost friends, possessions, and the security of familiar places and people at home, at school, or in the neighborhood. . . . Locations [of shelters] are usually undesirable, particularly with respect to children playing outside. Moreover, necessary shelter rules may strain a child and family life. For example, it is typical for no visitors to be allowed, and for children to be . . . accompanied at all times by a parent. [Masten, 1992]

Further, the parents are caught in a situation in which their autonomy and competence are always compromised (Seltser & Miller, 1993). Hence, they cannot really be parents—caregivers and tutors—to their school-age children. Moreover, a shelter is only a temporary solution to homelessness, requiring periodic upheaval as children move to alternative locations with a parent who is humiliated, depressed, and emotionally exhausted. Sometimes the child is sent to foster care or to some institution while the parent is treated separately. Thus three major risk factors—conflict, instability of relationships, and poverty—are glaringly present for homeless children.

Compared to their nonhomeless peers of similar economic and ethnic status, homeless children have fewer friends, more fears, more fights, more chronic illnesses, more changes of school, lower school attendance, and lower academic achievement (Ackerman et al., 1999; Buckner et al., 1999; Huth, 1997). During middle childhood, when school and friends become so important, about one-third of all homeless children are absent from school on any given day. Those in school are likely to be in special education or to be held back. The net result is that "many homeless youth are cut off for-

Fighting Homelessness Despite the anxiety evident in these children, this is a hopeful scene. The woman on the left, formerly homeless, is now living with her children in a stable community residence and is also studying for her high school degree, with the help of a college student. With secure housing and education or job training, many homeless families can become functional again.

ever from achievement in traditional school programs" (Huth, 1997).

In terms of long-term development, the most chilling result may be a loss of faith in life's possibilities. Even compared to other impoverished children, homeless children have lower aspirations, less hope, and more suspicion, expressing doubt that anyone will ever help them. And often they are right, especially regarding the most important support during childhood—the peer group. Virtually no homeless child can make school friends. The lack of continuity in their lives and their low self-esteem keep them from developing mutually supportive friendships. Even practical considerations, such as shelter rules about visiting and curfews, tend to make friendships impossible. Perhaps because of a lack of such support, clinical depression is common, striking almost one homeless child in every three (Bassuk & Rosenberg, 1990).

While the public may debate the root causes of, and the best solutions to, homelessness, it is apparent from a developmental perspective that something must be done immediately for every homeless child. Every month of education that a homeless child loses, and every blow to self-esteem that he or she suffers, may take years—or perhaps a lifetime—to overcome. For those who are interested in establishing public policies that offer a better future, providing education and permanent housing for homeless children is a good place to start (Nunez, 1996).

table **13.2**	**Strengths and Relationships That Help Children Under Stress**
Source	Strength
Individual child	Good intellectual functioning Appealing, sociable, easygoing disposition Self-efficacy, self-confidence, high self-esteem Talents (artistic, athletic, academic) Religious faith
Child's family	Close relationship to a caring parent figure Authoritative parenting: warmth, structure, high expectations Socioeconomic advantages Connections to extended supportive family networks
Other	Bonds to prosocial adults outside the family Connections to prosocial organizations (e.g., a church, temple, mosque, or settlement house) Attendance at an effective school with understanding teachers Stability and cohesiveness of neighborhood Supportive friendships

parent may not irreparably damage the child if other adults in the family give the child stability and nurturance; or if the school recognizes, praises, and encourages the child's competencies; or if the neighborhood cares for all its children. Community influences can counteract the effects of poverty, family stress, and even abuse (Garbarino et al., 1997).

Focus on Competency

If a child has several crucial strengths (see Table 13.2), he or she can "sustain reasonably good development" even in the face of serious problems (Masten & Coatsworth, 1998). Particularly important are various competencies—especially social, academic, and creative skills—which can help the child deflect or avoid many of the problems he or she may encounter at home or in the community (Conrad & Hammen, 1993).

There are several ways in which competence can make up for disabling factors. One is through self-esteem. If children feel confident in at least one area of their lives, they become able to see the rest of their lives in perspective. They can believe, for example, that despite how others might reject or belittle them, they are not worthless failures.

More practically, children with better-developed cognitive and social skills are able to employ coping strategies against their problems—perhaps by changing the conditions that brought about a problem in the first place or by restructuring their own reaction to the problem (Masten & Coatsworth, 1998). You learned from Chapter 12 that, during middle childhood, children develop metacognition and become more logical, an advance that allows them to think rationally about thinking. They can use this ability to convince themselves that "it's not my fault" or "when I am older, I will escape."

Because their cognitive abilities and, hence, their coping repertoires "increase and become more differentiated in middle childhood," older children may deal with the stresses of life better than children who are just beginning middle childhood (Aldwin, 1994). Thus, when a peer is suddenly antagonistic, a 6-year-old is likely to dissolve into tears or to launch a clumsy counterattack that merely brings further rejection. Older children are more adept at finding ways to disguise their hurt, keep a bully at bay, repair a broken friendship, or even make new friends to replace old ones (Compas et al., 1991).

Schools and teachers can play a significant role in the development of such competencies. School achievement can help all children, including those from seriously deprived backgrounds, to aspire beyond the limited horizons they may encounter in their daily lives. And in good schools, achievement is within the grasp of every child (except perhaps those with severe organic impairments) because good schools are characterized by strong leadership, warm teachers, and high expectations about the achievements of the children (Durlak, 1997).

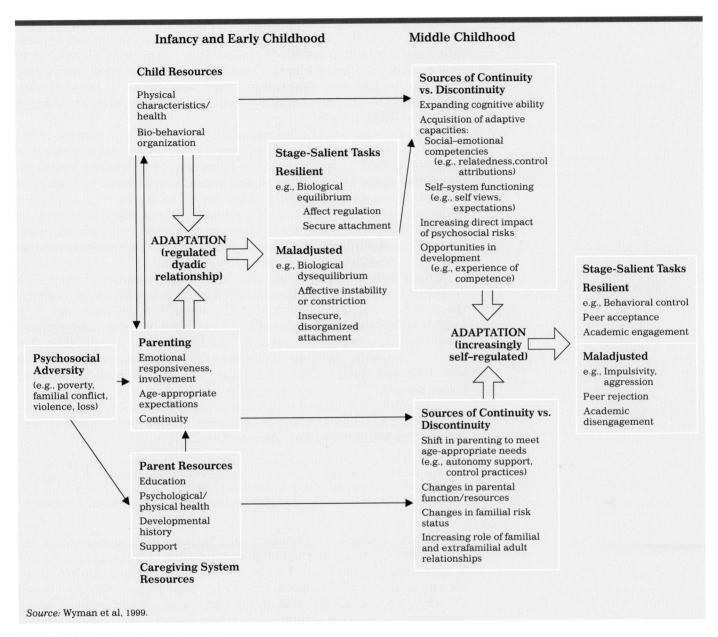

Source: Wyman et al, 1999.

Figure 13.2 An Organizational–Developmental Model of Resilience

Social Support

Another important element that helps children deal with problems—one we have already touched on—is the social support they receive (Garmezy, 1993). Ideally, a strong bond with a loving and firm parent can see a child through many difficulties. Even in war-torn or deeply impoverished neighborhoods, when a child is strongly attached to a parent, who in turn has been present consistently since the child's infancy, the child tends to be resilient (Masten & Coatsworth, 1998). An analysis of impoverished children living in very stressful conditions also found that parenting practices can be a buffer against adversity (Wyman et al., 1999). But as you can see from Figure 13.2, adaptation in middle childhood is increasingly a matter of the child's own ability to reach out for support.

Development research has repeatedly revealed that continuity is apparent from early childhood on: A child who was at risk at age 3 because of poor parenting, difficult temperament, poverty, and the like is probably still at risk at age 8 or 18. However, such risks remain potential, not actual, until or unless they erupt in violence, drug abuse, and the like. Although developmental research traces risk from age to age and generation to generation, a recent summary found that, overall, "discontinuities outweigh continuities" in risk and resilience (Rutter, 1998).

One of the benefits of the expanding social world of middle childhood is the availability of more potential sources of social support. For example, a child whose parents are fighting bitterly on their way to divorce may spend hours on the phone with a friend whose parents have successfully separated; may often be invited to dinner at a neighbor's house where family harmony still prevails; or may devote himself or herself to helping a teacher or a coach or to working with a community group. Grandparents, peers, and even pets are often very helpful to children in middle childhood (Borland et al., 1999).

Community members can also help. One example comes from Jonathan Kozol's (1991) study of children in the South Bronx. A young fatherless boy, whose mother had AIDS, found himself intrigued by a neighborhood man who was a poet. The boy often heard quotations from great literature; learned to read, especially admiring Edgar Allan Poe ("Did you know he grew up in the Bronx?"); and aspired to become a writer himself. Such hope for the future can sustain many a deprived young person.

An additional source of support is religion. Especially for children in difficult circumstances, religious faith itself can be psychologically protective. The South Bronx boy wrote to Kozol:

> No violence will there be in heaven. There will be no guns or drugs or IRS. You won't have to pay taxes. You'll recognize all the children who have died when they were little. Jesus will be good to them and play with them. At night he'll come and visit at your house. God will be fond of you. [quoted in Kozol, 1991]

School-age children, almost universally, develop their own theology, influenced by whatever formal religious education they might receive but by no means identical to it. This personal religion helps them structure life and deal with worldly problems (Coles, 1990; Hyde, 1990). An 8-year-old African American girl who, in the 1960s, was one of the first to enter a previously all-white school, remembers walking past a gauntlet of adults yelling insults:

> I was all alone, and those people were screaming, and suddenly I saw God smiling, and I smiled. A woman was standing there, and she shouted at me "Hey you little nigger, what are you smiling at?" I looked right up at her face, and I said "At God." Then she looked up at the sky, and then she looked at me, and she didn't call me any more names. [quoted in Coles, 1990]

In a way, this example illustrates many aspects of children's coping abilities, for it was not only faith but also a measure of self-confidence, social understanding, and skill at deflecting her own emotional reactions that enabled this child to overcome a very real threat.

Conclusion

We wish that all children could have an idyllic childhood, but that is never the case. Nor is a stress-free childhood necessary to a happy life.

Research on coping in middle childhood clearly suggests that as they grow older, most children develop ways to deal with all varieties of stress, from minor hassles to major traumatic events.

This realization can guide adults who seek to be of help. If the home situation is difficult, for instance, any adult, from a caring teacher to a loving grandparent, can step in and make a critical difference. If parents want to divorce, they should first figure out how to ensure that their children will receive the necessary material and emotional resources. Or if a child has a severe reading difficulty, developing the child's talents in some other area—math or baseball or music—may be as important to the child's overall well-being as tutoring to overcome the learning disability.

Within neighborhoods, the attitude that everyone is responsible for all the children's behavior can also improve life for individuals (Sampson et al., 1997). More broadly, measures designed to enhance the social context, perhaps by making violent neighborhoods safer or improving job opportunities in impoverished communities, can benefit school-age children substantially:

> Successful children remind us that children grow up in multiple contexts in families, schools, peer groups, baseball teams, religious organizations, and many other groups—and each context is a potential source of protective factors as well as risks. These children demonstrate that children are protected not only by the self-righting nature of development, but also by the actions of adults, by their own actions, by the nurturing of their assets, by opportunities to succeed, and by the experience of success. The behavior of adults often plays a critical role in children's risks, resources, opportunities, and resilience. Development is biased toward competence, but there is no such thing as an invulnerable child. If we allow the prevalence of known risk factors for development to rise while resources for children fall, we can expect the competent individual children and the human capital of the nation to suffer. [Masten & Coatsworth, 1998]

As you will see in the next three chapters, adolescence is a continuation of middle childhood, as well as a radical departure from it. Stresses and strains continue to accumulate, and "known risk factors," including drug availability and sexual urges, become more prevalent. Fortunately, for many young people protective resources and constructive coping also increase. Personal competencies, family support, and close friends get most children not only through childhood but also through adolescence undamaged. Indeed, the same factors help each of us throughout our development, as we overcome the problems, and build on the strengths, that characterized the first decade of our lives.

SUMMARY

AN EXPANDING SOCIAL WORLD

1. In middle childhood, children move away from their narrow social sphere and their unswerving self-satisfaction and enter a wide arena, as described by all developmental theories. Erikson, for example, calls this the time of industry, and Freud says that sexual concerns are latent.

2. School-age children develop a multifaceted view of social interactions, becoming increasingly aware of the complex personalities, motives, and emotions that underlie others' behavior. At the same time, they become better able to adjust their own behavior to interact appropriately with others.

3. Children also develop more sophisticated conceptions of themselves and their own behavior. As they become more knowledgeable about their personalities, emotions, abilities, and shortcomings, they evaluate themselves by comparing themselves with others. This contributes to greater focus on competence, more self-criticism, and diminished self-esteem.

THE PEER GROUP

4. Peer relationships provide opportunities for social growth because peers are on an equal footing with each other and must learn to adjust to each other accordingly. During the school years, children create their own subculture, with its own language, values, and codes of behavior. Quite specific norms for conflict and aggression are developed by each society of children.

5. Friendships become more selective and exclusive as children grow older. Psychologists, and children themselves, consider having a few close friends, or at least one best friend, an important indicator of psychosocial health.

6. Rejected and accepted children differ in many ways. One of the most important is how they interpret an ambiguous social situation—as a threat, an attack, an innocent mistake, or a friendly overture.

7. Bullying—repeated efforts by children to inflict harm on a particular child—seems to be universal. Among girls, victims tend to be shy, and bullies overassertive; among boys, victims are physically weaker, and bullies of above-average size. Over the years, victims may develop low self-esteem and bullies may become socially rejected and eventually criminal.

COPING WITH PROBLEMS

8. Almost every child has some difficulties at home, at school, or in the community. Most children cope quite well, as long as the problems are limited in duration and degree and do not stress daily life too much.

9. Families should provide support in middle childhood in five essential ways: basic sustenance, education, self-esteem,

nurturance of peer friendship, and harmony within a stable setting. The family style may range from open to closed, but it should be flexible enough to accommodate the child's unique temperament.

10. Divorce is not easy on children but need not cause permanent damage if family income remains stable and if satisfactory custody arrangements can be worked out.

11. How well particular children cope with the problems in their lives depends on the number and nature of the stresses they experience, the strengths of their various competencies, and the social support they receive.

KEY TERMS

industry versus
  inferiority (356)
social cognition (356)
peer group (357)
social comparison (358)
society of children (359)

aggressive-rejected
  children (361)
withdrawn-rejected
  children (361)
bullying (362)
family structure (368)

KEY QUESTIONS

1. How does a child's understanding of other people change during the school years, and what difference does this make for the child?

2. How does a child's self-understanding change from the preschool years through middle childhood?

3. Why are peer relationships particularly important during the school years?

4. What characteristics distinguish the society of children from the larger adult society?

5. How are the two types of rejected children different?

6. What are some of the consequences of bullying, for the victims and for the bullies?

7. What were the particulars, and the effects, of the antibullying program that was implemented in Norway?

8. What are the five essential ways a functional family nurtures school-age children?

9. How can school-age children be helped to cope with the stresses they encounter as they develop?

10. Why is divorce difficult for children, and how may its impact be reduced?

11. *In Your Experience* What were your specific individual and family characteristics? What cultural and community factors helped you cope during middle childhood? What factors tended to have the opposite effect?

BIOSOCIAL

Growth and Skills

During middle childhood, children grow more slowly than they did during infancy and toddlerhood or than they will during adolescence. Increased strength and lung capacity give children the endurance to improve their performance in skills such as swimming and running. Slower growth contributes to children's increasing bodily control, and children enjoying exercising their developing skills of coordination and balance. Which specific skills they master depends largely on culture, gender, and inherited ability.

Language

Children's increasing ability to understand the structures and possibilities of language enables them to extend the range of their cognitive powers and to become more analytical in their use of vocabulary. Most children develop proficiency in several language codes, and some become bilingual.

Special Needs

Many children have special learning needs that may originate in brain patterns but that express themselves in educational problems. Early recognition, targeted education, and psychological support help all children, from those with autism to the much milder instance of a specific learning disability.

COGNITIVE

Thinking

During middle childhood, children become better able to understand and learn, in part because of growth in their processing capacity, knowledge base, and memory capacity. At the same time, metacognition techniques enable children to organize their learning. Beginning at about age 7 or 8, children also develop the ability to understand logical principles, including the concepts of identity, reciprocity, and reversibility. Morality arises as a social construct, dependent on the example of parents and peers.

Education

Formal schooling begins worldwide, with the specifics of the curriculum depending on economic and societal factors. An individual child's learning success depends on the time allotted to each task, specific guided instruction from teachers and parents, and the overall values of the culture.

PSYCHOSOCIAL

Emotions and Personality Development

School-age children come to understand themselves and others, as well as what is right in their relations with others. The peer group becomes increasingly important as children become less dependent on their parents and more dependent on friends for help, loyalty, and sharing of mutual interests.

Parents and Problems

Parents continue to influence children, especially as they exacerbate or buffer problems in school and the community. During these years, families need to meet basic needs, encourage learning, develop self-esteem, nurture friendship, and—most important—provide harmony and stability. Parents in the midst of divorce may be deficient in all of these. Most single-parent, foster, or grandparent families are better than families in open conflict, but a family with two biological parents, both of whom are cooperative with each other and loving to the child, is generally best. Low family income, and particularly homelessness, add substantial stress in middle childhood. Fortunately, school-age children often develop competencies and skills that protect them somewhat against the stresses that almost all experience. Friends, family, school, and community can all be helpful in encouraging the resilience that many children manifest.

PART V

Adolescence

Adolescence is the period of transition from childhood to adulthood. It is probably the most challenging and complicated period of life to describe, to study, or to experience. The biological changes of puberty, which is the beginning of adolescence, are universal, but their expression, timing, and extent show enormous variety, depending on gender, genes, and nutrition. Cognitive development varies as well: many adolescents are egocentric, while others think logically, hypothetically, and theoretically. Psychosocial changes during this second decade of life show even greater diversity, as adolescents develop their own identities—choosing from a vast number of sexual, moral, political, and educational paths. Most of this diversity simply reflects differences in social and cultural contexts. But about one adolescent in four makes fateful choices that handicap, and sometimes destroy, the future.

Yet there is also a commonality to the adolescent experience. All adolescents are confronted with the same developmental tasks: they must adjust to their changing body sizes and shapes, to their awakening sexuality, and to new ways of thinking. They all strive for the emotional maturity and economic independence that characterize adulthood. As we will see in the next three chapters, the adolescent's efforts to come to grips with these tasks are often touched with confusion and poignancy.

Adolescence:
Biosocial Development

CHAPTER 14

During **adolescence**, roughly age 11 to 20, humans everywhere cross a great divide between childhood and adulthood—biosocially, cognitively, and socioculturally. No one would call this process easy. The biological aspect is uneven but occurs fairly quickly; the cognitive and psychosocial aspects typically take longer, lasting at least until age 18 and often until age 22, 25, or even 30. Adjusting to all the changes of adolescence can be difficult and stressful.

Adolescence is not defined by its problems, but all adolescents experience moments of awkwardness, confusion, anger, and depression; many make serious missteps on the path toward maturity; and some encounter obstacles that halt their progress completely. This chapter and the two that follow examine some of these problems, putting them into perspective.

However, the same developmental changes that cause difficulty also create excitement, challenge, and growth: "Adolescence in all industrial societies, and at all times during this century, constitutes a period of life that is full of [both] opportunity and risk" (Leffert & Petersen, 1995). The risk is real, but most adolescents seize the opportunity instead.

Seriously troubled adolescents are in the minority, and many "problems" of adolescence are actually more problematic for adults than for teenagers. For instance, the same music that troubles adults makes young people jump with joy; the telephoning that exasperates parents is a social lifeline for teenagers; the sexual awakening that many adults fear may be the beginning of thrilling intimacy. Any generalizations about adolescence, especially its turbulence, must be applied with care.

PUBERTY BEGINS

Puberty is a period of rapid physical growth and sexual maturation that ends childhood and begins adolescence, producing a person of adult size, shape, and sexual potential. Puberty is triggered by a chain of hormonal effects that bring on visible physical changes (see Table 14.1).

For girls, these visible changes include, in sequence, the onset of breast growth, the initial pubic hair, a peak growth spurt, widening of the hips, the first menstrual period, the completion of pubic-hair growth, and final breast development. For boys, the visible physical changes of puberty include, in approximate order, the initial pubic hair, growth of the testes, growth of the penis, the first ejaculation, a peak

table 14.1	Sequence of Puberty		
Girls		Approximate Average Age*	Boys
Ovaries increase production of estrogen and progesterone†		9	
Uterus and vagina begin to grow larger		9½	
Breast "bud" stage		10	Testes increase production of testosterone†
Pubic hair begins to appear		11	Testes and scrotum grow larger
Weight spurt begins		11½	
Peak height spurt		12	Pubic hair begins to appear
Peak muscle and organ growth (also, hips become noticeably wider)		12½	Penis growth begins
Menarche (first menstrual period)			
		13	Spermarche (first ejaculation)
			Weight spurt begins
First ovulation		13½	
		14	Peak height spurt
		14½	Peak muscle and organ growth (also, shoulders become noticeably broader)
Final pubic-hair pattern		15	Voice lowers
Full breast growth		16	Readily visible facial hair
		18	Final pubic-hair pattern

*Average ages are rough approximations, with many perfectly normal, healthy adolescents as much as 3 years ahead of or behind these ages. In addition, the sequence is somewhat variable.

†Estrogen, progesterone, and testosterone are hormones that influence sexual characteristics, including reproductive function. All three are also provided, in small amounts, by the adrenal glands in both sexes. Major production, however, occurs in the gonads, with marked male–female differences.

adolescence   The period of biological, cognitive, and psychosocial transition from childhood to adulthood, usually lasting a decade or so.

puberty   A period of rapid growth and sexual change that occurs in early adolescence and produces a person of adult size, shape, and sexual potential.

gonads   The pair of sex glands in humans. In girls, these are called ovaries; in boys, they are called testes or testicles.

growth spurt, voice deepening, beard development, and the completion of pubic-hair growth (Malina, 1990; Rutter, 1980).

Typically, growth and sexual maturation are complete 3 or 4 years after puberty begins, although some individuals gain an additional inch or two of height, and most gain additional fat and muscle over the next 10 years. Why and when does puberty start?

Hormones and Puberty

The biology of puberty begins with a hormonal signal from an area at the base of the brain called the *hypothalamus*. This signal stimulates the *pituitary gland* (located next to the hypothalamus) to produce hormones that then stimulate the *adrenal glands* (two small glands near the kidneys at both sides of the torso) and the **gonads,** or sex glands (the *ovaries* and *testes* or *testicles*). One hormone in particular, *GnRH (gonadotropin-*

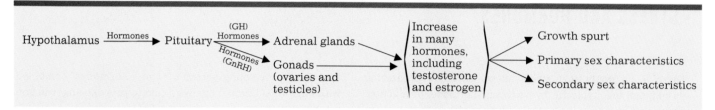

Figure 14.1 Biological Sequence of Puberty. Puberty begins with a hormonal signal from the hypothalamus to the pituitary gland. The pituitary, in turn, signals the adrenal glands and the ovaries or testes to produce more of their hormones.

releasing hormone), causes the gonads to dramatically increase the production of sex hormones, chiefly *estrogen* in girls and *testosterone* in boys. This increase, in turn, loops back to the hypothalamus and pituitary gland, causing them to produce more GH (growth hormone) as well as more GnRH, which causes the adrenal glands and gonads to produce even more sex hormones (see Figure 14.1).

Although testosterone is considered the male hormone and estrogen the female hormone, both boys and girls experience increased levels of both hormones at puberty. However, the rate of increase is sex-specific: Testosterone production skyrockets in boys, up to 18 times the level in childhood, but increases much less in girls. Estrogen production increases up to 8 times in girls but not nearly as much in boys (Malina & Bouchard, 1991). You will later see that changes in facial hair, voice quality, and breast size also occur in both sexes—and again, the difference is in degree.

As the opening paragraphs of this chapter make clear, adolescence is not usually a time of ongoing war between parents and children, or of violent emotional shifts, or of overpowering sexual drives. However, some increases in conflict, in moodiness, and in sexual urges are typical and merit explanation (Arnett, 1999).

Are hormonal changes responsible for the emotional changes of puberty, as well as for the physical changes? To some extent, they are (Golub, 1992; Richards, 1996; Susman, 1997):

- Rapidly increasing hormone levels, especially of testosterone, cause the more rapid arousal of emotions seen in teenagers.
  - Hormones affect the quick shifts in the extremes of emotions—from feeling great to suddenly feeling lousy—that seem typical.
  - For boys, hormonal increases lead to more thoughts about sex, as well as more masturbation.
  - For many girls, the ebb and flow of hormones during the menstrual cycle produce specific mood changes, from a positive mood at midcycle to sadness or anger a day or two before the next period.

All these hormonal shifts are lifelong, but they are more erratic and powerful, and less familiar and controllable, in puberty.

Nonetheless, detailed studies suggest that hormonal levels make a relatively small *direct* contribution to the daily emotional changes of puberty. A more potent hormonal

Raging Hormones? At this age, testosterone is suddenly flooding teenagers' bloodstreams, and sex is on their minds—a bawdy locker room joke will seem hilarious. For the most part, however, hormones await social triggers, and until something happens, these boys will remain emotionally neutral and socially detached. An unexpected team victory or defeat, or, for the boy on the left, the visible eruption of a pimple or a beard hair, could lead to an emotional explosion—sudden, exaggerated, and then gone a few hours later.

STRESS AND HORMONES

There is no doubt that stress affects hormone production throughout life, typically by reducing hormone production. Children under extreme stress grow more slowly, because production of growth hormones is reduced. Adult men and women are less likely to produce live sperm and fertile ova when they are under stress. Pregnant women have higher rates of miscarriage and premature labor when they are highly stressed. Accordingly, one might imagine that stress would delay the onset of puberty—but the opposite may be the case.

Many studies have found a correlation between early puberty and parent–adolescent strife. The traditional explanation always was that puberty caused the strife. More

specifically, the young person's "raging hormones" combined with emotional immaturity were said to provoke anger in and rejection by the parents.

Surprisingly, longitudinal research suggests that cause and effect may be reversed—that family conflict and stress may precede the early onset of puberty (Kim & Smith, 1998; Steinberg, 1988; Wierson et al., 1993), with the particulars that cause stress varying from culture to culture. For example, a New Zealand study found that girls experience earlier puberty when their parents are divorced (Moffitt et al., 1992); this was not found to be true in England (Richards, 1996). A Swedish study found that adopted girls from India typically began pu-

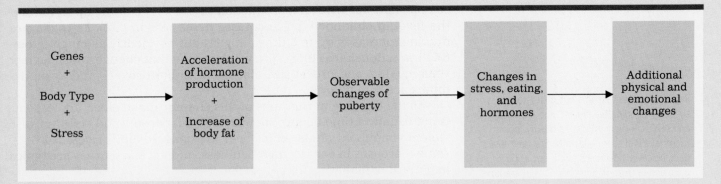

Figure 14.2 From Hormones in the Brain to Changes in the Body. Even this chart is a simplification of a complex interaction that includes genes, biological events, and psychological conditions every step of the way.

influence on the overall emotional tone of adolescence, both positive and negative, is *indirect,* via the psychological impact of the visible changes. And that impact, in turn, is powerfully influenced by the values and expectations of the developing person's family, peer group, and culture (Brooks-Gunn & Reiter, 1990; Nottelman et al., 1990).

In other words, hormones directly cause moods and emotions to change more quickly than before, but hormones have their greatest emotional impact indirectly, by causing visible signs such as the growth of breasts or beards. It is these signs, and the reactions they produce in other people, that cause most adolescent emotional reactions and counterreactions. The strength of all these reactions depends on the social context. Even the one change that is linked most directly to hormones, specifically thinking about sex, is powerfully affected by culture, which can shape such thoughts into enjoyable fantasies, shameful preoccupations, or an impetus to action.

berty at age 11½ years, which was earlier than the onset for girls in India (age 12½ for privileged girls and age 13½ for impoverished girls) and for native Swedish girls (age 13) (Proos et al., 1991). Again, family or community stress could be the underlying reason. Confirmation comes from research on animals, which shows that stress causes sudden increases in production of the hormones that initiate puberty. Rats, mice, and opossums under stress reach sexual maturity sooner than do their genetic relatives who have less stress (Warshofsky, 1999).

None of this proves that the correlation between puberty and family conflict results solely from stress. More likely, bio-

genetic and psychosocial factors interact. Stress can increase the production of hormones, a fact that may explain why many pubescent girls reach menarche during a stressful occasion in their lives; stress can also decrease hormone production, a fact that may explain why many young women experience irregular menstrual periods when they first go off to college (Veldhuis et al., 1997). Overall, as Figures 14.2 and 14.3 depict, biological events and psychological stresses are intertwined in the causes and consequences of puberty. It is widely accepted that stress has a powerful impact on all the hormones, but that the specifics depend on the duration, timing, and other aspects of stress (Sapolsky, 1994).

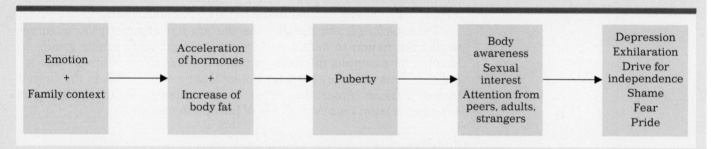

Figure 14.3 Biosocial Causes and Consequences of Puberty. The emotions caused by puberty are part of a chain of events that begin with genes and social context and end with a teenager who is proud or ashamed. At every step, the interplay of biological and psychological factors determines the emotions of the person.

When Do Changes Begin?

The visible changes of puberty, as you just read, are themselves triggered by an invisible sequence of hormone production, which typically begins a year or more before the first pubic hairs appear. But what starts the hormones? We know that the age of puberty is highly variable: Normal children begin to notice body changes at any time between the ages of 8 and 14, with the hormonal changes beginning a year or two earlier for girls than for boys. In addition to gender, three other factors play a role in timing. Two of them, genes and body type, are discussed below. The third factor, stress, is discussed in A Life-Span View.

Genes

menarche A female's first menstrual period.

Genetic influence is clearly seen in **menarche,** a girl's first menstrual period. The "normal" age of menarche varies widely, from 9 to 18 years. However, sisters reach menarche, on average, only 13 months apart,

An Awkward Age The normal variation in age of puberty is readily apparent in this junior high gym class in Texas.

❷ *Observational Quiz (see answer page 388):* *What three signs can you see that the boy in the foreground wants to be taller and the girl beside him wishes she were less conspicuous?*

and monozygotic twins typically differ by a mere 2.8 months. A daughter's age of menarche also is correlated with her mother's age of menarche, which occurred under quite different historical and familial circumstances (Golub, 1992). Other pubertal changes, for boys as well as for girls, also follow familial patterns (Brooks-Gunn, 1991).

Perhaps for genetic reasons, the average age of puberty varies somewhat from nation to nation and from ethnic group to ethnic group. In Europe, for example, the onset of puberty tends to be relatively late for Belgians and relatively early for Poles (Malina et al., 1988). In the United States, African Americans often begin puberty earlier, and Asian Americans later, than Americans of European ancestry.

Body Type

growth spurt The period of relatively sudden and rapid physical growth of every part of the body that occurs during puberty.

In general, stocky individuals experience puberty earlier than those with taller, thinner builds. The onset of puberty correlates with accumulation of body fat in both sexes, although it is more obvious in girls (Vizmanos & Marti-Henneberg, 2000). Menarche does not usually occur until a girl weighs about 100 pounds (about 45 kilograms). Females who have little body fat (either because they are severely malnourished or because they are serious athletes) menstruate later and more irregularly than the average girl. Those who are generally inactive (and thus have less muscle) menstruate earlier (Richards, 1996).

He's Outgrown His Shoes The typical body proportions of the young adolescent are particularly noticeable in this runner: long legs, long feet, and a relatively short torso.

In times of famine, puberty is typically delayed by several years (Golub, 1992). For instance, among teenagers in Kenya, those in impoverished rural communities experience puberty later than their urban agemates, by 3 years for boys and 2 years for girls (Kulin, 1993).

THE GROWTH SPURT

The **growth spurt** is just what the term suggests—a sudden, uneven, and somewhat unpredictable jump in the size of almost every part of the body. Growth proceeds from the extremities to the core. Adolescents' fingers and toes lengthen before hands and feet, and hands and feet lengthen before arms and legs. The torso is the last part to grow, so many pubescent children are tem-

❷ Especially for Educators: What are the practical implications of the physical changes of puberty when it comes to matters such as scheduling of classes and rules for proper School attire?

porarily big-footed, long-legged, and short-waisted, appearing to be "all legs and arms" (Hoffman, 1997).

Wider, Taller, Then Stronger

While the bones lengthen, the child eats more and gains weight more rapidly than before, to provide energy for the many changes taking place. As a result, fat accumulates. In fact, parents typically notice that their children are emptying their plates, cleaning out the refrigerator, and straining the seams of their clothes even before they notice that their children are growing taller.

By the end of middle childhood, usually between the ages of 10 and 12, all children become noticeably heavier, although exactly when, where, and how much fat accumulates depends partly on heredity, partly on diet and exercise, and partly on gender. Females gain more fat overall, so that about a fourth of their body weight is fat, almost double the average for boys (Daniluk, 1998). Sex differences in body fat are especially notable on the legs and hips, because evolution designed young adult females to have extra body fat to sustain pregnancy and lactation and designed young adult males to move swiftly in the hunt.

A height spurt follows soon after the start of the weight increase, burning up some of the stored fat and redistributing some of the rest. About a year or two later, a period of muscle increase occurs (Hoffman, 1997). As a consequence, the pudginess and clumsiness typical of early puberty generally disappears a few years later. Overall, boys increase in muscle strength by at least 150 percent (Armstrong & Welsman, 1997). This is particularly noticeable in boys' upper bodies: Between ages 13 and 18 years, male arm strength more than doubles (Beunen et al., 1988).

The typical girl gains about 38 pounds (17 kilograms) and 9⅝ inches (24 centimeters) between the ages of 10 and 14; the typical boy gains about 42 pounds (19 kilograms) and about 10 inches (25 centimeters) between the ages of 12 and 16. Girls typically gain the most weight in their thirteenth year, and boys in their fourteenth year (Malina & Bouchard, 1991). (See Appendix A.)

Note, however, that all these "typical" data are deceptive, because they are the average of many individual growth spurts, which occur at widely different ages for different children. At any age between 10 and 16, we can find some individuals who grow very little because their major growth spurt has not begun, some who grow very little because their spurt is already over, and some who are growing very rapidly. Thus, individual growth spurts are obviously much more rapid than the overall average: During the 12-month period of their greatest growth, many girls gain as much as 20 pounds (9 kilograms) and 3½ inches (9 centimeters), and many boys gain up to 26 pounds (12 kilograms) and 4 inches (10 centimeters) (Tanner, 1991). Most girls are unhappy with their increasing size while most boys are glad about theirs, which is one reason girls aged 13 to 18 are increasingly dissatisfied with their bodies while boys become more satisfied as they mature (Rosenblum & Lewis, 1999).

Proper Proportions

One of the last parts of the body to take final form is the head, which reaches adult size and shape several years after final adult shoe size is

Transitions These four adolescents, close in age, illustrate the discrepancy in timing that is typical at this age. No two people reach adult size and activity in every way simultaneously. Compare each of these pubescent individuals to a child or an adult, and you can see that each of them is in transition.

❓ *Observational Quiz (see answer page 390): What aspects of each person are ahead or behind in development?*

attained. To the embarrassment of many teenagers, their facial features, especially the ears, lips, and nose (which are markedly larger in adults than in children), grow before the skull itself takes on the larger, more oval shape typical of adults. Next time you see a 14-year-old covering his or her ears with a hat, or nose and mouth with a hand, remember that shame may be part of the reason.

At least as disturbing to some young people can be the fact that the two halves of the body do not always mature at the same rate; one foot, breast, testicle, or ear can be notably larger than the other. Fortunately, none of these anomalies persist very long. Once the growth process starts, every part of the anatomy reaches close to adult size, shape, and proportion in 3 or 4 years. (Of course, for an adolescent, a year or two spent waiting for one's body to take on normal proportions can seem like an eternity.)

A related concern for many adolescents is the wish that their bodies could develop "on time," which means at the same age as their peers (Dubas et al., 1991). Particularly difficult is early development for girls (a combination of shame and unwelcome sexual attention can lead to involvement with older boys) and late development for boys (who may be patronized or ostracized) (Downs, 1990; Graber et al., 1994).

Organ Growth

While the torso grows, internal organs also grow. Over the course of adolescence, the lungs increase in size and capacity, actually tripling in weight. Consequently, the adolescent breathes more deeply and slowly than a child (a 10-year-old breathes about 22 times a minute, while an 18-year-old breathes about 18 times). The heart doubles in size, and the heart rate decreases, slowing from an average of 92 beats per minute at age 10 to 82 at age 18. In addition, the total volume of blood increases (Malina & Bouchard, 1991).

❗ *Answer to Observational Quiz (from page 386): He is on his tip-toes, his arms stretch their longest, and even his hairstyle adds an inch or two. The girl beside him has her feet flat and wide apart, her T-shirt big and loose, and her hair as short and unfeminine as she can make it. If you noticed that his #23 Bulls shirt is Michael Jordan's number, give yourself extra credit.*

These changes increase physical endurance, making it possible for many teenagers to run for miles or dance for hours without stopping to rest. Note, however, that the more visible spurts of weight and height occur before the less visible spurts of muscles and organs. This means that athletic training and weight lifting for an adolescent should be designed to match the young person's size of a year or so earlier.

"Yes, when I was your age, all my friends used drugs, but they were all acne medications."

Cohort Differences The biological changes of puberty are universal, apparent in every culture and century. How individuals react, however, varies tremendously, from pride to shame, celebration to emotional problems.

Invitation to My Girl What do teenaged boys and girls do when adults are not around? Neither sex nor drugs tops the list. Favorite activities are talking, listening to music, and, as shown here, eating. Three aspects of teenage culture in the United States are evident: High-fat finger foods are preferred, pizza is the most common group meal, and boys enjoy watching girls eat.

Exhaustion and injury, as a result of overuse, occur when demands on a young person's body do not take this muscle and organ growth lag into account (Armstrong & Welsman, 1997).

These organic changes also increase the child's need for sleep, as well as change the day–night cycles. Because of hormonal shifts (especially the growth hormones) many teenagers crave sleep in the mornings and are wide awake late at night (Greydanus, 1997; Wolfson & Carskadon, 1998).

One organ system, the *lymphoid system,* which includes the tonsils and adenoids, actually decreases in size at adolescence. Having smaller tonsils and adenoids makes teenagers less susceptible to respiratory ailments. Mild asthma, for example, often switches off at puberty (Clark & Rees, 1996).

Finally, the hormones of puberty cause many relatively minor physical changes that are insignificant in the grand scheme but have substantial psychic impact. For instance, the oil, sweat, and odor glands of the skin become much more active. One result is acne, which occurs to some degree in about 90 percent of all boys and 80 percent of all girls (Greydanus, 1997). Another result is oilier hair and smellier bodies, which is one reason adolescents spend more money on shampoo and deodorants than does any other age group. The eyes also undergo a change: The eyeballs elongate, making many teenagers sufficiently nearsighted to require corrective lenses. All told, no part of the older adolescent's body functions or appears quite the same as it did a few years before.

Nutrition

The rapid body changes of puberty require fuel in the form of additional calories, as well as additional vitamins and minerals. In fact, the recommended daily intake of calories is higher for an active adolescent than for anyone else; the greatest calorie requirement occurs at about age 14 years for girls and 17 years for boys (Malina & Bouchard, 1991). During the growth spurt, the need for calcium, iron, and zinc (for both bone and muscle development) is about 50 percent greater than it was only 2 years earlier.

In developed nations, where high-quality food is sufficiently available, most adolescents meet their basic caloric needs most of the time, typically consuming four or more meals a day even without breakfast. However, puberty correlates with poor eating habits of all kinds—too much, too little, or the wrong kind (Cauffman & Steinberg, 1996). In fact, some are on their way to life-threatening eating disorders. One survey of middle school students found that 6 percent already induced vomiting or used laxatives to control their weight (Krowchuck et al., 1998). Such self-destructive behavior becomes more common by early adulthood, so this topic is discussed further in Chapter 17.

Even "normal" adolescents eat poorly. Only 27 percent of U.S. high school seniors consume the recommended five servings of fruits and vegetables a day, and 33 percent (23 percent of the girls and 41 percent of the

ATTITUDES ABOUT SEXUAL MATURITY

Obviously, how a particular adolescent responds to the changes in his or her body depends on many things, including an understanding of what is happening; conversations with parents and peers about puberty; timing of sexual maturity in relation to others in the peer group; and broader cultural values concerning sexual maturation.

In some cultures, for example, menstruation is heralded, with elaborate rituals, as a young woman's entry into adult status. Similar "rites of passage" occur to celebrate entry into manhood (Brooks-Gunn & Reiter, 1991). In the United States, reactions are more mixed. Newly menstruating girls report a combination of positive and negative feelings about menarche, including feelings of fear and distress mingled with a sense of maturity (Daniluk, 1998; Kaplan, 1997). Those who reach menarche earlier than their friends or who have relatively little information about it tend to be most upset; those who are well-informed and "on time" are more proud. The same may be true for boys reaching spermarche, with the latecomers most upset.

No matter what their personal attitudes about the sexual changes of puberty, almost all adolescents have a strong sense of privacy about them. Very few discuss their specific experiences of menarche or spermarche with friends, or with their parent of the other sex, until months later, if at all. Indeed, although most boys are proud to reach this point, few tell other boys the personal details of masturbation or ejaculation. They rarely confess unexpected or unwanted sexual arousal (caused by a photo, for instance) to another boy or a relative, even though such arousal is quite common. On their part, girls typically promise to tell all their close friends when menarche arrives, but become reticent when the actual event happens. Most girls want their

A Rite of Passage Cultures and families teach their youths whether puberty is shameful, prideful, or neither. Traditional religious celebrations to mark the passage from childhood to adulthood are now rare in mainstream culture, although the Sweet Sixteen, the gang initiation, and even the high school graduation have elements of it. However, many traditional groups still follow practices, such as that shown here among the Apache people, to guide the young person into the new status, with expectations for spiritual, intellectual, and social maturity.

mothers to provide practical advice—not generalities about "becoming a woman"—and they would prefer that their fathers not be informed at all. If the father is told, they hope

family, and society as much as, or more than, from the individual. This realization should make us all more sympathetic to the young person's worries about appearing attractive.

Breasts

For most girls, the first sign of puberty is the "bud" stage of breast growth, when a small accumulation of fat causes a slight rise around the nipples. From then on, breasts develop gradually, with full breast growth reached when almost all the other changes of puberty are completed (Malina, 1990). Because our culture misguidedly takes breast development to be symbolic of womanhood, small-breasted girls often feel "cheated," even disfigured; large-breasted girls attract unwanted stares and embarrassing remarks. No wonder some bras

he makes no comments, even congratulatory ones (Koff & Rierdan, 1995).

Given this variability and secrecy, some of the best information about the particular thoughts and reactions to sexual maturity, in earlier decades and today, comes from popular literature. An autobiographical account is provided in Frank McCourt's best-seller, *Angela's Ashes*:

I know about the excitement and I know it's a sin but how can it be a sin if it comes to me in a dream where American girls pose in swimming suits on the screen at the Lyric Cinema and I wake up pushing and pumping? It's a sin when you're wide awake and going at yourself the way the boys talked about it in Leamy's schoolyard after Mr. O'Dea roared the Sixth Commandment at us, Thou Shalt Not Commit Adultery, which means impure thoughts, impure words, impure deeds, and that's what adultery is, Dirty Things in General. . . .

Oh, boys, the devil wants your souls. He wants you with him in hell and know this, that every time you interfere with yourself, every time you succumb to the vile sin of self-abuse you not only nail Christ to the cross you take another step closer to hell itself. Retreat from the abyss, boys. Resist the devil and keep your hands to yourself.

I can't stop interfering with myself. I pray . . . I'll never do it again but I can't help myself and swear I'll go to confession and after that, surely after that, I'll never never do it again. I don't want to go to hell with devils chasing me for eternity jabbing me with hot pitchforks. [McCourt, 1996]

A fictional version of menarche appears in *She's Come Undone*. After a fight between her parents, the protagonist goes bike riding for hours. When she comes back home, she sees her mother in the kitchen:

She told me she didn't want to talk about anything right now . . .

Something about my pink shorts made her stop.

"What?" I said.

She was staring down there at me.

I saw and felt it at the same time: the dark red blotch of blood.

"That's great, Dolores. Thanks a lot," Ma said, her face crumpling in tears. "That's just what I need right now." [Lamb, 1993]

Fortunately, in the United States and elsewhere, attitudes toward spermarche and menarche have changed over the past decades, and accounts like these are less likely today.

As best we can determine, young people face these events without the fearful anxiety, embarrassment, or guilt that their parents had. This fact is illustrated by a recent example involving a 13-year-old who, happening to be away from home at menarche, called her mother in tears to announce the event. Her mother, remembering her own experience and mindful of the shame and misunderstanding that generations of women have experienced regarding menstruation, immediately reassured her about the glory of womanhood, the joy of fertility, the renewal of the monthly cycle, the evidence of health (since menstruation prevents disease and prepares the uterus for pregnancy), and so on. "I know all that," her daughter protested impatiently. "I'm glad I got my period. I'm crying because this means I won't grow much more, and I want to be tall!"

❶ *Answer to Observational Quiz (from page 391):* Braces. When faces reach adult size, jaws do, too, and few early adolescents have perfectly aligned teeth. Whether or not to do anything about this, of course, is a cultural, not a biological issue.

are padded to enlarge, others are advertised as "minimizers," and the most common major cosmetic surgery is that which increases or decreases breast size.

In boys, as well as girls, the diameter of the areola (the dark area around the nipple) increases during puberty. Much to their consternation, about 65 percent of all adolescent boys experience some breast enlargement (typically in midpuberty) (Behrman, 1992). However, their worry is usually short-lived, since this enlargement normally disappears by age 16.

Breasts are so closely connected in our minds with sex and reproduction that they are mistakenly considered part of reproductive ability. That is false: Breasts are secondary sexual characteristics; they can be absent completely with no effect on conception, pregnancy, or birth.

BODY IMAGE

The physiological changes of puberty necessitate a drastic revision of adolescents' **body image,** that is, their mental conception of, and attitude toward, their physical appearance. According to many psychologists, developing a healthy body image is an integral part of becoming an adult (Erikson, 1968; Simmons & Blythe, 1987). Indeed, one researcher states that "body image lies at the heart of adolescence" (Ferron, 1997). Adolescents need to appreciate their bodies "not simply as an object, but as a lived-in subject which is perceived as part of their being" (Richards, 1996). However, few adolescents are satisfied with their physiques; most imagine that their bodies are far less attractive than they actually are. In fact, body image is a matter of attitude, not reality; even seemingly attractive teenagers can have a distorted body image (Rosenblum & Lewis, 1999).

This negative self-appraisal can have a major impact on self-esteem. Although self-esteem is obviously influenced by success in athletics, academics, friendship, or other areas that the adolescent considers significant, a teenager's assessment of his or her appearance is the most important determinant. In explaining why, for teenagers, "self-esteem is only skin deep," one researcher notes that

> the domain of physical appearance . . . is an omnipresent feature of the self, always on display for others and for the self to observe. In contrast, one's adequacy in such domains as scholastic or athletic competence, peer social acceptance, conduct, or morality is not constantly open to evaluation, but rather is more context specific. Moreover, one has more control over whether, when, and how such characteristics [such as having good grades] will be revealed. [Harter, 1993]

As a result of this intense focus on physical appearance, many adolescents spend hours examining themselves in front of a mirror—worrying about their complexions, about how their hairstyles affect the shape of their faces, about whether the fit of their clothes makes them look alluring or cool. Some teenagers exercise or diet with obsessive intensity (perhaps lifting weights to build specific muscles or weighing food to the gram to better calculate calories).

At one time or another, almost every American girl undereats, sometimes drastically, to be thinner. In one study, girls age 14 to 18 typically wanted to be about 12 pounds lighter than they were (Brooks-Gunn et al., 1989). Amazingly, this held true across the board—regardless of the girls' maturation status, height, or exercise level (see Table 14.2). For example, girls who matured late, and thus had relatively thin, girlish bodies, wanted to lose almost as many pounds as girls with more womanly shapes who had matured on time.

Far from Perfect Many teenagers sacrifice time, money, and health to attain the lean look of the female model or the muscled physique of the macho movie star. Even teenagers who already have attractive bodies are often highly self-critical, while those who inherit a shape or size that is far from the cultural ideal are likely to be excessively self-conscious and depressed.

Similarly, competitive swimmers, whose bodies were quite muscular and who needed some fat to help them with buoyancy and endurance, wanted to lose weight just as much as nonathletes, who had somewhat more fat on their bodies and less reason to need it. Even the thinnest group, late-maturing girls who practiced daily in professional dance schools, wished they weighed 10 pounds less.

Boys are also vulnerable. Roughly 5 percent of male high school seniors use steroids to build up their muscles

(Johnston et al., 1998), ranging from about 9 percent of those in West Virginia to 2 percent in Hawaii (*MMWR*, 1998, August 4). These young men risk a variety of serious health problems, especially if they obtain the drugs illegally and "stack" one drug with another, as many do. One misguided motivation for taking steroids may be to excel at sports, but a survey found that one-third of steroid users did not participate at all in interscholastic athletics; they were apparently taking steroids solely for appearance (Johnston et al., 1989). Boys who do not take drugs nonetheless may lift weights or do pushups in an attempt to change their physiques.

Before dismissing adolescents' preoccupation with their body image as narcissistic, we should recognize that their concern is, in part, a response to the reactions of other people. Parents and siblings sometimes make memorable and mortifying comments about the growing child's appearance: "You look like a cow" (or bear or gorilla) or "You're flat as a board" or "What's that peach fuzz on your face?"

Strangers, too, target adolescents for unwanted and disconcerting remarks. Pubescent girls suddenly hear whistles, catcalls, and lewd suggestions; boys, depending on their level of maturation, often find themselves labeled as studs or wimps and find that rough-and-tumble play becomes more a test of strength with an aggressive undercurrent at puberty (Smith, 1997).

The concern with physique dominates the peer culture, particularly during early adolescence (Harter, 1993). Unattractive teenagers tend to have fewer friends—of either sex. And attractiveness is a sexual lure, especially during adolescence. For girls, those with more body fat have fewer dates or boyfriends than their thinner classmates (Halpern et al., 1999). For boys, larger bodies correlate with more aggression—partly directed against those boys who are not as well developed (Tremblay et al., 1998).

Adolescents also receive powerful messages from the broader social environment. Media images of handsome faces and beautiful bodies are used to sell almost everything, from clothes and cosmetics to luncheon meats and auto parts. These images reinforce the cultural stereotype that men should be tall and muscular, that women should be thin and shapely, and—at least in North America and western Europe—that both should have facial features that suggest Anglo ancestors.

Obviously, few real bodies fit this model. Not only many individuals but entire ethnic groups are genetically endowed with shorter stature, broader hips, or chunkier bodies than this cultural ideal projects. Often these genetic differences are latent during childhood, before hormones produce the adult body type the person is destined to have. This means that many young adolescents suddenly must come to terms with a body form, inherited from their ancestors, quite unlike that of the fashion models, sports heroes, and movie stars they idolize. They stare at their emerging self, with fascination and horror, in the mirror every morning (posing, turning, wetting down an unruly lock of hair, changing clothes again just when it is time to leave). As one father complained, "Whenever they talk to us, they won't even look at us if a mirror is close by, or even if a window is nearby. They will invariably look right by us at whatever might project an image of themselves" (Garvin, 1994).

Teenagers' concern about their body image should not be taken lightly. For most adolescents, *thinking* that they look terrible makes them feel terrible—even depressed (McKinley, 1999). Instead of ignoring or belittling the adolescent's self-preoccupation, adults might provide whatever practical help seems warranted—such as new clothing, encouragement to exercise, or medical treatment for acne. Understanding instead of derision could have far-reaching benefits, not only for body image but also for self-esteem, social acceptance, and overall enjoyment of life.

body image A person's concept of how his or her body appears. This self-evaluation may be quite different from the opinions of others or from any objective measures.

table 14.2	Adolescent Girls' Actual and Desired Weights*			
	Girls Who Matured On Time (weight in pounds)		Girls Who Matured Late (weight in pounds)	
	Actual	Desired	Actual	Desired
Dancers	116	102	108	98
Swimmers	130	117	128	114
Nonathletes	125	114	121	111

*For all six groups, average height was between 5'4" and 5'5½".
Source: Brooks-Gunn et al., 1989.

A Cultural Ideal At age 15, figure skater Michelle Kwan, from California, won the American Ladies National and World Championship titles. At 17 she won the Olympic silver medal but lost the gold to teammate Tara Lipinski, then 15. The combination of grace, strength, and slimness that she and other young female skaters and gymnasts exemplify is admired even more than the accomplishments of medalists in other Olympic events. This idealization may, however, be the downfall of many normally developing adolescent girls.

Why Shave? Facial hair is often considered a sign of virility, which explains why many young men shave regularly before doing so seems warranted. However, since the act of shaving may signal the young male's adult interests and urges, parents should not ridicule it, even when it involves little more than fuzz.

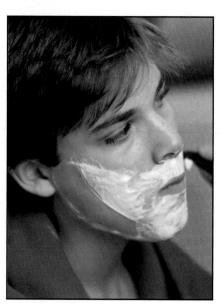

Voice and Hair

Another secondary sex characteristic is the voice, which becomes lower as the larynx grows. This change is most noticeable in boys. (Even more noticeable, much to the chagrin of the young adolescent male, is an occasional loss of voice control that throws his newly acquired baritone into a high squeak.) Girls also develop somewhat lower voices, the underlying reason people think a low, throaty female voice is "sexy."

During puberty, existing hair on the head, arms, and legs becomes coarser and darker, and new hair grows under the arms, on the face, and in the groin area. Visible facial hair and body hair are generally considered distinct signs of manliness in American society. This notion is mistaken, because hairiness is inherited. How often a man needs to shave, or how hairy his chest is, is determined primarily by his genes, not his virility. Further, during puberty all girls develop some light facial hair, as well as more noticeable hair on their arms and legs, with the specifics of color and density more genetic than hormonal.

HEALTH AND HAZARDS

In many ways, adolescence is a healthy time. The minor illnesses of childhood (such as flu, colds, earaches, and high fevers) become much less common, because inoculations and years of exposure have increased immunity. The two main killers of adults, heart disease and cancer, are rare: A 15-year-old's chance of dying from them is only one-third that of a 30-year-old and one-hundredth that of a 60-year-old.

However, while diseases are relatively uncommon, adolescents are at risk for health hazards of a different kind—especially as they gain increasing independence and make more of their own decisions. Many such hazards are discussed in the next two chapters, including risk taking, sexually transmitted diseases, pregnancy, suicide, and delinquency. Here, we will look at sexual abuse and abuse of alcohol, tobacco, and other drugs.

Sexual Abuse: Special Vulnerability in Adolescence

The definition of *sexual abuse* is quite comprehensive: any situation in which one person engages another person in a sexual activity, whether verbal or physical, without that person's freely given consent. Since children and younger adolescents are vulnerable to the power of adults and have little (if any) understanding of the implications of sexual activity, they are legally incapable of freely consenting to sexual acts. (The "age of consent" was only 10 in the nineteenth-century United States; today it varies from 14 to 18, depending on state law) (Donovan, 1997). Under that age, even voluntary sexual intercourse between, say, a 15-year-old girl and a 19-year-old man can be considered statutory rape.

childhood sexual abuse Any activity in which an adult uses a child for his or her own sexual stimulation or pleasure—even if the use does not involve physical contact. Child pornography, fondling, and lewd comments by strangers are all examples of childhood sexual abuse.

Thus, **childhood sexual abuse** is defined as any erotic activity that arouses an adult and excites, shames, or confuses a young person—whether or not the victim protests and whether or not genital contact is involved. Under this definition, sexual abuse is very common. Teasing a child in a sexualized manner, photographing a young person in erotic poses, intrusively questioning a young adolescent about his or her developing body, and invading the privacy of a child's bathing, dressing, or sleeping routines—especially once puberty begins—can all be sexually abusive. Even when the definition is more narrow—"forced to touch an adult or older child or forcibly touched by an older adult or older child in a sexual way"—30 percent of mothers and 9 percent of fathers polled nationwide had been abused as children (Gallup, 1995).

As with other forms of maltreatment, the harm from any particular act of sexual abuse increases the more it is repeated, the more it distorts adult–child relationships, and the more it impairs the child's ability to develop normally (Stevenson, 1999). In particular, repeated childhood sexual abuse by a trusted adult has the potential to permanently damage the person's ability, years later, to establish a warm, trusting, and intimate relationship. Whether this potential is realized depends on many factors, but, as with any other serious risk, the best course is to avoid it.

Sexual victimization in adolescence is often the continuation of less blatant childhood abuse. It may begin with fondling, explicit nudity, or suggestive comments—all of which tend to confuse a preschooler or young school-age child. Then, in late childhood or early adolescence, such sexualized adult–child interaction may escalate, with onset typically between ages 8 and 12 (Stewart, 1997).

Overt force is seldom involved, because the perpetrator is usually in a position of dominance over the child. The victim is especially powerless when she is a pubescent girl and the perpetrator is her own father. Although the victim may have confused feelings about the sexual contact, and may believe the reassurances or accusations she receives from the perpetrator ("You know you like it"), there is no question that a sexual father–daughter relationship is victimization. Slightly older adolescent girls are prime targets for victimization by older relatives, strangers, and especially young men they know. In a survey of young women of four ethnicities in the United States (African, Native, Mexican,

❓ **Especially for Social Workers:** What signs might indicate that a young person is being sexually abused?

and European American), about one-third of each group reported sexual abuse; one-fifth of these respondents had been raped (Roosa et al., 1999). Young Canadian women report similarly high rates (De Keseredy & Schwarts, 1998).

The *meaning* of being sexually victimized may be especially disturbing for older children and adolescents compared to younger children. At a time when they want to take pride in changes in their bodies, as they become increasingly self-aware and attracted to peers, sexual victimization can turn the world upside down. Indeed, adolescents often react to such maltreatment in ways that younger children rarely do—with self-destructive behavior (such as suicide, drug abuse, or running away) or with counterattack (such as vandalism or violence, aimed at society or directly at the perpetrator) (Ewing, 1990).

This is just as true for boys as for girls. In addition to bearing the stigma of unwelcome sexual activity, a molested boy is likely to feel shame at being weak and unable to defend himself and is also likely to worry that he is homosexual—all contrary to the macho image that many young adolescent boys strive to attain. The male perpetrator does not necessarily consider himself homosexual, nor is a boy's involvement a true indication of his sexual orientation. However, when the boy is, in fact, gay and is abused for it, the shame escalates. And when the sexual abuse of a boy occurs at home, typically by his father or stepfather, the problems of vulnerability and loss of self-esteem are multiplied (Finkelhor, 1994).

Although most abusers are male, about 20 percent of all sexual abusers are female (Bagley & Thurston, 1996). Such abuse can be sexual teasing and fondling, which evokes confusion and shame, or more blatant abuse. Boys obviously are spared the problems of unwanted pregnancy that many sexually abused girls experience, but they often turn their anger outward. An estimated 30 to 50 percent of child molesters are adolescent boys who had been abused themselves (Jones et al., 1999).

Alcohol, Tobacco, and Other Drugs

drug abuse   The ingestion of a drug to the extent that it impairs the user's well-being.

drug addiction   A person's dependence on a drug or a behavior in order to feel physically or psychologically at ease.

drug use   The ingestion of a drug, regardless of the amount or effect of ingestion.

The topic of drugs is a lightning rod for distorted statistics, latent prejudice, and murky thinking. Let us try to bring some clarity, beginning with clear definitions. **Drug abuse** is the ingestion of any drug to the extent that it impairs the user's well-being, either biologically or psychosocially, significantly more than it helps the person. By this definition, even prescribed drugs can be abused. **Drug addiction** occurs when the person craves more of a drug in order to feel physically or psychologically at ease. **Drug use** is simply the ingestion of a drug, regardless of the amount or effect of ingestion.

Note that the *abuse* of any drug, including alcohol and prescribed or off-the-shelf medicines, always upsets physical and psychological development, whether or not that abuse becomes addictive. Both addiction and abuse entail many complications, including death, and both are much more likely to emerge full-force in early and middle adulthood than during adolescence. For that reason, they are discussed in Chapter 20. Abuse of drugs is always harmful, but use is not necessarily bad and it may be legal (as caffeine and alcohol are).

The *use* of drugs is sometimes harmful, sometimes not, depending on the maturation of the drug user as well as on the reason for the use (Gerstein & Green, 1993). Use before age 18 is the topic here.

❷ **Especially for Educators:** How should you teach teenagers to avoid drugs? Specifically, which of the following four strategies would be best to prevent drug abuse in early adolescence: teaching by example, giving informative lectures, having open discussions, or remaining silent on the topic (relying on adolescents to discover lessons through experience)?

Figure 14.5 Drug Use Is Climbing A decade-long decline in regular drug use among U.S. high school seniors came to an end in 1992. This is so for both legal and illegal drugs; thus, it seems that drinking alcohol and smoking cigarettes are affected by the same cohort conditions as swallowing pills or smoking marijuana (or snorting cocaine or shooting heroin, shown here as part of "illicit drugs"). The cohort factor that seems most closely related to the recent upsurge in adolescent drug use is a decline in teenagers' belief that drug use is harmful.

Disquieting Trends

Most adolescents in most nations use drugs, as chronicled by many studies (Silbereisen et al., 1995). One of the most notable of these studies is an annual, detailed, confidential survey of nearly 50,000 American eighth-, tenth-, and twelfth-grade students from more than 400 high schools throughout the United States. Since its inception in 1975, this survey has consistently shown that more than 8 out of 10 seniors had drunk alcohol (more than a few sips), 2 out of 3 had smoked at least one cigarette, and close to half (ranging from 66 percent in 1981 to 41 percent in 1992) had tried at least one illegal drug (Johnston et al., 1999).

More Frequent Use. The rates just mentioned refer to "lifetime prevalence." They include instances of one-time-only experimentation. More troubling are data on use "within the past 30 days." The regular (30-day) use of most drugs (except cocaine) declined during the 1980s and then, in the early 1990s, began to increase (see Figure 14.5). From 1991 to 1999, for example, the regular use of marijuana rose significantly for all age groups, reaching about 23 percent in 1997–1999 among twelfth-graders. There were also increases in the regular use of other illegal drugs (hallucinogens, including LSD and PCP, nonprescription stimulants, cocaine, heroin, and so on), from a low of 6 percent in 1992 to a high of 11 percent in 1998.

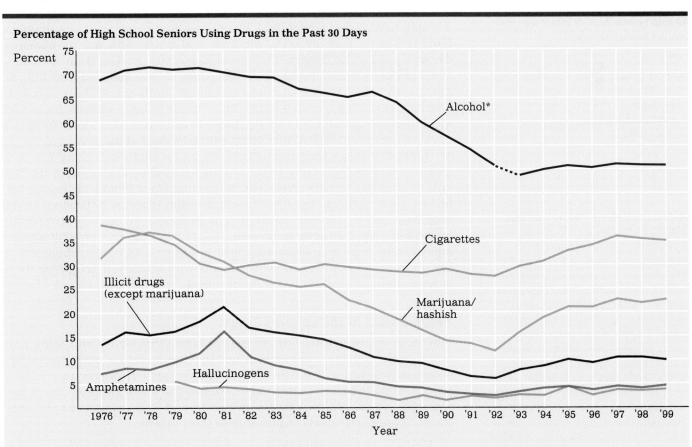

Percentage of High School Seniors Using Drugs in the Past 30 Days

*The 1993 alcohol questionnaire was revised to say "more than a few sips"; hence, the dashed part of the graph to indicate new quantity.
Source: Adapted from Johnston et al., 1999.

Then and Now This boy is shown at age 13, in 1986, when he was living in a German home for troubled boys. While developmental researchers have witnessed many young adolescents who defy the odds, this chilling photo includes four signs that this boy might be headed for trouble.

❓ *Observational Quiz (see answer page 404): What are these warning signs?*

gateway drugs Drugs—usually tobacco, alcohol, and marijuana—whose use increases the risk that a person will later use harder drugs, such as cocaine and heroin.

❗ **Response for Social Workers (from page 398):** Although some sexually abused children are also physically abused or neglected, some seem quite well cared for. Therefore, an unusually devoted or protective father who wants to keep his daughter away from the boys or who gives her expensive presents may not be as wonderful as he seems. Similarly, any adolescent girl or boy who is self-destructive, with drugs, mutilation, or suicide attempts, may be a victim of abuse. Finally, most sexually abused adolescents are ashamed and thus reticent to talk about their family relationships. None of these signs proves abuse, of course, but given the frequency of sexual abuse in early adolescence, further exploration is recommended when any of these signs appear.

Younger and Younger. A particularly disquieting feature of the 1999 school survey is the early onset of drug use. About 52 percent of all eighth-graders had already had at least one alcoholic drink; 44 percent had smoked at least one cigarette; and about 22 percent had tried marijuana, more than twice as many as in the 1991 survey. Repeated use of these drugs by age 13 or so is also on the rise. Between 1991 and 1999, the percentage of eighth-graders who had smoked cigarettes within the past 30 days rose from 14 to 19 percent, and the percentage who had smoked marijuana within the past 30 days tripled from 3 to 10 percent (Johnston et al., 1999). Other research confirms that more younger adolescents are using drugs than ever before. (See the Changing Policy box.)

Some developmentalists hesitate to condemn every instance of drug use, especially among high school seniors or college students, since use does not always lead to abuse and addiction (Moffitt, 1993). In fact, one 15-year longitudinal study found that 3-year-olds who were relatively well adjusted and well loved were likely to experiment with drugs by age 18. For these "experimenters" (in the researcher's formulation), drug use had no harmful effects; they were "psychologically healthy, sociable, and reasonably inquisitive individuals." By contrast, the 3-year-olds who were tense, distressed, and insecure became teenagers who either abused drugs or avoided them completely. Both the "frequent users" and the "abstainers" showed signs of psychological problems, although drug use did not predict adjustment in every case (Shedler & Block, 1990).

Despite mixed opinions about drug use in late adolescence, every developmentalist is alarmed by drug use among very young teenagers. One reason is that tobacco, alcohol, and marijuana act as **gateway drugs,** opening the door to the use of harder drugs (Gerstein & Green, 1993). To be specific, teenagers who begin to use tobacco, alcohol, or marijuana before the ninth grade are significantly more likely to use illegal drugs in high school and are more likely to have serious drug- and alcohol-abuse problems later on. Early drug use is also likely to make preexisting psychological problems worse (Wilens et al., 1997).

Indeed, a large longitudinal survey found that early drug use is a gateway to a wide variety of destructive activities and conditions, not only drug abuse but also risky sex, alienation from school, antisocial behavior, poor physical health, and depression (Kandel & Davies, 1996). Similarly, in the 15-year study just mentioned, among children with longstanding personality difficulties, those who had tried marijuana by age 14 were more maladjusted, more unhappy, and more rebellious at age 18 than those with similar problems who remained drug-free until at least high school (Shedler & Block, 1990).

Health Impact of the Gateway Drugs

The early use of gateway drugs makes later drug abuse and addiction more likely, but that outcome is not inevitable. Some early users become early quitters or never become heavy users. However, in addition to increasing the risk of later harm, each of the three gateway drugs has a strong and immediate impact on health and well-being; younger adolescents are particularly vulnerable to their effects.

Tobacco. Tobacco use decreases food consumption and interferes with the absorption of nutrients, both of which can limit the growth spurt.

Figure 14.6 Current Cigarette Use Among Ninth-to Twelfth-Graders. As you can see, cigarette use among U.S. high school students is increasing rapidly. The overall average of 35 percent for females and 38 percent for males is substantially above the average for adults.

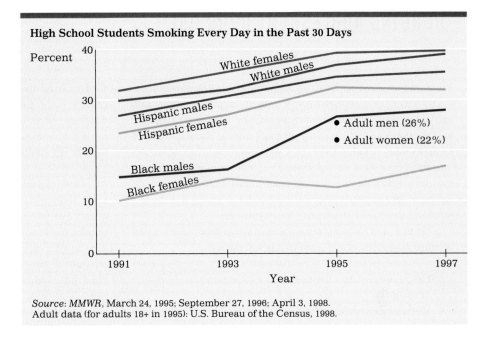

High School Students Smoking Every Day in the Past 30 Days

Source: MMWR, March 24, 1995; September 27, 1996; April 3, 1998.
Adult data (for adults 18+ in 1995): U.S. Bureau of the Census, 1998.

Young steady smokers are significantly shorter and smaller than they would have been if they had not started smoking until they were fully grown. Cigarette smoking markedly reduces fertility, which means the entire sexual and reproductive maturation process is probably impeded (Fiscella et al., 1998).

In addition, nicotine, the toxic chemical found in tobacco, is probably the most physically addictive drug of all, and the great majority of adolescents who become regular smokers are quickly hooked. Proof of this comes from the reports of young people, age 10 to 18 years, who had smoked at least one cigarette a day for the previous 30 days (see Figure 14.6). Most of them (74 percent) said that they smoked partly because "it's really hard to quit" (*MMWR*, October 21, 1994).

Alcohol. Alcohol consumption is especially destructive during adolescence. The primary reason is that, even in small doses, alcohol loosens inhibitions and impairs judgment—a dangerous effect in a person already psychologically off balance because of ongoing physical, sexual, and emotional changes. A survey of 46,000 high school students, most of them "middle American" (middle-class, midwestern), compared teenagers who had drunk alcohol six or more times in the previous month with teens who never or rarely drank (Bensen, 1997). The "drinkers" were:

- More than twice as likely to be sexually active (70 percent compared with 32 percent)
- More than twice as likely to engage in antisocial behaviors such as stealing, fighting in groups, and vandalizing property (49 percent compared with 19 percent)
- Almost four times as likely to be excessively absent from school (23 percent compared with 6 percent)
- More likely to ride in a car with a driver who has been drinking (86 percent compared with 56 percent)

❶ Response for Educators (from page 399): All these strategies make some sense, and each of them might backfire. If the "example" smokes or drinks, if the information is alarmist or inaccurate, if the open discussions include popular students defending drug use, or if silence implies consent, the result may be more and earlier drug use. Remember that because adolescents admire honesty, respond to caring, and abhor hypocrisy, any strategy must incorporate these factors. Another tip—sometimes an antidrug peer, a few years older, earns the most respect and trust.

CURBING ADOLESCENT DRUG USE

What can be done about drug use among adolescents, particularly young adolescents? As long as drugs are available and are not perceived as extremely damaging, most young people will try them and many will eventually abuse them. One goal, then, as most developmentalists see it, is to delay drug experimentation as long as possible. This increases the odds that the developing person will be realistically informed and will have the reasoning ability to limit—and perhaps avoid—destructive drugs in dangerous circumstances.

To this end, a wide array of measures have been tried. Among those that are at least partly effective are:

- Health education classes that honestly portray the risks of drug use
- Harsher punishments for store owners who sell alcohol or cigarettes to minors
- Higher prices of alcohol and cigarettes
- Drunk-driving laws that are strictly enforced
- Better parent–child communication about drugs

Collectively, these measures do indeed postpone and decrease drug use and prevent or diminish serious consequences when experimentation occurs. Cigarette smoking among U.S. eighth-graders is decreasing; it fell from 21 percent to 17 percent between 1996 and 1999 (Johnston et al., 1999).

One important factor is parental attitudes. Many parents are silent or poorly informed about the hazards of various drugs. Worse, many parents model the wrong behavior. One extensive New Zealand study found that half the parents allowed their very young children (age 9 or younger) to have an occasional sip of their alcoholic drinks, and these were the children most likely to become alcoholic by age 18 (Casswell, 1996).

A study in Scotland found that parents of middle-school children were most worried about illegal drugs, somewhat resigned about early smoking and drinking, and oblivious to the dangers of solvent sniffing. In fact, the actual prevalence of these three categories during middle school—rare, common,

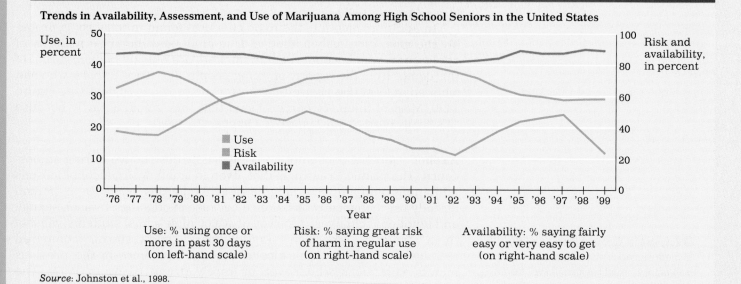

Trends in Availability, Assessment, and Use of Marijuana Among High School Seniors in the United States

Use: % using once or more in past 30 days (on left-hand scale)

Risk: % saying great risk of harm in regular use (on right-hand scale)

Availability: % saying fairly easy or very easy to get (on right-hand scale)

Source: Johnston et al., 1998.

Figure 14.7 Not Supply and Demand, but Attitude and Action. Marijuana has been easily available to almost nine out of ten U.S. high school seniors over the past 25 years, but actual pot smoking is closely related to perception of risk, not to supply. These are patterns for high school seniors, a group most likely to be affected by their peers' attitudes. Adults and addicts are not as vulnerable to shifts in attitudes, except, perhaps, if those changing attitudes are their own.

and extremely dangerous, respectively—were opposite from the parents' levels of concern (Boyland et al, 1998).

The same kind of gap between adult concepts and early adolescent needs is shown in one of the most popular and costly drug education programs in the United States. In Project D.A.R.E. (Drug Abuse Resistance Education), police officers go into classrooms from kindergarten through high school to present a curriculum that emphasizes the harmfulness of drugs, including videos of the frightening consequences of illegal drug abuse. Parents, politicians, and police departments like the program, funding it generously and extensively; but longitudinal research has found that the only benefit is a short-term increase in knowledge about specific drugs.

Students who experience D.A.R.E. are no more likely to abstain from drugs over the high school years than those who do not (Clayton et al., 1996; Ennett et al., 1994; Wysong et al., 1994). Is there some long-term "sleeper" effect, protecting D.A.R.E. recipients in young adulthood? No. In fact, 10 years later, the only difference between two groups of young people who were similar except that one group had experienced D.A.R.E. and the other had not was slightly lower self-esteem in those who had learned about drug abuse from a D.A.R.E. police officer (Lynam et al., 1999). Attitudes about the self changed for the worse; attitudes toward drugs were not affected.

The importance of a young person's attitude as a prelude to drug use is indicated in Figure 14.7, which shows that the actual use of marijuana follows overall shifts in the perception of the dangers of the drug by about a year (Johnston et al., 1998). Attitudes, in turn, are powerfully affected by national and local policies, as well as by personal experience. The importance of the macrosystem is indicated by trends in many nations of western Europe, where young people increasingly used drugs throughout the 1980s—the same years when adolescents in the United States were turning away from drugs (Silbereisen et al., 1995).

Unfortunately, antidrug attitudes softened markedly among young Americans during the 1990s, perhaps because each cohort goes through **generational forgetting**—that is, each generation forgets to communicate to the next one the hard lessons it learned through personal experience. In the case of drugs, generational forgetting renders each generation oblivious to the harm of drug use as directly witnessed by the cohort that preceded it. For example, generational learning is probably the reason heroin was abused less frequently in the 1980s than in the 1970s, but generational forgetting may be the reason heroin now seems to be experiencing a comeback. For the same reason, crack use, which declined markedly in the 1990s, may be increasing again (Johnston et al., 1998).

Tobacco is the most worrisome drug here. Despite massive publicity, attitudes have not changed much. Older adolescents have a higher smoking rate than any age group of adults, a trend apparent worldwide. In the United States, many younger adolescents answer "no great risk" when asked, "How much do you think people risk harming themselves (physically or in other ways) if they smoke one or more packs of cigarettes per day?" (See Figure 14.8.) The chief investigator of the high school survey comments: "That's virtually a question with a right-or-wrong answer, and nearly half of these 13- and 14-year-olds get it wrong" (Johnston, 1998).

If too many young adolescents see a certain drug's use as harmless, tomorrow's young adults may have "their own epidemic" of drug addiction (Wren, 1996).

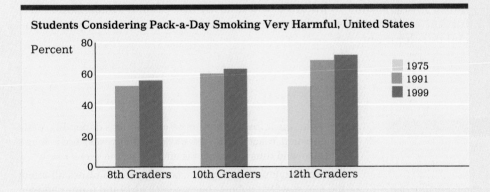

Students Considering Pack-a-Day Smoking Very Harmful, United States

Legend: 1975, 1991, 1999

Figure 14.8 Slow Progress. The trends are in the right direction, in that with age and time, more adolescents see smoking as harmful. However, since doctors and researchers universally know that tobacco is a leading cause of early death, it is astonishing that even in 1999, one-third of students in the United States denied this reality, with eighth-graders particularly willing to ignore possible harm.

generational forgetting The tendency of each new generation to ignore lessons learned by the previous cohort. For example, the hazards of crack were well known a decade ago, but today's teenagers are less aware of them.

Celebrating Alcohol These young people in a Florida motel room, rejoicing in their beer, have temporarily—and artificially—overcome the awkwardness and unease that most teenagers feel with each other.

❶ *Answer to Observational Quiz (from page 400): The cigarette smoked down to the filter suggests that he has gone through the first "gate," and within the next 4 years he may well use cocaine and heroin; his shirt suggests that he considers women solely as sex objects; his expression implies that he suspects everyone, perhaps with good reason. The fourth sign, the injury on his forehead, could mean that he has been regularly battered, perhaps causing brain damage, or that he had just one unfortunate encounter with a stationary object. This photo is suggestive; a detailed case history as he approaches age 30 might relieve our concern—or trouble us even more.*

Marijuana. The third of the gateway drugs, marijuana, seriously slows down thinking processes, particularly those related to memory and abstract reasoning. Such impairment is especially problematic in early adolescence, when academic learning requires greater memory and a higher level of abstract thinking.

In addition, over time, repeated marijuana "mellowness" may turn into a general lack of motivation and indifference toward the future. The result is apathy at the very time that young people should be focusing their energy on meeting the challenges of growing up. This explains the results of a longitudinal study in which children who became marijuana users experienced a developmental slowdown in adulthood. They were later than their peers to graduate from college, to obtain steady employment, and to marry (Brook et al., 1999).

Early drug use impairs the acquisition of knowledge, the ability to reflect on that knowledge, and the growth of mature judgment that leads to reasoned conclusions. The same cognitive impairment and social ineptness that are caused by early drug *use* play a role later by increasing the chances of drug *abuse* and addiction.

Centuries ago puberty did not occur until the later teens, when the adolescent mind and social context may have been ready for the challenges of sexual awakening and the growth spurt. Today, however, when puberty begins at age 11 or 12, young people may not be cognitively or socially capable of the autonomy their bodies seek. Fortunately, the social context can make a difference in how teenagers respond to their biological growth. Education and social pressures still guide young people in positive and healthy directions. These issues are further explored in the next two chapters, on cognitive and psychosocial development.

SUMMARY

PUBERTY BEGINS

1. The sequence of pubertal events is the same for young people of both sexes and in every culture, but the timing of puberty varies considerably. Normal children experience their first body changes sometime between the ages of 8 and 14.

2. Puberty is initiated by the production of hormones in the brain. Four of the most important hormones are gonadotropin-releasing hormone, growth hormone, testosterone, and estrogen. While performing their biological functions, these hormones can make adolescents' moods more volatile.

However, the impact of hormones on emotions depends greatly on personal reactions to the obvious changes in body shape and size, and thus the impact is affected by the social context.

3. The individual's sex, genes, body type, and stress all affect the age at which puberty begins, with girls and fatter children reaching puberty ahead of boys and leaner children.

THE GROWTH SPURT

4. The growth spurt—first in weight, then in height—provides the first obvious evidence of puberty, although some hormonal changes precede it. During the year of fastest growth, some girls gain up to 20 pounds (9 kg) and grow about

3½ inches (9 centimeters), and some boys gain up to 26 pounds (12 kg) and grow about 4 inches (10 centimeters).

5. The growth spurt usually affects the extremities first and then proceeds toward the torso. By the end of puberty, the lungs and heart have also increased in size and capacity. During the period of greatest growth, the body often appears misproportioned, since various parts of the body begin growth at different times.

6. To fuel the growth of puberty, adolescents experience increasing nutritional demands for vitamins and minerals as well as for calories—more than at any other period of life. Too much salt, too little iron, and not enough vegetables are common problems.

SEXUAL CHARACTERISTICS

7. During puberty, all the primary sex characteristics (sex organs) grow larger as the young person becomes sexually mature. Menarche in girls and spermarche in boys are the events usually taken to indicate reproductive potential, although full fertility is not reached until years after these initial signs of maturation.

8. Both sexes also experience changes in the secondary sex characteristics (breasts, voice, and facial and body hair)—although there are obvious differences in the typical development of males and females.

HEALTH AND HAZARDS

9. Coming at a time when the child is confronted with the physical changes of puberty and their psychological impact, sexual abuse in adolescence can be particularly devastating. The effects of sexual abuse largely depend on the nature of the abuse, its duration, and the adolescent's relationship to the abuser. Sexually abused adolescents may become depressed, drug-addicted, or abusers themselves.

10. Drug use or experimentation occurs among most adolescents, with almost every teenager knowing how to obtain cigarettes, beer, and other drugs. In the United States, drug use is increasing, after a long period of decline, and first-time drug users are younger.

11. Addiction, particularly to cigarettes, is a risk that seems to be underestimated by society and by teenagers themselves. However, laws, memories, and attitudes can and do change from generation to generation, so drug use by the next cohort may be markedly reduced or increased, depending on the social context.

KEY TERMS

adolescence (381)
puberty (381)
gonads (382)
menarche (385)
growth spurt (386)
primary sex
   characteristics (391)
spermarche (391)
secondary sex
   characteristics (391)

body image (394)
childhood sexual abuse
   (397)
drug abuse (398)
drug addiction (398)
drug use (398)
gateway drugs (400)
generational forgetting
   (403)

KEY QUESTIONS

1. What is the usual sequence of biological changes during puberty?

2. What factors trigger the onset of puberty?

3. How does the age at which puberty begins affect the adolescent, socially and emotionally?

4. What are the main changes that characterize the growth spurt?

5. How do the nutritional needs of adolescents differ from those of younger and older individuals?

6. How are the sexual maturation of males and that of females similar, and how are they different?

7. How is an adolescent's body image related to the development of self-esteem?

8. What are the potential consequences of sexual abuse in adolescence?

9. What are the reasons underlying increased adolescent use of some drugs and experimentation at an earlier age?

10. How might drug use be harmful to adolescents, even if the drug is legal?

11. *In Your Experience* How did the attitudes of your family, friends, and others affect your experience of puberty?

Adolescence:
Cognitive Development

Talking with a 16-year-old about international politics, the latest rage in music, or the meaning of life is obviously quite different from having conversations on the same topics with an 8-year-old. Thanks to major advances in their cognitive abilities, adolescents are increasingly aware of both world concerns and personal needs—others' as well as their own—and they are more adult in their use of analysis, logic, and reason.

However, as thinking develops and knowledge increases, young people become more vulnerable to ideas, speculations, and insights that are troubling or even dangerous. They may appear tough-minded; at least, their frequent sarcasm, cynicism, and arrogance give this impression. But the opposite is more likely true. Adolescents are naive, idealistic, troubled by their own introspections, and supersensitive to criticism, real or imagined.

ADOLESCENT THOUGHT

Every basic skill of thinking, learning, and remembering continues to progress during adolescence. Selective attention becomes more skillfully deployed, enabling students to do homework when they are surrounded by peers or blaring music (or both) *if* motivation is high. Expanded memory skills and a growing knowledge base allow adolescents to connect new ideas and concepts to old ones. Metamemory and metacognition help them become better students. This, in turn, deepens adolescents' understanding of calculus and chemistry, fads and friendship, and everything else they set their minds to.

Language mastery continues as well. Vocabulary grows and the nuances of grammar become better understood. Many adolescents develop a personal style in their writing and speech; poets, diarists, and debaters emerge in every high school classroom. However, ongoing maturation of these cognitive skills (already described in Chapter 12) does not capture the essence of adolescent thought. Something new emerges (Lutz & Sternberg, 1999; Moshman, 1998).

New Intellectual Powers

Piaget thought adolescents begin to reach **formal operational thought.** In his theory, formal operational thought is the fourth and final stage of cognitive development, arising from a combination of maturation and

formal operational thought In Piaget's theory, the fourth and final stage of cognitive development; arises from combination of maturation and experience.

experience (Inhelder & Piaget, 1958). Information-processing theorists likewise see a new and higher level of cognition, the result of accumulated improvements in cognitive processing and memory. Similarly, sociocultural theorists point to intellectual advances that result from entering secondary school, where such things as specialized teachers, changing classes, and long-term homework assignments constitute a new culture of learning. Indeed, almost all developmentalists agree that adolescent thought is qualitatively different from children's thought.

For many developmentalists, the single most distinguishing feature of adolescent thought is the capacity to think of *possibility*, not just reality. This capacity becomes their first reaction to a problem. Adolescents "start with possible solutions and progress to determine which is the real solution" (Lutz & Sternberg, 1999). As a result, adolescents think "outside the box" of tradition. They can analyze probabilities, realizing that something that is probable is possible, not inevitable (Falk & Wilkening, 1998). John Flavell and his colleagues (1993) describe this development as follows:

Weather Forecasting: Predicting the Possible
Thanks to a satellite feed from high-tech computers and monitors, these students are learning the art and science of weather forecasting. Such education is well suited to the adolescent mind. In their expansive knowledge of relevant factors, ability to remember several interrelated variables, and capacity to imagine possibilities, adolescents' thinking is quite different from that of younger children.

> The elementary school child's characteristic approach to many conceptual problems is . . . an earthbound, concrete, practical-minded sort of problem-solving approach, one that persistently fixates on the perceptible and inferable reality right there in front of him. . . . The child usually begins with reality and moves reluctantly, if at all, to possibility; . . . the adolescent or adult is more apt to begin with possibility and only subsequently proceed to reality. . . . Reality is seen as that particular portion of the much wider world of possibility that happens to exist or hold true in a given problem situation.

This ability to think in terms of possibility allows adolescents to fantasize, speculate, and hypothesize more readily and on a far grander scale than children, who are still tied to the tangible reality of the here and now. Adolescents can, and do, break free from the earthbound, traditional reasoning of the schoolchild, soaring into contradictory notions and ethereal dreams quite apart from conventional wisdom.

Hypothetical Thinking

hypothetical thought Thought that involves propositions and possibilities that may or may not reflect reality.

Adolescents demonstrate a capacity for **hypothetical thought,** that is, thought that involves reasoning about propositions that may or may not reflect reality. For younger children, imagined possibilities (such as in pretend play) are always tied to the everyday world as they know or wish it to be. For adolescents, possibility takes on a life of its own. "Here and now" is only one of many alternatives that include not only "there and then" but also "long, long ago," "nowhere," "not yet," and "never."

The adolescent's ability to ignore the real and think about the possible is clear in this hypothetical example: If an impoverished college student were offered $100 to argue in favor of the view that government should *never* give or lend money to impoverished college students, probably he or she could earn the money by providing a convincing (if insincere) argument. This demonstrates that the college student has mastered the skill of hypothetical thought. By contrast, school-age children have great difficulty arguing against their personal beliefs, espe-

❷ Especially for Parents: Suppose your 14-year-old child argues a position you think is completely irrational—that it would be best to leave school at 16, or that all religious leaders are greedy for money, or some such argument. What is the best way to convince him or her otherwise?

Abstraction Way Beyond Counting on Fingers and Toes This high school student explains a calculus problem, a behavior that requires a level of hypothetical and abstract thought beyond that of any concrete operational child—and of most adults. At the beginning of concrete operational thought, children need blocks, coins, and other tangible objects to help them understand math. By later adolescence, in the full flower of formal operational thought, such practical and concrete illustrations are irrelevant.

cially if those personal beliefs arise from their own situation. An 8-year-old would find it almost impossible to explain why parents should *not* give birthday presents to their children, even if the child knew this argument was "just pretend" (Flavell at al., 1993).

This newfound ability is one reason why adolescence is a time of agonized reflection about the world and one's place in it. Such reflection can lead to novel, provocative, and sometimes frightening thoughts. God and religion come up for analysis; the meaning of life is open to question; the misdeeds and moral failings of national heroes and one's own parents take on heavy significance. For many teenagers, reflection about any serious issue becomes a complicated and wrenching process. The complications were illustrated on a personal level by one high school student who wanted to keep her friend from making a life-threatening decision but did not want to judge her, because

> to . . . judge [someone] means that whatever you are saying is right and you know what's right. You know it's right for them and you know it's right in every situation. [But] you can't know if you are right. Maybe you are right. But then, right in what way? [quoted in Gilligan et al., 1990]

Although adolescents are not always sure what is "right in what way," they are quick to see what is "wrong." Unlike children, they do not accept current conditions because "that's how things are." Instead, they criticize what is, precisely because they can imagine how things could be, would be, should be in a world in which justice was realized, people were always sincere, and the meaning of human life was truly recognized. This is hypothetical thinking at its best.

Deductive Reasoning

As you saw in Chapter 12, during the school years, children increasingly use their accumulated knowledge of facts, as well as their personal experience, to reach conclusions. In essence, their reasoning goes like this: "If it walks like a duck and quacks like a duck, then it must be a duck." Such reasoning from particulars ("walks like" and "quacks like") to a general conclusion ("it's a duck") is called **inductive reasoning.**

During adolescence, as young people develop their capacity to think hypothetically, they soon become more capable of **deductive reasoning**

inductive reasoning Reasoning from one or more specific experiences or facts to a general conclusion.

deductive reasoning Reasoning from a general statement or principle, through logical steps, to a specific conclusion.

Deductive Reasoning High school chemistry classes, such as the one above, first teach students the general principles and then ask them to test the principles with specific substances. There is no way a student could simply be given these materials and told to figure out some generalities, as a teacher of 8-year-olds, with much simpler and safer substances, might do. Younger children think inductively; these students think deductively as well.

Chess is another example of deductive thinking. Unlike simple games of chance, which younger children enjoy, chess requires some general principles, such as protecting your king, focusing on the center, and changing strategies as the game progresses.

❓ *Observational Quiz (see answer page 413): Beyond the intellectual challenge of chemistry or chess, what other type of problem do these adolescents seem to be solving?*

❗ **Response for Parents (from page 408):**
Since adolescents love the game of thinking and are adept at hypothetical thinking, the first thing to remember is not to take the words too seriously or too personally. Part of the fun of the adolescent years is taking an idea to its hypothetical and deductive extreme—and shocking parents in the process. So listen, provide alternative perspectives and facts, but don't get too upset. Opinions change rapidly during these years.

Figure 15.1 Bottom Up or Top Down? Children are more likely to draw conclusions on the basis of their own experiences and what they have been told, as you might expect from concrete operational thinkers. This is called inductive, or bottom-up, reasoning. Adolescents can think deductively, from the top down. One way to remember this distinction is that *in*ductive reasoning begins inside the problem; *de*ductive reasoning begins *de*tached from it. Since adolescents focus on the possible and the hypothetical, they are much more able to detach from reality.

(Moshman, 1998). That is, they can begin with a general premise or theory, reason through one or more logical steps to draw a specific conclusion, and then test the validity of that conclusion. Deduction is reasoning from the general to the specific: "If it's a duck, it will walk and quack like a duck" (see Figure 15.1). Its development is discussed in more detail in the Research Report.

Piaget's Balance Experiment

Piaget devised a number of famous tasks involving scientific principles to study the reasoning of children of various ages. In one experiment, shown in Figure 15.3, children were asked to balance a scale with weights that could be hooked onto the scale's arms (Piaget & Inhelder, 1958). Mastering this problem requires realizing that the heaviness of the weights and their distance from the center interact to affect balance. This understanding is completely beyond the ability of 3- to 5-year-olds, who, in Piaget's research, randomly hung different weights on different hooks.

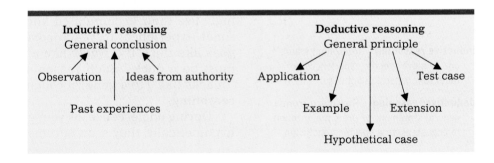

DEDUCTIVE REASONING: ARE DOLPHINS FISH?

To see the developmental progression from inductive to deductive reasoning more clearly, let's look at how children of various ages might try to figure out what class of animals dolphins belong to. Preschoolers are quick to believe that dolphins are fish—because dolphins, like fish, live in the water. Moreover, a preschooler might become angry at any suggestion that these obviously fishlike creatures are *not* fish. They center on appearance and stubbornly stick to their conclusion.

School-age children might have heard their teachers say that dolphins are mammals and might have noticed that dolphins breathe air. Accordingly, with those two bits of evidence, they might induce from the two facts they know (that teachers have knowledge and that dolphins breathe air) that dolphins are indeed mammals rather than fish. With the arrogance typical of an absolutist thinker (that is, a thinker who sees things as yes or no, true or false), the schoolchild might lord it over any younger child so foolish as to disagree.

In contrast, adolescents are likely to consider many alternative hypotheses, recognizing that until the evidence is in, things are "maybe," not yes or no, "possible," not true or false. Thus dolphins could be some form of fish, or mammal, or reptile, or even a bizarre type of bird (a distant relative of the penguin?). Acting logically on a teacher's statement that dolphins are mammals, adolescents might search for the general principle that distinguishes mammals from other biological classes—perhaps looking in a dictionary or an encyclopedia. Not only would they question whatever their teacher said; they would actually hope they could prove their teacher wrong. They would find that the root word for mammal is *mamma* (Latin for "breast") and that the definition is that mammals suckle their young.

That would lead our adolescents to reason that "if dolphins are mammals, then they nurse their young." And so they would seek evidence that mother dolphins do, or do not, suckle their pups, and they would ignore irrelevant data (such as that dolphins swim like fish or breathe air or have lateral fins that look like vestigial wings). Their deductive reasoning would have proceeded from the general principle (which may or may not agree with received wisdom or with everyday observation) to the specific application, rather than vice versa.

Illustrating this switch are the results of an experiment that tested belief in freedom of religion (Helwig, 1995). When asked, a group of seventh-graders, eleventh-graders, and college students in northern California all endorsed the principle (in the U.S. Constitution's Bill of Rights) of "free exercise of religion." Then this easy endorsement was put to the test, with questions such as "What if a particular religion refused to allow low-income people to become priests?" Almost all (94 percent) of the seventh-graders abandoned freedom of religion under those circumstances, but few (19 percent) of the eleventh-graders switched their thinking. They stood their ground—as one might expect for inductive thinkers.

If you are wondering if such firm adherence to principle is always a good thing, you will be interested to know that some psychologists contend that adults can reach a less absolutist stage *after* Piaget's formal operational stage. This fifth stage might be attained in college and is described in Chapter 18. In the study just mentioned, the college students were more aware than the high school students of the conflict between two general principles: religious freedom and economic justice. Consequently, 38 percent thought equal opportunity was more important, and 62 percent stuck to freedom of religion as the overriding idea (see Figure 15.2).

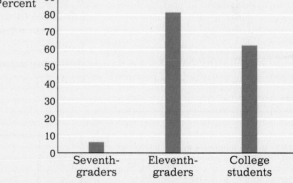

School-age Children and Adolescents Who Endorse Freedom of Religion—No Matter What

Source: Helwig, 1995.

Figure 15.2 Adherence to Principle. High school students are more capable of inductive reasoning than are middle schoolers, as shown by the fact that a much higher percentage of eleventh-graders were able to perceive religious freedom as a basic principle and to cling to it no matter what conflicting circumstances were proposed by the researcher. (College students were more aware that one of those conflicting circumstances might in itself represent a basic principle, so they were more likely than the eleventh-graders to temper their adherence to religious freedom.)

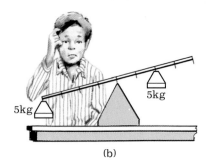

(a)

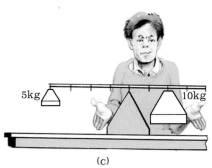

(b)

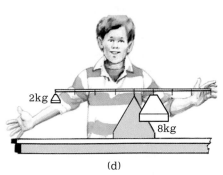

(c)

2kg   8kg

(d)

Figure 15.3 How to Balance a Beam. Piaget's balance-scale test of formal reasoning, as it is attempted by (a) a 4-year-old, (b) a 7-year-old, (c) a 10-year-old, and (d) a 14-year-old. The key to balancing the scale is to make weight times distance from the center equal on both sides of the center; the realization of that principle requires formal operational thought.

It's All About Me Personal perceptions cloud judgment at every age. However, egocentrism is particularly apparent in adolescence, when the discovery of self is not yet balanced by a deeper understanding of the breadth of human experience.

Piaget found that by age 7 children realized that the scale could be balanced by putting the same amount of weight on both arms, but they didn't realize that the distance of the weights from the center of the scale is also important. By age 10, near the end of the concrete operational stage, children often realized the importance of the weights' locations on the arms, but their efforts to coordinate weight and distance from the center to balance the scale involved trial-and-error experimentation, not logical deduction.

Finally, by about age 13 or 14, some children hypothesized that there is a direct relationship between a weight's distance from the center of the scale and the effect it has on a balance. By systematically testing this hypothesis, they correctly formulated the mathematical relation between weight and distance from the center and could solve the balance problem accurately and efficiently. Piaget attributed each of these advances to the intellectual growth from one cognitive stage to the next-higher one.

Hypothetical thought and deductive reasoning should make the adolescent a more flexible, resourceful thinker. And, in fact, they do—for some adolescents, some of the time. However, some adolescents—and adults—do quite poorly on standard tests of deductive reasoning skills, such as the balance-scale task. The cognitive gains of formal operational thought are not always accomplished during adolescence, nor are they necessarily acquired by all people.

Moreover, a teenager who can easily use deductive reasoning to figure out a mathematics problem may have great difficulty in deducing the solution to a problem in biology, or in assessing the ethics of various approaches to national health insurance, or in determining the most effective way to deal with a complex human dilemma. In other words, adolescents appear to apply formal logic to some situations but not to others. It seems that each individual's intellect, experiences, talents, and interests affect his or her thinking at least as much as the ability to reason formally.

Past education and historical conditions also have an effect. Research assessing 10- to 15-year-old students on Piaget's tests of formal operational thought has traditionally reported substantial variation. One careful assessment of 13- to 15-year-olds in France found

● *Answer to Observational Quiz (from page 410):* Both photos show partners who must collaborate in order to produce the desired outcome. How to work with another adolescent is the most urgent curriculum of all during the secondary school years, requiring speculation, strategy, and study of each individual case—particularly evident as the boy tries to understand why the girl is smiling as she moves her queen.

about one-third at the concrete level, one-third at an intermediate level, and one-third at a formal level. The same tests were repeated on a similar group of French students more than 10 years later. Contextual changes had had an impact. Scores had risen, with variation from test to test, such that more than half were at the formal level. However, about a sixth were still at concrete operational thought (Flieller, 1999).

Thinking About Oneself

Adolescents frequently practice their new thinking skills on themselves, a process that makes even those who reach formal thinking lose some of their new detachment. They worry about how they are regarded by others; they try to sort out their own conflicting feelings about parents, school, and close friends; they think deeply but not always realistically about their future possibilities; they reflect, at length, on each day's experiences. Analyzing their private thoughts and feelings, forecasting their future, and reflecting on their experiences underlie the greater reflection and self-awareness—and enhanced capacity for self-centeredness—that distinguish adolescence. (See the In Person box.)

All these new ventures in introspection are an essential part of the adolescent's expanding self-awareness. However, they are often distorted by **adolescent egocentrism** (remember, from Chapter 9, that "egocentric" means "self at the center"), a self-view in which adolescents regard themselves as much more socially significant than they actually are (Elkind, 1967, 1984). Younger adolescents tend to hypothesize about what others might be thinking (especially about them) and then egocentrically take their hypotheses to be fact—a kind of deductive reasoning that can lead to very false conclusions.

adolescent egocentrism A characteristic of adolescent thinking that sometimes leads young people to focus on themselves to the exclusion of others, believing, for example, that their thoughts, feelings, or experiences are unique.

Boys Do It, Too Although it is generally girls who are considered to be overly aware of minor flaws in their complexion or attire, the truth is that adolescent boys also pay exaggerated attention to their appearance. The cognitive capacity to think about oneself in egocentric terms makes many young people of both sexes spend hours combing their hair, adjusting their clothing, and searching for blemishes.

invincibility fable The fiction, fostered by adolescent egocentrism, that one is immune to common dangers, such as those associated with unprotected sex, drug abuse, or high-speed driving.

personal fable The egocentric idea, held by many adolescents, that one is destined for fame and fortune and/or great accomplishments.

Several false assumptions that characterize adolescent egocentrism have special names. One is the **invincibility fable**, by which young people feel that they will never fall victim, as others do, to dangerous behavior. Adults find evidence of the invincibility fable in, among other things, teenagers' high rates of smoking (despite awareness of the health risks of tobacco), unsafe sexual behavior (despite risks of pregnancy and of sexually transmitted diseases), and dangerous driving (despite mandated driver education). Invincibility leads to a foolish sense of security, and sometimes to disastrous risks.

Another false conclusion resulting from adolescent egocentrism is the **personal fable**, through which adolescents imagine their own lives as unique, heroic, or even mythical. They perceive themselves as different from others, distinguished by unusual experiences, perspectives, and values. Sometimes adolescents see themselves as destined for

IN PERSON

BETHANY AND JIM

Whether they are trying to understand the external world or themselves, adolescents are capable of a type of thinking vastly different from that of elementary school children. However, this new thinking is unpredictable: Teenagers' mastery of hypothetical thought and deductive reasoning is not always apparent, and their introspections can cause them to leap in the wrong direction.

This unevenness was well demonstrated by my eldest daughter, Bethany, whose newfound perspectives on art and history made her absolutely certain that she wanted to visit the Metropolitan Museum of Art. It was a humid midsummer afternoon, and all her friends were out of town, so she prevailed on me to go with her. I was ready in 5 minutes but, because she was in her midteens, it took her much longer.

In fact, we left the house so late that I was concerned the museum would close soon after we got there. Hence, I was relieved that our subway train arrived quickly and moved us rapidly to our stop. But when we climbed up to street level from the station, we saw a sudden downpour. Bethany became angry—at *me!*

She: You didn't bring an umbrella? You should have known.
Me: It's okay—we'll walk quickly. It's a warm rain.
She: But we'll get all wet.
Me: It's okay. We'll dry.
She: But people will see us with our hair all wet.
Me: Honey, no one cares what we look like. And we won't see anyone we know.
She: That's okay for you to say. You're already married.

I was mystified. "Do you think you are going to meet your future husband here?"

"No," she said, with an exasperated scowl that suggested I understood nothing. "People will look at me and think, 'She'll never find a husband looking like that!' "

Bethany's quickness to criticize me, and her egocentric concern with an imaginary audience who might judge her future possibilities, is echoed in almost every other teenager. Another example is reported by a father, himself a therapist:

The best way I can describe what happens [during adolescence] is to relate how I first noticed the change in my son. He was about 13 years of age. One afternoon he and I were riding in a car on a four-lane highway which circles Boston, Massachusetts. I was driving 65 miles an hour in a 55 mile zone.

He suddenly turned toward me and shouted, "Dad!"

I was startled and responded by saying, "What is it, Jim!"

Then there was this pause as he folded his arms and turned slowly in my direction and said, "Dad, do you realize how fast you are driving this car?"

I was obviously embarrassed because after all, I did not want my son to notice that on occasion I break the law! I was able to put this over on him up to this age in his life. But more than that, I was taken back by the new tone in his voice! I had not heard that before. It was a command, not a question!

Anyway, he was asking the question so I simply turned and said, "Oh, I'm doing 65 miles per hour!" (as if I didn't know it).

He then came right back at me and said, *"Dad!* Do you know what the speed limit is on this highway?"

Now my ego was hurt and I wanted to attack! This little voice in the back of my head was saying, "Here comes early adolescent behavior, wipe it out now!"

honor and glory, perhaps by discovering a cure for cancer, authoring a masterpiece, or influencing the social order. As one high school student expressed it, her goal is to

affect . . . as many people as possible. . . . I see myself in a big way saying big things. I see myself going to school for a long time and learning a lot. I want to write a book that is very, very solid and hard, to say "No, you are wrong." So that I can give it to the President and say, Look, Mr. President, you are wrong and you are going to hurt all these people and you are going to hurt yourself. I want to say something big. I want to change the world. [Gilligan et al., 1990]

Well, he was right, so I kept cool and responded by saying, "Yes, Jim, it's 55 miles an hour."

He then said, "*Dad!* Do you realize that you are traveling 10 miles over the speed limit!" I handled this one with calm because it at least indicated that he could add and subtract!

He continued, "*Dad!* Don't you care about my life at all! Do you have any idea of how many thousands of people lose their lives every year on our nation's highways who exceed the speed limit!"

Now I was beginning to get angry and I responded by saying, "Look, Jim, I have no idea how many people are killed every year, you were right I shouldn't have been speeding; I promise I won't ever do it again, so let us just forget it!"

Not being satisfied, he continued, "*Dad!* Any idea what would happen if the front wheel of this car came off doing 65 miles per hour, how many lives you might jeopardize!"

He kept on with this for another 10 minutes until I finally got him quiet for about 20 seconds! Then he came back at me and said, "Dad! I've been thinking about this."

Once he said that, I knew I was in deep trouble! You see, my son was so easy to deal with before he started *to think!* Who told him he had a right to start *thinking!* Before this all happened he would ask, *why,* and I would simply give him the answer and it was good enough! [Garvin, 1994]

Note that both Bethany and Jim were focused on future possibilities, just as one might expect. And both followed an idea, albeit an egocentric one, to a logical conclusion. But don't let these examples leave the wrong impression. Teenagers are not always egocentric and illogical, by any means. At age 17, Bethany wrote about her art:

Just as the mind, on seeing letters, must grab them and process them as words, so I must grab whatever materials are about and process my notions into images . . . struggling to draw certain lines intensifies their loveliness for me, creates a fascination with, say, the line of a dancer's body, a cat's back, a blowing blade of grass. . . . It has always been my sketchbook I grab when I feel too outraged and helpless to do anything but scream. Now I am trying to form a connection with the external world by drawing it. I am experimenting with difficult media, . . . sketching more varied objects and scenes.

Here, Bethany is clearly self-aware and analytic, thinking about the underlying import of her artistic interest and using it to expand her "connection with the external world," far beyond the limits of egocentrism.

In trying to arrive at a balanced view of teenagers' thinking, in which moments of adult insight are juxtaposed with childish reasoning, we cannot expect too much or too little. I would agree that

from early adolescence on, thinking tends to involve abstract rather than merely concrete representation; to become multidimensional rather than limited to a single issue; to become relative rather than absolute in the conception of knowledge; and to become self-reflective and self-aware. . . . [But] it is probably safest to assume that these shifts represent potential accomplishments for most adolescents rather than typical everyday thinking. [Keating, 1990]

imaginary audience The egocentric idea, held by many adolescents, that others are intensely interested in them, especially in their appearance and behavior.

A third false conclusion stemming from egocentrism is called the **imaginary audience.** This arises from many adolescents' assumption that other people are as intently interested in them as they themselves are. As a result, they tend to fantasize about how others react to their appearance and behavior. At times, the imaginary audience can cause teenagers to enter a crowded room as if they believe themselves to be the most attractive human beings alive. More often, though, they cringe from any attention, because they view something as trivial as a slight facial blemish or a spot on a shirt as an unbearable embarrassment that everyone will notice and judge.

The Thrill of the Fast Life These boys ride on top of high-speed trains and risk falling or hitting live electrical wires. Some die every year.

❷ Observational Quiz (see answer page 418): *What culture do you think these boys are from?*

person–environment fit   The degree to which a particular environment is conducive to the growth of a particular individual.

The acute self-consciousness resulting from the imaginary audience reveals that young people are not relaxed with the broader social world. This is one reason many seem obsessed with their hair, clothing, and so on, before going out in public. It also explains their need to fit in with their peer group, who presumably judge every visible nuance of their appearance and behavior. No wonder, then, that one adolescent explained,

I would like to be able to fly if everyone else did; otherwise it would be rather conspicuous. [quoted in Steinberg, 1993]

Overall, adolescent egocentrism suggests that intense reflection about thoughts, feelings, and motives is a mixed blessing. It enables adolescents to consider their lives more thoughtfully but often at the cost of great self-criticism.

SCHOOLS, LEARNING, AND THE ADOLESCENT MIND

Given the cognitive changes that adolescents typically experience, what kind of school would best foster their intellectual growth? That straightforward question has no single answer. The problem is that the optimum **person–environment fit**—that is, the best setting for an individual's personal growth—depends not only on the individual's developmental stage, cognitive strengths, and learning style but also on the society's traditions, educational objectives, and future needs. These vary substantially from person to person, place to place, and time to time.

The Adolescent Mind in the School Setting

As their ability to think hypothetically and abstractly starts to emerge, adolescents begin to abandon simplistic, concrete thinking and to construct more imaginative, comprehensive, and complex worldviews, as you have just seen. Consequently, they become increasingly interested in the opinions and judgments of others—adults as well as peers—from a variety of backgrounds. At the same time, they are ready, even eager, to question every idea, sometimes with an egocentrism that is stunning. As one high school student of mine said of the theory of relativity, "That's just Einstein's opinion. I have my own opinion, and I don't agree with him."

Teenagers' self-consciousness makes them highly sensitive to actual or anticipated criticism. This combination of openness and sensitivity puts them in an emotional bind: They are eager for lively intellectual interaction but highly vulnerable to self-doubt. The brash young man who is ready to challenge the ideas of any dead thinker may also avoid coming to class after the teacher has made a wisecrack at his expense.

Similarly, how much students study, and how much they learn, is clearly affected by their attitudes about school. In general, if they think they are being judged on their performance, when they realize they cannot always shine they may stop studying, claiming, "I didn't try" rather than risk being judged as stupid (Dweck, 1999). In a study of high school students of varied ability in eight communities, those who initially thought achievement depended on others or on fate, rather than on their own efforts, tended to have disengaged from class after a year (no longer doing the homework, asking questions, and so on)—a progression from attitude to action that occurred no matter what their true potential was (Glasgow et al., 1997).

Knowing these teenage tendencies, we might expect high schools to encourage supportive interaction among students and, especially, between teachers and students. Ideally, in offering support, teachers would find ways to build up each student's self-confidence. Too often, however, the opposite is the case. Instead of an appropriate person–environment fit, a **volatile mismatch** forms between many adolescents and their schools (Carnegie Council, 1989). Compared to elementary schools, most secondary schools have more rigid behavioral demands, intensified competition, and more punitive grading practices, as well as less individualized attention and procedures.

Secondary school teachers tend to consider themselves less effective (and their students tend to see them as less friendly, less caring, and less helpful) than teachers in elementary schools. And they are right: Achievement typically drops when a student enters middle school (Eccles et al., 1996). Middle school, especially for the first year or two, is also likely to be a dangerous place, with higher rates of student injuries (Miller & Spicer, 1998). (See Figure 15.4.)

By the end of the high school years, injuries decrease and achievement rises again. Among other reasons, the lowest achievers have dropped out, the students have become intellectually more mature, and the person–environment fit improves when the older students can choose their courses, lead various clubs, and so on.

Culture and Schools

Proper person–environment fit requires a good understanding not only of the developmental stage of the person but also of the requirements of the culture. The fact that educational goals (and therefore educational

volatile mismatch The potentially explosive situation that arises when teenagers' individual needs—intellectual, emotional, social—do not match the size, routine, and structure of their schools.

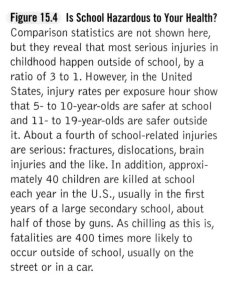

Figure 15.4 Is School Hazardous to Your Health? Comparison statistics are not shown here, but they reveal that most serious injuries in childhood happen outside of school, by a ratio of 3 to 1. However, in the United States, injury rates per exposure hour show that 5- to 10-year-olds are safer at school and 11- to 19-year-olds are safer outside it. About a fourth of school-related injuries are serious: fractures, dislocations, brain injuries and the like. In addition, approximately 40 children are killed at school each year in the U.S., usually in the first years of a large secondary school, about half of those by guns. As chilling as this is, fatalities are 400 times more likely to occur outside of school, usually on the street or in a car.

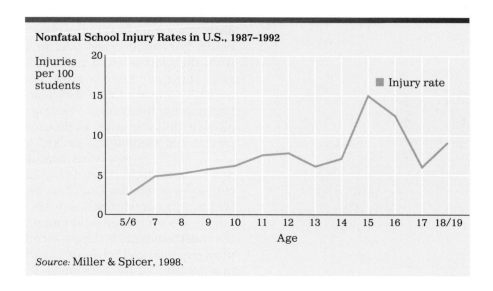

Nonfatal School Injury Rates in U.S., 1987–1992

Injuries per 100 students

■ Injury rate

Age: 5/6 7 8 9 10 11 12 13 14 15 16 17 18/19

Source: Miller & Spicer, 1998.

② Especially for Teachers: How would you use your knowledge of the adolescent mind to teach, say, a foreign language?

❶ Answer to Observational Quiz (from page 416): *Risk taking during adolescence is common in every culture, and it has been a sign of status and independence in every nation and every century, as stories of brave knights fighting fire-breathing dragons attest. It is very difficult to deduce from the countryside, the technology, or these teenagers' appearance where they are. The answer is Brazil, where such boys are so common they have a name:* surfistas.

content) differ by culture was convincingly expressed by Native Americans in colonial America in the year 1744. Members of the Council of Five Nations politely declined the offer of scholarships for their young men to William and Mary College, with the following statement:

> You who are wise must know, that different nations have different conceptions of things; and you will therefore not take it amiss if our ideas of this kind of education happen not to be the same with yours. We have had some experience of it; several of our young people were formerly brought up at the college of the northern provinces; they were instructed in all your sciences; but when they came back to us . . . [they were] ignorant of every means of living in the woods . . . neither fit for hunters, warriors, or counselors; they were totally good for nothing. We are, however, not the less obliged by your kind offer . . . and to show our grateful sense of it, if the gentlemen of Virginia will send us a dozen of their sons, we will take great care of their education, instruct them in all we know, and make men of them. [Drake, cited in Rogoff, 1990]

The goals of education in the United States have changed dramatically over the centuries, although "every means of living in the woods" is not yet part of the typical curriculum. Cohort differences in goals are apparent. At the beginning of the twentieth century, young men needed "vocational training for the sort of employment that likely awaited them" on the assembly line, on the farm, or in the retail store (West, 1996). As the twenty-first century begins, women, as well as men, require computer literacy, scientific understanding, and critical thinking skills.

Further, ethnic diversity and geographic differences in learning goals are widespread and deep. Communities, schools within communities, and even teachers within schools diverge and conflict, as evidenced by the criticism of public schools by those educated in private or parochial schools, and vice versa, and by the always divisive debates on public school funding. "Disagreements over the goals and strategies of education are virtually guaranteed" (West, 1996), perhaps especially in the United States but certainly in other nations as well. One example is the high school completion rate, which ranges from 100 percent in Norway and Belgium to 26 percent in Mexico (see Figure 15.5). National priorities are reflected in such national differences.

Competition and Individual Learning

One debate concerns the extent to which academic grades should be based on individual test performance, with students ranked against each other from best in the class to worst. This competitive style of education has some drawbacks in elementary school (as you remember from the discussion of norm-referenced testing in Chapter 12), but it gets worse as children grow older and become more self-conscious—painfully aware of how they compare to their peers and almost never happy with themselves. Failing students experience embarrassment along with low grades, while exceptionally good students risk being ostracized as "brainiacs," "geeks," or "nerds."

In overly competitive conditions, many students—especially girls and students from minority backgrounds—find it easier, and psychologically safer, not to try. They thus avoid the pain of either success or failure. Within schools, students are tracked; between schools, college acceptances are compared; and among schools and colleges. Competition for the "best" students is fierce—academic and sports scholarships go to the most capable, and the least capable drop out or settle for the form of education without the substance. For example, many students are passed

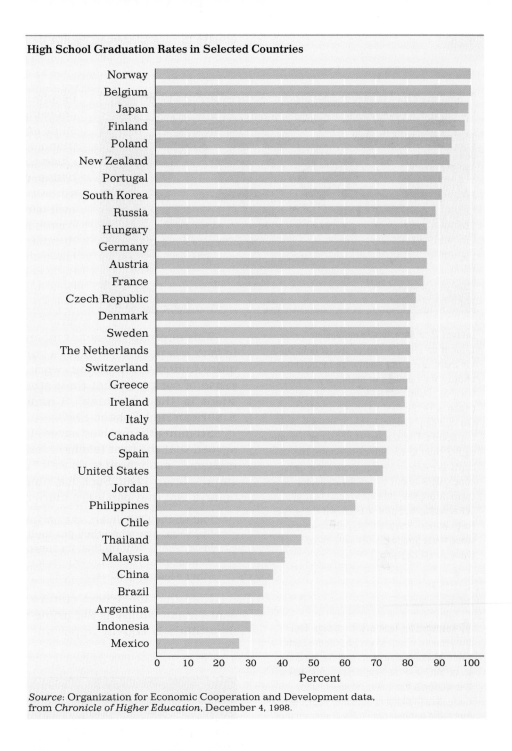

High School Graduation Rates in Selected Countries

Figure 15.5 Educational Priorities. Many other countries now attach more importance to education than the United States does. Whereas the United States once led the world in high school completion, it now lags behind 23 other industrialized nations.

Source: Organization for Economic Cooperation and Development data, from *Chronicle of Higher Education*, December 4, 1998.

along because of *social promotion,* the practice of promoting and even graduating a student who has not accomplished the basic achievements expected of students.

Standards and Group Learning

One possible antidote to the stress of individual competition is to encourage team research projects, in-class discussion groups, and after-school study groups—all of which allow students to succeed if they cooperate. Because accomplishing the learning task requires that students assist rather than surpass their peers, the social interaction that teenagers cherish is actually used constructively to enhance education.

Adolescents can become excited about learning when conditions foster enthusiasm. An example comes from science fairs, for which "students

419

Lessons Their Ancestors Never Studied
Education today prepares students to think for themselves, not memorize facts. This photo shows a class in prehistory, in contrast to traditional history classes, which began with the first written texts. Note also the "hidden" curriculum—in the way learning occurs. The teacher is acting as a guide rather than as an authority figure. The students are encouraged to draw their own conclusions about the evidence before them. Moreover, this interracial school is in Johannesburg, South Africa. All these features impart lessons that, presumably, will serve these young people well in the twenty-first century.

❗ **Response for Teachers (from page 418):**
Immersion, which works well in the early years, might not work so well during adolescence, since self-criticism might make the students too quiet. However, since deductive thinking is possible, you could teach the general principles of grammar or pronunciation, for instance, much better at this time than during younger years. In any case, you would want to provide high standards and lots of encouragement, as well as many opportunities for the students to help each other.

Does This Look Like Your High School?
Probably not, if your diploma is from before 1980.
❓ *Observational Quiz (see answer page 422):*
Which four features of this classroom are relatively new, and which four features have been characteristic for decades?

become deeply involved in a project of their choosing, conducting research, analyzing results, and presenting findings in a professional manner" (Dreyer, 1994). Other examples include the school play; the school band; the debating, chess, and math teams; and the various athletic teams. All these require—and get— avid participation, extensive practice of various cognitive skills, and an intensity that contrasts dramatically with the apathy apparent in some classrooms. In all these examples, the goal is to be excellent at the task, not necessarily better than one's classmates, and that goal is reached at least in part through the advancement of abstract, analytic, formal thinking.

This approach does not mean lower standards—quite the opposite, in fact. It is possible to offer "a curriculum of substance, courses that require students to do serious work . . . [and] teachers who are conveying a sense of caring so that their students feel that their teachers share a stake in their learning" (Commission on the Restructuring of the American High School, 1996).

Students themselves agree. One study of 300 tenth-grade students agreed that the best teachers "take pupils seriously," "have confidence in them," "push them to do well," and "make it easier for them to understand" (Tatar, 1998). Such learning enhances self-esteem. Students who believe that they can learn more if they put forth effort

> told us they felt smart, not only when they were striving to master new tasks, but also when they put their knowledge to work to help their peers learn. Thus within this framework, rather than being rivals for self-esteem, peers can gain self-esteem by cooperating and by facilitating each other's learning. [Dweck, 1999]

Note that the school culture and climate, rather than the adolescent's innate ability, is the prime ingredient for success. Often, the family attitude is equally important. A study of talented teenagers found

that predicting which ones would be successful depended on discovering who was willing and able to devote themselves to the *work*, not to the competition. Only when families and schools made this possible, and when peers did not become distractions, did the talented teenagers succeed (Csikszentmihalyi et al., 1993).

Similarly, a study of Latino 15-year-olds at risk for dropping out found that school practices and family involvement were more significant than the adolescents' innate ability. Although all the schools and parents said they wanted the youths to graduate, many schools used tracking and testing that made learning difficult. Many parents were unaware of the specific impact of class placement on their children (Romo & Falbo, 1996).

Unsafe at School An agony of grief and fear is apparent in these girls' faces as they leave Columbine High School in Littleton, Colorado, on the day of the worst school shooting in American history. According to writings and tapes the gunmen left behind, the massacre was an extreme reaction to their feelings of being ostracized by the school's "jocks." The culture of a school can foster powerful feelings of rejection that some students may be unable to deal with appropriately.

Cultural Diversity and the School Climate

Cooperative learning in secondary school often gives students their first extended exposure to people of differing backgrounds—economic, ethnic, religious, or racial—and thus to ideas, assumptions, and viewpoints that contrast with their own. In a cooperative setting, these differences can expand learning opportunities, bringing new perspectives that are both exciting and enriching.

In a competitive setting, however, these differences can lead to rivalry, social separation, and open hostility. Under such conditions, "others' misfortunes feed students' self-esteem," creating

a system of winners and losers, where there are a few winners at the top and a large number of losers under them. Many groups of adolescents have, understandably, rebelled against this by creating their own rule system in which working hard and getting good grades meet with strong disapproval. Through peer pressure, they seek to eliminate the winners. Then those who would have been the losers no longer stand apart. [Dweck, 1999]

One cause of the recent rash of shootings by middle and high school adolescents, at Columbine High School in Littleton, Colorado, and elsewhere, is the social climate of the school. If the administration as well as the student body foster anger and shame among the school's "losers," tragedy may ultimately result. As one social scientist comments,

Some apparently sensible interventions could produce negative or even disastrous consequences, depending on what is actually going on in the school. . . . A few days after the Columbine tragedy, my 16-year-old grandson came home from high school and said, "Guess what? The principal sent around a notice asking us to report any kids who are dressing strangely, behaving weirdly, appear to be loners, or out of it."

. . . The principal is shining his spotlight on the wrong part of the equation. Here's why: From my classroom research, I have found that the social atmosphere in most schools is competitive, cliquish, and exclusionary. The majority of teenagers I have interviewed agonize over the fact that there is a general atmosphere of taunting and rejection among their peers that makes the high school experience an unpleasant one. For many, it is worse than unpleasant—they describe it as a living hell, where they are in the out-group and feel insecure, unpopular, put-down, and picked on. By asking the "normal" students to point out the "strange" ones, my grandson's high school principal is unwittingly making a bad situation worse by implicitly sanctioning the rejection and exclusion of a sizable group of students whose only sin is unpopularity. [Aronson, 2000]

The demographics of the future tell us that migration from one nation to another will continue to accelerate and that the United States

Figure 15.6 Changing Proportions. As the numbers of minority youths rise, the proportions of the population shift, with more Latino and Asian youths than a generation ago. Projections suggest that these trends will continue, so future professionals who work with teenagers will find almost as many "minority" as majority teens. By the year 2040, the "majority" may be one of the minorities.

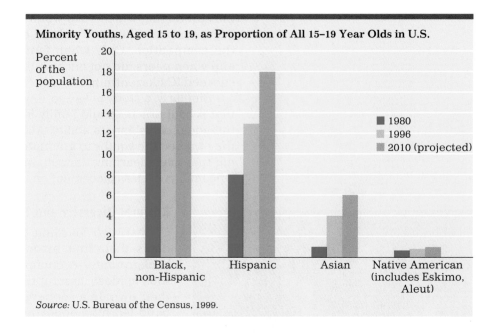

Minority Youths, Aged 15 to 19, as Proportion of All 15–19 Year Olds in U.S.

Source: U.S. Bureau of the Census, 1999.

❶ *Answer to Observational Quiz (from page 420): The most important innovation is cooperative learning. Once, individual desks were in rows, and passing a note to a classmate was a serious offense. Now, shared problem solving is considered the best way to engage adolescent minds. Other innovations include the high-speed calculators, the teacher's computer, and—at least to some extent—the multiethnic, multi-immigrant students. As for what remains the same, the list could be very long, including a tendency toward sex segregation, the old-fashioned blackboard, the old classroom itself, and the poster that makes Africa seem like one nation, similar to Mexico or Japan.*

(and many other nations) will become increasingly multiethnic (see Figure 15.6). Young people will benefit from a better understanding of other groups and from measuring themselves against standards, rather than against their peers. Virtually all developmentalists agree with this ideal, although there is still debate about when and to what extent our evolutionary history predisposes the species to competition or cooperation (Kagen, 1998).

ADOLESCENT DECISION MAKING

An understanding of adolescent thinking—formal, hypothetical, and egocentric—is important for a very practical reason (Hamburg, 1991). For the first time in their lives, teenagers are in a position to make personal decisions and independent choices that have far-reaching consequences for their future. They can decide, for example, what and how diligently to study, whether and where to go to college, whom to befriend, what career to pursue, whether to become sexually active, whether to use drugs, and whether to take a part-time job (see the Changing Policy box).

Because they think about possibilities, not practicalities, and because egocentricism makes it hard to plan ahead and then choose the current path that will make the plans a reality, few adolescents actually decide such matters in a rational, explore-all-the-options manner.

Specifically, college enrollment usually follows a pattern set years before. Teenagers in the academic track at high school usually attend the best colleges they can get into and pay for, and those in the basic courses rarely stay in school long enough, or learn well enough, for further education. Family background, not individual potential, is the main determinant.

Similarly, selecting a vocation on the basis of one's interests, talents, and values is much less common than taking whatever job is available, seeking the best pay scale and work requirements. (Deliberate career

SCHOOL AND PART-TIME EMPLOYMENT

Attitudes and practices regarding jobs and school vary a great deal from country to country (Hamilton & Wolfgang, 1996):

- In some nations, such as Japan, almost no adolescent is employed or even does significant chores at home, because the family and culture agree that the adolescent's main work is to study.

- In other nations, including several in Europe, many older adolescents have jobs that are an integral part of their school curriculum. Germany is a prime example.

- In still other nations, including the United States, such school-to-work partnerships are relatively rare, although when implementation includes changing the school schedule and curriculum, participants are more likely to graduate and continue their education (Stern, 1997).

Almost all North American adolescents gain nonacademic experience in the job market—after school, on weekends, or during the summer—earning not only substantial spending money but also status in the eyes of their peers and respect from their parents (Mortimer et al., 1994). Indeed, parents strongly approve of youth employment, citing increased responsibility, better money management, raised confidence, and work-related skills as benefits.

However, in today's job market meaningful jobs are rare. Most research finds that, especially when adolescents are employed more than 15 hours a week, having a job means less time for study, lower grades, and a negative attitude: Adolescents conclude that work is routinely dull and that working hard is "a little bit crazy" (Greenberger & Steinberg, 1986). Moreover, the money earned usually goes to clothes, entertainment, cars, alcohol, and drugs—not to basic household necessities or savings accounts (Bachman & Schulenberg, 1993; Mortimer et al., 1996; Steinberg & Dornbusch, 1991).

Solid data come from long-term research in the United States comparing teenagers who work long hours and those who do not. Even from one year to the next, having a job pulls down the grade-point average (Steinberg, 1993). Adults who were employed extensively as teenagers are more likely to use drugs and less likely to feel connected to their families. There is one possible benefit: If someone had a stable work history (such as the same job and schedule for months or years) during adolescence, he or she is more likely to have a stable work history in adulthood (Mihalic & Elliott, 1997). In general, however, adolescents work for the wrong reasons, sometimes unwittingly encouraged by parents and teachers (Steinberg, 1996).

Provocative international data from European nations show a negative correlation between hours of employment after school and learning in school (Kelly, 1998). Such correlations do not prove causation, but it is curious that U.S. fourth-graders, who obviously do not have jobs, score much closer to their European peers on standardized tests than U.S. twelfth-graders do.

Any such comparison evokes dozens of questions, caveats, and complications. For example, the five top-scoring nations on the Third International Mathematics and Science Study (TIMSS) are all small European nations where generous federal funding of education and health, not less adolescent part-time employment, may be the real cause of academic achievement. Teenagers in the United States spend less time on homework, more time with friends, and less time in school activities as well as more time at work; any of these factors may affect achievement. It is also the case that students who work longer hours often had below-average grades before they took their jobs. Nevertheless, it is no longer safe to say, as the U.S. National Commission on Youth did in 1980, that part-time jobs foster responsibility, good work habits, and academic motivation in high school students (Kelly, 1998).

Laughing on the Job These high school students are working in an automobile factory.

❷ *Observational Quiz (see answer page 424):* *Where is the likely location?*

Which College, Where? As a 17-year-old basketball star, high school senior Niesha Butler had a critical decision to make—which of hundreds of colleges to choose. Her top list included Harvard, Virginia, Notre Dame, and Georgia Tech—although she also thought of skipping college and turning pro because "if the money is there, why not?" That was a possibility her parents—who had banned television from their home years before—would not let her consider. She chose Georgia Tech, where she has a full scholarship and receives living expenses.

❶ *Answer to Observational Quiz (from page 423):* The main clue is that Germany is one of the few nations that has an apprenticeship program that includes manufacturing, in this case, a BMW plant. In some nations (such as Japan), few high school students work, and in others (such as the United States), they work in fast-food or other service-oriented jobs.

decisions may come in adulthood, as Chapter 19 explains.) Employment is usually found through friends or family—not through a methodical search of career possibilities. Finally, 18- to 21-year-olds have a notoriously poor voting record, another fact suggesting that independent commitments and choices are rarely made in adolescence.

Thus, until adulthood, most people do not make major decisions on their own. They are more likely to be moved along by parents, teachers, cultural values, or stuck by inertia. However, when it comes to matters of personal lifestyle, decisions *are* made, though not always what adolescents' elders would wish. This is most clearly shown when the decisions involve sex.

Choosing Risky Sex

Sexual interest during adolescence is a normal (even essential) part of development. How that interest is expressed depends on a host of factors, including biology and culture, family and friends. In fact, we could easily have discussed this topic in Chapter 14, on biosocial development, or in Chapter 16, on psychosocial development. But sexual arousal and activity are not just a biosocial reaction to hormones or a psychosocial reaction to peer pressure. They are also a reaction to mental processes (which is why one wag has said that "the most important sexual organ is between the ears"). Study after study confirm that beliefs, values, and reasoning processes affect what kind of sexual activity adolescents engage in, when they do so, and with whom. For this reason, our major discussion of adolescent sexuality is here, in the chapter on cognitive development.

The benefits of sexual activity are obvious. Pleasure, intimacy, and sexual release are among the most compelling drives of the human species. However, the risks are not so obvious. There are two apparent risks with sexual behavior—disease and unwanted pregnancy—that teenagers seem less aware of than adults, and a third—intense commitment—that is a hidden problem.

Sexually Transmitted Diseases

Sexually active teenagers have higher rates of gonorrhea, genital herpes, syphilis, and chlamydia—the most common **sexually transmitted diseases (STDs)**—than any other age group. This is true worldwide, although the absolute rates of STDs are actually higher among 20- to 24-year-olds because many teenagers are not sexually active and thus are less likely to contract an STD (Panchaud et al., 2000). Few cases of STDs are serious if promptly treated, but untreated STDs can cause lifelong sterility and life-threatening complications. Sexually active adolescents also risk exposure to the HIV virus, a risk that increases if a person:

- Is already infected with other STDs
- Has more than one partner within a year
- Does not use condoms during intercourse

All three of these conditions are common among teenagers and their sex partners (who often are unmarried young adults), making them the most likely to catch the virus. To be specific, recent data reveal that, by their senior year of high school, 21 percent of U.S. teenagers have already had four or more sexual partners and that only half used a condom at last intercourse (*MMWR*, August 14, 1998).

Unwanted Pregnancy

The second developmental risk for adolescents is unwanted pregnancy. Note that pregnancy itself is not the problem. Teenagers today actually have far fewer pregnancies than adults in their 20s and far fewer than teenagers did 35 years ago. This is true in virtually every nation, which is one reason the world's birth rate has dropped in recent decades from about four children per woman to about two. In the United States, the birth rate per 1,000 teenagers aged 15 to 19 fell from 90 in 1960 to 51 in 1998.

However, in 1960, few adults considered teen birth a major problem, because 80 percent of teenage mothers were married, and most of them wanted their babies because they expected to be full-time homemakers. Today the reverse is true: 80 percent of teenage mothers are unmarried. Almost no teen—married or not—wanted to become pregnant (teenagers' abortion rate is twice that of women in their 30s). In the United States, almost half of all teenage pregnancies are terminated, either through miscarriage (13 percent) or through induced abortion (33 percent). The remaining pregnancies are carried to term. In most other nations, the abortion rate for unmarried teenagers is much higher, at 50 to 70 percent (Singh & Darroch, 2000).

Both the teenage mother and her child are likely to experience a wealth of problems not only during pregnancy and at birth but also for decades beyond (Hardy et al., 1998). For the mothers, teenage parenthood slows educational and vocational achievement and restricts social and personal growth. No matter what a teenager's level of family support, income, or intellectual capacity, becoming a mother reduces eventual academic achievement by 3 years, on average (Klepinger et al., 1995). It also reduces her chance of employment and marriage, and, if she marries because she is pregnant, it increases her chances of being

sexually transmitted disease (STD) A disease spread by sexual contact. Such diseases include syphilis, gonorrhea, herpes, chlamydia, and AIDS.

Better Protection For decades, sex educators have bemoaned the fact that teenage girls have been considered solely responsible for practicing birth control. However, as this poster suggests, the AIDS epidemic has changed advertising and individual practice, with clear results. Almost half of all sexually active boys use condoms regularly, and the rate of teen pregnancy has been decreasing since the late 1980s.

❓ **Especially for Social Workers:** Suppose you are approached by a 14-year-old girl who thinks she is pregnant. She asks you to tell her what to do. What should you say?

abused, abandoned, or eventually divorced (Harris & Furstenberg, 1997; Waite & Lillard, 1991).

The likely consequences for the child are even more troublesome. Babies of teenagers have a higher risk of prenatal and birth complications, including low birthweight and brain damage, than do infants from the same ethnic communities and educational backgrounds whose mothers are older. And, as they develop, children born to young mothers experience more mistreatment of all kinds and less educational success of any kind. In adolescence, they are more likely to become drug abusers, delinquents, dropouts, and—against their mothers' advice—parents themselves (Fergusson & Woodward, 1999; Hardy et al., 1998; Hoffman et al., 1993).

The Danger of Intense Commitment

Adolescents, boys as well as girls, who engage in early sexual activity face one more risk. To see this third risk, we must first realize that most young people, like adults of every age, believe sex should occur only within a committed, loving relationship. This has been found through research in many nations, including the Netherlands, where a cultural attitude of sexual freedom is combined with extensive sexual education and a social climate that allows scientists to examine a large cross section of adolescent attitudes about sex. Because of this openness, the data on Dutch teenagers are probably accurate. The results of one recent study are shown in Tables 15.1 and 15.2.

Most of the teenagers believed that sexual intercourse was permissible only in a steady relationship (74 percent) or only in marriage (1 percent); one-fourth said casual coitus is sometimes acceptable if it is what both persons want. Their own behavior as they approached adulthood was even more conservative: Only 11 percent of those aged 18 to 19 were in a casual coital relationship (Ravesloot, 1995).

From a developmental perspective, the fact that teenagers associate sex with commitment is good for many reasons. Commitment reduces the other two risks already described, the spread of STDs and unwanted pregnancy. However, intimate commitment may create a third risk, especially for younger adolescents: an intensity that is difficult to handle. For one thing, breaking up is emotionally draining, one cause of adolescent depression and suicide (discussed in Chapter 16). Alternatively, intimate relationships can linger on and on, becoming restrictive of

table **15.1**	When Is Sexual Intercourse Permissible? Attitudes of Dutch Adolescents, Aged 16 to 17 Years		
	Boys	Girls	Average
In casual relationship	37%	14%	25%
Only in steady relationship	63	84	74
Only in marriage	0	2	1

Source: Ravesloot, 1995.

table **15.2**	**What Kind of Relationship Do You Currently Have? Actual Situations of Dutch Adolescents, Aged 18 to 19 Years**
Type of Relationship	Percentage of Adolescents in Such a Relationship
No sexual relationship	14%
Casual, no intercourse	10
Casual, includes intercourse	11
Steady, no intercourse	15
Committed, includes intercourse	50

Source: Ravesloot, 1995.

❶ **Response for Social Workers (from page 425):** Remember that at this age people think egocentrically and not very logically. Hence, you need to realize that her biggest worries may be the immediate ones, such as what her parents will say or whether birth will be difficult, not the long-range ones about how she might raise a child or how she can prevent another pregnancy. And she might not really *be* pregnant. So your job is not only to provide practical help (get her to a clinic) but to expand her thinking. Be aware that her family is the most likely source of support but that incest or rape is a real possibility. Very few 14-year-olds plan to become pregnant.

personal growth. Other activities—such as friendships with peers, concentration on academics, and the pursuit of individual interests—are curtailed, with obvious negative consequences.

All this suggests that an early sexual relationship—even with commitment—may cause young people more psychosocial complications than they are developmentally prepared to undertake.

Making Decisions About Sex

For many adolescents, behavior that adults would consider foolhardy—not just risky sex but also drug and alcohol use, breaking the law, skipping school—is a proven way to gain status, bond with friends, and free the emotions (Lightfoot, 1997). In other words, decisions that seem irrational are not necessarily so—at least for the moment. The problems occur later, and the sudden rush of hormones, their new freedom, and immediate stresses cause many adolescents to disconnect their minds from their behavior, their attitudes from their actions. Let us look at how this phenomenon pertains to decision making about sex.

Some people might be surprised that more than one-third of the older Dutch teens in the study cited in Tables 15.1 and 15.2 were not having sexual intercourse. After all, aren't adolescents sexually interested from the moment puberty begins? Don't most have at least one sexual experience by age 17? Isn't sex before marriage widely acceptable? Yes, yes, and yes.

Nevertheless, attitudes do not lead to actions: Worldwide, most adolescents under age 16 are still virgins, those who have sex early in adolescence typically are pressured (or even forced) to do so, and rates of intercourse for older teens are lower than those for unmarried adults. In most Western nations, most (80 percent) 19-year-olds have had sex, but even at this ripe old age, the rates of sexual activity are lower than those for young adults.

This raises the question: Why are the rates of STDs and unwanted pregnancy higher among adolescents than among single adults—even though the adults are more active sexually? Information about and protection from STDs and pregnancy are available to teenagers in every developed nation. The problem, as various studies have found, is that understanding the basic facts of sexuality does not necessarily lead to responsible and cautious sexual behavior. Nor do adolescents always

Imagine the Pleasure As adults try to warn adolescents of the dangers of early sex, they must also recognize the joys of young love. If they don't, their advice is likely to be rejected as either hypocritical or ignorant.

learn from their mistakes: After being treated for an STD, they are two to three times more likely than adults to become reinfected (Bates, 1995), and about a fifth of all teenage mothers have more than one child. In many developing nations, contraception is less available; but there, too, the number of *married* teenagers who wish to limit or space out their children but do not use contraception is much greater than the number of married women age 20 and older from the same nations whose need for contraception is not met (McDevitt, 1998).

Why is it that knowing the sexual facts does not always lead to responsible adolescent sexual behavior? To answer, we must remember how typical younger adolescents think. As you have seen, adolescents of, say, age 11 to 15 are only beginning to acquire the reasoning skills needed for mature decision making. Thus, they find it difficult to envision all the possible alternatives or scenarios and then choose the best one.

Instead, most sexually naive teenagers tend to focus on immediate considerations (on the difficulty or inconvenience of using contraception, for example) and fail to consider fully future possibilities (such as pregnancy, abortion, and parenthood). This is exactly what we might expect from individuals whose formal logical powers are very new, who reason with adolescent egocentrism, and who have had little personal experience with intimate discussions concerning sexual behavior. Further, the risks of sex—as well as of drugs and alcohol, which often accompany sex (Santelli et al., 1998)—are seen in a positive light by those for whom foolhardy behavior is considered socially bonding and emotionally freeing (Lightfoot, 1997).

This failure to think through *all the possible consequences* helps explain an interesting finding: Although few teenage girls actually try to become pregnant, most who do not practice contraception believe that having a baby would not be so bad (Hanson et al., 1987; Manlove, 1997). This view is captured in the response of an eighth-grader who said she did *not* want to become pregnant. Then she was asked what her reaction would be if she inadvertently became a mother in the near future. She said:

> I think having a baby would really make me a little happier because it would make me have something of him, . . . I know I'm young and everything, but I know I could take care of it because my mother had me when she was young. I am just about the same age [as] when she got pregnant. And she did okay, I'm here. [quoted in Taylor et al., 1995]

Unfortunately, in the eleventh grade this girl actually had a baby and dropped out of school. And, in spite of her assurance that she could "take care of it," she was forced to give up custody because she was unable to care for her child properly. Motherhood did not make her "a little happier"—just the opposite, in fact.

The Need for Better Sex Education

How can adolescents be helped to make more rational and timely decisions? A first step, according to many experts, is for adults to be more rational in *their* thinking. As you saw in Chapter 14, drug education that includes scare tactics that adolescents perceive as false are supported by adults but fail to influence teenagers. The same is true for sex education. (See A Life-Span View.)

Given the urgency of the sex drive, adolescents need more than "just the facts" to guide them. They need to develop the attitudes, values, and social skills that will help them refrain from sexual intercourse until they are wise enough to understand, and mature enough to take responsibility for, the consequences.

Many school systems are revising their sex education programs to make them more practical, focused on social interaction. This is occurring worldwide, even in nations such as France and Sweden, which have many fewer pregnancies among 15- to 19-year-olds (22 and 27 per 1,000, respectively) than do Canada and the United States (50 and 90 per 1,000, respectively); see Table 15.3 (Singh & Darroch, 2000). In the United States,

Different Rates Around the World These are rates of confirmed pregnancies (and thus do not include early miscarriages) per 1,000 women aged 15 to 19, between 1994 and 1996. In most nations, both pregnancy rates and birth rates decreased between 1995 and 2000.

table 15.3	Teenage Pregnancy Rates and Birth Rates in Selected Countries	
	Pregnancy Rate	Birth Rate
	(Per 1,000 Women Aged 15 to 19)	
Australia	—	22
Canada	50	26
Denmark	25	10
England	53	33
France	22	12
Hungary	63	32
Iceland	42	25
Japan	—	4
New Zealand	59	38
Norway	35	15
Sweden	27	9
United States	91	60

Source: Singh & Darroch, 2000.

WHICH GENERATION BEST UNDERSTANDS SEX?

Adults need to recognize that, like teenagers, they themselves are not immune to irrational sexual choices. Many 30- or 40-year-old new mothers are overwhelmed by the unexpected demands a baby brings, and adolescents are quick to notice. As one 18-year-old mother explained:

I've got an aunt who's 44, and she's got a 3-year-old, so I see a lot of these teenage moms better than her. Because I think teenage moms—we all share energy. We've got a lot more energy than a 30- or 40-year-old woman. She throws her kid in front of the TV and expects that to entertain him because her body's old. She really does not have enough energy to be chasing him. Or going to the grocery store with him kills her. It's just, that's all the energy she'll have for the entire day. The zoo is extremely hard on her. I think we're all very lucky that we have our bodies that are young. [quoted in Higginson, 1998]

Thus, the difference between a teen mother and an older mother is not necessarily rational risk assessment but adequate social support. The baby's father and other relatives are understandably more willing and able to help the older mother. Yet teens greatly need such help. For instance, one study found that an intensive support system, of caseworkers and parenting programs that worked with (not against) the families of pregnant teenagers, reduced the rates of school dropouts and repeat pregnancy (Soloman & Liefeld, 1998). Another ongoing study found that home visits made by nurses to a group of high-risk teenage mothers were correlated with a substantial reduction in the incidence of child abuse and an improvement in the mothers' health and income over a 15-year follow-up (Olds et al., 1999).

Such support would have had greater impact years earlier. Parents should educate their children about sex long before the need to support a pregnant teen arises. Some of that education occurs with explicit conversation that communicates not only by what is said but also by how it is said

(Whitaker et al., 1999). In addition, and probably more important, parents' overall relationships with their children and with each other, as well as their religious convictions and social values regarding sex, health, and each child's future, all have an effect (Hanson et al., 1987).

When it comes to the particulars, few parents are adequate sex educators. For one thing, they are too late. Many parents do not begin discussing sexual issues until long after the children have been informed, or misinformed, by friends, intuition, television, or personal experience. Adolescents who learn about sex at home learn mainly from their older siblings and almost never from their parents (Ansuini et al., 1996).

For another, parents fool themselves. For example, one mother confidently explained, "If you spend a lot of time talking with your children . . . they know how we feel about it [premarital intercourse]. As a result, we don't have any major conflict at all." In truth, however, conflicts about sex in this particular family were avoided not by communication but by silence. Their sexually active daughter never told her parents, because "they simply do not want to know." Consequently, her parents remained ignorant; her father hoped she would not get herself "dishonored," and her mother believed it was still too early for any serious relationship (du Bois-Reymond, 1995).

In another study, mothers were asked whether their teens had had sex and then the teens were asked for the truth. The difference between the two sets of replies was astounding (see Figure 15.7). For instance, 35 percent of 14-year-olds were sexually active, but only 14 percent of mothers knew it.

In this study, mothers who were more religious and more disapproving of teen sex were less likely to know when their children were sexually active (Jaccard et al., 1998). Did these young people avoid the discussion because they already knew their parents' attitudes? No. Few teenagers accurately assessed their mothers' attitudes on a variety of sexual issues—

90 percent of schools teach communication regarding health issues, and 48 percent teach the correct use of condoms (*MMWR,* September 11, 1998). Explicit instruction is important. Teens are more likely to use condoms, for instance, if they have specific knowledge about exactly when and how to wear them than if they merely have a general knowledge about the dangers of sexually transmitted disease (Sheeran et al., 1999).

particularly on the practical consequences of pregnancy (such as having to quit school or marry the wrong person).

Fully 72 percent of the mothers reported that they had talked with their teens at least once about sex, but only 45 percent of the teens agreed (Jaccard et al., 1998). Thus, 27 percent of mother–child pairs did not agree about whether or not they talked about sex.

An added problem is that many parents are themselves uninformed. This is especially likely if the parents' teenage years occurred

- Before the threat of AIDS
- Before the newer forms of contraception (Implants and injections are now the most common contraception pre-

scriptions among teenagers, and the Pill and the diaphragm are considered old-fashioned.)

- Before "good" girls were sexually interested or "real" boys were sexually careful
- Before sexual activity was an acceptable topic of conversation between partners and generations

This final item may be the most important. Although many parents were sexually active before marriage, they conducted their activity in secret and shame. This makes it hard for them to discuss the matter openly with their children (Daniluk, 1998; Ravesloot, 1995). It should be no surprise, then, that most sex education occurs outside the home.

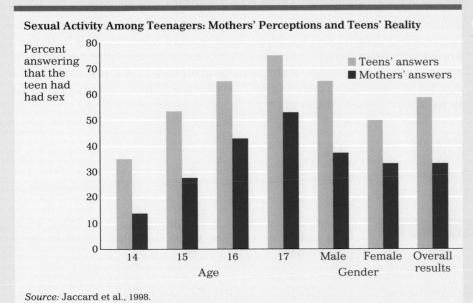

Sexual Activity Among Teenagers: Mothers' Perceptions and Teens' Reality

Source: Jaccard et al., 1998.

Figure 15.7 Mother Doesn't Always Know. This graph shows the discrepancy between the answers mothers gave to "Is your child sexually active?" and the answers teenagers gave when asked for the truth. Notice which age group and gender had the largest gaps—the younger teens and the boys.

Educational efforts are having an impact, according to many surveys. In the United States between 1991 and 1997, the teen birth rate declined 12 percent; the rate of sexual activity among high school girls fell 6 percent; the abortion rate fell by 30 percent; and the percentage of girls using contraception for their first sexual encounter increased from 65 percent in the late 1980s to 78 percent in 1995. Boys also reported less sexual activity and more use of condoms (Donovan, 1997; Kahn et al., 1999; *MMWR,* September 18, 1998).

The boys' increase in condom use parallels a change in attitudes and sexual communication. For example, in 1988, only 28 percent of young men strongly disagreed that "it would be embarrassing" to discuss using a condom with a girl before having sex. Seven years later, the number strongly disagreeing almost doubled, to 47 percent (Murphy & Boggess, 1998).

It would be naive to attribute all these shifts to cognitive advances and even more naive to trumpet sex education as the cause. Improved contraception and better opportunities and education for young women certainly contribute to the decline of teen births. Cultural differences between nations are so large that an individual's classroom experience with sex education is only part of the picture. As a review of the declines in teen pregnancy, abortion, and birth rates in forty-six countries concludes:

> Broad societal changes, as well as cross-cutting socioeconomic, political, and cultural characteristics of individual countries, play an important role in explaining recent trends. These factors include the greater importance ascribed to educational achievement, the increased motivation among young people to delay pregnancy and childbearing in order to achieve higher education levels and to gain job skills before forming a family, as well as improvements in knowledge of and access to the means of preventing unplanned pregnancy. [Singh & Darroch, 2000]

Nonetheless, notice how many factors relate to education. Advances in teenagers' thoughts and attitudes about sex are affecting their behavior, and improvement is evident. Facilitating more mature cognition is one way to help teenagers avoid the serious problems that sometimes derail normal development, creating an unexpected detour or even standstill in progress through these years.

SUMMARY

ADOLESCENT THOUGHT

1. Unlike younger children, whose thoughts are tied to tangible reality, adolescents can build formal systems and general theories that transcend (and sometimes ignore) practical experience. Their reasoning can be formal and abstract, rather than empirical and concrete. This ability also enables them to consider abstract principles, such as those concerning love, justice, and the meaning of human life.

2. Among the specific characteristics of formal operational thought is the ability to think hypothetically and reason deductively. Adolescents can imagine a general principle that might be true and then deduce specific ideas that follow from that generality. Teenagers do not always think at this advanced level, however.

3. Adolescent thought is marked, and sometimes marred, by egocentrism, exemplified by the invincibility and personal fables. Egocentrism also helps account for the self-

consciousness that is typical during this phase of life, when an imaginary audience seems to evaluate the teenager's every move.

SCHOOLS, LEARNING, AND THE ADOLESCENT MIND

4. Adolescence is typically a period of both openness and fear, when adolescents find themselves eager for intellectual stimulation but highly vulnerable to self-doubt. Many students entering secondary school feel less competent, less conscientious, and less motivated than they did in elementary school.

5. Compared with elementary schools, most secondary schools have more rigid behavioral demands, more intense competition, and less individualized attention and procedures. This impedes the proper match between the student's characteristics and the school structure.

6. The culture and the context of the school can support adolescent learning. Schools that have high standards and coop-

erative learning are likely to produce academic growth in all students.

7. Part-time employment can distract adolescents from their schoolwork, especially if the job is routine, provides easy pocket money, and is not connected to the school program.

ADOLESCENT DECISION MAKING

8. Adolescents have mixed abilities with regard to decision making. On the one hand, adolescence witnesses the growth of many cognitive skills that are essential to good judgment. On the other hand, judgment skills alone do not lead to good decisions.

9. Cognitive and motivational factors can make it difficult for teenagers to make good judgments about their sexual activity, as reflected in the high rates of sexually transmitted diseases and unwanted pregnancy during adolescence.

10. Family contexts and parental support can reduce the incidence of premature sexual activity, risky sexual behavior, and teen pregnancy. Unfortunately, few parents are timely and well-informed sex educators.

11. New, more practical sex education programs that are focused on social interaction may be succeeding, as shown by less sexual activity, more condom use, and fewer unwanted births in the past decade.

KEY QUESTIONS

1. What is the crucial difference between concrete operational thought and formal operational thought?

2. What is deductive reasoning, and how does it compare with the inductive reasoning of the younger child?

3. What are some of the characteristics of adolescent egocentrism?

4. Describe competitive and cooperative learning, giving the advantages and disadvantages of each style of education.

5. How should schools be organized to foster better academic success and supportive social interaction among teens?

6. What are the advantages and disadvantages of adolescent employment?

7. What are the risks of sexual activity during adolescence?

8. What are the most important aspects of sex education?

9. *In Your Experience* Who and what were your worst and best sources of information about sexuality? Discuss your parents, peers, school, books, and any others that were relevant.

KEY TERMS

formal operational
  thought (407)
hypothetical thought (408)
inductive reasoning (409)
deductive reasoning (409)
adolescent egocentrism
  (413)
invincibility fable (413)

personal fable (413)
imaginary audience (415)
person–environment fit
  (416)
volatile mismatch (417)
sexually transmitted
  disease (STD) (425)

Adolescence:
Psychosocial Development

Adolescence starts when the physical changes of puberty transform a childish body into an adult one (see Chapter 14). Then the cognitive changes of adolescence enable the young person to move beyond concrete thought, to think abstractly and hypothetically (see Chapter 15). However, the psychosocial changes—relating to parents with new independence, to friends with new intimacy, to society with new commitment, and to oneself with new understanding—are the critical ones that bring the young person to adulthood. Becoming an adult is not a matter of size or intellect; it requires social maturity.

THE SELF AND IDENTITY

Psychosocial development during adolescence is best understood as a quest for self-understanding, for answers to the question "Who am I?" The momentous changes that occur during the teen years—growth spurt, sexual awakening, less personal schools, more intimate friendships, and risk taking—all challenge the adolescent to find his or her **identity,** his or her unique and consistent self-definition (Kroger, 2000; Larson & Ham, 1993).

The first step in the identity process is to establish the integrity of personality—that is, to align emotions, thinking, and behavior to be consistent no matter what the place, time, circumstances, or social relationship. "Two-faced," "wishy-washy," and "hypocritical" are among the worst accusations one adolescent can throw at another, in part because integrity is fervently sought but is frustratingly elusive.

Younger children describe themselves primarily in terms of their skills in school, with friends, and perhaps on the athletic field. But adolescents distinguish their scholastic competence from other aspects of who they are; in addition, they think of their job skills, romantic appeal, moral conduct, and peer acceptance (Harter, 1993). They also begin to ponder career options, political identification, religious commitment, and sexual ethics, questioning how these values fit together with expectations for the future and the beliefs acquired in the past.

As they deal with these increasingly diverse and complex aspects of selfhood, adolescents confront the psychosocial challenge referred to by Erik Erikson as **identity versus role confusion.** For developmentalists like Erikson, the search for identity leads to the primary crisis of adolescence—a crisis in which the young person struggles to reconcile a quest

ALL SHE DID WAS CUT HER HAIR

Erikson's linking of past and future is particularly difficult when one's expectations of living by the democratic ideal are thwarted by social prejudice and institutionalized racism. As a result, "many ethnic minority youth . . . may have to deny large parts of themselves to survive, may internalize negative images of their group, and [consequently] may fail to adopt an ethnic cultural identity" (Hill et al., 1994). In some cases, minority youths adopt a negative identity—rejecting wholesale the traditions of both their ethnic group and the majority culture.

Such resistance to external control may be seen in one 15-year-old's haircut, a decision she made in defiance of her childhood tradition:

> For years, I needed my mom's help to twist my long, thick hair, which fell nearly halfway down my back, into a braid or even a ponytail. I hated that morning ritual because it made me feel helpless. I hated the long hours it took to wash and dry my hair.
>
> I wanted to feel free and independent . . . I wanted a haircut.
>
> But I couldn't make myself do it. A haircut was a big decision. My hair was more than just a bunch of dead cells. It was a symbol of control.
>
> For my parents and relatives, long hair is considered an essential part of being a woman. Especially for "good Indian girls."
>
> Most of my friends didn't want me to go short, either. I'm not sure why. Maybe they were like me, afraid of change. Somewhere inside, I believed that the really beautiful women had long hair. I remembered someone

saying that college guys liked women with long hair. (And college is the place where you meet your husband.) [Chikkatur, 1997]

Torn by all these conflicts, one day this young woman decided and—before she told her family or changed her mind—had her hair cut. For the next month, as all her relatives criticized her, she alternated between thinking she had made a "huge mistake" and being "glad I cut my hair." She considered her haircut a symbol of her independence, not only from her family but also from the majority culture's expectations about beauty, marriage, and sexual orientation. She challenged both cultures by finally concluding "that being beautiful has nothing to do with the length of my hair and that a short cut has nothing to do with being gay or straight."

More often than choosing independence, as this young woman did, African American, Native American, Mexican American, and Asian American adolescents choose foreclosed identity, and they do so more readily than European Americans (Phinney, 1990; Rotheram-Borus & Wyche, 1994; Streitmatter, 1988). The searching process itself may be too difficult when criticism from one's own group or from the majority group is evoked (or assumed) by every action.

Peers, themselves torn by similar conflicts, can be very critical. Minority-group members may be branded "oreos," "bananas," or "apples"—colorful on the outside but white inside. Whites who associate with blacks may be called "gray," or those who associate with Indians may be said to have "gone native." And these are the kinder comments.

Parents

generation gap The distance between generations in values, behaviors, and knowledge.

Adolescence is often characterized as a time of waning adult influence, when the values and behaviors of young people are said to become increasingly distant and detached from those of their parents and other adults. According to all reports, however, the **generation gap,** as the distance between the younger generation and the older one has been called, is not necessarily wide. In fact, younger and older generations have very similar values and aspirations. This is especially true when adolescents are compared not with adults in general but with their own parents (Holmbeck et al., 1995; Steinberg, 1990). An exception occurs when the parents grew up in a very different place and time, such as in a rural region of a developing nation, and the teenager is growing up in a big city in a developed nation (Harris, 1998).

The fact that the generation gap is typically small by objective measures does not mean all is harmonious at home. In fact, each generation

generational stake   The need of each generation to view family interactions from its own perspective, because each has a different investment in the family scenario.

Generational Stake This is a family: father, daughter, and mother.
❓ *Observational Quiz (see answer page 443): From facial expressions and body positions, and from the hypothesis of the generational stake, what can you infer about the relationships among these three?*

bickering   Petty, peevish arguing, usually repeated and ongoing. Bickering is typical in early adolescence.

🔴 **Response for Parents (from page 439):**
Most arguments are petty, involving disagreements about personal habits, style, and taste. Obviously, these issues are not the most important in the long run; too much bickering might cut off communication when it is really needed. Therefore, wise parents keep careful watch on health and safety issues and leave style alone. For instance, parents might let a son have an earring but not a cigarette, or they might allow a daughter to listen to her own music but make sure she travels with sober girlfriends when she goes out.

has its own distinct **generational stake** (Bengston, 1975). That is, each generation has a natural tendency to interpret parent–adolescent interactions from the viewpoint of its own position in the family. Parents have a stake in believing that all is well and that their children are basically loyal to the family despite a superficial show of rebellion. Adolescents have a stake in believing that their parents are limited, old-fashioned, and out of touch. This divergence occurs for good reason, since human evolution requires that adolescents break free from parental restraints to find their own mates and peers (Weisfeld, 1999).

Parents' concern about continuity of their own values leads them to minimize whatever friction occurs between the two generations. They blame problems on hormones or peer influences, rather than on anything long-lasting. Adolescents, in contrast, want to shed parental restraints and forge their own independent identities, so they exaggerate intergenerational problems. Consider a conflict about a curfew. A parent may see it merely as a problem of management, the latest version of trying to get the child to bed on time, but a teenager may consider it evidence of the parents' outmoded values or lack of trust. On a deeper level, teenagers may see parental rules as an attempt to control and dominate; parents may see them as an attempt to love and protect. No wonder they disagree about some specifics.

Parent–Adolescent Conflict

As long as parents and adolescents live under the same roof, a certain amount of conflict occurs in most families when the young person's drive for independence clashes with the parents' tradition of control. The extent of the conflict depends on many factors, including the child's age and gender and the cultural context.

Parent–adolescent conflict typically emerges in early adolescence, particularly with daughters who mature early and with mothers more than fathers (Arnett, 1999; Caspi et al., 1993; Montemayor, 1986). The reason younger adolescent girls and mothers are conflict-prone is easy to understand, once you know what the typical issues are. **Bickering** (repeated, petty arguments, more like nagging than fighting) occurs about habits of daily life—hair, neatness, and clothing issues, for example—that traditionally fall under the mother's supervision. These issues are also ones that girls had been more pressured about, and more docile about, than boys, making a daughter's rebellion more surprising and more noticeable to the parents. In addition, most parents curb their daughters' freedom more than their sons', thus evoking resistance. And it is the relatively young adolescent who feels compelled to make a statement—with green hair or blaring music—to establish in unmistakable terms that a new stage has arrived. Bickering follows.

Adolescents—both male and female—generally believe that they should be granted the privileges of adult status much earlier, and more extensively, than parents do (Holmbeck & O'Donnell, 1991). This dispute over status and age stems from the generational stake. Twelve-year-olds believe that controversies between themselves and their parents involve basic values such as personal privacy and freedom, which ought not to be interfered with by parents. Parents believe that the same issues (sleeping late on weekends, engaging in long telephone conversations, wearing

Talking and Listening One of the biggest issues between adolescents and parents is "You don't listen to me." Unlike when she was a little girl (see photo on mantel), this teenager keeps many of her opinions and experiences from her mother. In fact, she considers herself good when she does not shout, walk away, or cover her ears when her mother talks. Meanwhile, her mother remembers when "listening" meant responding, discussing, and finally obeying.

parental monitoring Parental awareness of what one's children are doing, where, and with whom.

tight or torn clothing, and leaving one's room in a mess) ought to be within their authority, since they have the child's well-being at heart. Few parents can resist making a critical comment about the dirty socks on the floor, and few adolescents can calmly listen to "expressions of concern" without feeling they are unfairly judged (Smetana & Asquith, 1994).

An ethnic variation is found in the *timing* of parent–child conflict. For Chinese, Korean, and Mexican American teens, stormy relations with parents may not surface until late in adolescence. It may be that because these cultures encourage dependency in children and emphasize family closeness, the typical teenager's quest for autonomy is delayed (Greenberger & Chen, 1996; Molina & Chassin, 1996).

Interesting as these variations are, we should stress that adolescents have *never* been found to benefit from families that are permissive to the point of laxness *or* strict to the point of abuse. The ethnic differences we are discussing occur within the range of normal authoritative and authoritarian parenting (see Chapter 10), not at the extremes. Families that are high in conflict, or parent–child relationships that are low in support, are almost always hard on the adolescent, no matter what the family structure or culture (Demo & Acock, 1996). If conflict reaches the point where the adolescent becomes a runaway or, more often, a throwaway—kicked out of the house—disaster is likely to follow in the form of suicide, indiscriminate sex, drug abuse, or violence of every kind (Yoder et al., 1998).

Other Family Qualities

Conflict is only one of the dimensions of the parent–teenager relationship that has been studied. Other aspects include:

- Communication (Can they talk openly with one another?)
- Support (Do they rely on one another?)
- Connectiveness (How close are they?)
- Control (Do parents encourage or limit autonomy?)

These four elements vary a great deal from family to family. No researcher doubts that communication and support are beneficial, if not essential; hundreds of studies throughout the world confirm their importance. However, the connection and control exercised by parents seems especially crucial to adolescents' development.

Control. The degree to which a close family exercises control, restricting the adolescent's autonomy, is an especially tricky aspect of family functioning. On the one hand, some steps to limit freedom are beneficial. A powerful deterrent for delinquency, risky sex, and drug abuse is **parental monitoring,** that is, parental vigilance regarding where one's child is and what he or she is doing and with whom (Fletcher et al., 1995; Patterson et al., 1989; Rogers, 1999; Sampson & Laub, 1993). Such monitoring helps limit access to alcohol, drugs, and guns by keeping the adolescent in places the parent allows.

Other sources of monitoring are people in the community: neighbors, store owners, and so on. Since many delinquent acts occur in late afternoon, between the closing school bell and the evening meal, after-school programs with adult supervision, particularly sports leagues or drama workshops that are attractive and available for boys as well as

A Guiding Hand Organized extracurricular activities, with appropriate adult supervision, supplement parental monitoring as a way of helping adolescents stay out of trouble. Note, however, the front row is 70 percent female, and the cluster at the back is 80 percent male. Boys are particularly likely to rebel against organized, coed after-school programs.

❶ Answer to Observational Quiz (from page 441): *The father's satisfied smile and his relaxed position, leaning back in his chair, suggest he is proud and happy. The mother also seems content, but she has her eyes on, her arm around, and her body leaning toward her daughter. Meanwhile, the daughter's expression is quizzical, even disbelieving, and her shoulders, arms, and legs all suggest she is keeping to herself, not about to defer to her parents. As a good scientist, you know that nothing can be proved on the basis of one snapshot, but you also know that these gestures and positions are in accord with the generational-stake hypothesis—fathers want to be proud of their families, mothers want to keep their children close, and adolescents want to be independent. Hence, this moment is typical of thousands of other parent–adolescent interactions.*

girls, can make a decided difference (Levin, 1999). Community closeness, which allows neighbors to know which teenagers might be getting into trouble and who their parents are, significantly decreases delinquency (Sampson, 1997).

On the other hand, too much parental interference and control is a strong predictor of adolescent depression. Adolescents apparently need some freedom in order to feel good about themselves (Barber et al., 1997). Obviously, parents need to find some middle ground, expressing involvement without interference, concern without restriction. Psychological intrusiveness, when parents not only know where the child is but also make the child feel guilty and anxious about his or her behavior, may make the child unhappy and sometimes rebellious (Larson & Gillman, 1999). The particulars depend on the culture, on the siblings, and on the inherited personalities of the individuals (Rowe, 1994).

All told, however, parent–teen relationships are typically supportive during adolescence, which is fortunate since family connection underlies psychological functioning. Some conflict is common, typically occurring in early adolescence and centering on day-to-day details like the adolescent's musical tastes, domestic neatness, and sleeping habits, not on world politics or moral issues (Barber, 1994).

Peers

Friendships, already prominent in middle childhood, become even more influential during early adolescence (Erwin, 1998; Harris, 1998). From hanging out with a large group in the schoolyard or at the mall to having whispered phone conversations with a trusted confidant or with a romantic partner, relations with peers are vital to the transition from childhood to adulthood.

Adolescents help each other negotiate the tasks and trials of growing up in many ways. As B. Bradford Brown (1990) explains, "Teenagers construct a peer system that reflects their growing psychological, biological,

Peer Pressure Peers give each other welcome guidance regarding what to wear, as shown by these two groups of friends. Although there may have been some early-morning phone consultation regarding who was wearing what, the overall fashion mode in both cases—"black with chains" and "casual prep"—was a foregone conclusion.

and social-cognitive maturity and helps them adapt to the social ecology of adolescence." Among the special functions performed by peer relationships and close friendships, Brown finds the following four most noteworthy:

- *Pubertal self-help.* Physical changes confront the young person with new feelings, experiences, and challenges to self-esteem. Peers provide both information and the companionship of those who are going through the same changes, able to listen to concerns and provide specific advice as few adults can.

- *Social support.* Friends provide social protection against the turmoil of the social ecology of adolescence, such as the transition to the larger, more impersonal middle and junior high schools, with heterogeneous student populations and fewer nurturant adults. As Brown (1990) observes, "Major changes in peer groups can be seen as efforts to cope with the new school structure thrust on youngsters at adolescence. The depersonalized and complex routine of secondary school increases the young teenager's need for sources of social support and informal exchanges."

- *Identity formation.* The peer group aids the search for self-understanding and identity by functioning as a mirror that reflects dispositions, interests, and capabilities. Superficial identity is often a first step, which explains why many groups watch the same TV shows, wear the same shoes, dance with the same moves to the same music, and so on. As adolescents associate themselves with this or that subgroup (the jocks, the brains, or the druggies, for instance), they are rejecting other subgroups—and the particular self-definitions that would go with them.

- *Values clarification.* Friends are a sounding board for exploring and defining values and aspirations. By experimenting with viewpoints, philosophies, and attitudes toward themselves and the world, with others who are willing to listen, argue, and agree, adolescents begin to discover which values are truest to them.

Because of the nature and importance of these four functions, loyalty and intimacy are critical (Berndt & Savin-Williams, 1992; Newcomb & Bagwell, 1995). Friends are obligated to stand up for each other, must never speak behind each other's backs, and need to share personal thoughts and feelings without ridicule or betrayal of trust. As one eighth-grader expressed very simply:

> I can tell Karen things and she helps me talk. If we have problems at school, we work them out together. And she doesn't laugh at me if I do something weird—she accepts me for who I am. [quoted in Berndt & Perry, 1990]

Such intimacy and trust are obviously very personal, not easily replaced. Most adolescent friendships are quite durable, with more stability from year to year than at younger ages (Degirmencioglu, 1998; Erwin, 1998).

Peer Pressure

peer pressure Social pressure to conform with one's friends or contemporaries in behavior, dress, and attitude; usually considered negative, as when adolescent peers encourage each other to defy adult standards.

The four peer functions just listed are constructive ones; for that reason, they are contrary to the notion of **peer pressure,** the idea that peers force adolescents to do things that they otherwise would not do. The idea of peer pressure is not completely false, but it is exaggerated in three ways:

- The pressure to conform to peers is strong only for a few years; it rises dramatically in early adolescence, but only until about age 14. Then it declines (Coleman & Hendry, 1990).
- Peer-group conformity can be constructive. It eases the transition for a young person who is trying to abandon childish modes of behavior, including dependence on parents, but who is not yet ready for full independence.
- Peer standards are not necessarily negative. Generally, peer-group membership, even more than close friendship, promotes higher grades and prosocial behavior and eases distress and antisocial behavior (Wentzel & Caldwell, 1997). Peers encourage each other to join sports teams, study for exams, avoid smoking, apply to colleges, and so on.

The reality that peer pressure can be positive does not negate another reality: Young people sometimes lead each other into trouble. When no adults are present, the excitement of being together and the desire to defy adult restrictions can result in risky, forbidden, and destructive behavior (Dishion et al., 1995; Lightfoot, 1997). Peer pressure is particularly likely to be negative in periods of uncertainty. For example, young people are more likely to admire aggressive boys when they themselves are new to a school, are experiencing the physical changes of puberty, and are uncomfortable with heterosexual attraction—as they might be in the first months of middle school (Bukowski et al., 2000).

Peers sometimes influence friends who are ambivalent about their values and activities but not those who are already set on a particular path (Vitaro et al., 1997). Indeed, peers choose each other; teenagers associate with other teenagers whose values and interests they share. Collectively, however, they may sometimes become involved in escapades that none of them would engage in alone. The reason for their behavior is not peer pressure but peer solidarity. As one adolescent described it:

> The idea of peer pressure is a lot of bunk. What I heard about peer pressure all the way through school is that someone is going to walk up to me and say "Here, drink this and you'll be cool." It wasn't like that at all. You go somewhere and everyone else would be doing it and you'd think, "Hey, everyone else is doing it and they seem to be having a good time—now why wouldn't I do this?" In that sense, the preparation of the powers that be, the lessons that they tried to drill into me, they were completely off. They had no idea what we are up against. [Lightfoot, 1997]

Fortunately, most peer-inspired misbehavior is a short-lived experiment rather than a foreshadowing of long-term delinquency. The teenager who argues that he or she must engage in a particular activity, dress a certain way, or hang out in certain parts of town because "everyone else does it" is trying to lighten the burden of responsibility for some demeanor, style, or philosophy that she or he is trying out. In a way, therefore, "peer pressure" acts as a buffer between the relatively dependent world of childhood and the relatively independent world of young adulthood.

The Peer Group for Immigrants

Conflict between peers and family is likely to arise in ethnic groups that revere closeness to family, respect for elders, and self-sacrifice for the sake of kin (Harrison et al., 1990). This ideal clashes with the peer-group emphasis on adolescent freedom and self-determination.

This is potentially problematic for immigrants, because the adolescent's physical and cognitive drives hit full force several years before they would in traditional societies, where puberty occurs later and the age for marriage and adult work follow soon after (Markstrom-Adams & Spencer, 1994). For many immigrant families, the normal strain between the generations is thus extended for several years longer than it would be in traditional cultures. Some minority adolescents (mostly girls) give in to parental control (perhaps docilely living at home until an early marriage), while others (mostly boys) rebel completely (perhaps leaving home in a fury). Some join a delinquent group, typically consisting of other boys from the same ethnic group. In this case, peers provide an identity that comes complete with codes of behavior, standards of dress, and social bonding experiences. Such groups are common in immigrant communities living in multiethnic cities (Johnson-Powell & Yamamoto, 1997; Wong, 1999) and actually make psychological sense as a transition experience.

In a desperate attempt to deal with the severe generation gap that arises in many minority families, the parents may send the adolescent back to the grandparents' traditional home, to the original nation, to a more isolated community, or, if those are impossible, to a specialized school, perhaps only for children of that sex, religion, and ethnicity. In all these cases, the teenager's self-actualizing search for identity is sacrificed or at least postponed.

The Same but Different Traditionally, minority identity in the United States focused on race, with young people of color needing to find their place in a white world. Currently, however, the issue has broadened to be seen as ethnic, not racial. These two California high school students look physically similar but are from very different backgrounds: one is from Cambodia and the other from Mexico. Each is finding her own bicultural identity. Their backgrounds differ, but the search is universal; many adolescents of European descent also struggle with issues of heritage and self.

In the United States, virtually no adolescent is able to associate only with peers of the exact same background (even if he or she wanted to), because every individual has somewhat different roots. In the long term, most psychologists would consider this liberating. But in the immediate context, establishing ethnic identity is not easy. Minority individuals take years—even decades—to sort through the divergent historical roots, gender roles, peer loyalties, vocational aspirations, religious beliefs, and political values of cultures that surround them (Staples & Johnson, 1993). Young Asian Americans are now found to follow the same sequence as other groups:

- Foreclosure on traditional ancestral values
- Rejection of tradition in favor of mainstream values
- Moratorium
- Identity achievement by connecting with other young Asian Americans
[Tse, 1999; Ying & Lee, 1999]

Notice that the final step includes both rejection of parental traditions and solidarity with a peer group that shares some of the same traditional background. In almost every other situation, adolescents also choose peers who will help with their particular problems and remain highly critical of other peers who have a different set of habits and values.

Boys and Girls Together

During most of early and middle childhood, voluntary segregation of the sexes is common (Maccoby, 1998). Then, as puberty begins, boys and girls begin to notice one another in a new way. However, given the diversity of sex roles in today's world, developing a sexual identity and then expressing it with a partner are almost impossible to do without friends (see the Research Report on page 448). Usually, the first sign of heterosexual attraction is not an overt, positive interest but a seeming dislike (see Table 16.2). The pace of the change depends on several factors, which vary from culture to culture. One factor is the biology of puberty, with early maturers likely to be first to reach out to the other sex. This is one reason Asian Americans are less likely to date, have sex, or give birth during adolescence: They tend to mature more slowly. More powerful is the influence of culture and peers who may push a given teenager to date, dance, or whatever. Parents are another strong influence; the closeness of their supervision and the personal example they

A Foursome, Not a Twosome When teenagers first start forming couples, they often spend time with other couples to ease the uncertainty about what to say, when to touch, and so on. Interestingly, it is not unusual for a breakup in one couple to trigger a breakup in the other, often with a new alliance between the same individuals.

table **16.2**	**Typical Adolescent Responses to the Opposite Sex***	
	From Girls	From Boys
Age 11	"Boys are a sort of disease."	"Girls are a pin prick in the side."
Age 13	"Boys are stupid although important to us."	"Girls are great enemies."
Age 15	"Boys are strange—they hate you if you're ugly and brainy but love you if you are pretty but dumb."	"Girls are the main objective."
Age 16	"Boys are a pleasant change from the girls."	"Girls have their good and bad points—fortunately, the good outnumber the bad."

*The quotations come from a study of adolescents in New Zealand.
Source: Kroger, 1989.

FINDING A PARTNER: STEP BY STEP

The progression of heterosexual involvement, first described almost 40 years ago (Dunphy, 1963), follows this general pattern:

- Groups of friends, exclusively one sex or the other
- A loose association of a girls' group and a boys' group, with all interactions very public
- A smaller, mixed-sex group, formed from the more advanced members of the larger association
- A final peeling off of heterosexual couples, with private intimacies

Cultural patterns affect the timing and manifestation of these stages, but the basic sequence seems biologically based and hence consistent across the centuries, cultures, and even species (Weisfeld, 1999). In modern developed nations, when puberty begins at about age 12 and marriage does not occur until a decade or two later, each of these stages typically lasts several years, with exclusive same-sex groups dominant in elementary school and heterosexual couples in later high school or college.

The overall sequence of sexual friendship patterns was documented in a study of students in a large, multiethnic public school outside Chicago (Richards et al., 1998). These students were beeped at random times of the day or evening and asked to record whom they were with, how they felt at the moment, and what they were thinking. As they got older, these adolescents gradually spent more time with the other sex and enjoyed it more: Freshmen were happiest when they were with companions of their own sex or in mixed-sex groups, while juniors and seniors were happiest when with one member of the other sex.

To get a sense of the time adolescents spend with peers, look at Figure 16.1. In the fifth and sixth grades, when they were on the edge of adolescence, children spent about 1 percent of their waking time (less than an hour a week) with the

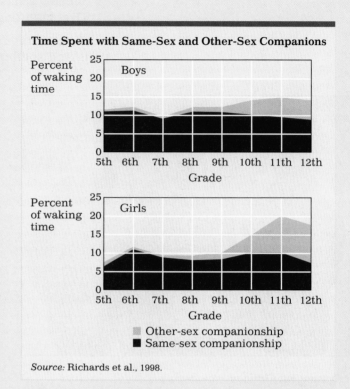

Time Spent with Same-Sex and Other-Sex Companions

Source: Richards et al., 1998.

Figure 16.1 We'll Still Be Friends. Through adolescence, young people spend increasing amounts of time with peers of the opposite sex, while almost maintaining the amounts of time spent with same-sex friends. Note, though, that older girls spend much more of their time with opposite-sex friends than older boys do.

other sex. (Classroom time was not counted.) By the eleventh grade, however, boys were spending 5 hours a week with girls, and girls about 10 hours with boys. (The numbers are not equal because for some of the girls, most mixed-sex time was in groups that included more girls than boys, and for others, most

set have a substantial impact. The final factor is the availability of someone in a setting that allows sexual interaction. Availability may hinge on quite personal characteristics, such as appearance and boldness. For all these reasons, some teenagers are much more advanced romantically than their classmates—or even than some 20-year-olds.

Overall, then, peers aid every major task of adolescence—from adjusting to the physical changes of puberty, to searching for identity, to forming romantic attachments. These findings help to put the notion of

"We slam danced 'til dawn, then we both got tattoos and had our noses pierced. It was so romantic"

Some Enchanted Evening In every generation, shared experiences bring couples closer together. The nature of those experiences varies from cohort to cohort and culture to culture.

of it was with older boys.) Related research found that these older adolescents spent about as much time thinking about the other sex as actually interacting (Richards et al., 1998). Obviously, heterosexual relationships are time-consuming and thought-provoking—something parents do not seem to understand and peers love to discuss.

The need to talk about the other sex is one reason adolescents continue to spend time with same-sex peers even after romantic relationships develop. One reason such talk is essential is that same-sex friends are chosen for their loyalty, but heterosexual intimacy is fraught with problems, espe-

cially the likelihood of rejection (Fischer, 1996; Furman & Wehner, 1994). Typically, early romances are intense but soon over (Feiring, 1996). Having supportive friends to cushion the pain, offer reassurance and solace, and validate emotions and self-worth is essential when rejection does occur.

For those adolescents who are gay or lesbian, added complications usually slow down romantic attachments. To begin with, there is the problem of realizing that one is, in fact, homosexual. One study of more than 3,000 ninth- to twelfth-grade teenagers found that only 0.5 percent identified themselves (confidentially) as gay or lesbian (Garofolo et al., 1999). Since estimates of the actual proportion of adult homosexuals range from 2 to 10 percent (depending on definitions), obviously many of these teenagers had not yet recognized their sexual orientation. Even including those who said they were bisexual (2 percent) and "not sure" (1.3 percent) did not bring the total to the probable 5 percent. Once a young person identifies as homosexual, other problems arise, including the difficulty of finding both romantic partners and loyal friends in whom to confide.

Especially in homophobic cultures, many young men with homosexual feelings deny these feelings altogether or try to change or conceal them by becoming heterosexually involved. Similarly, many young women who will later identify themselves as lesbian spend their teenage years relatively oblivious to, or in denial of, their sexual urges. One difference between the sexes here is that lesbian adolescents find it easier to establish strong friendships with same-sex heterosexual peers than homosexual teenage boys do. The probable reason is that female friendships generally tend to be close and intimate, whereas males are often wary of close friendships with other males, especially those whose sexual orientation is in doubt. In many cases, a homosexual boy's best friend is a girl, who is more at ease with his sexuality than a same-sex peer might be (D'Augelli & Hershberger, 1993; Savin-Williams, 1995).

peer pressure in perspective. Peers are more likely to complement the influence of parents during adolescence than to pull in the opposite direction and are more likely to moderate the push toward sexual intimacy than to prevent or rush it. The friendless adolescent is much more fragile than the one whose friends dress or talk in ways distinct from the parent's or culture's customs. As you will soon see, family and friends are both crucial in cushioning the serious emotional problems of adolescence, particularly depression and anger, which can lead to suicide or violent crime.

449

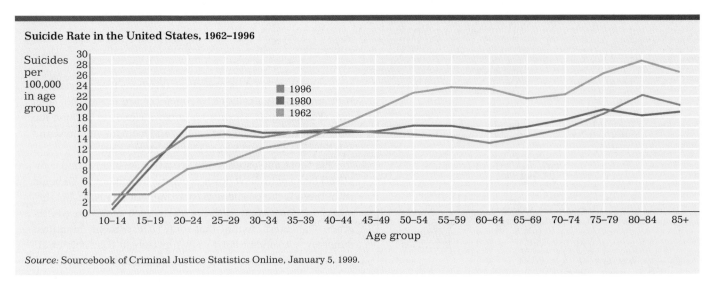

Suicide Rate in the United States, 1962–1996

Suicides per 100,000 in age group

1996
1980
1962

Age group

Source: Sourcebook of Criminal Justice Statistics Online, January 5, 1999.

Figure 16.2 So Much to Live For. A historical look at U.S. suicide statistics reveals two trends. First, although their rate is still below that of adults, teenagers are three times as likely to take their own lives as they once were. Second, this increase in teen suicide is part of a life-span trend. Whereas rates used to rise in middle age, today young adults are more suicidal and older adults less so. Among the possible reasons are that drug abuse, increased parental divorce, and other factors have made adolescence more problematic and that better health care and pension plans have made the later years easier.

❷ **Especially for Teachers:** Imagine that you teach more than 100 adolescents a semester and that you have no time for intense suicide prevention for everyone. Which of the following students would you be sure to talk privately with: a girl who is discouraged because she keeps getting average grades; a boy whose grade fell from an A to a D; a girl who has a light scratch across her wrist; a boy who plays on the basketball team, which just lost an important game?

suicidal ideation   Thinking about suicide, usually with some serious emotional and intellectual overtones.

ADOLESCENT SUICIDE

From a life-span perspective, teenagers are just beginning to explore life's possibilities. Even if they experience some troubling event—failing a class, ending a romance, fighting with a parent—surely they must realize that better days lie ahead. Not always. This logical perspective is not shared by suicidal adolescents, who are so overwhelmed with pain or anger that, for a few perilous hours or days, death seems their only solution.

But before discussing this issue, we need to destroy a prejudice: Adolescents under age 20 are much less likely to kill themselves than adults are. This is true now and was true in previous years, in North America and worldwide. Look at data for the United States, where year-by-year records are kept (see Figure 16.2).

These statistics run counter to the popular misconception that teenagers kill themselves at a high rate. Why does this mistaken idea persist? Four reasons account for it:

- The rate, low as it is, is triple the rate in 1960.
- Statistics often lump adolescents and young adults together, and 20- to 24-year-olds typically have a much higher suicide rate.
- Every adolescent suicide, particularly that of younger adolescents (298 children age 10 to 14 killed themselves in the United States in 1996; see Figure 16.3) is shocking and grabs our attention. Suicide in late adulthood, by contrast, rarely attracts publicity.
- Social prejudice tends to consider teenagers as problems, hence distorting the evidence. [Kachur et al., 1995; Males, 1996]

Suicidal Ideation

Since actual suicide is not common, why focus on this topic? Part of the reason is that adolescents think about suicide often—one of many signs that depression is prevalent during these years. A review of studies from many nations finds that **suicidal ideation**—that is, thinking about committing suicide—is so common among high school students that it might be considered normal (Diekstra, 1995).

In these studies, the rate of suicidal ideation ranged from 15 to 53 percent. The reason for that wide range seems more closely related to

Figure 16.3 Why? Suicide rates for adolescents have been rising over the past two decades, while rates for older individuals have been decreasing. Note, for example, that the rate for the youngest adolescents has doubled in that time, a cause for great concern.

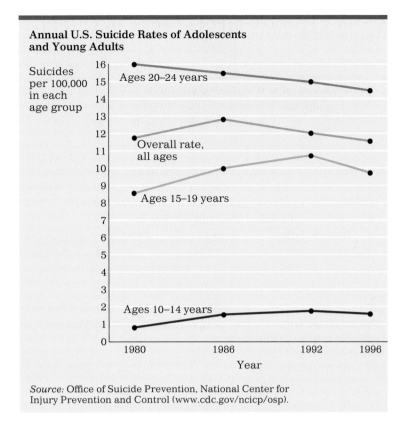

Annual U.S. Suicide Rates of Adolescents and Young Adults

Source: Office of Suicide Prevention, National Center for Injury Prevention and Control (www.cdc.gov/ncicp/osp).

the specifics of the research—for example, whether adolescents were asked if they had "ever" seriously thought about suicide or if they had done so "in the past year"—than to the specifics of the culture. In the United States, when high school students were asked about only one year, the rates were disturbingly high, especially among the younger girls (see Table 16.3). Research from many nations also finds that

table **16.3**	**Suicidal Ideation and Parasuicide, United States, 1998**			
	Seriously Considered Attempting Suicide	Planned Suicide	Parasuicide (Attempted Suicide)	Actual Suicide (Ages 14–18)
Overall	**21%**	**16%**	**8%**	**Less than .01% (about 9 per 100,000)**
Girls: 9th grade	29	20	15	
10th grade	30	24	14	**About 3 per 100,000**
11th grade	26	21	11	
12th grade	24	15	6	
Boys: 9th grade	16	13	6	
10th grade	15	11	4	**About 15 per 100,000**
11th grade	17	14	4	
12th grade	14	11	4	

Source: MMWR, August 14, 1998, based on a survey of 1,600 students from 23 states; actual suicide estimated from U.S. Bureau of the Census, 1998.

GENDER AND NATIONAL DIFFERENCES IN SUICIDE

At every age, the parasuicide rate is higher for females than for males. And at every age, the actual suicide rate is higher for males than for females. One reason is that when males attempt suicide, they use more lethal means—guns rather than pills—and hence it is harder to rescue them.

Males are more likely to commit suicide, and less likely to attempt it, in every nation of the world, but cultural factors influence age differences. As you can see from Figure 16.4, the data disprove at least one myth about adolescent suicide: The Japanese do not have the highest rate. Japan's teen suicide rate is actually among the lowest.

Cultural differences are even more apparent in subgroups within a larger society. In the United States, Native American teenagers have a suicide ideation and completion rate about twice the national norm. Among this group, protective factors, including being able to discuss problems with friends and being connected with family, are more potent at preventing suicide than risk factors (drug use, knowing someone who killed themselves) are at causing it (Borowsky et al., 1999).

In Australia, aboriginal youth are particularly vulnerable, in part because of cultural romanticism regarding sui-

Figure 16.4 International Suicide Rates. Comparing international suicide rates for adolescents is very difficult, in part because few nations report separate statistics for ages 15 to 19 and in part because rates rise or fall depending on historical factors, so the nations shown as having relatively high rates here may not have high rates in the year 2005. This chart does show, however, that a young man's risk of suicide depends more on his cultural context than on his age and sex.

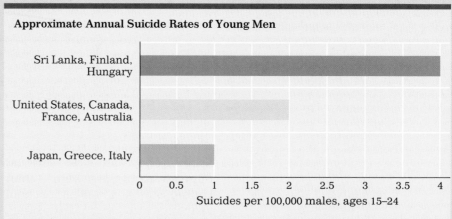

Approximate Annual Suicide Rates of Young Men

Suicides per 100,000 males, ages 15–24

Source: World Health Organization, 1995.

parasuicide A deliberate act of self-destruction that does not end in death. Parasuicide can be fleeting, such as a small knife mark on the wrist, or potentially lethal, such as swallowing an entire bottle of pills.

❶ Response for Teachers (from page 450): The first and the last youngsters are probably fine. Average grades are less worrisome than very high or very low grades, and being on a team is usually protection against isolation and serious drug taking. The middle two are more troubling—a sudden drop in grades or change in personality is a worrisome sign, and any form of parasuicide is a cry for help.

depression suddenly increases at puberty, especially among females (Cole et al., 1999; DeMan, 1999; Flisher, 1999; Wichstrom, 1999).

Parasuicide and Prevention

As you can see from the table, not only is suicidal ideation high in adolescence, but so is **parasuicide** (any deliberate act of self-destruction that does not result in death), with an international rate of between 6 and 20 percent.

Experts prefer the word "parasuicide" over "attempted suicide" or "failed suicide" because this term does not judge severity or intention (Diekstra et al., 1995). Particularly in adolescence, most self-destructive acts are carried out in a state of extreme emotional agitation and confusion. This means that intent may not be clear even to the self-destructive

"Fire Prevention" Depression can be an occasional feature of normal adolescence. When it is sustained, or when it is accompanied by loss of interest in social relationships or decline in school achievement, it may be a sign that the adolescent is at risk for suicide. Those around the troubled teen should take this seriously and take preventive action.

suicidal thoughts, talk, and attempts in other adolescents (Joiner, 1999).

For all of us, however, suicidal ideation and attempted suicide are "late clues," usually preceded by other signals that help is needed (Faberow, 1994). Reading these clues is everyone's "moral responsibility, something akin to omnipresent fire prevention" (Shneidman & Mandelkorn, 1994).

This moral responsibility extends to people at every point in the life span. Parents and teachers, as well as peers, can usually see the signs of teen suicide if they are alert to them. At every age, chronic depression, death of a close friend, drug abuse, loneliness, social rejection, and homosexuality correlate with suicide ideation and completion (Brent et al., 1999; Cochran & Mays, 2000; Faberow, 1994). This overall pattern helps to explain why older adult men in the United States who are widowers and now live alone are at high risk—and, again, alert family members of all ages can intervene. As with most problems that become apparent at every point in life, the social context in any culture can prevent or provoke the most destructive manifestations, from child neglect to adolescent drug abuse to suicide.

cide (Reser, 1998). Romanticism also underlies many **cluster suicides,** when a particular town or school sentimentalizes the "tragic end" of a teen suicide. Such publicity can trigger

cluster suicide A group of suicides that occur in the same community, school, or time period.

Which ethnic group's teenagers are most and least likely to commit suicide? In the spaces below, rank from 1 to 10 the following ethnic groups for suicide rates of their teens ages 15–19. See actual rankings and rates in Table 16.4.

	Males	Females
European American	___	___
African American	___	___
Hispanic American	___	___
Asian American	___	___
Native American	___	___

individuals themselves. Many who make a potentially lethal attempt not only are relieved that they did not die but soon wonder what they could possibly have been thinking.

Whether or not suicidal ideation eventually leads to a plan, a parasuicide, and then death depends on a multitude of factors that vary from community to community. In adolescence, five of the most influential are:

- Availability of lethal means, especially guns
- Parental supervision
- Alcohol and other drugs
- Gender
- Attitudes about suicide in the culture

We discuss the last two factors in A Life-Span View.

Rank for Teenagers Only Female suicide rates are always lower than male rates in every ethnic and age group, but the male–female ratio varies from six to one for African Americans to three to one for Asian Americans. Not shown here are variations by age, which also can be substantial. For example, among persons age 50 to 80, the Native American rates are lower than those of any other group, and the European American rates are higher.

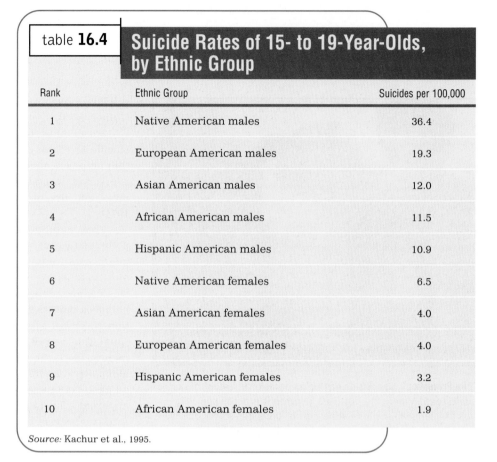

table **16.4**	Suicide Rates of 15- to 19-Year-Olds, by Ethnic Group	
Rank	Ethnic Group	Suicides per 100,000
1	Native American males	36.4
2	European American males	19.3
3	Asian American males	12.0
4	African American males	11.5
5	Hispanic American males	10.9
6	Native American females	6.5
7	Asian American females	4.0
8	European American females	4.0
9	Hispanic American females	3.2
10	African American females	1.9

Source: Kachur et al., 1995.

Figure 16.5 Boys Will Be Boys? While these data come from only one group—boys in a Wisconsin town—they exhibit two characteristics that are found no matter where such data are collected. First, the average number of police contacts per individual rises and then falls between ages 10 and 20. Second, almost every American boy has had nearly three police contacts (which often result in a warning, not an arrest) by age 20. Of course, not every transgressor is caught every time: The actual average number of delinquent acts is much higher.

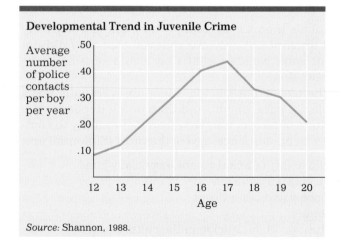

Developmental Trend in Juvenile Crime

Source: Shannon, 1988.

The first three factors make clear why the rate of youth suicide in North America and Europe has tripled since 1960: Adolescents have more guns, less adult supervision, and more alcohol and drugs because many parents are divorced, single, or working outside the home. In the United States, accessibility of guns is a major culprit; adolescent gunshot suicide increased by about 50 percent between 1980 and 1995. This accounts for virtually all of the recent increases (Kachur et al., 1995; Sickmund et al., 1997).

BREAKING THE LAW

Suicide is one indication of the emotional stress that many adolescents feel. Many psychologists believe that another indication is adolescent crime. Worldwide police statistics on arrests show that arrests are more likely to occur in the second decade of life than at any other time. More specifically, arrest rates rise rapidly at about age 12, peak at about age 16, and then decline slowly with every passing year (Rutter, 1998; Shoemaker, 1996; Smith, 1995; see Figure 16.5). In the United States, 44 percent of all arrests for serious crimes (crimes of violence, arson, or theft involving thousands of dollars) are of persons between the ages of 10 and 20 (Maguire & Pastore, 1997).

incidence How often a particular behavior or circumstance occurs.

prevalence How widespread within a population a particular behavior or circumstance is.

Incidence and Prevalence

The statistics in the preceding paragraph are **incidence** data; they are obtained by determining how all official arrests are distributed among the various age groups of arrestees. They tell us that adolescents have the highest criminal arrest rates, but they cannot tell us the **prevalence** of adolescent crime—that is, how widespread lawbreaking is among adolescents.

Suppose that, as some contend, a small minority of repeat offenders commit almost all the crimes. In this case, even though the incidence of adolescent crime might be high, the prevalence of lawbreaking would be quite low: Many adolescent crimes (high incidence) would then be committed by only a few lawbreakers (low prevalence) (Farrington, 1994). If this were true, and if adolescents on the path to a criminal career could be spotted early and then imprisoned, the *incidence* of adolescent crime would plummet, because those few potential multiple offenders could no longer commit their many crimes. Indeed, this supposition and strategy lead to attempts to "crack down" and "put away" young criminals.

However, such attempts do not work, because the supposition is false: Adolescents are far less often career criminals than adults are. Juveniles are mostly experimenters; they have not yet settled on any career, not even crime. Most have no more than one serious brush with the law, and even chronic offenders typically have a mix of offenses—some minor, some serious, and usually only one violent crime. In fact, of every 1,000 youths who are arrested at least once, only 13 (1.3 percent) have committed more than one violent offense. In other words, serious adolescent crimes are committed by many one-time offenders rather than by a few multiple offenders. The high incidence of adolescent crime is caused by its high prevalence, not by a few very active delinquents (Snyder, 1997).

The actual prevalence of adolescent crime is even greater than official records report, especially if all acts of "juvenile delinquency" (major or minor lawbreaking by youths under age 18) are considered (Rutter et al., 1999). Two reasons that actual prevalence rates are higher than arrest statistics indicate are that many crimes never come to the attention of the police, and that many police officers do not arrest a young first-time offender. As an example, according to one confidential survey, only 20 percent of adolescents who were self-admitted repeat offenders had been arrested even once (Henggeler, 1989).

Partly because few young offenders are arrested, law enforcement data on the gender and ethnic prevalences of delinquency are questionable (Rutter et al., 1999). Official U.S. juvenile arrest statistics show that males are three times as likely to be arrested as females, that African Americans are three times as likely to be arrested as European Americans, and that European Americans are three times as likely to be arrested as Asian Americans (U.S. Department of Justice, 1998). But longitudinal studies that ask teenagers, confidentially, about their own misbehavior find that most admit breaking the law in ways that could have led to arrest. Such confidential studies find much smaller gender and ethnic differences than those reflected in official arrest data.

When all illegal acts—including such minor infractions as underage drinking; disorderly conduct; breaking a community curfew; playing

❓ **Especially for Social Scientists:** Crime prevention is a hot political issue, but few people understand a developmental perspective. If you had unlimited funds to do research in one small town, with the goal of delinquency prevention, would you begin with police data, school records, parent reports, or interviews with teenagers? Would your study be longitudinal or cross-sectional? Would you have a control group?

PREVENTING A LIFE OF CRIME

A useful distinction can be made between the many lawbreakers who are **adolescent-limited offenders,** whose criminal activity stops by age 21, and the few who are **life-course-persistent offenders,** who later become career criminals (Moffitt, 1997).

Most life-course-persistent offenders are recognizable long before adulthood. They are among the earliest of their cohort to have sex, drink alcohol, and smoke cigarettes; are among the least involved in school activities and most involved in "hanging out" with older, lawbreaking youths; and are arrested many times for increasingly serious offenses throughout their teen years. They are antisocial in preschool and elementary school. Even earlier, they show signs of brain damage—perhaps being slow to express ideas in language, or being hyperactive, or having poor emotional control (Farrington, 1994; Rutter et al., 1998; Sampson et al., 1997).

While such youngsters are at high risk and while almost all career criminals have this ominous history, only about half of the children with these characteristics become serious criminals. Intervention measures—a particularly cohesive neighborhood, an especially effective school, a supportive peer group, a stable family, or a best friend who discourages crime—can halt the progression in early adolescence (Yoshikawa, 1994). If this fails, or if neighborhood, school, and peers all encourage serious crime, then intensive intervention that teaches life-course-persistent teenagers new ways of coping with their long-standing biological, cognitive, and psychosocial problems may help, especially if parents and teachers are taught as well (Rutter et al., 1998).

adolescent-limited offender   A juvenile delinquent who is likely to become law-abiding once adulthood is attained.

life-course-persistent offender   A juvenile delinquent who is likely to continue a pattern of lawbreaking even when adolescence is over. Such individuals usually started their pattern before the teen years.

In general, a developmental perspective always emphasizes primary prevention:

> Rather than waiting until violence has been learned and practiced, and then devoting increased resources to hiring policemen, building more prisons, and sentencing three-time offenders to life imprisonment, it would be more effective to redirect the resources to early violence prevention programs, particularly for young children and early adolescents. [Slaby & Eron, 1994]

Intensive, residential incarceration in a prison or reform school is needed only for a few. For most delinquents, sending them away from home and neighborhood weakens the protective social bonds that most offenders have (Sampson & Laub, 1993). Prison can actually breed delinquency if it means confining teenagers among peers who prize possessions more than people and who survive by means of deceit and self-centeredness rather than trust.

Researchers began to look for early signs of risk for life-course-persistent delinquency several years ago. They stopped because labeling a particular young boy (maleness was one of the risk factors) "high risk" would stigmatize the innocent and would unfairly target minorities, children of single mothers, and the poor (other risk factors). Obviously, such sociological categories are unfair when used to predict the future of individuals.

Nonetheless, some individuals (not groups) show neurological, genetic, and attachment signs of later violent crime (Moffitt, 1993). Children who have been abused or neglected, who have few friends, who are early substance users, or who are bullies are at higher risk (Rutter et al., 1998; Woodward & Fergusson, 1999). We can make fairly accurate risk assessments by age 10, but if early diagnosis leads to early punishment, it obviously is wrong. If, instead, it leads to early prevention, it may save what would otherwise be wasted lives.

hooky; ticket or fare cheating at a movie, stadium, club, or train; and underage buying of cigarettes—are included, virtually every adolescent is a repeat offender. In addition, most self-report studies (at least in North America, Great Britain, Australia, and New Zealand) reveal

Protection or Prejudice? Many question whether adolescent arrest statistics accurately reflect the true ethnic and gender ratios of juvenile delinquents.

❷ *Observational Quiz (see answer page 458): From what you see here, what raised the officers' suspicion, what was the crime, and what is the punishment?*

that more serious crimes—such as property damage, stealing, causing bodily harm, and buying or selling illegal drugs—are also common, being committed at least once before age 20 by more than half of all boys, with lower rates for girls (Rutter et al., 1998). Thus, again, prevalence is high for both minor infractions and more serious crimes. As one researcher concludes, "Numerous rigorous self-report studies of representative samples have now documented that it is statistically aberrant to refrain from crime during adolescence" (Moffitt, 1997).

The victims of adolescent crime also tend to be teenagers—a fact that is much more apparent in confidential surveys than in official statistics. The overall victimization rate of adolescents is two to three times that of adults, and the victimization rate for violent crimes (assault, rape, murder) shows an even greater ratio of teenagers compared to adults (Hashima & Finkelhor, 1997). (See Appendix A.)

Research in the United States, Britain, and Iceland finds that a major risk factor for becoming a violent criminal is being a victim of violence, and vice versa (Bjarnason et al., 1999). Perhaps as a consequence, teenagers who carry a weapon are likely to view doing so as defensive. Unfortunately, offense and defense usually go hand in hand, making homicide the leading nonaccidental cause of teenage death. (See the Changing Policy box.)

CONCLUSION

As this unit (Chapters 14–16) draws to a close, let us look again quickly at the period from age 10 to age 20. Except perhaps for the very first months of life, no other developmental period is characterized by such multifaceted and compelling biological changes. Nor are developing

❶ **Response for Social Scientists (from page 455):** The answers to the last two questions are easy: Given that life-course-persistent and adolescent-limited delinquency look similar, you need a longitudinal study. And given that many solutions have been tried but are unproved, you would need a control group. The first question is harder—where to start. Inaccuracies and omissions would come from all four sources. Perhaps the best way is to begin not with teenagers but with elementary school children.

❶ *Answer to Observational Quiz (from page 457):* *If you think the brown bag raised the suspicion, you are wrong, because the same bag carried by a girl, especially a middle-class girl in her suburban neighborhood, would go unnoticed. Even a group of girls, or of middle-class boys, might not attract attention. If you thought the crime was beer purchased underage, you may be partly correct, but how does that explain why the officers seem to be checking everyone's I.D.? And if you thought the punishment is kneeling on the ground, with hands clasped behind the neck and feet crossed, let's hope that this is the whole story and that arrest and imprisonment are not in these young men's future.*

persons at any other age likely to experience a more fascinating, unnerving, and potentially confusing sequence of intellectual and social transitions. The adolescent's developmental tasks—to reach adult size and sexuality, to adjust to changed educational expectations and intellectual patterns, to develop autonomy from parents and intimacy with friends, to achieve a sense of identity and purpose—are too complex to be accomplished without surprises. No wonder every young person, in every family and culture, experiences disruption of some sort (Arnett, 1999; Kroger, 2000; Schlegal & Barry, 1991).

As you have seen, most adolescents, most families, and most cultures survive this transition fairly well. Parents and children bicker and fight, but they still respect and love each other. Teenagers skip school, eat unwisely, drink too much, experiment with drugs, break laws, feel depressed, rush into sexual activity, conform to peer pressure, disregard their parents' wishes—but all these behaviors typically stay within limits. They do not occur too often or last too long; they do not lead to lifelong or life-threatening harm. For most young people, the teenage years overall are happy ones, during which they escape potentially serious problems and discover the rewards of maturity.

Unfortunately, while all adolescents have some minor difficulties, those with at least one serious problem often have several others as well (Cairns & Cairns, 1994). For instance, girls who become mothers by age 16 are also more likely to be from troubled families, to leave school, and to experiment with hard drugs. Boys who become chronic criminals also tend to be alienated from their families, failing in school, drug abusing, and brain-damaged (Rutter et al., 1998). Suicidal adolescents typically have been heartbreakingly lonely and seriously depressed for years with inadequate social support from family and friends (Flisher, 1999).

In almost every case, these problems stem from earlier developmental events. They begin with genetic vulnerability and prenatal insults and continue with family disruptions and discord in early childhood and then with learning disabilities and aggressive or withdrawn behavior in elementary school—all within a community and culture that does not provide adequate intervention. With the inevitable stresses of puberty, problems become worse, more obvious, and more resistant to change.

Fortunately, an encouraging theme emerges: No developmental path is set in stone by previous events; adolescents are, by nature, innovators, idealists, and risk takers, open to new patterns, goals, and lifestyles. Research on effective schools, on teenage sex, on the positive role of friendship, and on identity achievement shows that every problem can be adolescent-limited. Young people can find a path that leads them away from the restrictions and burdens of their past, alive and ready for their future. That path leads to adulthood, as the next chapters describe.

SUMMARY

THE SELF AND IDENTITY

1. According to Erikson, the psychosocial crisis of adolescence is identity versus role confusion. Ideally, adolescents resolve this crisis by developing both their own uniqueness and their relationship to the larger society, establishing a sexual, political, moral, and vocational identity in the process.

2. Sometimes the pressure to resolve the identity crisis is too great, and instead of exploring alternative roles, young people foreclose on their options, taking on someone else's values wholesale. They may foreclose the search by seizing on their parents' values, or they may choose the values of a cult or hero.

3. Others may take on a negative identity, defying the expectations of family and community. Some teenagers experience identity diffusion, making few commitments to goals, principles, or a particular self-definition. Many young people declare a moratorium, deciding to wait before settling on a mature identity.

4. In industrial and postindustrial societies, social change is rapid, and identity possibilities are endless. Consequently, identity achievement can be more difficult, especially for those—such as members of minority groups—who are caught between divergent cultural patterns.

FAMILY AND FRIENDS

5. Parents are an important influence on adolescents: The generation gap within families is usually not very large, especially with regard to basic values. Children tend not to stray too far from parental beliefs and ideals, and parents have a personal stake in minimizing whatever conflicts there are.

6. Conflict can emerge in parent–adolescent relationships, however, typically arising in early adolescence and taking the form of bickering over such matters as hair, neatness, and clothing.

7. In addition to conflict, other important aspects of the parent–adolescent relationship are communication, support, connectiveness, and, especially, control.

8. The peer group is a vital source of information and encouragement. The adolescent subculture provides a buffer between the world of children and the world of adults, allowing, for example, a social context for the beginning of heterosexual relationships. Although peer pressure can lead adolescents into trouble, its influence is often constructive.

9. While most close friendships in early adolescence are with members of the same sex, by late adolescence friendships typically include members of the opposite sex, as romantic relationships begin to develop. These relationships augment, rather than replace, same-sex friendships.

ADOLESCENT SUICIDE

10. Suicidal ideation is fairly common among high school students, with a small minority engaging in deliberate acts of self-destruction (parasuicide). Wide variation in teenage suicide rates is evident among ethnic and national groups, but, worldwide, girls are more likely to attempt suicide, boys are more likely to complete it, and teenagers are less likely to kill themselves than adults are.

BREAKING THE LAW

11. Lawbreaking is more common in adolescence than in any other period of the life span. Almost all adolescents engage in some delinquency, but relatively few are arrested and even fewer become life-course-persistent criminals. Adolescents are often victims of crimes as well.

12. Prevention of adolescent crime includes identifying children at risk, who have few friends, are early substance abusers, are bullies, or are abused or neglected. Not all adolescent lawbreakers are equally troubled, and the most effective intervention occurs years before a violent offense is committed.

CONCLUSION

13. Adolescence, even more than other stages of life, offers opportunities for growth as well as destruction. If the groundwork has been well laid, most developing persons are adequately prepared for adulthood.

KEY TERMS

identity (435)
identity versus role confusion (435)
identity achievement (436)
foreclosure (436)
negative identity (436)
identity diffusion (436)
identity moratorium (437)
generation gap (440)
generational stake (441)
bickering (441)

parental monitoring (442)
peer pressure (445)
suicidal ideation (450)
parasuicide (452)
cluster suicide (453)
incidence (455)
prevalence (455)
adolescent-limited offender (456)
life-course-persistent offender (456)

KEY QUESTIONS

1. What is the difference between foreclosure and negative identity?

2. What is the difference between identity diffusion and moratorium?

3. In what ways can a society or culture help adolescents form their identities?

4. Why is identity formation especially difficult for minority-group adolescents?

5. What factors correlate with parent–adolescent conflict? Why does each lead to disruption?

6. How do peer and friendship groups aid teenagers?

7. What is peer pressure, and how does it affect most adolescents' behavior?

8. What gender differences in suicidal ideation, parasuicide, and completed suicide exist? What might explain these differences?

9. What do the incidence and prevalence of delinquency tell us about preventing serious crime?

10. How and why do public attitudes about adolescent suicide and adolescent crime differ from the facts?

11. *In Your Experience* Was your adolescence difficult, dangerous, and self-destructive? Why or why not?

BIOSOCIAL

Physical Growth

Sometime between the ages of 8 and 14, puberty begins with increases in various hormones that trigger a host of changes. Within a year of the hormonal increases, the first perceptible physical changes appear—enlargement of the girl's breasts and the boy's testes. About a year later, a growth spurt begins, when boys and girls gain in height, weight, and musculature.

Sexual Maturation

Toward the end of puberty, menarche in girls and ejaculation in boys signal reproductive potential. On the whole, males become taller than females and develop deeper voices and characteristic patterns of facial and body hair. Females become wider at the hips; breast development continues for several years. The growing bodies of adolescents trigger much stress and confusion, especially if changes occur much earlier or later than one's peers, or if the family and culture are not supportive. Some teenagers, especially girls, become vulnerable to sexual abuse and/or unhealthy dieting. Others, especially boys, use drugs at an age or dose that is harmful to healthy growth.

COGNITIVE

Adolescent Thinking

Adolescent thought can deal with the possible as well as the actual, thanks to a newly emerging ability to think hypothetically, to reason deductively, and to explain theoretically. At the same time, adolescent egocentrism, along with feelings of uniqueness and invincibility, can cloud teenagers' judgment, as well as make them extraordinarily self-absorbed.

Education

The specific intellectual advancement of each teenager depends greatly on education. Each culture and each school emphasizes different subjects, values, and modes of thinking, a variation that makes some adolescents much more sophisticated in their thoughts and behavior than others. The interplay between education and egocentrism helps explain why some teenagers are at greater risk for STDs, AIDS, and pregnancy than others. Newer forms of sex education that take into account the teenager's need for social interaction and practical experience have successfully reduced adolescent pregnancy and increased condom use.

PSYCHOSOCIAL

Identity

One of the major goals of adolescence is self-understanding and then identity achievement. Achieving identity can be affected by personal factors—including relationships with family and peers—the nature of the society, and the economic and political circumstances of the times. Identity achievement can be especially problematic for members of a minority group in a multiethnic society.

Peers and Parents

The peer group becomes increasingly important in fostering independence and interaction, particularly with members of the other sex. Parents and young adolescents are often at odds over issues centering on the child's increased assertiveness or lack of self-discipline. These difficulties usually diminish as teenagers become more mature and parents allow more autonomy. Depression and thoughts about suicide are common in adolescence, especially among girls, although boys are more likely to actually complete a suicide. Despite common beliefs to the contrary, teenagers are less likely to commit suicide or, for that matter, to abuse drugs or give birth than young adults are. While most adolescents break the law in some way, the minority who commit serious crimes often come from a troubled family and a debilitating social context. More supportive communities can moderate these problems, and a responsive and aware pattern of child rearing can prevent serious delinquency.

PART VI

Early Adulthood

As young children, we look forward to the day when we will be "all grown up," imagining that when we attain adult size, we will automatically master the roles, privileges, and responsibilities of adulthood. As young teenagers, we likewise impatiently await our high school graduation or 18th or 21st birthday. We assume that independence, and the competence to cope with it, will be bestowed when we arrive at these "official" milestones.

But young adults, who must make their own decisions about career goals, intimate relationships, social commitments, and moral conduct, usually find these aspects of independence, though exciting, far from easy. This is especially true today because the array of lifestyle choices seems so vast and varied. No matter which roles young adults choose or how thoughtfully and eagerly they strive to play them, they are bound to be confronted with stresses, setbacks, and second thoughts. Today's 20-year-olds often postpone marriage or parenthood for a decade or more. Yet for most young adults, problems faced and solved, and limitations accepted or overcome, make the years from ages 20 to 35 exhilarating. Young adults often feel they are living to the fullest. The next three chapters describe how they cope with the engrossing, multidimensional realities of early adulthood.

Early Adulthood:
Biosocial Development

CHAPTER 17

In terms of biosocial development, early adulthood, from age 20 to roughly age 35, can be considered the prime of life. Bodies are stronger, taller, and healthier than during any other period. The beginning of young adulthood is the best time for hard physical work, for problem-free reproduction, and for peak athletic performance. Although some physiological declines are evident by age 30 or so, during young adulthood most real declines in health and strength are caused not by "normal aging," but by poor choices. Both normal and unusual development are described in this chapter.

GROWTH, STRENGTH, AND HEALTH

Girls usually reach their maximum height by age 16 and boys by age 18, with the exception of a few late-maturing boys who undergo final skeletal growth in their early 20s (Berhman, 1992). Muscle growth and fat accumulation continue into the early 20s, when women attain their full breast and hip size and men reach full shoulder and upper-arm size.

Because more of their body mass is composed of muscle, not fat, men are typically stronger than women. For both sexes, however, physical strength generally increases during the 20s, reaches a peak at about age 30, and then decreases (Sinclair, 1989). Young adults are better than any other age group at, say, running up a flight of stairs, lifting a heavy load, or gripping an object with maximum force.

All the body systems, including the digestive, respiratory, circulatory, and sexual-reproductive systems, function at an optimum level in young adulthood. Consequently, visits to the doctor between ages 15 and 44 are less than half what they will be later in life (National Center for Health Statistics, 1999). To be specific, the typical younger man sees a doctor three times a year, compared to an older man's ten visits; for women, the comparable numbers are six and eleven. Those young adult visits are not usually because of sickness, but because of injuries (often drug- or sports-related) or pregnancy. Even the common cold is less frequent in early adulthood than in any other part of the life span.

These findings are for the United States, where about a third of young adults have no health insurance. This is not the principal reason for the age difference, however. In a mammoth survey, 73 percent of young adults rated their health as very good or excellent, and only 5 percent rated it as fair or poor (Benson & Marano, 1994).

The older a person is, the longer it takes for homeostatic adjustments to occur, making it harder for older bodies to adapt to, and recover from, physical stress. Imagine that a younger and an older athlete, both equally fit, compete at the same intensity for the same duration. Then the older adult's heart rate, breathing, blood pH (acidity), and blood glucose (sugar) will take longer to reach peak levels and longer still to return to normal when the game is over. Similarly, older adults have more difficulty adjusting to work that is physiologically stressful.

These changes might mean that the average 35-year-old can no longer skip a night's sleep and still function adequately or can no longer bounce back quickly from a day of unusually heavy exertion. Such effects are apparent even during early adulthood; by late adulthood, less efficient homeostasis is obvious in dozens of ways, affecting each organ as well as overall functioning, and making overheating or a chill or exertion a potentially lethal event (Holliday, 1995).

The ability to bounce back from exertion is often a matter of concern in sexual activity, particularly for men who equate speed of recovery after orgasm and sexual vigor. As with many other aspects of homeostasis, however, some age-related accommodations are all that is needed. (See A Life-Span View.)

Reserve Capacity

This overall senescence and slowdown might seem frightening to college students just at the start of early adulthood. Fortunately, the subjective experience of senescence is much less daunting than one might imagine from the data on the body's decline with age. In normal day-to-day life, most adults of all ages feel that their bodies are quite strong and capable, not much less efficient than they were 10 years earlier. And for the most part, this perception is correct, not simply wishful thinking.

In fact, if they maintain their bodies adequately, most adults can function quite well until at least age 70. The reason is that the declines of aging affect **organ reserve,** the extra capacity that each organ has for responding to unusually stressful events or conditions that demand intense or prolonged effort (Fries & Crapo, 1981; Holliday, 1995). We seldom need this capacity, so gradual deficits in organ reserve go unnoticed. Thus, although 50-year-olds are somewhat slower than 20-year-olds at, say, running up several flights of stairs (because the reserve capacity of their hearts and lungs is not as great as it once was), they move from place to place with nearly equal ease in normal activity. Similarly, while a pregnant woman in her late 30s might find her kidneys or her blood pressure or her lung capacity more noticeably affected than when she was pregnant in her early 20s, she also finds that when she is not pregnant, these organs function very well.

Our bodies have a kind of muscle reserve as well. Few adults develop, or ever need to use, all the muscle capacity that they could attain during their years of peak strength. Maximum strength *potential* typically begins to decline at about age 30, with leg muscles affected more than arms and hands. However, this occurs so gradually that 50-year-olds can expect to retain 90 percent of the strength they had at age 20, and the 10 percent that is lost is rarely missed (McArdle et al., 1991).

organ reserve The extra capacity of the heart, lungs, and other organs that makes it possible for the body to withstand moments of intense or prolonged stress. With age, organ reserve is gradually depleted, but the rate of depletion depends on the individual's general state of health.

Man of Steel Declines in physical strength are irrelevant in modern-day occupations, even in the steel industry, where brute strength and unflagging endurance were once essential. Today's hard-hatted steel workers can perform most of their jobs with their fingertips.

A LIFE-SPAN VIEW

SEX IN BODY AND MIND

At every age, both male and female bodies follow a similar sequence of sexual activation: arousal, peak excitement, release through orgasm, refraction, and recovery, although there are sex differences as well. During the early years of manhood, sexual arousal and excitement (which includes both a faster heartbeat and penile erection) can occur very quickly and in response not only to a receptive partner but also to many other stimuli—even an idea, a photograph, or a passing remark. Typically, orgasm during sexual activity also occurs fairly quickly.

For both younger and older men, orgasm usually is followed by a refractory period, during which sexual arousal is not possible. For some young men, the refractory period may be very brief—a matter of minutes. Older men often need more explicit or prolonged stimulation to initiate sexual desire and excitement (Everaerd et al., 2000). In addition, as men age, more time elapses between the beginning of excitement and full erection, between erection and ejaculation, and between orgasm and the end of the refractory period, which may last for hours.

That these changes are in part physiological, not merely psychological or social, is suggested by research on lower animals such as rats and monkeys. When caged with a receptive female, young male rats are twice as sexually active as middle-aged rats, which, in turn, are more active than older rats, some of whom fail to mate at all (Hokao et al., 1993). As with all age-related biological patterns, the overall slowing down is universal, but the rate of decline varies. Specific events (such as a new sex partner) can temporarily speed up responses, in rats as well as in humans.

Age-related trends in sexual responsiveness are not as clear-cut for women (or female rats) as they are for men (Masters et al., 1994). In general, however, it seems that, as women mature from early adolescence toward middle adulthood, arousal and orgasm during lovemaking become more likely to occur (Rutter & Rutter, 1993). Since female bodies are similar to male bodies in other age-related ways, developmentalists are puzzled by the disparity in male and female patterns. Why are 40-year-old men slowing down sexually while 40-year-old women seem to be speeding up?

Several explanations have been suggested. It may be that the age-related slowing of the man's responses makes the sex act last longer. No longer troubled by premature ejaculation,

he has more time to give his partner the stimulation she needs to reach orgasm, so her sexual response increases in reaction to his slowdown. A related possible explanation for a woman's increased sexual responsiveness may be that, with experience, both partners have learned which aspects of their lovemaking intensify the woman's sexual responses and have come to focus on them.

Another explanation is primarily cultural. In most nations, young men are taught to be lustful, sex-driven, and uncontrolled, so their sexual expression at first is rapid and self-centered, only gradually accommodating the emotional aspects of a relationship. Their repeated orgasms are seen as "great sex" because they have been conditioned to believe that "more is better." Young women, by contrast, are taught that sex is "violent, victimizing, and reflective of individual morality" (Lear, 1997), so they are conditioned to say no to men, repressing their own desire and overemphasizing control of the entire experience. As a result, it may take years for women to acknowledge and appreciate their sexuality, and consequently to experience orgasm on a regular basis (Daniluk, 1998). This means that healthy sexuality emerges later in a woman's life, preceded by much "unlearning" (Johnston, 1997).

A final possible explanation comes from the ethological perspective (Weisfeld, 1998). According to this theory, males have more children, and hence pass on their genes more often (an evolutionary goal), if they are sexually promiscuous; in contrast, women need to restrain their sexual urges in young adulthood in order to concentrate on successful pregnancy, birth, breast-feeding, and child care. Therefore, as aging makes reproduction less likely for women, their sexual passions can increase.

No matter which explanation makes most sense to you, they all confirm a generality that applies to every aspect of physiological change during adulthood. How a person thinks about whatever changes he or she experiences is as important as the objective reality of physiological decline. Indeed, the "social and cultural environment determine sexual expression and the meaning of sexual experience," with genital arousal not necessarily connected to the subjective experience of sexual desire or pleasure, which is not reliably correlated with chronological age (Everaerd et al., 2000). When it comes to sex, how old you are is not as important as where you have been and whom you are with.

table **17.2**	**Heart Functioning**				
	Age				
	20s	30s	40s	50s	60s
Average maximum heart rate					
Men	195	190	182	175	162
Women	188	185	178	172	152
Average resting heart rate					
Men	75	75	75	75	75
Women	72	72	72	72	70

Source: Brooks & Fahey, 1984.

Consequently, in developed countries, where hard manual work is not a daily necessity, a healthy 50-year-old can perform virtually all the physical tasks of everyday living as well as a 20-year-old can. Moreover, since few adults today develop their full muscle potential, it is quite possible for a 50-year-old who begins working out to become stronger than ever.

The most important muscle of all, the heart, shows a similar pattern. The average maximum heart rate—the number of times the heart can beat per minute under extreme stress—declines steadily as the heart's reserve capacity is reduced with age. But the resting heart rate remains very stable, as can be seen in Table 17.2. Once again, although peak performance declines, normal functioning is not affected by aging until late adulthood.

Even in the smaller changes of aging, such as the wearing down of the teeth or loss of cartilage in the knees, serious reductions are not normally reached until late adulthood. As one expert explains, "A remarkable feature of aging is that various organs and structures have evolved to 'last a lifetime'" (Holliday, 1995). Thus, age-related biological changes during the first decades of adulthood are normally of little consequence. There are two notable exceptions to this generalization: athletic performance and reproduction.

Sports Stars and the Rest of Us

Minor differences in strength, reaction time, and lung efficiency can have a significant impact on professional athletes—as well as on serious weekend players. Athletic performance peaks somewhere between ages 15 and 35, with variations occurring not only person by person and sport by sport but also skill by skill within a single sport (Ericsson, 1990).

For example, a detailed study (Schultz et al., 1994) of the records of every professional baseball player who was active in 1965 and played for 10 or more years found that overall performance on various skills rose fairly quickly from age 19 to about age 27 and then declined. Within this general performance curve, variations were noted. Stolen bases, for example, peaked at age 27, pitching wins at age 28, earned run average at age 29, and fielding percentage (which is enhanced by experience) at age 30.

Roberto Alomar, Top Athlete at 33 Professional athletes are one of the few groups for whom the bodily declines of early adulthood may have significant consequences. However, depending on the sport and the particular skills involved, the benefits of experience and vigorous conditioning may permit superior athletes to perform at the top of their games well into their 30s.

On most skills, elite players, particularly Hall-of-Famers, peaked somewhat later than players of average ability. The superstars also sustained their high level of performance longer. The reason was probably not that their bodies were unusually quick or skilled, but that their experience enhanced their cognition and thus made them better players. Other research finds that superior performance does not correlate with the small differences in reaction time or specific skill among the members of any group of professional athletes (Shea & Powell, 1996). Instead, something more cerebral probably makes the final, crucial difference.

In general, performance in sports that demand vigorous gross motor skills peaks in the 20s; in those that demand fine motor skills, in the 30s; but in both types, ten years or so of preparation are needed to become a superstar. As a result, "peak performance is attained many years after peak physical maturity is reached" (Ericsson, 1996).

The authors of the baseball study offer a consoling thought for those of us who are on "the downward slope of the performance curve": Since few people are so fit that they achieve their peak levels in their 20s, their best performance could still lie ahead (Schultz et al., 1994).

There is another consolation, for athletes as well as for everyone else: The impact of aging depends on lifestyle, on the decisions made each day about consumption and exertion. Maintaining good health habits and a rigorous training schedule extends the years of high-level performance. For instance, in sedentary people, heart-lung capacity diminishes at about 10 percent per decade after age 25. However, for those who exercise regularly, the decline is much slower—between 2 and 5 percent per decade (Hagberg, 1987).

Indeed, conditioned older athletes perform so much better than most unconditioned younger persons that they are an inspiration, not a discouraging example of inevitable physical decline. Practiced marathoners in their 60s have run 26 miles at under 8 minutes a mile, while many sedentary 20- and 30-year-olds can't even run around the block. If these young adult couch-potatoes began walking briskly for a few hours a week, running a few miles would eventually be no problem.

THE SEXUAL-REPRODUCTIVE SYSTEM

The 20s and 30s are the most likely time for adults to enter a long-term sexual relationship and to decide to have children. Biological changes are pervasive in the sexual-reproductive system during young adulthood. These changes have very little effect on sexual pleasure, but they do affect the probability and frequency of parenthood.

Sex and Contraception

In both men and women, sexual responsiveness, sexual preferences, and sexual orientation vary for many reasons—innate predisposition, childhood experiences, and cultural taboos among them, as well as daily circumstances, such as sexual opportunities, stress, and fatigue (Everaerd et al., 2000). Even sexual intercourse, or coitus, though it may seem straightforward, is complicated by many factors:

Coitus is undertaken not only for pleasure and procreation but also to degrade, control and dominate, to punish and to hurt, to overcome loneliness and boredom, to rebel against authority, to establish sexual competence, or to show that sexual access was possible (to "score") for duty, for adventure, to obtain favors such as a better position or role in life, or even for livelihood. [Levin, 1994]

As you remember from Chapter 15, most, but by no means all, young adults in developed nations have their first experiences with sexual intercourse by age 18. In early adulthood, sexual activity increases in both prevalence and incidence, with fewer people remaining virgins and more people regularly engaging in sexual intercourse. The issue that first arose in adolescence—the need for protection against sexually transmitted diseases (STDs) and unwanted pregnancy—is more likely to be discussed and dealt with by young adults. For example, in a survey of college students (Lear, 1997), one young man said.:

> I actually have psyched myself out about it. I'll do the old "1 in 150. You may not get AIDS but you could get something else really nasty. Not all STDs are curable. Even if they are, they are not that fun." And so I just was like, "Save yourself the anguish and take 2 seconds [to put on a condom]." [Lear, 1997]

Note that this young man is using his formal operational thinking, balancing benefits and costs of condom use and even considering the odds that one sexual partner in 150 will be HIV-positive. And one young woman explained:

> If you might have sex with them, you might as well be open about it. You're gonna be naked. If they're gonna be standing there naked with someone else, I don't think it's gonna be that serious of an issue to bring a condom. I figure if they're gonna be that open with somebody, then you might as well be open all the way with everything else. [Lear, 1997]

These statements do not mean that young adults always use protection or that discussion about birth control is never awkward, last-minute, or unsuccessful. However, with maturity, individuals are more likely to be in a committed relationship and to recognize their responsibilities as adults. In every nation of the world, the percentage of women who are at risk for unplanned pregnancy but who do not use contraception is much lower in early adulthood than in late adolescence (Glei, 1999; see Figure 17.2). Contraceptive use increases and abortion decreases over the years of early adulthood, as people become more likely to think and plan.

Figure 17.2 Failure to Use Contraception. This chart shows the percentages of sexually active women in various age groups in the United States who do not want to get pregnant but do not consistently use contraception.

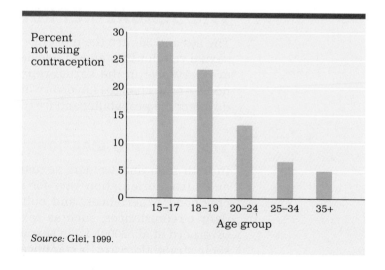

Source: Glei, 1999.

Fertility

Most young adults worry more about having children too soon than about waiting too long. In theory, they are right: Many women can bear a first child in their 40s, and many men can procreate at any age. They are right in practice, as well, especially with regard to such critical variables as marital stability, parental maturity, and financial well-being. The last factor is particularly salient today, unlike a century ago. To raise just one child from birth to age 18, the average U.S. family spends about $150,000. In general, older couples are financially better equipped to become parents. (See Table 17.3.)

However, advanced age is a disadvantage when it comes to fertility, the most basic prerequisite for parenthood. Overall, about 15 percent of all couples experience **infertility,** which is usually defined as the failure to conceive a child after a year or more of intercourse without contraception. The older a couple is, the more likely they are to experience infertility. About one couple in twenty is infertile when the woman is in her early 20s, one in seven has this problem when the woman is in her early 30s. Of those who try to conceive when the woman is in her 40s, about half fail and a higher proportion of the "successful" pregnancies end in miscarriage, stillbirth, or other reproductive problems (Barbieri, 1999).

Male Infertility

Men can be infertile for dozens of reasons. The most common is that they do not produce a sufficient number of live, motile (active) sperm; this is the primary cause of infertility in one-fourth of all infertile couples (Barbieri, 1999). Actually, in each ejaculate, every normal man produces millions of sperm that are dead, malformed, or of low motility, but

A Mature Commitment Today the promise "To have and to hold" is one that often is not made until after age 30. Although this postponement of marriage may increase the chances of marital success, to many couples it may also increase the chances of infertility.

❷ *Observational Quiz (answer on page 474):* What are three signs that this couple are closer to age 40 than to age 20?

infertility The lack of a successful pregnancy after one year of regular intercourse without contraception.

❷ **Especially for Couples:** What can be done, without seeing a doctor, to enhance fertility?

Biology Versus the Bank Account Family income (which includes the incomes of all the wage earners in the household) more than doubles from age 20 to age 40. No wonder, then, that many contemporary couples decide to wait until both have finished their education and become established in their careers before they have a baby.

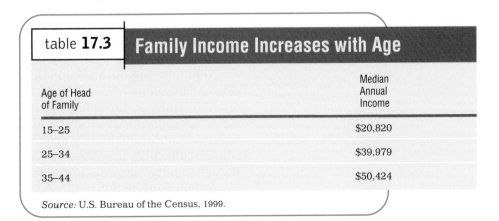

table **17.3**	**Family Income Increases with Age**
Age of Head of Family	Median Annual Income
15–25	$20,820
25–34	$39,979
35–44	$50,424

Source: U.S. Bureau of the Census, 1999.

❶ *Answer to Observational Quiz (from page 473):* *Some physical signs are apparent: He has less hair on his head and she has more fat on her arms than most 20-year-old newlyweds would have. The cultural context is a less precise but more powerful clue: Their hairstyles, clothing choices, outdoor wedding, and Bible-carrying priest are all more common among mature couples than among younger ones.*

he also produces more than 80 million sperm that are alive and swimming. Even a man who produces as few as 20 million sperm per ejaculate, only a third of which are normal in shape and movement, can usually still impregnate a woman (Mortimer, 1994).

As men grow older, the number, shape, and motility of their sperm decline. Men over age 40 take three times longer (measured by months of sexual activity before conception occurs) to produce a pregnancy than men under age 25 (Seibel, 1993). Sometimes the solution to such age-related reductions in sperm count is actually less, rather than more, sex: Waiting at least three days between ejaculations is advisable to allow the sperm count to rise (Mortimer, 1994).

Senescence is not the only factor that directly affects sperm production. Sperm develop and mature in the testes, in long threadlike tubes, over a period of 74 days. Thus, at any given moment, billions of sperm are in the process of development. Anything that impairs normal body functioning (such as a high fever, radiation, prescription drugs, environmental toxins, unusual stress, drug abuse, alcoholism, or cigarette smoking) reduces the number, shape, and motility of the sperm for several months (Seibel, 1993). Although such impairment is not necessarily age-related, age is often a factor: Since the incidence of illness, radiation treatment, and use of prescription medicine rises with age, the chances of a man's fertility being reduced for this reason increase with age.

Female Infertility

Women can be infertile for many reasons as well. These include drug use and all the conditions cited earlier that impair normal body functioning, plus two additional ones: being underweight and being obese (Seibel, 1993). Each of these conditions contributes to the most common underlying reason for female infertility: failure to ovulate—that is, to release an egg from the ovary. Ovulation is also age-related: It is most regular when a woman is in her 20s and then gradually becomes more erratic. As middle age approaches, women experience some menstrual cycles with no ovulation and other cycles in which several eggs are released. Thus, women in their late 30s not only take longer to conceive but also are more likely to have twins when they do.

Women's other common fertility problem (the primary cause for 22 percent of infertile couples) is blocked Fallopian tubes. This blockage is often caused by **pelvic inflammatory disease (PID),** which occurs when infections of the female organs are not treated promptly. Note that blocked Fallopian tubes are not caused directly by senescence (even in late adulthood, most women's Fallopian tubes are still open). But if a woman is sexually active with a number of partners over a number of years, she is more likely to contract a sexually transmitted disease, such as gonorrhea or chlamydia, which can cause PID. Thus, the incidence of this fertility problem rises steadily with age.

pelvic inflammatory disease (PID)   A common result of recurring pelvic infections in women. Pelvic inflammatory disease often leads to blocked Fallopian tubes, which, in turn, can lead to infertility.

Another common problem, again age-related but not directly age-caused, is *endometriosis,* in which fragments of the uterine lining grow on the surface of the ovaries or the Fallopian tubes. Endometriosis can block the reproductive tract. It is most common after age 25, and about a third of those who have it are infertile (Davajan & Israel, 1991). A final cause of infertility in women is uterine problems, such as infections and fibrous tumors ("fibroids"), that prevent implantation.

As you can see, for both sexes, successful conception gradually becomes more difficult with each passing year. Most physicians recom-

! Response for Couples (from page 473):
Good health practices make a big difference. Avoid drugs, eat a balanced diet, don't get sick, and relax. These solve about half of all fertility problems. However, time is crucial—especially if a couple is over age 30—so don't wait too long to seek medical help.

mend that would-be mothers begin their efforts at conception before age 30 and would-be fathers, before age 40. These recommendations are intended not only to increase the likelihood of conception but also to reduce the incidence of problems with pregnancy and birth.

Nevertheless, the relationship between age and infertility should not be exaggerated. Age is rarely the primary cause of complications with conception, pregnancy, or birth until age 40 or later. Adults who wait until their 30s and then find conception difficult might have had the same problem if they had started trying 10 years earlier.

Medical Advances

Many fertility problems can be solved by modern medical techniques, all of which raise ethical questions that each person involved must confront (see the In Person box). Minor physical abnormalities that cause infertility in the male (such as varicoceles, or varicose veins, in the testes and partially blocked genital ducts) are often correctable through surgery. In women, an inability to ovulate can usually be treated with drugs to stimulate ovulation, and blocked Fallopian tubes can often be opened surgically. Surgery may also help when endometriosis or fibroids interfere with conception.

in vitro fertilization (IVF) A technique in which ova (egg cells) are surgically removed from a woman and fertilized with sperm in the laboratory. After the original fertilized cells (the zygotes) have divided several times, they are inserted into a woman's uterus.

Another possibility is **in vitro fertilization (IVF)**, in which ova are surgically removed from the ovaries, fertilized by sperm in the laboratory, and allowed to divide until the zygote reaches the eight- or sixteen-cell stage. In vitro fertilization sidesteps problems not only with ovulation but also with low sperm count: In the laboratory a technician can insert one sperm into one ovum, thus avoiding the need for millions of sperm per ejaculate. The resulting zygotes are then inserted directly into the uterus (avoiding the journey through the Fallopian tubes) with the hope that one or more will become implanted. Embryos can also be frozen for later use. Since 1978, when the first "test-tube" baby was born, an estimated 300,000 babies have been born using IVF, 10,000 of them involving single-sperm injection (Djerassi, 1999).

Other techniques include *GIFT* (gamete intra-Fallopian transfer) and *ZIFT* (zygote intra-Fallopian transfer), which involve inserting either

Medical Miracles Although they obviously differ in age, brothers David and Nicholas might be called "twins," since they were conceived at the same time. Because their mother had a blocked Fallopian tube that prevented normal conception, the boys' parents turned to IVF. One of the embryos that resulted from the procedure (David) was used immediately; another embryo (Nicholas) was kept frozen and then used about a year later.

WHOSE BABY IS IT?

Many new questions are raised by alternative paths to reproduction. At the broadest level are questions regarding rights and obligations, such as:

- Should third-party donors, whether of sperm, ova, or wombs, have any parental rights?
- Should access to alternative reproduction be equally available to everyone, no matter what their marital status, sexual orientation, lifestyle, age, or motives for wanting a baby?
- Does an embryo conceived in vitro have a right to be implanted rather than frozen and destroyed after five years (as law in England requires)?
- If a woman, through alternative reproduction, conceives so many embryos that they probably cannot survive, is she obligated to abort some of them to save the others?
- Do children have the right to know if the parents who raise them are not their biological parents?
- Does society, in the form of laws, religious prohibitions, or medical ethics, have any right to allow or forbid the creation on any potential embryo conceived through alternative means?

Compassionate, thoughtful people—including developmentalists—differ widely in their responses to these legal and ethical issues. However, all agree that the answer to the question "Whose baby is it?" includes not just the mother or father but also the society that developed the laws and procedures that allowed the birth of infants who could not even have been conceived a few decades ago.

Alternative reproduction also gives rise to economic questions. Even though infertility is more common among poorer adults, fertility options become more readily available as income rises. In the United States, the average cost of having a baby through IVF, ZIFT, or GIFT is about $30,000, which puts those procedures beyond the reach of many couples (Barbieri, 1999). In other countries, national medical care covers some of the costs, which means doctors decide who qualifies for the procedure. It is easy to conclude that as long as there are millions of poor, neglected children in the world, no one should insist on having their own offspring.

Similar economic issues can be raised about becoming a surrogate mother or relinquishing a newborn for adoption. It is usually low-income, unmarried women who carry a fetus for someone else, in exchange for expenses and a fee. And when adoption takes place across national borders, children from poor, politically unstable regions are transferred to families in wealthier, more powerful communities. International adoptions cost between $15,000 and $50,000, with almost all of that money going to lawyers, adoption agencies, temporary guardians, government officials, airfare, and other expenses, and almost none to birth parents (Rosenthal, 1996). (Of course, both sets of parents usually believe that children who are adopted from poor nations to be raised in wealthy ones are much better off.)

One final question: Should laws, medical ethics, and contemporary culture encourage infertile individuals to willingly, even obsessively, incur great financial cost (as well as psychic stress and, sometimes, physical pain) in attempting to have their own biological children?

The following quotes attest to the devastating effect that infertility can have on the individual:

> Infertility takes the whole person. I used to feel attractive; I used to feel like I had a wonderful personality; I used to feel like I was smart; I used to feel like I could have a child if I wanted a child. And now all those things are shattered. [quoted in Sandelowski, 1993]

sperm and unfertilized ova (gametes) or fertilized ova (zygotes) directly into a Fallopian tube. IVF has a success rate of one baby in six attempts, and GIFT and ZIFT have even better success rates, about one in four attempts (Barbieri, 1999).

THREE HEALTH PROBLEMS

Although the picture of physical development and health in early adulthood has been fairly positive so far, this time of life is not trouble-free. A number of illnesses that appear in middle or late adulthood—such as cancer, cirrhosis of the liver, and coronary heart disease—gain a toehold

I just cannot imagine ever feeling good about anything again. I do not even know if my husband will stay with me when he realizes that children are not an option for us. My guess is he will find someone else who will be able to give him a baby. Since I cannot do that, I cannot imagine that he would be happy with me. I am not happy with me. [quoted in Deveraux & Hammerman, 1998]

The obsessive quest for offspring is given a sharper edge by the largely overlooked statistics that about one-third of all *untreated* infertile couples eventually produce their own biological babies and about half of all *treated* couples remain barren. But do not be too quick to criticize those who pursue their unconventional, irrational, and perhaps selfish quest for parenthood. In addition to the sociocultural assumptions and cognitive processes that encourage contemporary couples to seek alternative means of conception, the human species has a powerful biological impulse to pass genes on to the next generation. As one infertile woman explained:

When you take away being able to have a child biologically, it is like having to face death—almost like having half of you die. Having kids is the main way that people deal with the fact that they are mortal. [quoted in Hodder, 1997]

There is a genetic imperative to procreate, an urge that is crucial to the survival of the species (Barkow et al., 1992; Buss, 1994). As epigenetic systems theory (discussed in Chapter 2) would explain, not everyone feels this biological need, nor should everyone have children. But those who are fertile, or who are happily child-free, may be too judgmental about other people's reactions to "one of nature's cruelest tricks, infertility" (Cooper-Hilbert, 1998). We will see in Chapter 19, that biological parenthood is far from the only, or even the best, route to a productive, happy adulthood. But at this point in our culture, we should not be surprised that many adults believe it is.

The New Arrivals In many ways, this is a common sight. Like proud new parents everywhere, these adults from Maine discuss feeding schedules, diapers, and other baby-related topics as they give the newest members of (*from* left to right) the Watts, Diamond, and Wood families some fresh air.

❷ *Observational Quiz (see answer page 478): Looking closely at the three babies for clues, can you guess how far these parents are from their hometown?*

in early adulthood, although the symptoms are not yet apparent. They are discussed in Chapter 20. Here we address three health hazards that can gain not just a toehold but a stranglehold: drug abuse, destructive dieting, and violence.

Drug Abuse and Addiction

Older adolescents and young adults are the "chief initiators and heaviest users" of drugs and therefore those most at risk for serious drug problems (Robins, 1995). Remember from Chapter 14 that *drug abuse* is defined as using a drug in a quantity or a manner that is harmful to physical, cognitive, or psychosocial well-being.

drug addiction A condition of drug dependence such that the absence of the given drug in the individual's system produces a drive—physiological, psychological, or both—to ingest more of the drug.

It is not always easy to differentiate *use* and *abuse*, because one-time or occasional use can constitute abuse. A person might drink several beers and wreck a car, or eat a marijuana brownie and skip a final exam, or smoke crack and assault a friend, all of which would be abuse—not because of quantity or frequency but because of consequences. More often, however, abuse entails frequent use (such as a regular pattern of pot smoking or cocaine snorting) and high doses (for instance, consuming five or more drinks in a row) that impair the body, the mind, and/or social interaction.

Drug addiction is measured by the need for more of a drug. When the temporary absence or inadequate amount of a drug in a person's body causes a craving for more of the drug in order to satisfy a physiological need (to stop the shakes, to settle one's stomach, to get to sleep) or a psychological need (to quiet fears, to lift depression), those withdrawal symptoms are the telltale indication of addiction. Although many abusers are addicts and vice versa, the link is imperfect: Some abusers are not addicted, and some addicts are not drug abusers, as millions of habitual coffee drinkers prove. (Even caffeine addiction can become abuse if too much of it jangles the nerves or speeds up the heart.)

Drug use that begins before age 18 often becomes abusive and sometimes addictive between ages 19 and 23. The late teens and early 20s are the time of heaviest alcohol and marijuana consumption. The greatest use of other drugs, including cocaine, occurs at about age 23. A longitudinal study found that drug use often eases before age 30: 69 percent of the marijuana smokers and 67 percent of the cocaine users had quit by that age, as had 11 percent of the drinkers (Chen & Kandal, 1995).

In general, young adults are more likely to be addicts than are adolescents or older adults; men use and abuse drugs at a higher rate than women; and European and Hispanic Americans are more likely to use drugs than are African or Asian Americans.

College undergraduates are particularly vulnerable. For example, in one survey of undergraduates conducted at 104 colleges of all sizes in every region of the United States, 48 percent of the men and 30 percent of the women had consumed five or more drinks in a row at least once in the month preceding the survey, 10 percent had used marijuana, and 1 percent had used cocaine. When asked about the entire year, 25 percent had used marijuana and 6 percent had used cocaine (Presley et al., 1995).

Many of these college students admitted that their drug or alcohol use had had harmful consequences within the past year (see Table 17.4). Further, 11 percent thought that they might have an alcohol or drug problem, and 8 percent of the men and 4 percent of the women had tried to stop their own drug abuse and had failed—an ominous sign of addiction.

Why are the rates so high in the early years of young adulthood? Remember from Chapter 3 that the genetic temperament of those most likely to misuse drugs includes attraction to excitement, intolerance of frustration, and vulnerability to depression. These traits are inherited, but their expression depends on age: they increase in adolescence and early adulthood.

In addition, for many young adults, the social context encourages drug use and abuse. Young adults, no longer supervised or even observed by their parents, are free to make their own choices. At the same time, they experience stresses that drugs may temporarily relieve: not only the pressures to complete an education, establish a career, and find a mate but also the more immediate need to feel sophisticated and socially at ease.

❶ *Answer to Observational Quiz (from page 477):* About 7,000 miles. The crucial clue is the fact that the babies are all Chinese girls. This clue might make you look closely at the architecture and the stroller designs and to consider the age of the adults. This photo was taken in 1998 outside the White Swan Hotel in Guangzhou, China, and these adopted infants would soon fly to Maine with their new parents.

table **17.4**	Percentage of college students who use drugs and alcohol who have also, as a result. . . .	
Been hung over		60%
Been nauseous		48
Done things they regretted		37
Driven under the influence		33
Been arrested for driving while intoxicated		2
Gotten into a fight		30
Missed a class		27
Lost memory		25
Performed poorly on a test		20
Gotten physically hurt		15
Been taken advantage of, sexually		
Men		8
Women		10
Taken advantage of someone else, sexually		
Men		11
Women		2
Thought of suicide		5
Tried suicide		1

Source: Presley et al., 1995.

Also encouraging drug use are certain group activities—large parties, rock concerts, spectator sports—at which excessive drug use is tolerated and even expected, sometimes by one's own companions. Indeed, a careful longitudinal study found that the single most important correlate of drug use among young adults—even more important than life stress, temperament, and personal attitudes—was having friends who used drugs (Jessor et al., 1991). Enlisting in the military also put young adults at risk until a recent change of policy began to discourage drug use: In 1990, drug use was higher among soldiers than among civilians; by 1997, it was only half as high (Ammerman et al., 1999).

Finally, young adults are least likely to experience the most powerful deterrent to serious drug and alcohol abuse: religious faith and practice (Brunswick et al., 1992). People in their 20s are less likely to join religious groups, attend services, and pray than are people of any other age (Gallup, 1996).

For all these reasons, both abuse and addiction increase from about age 18 to age 26. The harm done can be substantial: Compared to others their age, young adult drug users are more likely to avoid, flunk out of, or drop out of college; to be employed below their potential and then lose or quit those jobs; to be involved in transitory, uncommitted sexual relationships; to die violently; and to suffer from serious eating disorders.

Young and Foolish? For some young adults, social camaraderie demands drinking to the point of being "blasted," "wasted," "plastered," and sometimes, quite literally, "smashed." This form of socializing was once considered a "male thing," but in recent years it has been taken up by young women at an alarming rate, particularly on college campuses.

Dieting as a Disease

Homeostasis works to maintain the body's weight just as it does to maintain the level of oxygen in the blood or the body's temperature. Obvious mechanisms such as pangs of hunger and the feeling of fullness, and less obvious ones such as fluctuations in hormonal levels and neurotransmitter activity, regulate the urge to eat. Healthy and active adults and children automatically tend to consume sufficient calories to maintain their required energy level.

In addition, many scientists believe that each person has a certain **set point**—that is, a particular body weight that the individual's homeostatic processes strive to maintain (Schlundt & Johnson, 1990). A person's set point is powerfully influenced by genes, which strongly affect metabolism as well as the storage and distribution of body fat. Environmental factors, particularly those that establish childhood eating habits, affect the set point as well.

The set point is not rigidly fixed, however. Throughout adulthood, it can change somewhat through the effects of diet, age, illness, hormones, and exercise, a potential that makes some experts think the term "settling point"—referring to the tendency of a person's weight to settle at a certain point—is more accurate (Bouchard & Bray, 1996).

Recognizing that everyone has his or her own natural weight, medical experts now maintain that people can vary by 20 pounds or so from other people of the same height and still be healthy. To assess whether a person is too thin or too fat, clinicians calculate **body mass index (BMI)**, the ratio of a person's weight in kilograms divided by his or her height in meters squared (see page 302 and Table 17.5). A healthy BMI is somewhere between 19 and 25.

set point   A particular body weight that an individual's homeostatic processes strive to maintain.

body mass index (BMI)   The ratio of a person's weight in kilograms divided by his or her height in meters squared.

Adult BMI   Overall, the BMI for both men and women should be between 19 and 25, with more muscular people on the higher end of that range and less muscular people on the lower end (since muscle weighs more than fat). Below 18 is considered anorexic; 30 or above is considered obese. The World Health Organization has set a BMI of 35 as severely obese. For more information on standards, exercises, and calculations, check the National Heart, Lung and Blood Institute's Web site at www.nhlbi.nih.gov.

table 17.5	**Body Mass Index (BMI)**

To calculate your BMI: Find your height, then look across that row. Your BMI is at the top of the column that contains your weight.

BMI	19	20	21	22	23	24	25	26	27	28	29	30	35	40
Height							*Weight (pounds)*							
4'10"	91	96	100	105	110	115	119	124	129	134	138	143	167	191
4'11"	94	99	104	109	114	119	124	128	133	138	143	148	173	198
5'0"	97	102	107	112	118	123	128	133	138	143	148	153	179	204
5'1"	100	106	111	116	122	127	132	137	143	148	153	158	185	211
5'2"	104	109	115	120	126	131	136	142	147	153	158	164	191	218
5'3"	107	113	118	124	130	135	141	146	152	158	163	169	197	225
5'4"	110	116	122	128	134	140	145	151	157	163	169	174	204	232
5'5"	114	120	126	132	138	144	150	156	162	168	174	180	210	240
5'6"	118	124	130	136	142	148	155	161	167	173	179	186	216	247
5'7"	121	127	134	140	146	153	159	166	172	178	185	191	223	255
5'8"	125	131	138	144	151	158	164	171	177	184	190	197	230	262
5'9"	128	135	142	149	155	162	169	176	182	189	196	203	236	270
5'10"	132	139	146	153	160	167	174	181	188	195	202	207	243	278
5'11"	136	143	150	157	165	172	179	186	193	200	208	215	250	286
6'0"	140	147	154	162	169	177	184	191	199	206	213	221	258	294
6'1"	144	151	159	166	174	182	189	197	204	212	219	227	265	302
6'2"	148	155	163	171	179	186	194	202	210	218	225	233	272	311
6'3"	152	160	168	176	184	192	200	208	216	224	232	240	279	319
6'4"	156	164	172	180	189	197	205	213	221	230	238	246	287	328
			Normal						*Overweight*				*Obese*	

Source: National Heart, Lung and Blood Institute.

anorexia nervosa A serious eating disorder in which a person restricts eating to the point of emaciation and possible starvation. Most victims are high-achieving females in early puberty or early adulthood.

bulimia nervosa An eating disorder in which the person, usually female, engages repeatedly in episodes of binge eating followed by purging through induced vomiting or use of laxatives.

Cultural norms and specifics of the social context may undermine the body's natural tendency toward maintaining a healthy weight, as the Changing Policy box explains. Some dieters, especially those who are young and well educated, develop an obsession with food and weight control that turns into a serious eating disorder.

One such problem is **anorexia nervosa,** an affliction characterized by self-starvation, sometimes to the point of death. Typically, a high-achieving female in early adulthood (or sometimes in early puberty) restricts her eating so severely that her BMI goes below 18. She may weigh a bony 80 pounds or less but still be exercising and complaining about being fat. Approximately 1 percent of young adult and adolescent females are anorexic (DSM-IV, 1994).

About three times as common as anorexia, especially among young female adults, is the other major eating disorder of our time, **bulimia nervosa.** This condition involves compulsive binge eating followed by purging through either vomiting or inducing diarrhea by taking massive doses of laxatives. Such behaviors are performed on occasion by many young adult women; some studies find that half of all college women have binged and purged at least once (Fairburn & Wilson, 1993), while other research finds bulimia present in virtually every city (but not every rural area) of the world (Nassar, 1997).

To warrant a clinical diagnosis of bulimia, bingeing and purging must occur at least once a week for three months, and the person must have uncontrollable urges to overeat and must show a distorted self-judgment based on misperceived body size. Between 1 and 3 percent of women in the United States are clinically bulimic during early adulthood (DSM-IV, 1994). People who suffer from bulimia are usually close to normal in weight and therefore unlikely to starve to death. However, they can experience serious health problems, including severe damage to the gastrointestinal system and cardiac arrest from the strain of electrolyte imbalance (Hsu, 1990).

College women are at particular risk for eating disorders, and college athletes—who, in theory at least, should be most concerned about health and fitness—are even more vulnerable than others (Cohn & Adler, 1992; Thompson & Sherman, 1993). Male athletes—especially wrestlers, rowers, and swimmers—are vulnerable as well.

Why are women particularly likely to be caught up in such destructive self-sabotage? Each theory of development offers an explanation:

- A *psychoanalytic* hypothesis is that women develop eating disorders because of a conflict with their mothers, who provided their first nourishment and from whom the daughters cannot psychically separate.
- *Learning theory* notes that for some people with low self-esteem, fasting, bingeing, and purging "have powerful effects as immediate reinforcers—that is, [as means of] relieving states of emotional distress and tension" (Gordon, 1990), thus setting up a destructive stimulus–response chain.
- One *cognitive* explanation is that as women compete with men in business and industry, they want to project a strong, self-controlled, masculine image antithetical to the buxom, fleshy body of the ideal woman of the past.
- *Sociocultural* explanations include the contemporary cultural pressure to be "slim and trim" and model-like—a pressure that seems to be felt particularly by unmarried young women seeking autonomy from their parents, especially when the parents espouse traditional values (Nasser, 1997).

EATING HABITS AND COHORT INFLUENCES

Each era has particular health habits and diseases that arise from aspects peculiar to that time and place. The three health problems detailed in this section of the chapter—drug use, excessive dieting, and violence—are very closely connected to current social attitudes. A hundred years ago, women almost never smoked tobacco and always tried to eat enough to fill out their bodies—and thus were saved from two serious health problems. In those days, "childbed fever" was a potentially deadly problem with a simple cause: the "modern" desire to have a doctor help with the birth of a baby combined with the common practice among doctors of delivering several babies in a day without ever washing their hands in between. Another dreaded illness was "consumption," or tuberculosis, the main symptom of which was extreme thinness and the main cause of which was urban life.

These two problems are rare now. Instead, many people each day eat substantially more or less than homeostatic controls call for. For example, the notion that the ideal body is virtually "fat-free" causes many young adult women to strive for an elusive and unhealthy thinness, with a BMI far below the healthy range. Such striving is now common in nearly all developed nations, most of which are gripped by a cultural, media-fueled obsession with female thinness.

Women in the United States of European ancestry seem particularly vulnerable to this obsession (Cash & Henry, 1995). However, as urbanization, Americanization, and the proliferation of chain restaurants selling high-calorie fast food have touched nation after nation, excessive dieting has become a common problem among young women in Egypt, Russia, Japan, Brazil, and many other nations (Nasser, 1997). (Men are more likely to wish they were taller and heavier [Mintz & Kashubeck, 1999].)

Many women attempt to lose weight because they needlessly feel dissatisfied with their bodies. A U.S. survey of 15,000 women, for example, found that 44 percent of those be-

Distorted Body Image The image in this trick mirror may be closer to the young woman's sense of her body than what she sees when she views herself in a true mirror. At some point in her development, almost every young woman in today's developed nations considers herself too fat.

■ An *epigenetic systems* explanation notes that girls who are overwhelmed with the stresses of puberty may discover that self-starvation makes their menstrual periods cease, their sexual hormones decrease, and their curves disappear—all of which relieve the pressures to marry and reproduce. Especially if such a girl is genetically susceptible to depression or addiction, an eating disorder may develop.

No matter what the explanation, it seems clear that for many of today's young women, dieting is a disease and that during the young adult years, when women should be at their peak of health, many risk serious illness by acting on distorted ideas of how their bodies should appear.

tween the ages of 17 and 60 were currently dieting. On average, they hoped to lose 30 pounds (14 kilograms)—a goal that, if attained, would have made most of them underweight (Williamson et al., 1992). Another survey of dieting women in North America found that almost half of them had a body mass index under 25—and thus were not at all overweight. Those who were young, well-educated, and employed were the ones most likely to diet *and* the least likely to need to (Biener & Heaton, 1995). Not every woman is dieting, but the average woman aged 17 to 28 would like to be 8 pounds lighter (and the average man would like to weigh 5 pounds more) (Mintz & Kashubeck, 1999).

When a person's self-selected target weight is substantially lower than the natural, healthy weight sought by the body's homeostatic mechanisms, the almost inevitable result is failure and frustration. In addition, the disturbances in natural equilibrium that this kind of dieting creates seem to make becoming overweight more likely later in life. Millions of young women share a self-defeating set of circumstances: feeling fat, reading diet books, dieting, doing spot exercises, losing weight, and then, as their bodies attempt to compensate, regaining weight, which leads to increased health risks (see Chapter 20), unhappiness, and a new obsessive-compulsive cycle. As one expert explains:

> It is as if women wear blinders to shut out half the truth about diets. On the one hand, women know how to lose weight—and they do so. In any room filled with chronic dieters, you will find them all knowledgeable about calories and nutrition. Dieters are not short on information on "proper eating." They know everything possible about all kinds of diets, from the liquid protein to the "sensible," moderate balanced diets. Most women have been on numerous and varied diets and lost weight on all of them. This is the part they remember. The second half of the experience—gaining back more than they lost—is routinely forgotten. [Gutwill, 1994]

Repeated dieting can in itself be very unhealthy, especially when it involves crash diets. Nearly all of these drastic regimens result in nutritional imbalance, energy loss, and vulnerability to disease. For many dieters, the health consequences are even more serious when they become dependent on diet drugs (Zerbe, 1993). Although men are more often addicted to the immediate physiological release of various drugs, women seek the appetite suppression and energy boost of stimulants, a high that builds for weeks, not hours. Long-term use of these drugs may result in insomnia, tenseness, anxiety, and, in megadoses, psychosis.

Can society change this unhealthy situation? Yes. As the dangers of eating disorders become more widely known, women in the United States aged 20 to 34 are less likely to be too thin. Having a BMI below 19 has become less prevalent, dropping from 16 percent in 1960 to a mere 8 percent recently (National Center for Health Statistics, 1999). Unfortunately, over the same time period, the number of women who are obese has increased. This is especially true in middle adulthood, as discussed in Chapter 20. Obviously, culture and public policy have not yet changed enough so that most people are happily maintaining a healthy weight.

Violence

While more women than men are afflicted by excessive dieting and eating disorders, young men are at greater risk of violence, and thus of death by accident, homicide, or suicide. As one male expert explains:

> Few people would consider male gender socialization to be a public health issue . . . yet there is considerable evidence to support such a pronouncement, evidence that links sexual abuse and a vast array of interpersonally abusive and violent behavior to the process by which male children, male adolescents, and young men are socialized into masculinity. [Lisak, 1997]

How much violent behavior is the result of "male gender socialization" and how much is hormonal is a matter of debate, but there is no doubt that far more males than females die violently. Moreover, relative to all other age groups, young adult males are at increased risk for virtually every kind of violent death, from car crashes to gang shoot-outs, from jumping off roofs to overdosing on drugs. More specifically, between the ages of 15 and 35, one U. S. male in every fifty dies violently (U.S. Bureau of the Census, 1999).

Violent death rates among young men in Canada, Mexico, and Chile are as high as in the United States. The specific mixture of suicides, homicides, and accidents varies from country to country, with Canada, for example, having far more suicides than homicides (Leenaars & Lester, 1995). Most European and Asian countries have somewhat lower rates of violent death among young men. Age-specific data are unavailable for most Middle Eastern and African nations. However, worldwide, every nation or city that tallies such statistics finds that young men in their early 20s are at least twice as likely to die from violence as from disease or famine, and are more likely to die violently than women of their own age and national group, with a sex ratio ranging from 3:1 to 10:1. (See the breakdown given in the Research Report.)

Many experts believe that social values are at the root of the problem. When "young men achieve masculinity through 'manhood rituals' involving violence, alcohol consumption, high-risk activities and sexual conquest," they obviously hurt other people, including other young men, but the victims are often themselves (Brooks, 1997). A society that turns positive masculine tendencies such as courage, independence, and competitiveness (all of which might have an evolutionary biological basis) into such negative male traits as recklessness, callousness, and "an egocentric and often obsessive need to be dominant and to win" is bound to suffer violent consequences (Miedzian, 1991).

Social values change. For example, in 1980 in the United States, a 16-year-old boy had more than 1 chance in 150 of dying in a motor-vehicle accident before he reached age 25, most likely because he or a friend was driving drunk. Between then and 1993, public anger and sorrow led to a series of steps to reduce drunk driving, among them intensified driver education, public service announcements, activism by private groups such as MADD and SADD (Mothers/Students Against Drunk Driving), peer pressure to appoint designated drivers when groups of friends go out drinking, and the enforcement of various pertinent laws (which doubled the national arrest rate for driving while intoxicated). Partly as a result, the automobile crash rate involving young drunk men fell by half between 1980 and 1997, as did the motor-vehicle death rate of young men (U.S. Bureau of the Census, 1999). Various social pressures and policies have translated into far less danger when young men take the wheel,

Who, Where, and When? The sad reality is that this could be young men in almost any place or time. In fact, this photo was taken in southern France on June 14, 1998, the night *before* the World Cup soccer match between England and Tunisia. Street fighting—such as this between supporters of the two teams, which led to 80 arrests, hundreds of wounded, but, fortunately, no deaths—is common among teenage boys in blue jeans, no matter what their ethnicity. The only comforting truth is that most of those rioting young men are adolescent-limited criminals, unlikely to persist in violent crime after they reach adulthood.

MALE VIOLENCE AND THE SOCIAL CONTEXT

Young men worldwide are more likely to engage in unnecessary bravado and irrational risk taking than young women or older adults are. However, the chances that a particular young man will die a violent death, and which specific type of death he risks, depend on many factors within him and within his family, neighborhood, and culture. Maleness is much more hazardous in some social settings than in others.

This variability is apparent in international comparisons of homicide rates (see Figure 17.3). One reason for these differences is the variation in the cultural ideal of a "real man." Some cultures, for example, encourage young men to master the art of gentlemanly compromise, while others propel them to exhibit an uncompromising bravado. Family discipline techniques, school curricula, television heroes, religious values, and alcohol availability also vary markedly from nation to nation and from subculture to subculture, and these differences affect the predisposition of young men to various expressions of violence (Rutter et al., 1998).

An additional contextual factor frequently cited for the variation in homicide rates is the availability of firearms. In 1993 in the United States, 42 percent of all adults reported that there was at least one gun in their home (U.S. Bureau of Justice Statistics, 1995). In theory, guns are equally available to all adults in the family, but young adult males are the most likely to use them and to be injured by them. Overall, the firearm-death rate in the United States is highest for both sexes between ages 20 and 24, with the rate among young men almost eight times higher than that among young women (U.S. Bureau of the Census, 1999).

One notable ethnic variation in violent death is that homicide is the leading cause of death for young African American and Latino men, while among European American men, accidents are the number-one cause. The reason is primarily economic: white young men are more likely to be middle-class and living in the suburbs, and hence are more likely to own and drive a car—a potentially dangerous tool. By contrast, daily life for many young men of color includes survival in the overcrowded, crime-torn, drug-infested, and job-poor inner city—where violent

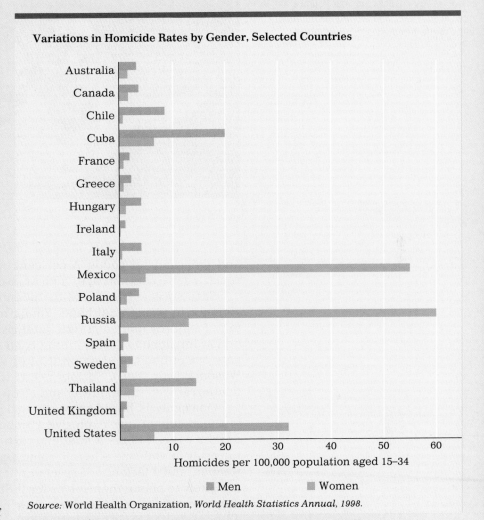

Variations in Homicide Rates by Gender, Selected Countries

Homicides per 100,000 population aged 15–34

■ Men ■ Women

Source: World Health Organization, *World Health Statistics Annual, 1998.*

Figure 17.3 Murder Risk Varies. What conclusions can you draw from the national and gender variations in homicide rates shown here? The text provides some answers.

impulses can intensify to the breaking point, turning minor disagreements between friends into deadly confrontations. Indeed, a newborn male of African descent born in the United States has one chance in twenty-five of being murdered before reaching age 75 (U.S. Bureau of the Census, 1999). Many researchers are working to understand how to reduce the homicide rate among those who are at greatest risk (Rutter et al., 1998).

Whatever the economic, cultural, or other explanations for national and ethnic differences in rates of violent death, the fact that such variations occur makes one conclusion obvious: It is not maleness per se that puts a young man at risk. Instead, it is a lethal combination of biological factors and cultural values that encourages young men to act, or not act, in ways that risk violent injury and death (Wilson & Daly, 1993).

Thrill Seeker Would you pay $200 to jump out of a helicopter with a bungee cord around your middle? If your immediate answer is yes, chances are that you are male, in your 20s, and already testing the limits of life-threatening entertainment.

and thousands of young Americans who would have died now live to reach a more cautious age, such as 25 or 30.

Such success highlights the possibility of solving other problems of violence in young adulthood. Young men still drink too much and still take foolhardy and sometime fatal risks, drowning because they drink and swim alone at night, killing each other when a drunken argument gets out of hand, and so on (Cotten et al., 1994; Howland et al., 1995; Wilson & Daly, 1993). Society needs to figure out how to make violent deaths rare, on the highway and elsewhere.

One analysis, based on psychological research, finds that aggression is the result of an "explosive combination" of high self-esteem and dashed expectations: A sudden crash of the self-concept is more likely to result in violence when it coincides with the presence of alcohol, a weapon, and a lack of self-restraint (Baumeister & Boden, 1998). Women are likely to blame themselves for their problems, so they diet, they cry, they become quiet. Men think they must become taller, stronger, and all-powerful, so their frustration erupts against others.

Gender is not necessarily protective: Many young women die violently, many young men develop abnormal eating habits, and many young adults of both sexes abuse drugs. However, all three hazards spring partly from cultural pressures to match a particular stereotype, and these pressures affect men and women in divergent ways. Women are vulnerable to low self-esteem and extreme self-control, making them more likely to diet excessively. Men are vulnerable to artificially high expectations and to a lack of self-restraint, making them more likely to be violent and impulsive. With maturity, both types of problems are moderated.

Given the grimness of the three problems we have been considering, we should end this chapter with an encouraging reminder that destructive behaviors are evident in only a minority of young adults. Most young people, no matter what their ethnic group, economic status, or gender, become increasingly capable of understanding and coping with difficulties in their lives during their prime years. The next two chapters provide the details about this dawning maturity.

Over the course of adulthood, many changes occur in our thinking processes. How much we know, how fast we think, what we think about, how efficiently we process new information, how deeply or reflectively we relate new experiences to previous ones, which intellectual skills we use—all this changes from the omnivorous questioning of adolescence to the more mature cognition of adulthood. Unlike the relatively straightforward cognitive growth of childhood and adolescence, these changes are multidirectional: Some abilities improve, others wane, and some remain stable.

Adult thinking is multicontextual as well. Instead of originating primarily in the classroom, it is fostered by many situations: finding and keeping a job or a mate, protecting and guiding a child or a friend, and making decisions about matters ranging from whether or not to have an abortion to whether or not to buy a new automobile.

Understanding adult cognitive development thus involves appreciating how thinking and reasoning reflect the interplay of gains and losses throughout the life span (Dixon, 1999). Obviously, the life-span perspective, first explained in Chapter 1, is needed here. The study of adult cognition must be multidisciplinary, only loosely connected to chronological age.

In fact, developmental theorists have used at least three different approaches to explain the cognitive changes that occur throughout adulthood:

- The *postformal approach* picks up where Piaget left off, emphasizing the possible emergence of a new stage of thinking and reasoning in adulthood that builds on the skills of formal operational thinking.
- The *psychometric approach* analyzes components of intelligence such as those measured by IQ tests, specifically describing which components improve or decline during adulthood.
- The *information-processing approach* studies the encoding, storage, and retrieval of information throughout life, considering whether the efficiency of these processes changes as the individual grows older.

All three approaches provide valuable insights into cognitive development across adulthood, from age 20 to age 100. However, to examine all three in each of the adult cognitive chapters (18, 21, and 24) would be repetitive and confusing. Therefore, in this chapter, our primary focus will be on the postformal approach. In Chapter 21 the psychometric approach will be emphasized, and Chapter 24 will consider information processing. Each of these three chapters will also look at some age-related influences on cognitive abilities, such as college education in this chapter.

POSTFORMAL THOUGHT

Adult thinking differs from adolescent thinking in many ways. Adolescents try to distill universal truths, develop topical arguments, and think about resolving the world's problems in terms of rational absolutes. Adult thinking is more personal, practical, and integrative. Consequently, adults are less inclined toward the playful "game of thinking" (see Chapter 15), because their intellectual skills become enlisted in the occupational and interpersonal demands that shape adult life.

Adults don't want to stay up all night to argue, winning points in debate; they want to figure out what to do next and why. Most adults learn to accept, and adapt to, the contradictions and inconsistencies of everyday experience, rather than decrying them or trying to resolve them definitively. Indeed, one hallmark of mature adult thinking is the realization that most of life's answers are provisional, not necessarily permanent. As Gisela Labouvie-Vief (1992) explains, adult thinking

> is less and less considered a purely objective, impersonal, and rational activity. Instead, it embraces dimensions that are subjective, interpersonal, and nonrational. By establishing a dialogue with those dimensions, thinking becomes rebalanced . . .

Taken together, these characteristics of adult thinking are referred to as **postformal thought**, the combination of a new "ordering of formal operations" with a "necessary subjectivity" (Sinnott, 1998).

postformal thought   A type of adult thinking that is suited to solving real-world problems. Postformal thought is less abstract and absolute than formal thought, more adaptive to life's inconsistencies, and more dialectical—capable of combining contradictory elements into a comprehensive whole.

Subjective Experience

A distinction can be made between *subjective* and *objective* thinking. Subjective thought arises from the personal experiences and perceptions of an individual; objective thought follows abstract, impersonal logic. Traditional models of advanced thought devalued subjective feelings, personal faith, and emotional experience and valued (or overvalued) objective, logical thinking.

Of course, objective thinking is a much-needed corrective to subjective thinking that is prejudiced, narrow, and highly emotional. The scientific method itself attempts to overcome the biases of traditional, culture-bound perspectives, encouraging scientists to base conclusions on objective data that can be verified through replication. In everyday life, this objective thinking may be adaptive for the schoolchild, the adolescent, and the "novice adult," because it permits them to "categorize experience in a stable and reliable way." However, purely objective, logical thinking becomes maladaptive in trying to understand, and deal with, the complexities and commitments of the adult world (Labouvie-Vief, 1985).

For the adult, subjective feelings and personal experiences must be taken into account, or the result will be reasoning that is "limited, closed, rigidified in relation to the complex human dimensions of everyday experience" (Sinnott, 1998). Truly mature thought involves the interaction between the abstract, objective forms of processing and the expressive, subjective forms that arise from sensitivity to context. Note that adult thought does not abandon objectivity; instead, "postformal logic combines subjectivity and objectivity" (Sinnott, 1998).

Cognitive Flexibility

An additional dimension of postformal thought is understanding that each person's perspective is only one of many potentially valid views and that knowledge is not necessarily absolute or fixed (Sinnott, 1998). A contextual awareness emerges that helps us recognize that life entails inconsistencies, including the inconsistencies between intellectual analysis and emotional realities. Living life to the fullest often requires a relativistic, flexible perspective.

To demonstrate the development of this form of thought, Labouvie-Vief and her colleagues presented subjects between the ages of 10 and 40 with brief narratives that tested problem-solving logic. Because the researchers were more interested in their subjects' problem-solving approach than in their specific solutions, the tests were designed to be superficially simple and logical but to allow for deeper interpretations outside the straightforward propositions of the text. One such story went as follows:

> John is known to be a heavy drinker, especially when he goes to parties. Mary, John's wife, warns him that if he comes home drunk one more time, she will leave him and take the children. Tonight John is out late at an office party. John comes home drunk.—Does Mary leave John?

In arriving at their answers, all the young adolescents and many of the older ones reasoned strictly according to the basic premise of the story: In the case of the drunken husband, it was evident to them that Mary would leave John because that is what she said she would do. Older respondents recognized the explicit logic of the story, but they resisted the narrative's limited logical premise and explored the real-life possibilities and contextual circumstances that might apply—whether, for example, Mary's warning was a plea rather than a final ultimatum, whether John was apologetic or abusive upon his return home, whether Mary had somewhere to go if she left John, what the history of their relationship might be, and so forth. At the most advanced level, adults tried to "engage in an active dialogue" with the text, forming multiple perspectives as a result (Adams & Labouvie-Vief, 1986). This appreciation and reconciliation of both objective and subjective approaches to real-life problems are the hallmarks of adult adaptive thought.

Within this overall pattern of cognitive progression, other research finds that the difference between the reasoning maturity of adolescents and that of young adults is particularly apparent when the problems to be solved are emotionally charged. In such cases, younger thinkers exhibit lower levels of reasoning, even when they have demonstrated reasoning ability equal to that of young adults on problems with less emotional content. (See the Research Report.)

Dialectical Thought

Cognitive flexibility, at its best, reaches the level of **dialectical thought,** perhaps the most advanced process of cognition (Basseches, 1984, 1989; Riegel, 1975). The word "dialectical" refers to the philosophical concept (first developed by the German philosopher Georg W. F. Hegel in the late eighteenth/early nineteenth century) that every idea, every truth, bears within itself the suggestion of the opposite idea or truth.

In terms used by philosophers, each new idea, or **thesis,** implies an opposing idea, or **antithesis.** Dialectical thinking involves considering

dialectical thought Thought that is characterized by ongoing awareness of pros and cons, advantages and disadvantages, and possibilities and limitations. In daily life, dialectical thinking involves incorporating beliefs and experiences with all the contradictions and inconsistencies of life.

thesis A proposition or statement of belief; the first stage of the dialectical process.

antithesis A proposition or statement of belief that opposes the thesis; the second stage of the dialectical process.

DO EMOTIONS CLOUD YOUR THINKING?

In a study of the effect of emotions on reasoning ability (Blanchard-Fields, 1986), adolescents, young adults, and middle-aged adults were presented with several reasoning tasks that varied in emotional intensity. Each task involved accounts of a fictional event presented from two conflicting points of view. One pair of accounts told of a war between "North Livia" and "South Livia" as reported by a partisan historian for each of the opposing sides. Another pair of accounts related a teenage boy's unwilling visit to his grandparents, with one version presented by the boy's parents (who said that they had reasoned with their son and convinced him to go) and the other by the boy himself (who said that his parents had lectured him on his duty and had forced him to go).

After the participants in this study read these accounts, they were asked questions regarding what the conflict was about, who was to blame, how the conflict was resolved, and who emerged the winner. They were also asked to explain how the discrepancies in the conflicting accounts arose. (A typical discrepancy in the war task was the assertion by the North Livian historian that a particular battle had turned the tide "heavily in favor of the North," while the historian for South Livia described the same battle as a "minor" setback for the South. Among the discrepancies in the visit task was the boy's assertion that, although he was as polite as possible at his grandparents', he was bored and felt forced into everything he did while there—versus his parents' perception that he had a good time and enjoyed "the family closeness.")

Responses were scored on the basis of six levels of reasoning, ranging from level 1, an absolutist approach in which only one perspective was recognized as correct, through a mid-level recognition of interpretive discrepancies and weakening insistence on external truth (level 3), to level 6, a multiple-perspectives stance that recognized the need to "weigh discrepant sources of information in order to arrive at the best answer for the particular situation." Despite variation within age groups on levels of reasoning, only 16 percent of adolescents scored above level 3, compared with 36 percent of young adults and 61 percent of middle-aged adults.

Particularly striking was the difference in adolescents' and young adults' reasoning on the emotionally charged problem of the visit (see Figure 18.1). The adolescent participants actually reasoned worse on that task, which engaged their personal emotions, than they did on the less emotionally arousing war task, on which their reasoning was virtually as good as the young adults'. According to the author of this study,

> The more emotionally [intense] context appeared to be more disruptive for the younger than for older thinkers,

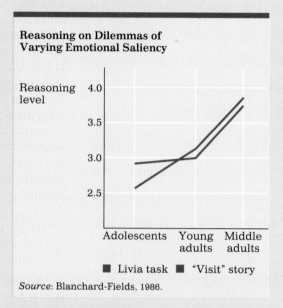

Reasoning on Dilemmas of Varying Emotional Saliency

■ Livia task ■ "Visit" story

Source: Blanchard-Fields, 1986.

Figure 18.1 Cognition and Emotion. In the Blanchard-Fields study of age-related reasoning on social dilemmas, older, more mature thinkers scored higher because they were better able to take into account the interpretive biases of each party's version of events. As you can see, this was especially true when the social dilemma was emotionally charged.

thus affecting their performance, particularly their ability to differentiate an event from its interpretation. . . . Developmentally mature adults are able to account for subjective factors in their thinking. This is in contrast with youthful thinkers, who assume that thinking is based on an objective structure of reality that is juxtaposed to subjectivity. Instead of resulting in more "objective" conclusions and resolutions of reasoning dilemmas, this form of thinking tends to maximize the chances of subjective errors. Therefore, maturity in thinking is not just a return to more subjective modes of thinking. Instead, by accounting for subjectivity, the mature adult becomes a more objective and powerful thinker. [Blanchard-Fields, 1986]

More recently, a team of researchers confirmed that older adults regulate their emotions better than younger ones—not denying negative feelings, but keeping them in check (Gross et al., 1997). Older adults experience deep and complex emotions, but they are less cognitively and physiologically overwhelmed by them. As a result, "despite loss and physical decline, adults enjoy good mental health and positive life satisfaction well into old age" (Carstensen & Charles, 1998).

synthesis The reconciliation of thesis and antithesis into a new and more comprehensive level of truth; the third stage of the dialectical process.

both these poles of an idea simultaneously and then forging them into a **synthesis**—that is, a new idea that integrates both the original idea and its opposite. The idea of the dialectical process also emphasizes that, because ideas are always initiating new syntheses, constant change is inevitable, and the dialectical process is continual.

Moreover, because each new synthesis is a deepening and refinement of the idea that initiated it, dialectical change results in developmental growth. This idea is also suggested by recent research in physics, which emphasizes the ever-changing, always adaptive character of all natural systems (Sinnott, 1998).

For our purposes here, we may say that in daily life, dialectical thinking involves the constant integration of one's beliefs and experiences with all the contradictions and inconsistencies that one encounters. The result of dialectical thinking is a continuously evolving view of oneself and the world, a view that recognizes that few, if any, of life's most important questions have single, unchangeable, correct answers.

This does not mean that dialectical thinkers adopt the idea that "everything is relative" and stop there, unable to commit themselves to broader values. On the contrary, a dialectic view explicitly recognizes the limitations of extremely relativistic positions, such as "If you think it is true, then it's true for you" (Leadbeater, 1986). Truly dialectical thinkers, in fact, acknowledge both the subjective nature of reality *and* the need to make firm commitments to values that they realize will change over time. They recognize that while many viewpoints may be potentially valid, some can be better justified or defended than others and thus provide a better basis for thoughtful decisions. Commitment to one course of action is essential, even as a person realizes that other actions could have been taken instead.

One Woman's Dialectical Journey In dialectical thinking, an individual develops new thoughts that seem opposed to his or her original thinking. Eventually, a new cognitive pattern incorporates both the original idea and the opposing one. In 1994, Carolyn McCarthy thought of herself primarily as a wife, mother, nurse (thesis)—until her husband was senselessly murdered, and her son seriously wounded, by a gunman who went on a shooting rampage with an assault rifle on a Long Island commuter train. She then began questioning many of the basic assumptions of her life and of the social order (antithesis). In particular, she opposed her congressman—whom she, as a lifelong Republican, had previously supported—because he was against gun control. This led to a synthesis in which she herself ran for Congress, as a Democrat, winning the seat to become a public advocate for a much wider community.

❓ *Observational Quiz (answer on page 495): What event is Rep. McCarthy promoting?*

Is Honesty Best?

Let us look at a simple example of how the dialectical process might work. Take the aphorism "Honesty is the best policy," which many people accept uncritically. A dialectical thinker, too, might begin by agreeing with this thesis but would then consider the opposite idea: that honesty may cause hurt feelings or foolish behavior or destructive emotions, so it may not be the best policy. From these opposites, a dialectical thinker might synthesize a new idea: that honesty is a desirable goal in human relationships because it fosters trust and intimacy, but honesty should not undermine respect for the other person.

The dialectical process does not stop here, however, for this new synthesis is itself constantly refined by new real-life situations. Does "respect for the other person" mean complimenting someone for a mediocre achievement that he or she worked hard to attain? In true postformal thinking, this question has several "right" answers, depending on whether the person in question is a child or an adult, has achieved a "personal best" or can improve, is spurred on by constructive criticism or is discouraged by it, and so on.

A LIFE-SPAN VIEW

THE DEVELOPMENT OF FAITH

Thinking about religious matters is an aspect of adult cognitive development that has interested some researchers. Like morality, faith is more than a cognitive process: It involves practice as well as preaching, and it arises from religious experience as well as religious education. Nonetheless, one view of faith is as a developmental process; as a person has more experience trying to reconcile religion with daily life, his or her faith may reach higher levels.

The most detailed description of the development of faith came from James Fowler (1981, 1986), who delineated six stages of faith. It should be noted that when Fowler describes "faith," he does not necessarily mean religious faith. He agrees with Paul Tillich (1958) that all humans need to have faith in something, whether that something is a god figure, philosophical principles, country, or simply oneself. Faith gives humans a reason for living their daily lives, a way of understanding the past, a hope for the future. It is whatever each person really cares about, his or her "ultimate concern," in Tillich's words.

Stage 1: Intuitive-Projective Faith

At stage 1, faith is magical, illogical, imaginative, and filled with fantasy, especially about the power of God and the mysteries of birth and death. It is typical of children ages 3 to 7.

Stage 2: Mythic-Literal Faith

At this stage, the individual takes the myths and stories of religion literally and believes simplistically in the power of symbols. In a religious context, this stage usually involves reciprocity: God sees to it that those who follow His laws are rewarded and that those who do not are punished. Stage 2 is typical of middle childhood, but it also characterizes some adults. For example, Fowler cites the case of a woman who says extra prayers at every opportunity, in order to put them "in the bank." She thinks that whenever she needs divine help, she can withdraw some of her accumulated credit.

Stage 3: Synthetic-Conventional Faith

A nonintellectual, tacit acceptance of cultural or religious values in the context of interpersonal relationships is typical of stage 3. It coordinates the individual's involvements in a complex social world, providing a sense of identity and adding significance to the rituals and symbols of daily life. For example, Fowler describes one man who puts his faith in his relationship with his family, a man whose personal rules include "being truthful with my family. Not trying to cheat them out of anything. . . . I'm not saying that God or anybody else set my rules. I really don't know. It's what I feel is right." Because of his commitment to his family, he has learned to accept the "rat race" of his daily work. Such responses are typical of this conformist stage of faith, which is conventional, reflects concern about other people, and values "what feels right" over what makes intellectual sense.

Stage 4: Individual-Reflective Faith

In stage 4, faith is characterized by intellectual detachment from the values of the culture and from the approval of significant other people. The experience of college can be a springboard to stage 4 as the young person learns to question the authority of parents, teachers, and other powerful figures and to rely instead on his or her own understanding of the world. An unexpected experience in adulthood, such as divorce, the loss of a job, or the death of a child, can also lead to stage 4. The adult's understanding of faith ceases to be a matter of acceptance of the usual order of things and becomes an active commitment to a life goal and lifestyle that differs from those of many other people.

Fowler's example of someone at the fourth stage of faith is Jack, whose time in the army allowed him to know people from other backgrounds and gradually to develop a personal philosophy. Jack explains:

> I began to see that the prejudice against blacks that I had been taught, and that everybody in the projects where I grew up believed in, was wrong. I began to see that us poor whites being pitted against poor blacks worked only to the advantage of the wealthy and powerful. For the first time I began to think politically. I began to have a kind of philosophy.

Jack's ability to articulate his own values, distinct from those of family, friends, and culture, makes his faith individual-reflective.

Stage 5: Conjunctive Faith

This type of faith incorporates both powerful unconscious ideas (such as the power of prayer and the love of God) and rational, conscious values (such as the worth of life compared with that of property) and is characterized by a willingness to accept contradictions. It involves a synthesis of the magical understanding of symbols and myths that characterized stage 2 and the conceptual clarity of stage 4.

Fowler cites one woman at this stage who believes strongly in God, but adds, "I don't think it matters a bit what you call it. I think some people are so fed up with the word God that you can't talk to them about God." Her recognition that the word "God" may be distracting and misleading is typical of the ability of the stage-5 thinker to articulate paradoxes and contradictions in faith. Also typical of this stage is an openness to new truths; this woman explains her beliefs by referring to Jesus, George Fox, Krishnamurti, and Carl Jung. Fowler says this cosmic perspective rarely comes before middle age.

Stage 6: Universalizing Faith

People at stage 6 have a powerful vision of universal compassion, justice, and love that compels them to live their lives in a way that, to most other people, seems either saintly or foolish. They put their own personal welfare aside, and sometimes even sacrifice their lives, in an effort to enunciate universal values. Often, a transforming experience converts an adult to stage 6, as happened to Moses when he saw the burning bush and to Muhammad, Buddha, and St. Paul. Fowler mentions some twentieth-century people who have reached this level, among them Mohandas Gandhi, Martin Luther King, Jr., and Mother Teresa, all of whom radically redefined their lives after a particular experience produced a new understanding of human community. Clearly, anyone who reaches stage 6 of faith is an exceedingly rare individual.

Faith and Progress

Indeed, the scarcity of people at the upper stages of Fowler's hierarchy might make one wonder how useful it is. Moreover, it may be galling to read that there are "higher" stages of faith than most adults are likely to reach—especially when some of the "lower" levels of thinking can be seen as no less valid than the "higher" levels. Describing levels of faith seems to imply values about the nature and object of belief. Further, a more intuitive personalized form of spiritual belief may be more reflective of deep religious experience than are the more abstract later stages of faith outlined by Fowler (Reich, 1993).

In Fowler's defense, it should be noted that he never explicitly says that the higher stages are better. In fact, he explains:

> Each stage has its proper time of ascendancy. For persons in a given stage at the right time for their lives, the task is the full realization and integration of the strengths and graces of that stage rather than rushing on to the next stage. Each stage has the potential for wholeness, grace and integrity, and for strengths sufficient for either life's blows or blessings. [Fowler, 1981]

If Fowler is correct, faith, like other aspects of cognition, may progress from a quite simple, self-centered, one-sided perspective to a more complex, altruistic, and multisided view.

An understanding of the stages of the development of faith begins with the realization that levels of spiritual reasoning are not measured in terms of religious doctrine. Mother Teresa

An Expression of Faith In any group of worshippers, be they in a mosque, temple, or church, (including a mega-church like the Crystal Cathedral, shown here), some will be at Fowler's first stages of faith and some will be in the final one, depending on their experiences and maturation, not on their devotion to particular items of creed or ritual.

was probably at Fowler's highest stage, but not all Roman Catholics share her convictions. Similarly, in any group of worshippers, be they in a mosque, synagogue, or church, some will be at the first stages of faith and some will be in the final one, depending on their experiences and maturation, not on their devotion to particular elements of belief or ritual.

Although Fowler's particular stages are not accepted by everyone, the role of religion in human development is now widely accepted, especially when people are confronted with "unsettling life situations" (Day & Naedts, 1999). Faith, apparently, is one way people combat stress, overcome adversity, and analyze challenges. And, like almost all forms of thinking and analyzing, faith is not static but changes as life does, with values shifting as experience accumulates (Rest et al., 1999).

thought things were pretty relative, that I can't tell you what to do and you can't tell me what to do, because you've got your conscience and I've got mine." But at age 25, she held these views:

> Just seeing more of life [led me to recognize] that there are an awful lot of things that are common among people. There are certain things that . . . promote a better life and better relationships and more personal fulfillment than other things, and . . . you would call [those things] morally right . . . I have a very strong sense of being responsible to the world, that I can't just live for my enjoyment, but just the fact of being in the world gives me an obligation to do what I can to make the world a better place to live in, no matter how small a scale that may be on. [Gilligan & Murphy, 1979]

According to Gilligan, adulthood involves new forms of moral thought because life experience poses more complex moral dilemmas than Kohlberg's story about Heinz (discussed in Chapter 15). In one case, a young district attorney interviewed by Gilligan had to decide whether to prosecute a gang member who was probably innocent of the current charges against him but was undoubtedly guilty of other crimes he had gotten away with (Gilligan et al., 1990). Should the gang member be prosecuted on the basis of flimsy, perhaps perjured evidence? Suppose he was unlikely to be able to afford a good attorney who could effectively defend him? Would justice be served if he were convicted in this manner, or would the system be corrupted?

Experiences like this, together with the capacity for asking deeper questions about such dilemmas, cause many young adults to retreat from the certainty they had formerly felt about the purely logical analysis of moral questions. They realize that determining the "right thing to do" is often highly ambiguous and uncertain, and possibly unknowable.

Conflict and Commitment

Out of the uncertainties caused by questioning, probing, and reworking ethical principles in light of the complexities of life experience, many adults forge new principles that guide their decisions, at least for the moment. In true dialectical fashion, people realize that they must make a moral commitment at certain moments of their lives. Each choice made is seen as the best decision possible at the time, even though people realize that other choices could be made as new syntheses emerge. In this way, continuous cognitive change results in less moral absolutism but fosters true moral growth.

Defining Issues Test (DIT) A series of questions developed by James Rest and designed to assess respondents' level of moral development by having them rank possible solutions to moral dilemmas.

The current approach to research on moral issues comes from a group of scientists led by James Rest, who developed the **Defining Issues Test (DIT)**, a series of questions about moral dilemmas. For example, in one of the most recent stories that elicit moral thinking, people are given one specific example of a reporter who must decide whether or not to publish some old personal information that will damage a political candidate. Instead of simply considering an open-ended question, respondents must rank possible answers, from personal benefits ("credit for investigative reporting") to higher goals ("What would best serve society?"). This method makes it easier to relate moral development to other aspects of adult cognition and life satisfaction (Schiller, 1998). In general, scores on the DIT rise with age and with each year of college education, as people become less doctrinaire and more flexible in their attitudes on moral issues (Rest et al., 1999).

COGNITIVE GROWTH AND HIGHER EDUCATION

Of particular interest to many developmental researchers, and to readers of this text, is the relationship between college education and adult thinking processes. Although most people today attend college to secure a better job and to learn specific skills (especially to prepare for careers in the new knowledge and service industries, such as Internet businesses and health care), the stated goal of most colleges and universities is the intellectual development of their students (Barnett, 1994). How successful are educational institutions in this objective? Do people think deeper and better because they have been to college? To be more specific, is there any sign that higher education makes them more likely to reach postformal thinking, combining the practical and the theoretical in a flexible, dialectical way?

College: Is It Worth It? As an investment strategy, yes. Over a lifetime, the typical college graduate earns half a million dollars more than the typical high school graduate. But the real payoff for parents may come in the cognitive blossoming they witness in their children between matriculation and graduation day.

The Effects of College

There is no doubt that, in general, education powerfully influences cognitive development. Years of education are strongly correlated with virtually every measure of adult cognition, even more so than such other powerful variables as age and socioeconomic status. College education not only improves students' verbal and quantitative skills and their knowledge of specific subject areas but also enhances the flexibility and resourcefulness of their reasoning abilities. In the words of one review of the research:

> Compared to freshmen, seniors have better oral and written communication skills, are better abstract reasoners or critical thinkers, are more skilled at using reason and evidence to address ill-structured problems for which there are no verifiably correct answers, have greater intellectual flexibility in that they are better able to understand more than one side of a complex issue, and can develop more sophisticated abstract frameworks to deal with complexity. [Pascarella & Terenzini, 1991]

The same findings appear even when age differences among the students are controlled for. This means that the expected maturity from age 18 to 22 is *not* the main reason the seniors outscore freshmen but that a very similar cognitive growth occurs in four years for the student who entered college at age 17 or age 22. Similarly, preexisting factors—such as family background and academic preparation—that might influence the cognitive growth of those young adults who go on to college are not the main reason higher education accelerates cognition. Significant cognitive advancement over a 4- to 5-year period of young adulthood occurs because of college itself.

The uncertainty is not whether college advances thinking (it does), but which aspect of college is the primary catalyst for cognitive growth. Is it the academic work, the encounter with new ideas, or the discussion with peers that is the primary stimulus? Research has no conclusive answer.

College education does more than deepen thinking. It also leads people to become more tolerant of political, social, and religious views that differ from their own and to be more flexible and realistic in their attitudes (Pascarella & Terenzini, 1991; Rest et al., 1999). Some research has even found a year-by-year progression in this process. It begins with the first year of college, when students believe that clear and perfect truths exist. Many first-year students are disturbed if they do not discover those truths

❓ Especially for College Students and Professors: Given the effects of college, would it be better for a student to study abroad in the first year or last year of a college education?

table **18.1**	**Scheme of Cognitive and Ethical Development**	
Dualism Modified	Position 1	Authorities know, and if we work hard, read every word, and learn Right Answers, all will be well.
	Transition	But what about those Others I hear about? And different opinions? And Uncertainties? Some of our own Authorities disagree with each other or don't seem to know, and some give us problems instead of Answers.
	Position 2	True Authorities must be Right, the others are frauds. We remain Right. Others must be different and Wrong. Good Authorities give us problems so we can learn to find the Right Answer by our own independent thought.
	Transition	But even Good Authorities admit they don't know all the answers *yet!*
	Position 3	Then some uncertainties and different opinions are real and legitimate *temporarily*, even for Authorities. They're working on them to get to the Truth.
	Transition	But there are *so many* things they don't know the Answers to! And they won't for a long time.
Relativism Discovered	*Position 4a*	Where Authorities don't know the Right Answers, everyone has a right to his own opinion; no one is wrong!
	Transition *(and/or)*	But some of my friends ask me to support my opinions with facts and reasons.
	Transition	Then what right have They to grade us? About what?
	Position 4b	In certain courses Authorities are not asking for the Right Answer. They want us to *think* about things in a certain way, *supporting* opinion with data. That's what they grade us on.
	Transition	But this "way" seems to *work* in most courses, and even outside them.
	Position 5	Then *all* thinking must be like this, even for Them. Everything is relative but not equally valid. You have to understand how each context works. Theories are not Truth but metaphors to interpret data with. You have to think about your thinking.
	Transition	But if everything is relative, am I relative too? How can I know I'm making the Right Choice?
	Position 6	I see I'm going to have to make my own decisions in an uncertain world with no one to tell me I'm Right.
	Transition	I'm lost if I don't. When I decide on my career (or marriage or values), everything will straighten out.
Commitments in Relativism Developed	Position 7	Well, I've made my first Commitment!
	Transition	Why didn't that settle everything?
	Position 8	I've made several commitments. I've got to balance them—how many, how deep? How certain, how tentative?
	Transition	Things are getting contradictory. I can't make logical sense out of life's dilemmas.
	Position 9	This is how life will be. I must be wholehearted while tentative, fight for my values yet respect others, believe my deepest values right yet be ready to learn. I see that I shall be retracing this whole journey over and over—but, I hope, more wisely.

Source: Perry, 1981.

or if their professors do not provide them. This phase is followed by a wholesale questioning of personal and social values and of the idea of truth itself. Finally, after carefully considering many opposing ideas, students become committed to certain values, at the same time realizing the need to remain open-minded (Clinchy, 1993; King & Kitchener, 1994).

Several teams of researchers have described this sequence. Obviously, it is a process, not necessarily a step-by-step, freshman-sophomore-junior-senior movement. In fact, for many students, the final stages are not reached until after graduation, when all the academic learning gels with time and practice (Silverman & Casazza, 2000).

This progression was first described in a classic study of Harvard University students by William Perry. As you can see from Table 18.1, Perry found that, over the course of their college careers, the thinking of his subjects progressed through nine levels of complexity, going from a

● Response for College Students and
Professors (from page 499): Since one result
of college is that students become more
open to other perspectives while developing
their commitment to their own values, foreign study might be most beneficial after
several years of college. If they study
abroad too early, some students might
either be too narrowly patriotic (they are not
yet open) or too quick to reject everything
about their national heritage (they have not
yet developed their own commitments).

simplistic either/or dualism (one is either right or wrong, a success or a
failure) to a relativism that recognized a multiplicity of perspectives.
Position 5, which recognizes that knowledge and values (including those
of authorities) are relative but not equally valid, is pivotal in this developmental scheme. According to Perry, this progression is a product of the
college environment: When students reach a new level, their peers, professors, reading, or classwork stimulates new questions that open the
way to the next level. Perry (1981) acknowledged that this developmental
process does not end with college, but continues throughout adulthood.

These findings do not mean that students necessarily switch from
conservative to liberal values during their college years. In fact, the difference involves not so much a change in attitudes as a change in the way
one's attitudes are held—namely, with greater confidence and tolerance.
College experience seems to make people more accepting of other people's attitudes and ideas because it makes people feel less threatened by
them. Research that focuses specifically on dialectical reasoning suggests
that the more years of higher education a person has, the deeper and
more dialectical that person's reasoning is likely to become.

The College Student of Today

You may have noticed that Perry's study was published in 1981. You also
know that cohort effects are powerful. Consequently, today's college
students might be different from those of a decade or two ago—and, indeed, in at least one crucial way, they *are* different. Over the past two
decades in the United States, college students have become less concerned about developing a philosophy of life and more concerned about
securing a good job (Levine & Cureton, 1998) (see Figure 18.2).

**Figure 18.2 Personal Aspirations Overwhelm
Philosophy and Politics.** The American
Council on Education began surveying college freshmen in 1966. Over the decades,
students have gradually become more
interested in their personal success and less
concerned about larger issues of developing
a philosophy and acting on it. For example,
keeping up to date on politics was important to 58 percent in 1966 but to fewer
than half as many (27 percent) in 1998.
Whether the college experience will change
the perspective of entering students or
students (and the culture) will change the
college experience is not clear. We do know,
however, that historical shifts mean that
college is not what it was in 1960; nor are
students the same as they were.

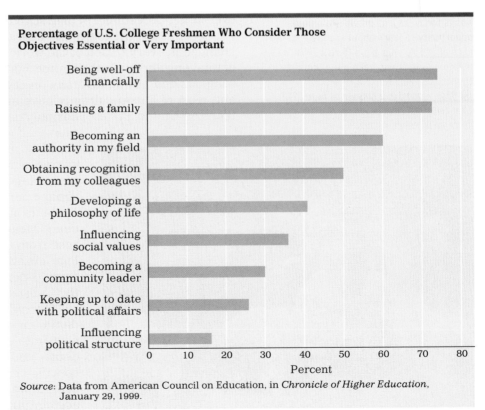

Percentage of U.S. College Freshmen Who Consider Those
Objectives Essential or Very Important

Source: Data from American Council on Education, in *Chronicle of Higher Education*,
January 29, 1999.

table 18.2	More Young Adults Go to College	
Year	Percentage of High School Graduates Going On to College	Male–Female Ratio (For every 100 entering freshmen, how many freshwomen are there?)
1960	45%	74
1970	52	88
1980	49	111
1990	60	107
1997	67	110

The percentage of high school graduates who go on to college has increased from less than half before 1970 to more than two-thirds today. The sex ratio reveals another interesting change: In 1960, parents were reluctant to send their daughters on to higher learning. That shifted about 20 years ago, and now more college students are female than male.
Source: U.S. Bureau of the Census, 1999.

Beyond this basic change in the approach to higher education, what are the contextual differences between today's college students and those of previous years? First, the sheer number of students receiving higher education has multiplied significantly in virtually every country worldwide. For example, when India gained its independence from Britain in 1948, only 100,000 students were in college; in the 1990s, 4 million Indians were—an increase of 4,000 percent (Altbach, 1998). Other nations also increased their college populations, with the United States enrolling an ever-larger percentage of high school graduates (see Table 18.2).

Second, the demographic characteristics of the student body have changed in every nation of the world, with more women (now 57 percent of total enrollment in the United States), more older students, and more religious and ethnic diversity on college campuses. Canada, Australia, and most of Europe already have an even higher female-to-male ratio than the United States; Germany is the only Western nation with more men than women in college (Bulmahn, 1999).

Most of this demographic change has occurred since 1980. In the United States, the percentage of Hispanic students has doubled (from 4 percent to 8 percent) and that of Asian students has tripled (from 2.4 percent to 7 percent). Meanwhile, African American students rose from 8 percent to 11 percent of total college enrollment, and Native Americans rose from .6 percent to .9 percent (U.S. Bureau of the Census, 1999).

Overall, there are more low-income students, more students who are parents, more part-time students, more nonresidential students, and more students who choose quite specific career-based curricula (computer programming, health services, engineering, accounting, business) rather than a broad lib-

A Meeting of the Minds For many young adults today, college provides a unique opportunity to learn about the life experience of people who are different from themselves in ethnic, religious, socioeconomic, and cultural background.

❓ *Observational Quiz (answer on page 504):* *What behavioral clues do you see that these students are in college, not high school?*

eral arts education. In response, institutions of higher learning have themselves become more diverse in both curricula and staff. Worldwide, college has changed from an activity of the elite to one of the masses. Many students—estimated at 4 million each year—travel abroad to matriculate at a university in a foreign nation (Altbach, 1998). Millions more take a semester or two to study in another country.

Another change is in the nature of student activities. As colleges become more diverse, more and more college student organizations are specifically organized for one interest group or another. For example, a small college might have one organization for Latino students, another for the African Americans. A large campus might have separate organizations for those of Mexican, Dominican, Caribbean, and West African origins (Levine & Cureton, 1998). Most campuses also have organizations for people of specific sexual orientations or religious affiliations.

Related to this separateness is a suspicion of political groups that focus on universal issues that have no direct impact on college life (Levine & Cureton, 1998). One reason for this cynicism is that each generation's outlook is shaped by the political events of their teenage years. Many contemporary college students remember the Persian Gulf War, the Rodney King verdict, the global spread of the AIDS epidemic, the civil wars in the Balkans, East Timor, and Central Africa, the economic collapse of Russia, and the economic difficulties of Japan. These salient events all lead in the same direction: This generation tends to be suspicious of politicians, governments, and philosophies, as Figure 18.2 demonstrates.

In another major change, most of today's college students work at least part time during their college years, worry about paying back college loans, and take more than 4 years to complete a degree. Few live on campus throughout their education, making the informal late-night debate much less common than it once was. As a result, the impetus for cognitive growth depends more on the classroom, less on the dorm room.

Restructuring the University

In response to all these developments, and often pushed by political and financial pressures, many educators are reorganizing the college experience to deliver skills, knowledge, and advanced thinking more efficiently. Is such reform and reorganization feasible? Several analysts believe so. For example:

> Effective expert teachers . . . can create the necessary chaos for the flexible change that must accompany learning. [Sinnott & Johnson, 1996]

> [H]igher education is obliged both to produce a dislocation among its students and to enable them, not just to tolerate the dislocation but to live effectively through it. [Barnett, 2000]

> Undergraduate learning would be enhanced by problem-centered learning and participation in knowledge discovery. [Rowley et al., 1998]

Whether, when, or where this enhancement occurs is not proven—at least not objectively. Subjectively, however, the best evidence may be the choices made by young adults themselves. Students in ever-increasing numbers seek a college education and value the instruction they get (Levine & Cureton, 1998). As an institution, college is increasingly becoming part of the typical cognitive progression of adults. The

CHEATING

CHANGING POLICY

Some newspaper headlines report that cheating is rampant among college students. For instance, a recent story in the *Chronicle of Higher Education* was titled "Cheating Is Reaching Epidemic Proportions Worldwide, Researchers Say" (Desruisseaux, 1998). Actual research suggests that

■ Almost every student knows of instances of cheating.
■ Almost no student who witnesses cheating reports it to college authorities.
■ About 1 student in 12 actually believes that cheating is necessary.

This last statistic is the most disturbing to professors, who usually see cheating as an insult to the learning process, an assault on academic integrity. Added to this problem is that students who are more closely connected to their academic institutions—those young full-time students living on campus at universities—are more likely to accept cheating than are students who commute (see Table 18.3).

The research data may actually underestimate the frequency of cheating. Indeed, another study found that, while few students approve of cheating, 20 percent admit having cheated at least three times, and almost 80 percent are aware of incidents when other students have cheated (McCabe & Trevino, 1996). Moreover, many students have a much more limited definition of cheating than professors, including yours truly (Dr. Berger), have. While almost everyone realizes that copying someone else's answers or sneaking a page of answers into a final exam is cheating, many students seem oblivious to the rules defining plagiarism, to the guilt of the person who allows another to copy from him or her, or to the limits of cooperation in doing homework.

The reality of this cultural gap was forcefully brought home to me when I realized that three students had given identical answers on the essay portion of a test. Instead of simply failing the offenders and stating the college's policy about cheating, I passed out an anonymous questionnaire. In the next class, I reported the data, divided the students into groups, and told each group to figure out what I should do and to choose a spokesperson who would report their conclusions. Then I left the room. The results included these findings:

■ 35 percent knew that cheating was going on in the class
■ 52 percent strongly suspected it
■ 13 percent thought there was no cheating

My first surprise was that so many knew about cheating but none had told me. When the summarizers reported the results of the discussion groups, I got another surprise: They did not share my horror of cheating. Some of the noncheaters felt superior to the cheaters (they are "only hurting themselves"). Some expressed ethnic prejudice (they "whisper things in their language"). Some believed that cheating was necessary ("Your tests are too hard") and benign (we should "help our friends"). Some even thought I was not very troubled by cheating. One student later told me privately that she had seen cheating and decided not to say anything to me because she thought I must have seen it but either didn't care or was afraid to do anything about it.

Using postformal thinking, I realized that my cultural system (in this case, the academic system) considers cheating an attack on the education that I expect all students to cherish. But my students' value system may encourage cooperation in order to cope with institutions that penalize the culturally different and the educationally underprepared. Someone who has that value system might consider "cheating" to be helping a friend or doing whatever is needed to get a diploma and a job. Indeed, research finds that cheaters are more likely to believe that the purpose of school is to get good grades, not to learn (Anderman et al.,

❶ Answer to Observational Quiz (from page 502): *Their age is a giveaway, but that is not a behavioral clue. A better answer refers to their clothing, hairstyles, activities, and body positions— each quite different. College encourages each person to make his or her own choices. The physical distance between one student and another also suggests that they are establishing independence. High school students would more likely cluster closely together, wearing very similar shoes and shirts.*

crucial factors for cognitive change are not the college's overall philosophy (religious or secular), funding (public or private), size (under 1,000 or more than 20,000 students), but the particular "interactions between students and teachers and among the students themselves" (Silverman & Casazza, 2000). Peer tutoring, structured group learning, reflective teaching, and many other aspects of the campus milieu—over several years—foster higher, dialectical thought.

table **18.3**	"Some Forms of Cheating Are Necessary to Get the Grades I Want": College Students Who Agree

Student Characteristics	Percentage Agreeing
All students	8%
Type of institution	
Two-year colleges	5
Four-year institutions	9
Universities	11
Attendance	
Full-time	9
Part-time	3
Gender	
Men	10
Women	5
Resident status	
Residence hall or fraternity	11
Commuter	6
Age	
25 or younger	10
Over 25	3

Source: Data cited in McCabe & Trevino, 1996.

spective, a new synthesis can be found. After my students and I listened to each other's viewpoints, they helped me become much more explicit about my requirements and the reasons for them and helped me signal that cheating was not acceptable to me. (I required students to sit farther apart from each other, I used alternate versions of the tests, and I required more creative written work, with assignments that changed each semester.) Now, when a student cheats, instead of angrily taking offense, I call the cheater and anyone who helped him or her into my office to discuss what they did wrong. The usual consequence is an F on the assignment for all involved, but also the chance to pass the course by submitting their own work for the rest of the semester.

Academia is one dynamic system among many. As a professor working in that system, I choose to uphold its values, customs, and assumptions, and I make them clear to my students. But I no longer assume that this system is the only, the correct, or the obvious one; nor do I assume that anyone who does not uphold it in the way that I consider best is malevolent or a fool. Instead, I explain my values and procedures, listen to students' comments (partly because of the system, most endorse my policies), and then begin teaching and learning.

1998). From that perspective, copying someone else's homework would be quite permissible.

This belief is antithetical to my belief, but dialectical theory suggests that, once both sides understand each other's per-

Thus, as you may already have personally concluded, the college years are a potentially significant period of cognitive growth. College can be a catalyst for mature thought, no matter how old the student is. From orientation week to graduation day, you are learning not only the information and issues pertaining to your major and other curricular topics but also how to think and reason more deeply, reflectively, and broadly.

A CASE OF COGNITIVE MATURITY

A study of adult psychosocial development (Kotre, 1984) described the life of a woman called Dorothy Woodson. She was the last of seven children, born to a poor rural family who, she thought, never loved her. She grew up feeling "horribly ugly," stupid, and neglected, and her perspective on life as she approached adulthood was constricted and bleak. She had no confidence in herself or any plans for the future. As she later said of herself, "Inside I was very fearful and uncertain. I always wanted somebody just to hold my hand through something. I didn't want to do anything by myself."

Dorothy's early adulthood reinforced her narrow view of life. At 18 she married a man on whom she felt desperately dependent but who rarely seemed to care about her. Within a year her first baby was born, weighing only 3 pounds. Neither her family nor her husband seemed very interested in the baby, and they gave Dorothy no help or encouragement in the difficult task of caring for a premature child. The infant developed slowly and died before his first birthday. Her second child, born soon after that, was "an extremely beautiful and precious" girl named Diana.

Shortly after Diana's birth, Dorothy's husband moved to a city 200 miles away, leaving Dorothy alone with their daughter and afraid to protest his absence or to follow him. At one point, when Diana was 2, Dorothy was desperate to see her husband and went to visit him, leaving Diana with a 13-year-old baby-sitter. The sitter's inexperience led to a tragic accident that killed Diana.

Not surprisingly, Dorothy's childhood experiences, her empty marriage, and the deaths of her first two children numbed her in many ways. Dorothy's view of life was shallow and pessimistic. She just barely managed to get through each day and was not at all inclined to make commitments or try to build any kind of future for herself. When she had her third child, she thought, "You're just going to die anyway; I'm not going to love you."

Gradually, however, Dorothy began to develop a new perspective on herself and her life. With the help of a friend, she became involved with a religious community, where she found not only emotional support but also encouragement to read and study. The real turning point for Dorothy came when she found a mentor who spurred and nurtured her intellectual and spiritual growth:

> I began to discuss my thoughts with him. He made me aware of studying critically. He started me wondering about a lot of things. He planted a lot of seeds in my mind, things I never even considered or aspired to. He would question me about everything and make me think about how I really felt, my gut reaction to things rather than parroting what I thought somebody wanted to hear. That opened up a whole new world for me.

As a result of this cognitive awakening, Dorothy began to see herself as worthwhile and her life as meaningful. More particularly, she began to clarify her values and to see personal issues in a much fuller dimension.

This is not to suggest that Dorothy's whole life suddenly changed for the better. To the contrary, she was faced with continual struggle—with the self-doubt and pain that she carried from the past; with the difficulties of raising a child alone; with the tedium of the jobs necessitated by her lack of formal education; with disillusionment in personal relationships; with various medical crises. What did change were the depth and complexity of the thinking she brought to these struggles. Listening to her speak of her life, and especially of her son, one is struck by the sense of balance she eventually achieved:

COGNITIVE GROWTH AND LIFE EVENTS

Research on one final topic relating to cognition in early adulthood is spotty, but the tentative conclusions are intriguing, especially from a developmental perspective. It has been suggested that many life events, or

I feel life is a process and that your experiences bad or good, specifically bad experiences, can either build character or destroy character. And if individuals are seeking a higher good or a higher reason for life, then the experiences will add to their character and add to their life. . . . One of my thoughts is that I've got to make every day count with my son. I mean every day. Not a day should pass that he's not loved and that his ideas and he as a person are not acknowledged and guided in some way. . . . I see family traits that I have, that I've seen in my sisters and my mother and my son. It's like ancestral influences I'm trying to overcome and replace with stronger, more transcendental values. I guess that's what I'm trying to do with him, to let him see that I've passed things on to him—and his dad has too. He's got some pretty good stuff from both of us, but he's got some weaknesses too. If he doesn't focus on them and just concentrates on those strong areas and replaces the weak areas with the creative things he likes to do, then he's going to be that much more valuable to society. . . . He's turning out to be such a fine, fine individual that I want to be a part of that and his posterity. . . . I guess what I'm saying is that there is a reason to fight for life.

Thus, certain key experiences enabled Dorothy to break through her self-defeating, helpless view of herself and to experience considerable cognitive growth. Her view of life, of parenthood, and of her role in the larger society became more complex and at the same time more adaptive and more responsive to the contradictions inherent in personal experience. She also demonstrates a more general possibility: Once adults understand the pain of their past experiences, they are able to say, "The damage stops here," and become a living buffer for the next generation (Kotre & Kotre, 1998).

Case studies, of course, do not prove general trends: they simply indicate what can sometimes happen. However, longitudinal studies that include many cases point in the same general direction. With some exceptions, the general movement of a person's thinking about his or her own life in adulthood is toward a more responsible and committed view of the world (Haan, 1985; Labouvie-Vief, 1992; Vaillant, 1977, 1993).

As with cognitive development earlier in life, such progression depends on context and on the person's interpretation of events. A common element of many life stories in which the person emerges stronger and wiser is what some researchers call a redemptive sequence. For example, individuals explain that the death of a father led to a closer family, a bad marriage led to a good marriage, or drug addiction led to a healthier lifestyle (McAdams et al., 1998). The key in such stories is the dialectical perspective, which enables the person to see the redeeming aspect of the disastrous situation.

Much more longitudinal research needs to be done before firm conclusions can be drawn. However, the general theme of this chapter seems plausible. As people move from late adolescence toward middle adulthood, the interplay between thought and experience, between the logic of formal operational intelligence and the sometimes erratic, sometimes confusing challenges of daily life, between exposure to many viewpoints and the need to take a stand in one's own life, may propel adults to new, postformal styles of thought. As both catalyst and consequence of postformal thinking, "humans balance mind, heart, soul, and the needs of others over time" (Sinnott, 1998). They may recognize and adjust to the contradictions and conflicts of adulthood—conflicts whose nature becomes more apparent in the next chapter.

specific notable occurrences, can trigger new patterns of thinking and thus further cognitive development.

One researcher asked adults how their thought had changed over time. Among the answers were: "I learned . . . how to love and relax; what was important in life; there is more than one right way to do

Life's Changes, Large and Small Life events—both the commonplace and the catastrophic—can lead to new patterns of thinking. In some cases, for example, traveling to another land can begin a series of cognitive shifts that deepens the individual's perspective about the human race. In other cases, being a victim or observer of a hurricane or other disaster can radically alter one's perspective on the meaning of one's own life, or of life itself.

things." And how did they learn it? "By having a family . . . by almost losing my job." This scholar concludes:

> Spurred by everyday social encounters, fresh from the everyday problem-solving tasks of creating a marriage, a long-term friendship, a parent–child relationship, an organization, a social role, a self . . . , the midlife adult seems to use assimilation and accommodation to become skilled in new ways of filtering life with a new postformal logic that combines subjectivity and objectivity. [Sinnott, 1998]

Parenthood is a prime example. From the birth of a first child, which tends to make both parents feel more "adult"—thinking about themselves and their responsibilities differently—through the unexpected issues raised by adolescent children, parenthood is undoubtedly an impetus for cognitive growth (McAdams et al., 1998). Other life events may also make people think more deeply about the nature and meaning of their lives and their relationships with others. A new intimate relationship or the end of an old one, a job promotion or dismissal, victimization by or prevention of a violent crime, exposure to a radically different lifestyle, an intense religious experience or in-depth psychotherapy, the serious illness or death of a loved one—all these experiences may give rise to cognitive disequilibrium and reflection. This, in turn, can result in a new view of oneself and the meaning of one's life.

Evidence for this type of cognitive growth abounds in biographical and autobiographical literature and in personal experience. Every reader of this book probably knows someone (or may actually be that someone) who seemed to have a narrow, shallow outlook on the world in early adulthood but who developed a broader, deeper perspective as experiences and insight accumulated. The In Person box on page 506 presents one case study in such cognitive growth. Your own life is another case study.

SUMMARY

POSTFORMAL THOUGHT

1. Adult cognition can be studied in several ways: from a postformal perspective, from a psychometric perspective, or from an information-processing perspective. This chapter focuses on the postformal perspective.

2. Many researchers believe that, in adulthood, the complex and often ambiguous or conflicting demands of daily life produce a new type of thinking, called postformal thought. This is well suited to coping with problems that may have no correct solutions. Postformal thought is adaptive, integrating thinking processes and experience in a contextual awareness.

3. At its most advanced, postformal thinking may be characterized as dialectical, capable of recognizing and synthesizing complexities and contradictions. Instead of seeking absolute, immutable trust, dialectical thought leads to a flexible, ever-changing approach.

4. Although postformal thinking is sometimes described as a stage, it is not the same kind of universal, age-related stage that Piaget described for earlier cognitive growth. Its appearance is more gradual and is dependent on particular experiences and education rather than on a universal, chronologically determined restructuring of mental processes.

ADULT MORAL REASONING

5. Thinking about questions of morality, faith, and ethics may also progress in adulthood, along the lines of postformal thought. For example, Gilligan suggests that men as well as women come to recognize the limitations of basing moral reasoning solely on abstract principles or personal concerns and try to integrate the two with life experience to forge a more reflective, less absolute moral awareness.

6. As people mature, life confronts them with ethical decisions. Adults realize they must make choices and commitments to moral values, even as they acknowledge that those values may not be universal absolutes.

COGNITIVE GROWTH AND HIGHER EDUCATION

7. College education tends to make people more flexible, thoughtful, and tolerant because it encourages them to feel less threatened by conflicting views. They become less inclined to seek absolute truths from authorities and increasingly acknowledge that knowledge and values are relative (though not equally valid).

8. College students today are different from earlier cohorts in many ways. In almost every nation of the world, not only has the sheer numbers of students increased, but more students are female, ethnic minorities, part-time, commuter, older, and concerned about their financial futures.

9. College education heightens cognitive skills regardless of where one goes to school, but factors like teacher–student interaction and student involvement in learning affect the extent of cognitive growth. It takes time for new thought patterns to develop—sometimes four years of college, sometimes more.

COGNITIVE GROWTH AND LIFE EVENTS

10. Life events also promote cognitive growth in many people. Notable life events, such as parenthood or job loss, may trigger new patterns of thinking that enhance cognitive development.

KEY TERMS

postformal thought (490)
dialectical thought (491)
thesis (491)
antithesis (491)

synthesis (493)
Defining Issues Test (DIT) (498)

KEY QUESTIONS

1. What are three approaches to the study of adult cognition?

2. What are the main characteristics of postformal thinking?

3. How does the emotional intensity of a problem affect the reasoning ability of individuals of different ages?

4. Show how an example from the text (honesty or a love affair) illustrates thesis, antithesis, and synthesis.

5. Describe your own example of dialectical reasoning, other than honesty and the end of a love affair.

6. Is postformal thinking a stage in the Piagetian sense of the term? Why or why not?

7. How does the moral thinking of adults differ from that of children and adolescents? Why?

8. According to research, how does college education affect the way people think?

9. What are the main differences between college students today and 30 years ago?

10. How might significant life events affect cognitive development?

11. *In Your Experience* What changes have you noticed in your values or thought processes between the time you entered college and now?

Early Adulthood:
Psychosocial Development

CHAPTER 19

In terms of psychosocial development, the hallmark of contemporary adult life is diversity. No longer limited by the pace of biological maturation or bound by parental restrictions, adults choose their own paths—and the array of choices for career, marriage, parenthood, lifestyle, and friendship is mind-boggling.

How do adults make their choices? One way is to try to figure out, within all the choices and restrictions presented by their culture and cohort, how best to meet their basic human needs. Thus, to sort out the various paths through adulthood, we first describe the two psychosocial needs that underlie and organize the complexity and diversity of life.

THE TASKS OF ADULTHOOD

What do adults seek in their personal and social development? Most theorists recognize two basic needs. The descriptive terms vary: affiliation and achievement, or affection and instrumentality, or interdependence and independence, or communion and agency (Bakan, 1966). Sigmund Freud (1935) put the same duality quite simply, explaining that a healthy adult is one who can "love and work."

The most elaborate hierarchy of needs was described by Abraham Maslow (1968), who said that, after basic needs for survival and sustenance are met, adults next seek "love and belonging" and then "success and esteem." Although these formulations differ in subtle ways, they all highlight the two drives that are inborn in every adult: to connect with other people in mutually nurturing relationships and to accomplish something themselves.

Perhaps the clearest statement from a development perspective comes from Erik Erikson, who wrote of intimacy and generativity. To be specific, Erikson maintains that after resolving the adolescent identity crisis, young adults next confront **intimacy versus isolation.** This arises from the powerful drive to share one's personal life with someone else, a drive that, if unfulfilled, carries the risk of profound aloneness. As Erikson (1963) explains:

> The young adult, emerging from the search for and the insistence on identity, is eager and willing to fuse his identity with others. He is ready for intimacy, that is, the capacity to commit himself to concrete affiliations and partnerships and to develop the ethical strength to abide by such commitments, even though they call for significant sacrifices and compromises.

intimacy versus isolation   The sixth of Erikson's eight stages of development. Adults seek to find someone with whom to share their lives, in an enduring and self-sacrificing commitment. Without such commitment, they risk profound aloneness, isolated from their fellow humans.

generativity versus stagnation
Erikson's seventh stage of development, in which adults seek to be productive through vocation, avocation, or child rearing. Without such productive work, adults stop developing and growing.

Many Words for One Concept

Affiliation	Achievement
Affection	Instrumentality
Interdependence	Independence
Communion	Agency
Love	Work
Love and belonging	Success and esteem
Intimacy	Generativity

The seventh stage described by Erikson is **generativity versus stagnation,** when the person needs to be productive in some meaningful way, usually through work or parenthood. Without a sense of generativity, says Erikson, life is empty and purposeless and adults are filled with "a pervading sense of stagnation and personal impoverishment" (Erikson, 1963).

Ages and Stages

Fifty years ago or so, the pursuit of intimacy and generativity, as well as adult development overall, seemed to follow the progression of stages described by Erikson. The typical middle-class, mid-century man chose his lifetime occupation and finished his education by his early 20s (identity), married, bought a house, and had children by age 30 (intimacy), and then devoted himself to climbing the career ladder in order to be "a good provider" (generativity). At that time, the typical middle-class woman attained intimacy through marrying in her early 20s and having several children by age 30, and then achieved generativity through her work as wife, mother, and homemaker. The specific steps of her life career depended primarily on the age of her offspring. These stages of development seemed so nearly inevitable that many social scientists confidently constructed their view of adult development around them (see Table 19.1).

Such patterns were visible to sociologists and psychologists, who were usually middle-class, white, and male, from North America or western Europe. However, matching one particular age with one partic-

table 19.1   Levinson's Stages of Adulthood

Early Adult Transition Ages 17 to 22	Leave adolescence, make preliminary choices for adult life.
Entering the Adult World Ages 22 to 28	Initial choices in love, occupation, friendship, values, lifestyle.
Age 30 Transition Ages 28 to 33	Changes in life structure. Either a moderate change or, more often, a severe and stressful crisis.
Settling Down Ages 33 to 40	Establish a niche in society, progress on a timetable, in both family and career accomplishments.
Midlife Transition Ages 40 to 45	Life structure comes into question, usually a time of crisis in the meaning, direction, and value of each person's life. Neglected parts of the self (talents, desires, aspirations) seek expression.
Entering Middle Adulthood Ages 45 to 50	Choices must be made, a new life structure formed. Person must commit to new tasks.

Source: Levinson, 1978.

ular stage of adult development is now seen as needlessly narrow and insensitive. Both intimacy and generativity take various forms throughout adulthood (Wrightsman, 1994). Adult lives "are less orderly and predictable than stage models suggest" (McAdams & de St. Aubin, 1998). In some cultures, marriage and emotional control are still considered the signs of adulthood; in others (notably the United States), financial independence is the mark of adult status (Arnett, 1998).

The Social Clock

social clock   Refers to the idea that the stages of life, and the behaviors "appropriate" to them, are set by social standards rather than by biological maturation. For instance, "middle age" begins when the culture believes it does, rather than at a particular age in all societies.

Although few developmentalists now endorse a strict stage view of adulthood, even fewer abandon ages and stages completely. Adult development still seems affected by a **social clock**, a culturally set timetable that establishes when various events and endeavors in life are appropriate. Each culture, each subculture, and every historical period sets its own social clock. Various norms govern the "best" age to become independent of one's parents, to finish schooling, to establish a career, to have children, and so on (Keith, 1990; Settersten & Hagestad, 1996).

Internationally, social-clock norms vary in both scope and rigidity. Societies in developed regions tend to be quite age-stratified, in that certain privileges, responsibilities, and expectations are associated with reaching a certain age. There is a legal age for driving, drinking, voting, getting married, and even signing a mortgage on a home. There is an expected age for marriage, first baby, completion of childbearing, grandparenthood, and so on. The specific ages change over time, but age itself remains significant. For example, fifty years ago, a woman was expected to begin having children at age 19 and to finish by age 30; now, 30 is an acceptable age at which to give birth to one's first child.

Societies in less developed regions are much less age-stratified, partly because fewer people survive to late adulthood. In these societies,

Resetting the Social Clock Social-clock settings in developed nations tend to be notably different from those in developing nations. In developed countries, for example, the social clock now permits grandmothers to be college graduates and discourages teenagers from becoming mothers. This is in marked contrast to developing nations such as Indonesia, where grandmothers never go to college and young teenagers, like this Javanese girl, often become mothers.

❷ *Observational Quiz (see answer page 514): Although these mother–daughter pairs are separated by 6,000 miles and at least 30 years, they display two similarities that are universal to close relationships of every kind. What are they?*

A Woman Now Two young girls participate in the traditional coming-of-age ceremony in Japan. Their kimonos and hairstyles are elaborate and traditional, as is the sake they drink. This is part of the ceremony signifying passage from girlhood to womanhood.

❓ *Observational Quiz (see answer page 516): At what age do you think this event occurs in Japan—15, 16, 18, or 20?*

status differences related to age may be recognized (people are more respected if they have accumulated property or grandchildren, for instance), but the idea that 30- to 40-year-olds have something in common that 20-year-olds do not is incomprehensible (Keith et al., 1994). Every person tries to move ahead on the developmental path as quickly as possible, so a married 18-year-old who postpones motherhood because she does not feel ready for it would be considered foolish.

A primary influence on this cultural-clock setting is socioeconomic status (SES): The lower a person's SES, the sooner he or she is expected to reach life's major milestones, from becoming independent to becoming "old." The influence of socioeconomic status is particularly apparent for women. Even in developed nations, women from low-SES backgrounds are still pressured to marry by age 18 and to finish childbearing by age 30, while women from high-SES backgrounds may not feel pressure to marry until age 30 or to finish childbearing until age 40. The social clock still ticks, worldwide. Although reproductive techniques make motherhood at age 50 possible, women (but not men) are considered too old to have a baby at that age.

SES has an even more powerful influence on social-clock settings in some other countries. In poor South American nations, for instance, marriage is legal at age 12 for females and 14 for males; more than half of all brides in Brazil, Ecuador, Paraguay, and Venezuela are under age 22. By contrast, men and women in Germany cannot legally marry until they are at least 18. Most wait much longer, with the median age of marriage being 27 for women and 29 for men (United Nations, 1995).

Specific ages differ, but the themes of intimacy and generativity are apparent at every age and in every culture. The prescribed ages for taking on adult roles still cluster in early adulthood, and intimacy (lifelong friendship, commitment to a partner) and generativity (starting a family, beginning a career) are much more common between ages 20 and 35 than later. Accordingly, these two themes are both discussed in this chapter. (Ongoing processes of intimacy and generativity, especially in family relationships and work patterns, are described further in Chapter 22.)

INTIMACY

To meet the need for intimacy (affiliation, affection, interdependence, communion, belonging, love), an adult may become a friend, lover, spouse, or all three. These various intimate relationships have much in common—not only the psychic needs they satisfy but also the behaviors they require. They all involve a progression, from initial attraction to close connection and then to ongoing commitment. Each role demands some personal sacrifice, a giving of oneself, an openness and vulnerability that bring deeper self-understanding and therefore shatter the isolation caused by too much self-protection. As Erikson explains, the young adult must

❗ *Answer to Observational Quiz (from page 513): Physical touching (note their hands) and physical synchrony (note their bodies leaning toward each other).*

face the fear of ego loss in situations which call for self-abandon: in the solidarity of close affiliations . . . sexual unions, in close friendship and in physical combat, in experiences of inspiration by teachers and of intuition from the recesses of the self. The avoidance of such experiences . . . may lead to a deep sense of isolation and consequent self-absorption. [Erikson, 1963]

Two primary sources of intimacy in early adulthood are close friendship and romantic partnership. (A third source, ongoing family ties across the generations, is discussed in Chapter 22.) First we look at friendship, a bond that is almost universal in early adulthood.

Friendship

Throughout life, friends are even better than family members as buffers against stress, as guides to self-awareness, and as sources of positive feelings (Antonucci, 1990; Bukowski et al., 1996). Personal choice is one reason. We do not choose our siblings, cousins, parents, or even children, but we do choose (and are chosen by) our friends. Friends choose each other for the very qualities (understanding, tolerance, loyalty, affection, humor) that make them good companions, trustworthy confidants, and reliable sources of emotional support.

The fact that friendship ties are voluntary, in contrast to the obligatory basis of family ties, makes close friendship a validation of personal worthiness. We earn our friends, and they choose to be close to us; no wonder having close friends is positively correlated with happiness and self-esteem (Allan, 1989; Fehr, 1996).

Although friends are important throughout life, the beginning of young adulthood is the prime time to solidify existing friendships and make new ones. There are two good reasons for this, especially with our culture's current social clock. First, most young adults try to postpone overriding commitments (such as marriage and small children). Second, because today's elderly are healthier, few young adults must provide care for aging parents, and most can therefore be independent. This absence of family obligations allows young adults time to form extensive and varied social networks, at college or at work, among political, cultural, athletic, or religious groups, even on vacation or waiting for a bus. Within this wide array of social opportunities, each adult selects acquaintances who provide companionship, information, advice, and sympathy.

A wide social network, typically formed in early adulthood, is a start. Without exposure, new friendships cannot begin. But what moves acquaintanceship forward to become close friendship? For friendship as for romance, four factors act as **gateways to attraction:**

gateways to attraction The various qualities, such as appearance and proximity, that are prerequisites for the formation of close friendships and intimate relationships.

- Physical attractiveness (even in platonic same-sex relationships)
- Apparent availability (demonstrated in willingness to chat, to do things together)
- Absence of "exclusion criteria" (no characteristics are completely unacceptable)
- Frequent exposure [Fehr, 1996]

The first two factors on this list are self-explanatory. The third, exclusion criteria, is noteworthy for its variability. Some people do not care very much about a friend's religion or politics, whereas other people would exclude from their inner circle someone who was not, say, a fundamentalist Christian or a practicing Muslim or a political liberal. Some people do not care about another's personal habits or demographic traits, but others would exclude anyone who, say, smoked cigarettes or was homosexual or was too stupid, too fat, or too old.

The point with exclusion criteria is not that people want close friends exactly like them or that people are intolerant of others' values or actions. In fact, most people appreciate diversity and accept a wide variety of human choices. However, when it comes to our close confidants, each

GENDER DIFFERENCES IN FRIENDSHIP

In friendships, men and women tend to differ—in what they do together, in what they say to each other, and in how they feel about each other (Fehr, 1996). Men friends share activities and interests; women friends are more intimate and emotional, providing shared confidences and practical assistance in times of crisis.

One sign of this gender difference is in conversations. Female friends engage in self-disclosing talk—secrets from their past, health problems, difficulties with their romantic or family relationships. Those conversations are the heart of the friendship. Male friends tend to talk about external matters—sports, work, politics, cars—and conversation is peripheral:

Men's adult friendships . . . are often geared toward accomplishing things and having something to show for their time spent together—practical problems solved, the house painted or the deck completed, wildlife netted, cars washed or tuned, tennis, basketball, poker, or music played, and so on. Shared talk may occur during these pursuits, but it is not the principal focus. [Rawlins, 1992]

As a result of these basic gender differences, men and women have different expectations. Women expect to reveal their weaknesses and problems to friends and receive an attentive and sympathetic ear and, if necessary, a shoulder to cry on. Men are less likely to talk about their weaknesses and problems, but, when they do discuss them, they expect practical advice rather than sympathy (Tannen, 1990).

Indeed, men's conversations, much more than women's, are meant to showcase their strengths and expertise, whether it involves their ability to do their job, their knowledge of the latest advances in computer technology, or their insight into why this or that team will never make it into the playoffs. In short, whereas friendship helps women cope with problems via shared fears, sorrows, and disappointments, it helps men maintain a favorable self-concept.

Such Good Friends Friendship patterns vary from person to person, of course, and gender stereotypes regarding these patterns are often wide of the mark. Nonetheless, on the whole, friendships between men tend to take a different direction than those between women. Men typically do things together—with outdoor activities frequently preferred, especially if they lend themselves to showing off and friendly bragging. Women, on the other hand, tend to spend more time in intimate conversation, perhaps commiserating about their problems rather than calling attention to their accomplishments.

❶ *Answer to Observational Quiz (from page 514):* *The most obvious clue—that the girls look like teenagers—is misleading. Remembering that the social clock is slower in developed nations and that Asian adolescents mature relatively late, you might accurately guess age 20, 5 years after Quinzeana, the similar Latina occasion, and 4 years after the European American "Sweet Sixteen."*

of us has two or three basic filters that are used to exclude certain groups of people. We allow variation in those traits that are not central to our own being, but we require similarity in whatever traits are most central to our self-concept.

The fourth factor is surprisingly powerful. The lifelong friends people make in college are more likely to be those who chanced to sit next to them in class rather than 15 seats away or who lived on their floor of a dorm rather than on the floor above. Work acquaintances are more likely to become friends if they happen to ride the same bus home day after day. Chance encounters that lead to repeated interactions are the basis for many lifelong relationships.

In part because they are open to new acquaintances and are exposed to many other people who are at the same stage of their lives, people in their early 20s almost never feel bereft of friendship. One

As a result, men's friendships are tinged with open competition, reflected in frequent teasing and needling. The willingness to embarrass each other is a way of indicating the solidity of the friendship (Sharkey, 1993). In fact, in many cultures a close friendship gives men permission to call each other names that normally would be insulting, to play tricks on each other, to borrow money or other things—to trespass beyond the boundaries that would be set among mere acquaintances (Krappmann, 1996). Men handle this rivalry with some care. In the words of one: "I'm sure each of us wants to gain greater status in the eyes of the other . . . but I can't think of any competition where one comes out a winner and the other a loser" (Rawlins, 1992).

Many social scientists have asked why men's friendships seem so much less intimate than women's. One reason is that intimacy is grounded in mutual vulnerability, a characteristic that is discouraged by the cultural pressure on men to be strong and hide their weaknesses and fears. Another reason is that, from childhood, boys seem inclined to be more active and girls more verbal, and this early difference may lay the groundwork for interaction patterns in adulthood (Fehr, 1996; Maccoby, 1998). A third reason is homophobia: Many men avoid any expression of affection toward other men because they fear its association with homosexuality.

Ironically, the most open expressions of affection between men tend to occur in situations where they are banded together in the name of aggression, such as competitive athletics or military combat—situations in which few people would question a man's masculinity. The butt-slapping or body-slamming that follows a sports victory, or the crying in a buddy's arms that follows a battlefield loss, would never occur in everyday male friendship.

Cross-sex friendships allow men and women to learn about their common humanity, as well as to gain skills usually "reserved" for the other sex—from cooking to car repair, from money management to child care. Further, to the extent that men and women do indeed have separate experiences and perceptions, cross-sex friendships expand each partner's perspective. Of course, men and women also have much in common. Similarities are often the reason a particular male–female friendship thrives (Canary & Emmers-Sommer, 1997).

However, cross-sex friendships pose special problems. For example, a woman might be genuinely upset by good-natured teasing (the kind her male friend exchanges with his male friends), while a man might be frustrated that his female friend continues to talk about her problems rather than taking his advice on how to solve them. An additional complicating factor is that cross-sex friendships are both "enriched and plagued by fluctuating and unclear sexual boundaries" (Swain, 1992). Men may try to sexualize a platonic friendship, while women may be offended if a friend crosses a sexual boundary.

Ambiguity about sexual feelings can lead to confusion and tension. Even if sexual attraction does not arise, both may still have difficulty explaining the asexual nature of their relationship to others. This awkwardness can kill the friendship, particularly if one of them is romantically involved with someone else or if they have a superior–subordinate work relationship, such as boss and secretary, doctor and nurse, professor and graduate assistant (O'Meara, 1989, 1994). Few people, for instance, believe that a manager can be "just good friends" with a subordinate who is of the opposite sex, especially if he is her secretary.

study found, for example, that 98 percent of young adults said they had at least one close friend (Jessor et al., 1991). Those who live alone are particularly likely to develop an extensive friendship circle and to spend as much time with their friends as they do alone. During early adulthood, both men and women tend to be more satisfied with the size and functioning of their friendship networks than with almost any other part of their lives.

The Best Friendships

Men and women tend to develop somewhat different friendship patterns (see the In Person box), but every friendship pattern has advantages. Cross-sex friendship benefits both sexes but is hazardous for other relationships. The typical female–female friendship pattern may

❓ **Especially for Young Men:** Why would you want at least one close friend who is a woman?

People sometimes talk and act as though love between two adults were a simple, universally understood experience—as though the Beatles lyric "All you need is love" said it all. In fact, over the life span, love takes many forms. Personal preferences, mutual interactions, developmental stages, gender differences, socioeconomic forces, and historical and cultural context—all make love complex and often confusing (Fehr, 1983; Sternberg & Barnes, 1988).

To untangle this complexity, Robert Sternberg explains that love does not have one simple form but instead has three distinct components: (1) passion, (2) intimacy, and (3) commitment. Sternberg believes that the relative presence or absence of these three components gives rise to seven different forms of love (see Table 19.2). Further, he finds that the emergence and prominence of each of these components tend to follow a common developmental pattern as a relationship matures.

As many researchers have found, passion generally is highest early in a relationship. This is the period of "falling in love," an intense physical, cognitive, and emotional onslaught characterized by excitement, ecstasy, and euphoria. Such moonstruck joy is often a bittersweet business, however, beset with uncertainties about intimacy and commitment and "fueled by a sprinkling of hope and a large dollop of loneliness, mourning, jealousy and terror" (Hatfield, 1988).

The truth is that, early in a relationship, while physical intimacy and feelings of closeness may be strong, the level of true emotional intimacy is not high. Indeed, research finds a negative correlation between passionate love and several characteristics of intimacy, including openness, honesty, and trust (Aron & Westbay, 1996). The probable reason for this

table **19.2**	**Sternberg's Seven Forms of Love**		
	Passion	Intimacy	Commitment
Liking		•	
Infatuation	•		
Empty love			•
Romantic love	•	•	
Fatuous love	•		•
Companionate love		•	•
Consummate love	•	•	•

Source: Sternberg, 1988.

❶ **Response for Young Men (from page 517):** Not for sex! Women friends are particularly responsive to deep conversations about family relationships, personal weaknesses, and emotional confusion. But women friends might be offended by sexual advances, bragging, or advice-giving. Save these for a potential romance.

be better for meeting intimacy needs. Although women may be criticized for gossiping, spilling secrets, or simply spending too much time on the phone with their friends (Allan, 1989), female friendship reduces the loneliness and self-absorption that is the danger of the intimacy versus isolation stage.

The male–male pattern of keeping emotional distance while sharing information, activities, and assistance may be the most effective and efficient, especially in the workplace. In fact, in the work setting, where "the shifting sands of promotion and demotion render some friends expendable," a woman's tendency to seek mutual loyalty among confidants who know each other's secrets can undermine her job performance (Rawlins, 1992). Women may be handicapped vocationally if they cannot treat their work colleagues with some distance and dispatch, just as men may be handicapped psychologically if they cannot share their problems with their personal friends.

Perhaps the best solution is for young adults to have several close friendships, each meeting different needs. This solution is, in fact, the

early lack of emotional intimacy is that the partners have not shared enough experiences and emotions to be able to understand each other very well. Nor have they gained the firm sense of commitment that comes when various obstacles have been overcome together.

As intimacy continues through time, the third aspect of love, commitment, is gradually established, expressed, and strengthened. Commitment grows through a series of day-to-day decisions to spend time together, to care for each other, to share possessions, and to overcome problems even when that involves some personal sacrifice. Devotion and mutual dependence are among the dominant traits of commitment (Aron & Westbay, 1996). Signs of commitment range from formal acknowledgments, such as engagement rings, weddings, and childbearing, to the routine aspects of daily life—from shared morning meals to shared checking accounts, from working out compromises about leisure activities to working out a division of household tasks.

As you can see from the table, the Western ideal holds that when commitment is added to passion and intimacy, the result is consummate love. For developmental reasons, however, this ideal is difficult to achieve. In large measure, passion is fueled by unfamiliarity, unexpectedness, uncertainty, and risk. Consequently, the growing familiarity and security that contribute to intimacy may dampen passion. In the beginning of passion, a reciprocated touch of the hand, a certain smile, or a mere glance at the lover's body will produce sexual excitement. As lovers get used to their physical relationship, maintaining the same level of arousal would require increasing degrees of physical, psychological, and fantasy stimulation.

In the same way, early in a relationship, the simplest shared confidence can trigger a rush of feelings of trust, but once a certain level of intimacy is taken for granted, deeper sharing is required to promote similarly intense feelings of togetherness. In other words, with time, passion tends to fade and intimacy tends to grow and then stabilize, even as commitment develops (Sternberg, 1988). This developmental pattern is true over the years for all types of couples: married, unmarried, and remarried, heterosexual and homosexual, young and old (Ganong & Coleman, 1994; Kurdek, 1992).

Recognizing the dynamic nature of love relationships—their continually changing boundaries, demands, and satisfactions—is key to making them endure. As Sternberg (1988) notes:

> "Living happily every after" need not be a myth, but if it is to be a reality, the happiness must be based upon different configurations of mutual feelings at various times in a relationship. Couples who expect their passion to last forever, or their intimacy to remain unchallenged, are in for disappointment. The theory suggests that we must constantly work at understanding, building, and rebuilding our love relationships. Relationships are constructions, and they decay over time if they are not maintained and improved. We cannot expect a relationship simply to take care of itself, any more than we can expect that of a building. Rather, we must take responsibility for making our relationships the best they can be.

one toward which most young adults strive, and it increasingly includes friendships with members of both genders.

The Development of Love and Marriage

Although having close friends is one important way to satisfy the need for affiliation, having an intimate relationship with a mate is an even more important goal for most adults. Humans try to find one partner, one "significant other," one person with whom to bond throughout life—a highly complex undertaking (see the Research Report).

Living Together

cohabitation An arrangement in which adults of the opposite sex are not married but live together in a committed sexual relationship.

Traditionally, the signs of anticipated partnership included engagement ring, wedding announcement, and honeymoon plans. In contemporary times, many couples take their first step toward commitment by living together, an arrangement called **cohabitation**.

Cohabitation is not just for the young. In some cultures—Sweden, Jamaica, and Puerto Rico among them—cohabitation is the norm throughout adulthood. In the United States, middle-aged and older adults who are divorced or widowed often cohabit, although our focus in this chapter is on cohabitation among young adults. Slightly more than half of all women aged 25 to 40 in the United States have lived with a man outside marriage. Most of them later marry their partner, but at any given time, about 10 percent of all unmarried young women are currently cohabiting and another 10 percent have broken up with their former live-in partner (U.S. Bureau of the Census, 1998). Thus, cohabitation is increasingly common, especially in the decade or so when most young adults are independent from their parents but not yet married.

But cohabitation does not necessarily benefit the participants, either while they are cohabiting or after they get married. A study of 18,000 adults in 17 nations found that cohabitants were much less happy, less healthy, and less satisfied with their financial status than married people were. Cohabitants were happier than single, never-married adults of the same age and sex, but not by much (Stack & Eshleman, 1998).

Two other studies, each with a specific longitudinal sample, suggest that cohabitants may be even unhappier than single adults. One, focusing on 25- to 31-year-olds in New Jersey, found that cohabitants were no more depressed than single adults but were much more likely to have serious problems with alcohol. This was especially true for young men who felt pressure to marry but cohabited instead, partly because of financial problems (Horwitz & White, 1998).

The other study, looking at 21-year-olds in New Zealand, found that cohabitants were three times as likely to be physically abusive with each other than either dating or married 21-year-olds from the same cohort (Maydol et al., 1998). The contrast with the dating couples held true even when a dozen possibly confounding background or demographic factors (such as income and education) were taken into account.

Living with a Same-Sex Partner

Long-term homosexual cohabitation, once rare or hidden, is now more common and open. An estimated 2 to 5 percent of all adults in the United States spend part of adulthood in gay or lesbian partnerships (Laumann et al., 1994), choosing such commitments either exclusively or in a sequence that includes heterosexual relationships.

Most jurisdictions do not permit homosexual couples to formally declare their mutual commitment, but even when it is allowed, many couples do not take that step—probably for reasons similar to those of heterosexual couples who choose to live together unmarried. Researchers have been unable to compare a sample of married or cohabiting heterosexual couples with a similar sample of gay and lesbian couples. However, research that has been done suggests that homosexual couples have the same relationship problems as heterosexual couples, especially in how relationship quality and acceptance by friends and families affect satisfaction and commitment over the years (Kurdek, 1998). Being appreciated and supported by others benefits every kind of couple.

Marriage

In much of the world, marriage is not what it once was—a desirable legal and religious arrangement sought as the *exclusive* avenue for sex-

❷ **Especially for Social Scientists:** Suppose your 30-year-old Canadian friend, never married, says, "Look at the statistics. If I marry now, there is a 50–50 chance I will get divorced." What three statistical facts, found in the next few pages, allow you to insist, "Your odds of divorce are much lower"?

ual expression, the *only* legitimate prelude for childbearing, and a *lifelong* source of intimacy and support. Among the U.S. statistics that highlight changes in the nature of marriage are the following:

- The proportion of adults who are unmarried is higher than in the previous 100 years.
- Only 10 percent of brides are virgins.
- Nearly one-half of all first births are to single mothers, who are increasingly unlikely to marry the fathers.
- At least another 20 percent of first births are conceived before marriage.
- The divorce rate is 49 percent of the marriage rate.
- The rate of first marriages in young adulthood is the lowest in 50 years. [Bachu, 1999; Zavodny, 1999]

Indeed, in the United States, most adults aged 20 to 30 are not yet married (60 percent) or are already divorced (3 percent) (U.S. Bureau of the Census, 1999). Adults in many developed nations now spend, on average, half of the years between ages 20 and 40 unmarried.

Nevertheless, marriage remains the most enduring evidence of a couple's commitment, celebrated in every culture of the world by a wedding ceremony complete with special words, clothes, blessings, food, drink, and, usually, many guests and great expense. The hoped-for outcome is a love that deepens over the years, cemented by events such as bearing and raising children, weathering economic and emotional turbulence, surviving serious illnesses or other setbacks, and sharing social and financial commitments. Ideally, the marriage is mutually beneficial, with each spouse taking distinct and complementary roles, both strengthened by their relationship.

Many experts and laypeople have tried to figure out what makes a marriage achieve this ideal. One developmental factor is the maturity of the partners. In general, the younger the bride and groom, the less

The New Matchmaker Once, almost every adult married before age 30, pressured by parents, religious institutions, and the social clock to do so. Their parents or a matchmaker often chose their mate. Now many young adults begin a traditional married life, others live together anticipating such a life, and still others explore interpersonal partnership in unconventional ways. In this "Internet cafe" in Beijing, as elsewhere in the world, the World Wide Web has replaced the church social, the college mixer, and parental introductions as a way of bringing young singles together.

likely their marriage is to succeed (Greenstein, 1995). That may be because, as Erikson points out, intimacy is hard to establish until identity is secure. Many older adolescents and young adults are still establishing their values and roles, which means that a young couple might find their values and roles diverging as they mature.

Further, compromise and interdependence are difficult until a person knows his own identity and what a long-term commitment to another entails. In a series of studies, college students who were less advanced on Erikson's identity and intimacy stages tended to define love in terms of passion rather than intimacy or commitment—butterflies and excitement rather than openness, trust, and loyalty (Aron & Westbay, 1996).

Nevertheless, international research finds that marriage makes people happier, healthier, and richer, so nations in which adults wait too long to get married tend to be nations where people overall are less happy (Stack & Eshleman, 1998). Thus, premature marriage is more likely to end in divorce, but marriage too long postponed is also likely to reduce overall happiness.

homogamy   As used by developmentalists, the term refers to marriage between individuals who tend to be similar with respect to such variables as attitudes, interests, goals, SES, religion, ethnic background, and local origin.

heterogamy   As used by developmentalists, the term refers to marriage between individuals who tend to be dissimilar with respect to such variables as attitudes, interests, goals, SES, religion, ethnic background, and local origin.

social homogamy   The similarity with which a couple regard leisure interests and role preferences.

Homogamy   One factor influencing marital success is the degree to which a couple is homogamous or heterogamous. When studying various cultures around the world, anthropologists draw a distinction between **homogamy,** that is, marriage within the same tribe or ethnic group, and **heterogamy,** or marriage outside the group. Traditionally, homogamy meant marriage between people of the same cohort, religion, SES, ethnicity, and education. For contemporary marriages, homogamy and heterogamy refer to similarity in interests, attitudes, and goals (Cramer, 1998). In general, the more homogamous a marriage is, the more likely it is to succeed, partly because similarity reduces the potential for tension and disagreement.

One study of 168 young couples found that **social homogamy,** defined as similarity in leisure interests and role preferences, is particularly important to marital success (Houts et al., 1996). For instance, if both spouses enjoyed (or hated), say, picnicking, dancing, swimming, going to the movies, listening to music, eating out, or entertaining friends, the partners tended to be more "in love" and more committed to the relationship. Similarly, if both agreed on who should make meals, pay bills, buy groceries, and so on, then ambivalence and conflict were reduced.

However, once again, finding the right degree of homogamy is difficult. The authors of the study of social homogamy criticize the idea that "finding a mate compatible on many dimensions is an achievable goal." In reality, "individuals who are seeking a compatible mate must make many compromises if they are to marry at all," because a high level of marital homogamy is extremely rare (Houts et al., 1996). According to their research, the odds of finding someone who shares a similar interest in at least three of one's favorite leisure activities and holds a similar view regarding at least three of one's most important role preferences is less than 1 percent. Most successful couples share a few crucial values or interests and learn to compromise, adjust, or agree to disagree about the rest.

Marital Equity   Another factor affecting the fate of a marriage is *marital equity,* the extent to which the two partners perceive a rough equality in the partnership. According to one theory, called *exchange theory,*

Sorting Things Out The kind of gender equity shown here presages fewer wars between the sexes in future years.

marriage is an arrangement in which each person contributes something useful to the other, something the other would find difficult to attain alone (Edwards, 1969). The marriage becomes a stable and happy one when both partners consider the exchange fair. Historically, the two sexes traded quite gender-specific commodities: Men provided social status and financial security, while women provided home-making, sex, and children (Townsend, 1998).

In many modern marriages, however, the equity that is sought is not exchange, but shared contributions of a similar kind: Instead of husbands earning all the money and wives doing all the domestic work, both are now expected to do both. Similarly, both partners expect sensitivity to their needs and equality regarding dependence, sexual desire, shared confidences, and so on. Despite this ideal, few marriages are actually equal, nor do spouses expect that each will do half the work (Risman & Johnson-Sumerford, 1998). Couples can be happy with various combinations of housework, child care, paid employment, and so on. What matters most is the perception of fairness, not measurable equality (Sanchez, 1994; Wilke et al., 1998).

One final attitudinal factor predicts marital satisfaction: the notion that a marital relationship is a work in progress, that both partners contribute to better communication, conflict resolution, and so on. The effort put into a marriage reduces the strains put on it (such things as moodiness, jealousy, drug use, hurt feelings, irritating habits) and thus improves quality over time (Myers & Booth, 1999).

Divorce

Throughout this book, we adopt a contextual view of development, which enables us to recognize that many events that seem isolated, personal, and transitory are actually interconnected, socially mediated, and enduring in their consequences. Divorce is a prime example. Marriages do not end in a social vacuum but, rather, are influenced by

Figure 19.1 Divorce Rates Still High That the divorce rate has leveled off in recent years in the United States can be seen as an encouraging sign—except for the fact that the leveling-off has occurred at close to one divorce for every two marriages, a rate that is higher than that of any other nation in the world.

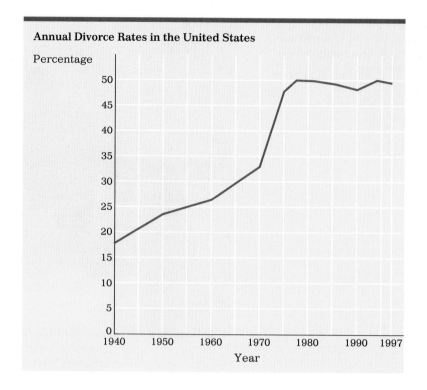

Annual Divorce Rates in the United States

factors in the overall social context as well as in the immediate family context, affecting the lives of many people for years (White, 1990).

One indication of the impact of the social context is the wide variation in divorce rates (defined simply as the number of marriages divided by the number of divorces) from nation to nation. The United States has the highest rate of any major country: Almost one out of every two marriages ends in divorce. Many other industrialized countries (including Canada, Sweden, Great Britain, and Australia) have a divorce rate of about one in three, while others (including Japan, Italy, Israel, and Spain) have markedly lower rates, with fewer than one in five marriages ending in divorce (U.S. Bureau of the Census, 1996).

Historical variations are as marked as national ones. Worldwide, divorce rates increased over most of the past 50 years but have stabilized recently. In England, for example, the divorce rate more than doubled between 1970 and 1980 but has since increased by less than 10 percent. In the Netherlands, the rate of divorce tripled between 1970 and 1992 (though it is still less than half the U.S. rate) and then leveled off. This worldwide trend is particularly apparent in the United States (see Figure 19.1), where a rapid increase that began in the 1970s reached a high of about 50 percent in 1980 and has hovered near that level ever since, partly because the marriage rate itself has declined.

The Role of Expectations

Many developmentalists believe that an underlying explanation for the declining marriage rates and increasing divorce rates is a cognitive shift that has led people to expect a great deal more from their marriage partner than spouses in the past did (Glenn, 1999). In earlier decades firm and separate gender roles meant that each spouse had to depend on the other. Women had to cook, clean, and raise children, while men had to provide the income. Because men were lost in the kitchen and women were unable to earn a living, they needed each other to maintain their family home. Today, marriage partners have a much more flexible view of marriage roles and responsibilities but expect each other to be friends, lovers, and confidants as well as wage earners and caregivers.

Ironically, while couples expect more from a relationship than couples once did, they devote less of themselves to a marriage. The solution to this dilemma may not be to raise expectations *for* oneself but to raise expectations *of* oneself, replacing the "unfettered pursuit of self-interest" with a willingness to "commit fully to the marriage and make the sacrifices and investments needed to make it succeed" (Glenn, 1996). Marital quality is enhanced if each partner idealizes the other's positive qualities. Such "positive illusions" may lead directly to a very real, long-lasting happiness (Murray et al., 1996).

Uncoupling

How does divorce affect development? Initially, divorce is usually worse than anticipated for men, women, and children in almost every way—health, happiness, self-esteem, financial stability, social interaction, and achievement. The longer a couple has been together, the more intimate they once were, and the more commitments they shared (such as joint property, mutual friends, and, most important, children), the more stress a breakup brings.

There are two reasons problems are worse than anticipated. First, before the breakup, unhappy partners focus on what is missing in their relationship and are "hardly aware of needs currently being well served" (Glenn, 1991). Thus, when they do separate, they lose benefits they never knew they had. Second, emotional entanglement almost inevitably increases the longer a couple is together: Feuding as well as friendly ex-partners often experience ongoing currents of emotion (hate, love, resentment, jealousy) after the breakup (Madden-Derdich & Arditti, 1999).

Of course, some relationships are so destructive or downright abusive (see A Life-Span View) that a breakup is a welcome relief. And sometimes every aspect of love—passion, intimacy, and commitment—dies long before a formal breakup, minimizing the pain of separation. Nonetheless, ending a long-term marital relationship is almost always difficult.

The Developmental Pattern of Divorce

Each divorce, just like each relationship, is unique. However, there are surprisingly many common features as well. In the first year of divorce, many ex-spouses become even angrier and more bitter than in the last months of the marriage, and most children become difficult. This is not entirely their fault: An adversarial legal system fosters conflict over alimony, property, and child custody. Then, too, the psychological need to preserve self-esteem despite a "failed" marriage almost requires that each former spouse direct fury and blame at the other.

Another first-year adjustment problem is that the ex-spouses' social circle usually shrinks: Former couple friends and in-laws find it difficult to remain on good terms with both halves of a severed couple; neighborhood friends are lost when one or both spouses move away; casual friends and work colleagues distance themselves when the newly

❶ Response for Social Scientists (from page 521): First, no other nation has a divorce rate as high as the United States. Second, even the 50–50 divorce rate in the United States comes from dividing the number of divorces by the number of marriages. Since some people get married and divorced many times, that minority provides data that drives up the ratio and skews the average. (Actually, even in the United States, only one *first* marriage in three—not one in two—ends in divorce.) Finally, since you have read that teenage marriages are particularly like to end, you can deduce that older brides and grooms are less likely to divorce. The odds of your friend getting divorced are only about one in five, as long as the couple have established a fair degree of social homogamy.

SPOUSE ABUSE

Violence in intimate relationships is very common. Surveys in the United States and Canada find that each year about 12 percent of all spouses push, grab, shove, or slap their partner and that between 1 and 3 percent use more extreme measures: hitting, kicking, beating up, or making threats with a knife or a gun (Dutton, 1992; Straus & Gelles, 1990). Such estimates depend on self-report and are considered low, especially if one remembers who is unlikely to answer surveys—young adults who are low-income or immigrants or both. Because they don't answer surveys as often as older, more established adults do, they are underrepresented in national data. More localized, intense studies find that precisely such individuals are likely to be in abusive relationships. For example, one recent study of women in South Carolina who were relatively poor found that 38 percent had at some point experienced physical violence in a sexual relationship (Coker et al., 2000). Abuse is especially common among cohabiting young couples, whether heterosexual, gay, or lesbian.

What leads to such harmful behavior between people who supposedly love each other? Many contributing factors have been identified, including social pressures that create stress, cultural values that condone violence, personality pathologies (such as poor impulse control), and drug and alcohol addiction (Gelles, 1993; McKenry et al., 1995; O'Leary, 1993; Straus & Yodanis, 1996; Yllo, 1993). From a developmental perspective, one critical factor is a history of child maltreatment. The child who is physically punished, often and harshly, who is sexually abused, or who witnesses regular spousal assault is at increased risk of becoming an abuser or a victim (Straus & Yodanis, 1996). Note that "merely" witnessing domestic abuse puts a child at risk for emotional and intellec-

tual problems in childhood and for violent behavior throughout life (Osofsky, 1999).

Common Couple Violence

A more detailed examination of spouse abuse reveals that it occurs in two forms (Johnson, 1995). The first form of spouse abuse is called **common couple violence.** This form of abuse entails outbursts of yelling, insulting, and physical attack, but it is not part of a systematic campaign of dominance. The perpetrators of couple violence are as likely to be women as men, with both partners sometimes becoming involved in violent arguments. Indeed, in many cultural groups, some interspousal violence is acceptable. In other cultures, it is less acceptable but still not rare. For example, one cross-sectional survey of Canadian women found that 11 percent experienced interpersonal conflict but not systematic abuse (Macmillan & Gartner, 1999).

Common couple violence can sometimes evolve into worse abuse, but more often the couple gradually learns more constructive ways to resolve conflicts, on their own or through marriage counseling. Since everyone—men, women, and children—suffers, help is sorely needed. Happily, in common couple violence, there is hope for the relationship.

Patriarchal Terrorism

There is almost no hope, however, when couples are locked in the second type of spousal abuse: **patriarchal terrorism**

common couple violence A form of abuse in which one or both partners of a couple engage in outbursts of verbal and physical attack.

divorced person becomes emotionally needy. The cumulative result is the loss of vital support at a time of high vulnerability.

Given all this, it is not surprising that newly divorced people are more prone to loneliness, disequilibrium, promiscuous sexual behavior, and erratic patterns of eating, sleeping, working, and drug and alcohol use. In most cases, such effects generally dissipate within a few years (Larson et al., 1995). Nonetheless, surveys from many nations find that single divorced adults of every age are least likely to be "very happy" with their lives, not only when they are compared to married people but also when they are compared to never-married or widowed adults (Stack & Eshleman, 1998).

Why does this effect last for years? Divorced individuals who do not remarry generally have less income (especially true for women with children) and a smaller social circle (especially true for men) than their never-divorced peers. Even when those factors are taken into account,

(Johnson, 1995). Patriarchal terrorism occurs when one partner, almost always the man, uses a range of methods to isolate, degrade, and punish the other. Patriarchal terrorism leads to the *battered-wife syndrome*, in which the woman is not only beaten but also psychologically and socially broken. She lives in perpetual fear and self-loathing, without friends or family to turn to, increasingly vulnerable to permanent injury and death. In nearly all cases, patriarchal terrorism becomes more extreme the longer the relationship endures, because the cycle of violence and submission feeds on itself. Each act that renders the wife helpless adds to the man's feeling of control and the woman's feeling that she cannot, must not, fight back.

In the Canadian study mentioned earlier, fewer than 2 percent of the women experienced this "qualitatively different" systematic abuse, but they were also more likely to respond yes to questions of coercive control, such as:

■ Partner is jealous and doesn't want you to talk to other men.

■ Partner tries to limit your contact with family and friends.

■ Partner insists on knowing who you are with and where you are at all times. [Macmillan & Gartner, 1999]

Many people find it difficult to understand why a woman would stay in such a relationship. There are two prime reasons: She has been conditioned, step by step, to accept the

patriarchal terrorism The form of spouse abuse in which the husband uses violent methods of accelerating intensity to isolate, degrade, and punish the wife.

abuse, and she has been systematically isolated from those who might encourage her to leave. In addition, if the couple have children, the husband typically uses them as hostages by threatening to kill them if the woman leaves. In many cases, such threats eventually backfire, as mothers who endure abuse themselves finally become brave enough to leave when the damage to the children is glaringly obvious.

A battered wife cannot break the cycle of abuse on her own. Her escape requires outside assistance. Such intervention has become increasingly available over the past twenty years. Recognition of patriarchal terrorism in the United States has led to a much tougher approach by law enforcement agencies, with police more likely to arrest perpetrators of domestic violence and judges more likely to issue and enforce orders of protection. It has also led to a network of shelters for battered women and their children (Carter et al., 1999). These shelters provide a haven from violence and, more important, intensive counseling and assistance to repair a woman's emotional damage and to protect her from further abuse.

Of course, primary prevention would be more effective over the long term. Educating children and protecting them from violence, counteracting the poverty and deprivation that underlies abuse, treating the alcoholism that often fuels it—all these are wise measures. From a life-span perspective, family examples and then family connections can protect individuals from getting caught in the downward spiral of patriarchal terrorism. Serious abuse is particularly likely to occur among younger adults in common-law marriages. That means that, unless both partners are able to stop common couple violence, the time to get out of a bad relationship is early on, before serious damage is done.

however, those who are divorced, especially if they have been divorced more than once, have higher rates of depression and poor health (Cramer, 1998; Larson et al., 1995).

Divorced, with Children

Children make adjustment to divorce more problematic. Especially in the first year or two, children often become more demanding, disrespectful, or depressed (Morrison & Coiro, 1999). Children also add financial pressure, require ex-spouses to compromise about visitation, and visibly remind both parents what might have been (or what actually used to be). Finally, children make remarriage less likely.

The financial burden of child rearing usually falls heaviest on the parent who is awarded legal custody, most often the mother. Some of this disparity is caused by fathers who provide no child support at all—

that is, about 40 percent of all divorced fathers. Recent legal measures against "deadbeat dads"—garnishing wages, withholding a driver's license, interstate and even international enforcement, and occasionally imprisonment—are addressing this problem (Beller & Graham, 1993). In fairness, those men who are most delinquent have the least money themselves. One detailed study found that two-thirds of the fathers who earned more than $20,000 a year paid full child support, but only 22 percent of those who earned less than $10,000 did (Meyer & Bartfeld, 1996). Other research suggests that state laws and enforcement are more to blame than fathers are. For instance, 85 percent of divorced fathers in Vermont have court-ordered collection, and 42 percent of them pay. In Illinois, the numbers are only 30 percent and 12 percent (Children's Defense Fund, 1999) (see Appendix A).

Even if both parents contribute as much to child rearing as they did before the divorce, it is not enough, because two residences are costly, and the saving from shared shopping, meal preparation, and child care disappears.

Custodial parents usually lose income and free time, but noncustodial parents suffer too: They lose the intimate bonds formed through daily and nightly interactions. This physical and psychic distance is particularly distressing for many contemporary fathers who had been active parents since their children were born. Few of them maintain intimate relationships with their noncustodial children (Arendell, 1995). Compounding the problem is that children's interests and emotional needs always change as they mature. Parents cannot adjust to the nuances of these changes without frequent, ongoing interaction with the child.

Many custodial mothers express their financial and social dissatisfaction by limiting the father's physical and emotional access to the child. This is destructive, because children do best with an involved, authoritative father who helps with homework, pays expenses, provides guidance and discipline consistent with the mother's caregiving, and spends more than a few hours at a time with the child. Mere father contact, especially when limited to fun and food, does not necessarily help in the man's or the children's long-term adjustment (Amato & Rivera, 1999).

GENERATIVITY

Like the desire for intimacy, the motivation to achieve—or the drive to be generative—is a powerful theme of adulthood. The observable expression of this motive varies a great deal. Some individuals and some cultures are highly competitive, seeking individual achievement; others are very cooperative, seeking group success. Some seek tangible signs of status, while others strive for less materialistic attainments. Some emphasize authority at the workplace; others seek respect from children, grandchildren, and the community.

Every adult needs to feel successful at something that makes his or her life seem productive and meaningful. That much is universal. However, adults meet this need for achievement in many ways.

The Importance of Work

From a developmental perspective, a paycheck is only one of the many possible benefits of employment. Work provides a structure for daily life, a setting for human interaction, a source of status and fulfillment.

❓ **Especially for Employers:** Suppose you want to keep a particular new trainee working for you. What incentives should you offer?

Even more crucial, work can satisfy generativity needs. It does so by allowing people:

- To develop and use their personal skills and talents
- To express their unique creative energy
- To aid and advise co-workers, as a mentor or friend
- To contribute to the community by providing goods or services

The pleasure of "a job well done" is universal. Research from many cultures confirms that job satisfaction correlates more with challenge, creativity, and productivity than with high pay and easy work (Myers, 1993; Wicker & August, 1995). In fact, those who work primarily for the money are least likely to enjoy their jobs. A satisfactory job, then, may be more than an economic necessity; it is a developmental imperative.

The Pattern of Work in the 1950s

As recently as the 1950s in the industrialized world, finding the right job seemed a fairly straightforward developmental task, following a culturally prescribed pattern. As described by the then-leading theorist of life-span vocational development, the typical career cycle had four stages: exploration, establishment, maintenance, and decline (retirement) (Super, 1957).

In early adulthood, a person was expected to explore the vocational possibilities, decide on a lifelong occupation, get the necessary training, and then, by age 25, establish a "permanent position" (Super & Thompson, 1981). Maintaining the same vocation, usually with the same employer, the individual was expected to climb, step by step, up the career ladder—achieving predictable advancements gained at predictable times. A worker followed one vocational path, steadily increasing seniority, responsibility, and salary and ending up with "forty years and a gold watch" at age 65 (Vondracek & Kawasaki, 1995).

This pattern suited the stable and not very demanding low-tech job market of the 1950s. Most men worked in manufacturing or sales in large companies or family businesses, and a sizable minority still worked on farms. Most jobs, particularly in manufacturing, "required low levels of expertise, so that employees became interchangeable," easily trained or replaced (Caruso, 1992). Consequently, young men tried to obtain a basic education and then find an employer or a union that would guarantee security, income, and eventually a pension.

For the vast majority of young women in 1950, a "career" meant marriage, children, and housekeeping. The task for them in early adulthood was to find a husband with a steady job so that they could be model homemakers.

Obviously, not everyone followed this pattern. Many workers found this lockstep approach to the career path unsuitable, and most nonwhite workers simply found such careers unavailable (Leong, 1995). But the structure of the job market endorsed this pattern as the natural one, with guidelines for promotion, health benefits, and retirement all drawn up with the stable, employed man in mind.

New Patterns of Work

In the twenty-first century, every aspect of the employment scene—the work, the workers, the employers, and the typical career sequence—is changing. As the authors of one international study note:

> Not only the context of work is rapidly changing, but also "work" itself [involves] new production concepts (for example, team-based work, lean production methods, telework), the flexible workforce concept, the 24-hour economy . . . [Kompier & Cooper, 1999]

Much of this change is a consequence of an altered world economy. In the poorest regions of the world, the shift is from agriculture to industry, as multinational corporations seek cheap labor. Developed nations, meanwhile, are shifting from industry-based economies to information and service economies (Chmiel, 1998).

Indicative of this restructuring is the fact that by 2005 the manufacturing and mining components of the U.S. economy are expected to shrink by a third from their already reduced levels. Rapid expansion will occur in jobs that require the worker to provide information, a service, or treatment rather than a particular product. Among the fastest-growing occupations are physical or occupational therapist, human service worker, computer engineer, home health caregiver, systems analyst, medical assistant, paralegal, and special-education teacher (U.S. Bureau of Labor Statistics, 1997).

Vocational shifts make it hard for any young adult to plan a career. Certain job categories appear or disappear, seemingly overnight; educational requirements for work shift every few years; and corporate strategies such as downsizing, leveling, outsourcing, and merging are standard practice. Consequently, no individual can expect a linear, secure career path, and the income gap between those with knowledge and expertise and those without will widen (Nelson, 1995). Half of all workers in the United States now use computers on the job, virtually all of which use programs that have been invented or updated in the past three years (U.S. Bureau of the Census, 1999).

Today's knowledge and expertise, however, may be obsolete tomorrow. Automation and reorganization of various industries mean that every few years workers must learn new skills. Usually these skills are quite specific to each job, but they build on overarching abilities, including decision making, memory for meaningful sequences, cooperation with co-workers, and problem solving (Chmiel, 1998). Whether or not a young worker has these abilities and whether or not work experience strengthens them depend on many factors, including higher education and job training. People in their 20s should not prepare only for one specific job but instead should seek those educational and vocational settings that foster a variety of psychosocial and cognitive skills (Anderson, 1995).

The pacing and timing of jobs vary as well. Once the workday was confined to the hours of 9 to 5 on weekdays, but now it is expanding and shifting as people want and need various services 24 hours a day, seven days a week. Further, the pace of production is changing, with moments or days of peak demand alternating with slack times. All this requires more flexibility and adjustment on the part of workers, who must counter the stress of heavy demands on their time and effort (Geurts & Gründemann, 1999). Even with increased hours of work for both men and women, there is no longer much job security, adding to the stress that many families feel (Ryan, 1998).

Diversity in the Workplace

Beyond changes in the work itself, another major change is in the diversity of the work force. Whereas once very few women were employed

❶ **Response for Employers (from page 528):** Money won't do it. Although everyone would like more money, employees are rightly concerned with obtaining recognition and respect for their personal contributions and family pressures. This is particularly true for women and minorities, who are wary of discrimination and are fearful that their jobs might disappear. Employers will have the least turnover if they foster a work culture in which each employee is needed and valued and workers are able to structure their work (hours, location, and benefits) to meet family obligations.

Man's Work, Woman's Work In the modern workplace, sex segregation is more likely at the lower end of the pay scale than nearer the top. While there are many more female lawyers and male teachers than there were even twenty years ago, few women today are big-rig truck drivers and almost no men are hotel housekeepers.

outside the home, in developed nations almost half the civilian labor force is now female: 40 percent in Japan, 45 percent in Canada and England, 46 percent in the United States, and 48 percent in Sweden (U.S. Bureau of Labor Statistics, 1998).

Gender diversity is spreading throughout the occupations. In the United States in 1997, for example, more than one-fourth of all the lawyers, physicians, computer scientists, and chemists were female. Some occupations continue to be sex-segregated; 93 percent of the registered nurses in the United States are female and 97 percent of the firefighters are male. Even in these occupations, however, the sex barriers are decreasing: twice as many men are nurses, and twice as many women are firefighters, as 15 years ago (U.S. Bureau of the Census, 1998).

Ethnic diversity in the workplace is increasing in every developed nation except France. For example, in the United States between 1980 and 1997, more than twice as many Hispanics were employed (from 5.5 million to 13 million), and the number of Asians in the work force doubled as well. Between 1980 and 1995, the number of employed African Americans rose from 9 million to 14 million (U.S. Bureau of Labor Statistics, 1992, 1998).

A major reason for this increased diversity is that immigrants have become a larger proportion of the labor force: 25 percent in Australia, 19 percent in Canada, 9 percent in the United States, Austria, and Germany, 3 percent in England and Italy. Even in Japan, where formerly no immigrants were employed, 1 percent of the work force was born elsewhere (U.S. Bureau of the Census, 1996).

The underlying reason is that people are more willing to move where work is available, and they can do so more easily, by spending just a few hours on an airplane. Between 1991 and 1997, more than 7 million immigrants, most of them of working age, entered the United States; this number over a 7-year period was about the same as the number who had immigrated over the 30 years from 1940 to 1970. During those 7 years, 58 nations each sent at least 10,000 immigrants to the United States, with the most immigrants coming from Mexico, the former Soviet Union, the Philippines, Vietnam, China, and the Dominican Republic (U.S. Bureau of the Census, 1999).

Implications for Development

What do these changes mean for today's workers, particularly for young adults just entering the world of work? First, no one should expect to climb one specific career ladder, rung by rung, for 40 years. Instead of training for a job or a career that will last a lifetime, young adults need advanced skills, particularly in communication, logical thought, and human relations, that will enable them to be flexible, mastering new tasks, working with new people, and changing jobs often.

Every adult should expect to be retrained and transferred within a restructuring company, to quit or be fired when an employer downsizes, to start his or her own small business, or to be hired by an employer in an industry that did not exist a decade ago. Instead of a smooth career path, almost every young adult will experience several periods of unemployment, self-employment, temporary work, or further education, and most middle-aged workers will have at least one such episode as well. The median interval a U.S. worker stays with the same employer is 3½ years, which means that the average employee works for a dozen companies—and usually holds several distinct job titles—between age 20 and retirement (U.S. Bureau of the Census, 1999).

Some Gender Barriers Fall Typical in many ways of today's labor force, these two workers in a food processing plant check quality rather than perform manual labor, as their counterparts fifty years ago did. The other major difference is that their historical counterparts were almost always married white men. In large companies today, almost half of the employees are female and/or nonwhite, except at top management, where a glass ceiling keeps boardrooms almost exclusively male and white.

The second implication, arising from the growing diversity of the workplace, is the need for sensitivity to cultural differences. The potential tension between the culture of the employee and the culture of the organization must be recognized and reconciled (Leong & Brown, 1995). For example, one organization might expect workers to follow a hierarchical chain of command and to use formal channels of communication, and another might expect free-wheeling teamwork and open cooperation across job titles. Depending on their particular personality and cultural background, certain workers might find one or the other of these two approaches incompatible with their own style of interaction. Similarly, cultural attitudes regarding punctuality, appropriate attire, and cross-sex interaction may differ from those endorsed by the organization. Immigrant women often find this situation particularly hard, for many developing nations foster restrictive and subservient female roles but many developed nations demand that women employees be assertive and vocal (Espin, 1999).

The cultural values and assumptions that workers bring to the job need to be recognized and appreciated. Then such patterns should be incorporated when they are beneficial and respectfully revised when they are not. In fact, work teams function best when members have a variety of talents and backgrounds, although such teams do not necessarily make workers happy and relaxed (Chmiel, 1998; Senior, 1997).

glass ceiling An invisible barrier experienced by many women in male-dominated occupations—and by many minority workers in majority-dominated occupations—that halts promotion and undercuts their power at a certain managerial level.

Another implication of the rapidly changing job picture is that women, ethnic minorities, and immigrants may experience difficulty in breaking through the **glass ceiling,** the invisible barrier to career advancement that has little to do with the individual's skills and abilities but a great deal to do with cultural assumptions and biases. The glass ceiling is easy to demonstrate in the overall work scene. For example, of the 800,000 managers of marketing, advertising, and public relations in the United States in 1998, only 4 percent were African Americans, only 3 percent were Hispanic Americans, and only 39 percent were women (U.S. Bureau of the Census, 1999). Women, minority-group members, and those who have physical disabilities are likely to be held to higher-than-normal performance standards with regard to promotion (Biernat & Kobrynowicz, 1997).

As obvious as the glass ceiling is in population statistics, it is usually invisible to the individual, who is denied promotion because of inadequate personality, experience, commitment, and the like. The increasing flux of the job market, diminishing job security, decreasing affirmative action, and the need for employees to switch jobs and career tracks fairly frequently—all make it easy for employers to conceal discrimination against workers for reasons other than competence.

Generally, new employees of whatever background or gender are likely to succeed to the extent that they reach out to not just one but several experienced co-workers for advice and support (Feij et al., 1995; Hesketh, 1995; Wood & Bandura, 1996). A company that encourages such mentoring is more likely to retain employees.

Success at work requires the same human relations skills needed in friendship and marriage. According to employers, only 9 percent of all dismissed new employees lost their jobs because they could not learn the work. The other 91 percent were fired because of attitude, absenteeism, or inability to adapt to the work environment (Cascio, 1995).

Gender Roles in Work and Family

Generativity, as has been explained, occurs in two major ways: through employment and parenthood. Whereas once men chose to have jobs and women chose to have children, both sexes now do both—and men and women must make a major adjustment as result. In the first decades of the century, custom (and sometimes law) dictated that married women were to be full-time housewives and mothers. In some professions, including teaching, female employees were required to quit as soon as they married; in others, being married was an automatic bar to women's employment. Husbands, by contrast, were designated by society as "the family breadwinner," happily avoiding baby care and housework, bragging that they had never changed a diaper, scrubbed an oven, or even boiled an egg. By 1950 in the United States, only 12 percent of the married mothers of young children were in the labor force but 99 percent of their husbands (aged 24–44) were (Cabrera et al., 2000).

Compare that with the picture in the United States today, when most married mothers are in the labor force, including 77 percent of those whose youngest child was in school and 61 percent who had a child under age 3 (U.S. Bureau of the Census, 1999). Almost all (96 percent) of their husbands were in the labor force as well, but most also shared domestic tasks with their wives, sometimes providing a major portion of child care. In fact, in the happiest couples, neither spouse works either very long hours (more than 60 a week) or very few hours.

Contributing to the War Effort In the early 1940s, the pressures of the wartime economy and a shortage of male workers led to the mass hiring of women. This young adult was happily employed as a welder in a shipyard in 1943. Three years later, she, like most other women who had been wartime workers, was out of the labor force and considered suited only for the role of wife and mother.

WHICH PARENT DOES WHAT, AND WHEN?

Family logistics—coordinating births, job changes, further training, relocations, housework, child care, work schedules, medical leave, vacations, and such specifics as who will dress Mary, mop up Johnny's spilled milk, and feed the baby just as the phone is ringing and the car-pool driver is honking—require a level of mutual agreement and planning that was unnecessary in earlier generations. As one researcher explains:

> Given the current economic climate, everyone's use of time and the ways of organizing work and family relationships are changing. The rapid expansion of the service sector and the growing reliance on contingent workers mean that more and more parents will move away from the conventional 8-hour, 5-day per week job. This structural transformation complicates the mutual negotiation of work and family roles, and it implies that strategies for juggling multiple roles will have to become more creative. [Brayfield, 1995]

In many families, the father is expected to do a major portion of child care, and about one-third of all dual-earner families schedule their hours so the father can provide child care while the mother works (Presser, 2000). However, this logical solution succeeds only for day or evening work, not when either parent works a night shift. Although couples without young children do not suffer from a night schedule, those with small children and night-time jobs are at high risk of divorce (see Figure 19.2). One reason is that the marital relationship, like the parental relationship, requires time. As one woman explained:

> Right now I feel torn between a rock and a hard place—my husband and I work opposite shifts, so we do not have to put our children in day care. Now, however, my husband claims opposite shifts [are] putting a strain on our marriage. . . . It is very stressful. [Quoted in Glass, 1998]

Another reason is more practical: A sleep-deprived parent who tries to work while the children are awake is often cranky and impatient.

In the family context, creativity means finding the best solution for the particular family in question. Some succeed by following traditional gender roles; others practice equity in all aspects; and still others switch traditional gender roles, with the wife acting as the primary wage earner and the husband becoming a stay-at-home dad. In all cases, each spouse needs to be able to take on the other's tasks when necessary and to recognize that no particular pattern is inevitably beneficial or harmful. Over the decades in any family, new babies

'Bye, Mom! Seeing the breadwinner off to work was a photographic cliché 50 years ago—except that Mom and Dad played opposite roles. Today an estimated one in ten two-parent families, like this one, include a father who works inside the home and a mother who works outside it. Usually the children and the marriage have at least as good a chance at success with this new pattern as with the traditional one.

arrive and older children grow up, job opportunities emerge or disappear, financial burdens increase or decrease. If, at each stage along the way, both spouses are able to appreciate each other's contributions and to adjust their roles as needed instead of clinging to a rigid pattern or resenting an unequal partnership, the family is more likely to thrive.

There are some signs that today's younger couples may be approaching this goal. In one study of young two-income families, the wives logged an average of 26 hours a week on domestic work and 42 hours on the job, while the husbands worked 21 hours at home (including car and yard care) and 48½ on the job (Barnett & Rivers, 1996). In general, wives perform a disproportionate share of domestic labor in a first mar-

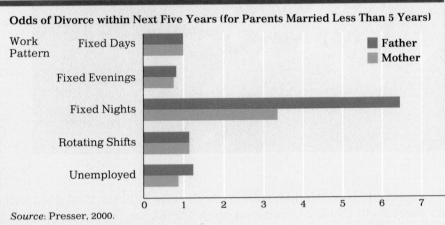

Odds of Divorce within Next Five Years (for Parents Married Less Than 5 Years)

Work Pattern	
Fixed Days	
Fixed Evenings	
Fixed Nights	
Rotating Shifts	
Unemployed	

■ Father
■ Mother

0 1 2 3 4 5 6 7

Source: Presser, 2000.

❓ *Observational Quiz (answer on page 538): Looking closely at the graph, can you say what effect parental unemployment has on a marriage with small children?*

Figure 19.2 Parents' Work Schedules and the Risk of Divorce. Both the wife's and the husband's work schedules affect their chances of getting divorced. To interpret this graph, you need to know that the odds of divorce are set at a baseline of 1.0 for those who are working "fixed days" (that is, most work hours occur between 8 a.m. and 4 p.m.). The odds of divorce for other couples are higher or lower than 1, depending on whether the risk is greater or less than that of the fixed-days group.

This study was longitudinal, measuring work schedules of 3,476 married couples over 5 years. Of those who initially had been married less than 5 years, 21 percent had divorced; of those who had been married more than 5 years, 8 percent had divorced.

riage with several children, and work is more fairly distributed when the spouses are college-educated, previously married, and/or African American (Orbuch & Custer, 1995; Pittman & Blanchard, 1996).

A kind of marital inequity increasingly common occurs when the wife earns more, and is more committed to her career, than the husband. This inequality is particularly devastating among men who are blue-collar workers or men who are immigrants (Espin, 1999; Orbuch & Custer, 1995; Staines et al., 1986).

Conversely, a man's substantially higher career status may facilitate his wife's vocational rise (perhaps allowing her to finance more education or to find work through his contacts) or it may lead her to depart from the job market completely. In many marriages, one spouse supports the other's education or career climb, and then, years later, the situation is reversed, resulting in equity over the long term rather than at any particular stage. When children are small, many couples seem to choose to have the father seek promotion, a second job, and higher wages, while the mother seeks work with less performance pressure (Gorman, 1999).

Looking to families in the future, the larger social context is crucial. Many institutions that have been following policies based on the typical family of 1960 must adjust to current patterns. Large corporations and employers already differ markedly in how "family-friendly" they are, with some having flextime, subsidized day care, personal leave to discharge family responsibilities, voluntary overtime, health benefits that include preventive care and coverage for all family members, and so on.

Nations vary on these factors as well. Some provide their citizens with free child care, universal health benefits, and paid maternity leave; others mandate that employers provide such benefits. Others, including the United States, furnish only minimal support, such as the first "family leave" law passed in 1993, which required employers to offer maternity leave—but for only 12 weeks, without pay. National variations obviously have deep cultural and political roots, with values implicit in every law and custom that affect family life and with potential for adjustment as work patterns change. Many developmentalists would agree with John Snarey, author of a four-generation study of fatherhood and generativity, who hopes for a more supportive social context in the future. Snarey (1993) concludes:

. . . as more childrearing fathers and mothers launch their children from the nest and begin to take on positions of broader responsibility, they will draw on their generative values to promote positive institutional changes . . . enlightened workplace policies which acknowledge the priority of family life and promote the common good of children, parents, and society as a whole.

What's Wrong with This Picture? The beaming man is obviously a proud and responsive father, old enough (33 years) to take his responsibilities seriously. A close look at his 22-month-old daughter suggests that he is doing a good job: She is delighted at the game he is playing with the ball, and he has moved his tall body way down, to be exactly at face level with her. Another fact also makes bonding easier: She is the biological child of these two young adults. So in terms of child and adult development, everything is right with this picture—but some people might be troubled by one detail: Neither parent has a wedding ring. They have never married.

❶ *Answer to Observational Quiz (from page 537): The effect of unemployment is not large, but it is significant. If the father is unemployed, the marriage is more likely to break apart; but if the mother is unemployed, the marriage is more likely to stay together. Reasons for this gender difference are many—but that is a matter of interpretation, not observation.*

Expectations for stepparenthood are rarely fulfilled. If all goes well, the stepparent usually becomes a close friend, an "intimate outsider," who nonetheless remains much more distant from the stepchild's personal life than he or she initially imagined would be the case (Hetherington & Clingempeel, 1992). Indeed, many stepchildren are fiercely loyal to the absent parent, sabotaging any newcomer's effort to fill the traditional parental role, perhaps by directly challenging authority ("You're not my real father, so don't tell me what to do") or by continually intruding on the couple's privacy or by evoking guilt by getting hurt, sick, lost, drunk, or arrested (Pasley & Ilhinger-Tallman, 1987).

Such childish reactions, often unconscious, may cause the stepparent, or both parents, to overreact in ways that further alienate the child. Even if the stepparent is patient and understanding, children take years to adjust to the new family dynamics necessitated by the inclusion of a new adult. It might take even longer before the children express appreciation and affection. The dilemmas of stepparenting are reflected in one stepfather's advice for taking on stepchildren:

> Don't ever expect to replace the natural father in their eyes; win their respect; treat them as your own; love them and discipline them as your own; let nothing come between you and your woman—especially the kids. [quoted in Giles-Sims & Crosbie-Burnett, 1989]

Some foster and older adopted children are likewise attached to their birth parents, an attachment that can be especially volatile because of the destructive treatment many of them have experienced. Other children present the opposite problem: They were never attached to anyone, were always distrustful, and thus rebuff the foster and adoptive parents' attempts to win them over. Attachment between foster parents and children is further hampered because they realize that their bond can be suddenly severed for reasons that have nothing to do with the quality of care. Foster families can be broken if the biological mother completes a drug treatment program and thus qualifies for another attempt at custodial motherhood, or even by a policy shift at the child welfare agency or the mayor's office that requires placing the child somewhere else.

Stepparents face different but equally significant threats to their relationship with their children (Papernow, 1993). One potential problem is divorce, which occurs in about half of all marriages involving stepchildren. Usually such divorces halt the children's relationship with their ex-stepparents, who have no legal rights regarding them, no matter how strong or long-lasting the emotional bond has been. Another potential problem is that the child's other biological parent may take over custody, formally or informally, legally or not. These various realities make both stepparents and foster parents less likely to invest themselves completely in the parent–child relationship.

Adoptive families have an advantage here: They are legally connected for life. Nevertheless, during adolescence, their emotional bonds may abruptly stretch and loosen, for many adoptive children become intensely rebellious and rejecting of family control, even as they insist on information about, or reunification with, their birth parents. Their reasons—whether to test their parents' devotion or to follow the lead of their genetic temperament or to discover their roots or to establish an identity independent from their adoptive family—are understandable. But the result is often a painful demonstration that the parent–child relationship is more fragile than the law pretends (Rosenberg, 1992).

One sign of the difficulties with parent–child attachments in all three situations is that stepchildren, foster children, and adoptive children tend to leave home—running away, marrying, joining the military, being sent away to school, or moving out on their own—earlier than adolescents living with one or both biological parents (Aquilino, 1991; Goldscheider & Goldscheider, 1998). Early home-leaving is particularly likely for adopted children, as they seek their own identity distinct from parental expectations.

All these potential complications certainly make nonbiological parenthood riskier than it is generally pictured to be. However, we must not exaggerate the difficulties. Most adoptive and foster parents cherish their parenting experiences so much that they try for more of the same, typically seeking a second child within a few years after the arrival of the first. Similarly, once stepparents realize that they cannot fill the shoes of the absent biological parent, they usually find satisfaction in the role they do play. On their part, the children usually reciprocate, if not immediately, then later on when they have a clearer understanding of the voluntary sacrifices their nonbiological parents have made (Keshet, 1988; Rosenberg, 1992).

Indeed, for some stepparents, foster parents, and adoptive parents, the rewards of their work go beyond the immediate household. This is exemplified in the reflections of one American mother of an adopted Korean child, who writes of her deepened understanding of the "global family" and of the bonds that connect one human being with another:

> We [adoptive parents], like these children whom we claim so adamantly as our kids, have deeper roots than we knew, an enlarged sense of family, another place in the heart, and a rich and varied history of facing life issues we would never have encountered without them. . . . I hear news about the mudslide [in Brazil, that buried the shacks of 50 families], or the orphans or the starving children, with a refrain at the end: These could be my kids. [Register, 1991]

Perhaps even more than biological parenthood, alternative routes to parenthood tend to make adults more humble, less self-absorbed, and more aware of the problems facing children everywhere. When this occurs, adults become true exemplars of generativity as Erikson and others (1986) described it, characterized by the virtue that is, perhaps, the most important of all—caring for others.

SUMMARY

THE TASKS OF ADULTHOOD

1. Adult development is remarkably diverse, yet it appears to be characterized by two basic needs. The first need is for intimacy, achieved through friendships and love relationships. The second is for generativity, usually achieved through satisfying work and/or parenthood.

2. Traditional patterns of development that followed specific age-related stages have been replaced to a large extent by more varied and flexible patterns. The culturally set social clock still influences behavior but less profoundly than it used to.

INTIMACY

3. During early adulthood, a primary source of intimacy is friendship, with notably different needs being served by men's and women's same-sex friendships. Cross-sex friendships present unique challenges and benefits.

4. For most people, the deepest source of intimacy is found through sexual bonding with a mate, a bonding that frequently involves cohabitation and/or marriage. High expectations are sometimes fulfilled, but about half the time the outcome is divorce.

5. Of the many factors that can affect the success or failure of a marriage, three are particularly notable: the age of the partners at marriage; the similarity of their background, values, and interests; and the couple's perception of the degree of equity in the marriage.

6. The divorce rate has risen dramatically over the past 50 years. Divorce is emotionally draining on both partners and is particularly difficult for those who have children. While some divorced parents manage to maintain good relationships with each other and with their children, more typically mothers have more work and less money than before, and fathers become estranged from their children.

GENERATIVITY

7. For most adults, work is an important source of satisfaction and esteem, as the pleasure of a job well done helps meet the need to be generative. Work is also an outlet for self-expression, a source of status, and a context for mentoring—all of which are generative.

8. Significant new patterns are emerging in today's world of work. A shift from a manufacturing- to a service-based economy means workers must acquire flexible skills that will enable them to perform a variety of different jobs over their careers. Knowledge, not manual skills, is now demanded by employers. Increased diversity in the workplace also creates a need for cultural sensitivity between employer and employee.

9. Changing gender roles have brought about significant shifts in the demographics of working women. Most parents today are part of dual-earner, dual-caregiving couples, facing both benefits and problems that traditional families did not have.

10. Parenthood is the other common expression of generativity. The specific challenges and satisfactions that parents experience depend in part on the child's stage of development. Nonbiological parents experience the same challenges and satisfactions as biological parents, but they also are likely to be faced with special problems.

KEY TERMS

intimacy versus isolation (511)
generativity versus stagnation (512)
social clock (513)
gateways to attraction (515)
cohabitation (519)
homogamy (522)

heterogamy (522)
social homogamy (522)
common couple violence (526)
patriarchal terrorism (527)
glass ceiling (533)
role overload (534)
role buffering (534)

KEY QUESTIONS

1. Describe the two basic needs of adulthood, using the words of several theorists as well as your own descriptions.

2. How does the social clock affect life choices for both high-income and low-income adults?

3. What factors do young adults consider when they form friendships?

4. What are the similarities and differences between cohabitation and marriage?

5. What facts suggest that marriage no longer is the preferred solution to the intimacy needs of young people in their 20s?

6. Compared to 50 years ago, what makes divorce more likely to occur today?

7. What are the gender diffrences and similarities in life after divorce?

8. Beyond supplying income, why is work important?

9. What major changes are occurring in the nature of work and careers?

10. How does diversity in the workplace affect the workers—members of the majority as well as members of minorities?

11. What work and family issues must be confronted in a dual-income family?

12. What special problems are often associated with alternative forms of parenthood?

13. *In Your Experience* Did your parents' marital and employment status affect you? How would you have fared if they had chosen other marriage or work patterns?

BIOSOCIAL

Growth, Strength, and Health

Noticeable increases in height have stopped by age 20, but increases in muscle strength continue until about age 30. All body systems and senses function at optimal levels as the individual enters adulthood, and declines in organ reserve and sensory acuity are so gradual that the onset of senescence is rarely noticed.

Sex and Gender Differences

For both sexes, sexual responsiveness remains high in early adulthood: the only notable changes are that men experience some slowing of their responses with age and women become more likely to experience orgasm. In both sexes, problems with fertility increase with age. While disease is rare, the years of early adulthood are peak times for hazards that are chosen by individuals and encouraged by the culture, specifically drug abuse, violent death (particularly for men), and destructive dieting (particularly for women).

COGNITIVE

Adult Thinking

As an individual takes on the responsibilities and commitments of adult life, thinking may become more adaptive, practical, and dialectical to take into account the inconsistencies and complexities encountered in daily experiences. Partly as a result, moral thinking becomes deeper and religious faith becomes more reflective, with more appreciation of diverse viewpoints and also more commitment to one's own convictions.

The Effects of College

College students today are more often part-time and older than they were 40 years ago, when the first research on higher education was reported. The majority of college students are now female, and a higher proportion is from minority groups. Moreover, most college students are more concerned about their current financial status and their future careers. Nevertheless, college education still seems to foster openness to new ideas as well as higher lifetime earnings.

Life experiences—marriage, childbirth, promotion, job loss, and dramatic events of every kind—can also foster cognitive growth.

PSYCHOSOCIAL

Intimacy

The need for affiliation is fulfilled by friends and, often, by a romantic commitment to a partner. Friendships are important throughout adulthood but are particularly so for individuals who are single. The developmental course of marriage depends on several factors, including the presence and age of children and whether the interests and needs of the partners converge or diverge over time. Divorce, if it is to occur, is powerfully affected by cultural pressures.

Generativity

The need for achievement can be met both by finding satisfying work and by parenthood, including several types of nonbiological parenthood. The labor market is changing radically and individuals should expect to experience several job changes and an increasing need for knowledge and flexibility within a diverse group of co-workers.

Traditional biological parenthood is one way adults achieve generativity. An increasing number become nonbiological parents, with similar rewards but additional stresses compared to traditional child rearing.

PART VII

Middle Adulthood

Popular conceptions of middle adulthood are riddled with clichés like "mid-life crisis," "middle-aged spread," and "autumn years" that conjure up a sense of dullness, resignation, and perhaps a touch of despair. Yet the tone of these clichés is far from reflecting the truth of the development that can and often does occur between the ages of 35 and 64. Many adults feel healthier, smarter, more pleased with themselves and their lives during these three decades than they ever did.

Of course, such a rosy picture does not apply to everyone. Some middle-aged adults are burdened by health problems, or a decline in intellectual powers, or unexpected responsibilities for aged parents or adult children. Some feel trapped by choices made in early adulthood. But the underlying theme of the next three chapters is that in middle age, the quality of life is directly related to perceptions and decisions, sometimes new ones, about how to live it. There are still many turning points ahead where new directions can be set, new doors opened, and a healthier and happier life story written.

Middle Adulthood:
Biosocial Development

In Chapter 17 we saw that the effects of aging are barely perceptible at first. During middle age, that changes: No adult can ignore aging skin, muscles, and sensations. Fortunately, adults remedy, reverse, or compensate for many of these physiological declines, and even recognize that some changes may be for the better. Aging is inevitable, but not inevitably bad.

NORMAL CHANGES IN MIDDLE ADULTHOOD

As people advance toward age 65, signs of aging abound. Hair usually turns gray and gets thinner; skin becomes drier and more wrinkled; middle-age spread appears as stomach muscles weaken; pockets of fat settle on various parts of the body—most noticeably around the abdomen, but also on the upper arms, the buttocks, the eyelids, and the chin.

People even get shorter. Back muscles, connective tissue, and bones lose strength, making the vertebrae in the spine collapse somewhat. This causes notable height loss (about an inch, or 2 to 3 centimeters) by age 65 (Merrill & Verbrugge, 1999).

In addition, overeating and lack of exercise make many people noticeably overweight, more commonly in middle age than during any other period of life. With the exception of excessive weight, midlife changes in appearance do not impair health. Self-image, however, can be substantially affected, particularly for women (Katchadourian, 1987). How important this link is for a particular person depends partly on how closely the culture connects youth and attractiveness, and how strongly affected the individual is by cultural values. (See the In Person box.)

The Senses

Sometime during middle age, virtually all adults notice that their sense organs function less well. Age-related deficits are most obvious in the two crucial sensory systems: hearing and vision (Kline & Scialfa, 1996).

Hearing

The hearing losses that adults experience involve three biological factors: sex, genes, and age. We will discuss each of these in turn.

WHEN YOU SEE YOURSELF IN THE MIRROR

In Western cultures, youthful beauty is a premium for women. Its fading in middle age can be very distressing. The French writer Simone de Beauvoir probably spoke for many middle-aged women of her cohort when she confessed in her 50s:

> I loathe my appearance now: the eyebrows slipped down toward the eyes, the bags underneath, and the air of sadness around the mouth that wrinkles always bring. Perhaps the people I pass in the street see merely a woman . . . who simply looks her age, no more, or less. But when I look I see my face as it was, attacked by the pox of time for which there is no cure. [de Beauvoir, 1964]

Most developmentalists would find these feelings both understandable and unfortunate. As we will see throughout the rest of this book, the overall impact of aging depends in large measure on the individual's attitude toward growing old. Regarding "the pox of time," many developmentalists might wish that both men and women held a view closer to the one expressed by Germaine Greer, an Australian writer who entered middle age two decades after de Beauvoir did. An advocate of the self-affirming ideas of the women's movement, Greer declared:

> Now, at last, we [middle-aged women] can escape from the consciousness of glamour; we can really listen to what people are saying, without worrying whether we look pretty doing it. . . . We ought to be turning ourselves loose, freeing ourselves from inauthentic ideas of beauty, from discomfort borne in order to be beautiful. [Greer, 1986]

This is not to suggest that developmentalists are in favor of people just "letting themselves go" in middle age. On the contrary, the benefits of staying physically fit are much more than cosmetic. In fact, women are more concerned about appearance and more likely to diet—both considered destructive—but also less likely to be overweight or to die prematurely than men. Developmentalists hope that both sexes might achieve a more balanced view of the changes of aging, one that is, literally and figuratively, more than skin deep. As the sociocultural perspective reminds us, we all are

"Old Is Ugly"? The message of these ads is clear: Old is considered ugly. American women are bombarded daily with similar messages from all the media, instilling in them the idea that they have two choices, to fight age or be unattractive—a lose-lose proposition.

affected by the attitudes and values that pervade our culture and historical period, but we can choose whether to accept or to modify these values. As the baby-boomers move into middle age, many experts believe that Western culture may be more realistic, and less prejudiced, concerning aging.

Ironically, the acceptance of one's aging body often occurs because being alive and old is better than being dead, once the fate half of humanity experienced before age 65. Letty Cottin Pogrebin may have spoken for today's baby-boomers when she wrote about reaching "the far side of 50,"

> These days I'm into the truth and the truth is I'm not crazy about my looks but I can live with them. . . . After the third funeral . . . I vowed to set my priorities straight before some fatal illness did it for me. Since then I have been trying to focus on the things that really matter. And I can assure you that being able to wear a bikini isn't one of them. [Pogrebin, 1996]

First, gender differences are notable in middle age. Women typically do not show hearing deficits until around age 50. Men begin to show some deficits by age 30, and they lose hearing twice as fast as women (Pearson et al., 1995).

Second, although some genetic hearing losses are unrelated to age (even children can be genetically hard of hearing), usually genes and age interact, with genes determining how quickly hearing loss becomes

Hard Rocking, Hard of Hearing Les Claypool is an example of the dangers posed by prolonged exposure to loud noise. Night after night of high-decibel rocking with his band, Primus, has damaged his hearing. When this photo was taken in 1999, Claypool was not only performing but also protecting his remaining hearing. He is active with H.E.A.R—Hearing Education and Awareness for Rockers.

apparent. Already by age 50 some individuals show signs of hearing loss, frequently asking others to repeat themselves or turning the TV up so loud that others complain.

Finally, some age-related hearing loss is not genetic; it is the result of prolonged exposure to noise. Each assault on the eardrums does a tiny bit of damage. Many young adults perform very noisy work for long periods without ear protection or habitually listen to music at ear-splitting levels, unaware of the hearing deficits they are developing. By middle adulthood, everyone who repeatedly heard painfully loud sounds when they were younger has noticeable hearing loss.

With all age-related hearing changes, the ability to distinguish pure tones declines faster than the ability to hear conversation. Consequently, the first sign may be the inability to hear a doorbell or a telephone ringing in the next room. Because such pure tones are missed first, speech sounds can usually be understood until late adulthood (see Table 20.1). When difficulty in hearing speech becomes evident, it first involves high-frequency noises, as when a woman or small child talks rapidly (Meisami, 1994).

Fortunately, deafness is rare in middle adulthood, and observable hearing losses are easy to remedy. Minor accommodation, such as asking others to speak up or adjusting the ring of the telephone, is usually sufficient. Middle-aged people who want to have an important talk need to choose a location for it, because background noises that accompany conversation (in a restaurant, for instance) are harder to ignore with age, even if pure-tone hearing is good (Tun, 1998). To correct more serious loss, today's tiny, digitally programmed hearing aids are much more efficient than the devices available

table **20.1**	Hearing Loss at Age 50		
		Men	Women
Can understand even a whisper		65%	75%
Can understand soft conversation but cannot understand a whisper		28%	22%
Can understand loud conversation but cannot understand soft conversation		5%	2%
Cannot understand even loud conversation		2%	1%

even a few years ago. Various telecommunication devices for the deaf (TDDs) are available, permitting additional decades of nearly normal hearing (Tyler & Schum, 1995).

Vision

The standard measure of visual acuity—the ability to focus on objects at various distances—shows more variation from person to person within every decade of adulthood than measures of auditory ability do. The main reason for this variability is that, after puberty, genes have a much greater effect on focusing ability than age does.

By late middle age, however, adults are likely to need corrective lenses. The kind of correction needed depends primarily on changes in the shape of the cornea. People who require glasses before age 20 tend to be nearsighted; that is, they have difficulty in distance viewing, because the cornea is too curved, like part of a ball. With time, the cornea becomes flatter, making adults over age 50 farsighted and likely to require glasses for reading. In addition, by age 35, a 50 percent reduction in elasticity impedes the ability of the lens to change focus from near to far and back (Merrill & Verbrugge, 1999). As a result, at some point in middle age, when flexibility declines, many people who always wore glasses now need bifocals, or two different pairs of glasses. Contact lenses alone no longer suffice. Many who never needed glasses now use them, for magnification or for focusing on fine print.

Other aspects of vision also decline steadily with age (Kline & Scialfa, 1996; Meisami, 1994). Among them are:

- Depth perception
- Eye-muscle resilience
- Color sensitivity
- Adaptation to darkness

Loss of Vision Having always had 20/20 vision, Kirby Puckett, a ten-time all-star outfielder, never felt the need to have an eye exam. At the age of 34, he awoke one morning to discover a permanent black spot in the vision of his right eye. It was his first manifestation of glaucoma, and the end of his baseball career. Mr. Puckett is now an activist for increased awareness of glaucoma, a disease that is most prevalent among African Americans and that can be easily detected in its earliest stages by a simple test.

glaucoma   An eye disease, increasingly common after age 40, that begins without apparent symptoms and often causes eventual blindness. Early detection and treatment can prevent vision impairment from glaucoma.

Each of these changes can affect daily life. Decreasing depth perception makes people more likely to misstep going up and down stairs. Eye-muscle weakness makes it harder to focus on small print for several hours. Decreased color vision (especially for blue, green, and violet) means that clothes no longer match as well and multicolored signs are harder to read. Slower dark adaptation increases the time it takes to distinguish shapes in a dark room after coming in from sunlight or, more ominously, to see the edge of the road at night after the momentary blindness caused by oncoming headlights.

All four of these changes are apparent after age 50, but they usually do not become very severe for another decade or two. Serious accidents, either in a fall or while driving a car, are much more common in late adolescence (when risk taking peaks) or late adulthood (when vision gets worse) than in middle adulthood, when most people are sufficiently cautious to compensate for minor visual losses (Merrill & Verbrugge, 1999).

However, one vision problem that often begins in middle age, **glaucoma**, can be very serious. Glaucoma is a hardening of the eyeball due to an increase of fluid within it. This hardening puts pressure on the optic nerve, damaging it. Glaucoma becomes increasingly common after age 40, and it is the leading cause of blindness by age 70 in the United States, Canada, and Great Britain, especially among people of African descent (Wilson, 1989). Serious consequences can usually be prevented by early treatment, but, unfortunately, glaucoma presents no obvious warning signs to the individual. A simple optometric test (a puff of air to detect increasing pressure within the eyeball) for glaucoma should be part of routine health care for every middle-aged person.

Vital Body Systems

The systemic declines noted in Chapter 17 continue in middle age, reducing organ reserve in the lungs, heart, digestive system, and so forth. People gradually become more vulnerable to chronic disease (see Table 20.2). Declines are also evident in the immune system, which defends the body against external threats, (such as bacteria, parasites, and viruses), and against internal threats (such as cancer).

In some ways the immune system is actually stronger: Specific immunity from past diseases has accumulated, making most viruses, flu, and even the common cold less likely. However, once an invader overcomes the initial immunity, recovery from everything from chickenpox to major surgery, takes longer. The aging immune system is also more likely to mistake the person's own body cells as foreign and launch an internal attack, causing **autoimmune diseases** such as rheumatoid arthritis and lupus (Merrill & Verbrugge, 1999; Miller, 1996; Sternberg, 1994).

autoimmune diseases Illnesses that occur because the immune system malfunctions, reacting to the person's own body cells as if they were foreign invaders. The body attacks itself, causing lupus, rheumatoid arthritis, some allergies, and other diseases.

The ages shown in this table for the stages of chronic diseases are only averages. A person could follow the progressions of each disease from start to finish more rapidly and die by age 40, or the progress could be more gradual, with a 70-year-old still in the subclinical stages.

table **20.2**	**The Increments of Chronic Disease**					
Age Stage	Atherosclerosis (Hardening of Arteries)	Cancer	Arthritis	Diabetes	Emphysema	Cirrhosis
20 Start	Elevated cholesterol	Carcinogen exposure	Abnormal cartilage staining	Obesity, genetic susceptibility	Smoker	Drinker
30 Discernible	Small lesions on arteriogram	Cellular metaplasia*	Slight joint space narrowing	Abnormal glucose tolerance	Mild airway obstruction	Fatty liver on biopsy
40 Subclinical	Larger lesions on arteriogram	Increasing metaplasia	Bone spurs	Elevated blood glucose	Decrease in surface area and elasticity of lung tissue	Enlarged liver
50 Threshold	Leg pain on exercise	Carcinoma *in situ*	Mild articular pain	Sugar in urine	Shortness of breath	Upper GI hemorrage
60 Severe	Angina pectoris	Clinical cancer	Moderate articular pain	Drugs required to lower blood glucose	Recurrent hospitalization	Fluid in the abdomen
70 End	Stroke, heart attack	Cancer spreads from site of origin	Disabled	Blindness; nerve and kidney damage	Intractable oxygen debt	Jaundice; hepatic coma
Prevention or Postponement	No cigarettes; normal weight; exercise	No cigarettes; limit pollution; diet; early detection	Normal weight; exercise; minimize stress on joints	Normal weight; exercise; diet	No cigarettes; exercise; limit pollution	No heavy drinking; diet

*Abnormal replacement of one type of cell by another.
Source: Adapted from Fries & Crapo, 1981.

For most middle-aged people, none of these systemic changes is critical. Thanks to better health habits and disease prevention, deaths among the middle-aged have declined dramatically, especially from the two leading killers, heart disease and cancer. Specifically, since 1940, despite the advent of AIDS (the most common deadly disease among people aged 25 to 44 during the 1990s), the North American death rate during middle age has been cut in half.

Current estimates are that 80 percent of all United States adults alive at age 35 will still be alive at age 65 (U.S. Bureau of the Census, 1998). In other nations (including Japan, Canada, and western Europe), middle age is even more healthy, while in the poorest nations, less than half the people survive middle age. Afghanistan, Cambodia, Kenya, and Tanzania are among the nations where most people die before age 60.

HEALTH HABITS OVER THE YEARS

As signs from their bodies, advice from their doctors, and birthdays that end with a zero drive home the reality of aging, middle-aged adults often improve their health habits (Katchadourian, 1987; Siegler et al., 1999). For example, among the middle-aged in the United States, 30 percent of the men and 24 percent of the women are currently smokers, but another 30 percent of men and 20 percent of women have quit smoking (National Center for Health Statistics, 1995; U.S. Bureau of the Census, 1998). Many middle-aged adults also moderate their consumption of fatty foods and alcohol and give up illegal drugs. Even serious injuries are less likely.

These improvements may reflect a greater wisdom, or at least a greater inclination toward caution and moderation. They also reflect a historical shift that is not directly age-related. For example, since 1980, among adults of any age, smoking in the United States has declined, and the average quantity of hard liquor (excluding beer and wine) consumed per adult has decreased by 40 percent. Consumption of red meat is down about 10 percent; of whole milk, down 50 percent; of fruits and vegetables, up 25 percent; and of flour and cereal, up 50 percent (U.S. Bureau of the Census, 1998).

If every 40-year-old ate better, exercised more, and did not smoke, the majority of this age group would live to at least age 80 and, in many cases, to age 90 or even 100. The Harvard School of Public Health has determined that 65 percent of all cancer deaths are attributable to lifestyle, specifically smoking (30 percent), poor diet and obesity (30 percent), and lack of exercise (5 percent) (Willett & Trichopoulos, 1996). Not just survival is at stake. As one review of health in midlife concludes: "For most conditions and diseases, it's the way we live our lives that has the greatest influence on delaying and preventing physiological decline" (Merrill & Verbrugge, 1999).

The research on smoking is most detailed and universally accepted by the scientific community and even by the cigarette manufacturers (see the Research Report). The success of efforts over the past 40 years to discourage smoking—from scientific hypotheses to research conclusions to public service announcements to legal restrictions to individual behavior change—is a hopeful sign for other unhealthy habits. Now let us look at the more surprising, puzzling, or controversial lifestyle factors.

"Structurally, you're sound. It's your facade that's crumbling."

A Major Overhaul In addition to maintaining better health habits, such as cutting down on fatty foods and not smoking, many middle-aged people are coming to realize the benefits of active conditioning. A moderate diet and a program of regular exercise can produce wonders of restoration, even for a facade like this.

SMOKING AND HEALTH

In the United States, about 30 percent of all middle-aged men and 24 percent of all middle-aged women smoke cigarettes, at significant peril to their health. Canadian smoking rates in middle age are similar, at about 31 percent of men and 29 percent of women (Pechman et al., 1998). Death rates for lung cancer (by far the leading cause of cancer death) reflect smoking patterns of several decades earlier. Since fewer North American men now smoke than did 50 years ago, the 35- to 65-year-old male lung cancer death rate is down 20 percent from the 1980 peak (see Appendix A). At the same time, the worldwide lung cancer death rate for women is still rising, having increased in the United States by 20 percent between 1980 and 1995 (U.S. Bureau of the Census, 1998). Female lung cancer deaths are now higher than deaths from breast, uterine, and ovarian cancers combined, a marked contrast to 50 years ago, when breast cancer killed twice as many women as lung cancer (U.S. Bureau of the Census, 1998). Worldwide, tobacco use is expected to cause more deaths in the year 2020 than any single disease (Michaud, 1999).

Smoking increases the rate of most other serious diseases, including cancer of the bladder, kidney, mouth, and stomach, as well as heart disease, stroke, pneumonia, and emphysema. Marijuana, low-nicotine cigarettes, cigars, bidis (flavored cigarettes), and chewing tobacco all increase these diseases as well, although researchers are uncertain whether they are equally, more, or less harmful than regular cigarettes. Second-hand smoke is also dangerous. Nonsmokers married to smokers have a 30 percent higher risk of lung cancer than nonsmokers married to nonsmokers (Brownson et al., 1992). Stroke statistics are even more ominous. According to an Australian study of people middle-aged and older, if your spouse smokes, you are twice as likely to suffer a stroke (You et al., 1999).

All smoking diseases are dose- and duration-sensitive: A middle-aged man who smoked two packs a day for 40 years is three times as likely to die of lung cancer as a contemporary who smoked one pack a day for 30 years. At any age, a person who quits smoking reduces his or her health risk substantially; middle age is the most common time to quit (Pechmann et al., 1998).

Although African American smokers tend to begin smoking later and to smoke fewer cigarettes than European Americans, they are more likely to die of smoking-related causes. This difference is probably caused by behavior, not by genes. To be specific, 90 percent of black smokers (compared with 30 percent of white smokers) smoke menthol cigarettes, which deliver more nicotine and presumably more of all the other carcinogens in tobacco than do regular cigarettes (McCarthy et al., 1995).

The importance of culture and cohort, rather than genes, is further shown in the fact that the smoking rates in most European nations have not dropped, as the North American rate has. Indeed, about 50 percent of men and 30 percent of women in Germany, Denmark, Poland, Holland, Switzerland, and Spain are smokers (United Nations, 1991). The joke in France is that the best way to stop smoking is to take a trip to the United States.

In developing nations the news is even worse. The rates for males in China, Argentina, and Indonesia, are 55, 58, and 75 percent, respectively—much higher than the rate for North Americans whose ancestors came from those nations.

The wide variations, from nation to nation, cohort to cohort, and group to group show that this particular habit is not merely a matter of personal choice but also a matter of social norms. As those norms change, smoking can decrease and health can improve. This is an encouraging sign for public health advocates, who would like to see similar successes with diet and exercise (Kaplan, 2000).

Times Change—for the Better Health, as much as any aspect of life, is affected by social norms. At mid-century, smoking was the "thing to do," and the dancing Old Gold cigarette packs shown here were typical of cigarette advertising that dominated every medium, including television, in the 1950s. An immediate result of such promotion was the highest rate of cigarette smoking in American history, followed 30 years later by the highest rates of lung cancer. Today, "smoke-free" is in, and the rate of smoking among adults has dropped by half.

Alcohol

Contrary to the traditional assumptions of temperance advocates, adults who drink wine, beer, spirits, or other alcohol *in moderation*—no more than two servings a day—tend to live longer than those who never drink (Berger et al., 1999). The major benefit is a reduction in coronary heart disease. One possible reason is that alcohol increases the blood's supply of HDL (high-density lipoprotein), often referred to as "good cholesterol." HDL is instrumental in reducing LDL (low density lipoprotein), the "bad" cholesterol that causes clogged arteries and blood clots (Wannamethee & Shaper, 1999). Small amounts of alcohol, taken with food, may also reduce tension and aid digestion. Moderate drinkers tend to experience less stress and less depression than either abstainers or heavy drinkers (Lipton, 1994).

Whatever the potential health benefits, however, alcohol comes with notable risks. Many people do not (perhaps cannot) drink in moderation, and middle-aged people are particularly vulnerable to chronic alcohol abuse, with alcohol dependence being most common at about age 40 (Cahalan, 1991). Heavy daily drinking over the years is the main cause of cirrhosis of the liver, which kills 14,000 middle-aged adults in the United States each year.

Excessive alcohol use stresses the heart and stomach, destroys brain cells, hastens the calcium loss that causes osteoporosis, decreases fertility, and increases the risk of many forms of cancer, including breast cancer. Even moderate alcohol consumption poses a health risk if it increases cigarette smoking and overeating. More immediately, drinking accompanies almost half of all fatal accidents, suicides, and homicides.

All told, alcohol consumption, in one form or another, is responsible for about 108,000 deaths in the United States each year, which is 5 percent of total mortality (Archer et al., 1995). Worldwide, alcohol is one of the leading causes of the **global disease burden,** which combines indicators of premature death with indicators of disability worldwide. Especially because excessive drinkers tend to be relatively young, the global burden of disease is adversely affected by this drug (Michaud, 1999). A longitudinal study of 6,000 Scottish men found that those who initially said they consumed five drinks a day were, 21 years later, almost twice as likely to be dead as the other subjects, and those who had two or three drinks a day were one-third more likely to die—not from heart disease, but from almost everything else (Hart et al., 1999). Thus, the fact that moderate drinking has health benefits should not delude anyone: For many adults (not only alcoholics), alcohol is a major health risk.

global disease burden A measure that combines indicators of premature death with indicators of disability. This measure can be calculated for the entire world, which makes it a global number.

Nutrition

Can you eat your way to health? Probably not. The popular press often touts specific foods or nutrients as preventing, or causing, major problems. Most of the nutritional research that makes headlines is not yet accepted by the scientific community. However, at least two conclusions have been proven in study after study: Avoid too much fat, and get enough fiber.

Adults in industrialized countries typically consume about 40 percent of their daily calories in the form of fat, much of it animal fat (in whole milk, cheese, butter, beef, pork, and egg yolks). Animal fat is high in cholesterol and is a major contributor to coronary heart disease, par-

Learning Healthy Eating This session between a dietitian and a heart-attack patient illustrates two factors that powerfully correlate with a healthy diet. The first is one-on-one training, with a knowledgeable professional able to individualize and specify nutritional advice. The second, unfortunately, is that it often takes a brush with death to make people examine and alter their lifestyle.

ticularly in middle age, and to several types of cancer. Adults should get less than 30 percent of their calories from fat, but this ideal is achieved by only 37.5 percent of all U.S. adults (U.S. Bureau of the Census, 1998).

High-fiber diets make several forms of cancer, particularly colon cancer, less likely. Further, vegetables and fruits also contain vitamins and minerals that seem to reduce the risk of virtually every serious disease. Grain and cereals, particularly whole grains such as oatmeal and brown rice, increase overall health, at least in women (Jacobs et al., 1999).

It is recommended that adults increase their consumption of fiber to more than 30 grams per day, including at least five daily servings of fruits and vegetables. North American adults currently consume only about 20 grams a day of fiber. Only 17 percent of people in the United States had two or more servings of fruit per day in 1996, and only 32 percent had three or more servings of vegetables (U.S. Bureau of the Census, 1998).

Obesity

About two of every three residents of the United States between the ages of 35 and 65 are overweight (a body mass index of 25 to 30), with 2 percent of the men and 1 percent of the women actually obese (a BMI of 30 or more; see Appendix A) (National Center for Health Statistics, 1999). Defining obesity as a BMI of 30 or more means that a person who is 5 feet, 8 inches tall and weighs 200 pounds is considered barely obese.

Forty years ago, U.S. residents who were then middle-aged were less likely to be obese. When people who are now 60 were in their 20s, only 8 percent were overweight. Americans are getting fatter, and are much fatter than their parents and grandparents ever were. Similar trends are apparent in Central and South America, in Europe, and in Asia. Thus, most people are fatter than their ancestors and fatter than they themselves once were. This weight increase is bad news, because obesity is a risk factor in heart disease, diabetes, and stroke, and it contributes to arthritis, the most common disability among older adults.

While these dangers of obesity have long been known, it was generally assumed that being "somewhat" overweight was harmless. However, many experts now believe that even those who are only slightly overweight increase their risk of virtually every cause of disease, disability, and death (Oster et al., 1999). Even mood is affected. Women are more likely to be depressed, even suicidal, if they are overweight. Men are more likely to be depressed if they are underweight (a BMI below 21) (Carpenter et al., 2000). This depression in men may be a direct result of their thinness, or an indirect result, in that marriage tends to make men happier and heavier, and most thin men are not married. As Chapter 17 explains, for women, being too thin or being too worried about a few extra pounds can be destructive.

If even a little extra fat is hazardous to health, then everyone needs to eat less than they did in younger years. The reason is that between ages 20 and 50 metabolism normally slows down by a third, which means that merely eating at the same level would cause ballooning weight gain over the decades. As metabolism decreases, so does efficient oxygen consumption and quick recuperation after stress and exercise. This age-related slowdown is another reason to avoid slowing down the body even more by being overweight (Merrill & Verbrugge, 1999).

We should add that the harmful consequences of a BMI between 25 and 30 is controversial, with some suggesting that people who are short, elderly, African, Latino, or Asian American are unharmed unless they become truly obese (Strawbridge et al., 2000). But all the experts agree that every adult should exercise more.

Exercise

When middle-aged people think about losing weight, they think of eating less. Unfortunately, they often forget the other step, exercising more. Both steps are necessary to attain a healthy weight. In fact, this second step is more important (Sallis & Owen, 1999). Activity burns calories, but that is only a start: It also reduces serious illness and death. Simply walking briskly for 30 minutes a day makes people live longer and healthier (Lemaitre et al., 1999; Siegel et al., 1995). Activity (by swimming, jogging, bicycling, and the like) leads to proven increases in heart and lung capacity, HDL, and metabolism and to proven decreases in blood pressure, LDL, and of course, weight.

Even if weight remains the same, vigorous exercise reduces the ratio of body fat to body weight, with significant health benefits. For example, an 8-year study of 72,488 middle-aged women found that those who walked briskly for a total of 3 hours a week were one-third less likely to have heart attacks than were inactive women of the same age, education, diet, smoking status, and weight (Manson et al., 1999). In this study, to determine whether exercise was more important than weight, groups of women of the same weight, but varying activity rates, were compared. In the general population, active and inactive people usually do not weigh the same, because exercise is the best method of weight reduction: It burns calories, decreases appetite, and increases metabolism for hours after a workout (Going et al., 1994).

An additional advantage of both vigorous and more modest exercise, especially in middle-aged and older people, is enhanced cognitive functioning, probably because of improved blood circulation to the brain (Stones & Kozma, 1996). Perhaps for this reason, exercise decreases depression and hostility, making a person psychologically healthier as well as physically more fit.

Unfortunately, even modest regular exercise is beyond a third of all middle-aged adults, according to a 1996 U.S. Surgeon General's re-

Balance and Stretch Exercise used to mean simply moving fast, long, and hard enough to work up a sweat. Now we realize that stretching, lifting and holding weights, and maintaining balance are as important as simply moving the whole body. Ideally, then, an adult's exercise routine includes more varied activities than walking several blocks and playing on a weekend softball team.

❷ *Observational Quiz (see answer page 556): Which of these people do you think is gaining most benefit from this aerobics class?*

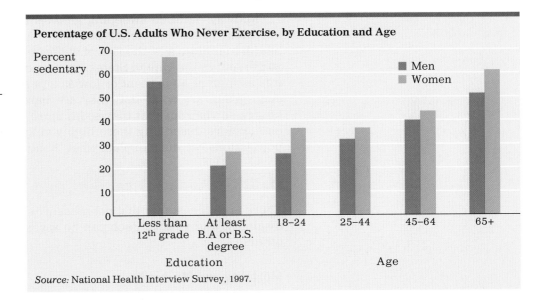

Figure 20.1 The Nonmovers. These are the percentages of U.S. adults who never engage in any physical activity—walking, gardening, or anything else—for at least 20 minutes several days a week. It is not surprising that weight and disease increase with age and are higher among those with less education.

❷ *Observational Quiz (see answer page 557): Which age group has the greatest gender differences? Which has the least?*

Percentage of U.S. Adults Who Never Exercise, by Education and Age

Source: National Health Interview Survey, 1997.

❶ **Response for Doctors and Nurses (from page 550):** Obviously, much depends on the specific patient. Overall, however, far more people develop disease or die because of years of poor health habits than because of various illnesses not spotted early. With some exceptions, age 35 is too early to detect incipient cancers or circulatory problems, but it's prime time for stopping cigarette smoking, curbing alcohol abuse, and improving exercise and diet.

port (see Figure 20.1). Since physical activity has been proven to make people look better, feel better, and stay healthier, the puzzle is why most adults still prefer sitting for hours in front of the TV to going for a swim, a run, or a walk.

VARIATIONS IN HEALTH

Thus far we have been describing the "average" or "typical" middle-aged adult, based on numbers from one or more populous nations. But statistics about health in midlife are generalities that veil many variations. For example, relatively well-educated, financially secure, urban-dwelling individuals tend to live longer, avoid chronic illness or disability, and feel healthier than do adults of the same sex and ethnicity who have less education and money and who live in rural areas. This holds true for every nation.

Further, within every nation, certain regions seem healthier than others: In the United States, middle-aged people living in the West and Midwest are healthier than those in the South and the Middle Atlantic region; in Canada, those in Ontario are healthiest; in Great Britain, health among the middle-aged tends to improve as one moves from north to south.

The reasons for such differences among people of the same age range from the overall quality of the environment and of health care to personal factors that characterize particular individuals. For example, genetic, dietary, religious, socioeconomic, medical, and cultural patterns may explain why fatal heart attacks are more than twice as common in Mississippi and West Virginia as in Utah and Colorado; they may also explain why some particular persons in Mississippi are highly unlikely to have a heart attack, while some other particular persons in Colorado are at very high risk (Smith, 1987; U.S. Bureau of the Census, 1998). One factor is, not just which state a person lives in, but which particular community: In the United States, almost every region has some counties where the premature death rate is four times as high as that of another county less than 100 miles away (Mansfield et al., 1999).

Midway between sweeping generalizations and specific cases, we find many fascinating details about how ethnicity, income, and sex affect health in middle age: the risk of dying between ages 35 and 65 averages 20 percent in the United States, but for some specific clusters of people, it is as high as 50 percent or low as 2 percent. Some of the survivors in each group are so ill that they are barely alive; others are hale and hearty, so vigorous that they seem more like 20-year-olds than 60-year-olds. Before describing these highly vulnerable or relatively protected populations, we must explain what "health" and "illness" mean.

Death, Disease, Disability, and Vitality

There are at least four distinct measures of health: mortality, morbidity, disability, and vitality. Each can be assessed quite separately from the others.

Mortality and Morbidity

mortality   Death. As a measure of health, mortality usually refers to the number of deaths each year per 1,000 members of a given population.

The most solid indicator of the health of a given age group is its rate of **mortality**, as measured by the number of deaths each year per 1,000 individuals. Mortality statistics are based on legally required death certificates, which indicate the age, the sex, and the immediate cause of death. This measure allows valid international and historical comparisons.

morbidity   Disease. As a measure of health, morbidity refers to the rate of diseases of all kinds in a given population.

A much more comprehensive measure of health is **morbidity**, or the incidence of illness. Morbidity includes disease of all kinds. Morbidity can be *acute*, that is, sudden and severe, ending in either death or recovery, or it can be *chronic*, extending over a long period, even over a lifetime. International indicators of morbidity reveal some interesting data not seen in mortality statistics, such as the fact that depression and schizophrenia cause significant morbidity worldwide (Michaud, 1999).

Disability

To truly portray a person's overall health, we must broaden the picture to include not only whether a person is alive and not seriously sick, but also how satisfying his or her life is. Thus, to measure quality of life, we need two additional measures: disability and vitality.

disability   Lack of ability to do some basic activity. As a measure of health, disability refers to the portion of the population who cannot perform activities that most others can.

Disability refers to a person's long-term inability to act in "necessary, expected, and personally desired ways" (Verbrugge, 1994). Limitation in normal function, not the degree or type of illness, is the measure of disability (Merrill & Verbrugge, 1999). A victim of heart disease, for example, might be unable to walk more than a block without having to rest. This would be a serious disability for a person who has always walked for work or leisure, but not a disability for someone who never walked more than a few steps at a time anyway.

Disease does not always lead to disability even if that disease temporarily results in serious impairment. The crucial question is whether the impairment is temporary or is part of a process of functional impairment. Indeed, instead of experiencing disability, some people with heart disease become able to walk longer and faster than they did before becoming ill, either because of medical intervention (such as a pacemaker) or rehabilitation (a new exercise routine).

Disability is more costly to society than mortality or morbidity, because when a person is unable to perform the tasks of daily life, society loses an active member and often must provide a caregiver or special

❶ *Answer to Observational Quiz (from page 554):* Not the woman in black, who may be the star of the class but who already looks young and trim. Look for those who need exercise most—the middle-aged people who are gaining weight in the midsection and who tend not to exercise it off. By this criterion, the real hero of this class is probably the man half-hidden on the left.

❶ *Answer to Observational Quiz (from page 555):* Greatest are the young adults, aged 18–34, and least are the middle-aged, aged 35–64. Why? (Answer not found in the margins, but you may speculate on the basis of the text.)

vitality A measure of health that refers to how healthy and energetic—physically, intellectually, and socially—an individual actually feels.

quality-adjusted life years (QALYs) A way of comparing mere survival without vitality to survival with health. QALYs indicate how many years of full vitality are lost to a particular physical disease or disability. Expressed in terms of life expectancy as adjusted for quality of life.

equipment. In the United States during the 1990s, the average person had 15 disability days per year, when he or she could not work, go to school, or otherwise function in the usual way (U.S. Bureau of the Census, 1998).

That statistic alone indicates that disability is a serious social problem. Since rates of disability increase with age and more people are living longer, the next century may bring lower mortality but higher disability. The specter of fewer and fewer able people caring for more and more disabled elderly individuals is a frightening one. Fortunately, another set of statistics indicates that historical improvements in exercise, diet, and other health-related behaviors actually reduce the proportion of people who are disabled. To pick one specific, in 1984, of all U.S. residents aged 50 to 65, one in six had difficulty walking three city blocks—a serious disability for most people. Ten years later, only one in eight had this problem (Freedman & Martin, 1998).

Vitality

The final measure of health, **vitality**, refers to how healthy and energetic—physically, intellectually, and socially—an individual actually feels. Vitality is *joie de vivre*, the zest for living, the love of life. Vitality is a subjective measure (some people say their health is very good even when they have several chronic diseases and obvious disabilities), but for that very reason, vitality is probably more important to quality of life than any other measure (Stewart & King, 1994).

Most experts, as well as the general public, now agree that the goal of medicine should be extending and improving vitality rather than simply postponing mortality, preventing morbidity, or remediating disability. Indeed, the motto of those who study aging is to "add life to years" not just to "add years to life" (Timiras, 1994).

The concept of **quality-adjusted life years,** or **QALYs,** is a way of comparing mere survival without vitality to survival with health. QALYs indicate how many years of full vitality are lost to a particular physical disease or disability. The first part of the calculation is fairly simple: If a person dies prematurely, before the average expected life span, then a certain number of years are completely lost. For example, if a young man is statistically expected to live to be 80 but is shot and killed at age 20, then 60 quality of life years are lost.

The second part of the calculation is more difficult, because it measures how much a particular condition diminishes the quality of the person's remaining life. If a 20-year-old is shot and disabled—perhaps brain-injured—but not killed, then each year might be judged to provide only a third of the expected quality of life, and thus 40 QALYs would be lost by age 80. Or if a 20-year-old is shot, undergoes a year-long recovery that is so painful and disabling that his QALY is only one-fourth of full vitality, and then recovers completely to live a healthy life until age 80, his total QALY would be 50 years and 3 months.

If we weigh the benefits of any particular health procedure, both in extending life and reducing disability, against the human and financial costs of decreasing vitality or increasing disability, then some new conclusions about preventive medicine emerge (Kaplan, 2000). Annual mammograms between ages 40 and 50 or surgery for prostate cancer may extend life by a few days, on average, but substantially reduce the quality of life and, in that light, could be considered harmful rather than helpful when QALYs are calculated.

As you can imagine, calculating how much quality of life is reduced by any particular circumstance is difficult. For example, this chapter begins with a description of changes in appearance. For some people, quality of life is affected by appearance, and they gladly incur the expense and pain of a face-lift rather than live 20 years or so with a visibly aging face. Others are not affected by appearance at all.

We may need to reassess our approach to disease prevention (Kaplan, 2000). If we focus merely on mortality, morbidity, and disability, then prevention comes late, perhaps saving the seriously ill from dying (tertiary prevention) or spotting and reducing high cholesterol levels (secondary prevention). But if the goal is vitality, then more exercise, improved nutrition, and reduced tobacco use add quality of life years before the first hints of heart disease, cancer, and many other health problems appear. A well-equipped exercise room available free to every employee may be a more cost-effective way for companies to increase health than free X-rays or flu shots.

Ethnicity and Health

Ethnicity, with its attendant genetic and cultural factors, is a powerful influence on all four measures of health in middle age. Mortality data on the five ethnic groups recognized by the U.S. Bureau of the Census make the point clearly: Between the ages of 45 and 55, African Americans die at twice the rate of European Americans, who themselves die at twice the rate of Asian Americans. Native Americans have about a 20 percent higher death rate and Hispanic Americans a 20 percent lower rate than the overall average (see Figure 20.2).

In general, morbidity and disability follow the same ethnic patterns in middle age as does mortality, with people of African descent most likely to be sick and disabled. These patterns are further reflected in self-reports of health status (see Figure 20.3).

Figure 20.2 Death Rates in Middle Age. Racial differences in death rates are probably caused more by environmental factors than by heredity. (Note the rates for Native Americans and Asian Americans, who are quite similar genetically.) Sex differences are more marked than racial differences. Some believe that a biological explanation (the second X chromosome or female hormones) underlies women's lower death rates. Others favor social and psychological factors.

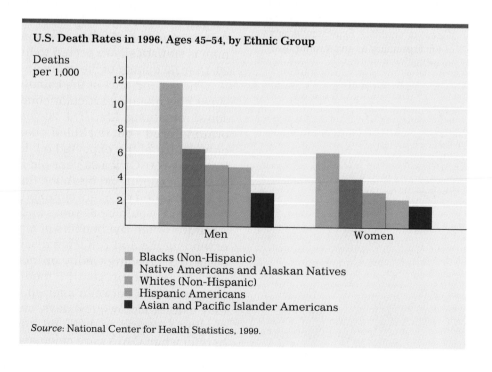

Source: National Center for Health Statistics, 1999.

Figure 20.3 Fair or Poor Health. Asking people about their health reveals that men and women differ, but ethnic groups differ far more. The 1999 data reveal improvements for whites, blacks, and Hispanics, but not for Asian Americans or Native Americans

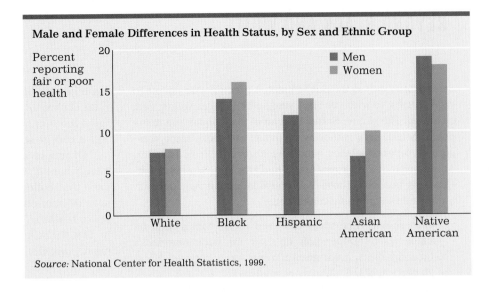

Male and Female Differences in Health Status, by Sex and Ethnic Group

Percent reporting fair or poor health

- Men
- Women

White, Black, Hispanic, Asian American, Native American

Source: National Center for Health Statistics, 1999.

Each specific ethnic group within each of these five broad ethnic categories has its own pattern. Among middle-aged Hispanics, for instance, the death rate of Cuban Americans is quite low, while that of Puerto Ricans is relatively high. Among Asians, Japanese Americans tend to live longer than Filipino Americans. Differences in socioeconomic status (SES) seem the most plausible explanation, since Puerto Ricans and Filipinos tend to have lower incomes than do the other two groups.

One intragroup difference does not follow SES patterns: Recent North American immigrants are healthier than long-time residents of the same age and ethnicity (Abraido-Lanza et al., 1999; Scribner, 1996; Singh & Yu, 1996). Several factors may explain this difference:

- Self-selection; only the hardiest individuals emigrate
- Health habits, particularly with regard to alcohol, other drugs, exercise, and diet
- Optimism
- Family communication and support

Healthy Families For every American ethnic group, health is affected by two cultures. For example, overall, the death rate of Japanese Americans is lower than that of most other Americans, but it is higher than that of Japanese who have not emigrated. Every ethnic group also has certain illnesses to which it is particularly or rarely prone. For the Japanese, the rate of heart disease is quite low but the rate of stomach cancer is quite high.

BEYOND BLACK AND WHITE

Scientists as well as the public habitually categorize people in racial terms, as white or black and sometimes as yellow, red, or brown. The United States Bureau of the Census and many public health data-gathering agencies use those same categories, currently labeled white; black; Asian/Pacific Islander; American Indian/Eskimo/Aleut; and Hispanic. However, categorizing people in those five groups is increasingly difficult, as these three questions make clear:

1. How should Americans of mixed racial background be categorized? Depending on how far back one looks (grandparents, great-grandparents, etc.), between 2 and 20 percent of U.S. infants are multiracial.

2. How should people from India and the Middle East be categorized? These people were all considered white by the U.S. government until recently, when Indians were reclassified as Asian (even though their skin coloring is quite different from that of other Asians, such as the Japanese). In England, these groups always were, and still are, classified as nonwhite.

3. Why are ethnic subgroups often listed for each of the four nonwhite categories, whereas "white" is usually only one category? This subdivision makes little sense genetically, because there are more differences between "white" groups such as Finns and Greeks than between Cubans and Puerto Ricans or between North American and Caribbean people of African descent. [Bhopal & Donaldson, 1998]

Reliance on racial categories leads too many scientists to make the mistake of looking at genes and ancestral culture as the main explanations for group differences in health. In fact, current education, SES, and the pressures and opportunities provided by the larger society have more influence on health than genes do. Within racial categories, these factors make a substantial difference. This is true in every nation, but it is particularly obvious in a nation where most people have the same genetic background. For example, in the Netherlands, rates of chronic lung disease, heart disease, and diabetes are three times as high among the least educated as among those with a college education (Mackenbach et al., 1996).

Of course, education correlates with awareness of good health habits. That is a partial explanation for the difference that college makes. Much more significant, however, are the emotional stresses, missed opportunities, and barriers to health care that accompany low SES. A detailed study in the Netherlands found that material factors (employment, income) affected health more than did personal

A Race-Based Health Gap? A nurse checks blood pressure at a clinic in an urban setting.

❓ *Observational Quiz (see answer page 562): Looking closely, can you see at least four examples of the many reasons the average middle-aged African American is less healthy than peers of other ethnic groups?*

Note that all these explanations suggest that differences in health are not primarily genetic. Even among groups who have been in the United States for 100 or more years, cultural habits undoubtedly affect mortality and morbidity (see the Changing Policy box). Likewise, the incidence of skin cancer is much higher among European Americans than among any other American group, not only because their genetic makeup gives them less protective melanin in their skin but also because their culture approves of the "healthy" look of a sun-

choices (alcohol abuse, high BMI, low exercise) (Schrijvers et al., 1999).

Now, let us compare the two groups that are considered racial opposites, "black" and "white." At almost every age and on virtually every measure, people who are considered white are healthier than people who are considered black (Council of Economic Advisors, 1998). Curiously, however, the age of the person markedly affects this racial difference. The greatest mortality gap occurs in the early 40s when U.S. blacks are three times as likely to die as whites. Then the gap narrows again. In fact, by age 85, the gap completely disappears, a phenomenon called the *racial crossover*. If anything, at the very oldest ages, blacks are less likely to die than whites, irrespective of SES (Corti et al., 1999; Guralnik, 1993; Sorlie et al., 1995).

Of the many possible explanations for this pattern, genes and ancestry are the least compelling, since genetic predisposition and African heritage do not affect the middle-aged much differently than they affect children or the elderly (Markides & Black, 1996). A more plausible explanation is that extrinsic factors, particularly prejudice and poverty, do more direct damage between ages 15 and 65 than at earlier and later ages. Younger children and the elderly may escape the full brunt of discrimination, because they are not in the labor force and not expected to protect their families.

The greater impact of racial prejudice in middle age might explain another curious statistic: The mortality rate of black men aged 25 to 44 was found to be four times higher if they live in a very segregated neighborhood rather than in a mostly white neighborhood. This effect was apparent (although not as large) for black women as well, but not for the elderly of any race or sex. Even when people of the same income were compared, black men in this age group were three times as likely to die if their neighborhood was more than 70 percent black than if it was less than 10 percent black (Jackson et al., 2000).

Support for the idea that racial prejudice affects personal health comes from a study of adults of West African ancestry. Blood pressure was measured among seven groups: three in Africa, three in the Caribbean, and one in the United States. Rates of hypertension (high blood pressure) rose as adults grew up farther away from rural Africa; only 15 percent of those living in rural Cameroon had a blood pressure reading of 140/90 or higher, compared with 33 percent of the African Americans in Chicago. The readings of those in the Caribbean were midway between the Chicago and Cameroon readings (Cooper et al., 1997).

As another example, the incidence of breast cancer in middle-aged African American women is slightly less than in European American women, but their death rate from breast cancer is 46 percent higher, a racial gap that has actually increased over the past 40 years (National Center for Health Statistics, 1999). Factors related to education, income, and racism (such as routine screening, awareness of the early signs of cancer, and access to excellent health care once cancer is found) seem more plausible explanations of this discrepancy than any possible genetic differences (Schoenbaum & Waidman, 1997).

None of this research denies that ethnicity is sometimes relevant to health. Ancestry, recent history, habits, community, and social stresses all affect health, and knowing which groups of people are likely to have which early symptoms and potential hazards often guides diagnosis. Thus, African Americans should be regularly screened for glaucoma, Native Americans for diabetes, European American women for osteoporosis, and so on. However, racial categories—especially when they are thought to index genetic categories—mislead more often than they cure. "White" and "black" are sometimes useful descriptions in everyday language—to indicate the color of ink on paper, say, or as a metaphor for opposites—but, they are distortions when it comes to public health.

tan. Although genetic factors are part of the explanation for ethnic differences, they are not the major part.

Sex Differences in Health

As you can see from Figure 20.2, mortality rates in middle age continue to favor females, with men twice as likely to die of any cause and three times as likely to die of heart disease. Not until age 85 are the death

Diagnostic Differences Until recently, heart disease was regarded by most doctors as a man's disease, and diagnostic procedures such as the stress test shown here were performed almost exclusively on men. As a result, heart disease tended not to be recognized in women until it had reached an advanced stage.

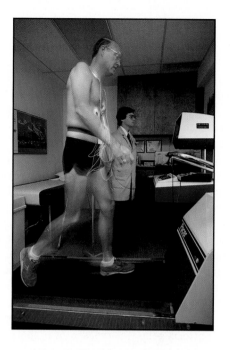

rates equivalent. However, chronic morbidity and disabling conditions show a contrary trend: Beginning in middle age, women have higher disease and disability rates than men.

There are many plausible hypotheses for the health differences between the sexes. Most people first think about biological sex as the explanation—something to do with the second X chromosome, or of female hormones, or having internal sex organs. The underlying assumption is that male and female are considered opposites, so biology should explain *all* observed differences.

But biology fails to explain certain historical statistics. In most nations in the nineteenth century (and in some nations today), women were more likely to die young than men were. And as recently as 1940 in England, Wales, and the United States, middle-aged men and women were equally likely to die not only of heart disease but also of other causes (Nikiforov & Mamaev, 1998). Such data make us look beyond biology and genetics. Could health practices explain the gender differences we now see? Yes: Men are more likely to smoke, drink, be overweight, repress their emotions, and ignore their medical symptoms—so they die sooner, not because of their maleness per se, but because males in developed nations are likely to engage in these behaviors.

That explains the sex difference in mortality, but why are women more likely to experience morbidity and disability? Perhaps the bias of medicine holds an answer. The facts that middle-aged men are more likely to experience sudden, fatal disease and that women of the same age are more likely to experience chronic, disabling illnesses produce another unfortunate gender difference: "Even though women make up the primary patient load for health care professionals . . . men have been the primary subjects of medical research" (Parrott & Condit, 1996).

This gender bias is not the result of deliberate sexism. Rather, the traditional focus in the medical community has been on acute illnesses rather than chronic conditions, on preventing death rather than avoiding disability. Thus, relatively little research has been devoted to such diseases as arthritis, osteoporosis, lupus, and migraine headaches—each of which is a common chronic condition that affects far more women than men, but none of which typically produces sudden death. A related cause is that key longitudinal and large-scale studies of heart disease have excluded women, partly because women are less likely to die in middle age (although the overall rate of heart disease is higher for women than for men). As a result, women with heart disease are less likely to receive specific diagnostic and therapeutic procedures.

Doctors, just like other Americans, do not believe their behavior reflects sexism, racism, or any other form of prejudice. However, it is hard for any human to be completely free of bias (Davidio & Gaertner, 1999). In one study, researchers asked more than 700 physicians to recommend treatment for eight heart patients. The doctors were shown the

❶ Answer to Observational Quiz (from page 560): *A disproportionate number of African Americans are overweight, poor, urban-dwelling, and reliant on health care from public clinics, not from their own private doctors. Another significant difference is harder to see, because it is shown here by its absence: all men, but especially African American men, are less likely than women to get preventive screening, even for ailments to which they are particularly susceptible, including glaucoma, prostate cancer, and high blood pressure.*

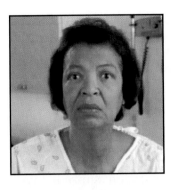

All Equally Sick? These photographs were used in a study that assessed physicians' biases in recommending treatment (Schulman et al., 1999). These supposed "heart patients" were described as identical in occupation, symptoms, and every other respect except age, race, and sex. However, the physician subjects who looked at the photos and the fictitious medical charts that accompanied them did not make identical recommendations. The appropriate treatment for the supposed symptoms would be catheterization; but for the younger, white, or male patients, catheterization was recommended 90, 91, and 91 percent of the time; for the older, female, or black patients, 86, 85, and 85 percent of the time. Are you surprised that the bias differences were less than 10 percent? Or are you surprised that physician bias existed at all?

menopause The time in middle age, usually around age 50, when a woman's menstrual periods cease completely and the production of estrogen drops considerably. Strictly speaking, menopause is dated 1 year after a woman's last menstrual period.

patients' photographs and told that they all had identical symptoms, insurance policies, and background. Actually, all eight "patients" were actors who differed only in sex, race, and stated age (55 or 70). The treatment recommended by the subjects (the physicians) was a matter of judgment, with even the middle-aged white male sometimes not being recommended for catheterization. Nevertheless, some slight anti-female and anti-black bias was detected (Schulman et al., 1999). Such bias is a problem in health care, although other factors (such as patients' lifestyles and attitudes toward medical care) are probably more important overall.

THE SEXUAL-REPRODUCTIVE SYSTEM

Both sexes experience similar changes in their sexual-reproductive systems. With age, sexual responses gradually become slower and less distinct, and reproduction less likely. For both sexes, attitudes are more important than biology in assessing the impact of these changes. However, let us begin with the one change that clearly originates with biology and affects one sex and not the other: menopause.

The Climacteric

Sometime between ages 42 and 58 (the average age is 51), women usually reach **menopause**. Ovulation and menstruation stop and the production of several hormones, especially estrogen, progesterone, and testosterone, drops. Strictly speaking, menopause is dated 1 year after a woman's last menstrual period (Carlson et al., 1996).

climacteric   Refers to the various biological and psychological changes that accompany menopause.

The term "menopause" is also sometimes loosely used to refer to the **climacteric**, a phase preceding actual menopause and lasting about 6 years, during which the woman's body adjusts to much lower levels of estrogen. This adjustment is marked by a variety of biological and psychological symptoms (Avis, 1999).

Symptoms of the Climacteric

The first symptom of the climacteric is typically shorter menstrual cycles. Then, toward the end of her 40s, the timing of a woman's periods becomes erratic, the duration variable, and ovulation unpredictable. Instead of occurring midcycle as in earlier years, ovulation sometimes occurs quite early or late in a cycle; sometimes several ova are released, sometimes none. This explains why some women who thought they knew their body's rhythm well enough to avoid both pregnancy and contraception find themselves with a "change of life" baby or twins (Carlson et al., 1996).

The most obvious symptoms of the climacteric are *hot flashes* (suddenly feeling hot), *hot flushes* (suddenly looking hot), and *cold sweats* (feeling cold and clammy). These symptoms are all caused by *vasomotor instability*, that is, a temporary disruption in the body's homeostatic mechanism that constricts or dilates the blood vessels to maintain body temperature.

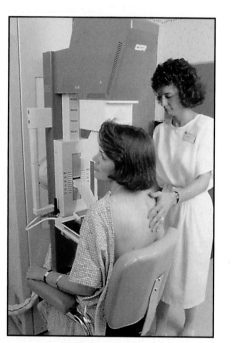

Once a Year While menopause brings relief from possible complications of birth control, pregnancy, and menstruation, it also brings increased risk for heart disease, osteoporosis, and breast cancer. Fortunately, preventive medicine can halt most problems before they do serious damage. Unfortunately, many women do not get the care they need until symptoms emerge. Less than half of all American women over age 50 get their annual mammograms, even though doing so would save thousands of lives.

osteoporosis   A loss of calcium that makes bone more porous and fragile. It occurs somewhat in everyone with aging, but serious osteoporosis is more common in elderly women than men. Osteoporosis is the main reason the elderly suffer broken hip bones much more often than the young.

Vasomotor instability varies widely in severity: Of every five menopausal women, these sudden changes in body temperature are very bothersome to one, not a problem for three, and not even noticed by one (Avis, 1999). Lower estrogen levels produce many other changes in the female body, including drier skin, less vaginal lubrication during sexual arousal, and loss of some breast tissue, again with substantial variation.

Two changes caused by reduced estrogen levels pose serious health risks. One is loss of bone calcium, which can eventually lead to **osteoporosis**, a porosity and brittleness of the bones that makes them break easily. The other is an increase of fat deposits in the arteries, which sets the stage for coronary heart disease. Osteoporosis and coronary heart disease are each experienced by about half of all women who survive to late adulthood.

Many women also find that, in the climacteric, their moods change inexplicably from day to day. Usually this moodiness is blamed directly on the hormonal changes, but it is probably caused indirectly by the exhaustion that occurs if hot flashes interrupt sleep night after night. Clinical depression is rare during menopause, except in women who already have a history of depression (Avis, 1999).

All these symptoms are variable. The sudden onset of menopause caused by a hysterectomy (surgical removal of the uterus) is more likely to produce marked symptoms than natural menopause, for both biological and psychosocial reasons. About one in three women in the United States has a hysterectomy sometime in her life, not necessarily before menopause (U.S. Bureau of the Census, 1998).

How troubling natural menopause is depends on the social context. Some cultures value a woman's reproductive capacity more than others, and medical views have changed dramatically over time (Daniluk, 1998). The Western medical profession traditionally applied a sickness model to menopause, describing menopausal women as "diseased, sexless, irritable, and depressed" (Golub, 1992). Such negative views created a self-fulfilling prophecy, leading women to focus unduly on the symptoms of menopause, fearing the worst and having their fears confirmed by their physicians.

Hormone Replacement Therapy

Today, menopause is no longer regarded as a disease, nor are its symptoms usually regarded as overwhelming. In the United States, only about 10 percent of all women going through natural menopause, as well as about 90 percent going through surgically induced menopause, experience symptoms severe enough that estrogen replacement is indicated. In most cases, this treatment is in the form of **hormone replacement therapy (HRT)**, in which the woman takes periodic doses of progesterone as well as daily doses of estrogen (Bellantoni & Blackman, 1996).

Continued use of HRT beyond menopause can have a number of health benefits, reducing by more than half the incidence of hip fractures (now experienced by a third of all women who reach age 90) (Carlson et al., 1996; Grodstein et al., 1996). Longitudinal research finds another benefit of long-term HRT: reduced risk of Alzheimer's disease, with those taking estrogen for 15 years or more particularly likely to benefit (Kawas et al., 1997).

However, HRT is not risk-free. Hormone supplements may increase the risk of some forms of cancer, particularly breast cancer, although not by much (Schairer et al., 2000). Solid evidence regarding HRT use for 20 years or more is not yet available. Many 50-year-olds wonder if unforeseen disaster might occur at age 80 if they take synthetic hormones all those years. Certainly every woman, whether or not she takes estrogen, should lower her risk of osteoporosis by a lifetime of healthy habits, such as eating a low-fat, high-calcium diet, avoiding cigarettes, and engaging in regular weight-bearing exercise.

Decisions regarding the use of HRT require specific risk analysis. Osteoporosis, for example, is most prevalent in small-framed women of European descent. These women need to check their bone density, because HRT may reduce their risk of disease substantially. Many physicians now recommend HRT for all menopausal women, unless there are counterindications. Medical opinion is "definitely turning in favor" of HRT from menopause throughout late adulthood (Carlson et al., 1996).

hormone replacement therapy (HRT)
Treatment to compensate for hormone reduction at menopause or following surgical removal of the ovaries. Such treatment, which usually involves estrogen and progesterone, minimizes menopausal symptoms and diminishes the risk of heart disease and osteoporosis in later adulthood.

Age-Related Changes in Sexual Expression

The usual way to measure sexual activity is in frequency of intercourse and orgasm. By this measure, sexual expression declines gradually throughout adulthood. There are many individual differences, including some middle-aged people who stop having intercourse altogether and others who continue to have intercourse daily.

MENOPAUSE AND THE MIND

Menopause signals the loss of reproductive potential. Is this, in itself, stressful and depressing? Traditionally, women attained social status directly from their role as mother: The more children a couple had, the more fortunate they were considered to be. In those circumstances, menopause had substantial psychological impact. Especially if a couple had only one or two children, menopause meant the sad "closing of the gates" of reproduction, as psychoanalyst Helene Deutsch (1945) once described it.

Today, however, the end of childbearing is now determined less by age than by personal factors, such as the number of children a woman already has or the couple's financial situation. In fact, the end of childbearing often occurs through a conscious decision long before reproduction becomes biologically impossible. More than half of all North American couples in which the woman is between the ages of 35 and 44 have chosen to become surgically sterile, via either a vasectomy or tubal ligation. In fact, a Canadian study found that of women as young as 30, 33 percent had already been sterilized, 40 percent were using reversible contraception, and only 27 percent were not using any contraception—some because they were not sexually active, others because they were already pregnant, and a few because they wanted to get pregnant (Martin & Wu, 2000). Similarly, a U.S. survey found that only 4 percent of women aged 15–44 were not using contraception because they hoped to become pregnant (U.S. Bureau of the Census, 1999). Thus, the "loss of reproductive potential" is welcomed more than mourned.

At about age 50, when menstruation ceases and sexual activity no longer entails fear of pregnancy and the inconveniences of contraception, few women have regrets about children not born. In some nations—Greece and India among them—menopause is liberating, because potentially fertile women are sheltered and chaperoned, but postmenopausal women are free to do as they please (Avis, 1999). Even in developed nations, menopause may signal an increase in sexual activity and enjoyment. At least one study found that, two years after a hysterectomy, women had increased the frequency of sexual intercourse and orgasm by 10 percent (Rhodes et al., 1999).

Male Menopause?

For men, there is no sudden drop in reproductive ability or hormonal levels, as there is with women. Thus, physiologically, men experience nothing like the female climacteric. Most men continue to produce sperm indefinitely. Although there are important age-related declines in the number and motility of sperm (see Chapter 17), men are theoretically (and in some cases, actually) able to father a child in late adulthood. Similarly, the average levels of testosterone and other hormones decline gradually, not suddenly, with age (Mobbs, 1996).

Strictly speaking, then, there is no "male menopause." However, this phrase may have been coined to refer to another phenomenon: Testosterone dips markedly if a man becomes sexually inactive or unusually worried, as might happen if he were faced with unemployment, marital problems, serious illness, or unwanted retirement. Levels of testosterone correlate with levels of sexual desire and speed of sexual responses, so a man with low testosterone might find himself unable to have an erection when he wanted to. Thus, the effects of this dip, especially when added to age-related declines, may make a man highly anxious about his sexual virility, which, in turn, reduces his testosterone level even more. This seems like menopause, that is, a sudden drop in reproductive potential.

The opposite can occur: A man of any age who lands a new, ego-enhancing job or adds some novelty to his sex life may experience a rise in self-esteem, and consequently rising testosterone and desire. Various drugs, most recently Viagra, trigger the same set of responses. Underlying such situational peaks and valleys, however, is a steady, gradual decline. And underlying some men's need for a new and younger wife, or an expensive and possibly dangerous drug, is their unhappiness with the sexual consequences of growing older.

Changes in Men and Women

Even for the sexually active, the specifics change, especially for men. Sexual stimulation takes longer and needs to be more direct than at earlier ages. Further, as Herant Katchadourian (1987), a physician who studies sexuality, writes about men, "Orgasmic reactions become less intense with age . . . contractions are fewer, ejaculation is less vigorous, and the volume of the ejaculate is smaller."

You're Only As Old As You Feel Throughout adulthood, continued, pleasurable sexual experiences depend much less on the partners' age than on their attitudes toward each other and toward sex itself. As many experts have noted, the most important human sexual organ is the brain.

To a 20-year-old male, such prospects in the distant future may seem dismaying, but to the man actually experiencing these differences, the reality is much less troubling. A study of middle-aged men found that, although their levels of desire and their frequency of ejaculation decreased with age, almost all were satisfied with their sex lives (McKinlay & Feldman, 1994).

Not until age 60 or so do more men agree rather than disagree with the statement that "men's sexual interest declines with age." Even then, most 60-year-olds are satisfied with their sex lives, although the minority who are very dissatisfied doubled from about 5 percent throughout middle age to about 10 percent after age 60 (McKinlay & Feldman, 1994).

Changes in women's orgasmic ability are harder to measure, but many researchers think a woman's eroticism is at least as strong in middle age as in early adulthood. As one group reports:

> The woman's capacity for orgasm is not impaired in any way by aging as long as there is no other health problem complicating the picture. In fact, many women report being more easily orgasmic in their post-menopausal years than they were previously, although this effect may relate more to psychosocial components of sexual responsivity (e.g., no worries about becoming pregnant) than to biological factors. [Masters et al., 1994]

Couple Changes

One final fact seems to be suggested by the research: Sex is usually the result of social interaction. Middle-aged couples do not move from active, happy sex lives to troubled or nonexistent ones unless their relationship is plagued by other problems. It is quite "possible to compensate for these changes in sexual development if one does not panic and engage in a struggle to continue sex in exactly the same way as in the younger years or cling to traditional sex roles" (Pedersen, 1998). Emotional problems, physical illness, and numerous medications can affect sexual performance, particularly in men; but a satisfactory sex life is possible for most loving couples, at any age. If a couple was never comfortable with their sexual interaction, however, the onset of middle age can be used as an excuse to stop trying.

Throughout life, it seems that sexual activity itself helps promote sexual interest and excitement; correspondingly, absence of sexual activity results in lower levels of sex hormones and a loss of sexual interest. One thing that improves is a person's willingness to acknowledge his or her sexual needs. Some homosexual individuals, even married ones, come "out of the closet" during middle age, and some heterosexual individuals, for the first time, talk to their partner about their sexual desires.

As we saw in the chapters on early adulthood, as adults grow older, biosocial development is less indexed by chronological age than it was in childhood. Personal choices become increasingly important in affecting the course of development in sexuality and many other areas. In the next chapter, we will see that choice can influence the development of our intellectual skills as well. At least in some abilities, we can choose to be smarter, wiser, or more expert, and then take action to become so.

SUMMARY

NORMAL CHANGES IN MIDDLE ADULTHOOD

1. A person's appearance undergoes gradual but notable changes as middle age progresses, including more wrinkles, less hair, and new fat, particularly on the abdomen. With the exception of excessive weight gain, changes in appearance have little impact on health.

2. Hearing gradually becomes less acute, with noticeable losses being more likely for high-frequency sounds, particularly in men. Vision also becomes less sharp with age. Two particular difficulties for many middle-aged people are reading small print and adjusting to glare at night. For the most part, these sensory changes are inconsequential; blindness and deafness are rare in middle age.

3. During middle age, declines in all the body's systems become apparent, but generally they are not sufficient to impair normal functioning. Overall, health is generally quite good, with the death rate for today's middle-aged adults being significantly lower than for earlier cohorts.

HEALTH HABITS OVER THE YEARS

4. Although there is evidence that middle-aged Americans today are more conscious of good health habits, many people still put their health at risk by smoking cigarettes, drinking alcohol excessively, eating poorly, gaining weight, and maintaining a sedentary lifestyle.

VARIATIONS IN HEALTH

5. Variations in health—which can be measured in terms of mortality, morbidity, disability, and vitality—arise from a combination of many factors, chief among them race, ethnicity, socioeconomic status, and gender. Quality-adjusted life years are more important than mere survival.

6. Both genetic and cultural factors affect the overall health of various ethnic groups to a large extent, but social and psychological factors may be even more influential. Members of certain ethnic groups in certain settings are much more prone to health risks, and inadequate medical care and neighborhood characteristics affect minorities adversely.

7. Beginning in middle age, women have higher morbidity and disability rates than men. One reason for this difference may be a gender bias in health research that has favored the study of acute illness. More research studies today, though, are examining patterns of illness among women.

THE SEXUAL-REPRODUCTIVE SYSTEM

8. At menopause, as a woman's menstrual cycle stops, ovulation ceases and levels of estrogen are markedly reduced. This hormonal change produces various symptoms and possible problems, although most women find the experience of menopause much less troubling than they had expected it to be. Hormone replacement therapy has been shown to have health benefits for postmenopausal women, although it has risks as well.

9. As sexual responses slow down with age, many couples find that they engage in intercourse less often. However, satisfying sexual relationships can, and often do, continue throughout adulthood.

KEY TERMS

glaucoma (548)

autoimmune diseases (549)

global disease burden (552)

mortality (556)

morbidity (556)

disability (556)

vitality (557)

QALYs (quality-adjusted life years) (557)

menopause (563)

climacteric (564)

osteoporosis (564)

hormone replacement therapy (HRT) (565)

KEY QUESTIONS

1. What changes in appearance typically occur during middle age, and what is their impact?

2. List three reasons one person might have a greater hearing loss than another in middle adulthood.

3. What are the likely changes in a person's vision during middle adulthood?

4. How do changes in the immune system affect people as they grow older?

5. What is the effect of alcohol on a person's risk of mortality?

6. Why are people more likely to become overweight with age?

7. How does obesity affect physical and psychological health?

8. How does health vary between and within ethnic groups?

9. What are the major differences in health between middle-aged men and women, and what explains these differences?

10. Why might a woman welcome menopause?

11. How do age and other factors affect a typical couple's sex life?

12. *In Your Experience* Would you be more troubled to learn that your parents (or grandparents) were no longer sexually active or to learn the details of their sexual urges, passions, and activities? Why?

Middle Adulthood: Cognitive Development

CHAPTER 21

The main topic of this chapter is adult cognitive development as measured by various tests of achievement. For more than a century, developmentalists have used this psychometric approach to study intelligence. However, the consensus among researchers changes every few decades, from the pronouncement that intelligence declines with age to the assertion that it rises, from the conviction that genes cause change in cognitive ability to the opposite belief, that life circumstances are critical; from the concept that intelligence is a single general trait to the idea that many distinct intelligences exist.

Each of these conclusions was based on the results of studies that were later called into question by other research. Into this soup of contradictory findings came a theory, the life-span perspective. As you remember from Chapter 1, the life-span perspective allows a highly complex and variable view of human development, a way to "organize" the conflicting data regarding adult cognition. Once the theory emerged, it, like any other good development theory, clarified observations and suggested future directions.

Intellectual growth is difficult to understand without the life-span view that it is multidimensional, multidirectional, contextual, and plastic. To understand the patterns of adult cognition as measured by tests of intelligence, and to present vivid examples of each of these four aspects of the life-span perspective, we will discuss them in turn.

MULTIDIMENSIONAL INTELLIGENCE: NOT ONE, BUT MANY

Historically, psychologists as well as laypeople have thought of intelligence as a single entity, a certain ability that people possess in greater or lesser amounts. In this vein, a leading theoretician, Charles Spearman (1927), argued for the concept of **general intelligence,** which he called *g*. Although it cannot be measured directly, Spearman contended that *g* can be inferred from various abilities that can be tested, such as vocabulary, memory, and reasoning. A person can then be assigned one overall IQ score, a number that indicates whether the person is properly called a genius, average, retarded, and so on (explained in more detail in Chapter 11).

The idea that there is a single quality called "intelligence" continues to influence thinking on this subject. However, virtually every psychologist

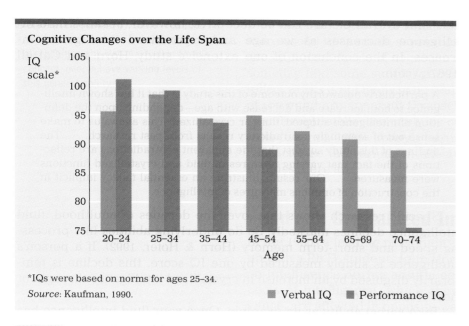

Cognitive Changes over the Life Span

IQ scale*

*IQs were based on norms for ages 25–34.
Source: Kaufman, 1990.

■ Verbal IQ   ■ Performance IQ

Figure 21.1 Verbal IQ Versus Performance IQ. Whether intellectual abilities increase or decline over the years of adulthood depends on which ability is measured—as is apparent to every older adult whose knowledge of history far overshadows that of their teenage grandchildren, who nonetheless can beat their elders four times over at a video game. Even clusters of abilities, such as those of crystallized versus fluid intelligence, or the Verbal items of the Wechsler (green) versus the Performance items (blue), follow distinct developmental patterns.

? Especially for Prospective Parents: In terms of the intellectual challenge, what type of intelligence is most needed for effective parenthood?

❶ Answer to Observational Quiz (from page 573): *The pressure is on him, as is made clear by the test giver's timekeeping (he is looking at his watch), clothing (his white shirt and tie are signs of formal high status), and sex (men often feel more pressure when performing in front of other men). In addition, the test item, block design, is an abstract, out-of-context measure of performance IQ, which usually declines with age.*

(vocabulary, information, and the like) and Performance (puzzles, visual perception, and so forth). As you can see from the cross-sectional data in Figure 21.1, Verbal IQ remains in the average range throughout adulthood, with small fluctuations and only a minimal decline from the early 20s to the early 70s. Since cross-sectional data can give an exaggerated picture of decline, even these small declines might be reversed if subjects in the younger age groups were followed longitudinally. In contrast, Performance IQ falls markedly over the course of adulthood, dropping by an average of 25 points, from around 101 to 76 (nearly the level of mental retardation), because Performance IQ measures the processes of learning, not the products.

Of course, the crucial question is, "What is the practical importance of this distinction?" Solid evidence is hard to find, but theoretically a person could increase his or her intelligence by shifting the emphasis from process to product (Salthouse, 1999). Whether or not this actually occurs depends on measures of practical intelligence, as we will now see.

Sternberg's Three Forms of Intelligence

Another way to categorize many dimensions of intelligence is to look at the uses to which cognition is put. As we noted in Chapter 12, Robert Sternberg (1988) has proposed that intelligence appears in three fundamental forms: the *analytic*, the *creative*, and the *practical*.

Analytic Intelligence

The analytic, or academic, aspect consists of mental processes that foster efficient learning, remembering, and thinking. These include planning, strategy selection, attention, and information processing, as well as verbal and logical skills. Such skills and talents are particularly valued at the beginning of adulthood—that is, in college, in graduate school, and in job training. Multiple-choice tests, with one and only one right answer, reward analytic intelligence.

Creative Intelligence

A second aspect of intelligence, creativity, involves the capacity to be intellectually flexible and innovative when dealing with new situations. Creative intelligence is prized whenever life circumstances change or new challenges arise. Over the long run, creativity is a better predictor of accomplishment than traditional measures of IQ (Csikszentmihalyi, 1996), although at first some manifestations of creativity are so innovative and out of touch with the culture that the creator is the object of scorn, legal action, or—worst of all—complete indifference (Sternberg, 1999).

Different Forms of Intelligence Both these adults at work—a scientist investigating the genetics of breast cancer and a Turkese helmsman navigating the South Pacific without instruments—demonstrate highly specialized intellectual abilities. Imagine the difficulty of trying to create a single IQ test that would allow both individuals to demonstrate their intelligence equally. Similar though less obvious disparities exist among those whose minds are unusually creative, analytic, or practical and likewise pose a problem in adequately assessing IQ.

practical intelligence The intellectual skills used in everyday problem solving.

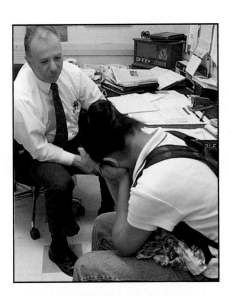

Practical Advice Needed What kinds of abilities are needed to listen to, understand, and advise the diverse adolescent population of a large urban school? Whatever the abilities might be, they spring from long hours of practical experience, not primarily from abstract learning.

Indeed, creative thinking is always *divergent* rather than *convergent,* which means that creative people find diverse, innovative, and unusual solutions to problems and ways to accomplish tasks, rather than relying on the solution that has always been considered the right one. Curiously, one of the situations where creativity is most evident is in problems that require adults to use several steps of arithmetic—the best way to maximize costs and benefits in buying groceries to feed a family, or to choose a health insurance policy, or to get several people from one place to another (determining, for example, who should take which car or bus along which route at what time of day). Each culture values creativity in some domains more than others, which affects the success or scorn that creative individuals experience (Garnham & Oakhill, 1994).

Practical Intelligence

A third aspect, **practical intelligence,** involves the capacity to adapt one's behavior to the contextual demands of a given situation. This capacity includes an accurate grasp of the expectations and needs of the people involved and an awareness of the particular skills that are called for, along with the ability to meet these demands effectively.

Such practical intelligence is particularly essential for managing the conflicting personalities in a family or for convincing members of an organization (business, social group, school) to do something. Without practical intelligence, a solution that is ideal according to analytic intelligence will fail miserably, because it will encounter resistance:

> When managers try to introduce decisions that are incompatible with the culture, the organization's members refuse to endorse them, predict that they will fail, and may balk at attempts to implement them. [Beach et al., 1997]

Some people might say that practical intelligence is learned in "the school of hard knocks"—that it is "street smarts," not "book smarts." Practical intelligence is particularly valued by people in middle adulthood. Certainly, most adults do not occupy their time trying to define obscure words or deduce the next element in a number sequence (analytic intelligence). Nor do they try to figure out new ways to play music, structure local government, or write a poem (creative intelligence). Instead they try to solve the real-world challenges of

OLDER TYPISTS, RESTAURANT WORKERS, AND BANK MANAGERS

Evidence for a slowing down of fluid intelligence in the later adult years does not tell the whole story of cognitive change, because adults often find ways to compensate for their loss of speed and capacity for abstract analysis. Indeed, many researchers believe that a hallmark of successful aging is the ability to use intellectual strengths strategically to compensate for declining capacities (Dixon, 1992). Paul Baltes and his colleagues call this strategy *selective optimization with compensation,* and they believe that it accounts for the ability of many older adults to maintain the performance levels of their younger years (Baltes et al., 1998). This kind of adaptive competence can be found not just in research laboratories but in everyday workplaces and recreational settings as well.

Consider waiting on tables in a restaurant, a job that demands a wide range of cognitive skills, including knowledge of menu items, memory for ordering and delivery procedures, simultaneous management of several tables (each at a different stage of the meal), the ability to combine, order, and prioritize various tasks, and the monitoring of social relations with customers and co-workers—as well as physical stamina! Adolescents and young adults in these roles have an advantage over older adults in their physical dexterity and endurance and in their cognitive speed and flexibility, and this may explain why restaurant managers sometimes prefer younger employees. But are older employees less efficient, or do they have ways of compensating for the declines they experience?

Marion Perlmutter and her colleagues sought an answer to this question by identifying the skills required for successful performance in restaurant work and then assessing these

Hire This Woman If you were opening a restaurant and if this woman is typical of her age group, she would be your ideal employee: cheerful, efficient, and reliable. Unfortunately for you, she would probably not be for hire: Older workers tend to stay in the same job for years, if possible, while younger workers are quicker to complain, quit, or be fired.

skills in a sample of 64 restaurant and cafeteria employees who varied in age and prior work experience (Perlmutter et al., 1990). These workers were assessed on tests of memory ability, physical strength and dexterity, knowledge of the technical and organizational requirements of the job, and social capacities. They were also observed during different periods of the workday, such as during rush and nonrush hours, to de-

❶ **Response for Prospective Parents (from page 574):** Since parenthood demands flexibility and patience, Sternberg's practical intelligence or Gardner's social-understanding is probably most needed. Anything that involves finding a single correct answer, such as analytic or mathematical intelligence, would not be much help.

managing a home, advancing a career, balancing family finances, and analyzing information from media, mail, and the Internet, as well as addressing the needs of family members, neighbors, and colleagues.

Solving practical problems involves the kinds of intellectual abilities and knowledge that most adults consider to be increasingly important as they mature (Sternberg et al., 1995). Most also think that they steadily improve in this aspect of intelligence even into old age. One study found that 76 percent of older adults believed that their thinking abilities had improved with age, and only 4 percent thought that they had declined (Williams et al., 1983). When asked about evidence for overall decline in IQ, the respondents explained that they

termine their effectiveness. Perlmutter and her colleagues wanted to know if younger and older employees differed in their overall job performance—and if so, whether this difference was due to physical and cognitive skills, work experience, or both.

They were surprised to discover that, independent of age, the amount of prior work experience had little impact on the employees' work performance or on their physical or cognitive skills. Apparently, after one has learned the basic requirements of the job, additional experience does not necessarily yield better performance (Ceci & Cornelius, 1990). However, the employees' age (independent of prior experience) made a significant difference. Younger workers, as expected, had better physical skills, better memory abilities, and greater efficiency in computation (as when calculating the check). Nevertheless, when the two groups were compared on their work performance, older employees outperformed their younger counterparts in the number of customers served, during both rush and nonrush periods.

Perlmutter found that this was consistent with the reports of some of the restaurant managers she interviewed. For example, she noted,

> it was consistently reported that older workers chunk tasks to save steps by combining orders for several customers at several tables and/or by employing time management strategies such as preparing checks while waiting for food delivery. . . . Although younger experienced food servers may have the knowledge and skills necessary for such organization and chunking, they do not seem to use the skills as often, perhaps because they do not believe they need to.

Thus, older employees devised cognitive strategies to compensate for the narrowing of some of their other job-related skills. These researchers concluded that "this evidence of adaptive competence in adulthood represents functional improvements that probably are common, particularly in the workplace."

Indeed, this appears to be the case. Salthouse (1984) found, for example, that older skilled typists could perform at speeds comparable to younger typists, but they used different strategies to attain the same result. Specifically, they read ahead and developed a longer mental span of letters to be typed, in order to compensate for age-related declines in their perceptual and motor skills.

Similar results were found in a study of bank employees aged 24 to 58. Of the older workers, those who were most successful (measured by authority, salary, and ratings) were not necessarily the ones who scored highest on standard measures of intelligence, but they did score well on a measure of practical intelligence of bank management. The author of this study cautions against using either age or psychometric tests to assess ability in middle-aged workers. Practical, everyday assessment is more pertinent (Colonia-Willner, 1998). Through selective optimization with compensation, older adults can maintain their performance levels. They find strategies that are well suited to the changes taking place in their cognitive capacities.

were talking not about IQ tests but about practical intelligence. Whether such improvement actually occurs or is wishful thinking is a matter of debate. However, the scientific community accepts the "considerable evidence" that older adults function well and that the cognitive declines demonstrated in the lab do not have as negative an impact on everyday domains as one would expect (Park, 1999), as the Research Report demonstrates.

Thus, many middle-aged and older adults believe that they once were foolish when it came to love or money, or naive in human relations, or ignorant about career management, but that gradually their practical intelligence improved.

THE FALL AND RISE OF IQ

For most of the twentieth century, psychologists were convinced that intelligence improves every year of childhood, reaches a peak in adolescence, and then gradually declines during adulthood (Woodruff-Pak, 1989). This belief was based on what seemed to be solid evidence. For instance, the United States Army tested the intelligence of all literate draftees in World War I. When the test scores of men of various ages were compared, one conclusion seemed obvious: The average male reached an intellectual peak at about age 18, stayed at that level until his mid-20s, and then began to decline (Yerkes, 1923).

Similar results came from a classic study of 1,191 individuals, aged 10 to 60, all from 19 carefully selected, insular New England villages. (The purpose of sampling isolated villages was to find a group of subjects who differed in age but were similar in ethnicity and life experience.) IQ tests of this group showed intellectual ability declining after a peak between ages 18 and 21, with the average 55-year-old scoring the same as the average 14-year-old (Jones & Conrad, 1933). The case for age-related decline in intelligence was considered proven.

Then two psychologists, Nancy Bayley and Melita Oden (1955), began to analyze the adult development of the children originally selected by Lewis Terman in 1921 for his study of child geniuses. (This group has been studied by a succession of researchers over the past 80 years.) Bayley knew that in previous cross-sectional studies, "the invariable findings had indicated that most intellectual functions decrease after about 21 years of age" (Bayley, 1966). She found instead that on several tests of concept mastery, the scores of these gifted individuals increased between ages 20 and 50.

Bayley followed this clue by retesting a more typical group of adults who had also been tested as children. These subjects, as members of the Berkeley Growth Study, had been selected in infancy to be representative of the infant population of Berkeley, California. Results again showed a general increase in intellectual functioning from childhood through young adulthood. Instead of reaching a plateau at age 21, the typical 36-year-old was still improving on the most important subtests of the Wechsler Adult Intelligence Scale (WAIS), vocabulary, comprehension, and information. Bayley (1966) concluded that "intellectual potential for continued learning is unimpaired through 36 years."

Why did Bayley find such a different pattern of intellectual aging? Recall that her study used a *longitudinal* design (in which the same people are tested repeatedly as they grow older) whereas earlier studies were *cross-sectional* (testing groups of people who are similar in every important aspect but the one being studied). As we saw in Chapter 1, cross-sectional research can yield a misleading picture of adult development, not only because it is impossible to select adults who are simi-

Smart Enough for the Trenches? These young men were drafted to fight in World War I. Younger men (about age 17 or 18) did better on the military's intelligence tests than slightly older ones.
❓ *Observational Quiz (see answer page 583): Beyond the test itself, what conditions of the testing favored the teenaged men?*

lar to each other in every important aspect except age but also because each cohort has a unique history of life experiences. Adults who grew up during the Great Depression, for example, or during World War II acquired different cognitive skills than younger cohorts who grew up during the 1950s, say, or the 1990s. Among other influences, the quality of public education, the variety of cultural opportunities, and the expanded supply of information from newspapers, radio, TV, and the World Wide Web have provided advantages to later-born cohorts. Even more significant, elderly adults who grew up early in the twentieth century, when most children quit school by eighth grade, are likely to differ intellectually from those who grew up later, when a high school education was more normative, or even later, when many people went to college.

However, longitudinal research has problems, too. By studying the same individuals repeatedly over many years, the scientist is giving a certain group repeated practice on whatever tests are used, so the longitudinal rise in IQ scores might reflect practice rather than a true increase. Further, people who move away, get sick, or have other life problems are more likely to drop out of a longitudinal study, so the remaining subjects may be a self-selected sample. Finally, longitudinal research, by definition, takes a long time. To study adult intelligence from age 20 to 80 would require 60 years of diligence and patience.

These competing methodological problems led cross-sectional experts to believe that adult intelligence fell over the years (with crystallized intelligence temporarily masking a drop in learning ability) and longitudinal experts to insist that it rose. Into this controversy, with a new research method to settle the issue, came a graduate student named K. Warner Schaie.

In 1956, as part of his doctoral research, Schaie tested a cross-sectional sample of 500 adults aged 20 to 50 on five "primary mental abilities": verbal meaning (vocabulary comprehension), spatial orientation, inductive reasoning, number ability, and word fluency. His initial cross-sectional results showed some gradual decline in ability with age, as he expected. However, he decided to retest his initial sample 7 years later. He also tested a new group of adults at each age interval, and then he followed this new group longitudinally as well, from 1963 to 1991. By comparing the scores of the retested individuals with their own earlier scores (longitudinal) and with the scores of the new group (cross-sectional), he could get a more accurate view of development than either method alone would provide. The new method, called *cross-sequential*, is illustrated in Figure 21.2. The cross-age comparisons made possible by this accumulation of longitudinal and cross-sectional data over many years allow analysis of possible effects of retesting, cohort differences, and other influences on adult changes in intelligence.

The results of Schaie's research, known as the *Seattle Longitudinal Study* (Schaie, 1983), confirmed and extended what others had found many years earlier: Most people improve in primary mental abilities during most of adulthood. However, each particular ability showed a different pattern. As shown in Figure 21.2, cognitive abilities are more likely to increase than decrease from age 20 until the late 50s. The only

exception is number ability, which begins to shift slightly downward by age 40. After age 60, decreases at 7-year intervals are statistically significant but small throughout. In his most recent follow-up Schaie wrote, "It is not until the 80s are reached that the average older adult will fall below the middle range of performance for young adults" (Schaie, 1996).

Because of the carefulness of his design, Schaie was able to go further than simply document changes in the five primary abilities. He found that some activities, such as doing challenging work and being married to an intellectually stimulating partner, would tend to increase scores and other factors, such as divorce or death of a spouse, would decrease them. In fact, the fastest drop of all occurred among widows who were full-time homemakers. He then gave special training to a group of 60-year-olds who had shown marked declines in spatial or reasoning skills. After 5 hours of one-on-one training, 40 percent of them improved to the level at which they had been 14 years earlier.

Schaie's research and many other studies have proved that intellectual abilities in adulthood can rise, fall, stay the same, and then rise and fall again. Schaie's demonstration of the multidirectionality of intelligence has been replicated many times and with diverse subjects. One of the most recent was with monozygotic and dizygotic twins, born in Sweden and now studied at ages 41 to 84. The results are markedly similar, revealing, "vast individual differences in the aging process, the extent and nature of which depend on the phenotype in question." The cross-sequential method is "a powerful tool for investigating life span development" (Finkel et al., 1998).

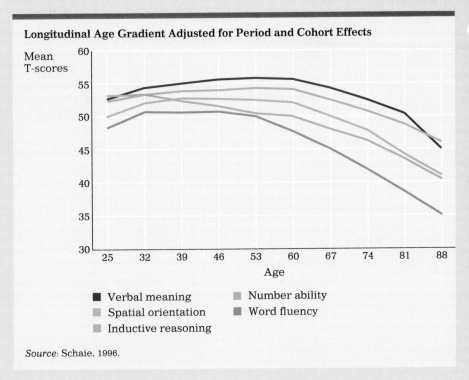

Longitudinal Age Gradient Adjusted for Period and Cohort Effects

- ■ Verbal meaning
- Spatial orientation
- Inductive reasoning
- Number ability
- ■ Word fluency

Source: Schaie, 1996.

Figure 21.2 Age Differences in Intellectual Abilities. Cross-sectional data on intellectual abilities at various ages would show much steeper declines than those shown here; longitudinal research, in contrast, would show more notable rises. Because Schaie's research is cross-sequential, the trajectories it depicts are more revealing. In part, this is because the methodology takes into account the cohort and historical effects and thus holds educational experiences constant. As you can see in this more accurate reflection of intellectual development, the age-related differences from age 25 to 60 are very small.

The portrayal of adult intelligence as multidimensional, multidirectional, and individually variable can seem terribly abstract when it is based on group averages. But individual profiles of intellectual change can be separated out from group trends, allowing growth, decline, and stable functioning to be examined on a case-by-case basis. Case studies like these reveal that the reasons for intellectual growth or decline are complex and multifaceted, based on the unique experiences of adult life.

Using data from his Seattle Longitudinal Study, K. Warner Schaie (1989) has provided the following portrayals of changes in word recognition (a measure of crystallized intelligence) in two pairs of adults of comparable age. More important, information about each person's occupation, health, marital status, and significant life events was used to assess why patterns of growth, decline, or stability in intelligence emerged.

The first two profiles [Figure 21.3a] represent two . . . women who throughout life functioned at very different levels. Subject 155510 is a high school graduate who has been a homemaker all of her adult life and whose husband is still alive and well-functioning. She started our testing program at a rather low level, but her performance had had a clear upward trend. The comparison participant subject (154503) had been professionally active as a teacher. Her performance remained fairly level and above the population average until her early sixties. Since that time she has been divorced and retired from her teaching job; her performance in 1984 dropped to an extremely low level, which may reflect her experiential losses but could also be a function of increasing health problems.

The second pair of profiles [Figure 21.3b] shows the 28-year performance of two . . . men now in their eighties. Subject 153003, who started out somewhat below the population average, completed only grade school and worked as a purchasing agent prior to his retirement. He showed virtually stable performance until the late sixties; his performance actually increased after he retired, but he is beginning to experience health problems and has recently become a widower, and his latest assessment was

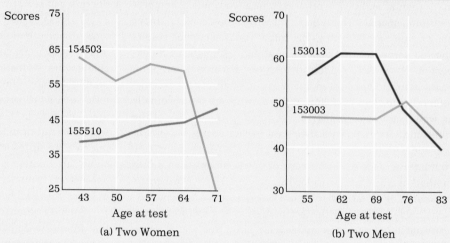

Source: Schaie, 1989.

(a) Two Women (b) Two Men

Figure 21.3 Two Profiles of Word Recognition Ability. These figures index changes in word recognition scores (which are used as a measure of crystallized intelligence) for two pairs of comparable adults over time. Notice how distinctly different the profiles of individual change for each person are—even though each is the same age and part of the same birth cohort. These differences underscore how much intellectual change in adulthood is affected by occupational, marital, health, and other experiences that vary from one person to another.

below the earlier stable level. By contrast, subject 153013, a high school graduate who held mostly clerical types of jobs, showed gain until the early sixties and stability over the next assessment interval. By age 76, however, he showed substantial decrement that continued through the last assessment, which occurred less than a year prior to his death.

Looking at the relative scores of each pair of subjects at their first testing, no one could have predicted their later-life intellectual performance, even if one knew the overall trends in group averages that occur with increasing age. The influences of education, occupation, and idiosyncratic events like divorce, health problems, and the death of a spouse contributed to unique profiles of intellectual change. The lesson: Intellectual changes are woven into the changing life circumstances that each individual experiences during the adult years, resulting in variations in intellectual development that defy precise prediction.

relating to people, to things, and to data. The study's main conclusion was:

> As the adults in the study grew older, the level of complexity of their paid work continued to affect the level of their intellectual functioning as it had when they were 20 and 30 years younger. Doing paid work that is substantially complex appears to raise the level of participants' intellectual functioning; doing paid work that is not intellectually challenging appears to decrease their level of intellectual functioning. Furthermore, the positive effect. . . appears even greater for older than for somewhat younger workers . . . [and is] the same [for] women as for men. [Schooler et al., 1999]

Educational level, income, health, personality, and marital status also contribute to individual differences in intellectual aging: Being well educated, financially secure, physically active, and happily married to a stimulating spouse has intellectual as well as emotional benefits. These results have been shown in longitudinal research among French- and English-speaking Canadians (Arbuckle et al., 1998) as well as in the United States (Schaie, 1996).

The importance of context emphasizes again the specifics of cohort. The clearest evidence for cohort differences in the patterns of cognitive growth has come, once again, from the Seattle Longitudinal Study. As you can see in Figure 21.4, each successive cohort (born at 7-year intervals from 1889 to 1966) scored higher in the two abilities currently most prized among educators, Verbal Memory and Inductive Reasoning. The most probable explanation for these results is that the later cohorts had more years of schooling and were more likely to have had teachers who encouraged them to think and express their own ideas, rather than to memorize facts and others' opinions, as teachers of earlier cohorts tended to do. These cohort improvements are reflected in scores on IQ tests as well, which showed a steady upward drift over most of the twentieth century in every nation (Flynn, 1999; Neisser et al., 1996).

❶ Answer to Observational Quiz (from page 580): *Sitting on the floor with no back support, with a test paper at a distance on your lap, and with a sergeant standing over you holding a stopwatch—all are enough to rattle anyone, especially people over 18.*

Figure 21.4 Cohort Differences in Intellectual Abilities. Schaie's multicohort, multiperiod research enables him to compare adult intellectual abilities among people born in 1903 and every 7 years after that, including those who are young adults today.
❷ Observational Quiz (see answer page 585): *Which abilities have improved over the decades?*

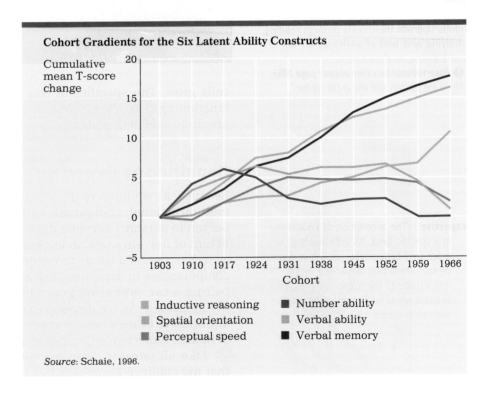

Source: Schaie, 1996.

THE IMPORTANCE OF KNOWING HOW TO PLAY

What are the implications of the research on intelligence and expertise? The fact that intelligence rises and falls with training and experience means that many workers can learn new skills and develop new habits if given the proper training. It is generally agreed that age is not the reason that a person is less able to do a job. Technical changes, such as new computer programs, make young college graduates more employable than older workers—not because of any age-related intelligence, but because of past experience with computers. To address such ever-changing workplace requirements, a plethora of employee training programs are available, and about half of all adults are engaged in them at any particular time (see Figure 21.5).

More important, middle-aged adults are now seen as still able to make choices about how to live the rest of their lives and spend their time. We saw in Chapter 20 that as many adults have chosen to quit smoking (perhaps the most difficult addictive habit to break) as are still smoking. We will see in Chapter 22 that middle-aged adults must shift in the way they react to their grown children and aged parents. Another important example of such change is how adults choose to use their leisure time. The research on adult intelligence suggests that every aspect of life—from political values to social patterns, from the words we use to the routines we follow—can change. However, the research on expertise suggests that such change does not happen quickly, merely as a new decision, but is the result of years of effort and practice.

This pattern is apparent in how adults regard their leisure time, a topic of considerable interest to developmentalists. The cohort that grew up during the Great Depression emphasized the importance of hard work (Kleiber, 1999). All their lives, having a job and earning a paycheck were very important, and many saw retirement as something to be dreaded or as a time to take on a new job, a new career, a new productive task. As you will see in later chapters, many of today's elderly have found creative ways to stay busy. However, relaxing, taking life easy, enjoying each day, is difficult for some people who grew up when leisure meant laziness and laziness was social sin. Yet, particularly in middle age, the anti-leisure mentality can be destructive. As one scholar writes:

> Relaxation can have the momentary value of enabling one to adjust effectively to circumstances throughout life, but its existential value is especially important during midlife. Pausing and relaxing thoroughly provides the psychological distance necessary to make judgments and effective decisions about what is worth doing next and about how best to use the life that is left to live. [Kleiber, 1999]

Although it is true that people learn best the tasks they focus their minds on, it is also true that a balance of academic, creative, and practical intelligence is most likely to carry a person through life successfully. That means that even playful activities are useful in development. Not only is this apparent at

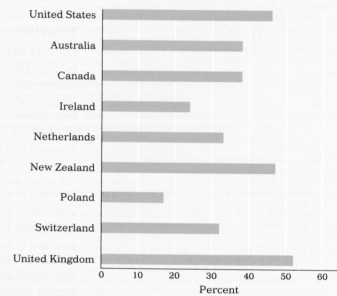

Percentage of Adults in Job-Related Continuing Education, Selected Countries

Source: Organization for Economic Cooperation and Development, Paris, *Education at a Glance*, annual.

Figure 21.5 Continuing Education. This chart shows the percentage of adults in certain countries who are enrolled in continuing education related to their work, either through their employment or on their own.

the end of life and in the middle of it, but it also seems true in the college years. One indicator of success in college is academic achievement, and one hypothesis is that extracurricular activities undercut study time. But longitudinal study of more than 7,000 college seniors found that those who engaged in more activities had grade point averages as good as or better than those of students who avoided all sports, clubs, and the like (Camp, 1990). This is not to say that a person should go too far in the other direction, avoiding all intellectual pursuits. It does mean that making good choices—not necessarily the same ones that previous generations made—leads to a fuller intellectual as well as social life. This becomes clearer with time, as a person realizes that he or she cannot be equally successful at everything. As one father explained poetically:

I told my son: triage
Is the main art of aging.
At midlife, everything
Sings of it. In law
Or healing, learning or play,
Buying or selling—above all
In remembering—the rule is
Cut losses, let profits ring.

Specifics rise and fall
By selection, which is triage;
Even the beautiful,
Gleaming as if timeless—
A standing wave in the flood
That washes away—
Is a species of survival.

[Hamil, 1991]

SUMMARY

1. The life-span perspective encourages us to realize that adult cognitive development is multidimensional, multidirectional, contextual, and plastic.

MULTIDIMENSIONAL INTELLIGENCE: NOT ONE, BUT MANY

2. The evidence does not support the idea that there is one general entity called intelligence that people have in greater or lesser quantity. Most researchers now think that there are several distinct intelligences, not just a single entity of general intelligence.

3. Cattell and Horn concluded that while crystallized intelligence, which is based on accumulated knowledge, increases with time, one's fluid, flexible reasoning skills inevitably decline with age.

4. Sternberg proposed three fundamental forms of intelligence: analytic, creative, and practical. Most adults believe that while analytic and creative abilities decline with age, their practical intelligence improves as they grow older, and research supports this belief.

5. Gardner identified eight intelligences: linguistic, logical-mathematical, musical, spatial, body-kinesthetic, naturalistic, social-understanding, and self-understanding. The individual's genetic heritage and culture influence which of these intelligences are more highly developed.

MULTIDIRECTIONAL INTELLIGENCE: NOT JUST INCREASE OR DECREASE

6. Adult intellectual competence is multidirectional, with some abilities (such as short-term memory) declining with age but others (such as vocabulary) increasing.

CONTEXTUAL INTELLIGENCE: WHERE YOU ARE AND WHERE YOU WERE

7. Each individual's cognitive development is unique, varying with his or her genetic heritage and cultural context, in adulthood as well as in childhood. Contextual variations influence cohort differences in patterns of cognitive growth.

PLASTIC INTELLECTUAL CHANGE

8. Plasticity refers to the fact that cognitive abilities can be molded by many factors, particularly education or training.

9. As people grow older, they may become more expert in whatever types of intelligence or skills they choose to develop. Meanwhile, abilities that are not exercised may fall into decline.

10. In addition to being more experienced, experts are better thinkers than novices because they are more intuitive; their cognitive processes are automatic, often seeming to require little conscious thought; they use more and better strategies to perform whatever task is required; and they are more flexible.

KEY TERMS

general intelligence *(g)* (571)

fluid intelligence (572)

crystallized intelligence (572)

practical intelligence (575)

plasticity (584)

expertise (584)

expert (585)

KEY QUESTIONS

1. What four aspects of cognitive growth are highlighted by the life-span perspective?

2. How is fluid intelligence different from crystallized intelligence? How does each change in adulthood?

3. How do Sternberg's three fundamental forms of intelligence—analytic, creative, and practical—tend to vary with age?

4. Which of Gardner's eight intelligences tend to increase during adulthood in North America, and why?

5. How and why do context and cohort affect patterns of cognitive growth?

6. How is plasticity of cognitive development related to education?

7. What are the differences between an expert and a novice?

8. *In Your Experience* What changes in your own intelligence have occurred in the past 10 years?

Middle Adulthood: Psychosocial Development

Although no dramatic biological shifts occur to signal it, middle age begins at about age 35. Midlife is about age 40, because at that point, the average adult has about as many years of life ahead as have already passed. For most people, **middle age** is the longest period, lasting 30 years—from age 35 to age 65.

Midlife is sometimes portrayed as a time of crisis. However, continuities of love relationships, family commitments, work involvements, and personality patterns often seem more salient during middle age than any crisis that may occur. As at other periods, both change and continuity are apparent.

CHANGES DURING MIDDLE AGE

A number of potentially troubling personal changes cluster in the 40s. The most obvious is simply that the social clock signals that one is growing old. Beginning with the "Big Four-O," birthdays are seen in a new perspective—not time already lived but time remaining to live. This perceptual shift is often highlighted by the death or serious illness either of a close relative from the next-older generation—perhaps a parent or an aunt or uncle—or of a friend or colleague, possibly only a few years older than oneself. Such events bring not only feelings of personal loss but also thoughts about one's own mortality (Katchadourian, 1987).

For many parents, an additional source of midlife upheaval is the need to make important, and not always easy, adjustments. When children become teenagers, they start demanding greater independence and sexual freedom, putting their parents' authority and values to the test. No sooner have parents adjusted to these changes than their children set out on their own as young adults, perhaps first distancing themselves and then needing a new type of nurturance and closeness when they turn their parents into parents-in-law and grandparents.

Further, for many adults, middle age is a time to reexamine earlier choices regarding intimacy and generativity. Those who thought that they had ample time to accomplish certain life goals suddenly see the door to the future closing. Some reassess the balance between work and family. For example, those who have been single-mindedly pursuing a career often become concerned about the loved ones they have neglected; those who have devoted themselves to child rearing often worry about what they will do when their children are gone. Marriages

Forty Can Be Fabulous As these birthday greetings suggest, the advent of middle age is assumed to be a source of high anxiety and turmoil. For most people, however, the actual experience of middle age is not strikingly different from that of early adulthood and seldom produces anything like the proverbial "midlife crisis."

middle age   The years from age 35 to age 65.

sandwich generation   The generation "in between," having both grown children and elderly parents. Many middle-aged people feel pressured by the needs and demands of their adult children on the one hand and of their elderly (and perhaps ailing or widowed) parents on the other.

midlife crisis   A period of unusual anxiety, radical reexamination, and sudden transformation that is widely associated with middle age but which actually has more to do with developmental history than with chronological age.

may also be examined, perhaps with the thought that middle age is the last chance for divorce and re-marriage. Elderly parents sometimes become frail, needing care from their middle-aged children. Under some circumstances, family ties can become quite burdensome. Because of their position in the generational hierarchy, the middle-aged are expected to help both older and younger generations of their family. Squeezed from both sides, the middle-aged have been called the **sandwich generation** (see A Life-Span View).

All these midlife shifts are recognized by most developmentalists who study adulthood. However, few developmentalists today believe that such changes commonly produce a **midlife crisis,** defined as a period of unusual anxiety, radical reexamination, and sudden transformation (Hunter & Sundel, 1989; Wrightsman, 1994). Like other periods of life, midlife brings some blessings, some challenges, some problems. A wealth of research reveals a great deal of variability among people the same age and a great deal of continuity within each individual.

In short, how people react to the challenges and changes of middle adulthood has much more to do with their overall developmental history than with calendar milestones. As two experts in the psychology of aging comment, chronological age, as a predictor of development, is like "an initially appealing false lover who tells you everything and nothing" (Birren & Schroots, 1996).

PERSONALITY THROUGHOUT ADULTHOOD

Throughout adulthood, the major source of developmental continuity is the stability of personality. Paradoxically, the stability of personality is also a major reason for developmental discontinuity when it occurs. Our personality traits lead us to seek, interpret, and then react to life events in ways that are distinctly our own. As two leading researchers explain:

> People undoubtedly do change across the life span. Marriages end in divorce, professional careers are started in mid-life, fashions and attitudes change with the times. Yet often the same traits can be seen in new guises: Intellectual curiosity merely shifts from one field to another, avid gardening replaces avid tennis, one abusive relationship is followed by another. Many of these changes are best regarded as variations on the "uniform tune" played by individuals' enduring dispositions. [McCrae & Costa, 1994]

To better understand this point, we need to draw a distinction between the basic personality traits that seem stable throughout life and the variable expression of them.

THE SANDWICH GENERATION

The term *sandwich generation* evokes an image of two slices of bread with a substantial filling—meat, jam, peanut butter, cheese—in the middle. The analogy to the substantial middle generation squeezed by obligations to those younger and older is vivid, but not always appropriate. However, the term captures the feeling of obligation to both generations that is often deeply felt by middle-aged people who are both children and parents.

Middle-aged adults are often particularly surprised by the need to care for their young adult children long after they thought the nest would be empty. In fact, instead of flying away, many young adults stay on or return. This phenomenon has prompted one observer to describe the "swollen nest" phase of life, an uncomfortable period that often follows the child-rearing phase (Ginn & Arber, 1994).

At any given moment, almost half of all middle-aged parents have at least one child still living with them. This is especially likely when the parents are in good health and when the children are financially needy—such as when they are unemployed or single parents (Whittington & Peters, 1996; Nilsson & Strandh, 1999). In such households, parents continue to pay most of the bills and to do most of the housework, with the nesting children seldom contributing substantially to either (Ward & Spitze, 1996). Neither generation is particularly happy living in a swollen nest. Parents, especially, regard independent living as the natural order of things, and both generations feel the loss of privacy and the increase in conflict that sharing a household entails (Alwin, 1996; White & Rogers, 1997).

The other side of the sandwich represents the need to care for elderly relatives. This is nothing new, particularly for middle-aged women. Typically, one member of the middle generation, usually a daughter, takes on the task of kinkeeping and caregiving. However, compared to earlier times, the kinkeeper role is less voluntary and more disruptive. Many middle-aged women are employed and they have fewer siblings, making it less likely that a sister with both the time and temperament for full-time caregiving will naturally emerge.

Thus, when an elderly person needs ongoing care, often a daughter feels she must quit her job, or a daughter-in-law is recruited to provide care, or a son is the only adult child available to take on the role, or a granddaughter puts her own life on hold. None of these circumstances seems a part of the natural rhythm of life, so all are seen as an interruption, a burden, a developmental halt. Daughters-in-law are particularly likely to feel unfairly burdened with elder care (Ingersol-Dayton & Starrels, 1996). (Care of the elderly is discussed in more detail in Chapter 25.)

An added stress occurs when the adult children who are living with their parents have serious disabilities (Roberto, 1993). This situation has become more common, for two reasons. First, medical advances have saved the lives of many such children who, 30 years ago, would have died. Second, as society has come to recognize the human and economic costs

Mother, Father, and Son Outsiders might pity this family because the 40-year-old son has cerebral palsy and is dependent on his parents. However, these three are accustomed to their caregiving interactions, gain comfort from their roles, and are satisfied with their relationship.

of large institutions, many such places have closed, so more disabled children stay at home.

As you can imagine, any of the above problems might make middle-aged adults feel squeezed. However, to some extent, having many roles to fill increases a middle-aged person's life satisfaction. For example, it has long been assumed that middle-aged women were overburdened if they were simultaneously employee, wife, mother of a child still at home, and daughter of a parent who needed assistance. But research has revealed that this is not necessarily the case. Especially if the roles are important to the woman, if her relationships with the various people are satisfying, and if the time requirements are not overwhelming, filling many roles is a source of satisfaction (Lawrence et al., 1998; Matire et al., 2000). Furthermore, overwhelming demands are unusual in middle age, for three reasons:

- Although young adult children living at home may not contribute much to the household, their independence reduces the ongoing burden they represent.
- Disabled adults usually require less care than when they were children, so their parents have adjusted to the task.
- Major caregiving of the very oldest is often borne by other older adults—spouses, siblings, friends, or children who themselves are older than 65.

Therefore, middle-aged adults are less "caught in a web of generational obligation" than buoyed by the rewards of each role (Soldo, 1996; Stephens et al., 1994). Most of them experience pleasure in their maturing children, take comfort in their closer relationships with their active and healthy parents, and find satisfaction with their family relationships overall. The sandwich generation is not really the filling in the middle after all—another example of the many myths surrounding middle age.

Stable Traits: The Big Five

Big Five The five basic clusters of personality traits that remain quite stable throughout adulthood: extroversion, agreeableness, conscientiousness, neuroticism, and openness.

Extensive longitudinal and cross-sectional research among men and women of many nations and ethnicities finds five basic clusters of personality traits—referred to as the **Big Five**—that remain quite stable throughout adulthood (Costa & McCrae, 1999; Digman, 1990). The Big Five have emerged from factor analysis of personality traits in many cultures. Such analysis has demonstrated that "all human beings are of one species" when it comes to personality structure (McCrae et al., 1999). Although various experts use somewhat different terms to describe these clusters, there is a consensus that the Big Five can be summarized as follows:

- Neuroticism—anxious, moody, and self-punishing
- Extroversion—outgoing, assertive, and active
- Openness—imaginative, curious, artistic, open to new experiences
- Agreeableness—kind, helpful, and easygoing
- Conscientiousness—organized, deliberate, and conforming

You can estimate the degree to which your own personality reflects each of the Big Five characteristics in Figure 22.1.

Whether a given individual ranks high or low in each of the Big Five is determined by the interacting influences of genes, culture, early child rearing, and the experiences and choices made during late adolescence and early adulthood. The strength of these Big Five traits may fluctuate for anyone under age 30, because the social context and personal choices of adolescence and young adulthood evoke new personality patterns that were not apparent in early childhood. However, by about age 30, the Big Five usually become quite stable, and they remain so throughout the life span.

ecological niche The particular lifestyle and social context adults settle into that are compatible with their individual personality needs and interests.

One reason for this stability is genetic. Genes do not always manifest themselves in infancy, but by early adulthood, genetic personality traits are usually evident. Another influence on personality stability is the fact that by age 30, most people have created and settled into an **ecological niche.** This niche is their chosen lifestyle and social context, including vocation, mate, neighborhood, and daily routines. The fact that people choose surroundings to suit their temperament has led two personality researchers to quip, "Ask not how life's experiences change personality; ask instead how personality shapes lives" (McCrae & Costa, 1990). (See the In Person box.)

Figure 22.1 Big Five Self-Assessment. Estimate your own personality on the Big Five traits. Rate yourself on each characteristic, from 1 to 5, with 1 as very low, 5 as very high, and 3 as middling. This simple self-report is not a valid measure, but most research in personality asks people to assess their own traits in a similar way. (Typically, each characteristic is revealed by asking subjects how strongly they agree with various statements. For example, somebody high in neuroticism might agree strongly with the statement "I wonder if other people like me" and disagree strongly with the statement "I never blame myself for my past mistakes.")

❷ *Observational Quiz (see answer page 596):* *How do your scores change over time?*

Trait cluster	10 years ago	Now	10 years from now
Neuroticism			
Extroversion			
Openness			
Agreeableness			
Conscientiousness			

PERSONALITIES THROUGHOUT LIFE

Some simplified examples will illustrate how an ecological niche interacts with personality. By age 30, those high in extroversion have likely found mates who share their outgoingness, or at least encourage it. They have established a busy social life with a wide circle of friends and acquaintances; their jobs allow them to interact with many people, perhaps in sales, politics, or public relations. Similarly, the details of their lifestyle foster social contact: They may have phones in every room, which would ring often (with call-waiting and call-transfer features, as well as cell phones and answering machines), as well as at least one active e-mail account. They probably live in a busy neighborhood, belong to an amateur sports league or social club, volunteer at their local community center, and engage in occasional group adventures such as mountain hiking or bicycle touring.

By contrast, those fairly high in neuroticism, with their anxiety and moodiness, are likely to choose a vocation that draws on their general apprehensiveness and vigilance against things going wrong—perhaps as a contract lawyer, a corrections officer, a cost accountant, a proofreader. They tend to expect the worst from their jobs, their mates, their children, and themselves, and this very expectation creates antagonism, as "people with negative self-views consistently enact behaviors that alienate the people around them" (Swann et al., 1992). Further, their fearfulness makes them afraid to take a new job or travel to a new place or join a new group of people. Thus they may become stuck in a cycle of self-pity, a life pattern that may, in itself, perpetuate unhappiness and further alienate others. In fact, neuroticism is the personality trait that best predicts unhappiness in marriage (Bouchard et al., 1999).

The genetic as well as the contextual continuity of personality also helps explain the lifestyle of those adults whose lives are in constant flux, with frequent changes of jobs, residences, and relationships. Such restless churning may seem to indicate an unstable personality, but it is actually typical of someone who is strong and stable on the Big Five trait of openness to new experiences. If such a person is also high in extroversion, low in conscientiousness, and not very easygoing, that individual may be particularly vulnerable to a midlife crisis. Being strong and stable in the openness trait may also be related to a propensity for divorce, particularly for women (Jockin et al., 1996).

This research suggests that we are who are we are, even when buffeted by events and burnished by time. To illustrate this insight, I will try to apply it to myself. When I was a girl in the Midwest, several older relatives said I was smart, so I should become a teacher. I said, "Never," recognizing that they were stereotyping me on the basis of gender. What did I want to become instead? Perhaps a great poet, perhaps a missionary, perhaps a doctor who traveled by dogsled. In college, my first major was English, my second was Asian history, my third (after I transferred from Stanford University to Harvard) was international relations. I was clearly so low on neuroticism (as defined in the Big Five) that I might be foolhardy, so

Niche-Picking The Marine sergeant in the top photo and the park ranger below have much in common. Both are middle-aged women, serving their country in uniform. However, if their expressions here are at all indicative, they have quite different personality traits, and each has picked a vocational niche that is compatible with those traits and reinforces them—a niche in which the other would probably feel quite out of place.

open to new experiences that I did not stay put. I wanted to rebel against conventional wisdom, as many other members of my cohort (who came of age in the 1960s) did.

It was actually my desire to change the world that led me to teaching—as the first Harvard student to do practice teaching in the Boston public schools. Several degrees and several decades later, I find that I am fulfilling some of my childhood impulses—as a textbook author, not a poet; as a college teacher, not a missionary; as a Ph.D., not an M.D. I can now see that the traits of my young adulthood—low on neuroticism, high on openness—led me to New York City. Although I had lived in seven homes in four states by age 18, it probably is no surprise to anyone but me that I settled down by age 30 and have had the same work, the same husband, and the same home since then. Any sign of a midlife crisis? Right at about age 40, I had my fourth child and taught one course in Sing Sing prison—both a bit unusual, but very much in character for me.

Developmental Changes in Personality

In large-scale cross-cultural research, the stability of the Big Five is impressive. However, research on personality occasionally reveals "quite dramatic interindividual differences" in the direction and pace of personality change (Jones & Meredith, 1996). Certain traits, such as warmth toward others and confidence about oneself, are particularly likely to show marked individual patterns.

For everyone at every age, the environment continues to play a significant role. Most adults select an ecological niche that reinforces their basic temperament, but significant changes in that niche can produce changes in personality (Loehlin, 1992). Such transformations are particularly likely when life circumstances are altered dramatically—perhaps by divorce or the death of a spouse, a new marriage or career, recovery from a longstanding addiction, or a move to a nation with a "foreign" culture. A new set of values, as in a religious conversion, or a new point of view, as when a depressed person begins to respond to antidepressant medication and cognitive therapy, can also produce change. Sometimes one change leads to another. For instance, newly divorced women are more likely to go to college than other women their age, while married middle-aged women who go to college are more likely to divorce.

Age-related shifts in the typical adult personality also occur. The cumulative impact of living a life often leads to self-improvement and greater generativity, especially from about age 30 to 65 (Jones & Meredith, 1996; McAdams et al., 1993; Peterson & Stewart, 1993). The grandparent may be much more patient with small children than he or she was as a parent; the workaholic becomes more involved in church or community affairs; the homebody seeks to enter the work force.

These three examples would probably be seen as improvements by most readers of this book. However, some traits are more valued in certain cultures than others, such as conscientiousness in China, extroversion in Australia, and openness in the United States (McCrae et al., 1999; de Raad et al., 1999). (See Figure 22.2.)

Gender Convergence

In many cultures, rigid gender roles loosen during middle age, allowing both men and women to explore feelings and behaviors previously reserved for the other sex. In fact, some scholars speculate that there may be a **gender crossover** of personality traits (Gutmann, 1994; Huyck, 1999). Overall, whether there is a true crossover (switching

❶ *Answer to Observational Quiz (from page 594):* Any answer is correct, as long as it is based on a reasonably accurate measurement of each trait before and after the present. Scores expressed in numbers (for example, 2 points for an increase in agreeableness between now and 10 years from now) reflect more careful observation than generalities such as "I got better." Interestingly, most people's scores change very little over the decades.

gender crossover The idea that each sex takes on the other sex's roles and traits in later life. This idea is disputed, but there is no doubt that maleness and femaleness become less salient in middle age.

Figure 22.2 Is It "Creativity" or "Rebellion"? The Big Five personality structure is apparent in humans of many cultures. However, the particular terms used to describe each trait vary, depending on the values of the society. The most divergent descriptions are for "openness," which is regarded more highly in the United States than in Italy. Accordingly, a person high in openness is described in more positive terms in English, while a low degree of openness is referred to more favorably in Italian. (Italian descriptors are back-translated from a version of the personality test developed and validated within Italy by native Italians.)

	English descriptors	Italian descriptors
High on openness	Creative, intellectual, imaginative, philosophical, artistic, inventive, intelligent, innovative	Nonconformist, rebellious, progressive, innovative, original, revolutionary, extravagant, ironical
Low on openness	Uncreative, unimaginative, unintellectual, simple, unintelligent, imperceptive, shallow, unsophisticated	Traditional, devoted, conservative, conventional, obedient, servile, religious, Puritan

Source: McCrae et al., 1999.

Gender Convergence Two generations ago, a man in an apron at home was usually an object of ridicule. The fact that this father seems perfectly at ease in his may be a sign that he is experiencing gender convergence, or it may simply reflect the gradual loosening of gender roles that has been occurring over the decades.

roles), a convergence (coming together), or simply a historical shift (with everyone becoming less sex-typed) is still a matter for debate. However, compared to when they were younger, many middle-aged women are more self-confident, while middle-aged men are often able to express tenderness or sadness more openly. The young man who was a warrior becomes a peacemaker, and the obedient housewife becomes an assertive grandmother or, in some cultures, a malevolent witch (Gutmann, 1994).

One explanation for this shift is biosocial. To some extent, the male tendency toward aggressiveness and dominance and the female tendency toward passiveness and nurturance are influenced by the sex hormones, as part of an adaptive process that is essential in the early years of mate selection and child rearing (Rossi, 1994). Then, in midlife, reduced levels of their respective sex hormones may free both men and women from narrow gender roles, allowing them to express previously suppressed traits. Similarly, at middle age, less restrictive cultural roles may allow some gender crossover (Holmes & Holmes, 1995).

Another explanation for this phenomenon originated in the work of Carl Jung (1933), a psychoanalyst who believed that everyone has both a masculine and a feminine side but that, because of societal pressures, young adults develop only those traits that "belong" to their own gender. Thus, women strive to be more tender and deferential than they might naturally be, while men try to be brave and assertive even when they feel afraid.

This gender difference is reinforced by the traditional arrangement that puts young mothers at home with small children (who need every ounce of nurturance an adult can muster) and fathers in the workplace (where self-assertion is needed to compete for critical increments of power and money). Both parents thus are pushed into traditional gender roles by the "chronic state of emergency" that is part of the "parental imperative" (Gutmann, 1987).

According to Jung, in middle age, adults finally become more reflective. They realize that

> . . . the achievements which society rewards are won at the cost of a diminution of personality. Many—far too many—aspects of life which should have been experienced lie in the lumber-room among dusty memories. [Jung, 1993]

Thus, middle-aged adults of both sexes explore the *shadow side* of their personality—women, their repressed masculine traits, and men, their repressed feminine traits.

While these biosocial and psychoanalytic explanations of gender convergence are intriguing, longitudinal survey research suggests a third explanation, a historical one. It is true that many middle-aged and older individuals become less tightly bound by gender restrictions than they were when they were younger. However, each decade of the twentieth century, in almost every nation, has witnessed a broadening of gender roles for everyone at every stage of life.

Thus, adults of all ages may have experienced some gender crossover, but older adults who vividly remember more rigid sexism are more conscious of the shift. The current cohort of middle-aged adults seems less marked in their convergence of sex roles than the previous cohort was, perhaps because male and female roles were less sharply defined for them than they had been for previous generations (Helson et al., 1995; Moen, 1996).

FAMILY DYNAMICS IN MIDDLE ADULTHOOD

It is hard to overestimate the importance of the family. It is a "problem-solving system" (Wilson et al., 1995) that "persists over time . . . as households wax and wane" (Troll, 1996). Although composed of individuals, each family transcends any one person. Families raise children, care for the sick, provide resources for all members, and create a family culture that gives meaning to and provides role models for personal aspirations and decisions.

No other group system has replaced the family, in any nation or century. This does not mean that families always do their job or always do it well. Some adults wisely keep their distance from their blood relatives and may be accepted as "fictive kin" in a family system that is not legally or biologically their own. Nonetheless, family ties seem as crucial in the twenty-first century as in the nineteenth or twentieth.

Where do middle-aged adults fit into the family picture? Right in the center, often as the linchpin that holds it all together. They are the cohort bridge, the "generation in the middle," between aging parents and adult children. Often they have grandchildren and sometimes grandparents as well, meaning that they are in the middle of five generations.

All Adults Now Years after the nest has emptied, the links between parents and their adult children generally remain strong, with frequent communication between the generations and regular visits. In many cases, the relative independence of the two generations works to make their relations smoother than they were when everyone was sharing the same household.

❓ *Observational Quiz (see answer page 600): Members of the middle generation prefer to visit their elderly parents at their home, rather than have the elders live with them. Can you see three signs that this is probably the case here?*

It is easy to underestimate the critical role of family dynamics for the middle generation in modern Western cultures because middle-aged people usually do not live with family members, except perhaps their own spouse. The role of the middle-aged is sometimes ignored because *family* is sometimes confused with *household*—that is, people who eat and sleep together in the same dwelling. In comparison with the traditional extended family found in many other cultures (in which several generations live under the same roof and are intensely involved in one another's lives), the various generations of the modern family seem geographically remote from one another.

However, the fact that several generations no longer sleep under the same roof does not mean that family ties are weak. In every nation that has been studied, relatives are typically in frequent contact, even when they live at a distance. They stay in touch by telephoning and visiting, and they provide each other with substantial help, ranging from advice and emotional support to gifts, loans, baby-sitting, home repair, and health care (Barresi & Menon, 1990; Crimmins & Ingegneri, 1990; Farkas & Hogan, 1995). Indeed, while it is tempting to idealize the traditional large household, the truth is that many contemporary family members are more supportive of each other, experiencing less tension and discord, when they live apart than when they live together (Coward et al., 1992; Fry, 1995; Umberson, 1992).

The generation most capable of providing the kind of support that family members need is the middle-aged, because they are physically healthy, cognitively practical, psychosocially generative, and, usually, without small children of their own. Often, someone in the middle generation becomes the family's **kinkeeper,** the one who ensures that relatives keep in touch, who plans and hosts family get-togethers, who provides help in times of illness or other crisis. Most kinkeepers are

kinkeeper   The person who celebrates family achievements, gathers the family together, and keeps in touch with family members who no longer live nearby.

Closer Than Ever Many adults find their understanding and love of their parents increasing as they themselves become older. Mother–daughter and father–son relationships are particularly likely to become closer than they were when the child was an adolescent.

❷ *Observational Quiz (see answer page 601):* *What three signs suggest that these women are mother and daughter, not a frail elderly person and a friend?*

familism   The idea that family members should support each other because family unity is more important than individual freedom and success.

Figure 22.3 Why the Difference? The fact that more elderly nonwhites than whites live with their grown children is a commendable expression of family support. However, familism can reduce the independence of the middle generation and weaken the bond between husband and wife. The reason for these ethnic differences may be a practical one: Because of historical discrimination, fewer older minorities reach late adulthood (so traditional values are not as often put to a practical test), and those who do are less able to afford to live on their own.

women, although middle-aged men sometimes take on this role. Now we will look at each of the kin categories.

Aging Parents

The relationship between most middle-aged adults and their parents improves with time. One reason is that, as adult children mature, they develop a more balanced view of the relationship as a whole, especially with regard to their years of growing up. The perspective of time can lead to a measure of forgiveness, as both generations acknowledge past mistakes in their relationships. This is especially true as adults gain a firsthand understanding of the pressures of parenthood.

The improvement in the relationship between adult children and their aging parents is particularly likely to occur today, because most of the elderly are healthy, active, and independent. They typically prefer not to live with their adult children, and most of them can afford to live on their own. The resulting freedom and privacy enhance the relationship between the two generations.

Positive relationships between the middle and older generations are also apparent in subcultures in which co-residence is still the custom. For example, Hispanic and Asian Americans are likely to live in three-generation families, for the most part harmoniously. When a conflict does arise, the source is usually either a very dependent and demanding elderly person or a rebellious teenager, not the generation in the middle (Johnson, 1995; Mindel et al., 1988).

Whether or not middle-aged adults and their parents live together depends mostly on the basic value called **familism,** the belief that family members should be close and supportive of one another, even if that means sacrificing some individual freedom and success. Practical considerations, such as health and finances, influence the decision, but when familism is weak, ways are found to avoid co-residence while still providing support (Burr & Mutchler, 1999). Generally, familism is stronger among ethnic minority groups than among the white majority (see Figure 22.3).

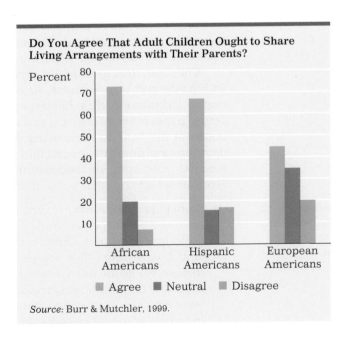

Do You Agree That Adult Children Ought to Share Living Arrangements with Their Parents?

■ Agree   ■ Neutral   ■ Disagree

Source: Burr & Mutchler, 1999.

Adult Children

Parents generally maintain close relationships with their children, even when the latter are fully grown, independent, and living away from the family home. One in-depth, longitudinal study of four generations found that "most mothers and daughters had stormy relationships during the daughter's adolescence but close and friendly ones once the daughters left home, whether or not the daughters married" (Troll, 1996).

A seven-nation survey of thousands of middle-aged adults found that the majority (75 percent) communicated with their adult children several times a week; only a tiny minority (less than 5 percent) got in touch only once a year or less. Most adults of both sexes and both generations said that they would turn to each other for help in every situation, from emotional problems to furniture arranging (Farkas & Hogan, 1995).

Typically, financial help and a variety of other support services (from home repair to laundry) flow more freely from middle-aged parents to young adults than in the other direction. However, parents benefit from their generosity in less tangible ways. They usually take great pride in their adult children's accomplishments, and their self-esteem is enhanced by the fact that their offspring are well-functioning adults (Keyes & Ruff, 1999).

Middle-aged parents also benefit from the younger generation's ability to serve as a source of information and advice about new developments in the culture. Many a middle-aged woman has gone to college because her adult children urged her to; many a middle-aged man takes better care of himself because his adult children advised—or nagged—him to.

Grandchildren

Grandparenthood begins most often in middle age, although its timing and prevalence obviously vary from culture to culture, cohort to cohort, and person to person. In the United States, more than two out of every three adults become grandparents sometime between age 40 and 65. Another smaller group become grandparents "off-time," typically before age 40 (about 10 percent overall) or occasionally after age 65. The rest will never become grandparents, usually because they themselves have no children (about 15 percent).

When the first grandchild arrives, almost every grandparent reacts with pride and wonderment. As one grandfather exulted, "Now I'm immortal." However, while becoming a grandparent is an affirmation, the actual experience of being a grandparent is much more variable, ranging from fulfilling to frustrating, from pivotal to peripheral. Generally, ongoing grandparent–grandchild relationships take one of three forms: remote, involved, or companionate (Cherlin & Furstenberg, 1986; Gratton & Haber, 1996).

- **Remote grandparents** are emotionally distant but esteemed elders who are honored, respected, and obeyed by children, grandchildren, and great-grandchildren. Often, remote grandparents control the family land, business, or other wealth. Even when they do not, they may see themselves as the patriarch or matriarch of the family heritage, responsible for maintaining traditional values. Remote grandparents were typical a century ago in the United States and are still prevalent in some traditional cultures.

❶ *Answer to Observational Quiz (from page 598):* The elderly father is wearing shoes and a shirt that a person is more likely to wear at home than on a visit; the foliage and small, enclosed patio suggest that the setting is a senior citizens' residence in a Sunbelt community; and the son (or son-in-law) is sitting in a chair without armrests or a back—unlikely if this were his home.

❷ **Especially for Social Workers:** If a client of yours is an elderly immigrant widower who is not proficient in English, would you recommend that he move in with his grandchildren or seek companionship among people his own age?

remote grandparents Grandparents who are distant but who are honored, respected, and obeyed by the younger generations in their families.

At Grandma's The Hispanic and Korean cultures from which these children's parents come traditionally endorse the involved-grandparent role—and the children's grandmother, who provides their daily care, seems to thrive in filling that role.

involved grandparents Grandparents who remain active in the everyday activities of their grandchildren, seeing them daily.

companionate grandparents Grandparents whose relationships with their children and grandchildren are characterized by independence and friendship, with visits occurring by the grandparents' choice.

❶ *Answer to Observational Quiz (from page 599):* Despite differences in shape and age, they dress alike, both in a family favorite color, with white stockings, black shoes, and gold earrings. They also look as if they share genes, as shown by their teeth, eyeglasses, and coloring. Finally, and most important, the daughter's hands, facial expression, and body position indicate that she really loves this old woman.

■ **Involved grandparents** are active in the day-to-day life of the grandchildren. Involved grandparents live in or near the grandchildren's household and see them daily. This pattern was prevalent among grandparents for most of the twentieth century, but it is relatively rare today, at least among grandparents who were born in the United States.

■ **Companionate grandparents** are independent and autonomous, maintaining a separate household and their own lifestyle. Such grandparents choose how generational interaction occurs, which grandchildren get the most attention, when and how long to baby-sit. They play with and even "spoil" their grandchildren, but they do not discipline them—especially in ways, or for reasons, that the parents would not.

Most grandparents today seek the companionate role in that they "strive for love and friendship rather than demand respect and obedience" (Gratton & Haber, 1996). A major reason is that grandparents now are independent, living in their own households with their own values, social lives, and jobs (middle-aged grandmothers are usually employed these days).

Most grandparents are quite comfortable with the companionate role: They like to boast about their grandchildren's achievements, display their photographs in their living rooms, and provide their grandchildren with fun, treats, and laughter—and leave the responsibilities to the parents (Erikson et al., 1986). As one grandparent confessed, "Glad to see them come and glad to see them go." In fact, among contemporary adults, companionate grandparents generally enjoy grandparenting more than remote grandparents (who are likely to be frustrated if they cannot maintain family rules and traditions) and more than involved grandparents (who may feel overburdened by the demands of their involvement) (Jendrek, 1994; Shore & Hayslip, 1994; Thomas, 1986).

Diversity in Grandparenting

These generalities should not obscure the tremendous diversity of grandparent–grandchild relationships. Some of this diversity results from differences in personality, ethnic traditions, and national background. Many immigrant grandparents take an involved role with their grandchildren, especially when all the family members speak a common language (Perez, 1994). Of all U.S. households, only 4 percent of those with a native-born head of household include grandchildren. By contrast, 25 percent of those households with a Mexican-born head, 18 percent of those headed by an Asian refugee, and 15 percent of those headed by someone born in the Caribbean include three or four generations (Glick et al., 1997).

Another factor contributing to diversity in grandparenting is the developmental stage of all three generations. Generally, the grandparent–grandchild bond is closer if:

- The grandchild is relatively young
- The parent is the first sibling to have children
- The grandparent is neither too young nor too old—retired but not physically impaired.

Many developmentalists are saddened at the trend toward relatively uninvolved grandparenting. It provides more independence for each generation and protects everyone from unwelcome closeness (Gratton & Haber, 1996; Thompson et al., 1989), but at a price: Every generation can suffer when distance diminishes the sense of generational continuity and interdependence.

This is particularly true among immigrant and minority groups, in which grandparents transmit "the values, beliefs, language, and customs" that allow each new generation to understand its cultural heritage (Silverstein & Chen, 1999). In adolescence and adulthood, many grandchildren of immigrants no longer respect or obey their grandparents. Teenagers believe that their grandparents' emphasis on the ways of the old country undercuts their own attempt to adjust to the new country, and the grandparents themselves neither listen nor understand (Kolland, 1994). This causes distress on all sides, particularly for the involved grandparent whose identity is tied to the development of the new generation. As one 60-year-old immigrant Cambodian woman explained:

> I'm afraid they might not be what I want them to be because in this country the children are very unpredictable. . . . I don't like to talk too much, because the more you talk the less respect they have toward you. [quoted in Detzner, 1996]

Another type of diversity in grandparenting occurs when the grandparents take on some of the parenting responsibility because they have no choice (see the Research Report on page 604).

Partners

Having an intimate relationship over the years of middle adulthood is a source of happiness, comfort, and self-respect. For the majority of middle-aged adults, their most intimate relationship is with their spouse, who is also their closest friend. For a growing minority of divorced or never-married middle-aged adults, intimacy is achieved through cohabitation with a partner. In the 1990s, of all adults not currently married in the United States, as many 35- to 65-year-olds were living with opposite-sex mates as 20- to 35-year-olds. The number of gay and lesbian middle-aged couples living together also seems to be increasing (Chevan, 1996; Huyck, 1995).

❶ **Response for Social Workers (from page 600):** Your client is likely to seek a remote grandparent role, and the children and grandchildren are likely to balk at taking him in. It would be better to find him a senior center with contemporaries of the same ethnicity. Since the client is a widower, not a widow, remarriage is likely and is often very satisfying.

Many of the remaining single middle-aged adults find intimacy in a close romantic relationship that does not include sharing a home. Research on the exact developmental impact of these nonmarital relationships in middle age is sparse. However, much is known about the close relationship that has been most intensively studied: marriage in middle age.

Marriage

As already detailed in Chapter 19, throughout adulthood, in every nation, marriage is the family relationship that seems most closely linked to personal happiness, health, and companionship. This does not mean, however, that single people are necessarily unhappy or that married people are necessarily happy.

Some research indicates that, after a dip in the first decade or so, marital happiness gradually increases (Glenn, 1991). One possible reason is financial. Overall, money is a major source of marital tension, but by the time children leave home, financial pressures have usually lessened. In addition, once the "chronic emergency" of raising young children subsides, disputes over equity in domestic work become less frequent and bitter. The children's growing independence means fewer judgment calls about which the parents might disagree and provides more opportunities for a sense of parental accomplishment. Further, many couples have adjusted their work lives to have adequate—but not too much—time for the marriage relationship (Becker & Moen, 1999).

Enjoying the Empty Nest During the empty-nest period, many middle-aged parents regain their freedom to frolic, invigorating their marriage with renewed closeness and the sharing of activities that the earlier demands of work and family life may have curtailed.

As a qualification to all this good news, it should be noted that one other reason research on long-term marriages generally finds higher levels of satisfaction is that many unhappy marriages end before they can become long-term. Thus, any survey of long-term marriages involves a selective sample. Further, some research finds that the happiness of marriage partners overall is decreasing, so that what seemed like happy "golden years" for the older generation may no longer be the pattern for today's married young adults (Glenn, 1999).

RESEARCH REPORT

GRANDPARENTS AS SURROGATE PARENTS

Although most grandparents today are peripheral to their grandchildren's day-to-day lives, a range of social problems sometimes catapult grandparents into an extremely involved role. If the parents are poor, young, unemployed, drug- or alcohol-addicted, single, or newly divorced, grandparents may become **surrogate parents.** They take over the work, the cost, and the worry of raising the children. In 1998, almost 6 percent of all children in the United States were living with their grandparents, most of them with a single parent as well but 2 percent without any parent present (U.S. Bureau of the Census, 1999). Note that this statistic refers to the children: Since most grandparents have several grandchildren, it is estimated that about 20 percent of all grandparents spend at least some time providing a major portion of the care of at least one grandchild.

Children who need intensive involvement are particularly likely to be sent to Grandma: Drug-affected infants or rebellious school-age boys, for example, are more likely to live with grandparents than normal preschool girls are. If the parents are adjudicated as neglectful or abusive, this becomes *kinship care* (see Chapter 8), with some compensation from the state. More often the grandparents take over out of necessity, with no compensation and with increased stress and less joy (Bowers & Myers, 1999).

Many middle-aged and older grandparents provide excellent surrogate care, furnishing the stability, guidance, and patience that distressed parents lack (Solomon & Marx, 1995). In fact, children of single parents generally benefit in many ways from living with a grandparent, because the grandparent relieves some of the stress and loneliness that single parents feel (Hinton et al., 1995). But this caregiving can impair the grandparent's own health and well-being, increasing the risk of illness as well as marital problems (Jendrek, 1994; Minkler & Roe, 1996; Shore & Hayslip, 1994). Surrogate parenting takes a particularly heavy toll if it lasts for years or even for generations,

especially among families already burdened by poverty. As one 53-year-old great-grandmother lamented:

> I have been taking care of all these kids for a mighty long time. Sandy [her daughter] needs so much help with her children. LaShawn [her granddaughter] I raised from a baby. Now she got two kids and I'm doing it again. I bathe, feed them, and everything. Three generations I raised. Lord Almighty! I'm tired, tired, tired. Sick too . . . [quoted in Burton, 1995]

More than one in three grandparents witnesses the divorce of their adult child. Following a divorce involving children, how do the grandparents' lives change? If the adult child has custody of the grandchildren, the older generation typically provides emergency housing, extra baby-sitting, financial support, and sometimes surrogate parenting. The parents of the noncustodial ex-spouse are often completely shut out of the grandchildren's lives unless their biological child has an excellent relationship with the ex-spouse and the other grandparents.

If grandparents are shut out, they may sue for visitation rights. Since 1970, every state in the United States has enacted laws that require continuation of a close relationship already formed if a child has lived with the grandparent. Some states go much further, mandating grandparent visitation rights even if the grandchild has never had a relationship with the grandparent, even if the parents were never married, and even if both parents oppose it. In other states, the courts are much more restrictive, ruling that grandparents must prove that the child will benefit sufficiently to overrule the parents' wishes (Hartfield, 1996).

Developmentalists are on both sides of this dilemma. Intergenerational nurturance is an important mainstay for many grandparents and grandchildren, but a biological connection does not necessarily mean that a relationship benefits the child. Not every child needs every grandparent. Just as with parents, some grandparents are destructive. In the emotional heat of divorce, it is difficult to decide whether a grandparent is a blessing or is making matters worse.

surrogate parents The role some grandparents play for their grandchildren due to their children's extreme social problems.

Divorce and Remarriage

Overall, the reasons for divorce in middle adulthood, and the problems it causes, are similar to those associated with divorce in early adulthood (see Chapter 19). However, divorce in middle adulthood is generally more difficult, because it usually occurs after years of marriage or after a second marriage and thus increases the loss of self-esteem.

Most divorced people remarry—on average, within 5 years of being divorced. In fact, in the United States, divorced people are more likely to marry than single people who are the same age. Almost half of all marriages (46 percent) are remarriages for at least one of the spouses. Remarriage is more likely if the divorced person is relatively young, in part because there are more potential partners still available; the typical remarrying bride is age 34 and the typical groom is age 37 (see the Changing Policy box on pages 606–607). Thus, a sizable percentage of middle-aged adults—far more men than women—are in the early years of their second marriage.

Remarriage often brings initial happiness and other benefits: divorced women typically become financially more secure, and divorced men typically become healthier and more sociable after they marry a new partner. In terms of parenthood, remarriage for men, in particular, often leads to new relationships with the younger generation through new bonds with custodial stepchildren or the birth of a baby. Having a baby together typically strengthens the second marriage while loosening the holdover emotional bonds of the first.

Popular wisdom to the contrary, however, there is no guarantee that love is better the second time around. Compared with people in first marriages, remarried people are more likely to describe their marriages as either very happy or quite unhappy, with less middle ground (Ganong & Coleman, 1994).

It may also be that some individuals are temperamentally prone to divorce (perhaps by virtue of being unusually impatient, dissatisfied, or adventurous) while others are more likely to stick it out, perhaps for religious or personality reasons. In general, the more often a person has been married, the more likely his or her current marriage is to end in divorce. For such people, divorce may be much less troublesome than having to accept a mate as he or she is. They are also more likely to divorce again (U.S. Bureau of the Census, 1999).

When developmentalists take a life-span approach, they become increasingly aware of the many ways adults find to satisfy their needs for intimacy. It is not healthy—emotionally or physically—to be without a confidante for too long. Although adults usually find this partner in a spouse, many people instead have a close friend, a lover who does not live with them, a dependent relationship with a young adult child (often a son among Asians, a daughter among Americans), or even a group such as people at work, at church, at school, or in the neighborhood. Most of these affectionate bonds are discussed elsewhere in this text. Now let us look, once again, at the world of work.

WORK

For many middle-aged adults, work is a major part of life. As we saw in Chapter 19, work provides friendship, status, structure, and esteem, as well as a paycheck. As also described in that chapter, work and the workplace are changing, with more gender and ethnic diversity, more emphasis on teamwork and knowledge, more relocation and working at home, and less stability and security.

SUPPLY AND DEMAND IN THE MIDDLE-AGE MARRIAGE MARKET

Middle-aged women are disadvantaged, when it comes to finding a marriage partner, for three reasons:

- Middle-aged men tend to marry younger women.
- Men die at younger ages.
- Few marriages take place between a younger man and an older woman.

All this makes the numbers work against middle-aged women. For example, in 1998, of all married men in the United States aged 35 to 44, 25 percent had a wife under age 35 and only 2 percent had a wife over age 44 (U.S. Bureau of the Census, 1999). As long as men marry women in their own age group or a decade younger, then all divorced and never-married middle-aged men will have three times as many possible partners as their female contemporaries have.

This unevenness varies from subgroup to subgroup. Partly because single men are more likely to immigrate than single women, Hispanic women already in the United States can be more selective in seeking a marriage partner of their own ethnicity: 54 percent of all unmarried Spanish-surnamed adults living in the United States are men. Of course, this means that unmarried women still living in Mexico, Puerto Rico, Cuba, and South America are at an additional disadvantage.

By contrast, the marriage odds are stacked against African American women. First, because of higher male mortality in childhood and adolescence, only 46 percent of African American adults are men. Second, 8 percent of all black grooms marry nonblack women, while only 4 percent of

Waiting to Exhale Many men complained that this movie portrayed them unfairly. However, as in *The First Wives Club* and *Thelma and Louise,* a Hollywood distortion can capture an emotional truth: When men are scarce, insensitive, or abusive, women depend on one another.

black brides marry outside their race. Finally, for every group, marriages are more likely between people of equal educational status or involve a man with more education than his wife. This bias works against all educated women (remember, since about 1970, more women than men attend college)

In middle adulthood, diversity and teamwork continue, but job security usually increases. During their 30s and 40s, more than 80 percent of all U.S. adults are employed (with similar percentages for men and women, parents or not). Most of them have worked for the same employer for at least 10 years and have found work that satisfies them, or at least meets their basic needs. One statistic that bears this out is that employees in their early 50s are a third less likely to be actively seeking a new job than employees in their early 30s (U.S. Bureau of the Census, 1999). Generally, middle-aged workers stay put, with good attendance records, to the satisfaction of their employers. Beyond this increased stability, most work-related issues are similar for workers of every age. One thing that does evolve, between ages 35 and 65, however, is the balance among work, family, and self.

but is particularly pronounced among African Americans, since twice as many black women as black men attain a B.A. degree.

What should an adult woman do if the marriage market is biased against her? Fifty years ago, the answer was either to live at home, caring for aging parents and working at a job that did not fully engage her potential, or to "settle" for marriage to a man she did not love, becoming a wife and mother whose own ambitions never were expressed. Even the very bright women of that cohort found themselves in that disap-

pointing situation more often than the men did (Holahan et al., 1999). But as a result of social changes, more women now go to college, have careers, and raise children—without being wives. Marriage rates are down, and single-parenthood rates are up (see Table 22.1). Was society better off when married women had more children and unmarried ones had few? Generally women today express higher satisfaction now that they have more personal freedom. Surveys do not make it clear whether men, aging parents, and young children are also better off.

table 22.1	**Percentage of Family Households Headed by a Woman**			
	White	Black	Asian	Hispanic
1960	8.7	22	—	—
1980	12	40	11	20
1998	14	47	12	23

These data are from the U.S. Bureau of the Census, which uses these ethnic categories. The overall male-to-female ratio during middle age has actually become more nearly equal in the past decades (because fewer men die prematurely than once did), but women are less likely to feel they must be married to raise children.

Workaholics

During early adulthood, the demands of the workplace combine with each individual's own demands and aspirations for promotion, income, success, and authority. This combination often becomes an irresistible whirlpool, creating "workaholics" who are addicted to long and hard work—just what the current marketplace, with its high-speed schedules, tight deadlines, "just in time" production, and customer demands, expects and rewards. The new order of the workplace puts stress on workers, who sometimes adjust and sometimes do not (Geurts & Grundmann, 1999).

Indeed, today's employers might be described as greedy. Many corporations want and even require employees to work more than 40 hours a week, including some evenings and weekends (Hochschild, 1997). This may have always been true for employed men; but now women have their own demanding jobs, and they expect any adult who shares their home (husband, mother, or sibling) to do housework and child care. Most married men do much more of this work than their own fathers did, although not as much as their wives (Barnett & Rivers, 1999).

Scaling Back

By middle adulthood, many workers begin to balance their work lives with other concerns. Perhaps the most remarkable shift is that which occurs in married couples with children. According to one study of dual-earner couples, in the "establishment" stage of marriage (aged 35 to 54, with children), both men and women figure out ways to combine work and parenthood. Often they engage in *scaling back*, deliberately putting less than full effort into employment (Becker & Moen, 1999).

Scaling back is typically a conscious, shared decision to place limits on work hours or responsibilities, which may include refusing jobs that require travel or weekend work. When limits cannot be placed, one spouse may choose to work part time. This strategy is less used in the United States than in nations such as Sweden, where part-timers are better paid and are given more responsibility (Drobnic et al., 1999).

Another scaling-back strategy is for both partners to be employed full time, but for one person to designate their work as a "job" to earn money, while the other has a lower-paying "career." This is a particularly useful strategy if the man earns less than the woman, because she can pay the bills without feeling that she is devoting herself to her work and abandoning her role as wife and mother. As one married woman said:

> We began to realize . . . that my job was going to be the primary job. He tried to work at other jobs during the year, but he wasn't at all happy. So I told him at that point that he had to try to make a go at a career in coaching. Fortunately, he found a part-time job at a college 40 miles away. He hardly earned anything. It was probably less than our babysitting costs. In the meantime, my job was going very well. [quoted in Becker & Moen, 1999]

In another scaling-back strategy, the couple take turns, with one working at full speed while the other does most of the housework and child care. Unlike in earlier times, when men always were breadwinners and women always were homemakers, today's couples who use this strategy acknowledge that their roles may switch off. Many men as well as women who devote most of their time to family care specifically talk about the time when they will resume their career path.

In fact, all these scaling-back strategies are joint decisions, protecting work and family from unreasonable demands. Interestingly, housework is the one aspect of life that gets shortchanged. For many couples, if both are working, then less housework gets done, and if one is not working, then that spouse (man or woman) does more of the household tasks (Szinovacz, 2000).

Middle age is a time when individual workers, as well as married couples, sometimes shift their priorities. One such shift occurs when an employee achieves a certain status or expertise, and is in a position to become a **mentor**—that is, someone who guides an inexperienced

mentor   A guide or teacher who helps an inexperienced person through example, shared activities, or explicit advice.

Figure 22.4 Opting Out of the Work Force
In many developed nations, increasing proportions of the work force are choosing to retire or stop working full time before age 65. Such decisions are based on assessments of financial security and on shifts in priorities.

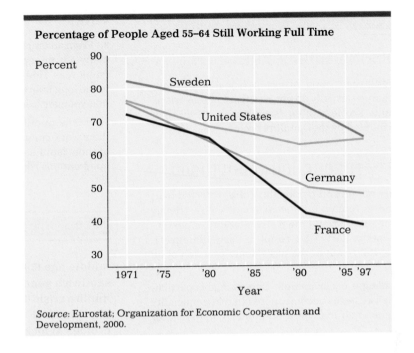

Percentage of People Aged 55–64 Still Working Full Time

Source: Eurostat; Organization for Economic Cooperation and Development, 2000.

worker. Ideally, the mentor teaches not only the job but also the culture of the workplace, helping the new worker learn the ropes, make friends, and dress properly. In developmental terms, a mentor becomes able to put aside his or her self-centered concerns in order to help someone else; this change is more likely in mid-career than at the start (Vaillant, 1993).

In midlife, "more free time and financial security often provide ideal conditions for self-expression" (Kleiber, 1999). According to this scholar, many people experience a "life-changing catalyst" in their work lives during middle age. This catalyst could be an unexpectedly lost job or new work offer, an attained or denied promotion, or any other work event that pushes them to rethink their priorities.

Such rethinking can lead to a reassessment of the value of employment as such, and then to a decision to retire. Now that forced retirement is illegal in most jobs and in most nations, more and more workers are actually deciding to retire before age 65, pushed out not by their employers or by failing health, but by their own financial assessments and future plans. Indeed, in a change that occurred over the past 30 years, more than half of all the adults aged 55 to 64 in France and Germany are no longer working full time (see Figure 22.4).

Exactly what older adults do when they stop working is discussed in the next trio of chapters, although much of the planning begins as early as age 50 or even 40. As those chapters explain, older adults keep busy, happy, and active.

SUMMARY

CHANGES DURING MIDDLE AGE

1. Although middle age often brings personal and family changes, these changes usually do not lead to a "midlife crisis." Middle-aged adults are less often "sandwiched in" by their obligations than fulfilled by their multiple roles.

PERSONALITY THROUGHOUT ADULTHOOD

2. After about age 30, several personality traits, referred to as the Big Five, tend to remain quite stable, and these strongly influence the course of development. The stability of personality is partly genetic, partly the result of early life experiences, and partly the result of the individual's creation of an ecological niche.

3. Personality changes occur as well. One change is particularly notable: The two sexes become more alike in personality traits. This phenomenon may be a hormonal, contextual, or cohort effect.

FAMILY DYNAMICS IN MIDDLE ADULTHOOD

4. The middle generation often plays a critical role within the family, providing emotional and material support to older and younger family members and serving as the link that connects one relative to another. Middle-aged adults generally find that their relationships with their own parents and with their young adult children improve.

5. Middle adulthood is the time people are likely to become first-time grandparents. Grandparents commonly take the role of remote, involved, or companionate figures in their grandchildren's lives, with grandparents in today's society typically less involved with the younger generation than they were in the past.

6. A small but increasing number of grandparents act as surrogate parents to their grandchildren, raising them full time because their parents are unable to do so. This is sometimes the best solution for the children, but it adds to the stress on the grandparent.

7. Most middle-aged adults are involved in a satisfying intimate relationship, usually through marriage. Adults whose marriages have survived to middle age generally are happily wed, deriving a strong sense of self-esteem from their marriage. Decreasing family and work responsibilities may allow a couple to devote more time to each other.

8. When a marriage ends through divorce in middle age, the experience may be more difficult than at an earlier phase of life because middle-aged people are less likely to find new partners. This is particularly true for women.

WORK

9. From an employer's perspective, middle-aged workers have many advantages: They are more conscientious and steadier employees. However, they are less likely to devote themselves to the long hours, promotion opportunities, and time pressures that younger workers tolerate.

10. Many middle-aged workers have learned to scale back their work commitments in order to accommodate the needs of their families. An increasing number of workers in developed nations retire before age 65.

KEY TERMS

middle age (591)
sandwich generation (592)
midlife crisis (592)
Big Five (594)
ecological niche (594)
gender crossover (596)
kinkeeper (598)
familism (599)

remote grandparents (600)
involved grandparents (601)
companionate grandparents (601)
surrogate parents (604)
mentor (608)

KEY QUESTIONS

1. What factors might cause a midlife crisis?

2. What changes might occur in the five trait clusters in personality?

3. Give an example (other than the one in the text) of the way one's ecological niche contributes to stability of personality.

4. How might men and women be affected differently by middle age?

5. How does the relationship between children and elderly parents typically change when the children reach middle age?

6. How does the relationship between parents and children change when the children reach adulthood?

7. How has grandparenthood changed over the past 100 years?

8. How does the marriage relationship change over the decades?

9. How do middle-aged adults cope with divorce—their own and that of their adult child?

10. What are the differences between work in middle age and work in young adulthood?

11. *In Your Experience* Describe a relationship that you know of in which a middle-aged person and a younger adult learned from each other.

BIOSOCIAL

Normal Changes

Changes in the appearance of the skin, hair, and body shape are benign, but can be disconcerting. Losses of acuity in hearing and vision are usually gradual, and most individuals learn to compensate quite easily. Overall wellness is influenced by such variables as sex, ethnicity, SES, and long-term health habits. Genetics clearly play a role as well, but social context and individual choice are more powerful influences on vitality and morbidity than heredity in middle age.

The Sexual Reproductive System

During their late 40s and early 50s, women experience the climacteric, when their body adjusts to changing hormonal levels. Menopause signals the end of a woman's reproductive potential, as well as the beginning of reduced natural hormones. Men experience no comparable dramatic decline in hormones or reproductive ability, but the gradual diminution of their sexual responses continues. Both sexes adjust to changes in their sexual interaction.

COGNITIVE

Adult Intelligence

Some intellectual abilities improve with age, while others decline. Typically, fluid intelligence decreases, and crystallized intelligence increases. Reaction time and speed of thinking slow down; practical intelligence deepens. Overall, cohort differences and individual variations are more important influences on the development of adult intelligence than age alone.

Expertise

Adult intelligence tends to flourish in areas of the individual's particular interests, because motivation leads to years of practice and involvement. The result is the development of expertise, characterized by cognitive processes that are intuitive, automatic, and flexible. Each adult becomes an expert at tasks that were once difficult and mysterious, becoming a good cook or a careful driver or an expert surgeon, author, or chess player.

PSYCHOSOCIAL

Changes During Middle Age

Middle age is characterized by more stability than change in personality, as the Big Five personality traits combine with each person's construction of an ecological niche to engender continuity. Personality changes that do occur, such as a narrowing of the gap between masculine and feminine personality traits, result from historical shifts and personal efforts at self-improvement.

Family Dynamics in Middle Age

Middle-aged adults usually have rewarding relationships with their adult children and grandchildren, without the stress that responsibility for child rearing creates. Marriages tend to become less conflicted. Usually the oldest generation does not require extensive caregiving. However, some middle-aged adults are called on to meet the caregiving and financial needs of both the older and younger generations.

Work

Work continues to be an important source of both stress and status in middle age. One of the improvements that occur over the decades of adulthood is that many adults learn how to coordinate the demands of a partner, children, and an employer. A balance of life—which means intense work for some people at some times and early retirement for others—is more likely to be reached in middle age.

PART VIII

Late Adulthood

What emotions do you anticipate experiencing as you read about development in late adulthood? Given the myths that abound regarding old age, you may well expect to feel discomfort, depression, resignation, and sorrow. Certainly there are instances in the next three chapters when such emotions would be appropriate. However, your most frequent emotion in learning about late adulthood is likely to be surprise. For example, you will learn in Chapter 23 that most centenarians are active, alert, and happy; in Chapter 24, that marked intellectual decline is the fate of only a minority of the elderly, who are sometimes victims of conditions that can be prevented; in Chapter 25, that relationships between the older and younger generations are neither as close as some sentimentalists idealize them to be nor as distant as some critics claim. Overall, late adulthood is much more a continuation of earlier patterns than a break from them, and, instead of falling into a period of lonely isolation, most older adults become more social and independent than ever.

Nevertheless, this period of life, more than any other, seems to be a magnet for misinformation and prejudice. Why is this so? Think about this question when the facts, theories, and research of the next three chapters are not what you expected them to be.

Late Adulthood:
Biosocial Development

We now begin our study of the last decades of life, from age 65 or so until death. As in the book's preceding parts, this first of the trio of chapters in Part VIII describes physiological changes—in the senses, the vital organs, morbidity, and mortality—and the next two chapters describe cognitive and social changes. If the thought of reading about this period of life evokes feelings of dread, doom, or even a simple lack of interest, you will be reassured to realize that knowledge usually softens the negative emotions that many people—including many of the elderly themselves—have about this period (Palmore, 1998). The quiz below will help you comprehend this point.

1. The proportion of the United States population over age 65 is about
   a. 3 percent
   b. 13 percent
   c. 25 percent
   d. 33 percent

2. The proportion of the world population over age 65 is about
   a. 2 percent
   b. 7 percent
   c. 12 percent
   d. 20 percent

3. Happiness in older people is:
   a. rare
   b. about the same as in younger adults
   c. much *less* common than in younger adults
   d. much *more* common than in younger adults

4. The senses that tend to weaken in old age are
   a. sight and hearing
   b. taste and smell
   c. varied: senses improve in some people, decline in others
   d. all five senses

5. The automobile accident rate per licensed driver over age 65 is
   a. higher than the rate for those under 65
   b. about the same as the rate for those under age 65
   c. lower than the rate for those under age 65
   d. unknown, because such statistics are not recorded

6. Of all North Americans over age 65, the proportion who are in nursing homes and hospitals is about
    a. 5 percent
    b. 10 percent
    c. 25 percent
    d. 50 percent

7. Compared to that of younger people, the reaction time of older people is
    a. slower
    b. about the same
    c. faster
    d. slower for men, faster for women

8. Lung capacity
    a. tends to decline with age
    b. stays the same among nonsmokers as they age
    c. tends to increase among healthy old people
    d. is unrelated to age

9. The most common living arrangement for a person over age 65 in the United States is
    a. with a husband or wife
    b. with a grown child
    c. alone
    d. with an unrelated elderly person

10. Compared to people under age 65, an older adult's chance of being a crime victim is
    a. lower
    b. about the same
    c. higher
    d. lower for men, higher for women

This quiz is adapted from a much larger one called *Facts on Aging*, first published in 1977, used by thousands of instructors and students, and revised and republished in 1998 (Palmore, 1977, 1998).

As you read this chapter, you will find the answers to the ten questions (1, p. 619; 2, p. 619; 3, p. 643; 4, p. 622; 5, p. 626; 6, p. 619; 7, p. 626; 8, p. 621; 9, p. 620; 10, p. 625). Typical college students get more than half wrong, sometimes because they simply don't know the correct answer, but usually because their prejudices—more often negative than positive—about aging overwhelm them, as we will now explain (Palmore, 1998).

AGEISM

Two leading scientists who study old age note that:

> Common beliefs about the aging process result in negative stereotypes—oversimplified and biased views of what old people are like. The "typical" old person is often viewed as uninterested in (and incapable of) sex, on the road to (if not arrived at) senility, conservative and rigid. The stereotype would have us believe that old people are tired and cranky, passive, without energy, weak, and dependent on others. [Schaie & Willis, 1996]

ageism A term that refers to prejudice against the aged. Like racism and sexism, ageism works to prevent elderly people from being as happy and productive as they could be.

All these stereotypes about old people are false. They arise from a widespread prejudice called **ageism,** the tendency to categorize and judge people solely on the basis of their chronological age. Similar to racism and

Ageism on the Decline A cross-section of the U.S. population like these people about to visit the Statue of Liberty, always includes some old, some young, and some in between. In the future, however, when the baby-boomers reach old age, a representative sample of the population will, proportionally, include a great many more of the elderly than are present here. As the elderly become an ever-increasing proportion of the general population, we predict that the culture will place less emphasis on youth. Ageism may fade considerably.

gerontology The study of old age. This is one of the fastest-growing special fields in the social sciences.

demography The study of populations, including descriptive statistics regarding age, sex, and other characteristics of various groups.

sexism, ageism "is a way of pigeon-holing people and not allowing them to be individuals with unique ways of living their lives" (Butler et al., 1991).

Ageism can target people of any age. Teenagers, for example, are frequently branded as being irresponsible and trouble-prone. Many cities have curfew laws that apply only to teenagers, a manifestation of ageism that unfairly restricts law-abiding adolescents. Imagine the outcry if curfews applied only to all male teenagers or to all nonwhite teenagers, and you can see the similarity to sexism and racism. Although it affects people of all ages, ageism probably does most damage when it targets the old, because it permits policies and attitudes that reduce pride, activity, and social involvement. Teenagers usually rebel against ageism; the elderly are more likely to accept it.

Fortunately, this picture is changing, primarily for two reasons. One reason is the recent advances made in **gerontology,** the scientific study of old age. New theoretical perspectives have pointed to ways in which aging has become a social construction that distorts reality (Riley et al., 1994). As one gerontologist wrote: "If anything has remained constant, it has been the perception of older people as elderly others, rather than as the embodiment of our future selves. That divisive view will be singularly anachronistic in the new millennium" (Blaikie, 1999).

The second reason is the data produced by **demography,** which is the study of population characteristics. In a major demographic shift (described in detail in A Life-Span View), there are many more elderly people today than there once were, making it harder to stereotype them all. This is true on a personal basis as well. Nowadays, almost everyone has several relatives who have survived to age 60, 70, 80, or more. It is obvious that each is unlike the other—some impaired, some doing very well.

A LIFE SPAN VIEW

THE SHAPE OF DEMOGRAPHY

Until recently, ageism was acceptable because the elderly were less than 5 percent of the total population—too few, with too little political or economic clout, to prevent stereotyping by younger, more populous generations. Demeaning clichés such as "second childhood," "dirty old man," and "doddering," or patronizing compliments such as "spry" and "having all his or her marbles," were used to stereotype and dismiss those few who survived to age 80 or so.

This unequal age distribution was reflected in the charts used by demographers to sort and stack populations according to age groups, with the youngest at the bottom and the oldest at the top. Over the past century, the resulting picture was usually a *demographic pyramid,* as seen in Figure 1.4 on page 9.

There were two reasons the population took on this pyramid, or wedding-cake, shape. First, each generation of young adults gave birth to more than enough children to replace themselves, typically four or more per family, thereby creating larger levels of younger people at the bottom of the pyramid. Second, before immunization, antibiotics, or even modern sanitation came into being, a sizable portion of each cohort died before advancing to the next level of the pyramid, with death rates particularly high among those under age 5 and over age 50 (Masoro, 1999). This explains why, in 1920, each five-year cohort from middle age on was about 20 percent smaller than the next-younger age group (as the pyramid on the left in Figure 1.4 shows).

Today, however, because of falling birth rates and increased longevity, the population pyramid is becoming square. Currently, many cohorts are less than 5 percent larger or smaller than the neighboring cohort (as the squarish pyramid on the right in Figure 1.4 shows). A similar pattern is found in every developed nation, even more notably in Spain, Italy, and Japan than in the United States. The two age clusters that deviate from this pattern can be explained by unusual events: the Great Depression and World War II, which resulted in a dramatic drop in the number of babies born between 1930 and 1945, and postwar prosperity, which led to a baby boom between 1947 and 1964.

Unless another unusual event occurs, such as a dramatic change in birth rate or an enormous wave of immigration, demographers will soon chart not a pyramid but a square or rectangle for North America. Members of each generation will replace only themselves, and most of them will live to age 80 or more. This is already beginning to happen: The top three cohorts (ages 75–79, 80–84, and 85 and over) now constitute the fastest-growing age group worldwide, having increased in the United States from slightly more than 1 million in 1900 to 17 million in 2000.

The proportion in other nations varies. In some developing nations (for example, Afghanistan, Angola, Ethiopia, and Syria), less than 3 percent of the population is over age 65. But if the trends of the past 20 years continue, the proportion of those over 65 will double worldwide, from the current 7 percent to 15 percent, by 2030. The world pyramid will also look more like a square.

A longer average life span leads directly to fewer births: Japan has the longest average life span (age 80) and the lowest birth rate (less than 1.5 per woman) of all nations with large populations. The only region of the world where couples still want four or more children is sub-Saharan Africa, which is also the region with the highest infant and young adult mortality rates (Tsui et al., 1997).

These demographic shifts affect everyone of every age. As birth rates fall, young adults postpone life transitions, such as completing their education, selecting a mate, and having a first child. For most people in the nineteenth century, all three of these milestones were passed by age 18. Today they are not reached until age 21, 30, or even later. Because adults have fewer children, most children born today will have one sibling or none, but they will have several living great-grandparents—unlike children a generation or two ago, who had many siblings and dozens of cousins but none of their eight great-grandparents. These changes may directly (not just via culture) increase the life span; over the past century at least, women who had fewer children, and who gave birth relatively late in life, lived longer than those who had several children before age 30 (Warshofsky, 1999).

As the average life span increases, most people will plan for decades of healthy retirement before they become really old, accumulating pensions and making travel plans during middle age. In the United States, the average age of retirement has already dropped, on average, from age 65 to 62. In some European nations the retirement age is even lower (Guillemard & Rein, 1993; Quadagno & Hardy, 1996). We are moving toward a day when the population will be divided into thirds, with only the middle third, aged 30 to 60, active full time in the labor force. Whether this prospect is viewed with dread, delight, or indifference depends on how ageist a person is.

Further, the proportion of the world's population that is over age 65 has grown from 2 percent in 1900 to 7 percent today *(question 2).* In developed nations, the proportion is even larger—13 percent of the population in the United States *(question 1),* Canada, and Australia, more than 16 percent in Japan, Italy, and Great Britain. These numbers help to keep political leaders, media publicists, and business executives from underestimating the political and economic influence of the old.

Interpretation of this demographic shift may reveal the ageism of the interpreter. Some people stress the increasing *numbers* of people over age 65 (between 1900 and 2000, from about 3 million to 35 million in the United States) instead of *proportions* (from 4 to 13 percent of the population). A focus on the 12-fold increase in numbers conveys the impression that the legions of elderly people will soon overburden us all.

Answering "c" or "d" on questions 1 and 2 of the quiz probably indicates a negative stereotype. Those who overestimate the proportions of the elderly are also likely to overestimate the percentage who are weak and dependent on others or actually in long-term care institutions. The actual proportion of the elderly who are in nursing homes and hospitals is only 5 percent at any given time *(question 6).*

Similarly, the topics that gerontologists choose to study may reflect ageism. At the end of this chapter you will read about the very, very old, who have been idealized as well as feared. Some of the research on this cohort may be ageist as well. In truth, the relationship among dependence, independence, and age is much more complex than most people realize.

Dependents and Independence

Each society has a certain number of self-sufficient, productive adults and a certain number of dependents—that is, people who do not contribute to society but instead need to be taken care of. Traditionally, the **dependency ratio** is calculated by comparing the number of the population who are between ages 15 and 64 to the number who are 14 or younger and 65 or over. If the first number (the workers) is higher than the second number (the dependents), then the burden on the middle generation is not considered too heavy.

dependency ratio   The ratio of self-sufficient, productive adults to dependents—children and the elderly.

In most industrialized countries, the current dependency ratio, about two independent adults for every dependent person, is better than it has been for a century, as a result of the declining birth rate since 1970 and the small cohort just entering late adulthood. In the poorest developing nations, the large numbers of children make the current ratio about 1:1 (see Appendix A). The youth portion of the dependency ratio will soon improve in poor nations because the birth rate is declining, and the old-age portion will worsen because more people will live to age 80 or 90.

What will happen as more and more people live past working age? Some experts warn about the potentially catastrophic consequences of increased costs for the medical care of the elderly and of decreased public funds for the needs of the younger generation (Howe, 1995). Especially if the young continue to enter the labor market later and the old continue to exit earlier, the entire tax and caregiving burden may fall on the shoulders of the shrinking middle cohort. Will they revolt, refusing to support either the old or young? Will employed adults privately provide minimal care for their own parents and own children and vote against public funding for Medicare, day care, health insurance, or even education for everyone else?

Fortunately, such political self-interest is far from inevitable: In several European nations, the increasing numbers of the elderly have led to social policies that benefit all the generations, such as publicly funded health care, continuing education, and multigenerational housing within the community (Pampel, 1994). Even the basic assumption that people over age 65 are "dependent" may be misguided. Most members of this age group are in fact independent, not only providing for their own daily care and living expenses but still contributing to society. The elderly are more likely than those under age 60 to vote, obey the law, participate in community and religious groups, and donate money and time to help others (Posner, 1995).

Obviously, the idea that most of the elderly are frail is mistaken. Only about 5 percent, usually the oldest-old, live in nursing homes, about another third (usually widows) live alone, about 20 percent live with grown children, and the rest (the largest number) live with a husband or wife *(question 9)*. Generally, such couples take care of each other as they always have and are not particularly dependent on anyone else.

Variability in Aging

young-old   Healthy, vigorous, financially secure older adults (generally, those under age 75) who are well integrated into the lives of their families and their communities.

old-old   Older adults (generally over age 75) who suffer from physical, mental, or social deficits.

oldest-old   Elderly adults (generally, those over age 85) who are dependent on others for almost everything, requiring supportive services such as nursing homes and hospital stays.

In fact, dependency is usual for only a small group of the aged. Gerontologists distinguish among the **young-old**, the **old-old**, and the **oldest-old**, a distinction based not exclusively on age but also on characteristics related to health and social well-being (Zarit, 1996). The *young-old* are "healthy and vigorous, relatively well-off financially, well integrated into the lives of their families and communities, and politically active." The *old-old* suffer "major physical, mental, or social losses" (Neugarten & Neugarten, 1986), although they still have strengths in some of these areas. The *oldest-old* are dependent on others for almost everything. They are a small minority of those over age 65, but they are most noticeable because they require intense supportive services or live in nursing homes or hospitals. In general, the young-old are those under age 75 and the oldest-old are those over age 85. Age is not an accurate predictor of dependency, however, so some gerontologists use terms that make no reference to chronological age: *optimal aging, usual aging,* and *impaired aging* (Powell, 1994).

It is overly optimistic (and probably ageist) to expect every elderly person to be optimal, and it is obviously prejudiced to expect all old people to be impaired. The question then becomes, "What is the usual aging process?"

PRIMARY AGING

primary aging   The universal and irreversible physical changes that occur to living creatures as they grow older.

secondary aging   The specific physical illnesses or conditions that are more common in aging but are caused by health habits, genes, and other influences that vary from person to person.

It is useful to distinguish between **primary aging**, which encompasses all the irreversible and universal changes that occur with time, and **secondary aging**, which refers to those changes that are caused by particular conditions or illnesses. Although secondary aging correlates with age, it is not directly caused by age. Secondary aging is selective, and it may be prevented, remedied, or even reversed.

Primary aging includes all the processes of *senescence* that were described in Chapters 17 and 20. Every part of the body slows down, from speech to heart rate, from speed of walking to speed of thinking, from reaction time to reading time. This overall slowdown is a universal result of aging. (Its implications are discussed in the next chapter.)

Every body system also becomes less efficient with age, with a gradual reduction in capacity and organ reserve. The heart pumps less blood per beat, the arteries harden, the digestive organs become less efficient, the lungs lose capacity (*question 8;* see Chapter 20 for details), sexual responses become slower, sleep becomes less sound, and so on. While this decline occurs over several decades, its pace speeds up in later life (Kanungo, 1994). Many of the specific consequences are actually aspects of secondary aging and will be discussed later. However, changes in how people look and how they perceive the world are universal.

Changes in Appearance

As time passes, primary aging makes everyone look older. Middle-aged adults may try to stave off the inevitable by wearing the latest clothing styles, moisturizing their skin, and coloring their hair, but primary aging is eventually beyond concealment. The skin is often the first sign: It becomes drier, thinner, and less elastic; wrinkles and visible blood vessels and pockets of fat appear (Whitbourne, 1996). In addition, dark patches known as "age spots" are seen on the skin of about 25 percent of adults by age 60, about 70 percent by age 80, and almost everyone by age 100.

The hair also undergoes obvious changes, growing thinner and grayer and, in many people, eventually becoming white or disappearing completely. Interestingly, loss of hair pigment is the physical change that correlates most closely with chronological age. It is a clearer index to a person's age than skin changes, hearing acuity, blood pressure, heart size, or vital capacity (Balin, 1994). While gray hair indicates age, it does not correlate with impairment.

Other visible physical changes in late adulthood include alteration of overall body height, shape, and weight (Masoro, 1999). Most older people are more than an inch shorter than they were in early adulthood, because, as noted in Chapter 20, the vertebrae begin settling closer together in middle age. Further, the muscles that hold the vertebrae become less flexible, making it harder to stand as straight as in earlier years. Body shape is affected by redistribution of fat, disappearing from the arms, legs, and upper face and collecting in the torso (especially the abdomen) and the lower face (especially the jowls and chin).

Closely related is a reduction in flexibility of the joints: As muscles stiffen and atrophy, so does the range of motion in, for example, kicking from the knee, swinging the arms, and turning the torso (Masoro, 1999). For both sexes, the reduction in muscle strength and flexibility is especially apparent in the legs, necessitating a slower, stiffer gait and sometimes a cane or walker to counteract unsteadiness.

Older adults often weigh less than they did at age 50 or so, partly because of a reduction in muscle tissue, which is relatively dense and heavy. This difference is particularly notable in men, who have relatively more muscle and less body fat than women.

Another reason older people weigh less is a loss of bone calcium, which makes bones more porous and fragile. Most women lose bone at a rate of about 1 to 2 percent per year after menopause; men lose bone as well, although at a slower rate. This causes some older people to stoop instead of standing up straight; it is the main reason a fall is likely to result in a broken bone.

Note that weight reduction is not usually a good sign. Losing weight meant less fat and better health in the younger years, but now it means less muscle, thinner bone, and greater risk.

Misleading Appearances This couple may no longer be able to take carefree strolls hand in hand, but that does not mean that romance no longer beats in their hearts. Assumptions based on appearance alone are at the root of ageism, just as they are with racism.

❓ *Observational Quiz (see answer page 623): Who has the more useful walker? Find three reasons for your answer.*

DO YOU SEE WHO I SEE?

Changes in appearance can have serious social and psychological consequences. In an ageist society, those who look old are treated as old, in a stereotyped way. Using "elderspeak" with older people makes them feel—and eventually become—less competent; taking care of them by doing things they could do for themselves reduces their sense of self-worth; criticizing them for trying to look younger undercuts their attempt to deflect the prejudice they experience. Children are quick to see the elderly as old-fashioned; they may ask their own grandparents what life was like before electricity or automobiles.

Yet most older people consider their personalities, values, and attitudes quite stable and, except for acknowledging that they may have slowed down a bit, do not feel that much has changed in them (Troll & Skaff, 1997). One researcher described a nursing home resident who:

> when asked whether she had changed much over the years, extracted a photo from a stack in her dresser drawer, one taken when she was in her early twenties, and said, "That's me, but I changed a little." She had indeed changed. She was now neither curvaceous nor animated, but was physically distorted from crippling arthritis and sullen from pain. To herself, however, she was still the same person she had always been. [Tobin, 1996]

When older people see a recent photograph of themselves, or catch an unguarded glimpse in the mirror, or merely notice how others treat them, they are surprised, even in late-late adulthood. As one 92-year-old woman described this reaction:

> There's this feeling of being out of one's skin. The feeling that you are not in your own body. . . . Whenever I'm walking downtown, and I see my reflection in a store window, I'm shocked at how old it is. I never think of myself that way. [quoted in Kaufman, 1986]

Similar feelings were expressed by a man, also 92, who needed a cane to get around:

> I look like a cripple. I'm not a cripple mentally. I don't feel that way. But I am physically. I hate it. . . . You know, when I hear people, particularly gals and ladies, their heels hitting the pavement . . . I feel so lacking in assurance—why can't I walk that way? . . . I have the same attitude now, toward life and living, as I did 30 years ago. That's why this idea of not being able to walk along with other people—it hurts my ego. Because inside, that's not really me. [quoted in Kaufman, 1986]

If elderly people associate their appearance with their identity, or if they depend on the reactions of others to validate their self-concept (as we all do sometimes), then the realization that they look like, move like, or are treated like old people may make them act and think in accordance with the ageist stereotype—with harmful consequences to themselves.

The implications of these age-related changes in appearance are discussed in the In Person box.

Dulling of the Senses

❓ Especially for Young Adults: Should you always speak louder and slower when talking to a senior citizen?

For many of the healthy elderly, the most troubling part of aging is not how they appear to others but how they connect with others. Social connection depends primarily on the use of the senses, all of which become less sharp with each decade (Meisami, 1994) *(question 4)*. This is probably as true for the sense of touch (particularly in the extremities), of taste (particularly for sour and bitter), and of smell as it is for the more critical senses of sight and hearing.

Up until a century ago, these sensory losses were often devastating: Many people who survived to old age were rendered isolated and vulnerable, particularly by their inability to see and hear. Today, however, food is processed so that it is less likely to spoil and cause digestive upset in a person who could not smell or taste the rot; smoke alarms and carbon monoxide alarms compensate for a diminished ability to

❶ *Answer to Observational Quiz (from page 621):* He does. The walkers themselves provide some clues, in that four wheels are more mobile (especially on curbs) than three, and his has a seat for resting while hers merely has a basket. Note that he is leaning into the walker, using it to help him navigate, while she seems to be merely pushing hers along.

cataracts A common eye disease among the elderly involving a thickening of the lens; it can cause distorted vision if left untreated.

glaucoma A disease of the eye that can destroy vision if left untreated. It involves hardening of the eyeball due to a fluid buildup within the eye.

senile macular degeneration A disease of the eye involving deterioration of the retina.

presbycusis Age-related hearing loss.

smell; and most of the visual and auditory losses of the aged can be corrected or at least remedied. This does not mean that the senses function as well as they did in earlier years. In fact, only 50 percent of old people pass an odor-discrimination test that 99 percent of 17-year-olds pass (Bornstein & Arterberey, 1999). But sensory losses need not be debilitating, as we will now see in the case of sight and hearing.

Vision

Although only 10 percent of the aged see well without corrective lenses, another 80 percent can see quite well with glasses. The remaining 10 percent have serious vision problems. This group (about 5 percent of those younger than age 80 and more than a third of those older than 80) usually has one of the three major eye diseases of the elderly: cataracts, glaucoma, and senile macular degeneration.

Cataracts involve a thickening of the lens that causes vision to become cloudy, opaque, and distorted. As early as age 50, about 10 percent of adults have such clouding, with 3 percent experiencing a partial loss of vision. By age 70, 30 percent have some visual loss because of cataracts. These losses are initially treatable with eyeglasses and then, as they get progressively worse, by a simple surgical procedure that is almost always successful (Meisami, 1994).

Glaucoma, a problem for 1 percent of those in their 70s and 10 percent of those in their 90s, involves damage to the optic nerve caused by pressure resulting from a buildup of fluid within the eye. This condition can be relieved with special eyedrops; if left untreated, it eventually destroys vision.

Senile macular degeneration is deterioration of the retina that affects one in twenty-five people between the ages of 66 and 74 and one in six of those age 75 and older. This condition is hard to treat medically and is therefore the leading cause of legal blindness. Fortunately, although many people with senile macular degeneration are legally blind, few are completely sightless. The little vision they have is enough for them to benefit from mobility training: They can learn how to use auditory and tactile cues (such as particular street noises, the contours of the sidewalk, the location of furniture in their rooms) to get around. Sometimes their daily activities are improved just by strong lighting and a powerful magnifying glass for reading. Those who are entirely unable to read can benefit from a computer that scans printed text and "speaks" the words, as well as audiotapes of books, magazines, and newspapers. In these and other ways, even the elderly whose vision is severely impaired can be helped to maintain independence.

Hearing

Presbycusis, or age-related hearing loss, affects about 40 percent of those aged 65 and older (Masoro, 1999). When people first notice a serious hearing problem, they usually ignore it, typically waiting 5 years or more to consult an audiologist.

Sometimes the audiologist concludes that the person must adjust to some hearing loss. This is the case with *tinnitis,* a buzzing or rhythmic ringing in the ears experienced by 10 percent of the elderly (Coni et al., 1992). The only treatment at the moment is surgery, which is not always successful. In many cases, people with tinnitis become accustomed to the ringing and learn to ignore it, just as a younger person might no longer notice the loud ticking of a clock.

Read My Lips When hearing begins to fade, listeners need to read lips in order to understand every syllable. Younger adults usually watch a speaker's eyes to catch nuances of emotion; older adults often watch the mouth to see what they cannot hear.

elderspeak A way of speaking to older adults that resembles baby talk, with simple and short sentences, exaggerated emphasis, a slower rate, higher pitch, and repetition.

Sometimes the audiologist can easily remedy the problem, as by removing impacted earwax. However, most often presbycusis can be remedied with a hearing aid, and this is where ageism starts to interfere. A third of the elderly could benefit, but less than 10 percent actually have hearing aids that they use every day (Mulrow, 1990).

Until 20 years ago, people refused to use hearing aids because they squeaked, distorted, and boomed. But with current technology, that is no longer true. Unfortunately, however, to avoid ageism, many people would rather miss the sounds of daily life than appear old.

Ironically, individuals who frequently mishear and misunderstand conversation are often considered not only old but doddering or even stupid and are excluded from social give-and-take. The hard-of-hearing are likely to withdraw socially and to suspect that inaudible conversations are about them (Busse, 1985). The net effect is that, much more than the visually impaired, "hard-of-hearing individuals are often mistakenly thought to be retarded or mentally ill . . . [and] are more subject to depression, demoralization, and even at times psychotic symptomology" (Butler et al., 1991).

In addition to mishearing conversation, other common hearing losses include errors in detecting where sound is coming from, in deciphering electronically transmitted speech (especially by the telephone), and in perceiving high-frequency sounds. This last problem begins with the inability to hear pure tones, such as that of a doorbell, and proceeds to difficulty in hearing speech, particularly consonants and the higher-pitched voices of women and children.

Practical steps to compensate involve both the listener and the speaker. The elderly person needs to look for clues in the speaker's lip movements and facial expressions. Meanwhile, the speaker needs to talk in a lower register and to enunciate more distinctly, to use pauses at the end of phrases to emphasize ideas, and to shut the window, turn off the radio, or otherwise avoid background noises. Repetition, logical pauses, and simple—but not necessarily short—sentences can improve comprehension (Kemper & Harden, 1999).

Sometimes younger adults automatically use **elderspeak** when they talk to older adults whom they do not know. Like baby talk, elderspeak uses simple and short sentences, exaggerated emphasis, slower talk, higher pitch, and repetition (See & Ryan, 1999). Given what you have read about hearing and aging, do you think elderspeak is helpful? Research has shown that some aspects of elderspeak actually make communication more difficult (Kemper & Harden, 1999). In fact, *lower* pitch is better than higher, and slower speech that stretches out the words rather than increasing the logical pauses actually reduces comprehension. If older adults recognize elderspeak as patronizing, especially when people exaggerate certain words, or call the elderly person "honey" or "dear," or use a nickname instead of a surname ("Johnny" instead of "Mr. White"), the result may be anger or, even worse, self-doubt.

This point raises a broader issue: How do people respond when other people try to provide help that they did not request? Surprisingly, unsolicited help is given more often to younger than to older adults.

● Response for Young Adults (from p. 622):
No. Some seniors hear well, and they would resent it.

Moreover, except when it involves suggestions about managing money, younger people are more resentful of such advice, whereas older people more often think of it as friendly (Smith & Goodnow, 1999). But be careful: If the unasked-for assistance implies a lack of respect for the older person's competence, resentment builds. "Patronizing communication" is stereotypical and unresponsive, and therefore not effective (See & Ryan, 1999).

Adjusting to Senescence

We noted earlier that aging may be optimal, usual, or impaired. For optimal functioning, body changes require active adjustment, not passive acceptance. Adjustment involves finding the right balance between maintaining normal activities and modifying routines to fit diminished capacities.

For the healthy young-old, modifications may be minor, such as eating smaller, more frequent meals and devoting more time to stretching and warmups before vigorous exercise. Some of the old-old need to conserve energy and effort, limiting themselves, beyond the basic routines of life, to only one or two activities—having lunch with a friend *or* working in the garden *or* visiting a grandchild.

Medical interventions should take place during optimal or usual aging, before it is too late. Thus, for example, knee or hip replacement should be done while the heart is still strong, and blood pressure must be lowered before a stroke. The same is true for lifestyle changes: Stopping smoking cannot reverse lung cancer once it has occurred; losing weight cannot erase diabetes; exercise is better at prevention than cure. All these are best done in early or middle adulthood, but a young-old person who undertakes them will still benefit.

As with adjustment to hearing losses, the critical factors are the older person's honest recognition of the problem and willingness to make the necessary changes. Two sets of statistics indicate that many elderly people meet these criteria. First, the aged are less likely to be victims of crime than are younger adults, in part because they become more cautious (see Figure 23.1) *(question 10)*. Second, the

Figure 23.1 Victims of Crime. As people grow older, they are less likely to be crime victims. These figures come from personal interviews in which repondents were asked whether they had been the victim of a crime such as assault, rape, or robbery in the past several months. This approach yields more accurate results than official crime statistics, because many crimes are never reported to the police.

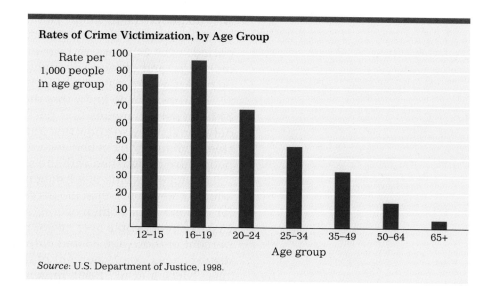

Rates of Crime Victimization, by Age Group

Rate per 1,000 people in age group

Source: U.S. Department of Justice, 1998.

Figure 23.2 Motor Vehicle Accidents. Caution seems to rise with age, as older drivers evidently take fewer risks behind the wheel.

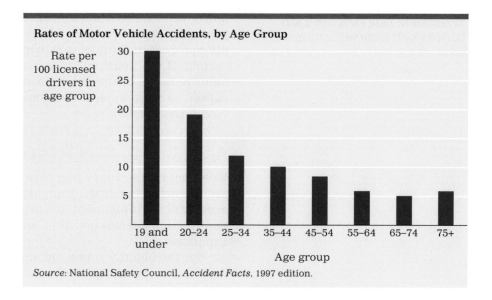

Rates of Motor Vehicle Accidents, by Age Group

Source: National Safety Council, *Accident Facts*, 1997 edition.

elderly are less likely to be the driver in a serious auto accident *(question 5)*: Reaction time is slower *(question 7)*, sign reading is difficult, and night vision is worse, but most drivers adjust—taking their time, traversing short and familiar routes, getting home before dark (see Figure 23.2).

Family and friends must adjust as well. For instance, adult children should be aware that a visit from one grandchild may be an invigorating experience, but a visit from several active youngsters at once may be exhausting, and baby-sitting for a whole weekend may be overwhelming. Similarly, conversation on an ordinary telephone or in a noisy restaurant may be frustrating or even impossible.

The need for adjustment by all involved is particularly apparent with sleep disorders, one of the most common complaints of the elderly.

Sleep: An Example of Adjustment

Why do people need sleep? How much sleep do they need? Does it matter if sleep occurs in one unbroken period each night; in several shorter periods over 24 hours; or over a week, with some late nights and early mornings, and other early nights and late mornings? Surprisingly, we do not know the answers.

However, we do know that depriving a person of sleep, even for one 24-hour period, makes that person irritable, confused, and sometimes delusional. We also know that adults of all ages average about 7 hours of sleep (not just lying in bed awake) in every 24-hour period but that many people are dissatisfied with the amount of sleep they get.

In fact, insomnia is a frequent complaint, particularly among older adults (Foley, 1995). Specific percentages range from "inadequate sleep" for 20 percent of women over age 80 in Norway, to "severe" insomnia for 23 percent of people over age 65 in Germany, to "trouble sleeping" for 35 percent of those age 65 and older in Great Britain, to "persistent sleep disturbances" for 75 percent of those over age 70 in China (Chiu et al., 1999; Nielson et al., 1998). In general, older adults spend more time in bed, take longer to fall asleep, spend less time in deep sleep, wake up often (about 10 times per night), take more naps, feel drowsy more often in the daytime, and, because of all this, are more distressed by their sleep patterns than younger adults are.

The response of many physicians to sleep complaints at any age is to prescribe narcotic drugs. This approach may be particularly harmful in late adulthood (Bromley, 1999; Ohayan et al., 1999). These drugs sometimes mask age-related physiological problems (such as sleep apnea and prostate enlargement) for which sleep disturbances are a symptom, not a cause. In addition, the usual narcotic dose is often too much for an older person's metabolism, causing very heavy sleep temporarily and then rebound wakefulness, with confusion, depression, impaired cognition, and even nighttime falls because of reduced motor control.

Actually, the root problem may be not biological but cognitive, not insomnia but the mistaken notion that everyone should "sleep like a baby." Most of the elderly awaken several times a night because of the need to urinate, to move the legs, to adjust the blankets. With advancing years, it is usual to experience less electrical activity in the brain during sleep, which means sleep is not as deep nor dreams as long (Masoro, 1999). Frequent waking and daily napping may be quite normal (Engle-Friedman & Bootzin, 1991).

In addition, daily body rhythms change with age, so most people naturally wake up earlier and are more alert in the morning than at night. For most of the elderly, taking too long to fall asleep is more troubling than getting up too early (Riedel & Lichstein, 1998), although family members may wonder why Grandpa is eating breakfast at 5:00 a.m. If insomnia does become a problem, substantial evidence supports cognitive therapy instead of drugs (see the Research Report).

SECONDARY AGING

The distinction between primary and secondary aging is intended to emphasize the fact that aging and disease are not synonymous. Indeed, most aged people, most of the time, consider their health to be good or excellent. In one survey of 1,600 elderly people, the majority said their health does not limit their activities at all, even though 62 percent had two or more chronic conditions such as arthritis and heart disease (Herzog, 1991).

Another survey also found that the old were similar to the young in estimation of days in poor health, although, as Table 23.1 shows, more of

table **23.1**	**Self-Reports of Physical and Mental Health**

	Average Number of Days "Not Good" in Past 30 Days			
Age	Physical Health		Mental Health	
		Missing Responses		*Missing Responses*
18–44	3.1 days	Less than 1%	5.3 days	Less than 1%
45–69	4.8	Less than 1%	5.3	Less than 1%
70+	6.0	8%	2.7	7.1%

Source: Schechter et al., 1999.

EDUCATION OR MEDICATION FOR INSOMNIA?

Many gerontologists now recommend cognitive, not pharmacological, solutions to insomnia in the elderly. One team of researchers (Riedel et al., 1995) hypothesized that sleep difficulties might occur because older adults do not realize that they need less sleep than younger adults do and that waking up several times during the night is normal. The researchers also hypothesized that older adults might sleep better, with greater satisfaction, if they practiced "sleep compression," limiting the time spent in bed to the amount of time actually needed for sleep.

To test these hypotheses, the researchers advertised for volunteers over age 65 to participate in a study of sleep patterns, with each participant receiving $100. Of the 234 people who responded to the ad, almost half were eliminated, either because they changed their minds about participating once they learned more about the experiment or because those with disabilities or medications that might affect sleep were excluded. The remaining 125 participants were asked to report data on their sleep for a week, including when they fell asleep and woke up during the night, total time spent in bed, and, on a scale of 1 to 10, how satisfied they were with their sleep each night.

At the end of the week, based on the data, 75 participants qualified as insomniacs. They averaged only 5 hours of sleep per night, even though they spent 7½ hours in bed. They rated their sleep satisfaction at only 3.5. This was in marked contrast to the 50 noninsomniac elderly, who slept almost 7 hours a night, spent less than an hour awake in bed, and rated their sleep satisfaction at 8, on average.

The researchers then divided the insomniacs into three groups of 25. The groups were roughly equivalent in age, sex ratio, and sleep profiles. Two of the groups, the *experimental* groups, received the special experimental treatment, while the third group, the *control* group, received no special treatment. Both experimental groups viewed a 15-minute video that explained normal age-related sleep patterns and suggested that insomniacs should compress their total time in bed (by going to bed later, getting up earlier, or both). They were also given a brochure that outlined the video's main ideas. After viewing the video a second time, participants were given a quiz about it, to reinforce the message as well as to confirm that they understood it. (They did.)

Members of one experimental group also received four weekly sessions of sleep counseling, including a personalized schedule for sleep compression. At the conclusion of the experimental program, all three groups recorded their sleep patterns, and did so again 2 months later.

Note that these researchers followed standard experimental practice, as described in Chapter 1. First, they measured the variable of interest, the *dependent variable* (in this case, sleep patterns). Next they administered some special treatment, the *independent variable* (in this case, education and counseling). Then they measured the dependent variable again to see if any change had occurred. As Table 23.2 illustrates, both experimental groups showed more improvement than the control group did. The researchers' hypothesis was confirmed by the evidence they gathered: The elderly can reduce insomnia if they understand the normal sleep patterns of old age and practice sleep compression.

Two unstated aspects of this experiment undoubtedly added to its impact. First, the participants were volunteers—they were motivated to improve. Second, the greatest increase in satisfaction (but not the greatest objective improvement) involved individual counseling. The elderly benefit from talking with someone who understands their personal problems. Other research also found that elderly people slept better after brief courses of psychotherapy accompanied by hints about not using the bed for reading or watching TV, keeping the bedroom's temperature down, and avoiding caffeine, alcohol, and heavy bedtime snacks (Morin, 1993).

the elderly did not respond (Schechter et al., 1999). How this lack of response is interpreted may indicate ageism: Were most of them ailing and reluctant to admit it, or were most of them well and offended by the question? Or was the interviewer less conscientious about getting a response?

Aging and Illness

Whether a particular elderly person is likely to be seriously ill, somewhat ailing, or in fine health depends primarily not on age but on genetics, past lifestyle, and current eating and exercise habits. Psychosocial

table **23.2**	**Remediation of Insomnia in Elders: Experimental Results**								
	Minutes Total Sleep			Minutes Awake in Bed			Satisfaction		
	Before	After	Increase	Before	After	Decrease	Before	After	Improvement
Video only	306	350	14%	92	48	48%	3.5	5.7	+2.2
Video and counseling	290	329	13%	68	32	53%	3.6	6.1	+2.5
Controls	314	340	8%	83	64	23%	3.8	4.8	+1.0

Source: Riedel et al., 1995.

From the perspective of a developmental psychologist, cognitive therapy is usually the best strategy, partly because the complaint is not too serious. Insomnia is less worrisome than sleeping too much. To be specific, sleeping less than 8 hours, or waking up too early, is less problematic than sleeping too much and too soundly, which may indicate depression, poor circulation, or other health problems.

Another experiment tested the efficacy of drugs, which are the usual treatment for insomnia in the elderly (Morin et al., 1999). Four groups of about 20 subjects were involved, all age 55 or older and with sleeping problems, as measured not only by their sleep diaries, self-reports, and a standard interview called the *Sleep Impairment Index* but also by records of their brain waves, breathing patterns, and limb movements made while they slept in a laboratory for 3 consecutive nights.

All four groups were given pills. Two groups got a sleep medication called temazepan (Restoril), and two groups got a placebo (a look-alike pill with no active medication). Two of the groups (one Restoril and one placebo) also received 8 weeks of psychotherapy, designed to change faulty beliefs about insomnia and to encourage several sleep-enhancing practices, such as going to bed only when sleepy and getting up at the same time each day.

On virtually all the follow-up measures (both subjective and objective), the combined group (counseling plus Restoril) did best, followed by the group that got psychotherapy plus placebo, then the group that received medication alone, then, worst, the group that got the placebo alone. Several months after treatment, the groups were measured again on the Sleep Impairment Index. About 45 percent still qualified as insomniacs, with significant differences depending on the treatment they had received. The people who still had insomnia were only 22 percent of those who had received therapy plus placebo, 25 percent who had had therapy plus medication, 44 percent who had had medication without therapy, and 86 percent who had received the placebo and no therapy.

To some extent, these results are typical of other therapeutic attempts. A small portion (25 percent in this case) do not improve even with the best treatments available, and at the other end of the spectrum, a small group (here 14 percent) become better merely because of time and the placebo effect. However, the most interesting result is that not only did most people eventually get better but that therapy *without* medication was as effective as therapy with medication.

Given the possible side effects of medication in late adulthood, this is very good news. Treating the mind—even for a short period—may best help both body and mind, not only for sleep disorders, but also for eating disorders, depression, and anxiety (in other research, not detailed here).

factors, particularly social support and feeling in control of daily life, as well as personality, are also influential. In fact, assertiveness to the point of "some kind of determined nastiness" bodes well for health, vitality, and survival itself (Tobin, 1996).

Nevertheless, it is undeniable that the incidence of chronic and acute diseases becomes greater with age. One reason for this connection between aging and disease is that the older a person is, the more likely it is that decades of smoking, heavy drinking, inactivity, overweight, or breathing polluted air have increased the risk of osteoporosis, heart disease, cancer, and other ailments.

Figure 23.3   Leading Causes of Death Among the Elderly. The death rate from the eight leading causes of death is significantly higher for elderly people than for younger people. This chart shows approximate ratios between the death rates for Americans aged 65 and older and those under 65. A finer analysis reveals some interesting age differences. For example, elderly pedestrians are much more likely to be killed in auto accidents than other adult pedestrians are, whereas younger adults are more likely to be killed in auto accidents when they are drivers or passengers.

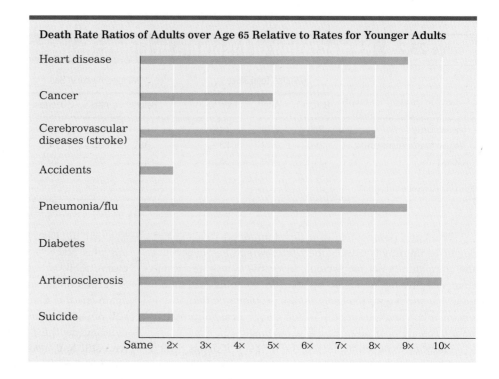

Death Rate Ratios of Adults over Age 65 Relative to Rates for Younger Adults

In addition to the cumulative risks of longstanding unhealthy habits, the body is more susceptible to disease because primary aging makes it less efficient. If a young person contracts pneumonia, for example, he or she almost always is fine again in a few weeks, but for a person already seriously weakened by senescence, pneumonia can cause death. Even the flu can kill, which is why flu shots are recommended for everyone over age 65 but not for healthy younger people.

In short, no one reaches age 100 disease-free. Older persons are more susceptible to disease, take longer to recover from illness, and are more likely to die of any given disease or infection (see Figure 23.3) (Arking, 1998). Although many of the very old are still able to take care of their basic needs within their social world, all have at least a few chronic illnesses, and many have daily medication, pacemakers, artificial hips, and the like (Alder, 1995).

Although no particular ailment, from the most common lethal diseases (heart disease and cancer) to the most common chronic conditions (arthritis, hearing impairment), is inevitable, every disease becomes more likely with every passing year. Many aged hearts are quite strong, but none are as strong as they were 50 years earlier. And while few people are diagnosed with cancer, autopsies of old people "usually reveal incipient or well-developed tumors, although they have not been the causes of death" (Holliday, 1995).

The most striking example of this is prostate cancer, which is evident upon autopsy in virtually every man who dies at age 80 or older but causes an old man's death less than once in a thousand instances. Likewise, breast cancer is far more common in the very old, when it grows more slowly than in younger women. It is a mistake to treat such cancers in the same way one would if the patient were 40 years old; the risk of acute morbidity caused by surgery needs to be balanced against the risk of mortality caused by slowly developing disease (Kaplan, 2000).

Dying Slowly Versus Dying Quickly

We cannot avoid aging, but we can extend living and shorten the process of dying. Although it is impossible to prevent the diseases that result from senescence, it is possible to postpone their onset. Ideally, say gerontologists, this will produce a **compression of morbidity**—that is, fewer days and months that an aged person is disabled or in pain.

James Fries (1994) illustrates the idea of the compression of morbidity with a hypothetical example of identical twin brothers (see Figure 23.4). Both have the same genetic vulnerabilities to disease and both are exposed to the same pathogens, but one "smokes like a chimney, is fat, doesn't exercise, and has a poor diet," while the other has "fairly good health habits." When both get pneumonia at about age 25 (environmental exposure), they recover quickly because their organ reserves and immune systems have only just begun to age.

However, both twins are genetically predisposed to other illnesses—emphysema, heart attack, stroke, and lung cancer. The foolish twin is sick from middle age on, with chronic disease. By his 70s, he has several serious illnesses. Meanwhile, his health-conscious brother has inherited the same conditions, but his lifestyle protects him. Indeed, by the time he dies, his genetic vulnerability to cancer has not yet manifested itself. The healthier twin spends much less time seriously ill before dying than does the sick twin, because less secondary aging occurs.

Compression of morbidity is a psychological as well as a biological blessing. A healthier person is likely to be intellectually alert and socially active—in other words, to be among those experiencing optimal

compression of morbidity A limiting of the time a person spends ill or infirm, accomplished by postponing illness or, once morbidity occurs, hastening death.

Figure 23.4   Primary and Secondary Aging. The interplay of primary and secondary aging is shown in this diagram of the illness and death of a hypothetical pair of monozygotic twins. Both are equally subject to certain illnesses—so both experience a bout of pneumonia at about age 25. Both also carry the same genetic clock, so they both die at age 80. However, genetic vulnerabilities to circulatory, heart, and lung problems affect each quite differently. The nonexercising smoker (top) suffers from an extended period of morbidity, as his various illnesses become manifest when his organ reserve is depleted, beginning at about age 45, and worsening over the next 30 years. By contrast, the healthy lifestyle of his twin (bottom) keeps disability and disease at bay until primary aging is well advanced. Indeed, he dies years before the emergence of lung cancer—which had been developing throughout late adulthood but was slowed by the strength of his organ reserve and immune system.

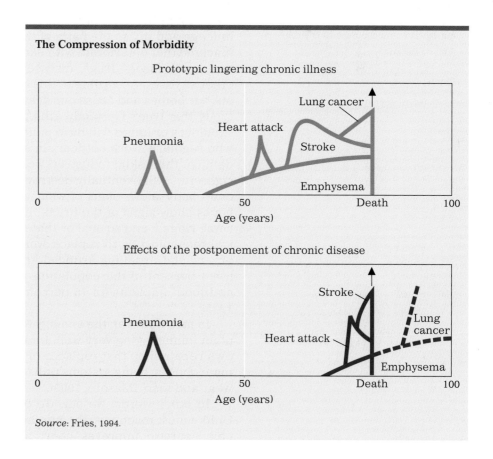

The Compression of Morbidity

Prototypic lingering chronic illness

Lung cancer

Heart attack

Pneumonia

Stroke

Emphysema

0   50   Death   100
Age (years)

Effects of the postponement of chronic disease

Stroke

Pneumonia

Heart attack

Lung cancer

Emphysema

0   50   Death   100
Age (years)

Source: Fries, 1994.

aging as a young-old person, not living the impaired life of the oldest-old. This compression of serious illness is one of the most powerful accomplishments of medical science over the past century. Improved prevention, detection, and, most important, treatment measures have meant that a typical old person today has made gains in several areas, living with less pain, more mobility, better vision, more and stronger teeth, sharper hearing, clearer thinking, enhanced vitality, and so on (Bunker et al., 1995). A healthier lifestyle among the middle-aged has reduced premature death related to heart disease, strokes, and cancer.

Reduction of secondary aging raises important questions regarding the primary aging process itself: What causes it, and can it, too, be markedly slowed?

CAUSES OF SENESCENCE

❓ Especially for Biologists: What are some immediate practical uses for research on the causes of aging?

Might we control aging so that late adulthood never brings frailty, senility, disability, and pain? Can death itself be postponed, allowing the average person to live 90 to 100 healthy years instead of 75 or 85? Underlying these questions is the fundamental one: Why does aging occur? As you will see, there are many intriguing answers. Some implicate our interactions with our contexts; some, our genetic makeup; and some, the simple passage of time (Clark, 1999; Holliday, 1995; Kanungo, 1994; Masoro, 1999).

Wear and Tear

wear-and-tear theory A theory of aging that states that the human body wears out by time and exposure to environmental stressors.

The oldest, most general, and most logical theory of aging is **wear and tear.** Just as the parts of an automobile begin giving out as the years and mileage add up, so the parts of the body can be thought of as parts of a machine that deteriorate with each year of exposure to pollution, radiation, toxic foods, drugs, diseases, repeated movements, and various other stresses. According to this theory, just by living our lives, we wear out our bodies and cause our deaths.

Is this true? Certainly athletes who put repeated stress on their shoulders or knees will have painful joints by middle adulthood; people who regularly work outdoors in strong sunlight without protection will damage their skin; industrial workers who inhale asbestos and smoke cigarettes will eventually destroy their lungs. By late adulthood, everyone's body shows signs of wear and tear as scars accumulate, broken bones show signs of the break, eyes get a little cloudy, fingernails become ridged, and so on. For that reason, one emphasis of modern medical technology is to replace worn-out parts—from transplanting vital organs and installing artificial knees and hips (now almost routine for the 4 percent of the population who require them) to fitting dentures and tooth implants (in 75 percent of those over age 65) (Bunker et al., 1995).

In fact, however, the analogy to a machine's wearing out does not explain human aging very well. In many respects, the human body has its own repair shop that replaces or mends damaged parts; "unlike inanimate objects, living systems utilize external matter and energy to repair wear and tear" (Masoro, 1999).

In other words, we eat, we breathe, we move, and we get better! Unlike most machines, the human body benefits from use. Regular aerobic exercise improves heart and lung functioning; sexual activity

Use It So You Don't Lose It Although wear-and-tear theory might predict otherwise, the single most critical failure of body functions that accelerates aging is loss of mobility. We now know that after a stroke or other mobility-restricting event, the best therapy is to start walking again.

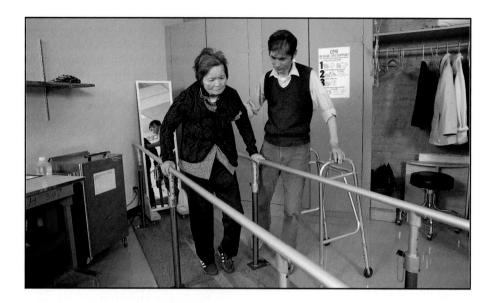

throughout adulthood stimulates the sexual-arousal system in old age; eating raw fruits and vegetables that require vigorous intestinal activity actually improves digestion.

The opposite is true as well: Inactivity breeds illness. We are more likely to rust out than to wear out; thus, the wear-and-tear theory applies to some diseases in some organs and body parts, but not to senescence overall. More promising theories of aging begin at the cellular level, recognizing that humans are not machines but living creatures, made up of millions of aging and regenerating cells.

Cellular Accidents

Too Much Sun The "beauty benefits" of devoted sunbathing are transient; the damage is cumulative. Age spots, wrinkles, and leathery skin texture associated with aging become exaggerated from lengthy exposure to the sun. Worse, prolonged sun exposure greatly increases the risk of skin cancer.

❷ *Observational Quiz (see answer page 635): Identify several signs visible in this photograph that this woman is high in socioeconomic status.*

Most cells of the human body continue to reproduce throughout life. An obvious example is the outer cells of the skin. Under normal conditions, these cells are entirely replaced every few years. When a cut or scrape happens, the process occurs within a few days. Blood and tissue cells also duplicate rapidly; cells of the ear, eye, and brain, more slowly (if at all). But new cells are being made every minute, each designed to be the exact copy of an old cell.

However, mutations in the cell structure often occur, as the result of "an ever growing number of chemical agents discharged in our environment, [and] . . . an increased possibility for the interaction of different toxicants" as well as radiation from the sun and other sources (Cooper et al., 1991). Mutations also occur in the normal process of DNA repair. When the genetic instructions for creating new cells become imperfect, the new cells are not quite exact copies of the old.

Over time, with the rapidly reproducing skin cells, for example, inexact replication results in slower replacement, benign growths, color changes, or skin cancer (Giacomoni & D'Alessio, 1996). Similarly, throughout the entire body, cellular imperfections and the declining ability to detect and correct them can result in harmless changes, small reductions in function, or fatal damage.

Free Radicals

One specific aspect of this theory (that cellular accidents cause aging) begins with the fact that electrons of certain body molecules can separate from their atoms. The resulting altered atoms are called *free radicals*. Such atoms are highly unstable because they have unpaired electrons; they are thus capable of reacting violently with other molecules, splitting them or tearing them apart.

The most damage occurs when free radicals of oxygen scramble DNA molecules. These **oxygen free radicals** produce errors in cell maintenance and repair that, over time, may cause cancer, diabetes, and arteriosclerosis. This process may be slowed down by certain **antioxidants** (substances that bind oxygen radicals, making them no longer freely damaging). Vitamins A, C, and E and the mineral selenium are all antioxidants, which is one reason a healthy diet slows the rate of various diseases. Ironically, high doses of antioxidants taken in pill form, not as food, may actually increase oxygen free radicals (Dothie & Bellizzi, 1999).

However, the accumulation of problems in DNA replication is inevitable. Increasing numbers of oxygen free radicals are reproduced during normal body growth and maintenance, in reaction to infections and inflammation of the intestinal tract and as a result of ultraviolet radiation (Holliday, 1995). It seems, then, that since oxygen free radicals damage cells, affect organs, and accelerate diseases, and since the number of such radicals in the body increases over time and with stress, the gradual accumulation of free-radical damage may be one cause of the aging process.

Some Encouragement

Not all findings about the causes of senescence are so discouraging. When the systems of the body function well, cellular damage is minimized by specific cells that destroy seriously damaged cells and take over the work that imperfect cells no longer perform. For example, three major enzymes are involved in the destruction of oxygen free radicals. In addition, antioxidants nullify the effects of oxygen free radicals by forming a bond with their unattached oxygen electrons. A gene called P53 responds to DNA damage by causing a flawed cell to self-destruct or at least to stop duplicating. Further, some normal processes may be protective, particularly via hormones. This is most apparent in women, who are defended against heart disease by estrogen and other hormones until the reproductive years are over. Postponing or limiting childbearing may extend life as well (Westendorp & Kirkwood, 1998).

In these and many other ways, the body makes use of natural protection and self-healing processes. Given a healthy lifestyle, cell errors accumulate slowly, causing little overall harm. Nevertheless, aging makes repair less efficient, errors more extensive, and critically important cells damaged, so that the body can no longer control or isolate the errors. Even the P53 gene can mutate, disabling its cancer-fighting potential (Pennisi, 1999). Worst of all, the immune system itself declines.

The Immune System

As noted in Chapter 20, the immune system recognizes foreign or abnormal substances in the circulatory system, isolates them, and destroys them. It does this mainly with two types of attack cells. **B cells** (so

---

oxygen free radicals   Atoms that, as a result of metabolic processes, have an unpaired electron. They produce errors in cell maintenance and repair that, over time, may cause cancer, diabetes, and arteriosclerosis.

antioxidants   Compounds that nullify the effects of oxygen free radicals by forming a bond with their unattached oxygen electron.

❶ **Response for Biologists (from page 632):** Although ageism and ambivalence limit the funding of research on the causes of aging, the applications include prevention of AIDS, cancer, senility, and physical damage from pollution—all urgent social priorities.

B cells   Cells manufactured in the bone marrow that create antibodies for isolating and destroying invading bacteria and viruses.

called because they are manufactured in the bone marrow) create antibodies to destroy specific invading bacteria and viruses. These antibodies remain in the system, which explains why we get measles, mumps, or specific strains of influenza only once. A second invasion by such specific disease microbes is immediately thwarted by B cells that are always at the ready.

The other type of attack cells, called **T cells** (manufactured by the thymus gland), produce substances that attack any kind of infected cells. T cells also help the B cells produce more efficient antibodies and strengthen other aspects of the immune system as well.

B cells and T cells specialize further, with some responding to antigens that the body has already experienced and others defending against new diseases and tumors. These two types of cells compose only part of the "very complex defense mechanism of the immune response"—a complexity necessitated by the fact that humans are "slow-breeding complex organisms continuously exposed to infection by rapidly growing pathogens or parasites" (Holliday, 1995). Among other components of the immune system are NK ("natural killer") cells and K ("killer") cells and white blood cells.

Many, though not all, aspects of the immune system become less efficient with age (Miller, 1996). The thymus gland begins to shrink during adolescence; by age 50, it is only 15 percent as big as it was at puberty. Partly for this reason, over the years of adulthood the production and power of T cells and B cells decline, as does the efficiency of the mechanisms that regulate them. These depletions are another reason why most forms of cancer become much more common with age and why various other illnesses—from a first bout of chicken pox to sudden food poisoning to the latest strain of influenza—are much more serious in an adult than in a child. By late adulthood, the flu can be fatal, because the immune system is too weak to launch an effective, speedy counterattack.

Additional support for the theory that the declining immune system permits aging as well as disease comes from research on AIDS, or *acquired immune deficiency syndrome*. HIV (human immunodeficiency virus) can be latent for many years after the person becomes infected with it, but it becomes much more destructive (and therefore reaches the point where it is called full-blown AIDS) once the cells of the immune system reach a certain low count (fewer than 200 CD4 cells) in the blood. Persons of any age who have AIDS experience some specific cancers and signs of dementia that usually do not occur until late adulthood. This is further evidence that the immune system's gradual loss of the ability to protect, defend, and repair damage to the body is key to the aging process.

Even in the absence of illness, individuals with stronger immune systems (measured by laboratory analysis of the T and B cells in the blood) outlive their contemporaries, suggesting that the decline in immunity may be, not merely an accompaniment of aging, but actually the cause of it (Miller, 1996). Other evidence comes from healthy centenarians, whose immune systems are slower but surprisingly strong (Franceschi et al., 1996) and chronically depressed people, who have fewer T cells and a higher rate of illness (Gutmann, 1996; Meeks et al., 2000).

The immune system may even explain sex differences in morbidity and mortality. Throughout life, females tend to have stronger immune systems than males: Their thymus gland is larger, and laboratory tests reveal that their immune responses are more efficient. This advantage may be a mixed blessing, however, because women are more vulnerable

T cells Cells created in the thymus that produce substances that attack infected cells in the body.

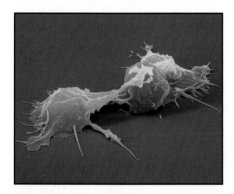

Normal Killers The immune system is always at war, attacking invading bacteria, viruses, and other destructive agents. Here two "natural killer" cells are overwhelming a leukemia cell. How healthy we are and how long we live are directly related to the strength and efficiency of our immune system.

❶ *Answer to Observational Quiz (from page 633): She is reading a newspaper, listening to an expensive Walkman, sitting on a hotel beach in Hawaii, and wearing fashionable sunglasses and swimsuit—all of which suggest that she should be too well informed to overexpose her skin to the sun.*

to autoimmune diseases such as rheumatoid arthritis and lupus erythematosus, in which an overactive immune system attacks the person's own body (Carlson et al., 1996). In very late adulthood, when immune-system functioning declines, women and men have similar vulnerability to disease.

The Genetics of Aging

Errors in cellular duplication seem to explain some primary aging, in that they are cumulative, universal, and pervasive, occurring in all the body systems. Similarly, a slowdown in the body's repair system would explain the increase in secondary aging over time, as whatever vulnerabilities a person's genes and life habits entail can no longer be contained once the immune system weakens.

However, neither of these two theories explains all the changes of aging that begin in early adulthood; nor do they account for the predictable acceleration of death that universally occurs with age; nor do they explain the variability in whether and when a person will experience a particular age-related disease. If cellular error and immune-system decline were the only factors involved in aging, we would expect that some individuals would show no signs at all of senescence until age 100 or more, while other unlucky ones would age quite suddenly at 30. This is not the case: Senescence accumulates in everyone at every point of the life span, with variation as to timing, duration, and type.

Maximums and Averages

Since wear and tear, cellular errors, and declining immunity are incomplete explanations, some theorists propose that aging is genetic in all species. In other words, aging is no mistake. It may be the normal, natural result of the genetic plan.

This theory begins with an obvious fact: Every living species has a genetically inherent **maximum life span.** The maximum life span is defined as the oldest age to which any member of a given species can live, even with protection against all the "extrinsic factors, such as nutrition, temperature, radiation, pollution, and . . . stress as well as intrinsic factors such as hormones and free radicals" (Kanungo, 1994). For instance, under ideal circumstances, the most that rats live is 4 years; rabbits, 13; tigers, 26;

maximum life span The oldest age to which members of a species can live, under ideal circumstances. For humans, that age is approximately 120 years.

The Oldest of All When she died in 1997, at age 122, Jeanne Calment of southern France was the oldest living person in the world, and one of the very few documented instances of someone's living out the maximum human life span.
❷ Observational Quiz *(see answer page 639): The photograph album signifies several factors that correlate with long life. What are they?*

average life expectancy The number of years the average newborn of a particular population group is likely to live. In humans, this age has tended to increase over time, primarily because fewer children die in infancy.

house cats, 30; brown bears, 37; chimpanzees, 55; Indian elephants, 70; finback whales, 80; humans, 122; giant tortoises, 180 (Clark, 1999).

Maximum life span is quite different from **average life expectancy,** which is how long the typical newborn of a particular population of a given species will live. In humans, average life expectancy varies according to the historical, cultural, and socioeconomic factors that cause death in childhood, adolescence, or middle age. In the United States today, average life expectancy at birth is about 74 years for men and 80 years for women. Americans who are already 65 years old, and thus no longer at risk of an early death, are expected to live to 81 if male and to 84 if female, and those who are already 90 can expect to live another 4 years. Sometime during the 90s the death rate actually stabilizes, so a person who is 105 is no more likely to die that year than a person who is only 95.

In ancient times, the average life expectancy was about 20 (because so many babies died). In 1900, in developed nations, it was about age 50. The reason for this improvement was not an increase in the maximum life span for the human species but the improved odds of survival to age 5, which raised the average.

As best we can tell from historical records, the maximum human life span a millennium or two ago was a few years past 100, just as it is today. (The biblical Methuselah's age, 969, was measured in "years" that had fewer days.) If childhood diseases, accidents, infections, warfare, childbirth, and famine had not killed so many early Greeks, Egyptians, and Chinese, most adults in those ancient civilizations would have reached old age, as a lucky few did then and as most now do. At that point, however, primary aging takes over. Those who survived to age 70 would have died of aging-related causes, as they do today. Just as we are genetically programmed to reach sexual maturity during the teen years, we may be genetically programmed to die during late adulthood.

Why Death May Be Genetic

Epigenetic systems theory (discussed in Chapter 2) provides several explanations for senescence. One is that since reproduction is essential for the survival of the species, it was genetically important for the human community to protect those who might have offspring. Thus, deaths should occur either very early in life (so society didn't expend food and energy raising children to puberty only to have them die) or after childbearing and child rearing, at age 50 or so. At that point, the genes not only could, but even should, allow various fatal diseases, in order not to waste resources on adults who were no longer able to produce the next generation.

The same results could have been achieved in a more straightforward manner, as a consequence of selective adaptation one person at a time. Early in life, genetic abnormalities (such as an extra chromosome) usually cause the organism to die before implantation, before birth, or almost certainly before parenthood. Thus, those genes are not passed on.

If a given mutation affects only older people, then that gene would be passed on to another generation. Parkinson's disease, Huntington's disease, Alzheimer's disease, Type II diabetes, coronary heart disease, and osteoporosis are among the many examples of genetic diseases that evolutionary processes would have no mechanism, or reason, to select against (Masoro, 1999). As a result, we all have inherited genes from our ancestors that cause us to survive to age 40 or so but then to become senescent, get sick, and die—each in our particular genetic way.

genetic clock According to one theory of aging, a regulatory mechanism in the DNA of cells regulates the aging process.

Progeria This 16-year-old South African boy, embraced by his 81-year-old grandmother, has progeria, a genetic disorder that produces accelerated aging, including baldness, wrinkled skin, arthritis, and heart and lung difficulties, and early death.

Hayflick limit The number of times a human cell is capable of dividing into two new cells. The limit for most human cells is approximately 50 divisions, suggesting that the life span is limited by our genetic program.

The Genetic Clock

Another explanation is that every human has not just genes for abnormalities, but also genes for normal aging. Does the DNA that directs the activity of every body cell also regulate aging, not as a mutation but as a proper function? Do all humans have a kind of **genetic clock,** triggering hormonal changes in the brain and regulating the cellular reproduction and repair process? As the genetic clock gradually "switches off" the genes that promote growth, it might switch on genes that promote aging. Senescence would then accelerate until one or more body systems could no longer function and natural death occurred.

Evidence for genetic regulation of aging comes from several genetic diseases that produce premature signs of aging and early death. Down syndrome, or trisomy 21, is the most common: People with this disorder who survive childhood almost always die by middle adulthood, with symptoms of heart disease and Alzheimer's disease (Masoro, 1999). Children born with a rare genetic disease called *progeria* have a normal infancy but by age 5 stop growing and begin to look like old people, with wrinkled skin and balding heads. Although their intellects and memories are normal for young people, they develop many signs of premature aging and die by their teens, usually of heart diseases typically found in the elderly (Clark, 1999).

The idea of a genetic clock that limits the life span is also supported by laboratory research, particularly the work of Leonard Hayflick (1994; Hayflick & Moorhead, 1961). Hayflick allowed cells taken from human embryos to age "under glass" by providing them with all the necessary nutrients for cell growth and protecting them from external stress or contamination. In such ideal conditions, it was believed, the cells would double again and again, forever. Instead, the cells stopped multiplying after about 50 divisions. Cells similarly cultured from children doubled fewer times than cells from embryos, and cells from adults divided fewer times than cells from children. The total number of cell divisions roughly correlates with the age of the donor, and it is never infinite.

This research has been repeated by hundreds of scientists, using many techniques and various types of cells from people and animals of various ages. The result is always that the cells stop replicating at a certain point, referred to as the **Hayflick limit.** Even in ideal conditions, the replication of cells of living creatures roughly equals that which occurs in the maximum life span of their particular species. Cells from people with progeria, Down syndrome, and similar genetic conditions do not double as many times as would be expected, given the age of the donors.

When the Hayflick limit is reached, the aged cells differ from young cells in many ways. One is that the very ends of the cells—called the telemeres—are much shorter. Thus, replications of the cells of the body are never—even without oxygen free radicals or other disruptive forces—perfect transcriptions.

CAN AGING BE STOPPED?

If aging results from cellular accidents or declining T cells or programmed senescence, then perhaps a gene, a chemical, or another mechanism can be found that alters the aging process. This has already been done in animals: Greatly reduced diet has slowed the aging process in monkeys and chimpanzees, lengthening life by about a third (Lane et al., 1999). Selective breeding of fruit flies has doubled the average life span (Masoro, 1999). In mice, chemicals have altered a defective P53 gene and halted cancer tumors (Foster et al., 1999). Could any of these developments be applied to humans?

There is no reason to rule out the possibility that people could live several decades longer than they now do—although the specifics might be different for our species than for mice and fruit flies. But more important, *should* it happen for humans? Is a greatly extended life span what people want? (See the Changing Policy box.)

Human Evidence and Questions

Most scientists now believe that aging occurs on the cellular level, with genes at least partly responsible. However, very few researchers believe that, except in rare cases such as progeria, aging is directly controlled by one or several particular genes. This means that human aging probably cannot be halted or slowed with a specific vitamin or via genetic engineering. The causes of primary aging, as well as the specific diseases of secondary aging, are the result of "multiple cellular pathways," with no one factor acting in isolation (Cristofalo, 1996).

Far more research is focused on preventing heart disease, AIDS, cancer, mental illness, or violent crime than on adding a decade or more to life (Holliday, 1999). Yet even though prevention of aging is not a top research priority, we have learned how diseases related to secondary aging can be prevented or slowed, health can be increased, and average life expectancy can be extended.

An analysis of death rates in Sweden, where universal health care has been excellent for decades and where accurate death records have been available for a century, shows a steady increase in average life expectancy (Vaupel & Lundstrom, 1994). Not only are fewer Swedish babies and children dying, but older people are living longer. At age 95, the number of remaining years for an average Swede was about 2 years in 1945 and is about 3 now. The authors of this study conclude:

> The available evidence, taken together, suggests that, if historical rates of progress in reducing mortality rates continue to prevail in the future, newborn children today can expect to live about 90 years on average. If, as health and biomedical knowledge develops, progress accelerates so that age-specific mortality rates come down at an average rate of about 2 percent per year, then the typical newborn today in developed countries will live to celebrate his or her 100th birthday. [Vaupel & Lundstrom, 1994]

Sweden is an example of effective life extension. Examples in the other direction include Russia, where epigenetic factors (especially stress and pollution) have shortened the average life span during the 1990s, and several nations of Africa, where AIDS kills young adults who would have survived a generation ago. Thus, although secondary aging is under human control, there is no guarantee that such control will work to our advantage.

The Centenarians

A centenarian is someone still alive after his or her 100th birthday. Do you hope to become one, as "the typical newborn today in developed countries" is expected to? There is no guarantee that the added years will be active, healthy, and happy instead of being a time of decrepitude,

❶ *Answer to Observational Quiz (from page 636):* Remember that the photos in the album were taken a century ago, when most girls were not photographed at all, much less photographed for posterity. Obviously, in her youth Madame Calment was wealthy, loved, appreciated, and educated. All four factors still make it less likely that a person will die young, although none of them guarantees long life.

SHOULD EVERYONE LIVE TO 100?

Research on the aging process has yielded substantial information on how mice, rats, and fruit flies can be made to live longer as well as some intriguing ideas about human DNA, immunity, and so on. However, none of this has immediate practical applications for most of us, and policy changes and research funds are not yet focused on ways of extending the human life span. Indeed, legislators are more concerned about bankrupting Social Security and the "high cost of dying" (issues discussed in Chapter 25). As for the general public, many people say they want to live longer, but few are willing to make personal sacrifices to accomplish that goal. To understand the obstacles involved, let's look at two areas: nutrition and exercise.

Nutrition

Obtaining good nutrition becomes more difficult with age, for several reasons. First, the need for vitamins and minerals increases, as the body becomes less efficient at digesting food and using its nutrients. Meanwhile, daily caloric requirements decrease by about 100 calories per decade after age 45, so the average 75-year-old should consume at least 10 percent fewer calories than at middle age in order to maintain weight and energy levels (Blumberg, 1996).

Because more nutrients need to be packed into fewer calories, a varied and healthful diet, emphasizing fresh fruits and vegetables, lean meats and fish, and complex carbohydrates (cereals and grains), is even more essential in late adulthood than earlier in life. For example, those elderly with clear deficits in B vitamins, particularly B_{12} and folic acid, are more likely to have memory deficiencies than those whose intake was adequate (Wahlin et al., 1996). Dehydration is a greater risk because aging cells hold water less efficiently, yet aging digestive systems need more water to function well.

In addition, because the senses of smell and taste diminish with age, food is less appealing, and hunger and thirst are less compelling. A number of external factors may also affect the nutrition of some old people:

- Poverty (high-quality nutrients are more expensive)
- Living alone (those who eat alone tend to eat quick, irregular meals)
- Dental problems (missing teeth and gum disease make people eat softer food and less of it)

Many of the elderly take drugs that affect nutritional requirements. For example, aspirin (taken daily by many who have arthritis) increases the need for vitamin C; antibiotics reduce the absorption of iron, calcium, and vitamin K; antacids reduce absorption of protein; oil-based laxatives deplete vitamins A and D (Lamy, 1994). Alcohol, especially in large amounts, depletes B vitamins, calcium, magnesium, and vitamin C (Wattis & Seymour, 1994). The caffeine in coffee, tea, and other drinks reduces the water in the body, making the elderly especially vulnerable to dehydration. The elderly are more likely to take daily vitamin pills than younger people are, sometimes taking megadoses that harm them more than help them (Lamy, 1994).

All this information has been known for decades, and most gerontologists and social workers are well aware of the possibility of malnutrition in the elderly. Programs to enable the impoverished elderly to get enough food, to provide free "meals on wheels" to everyone who applies, and to serve nutritious meals at senior centers, nursing homes, and hospitals are all an outgrowth of the public concern about the elderly who subsist on meager diets or even on pet food.

There is another nutritional concern—one that is less well known, less likely to gain political support, less often part of a program sponsored by hospitals and social workers. The concern is that, if we really are concerned about a long and healthy life for the elderly, we should reduce the daily caloric intake of the middle-aged. Animals live almost twice as long if they eat almost half as much. To be specific, when mice and rats are well nourished but consume only half as much food as rodents that eat freely, the restricted diet slows down growth, reproduction, senescence, and death (Pendergrass et al., 1995). Animals with reduced calories are stronger, more vital, and younger in appearance, as long as they consume adequate vitamins and minerals (Clark, 1999). Primates, including monkeys and chimpanzees, probably experience similar benefits (Lane et al., 1999; Ramsey et al., 1997). The implications for humans are discussed on the next page.

Exercise

The exercise story in old age is similar to the nutrition story: The elderly do it less but need it more, and research suggests they might do it differently. Even in the very old, physical activity benefits the cardiovascular, respiratory, digestive, and virtually all other body systems, although the pace of exercise must match the declines in heart and lung functioning. For some, this means that jogging replaces running; for others, that brisk walking replaces jogging; for still others, that strolling replaces brisk walking.

Nonetheless, regular exercise—three or more times a week for at least half an hour—is even more important in late adulthood than earlier to maintain the strength of the heart muscle and the lungs. Activities that involve continuous rhythmic movements for an extended period are more beneficial than those that require sudden, strenuous effort (Shephard, 1997).

Now, here is the surprise: Weight-lifting should be part of an elderly exercise routine. Although the elderly lose muscle at an increasingly rapid rate, they can retain or gain muscle rapidly if they undertake strength training, including working out with weights and machines that provide resistance (Felsenthal et al., 1994; Raloff, 1996). The result is usually not bulging muscles, but greater mobility, more lean body mass, greater leg strength, and thus fewer falls (and less damage if a fall occurs) and longer life. In fact, how well a person is able to move his or her lower body is one of the best predictors of vitality in old age.

It is almost never too late to improve muscle strength (Warshofsky, 1999). Reporting on a 10-week program of muscle training with frail nursing home residents between the ages of 72 and 98, Raloff (1996) notes: "Individuals more than doubled the strength of trained muscles and increased their stair-climbing power by 28 percent when they exercised their legs with resistance training three times a week."

Exercise for Life While most members of health clubs are adults in their 20s and 30s, the ones who benefit most are in their 70s and 80s. Rapid muscle gain, improved mobility, intellectual quickness, and longer life are all benefits from targeted strengthening in late adulthood.

Policy Implications

Now think of the gap between research, public policy, and practice. Fewer than 1 percent of those over age 50 currently eat a restricted diet (about 1,500 to 1,800 calories per day) or use resistance training to build their muscles. Reasons for this inaction abound, from laziness and a preference for comfort to a suspicion that measures that are effective for rats, monkeys, or the very frail oldest-old might not work for the majority of humans. Even deeper is an ambivalence: We do not want to grow old, so longevity is regarded with humor and doubt, not passionate dedication.

Most people do not act to extend their lives until time seems to be short. Public policies do not effectively encourage healthy eating (perhaps with a tax and warning signs for fast food, as now occurs for cigarettes) or encourage exercise (perhaps with free public stair-climbers, just as we now have free public toilets and escalators). It may be that most people prefer a comfortable, if not overly long, life and that public policy is merely giving people what they want. One scientist frames the issue well:

> An important question to ask about caloric restriction is what impact it may have on the quality of life. This is uniquely a human question, entirely subjective, and not one that can be answered directly from animal studies. Although all of the primates kept on restricted diets so far are certainly healthy, we cannot ask them how they feel about it. Would humans subjected to a calorically restricted diet be constantly hungry, spending all of their free time and energy thinking about food, and how to get it? Would we be constantly agitated and irritable because we're chronically hungry? To achieve an extended lifespan, would we have to reduce our total energy expenditure, forgoing many of the energy-expensive activities that enrich our lives? [Clark, 1999]

The human assessment of the costs and benefits is expressed differently by a gerontologist who himself has been on a 1,700-calorie-a-day diet for 10 years,

> I expect if I keep this up that it will add fifteen to twenty years to my life span. I think that diet is very healthy and it makes you feel better. I need less sleep. You have more energy, but you are a little hungry. But I'm a lot hungrier to live longer for knowledge, beauty, and justice, and things like that, than I am for angel food cake. So it's a good substitution. [Walford, quoted in Warshofsky, 1999]

Policies change when people change their minds and behavior, and then choose leaders who reflect their impulses. Personally, I have voted for several chubby political leaders, and I myself am neither skinny nor strong. Are you?

disability, and misery. Compression of morbidity is a goal attained by some people in some nations but not by everyone everywhere. Before deciding that you don't want to live past 80 without a guarantee of good health, consider what your life might be like if you lived to be 100.

Other Places, Other Stories

Westerners who traveled to remote regions of the world found three places—one in Georgia in the former Soviet Union, one in Pakistan, and one in Peru—that had large numbers of people who enjoyed unusual longevity. In these places, adulthood seemed not only long but also vigorous.

One researcher described the Abkhazia people in Georgia as follows:

> Most of the aged [those about age 90] work regularly. Almost all perform light tasks around the homestead, and quite a few work in the orchards and gardens, and care for domestic animals. Some even continue to chop wood and haul water. Close to 40 percent of the aged men and 30 percent of the aged women report good vision; that is, that they do not need glasses for any sort of work, including reading or threading a needle. Between 40 and 50 percent have reasonably good hearing. Most have their own teeth. Their posture is unusually erect, even into advanced age. Many take walks of more than two miles a day and swim in mountain streams. [Benet, 1974]

Among the people described in this report are a woman said to be over 130 who drinks a little vodka before breakfast and smokes a pack of cigarettes a day; a man who sired a child when he was 100; and another man who was a village storyteller with an excellent memory at a reported age of 148.

Longevity Three remote regions of the world are renowned for the longevity of their people. In Vilcabamba, Ecuador, *(a)* 87-year-old Jose Maria Roa stands on the mud from which he will make adobe for a new house, and *(d)* 102-year-old Micaela Quezada spins wool. In Abkhazia in the Republic of Georgia, companionship is an important part of late life, as shown by *(b)* Selekh Butka, 113, posing with his wife Marusya, 101, and *(c)* Ougula Lodara talking with two "younger" friends. Finally, Shah Bibi *(e)* at 98, and Galum Mohammad Shad *(f)*, at 100, from the Hunza area of Pakistan, spin wool and build houses. Alexander Leaf, the physician who studied these people, believes that the high social status and continued sense of usefulness of the very old in these cultures may be just as important in their longevity as the diet and exercise imposed by the geographical conditions in each region.

(a)   (b)   (c)

(d)   (e)   (f)

A more comprehensive study (Pitskhelauri, 1982) found that all the regions famous for long-lived people share four characteristics:

- Diet is moderate, consisting mostly of fresh vegetables and herbs, with little consumption of meat and fat. A prevailing belief is that it is better to leave the dining table a little bit hungry than too full.
- Work continues throughout life. In these rural areas, even very elderly adults help with farm work and household tasks, including child care.
- Family and community are important. All the long-lived are well integrated into families of several generations and interact frequently with friends and neighbors.
- Exercise and relaxation are part of the daily routine. Most of the long-lived take a stroll in the morning and another in the evening (often up and down mountains); most take a midday nap and socialize in the evening, telling stories and discussing the day's events.

Each of these communities is in a rural, mountainous region, at least 3,000 feet above sea level. This situation minimizes pollution and maximizes lung and heart fitness, since even walking provides aerobic exercise. Furthermore, in all three, the aged are respected, and strong traditions ensure that the elderly play an important social role. Perhaps these two factors—exercise and social respect—lengthen life.

Note, however, that these communities have no verifiable birth or marriage records from the nineteenth century. Beginning at about age 70, many people in these areas systematically exaggerate their age (Thorson, 1995). Persons who claim to be 100 years old may be much younger. In fact, probably every one of those people who claimed to be a centenarian was fibbing. And every researcher who believed them was vulnerable to a kind of ageism in reverse, the idea that life could be long and wonderful if only the ills of modern civilization could be avoided.

The Truth About Life After 100

Are you disappointed? Does this mean the testimonies are useless? No. Although the years are exaggerated, it is true that an unusual number of very old people thrive in these isolated areas of the world. While their genetic clocks almost certainly do not allow them to live to age 148, their habits and culture probably do allow many to reach 90.

An even more heartening discovery is that such people are not unusual. Excellent records in many developed countries reveal that an increasing number of people are reaching age 100 or more. Some of them are in very good health. And people over age 70—whether they are in excellent health or not—are generally just as happy and satisfied with their lives as younger adults (Myers et al., 2000) *(question 3)*. In fact, the oldest of all may be happier (Mroczek & Kolarz, 1998). As one woman explained:

> At 100, I have a sense of achievement and a sense of leisure as well. I'm not pushed as much as I was. Old age can be more relaxing and more contemplative. I'm enjoying it more than middle age. [quoted in Adler, 1995]

Researchers in western Europe, Japan, and North America find similarities between the centenarians in their research and those aged individuals in Peru, Pakistan, and Russia: moderate diet, hard work, an optimistic attitude, intellectual curiosity, and social involvement are likely to extend the life span. Sometimes morbidity, disability, and senility eventually set in, but sometimes a person celebrates a 100th birthday with energy, awareness, and joy (Adler, 1995; Hitt et al., 1999; Franceschi et al., 1996; Poon, 1992). Centenarians tend to have strong personalities and deep religious beliefs, and to be happier than younger adults.

They may even be healthier than people who are a little younger. People who live past 100 are more likely to have a shorter period of morbidity before death than younger people are. This encouraging finding is one reason the United States Health Care Financing Administration calculated the cost of medical care in the last 2 years of life as $22,600 for people who die at 70, but just $8,300 for people who die after age 100 (cited in Warshofsky, 1999).

Taken together, these and many other studies of the very old lead to a ready conclusion: If people reach late adulthood in good health, their attitudes and activities may be even more important in determining the length and quality of their remaining years than purely physiological factors are. There is no reason to assume that a human will be less happy, less alert, and less interested in life at age 90 than at age 30 or 60. Those of us who are still young might push back our own horizons, diminishing self-defeating ageism as we look toward our future.

SUMMARY

AGEISM

1. Prejudices about the elderly are common and destructive, because they result in the old living unnecessarily limited and isolated lives. Contrary to the stereotype, most of the aged are happy, quite healthy, and active. Fortunately, ageism is weakening as gerontologists work to provide a more comprehensive picture of old age and as the sheer number of the aged in the general population increases.

2. The dependency ratio expresses the relationship between the number of self-sufficient, productive adults and the number of children and elderly dependents. Although now lower than at any time in the past century, the dependency ratio is increasing in developed nations because more people are surviving past age 65, and it is decreasing in developing nations where fewer children are being born.

3. Gerontologists distinguish among the young-old, the old-old, and the oldest-old, according to each age group's relative degree of dependency. Another way to describe the aging process is to distinguish among optimal, usual, and impaired aging.

PRIMARY AGING

4. Primary aging occurs throughout the life span, even from birth. It involves the universal and irreversible physical changes that occur to all living organisms as they grow older.

5. The many apparent changes in skin, hair, and body shape that began earlier in adulthood continue. In addition, most older people are somewhat shorter and weigh less than they

did, and they walk more stiffly. Such changes in appearance can affect the self-concept of the older person.

6. Vision is almost always impaired by late adulthood: nine out of ten of the elderly need glasses. Those over age 80 are likely to experience at least one of the three major eye diseases of the elderly—cataracts, glaucoma, or senile macular degeneration. Most vision problems can be corrected or relieved.

7. Problems with hearing affect about a third of the elderly, often causing social isolation as well as feelings of rejection. Hearing aids are often avoided because they are seen as symbols of aging. This problem is worsened by younger people who use patronizing elderspeak.

8. The age-related declines of the major body systems and organ reserve eventually reach a point—different for everyone—at which some of the routines of daily life (such as sleep habits) need adjusting. Most of the elderly become more cautious and less likely to be victims of crime or automobile accidents.

SECONDARY AGING

9. Secondary aging involves changes caused by particular conditions or illnesses, which may correlate with age but are not the inevitable result of age.

10. The aging process is not synonymous with the disease process. We should not assume that illness is an expected, and thus an accepted, companion during the later years. Almost every elderly person does have some chronic ailment, but the incidence, severity, and specifics depend on the individual's health habits, environment, and genes.

11. Many gerontologists believe that postponement of the onset of various diseases associated with aging will add to a compression of morbidity, reducing the period of pain and disability before death. The result will be the extension not of the maximum human life span but of the period of vital, healthy aging.

CAUSES OF SENESCENCE

12. Many theories address the environmental and genetic causes of aging. One theory is that as we use our bodies we wear them out, just as a machine wears out with extended use. This wear-and-tear theory is refuted by research findings that activity promotes longer life and healthier aging.

13. Cellular theories of aging seem more plausible. The DNA duplication and repair processes are affected by radiation and other factors, leading to an accumulation of errors when new cells are made. Oxygen free radicals, which can produce errors in cell maintenance and repair, are suspected culprits in several chronic diseases.

14. The decline in the immune system may cause aging, as it contributes to elderly people's increasing vulnerability to disease. As the thymus shrinks and production of both B and T cells decreases, the body becomes less able to fight off disease.

15. The maximum human life span may be fixed by a genetic clock that switches the aging process on at some point. The theory that genes cause aging is buttressed by evidence that several conditions that are accompanied by premature aging, such as Down syndrome and progeria, are caused by genetic abnormalities.

16. Further evidence for programmed senescence is found in the Hayflick limit. Even in ideal conditions, cells in the laboratory stop reproducing themselves after a certain number of divisions. This number decreases as the age of the cell donor increases.

CAN AGING BE STOPPED?

17. Secondary aging is under human control, but the possibility of an extended human life span has potential drawbacks as well as advantages. Average life expectancy is increasing in some nations and decreasing in others.

18. In parts of the former Soviet Union, Pakistan, and Peru, large numbers of people seem to live to be very old. Moderate diet, high altitude, hard work, and traditional respect for the aged characterize all three places. Although such reports are exaggerated, even in developed nations centenarians are increasing in number and vitality.

KEY TERMS

ageism (616)
gerontology (617)
demography (617)
dependency ratio (619)
young-old (620)
old-old (620)
oldest-old (620)
primary aging (620)
secondary aging (620)
cataracts (623)
glaucoma (623)
senile macular degeneration (623)
presbycusis (623)

elderspeak (624)
compression of morbidity (631)
wear-and-tear theory (632)
oxygen free radicals (634)
antioxidants (634)
B cells (634)
T cells (635)
maximum life span (636)
average life expectancy (637)
genetic clock (638)
Hayflick limit (638)

KEY QUESTIONS

1. How is ageism comparable to racism or sexism?

2. Why is the increasing number of people living past the age of 65 less of a problem than some people imagine it to be?

3. What is the difference between primary aging and secondary aging?

4. What changes occur in the sense organs in old age, and how can they be ameliorated?

5. Explain each of the factors that affect how long a person is sick before he or she dies.

6. Evaluate the validity of the wear-and-tear explanation for senescence.

7. In what ways do the cellular theories of aging seem plausible?

8. What is the relationship between the immune system and aging?

9. How do genes contribute to the length of life?

10. Describe an epigenetic explanation for the the aging process.

11. What conclusions can be drawn from Hayflick's research?

12. What are some of the characteristics of people who live to a very old age?

13. *In Your Experience* Describe someone you know who looks much younger or older than they actually are. Is this discrepancy a result of their health habits, their genes, or your own ageism?

Late Adulthood:
Cognitive Development

As we saw in the two earlier chapters on cognition (18 and 21), during early and middle adulthood some cognitive abilities increase, others wane, and some remain stable. By late adulthood, however, decline predominates. The questions to be answered involve when, to whom, and why such decline occurs, not whether it happens.

Physical impairments, perceptual declines, decreases in energy, and slowed reaction time take an increasing toll on cognitive competence. Yet this is not the entire story. Years of experience and accumulated knowledge can help the old person face intellectual challenges, perhaps with deepening wisdom. Cognition in late adulthood becomes even more multidirectional and multicontextual than before, as well as more complex.

One complexity, as you remember from the previous chapter, is that aging may be classified as optimal, usual, or impaired. Severe impairment (dementia) is discussed in this chapter, followed by aspects of optimal aging. First we examine the usual aging process.

CHANGES IN INFORMATION PROCESSING

Although most intellectual abilities increase or remain stable throughout early and middle adulthood (as documented in Chapter 21), beyond age 60 everyone experiences some decrements. In K. Warner Schaie's Seattle Longitudinal Study, most adults began to decline in all five primary mental abilities (verbal meaning, spatial orientation, inductive reasoning, number ability, and word fluency), particularly in subtests that measured numeric ability or processing speed (Schaie, 1996).

Other research agrees (Powell, 1994). No one thinks as quickly or extensively at age 80 as they did at age 40, even though no 80-year-old is exactly like another (variability is even greater in old age), and some elders are more intelligent than some much younger people.

Even in a 4-year longitudinal study, which began with almost 900 relatively high-functioning, community-dwelling people in their 70s, 80s, and 90s, variability increased with age. Individuals showed "both greater-than-expected deterioration as well as less-than-expected deterioration (including improvement). This diversity persisted when participants with dementia or extreme scores were excluded" (Christensen et al., 1999). No one, neither the typical nor the atypical, is completely predictable.

Why and how do these variations and decrements occur? An information-processing approach, which examines input, processing, and output—specifically, how the human mind senses, perceives, stores, and retrieves information—provides some answers.

Sensory Register

We saw in Chapter 2 that the *sensory register* (also called the *sensory store*) holds incoming sensory information for a split second after it is received. Senescence causes small declines in the sensitivity and power of the brain capacity of the sensory register, making an older person less adept at repeating words he or she has just heard or retaining the afterimage of a visual display just seen. In general, this physiological decline is relatively slight and can be overcome by such tactics as asking others to speak more slowly or by looking longer and more intently at crucial images (Albert & Moss, 1996; Fozard, 1990; Poon, 1985).

However, in order for information to register, it must cross the *sensory threshold*. That is, the sensory systems must be able to detect the relevant sensations, and this is where a significant decline in input can occur. As a result of the declines of the five senses outlined in Chapter 23, some older people cannot register certain information—such as the details of objects in a dimly lit room or of a soft conversation spoken against a noisy background—because they can no longer detect the sensory stimuli, Such deficits are usually progressive: Eventually, even loud conversation or the major features of a poorly lit room may be missed.

What Did He Say? No one hears as well as they once did, an especially serious problem for the older members of the audience in this meeting about Medicare. Because we all use our preconceptions to fill in the gaps created by sensory failures, we are likely to appear, and even to be, more stupid than we could be.

These sensory losses can have a notable effect. For example, in a study that compared the cognitive abilities of individuals ranging in age from 70 to 100, the differences in visual and auditory acuity accounted for half the variance in cognitive scores (Lindenberger & Baltes, 1994). In other words, if one person scored 20 points higher on a given cognitive test than another, typically about 10 of those points could be attributed to the better sight or hearing of the "smarter" person.

Thus, while the sensory register itself declines only a small amount, the declines in sensory acuity can be large. In fact, one expert suggests that "sensory function may be a fundamental index of cognitive aging," which means that the simplest way to predict how much an older person has aged intellectually is to find out how much their vision and hearing have declined (Park, 1999). This variation in sensory abilities (described in Chapter 23) is one significant reason for the overall variation in adult intelligence.

Working Memory

Once information is perceived, it must be placed in *working memory* in order to be utilized. As discussed in Chapter 2, working memory (also called *short-term memory*) has two interrelated functions:

- It temporarily stores information so that it can be consciously used.
- It processes information that is currently in the conscious mind, using integrative reasoning, mental calculations, the drawing of inferences, and other cognitive processes.

Read Their Faces Do you think that these five people, aged 72 to 80, are amazed and bewildered by the Internet? Not at all. They are members of the Silver Stringers, a computer group that meets in the Milano Senior Center in Melrose, Massachusetts. They are scanning one of the Web sites they have created.

❷ *Observational Quiz (see answer page 650): In what two ways is this group compensating for the visual deficits of late adulthood?*

This means that working memory functions both as a temporary information repository and as an analytical processor. In terms of both storage and processing, working-memory capacity is smaller in late adulthood than earlier. Older individuals have particular difficulty holding several items of new information in mind while analyzing them in complex ways, especially when distracting material appears. For example, if an experimenter gives adults something to remember, such as a list of objects or a passage of poetry, and then distracts them by having them count backward by threes from 150 to 0, older adults recall far less of the initial material than younger adults do (Parkin, 1993). Other research also finds that increasing the number of things an adult must attend to, or must ignore, reduces performance even more in late adulthood than earlier (Li et al., 1998; Maylor & Lavia, 1998).

In sum, increased demands on the information-processing capability, whether caused by the complexity of the task or by distractions, strain the working memory of older adults. Information just added to the mind may be forgotten before it reaches long-term memory. In fact, of all the aspects of information processing, working memory is the component that shows the most substantial declines with age (Briggs et al., 1999; Craik, 1999).

Long-Term Memory: Linking Input and Output

Cognitive performance depends not only on the specifics of input and the capacity of working memory but also on the knowledge base—that is, the information already stored in long-term memory. Since memory lapses are elderly people's most common complaint and since accumulated knowledge is their most obvious asset, assessing the advantages and disadvantages of changes in long-term memory is crucial.

Knowledge Base

As discussed in Chapter 2, the *knowledge base* is the storehouse of all the information ever put into memory. In theory, we could store somewhere in our brains everything that ever happened to us, from experiences in the womb to the words we overheard yesterday in a conversation between two strangers. In reality, selective attention and selective memory allow most of this material to be forgotten.

In fact, stored memory is far from perfect: Even some things that are remembered are actually misremembered, with important details

❶ *Answer to Observational Quiz (from page 649):* *The computer has an extra-large monitor, and all five people are wearing eyeglasses. Another feature, which you may not be able to see, is that their Web site has a large typeface. Together, such devices allow their cognitive abilities to remain unscathed.*

explicit memory   Memory that is easy to retrieve, usually with words. Most explicit memory involves consciously learned words, data, and concepts.

implicit memory   Unconscious or automatic memory that is usually stored via habits, emotional responses, routine procedures, and various sensations.

Does She Need Her Shopping List? A shopping list may help when explicit memory fails. If this shopper wrote a list and then misplaced it, however, she could scan the store shelves and imagine her kitchen cupboards. Implicit memory would probably enable her to choose almost every item she needed.

forgotten or confused. At every age, "it is the rule rather than the exception for people to change, add, and delete things from a remembered event" (Engel, 1999).

What happens to the knowledge base with old age? Does it increase, since the person has experienced more? Or does it fade? When groups of older and younger adults are asked to recall something specific—including long-stored information, such as a famous event in world history, or something more recently learned, such as the date and time for an upcoming doctor's appointment—the younger adults usually perform better. Indeed, a major review of the accumulated research concluded that long-term as well as short-term memory are diminished in older adults (Light, 1996).

However, this conclusion must be qualified, especially in reference to the usual declines of long-term memory. Some knowledge, under particular circumstances, is much easier for older adults to retrieve than other kinds. Accuracy also varies, with distortion much more likely to occur for certain kinds of memories.

Implicit and Explicit Memory

Memory takes at least two distinct forms, each originating in a different area of the brain (Mayford et al., 1996; Schacter & Tulving, 1994).

Explicit memory involves words, data, concepts, and the like. Most of what is in explicit memory was consciously learned, usually being linked with verbal information already in mind. Often explicit memory items are repeated and reviewed so that they can be recalled later. Partly because of this rehearsal, the contents of explicit memory can usually be retrieved in response to questioning.

Implicit memory is a kind of unconscious or automatic memory involving habits, emotional responses, routine procedures, and the senses. For the most part, the contents of implicit memory are never deliberately memorized for later recall. Items in implicit memory are, accordingly, difficult to retrieve on demand. However, they are retrievable in other circumstances.

For example, if you were asked to describe the distinctive facial features of your best friend in third grade, you might find the task nearly impossible—but you could immediately recognize that friend in a class photograph. When Jean Piaget asked people how to crawl, most of them gave the wrong verbal directions. (Is it hands and feet, or elbows and knees? Which parts and pairs of the four limbs move together?) However, almost everyone can get down on the floor and correctly demonstrate crawling, because that ability is in implicit, not explicit, memory (Piaget, 1970).

Implicit memory is much less vulnerable to age-related deficits than explicit memory is (Craik, 1999). Indeed, on some tests of implicit memory, older adults who are intellectually sharp overall show no evidence of decline (Cherry & Stadler, 1995; Fastenau et al., 1996; Mitchell, 1993). This is partly related to automaticity, a concept mentioned in Chapters 12 and 21. Once a behavior becomes well learned, it becomes automatic and routine, easy to access when needed in context but beyond the verbal command of explicit memory.

The difference between explicit and implicit memory has been demonstrated (Howard & Howard, 1992). In a series of trials, subjects were told to expect an asterisk to appear in one of four boxes on a video screen in front of them. As soon as they saw it, they were to push a button under that box. Although they were not warned, in each series the asterisks appeared in a particular sequence, such that the same pattern was repeated 10 times. The older and younger adults recognized the patterns equally quickly. This was measured by how much faster they pushed the buttons toward the end of the trials (when they could anticipate where the asterisk would appear next) than at the beginning, before implicit memory had allowed them to perceive the patterns.

This age equality in implicit memory was not evident in explicit memory. When subjects were asked "What was the pattern?" older adults were less likely to describe the sequence correctly than younger adults. Thus, the memory for the pattern was in the older adults' implicit knowledge base but they did not readily recall it in response to explicit questions.

In everyday terms, this difference in implicit- and explicit-memory competence might be exhibited in an older adult's ability to remember how to perform a particular task—from preparing a complicated recipe to changing a flat tire—but inability to describe each action and decision as well as a younger person could. Most traditional long-term memory tests focus on explicit memory, failing to take into account the substantial implicit memory that an older adult might have (see A Life-Span View).

Other Aspects of Cognition

Memory is the springboard for cognition. New learning depends on working memory, and demonstration of intelligence depends on long-term memory. However, other aspects of cognition are also important. The ability to direct and regulate cognitive functioning, a task carried out by the **control processes** (also called *executive function*), may be the reason for variations in cognition. Control processes include storage mechanisms, retrieval strategies, selective attention, and logical analysis. In short, control processes are the ways people use their intellectual powers.

As with most other aspects of information processing, older adults seem less efficient at managing control processes. In particular, in their decision making, they seem not to gather and consider all relevant data. They are likely to rely on prior knowledge, general principles, and rules of thumb, applying them even when the specifics require additional information or new approaches.

Given a diagnosis of cancer, older adults are more likely to arrive at a treatment decision without getting a second opinion or seeking further information on medical options, benefits, and risks. This is a "top-down" strategy, using deductive rather than inductive reasoning (Meyer et al., 1995). Similar results are found for other medical decisions: Age correlates with less effective control processes (Zwair, 1999).

control processes That part of the information-processing system which regulates the analysis and flow of information. Memory and retrieval strategies, selective attention, and rules or strategies for problem solving are all useful control processes.

LONG AGO, BUT NOT FORGOTTEN

Long-term memory for past episodes may seem particularly impressive when an elderly person describes sensory details of an experience that occurred 50 or even 75 years ago. However, definitive research on long-term memory is almost impossible, because we cannot verify personal recollections with a large, representative sample of adults. One 80-year-old may describe her childhood in detail, and another may recount the story of his youthful courtship in a compelling narrative; but unless another informant confirms each specific recollection, the memories might be fantasies or, at least, inaccurate. What if some details are proven false? This would not prove that long-term memory fades markedly with age: Many younger adults cannot recollect events that happened last year, or even yesterday, with total accuracy.

In fact, for adults of any age, events that happened between ages 10 and 30 are remembered better than events earlier or later than that. Further, people of all ages are more likely to remember *what* happened and *how they felt* about it ("I was hit by a car," "I was put in jail," "I was frightened") than exactly *where* and *when* the particular event occurred. Especially common is **source amnesia:** not remembering who or what was the source of a specific fact, idea, or snippet of conversation (Craik, 1999).

Cross-sectional comparisons of people's memories of public events or facts is one way to assess long-term memory. Such a study was done for people's memories of the verdict in the O.J. Simpson murder trial; that study found that older and younger subjects were equally likely to have good, but not perfect, memories (Bluck et al., 1999). But the Simpson trial had taken place less than a year before the study. What about memory for events that occurred 5 or more years previously?

source amnesia   The inability to remember who or what was the source of a specific fact, idea, or snippet of conversation.

Asking about long-ago public events gives an advantage to adults of one cohort or another. For example, asking for t he names of the heads of state at the Yalta Conference favors people who were politically aware in 1945; asking for the names of the four Beatles gives an advantage to those who were teenagers in the 1960s; and asking for the names of the stars of the NBA in 1995 gives an edge to those who are relatively young, from the United States, and male. (If you are not in this category, you may not know that NBA stands for National Basketball Association.) Further, each of these examples favors people with particular interests—politics, music, and sports, respectively—and each cohort and age tends to have different interests. Overall, then, no test questions can equitably compare the long-term memory of the average 70-year-old, the average 40-year-old, and the average 15-year-old.

Another approach to assessing long-term memory is to measure knowledge that was learned in high school. Studies of school knowledge have shown neither remarkable durability nor significant deterioration in the old (Salthouse, 1991). One classic study compared memory of Spanish that had been studied in late adolescence but used very little in the years since. As might be expected, young adults who had studied Spanish within the past 3 years remembered it best. Thereafter, however, the amount of forgetting was very gradual, with the older persons who had studied Spanish 50 years earlier remembering about 80 percent of what the young adults who had studied it 5 years earlier remembered. The crucial variable was not how long ago the language had been studied, but how well the person had learned it in the first place: Those who had received As in Spanish 50 years earlier outscored those who had received Cs just 12 months before (Bahrick, 1984). This has interesting implications for students. If we want to remember something for the rest of our lives, we had better learn it well now.

One example relates to the tip-of-the-tongue phenomenon, when a person feels on the verge of retrieving some bit of information from memory—the name of a person or object, for example—but can't actually bring the information to mind. The tip-of-the-tongue experience becomes more common with age, beginning as early as the late 30s (Burke et al., 1991; Heine et al., 1999).

More to the point, strategies for tip-of-the-tongue retrieval worsen with age. Trying to recall the name of a childhood acquaintance, for example, a young adult might use effective strategies such as running through an alphabetical mental checklist or trying to associate the person in question with a specific context. In contrast, an older adult is more likely to say, "I forget the name" and then, "It will come to me," or, more ominously, "My memory is failing."

Where Are They Now? How well adults could answer questions about these three bands would depend largely on what cohort the adults belonged to and on how interested they were in pop music. This obvious fact points to the difficulty of constructing test items that equitably assess long-term memory in people of different ages.

❷ *Observational Quiz (see answer page 656): What are the names of these three bands? (The drum in the middle photo makes it too easy, so can you name all four members of that group?)*

Similar results have been found for long-term memory of basic math. Here older cohorts surpass younger cohorts, not because their fluid numerical ability is better (it is not) or because they themselves are as good at math as they were (they are not), but because their long-term memory for math learned conscientiously in the days when rapid recitation of the multiplication tables was a daily event compensates for their current deficits (Schaie, 1996).

Overall, then, memory is somewhat weaker in the elderly than the young, but when some particular kinds of memory are assessed, the elderly can hold their own. Much depends on the specifics of *what* is to be learned and remembered, *how*, and *when.* One example is a "lady of 100 years old who could still play (and win) Scrabble in three languages, even though she had marked difficulty remembering what she just had for lunch" (Parkin, 1993). Scrabble playing is a valuable skill that a few people cherish, but most do not. In a well-functioning human community, someone will know about Yalta, someone else will know about the Beatles, and someone else will know about professional basketball—and they will listen to one another when relevant and contribute their own expertise at other times.

If anyone wants to learn how to do something (implicit memory) that is rarely done today, such as chop wood, make a pie crust, or fix a broken clock, then watching an older person perform the task is a useful method. Certainly if younger people want to understand things that happened before they were born, or wish to learn about topics that they themselves never knew anything about, then asking an older adult is a good strategy.

❷ **Especially for Busy People:** When does "speed reading" make sense?

REASONS FOR AGE-RELATED CHANGES

Declines in cognitive functioning may be caused by primary aging, a consequence of inevitable neurophysiological and biological changes, or by secondary aging that is not necessarily associated with age. Or the causes may not be physiological at all. They may be psychosocial, including disparaging self-perceptions and diminished opportunities for learning. They may even simply reflect the specific techniques that scientists use to measure cognitive functioning. Let's look closely at all these sources of age-related changes in cognitive functioning, beginning with psychosocial factors, then examining problems with laboratory research, and concluding with a discussion of changes in the brain.

Stereotyping

For a person of any age, sex, or race, being stereotyped does most harm when the individual internalizes the prejudice and reacts with helplessness, self-doubt, or misplaced anger. This may happen when the elderly expect to lose their intellectual power. That is precisely what they expect, especially when assessing their own problems with memory (see Figure 24.1).

Under the influence of expectations, people aged 50 to 70 tend to overestimate the memory skills they had in young adulthood, selectively forgetting their earlier forgetfulness! As a result, older people are not very accurate in estimating their current memory losses, typically believing that the decline is greater than it actually is (Hanninen et al., 1994; Taylor et al., 1992). In fact, some research finds no correlation at all between an older person's self-assessment of his or her memory ability and an objective measure of it (Smith et al., 1996).

For the minority of the elderly who are in the early stages of senility, underestimating and even denial of memory loss is a problem, as we will describe later. More common is exaggeration of memory deficit. This in itself can create a loss of confidence that impairs memory (as every student who has panicked about an exam can testify). Confidence is further eroded when others interpret an older person's hesitant effort to recall as a sign of impaired memory and react accordingly. Elderspeak (as explained in Chapter 23), simplified content, and hesitancy to challenge or argue all lead to cognitive losses.

Are the aged aware that they handicap themselves? Probably not. But in one experiment, words that expressed either positive or negative ageism were flashed on a screen. The words disappeared so quickly that the subjects could not say what they were; in fact, the subjects didn't even know they had seen the words. Nonetheless, older adults performed better on cognitive tests after they saw words that reflected positive stereotypes (such as *guidance, wise, alert, sage, accomplished, learned, improving, creative, enlightened, insightful,* and *astute*) than after words that reflected negative stereotypes (such as *Alzheimer's, decline, dependent, senile, misplaces, dementia, dying, forgets, confused, decrepit, incompetent,* and *diseased*) (Levy, 1996).

When the same experiment was repeated with younger adults, no significant differences in test scores appeared. Apparently, negative stereotypes do damage only if a person identifies with them. The researcher concludes:

Two messages emerge from this research. The pessimistic one is that older individuals' memory capabilities can be damaged by self-stereotypes that are derived from a prevalent and insidious stereotype

Figure 24.1 Older People's Self-Ratings of Memory Decline. More than 400 community-dwelling Minnesotans, aged 55 to 97, were asked "How would you rate your memory in terms of the kinds of problems you have?" Very few older people rated their memory problems as major. Most acknowledged only "some minor problems" (#4), and about 10 percent of every age group believed they had "no problems" with memory (#7). None of the oldest considered memory a major problem. In data not shown here, the oldest were more likely to believe their memories had improved or stayed the same over the past 5 years, and the youngest group were more likely to have noticed recent decline. Perhaps, like gray hairs, memory problems are most noticeable, and frightening, when they first appear.

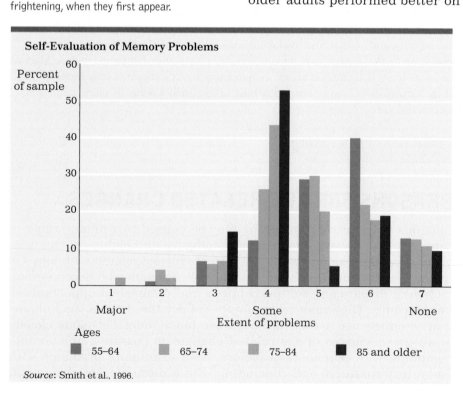

Self-Evaluation of Memory Problems

Percent of sample (vertical axis)
Extent of problems (horizontal axis): 1 Major ... 4 Some ... 7 None

Ages:
- 55–64
- 65–74
- 75–84
- 85 and older

Source: Smith et al., 1996.

about aging. Specifically, the stereotype that memory decline is inevitable can become a self-fulfilling prophecy. This research also offers an optimistic message. The findings indicate that memory decline is not inevitable. In fact, the studies show that memory performance can be enhanced in old age. [Levy, 1996]

The influence of stereotyping is further emphasized by a study that looked at cognitive decrements in two groups of people who are somewhat protected from ageist messages: mainland Chinese, who traditionally venerate the old, and the American deaf, whose lack of hearing reduces their exposure to ageist stereotypes (Levy & Langer, 1994). First, researchers assessed attitudes. Hearing Americans had the least positive views of aging, Chinese had the most positive, and deaf Americans were about midway between. Then they compared memory differences between old and young individuals from China, from the deaf community in North America, and from the hearing North American population. For hearing Americans, the memory gap between old and young was twice as great as that for deaf Americans and five times as great as that for the Chinese. It seems clear that negative cultural attitudes lead directly to impaired thinking in the elderly—quite apart from the effects of any neurological deficits caused by primary or secondary aging.

Problems with Laboratory Research

Some research procedures exaggerate cognitive declines because their designs inadvertently "stack the deck" against older people. In the typical laboratory experiment, subjects are given items to memorize within a specific time and then are tested on the accuracy and speed of their retrieval. Memory tests traditionally use items that are fairly meaningless, perhaps a string of unrelated words or numbers. Similarly, tests of intelligence are designed to be culture-neutral, so they, too, use very general—often vague—items.

Selecting such abstract measures places older persons at a disadvantage, because it eliminates **priming,** in which one event, clue, or past accomplishment is used to make it easier to remember the next one. Most experiments are constructed to exclude spontaneous priming, depriving older adults of a useful cognitive tool.

In other words, many tests focus on abstract explicit memory in order to get a "purer" measure of older adults' memory skills. But in so doing, they necessarily exclude implicit and contextual memory, as well as any benefit that a large knowledge base might provide. What some purists consider contamination (using familiar cues) might actually create a much more realistic and relevant measure (Smith et al., 1998).

Further, laboratory experiments do not reflect differences in context and motivation. Young college students are accustomed to learning material that is not immediately relevant to their lives. They are motivated and practiced at working effectively in an unfamiliar room to attain high scores on exams, even when they think they will never need that particular chemistry formula or history date again. Older adults, by contrast, may question the purpose of such learning. If they are conscious of ageist stereotypes, they may decide that the purpose is to prove them stupid, may expect not to do well, and may therefore not try very hard—allowing themselves the face-saving excuse "I didn't really care" or "It didn't really matter."

Clutter or Control? This man uses notes, photographs, and objects to help him remember, not just what he must do, but also what he likes to think about. Many older people are attached to specific personal memorabilia—a warning to any younger person who is tempted to organize Grandpa's things.

priming   Using one event, clue, or past accomplishment to make it easier to remember another one.

Changes in the Brain

Thus far, we have stressed that people are ageist and that ageism is unfair. That much is true, but those excuses do not tell the whole story. One scholar stresses the many ways the elderly cope with aging and the variability of their deficits. But he also explains:

> It is fashionable to dismiss as obsolete views of aging that bear connotations of loss, constraint, and acceptance and to propagate an expansive concept of active, "successful" aging that is modeled on ideals of youthful vigor and attractiveness. Neither traditional "deficit views" of aging nor their optimistic counterparts, however, can do justice to the multifaceted and to some extent even counterintuitive picture of development in later life that has emerged since the late 1980s from research on resilience and vulnerability in the elderly.
>
>   . . . the biological, social, and psychological processes of aging involve a multitude of aversive and irreversible changes in many domains of life and functioning. The fading of physiological and adaptive resources is an outstanding feature of biological aging. [Brandtstadter, 1999]

Let us look now at the specific impact that biological aging has on cognitive functioning.

Fewer Neurons, Slower Reactions

The brain in late adulthood is notably smaller than in early adulthood, losing at least 5 percent of its weight and 10 percent of its overall volume (Coffey et al., 1992). Much of this shrinkage is due to the fact that neurons die throughout life—and die at an increasing rate after about age 60. Although the precise effects of this accumulating cell death were not previously understood, experts assumed that "it could cause rather dramatic declines in cognitive abilities in the normal, healthy elderly. Additionally, it was assumed that these changes were inevitable and almost impossible to reverse" (Wickelgren, 1996). This is no longer assumed.

One brain change cannot be denied, however. The brain's communication processes become markedly slower beginning in the late 50s. The most obvious measure of this slowdown is reaction time: In every type of laboratory test (such as pushing a button in response to a light flashing on), the elderly react much more slowly than younger adults.

This brain slowdown is universal and age-related, and therefore part of primary aging. It can be traced partly to reduced production of the neurotransmitters—including dopamine, glucamate, acetylcholine, and serotonin—that allow nerve impulses to jump across the synapse from one neuron to another. Other aspects of the brain that decrease with age include the total volume of neural fluid, the speed of the cerebral blood flow, and the activation of various parts of the cortex—all of which affect reaction time (Albert & Moss, 1996; Glady et al., 1994; Scheibel, 1996).

Too Fast to Comprehend

How does speed affect cognitive competence? Is a slow thinker necessarily a less intelligent thinker? Not always, but quickness is related to brightness. Working memory is bound to shrink if processing slows down. If a person cannot process information or ideas quickly, then he or she cannot think about many facts or ideas at once, cannot sequentially analyze information, and cannot fully take in new information as soon as it arrives, because earlier information is still being processed. If you have ever complained about information overload or said, "Don't everyone talk at once," you understand this problem.

❶ *Answer to Observational Quiz (from page 653):* *The Tommy Dorsey Orchestra, the Beatles (from left to right: Paul McCartney, George Harrison, Ringo Starr, John Lennon), Pearl Jam.*

The result is that when thinking becomes slower, it also becomes simpler and shallower because important information gets lost (Salthouse, 1993). This hypothesis has been substantiated by various researchers who, in testing adults' ability to learn new materials, allowed adults of all ages additional time to study whatever material was to be learned.

Not surprisingly, extra time aided the cognitive performance of older subjects—but it helped the cognitive performance of younger subjects even more (Byron & Luszcz, 1996). In other words, the aged need more time simply to reach the level of younger adults, but if the younger adults are required to spend more time, they will further surpass their elders because they will learn better.

Brain Compensation

Researchers now recognize that intellectual activity is not directly related to size, weight, or number of brain cells, except in cases of extreme malformation, damage, or disease. In fact, when brain cells die, other cells routinely take over their function. In addition, the nerve fibers called dendrites (see Chapter 5) continue to grow, and the death of certain neurons allows the connections between neurons to become more extensive. This compensation might allow older adults to think as well as they once did, with the additional dendrites making up for the loss of neurons (Cotman & Neeper, 1996; Scheibel, 1996).

An astonishing recent discovery is that stem cells in the brains of humans (as well as in lower animals) can create new neurons (Barinaga, 1999). The rate of such cell creation is slower than the rate of cell death, so brain senescence is still relevant. It is not yet known how many new neurons the adult human brain produces, or under what circumstances. However, the discovery that it occurs at all shatters the old idea that human brains merely disintegrate, never rejuvenate, with age.

Another hopeful note is that the extent of cell death and brain shrinkage varies in different areas of the brain. Less loss occurs in the cerebral cortex (the "gray matter" where thinking occurs) than in lower portions of the brain (Albert & Moss, 1996). Even slowness is not so much a deficit as a delay: An older adult just needs more time to find the right answer.

Nevertheless, compensation is limited, because slower reactions are inevitable with age. This means that slower cognition is inevitable as well.

COGNITION IN DAILY LIFE

Most older adults acknowledge that one of the most salient changes associated with aging is cognitive decline, particularly memory failure. Thus, in a study of community-dwelling Australians aged 55 and older, only 29 percent reported no memory decline (Jorm et al., 1994). In the study already mentioned of community-dwelling Minnesotans between the ages of 55 and 97, only 12 percent claimed to have no memory problems (Smith et al., 1996).

Memory Losses in Daily Life

Surprisingly few older adults consider memory problems a significant handicap in their daily lives. They worry about memory lapses

- when they first appear at the beginning of late adulthood
- if they think senility is beginning

⊙ Response for Busy People (from page 653): Faster is not always better, and people who believe a stereotype and develop research to prove it often find what they expect. Therefore, take a skeptical view of any claim that is made about speed reading.

LABORATORY RESEARCH AND EVERYDAY LIFE

Since one of the problems with memory in late adulthood is that old people don't use some of the memory tricks that researchers have discovered, a logical approach to improving memory is to teach those strategies. In fact, however, this effort to improve control processes does not necessarily help (Cavanaugh, 1999).

In an experiment that highlighted the limitations of laboratory research, adults of various ages were taught a memory technique called the method of loci, in which the person creates a mental picture of bizarre locations in which the items to be remembered are "placed." Many of the older adults quietly resisted using the new method, even though the laboratory experiment required it and, within the narrow confines of the research conditions, the strategy ensured better recall. Instead, the older adults, to the detriment of their memory scores, used their own memory strategies or tried to combine theirs with the new technique. Half the gap between the memory scores of the older subjects and the younger ones could be traced directly to this noncompliance rather than to age-related decline (Verhaeghen & Marcoen, 1996).

Another series of experiments on tip-of-the-tongue forgetting began with three groups of subjects aged 18–24, 60–74, and 80–92 (Heine et al., 1999). All were relatively well educated: The young adults were usually in their junior year of college, and most of the older subjects were college gradu-

ates. None had serious health problems, such as a history of strokes or serious head injury, that might affect cognition.

Each subject was presented with 112 short definitions of uncommon words and was asked to say what the word was. At any time if they thought they knew the word but could not quite recall it, they were supposed to report a tip-of-the-tongue event. If they did not give the right answer immediately, they were given a related word as a clue (e.g., *salamander* for *chameleon*) or a spelling clue (e.g., c_ _ _ _ _ _ _ _). If they still hadn't gotten it, they were given a multiple-choice question, with the right word as well as three other words that were similar in meaning or spelling. Thus, for the word *grout*, the three foils were *glue, plaster,* and *glair.* Not surprisingly, almost everyone got the questions right eventually. The youngest and the very oldest got 84 percent correct; the 60- to 74-year-olds got 91 percent correct.

However, the researchers were particularly interested in how often the subjects reported tip-of-the-tongue phenomena. Here the oldest reported them most frequently and took longest to say the right answer (see Table 24.1). This was expected: The elderly were slowest and most forgetful, although they were equal to or better than the young in how many right answers they eventually guessed.

To learn whether laboratory evidence would be confirmed by real life the experimenters then asked the same subjects to keep a diary for 4 weeks. They were told to detail every tip-of-

Otherwise, they take memory problems in stride. Only 3 percent of the elderly surveyed in the Australian study thought that they had "major" problems with memory (Jorm et al., 1994). Older people readily report some problems, such as difficulty remembering names and phone numbers, but they also think that they are better than the young at remembering to pay bills, take medicine on time, and keep appointments (Cohen, 1993). In fact, they may be right (Park, 1999; Rendell & Thompson, 1999).

One classic study was designed to mimic the memory demands of daily life (Moscovitch, 1982). Older and younger adults (all living busy lives) were asked to call an answering service every day for 2 weeks at a designated time chosen by them. This assignment was selected partly because remembering appointments is something everyone must do in daily life. Only 20 percent of the younger adults remembered to make every call, but 90 percent of the older adults did.

Why the dramatic difference? Younger adults, it seems, were likely to put excessive trust in their memories ("I have an internal alarm that always goes off at the right time") and therefore were less likely to use mnemonic devices to jog their memories. Older adults, with a heightened awareness of the unreliability of memory, did use reminders, such as a note on the telephone or a shoe near the door.

The experimenters then attempted to increase forgetting. They required only one call per week at a time that the researchers designated

table **24.1**

	Laboratory Experiment			Real Life		
	Average number of tip-of-the-tongue experiences	Percentage eventually correct	Average time to guess correct answer	Average number of tip-of-the-tongue experiences	Average number of "pop-ups"	Percentage eventually correct
Young (aged 18–24)	23	100%	12 seconds	5	1.8	91%
Young-old (aged 60–74)	27	100%	13 seconds	7	3.6	95%
Old-old (aged 80–92)	33	100%	14½ seconds	9	5	98%

Source: Heine et al., 1999.

the-tongue experience they had in real life, describing what it was and what they did about it (e.g., ask someone else, use a memory strategy, or simply wait and hope the right answer popped up). The table shows that older people reported more tip-of-the-tongue events than younger adults but used a memory strategy less often. Instead they usually just waited for the right answer to "pop up." As expected, they had a bigger problem and a less effective solution. But note that older adults eventually remembered the forgotten name or word 98 percent of the time—more often than the two younger groups.

Four conclusions are apparent from this and several other studies:

- Mental processes slow down with age.
- The elderly do show memory declines.
- The elderly are less likely to use memory strategies.
- Even without strategies, memory in late adulthood is not as weak as anticipated or expected. [Cavanaugh, 1999; Hertzog et al., 1999]

The first two or three of these conclusions are not surprising. However, the fourth one has an interesting implication: Don't teach memory strategies to the elderly unless they want to learn them, not only because they may not use them but also because they may not *need* to use them.

and they made the subjects promise not to use any visible reminders. About half of both groups, old and young, failed to call at the appointed time. More old people would probably have forgotten, but some of them bent the rules, using a memory-priming measure (such as carrying the phone number in plain sight in their wallets), despite instructions to avoid visible reminders. One of the researchers concluded:

> With more effort, we are sure we can bring old people's memory to its knees . . . but that hardly seems to be the point of this research. The main lesson of this venture into the dangerous real world is that old people have learned from experience what we have so consistently shown in the laboratory—that their memory is getting somewhat poorer—and they have structured their environment to compensate. [Moscovitch, 1982]

Many other researchers have assessed memory in older adults, not only in traditional experiments but also in more novel experiments designed to accommodate the special abilities and needs of the elderly (see the Research Report). Almost invariably, the less artificial the circumstances, the better an older person remembers. As one series of studies concludes, "Older adults, in their everyday life, are capable of accurate and reliable performance of important tasks" (Rendell & Thompson, 1999).

Slowing Down the Slowdown

Older adults are slow to abandon old techniques and try new ones. They take longer to access information from their knowledge base. These facts are usually irrelevant in daily life, especially in familiar situations. As a noted scientist explains, the decisions that people make in everyday life are usually complex enough that

> decision time is controlled more by "appropriate programming" that uses our brains efficiently than by raw speed of information processing. . . . In most cases involving everyday activity, the young–old contrast should not be thought of as a contrast between a fast and a slow computer, but as a contrast between a fast computer with a limited library of programs and a slow computer with a large library. [Hunt, 1993]

As we saw in Chapter 21, a hallmark of successful aging is the capacity to compensate strategically for intellectual declines associated with aging—what Paul Baltes and his colleagues call "selective optimization with compensation" (Baltes, 1998). Using mnemonic devices and written reminders, allowing additional time for problem solving, repeating instructions that might be confusing, focusing only on meaningful cognitive tasks and ignoring those that are irrelevant—all are compensatory methods that many older adults use to optimize their strengths. These techniques keep the cognitive demands of daily life well within their intellectual capacity.

The general principle that compensation is possible is comforting when we consider that the number and proportion of elderly are increasing in virtually every nation, with those over age 85 the fastest-growing group. Even in the difficult circumstances of a nursing home, understanding the cognitive potential of the infirm elderly can bring about changes for the better in practice and policy (see the Changing Policy box).

Encouraging residents of nursing homes to think for themselves, as described in the box, is irrelevant for the 95 percent of those over age 65 who are not in nursing homes. However, study after study suggests that older people's attitude about themselves is a powerful influence on their cognition. It begins with their active pursuit of their physical health.

Although a slowing of thinking processes seems inevitable with age, it can actually often be halted or even reversed. For example, regular exercise improves blood flow in the brain, aiding cognition in many ways, including faster reaction time and improved memory. Exercise has these effects not only because blood flow is faster at the moment but also because the uptake of neurotransmitters and the branching of dendrites are accelerated (Cotman & Neeper, 1996).

In addition, cognitive stimulation, as when a person is challenged to understand and analyze new experiences, can cause dendrites to develop new connections. Marion Diamond, a leading neurobiologist, has found that when healthy rats are kept in enriched environments, such as large crates with many toys, aging does not reduce the number of cells in the cerebral cortex to any appreciable degree, and new dendrite connections develop. The old brain is still sufficiently "plastic" (that is, flexible) that new learning can occur. Diamond (1988) concludes:

> The results demonstrating cortical plasticity in the very aged animal contain both caution and promise for our aging human population. They caution us against entering into inactive life styles that reduce the sensory stimuli reaching our brains, and they provide hope, if we continue to stimulate our brains, for healthy mental activity throughout a lifetime.

PRACTICAL COMPETENCE IN A NURSING HOME

Research presents a fairly optimistic picture of cognitive functioning in late adulthood: Despite age-related declines in memory and abstract reasoning, older adults can continue to manage all the demands of everyday life. This picture is based largely on studies of healthy, well-educated older adults living independently in the community. Such adults are chosen as research subjects because they are cooperative, free of serious health problems, and capable of giving informed consent. But they may also provide an overly rosy view of cognitive functioning in old age.

Consider another group—the elderly residents of a nursing home. Quite clearly, their living conditions often do not foster the kinds of practical competencies that are experienced by older adults living independently. In fact "staff are trained in routinized delivery of physical and health care to residents that restricts opportunities for autonomous self-directed behavior" (Zavit et al., 1998).

The practical difficulties of running a large institution such as a hospital or nursing home mean that passive, dependent, and predictable behavior is encouraged more than independent or innovative actions. For example, residents who do not perform their own personal care or hygiene—who, say, just sit staring at their food when it is placed before them—are likely to receive help and attention from the staff. By contrast, those who manage for themselves are likely to be ignored.

Similarly, those who stick to the nursing home's schedules and routines are much more likely to be praised than are those who, against the rules, attempt to get a midnight snack, or want to go to a store on a day not designated as shopping day, or try to keep a pet in their room. When older patients ask for an explanation of some medicine or therapy or, worse, refuse to take a prescribed pill, they may be labeled as mentally impaired and disruptive and will be treated accordingly. (Interestingly, younger adults follow the doctor's orders precisely only about half the time, with noncompliance typically regarded as a sign of mental alertness, not defiance.) One review sums up, with frightening clarity, the conditions that prevailed in many nursing homes:

The individual . . . gives up control over the most mundane daily activities, when to sleep, wake, visit, perform toileting activities, bathe, and shop. The patient is exposed to infantilization and numbing bureaucratic and health routines that are of obscure purpose due to the invariably poor communication and misinformation given to placate the patient. Information is withheld or distorted under the assumption that it will not be understood or well-tolerated by the patient. [White & Janson, 1986]

All these contextual factors led directly to lack of intellectual stimulation and, consequently, to intellectual decline.

Declines in cognitive competence are intensified, if, in the name of protection from self-harm, the patient is subjected to physical restraints. As one report explains:

Far from protecting patients from harm, restraints inflict it. Physical risks include bed sores, infections, reduced circulation, muscle weakness, pneumonia, loss of appetite, and incontinence caused by immobility. . . . Psychosocial risks, more difficult to quantify, include humiliation, fear of abandonment, impairment to self-image, agitation, panic, and disorientation. [Collopy et al., 1991]

Research has found that when nursing-home residents are encouraged to manage on their own, many take more control over their activities, developing their own schedules and social lives as well as becoming more responsible for their daily care. Such an approach is called "therapeutic risk taking," allowing patients the freedom to make mistakes in order to preserve their physical and mental health (Aronson, 1994).

Some of the specifics are amazingly simple, from allowing the nursing-home resident to have a plant to explaining the reason for various medications. The more complex measures include allowing family members to visit at any time; allowing residents to have their own rooms, furniture, and personal effects; scheduling meals when a person wants them and serving what they want (which might be beer with lunch, or coffee after dinner—both routinely consumed by younger adults but almost always forbidden in nursing homes); and creating a setting that fosters interaction (not a series of rooms down a long hall, but living areas with accessible refrigerators).

All these measures foster intellectual development as well as psychosocial health. The most amazing evidence comes from Sweden, where elderly people in the early stages of dementia live in group homes of just five to seven residents, each with his or her own personal effects and keys. The residents care for themselves and each other and generally experience a much slower decline than people in traditional nursing homes (Malmberg & Zarit, 1993).

Policy is changing, as are architecture (homelike, not hospital-like) and staffing (not just medical caregivers), although improvements are not yet evident in every institution. If we want the oldest-old to retain their intellectual capacity, new designs for nursing homes are required (Baltes & Horgas, 1997).

"Given that AD is a condition involving multiple genetic, environmental, and pathological factors, there may be many therapeutic strategies that will be useful for delaying or slowing dementia" (Vickers et al., 2000).

Stages of Alzheimer's Disease

Alzheimer's disease usually runs through a progressive course of identifiable stages, beginning with general forgetfulness and ending in total mindlessness.

First Stage   Absentmindedness about recent events or newly acquired information, particularly the names of people and places, marks the first stage. Typically, a person in the first stage of the disease will put something away and shortly thereafter be unable to remember where it is. The person may also be unable to recall people's names after being introduced to them.

In this early stage, most people recognize that they have a memory problem and try to cope with it, writing down names, addresses, appointments, shopping lists, and other items much more often than they once did. This first state is often indistinguishable from *benign senescent forgetfulness,* the normal decline in explicit memory, described earlier (Powell, 1994).

Failure to remember a common word is a notable sign. One woman in the early stages described the problem:

> There is embarrassment when I want to say "ocean" and I can't think of the word. It depends on how comfortable I am with the person I'm talking with. Then I can ask, "What's that big water thing?" and they'll guess, "The ocean?" Then I say, "Oh yeah." [Synder, 1999]

Many people never progress beyond this first stage of dementia, remaining somewhat forgetful for the rest of their lives. On autopsy, many plaques and tangles are apparent in their cortexes, which confirms that they indeed had early Alzheimer's disease.

Second Stage   Confusion becomes more generalized, with noticeable deficits in concentration and short-term memory, in the second stage. Speech becomes aimless and repetitious, vocabulary is much more limited, and words are mixed up. A person might say "tunnel" when he means "bridge," for instance.

Someone at stage two is likely to read a newspaper article and forget it completely the next moment, or to put down her keys or glasses and within seconds have no idea where they could be. If the person is suspicious by nature, he may accuse others of having stolen what he himself has mislaid and forgotten. Then, "in the firm conviction of having been robbed, the patient starts hiding everything, but promptly forgets the hiding place. This reinforces the belief that thieves are at work" (Wirth, 1993).

Such personality changes tend to be longstanding traits, which become more pronounced the less they are controlled by rational thought. A person given to tidiness may become compulsively neat; a person with a quick temper may begin to display explosive rages; a person who is asocial may become even more withdrawn.

Memory loss in the second stage is sufficiently severe that many people forget they have a memory problem. Typical is the case of a man who, in stage one, began to run into financial problems because of his fading memory. In stage two, he was forced to turn over all his financial decisions to others, having no responsibility beyond putting his signature on documents. When asked if he was depressed, he replied that he didn't have any reason to be. He knew that he had had problems in the past, but now, he said, "I sign the papers. I'm in charge" (Foley, 1992).

Third Stage Memory loss becomes truly dangerous as well as debilitating in the third stage. Individuals can no longer manage their basic daily needs. They may take to eating a single food, such as bread, exclusively, or they may forget to eat entirely. Often they fail to dress properly, or at all, going out barefoot in winter or walking about the neighborhood naked. They are likely to turn away from a lighted stove or a hot iron and forget about it for the rest of the day, creating a fire hazard. They may go out on some errand and then lose track not only of the errand but also of the way back home. And they would not be able to ask neighbors for help because they wouldn't recognize them.

For some people with Alzheimer's, visual recognition is a major problem. The particular part of the brain that looks at an object and realizes that it is a *K,* a hat, or a person may become tangled before other parts, rendering the person more helpless and seemingly more incompetent than the overall decrements would indicate.

A Moment of Pleasure Can you live in the moment, as Alzheimer's forces these elderly patients to do? Musician Alicea Lewis believes that music activates part of the brain that does not require short-term memory or long-term planning, so she volunteers to play and sing in the Nashville Health Clinic.

Fourth Stage Patients need full-time care in the fourth stage. They cannot care for themselves or respond normally to others, sometimes becoming irrationally angry or paranoid. At the end, they can no longer put even a few words together to communicate. They cannot recognize even their closest loved ones. This is not necessarily because they do not remember them at all, but because the part of the brain that recognizes objects and faces has further deteriorated. A man might demand to see his wife but refuse to believe that the person before him is, indeed, his wife.

Fifth Stage People become completely mute in the fifth stage, failing to respond with any action or emotion at all. The final stage is death, which may come 10 to 15 years after stage one (Fromholt & Bruhn, 1998).

The Current Outlook

As people increasingly survive to old age, more and more will develop Alzheimer's disease, eventually living in a state of total dependency at the fourth and fifth stages. Thus, the victims of Alzheimer's disease include not only the patient but also the patient's family, who typically are the main source of care until the last stages of the disease. Compounding the demands of caregiving for family members are the requirements to express understanding and patience with a person who seems in good health but who cannot act or think yet can lash out in frustrated anger at a caregiver. It is not surprising if the caregiver also feels frustrated. One woman described her forgetfulness, and her appreciation of her husband, Joe:

> It seems Joe's having to do too much, but I can't do anything about it. He has to do all of the cooking. He fixes all the meals. I make the salad and set the table and do what I can to help. I used to do a lot of entertaining, and I'd take pride in setting a nice table. But now I don't even know on which side the fork or knife is supposed to go. I'll get the plates on and then I'll get the silverware. I'll ask Joe, "Where do these go?" He'll show me, but then I don't remember the next time. That's frustrating. Sometimes he must think I'm awfully stupid. I feel so dumb when I ask, "Where is my fork?" He'll answer, "It's right there." I've put it on the table half the time. It's just weird. The simplest things that I've done before, I can no longer do. Sometimes I can do these, though, and then I think he wonders if I'm just putting all of this on. [Synder, 1999]

No cure seems forthcoming, but scientists are learning many ways to postpone or slow the course of Alzheimer's disease. Estrogen replacement therapy seems to delay AD in women. Other research shows that, when taken in the early stages, drugs to stop the loss of certain brain chemicals can improve cognition for AD patients (Giacobini, 1995; Hagino et al., 1995). Overall, drug treatment for Alzheimer's disease is in the very beginning stages, but it is a promising start.

Two other types of treatment are even more promising, but more experimental. Both depend on diagnosis of Alzheimer's much earlier than previously, at stage one. One possibility is to slow the buildup of APP (amyloid precursor protein), which may contribute to the formation of amyloid plaques, which are the precursor to memory loss (Price et al., 1998). The other approach is group and family therapy that teaches the individuals and the caregivers ways to make the disease less devastating (Snyder, 1999).

Many Strokes

The second most common type of dementia is caused by a stroke or, more often, a series of many strokes, a condition called **multi-infarct dementia (MID)** (Fromholt & Bruhn, 1998). An *infarct* is a temporary obstruction of the blood vessels, which prevents sufficient oxygen from reaching a particular area of the brain. This causes the destruction of brain tissue, which produces such immediate symptoms as blurred vision, shaky or paralyzed limbs, slurred speech, and obvious mental confusion. In a so-called silent stroke, or ministroke, these manifestations typically disappear in hours or even minutes and are often so slight that the person is unaware that anything has happened. Nevertheless, brain damage has occurred.

The underlying cause of the blood-vessel obstructions that lead to MID is systemic arteriosclerosis (hardening of the arteries). People who have problems with their circulatory systems, including those with heart disease, hypertension, numbness or tingling in their extremities, and diabetes, are at risk for arteriosclerosis and MID. Therefore, measures to improve circulation (such as exercise) or to control hypertension and diabetes (such as diet and drugs) help to prevent MID or to slow or halt the progression of the disease.

MID causes about 15 percent of all cases of dementia in the United States. In combination with Alzheimer's disease, MID is part of the

⊕ Response for Genetic Counselors (from page 663): A general guideline for genetic counselors is to provide clients with whatever information they seek; but because of both the uncertainty and the devastation of Alzheimer's disease, the apoE4 test is not available at present. This may change (as was the case with the test for HIV) if early prevention and treatment become more effective.

multi-infarct dementia (MID) The form of dementia characterized by sporadic, and progressive, loss of intellectual functioning. The cause is repeated infarcts, or temporary obstructions of blood vessels, preventing sufficient blood from reaching the brain. Each infarct destroys some brain tissue. The underlying cause is an impaired circulatory system.

Figure 24.2 The Progression of Multi-Infarct Dementia and Alzheimer's Disease. As shown on this chart, cognitive decline is apparent in both Alzheimer's disease and multi-infarct dementia. However the pattern of decline for each disease is different. Victims of AD show steady, gradual decline, while those who suffer from MID get suddenly much worse, improve somewhat, and then experience another serious loss.

cause of another 25 percent. The progression of MID is quite different from that of Alzheimer's disease (see Figure 24.2). Sometimes the person with MID shows a sudden drop in intellectual functioning following an infarct. Then, as other neurons take over some of the functions of the damaged area, the person becomes better. Therapy to retrain the brain's automatic responses and to repair the damaged links between one neuron and another can sometimes restore the person to intellectual health.

However, as the name of the disease denotes, the multiple recurrences of infarcts make it harder and harder for the remaining parts of the brain to compensate. If heart disease, major stroke, diabetes, or another illness does not kill the MID victim, and if ministrokes continue to occur, the person's behavior eventually becomes indistinguishable from that of someone suffering from Alzheimer's disease. Autopsy reveals, however, that parts of the brain have been destroyed while other parts seem normal; the widespread proliferation of plaques and tangles characteristic of Alzheimer's disease is not present.

Subcortical Dementias

Many other dementias originate in the subcortex. Because they are below, not inside, the cortex, they do not directly involve thinking and memory. **Subcortical dementias** cause a progressive loss of motor control but initially leave the thinking processes intact. Among these dementias are Parkinson's disease, Huntington's disease, and multiple sclerosis. All these diseases lead to dementia, but all begin with a person in full possession of his or her mental faculties and with clear indications that a serious, chronic illness has taken hold in the body, not the mind.

In the later stages of subcortical dementia, a person's mental functioning varies considerably, depending on the time of day, the degree of stress, the specific activity, the social context, and the medical treatment. Further, in subcortical dementias, short-term memory and the ability to learn new material are usually much better than long-term memory, exactly the opposite of people with cortical degeneration (Derix, 1994).

The best known subcortical dementia is **Parkinson's disease,** which is initially marked by rigidity or tremor of the muscles, or both. Parkinson's produces degeneration of neurons in a brain region that produces dopamine, a neurotransmitter essential to normal brain functioning. Dementia is not evident until the destruction of brain cells reaches a certain threshold. It is likely that mental impairment occurs when, and only when, the normal ability of the brain to compensate for neuron loss becomes overwhelmed. Since cognitive reserve declines with age, it is not surprising that Parkinson's disease that begins after age 60 is more likely to lead to dementia than is the early-onset type (Edwards, 1993).

Among the factors implicated in Parkinson's disease are genetic vulnerability and certain viruses. This disease is most common in the

subcortical dementias Dementias, such as Parkinson's disease, Huntington's disease, and multiple sclerosis, that originate in the subcortex. These diseases begin with impairments in motor ability and produce cognitive impairment in later stages.

Parkinson's disease A chronic, progressive disease that is characterized by muscle tremors and rigidity, and sometimes dementia, caused by a reduction of dopamine production in the brain.

aged, but it is not exclusively an old person's illness: An estimated 8 percent of newly diagnosed individuals are under age 40. Treatment now includes daily doses of dopamine medication, which slows the course of the disease. Experimental treatment using cells from aborted fetuses to stimulate production of neurotransmitters in the brain shows promise but is very controversial.

Some of the many other diseases that can involve dementia affect the cortex first, impairing the person's mental processes while leaving motor skills intact. One of these is Pick's disease, which involves atrophy of the frontal and temporal lobes of the brain (Edwards, 1993). The initial symptoms of Pick's disease are personality changes, including loss of social skills and motivation, followed by loss of language and memory. Eventually the individual lapses into a completely vegetative state. Pick's disease is always fatal, running its course in two to fifteen years.

Various toxins and infectious agents can also affect the cortex. For instance, almost half of all AIDS patients develop a brain infection that produces dementia, as do many people in the last stages of syphilis. Consumption of beef infected with bovine spongiform encephalitis ("mad cow disease") leads to dementia and death, because of a slow-acting virus or a prion, a protein particle that acts as a disease agent (Collinge et al., 1996). When alcohol abuse is chronic, disruptions in the functioning of the central nervous system impair learning, reasoning, perception, and other mental processes, producing alcohol dementia. Over the long term, alcohol abuse can lead to Korsakoff's syndrome, with severe loss of short-term memory caused by lesions in the brain (Tarter, 1995).

Reversible Dementia

It is not uncommon for the elderly to be assumed to be suffering from one form of dementia or another when, in fact, their "symptomatic" behaviors are caused by some other factor, such as medication, alcohol abuse (short of Korsakoff's syndrome), mental illness, or depression. All of these can be treated once the problem is determined.

Overmedication

Noncompliance with the prescribed use of medications is a serious problem for many of the elderly (Higbee, 1994); it can lead to drug-related loss of intellectual functioning. Adults over 65, who represent about 13 percent of the U.S. population, use 30 percent of all the drugs prescribed and 50 percent of all drugs sold over the counter (Beizer, 1994). Drug interactions can produce symptoms of dementia, from confusion to psychotic behavior. An added problem is that the dosage of most prescription drugs is usually determined by tests on younger adults, yet the dosage that is appropriate for 30-year-olds may be an overdose for the elderly, whose ability to excrete excess drugs is impaired (Beizer, 1994).

Further, many of the drugs commonly taken by the elderly (such as most of those to reduce high blood pressure, to combat Parkinson's disease, or to relieve pain) can, by themselves, slow down mental processes. This is especially true if they are taken on an empty stomach or if a double dose is inadvertently taken. The solution is simple—moderation or elimination of the problem prescription—but this solution obviously requires that the specific problem first be recognized.

Which Pill Today? Most elderly have medicine cabinets that look like this one, crammed with prescribed and over-the-counter medications for a variety of chronic conditions. Overdoses or intermixings of these medications can produce symptoms that resemble dementia.

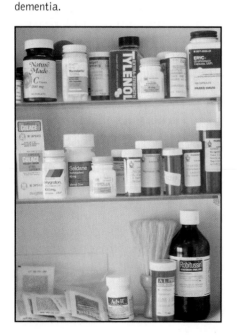

Psychological Illness

In general, psychological illnesses are less common in the elderly than in younger adults (Gatz et al., 1996). Nonetheless, about 10 percent of the elderly who are diagnosed as demented are actually experiencing psychological, rather than physiological, illness. In some cases, the person is merely unusually anxious (Scogin, 1998). As anyone who has taken a final exam under pressure knows, anxiety can make even a bright and healthy person forget important information.

For many older people, the anxiety that occurs when they arrive at a hospital or nursing home is sufficient to cause substantial disorientation and loss of memory. If the anxious new patient is tested immediately, a misdiagnosis of organic brain damage is possible. And if psychotropic medicine is overprescribed or overused, the result can be a person who seems continually demented (Sherman, 1994).

Depression in the elderly is also often misread as dementia. Although major depression is less common in late adulthood than earlier, many adults, at some time in their later years, experience symptoms of minor depression that are sufficiently debilitating to resemble those of dementia (Kasl-Godley et al., 1998). In clinical assessments of the elderly, even mild depression can diminish overall cognitive performance, even though it does not reduce underlying ability (Powell, 1994; Rabbitt et al., 1995). It is possible that some individuals become anxious or depressed because they notice signs of mental deterioration, or at least they think they do.

Throughout adulthood, however, it seems that depression causes intellectual decline and various health problems more often than vice versa (Meeks et al., 2000). In fact, one of the symptoms of depression in late adulthood is exaggerated attention to small memory losses. Quite the opposite reaction comes from people who truly suffer from dementia, who are often blithely unaware of their serious problems.

Depression in late adulthood, as at younger ages, is one of the most treatable mental illnesses. Psychotherapy and careful pharmacotherapy usually bring about noticeable improvement in a few weeks, and the pseudodementia disappears (Kasl-Godley et al., 1998). However, even more than at younger ages, most depressed older people are not treated because no one recognizes their depression as a curable disease. Instead, many caregivers consider depression a natural consequence of aging, or they confuse the symptoms with those of brain disease. If the depressed person has recently lost a loved one, the symptoms of depression may mistakenly be attributed to bereavement. It is normal for the elderly who are in mourning to be sad and to have difficulty eating and sleeping; but, unlike depression, bereavement does not normally involve strong feelings of guilt and self-deprecation, nor do its symptoms last longer than a few months.

One consequence of untreated depression among the elderly is a higher suicide rate for those over age 60 than for any other age group. Suicide rates in the United States are particularly high among white and Hispanic men and Asians of both sexes and very low

Dementia? Mental illness in the elderly often goes unrecognized and untreated because it is mistaken as a natural component of aging or as a sign of dementia.

❷ *Observational Quiz (see answer page 670):* *Can you see any indications that this woman's problem more likely arises from her concerns and her circumstances than from an inability to think at all?*

❶ *Answer to Observational Quiz (from page 669):*
The visible objects—ashtray, fan, hidden and small photographs, worn sofa cushion, too-large blouse— all suggest that the circumstances of her life are not ideal or even adequate to her needs. More telling are her facial expression, body position, and hands—all of which suggest that she is worried or sad, not mindless. Physical illness may also be a problem here if two symptoms suggested by this photo are actually present: recent weight loss and headache.

among African American women (see Appendix A). In many other nations—Canada, Chile, Hungary, France, and Japan, among them—the suicide rate for elderly men is higher than for any other age group.

In most cases, the precipitating event for suicide is a social loss, with retirement or widowhood being the most common precipitator, especially for men who live alone (Canetto, 1992). A related cause of suicide is illness, particularly cancer or illnesses that affect the brain, or the fear that normal symptoms of aging are the first sign of such an illness. As at every age, confusion brought on by alcohol or drugs increases the risk of suicide.

Reversible dementia can also be caused by brain injuries, brain tumors, and head injuries that result in an excess of fluid pressing on the brain. In these cases, surgery can often remedy the problem and restore normal cognitive functioning.

NEW COGNITIVE DEVELOPMENT IN LATER LIFE

So far in this chapter we have mainly considered possible declines in the intellectual functioning of older adults. What about positive changes? Can older adults develop new interests, new patterns of thought, a deeper wisdom? Many of the major theorists on human development believe that they can. For example, Erik Erikson finds that the older generation are more interested than others in the arts, in children, and in the whole of human experience. They are the "social witnesses" to life and thus are more aware of the interdependence of the generations (Erikson et al., 1986). Abraham Maslow maintains that older adults are much more likely than younger people to reach what he considers the highest stage of development—self-actualization—which includes heightened aesthetic, creative, philosophical, and spiritual understanding (Maslow, 1970). Development of the artistic spirit is described in the In Person box. The life review and wisdom, two developments that are more directly cognitive, are discussed below.

The Life Review

In old age, many older people become more reflective and philosophical than they once were. In most cases, this is personally centered. The individual attempts to put his or her life in perspective, assessing accomplishments and failures based on personal perceptions of the overall scheme of life.

life review   The examination of one's own past life that many elderly people engage in. According to Butler, the life review is therapeutic, for it helps the older person to come to grips with aging and death.

One form of this attempt to put one's life into perspective is called the **life review.** An older person recalls and recounts various aspects of his or her life, remembering the highs and lows and comparing the past with the present. In general, the life-review process helps elders connect their own lives with the future as they tell their stories to younger generations. At the same time, it renews links with past generations as a person remembers what parents, grandparents, and even great-grandparents did and thought. The individual's relationship to humanity, to nature, to the whole of life also becomes a topic of reflection, as various memories are revived, reinterpreted, and finally reintegrated to achieve a better understanding of the entire life course (Kotre, 1995).

One interesting aspect of the life review is that it is more social than solitary. Elderly people want to tell their stories to someone, and they

Many people seem to appreciate nature and aesthetic experiences in a deeper way as they get older. As one team of leading gerontologists explains:

> The elemental things of life—children, friendship, nature, human touching (physical and emotional), color, shape—assume greater significance as people sort out the more important from the less important. Old age can be a time of emotional sensory awareness and enjoyment. [Butler et al., 1991]

For many older people, this heightened appreciation leads to active expression. They may begin gardening, birdwatching, pottery, painting, or playing a musical instrument—and not simply because they have nothing better to do. The importance that creativity can have for some in old age is wonderfully expressed by a 79-year-old man, not famous, little educated, yet joyful at his workbench:

> This is the happiest time of my life. . . . I wish there was twenty-four hours in a day. Wuk hours, awake hours. Yew can keep y' sleep; plenty of time for that later on. . . . That's what I want all this here time for now—to make things. I draw and I paint too. . . . I don't copy anything. I make what I remember. I tarn wood. I paint the fields. As I say, I've niver bin so happy in my whole life and I only hope I last out. [quoted in Blythe, 1979]

For this man, as for many other older people, the impulse to create did not suddenly arise in late adulthood; it was present, although infrequently expressed, in earlier years. What does seem to occur in late adulthood is a deepening need to express and develop that impulse, perhaps because, as the years left to live become fewer, these people decide to defer their dream of creative expression no longer. Interestingly, the very circumstances of late adulthood can make artistic creation more significant.

One of the most famous examples of late creative development is Anna Moses, who was a farm wife and mother of 10. For most of her life, she expressed her artistic sensitivity by stitching quilts and doing embroidery during the long winters on the farm. At age 75, arthritis made needlework impossible, so she took to "dabbling in oil" instead. Four years later, three of her oil paintings, displayed in a local drugstore, caught the eye of a New York City art dealer who happened to be passing by. He bought them, drove to Anna Moses's house to buy 15 more, and began to exhibit them in the city. One year later, at age 80, "Grandma Moses" had her first one-woman show in New York, receiving international recognition for her unique "primitive" style. She continued to paint, "incredibly gaining in assurance and artistic discretion," into her 90s (Yglesias, 1980).

Reverence for Life When was the last time you sat down to focus all your attention on one pink flower? A heightened appreciation of nature sometimes characterizes the elderly, but rarely the young. Younger adults remind each other to wake up and smell the coffee; older adults take time to smell the roses.

For those who have been creative all their lives, old age is often a time of continuing productivity and even of renewed inspiration. Famous examples abound: Michelangelo painted the amazing frescoes in the Sistine Chapel at age 75; Giuseppe Verdi composed the opera *Falstaff* when he was 80; Frank Lloyd Wright completed the Guggenheim Museum in New York City, an innovative architectural masterpiece, when he was 91.

In a recent study of extraordinarily creative people, it was found that almost none of the subjects felt that their ability, their goals, or the quality of their work was much impaired with age. What had changed was their sense of urgency about their work, which was sharpened by their realization that fewer years lay ahead and that their energy and physical strength were diminishing (Csikszentmihalyi, 1996). As the researcher observed of these individuals, "In their seventies, eighties, and nineties, they may lack the fiery ambition of earlier years, but they are just as focused, efficient, and committed as before . . . perhaps more so."

prefer a story that is not theirs alone but the story of a family, a cohort, a people. Research finds that the stories told by elders are more interesting to listen to than similar stories told by younger people, perhaps because the elders have more time, more experiences, and more practice (Pratt & Rubens, 1991). It should be noted, however, that not every adult, old or young, can tell stories well. The authors of one study explain:

> Most of us can recall older family members or acquaintances from our youth who were legendary (sometimes, perhaps, notorious) as champion storytellers. These individuals shared important cultural and personal knowledge and information on a variety of topics with younger generations through the recounting of their own past experiences. Yet other adults may come to mind who were terrible storytellers. Clearly, adults vary dramatically in their capacities and motivation to engage in such adult storytelling with young persons. [Pratt et al., 1999]

Sometimes the life review takes the simple form of nostalgia, reminiscence, or storytelling, which may be quite helpful to the older person, although not always easy for others to listen to. Yet it may be crucial to the person's self-worth that others recognize the significance of these reminiscences. As Robert Butler and his colleagues explain:

> We have been taught that this nostalgia represents living in the past and a preoccupation with self and that it is generally boring, meaningless, and time-consuming. Yet as a natural healing process it represents one of the underlying human capacities on which all psychotherapy depends. The life review should be recognized as a necessary and healthy process in daily life as well as a useful tool in the mental health care of older people. [Butler et al., 1991]

In some cases, the reflectivity of old age may lead to, or intensify, attempts to put broader historical, social, and cultural contexts of life into perspective (Cohen, 1999). It is interesting to note that when Wayne Dennis (1966) studied the production of professionals in 16 fields, he found that in two of them—history and philosophy—production peaked when subjects were in their 60s and 70s. One notable example is Will and Ariel Durant's *The Story of Civilization*, a monumental, 10-volume history of civilization written mostly in late adulthood—which was followed by *The Lessons of History* and *Interpretations of Life*, published when the Durants were in their 80s.

Wisdom

Wisdom is one of the most positive attributes commonly associated with older people. Indeed, the idea that wisdom may be one of the benefits of old age has become a "hoped-for antidote to views that have cast the process of aging in terms of intellectual deficit and regression" (Labouvie-Vief, 1990).

The question is, What is wisdom, really, and is it a common feature of old age? Wisdom is clearly an elusive concept, and any definition of it is bound to be at least partly subjective. In addition, whether any given individual is perceived as wise depends very much on the immediate social context in which that person's thoughts or actions are being judged. Given these obstacles to definitional precision, one of the more comprehensive, all-purpose definitions of wisdom is that offered by Paul

Will They Remember? As her upraised finger indicates, this woman from the Inuit people of the Arctic expects these young children to heed her counsel. From their expressions, it seems that some of them may do so. Although research has not demonstrated that the elderly are necessarily wise, the proof may be in the practical, everyday context. If the young remember and reflect on the words of the old—which is more likely to happen in traditional cultures than in postmodern ones—then wisdom may be confirmed.

wisdom A cognitive perspective characterized by a broad, practical, comprehensive approach to life's problems, reflecting timeless truths rather than immediate expediency; said to be more common in the elderly than in the young.

Baltes, a developmentalist specializing in cognitive gerontology. Baltes defines **wisdom** as "expert knowledge in the fundamental pragmatics of life, permitting exceptional insight and judgment involving complex and uncertain matters of the human condition" (Baltes et al., 1992). Baltes and his colleagues argue that five features distinguish wisdom from other forms of human understanding (Dittmann-Kohli & Baltes, 1990):

- rich factual knowledge that concerns the broad topic of human experience
- knowledge of the "pragmatics of life"—that is, practical and procedural knowledge about the conditions of life and their variations
- a contextual approach to understanding life that takes into account its broader ecological, social, and historical dimensions
- acceptance of the uncertainty inherent in defining and solving life's problems and of the unpredictability of one's own future life course
- recognition of individual differences in values, goals, and priorities, leading to flexibility and relativism in tackling the contradictions of life experience

Wisdom thus involves elements of both the dialectical thinking that emerges in early adulthood and the refinement of thinking that comes with years of personal experience. But is wisdom a typical characteristic of older adults' thinking?

In one effort to study wisdom, Smith and Baltes (1990) asked 60 adults of various ages to assess the lives of four fictitious persons who each faced a difficult decision regarding the future. Here is an example of one story concerning a young adult:

> Elizabeth, 33 years old and a successful professional for 8 years, was recently offered a major promotion. Her new responsibilities would require an increased time commitment. She and her husband would also like to have children before it is too late. Elizabeth is considering the following options: She could plan to accept the promotion, or she could plan to start a family.

The other three stories concerned dilemmas about parental responsibilities at home, accepting early retirement, and intergenerational commitments. After hearing these stories, subjects were asked to formulate a course of action for each fictitious person and to think aloud as they did so, indicating when they thought additional information was needed about certain issues. Their responses were subsequently transcribed and rated by a panel of human-service professionals according to whether they exhibited the characteristics of wisdom described above.

Not unexpectedly, wisdom appeared to be in fairly short supply. Of the 240 responses to their hypothetical stories, Smith and Baltes found that only 5 percent were judged as truly wise. Somewhat more surprisingly, the distribution of responses judged to be wise was fairly even across young, middle-aged, and old adults in the sample. That is, wisdom was not reserved for later life but could be found at any phase of adulthood—depending, presumably, on the person's life experiences and reflective insight about them. More recent research likewise finds wisdom at many ages, although the very wise tend to be in late adulthood.

Another study makes clear the distinction between IQ, as measured by intelligence tests (described in Chapter 21), and wisdom (not labeled as such), as indicated by measures of such qualities as warm interactions with other people, humor in dealing with problems, and concern about other people rather than self-absorption (Vaillant & Davis, 2000). This study traced impoverished males who scored low (between 60 and 86) on

IQ tests as adolescents but who, by age 65, had good lives. For example, one boy was labeled "slovenly, tardy, and lazy" by his teacher, but he became involved with the Salvation Army and eventually became pastor first of a small parish, then of progressively larger ones. He loves "helping and teaching" people, and he is excellent at it. Wisely, he appreciates that his wife does the paperwork and math, and he is thrilled that all his children have attended college. Not everyone in this study eventually attained such success. However, approximately half the low-IQ subjects achieved levels of joy, depth, devotion, and caring that matched those attained by members of the same cohort who had much higher IQs.

On balance, then, it seems fair to conclude that the mental processes in late adulthood can be adaptive and creative, not necessarily as efficient as thinking at younger ages but more appropriate to the final period of life. An illustrative and exemplary case in point is the following poem, written by Henry Wadsworth Longfellow at age 80:

> But why, you ask me, should this tale be told?
> Of men grown old, or who are growing old?
> Ah, Nothing is too late
> Till the tired heart shall cease to palpitate;
> Cato learned Greek at eighty; Sophocles
> Wrote his grand *Oedipus,* and Simonides
> Bore off the prize of verse from his compeers,
> When each had numbered more than four score years,
> And Theophrastus, at four score and ten,
> Had just begun his *Characters of Men.*
> Chaucer, at Woodstock with the nightingales,
> At sixty wrote the *Canterbury Tales;*
> Goethe at Weimar, toiling to the last,
> Completed *Faust* when eighty years were past.
> These are indeed exceptions, but they show
> How far the gulf-stream of our youth may flow
> Into the arctic regions of our lives
> When little else than life itself survives.
> Shall we then sit us idly down and say
> The night hath come; it is no longer day?
> The night hath not yet come; we are not quite
> Cut off from labor by the failing light;
> Some work remains for us to do and dare;
> Even the oldest tree some fruit may bear;
> And as the evening twilight fades away
> The sky is filled with stars, invisible by day.

SUMMARY

CHANGES IN INFORMATION PROCESSING

1. Although thinking processes become slower and less sharp once a person reaches late adulthood, there is much individual variation in this decrement, and each particular cognitive ability shows a different rate of age-related decline.

2. The sensory register declines relatively little in late adulthood, although as the senses themselves become dulled, some material never reaches the sensory register. Working memory shows notable declines, especially when one must simultaneously store and process information in complex ways. One reason for this loss is that processing takes longer with age.

3. With increasing age, adults experience greater difficulty accessing information from both short- and long-term memory. However, knowledge stored in implicit memory is more easily retrieved than are the facts and concepts stored in explicit memory. Past knowledge is more accessible the more it was initially "overlearned" and subsequently used.

4. Control processes also are less effective with age, particularly when measured in laboratory tests of intellectual functioning. The two possible reasons for this deficit are either that

the aging brain is less capable of strategizing the best use of mental ability or that older persons do not know how to organize, memorize, and analyze information as well as they might.

REASONS FOR AGE-RELATED CHANGES

5. One reason older adults, on average, do not perform as well as younger adults on tests of cognitive functioning is that more of the older group have negative self-perceptions of their mental skills that undermine their motivation to succeed. Older adults' cognitive performance can be negatively affected by exposure to ageist stereotypes. Some laboratory research creates contexts that impede the efficient use of adult cognition.

6. With age, the brain's communication processes slow down, as measured by a notable decrease in reaction time in the elderly. When older adults are given more time to remember, analyze, and answer an intellectual problem, their performance improves markedly. Researchers have also found that both physical and intellectual activity can halt or reverse some of the cognitive slowdown that occurs in old age.

COGNITION IN DAILY LIFE

7. In daily life, most of the elderly are not seriously handicapped by cognitive difficulties. Usually, once they recognize problems in their memory or other intellectual abilities, they learn to compensate with selective optimization; that is, they learn to build on strengths and shore up weaknesses.

DEMENTIA

8. Dementia, whether it occurs in late adulthood or earlier, is characterized by memory loss—at first minor lapses, then more serious forgetfulness, and finally such extreme losses that recognition of closest family members fades.

9. The most common cause of dementia is Alzheimer's disease, an incurable ailment that becomes more prevalent with age. Genetic factors (especially the apoE4 gene) play a role in Alzheimer's disease, increasing the amyloid plaques that impair the brain. Drug therapy is beginning to offer some promise for the prevention and treatment of Alzheimer's disease.

10. Multi-infarct dementia is caused by a series of ministrokes that occur when impairment of blood circulation destroys portions of brain tissue. Measures to improve circulation and to control hypertension can prevent or slow the course of this form of dementia.

11. In addition to Alzheimer's disease and multi-infarct dementia, subcortical abnormalities, such as that leading to Parkinson's disease, are a leading cause of dementia. Other disorders that may lead to dementia are Pick's disease, alcoholism, and AIDS.

12. Dementia is sometimes mistakenly diagnosed when the individual is actually suffering from some other problem, such as overuse or misuse of medication or a psychological illness such as anxiety or depression.

NEW COGNITIVE DEVELOPMENT IN LATER LIFE

13. Many people become more responsive to nature, more interested in creative endeavors, and more philosophical as they grow older. The life review is a personal reflection that many older people undertake, remembering earlier experiences and putting their entire lives into perspective.

14. Wisdom is commonly thought to increase in life as a result of experience, but this idea has not been confirmed. Apparently, wisdom is not necessarily prevalent at any age.

KEY TERMS

explicit memory (650)
implicit memory (650)
control processes (651)
source amnesia (652)
priming (655)
dementia (662)
Alzheimer's disease (AD) (663)

multi-infarct dementia (MID) (666)
subcortical dementias (667)
Parkinson's disease (667)
life review (670)
wisdom (673)

KEY QUESTIONS

1. How is each part of the information-processing system—sensory register, working memory, knowledge base, and control processes—affected by age?

2. Compare age differences in explicit and implicit memory.

3. What are the problems with, and the conclusions derived from, research on long-term memory?

4. How do stereotypes about aging held by researchers, by cultures, and by individuals affect research on memory?

5. What are some physiological and some external reasons for age-related changes in cognition?

6. How true is it that everyone develops dementia if they live long enough?

7. What are the similarities of and differences between Alzheimer's disease and MID?

8. What prevents or causes the various types of dementia?

9. What are the purpose and the result of the life review?

10. *In Your Experience* When are you bored by, and when are you fascinated with, someone else's life story?

Late Adulthood:
Psychosocial Development

CHAPTER $\overset{\text{\Large 25}}{}$

Viewing development from age 65 on, one is struck by the vast array of possibilities and outcomes. As we saw in the previous two chapters, some people in their 70s or even 80s run marathons; others hardly move. Some write timeless poetry; others cannot think at all.

In psychosocial development as well, old age is less likely to level individual differences than to magnify them, expanding the diversity of human experience even more than in previous decades. As we try to comprehend the whole of human development, diversity brings complexity; we need ways to organize the multifaceted, multidirectional observations and data regarding late adulthood. We begin, therefore, with theories.

THEORIES OF LATE ADULTHOOD

Dozens of theories focus on development in late adulthood. To simplify, we will consider these theories in three clusters: self theories, stratification theories, and dynamic theories.

Self Theories

Self theories begin with the premise that adults make choices, confront problems, and interpret reality in such a way as to define, become, and express themselves as fully as possible. As Abraham Maslow (1968) described it, people attempt to *self-actualize,* to achieve their full potential. Self theories emphasize "human intentionality and the active part played by the individual in developing selfhood" (Marshall, 1996).

Integrity Versus Despair

The most comprehensive self theory came from Erik Erikson, who even in his 90s was still writing. The eighth and final stage of his theory of development is *integrity versus despair,* when older adults seek to integrate and unify their unique personal experiences with their vision of their community. Many develop pride and contentment with their past and present lives, as well as a "shared sense of 'we' within a communal mutuality" (Erikson et al., 1986). Others experience despair, "feeling that the time is now short, too short for the attempt to start another life and to try out alternate roads to recovery" (Erikson, 1963).

677

self theories   Theories of late adulthood that emphasize the core self, or the search to maintain one's integrity and identity.

As at every stage, tension between the two opposing aspects of the developmental crisis helps move the person toward a fuller understanding. In this eighth stage,

> life brings many, quite realistic reasons for experiencing despair: aspects of the present that cause unremitting pain; aspects of a future that are uncertain and frightening. And, of course, there remains inescapable death, that one aspect of the future which is both wholly certain and wholly unknowable. Thus, some despair must be acknowledged and integrated as a component of old age. [Erikson et al., 1986]

Ideally, the looming prospect of death brings a new view of survival, through children, grandchildren, and the human community as a whole, which allows a "life-affirming involvement" in the present.

Identity Theory

A second version of self theory actually originates in Erikson's fifth stage, *identity versus role confusion.* Erikson himself recognized that the search for identity was lifelong, that each new experience, each gain or loss, requires people to reassess and reassert their personal identity. This theme is evident in the work of other developmentalists as well (Cross & Markus, 1991; Kiecolt, 1994; Kroger, 2000; Whitbourne, 1996).

Identity is particularly challenged in late adulthood: The usual pillars of self-concept begin to crumble, specifically physical appearance, physical health, and employment (Kraus, 1999; Whitbourne, 1996). As a 70-year-old retired teacher said, "I know who I've been, but who am I now?" (quoted in Kroger, 2000).

According to Whitbourne (1996), the process of maintaining identity involves a combination of assimilation and accommodation (terms first used by Jean Piaget, as explained in Chapter 2). In *identity assimilation,* identity remains what it always was, and new experiences are incorporated, or assimilated, into it. Thus, the person maintains self-esteem by distorting reality and denying that anything has really changed that might affect him or her.

An assimilating older individual might "refuse to acknowledge the weaknesses of the cardiovascular system that may lead to disaster when a highly physically stressful activity is attempted. Or the individual may refuse to buy or use bifocals or hearing aids" (Whitbourne, 1996). This strategy results in high satisfaction and self-justification, with few self-doubts, although those who use it often react with anger at everyone and everything.

The opposite strategy is *identity accommodation,* in which people adapt to new experiences by changing their self-concept. Accommodating people begin the process by doubting their values, beliefs, and even themselves, sometimes so intensely that "self-doubting can be an extremely painful process" (Whitbourne, 1996).

Accommodating people might decide that all they have ever worked for is lost because, for example, grandchildren no longer go to church, take pride in their ethnic heritage, respect their elders, or—worst of all—listen to their grandparent. With too much accommodation, a person experiences something like the despair that Erikson wrote about—although not because of impending death, but because of changing circumstances.

The basic idea of identity theory is that people of all ages have a sense of who they are, but personal identity is challenged by the inevitable experiences of aging. As a result, a person might either assimilate (becoming very rigid, insisting on self-centered and narrow moral values) or accommodate (crumbling in the face of changing circumstances). Ideally, the person maintains a firm but flexible identity, not tilting too far in either direction despite the challenges of aging.

Selective Optimization

Paul Baltes emphasizes that people can choose to cope successfully with the undeniable physical and cognitive losses of late adulthood through "selective optimization with compensation," a concept central to self theories. As we saw in Chapter 21, the basic idea of this optimization is that individuals set their own goals, assess their own abilities, and then figure out how to accomplish what they want to achieve despite the limitations and declines of later life (Baltes et al., 1998).

As an example of this process, Arthur Rubinstein, a world-famous concert pianist who continued to perform in his 80s, explained that he limited his repertoire to pieces he knew he could perform well (selection) and that he practiced before a concert more than he might have when he was younger (optimization). And because he could no longer play fast passages at the brilliant tempos he once could, he deliberately played slow passages more slowly than he used to, thereby making his playing of the fast passages seem faster than it was (compensation) (Schroots, 1996).

More common examples are provided by the many elders who structure their lives so that they can do what they want and do it well. In a study of some of the strategies used by people over age 80, Johnson and Barer (1993) report a woman who did her food shopping at a distant store because it was near the end of the bus line, ensuring empty seats available for her and her groceries on the return trip. Similarly, a man who continued to drive a car "plots out the streets and plans his exact route in order to avoid getting lost, while another drives around the block rather than making a left turn at a busy intersection."

The readiness to make such selective changes is itself a measure of the strength of the self. People who have a strong sense of self-efficacy (Bandura, 1997) believe that they can master any situation life presents and thus can cope with the various events of aging.

Behavioral Genetics

In recent years, self theories have received substantial confirmation from behavioral genetics. Longitudinal studies of monozygotic and dizygotic twins find that, contrary to the logical idea that genetic influences weaken as life experiences accumulate, some inherited traits seem even more apparent in late adulthood than earlier. It seems that "when heritability changes with development, it increases" (Bergeman, 1997). Various life events—from how early a person retires to how often a person marries—seem to be affected at least as much by genetics as by life circumstances (Saudino et al., 1997).

The explanation for this, some developmentalists hypothesize, is that when older adults are unharnessed from family and work obligations, their temperament gains free rein and they can become more truly themselves. As one 103-year-old woman observed, "My core has stayed the same. Everything else has changed" (Troll & Skaff, 1997).

Obviously, certain events common in late adulthood seem beyond a person's control (such as the death of a close relative, a serious illness, or a sudden loss of income). But the frequency of such stressful

Selective Optimization with Compensation Max Roach has been a leading jazz drummer for over 50 years. His approach to his work at age 73 clearly reflects the idea of selective optimization with compensation: "I joined a health club . . . I thought I'd tune up, you know, tone up. Playing my instrument is a lot of exercise. All four limbs going. . . . I don't play the way I did back in the 52nd Street days. We were playing long, hard hours in all that smoke. It would kill me now if I played like I did then. Now I play concerts, and the show goes on for just an hour. But I'll tell you something: I'm ready to play until the sticks get too heavy for me to hold up."

events is caused—about a third of the time—by genetic factors that have been in place since conception (Bergeman, 1997). Even self-concept, including assessment of abilities, is partly genetic (McGue et al., 1993). For example, some people are inclined to think well of themselves, their parents, their potential, and so on, while others take the opposite view: The difference arises not primarily because their parents were actually loving or hostile, but because each person is always him- or herself, tending to have a particular outlook on childhood (and everything else).

Remember, however, that behavioral geneticists never claim that any aspect of the self is *entirely* genetic. Although there is much variation, depending on the person and the trait, usually between a third and a half of the variation in characteristics related to the self is genetic; the rest is the result of the environment (Bergeman, 1997).

Stratification Theories

A quite different perspective on late adulthood is proposed by those who endorse **stratification theories.** These theories maintain that social forces limit individual choice and direct life at every stage. Many believe that cultural forces become even more important but less supportive in old age (Smith & Baltes, 1999).

Stratification by Age

One form of stratification theory focuses on age stratification. Industrialized nations tend to segregate their oldest citizens, giving them limited roles and circumscribed opportunities in order to make way for upcoming generations. The elderly are induced or compelled to retire, offered fewer lifesaving medical treatments, and encouraged to live in housing restricted to their cohort.

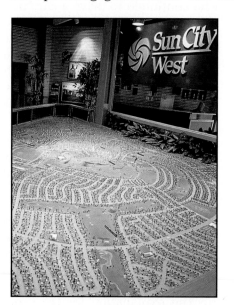

stratification theories   Theories emphasizing that social forces, particularly those related to a person's social stratum or social category, limit individual choices and affect the ability to function. In late adulthood, past stratification continues to limit life in various ways.

Hello in There   This model shows the homes of the 25,000 residents of Sun City West, Arizona, one of hundreds of retirement communities throughout the country, including the original Sun City, a larger community only 2 miles away. Although voluntary age segregation could be considered disengagement from the mixed-age communities where most people dwell, it does not necessarily lead to passivity. Most Sun City residents maintain active schedules of work and play as well as shopping, exercising, worshiping, and socializing, all within the security of the compound.

disengagement theory   The view that aging makes a person's social sphere increasingly narrow, resulting in role relinquishment, withdrawal, and passivity.

Disengagement Versus Activity The most controversial version of this age stratification process is **disengagement theory** (Cumming & Henry, 1961; Johnson & Barer, 1992), which holds that aging makes a person's social sphere increasingly narrow. Traditional roles become unavailable or unimportant; the social circle shrinks as friends die or move away; coworkers stop asking for help; children have families of their own. As adults reach their 60s, they anticipate and adjust to this narrowing of the social sphere by disengaging—relinquishing many of the roles they have played, withdrawing from society, and developing a passive style of interaction.

Disengagement theory provoked a storm of protest, particularly from gerontologists who insisted that older people need, want, and find

activity theory   The view that elderly people need to remain active in a variety of social spheres—with relatives, friends, and community groups—and become withdrawn only unwillingly, as a result of ageism.

new involvements and new friends to replace the ones they have lost because of retirement, relocation, or death. Some gerontologists developed an opposite theory, called **activity theory,** which holds that the elderly remain active in a variety of social spheres—with relatives, friends, and community groups. If the elderly do disengage and withdraw, activity theorists contend, they do so unwillingly (Hochschild, 1975; Rosow, 1985).

The dominant view is that the more active the elderly are and the more roles they play, the greater their life satisfaction and the longer their lives (Harlow & Cantor, 1996). According to activity theory, whenever age stratification leads to disengagement, it is the result of ageism and it should be discredited in the same way, and for the same reasons, that forced segregation by race or sex is discredited.

A more recent view of age stratification suggests that both disengagement theory and activity theory may be too extreme:

> Care providers have reported that their feelings are very mixed when trying to "activate" certain old people. The workers say that while they believe activity is good, they nevertheless have the feeling that they are doing something wrong when they try to drag some older people to various forms of social activity or activity therapy. [Tornstam, 1999–2000]

Rather than either disengaging or needing more activity, most older people become more selective in their social contacts, and are happier as a result (Charles & Carstensen, 1999). Age may change how a person thinks and behaves, so that to expect an older person to be as active as he or she once was is to fail to recognize the distinctive psychosocial role of the oldest generation.

Stratification by Gender and Race

All stratification theories focus on the ways in which people organize themselves—and are organized by society—according to their particular characteristics and circumstances. Age is one such powerful and limiting stratification category, and, especially in late adulthood, sex and race are two more.

Sexual Discrimination   *Feminist theory,* for example, draws attention to the values underlying the gender divisions promoted by society. Feminists are particularly concerned about late adulthood because "the study of aging, by sheer force of demography, is necessarily a woman's issue" (Ray, 1996). Currently in the United States, women make up nearly two-thirds of the population over age 65 and nearly three-fourths of the elderly poor. Feminist theorists point out that, since most social structures and economic policies have been established by men, women's perspectives and needs are devalued.

What might those needs be? Money and independence. Many older women became impoverished because of male-centered economic policies. One example is pension plans that are pegged to a lifetime of continuous employment. Another is medical insurance that pays more for acute illness than for chronic disease. In addition, because most men marry younger women and die at younger ages, there are far more widows than widowers (a ratio of 2:1 after age 80), and being unmarried doubles the risk of living in poverty and ill health (Rank, 1999).

Feminist theorists likewise note that because women are socialized to be nurturant, they are more likely than men to become caregivers for frail relatives (husband, siblings, or handicapped children), even if care-giving strains their own health. Indeed, in many ways, social policies and cultural values converge to make later life particularly burdensome for women (Barusch, 1994).

Racial Discrimination Another view of stratification comes from *critical race theory*, which sees race not as something inborn but rather as "a social construct whose practical utility is determined by a particular society or social system" (King & Williams, 1995). According to this theory, longstanding racism results in stratification along racial lines; it shapes experiences and attitudes for minorities as well as majorities, often without their conscious awareness (Bell, 1992). Remember that today's elderly were raised before 1950, when almost all nonwhite nations were ruled by Europeans and, in the United States, not only schools and the army but even hospitals and cemeteries were segregated. In those years, people of color were more likely to be poor, dependent, and less educated.

Decades of racial stratification resulted in poverty and frailty for minority elderly who were excluded from the economic mainstream. Even in late adulthood, they have less access to senior-citizen centers, nursing homes, and other social services and amenities (Skinner, 1995).

Dig Deeper A glance at this woman at her outdoor pump might evoke sympathy. Her home's lack of plumbing suggests that she is experiencing late adulthood in poverty, in a rural community that probably offers few social services. Her race and gender put her at additional risk of problems as she ages. However, a deeper understanding might reveal many strengths: religious faith, strong family ties, and gritty survival skills.

The consequences of past racial stratification take more subtle forms as well. For example, in North America many elderly homeowners can choose whether they want to sell their home for profit, live in it rent-free, or obtain a "reverse mortgage" (receiving a monthly payment in exchange for title to the house when they die). However, decades of housing discrimination mean that fewer elderly African Americans own their houses than European Americans do. Even when black people do own a home, it is usually worth less than homes owned by whites, including whites who had the same income level (Myers & Chung, 1996).

Better Female, Nonwhite, and Old? Many contemporary analysts argue that stratification theory unfairly stigmatizes women and minority groups, who often have remarkable strengths in late adulthood (Blakemore & Boneham, 1994). For instance, compared to European Americans, elderly African and Hispanic Americans are often nurtured by multigenerational families and churches. As a result of this familism, fewer are in nursing homes (Johnson, 1999). Similarly, because women are caregivers and kinkeepers, they are less likely than elderly men to be lonely and depressed (Barusch, 1994). One review finds that because men are socialized to be self-sufficient, they are more vulnerable in late adulthood than women are. As a result, "gender is more problematic for men than women" (Huyck, 1996).

As age stratification theory reminds us, cohort shifts will change the meaning of gender and ethnicity for future generations. Today's middle-aged women are employed at almost the same rate as men, so many of them will have their own retirement income. Being old and female will no longer mean being poor. A less beneficial cohort shift is that younger African Americans depend less on family and church; thus their social isolation may increase in late adulthood. The general principle of stratification theory, however, is that whatever restrictions are placed on a person in middle adulthood will continue to have an impact later on. Gender and race may no longer have so powerful an impact, but other factors—perhaps immigration status or language skill—may come to the fore.

Dynamic Theories

dynamic theories Theories that emphasize change and readjustment rather than either the ongoing self or the legacy of stratification. Each person's life is seen as an active, ever-changing, largely self-propelled process, occurring within specific social contexts that themselves are constantly changing.

continuity theory The theory that each person experiences the changes of late adulthood and behaves toward others in much the same way as at earlier periods of life.

As you can see, neither self theories nor stratification theories include all the variations and changes of late adulthood. **Dynamic theories,** in contrast, view each person's life as an active, ever-changing, largely self-propelled process, occurring within specific social contexts that themselves are constantly changing.

Continuity Theory

The best-known dynamic theory is called (somewhat ironically) **continuity theory;** it focuses on how selfhood is maintained throughout the social events and biological changes. Continuity theory "assumes that a primary goal of adult development is adaptive change, not homeostatic equilibrium" (Atchley, 1999).

One type of continuity comes from temperament. Reinforced by the ecological niches that individuals have carved out for themselves, the so-called Big Five personality traits (described in Chapter 22) are maintained throughout old age as they were in younger years. Therefore, reactions to any potentially disruptive problem reflect continuity more than change. Attitudes toward everything—drugs, sexuality, money, neatness, privacy, health, government—similarly reflect lifelong continuity (Binstock & Day, 1996).

In what way is continuity theory dynamic and not merely an extension of behavioral genetics? The explanation lies in the fact that people

Not So Easy Increasing the adult–child ratio in the classroom benefits children, but funding, commitment, and program management on the part of government and school officials are often lacking. As a result, older adults who volunteer in the schools tend to be an inadequately utilized resource.

❷ Observational Quiz (see answer page 685): What aspects of this photograph indicate that this school volunteer, though well intentioned, is not providing the kind of supportive, interactive, and ongoing help that these children need?

tend to display a genetic inclination toward continuity that nonetheless accommodates to whatever changing social context they find themselves in (Atchley, 1999). For example, one woman never had her own career because she was actively supportive of her wealthy husband. After his retirement, she and her husband traveled extensively. Such a change may seem like a break from earlier times, but the same core of herself, and the same social niche, were evident: She was still a companion to her wealthy husband on cruises and visits to exotic cities. Then two very disruptive events occurred: Her husband died, and illness made her housebound. Nonetheless, she continued in her social role, hiring someone to manage her money, donating to selected charities, and finding satisfaction in supervising her three hired caregivers. These were all dynamic responses, not stagnant ones.

A similar example of a person who maintained her core identity even while adjusting to changing circumstances is a retired home economics teacher. She continued helping other people—first by doing volunteer work in her community; then, when walking became impossible, by allowing high school seniors to interview her at home. She spent the last days of her life as a much-loved role model in a nursing home (Atchley, 1999).

The dynamic viewpoint stresses that the entire social system works toward continuity, even as elements of individual lives change. Thus, although the retired teacher's nursing home was located several miles from the town where she had formerly lived, she still had more visitors than any other resident and was admired by staff and residents for her cheerful determination to make the best of things. The specifics of the system are constantly changing in response to how aging affects the individuals, but the entire system continues to function to ensure continuity.

Epigenetic Systems Again

You have probably noticed that self theories echo psychoanalytic theories (Chapter 2), especially in the importance they place on childhood self-concept and identity. Similarly, social stratification theories apply many concepts from sociocultural theory (Chapter 2). Now you can also see that this stress on dynamic change is an extension of epigenetic systems theory (also discussed in Chapter 2), which attempts to incorporate all the genetic, childhood, and cultural forces into an ever-changing but always productive system.

Both self theories and stratification theories are contained within dynamic theories. Self theories emphasize that, even in old age, each person defines him- or herself. Stratification theories alert us to the power of social context and include insights from the social-cultural perspective. Adding to both, however, dynamic theories stress the fluctuations caused by self and context and by personal and historical changes. Putting it all together, one researcher wrote, "Human life can be considered as a dynamic system consisting of hierarchically ordered and interacting elements . . . genes, cells, and organs, . . . cognition, motivation, and emotion, . . . social and material contexts" (Staudinger, 1999).

KEEPING ACTIVE

One basis of disengagement theory was the observation that retirement—either voluntary or forced—often correlated with reduction of social connections. As we will now see, however, retirement is a much

● *Answer to Observational Quiz (from page 683):* *He has a name tag ("Hello"), but they do not; and none of the trio is writing, pointing, or talking, all of which suggest a lack of close, supportive interaction.*

more varied experience than disengagement theory suggests, and many older adults who no longer work find other ways to stay active.

Retirement

Many nations are making mandatory retirement illegal and postponing the age at which government pension payments begin (Bossé, 1998). In theory, these changes would mean that more people would continue to work, especially because the correlation between retirement and ill health is widely known: Almost everyone knows someone who quit work and died a few months later.

Instead, however, adults are retiring at younger and younger ages, some as early as age 55, most before age 65, and almost all by age 70—a change from previous decades (see Figure 25.1). Similar trends are apparent in every developing nation (Ilmarinen, 1995).

These statistics actually exaggerate employment after age 55 because temporary layoffs, part-time work, and self-employment are bridges to retirement (Moen, 1998). Those listed as employed after age 65 are usually self-employed or part-time workers; by age 70, almost no one is working full time for someone else. They retire by choice for many reasons, including the anticipation of a happy, work-free life (Bossé et al., 1996).

Not all is rosy for retirees. There are two main problems: health and money. First, early retirement is often the result of failing health (Mutchler et al., 1999). Retirement and ill health are correlated not because retirement causes sickness (as people sometimes thought), but because sickness causes retirement (Mutchler et al., 1999). Second, income typically falls with age, as inflation, health care, and even housing become more costly than expected. If people simply look at average life span (about age 76) and ignore the average life span for someone who is already age 65 (age 84), they may seriously underestimate how much money they need. Early retirement induced by a generous severance payout often means pleasure at age 60 but poverty by age 80 (Quadagno & Hardy, 1996).

Fortunately, more and more of the elderly find their own way to supplement their income: becoming self-employed, working part time, or

Figure 25.1 Time to Retire. For men, the biggest change in retirement patterns occurred between 1970 and 1980. Since then, the trend has been for men to begin thinking about retirement at age 55 and, in nearly all cases, to retire by age 65.

● *Observational Quiz (see answer page 687):* *In what ways are women's retirement rates similar to and different from men's?*

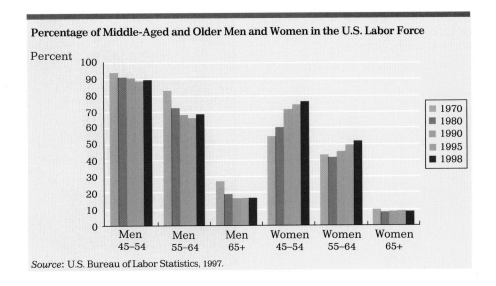

Percentage of Middle-Aged and Older Men and Women in the U.S. Labor Force

Source: U.S. Bureau of Labor Statistics, 1997.

performing unpaid work for family and friends in exchange for help, housing, and other necessities. The financial situation for widows and racial minorities is also improving, as pensions come closer to covering their needs. Overall, between 1980 and 1997 in the United States, the percentage of people over age 65 living in poverty fell from 15.7 percent to 10.5 percent. Even though minorities and widows have higher poverty rates than other groups, their situation has generally improved as well. This is most evident in the fastest-growing U.S. minority: 31 percent of elderly Hispanics were poor in 1980, but that figure fell to 24 percent in 1997 (U.S. Bureau of the Census, 1999).

Continuing Education

For many of the elderly, retirement offers an opportunity to pursue educational interests. During the 1990s in the United States, about one out of seven adults age 65 and older were enrolled in classes of some sort, ranging from courses in the practical arts to those leading to advanced college degrees (U.S. Bureau of the Census, 1999). Most of those under age 65 study for career advancement, but most (86 percent) elderly students are motivated by personal or social development. This can include a desire to develop hobbies, to manage investment income, or to understand their grandchildren (Jeanneret, 1995).

The eagerness of the elderly to learn is exemplified by the rapid growth of **Elderhostel,** a program in which people aged 55 and older live on college campuses and take special classes, usually during college vacation periods. Begun in New England in 1975 with 220 students, Elderhostel now operates at more than 2,000 sites throughout the United States and Canada, with an annual enrollment of more than 200,000 paying students (Elderhostel, 2000).

Thousands of other learning programs in the United States and Canada are filled with retirees. And in Europe, *Universities of the Third Age,* dedicated to older learners, have opened in a least a dozen na-

Elderhostel   A program in which people aged 55 and older live on college campuses and take special classes, usually during college vacation periods.

An Elderhostel Expedition Not all Elderhostel courses take place in the classroom. This group of U.S. students is on a three-week expedition studying the wildlife of Kangaroo Island, Australia.

tions. A survey in Norway found that 10 percent of those over age 67 had taken a course at one of these institutions in the past 3 years (Ingebretsen & Endestad, 1995).

Many elderly people hesitate to enter academic classes populated by mostly younger students. When they do so, however, they usually earn excellent grades because motivation, conscientiousness, and crystallized intelligence compensate for slower reactions and less fluid intelligence. They also enjoy the experience. One man surprised himself by taking drawing, painting, and Spanish classes at a community college, explaining:

> When I first retired, I couldn't wait to pack up and go to a warm climate and just goof off. But now, retirement is an enormous challenge. Once you start learning about yourself, you get the feeling that anything is possible. [quoted in Goldman, 1991]

Volunteer Work

Many older adults feel a strong commitment to their community and believe that older people should be of service to others. For example, when a cross section of nearly 3,000 Americans were asked whether older adults have an obligation to help others and serve the community, about twice as many older adults as younger adults strongly agreed; only 6 percent of those over age 60 strongly disagreed, compared to 12 percent of those under 60 (Herzog & House, 1991). Older adults are particularly likely to do volunteer work assisting the very young, the very old, or the sick, perhaps because of their perspective on life or because of their patience and experience. Interestingly, those who are recently retired are more likely to become involved in volunteer work than are those over age 75 (Caro & Bass, 1997; Guterbock & Fries, 1997).

Much of this volunteer work is informal. In stable neighborhoods that have a sizable number of elderly, the more capable residents often run errands, fix meals, repair broken appliances, and perform other services that generally make it possible for the disabled elderly to continue to live at home. Such neighborhood help is particularly notable among elderly African Americans. This is one reason that, as noted in Chapter 23, their crime victimization rate is much lower than that of young people, even though many of them live in deteriorating areas (Johnson, 1999).

The elderly also provide a good deal of care for family members. About 30 percent of the elderly provide regular personal care to an elderly relative, and 15 percent provide child care, again usually for relatives (Kincade et al., 1996).

About a third of the elderly are involved with more structured volunteering, often through churches, hospitals, or schools (U.S. Bureau of the Census, 1999). While this proportion is substantial, it is lower than volunteerism rates for younger adults with similar work and family obligations. In fact, those who are fully retired are less likely to volunteer than are those who are still working part time.

Self theories and stratification theories suggest that more of the elderly would do volunteer work if they recognized their own potential and if social agencies made an effort

Friend-to-Friend Some volunteer programs are trying a new approach known as "timedollars." Volunteer caregivers earn credits for the time they volunteer—visiting, shopping, doing housekeeping, providing transportation, and the like—and are then able to redeem those credits when they themselves are in need of services. Felina Mendoza, shown here visiting a man who is just home from the hospital, is a member of Friend-to-Friend, a timedollar program in Miami, Florida. Its 800 participants earn an average of 8,000 hours of service credits each month.

to match each person's talents with the needs of the community (Herzog & Morgan, 1993). That the elderly often do not recognize the service they can provide is reflected in the reaction one older woman had when she and her husband were asked to work with stroke victims:

> Of what possible use could we be, a seventyish couple who had none of the seemingly necessary skills, no knowledge of speech or physical therapy, no special social skills either?

Several months after this couple overcame their self-doubt and began the volunteer work, the woman wrote:

> The real question was [not] "What can we do?" [but] "What can we be?" Can we be warm, caring unstroke-damaged human beings, to meet . . . with stroke-damaged ones, exchanging concerns, playing word games, encouraging them to feel at ease, to talk and tease and laugh with us and with each other. . . . I wish everyone who feels so useless and lonely could have such a completely satisfying experience as Tom and I are having. [quoted in Vickery, 1978]

As in this example, the elderly themselves benefit from volunteering. One large study found that volunteers lived longer than those who did not volunteer (Musick et al., 1999). This was not merely a correlation between level of activity and health, because those who benefited most volunteered for only one organization. The reason may be that for the elderly, volunteering serves as a way to gain an important role and to be needed as well as "to construct an enhanced sense of purpose by doing things for others" (Bradley, 1999–2000). These goals are easier to accomplish if a person commits to just one organization and then makes him- or herself useful, even essential, to that group.

Political Involvement

By many measures, the elderly are more politically active than any other age group. Compared to younger people, they know more about national and local issues, write more letters to their elected representatives, vote in more elections, feel stronger about party loyalty, and belong to more groups that lobby for their interests (Torres-Gil, 1992). The only measurement of political participation on which they fall short is in door-to-door campaigning, although even here, many are active pavement pounders.

All this political participation translates into considerable power, especially when the elderly organize themselves into political action groups. The major U.S. organization representing the elderly is the American Association of Retired Persons (AARP), the largest organized interest group in the United States. In 1999,

Taking to the Streets This prominent women's movement leader urges her followers to demonstrate against a 1999 proposal that the Japanese government organize a small army. The U.S. government advocates the proposal, because the Japanese arms expansion before World War II is a distant memory for most Americans. Not so for Fuki Kushida, who, despite her age, speaks with considerable political force.

❓ *Observational Quiz (see answer page 692): How old do you think Fuki Kushida is? (Hint: Merely looking at the photograph will not help. Think about the caption.)*

AARP had a membership of more than 33 million (members must be over 50 but need not be retired), employed 52 congressional lobbyists, and involved more than 158,000 volunteers in various projects. The political influence of this organization is one reason Social Security has been called "the third rail" of domestic politics, fatal if touched by any politician who wants to cut its benefits.

Among other major senior organizations are the National Committee to Preserve Social Security and Medicare and the National Council for Senior Citizens (5 million members each) as well as the Gray Panthers (400,000 members). Dozens of smaller special-interest groups focus on issues of concern to elders (Binstock & Day, 1996).

All this political activism makes many younger adults suspect that senior citizens wield unprecedented power, which they use unfairly to advance their economic interests. This idea is inaccurate. True, elders tend to support financial assistance of all kinds for the aged, but most also understand wider social concerns and are willing to vote against the interests of their own age group if a greater good is at stake. When a tax on the Social Security income of wealthier elders was proposed in 1993, for example, the idea received more support from the old than from the young (Kosterlitz, 1993). Questions regarding generational equity—that is, whether each generation contributes and receives its fair share of society's wealth—can be asked about every age group (see the Changing Policy box).

Home, Sweet Home

One way many people stay busy is to maintain their home and yard. Typically, the amount of housework done by both men and women increases after retirement (Klieber, 1999; Szinovacz, 2000). Particularly strong is the impulse to do tasks that are *not* necessary household chores: gardening, redecorating, building, and, in some cases, moving. For a minority of the elderly, retirement means going to another place—to a Sunbelt state (18 percent of Florida's population was over age 65 in 2000) or back to a sunny homeland in the Caribbean, Mexico, or Africa.

Most elderly people, however, prefer to "age in place" (Pynoos & Golant, 1996), staying in the same home and never moving. When they do relocate, it is often within the same region so as to remain near their adult children, other family members, or old friends (Hobbs & Damon, 1996). If the children move too far away, however, most elders stay put—which helps to explain why the elderly population in such unlikely places as West Virginia, Maine, and Pennsylvania is above the national average.

One result of aging in place is that many of the elderly live alone. Some observers bemoan the demise of the extended family living under one roof. However, interviews and studies of the elderly themselves find that the majority of those living alone prefer it that way.

We should not confuse living arrangements with social support. In one multinational study, most respondents said they talk to family members regularly; 90 percent said they would solicit help or advice from another generation within their family if a problem arose (Farkas & Hogan, 1995). Thanks to the ease of communication and travel today, aging parents and middle-aged children typically stay in very close touch with each other even if they live a great distance apart (Bengston et al., 1996). It is no longer unusual for senior citizens to e-mail their children every day and to keep a guest room ready for an extended visit.

POVERTY, AGE, AND EQUITY

About 40 years ago, in his book *The Other America*, Michael Harrington painted a chilling picture of the extent of poverty among adults who were then above age 65:

> Fifty percent of the elderly exist below minimal standards of decency, and this is a figure much higher than that for any other age group. . . . We have given them bare survival, but not the means of living honorable and satisfying lives. [Harrington, 1962]

Harrington was right. One out of every three elderly residents of the United States was then living below the poverty line, and a substantial additional number were "near poor," at the edge of poverty. Health care was privately paid, which meant it was beyond the reach of many senior citizens.

Since that time, various economic, demographic, and political changes have raised both the personal income and the living standards of many elderly Americans. Social Security was extended to more people. A range of medical and social benefits were established for the aged, reducing the proportion of the elderly below the poverty line to about one in ten. The federal government in 1998 spent three times as much on the aged (mostly Medicare and Social Security) as on defense (U.S. Bureau of the Census, 1999). Many state and local governments offer the elderly a break on income tax, transportation, and so on. Many companies now offer pensions that afford a comfortable retirement and provide symbolic measures, such as discounts at fast-food restaurants.

Ironically, during the same years that the elderly in the United States were growing richer, children were growing poorer. In 1998, about one child in five (19 percent) lived below the poverty line compared with one in seven (15 percent) in 1970 (U.S. Bureau of the Census, 1999).

A backlash against this economic disparity has led to calls for *generational equity*, defined as equal contributions from, and fair benefits for, each generation. Some point out that the current distribution of benefits is particularly imbalanced for racial minorities, who tend to be overrepresented among the young and underrepresented among the old (see Figure 25.2).

One area that is frequently mentioned as a candidate for generational equity is health care: The outlay of public funds

Proportion of the U.S. Population Under Age 20 and Age 60 and Older, by Race

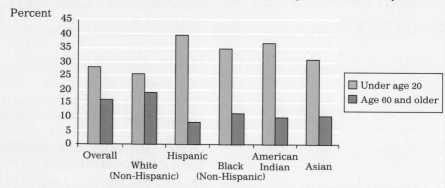

Figure 25.2 The Young and the Old. Racial discrimination sometimes results inadvertently from policies intended to be fair to all. For example, a decision to decrease funds for public schools in order to increase funding for senior citizens' health care is twice as likely to benefit non-Hispanic white seniors as other ethnic groups, while more nonwhite children are harmed. The population breakdown shown here is for the United States, but similar proportions hold for the entire world, with one exception: The continent with the most children is Africa, not Latin America (see Appendix A).

THE SOCIAL CONVOY

social convoy Collectively, the family members, friends, acquaintances, and even strangers who move through life with an individual.

The phrase **social convoy** highlights the truism that we travel our life course in the company of others. At various points, other people join and leave our convoy; but just like members of a wagon train headed west or a convoy of battleships crossing the high seas, we could never make the journey successfully alone. The special bonds formed as we journey help us in good times and bad. It is more pleasant to share triumphs with those who know how important the victory is. When our survival is threatened, it may be critical to have familiar confederates

for medical treatment and hospitalization of the aged results in inadequate preventive medicine in childhood and adolescence (Callahan, 1990). As one older researcher explains:

> We fear being overthrown by the next generation. . . . We fear not being cared for in our waning years. Greed, too, is involved, not only the financial greed that makes us overstay our years in a high-paying job or resist a reconsideration of government entitlements, but also greed for life, for the extra year or two that extraordinary medicine might bestow. The cost of those extra years may very well compromise medical care for the young. [Kotre, 1999–2000]

At their fiercest, critics argue that the young are soaked to enrich the old, that greedy elders are living off the regressive Social Security taxes that deplete the wages of younger workers, and that "age wars" will soon ensue unless we "cut the graybeards a smaller slice of the pie" (Becker, 1994).

Gerontologists believe that this framing of the problem is an "ideological smokescreen" that obscures the real needs of the poor, whatever age they are (Adams & Dominick, 1995). In fact, income inequality in the United States increases with age, with some of the elderly among the richest and others among the poorest (O'Rand, 1996). Most are in the middle, but even for them, the specter of poverty seems frighteningly close. Forty percent experience at least 1 year of poverty before age 90. This number increases to 90 percent of elderly African Americans who never completed high school (Rank & Hrischl, 1999).

Many of the most vulnerable older individuals, especially the widowed, the divorced, the nonwhite, and the physically frail, live alone in dangerous and dilapidated housing. In the United States in 1998, about 5 million women over age 75 lived alone, a higher proportion than any other group (U.S. Bureau of the Census, 1999). Thus, it is mistaken to imagine that the elderly are rich. Even the middle class have good reason to fear poverty if they live long enough.

Competition Between Generations Social Security is the only major public assistance that rises automatically with inflation—a fact not lost on many young adults who see their Social Security taxes rise and their educational benefits fall.

Moreover, implicit in a life-span view of human development is the realization that each age and cohort has its own particular and legitimate economic needs that other generations might fail to appreciate. For instance, whether day-care programs, low-interest loans for college, or entitlements for the elderly are the most important use of government funds depends largely on the immediate interests of one's own age group. Yet in the long term, each of these subsidies works to the betterment of all.

Taking a developmental view, then, each generation might balance its needs with those of the others. The interdependence of all generations must be seen in full perspective and addressed accordingly: Help for impoverished youth should not be found by depriving the old.

whom we have helped in the past. Having people who know who we once were helps us maintain our identity. Even strangers from the same cohort help us in this way, which is part of the reason many young adults grieved at Princess Diana's death and many older adults take comfort in the continued survival of elderly political figures and entertainers.

For older adults particularly, the social network's continuity over time is an important affirmation. Friends who "knew them when" are particularly valuable, as are family members who share a lifetime of experiences and commitments. We will begin our examination of the social convoy by looking at the closest relationship of all, the long-term marriage.

So Happy Together Research suggests that long-term marriages improve with age, and that many long-married older adults are happier with their partners than they were as newlyweds. This blissful couple, married over 40 years, would no doubt concur.

❶ *Answer to Observational Quiz (from page 688): She is 100 years old.*

Long-Term Marriages

For many older people, a spouse is the best buffer against many of the potential problems of old age. Most elders are married, and they tend to be healthier, wealthier, and happier than those who never married or who are divorced or widowed (Myers, 2000). When asked "What is your most important role in life?" almost half of a cross section of older adults said "spouse," compared to about a fourth who said "parent" and an eighth who said "grandparent" (Krauss, 1999).

Although some people marry or remarry in late adulthood, it is far more common for an elderly couple to have been together for decades. This raises an important question: Do marriage relationships change as people grow old? According to longitudinal as well as cross-sectional research, both continuity and discontinuity are apparent. The single best predictor of the nature of a marriage in its later stages is its nature early on: While the absolute levels of conflict, sexual activity, and emotional intensity drop over time, couples who start out relatively high or low on any of these dimensions tend to remain so as time goes by.

In some ways, marriage actually improves with time. One reason is the children, who grow from being the prime source of conflict for younger parents to being the prime source of pleasure for elderly parents (Levenson et al., 1993). Another reason is that all the shared contextual factors—living in the same community, raising the same children, and dealing with the same financial and spiritual circumstances—tend to change both partners in similar ways. This brings long-married couples closer together in personality, perspectives, and values (Caspi et al., 1992).

Even conflicts become less troublesome. One study that deliberately compared both happy and unhappy couples of various ages found that when the older couples discussed contentious issues, they expressed more warmth, humor, and respect than the younger couples did (Carstensen et al., 1995).

Generally, older spouses accept their mutual frailties, tending to each other's physical and psychological needs as best they can, usually with feelings of affection rather than of simple obligation. The affection that accompanies such caregiving was shown in a study which found that wives who cared for their dependent husbands usually felt closer to their spouses and less burdened by the experience in the later stages of caregiving than at the start (Seltzer & Li, 1996). This positive result was a direct consequence of being a spouse—rather than of simply being a female or of simply getting used to caregiving—because the same study also found that daughters providing care for aging parents felt more burdened and a greater emotional distance in the later stages of caregiving.

Our focus on mutual caregiving should not distort our understanding of late-life marriages. Intimacy, companionship, and even passionate love are part of the marital relationship for many older couples (Melton et al., 1995). When one happily married elderly couple were asked about their sex life, the husband responded:

> We have sex less frequently now, but it's satisfying to me. Now that we are both home, we could spend all our time in bed. But it's still more amorous when we go away. When we travel, it's like a second honeymoon.

His wife added:

> Sex has been important in our marriage, but not the most important. The most important thing has been our personal relationship, our fondness, respect, and friendship. [quoted in Wallerstein & Blakeslee, 1995]

Widowhood

Half of all married older adults will, obviously, experience the death of a spouse, the most serious stress that adults typically undergo. This is usually a woman's crisis: Women in the United States live 6 years longer than men on average, and husbands are typically 3 years older than their wives, so American wives average 9 years of widowhood. Of the more than 29 million Americans who were 65 or older in 1998, 8.4 million women were widows, while just over 2 million men were widowers (U.S. Bureau of the Census, 1999).

The death of a mate usually means not only the loss of a close friend and lover but also lower income, less status, a broken social circle, and disrupted daily routines. In addition, routines of meal preparation, visiting friends, taking walks, and even regular bedtimes typically falter, adding up to substantial physiological stress. Perhaps even more crucial for today's older widows—whose primary roles are likely to have been spouse, caregiver, and homemaker—is the loss of identity (DeGarmo & Kitson, 1996).

It is not surprising, then, that in the months following the death of their spouse, widows and widowers are more likely to be physically ill than their married contemporaries are. Widowers particularly are also at a markedly increased risk of death, either by suicide or by natural causes (Hemstrom, 1996; Osgood, 1992).

Gender Differences

In general, living without a spouse is somewhat easier for women than for men. Elderly women expect to outlive their husbands and make arrangements for some of the adjustments that widowhood will require. Men, by contrast, often buy insurance to protect their wives rather than thinking about how their own needs will be met if their wives die first. In addition, new widows usually have friends and neighbors who themselves are widows and who are ready to provide sympathy and support.

One longitudinal study found that over a 2-year period, morale went up in 39 percent and down in 33 percent of women whose husbands died. Men, however, often become less happy when their wives died: 42 percent dropped in morale (Atchley, 1999). The size of this sample was too small to claim that these results are statistically significant. Nonetheless, the findings are in accord with those of other quantitative research.

Another gender difference also makes adjustment more difficult for widowers. Many members of this cohort grew up with restrictive notions of masculine behavior. As a result, they tend to depend on their wives to perform the basic tasks of daily living (such as cooking and cleaning) and to provide emotional support and social interaction. When their wives die, they often find it hard to reveal their feelings of weakness and sorrow to another person, to ask for help, to care for themselves, or even to invite someone over to chat (Wilson, 1995).

Once they have gotten over their initial depression, many men discover that they are sought after by women who would happily fix their meals, clean their houses, and marry them, if possible. Indeed, widowers

Chorus Line What is in store for the elderly woman whose husband dies? Probably not a new man: unattached older males are "scarce as hen's teeth." Instead, female friends, such as these women sunning themselves in Miami Beach, are usually eager to welcome one more to their lineup. Notice the one man at the end (the only one not looking at the photographer).

SIBLINGS

One of the seldom-studied yet vital aspects of late adulthood is the relationship between siblings, who are often quite close in late adulthood (Cicirelli, 1995). In one study of 300 older adults, 77 percent considered at least one of their siblings to be "a close friend" (Connidis, 1994).

This is apparent in my own family. When my parents were in their 60s, living in Pennsylvania and thinking of retiring, they thought of moving to a Sunbelt state, particularly Arizona, where some of their friends had gone. In the end, however, they moved back to their childhood home state of Minnesota to be near their five living siblings. My phone conversations with them revealed more about sibling rivalry and support than I would have imagined.

At one point, two of my aunts, Beth and Laura, were so angry at each other that they stopped speaking. I saw them as old women in their 80s, both looking almost the same: overweight, with thick glasses, and walking with a cane. Dumbfounded that anyone in that condition could be so angry, I asked my mother what the argument was about. "It began long ago when Papa favored Laura," Mom said. "You have to remember, Laura is the pretty one [she had blue eyes and curly hair], and Beth has always been jealous." I am happy to report that, thanks to my elderly father's intervention, Beth and Laura resumed daily phone conversations several months before Laura died of cancer.

As in this example, closeness between siblings is not automatic: Rivalries rooted in childhood often continue throughout life (Greer, 1992). In some cases, the death of the parents, rather than freeing siblings from a lifelong rivalry, actually increases it. Even the death of a sibling does not nec-

essarily release the survivor from resentment or jealousy (Cicirelli, 1995).

More often, however, sibling conflicts fade and intimacy increases in late adulthood. One researcher described the usual pattern between siblings as an "hourglass effect": close during childhood, increasingly distant until middle adulthood, then gradually closer again as late adulthood progresses (Bedford, 1995). Siblings who respected and liked each other throughout adulthood but who never spent much time together often become confidants and may even live together again when a spouse dies. Relationships between sisters are likely to be particularly close.

The specifics of sibling relationships in late adulthood are strongly influenced by family values instilled in childhood. If the family encouraged the idea that one should "protect your sister" or "stick up for your brother," this value is likely to reemerge in old age, especially if frailty or loneliness threatens (Cicirelli, 1995).

Ironically, the life event most likely to bring siblings closer is death—of a parent, a spouse, or, most of all, a sibling. With such losses often comes appreciation of one's brothers and sisters. As one man, the youngest of six, explained:

> When our mother died, a big shift happened in our family. Instead of counting on Mom to arrange family gatherings or parties, we all realized we would have to do that ourselves. It's true that Emily [the oldest sibling] has become a "surrogate Mom" and takes responsibility for remembering all the birthdays and who would bring what for Thanksgiving dinner. But all of us feel closer. [quoted in Gold, 1996]

While relationships with younger generations are clearly positive, they also include tension and conflict. Almost all elders who have children and grandchildren devote time and attention to them, sometimes to the frustration of all parties. Few older adults stop parenting simply because their children are fully grown, independent, married, or parents themselves. As one 82-year-old woman succinctly put it: "No matter how old a mother is, she watches her middle-aged children for signs of improvement" (Scott-Maxwell, 1968).

Generally, the mother–daughter relationship is simultaneously close and vulnerable. For example, in one study of 48 mother–daughter pairs whose average ages were 76 and 44, respectively, 75 percent of the mothers and almost 60 percent of the daughters listed the other among the three most important persons in their lives. At the same time, 83 percent of the mothers and 100 percent of the daughters readily acknowledged having recently been "irritated, hurt, or annoyed" by the other. The mothers were more likely to blame someone else for the irritation ("Her husband kept on turning up the radio every time I turned it down"), and the daughters were more likely to blame their mother for intruding on their lives ("She tells me how to discipline my kids") (Fingerman, 1996).

Ideally, either the elders are willing to accept help gratefully, "minding their own business" about any complaints they might have, or the elders and their children are quite willing to keep their distance. The least satisfactory situations are when parents want assistance and feel entitled to criticize their children, or when children want to provide help and are critical of their parents (Pyke, 1999). Here is an example of the latter:

> *Father:* My daughter called up my wife and said, "You must sell your house." I have this heart condition, and my daughter doesn't want me to walk up a flight of stairs to go up to the bedroom. . . . So my wife says, "No. I'm never going to sell it. . . . I love the place we live in."
>
> *Daughter:* I've always been close to my mother, but it's only this last, well, maybe the last 2 years that I'm beginning to resent the fact that she lives in this big house and that I have to keep worrying about her and going there and making sure that they're all right. My dad is too ill to live in a big house, but she just doesn't want to give it up. . . . My mother refuses to leave the house, and I'm beginning to resent her selfishness; I really am. [quoted in Pyke, 1999]

A family can be very supportive or very independent, with either pattern welcomed in some families and resented in others. As a variation, a family can be high on assistance and contact without necessarily being high on warmth and affection. Both satisfaction and resentment depend more on emotional ties than on particulars of communication and help.

- Assistance arises both from need and from the ability to provide it.
- In-person contact depends mostly on geographic proximity.
- Affection is strongly influenced by a family's past history of mutual love and respect.
- Sons feel stronger obligation, while daughters feel stronger affection.
- Cultures and families vary markedly; there is no agreed-upon "right" way for the generations to interact.

Contrary to popular perceptions, since most of the elderly are quite capable of caring for themselves, assistance typically flows from the older generation to their children instead of vice versa. In fact, most elders are pleased to be able to buy things for their children and to help out occasionally with the grandchildren, and they do not expect large gifts in return, even if their financial circumstances should change (Hamon & Blieszner, 1990). The older generation also typically enjoys social contact with the younger generations, but most prefer the children to visit them at their invitation for a few hours rather than to come uninvited, stay too long, or expect the elders to do the traveling.

The price of intergenerational harmony may be intergenerational distance. This was clearly the case for one couple who felt that they were viewed as "outmoded and irrelevant" rather than "wise or expert":

> Our grandson just got married. They both have fancy taste and fancy plans, and they mean to have it all. When we asked about a baby, they said they wouldn't even think about having a child until they could afford a full-time nanny to raise it. Imagine planning to have children so that you won't have time to raise them! Whose children are they, anyway? Why have them? We love him so much, and we don't want to hurt him, so we didn't say anything. As long as we keep rather quiet, he thinks we're sweet and lovable—and rather silly. . . . [Erikson et al., 1986]

THE FRAIL ELDERLY

Remember from Chapter 23 that aging can be categorized as optimal, usual, or impaired. So far we have emphasized the majority of the elderly—either those aging in the usual way, alert and active, financially secure, supported by friendship and family ties, or those who are so successful that they gain new financial and social freedom. These two groups are quite different from the group we focus on now—the **frail elderly,** a group that includes the physically infirm, the very ill, and the cognitively impaired.

Beyond simple vulnerability and fragility, the crucial sign of frailty is an elderly person's inability to perform, safely and adequately, the various tasks of self-care. Gerontologists often refer to the **activities of daily life,** abbreviated **ADLs,** which consist of eating, bathing, toileting, dressing, and transferring between a bed and a chair. If a person needs assistance with even one of these five tasks, he or she may be considered frail, although for some purposes (such as medical insurance or research on dependency) frailty does not begin until a person is unable to perform three or more of them.

Equally important to independent living, if not more so, are the **instrumental activities of daily life,** or **IADLs,** actions that require some intellectual competence and forethought (Willis, 1996). As one might expect, specific IADLs vary somewhat from culture to culture. For most of the elderly in developed nations, IADLs include shopping for groceries, paying bills, driving a car, taking medications, and keeping appointments (see Table 25.1). In rural areas of other nations, feeding the chickens, cultivating the garden, mending clothes, getting water from the well, and baking bread might be among the culture's IADLs. Everywhere, however, the inability to perform such tasks can make a person sufficiently impaired that he or she becomes frail and dependent on others.

frail elderly   People over age 65 who are physically infirm, very ill, or cognitively impaired.

activities of daily life (ADLs)   Actions that are important to independent living, typically comprising five tasks: eating, bathing, toileting, dressing, and transferring from a bed to a chair. The inability to perform these tasks is a sign of frailty.

instrumental activities of daily life (IADLs)   Actions that are important to independent living and that require some intellectual competence and forethought. These are even more critical to self-sufficiency than ADLs.

An Activity of Daily Life Severe arthritis puts this woman in the category of the frail, meaning that she needs assistance with her ADLs. She is not frail of spirit, however, and with the help of an aide, she is able to live a robust and relatively independent life.

table **25.1**	**Instrumental Activities of Daily Life**
Domain	Exemplar Task
Managing medications	Determining how many doses of cough medicine can be taken in 24-hour period Completing a patient medical history form
Shopping for necessities	Ordering merchandise from a catalog Comparison of brands of a product
Managing one's finances	Comparison of Medigap Insurance Plans Completing tax return for income tax form
Using transportation	Computing taxi rates Interpreting driver's right-of-way laws
Using the telephone	Determining amount to pay from phone bill Determining emergency phone information
Maintaining one's household	Following instructions for operating a household appliance Comprehending appliance warranty
Meal preparation and nutrition	Evaluating nutritional information on food label Following recipe directions

Source: Willis, 1996.

Another Test The items in the right-hand column are taken from a questionnaire to assess IADL competence. As you can see, managing daily life is not easy; but most of the elderly do it well.

Increasing Prevalence of Frailty

Worldwide, the frail elderly are a minority. At any given moment, no more than a fifth of the world's senior citizens overall are frail by any measure, which means most of the elderly can manage their own daily care. However, in every nation, the number of frail elderly and the degree of their frailty are increasing, for four reasons:

- More people are reaching very old age. In the United States, for instance, the number of people aged 85 and older doubled in the 20 years from 1980 to 2000 (a time period when the number of teenagers actually fell), making the oldest age group the fastest-growing segment of the population. Those over age 65 are still only 7 percent of the world's population, compared to 30 percent under age 15; but this is nonetheless a sizable shift. In 1970, only 5 percent of the world's people were over 65, and 40 percent were under 15.
- Medical care now prolongs life. For example, a British study examined the last year of life over an 18-year period. An increasing proportion of those who died were over age 75 (54 percent in 1987 compared with 40 percent in 1969), were physically frail, and were in and out of hospitals in their last year of life (Seale & Cartwright, 1994). An active 70-year-old was far less likely to die peacefully at home in his sleep after 1980 than before.
- Health care emphasizes death postponement more than life enhancement. Since chronic problems—everything from Alzheimer's disease and arthritis to ulcers and varicose veins—are the ones that most commonly sap elderly people's strength, pride, and independence, the result of these medical priorities is increasing morbidity even as mortality rates fall.

■ Measures that could prevent or reduce impairment—such as adequate nutrition, safe housing, hearing aids, and hip replacements—do not necessarily reach the frailest elderly, who need them the most. Obtaining benefits requires some mobility, planning, initiative, and sometimes co-payment (especially for the most essential ones—housing, health, and food). This combination tends to exclude the poor, uneducated, or isolated, precisely those who are most likely to become frail (Estes et al., 1996). Without access to various benefits, a higher proportion of those who have no family advocates become both physically and mentally impaired (Skinner, 1995).

Age and Self-Efficacy

❓ Especially for Those Uncertain About Future Careers: Would you like to work in a nursing home?

Because we are focusing here on impairments and on the personal attitudes (self theories) and social structures (stratification barriers) that foster them, we need to remember the variability (dynamic systems) of later life: Even living until 100 or being female, nonwhite, or poor does not necessarily lead to frailty. Much depends on various personal, family, community, and cultural conditions. Further, cultural forces are increasingly important with age (Baltes et al., 1998), which means that any particular person who is both poor and frail may have first become culturally restricted and socially isolated and then become poor and frail as a result, rather than vice versa.

To better understand how a person avoids frailty, we need to look not only at demographics (such as stratification by race and gender) but also at self theory. An active drive for autonomy, control, and independence is one of the best defenses against becoming dependent. Correspondingly, loss of control invites further weaknesses in many domains (Miller & Lackman, 1999). As one team of researchers notes:

> To a sizable number of chronically ill older persons, their disability is of less salience than might be expected, because they can shift their priorities to other behavioral options. Perceived control and perceived self-efficacy are associated with positive health practices on the one hand, and with the absence of chronic disease and with good functional ability and self-perceived health on the other hand. [Deeg et al., 1996]

Essentially, when a disability occurs, a person can choose to overcome it, compensate for it, live with it, or dwell on it. Thus, a person who is becoming limited because of weakening leg muscles might start a daily regimen of strength training, might purchase a good walker, might adjust to the limitation (by staying on the first floor of the home, for example, rather than going upstairs or walking outside), or might become a chair-bound invalid, complaining, "I can't do anything anymore because I might fall."

In this example, working to remain mobile would be especially appropriate because a fear of falling is one of the best predictors of later functional decline (Tinetti & Powell, 1993), and lower body strength is one of the best predictors of avoiding dependency (Lewis, 1996). Similar choices are involved in virtually every disability, with each choice affecting the degree of frailty that ensues.

As the dynamic systems perspective reminds us, some people enter late adulthood with many protective buffers in place: family members

A LIFE-SPAN VIEW

BETWEEN OLD, FRAGILE, AND FRAIL—PROTECTIVE BUFFERS

Frailty is not automatically defined by either age or illness. Both advanced years and specific infirmities may make a person more fragile. However, neither condition necessarily makes a person frail, because the health and independence of the elderly depend not only on intrinsic impairment but also on extrinsic resources (Davies, 1991). Many elderly persons with health problems never become helpless because four protective factors—attitude, social network, physical setting, and financial resources—act as buffers. They prevent or postpone the progression from fragility to frailty.

Consider the hypothetical example of two 80-year-old childless widows who have the same good hearing but failing eyesight and advanced osteoporosis. One widow might live alone in an old, rundown house in an isolated neighborhood. Among the particulars of her residence and daily life are uneven hardwood floors covered with braided scatter rugs, a flight of steep stairs separating the bedroom and the kitchen, dimly lit rooms and hallways, and rumors of a recent robbery two blocks away. She hears every creak of the old house, listening in terror.

After falling and fracturing her wrist on the way to the toilet one night, she is now apprehensive about walking without help. She refuses to go downstairs to prepare meals. She never ventures outside and is afraid to answer the door or the phone. Further, she no longer tries to wash or dress herself, or even to eat as much as she should, citing some lingering pain in her fingers and her belief that "no one cares anyway."

Obviously, this widow is very frail, requiring ongoing care. At present, a home attendant comes every morning to bathe her and prepare the day's food, but the attendant is worried about the woman's depression. This is a valid concern, since suicide is more prevalent among the elderly than among any other age group and is particularly common among those over 75 who live alone. This widow is on the waiting list of a nursing home. There she is likely to become even more frail, since nursing homes often discourage independent functioning.

The other widow, by contrast, might have had the financial resources and foresight in middle age to have purchased, with two old friends, a large co-op apartment near a small shopping center. As all three are aging, they have reduced their vulnerability by outfitting their home with precautionary amenities such as bright lighting, sturdy furniture strategically placed to aid mobility, secure grab rails in the bathroom to ease bathing and toileting, wall-to-wall carpeting nailed to the floor, a telephone programmed to dial important numbers at the push of one button, a stove that automatically shuts off after a certain time, and a front door that buzzes until it is properly locked with the key.

In addition, all three women gladly compensate for each other's impairments: The one who sees best reads the fine print on all the medicine bottles, legal papers, and cooking directions; the one who is the sturdiest sweeps, mops, and vacuums; and our poorly sighted, osteoporotic widow, who has excellent hearing, responds to the phone, the doorbell, the alarm clock, the oven timer. All three regularly eat, converse, and laugh together—a practice that is good for the digestion as well as the spirit.

Unlike the first widow, who will soon be institutionalized, the second widow with the same physical problems is safe and happy in her apartment, caring for herself, socializing with friends, and shopping in the community. Her buffers will defend her against many factors that could otherwise be disabling. For example, she will be motivated, encouraged, and financially able to obtain good medical care and enabling accessories, such as corrective eyedrops and special glasses, or calcium supplements and a hip replacement, or even, if both major disabilities worsen, home delivery of audiotaped books and the purchase of a small, motorized wheelchair.

The lesson here is that a certain degree of fragility and vulnerability does not necessarily translate into an equivalent degree of frailty. Just as a fine crystal goblet—admired, lovingly handled, and carefully stored—is unlikely to break despite its fragility, so an older person, surrounded by crucial buffering, may not become frail.

and friends, past education and continued educational opportunity, work that gave them a good pension and continued work opportunities, and a lifetime of good health habits (see A Life-Span View). Others suffer every type of setback.

Caring for the Frail Elderly

Today, as in the past, most of the frail elderly are cared for by relatives. Indeed, of every ten North American elders who need some assistance, six depend exclusively on family and friends. The other four receive a combination of family and professional care, half within a nursing home and half in the community. Even those who are mentally incompetent as well as physically frail are usually cared for by family in the community; those in nursing homes are disproportionately widowed or never-married and without living children (Gordon & Stryker, 1996).

Ageless Love Many women today who reach age 35 hesitate to have a child because they worry they will not be alive when the child grows up. Such concerns are becoming outdated as more and more people live to age 80 and beyond. This Manitoban mother, who is 117, is cared for by her daughter, who was born when the mother was 49.

The tradition in the United States is that husbands and wives care for each other until it is no longer possible. By contrast, many other cultures stress the obligation of children to their parents rather than of the elderly to each other. In Korea, for instance, 80 percent of elderly people with dementia are cared for by daughters-in-law and only 7 percent by a spouse. This changes soon after immigration. In a similar group of Korean Americans, 40 percent of spouses and only 19 percent of daughters-in-law were the main caregivers (Youn et al., 1999).

Burdens and Benefits of Family Care

The demands of caring at home for a frail elderly relative should not be underestimated. In many cases, the caregiver must forgo all other activities, because the physical work and psychological stress are overwhelming. One daughter describes the strain she and her elderly father experienced when her mother developed Alzheimer's disease:

> I worked the entire time through four pregnancies . . . returning to work within six weeks of delivery. It was a piece of cake compared to trying to cope with a combative, frustrated adult who cannot dress, bathe, feed herself; who wanders constantly. A person faced with this situation . . . having to work a full day, raise a family, and take care of an "impaired" relative would be susceptible to suicide, "parent-abuse" . . . possibly murder.
>
> My father tried very hard to take care of her, but a man 84 years old cannot go without sleep, and cannot force her to take care of her personal cleanliness. Up until two years ago, she was taking care of the finances and household. Her signature was beautiful . . . now it's just a wavy line. An 84-year-old man does not learn to cook and balance the budget very easily, and he becomes bitter. He did not want to put her in the nursing homes he visited, and so he reluctantly sold his house and moved to a city he didn't like so that his children could help with her care. It has been a nightmare . . . she obviously belonged in a secondary-care facility because no one can give her 24-hr. care and still maintain their sanity and families. But the real victim is Dad . . . his meager income eaten away by the nursing home . . . separated from his wife of 50 years . . . stripped of his house, car, acquaintances . . . dignity. He is the real victim. [quoted in Lund, 1988]

Sometimes caregivers feel fulfilled by their experience because everyone else, from the care receiver and other family members to neighbors and community professionals, appreciates their efforts and relieves the burden as much as possible. Even when the care recipient has dementia and a caregiver has provided major care for years, only a third of all caregivers are depressed. All are at risk for depression, however, with feeling trapped and unappreciated being more pivotal than the particular behaviors of the older person (Alspaugh et al., 1999).

In most cases, the caregiver feels that his or her actions are reciprocation for nurturing received in youth. A notable exception to this is when the caregiver to a frail elder is a daughter-in-law; in this case, the caregiver is likely to give far more care than she ever received (Ingersol-Dayton & Starrels, 1996).

Even when caregiving is entered into with a strong sense of reciprocity, caregivers may soon feel unfairly burdened and resentful, for three reasons:

- If one relative seems to be doing the job, other family members tend to feel relief or jealousy. They do not do their share, especially in the way the primary caregiver prefers, which leads to resentment.
- Care receivers and caregivers often disagree about how much and what kind of care are needed. Does the caregiver have the right to set the daily schedule, regulate menus, arrange doctor's visits, and so forth? Disagreements are bound to cause strain between the frustrated caregiver and the self-assertive care receiver.
- Public agencies rarely provide services unless the need is obvious, by which time it may be too late. Especially needed are caregiver support groups and **respite care,** in which a professional caregiver takes over to give the family caregiver a break for a few hours each day or for an occasional weekend. These types of services are especially hard to obtain if the care receiver is cognitively impaired (Pearlin et al., 1996; Zarit et al., 1998).

As the Research Report explains, when caring for a frail elder does create feelings of resentment and entails social isolation, elder maltreatment sometimes results.

respite care An arrangement in which a professional caregiver takes over to give the family caregiver of a frail elderly person a break for a few hours each day or for an occasional weekend.

Nursing Homes

Many elders and their relatives feel that nursing homes should be avoided at all costs, usually because they believe that all nursing homes are horrible places (Pyke & Bergston, 1996). In fact, some nursing homes are horrible. The worst ones tend to be profit-making ventures in which most patients are subsidized entirely by Medicare. The only way for these institutions to turn a profit is to cut down on expenses. Consequently, they are staffed by overworked, poorly trained aides who provide minimal, often dehumanizing care. Understandably, family members who see nursing homes as a last resort often feel as guilty, depressed, and worried as they did before (Aneshensel et al., 1995).

Overall, however, the abuses that occurred in the 1950s and 1960s, when the sudden, unregulated expansion of the nursing-home industry triggered a rash of shoddy care and maltreatment, have been greatly reduced. Professionals are becoming involved in developing good nursing-home care, with the goal of helping each patient gain as much

ELDER ABUSE

For many reasons, the frail elderly are particularly vulnerable to abuse. Not only do they depend on others for their physical care, but they also are often confused about many things, from the names of those around them to the state of their finances. Further, many who are abused or neglected are ashamed to admit it; and even when they do, the accusation is sometimes dismissed as paranoid. Given all this, it seems certain that the rate of maltreatment for the frail elderly is much higher than that for elders overall, which "worldwide studies based on community surveys reveal [to be] about a 5% to 6% rate" (Wolf, 1998).

Although some of the substantiated maltreatment of the elderly is perpetrated by professional caregivers, con artists, and mean-spirited strangers, elder maltreatment is primarily a family affair. For example, a detailed study of every case of elder abuse in Illinois found that 87 percent of the perpetrators were family members, most often a middle-aged child (39 percent), sometimes another relative (24 percent), and least often a spouse (14 percent) (Hwalek et al., 1996).

An earlier survey in Boston, by contrast, found that spouses were most often the perpetrators (Pilleman & Finkelhor, 1988). One obvious reason for the difference is that spousal abuse is less likely to be reported and thus is not discovered unless someone visits every frail person in the community to assess whether he or she is being mistreated.

In many ways, elder abuse and neglect are similar to child and spouse maltreatment. For all ages, maltreatment ranges from direct physical attack to ongoing emotional neglect. For all ages, risk factors include social isolation and powerlessness of the victim, mental impairment or drug addiction of the perpetrator, and inadequate education and poverty within the household (Wolf, 1998).

There are differences as well. The typical case of elder maltreatment begins benignly, as an outgrowth of a mutual caregiving relationship within the family. For example, an elder may begin to financially assist someone of the younger generation, who then gradually takes control of and misuses more and more of the elder's assets; or a younger family member may assume care of an increasingly frail relative, only to become so overwhelmed by the task that gross neglect and abuse occur.

Occasionally, an elder who becomes mentally impaired also becomes the perpetrator of abuse. For example, one Chinese American woman, age 73, was admitted to the hospital with bruises and a broken wrist. On careful questioning, she admitted that her husband, suffering from Alzheimer's

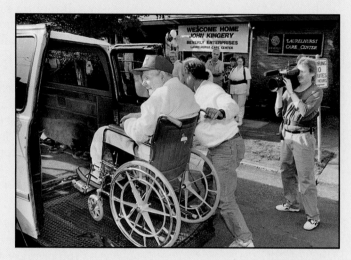

A Cycle of Abuse This elderly man was found alone, amnesiac and incontinent, tied in his wheelchair at an Idaho dog track. It was later discovered that his own 40-year-old daughter had abandoned him there, hundreds of miles from her home in Oregon, hoping to rid herself of the stress of having to take care of him. The daughter was put on trial on a variety of charges, but her defense describes the kind of tangled family dynamics that often surround elder abuse: The father has late-stage Alzheimer's disease, requiring extensive care and boundless patience, and the daughter says that she was sexually and physically abused by both parents when she was young. Until a year before this incident, she had not seen her father for 20 years. Then one day he arrived at her doorstep, needing help.

disease, had battered her when she tried to care for him (Elder Abuse Project, 1991).

These examples make it clear that elder abuse within the family must be diagnosed, treated, and prevented case by case. Typically, abuse is "only one component of a larger set of complicated problems," part of a complex "social, psychological, and economic equilibrium that has taken a lifetime to develop" (Hornick et al., 1992). Most elderly victims endure spousal abuse for years, too ashamed to report it and too dependent to leave (Harris, 1996).

The best solution would be the provision of extensive public and personal safety nets of support for those elderly who are frail or powerless, so that no one—caregiver or care receiver—gets to the point of abusing or being abused. If abuse does occur, a social worker, not simply a prosecutor, needs to tackle all the problems that emerge.

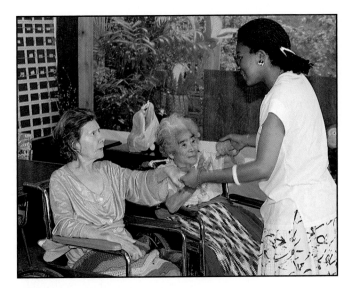

Help from My Friends Good nursing homes encourage residents to participate in regular physical exercise, and the best provide physical therapy and social activities. Both of these photographs illustrate this point. In the one on the left, a volunteer brings an attentive smile; in the one on the right, those who look more alert are also better able to exercise.

⚠ **Response for Those Uncertain About Future Careers (from page 700):** Why not? The demand for good workers will obviously increase as the population ages, and the working conditions will improve. An important problem is that quality varies, so you need to make sure you work in a home whose policies incorporate the view that the elderly can be quite capable, social, and independent.

independence, control, and self-respect as possible (Goldsmith, 1994; Gordon & Stryker, 1996).

Thus, it is possible to find good care if one knows what to look for and can afford it. The quality and suitability of nursing-home care can make the difference between the full, satisfying final years and a desolate closure. In fact, good care can even lead to a longer life and better family relationships.

A young adult named Rob related that his 98-year-old great-grandmother "began to fail. We had no idea why and thought, well, maybe she is growing old." The family reluctantly decided it was time to move her from her suburban home, where she had lived for decades, into a nursing home. Fortunately, the nursing home encouraged independence and did not assume that declines in functioning are always signs of "final failing." Indeed, the doctors there discovered that the woman's pacemaker was not working properly. As Rob explains,

> We were very concerned to have her undergo surgery at her age, but we finally agreed. . . . Soon she was back to being herself, a strong, spirited, energetic, independent woman. It was the pacemaker that was wearing out, not Great-grandmother. [quoted in Adler, 1995]

This story contains a lesson for us all, one that underlies many of the lessons learned throughout this book. Whenever an older person seems to be failing, or a preschooler is unusually aggressive, or a teenager is depressed, or an adult is overloaded with work and family, the tendency is to think that such problems "go with the territory" of being at a particular age. There is some truth in that, for all these possible problems are more common at the stages mentioned. However, the overall theme of the life-span perspective is that, at every age, people can be "strong, spirited, and energetic." We are all able to live life to the fullest no matter how young or old we are.

SUMMARY

THEORIES OF LATE ADULTHOOD

1. Several self theories hold that adults make personal choices in ways that allow them to become fully themselves. Erikson believed that individuals seek integrity that connects them to the human community. Identity theory suggests that people try to maintain a sense of themselves.

2. A dominant interpretation of the goal of later life is that selective optimization with compensation can help in adjusting to physical and cognitive decline. Genetic personality traits may continue to play a major role in the way late adulthood plays itself out.

3. Stratification theories maintain that social forces limit personal choices, especially the disengagement that may come with age. Lifelong stratification by gender or race may also limit an elder's ability to function well.

4. Dynamic theories see human development as an ever-changing process, influenced by social contexts, which themselves are constantly changing, as well as by genetic and historical factors that are unique to each person. For instance, continuity theory emphasizes that the changes that occur with age are much less disruptive than they might appear to be.

KEEPING ACTIVE

5. People are retiring at younger ages than ever before. Many retired people continue their education or perform volunteer work in their communities. Both of these activities enhance the health and well-being of the elderly and benefit the larger society.

6. The elderly are politically active and influential, which is one reason for their success in protecting their economic benefits. Fortunately, most older adults agree on the need for generational equity.

THE SOCIAL CONVOY

7. A spouse is the most important member of a person's social convoy. Older adults in longstanding marriages tend to be quite satisfied with their relationships and to safeguard each other's health. As a result, married elders tend to live longer, happier, and healthier lives than unmarried elders.

8. The death of a spouse is serious stress. Widowers are more likely to experience health problems but are more likely to remarry. Widows are more likely to have financial difficulties but also to find comfort through an expanded network of friends.

9. Friendship continues to be important in late adulthood, as a source of happiness and as a buffer against trouble. Particularly among the never-married or the no-longer-married, long-term friendships are particularly valued.

10. Many older people are part of multigenerational families, sometimes with two generations over age 60, each maintaining dependence as well as mutual support. Typically the young-old are more likely to give advice and assistance to younger and older generations than to receive it.

THE FRAIL ELDERLY

11. Many older people eventually become frail, unable to care for their daily needs. Those who are poor, female, and over age 85 are particularly likely to experience an extended period of frailty. As more people reach very old adulthood, the number needing help from family and society will increase.

12. The frail are usually cared for by a close relative—typically their spouse, daughter, or daughter-in-law. Despite the personal sacrifices this care entails, most relatives consider such care an expression of family commitment. Caring for a dependent and needy older person may lead to frustration, anger, and maltreatment.

13. For the elderly who enter a nursing home, the quality of their final years of life can vary enormously, depending on the quality of the home. The best homes recognize the individuality of the elderly and encourage their independence.

KEY TERMS

self theories (677)
stratification theories (680)
disengagement theory (680)
activity theory (681)
dynamic theories (683)
continuity theory (683)

Elderhostel (686)
social convoy (690)
frail elderly (698)
activities of daily life (ADLs) (698)
instrumental activities of daily life (IADLs) (698)
respite care (703)

KEY QUESTIONS

1. What are the similarities and differences between identity theory and behavioral genetics?

2. Compare the three types of stratification in late adulthood.

3. How can continuity theory be considered a dynamic systems theory?

4. What kinds of activities do older people undertake after they retire?

5. What changes typically occur in long-term marriages in late adulthood?

6. Compare the roles of friends and family in late adulthood.

7. How does reaction to the death of a spouse differ for men and women?

8. What factors affect the ability to perform ADLs and IADLs?

9. What accounts for the increasing prevalence of the frail elderly?

10. What problems might arise in caring for a frail elderly person?

11. *In Your Experience* What kinds of help are easiest for you to give? To receive?

BIOSOCIAL

Ageism

Ageism restricts the functioning of the elderly and makes younger people overestimate how many of the aged are impaired. All the same, primary aging is inevitable. Deficits in vision and hearing are widespread, although many elders can prevent or remedy the damage.

Secondary Aging

Because of declines in organ reserve, the immune system, and overall muscle strength, older adults are at greater risk of chronic and acute diseases, heart disease, and cancer. However, risk is also related to longstanding health habits and quality of health care.

Postponement of many of the illnesses linked with age is possible, allowing a "compression of morbidity." Research on the causes of aging indicates that genes play a prime role. Specific theories of aging related to the immune system, a "genetic clock," damage from free radicals, and cellular error are all plausible.

Those who live to age 90 or more are often surprisingly active, happy, and independent.

COGNITIVE

Changes in Information Processing

Memory fades in older age, but some aspects are more likely to show deficits. Working (or short-term) memory is the first to slow down; long-term memory is more durable.

Experimental testing of older adults reveals deficits in their ability to receive information, store it in memory, and organize and interpret it. These deficits may result from a decrease of neurotransmitters and blood flow in the brain, a drop in memory self-efficacy, and/or the influence of ageist expectations in the social context. In the tasks of real life, most older adults develop ways to compensate for memory loss and slower thinking.

Dementia

Dementia, with its progressive impairment of cognitive functioning, is not inevitable in old age but it does become more common, especially in the very old. Symptoms of dementia may be caused by Alzheimer's disease, problems in the circulatory system, other diseases, depression, or drugs. The underlying causes are primarily genetic or organic. Sometimes a temporary problem or mental illness is misdiagnosed as dementia.

New Cognitive Development

Many older individuals develop or intensify their aesthetic and philosophical interests and values in later life. An opportunity to remember and to recount the past, called life review, can be very useful.

PSYCHOSOCIAL

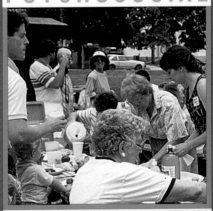

Theories of Late Adulthood

The variability of life in late adulthood is even greater than at other periods. Self theories, stratification theories, and dynamic life course theories all point to sources of variability.

Keeping Active

Elders usually remain active whether working or retired. Most find ways to expand their horizons after retirement, with education, volunteering, and political involvement.

The Social Convoy

Older adults' satisfaction with life depends in large part on continuing contact with friends and family. Generally, marital satisfaction continues to improve. The greatest source of social support is likely to be other elders, either relatives or friends, particularly those of longstanding importance.

The Frail Elderly

As people increasingly live to a very old age, the number needing assistance with the activities of daily life grows. Ideally, this assistance encourages elders to be as active and independent as possible. Most caregivers are other elderly people, who sometimes are overwhelmed with the stresses of their situation. Social support and recognition can reduce caregiver stress. Nursing homes and other modes of care are sometimes very helpful, sometimes not.

Death and Dying

E P I L O G U E

One goal of our study of human development, as outlined in Chapter 1, is to help each person realize his or her full potential. According to many developmental theorists, understanding death and dying is essential to reaching this goal. However, thinking about death is difficult, because "the complexity of life is mirrored in, and elaborated by, the complexity of dying, death, and bereavement" (deVries, 1999). Even more than at other periods of life, dying highlights cultural differences, ethical dilemmas, and spiritual practices, each of which is elusive and controversial, hard to pin down with definitive research. As this epilogue will make clear, there are no easy answers.

THE DYING PERSON'S EMOTIONS

Death can have many personal meanings. It can be seen as "a biological event, a rite of passage, an inevitability, a natural occurrence, a punishment, extinction, the enforcement of God's will, the absurd, separation, reunion . . . a reasonable cause for anger, depression, denial, repression, guilt, frustration, relief" (Kalish, 1985). This emotional gamut can occur within a single dying person. Contradictory emotions are normal and to be expected, as was first described in landmark research by Elisabeth Kübler-Ross (1969, 1975).

Talking with dying patients in a large Chicago hospital led Kübler-Ross to propose that, when they are told the truth by an honest and empathic listener, the dying go through five stages: *denial, anger, bargaining, depression,* and *acceptance.* This final emotion requires some explanation:

> Acceptance should not be mistaken for a happy stage. It is almost void of feelings. It is as if the pain had gone, the struggle is over, and there comes a time for "the final rest before the long journey," as one patient phrased it. This is also the time during which the family usually needs more help, understanding, and support than the patient. [Kübler-Ross, 1969]

Other researchers have *not* found the same sequence of stages. More typically, denial, anger, and depression appear and reappear, bargaining is a fleeting thought, and acceptance is elusive (Kastenbaum, 1992). However, all agree with Kübler-Ross that honest communication is essential. Only a few years ago, doctors sometimes told the patient's immediate family that the illness was terminal but explicitly instructed them not to tell the patient. The result of this "conspiracy of silence" was increased isolation and sorrow for both the patients and their families (Moller, 1996). In other instances, impending death was proclaimed in such an abrupt and insistent manner that all hope was destroyed. And sometimes the truth was hidden from everyone, allowing no time for preparation, reconciliation, or comfort (Nyland, 1994). Today, physicians are usually willing to tell patients of the probability of dying, but only if the patient asks directly (Kaplowitz et al., 1999). Being informed of impending death triggers emotional reactions that tend to vary with age, in both the dying person and the mourner (see A Life-Span View).

DECIDING HOW TO DIE

As the years accumulate, planning for death becomes more likely. Older people often draw up a will, reconcile with friends, and end each family visit with loving good-byes. Such preparations are not only normal; they are psychologically healthy. Even when merely imagining that they will die soon, adults of all ages can shift their priorities, no longer seeking new experiences and excitement but instead seeking emotional closeness and comfort (Fung et al., 1999).

Adults hope that they will die swiftly, with little pain and great dignity. However, this hope runs counter to modern medicine, which can hold off death with all manner of technological interventions and is even able to maintain organ functioning after brain death has occurred. Many people in hospitals or other medical institutions (where 80 percent of North Americans and 70 percent of Britons now die) undergo an extended period of confused semiconsciousness, attached to an assortment of machines, tubes, and intravenous drips. Often they die in pain, largely because analgesic medications are still underprescribed because of a misguided fear of causing addiction (Meier & Morrison, 1999).

Pain at life's end is particularly likely for the oldest-old patients in nursing homes, where even those dying of cancer may receive no pain medication at all (26 percent) or nothing stronger than Tylenol (16 percent), according to one study (Bernabei et al., 1998). Other physical discomforts (nausea, bedsores, constipation, shortness of breath), psychic terrors (nightmares and hallucinations brought on by pain medication), and fears that dignity will be lost and "medicine will take over their death" are almost inevitable (Cassel, 1996). However, such suffering can be averted through the concerted actions of the patient and his or her family, medical personnel, and society's policy makers.

The Patient and Family

There is a growing consensus, both in law and in hospital practice, that the ultimate authority regarding what measures are to be used in terminal cases should be the individual who must undergo those treatments. Some people, long before death is imminent, make a **living will,** a document that indicates what medical intervention they want if they become incapable of expressing those wishes. Others resist writing such a document, with low-income, younger, minority patients especially suspicious that advance statements might deprive them of life-support systems and even routine nursing care when they need them (Dubler, 1993).

The problem, of course, is that no one knows all the specifics of their dying when they are deciding whether to write a living will and, if they

living will   A document that indicates what medical intervention an individual wants if he or she becomes incapable of expressing those wishes.

EMOTIONAL REACTIONS TO DYING

As the life-span perspective would predict, the age of the dying person affects how he or she feels (Stillion, 1995; Wass, 1995):

- Young children, not understanding the concept of death, are usually angry and upset by the thought of separation from those they love. A dying child therefore needs constant companionship and reassurance. The developing cognitive competencies of the school-age child can lead the very ill young person to become absorbed with learning the facts about the illness, its treatment, and the "mechanics" of dying. Attempts to shield the child with half-truths ("This treatment will cure you"; "Grandma took a long trip") are inevitably discovered and powerfully resented.

- Adolescents tend to think not about the distant future but about the quality of life at present. Thus, for seriously ill adolescents, the effect of their condition on their appearance and social relationships may be of primary importance. Survivors may, egocentically, feel responsible.

- For the young adult, coping with dying often produces great rage and depression at the idea that, just as life is about to begin in earnest, it must end. The strength of these emotions, widespread and publicly acknowledged because of the AIDS epidemic, has led to changes in attitudes, in laws, and in drug research.

- For the middle-aged adult, death interrupts half-finished obligations and responsibilities. Most middle-aged people who know they are dying try to make sure that insurance policies, child-care responsibilities, and other matters are in good order.

- An older adult's feelings about dying depend a great deal on context. If one's spouse has already died, and if the terminal illness brings pain and infirmity, acceptance of death is comparatively easy.

The emotional response to death also depends on the age of the mourner. Little children, for example, are often angry that the dying person abandoned them and wonder whether they caused the death by their misbehavior. Such emotions are carried into adulthood, and another death may trigger childhood feelings of abandonment and guilt. Generally, it is somewhat easier to accept the death of an elderly, sick person than an unanticipated sudden death (such as when a parent loses a teenage child). The reason is that before the actual death, *anticipatory grief* reduces the shock, and there is time for reconciliation and apologies, if needed (Lehman et al., 1999; Zilberfein, 1999).

One emotion is particularly strong in those of any age who have witnessed the dying of someone else: fear of isolation and pain. This is a legitimate fear. Once people died at home, usually fairly quickly after a fatal illness struck, and family members were sad but accepting.

Medical advances made since 1950 have meant that many "heroic" measures, such as respirators, heart restarting, dialysis, and organ transplants, have prolonged life, increasing both pain and the time a dying person spends alone, surrounded by bright lights, warning beeps, and tubes, without familiar faces and sometimes with no human contact at all. As one physician explains: "The solitary death is now so well recognized that our society has organized against it, and well we should" (Nyland, 1994).

As you have read many times in this book, friends and family help people through all the difficult transitions of life. This is no less true for dying than for other changes, and sensitivity to the age-specific concerns is always needed.

do, what provisions to include in it. If a particular treatment—itself painful or debilitating—has only one chance in five of prolonging life, is its use merited? What about one chance in a hundred? Does it matter whether life is prolonged for only a few days instead of months or years? And if the patient survives, what quality of life—full mental and physical capacity, or something much less—is acceptable? Such quantitative and qualitative issues are at the heart of the decision to fight death or accept it, and opinions vary.

In the midst of the dying process, few patients are able to make a rational selection among the many options. Most doctors, by personality and training, use their specialized skills to stave off death. "The greater humility that should have come with greater knowledge is instead replaced by medical hubris: since we can do so much, there is no limit to what should be attempted—*today* and for *this patient*" (Nyland, 1994). To avoid these complications, each person should not only sign a living will but should also designate a proxy, someone who can make decisions for him or her on the spot if need be. There are three problems with proxy designations:

- Without explicit prior discussions, many proxies do not know what to conclude. For example, in some cultures, the role of a good wife is to do everything possible to prolong the life of a husband, even if she herself would not want life support when her own death is imminent (Hallenbeck & Goldstein, 1999).
- Family members may disagree with the proxy about such matters as how much suffering is acceptable, whether God would want the person to have a natural death (no life support) or a miracle (continuing use of a respirator even after irreversible coma), and whether "no expense spared" or "care for the survivors" is more important. Under the stress of the death watch, family members and friends sometimes differ bitterly and destructively.
- Even with an advance directive and a proxy, more than half the time such directives are ignored by hospital staff when an emergency arises (Teno et al., 1997).

Responsibility begins with the individual, extends to the family, but inevitably requires cooperation from health care personnel.

Medical Personnel

Almost everyone—healers, judges, theologians, and the general public—agrees that when organs fail in a terminally ill person who has experienced severe pain, fearful confusion, and loss of consciousness, medical personnel need not intervene to restore breathing or restart the heart. Allowing such a person to die is considered good medical practice. The order *DNR (do not resuscitate)* placed on a person's hospital chart usually indicates that the patient prefers to die naturally.

Similarly, it is becoming more common to provide the dying with ample morphine and other medication to reduce pain, even if thus improving the quality of their last days of life might hasten death. This is called **double effect**: The intended effect is pain reduction, and the secondary effect (hastening death) is acceptable according to medical ethics and most religions.

DNR orders and large doses of morphine can be a part of **palliative care**, which is care designed not to treat the illness but to "relieve physical, emotional, social, and spiritual pain and suffering . . . for patients and their families" (Sherman, 1999). Inadequate palliative care is the glaring weakness of modern medicine. Not even physical suffering is as well treated in the dying as in those expected to survive, so nausea, constipation, itchy skin, muscle aches, and other symptoms are common.

Further, very few doctors or nurses are trained to handle the psychological demands of palliative care for terminally ill patients and their families (Mezey et al., 1999). Half of all medical textbooks do not discuss care of the dying at all (Rabow et al., 2000). To combat this lack, a new institution called the **hospice** has been created, where medical and nonmedical staff work together to provide the best palliative care possible (see the Changing Policy box).

double effect   A situation in which medication has the intended effect of relieving a dying person's pain and the secondary effect of hastening death.

palliative care   Care designed not to treat an illness but to relieve the pain and suffering of the patient and his or her family.

hospice   An institution in which terminally ill patients receive palliative care.

THE HOSPICE

In London during the 1950s, a dedicated woman named Cecily Saunders opened the first modern hospice. In response to the dehumanization of the typical hospital death, hospices provide the dying with skilled medical care—which includes painkilling medication but shuns death-defying intervention—in a setting where their dignity as human beings, and that of their family members, is respected (Saunders, 1978).

In a hospice, both the dying person and the family are considered "the unit of care" (Lattanzi-Licht & Connor, 1995). Usually, family and friends are encouraged to visit at any time. Often, one family member or close friend, called a *lay primary caregiver,* provides much of the routine care. This arrangement makes the dying person feel less alone and helps the caregiver to feel involved rather than excluded, as would be the case in most hospital settings. When death comes, the staff continues to tend to the family's psychological and other needs.

In some cases, a dying person's home can become a hospice, allowing the individual the emotional comfort of familiar surroundings. In addition, having home as the hospice can actually prolong life, since the sick often contract infections and contagious diseases in hospitals. When hospice care is provided in the home, doctors and nurses visit regularly to give reassurance as well as medication and therapy and to instruct and comfort family members.

Hospices do not solve all the problems of dying. First, to be admitted, patients must be diagnosed as terminally ill; that is, they must have no reasonable chance of recovery, and death must be anticipated within 6 months or so. In the United States, insurance (public and private) does not pay for hospice care without such a diagnosis (Mezey et al., 1999). Second, patients must accept the diagnosis. Understandably, some prefer hope and one last operation, with odds against success, instead of waiting for death.

Third, hospice care does not meet all the needs of the dying and their families. One reason is cost: While the well-functioning hospice uses less high-technology equipment and fewer surgical procedures than a comparable hospital would, good hospice care is labor-intensive and skilled workers are expensive. All the care providers—doctors, nurses, psychologists, social workers, clergy, and aides—must be well trained and willing to take the time to provide individualized care around the clock. Almost no hospice has enough staff, on a permanent basis, to spend time with everyone who needs it.

Finally, hospices are much better prepared to meet the needs of young adult patients with cancer than older patients with combinations of illnesses that shorten life but do not necessarily bring death. More and more hospices are accepting the

A Better Way to Die A particularly appealing aspect of hospices is the attention they pay to the "extras" that make their patients' remaining days more pleasant, such as colorful bedclothes, fresh flowers, and frequent visits from volunteers. Here, a volunteer hospice worker holds the hand of a 92-year-old patient with terminal congestive heart failure.

latter type of patient—about a fourth of all hospice patients have a diagnosis other than cancer—but problems arise when persons do not die "on schedule" (Lattanzi-Licht & Connor, 1995).

Problems also occur at the other end of the life span, with children dying of cancer, as about 3,000 do in North America each year. Almost no hospices serve children, and only about 30 percent of these young patients are given good palliative care (Wolfe et al., 2000). The rest suffer pain and futile, debilitating treatment, in part because parents and oncologists never want to face the reality that a child's death has become inevitable. Respect for the suffering and emotions of the cancer patient is not always offered to adults who are old and alone or to members of minority groups (Hewitt & Simone, 1999)—and "children must now be added to this list" (Morgan, 2000).

Thus, hospice care benefits some, but by no means all, dying individuals. In the United States, only 17 percent of all deaths occur with hospice care. The availability of hospice care depends on the location, with hospices more common in England than the Netherlands (Zylicz, 1999) and more common in the western United States (especially Oregon) than in the Deep South. Increasingly, doctors and nurses now accept the basic (though difficult) hospice philosophy, seeing it as part of their mission to help the dying prepare for death and to keep the patient and the family informed and comfortable.

Community Policies

The third group that helps to determine whether or not a person will have a good death is the community as a whole. Each person's opinions and values are part of that community. When the cause is a chronic illness, "the actual death often occurs as a result of a conscious decision" made by someone (Mezey et al., 1999), and when the cause is sudden—such as a homicide, heart attack, or stroke—measures that could have prevented the death often seem obvious after the fact. Thus, cultural values and community practices are directly involved in almost every death. One way this involvement is manifested is through laws and policies. For example, in the United States, tobacco companies and gun manufacturers are sometimes charged with legal responsibility for deaths.

Most people now accept that a healthy lifestyle prolongs life, that certain behaviors are foolish and life-threatening, and that public health is the responsibility of the community. Values have shifted to accept that decisions made at the very end of life to reduce pain or turn off a respirator might be good medical practice. However, two practices still are fiercely controversial:

- **Physician-assisted suicide,** when a doctor provides the means for someone to end his or her own life
- **Voluntary euthanasia,** when, at the patient's request, someone else ends his or her life

Both practices are illegal almost everywhere in the world, but both occur almost everywhere. Very few instances of physician-assisted or -implemented death are discovered and prosecuted, and almost none result in punishment (Prado & Taylor, 1999). Many fear that tacit acceptance of these measures would put society at the top of a *slippery slope,* that allowing even a few such deaths would trigger an unstoppable landslide of unwarranted deaths. This fear seems groundless in the three localities that have gathered statistics, specifically Oregon, the Northern Territory of Australia, and the Netherlands (see the Research Report). One observer notes, "The slippery slope is itself a bit of a slippery customer, usually more a bit of suggestive rhetoric than a serious argument" (Griffiths, 1999).

THE SOCIAL CONTEXT OF DYING

Although death comes to everyone, perceptions of death are highly variable. Death has been denied, sought, feared, fought, and experienced by families, medical personnel, communities, and the dying themselves in quite different ways. As you might expect, religion and nationality are among the main reasons for these differences.

Death Around the World

In many African traditions, elders gain new status through death, joining the ancestors who watch over their descendants and the entire village. Accordingly, the entire village participates in each adult's funeral, preparing the body and providing food and money for the journey to the ancestral realm. Mourning one person's death allows all members of the community to celebrate their connection with one another and with their collective past (Opoku, 1989).

physician-assisted suicide   A situation in which a doctor provides the means for someone to end his or her own life.

voluntary euthanasia   A situation in which, at a patient's request, someone else ends his or her life.

❓ **Especially for Educators:** How might a teacher help a young child cope with death?

THE DUTCH EXPERIENCE WITH ASSISTED DYING

Assisted suicide and euthanasia are still illegal in the Netherlands, but in 1993 the Dutch legislature promised that doctors would not be prosecuted for such deaths *if* the dying person:

■ Is of sound mind and fully informed
■ Repeatedly requests assistance in dying
■ Experiences intolerable and hopeless suffering (either physical or psychological)

and *if* the physician, before the death:

■ Ascertains that no acceptable alternative treatment remains
■ Consults with another, independent physician
■ Reports the death as "unnatural" to authorities [Legemaate, 1999]

Some doctors in the Netherlands would prefer that medical, rather than legal, authorities review each case to make sure these guidelines have been met, but almost no Dutch professional advocates that euthanasia decisions be unexamined and private. They warn that secrecy can lead to abuse, especially in "countries which couple an absolute prohibition with an absolute lack of actual control" (Griffiths, 1999).

Data from the Netherlands in 1995 reveal that 42 percent of all deaths involved some kind of medical decision, although outright euthanasia is relatively rare:

■ Deaths with no medical decision: 58 percent
■ Deaths that included withholding futile treatment: 20 percent
■ Deaths that resulted from a secondary effect of essential pain medication: 19 percent
■ Deaths from euthanasia: 3 percent (usually from injection of barbiturates and muscle relaxants)
■ Deaths from assisted suicide: .3 percent (usually drinking a potion in the doctor's presence) (van der Wal & Van der Maas, 1999).

Almost always, the patient's own family doctor facilitates the death; each physician performs, on average, less than one euthanasia per year. Since all Dutch citizens are guaranteed coverage for any health care expenses, doctors have no incentive other than providing the best care for people they know well. Most are very careful, convincing their patients who request euthanasia that a better choice would be additional treatment, pain relief, and a natural death. As one explains:

The process and procedure take so much emotional energy that physicians hope that nature will take its course before matters reach the point where euthanasia is appropriate. I am grateful when patients die peacefully on their own and do not need euthanasia. Even if the time for euthanasia never comes, just the fact that the physician talks about it with the patient provides an assurance that makes dying a little easier. Patients know they will not be left alone in pain, they will not have to suffer unnecessarily, and they have the comfort of knowing their physician will be there for them no matter what. [quoted in Thomasma et al., 1999]

Such statements do not sway those who are opposed to euthanasia. Of particular concern is the possibility that in a larger nation than the Netherlands (which is about the size of Rhode Island) that does not have universal health care, doctors might be more likely to speed the deaths of those who are poor, disabled, female, elderly, or minority-group members (Prado & Taylor, 1999).

Evidence does not support this suspicion. Oregon has allowed physician-assisted suicide since 1998. In the first 2 years, of the 60,000 people who died in that state, less than .1 percent (43 people) were assisted suicides. Those 43 were somewhat younger, and more often white and male, than the average Oregon death. Most were dying of cancer and were already receiving palliative care (Sullivan et al., 2000).

Thus, the data undercut some of the arguments against assisted suicide. Still, two powerful questions remain.

■ Should humans be encouraged, or even allowed, to control their own death and avoid suffering? If a person feels physical or psychological pain, relief may come from palliative measures instead, including morphine, social support, therapy for depression, and an appreciation of the life lessons learned through suffering.
■ Is a request for assistance in dying really a plea for assistance in living? Communication, not lethal medication, may be the answer.

Last Rites This colorful Balinese funeral procession on its way to a Buddhist cremation is a marked contrast to the somber memorial service that is more common in the West. No matter what form it takes, community involvement in death and dying seems to benefit the living.

In many Muslim nations, death affirms faith in Allah. Islam teaches that the achievements, problems, and pleasures of this life are transitory and ephemeral; everyone should be mindful of, and ready for, death at any time. Therefore, caring for the dying is a holy reminder of mortality and of the happy life in the afterworld. Public and obvious lamenting over death is acceptable in men as well as women (Nobles & Sciarra, 2000). Specific rituals—including reciting prayers, washing the body, carrying the coffin, and attending the funeral—are performed by devout strangers as well as by relatives and friends (Gilanshah, 1993).

Among Buddhists, disease and death are among life's inevitable sufferings, which may bring enlightenment. The task of the dying individual is to gain insight from the experience, with a clear mind and calm acceptance (Truitner & Truitner, 1993). Family and friends help by preventing mind-altering medication or death-defying intervention.

Among Hindus and Sikhs, helping the dying to relinquish their ties to this world and prepare for the next is a particularly important obligation for the immediate family. A holy death is one that is welcomed by the dying person, who should be placed on the ground at the very last moment, chanting prayers and surrounded by family members who are also reciting sacred texts. Such a holy death is believed to ease entry into the next life. Two practices are critically important: knowing when someone will die so proper preparations can be made, and having the entire family "present when the soul leaves" (Firth, 1993).

Preparations for death are not emphasized in the Jewish tradition because hope for life should be sustained. For the same reason, the dying person should never be left alone. After death, the body is buried the next day, unembalmed and in a plain wooden coffin, to emphasize that physical preservation is not possible. The family is expected to mourn at home for a week and then to reduce social activities for a year out of respect and memory (Katz, 1993).

Many Christians believe that death is not an end, but the beginning of eternity in heaven or hell, and thus welcome or fear it. Particular customs, such as preserving the body for bodily resurrection or celebrating the "passing" with food and drink, vary from place to place, denomination to denomination, and nation to nation (Power, 1993). For instance, among Mexican Catholics, funerals bring relatives and neighbors together to view the body, not only for visible and vocal expressions of sorrow (especially from the immediate relatives) but also for conversation, food, acceptance of death, and anticipation of eventual resurrection (Younoszai, 1993). Among many North American Protestants, a funeral or memorial service is a more restrained, less noisy, and smaller affair—usually without the body or even the coffin visible. Finally, the 70 or so tribes of Native Americans vary in their customs, although all consider death an affirmation of community values (Broken Leg & Middleton, 1993).

In fact, culture often has more influence on variations in death practices than religion does. The place of death (home or hospital?), the mourners (only immediate family or a wide community?), and the disposal of the body (burial or cremation?) are issues of great importance (see Table E.1).

Country	Percentage Being Cremated
table E.1	**Cremation Rates in Selected Countries, 1990–1991**
Australia	47.20%
Canada	34.25
China	31.00
Commonwealth of Independent States (Russia et al.)	34.62
France	7.17
Great Britain	69.90
Italy	1.50
Japan	97.40
Netherlands	45.28
Spain	2.83
Sweden	62.70
Switzerland	59.72
United States	18.50

Source: Cremation Society of Britain, cited in Tappenden, 1996.

❓ *Observational Quiz (see answer page 719):* *Which nations have the highest and lowest rates of cremation? What do these two opposite nations have in common?*

Mourning customs also vary. One dramatic example occurs with widows, who at various times have been expected to die on their husband's funeral pyre (India), or to marry their husband's brother (the Middle East), or to get on with their social lives, keeping their emotions to themselves (North America) (Lopata, 1999).

Two universal themes underlie all this international diversity:

- Religious and spiritual concerns, downplayed in everyday life, often reemerge.
- Returning to one's roots, via either long-ignored rituals or an actual journey, is a common urge.

Both of these themes are evident in many writings, ranging from a scholarly book by a secular Jew who surprised even himself by attending services every day for a year after his father died (Wiesentier, 1998) to a review of research which concludes that many religious beliefs help people overcome death anxiety (Fins, 1999).

Exemplifying both trends is a study of a group of seriously ill people who had emigrated to Canada from India. As you can see from Figure E.1, generally the longer a person had been away from India, the stronger both the religious and homeland impulses became (Fry, 1999). In the words of one woman who had spent 22 years in Canada:

I long to die among my relatives in the old country. . . . I miss the music, the chantings, the smells and sounds and the ringing of the temple bells in my home town. I worry whether my own Hindu God will take me back or reject me because I am not a pure Hindu any more and have not been in communion with the elders of the Hindu faith for the years and years I have spent in Canada. [quoted in Fry, 1999]

Figure E.1 Strong Homeland and Religious Impulses. Open-ended interviews with seriously ill Indians who had emigrated to Canada found that the longer they had been away, the more important India and Hinduism became as they thought about their deaths.

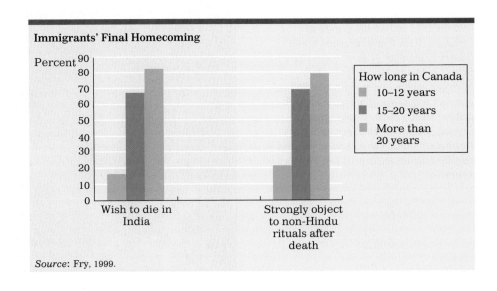

Immigrants' Final Homecoming

Source: Fry, 1999.

Saying Good-bye The quiet dignity of a cemetery helps many individuals experience all the emotions of bereavement—not only sadness but anger and acceptance as well. The obvious reality that death is a universal part of the human experience puts each person's private grief into perspective.

Helpless and Scared When a child loses a friend, especially to violence, adults need to help the child survive the emotional onslaught. Here Previn Brandon brings flowers to the door of Buell Elementary School in Mount Morris Township, Michigan, where 6-year-old Kayla Rolland was shot and killed by a first-grade classmate in March 2000. Previn's mother, Crystal, is demonstrating her awareness that human touch, comforting words, and tangible tributes make grief less overwhelming.

Bereavement

In recent times, mourning has become more private, less emotional, and less religious than formerly. Younger generations of all spiritual backgrounds are likely to prefer small memorial services after cremation, while older generations prefer burial after a traditional funeral (Hapslip et al., 1999; Tappenden, 1996).

What have these trends led to? According to a review of the research, one result is an increasing tendency toward social isolation for those who have just lost a loved one—exactly the opposite of a healthy reaction. Another result is physical illness, with many of the bereaved feeling sick more often in the days and months after a death. This sickness sometimes propels them to a doctor, not only for medication but also for sympathy and attention—exactly what a proper mourning period would have brought. Grief that lingers can even precipitate death, primarily from heart disease, cirrhosis, and, especially for men, suicide (Moller, 1996).

> Unexpressed grief also harms the larger community, particularly children: the funeral provides the setting in which both private sorrow and public loss can be both expressed and shared. . . . As a social ceremony, it serves to bring together the community. As such, it serves as an important vehicle of cultural transmission. The contemporary impulse to preclude funerals from society or to exclude children from funerals can also have unintended consequences. In addition to cutting children off from direct expressions of love, concern, and support at this time of family crisis, it may deprive them of the opportunity to learn about life's most basic fact—death. The social meaning and intrinsic value of human life itself, moreover, may be implicitly denied by the failure to acknowledge our mortality. [Fulton, 1995]

Healing is also particularly difficult if the bereaved are actively prevented from mourning in the way that they wish. In one case, emergency-room staff did not allow the mother of a 17-year-old boy who was killed in an auto crash to see her son's body until she, first, answered many questions and, second, promised not to "do anything silly." She writes:

I desperately needed to hold him, to look at him, to find out where he was hurting. These instincts don't die immediately with the child. The instinct to comfort and cuddle, to examine and inspect the wounds, to try to understand, most of all, to hold. But my lovely boy was draped on an altar, covered with a purple robe, and all expressions of love and care were denied to me. And I don't know when that wound will heal. [Awoonor-Renner, 1993]

In another case, the adult sons of a Lakota Native American man began chanting in his hospital room as soon as he died:

A nurse entered the room, heard the chants and called hospital security to remove "those drunken Indians." . . . A doctor arrived to announce that an autopsy should be performed . . . [although the] tribe was firmly opposed to autopsies. [Broken Leg & Middleton, 1993]

Recovery

What can others do to help the bereaved person? The first step is simply to be aware that powerful, complicated, and culturally diverse emotions are likely: A friend should listen, sympathize, and not ignore the mourner's pain. Touching the dead person, visiting the grave, lighting a candle, cherishing a memento, singing, wailing, sobbing, laughing—all might or might not be desired, depending on various traditions.

The second step is to understand that bereavement is often a lengthy process, demanding sympathy, honesty, and social support for months or even years. As time passes, the bereaved person should become involved in other activities but should not be expected to forget the person to whom he or she was attached. Once psychologists feared that expressions of grief were pathological if they continued for more than a few weeks, but we now know that flashbacks, unexpected tears, and other manifestations of sorrow may occur over long periods.

The AIDS Memorial Quilt Compiling a scrapbook of memorabilia, building a memorial garden, and designing and sewing a square on a quilt are among the many creative actions that fight the numbness after a loved one dies. When others acknowledge that "a special person lived and died," as occurred here at the display of the AIDS Memorial Quilt, survivors feel that someone's life had meaning.

② Observational Quiz (see answer page 721): *The impact of the AIDS quilt stems from its huge size, as its display on the Washington Mall attests: It forces the viewer to acknowledge that hundreds of thousands have died. Yet each panel of the quilt represents sorrow over one individual's death. What can you see that attests to that?*

CYBERSPACE GRIEF

The need to express grief in one's own way has been declared by grief counselors, affirmed by clergy, and published in numerous books and journals (e.g., *Omega: A Journal of Death and Dying*). Now anyone with Internet access can see this for themselves, via several World Wide Web sites devoted to memorial messages. As one example, Yahoo! Health offers on-line message boards under the heading "Mourning and Loss."

Many of those who post notices are younger people writing about parents, grandparents, and best friends. Three characteristics sometimes said to apply to young adults—cynicism, irreverence, and detachment—are conspicuous by their absence. Instead, faith and connection abound.

One daughter misses her father, who died in May 1999. Like many of her elders, she is sustained by her children:

I was told today "It's okay Mommy, Poppy is an angel now." You know, I believe you are. I feel your spirit around us, guiding us, loving us; and somehow I know there will come a day when we will feel like smiling again. I know this because it's what you would have wanted. So each summer, when the days are warm, the sky is blue and the sun is shining brightly . . . I will stop, and close my eyes and feel your spirit on the summer wind. And I Will Smile. I love you Herb. Always. [Virtual Memorial Garden, 2000]

Many postings are quite explicit about religion. One, about a 25-year-old who died suddenly in March 2000, explains:

Peter . . . meaning rock or stone. Pretty much says it all about this wonderful friend. He was strong as an ox, in anything he did. With loving his family, and friends, every relationship was solid. . . . Pete was always the life of the party, and he was usually the reason there was one. We will miss you dearly, Peter. Taken by a tragedy, we have to believe that God needed your help at this time. You will live through those who love you. [Virtual Memorial Garden, 2000]

As in this message, writing directly to the dead person seems to come easy in cyberspace. One message even says:

. . . if there is a "net" in heaven, please send email to me or chris or michael or josh! [Virtual Memorial Garden, 1997, quoted in Roberts, 1999]

Noteworthy among these memorials are messages from mourners that ordinarily are not given expression in traditional funeral services. Included are many parents grieving for their newborns, many young people mourning their cats or dogs, and unmarried adults grieving for romantic partners. These tributes "provide an excellent research opportunity for studying various issues related to death and dying" (Roberts, 1999). They confirm what more conventional research has found: Grief needs appropriate expression, which humans find in myriad ways.

It is also important to recognize that each culture, cohort, and generation imparts to its people distinct customs and values. Those who have been taught to bear grief stoically may be doubly distressed if they are advised to cry and cannot; conversely, those whose cultures expect loud wailing and rending of garments may become confused and resentful if they are told to hush. Particularly among younger people, grieving is sometimes aided today by an electronic letter to the dead (see the In Person box).

No matter what method is used to work through emotions of grief, the experience may give the living a deeper appreciation of themselves as well as of the value of human relationships. In fact, a theme frequently sounded is that we all need to learn lessons that mourners can teach. The most central of these is the value of intimate, caring relationships. As one counselor expresses it:

Rest in Peace? Among the most difficult deaths to accept, both by the dying and the living, are senseless, unexpected deaths long before old age. Here lies a young man shot and killed in gang retribution.

❶ *Answer to Observational Quiz (from page 719):*
Not only does each panel have a distinct design and color scheme, but many have names and symbols that testify to the life and death of one specific human being.

I often have heard phrases such as "I wish I had told him I loved him" or "I wish we could have resolved our differences earlier." There may be things we need to say, appreciations that need to be expressed, distances to bridge. . . . Loving and being loved is not just something that happens to us. It is a creative art that must be worked in a variety of ways. [Sanders, 1989]

It is fitting to end this book with just such a reminder of the creative work of loving. As first described in Chapter 1, the study of the process of human development is a science—a topic to be researched, understood, and explained in order to enhance human lives. But the process of actually living one's own life is an art as well as a science, with strands of love and sorrow and recovery that are woven into each person's unique tapestry. Death, when accepted, grief, when allowed expression, and bereavement, when it leads to a fuller appreciation of living, give added meaning to birth, growth, development, and all human relationships.

Appendix A
Supplemental Charts and Graphs

Often, examining specific data is useful, even fascinating, to developmental researchers. The particular numbers reveal trends and nuances not apparent from a more general view. For instance, many people mistakenly believe that the incidence of Down syndrome babies rises sharply for mothers over 35, or that even the tiniest newborns usually survive. With each chart in the following section you will probably see information not generally known.

A-1 Blood—Donated, Received, and Inherited

Blood types A and B are dominant traits, and type O is recessive. The percentages given in the first column of this chart represent the odds that a child born to the parents with the various combinations of genotypes will have the genotype given in the second column.

Genotypes of Parents*	Genotype of Offspring	Phenotype	Can Donate Blood To (Phenotype)	Can Receive Blood From (Phenotype)
AA + AA (100%) AA + AB (50%) AA + AO (50%) AB + AB (25%) AB + AO (25%) AO + AO (25%)	AA (inherits one A from each parent)	A	A or AB	A or O
AA + OO (100%) AB + OO (50%) AO + AO (50%) AO + OO (50%) AB + AO (25%) AB + BO (25%)	AO	A	A or AB	A or O
BB + BB (100%) AB + BB (50%) BB + BO (50%) AB + AB (25%) AB + BO (25%) BO + BO (25%)	BB	B	B or AB	B or O
BB + OO (100%) AB + OO (50%) BO + BO (50%) BO + OO (50%) AB + AO (25%) AB + BO (25%)	BO	B	B or AB	B or O
AA + BB (100%) AA + AB (50%) AA + BO (50%) AB + AB (50%) AB + BB (50%) AO + BB (50%) AB + BO (25%) AO + BO (25%)	AB	AB	AB only	A, B, AB, O ("universal recipient")
OO + OO (100%) AO + OO (50%) BO + OO (50%) AO + AO (25%) AO + BO (25%) BO + BO (25%)	OO	O	A, B, AB, O ("universal donor")	O only

*Blood type is not a sex-linked trait, so any of these pairs can be either mother-plus-father or father-plus-mother.
Source: Adapted from Hartl & Jones, 1999.

A-2 Common Genetic Diseases and Conditions

Name	Description	Prognosis	Probable Inheritance	Incidence*	Carrier Detection†	Prenatal Detection?
Alzheimer's disease	Loss of memory and increasing mental impairment.	Eventual death, often after years of dependency.	Additive.	Fewer than 1 in 100 middle-aged adults; 20 percent of all adults over age 80.	Yes, for some genes	No
Breast cancer	Tumors in breast that can spread.	With early treatment, most are cured. Without it, death within 3 years.	BRCA1 and BRCA2 genes seem dominant; other cases, multifactorial.	1 woman in 8 gets breast cancer.	Yes, for BRCA1 and BRCA2	No
Cleft palate, cleft lip	The two sides of the upper lip or palate are not joined.	Correctable by surgery.	Multifactorial.	1 baby in every 700. More common in Asian Americans and Native Americans.	No	Yes
Club foot	The foot and ankle are twisted.	Correctable by surgery.	Multifactorial.	1 baby in every 200. More common in boys.	No	Yes
Cystic fibrosis	Mucous obstructions, especially in lungs and digestive organs.	Most live to middle adulthood.	Recessive gene. Also spontaneous mutations.	1 European American in 2,500. 1 in 20 European Americans is a carrier.	Sometimes	Yes, in some cases
Diabetes	Abnormal sugar metabolism because of insufficient insulin.	Early onset fatal without insulin; for adult onset, variable risks.	Multifactorial. For adult onset, environment is crucial.	1 child in 500 is born diabetic. More common in Native Americans and African Americans. 1 elderly adult in 10 is diabetic.	No	No
Hemophilia	Absence of clotting factor in blood.	Death from internal bleeding. Blood transfusions reduce or prevent damage.	X-linked recessive. Also spontaneous mutations.	1 in 10,000 males. Royal families of England, Russia, and Germany had it.	Yes	Yes
Hydro-cephalus	Obstruction causes excess water in the brain.	Brain damage and death. Surgery sometimes makes normal life possible.	Multifactorial.	1 baby in every 100.	No	Yes

*Incidence statistics vary from country to country; those given here are for the United States. All these diseases can occur in any ethnic group. When certain groups have a high or low incidence, it is noted here.
†Studying the family tree can help geneticists spot a possible carrier of many genetic diseases or, in some cases, a definite carrier. However, here "Yes" means that a carrier can be detected even without knowledge of family history.

Name	Description	Prognosis	Probable Inheritance	Incidence*	Carrier Detection†	Prenatal Detection?
Muscular dystrophy (13 diseases)	Weakening of muscles.	Inability to walk, move; wasting away and sometimes death.	Duchenne's is X-linked; other forms are recessive or multifactorial.	1 in every 3,500 males develop Duchenne's; 10,000 Americans have some form of MD.	Yes, for some forms	Yes, for some forms
Neural-tube defects (open spine)	Anencephaly (parts of the brain missing) or spina bifida (lower spine not closed).	Anencephalic: severe retardation; spina bifida: poor lower body control.	Multifactorial; defect occurs in first weeks of pregnancy.	Anencephaly: 1 in 1,000 births; spina bifida: 3 in 1,000. More common in those of Welsh and Scottish descent.	No	Yes
Phenylketonuria (PKU)	Abnormal digestion of protein.	Mental retardation, hyperactivity. Preventable by diet.	Recessive.	1 in 10,000 births. 1 in 100 European Americans is a carrier. especially those of Norwegian and Irish descent.	Yes	Yes
Pyloric stenosis	Overgrowth of muscle in intestine.	Vomiting, loss of weight, eventual death. Correctable by surgery.	Multifactorial.	1 male in 200; 1 female in 1,000. Less common in African Americans.	No .	No
Sickle-cell anemia	Abnormal blood cells.	Possible painful "crisis"; heart and kidney failure. Treatable with drugs.	Recessive.	1 in 500 African Americans. 1 in 10 African Americans is a carrier, as is 1 in 20 Latinos.	Yes	Yes
Tay-Sachs disease	Enzyme disease.	Apparently healthy infant becomes progressively weaker, usually dying by age 5.	Recessive.	1 in 4,000 births. 1 in 30 American Jews and 1 in 20 French Canadians are carriers.	Yes	Yes
Thalassemia	Abnormal blood cells.	Paleness and listlessness, low resistance to infections.	Recessive.	1 in 10 Greek, Italian, Thai, and Indian Americans is a carrier.	Yes	Yes
Tourette syndrome	Uncontrollable tics, body jerking, verbal obscenities.	Often imperceptible in children; worsens with age.	Dominant.	1 in 500 births.	Sometimes	No

Sources: Mange & Mange, 1999; McKusick, 1994; National Academy of Sciences, 1994; Price et al., 1998; Rohman & Stratton, 1998.

A-3 Incidence of Down Syndrome: Estimated Risk by Maternal Age and Gestation

The odds of any given fetus, at the end of the first trimester, having three chromosomes at the 21st site (trisomy 21) and thus having Down syndrome is shown in the column 10 weeks. Every year of maternal age increases the incidence of trisomy 21. You can also see that, as pregnancy continues, more Down syndrome fetuses are aborted, either spontaneously or by choice. The number of Down syndrome infants born alive is only half the number who survived the first trimester. Although obviously the least risk is at age 20 (younger is even better), there is some comfort for the older mother. There is no year when the odds suddenly increase (age 35 is an arbitrary cut-off), and even at age 44, less than 4 percent of all newborns have Down syndrome. Other chromosomal abnormalities in fetuses also increase with mother's age, but the rate of spontaneous abortion is much higher, so births of babies with chromosomal defects is not the norm, even to women over age 40.

Age (yrs)	Gestation (weeks)			
	10	25	35	Births
20	1: 804	1,294	1,464	1,527
21	1: 793	1,277	1,445	1,507
22	1: 780	1,256	1,421	1,482
23	1: 762	1,227	1,389	1,448
24	1: 740	1,191	1,348	1,406
25	1: 712	1,146	1,297	1,352
26	1: 677	1,090	1,233	1,286
27	1: 635	1,022	1,157	1,206
28	1: 586	943	1,068	1,113
29	1: 531	855	967	1,008
30	1: 471	758	858	895
31	1: 409	658	745	776
32	1: 347	559	632	659
33	1: 288	464	525	547
34	1: 235	378	427	446
35	1: 187	302	342	356
36	1: 148	238	269	280
37	1: 115	185	209	218
38	1: 88	142	160	167
39	1: 67	108	122	128
40	1: 51	82	93	97
41	1: 38	62	70	73
42	1: 29	46	52	55
43	1: 21	35	39	41
44	1: 16	26	29	30

Source: Snijders & Nicolaides, 1996.

A-4 Birthweight and Mortality, United States, 1995

Note that, by far, the highest mortality is for infants born weighing less than 500 grams (that's 17 ounces, which is slightly more than a pound). Eighty-nine percent of those that live for a few hours (this does not include those who die during birth) die during the neonatal period, which is the first 28 days. Eighty-seven of the 635 tiny survivors died between one month and one year. This category of LBW newborns has not benefited from recent advances in medical care. Even with the best care, they are simply too immature to survive. By contrast, 1,000-gram infants are twice as likely to live as they were ten years ago.

Birth-weight	Live births	Infant deaths (first year)	Neonatal deaths (first 28 days)	Postneonatal deaths (day 29–365)	Infant mortality rate*	Percent decrease in mortality 1985–95
Less than 500 grams	5,703	5,155	5,068	87	903.9	− 1.9
500–749 grams	9,998	5,280	4,674	606	528.1	−31.0
750–999 grams	10,816	1,970	1,516	453	182.1	−55.2
1,000–1,249 grams	12,242	1,047	744	303	85.5	−55.8
1,250–1,499 grams	14,267	779	559	220	54.6	−49.7
1,500–1,999 grams	55,342	1,835	1,164	672	33.2	−39.4
2,000–2,499 grams	177,608	2,406	1,222	1,183	13.5	−35.0
2,500–2,999 grams	640,891	3,484	1,419	2,064	5.4	−30.3
3,000–3,499 grams	1,438,889	4,131	1,389	2,742	2.9	−33.3
3,500–3,999 grams	1,129,470	2,272	770	1,502	2.0	−34.5
4,000–4,499 grams	339,910	618	241	376	1.8	−35.7
4,500–4,999 grams	56,309	122	46	76	2.2	−43.2
5,000 grams or more	6,466	54	36	18	8.4	−42.7

*Rate is per 1,000 live births.
Source: Monthly Vital Statistics Report, 1998.

A-5 Recommended Childhood Immunization

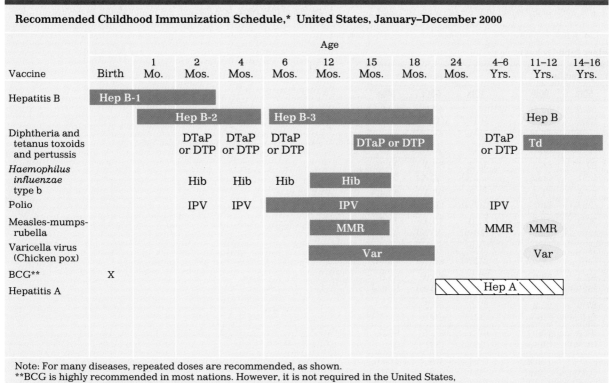

Recommended Childhood Immunization Schedule,* United States, January–December 2000

						Age						
Vaccine	Birth	1 Mo.	2 Mos.	4 Mos.	6 Mos.	12 Mos.	15 Mos.	18 Mos.	24 Mos.	4–6 Yrs.	11–12 Yrs.	14–16 Yrs.
Hepatitis B	Hep B-1		Hep B-2		Hep B-3						Hep B	
Diphtheria and tetanus toxoids and pertussis			DTaP or DTP	DTaP or DTP	DTaP or DTP		DTaP or DTP			DTaP or DTP	Td	
Haemophilus influenzae type b			Hib	Hib	Hib	Hib						
Polio			IPV	IPV	IPV					IPV		
Measles-mumps-rubella						MMR				MMR	MMR	
Varicella virus (Chicken pox)						Var					Var	
BCG**	X											
Hepatitis A										Hep A		

Note: For many diseases, repeated doses are recommended, as shown.
**BCG is highly recommended in most nations. However, it is not required in the United States, because the rate of tuberculosis is low.
Source: *Morbidity and Mortality Weekly Report*, January 21, 2000.

■ Range of acceptable ages for vaccination

⬭ Vaccines to be assessed and administered if necessary

◹ Recommended in selected areas

A-6 Height Gains from Birth to Age 18

The range of height (below) and weight (see Figure A-7) of children in the United States. The columns labeled "50th" (the fiftieth percentile) show the average; the columns labeled "90th" (the ninetieth percentile) show the size of children taller and heavier than 90 percent of their contemporaries; and the columns labeled "10th" (the tenth percentile) show the size of children who are taller than only 10 percent of their peers. Note that girls are slightly shorter, on average, than boys.

Length in Centimeters (and Inches)

AGE	Boys: percentiles			Girls: percentiles		
	10th	50th	90th	10th	50th	90th
Birth	47.5 (18¾)	50.5 (20)	53.5 (21)	46.5 (18¼)	49.9 (19¾)	52.0 (20½)
1 month	51.3 (20¼)	54.6 (21½)	57.7 (22¾)	50.2 (19¾)	53.5 (21)	56.1 (22)
3 months	57.7 (22¾)	61.1 (24)	64.5 (25½)	56.2 (22¼)	59.5 (23½)	62.7 (24¾)
6 months	64.4 (25¼)	67.8 (26¾)	71.3 (28)	62.6 (24¾)	65.9 (26)	69.4 (27¼)
9 months	69.1 (27¼)	72.3 (28½)	75.9 (30)	67.0 (26½)	70.4 (27¾)	74.0 (29¼)
12 months	72.8 (28¾)	76.1 (30)	79.8 (31½)	70.8 (27¾)	74.3 (29¼)	78.0 (30¾)
18 months	78.7 (31)	82.4 (32½)	86.6 (34)	77.2 (30½)	80.9 (31¾)	85.0 (33½)
24 months	83.5 (32¾)	87.6 (34½)	92.2 (36¼)	82.5 (32½)	86.5 (34)	90.8 (35¾)
3 years	90.3 (35½)	94.9 (37¼)	100.1 (39½)	89.3 (35¼)	94.1 (37)	99.0 (39)
4 years	97.3 (38¼)	102.9 (40½)	108.2 (42½)	96.4 (38)	101.6 (40)	106.6 (42)
5 years	103.7 (40¾)	109.9 (43¼)	115.4 (45½)	102.7 (40½)	108.4 (42¾)	113.8 (44¾)
6 years	109.6 (43¼)	116.1 (45¾)	121.9 (48)	108.4 (42¾)	114.6 (45)	120.8 (47½)
7 years	115.0 (45¼)	121.7 (48)	127.9 (50¼)	113.6 (44¾)	120.6 (47½)	127.6 (50¼)
8 years	120.2 (47¼)	127.0 (50)	133.6 (52½)	118.7 (46¾)	126.4 (49¾)	134.2 (52¾)
9 years	125.2 (49¼)	132.2 (52)	139.4 (55)	123.9 (48¾)	132.2 (52)	140.7 (55½)
10 years	130.1 (51¼)	137.5 (54¼)	145.5 (57¼)	129.5 (51)	138.3 (54½)	147.2 (58)
11 years	135.1 (53¼)	143.33 (56½)	152.1 (60)	135.6 (53½)	144.8 (57)	153.7 (60½)
12 years	140.3 (55¼)	149.7 (59)	159.4 (62¾)	142.3 (56)	151.5 (59¾)	160.0 (63)
13 years	145.8 (57½)	156.5 (61½)	167.0 (65¾)	148.0 (58¼)	157.1 (61¾)	165.3 (65)
14 years	151.8 (59¾)	63.1 (64¼)	173.8 (68½)	151.5 (59¾)	160.4 (63¼)	168.7 (66½)
15 years	158.2 (62¼)	169.0 (66½)	178.9 (70½)	153.2 (60¼)	161.8 (63¾)	170.5 (67¼)
16 years	163.9 (64½)	173.5 (68¼)	182.4 (71¾)	154.1 (60¾)	162.4 (64)	171.1 (67¼)
17 years	167.7 (66)	176.2 (69¼)	184.4 (72½)	155.1 (61)	163.1 (64¼)	171.2 (67½)
18 years	168.7 (66½)	176.8 (69½)	185.3 (73)	156.0 (61½)	163.7 (64½)	171.0 (67¼)

Source: These data are those of the National Center for Health Statistics (NCHS), Health Resources Administration, DHHS. They were based on studies of The Fels Research Institute, Yellow Springs, Ohio. These data were first made available with the help of William M. Moore, M.D., of Ross Laboratories, who supplied the conversion from metric measurements to approximate inches and pounds. This help is gratefully acknowledged.

A-7 Weight Gains from Birth to Age 18

Figures A-6 and A-7 present rough guidelines; a child might differ from these norms and be quite healthy and normal. However, if a particular child shows a discrepancy between height and weight (for instance, at the 90th percentile in height but only the 20th percentile in weight) or is much larger or smaller than most children the same age, a pediatrician should be alerted to see if disease, malnutrition, or genetic abnormality is part of the reason.

Weight in Kilograms (and Pounds)

AGE	Boys: percentiles			Girls: percentiles		
	10th	50th	90th	10th	50th	90th
Birth	2.78 (6¼)	3.27 (7¼)	3.82 (8½)	2.58 (5¾)	3.23 (7)	3.64 (8)
1 month	3.43 (7½)	4.29 (9½)	5.14 (11¼)	3.22 (7)	3.98 (8¾)	4.65 (10¼)
3 months	4.78 (10½)	5.98 (13¼)	7.14 (15¾)	4.47 (9¾)	5.40 (12)	6.39 (14)
6 months	6.61 (14½)	7.85 (17¼)	9.10 (20)	6.12 (13½)	7.21 (16)	8.38 (18½)
9 months	7.95 (17½)	9.18 (20¼)	10.49 (23¼)	7.34 (16¼)	8.56 (18¾)	9.83 (21¾)
12 months	8.84 (19½)	10.15 (22½)	11.54 (25½)	8.19 (18)	9.53 (21)	10.87 (24)
18 months	9.92 (21¾)	11.47 (25¼)	13.05 (28¾)	9.30 (20½)	10.82 (23¾)	12.30 (27)
24 months	10.85 (24)	12.59 (27¾)	14.29 (31½)	10.26 (22½)	11.90 (26¼)	13.57 (30)
3 years	12.58 (27¾)	14.62 (32¼)	16.95 (37¼)	12.26 (27)	14.10 (31)	16.54 (36½)
4 years	14.24 (31½)	16.69 (36¾)	19.32 (42½)	13.84 (30½)	15.96 (35¼)	18.93 (41¾)
5 years	15.96 (35¼)	18.67 (41¼)	21.70 (47¾)	15.26 (33¾)	17.66 (39)	21.23 (46¾)
6 years	17.72 (39)	20.69 (45½)	24.31 (53½)	16.72 (36¾)	19.52 (43)	23.89 (52¾)
7 years	19.53 (43)	22.85 (50¼)	27.36 (60¼)	18.39 (40½)	21.84 (48¼)	27.39 (60½)
8 years	21.39 (47¼)	25.30 (55¾)	31.06 (68½)	20.45 (45)	24.84 (54¾)	32.04 (70¾)
9 years	23.33 (51½)	28.13 (62)	35.57 (78½)	22.92 (50½)	28.46 (62¾)	37.60 (83)
10 years	25.52 (56¼)	31.44 (69¼)	40.80 (90)	25.76 (56¾)	32.55 (71¾)	43.70 (96¼)
11 years	28.17 (62)	35.30 (77¾)	46.57 (102¾)	28.97 (63¾)	36.95 (81½)	49.96 (110¼)
12 years	31.46 (69¼)	39.78 (87¾)	52.73 (116¼)	32.53 (71¼)	41.53 (91½)	55.99 (123½)
13 years	35.60 (78½)	44.95 (99)	59.12 (130¼)	36.35 (80¼)	46.10 (101¾)	61.45 (135½)
14 years	40.64 (89½)	50.77 (112)	65.57 (144½)	40.11 (88½)	50.28 (110¾)	66.04 (145½)
15 years	46.06 (101½)	56.71 (125)	71.91 (158½)	43.38 (95¾)	53.68 (118¼)	69.64 (153¼)
16 years	51.16 (112¾)	62.10 (137)	77.97 (172)	45.78 (101)	55.89 (123¼)	71.68 (158)
17 years	55.28 (121¾)	66.31 (146¼)	83.58 (184¼)	47.04 (103¾)	56.69 (125)	72.38 (159½)
18 years	57.89 (127½)	68.88 (151¾)	88.41 (195)	47.47 (104¾)	56.62 (124¾)	72.25 (159¼)

Source: Data are those of the National Center for Health Statistics, Health Resources Administration, DHHS, collected in its Health Examination Surveys.

A-8 DSM-IV Criteria for Conduct Disorder (CD), Attention-Deficit/Hyperactivity Disorder (ADHD), and Oppositional Defiant Disorder (ODD)

As you'll see below, the specific symptoms for these various disorders overlap. Many other childhood disorders also have some of the same symptoms. Differentiating one problem from another is the main purpose of DSM-IV. That is no easy task, which is one reason the book is now in its fourth major revision and contains 886 pages.

Diagnostic Criteria for Conduct Disorder

A. A repetitive and persistent pattern of behavior in which the basic rights of others or major age-appropriate societal norms or rules are violated, as manifested by the presence of three (or more) of the following criteria in the past 12 months, with at least one criterion present in the past 6 months:

Aggression to people and animals

(1) often bullies, threatens, or intimidates others
(2) often initiates physical fights
(3) has used a weapon that can cause serious physical harm to others (e.g., a bat, brick, broken bottle, knife, gun)
(4) has been physically cruel to people
(5) has been physically cruel to animals
(6) has stolen while confronting a victim (e.g., mugging, purse snatching, extortion, armed robbery)
(7) has forced someone into sexual activity

Destruction of property

(8) has deliberately engaged in fire setting with the intention of causing serious damage
(9) has deliberately destroyed others' property (other than by fire setting)

Deceitfulness or theft

(10) has broken into someone else's house, building, or car
(11) often lies to obtain goods or favors or to avoid obligations (i.e., "cons" others)
(12) has stolen items of nontrivial value without confronting a victim (e.g., shoplifting, but without breaking and entering; forgery)

Serious violations of rules

(13) often stays out at night despite parental prohibitions, beginning before age 13 years
(14) has run away from home overnight at least twice while living in parental or parental surrogate home (or once without returning for a lengthy period)
(15) is often truant from school, beginning before age 13 years

B. The disturbance in behavior causes clinically significant impairment in social, academic, or occupational functioning.

Diagnostic Criteria for Attention-Deficit/Hyperactivity Disorder

A. Either (1) or (2):
(1) Six (or more) of the following symptoms of **inattention** have persisted for at least 6 months to a degree that is maladaptive and inconsistent with developmental level:

Inattention
(a) often fails to give close attention to details or makes careless mistakes in schoolwork, work, or other activities
(b) often has difficulty sustaining attention in tasks or play activities
(c) often does not seem to listen when spoken to directly
(d) often does not follow through on instructions and fails to finish schoolwork, chores, or duties in the workplace (not due to oppositional behavior or failure to understand instructions)
(e) often has difficulty organizing tasks and activities
(f) often avoids, dislikes, or is reluctant to engage in tasks that require sustained mental effort (such as schoolwork or homework)
(g) often loses things necessary for tasks or activities (e.g., toys, school assignments, pencils, books, or tools)
(h) is often easily distracted by extraneous stimuli
(i) is often forgetful in daily activities

(2) Six (or more) of the following symptoms of **hyperactivity-impulsivity** have persisted for at least 6 months to a degree that is maladaptive and inconsistent with developmental level:

Hyperactivity
(a) often fidgets with hands or feet or squirms in seat
(b) often leaves seat in classroom or in other situations in which remaining seated is expected
(c) often runs about or climbs excessively in situations in which it is inappropriate (in adolescents or adults, may be limited to subjective feelings of restlessness)

(d) often has difficulty playing or engaging in leisure activities quietly

(e) is often "on the go" or often acts as if "driven by a motor"

(f) often talks excessively

Impulsivity

(g) often blurts out answers before questions have been completed

(h) often has difficulty awaiting turn

(i) often interrupts or intrudes on others (e.g., butts into conversations or games)

B. Some hyperactive-impulsive or inattentive symptoms that caused impairment were present before age 7 years.

C. Some impairment from the symptoms is present in two or more settings (e.g., at school [or work] and at home).

D. There must be clear evidence of clinically significant impairment in social, academic, or occupational functioning.

Diagnostic Criteria for Oppositional Defiant Disorder

A. A pattern of negativistic, hostile, and defiant behavior lasting at least 6 months, during which four (or more) of the following are present:

(1) often loses temper

(2) often argues with adults

(3) often actively defies or refuses to comply with adults' requests or rules

(4) often deliberately annoys people

(5) often blames others for his or her mistakes or misbehavior

(6) is often touchy or easily annoyed by others

(7) is often angry and resentful

(8) is often spiteful or vindictive

Note: Consider a criterion met only if the behavior occurs more frequently than is typically observed in individuals of comparable age and developmental level.

B. The disturbance in behavior causes clinically significant impairment in social, academic, or occupational functioning.

A-9 U.S. Children in Relatives' Care

The number of children living with relatives and no parents grew 51.5 percent between 1990 and 1998. Notice the big jump between 1993 and 1994. What factors do you think can account for that change? See Chapter 8 for a discussion of kinship care.

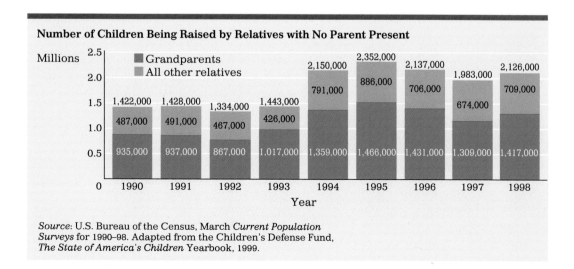

Number of Children Being Raised by Relatives with No Parent Present

Source: U.S. Bureau of the Census, March *Current Population Surveys* for 1990–98. Adapted from the Children's Defense Fund, *The State of America's Children* Yearbook, 1999.

A-10 Dependency Ratios in Selected Countries

This table shows projected data for 25 of the most populous nations of the world. A high proportion of children is more likely than a high proportion of old people to give a nation one of the worst dependency ratios, with only one adult to care for each child or elder. In the nations with the best ratios, two adults are available to care for each dependent. Since most people over age 64 actually care for themselves, the difference between the best and the worst ratios is even more pronounced than is indicated here.

Country	Total population (in millions)	Percentage under age 15	Percentage over age 64	Dependency ratio (approximate)
Algeria	31,788	36.4%	3.9%	60:40
Argentina	37,215	27.3	10.3	62:38
Australia	18,950	20.8	12.6	66:33
Bangladesh[†]	129,147	36.3	3.3	60:40
Brazil	173,791	29.4	5.3	65:35
Canada*	31,330	19.3	12.6	68:32
Chile	15,155	27.6	7.2	65:35
China*	1,256,168	25.1	7.0	68:32
Colombia	40,037	32.7	4.6	63:37
Cuba*	11,139	21.4	9.7	69:31
Egypt[†]	68,495	35.2	3.7	61:39
Ethiopia	60,967	46.3	2.8	51:49
France	59,126	18.5	16.1	65:35
Germany*	82,081	15.2	16.5	68:32
Ghana[†]	19,272	41.7	3.2	55:45
India	1,017,645	33.7	4.7	62:38
Indonesia	219,267	30.1	4.3	66:34
Italy*	56,687	14.2	18.2	68:32
Japan*	126,434	14.9	17.0	68:32
Mexico	102,027	34.8	4.3	61:39
Nigeria[†]	117,171	44.8	3.0	52:48
South Africa	43,982	34.1	4.6	61:39
Uganda[†]	23,452	51.2	2.2	47:53
United Kingdom	59,247	19.1	15.7	65:35
United States	274,943	21.4	12.6	66:34
World	6,073,099	30.0	6.9	63:37

*Best dependency ratio.
[†]Worst dependency ratio.
Source: U.S. Bureau of the Census, 1999.

A-11 Sexual Behaviors of U.S. High School Students: State-by-State Variations

These numbers, as high as they are, are actually lower than they were in the early 1990s.

Percentage of High School Students Who Reported Engaging in Sexual Behaviors

State	Ever had sexual intercourse			[1993]† [Total]	First sexual intercourse before age 13			Four or more sex partners during lifetime			[1993]† [Total]	Currently sexually active*			[1993]† [Total]
	Female	Male	Total		Female	Male	Total	Female	Male	Total		Female	Male	Total	
Arkansas	57.5	61.9	59.7		5.9	18.7	12.4	19.2	29.7	24.5		45.4	43.5	44.4	
Connecticut	42.3	44.4	43.5		3.3	5.9	4.7	10.0	13.0	11.7		33.4	31.6	32.7	
Hawaii	44.8	35.8	40.3	[44.3]	4.9	9.1	7.0	8.2	9.7	9.1	[11.4]	32.6	19.3	25.8	[28.7]
Iowa	39.2	46.3	42.8		2.0	5.6	3.8	13.4	11.9	12.7		31.5	34.3	33.0	
Kentucky	50.3	56.9	53.7		3.4	10.7	7.2	12.6	23.1	18.1		38.3	40.2	39.4	
Maine	50.1	52.9	51.6		4.3	9.2	6.8	11.9	13.2	12.5		38.3	34.0	36.2	
Massachusetts	42.4	46.8	44.7	[48.7]	4.2	9.8	7.1	10.6	14.8	12.7	[14.5]	31.8	30.0	31.0	[33.4]
Michigan	47.2	50.7	48.9		5.0	11.8	8.3	14.2	18.5	16.4		36.0	32.7	34.4	
Mississippi	64.5	74.9	69.5	[69.0]	8.5	34.7	21.2	19.7	44.1	31.4	[28.1]	49.2	55.1	52.1	[50.4]
Missouri	52.4	50.4	51.5		4.5	11.9	8.2	13.1	18.3	15.8		41.2	31.9	36.7	
Montana	44.4	47.3	45.9	[51.0]	4.1	9.0	6.5	14.5	16.6	15.5	[17.9]	33.1	29.8	31.5	[33.7]
Nevada	46.7	47.6	47.1	[58.4]	3.9	9.1	6.5	12.6	18.0	15.3	[23.0]	35.6	31.5	33.5	[39.7]
New York	37.0	45.4	41.2		3.2	11.7	7.4	8.0	17.4	12.6		27.9	30.5	29.2	
Ohio	47.4	49.9	48.7	[55.2]	4.7	14.2	9.4	13.0	20.1	16.6	[20.6]	35.3	32.9	34.2	[39.2]
Rhode Island	42.2	43.1	42.7		3.8	7.5	5.7	9.8	14.2	12.1		33.8	27.9	31.1	
South Carolina	59.1	64.0	61.5	[65.5]	9.3	22.5	15.8	20.1	29.9	25.0	[28.3]	43.4	41.0	42.3	[46.4]
South Dakota	43.1	39.4	41.2	[52.0]	3.9	6.1	5.0	14.5	12.9	13.7	[16.5]	30.3	26.9	28.6	[37.0]
Vermont	NA	NA	NA		4.3	9.5	7.0	9.8	13.3	11.6		31.5	29.6	30.6	
West Virginia	53.1	58.0	55.5	[63.1]	3.6	11.4	7.4	15.1	19.1	17.0	[22.4]	40.1	40.7	40.4	[45.6]
Wisconsin	38.7	43.7	41.3	[47.0]	4.2	6.8	5.5	11.4	11.4	11.4	[14.3]	30.5	27.0	28.7	[32.5]
Wyoming	44.0	45.9	45.0		4.3	8.2	6.2	16.3	17.5	16.9		32.4	28.8	30.6	

NA = Not available.
*Active in 3 months prior to survey.
†If available.
Source: Morbidity and Mortality Weekly Report, August 14, 1998 (Selected U.S. sites, Youth Risk Behavior Surveys, 1997.)

A-12 Rates of Births to Teenage Mothers: International Comparisons

Note that teens in the United States have far more babies than their counterparts in other developed countries.

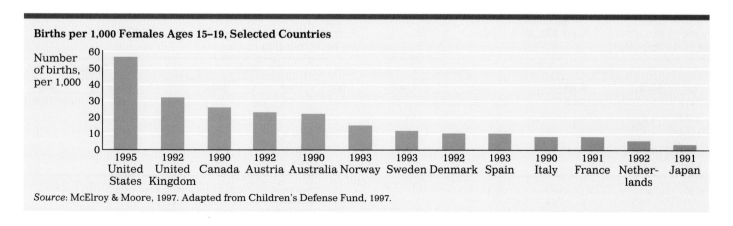

Births per 1,000 Females Ages 15–19, Selected Countries

Source: McElroy & Moore, 1997. Adapted from Children's Defense Fund, 1997.

A-13 Homicide Victim and Offender Rates,
Adolescents Compared to All Ages

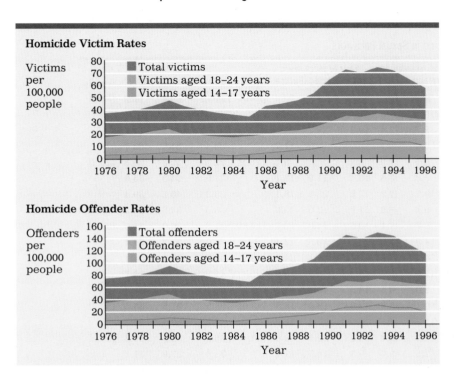

A-14 Homicide Victim and Offender Rates, by Race
and Gender, Ages 14–17

*Teenage boys are more often violent offenders than victims. The ratio of
victimization to offense has varied for teenage girls over the years.*

Homicide Victimization Rates per 100,000 Population
for 14–17-Year-Olds

	Male		Female	
Year	**White**	**Black**	**White**	**Black**
1976	3.7	24.6	2.2	6.4
1981	4.4	23.6	2.4	6.2
1986	4.2	27.4	2.3	6.6
1991	8.7	73.6	2.6	9.6
1996	8.4	53.3	2.1	8.9

Tabulations based on FBI Supplementary Homicide Reports and U.S.
Census Bureau, Current Population Reports.

Estimated Homicide Offending Rates per 100,000 Population
for 14–17-Year-Olds

	Male		Female	
Year	**White**	**Black**	**White**	**Black**
1976	10.4	72.4	1.3	10.3
1981	10.9	73.1	1.3	8.6
1986	12.3	72.2	1.1	5.6
1991	21.9	199.1	1.3	12.1
1996	17.4	134.8	1.7	7.8

Tabulations based on FBI Supplementary Homicide Reports and U.S.
Census Bureau, Current Population Reports. Rates include both
known perpetrators and estimated share of unidentified perpetrators.

A-15 Lung Cancer Death Rates: It's Not Just Genes and Gender

For lung cancer as well as most other diseases, the male death rate is markedly higher than the female death rate in the United States. Moreover, the death rate for African Americans is almost twice the average, and for Asian Americans it is almost half the average. Genes and gender do not explain these discrepancies, however. As you clan see, white women are at greater risk than Hispanic or

Native American men, and the rate for black men went down as the rate for some other groups rose. (These are "age-adjusted" rates, which means that they reflect the fact that more Asians reach old age and fewer Native Americans do. In other words, the sex and ethnic differences shown here are real—not artifacts of the age distribution.)

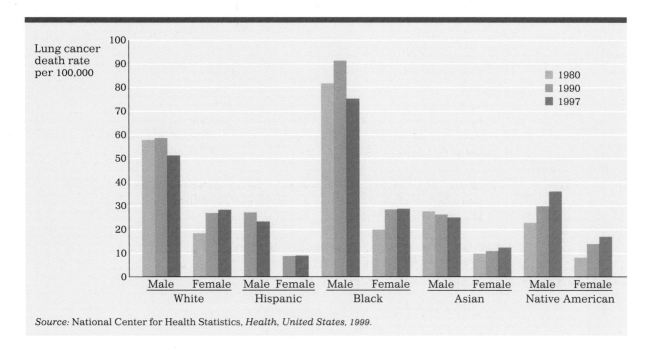

Source: National Center for Health Statistics, *Health, United States, 1999.*

A-16 Median Annual Income by Educational Attainment

Although there is some debate about the cognitive benefits of college education, there is no doubt about the financial benefits. No matter what a person's ethnicity or gender, a bachelor's degree more than doubles his or her income compared to that of someone who has not completed high school.

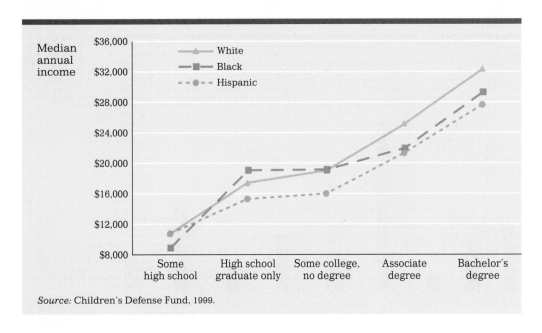

Source: Children's Defense Fund, 1999.

A-17 Child Support Enforcement, by State, 1996

	Number of cases	Percent with court order	Percent with collection	Rank
Alabama	387,817	56.7%	21.3%	26
Alaska	55,854	77.6	17.8	35
Arizona	272,058	32.0	13.9	48
Arkansas	137,633	69.6	27.8	12
California	2,469,826	46.2	17.2	37
Colorado	199,471	67.0	16.7	38
Connecticut	235,547	61.9	17.6	36
Delaware	56,159	73.1	28.3	11
District of Columbia	100,384	41.1	9.9	51
Florida	1,016,299	100.0	15.7	43
Georgia	519,240	55.6	20.1	31
Hawaii	58,610	50.9	23.6	19
Idaho	73,791	76.8	24.9	16
Illinois	730,397	30.2	11.8	50
Indiana	610,026	62.6	12.6	49
Iowa	195,321	77.9	20.2	30
Kansas	138,343	58.8	34.1	5
Kentucky	322,036	56.0	16.3	39
Louisiana	339,721	38.2	16.1	41
Maine	77,228	80.2	37.1	3
Maryland	379,687	71.6	22.7	23
Massachusetts	208,435	78.0	30.4	9
Michigan	1,561,364	47.3	16.1	41
Minnesota	239,443	77.6	41.2	2
Mississippi	271,119	45.3	14.5	45
Missouri	393,250	72.9	21.1	27
Montana	43,143	62.4	24.7	17
Nebraska	131,541	55.6	21.0	28
Nevada	80,474	60.5	22.9	21
New Hampshire	46,953	75.3	36.8	4
New Jersey	526,701	70.0	26.4	15
New Mexico	77,134	21.8	21.9	25
New York	1,298,272	59.7	16.3	39
North Carolina	463,252	49.2	22.6	24
North Dakota	43,856	69.5	23.8	18
Ohio	952,741	67.8	28.5	10
Oklahoma	118,331	56.3	19.5	34
Oregon	272,009	53.3	19.6	33
Pennsylvania	885,131	73.2	32.7	8
Rhode Island	69,182	56.4	14.8	44
South Carolina	220,475	45.4	26.8	14
South Dakota	31,831	91.8	33.0	7
Tennessee	495,124	45.6	14.2	46
Texas	833,181	46.4	20.1	31
Utah	114,244	71.4	21.0	28
Vermont	19,366	84.5	41.7	1
Virginia	386,669	62.0	23.0	20
Washington	374,935	85.9	33.7	6
West Virginia	110,966	46.7	22.8	22
Wisconsin	409,307	83.5	27.0	13
Wyoming	62,010	49.4	14.1	47
United States	19,115,887	59.1	20.4	

Source: Children's Defense Fund, 1999.

A-18 Better Health in Middle Age: Deaths Per 1,000 Adults

This table shows the number of deaths per 1,000 adults living in the United States in 1980, 1990, and 1997. Improvement is calculated by subtracting the rate in 1997 from the rate in 1980, and then expressing that difference as a percentage of the 1980 rate. Note that the greatest improvement is in middle age and that, although more people reach late adulthood, survival each year has not changed much: about 850 of every 1,000 90-year-olds survive each year.

Age range	Year			Improvement
	1980	1990	1997	
25–34	1.4	1.4	1.2	14%
35–44	2.8	2.3	2.0	29
45–54	5.8	4.7	4.3	26
55–64	13.5	12.0	10.6	21
65–74	29.9	26.5	25.1	16
75–84	66.9	60.1	57.3	14
85+	159.8	153.3	153.5	4

Source: National Center for Health Statistics,
Health, United States, 1999.

A-19 Old, Black, and Female: Triple Jeopardy? Apparently Not

It is sometimes said that to be old, female, and black in the United States puts a person in triple jeopardy, with three strikes against her. This may be true economically or physically (most older black women have few financial resources and many health problems), but it certainly is not true when it comes to state of mind. Severe depression, social isolation, and despair are highest among older white men, who have by far the highest rate of suicide.

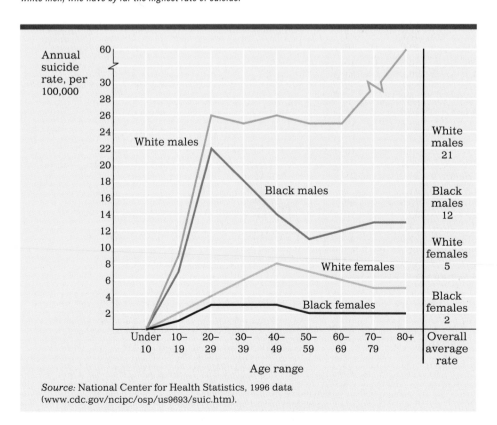

Source: National Center for Health Statistics, 1996 data
(www.cdc.gov/ncipc/osp/us9693/suic.htm).

Appendix B
More About Research Methods

The first part of this appendix details some pointers on how to go about gathering more information about development. The second part expands on Chapter 1's discussion of ways to ensure that research is valid.

LEARNING MORE

There are many ways to deepen your understanding of human development, including thinking about your own life and watching the children around you with careful attention to details of expression and behavior. Indeed, such thoughts may become second nature, as you realize how much there is to learn through reflection and observation. But we also urge more systematic research, and further book learning, as we will now explain.

Library Research

To read more about a particular topic, you need to focus on readings that are current and scholarly. For instance, if something in a popular magazine or newspaper catches your attention, remember that the writer may have sensationalized, exaggerated, or biased the reporting. You might first check what this text says about the topic, and then look at the references cited.

This is often a good strategy to begin effective library research. Start with current published material and then find material from the bibliographies that can fill you in on the background and historical context of many issues.

In addition, there are two collections of abstracts that review current articles from a variety of developmental journals:

Psychscan: Developmental Psychology is published four times a year by the American Psychological Association and includes abstracts of articles from almost 40 scholarly journals, from *Adolescence* to *Psychological Review*. Volume 20 covers the year 2000.

Child Development Abstracts and Bibliography is published three times a year by the Society for Research in Child Development and is organized topically by author. Included are not only journal articles in biology, cognition, education, personality, and theory, but also reviews of major books in the field. Volume 74 covers the year 2000. The online address is www.scrd.org.

To find the most current research, even before it appears in these abstracts, look at the most recent issues of the many research journals.

The two that cover all three domains (biosocial, cognitive, and psychosocial) are *Developmental Psychology,* published by the American Psychological Association (750 First St., NE, Washington, DC 20002), and *Child Development,* published by Blackwell Publishers for the Society for Research in Child Development. (Blackwell Publishers: 350 Main St., Malden, MA 02138; Society for Research in Child Development: University of Michigan, 505 East Huron St., Suite 301, Ann Arbor, MI 48104-1522.)

These suggestions are only a start. All of us who are professors hope you begin with one topic and soon lose track of time and subject, finding your interest drawn from one journal or book to another.

Learning Through Observation

Much can be learned by becoming more systematic in your observations of the children around you. One way to begin is to collect ten observations of different children, in differing contexts, during the semester. Each profile should be approximately one page and should cover the following four items.

1. *Describe the physical and social context.* You will want to describe where you are, what day and time it is, and how many people you are observing. The weather and age and gender of those who are being observed might also be relevant. For example

   Neighborhood playground on (street), at about 4 P.M. on (day, date), thirty children and ten adults present.
       OR
   Supermarket at (location) on Saturday morning (day, date), about 20 shoppers present.

2. *Describe the specific child who is the focus of your attention.* Estimate age, gender, and so on of the target child and anyone else who interacts with the child. Do not ask the age of the child until after the observation, if at all. Your goal is to conduct a naturalistic observation that is unobtrusive. For example

   Boy, about 7 years old, playing with four other boys, who seem a year or two older. All are dressed warmly (it is a cold day) in similar clothes.
       OR
   Girl, about 18 months old, in supermarket cart pushed by woman, about 30 years old. The cart is half full of groceries.

3. *Write down everything that the child does or says in three minutes.* (Use a watch with a second hand.) Record gestures, facial expressions, movements, and words. Accurate reporting is the goal, and three minutes becomes a surprisingly long time if you write down everything. For example

   Child runs away about 20 feet, returns, and says, "Try to catch me." Two boys look at him, but they do not move. Boy frowns. He runs away and comes back in ten seconds, stands about four feet away from the boys, and says, "Anyone want to play tag?" [And so on.]
       OR
   Child points to a package of Frosted Flakes cereal and makes a noise. (I could not hear if it was a word.) Mother says nothing and pushes the cart past the cereal. Child makes a whining noise, looks at the cereal, and kicks her left foot. Mother puts pacifier in child's mouth. [And so on.]

4. *Interpret what you just observed.* Is the child's behavior typical of children that age? Is the reaction of others helpful or not helpful? What values are being encouraged, and what skills are being mastered? What could have happened differently? This section is your opinion, but it must be based on the particulars you have just observed and on your knowledge of child development, ideally with specific reference to concepts (e.g. the first may be a rejected child, the second may be neglect of early language).

Structuring a Case Study

A case study is more elaborate and detailed than the observation report just described. You need to select one child (ask your instructor if family members can be used) and secure permission from the caregiver and, if the child is old enough, the child him- or herself. Explain that you are not going to report the name of the child, that the material is for your class, that the child or caregiver can stop the project at any time, and that they would be doing you a big favor in helping you learn about child development. Most people are quite happy to help in your education, if you explain this properly.

First, collect the information for your paper by using all the research methods you have learned. See a summary of these methods below.

1. *Naturalistic observation.* Ask the caregiver when the child is likely to be awake and active and observe the child for an hour during this time. Try to be as unobtrusive as possible: you are not there to play with, or care for, the child. If the child wants to play, explain that you must sit and write for now and that you will play later.

   Write down, minute by minute, everything the child does and that others do with the child. Try to be objective, focusing on behavior rather than interpretation. Thus, instead of writing "Jennifer was delighted when her father came home, and he dotes on her," you should write "5:33: Her father opened the door, Jennifer looked up, smiled, said 'dada,' and ran to him. He bent down, stretched out his arms, picked her up, and said, 'How's my little angel?' 5:34: He put her on his shoulders, and she said, 'Getty up, horsey.'"

After your observation, summarize the data in two ways: (1) Note the percentage of time spent in various activities. For instance, "Playing alone, 15 percent; playing with brother, 20 percent; crying, 3 percent." (2) Note the frequency of various behaviors: "Asked adult for something five times; adult granted request four times. Aggressive acts (punch, kick, etc.) directed at brother, 2; aggressive acts initiated by brother, 6." Making notations like these will help you evaluate and quantify your observations. Also, note any circumstances that might have made your observation atypical (e.g., "Jenny's mother said she hasn't been herself since she had the flu a week ago," or "Jenny kept trying to take my pen, so it was hard to write").

Note: Remember that a percentage can be found by dividing the total number of minutes spent on a specific activity by the total number of minutes you spent observing. For example, if, during your 45-minute observation, the child played by herself for periods of 2 minutes, 4 minutes, and 5 minutes, "playing alone" would total 11 minutes. Dividing 11 by 45 yields .244; thus the child spent 24 percent of the time playing alone.

2. *Informal interaction.* Interact with the child for at least half an hour. Your goal is to observe the child's personality and abilities in a relaxed setting. The particular activities you engage in will depend on the child's age and character. Most children enjoy playing games, reading books, drawing, and talking. Asking a younger child to show you his or her room and favorite toys is a good way to break the ice; asking an older child to show you the neighborhood can provide insights.

3. *Interview adults responsible for the child's care.* Keep these interviews loose and open-ended. Your goals are to learn (1) the child's history, especially any illnesses, stresses, or problems that might affect development; (2) the child's daily routine, including play patterns; (3) current problems that might affect the child; (4) a description of the child's character and personality, including special strengths and weaknesses.

You are just as interested in adult values and attitudes as in the facts; therefore, you might concentrate on conversing during the interview, perhaps writing down a few words. Then write down all you remember as soon as the interview has been completed.

4. *Testing the child.* Assess the child's perceptual, motor, language, and intellectual abilities by using specific test items you have planned in advance. The actual items you use will depend on the age of the child. For instance, you would test object permanence in an infant between 6 and 24 months old; you would test conservation in a child between 3 and 9 years old. Likewise, testing language abilities might involve babbling with an infant, counting words per sentence with a preschooler, and asking a school-age child to make up a story.

Second, write the report, using the following steps.

1. Begin by reporting relevant background information, including the child's birth date and sex, age and sex of siblings, economic and ethnic background of the family, and the educational and marital status of the parents.

2. Describe the child's biosocial, cognitive, and psychosocial development, citing supporting data from your research to substantiate any conclusions you have reached. Do *not* simply transcribe your interview, test, or observation data, although you can attach your notes as an appendix, if you wish.

3. Predict the child's development in the next year, the next five years, and the next ten years. List the strengths in the child, the family, and the community that you think will foster optimal development. Also note whatever potential problems you see (either in the child's current behavior or in the family and community support system) that may lead to future difficulties for the child. Include discussion of the reasons, either methodological or theoretical, that your predictions may not be completely accurate.

Finally, show your report to another classmate (your instructor may assign you to a peer mentor) and ask if you have been clear in your description and predictions. Discuss the child with your classmate to see if you should add more details to your report. Your revised case study should be typed and given to your professor who will evaluate it. If you wish, send Professor Berger a copy at Worth Publishers, 41 Madison Avenue, 36th floor, New York, NY 10010.

WAYS TO MAKE RESEARCH MORE VALID

As emphasized throughout this text, the study of development is a science. All social scientists use many methods to make their research more objective and therefore more valid. Several basic techniques are described in Chapter 1, including observation and experiments, correlation and statistical significance, independent and dependent variables, and cross-sectional, longitudinal, and cross-sequential research designs. Six additional terms or techniques pertaining to the validity of research are described here.

Population and Subjects

The entire group of people about whom a scientist wants to learn is called the **population.** Generally, a research population is quite large—not usually the world's entire population of 6 billion, but perhaps all the 4 million babies born in the United States during 1998, or all the 500,000 Japanese currently over age 65, or even all the 70,000 low-income fifth-graders attending New York City public schools in the year 2000. The particular individuals who are studied in a specific research project are called the **subjects.** Typically, the subjects reflect the characteristics of the population. Indeed, every published study reports who the subjects were and how they did, or did not, reflect the population.

Sample Size

To make statements about people in general, scientists study particular subjects chosen from the larger population. Each group of research subjects, called a **sample,** must be large enough to ensure that if a few extreme cases happen to be included, they do not distort the statistical picture the sample gives of the population. Suppose, for instance, that

researchers want to know the average age at which children begin to walk. Since they cannot include every infant in their study, they choose a sample of infants, determine the age of walking for each subject in the sample, and then calculate the sample average. If the sample is typical, the average walking age will be very close to the average for the entire infant population.

The importance of an adequate **sample size** can be seen if we assume, for the moment, that one of the infants in the sample had an undetected disability and did not walk until age 24 months. Assume also that all the other infants walked at 12 months, the current norm. If the sample size was less than 10 infants, then one late walker would add more than a month to the age at which the "average" child is said to walk. However, if the sample contained more than 500 children, the one abnormally late walker would not change the results by even one day.

Representative Sample

Data collected from one group of subjects may not be valid (that is, applicable and accurate) for other people who are different in some significant way, such as gender or ethnic background. Thus, every sample should be a **representative sample**—that is, should consist of people who are typical of the population the researchers wish to learn about. In a study of the average walking age, for example, the sample population should reflect—in terms of male/female ratio, socioeconomic and ethnic background, and other characteristics—the entire population of infants. Ideally, other factors might be taken into consideration as well. For instance, if there is some evidence that firstborn children walk earlier than later-born children, the sample should also be representative of the population's birth order.

The importance of representative sampling is revealed by its absence in two classic studies of age of walking for infants in the United States (Gesell, 1926; Shirley 1933). Both studies used a relatively small and unrepresentative sample (all the children were

population The entire group of individuals who are of particular concern in a scientific study, such as all the children of the world or all newborns who weigh less than 3 pounds.

subjects The people who are studied in a research project.

sample A group of individuals drawn from a specified population. A sample might be the low-birthweight babies born in four particular hospitals that are representative of all hospitals.

sample size The number of individuals who are being studied in a single sample in a research project.

representative sample A group of research subjects who reflect the relevant characteristics of the larger population whose attributes are under study.

European American and most were middle-class). Partly because the samples were not representative of the general population of infants, both studies arrived at an average walking age of 15 months. This is 3 months later than the current U.S. norm, which was obtained through research on a much larger, more representative sample that included some low-SES children and some children of African and Latino descent—groups known to have high proportions of early-walking children. Another reason the earlier studies found babies walking 3 months later is that infants 80 years ago received much less physical stimulation, so their motor skill development was slowed down. In other words, infants actually did start to walk somewhat later then (although not 3 months later, as would have been the case if they had been a representative group).

"Blind" Experimenters and Subjects

When experimenters have specific expectations about their research findings, those expectations can unintentionally affect the research results. As much as possible, therefore, the people who actually gather the data should be in a state of **"blindness"**—that is, they should be unaware of the purpose of the research.

Suppose we are testing the hypothesis that first-born infants walk sooner than later-borns. Ideally, the examiner who measures the subjects' walking ability should not know the hypothesis or the infants' age or birth order. The subjects of the research should also be kept blind to its purpose, especially when the subjects are older children or adults, who might be influenced by their own expectations.

Operational Definitions

When planning a study, researchers establish *operational definitions* of whatever phenomena they will be examining. That is, they define each variable in terms of specific, observable behavior that can be measured with precision. Even a simple variable, such as whether or not a toddler is walking, requires an operational definition. For example, does "walking" include steps taken while holding onto someone or something, or must the steps be taken without support? Is one unsteady step enough to meet the definition, or must the infant be able to move a certain distance without faltering? For a study on age of first walking to be meaningful, the researchers would need to resolve questions like these in a clear and thorough definition. In fact, the usual operational definition of walking is "takes at least three steps without holding on."

Understandably, operational definitions become much harder to establish when personality or intellectual variables are being studied. It is nonetheless essential that researchers who are investigating, say, "aggression" or "sharing" or "reading" define the trait in terms that are as precise and measurable as possible. Obviously, the more accurately operational definitions describe the variables to be examined, the more objective and valid the results of the study will be.

Experimental and Control Groups

To test a hypothesis adequately in an experiment, researchers gather data on two samples that are similar in every important way except one. They compare an **experimental group,** which receives some special experimental treatment, and a **control group,** which is matched to the experimental group in every respect but one: It does not receive the experimental treatment.

Suppose a research team hypothesizes that infants who are provided with regular exercise to strengthen their legs begin to walk earlier than babies who do not receive such exercise. In other words, they hypothesize that the independent variable of exercise affects the dependent variable of walking. To find out if this hypothesis is true, the researchers would first select two representative samples of children and examine both groups to make sure they are equivalent in motor skills, such as the ability to roll over and sit up. Then one sample (the experimental group) would receive daily "workouts" devoted to leg-strengthening between, say, their

blindness A situation in which data gatherers and their subjects are deliberately kept ignorant of the purpose of the research in order to avoid unintentionally biasing the results.

experimental group Research subjects who experience the special condition or treatment that is the crux of the research.

control group Research subjects who are comparable to those in the experimental group in every relevant dimension except that they do not experience the special condition or treatment that is the key variable of the experiment.

sixth and twelfth months; and the other sample (the control group) would get no special leg exercise. Results for the two groups would then be compared to test the hypothesis.

To put all this together with the techniques discussed in Chapter 1, a researcher might find 1,000 subjects *(sample size)*, randomly chosen from all babies *(population)* born throughout the United States on a particular day *(representative sample)* and visit them at home once a month from age 8 months to 18 months *(longitudinal research)*, seeing *(naturalistic observation)* which ones take three unaided steps *(operational definition)* at what age. Then, in follow-up research with a similar sample, two groups of subjects would be matched on every variable except one: The parents of half the babies *(experimental group)* would be shown how to exercise their infants' legs *(independent variable)* and be encouraged, perhaps even paid, to do this every day. These babies' age of walking *(dependent variable)* could be compared with that of the non-exercised babies *(control group)* by a researcher who doesn't know *(blind)* which babies are in which group. If differences between the groups emerge, they could be analyzed to see if they exceed random variability (that is, they could be tested for *statistical significance*).

Glossary

abuse Any action that is harmful (either physically or psychologically) to an individual's well-being. The severity of abuse depends on how much and how often it occurs and on the vulnerability of the victim. (p. 231)

achievement tests Tests designed to measure how much a person has learned in a specific subject area. (p. 310)

acquired immune deficiency syndrome (AIDS) The diseases and infections, many of them fatal, that result from the degradation of the immune system by HIV. (p. 110)

activities of daily life (ADLs) Actions that are important to independent living, typically comprising five tasks: eating, bathing, toileting, dressing, and transferring from a bed to a chair. The inability to perform these tasks is a sign of frailty. (p. 698)

activity theory The view that elderly people need to remain active in a variety of social spheres—with relatives, friends, and community groups—and become withdrawn only unwillingly, as a result of ageism. (p. 681)

additive gene One of a number of genes affecting a specific trait, each of which makes an active contribution to that trait. Skin color and height are determined by additive genes. (p. 77)

ADHD (attention-deficit hyperactivity disorder) A behavior problem characterized by excessive activity, an inability to concentrate, and impulsive, sometimes aggressive, behavior. (p. 319)

adolescence The period of biological, cognitive, and psychosocial transition from childhood to adulthood, usually lasting a decade or so. (p. 382)

adolescent egocentrism A characteristic of adolescent thinking that sometimes leads young people to focus on themselves to the exclusion of others, believing, for example, that their thoughts, feelings, or experiences are unique. (p. 413)

adolescent-limited offender A juvenile delinquent who is likely to become law-abiding once adulthood is attained. (p. 456)

affordance Each of the various opportunities for perception, action, and interaction that an object or place offers to any individual. (p. 160)

ageism A term that refers to prejudice against the aged. Like racism and sexism, ageism works to prevent elderly people from being as happy and productive as they could be. (p. 616)

age of viability The age (about 22 weeks after conception) at which a fetus can survive outside the mother's uterus if specialized medical care is available. (p. 101)

aggressive-rejected children Children who are actively rejected by their peer group because of their aggressive, confrontational behavior. (p. 361)

Alzheimer's disease (AD) The most common form of dementia, characterized by gradual deterioration of memory and personality and marked by plaques of B-amyloid protein and tangles in the brain. Alzheimer's disease is not part of the normal aging process. (p. 663)

anal stage Freud's second stage of psychosexual development, in which the anus becomes the main source of bodily pleasure and control of defecation and toilet training are therefore important activities. (p. 194)

androgyny A balance, within an individual, of male and female gender characteristics such that the individual feels comfortable in breaking through gender stereotypes; thus, for example, an androgynous male will feel comfortable being nurturant as well as being assertive. (p. 293)

anorexia nervosa A serious eating disorder in which a person restricts eating to the point of emaciation and possible starvation. Most victims are high-achieving females in early puberty or early adulthood. (p. 481)

anoxia A lack of oxygen that, if prolonged, can cause brain damage or death. (p. 122)

antioxidants Compounds that nullify the effects of oxygen free radicals by forming a bond with their unattached oxygen electron. (p. 634)

antisocial behavior An action, such as hitting, insulting, lying about, or taking from another person, that is intended to harm someone else. (p. 277)

antithesis A proposition or statement of belief that opposes the thesis; the second stage of the dialectical process. (p. 491)

Apgar scale A means of quickly assessing a newborn's body functioning. The baby's color, heart rate, reflexes, muscle tone, and respiratory effort are scored (from 0 to 2) 1 minute and 5 minutes after birth and compared with a standard for healthy babies (a perfect 10). (p. 118)

aptitude tests Tests designed to measure potential, rather than actual, accomplishment. (p. 310)

Asperger syndrome   A disorder in which a person masters verbal communication (sometimes very well) but has unusual difficulty with social perceptions and skills. (Also called *high-functioning autism*.) (p. 315)

asthma   A disorder characterized by chronic inflammation of the airways. (p. 306)

attachment   An enduring emotional connection between people that produces a desire for continual contact as well as feelings of distress during separation. (p. 206)

authoritarian parenting   A style of child rearing in which standards for proper behavior are high, misconduct is strictly punished, and parent–child communication is low. (p. 283)

authoritative parenting   A style of child rearing in which the parents set limits and provide guidance but are willing to listen to the child's ideas and make compromises. (p. 283)

autism   A disorder characterized by an inability or unwillingness to communicate with others, poor social skills, and diminished imagination. (p. 315)

autoimmune diseases   Illnesses that occur because the immune system malfunctions, reacting to the person's own body cells as if they were foreign invaders. The body attacks itself, causing lupus, rheumatoid arthritis, some allergies, and other diseases. (p. 549)

automatization   The process by which familiar and well-rehearsed mental activities become routine and automatic. (p. 330)

autonomy versus shame and doubt   Erikson's second stage of psychosocial development, in which the toddler struggles for self-control but feels shame and doubt about his or her abilities if it is not achieved. (p. 195)

average life expectancy   The number of years the average newborn of a particular population group is likely to live. In humans, this age has tended to increase over time, primarily because fewer children die in infancy. (p. 637)

axon   The single nerve fiber that extends from a neuron and transmits impulses from that neuron to the dendrites of other neurons. (p. 133)

babbling   The extended repetition of certain syllables, such as "ba-ba-ba," that begins at about 6 or 7 months of age. (p. 176)

baby talk   The special form of language that adults use when they talk to babies, with shorter, more emphatic sentences and higher, more melodious pitch. (Sometimes called *motherese*.) (p. 180)

B cells   Cells manufactured in the bone marrow that create antibodies for isolating and destroying invading bacteria and viruses. (p. 634)

behavioral genetics   The study of the effects of genes on behavior, including their effect on personality patterns, psychological disorders, and intellectual abilities. (p. 79)

behavioral teratogens   Teratogens that tend to harm the prenatal brain, affecting the future child's intellectual and emotional functioning. (p. 105)

bickering   Petty, peevish arguing, usually repeated and ongoing. Bickering is typical in early adolescence. (p. 441)

Big Five   The five basic clusters of personality traits that remain quite stable throughout adulthood: extroversion, agreeableness, conscientiousness, neuroticism, and openness. (p. 594)

bilingual education   An approach to teaching a second language that also advances knowledge in the first language. Instruction occurs, side by side, in two languages. (p. 347)

bilingual-bicultural education   An approach to teaching a second language that adds preservation of nonnative cultural symbols and strategies (such as in the way teaching occurs) to a bilingual program. (p. 347)

binocular vision   The ability to use both eyes together to focus on a single object. (p. 138)

biosocial domain   The part of human development that includes physical growth and development as well as the family, community, and cultural factors that affect that growth and development. (p. 5)

blindness   A situation in which data gatherers and their subjects are deliberately kept ignorant of the purpose of the research in order to avoid unintentionally biasing the results. (p. B-5)

body image   A person's concept of how his or her body appears. This self-evaluation may be quite different from the opinions of others or from any objective measures. (p. 395)

body mass index (BMI)   A measure of obesity determined by dividing weight in kilograms by height in meters square. (pp. 302, 480)

breathing reflex   A reflex that ensures an adequate supply of oxygen and the discharge of carbon dioxide by causing the individual to inhale and exhale. (p. 139)

bulimia nervosa   An eating disorder in which the person, usually female, engages repeatedly in episodes of binge eating followed by purging through induced vomiting or use of laxatives. (p. 481)

bullying   Repeated efforts by a child or group of children to inflict harm on another child through physical, verbal, or social attacks. (p. 362)

bullying aggression   Aggressive behavior in the form of an unprovoked physical or verbal attack on another person. (p. 278)

butterfly effect   The idea that a small action—such as the breeze caused by the flap of a butterfly's wings—may set off a series of powerful changes. (p. 7)

carrier   A person who has a gene in his or her genotype that is not evident as part of the phenotype. Carriers can pass such a gene on to their offspring. (p. 77)

case study   A research method that focuses on the life history, attitudes, behavior, and emotions of a single individual. (p. 26)

cataracts   A common eye disease among the elderly involving a thickening of the lens; it can cause distorted vision if left untreated. (p. 623)

centration   The tendency to focus on one way of thinking and perceiving, without acknowledging any alternatives. (p. 246)

cerebral palsy   A disorder that results from damage to the brain's motor centers, usually as a result of events during or before birth. People with cerebral palsy have difficulty with muscle control, which can affect speech or other body movements. (p. 122)

cesarean section   A means of childbirth in which the fetus is taken from the mother surgically, through an incision that extends from the mother's abdomen through the uterus. (p. 119)

child maltreatment   Any intentional harm or avoidable endangerment to anyone under age 18. (p. 231)

child with special needs   A child for whom learning new skills and developing friendships are hampered by a psychological or physical disorder. (p. 313)

childhood sexual abuse   Any activity in which an adult uses a child for his or her own sexual stimulation or pleasure—even if the use does not involve physical contact. Child pornography, fondling, and lewd comments by strangers are all examples of childhood sexual abuse. (p. 397)

chromosome   A carrier of genes; one of forty-six segments of DNA that together contain all human genes. (p. 70)

climacteric   Refers to the various biological and psychological changes that accompany menopause. (p. 564)

cluster suicide   A group of suicides that occur in the same community, school, or time period. (p. 453)

code-switching   A pragmatic communication skill that involves a person's switching from one form of language, such as dialect or slang, to another. (p. 345)

cognitive domain   The part of human development that includes all the mental processes through which the individual thinks, learns, and communicates, plus the institutions involved in learning and communicating. (p. 5)

cognitive equilibrium   A state of mental balance, in which a person's thoughts and assumptions about the world seem (at least to that person) not to clash with one another or with that person's experiences. (p. 48)

cognitive theory   A theory which holds that the way people think and understand the world shapes their perceptions, attitudes, and actions. (p. 47)

cohabitation   An arrangement in which adults of the opposite sex are not married but live together in a committed sexual relationship. (p. 519)

cohort   A group of people who, because they were born within a few years of one another, experience many of the same historical and social conditions. (p. 8)

common couple violence   A form of abuse in which one or both partners of a couple engage in outbursts of verbal and physical attack. (p. 526)

companionate grandparents   Grand-parents whose relationships with their children and grandchildren are characterized by independence and friendship, with visits occurring by the grandparents' choice. (p. 601)

compression of morbidity   A limiting of the time a person spends ill or infirm, accomplished by postponing illness or, once morbidity occurs, hastening death. (p. 631)

concrete operational thought   In Piaget's theory, the third period of cognitive development, in which a child can reason logically about concrete events and problems but cannot yet reason about abstract ideas and possibilities. (p. 332)

conditioning   Any learning process that occurs according to the laws of behaviorism or learning theory. This can be classical conditioning, in which one stimulus is associated with another, or operant conditioning, in which a response is gradually learned via reinforcement. (p. 42)

conservation   The concept that the total quantity, number, or amount of something is the same (preserved) no matter what the shape or configuration. (p. 247)

contact-maintaining behaviors   Behaviors that are intended to keep a person near another person to whom he or she is attached. (p. 206)

continuity theory   The theory that each person experiences the changes of late adulthood and behaves toward others in much the same way as at earlier periods of life. (p. 683)

control group   Research subjects who are comparable to those in the experimental group in every relevant dimension except that they do not experience the special condition or treatment that is the key variable of the experiment. (p. B-5)

control processes   That part of the information-processing system which regulates the analysis and flow of information. Memory and retrieval strategies, selective attention, and rules or strategies for problem solving are all useful control processes. (pp. 328, 651)

conventional moral reasoning   Kohlberg's term for the second level (stages 3 and 4) of moral thinking, in which the individual considers social standards and laws to be the primary arbiters of moral values. (p. 334)

corpus callosum   A network of nerves connecting the left and right hemispheres of the brain. (p. 223)

correlation   A relation between two variables such that one is likely (or unlikely) to occur when the other occurs or one is likely to increase (or decrease) in value when the other increases (or decreases). (p. 21)

cortex   The outer layer of the brain, about an eighth of an inch thick. This area is involved in the voluntary, cognitive aspects of the mind. (p. 136)

critical period   In prenatal development, the time when a particular organ or other body part is most susceptible to teratogenic damage. (p. 105)

cross-sectional research   A research design in which groups of people, each group different from the others in age but similar to them in other important ways, are compared. (p. 27)

cross-sequential research   A research design that combines cross-sectional and longitudinal research. Groups of people of different ages are studied over time, to distinguish differences related to age from differences related to historical period. (Also called *cohort-sequential research* or *time-sequential research*.) (p. 30)

crystallized intelligence   Those types of intellectual ability that reflect accumulated learning. Vocabulary and general information are examples. Some developmental psychologists think crystallized intelligence increases with age, while fluid intelligence declines. (p. 572)

culture   The set of shared values, assumptions, customs, and physical objects that are maintained by a group of people in a specific setting (a society) as a design for living daily life. (p. 11)

deductive reasoning   Reasoning from a general statement or principle, through logical steps, to a specific conclusion. (p. 409)

deferred imitation   The ability to witness, remember, and later copy a particular behavior. (p. 168)

Defining Issues Test (DIT)   A series of questions developed by James Rest and designed to assess respondents' level of moral development by having them rank possible solutions to moral dilemmas. (p. 498)

dementia   Irreversible loss of intellectual functioning caused by organic brain damage or disease. Dementia becomes more common with age, but even in the very old, dementia is abnormal and pathological. Sometimes dementia is misdiagnosed, since reversible conditions such as depression and drug overdose can cause the symptoms of dementia. (p. 662)

demography   The study of populations, including descriptive statistics regarding age, sex, and other characteristics of various groups. (p. 617)

dendrites   Nerve fibers that extend from a neuron and receive the impulses transmitted from other neurons via their axons. (p. 133)

dependency ratio   The ratio of self-sufficient, productive adults to dependents—children and the elderly. (p. 619)

dependent variable   The variable that might change as a result of changing or adding the independent variable in an experiment. (p. 23)

developmental biodynamics   Maturation of the developing person's ability to move through, and with, the environment, by means of crawling, running, grasping, and throwing. (p. 139)

developmental psychopathology   A field of psychology that applies the insights from studies of normal development to the study and treatment of childhood disorders. (p. 314)

developmental theory   A systematic set of principles and generalizations that explains development, generates hypotheses, and provides a framework for future research. (p. 38)

dialectical thought   Thought that is characterized by ongoing awareness of pros and cons, advantages and disadvantages, and possibilities and limitations. In daily life, dialectical thinking involves incorporating beliefs and experiences with all the contradictions and inconsistencies of life. (p. 491)

differential response   The idea that child-maltreatment reports should be separated into those that require immediate investigation, possibly leading to foster care and legal prosecution, and those that require supportive measures to encourage better parental care. (p. 236)

disability   Lack of ability to do some basic activity. As a measure of health, disability refers to the portion of the population who cannot perform activities that most others can. (p. 556)

disengagement theory   The view that aging makes a person's social sphere increasingly narrow, resulting in role relinquishment, withdrawal, and passivity. (p. 680)

dizygotic twins   Twins formed when two separate ova were fertilized by two separate sperm at roughly the same time. Such twins share about half their genes, like any other siblings. (p. 75)

dominant gene   The stronger of an interacting pair of genes. (p. 78)

double effect   A situation in which medication has the intended effect of relieving a dying person's pain and the secondary effect of hastening death. (p. 712)

drug abuse   The ingestion of a drug to the extent that it impairs the user's well-being. (p. 398)

drug addiction   A condition of drug dependence such that the absence of the given drug in the individual's system produces a drive—physiological, psychological, or both—to ingest more of the drug. (pp. 398, 478)

drug use   The ingestion of a drug, regardless of the amount or effect of ingestion. (p. 398)

DSM-IV   The fourth edition of the *Diagnostic and Statistical Manual of Mental Disorders*, developed by the American Psychiatric Association, which describes and distinguishes the symptoms of various emotional and behavioral disorders. (p. 314)

dynamic perception   Perception that arises from the movement of objects and changes in their positions. (p. 163)

dynamic theories   Theories that emphasize change and readjustment rather than either the ongoing self or the legacy of stratification. Each person's life is seen as an active, ever-changing, largely self-propelled process, occurring within specific social contexts that themselves are constantly changing. (p. 683)

dyscalcula   A specific learning disability involving unusual difficulty with math. (p. 318)

dyslexia   A specific learning disability involving unusual difficulty with reading. (p. 317)

eclectic perspective   A perspective whose adherents choose what seem to be the best, or most useful, elements from the various theories, instead of adhering to only a single perspective. (p. 65)

ecological niche   The particular lifestyle and social context adults settle into that are compatible with their individual personality needs and interests. (p. 594)

egocentrism   The tendency to perceive events and interpret experiences exclusively from one's own, self-centered, perspective. (p. 247)

Elderhostel A program in which people aged 55 and older live on college campuses and take special classes, usually during college vacation periods. (p. 686)

elderspeak A way of speaking to older adults that resembles baby talk, with simple and short sentences, exaggerated emphasis, a slower rate, higher pitch, and repetition. (p. 624)

Electra complex In the phallic stage of psychosexual development, the female version of the Oedipus complex: Girls have sexual feelings for their fathers and accompanying hostility toward their mothers. (p. 290)

emergent theories Relatively new comprehensive theories, formulated within the past 30 years, that bring together information from many disciplines but are not yet a coherent, comprehensive whole. (p. 38)

emotional regulation The ability to direct or modify one's feelings, particularly feelings of fear, frustration, and anger. Because of brain maturation, emotional regulation becomes more possible during the preschool years. (p. 275)

English as a second language (ESL) An approach to teaching English in which English is the only language of instruction for students who speak many other native languages. (p. 347)

environment All the nongenetic factors that can affect development—everything from the impact of the immediate cell environment on the genes themselves to the broader effects of nutrition, medical care, socioeconomic status, family dynamics, and the economic, political, and cultural contexts. (p. 70)

epigenetic systems theory A developmental theory that emphasizes the genetic origins of behavior but also stresses that genes, over time, are directly and systematically affected by many environmental forces. (p. 55)

ethnic group A collection of people who share certain background characteristics, such as national origin, religion, upbringing, and language, and who, as a result, tend to have similar beliefs, values, and cultural experiences. (p. 14)

ethology The study of behavior as it is related to the evolution and survival of a species. (p. 58)

experiment A research method in which the scientist deliberately causes changes in one variable (called the *independent variable*) and then observes and records the resulting changes in some other variable (called the *dependent variable*). (p. 23)

experimental group Research subjects who experience the special condition or treatment that is the crux of the research. (p. B-5)

expert Someone who is notably more skilled and knowledgeable about a specific intellectual topic or practical ability than the average person is. (p. 585)

expertise The acquisition of knowledge in a specific area. As individuals grow older, they concentrate their learning in certain areas that are of the most importance to them, becoming experts in these areas while remaining relative novices in others. (p. 584)

explicit memory Memory that is easy to retrieve, usually with words. Most explicit memory involves consciously learned words, data, and concepts. (p. 650)

familism The idea that family members should support each other because family unity is more important than individual freedom and success. (p. 599)

family structure The legal and genetic relationships between members of a particular family. (p. 368)

fast mapping Used by children to add words to their vocabulary, the process of hearing a word once or twice and then quickly defining it by categorizing it with other words. (p. 260)

fetal alcohol syndrome (FAS) A cluster of birth defects, including abnormal facial characteristics, slow physical growth, and retarded mental development, that is caused by the mother's drinking excessive quantities of alcohol when pregnant. (p. 112)

fine motor skills Physical skills involving small body movements, especially with the hands and fingers, such as picking up a coin or drawing. (p. 141)

5-to-7 shift A notable reorganization of the thinking process that occurs between ages 5 and 7, enabling the school-age child to reason and respond at a much more advanced level than the younger child. (p. 332)

fluid intelligence Those types of basic intelligence that make learning of all sorts quick and thorough. Underlying abilities such as short-term memory, abstract thought, and speed of thinking are all usually considered part of fluid intelligence. (p. 572)

foreclosure Erikson's term for premature identity formation, in which an adolescent adopts parents' or society's roles and values wholesale, without questioning and analysis. (p. 436)

formal code A form of speech used by children in school and in other formal situations; characterized by extensive vocabulary, complex syntax, lengthy sentences, and conformity to other middle-class norms for correct language. (Sometimes called *elaborated code*.) (p. 345)

formal operational thought In Piaget's theory, the fourth and final stage of cognitive development; arises from combination of maturation and experience. (p. 408)

foster care A legally sanctioned, publicly supported arrangement in which children are cared for by someone other than their biological parents. (p. 238)

fragile-*X* syndrome A disorder in which part of the X chromosome is attached to the rest of it by a very slim string of molecules; it is caused by a genetic abnormality and often produces mental deficiency. (p. 89)

frail elderly People over age 65 who are physically infirm, very ill, or cognitively impaired. (p. 698)

gamete A reproductive cell; that is, a cell that can reproduce a new individual if it combines with a gamete from the other sex. (p. 70)

gateway drugs Drugs—usually tobacco, alcohol, and marijuana—whose use increases the risk that a person will later use harder drugs, such as cocaine and heroin. (p. 400)

gateways to attraction   The various qualities, such as appearance and proximity, that are prerequisites for the formation of close friendships and intimate relationships. (p. 515)

gender crossover   The idea that each sex takes on the other sex's roles and traits in later life. This idea is disputed, but there is no doubt that maleness and femaleness become less salient in middle age. (p. 596)

gender differences   Cultural differences in the roles and behavior of the two sexes. (p. 287)

gene   The basic unit for the transmission of heredity instructions. (p. 70)

general intelligence (g)   The idea that intelligence is one basic trait, underlying all cognitive abilities. According to this concept, people have varying levels of this general ability. (p. 571)

generational forgetting   The tendency of each new generation to ignore lessons learned by the previous cohort. For example, the hazards of crack were well known a decade ago, but today's teenagers are less aware of them. (p. 403)

generational stake   The need of each generation to view family interactions from its own perspective, because each has a different investment in the family scenario. (p. 441)

generation gap   The distance between generations in values, behaviors, and knowledge. (p. 440)

generativity versus stagnation   Erikson's seventh stage of development, in which adults seek to be productive through vocation, avocation, or child rearing. Without such productive work, adults stop developing and growing. (p. 512)

genetic clock   According to one theory of aging, a regulatory mechanism in the DNA of cells regulates the aging process. (p. 638)

genetic code   The sequence of chemical compounds (called bases) that is held within DNA molecules and directs development, behavior, and form. (p. 71)

genetic counseling   Consultation and testing that enables individuals to learn about their genetic heritage, including conditions that might affect future children. (p. 92)

genetic imprinting   The tendency of certain genes to be expressed differently when they are inherited from the mother than when they are inherited from the father. (p. 79)

genotype   A person's entire genetic inheritance, including genes that are not expressed in the person. (p. 77)

germinal period   The first 2 weeks of development after conception; characterized by rapid cell division and the beginning of cell differentiation. (p. 98)

gerontology   The study of old age. This is one of the fastest-growing special fields in the social sciences. (p. 617)

glass ceiling   An invisible barrier experienced by many women in male-dominated occupations—and by many minority workers in majority-dominated occupations—that halts promotion and undercuts their power at a certain managerial level. (p. 533)

glaucoma   A disease of the eye that can destroy vision if left untreated. It involves hardening of the eyeball due to a fluid buildup within the eye. (pp. 548, 623)

global disease burden   A measure that combines indicators of premature death with indicators of disability. This measure can be calculated for the entire world, which makes it a global number. (p. 552)

goal-directed behavior   Purposeful action initiated by infants in anticipation of events that will fulfill their needs and wishes. (p. 173)

gonads   The pair of sex glands in humans. In girls, these are called ovaries; in boys, they are called testes or testicles. (p. 382)

goodness of fit   The degree to which a child's temperament matches the demands of his or her environment. (p. 201)

grand theories   Comprehensive theories that have inspired and directed thinking about development for decades but no longer seem as adequate as they once did. (p. 38)

graspability   The perception of whether or not an object is of the proper shape, size, texture, and distance to afford grasping or grabbing. (p. 161)

gross motor skills   Physical skills involving large body movements such as waving the arms, walking, and jumping. (p. 140)

growth spurt   The period of relatively sudden and rapid physical growth of every part of the body that occurs during puberty. (p. 386)

guided participation   A learning process in which an individual learns through social interaction with a "tutor" (a parent, a teacher, a more skilled peer) who offers assistance, structures opportunities, models strategies, and provides explicit instruction as needed. (pp. 54, 249)

habituation   The process of becoming so familiar with a particular stimulus that it no longer elicits the physiological responses it did when it was originally experienced. (p. 148)

Hayflick limit   The number of times a human cell is capable of dividing into two new cells. The limit for most human cells is approximately 50 divisions, suggesting that the life span is limited by our genetic program. (p. 638)

heredity   The specific genetic material that an organism inherits from its parents. (p. 70)

heterogamy   As used by developmentalists, the term refers to marriage between individuals who tend to be dissimilar with respect to such variables as attitudes, interests, goals, SES, religion, ethnic background, and local origin. (p. 522)

holophrase   A single word that expresses a complete thought. (p. 178)

homeostasis   The adjustment of the body's systems to keep physiological functions in a state of equilibrium. As the body ages, it takes longer for these homeostatic adjustments to occur, making it harder for older bodies to adapt to stresses. (p. 467)

homogamy As used by developmentalists, the term refers to marriage between individuals who tend to be similar with respect to such variables as attitudes, interests, goals, SES, religion, ethnic background, and local origin. (p. 522)

hormone replacement therapy (HRT) Treatment to compensate for hormone reduction at menopause or following surgical removal of the ovaries. Such treatment, which usually involves estrogen and progesterone, minimizes menopausal symptoms and diminishes the risk of heart disease and osteoporosis in later adulthood. (p. 565)

hospice An institution in which terminally ill patients receive palliative care. (p. 712)

Human Genome Project An international effort to map the complete human genetic code. (p. 71)

human immunodeficiency virus (HIV) A virus that gradually overwhelms the body's immune responses, leaving the individual defenseless against a host of pathologies that eventually manifest themselves as AIDS. (p. 110)

hypothesis A specific prediction that is stated in such a way that it can be tested and either proved or disproved. (p. 15)

hypothetical thought Thought that involves propositions and possibilities that may or may not reflect reality. (p. 408)

identification A defense mechanism that lets a person symbolically take on the role and attitudes of someone more powerful than himself or herself. (p. 290)

identity A consistent definition of one's self as a unique individual, in terms of roles, attitudes, beliefs, and aspirations. (p. 435)

identity The logical principle that certain characteristics of an object remain the same when other characteristics are changed. (p. 333)

identity achievement Erikson's term for attainment of identity, or the point at which a person understands who he or she is as a unique individual, in accord with past experiences and future plans. (p. 436)

identity diffusion The situation in which an adolescent does not seem to know or care what his or her identity is. (p. 436)

identity moratorium Erikson's term for a pause in identity formation that allows young people to explore alternatives without making final identity choices. (p. 437)

identity versus role confusion Erikson's term for the fifth stage of development, in which the person tries to figure out "Who am I?" but is confused as to which of many roles to adopt. (p. 435)

imaginary audience The egocentric idea, held by many adolescents, that others are intensely interested in them, especially in their appearance and behavior. (p. 415)

immunization A process that stimulates the body's own defensive (immune) system to defend against attack by a particular infectious disease. (p. 134)

implantation Beginning about a week after conception, the burrowing of the organism into the lining of the uterus, where it can be nourished and protected during growth. (p. 89)

implicit memory Unconscious or automatic memory that is usually stored via habits, emotional responses, routine procedures, and various sensations. (p. 650)

incidence How often a particular behavior or circumstance occurs. (p. 455)

inclusion An approach to educating children with special needs whereby they are included in the regular classroom while also receiving special individualized instruction, typically from a teacher or paraprofessional trained in special education. (p. 322)

independent variable The variable that is added or changed in an experiment. (p. 23)

inductive reasoning Reasoning from one or more specific experiences or facts to a general conclusion. (p. 409)

industry versus inferiority The fourth of Erikson's eight crises of psychosocial development, in which school-age children attempt to master many skills and develop a sense of themselves as either industrious and competent or incompetent and inferior. (p. 356)

infantile amnesia The inability, hypothesized by Freud, to remember anything that happened before the age of 2 years or anything but very important events that occurred before the age of 5. (p. 167)

infertility The lack of a successful pregnancy after one year of regular intercourse without contraception. (p. 473)

informal code A form of speech characterized by limited use of vocabulary and syntax; meaning is communicated by gestures, intonation, and shared understanding. (Sometimes called *restricted code*.) (p. 345)

information-processing theory A theory of learning that focuses on the steps of thinking—such as sorting, categorizing, storing, and retrieving—that are similar to the functions of a computer. (p. 328)

initiative versus guilt The third of Erikson's eight "crises" of psychosocial development, in which the preschool child eagerly begins new projects and activities—and feels guilt when his or her efforts result in failure or criticism. (p. 272)

injury control The practice of limiting the extent of injuries by planning ahead, controlling the circumstances, preventing certain dangerous activities, and adding safety features to other activities. (p. 226)

insecure attachment A caregiver–infant relationship characterized by the child's overdependence on, or lack of interest in, the caregiver and by a lack of confidence on the part of the child. (p. 207)

instrumental activities of daily life (IADLs) Actions that are important to independent living and that require some intellectual competence and forethought. These are even more critical to self-sufficiency than ADLs. (p. 698)

instrumental aggression Aggressive behavior whose purpose is to obtain or retain an object desired by another. (p. 278)

interaction effect The phenomenon in which a teratogen's potential for causing harm increases when it is combined with another teratogen or another risk factor. (p. 106)

intergenerational transmission   The assumption that mistreated children grow up to become abusive or neglectful parents themselves. This is less common than is generally supposed. (p. 235)

intimacy versus isolation   The sixth of Erikson's eight stages of development. Adults seek to find someone with whom to share their lives, in an enduring and self-sacrificing commitment. Without such commitment, they risk profound aloneness, isolated from their fellow humans. (p. 511)

invincibility fable   The fiction, fostered by adolescent egocentrism, that one is immune to common dangers, such as those associated with unprotected sex, drug abuse, or high-speed driving. (p. 413)

involved grandparents   Grandparents who remain active in the everyday activities of their grandchildren, seeing them daily. (p. 601)

in vitro fertilization (IVF)   A technique in which ova (egg cells) are surgically removed from a woman and fertilized with sperm in the laboratory. After the original fertilized cells (the zygotes) have divided several times, they are inserted into a woman's uterus. (p. 475)

IQ tests   Aptitude tests designed to measure a person's intelligence (which was originally defined as mental age divided by chronological age, times 100—hence, intelligence quotient, or IQ). (See below)
An example
Actual age of three children: 12, 12, 12
Mental ages of the three: 15, 12, 8
IQ of each of these three:
$15/12 = 1.25 \times 100 = 125$ (superior)
$12/12 = 1 \times 100 = 100$ (average)
$8/12 = .75 \times 100 = 75$ (slow learner) (p. 310)

kinkeeper   The person who celebrates family achievements, gathers the family together, and keeps in touch with family members who no longer live nearby. (p. 598)

kinship care   A form of foster care in which a relative of a maltreated child takes over from the abusive or neglectful parents. (p. 238)

knowledge base   A body of knowledge in a particular area that has been learned and on which additional learning can be based. (p. 331)

kwashiorkor   A disease resulting from a protein deficiency in children. The symptoms include thinning hair and bloating of the legs, face, and abdomen. (p. 153)

language acquisition device (LAD)   Chomsky's term for a brain structure or organization that he hypothesized was responsible for the innate human ability to acquire language, including the basic aspects of grammar. (p. 179)

launching event   Something that seems to start, or trigger, a particular happening. Launching events are used to study understanding of cause-and-effect relationships. (p. 170)

learning disability   Difficulty in mastering a specific cognitive skill that is not attributable to intellectual slowness, obvious impairment of the senses, lack of education, or family dysfunction. (p. 317)

learning theory   A grand theory of development, built on behaviorism, that focuses on the sequences and processes by which behavior is learned. (p. 42)

life-course-persistent offender   A juvenile delinquent who is likely to continue a pattern of lawbreaking even when adolescence is over. Such individuals usually started their pattern before the teen years. (p. 456)

life review   The examination of one's own past life that many elderly people engage in. According to Butler, the life review is therapeutic, for it helps the older person to come to grips with aging and death. (p. 670)

life-span perspective   A view of human development that takes into account all phases of life, not just childhood or adulthood. (p. 4)

little scientist   Piaget's term for the stage-five toddler (age 12 to 18 months), who actively experiments to learn about the properties of objects. (p. 174)

living will   A document that indicates what medical intervention an individual wants if he or she becomes incapable of expressing those wishes. (p. 710)

longitudinal research   A research design in which the same people are studied over a long time (which might range from months to decades) to measure both change and stability as they age. (p. 28)

long-term memory   The part of memory that stores information for days, months, or years. (p. 328)

low birthweight (LBW)   A birthweight of less than 5½ pounds (2,500 grams). (p. 112)

mainstreaming   An approach to educating children with special needs by putting them in the same "stream"—the general-education classroom—as all the other children, rather than segregating them. (p. 322)

marasmus   A disease that afflicts young infants suffering from severe malnutrition. Growth stops, body tissues waste away, and death may eventually occur. (p. 153)

maximum life span   The oldest age to which members of a species can live, under ideal circumstances. For humans, that age is approximately 120 years. (p. 636)

menarche   A female's first menstrual period. (p. 385)

menopause   The time in middle age, usually around age 50, when a woman's menstrual periods cease completely and the production of estrogen drops considerably. Strictly speaking, menopause is dated 1 year after a woman's last menstrual period. (p. 563)

mental combinations   Sequences of actions developed intellectually, before they are actively performed. Mental combinations are a characteristic of the toddlers at Piaget's stage six of sensorimotor intelligence. (p. 174)

mental retardation   Slow learning in all, or almost all, intellectual abilities. The degree of retardation is usually measured by an intelligence test. In young children, mental retardation is often called *pervasive developmental delay* to allow for the possibility that the child will catch up to normal, age-appropriate development. (p. 317)

mentor A guide or teacher who helps an inexperienced person through example, shared activities, or explicit advice. (p. 608)

metacognition The ability to evaluate a cognitive task to determine how best to accomplish it, and then to monitor one's performance—"thinking about thinking." (p. 330)

middle age The years from age 35 to age 65. (p. 591)

midlife crisis A period of unusual anxiety, radical reexamination, and sudden transformation that is widely associated with middle age but which actually has more to do with developmental history than with chronological age. (p. 592)

minitheories Theories that explain some specific area of development but that are not as general and comprehensive as grand theories. (p. 38)

modeling Part of social learning theory; in particular, the process whereby a person tries to imitate the behavior of someone else. Modeling occurs with minor actions, such as how someone laughs or what shoes he or she wears, but it also occurs in powerful ways, as when a male child identifies with his father as a role model. (p. 46)

molecular genetics The study of genetics at the molecular level, including the study of the chemical codes that constitute a particular molecule of DNA. (p. 81)

monozygotic twins Twins who have identical genes because they were formed from one zygote that split into two identical organisms very early in development. (p. 75)

morality of care Moral thought and behavior based on comparison, nurturance, and concern for the well-being of other people. This morality is said to be more common among girls and women. (p. 337)

morality of justice Moral thought and behavior based on depersonalized standards of right and wrong, with judgments based on abstractions, not relationships. This morality is said to be more common among boys and men. (p. 337)

morbidity Disease. As a measure of health, morbidity refers to the rate of diseases of all kinds in a given population. (p. 556)

mortality Death. As a measure of health, mortality usually refers to the number of deaths each year per 1,000 members of a given population. (p. 556)

multifactorial traits Characteristics produced by the interaction of genetic and environmental (or other) influences (rather than by genetic influences alone). (p. 77)

multi-infarct dementia (MID) The form of dementia characterized by sporadic, and progressive, loss of intellectual functioning. The cause is repeated infarcts, or temporary obstructions of blood vessels, preventing sufficient blood from reaching the brain. Each infarct destroys some brain tissue. The underlying cause is an impaired circulatory system. (p. 666)

myelination The process in which axons are coated with myelin, a fatty substance that speeds communication between neurons. (pp. 136, 222)

negative identity An identity that is taken on with rebellious defiance, simply because it is the opposite of whatever parents, or society, expect. (p. 436)

neglect Any inaction that harms or endangers a person. Neglect can involve physical needs (food, warmth) or psychological needs (love, language). (p. 231)

neural tube A fold of outer embryonic cells that appears about 3 weeks after conception and later develops into the central nervous system. (p. 98)

neuron A nerve cell of the central nervous system. Most neurons are in the brain. (p. 133)

neurotransmitter A brain chemical that carries information across the synaptic gap between one neuron and another. (p. 136)

norm A standard, or average, derived or developed for a specified group population. What is "normal" may not be what is ideal. (p. 143)

object permanence The realization that objects (including people) still exist even when they cannot be seen, touched, or heard. (p. 164)

Oedipus complex In the phallic stage of psychosexual development, the sexual desire that boys have for their mothers and the related hostility they have toward their fathers. (p. 289)

oldest-old Elderly adults (generally, those over age 85) who are dependent on others for almost everything, requiring supportive services such as nursing homes and hospital stays. (p. 620)

old-old Older adults (generally over age 75) who suffer from physical, mental, or social deficits. (p. 620)

oral stage Freud's term for the first stage of psychosexual development, in which the infant gains pleasure through sucking and biting. (p. 194)

organ reserve The extra capacity of the heart, lungs, and other organs that makes it possible for the body to withstand moments of intense or prolonged stress. With age, organ reserve is gradually depleted, but the rate of depletion depends on the individual's general state of health. (p. 468)

osteoporosis A loss of calcium that makes bone more porous and fragile. It occurs somewhat in everyone with aging, but serious osteoporosis is more common in elderly women than men. Osteoporosis is the main reason the elderly suffer broken hip bones much more often than the young. (p. 564)

otitis media A middle-ear infection that can impair hearing temporarily and therefore can impede language development and socialization if it continues too long in the first years of life. (p. 148)

overextension The application of a newly learned word to a variety of objects that may share a particular characteristic but are not in the general category described by that word. (Also called *overgeneralization*.) (p. 177)

overregularization The tendency to make a language more logical and "regular" than it actually is, which leads to mistaken application of the rules of grammar. (p. 263)

oxygen free radicals Atoms that, as a result of metabolic processes, have an unpaired electron. They produce errors in cell maintenance and repair that, over time, may cause cancer, diabetes, and arteriosclerosis. (p. 634)

palliative care   Care designed not to treat an illness but to relieve the pain and suffering of the patient and his or her family. (p. 712)

parasuicide   A deliberate act of self-destruction that does not end in death. Parasuicide can be fleeting, such as a small knife mark on the wrist, or potentially lethal, such as swallowing an entire bottle of pills. (p. 452)

parental monitoring   Parental awareness of what one's children are doing, where, and with whom. (p. 442)

parent–newborn bond   The strong feelings of attachment that arise between parents and their newborn infants. (p. 123)

Parkinson's disease   A chronic, progressive disease that is characterized by muscle tremors and rigidity, and sometimes dementia, caused by a reduction of dopamine production in the brain. (p. 667)

patriarchal terrorism   The form of spouse abuse in which the husband uses violent methods of accelerating intensity to isolate, degrade, and punish the wife. (p. 526)

peer group   A group of individuals of roughly the same age and social status who play, work, or learn together. (p. 357)

peer pressure   Social pressure to conform with one's friends or contemporaries in behavior, dress, and attitude; usually considered negative, as when adolescent peers encourage each other to defy adult standards. (p. 445)

pelvic inflammatory disease (PID)   A common result of recurring pelvic infections in women. Pelvic inflammatory disease often leads to blocked Fallopian tubes, which, in turn, can lead to infertility. (p. 474)

perception   The mental processing of sensory information. (p. 145)

period of the embryo   From approximately the third through the eighth week after conception, the period during which the rudimentary forms of all anatomical structures develop. (p. 98)

period of the fetus   From the ninth week after conception until birth, the period during which the organs grow in size and complexity. (p. 98)

permanency planning   The process of finding a long-term solution to the care of a child who has been abused. The plan for permanent care may involve adoption, return to a restored family, or long-term foster care. (p. 238)

permissive parenting   A style of child rearing in which the parents rarely punish, guide, or control their children but are nurturant and communicate well with their children. (p. 283)

personal fable   The egocentric idea, held by many adolescents, that one is destined for fame and fortune and/or great accomplishments. (p. 413)

personality   The emotions, behaviors, and attitudes that make an individual unique. (p. 193)

person–environment fit   The degree to which a particular environment is conducive to the growth of a particular individual. (p. 416)

phallic stage   The third stage of psychosexual development, occurring in early childhood, in which the penis becomes the focus of psychological concern as well as physiological pleasure. (p. 289)

phenotype   All the genetic traits, including physical characteristics and behavioral tendencies, that are expressed in a person. (p. 77)

phobia   An irrational fear that is strong enough to make a person try to avoid the feared object or experience. (p. 276)

physician-assisted suicide   A situation in which a doctor provides the means for someone to end his or her own life. (p. 714)

placenta   The organ that encases the embryo and connects its circulatory system with that of its mother. The placenta allows nourishment to flow to the embryo and wastes to flow away but maintains the separation of the two circulatory systems. (p. 101)

plasticity   In developmental psychology, a term used to indicate that a particular characteristic is shaped by many environmental influences. Many mental abilities, once thought to be firmly fixed before adulthood, are now known to have much more plasticity than was once believed. (pp. 4, 584)

polygenic traits   Characteristics produced by the interaction of many genes (rather than by a single gene). (p. 77)

population   The entire group of individuals who are of particular concern in a scientific study, such as all the children of the world or all newborns who weigh less than 3 pounds. (p. B-4)

postconventional moral reasoning   Kohlberg's term for the third and highest level (stages 5 and 6) of moral thinking, in which the individual follows moral principles that may supersede the standards of society or the wishes of the individual. (p. 334)

postformal thought   A type of adult thinking that is suited to solving real-world problems. Postformal thought is less abstract and absolute than formal thought, more adaptive to life's inconsistencies, and more dialectical—capable of combining contradictory elements into a comprehensive whole. (p. 490)

postpartum depression   The profound feeling of sadness and inadequacy that sometimes is experienced by new mothers, leading to an inability to eat, sleep, or care normally for their newborns. (p. 124)

practical intelligence   The intellectual skills used in everyday problem solving. (p. 575)

preconventional moral reasoning   Kohlberg's term for the first level (stages 1 and 2) of moral thinking, in which the individual reasons in terms of his or her own welfare. (p. 334)

preoperational thought   Piaget's term for the cognition of children between the ages of about 2 and 6, implying that such children have not yet learned to use logical principles in their thinking. (p. 246)

presbycusis   Age-related hearing loss. (p. 623)

preterm birth   Birth that occurs 3 weeks or more before the full term of pregnancy has elapsed, that is, at 35 or fewer weeks past conception rather than at the full term of about 38 weeks. (p. 113)

prevalence How widespread within a population a particular behavior or circumstance is. (p. 455)

primary aging The universal and irreversible physical changes that occur to living creatures as they grow older. (p. 620)

primary prevention An approach to a problem that is designed to prevent maltreatment (or other harm) from ever occurring. (p. 240)

primary sex characteristics The sex organs—those parts of the body that are directly involved in reproduction, including the vagina, uterus, ovaries, testicles, and penis. (p. 391)

priming Using one event, clue, or past accomplishment to make it easier to remember another one. (p. 655)

private speech The dialogue that occurs when one talks to oneself, either silently or out loud, to form thoughts and analyze ideas. (p. 252)

prosocial behavior An action, such as sharing, cooperating, or sympathizing, that is performed to benefit other people without the expectation of reward for oneself. (p. 277)

protein-calorie malnutrition A nutritional problem that results when a person does not consume enough nourishment to thrive. (p. 153)

proximity-seeking behaviors Behaviors that are intended to place a person close to another person to whom he or she is attached. (p. 206)

psychoanalytic theory A grand theory of human development that holds that irrational, unconscious forces, many of them originating in early childhood, underlie human behavior. (p. 39)

psychosocial domain The part of human development that includes emotions, personality characteristics, and relationships with other people—family, friends, lovers, and strangers. This domain also includes the larger community and the culture. (p. 5)

puberty A period of rapid growth and sexual change that occurs in early adolescence and produces a person of adult size, shape, and sexual potential. (p. 382)

quality-adjusted life years (QALYs) A way of comparing mere survival without vitality to survival with health. QALYs indicate how many years of full vitality are lost to a particular physical disease or disability. Expressed in terms of life expectancy as adjusted for quality of life. (p. 557)

race A social construction that originated with biological differences among people whose ancestors came from various regions of the world and whose social status was considered inferior or superior. Race is a misleading term; social scientists prefer to use ethnicity, national background, or culture instead. (p. 14)

reaction time The time it takes to respond to a particular stimulus. (p. 307)

reactive aggression Aggressive behavior that is an angry retaliation for some intentional or accidental act by another. (p. 278)

recessive gene The weaker of an interacting pair of genes. (p. 78)

reflexes Involuntary physical responses to stimuli. (p. 139)

reinforcement The process whereby a particular behavior is strengthened, making it more likely that the behavior will be repeated. (p. 46)

relational aggression Aggressive behavior that takes the form of insults or social rejection. (p. 278)

reminder session An experience that includes some aspect (a sight, a smell, a sound) of something to be remembered and thus serves to trigger the entire memory. (p. 167)

remote grandparents Grandparents who are distant but who are honored, respected, and obeyed by the younger generations in their families. (p. 600)

replicate To repeat a previous scientific study, at a different time and place but with the same research design and procedures, in order to verify that study's conclusions. (p. 15)

representative sample A group of research subjects who reflect the relevant characteristics of the larger population whose attributes are under study. (p. B-4)

resource room A designated room, equipped with special material and staffed by a trained teacher, where children with special needs spend part of their school day getting help with basic skills. (p. 322)

respite care An arrangement in which a professional caregiver takes over to give the family caregiver of a frail elderly person a break for a few hours each day or for an occasional weekend. (p. 703)

response A behavior (either instinctual or learned) that is elicited by a certain stimulus. (p. 42)

reversibility The logical principle that something that has been changed can be returned to its original state by reversing the process of change. (p. 334)

risk analysis The process of weighing the potential outcomes of a particular event, substance, or experience to determine the likelihood of harm. In teratology, the attempt to evaluate all the factors that can increase or decrease the likelihood that a particular teratogen will cause harm. (p. 105)

role buffering The common situation in dual-earner families in which one role that a parent plays reduces the disappointments that may occur in other roles. (p. 534)

role overload The stress of multiple obligations that may occur for a parent in a dual-earner family. (p. 534)

rooting reflex A reflex that helps babies find a nipple by causing them to turn their heads toward anything that brushes against their cheeks and to attempt to suck on it. (p. 140)

rough-and-tumble play Play such as wrestling, chasing, and hitting that mimics aggression but actually occurs purely in fun, with no intent to harm. (p. 279)

rubella A viral disease that, if contracted early during pregnancy, can harm the fetus, causing blindness, deafness, and damage to the central nervous system. (Sometimes called *German measles*.) (p. 107)

sample A group of individuals drawn from a specified population. A sample might be the low-birthweight babies born in four particular hospitals that are representative of all hospitals. (p. B-4)

sample size The number of individuals who are being studied in a single sample in a research project. (p. B-4)

sandwich generation The generation "in between," having both grown children and elderly parents. Many middle-aged people feel pressured by the needs and demands of their adult children on the one hand and of their elderly (and perhaps ailing or widowed) parents on the other. (p. 592)

scaffold To structure participation in learning encounters in order to foster a child's emerging capabilities. Scaffolds can be provided in many ways: by a mentor, by the objects or experiences of a culture, or by the child's past learning. (p. 252)

scientific method The principles and procedures used in the systematic pursuit of knowledge (formulating questions, testing hypotheses, and drawing conclusions), designed to reduce subjective reasoning, biased assumptions, and unfounded beliefs. (p. 15)

scientific observation The unobtrusive watching and recording of subjects' behavior, either in the laboratory or in a natural setting. (p. 19)

scientific study of human development The science that seeks to understand how and why people change, and how and why they remain the same, as they grow older. (p. 4)

scripts Skeletal outlines of the usual sequence of events during certain common, recurring experiences. (p. 256)

secondary aging The specific physical illnesses or conditions that are more common in aging but are caused by health habits, genes, and other influences that vary from person to person. (p. 620)

secondary prevention An approach to a problem that focuses on responding to the first symptoms or signs of risk. Secondary prevention can, and should, begin before the problem becomes severe. (p. 240)

secondary sex characteristics Body characteristics that are not directly involved in reproduction but that indicate sexual maturity, such as a man's beard or a woman's breasts. (p. 391)

secure attachment A caregiver–infant relationship that provides comfort and confidence, as evidenced first by the infant's attempts to be close to the caregiver and then by the infant's readiness to explore. (p. 207)

selective adaptation An aspect of evolution in which, over generations, genes for the traits that are most useful will become more frequent within individuals, making the survival of the species more likely. (p. 60)

selective attention The ability to concentrate on relevant information and ignore distractions. (p. 329)

self-awareness A person's sense of himself or herself as being distinct from other people. (p. 191)

self theories Theories of late adulthood that emphasize the core self, or the search to maintain one's integrity and identity. (p. 677)

senescence The state of physical decline, in which the body gradually becomes less strong and efficient with age. (p. 466)

senile macular degeneration A disease of the eye involving deterioration of the retina. (p. 623)

sensation The response of a sensory system when it detects a stimulus. People are not necessarily aware of sensations. (p. 145)

sensorimotor intelligence Piaget's term for the intelligence of infants during the first (sensorimotor) period of cognitive development, when babies think by using the senses and motor skills. (p. 171)

sensory register A memory system that functions for only a fraction of a second, retaining a fleeting impression of a stimulus on a particular sense organ. (p. 328)

separation anxiety An infant's fear of being left by his or her caregiver. (p. 188)

set point A particular body weight that an individual's home-ostatic processes strive to maintain. (p. 480)

sex differences Biological differences between males and females. (p. 287)

sexually transmitted disease (STD) A disease spread by sexual contact. Such diseases include syphilis, gonorrhea, herpes, chlamydia, and AIDS. (p. 425)

small for gestational age (SGA) A term applied to newborns who weigh substantially less than they should, given how much time has passed since conception. (Also called *small-for-dates*.) (p. 114)

social clock Refers to the idea that the stages of life, and the behaviors "appropriate" to them, are set by social standards rather than by biological maturation. For instance, "middle age" begins when the culture believes it does, rather than at a particular age in all societies. (p. 513)

social cognition A person's awareness and understanding of human personality, motives, emotions, intentions, and interactions. (p. 356)

social comparison The tendency to assess one's abilities, achievements, social status, and the like by measuring them against those of others, especially those of one's peers. (p. 358)

social construction An idea about the way things are, or should be, that is built more on the shared perceptions of members of a society than on objective reality. (p. 10)

social convoy Collectively, the family members, friends, acquaintances, and even strangers who move through life with an individual. (p. 690)

social homogamy The similarity with which a couple regard leisure interests and role preferences. (p. 522)

social learning A theory that learning occurs through observation and imitation of other people. (p. 46)

social mediation In regard to language, the use of speech as a tool to bridge the gap in understanding or knowledge between learner and tutor. (p. 252)

social referencing Looking to trusted adults for cues on how to interpret unfamiliar or ambiguous events. (p. 189)

social smile An infant's smile of pleasure in response to a human face or voice. (p. 188)

society of children The social culture of children, including the games, vocabulary, dress codes, and rules of behavior that characterize their interactions. (p. 359)

sociocultural theory A theory which holds that human development results from the dynamic interaction between developing persons and the surrounding culture, primarily as expressed by the parents and teachers who transmit it. (p. 51)

sociodramatic play Pretend play in which children act out various roles and themes in stories of their own creation. (p. 280)

socioeconomic status (SES) An indicator of social class that is based primarily on income, education, place of residence, and occupation. (p. 10)

source amnesia The inability to remember who or what was the source of a specific fact, idea, or snippet of conversation. (p. 652)

spermarche A male's first ejaculation of live sperm, whether through masturbation, a dream, or sexual contact with another person. (p. 391)

spontaneous abortion The naturally occurring termination of a pregnancy before the fetus is fully developed. (Also called *miscarriage*.) (p. 88)

stimulus An action or event that elicits a behavioral response. (p. 42)

stranger wariness A fear of unfamiliar people, exhibited (if at all) by infants over the age of about 6 months. (p. 188)

Strange Situation An experimental condition devised by Mary Ainsworth to assess an infant's attachment to a caregiver. The infant's behavior is observed in an unfamiliar room while the caregiver (usually the mother) and a stranger move in and out of the room. (p. 207)

stratification theories Theories emphasizing that social forces, particularly those related to a person's social stratum or social category, limit individual choices and affect the ability to function. In late adulthood, past stratification continues to limit life in various ways. (p. 680)

subcortical dementias Dementias, such as Parkinson's disease, Huntington's disease, and multiple sclerosis, that originate in the subcortex. These diseases begin with impairments in motor ability and produce cognitive impairment in later stages. (p. 667)

subjects The people who are studied in a research project. (p. 15)

sucking reflex A reflex that causes newborns to suck anything that touches their lips. (p. 140)

suicidal ideation Thinking about suicide, usually with some serious emotional and intellectual overtones. (p. 450)

superego The part of the personality that is self-critical and judgmental and that internalizes the moral standards set by parents and society. (p. 290)

surrogate parents The role some grandparents play for their grandchildren due to their children's extreme social problems. (p. 604)

survey A research method in which information is collected from a large number of people, through written questionnaires or personal interviews. (p. 24)

symbolic thinking Thinking that involves the use of words, gestures, pictures, or actions to represent ideas, things, or behaviors. (p. 246)

synapse The point at which the axon of one neuron meets the dendrites of another neuron. (p. 133)

synchrony Coordinated interaction between infant and parent (or other caregiver) in which each individual responds to and influences the other. (p. 203)

syndrome A cluster of distinct characteristics that tend to occur together in a given disorder. (p. 88)

synthesis The reconciliation of thesis and antithesis into a new and more comprehensive level of truth; the third stage of the dialectical process. (p. 493)

T cells Cells created in the thymus that produce substances that attack infected cells in the body. (p. 635)

temperament The set of innate tendencies, or dispositions, that underlie and affect each person's interactions with people, situations, and events. (p. 198)

teratogens Agents and conditions, including viruses, drugs, chemicals, stressors, and malnutrition, that can impair prenatal development and lead to birth defects or even death. (p. 105)

teratology The scientific study of birth defects caused by genetic or prenatal problems or by birth complications. (p. 105)

tertiary prevention An approach to a problem that is aimed at halting the harm after it occurs and treating the victim. Removing a child from the home, providing needed hospitalization or psychological counseling, and jailing the perpetrator are all examples of tertiary measures for child-maltreatment prevention. (p. 241)

theory of mind An understanding of human mental processes, that is, of one's own and others' emotions, perceptions, intentions, and thoughts. (p. 257)

thesis A proposition or statement of belief; the first stage of the dialectical process. (p. 491)

threshold effect The phenomenon in which a particular teratogen is relatively harmless in small doses but becomes harmful when exposure reaches a certain level (the threshold). (p. 106)

toddler A child, usually between the ages of 1 and 2, who has just begun to master the art of walking. (p. 141)

total immersion An approach to learning a second language in which the learner is placed in an environment where only the second language is spoken. (p. 346)

transient exuberance The great increase in the number of neurons, dendrites, and synapses that occurs in an infant's brain over the first 2 years of life. (p. 136)

trisomy-21 (Down syndrome) A syndrome that includes such symptoms as a rounded head, thick tongue, unusual eyes, heart abnormalities, and mental retardation. It results when there is an extra chromosome at the site of the twenty-first pair. (p. 88)

trust versus mistrust   Erikson's first stage of psychosocial development, in which the infant experiences the world either as secure and comfortable or as unpredictable and uncomfortable. (p. 195)

twenty-third pair   The chromosome pair that, in humans, determines the zygote's (and hence the person's) sex, among other things. (p. 72)

underextension   The use of a word to refer only to certain things, even though the word is generally applied more broadly by most people. (p. 177)

variable   Any quantity, characteristic, or action that can differ between individuals, situations, or groups, or even within one individual from moment to moment. (p. 18)

visual cliff   An apparent (but not actual) drop between one surface and another. The illusion of the cliff is created by connecting a transparent glass surface to an opaque patterned one, with the floor below the glass the same pattern as the opaque surface. (p. 161)

vitality   A measure of health that refers to how healthy and energetic—physically, intellectually, and socially—an individual actually feels. (p. 557)

volatile mismatch   The potentially explosive situation that arises when teenagers' individual needs—intellectual, emotional, social—do not match the size, routine, and structure of their schools. (p. 417)

voluntary euthanasia   A situation in which, at a patient's request, someone else ends his or her life. (p. 714)

wear-and-tear theory   A theory of aging that states that the human body wears out by time and exposure to environmental stressors. (p. 632)

wisdom   A cognitive perspective characterized by a broad, practical, comprehensive approach to life's problems, reflecting timeless truths rather than immediate expediency; said to be more common in the elderly than in the young. (p. 673)

withdrawn-rejected children   Children who are actively rejected by their peer group because of their withdrawn, anxious behavior. (p. 361)

working memory   The part of memory that handles current, conscious mental activity. (Also called *short-term memory*.) (p. 328)

X-linked genes   Genes that are on the X chromosome. (p. 78)

young-old   Healthy, vigorous, financially secure older adults (generally, those under age 75) who are well integrated into the lives of their families and their communities. (p. 620)

zone of proximal development (ZPD)   The range of skills, knowledge, and understanding that an individual cannot yet perform or comprehend on his or her own but could master with guidance; this is the arena where learning occurs. (pp. 56, 252)

zygote   The single cell formed from the fusing of a sperm and an ovum. (p. 70)

References

Aboud, Frances E. & Mendelson, Morton J. (1996). Determinants of friendship selection and quality: Developmental perspectives. In William M. Bukowski, Andrew F. Newcomb, & Willard W. Hartup (Eds.) *The company they keep: Friendship in childhood and adolescence*. Cambridge, UK: Cambridge University Press.

Abraído-Lanza, Ana F., Dohrenwend, Bruce P., Ng-Mak, Daisy S., & Turner, J. Blake. (1999). The Latino mortality paradox: A test of the "salmon bias" and healthy migrant hypotheses. *American Journal of Public Health, 89*, 1543–1548.

Achenbach, Thomas M., Howell, Catherine T., Quay, Herbert C., & Conners, C. Keith. (1991). National survey of problems and competencies among four- to sixteen-year-olds. *Monographs of the Society for Research in Child Development, 56* (Serial No. 225), 3.

Ackerman, Brian P., Kogos, Jen, Youngstrom, Eric, Schoff, Kristen, & Izard, Carroll. (1999). Family instability and the problem behaviors of children from economically disadvantaged families. *Developmental Psychology, 35*, 258–268.

Adams, Cynthia, & Labouvie-Vief, Gisela. (1986, November 20). Modes of knowing and language processing. Symposium on developmental dimensions of adult adaptation: Perspectives on mind, self, and emotion. Paper presented at the meeting of the Gerontological Association of America, Chicago.

Adams, G. R., Gullottra, T. P., & Montemayor, R. (1992). *Advances in adolescent development: Adolescent identity formation*. New York: Russell Sage.

Adams, Marilyn Jager. (1990). *Beginning to read: Thinking and learning about print*. Cambridge, MA: MIT Press.

Adams, Marilyn Jager, Treiman, Rebecca, & Pressley, Michael. (1998). Reading, writing, and literacy. In William, Damon, Irving E. Sigel & K. Anne Renninger (Eds.), *Handbook of Child Psychology, Volume Four: Child psychology in practice*. New York: Wiley.

Adams, Paul, & Dominick, Gary L. (1995). The old, the young, and the welfare state. *Generations, 14*, 38–42.

Adler, Lynn Peters. (1995). *Centenarians: The bonus years*. Santa Fe, NM: Health Press.

Adolph, Karen E. (1997). Learning in the development of infant locomotion. With commentary by Bennett I. Bertenthal & Steven M. Boker, by Eugene C. Goldfield and by Eleanor J. Gibson. *Monographs of the Society for Research in Child Development, 62*.

Adolph, K.E., Eppler, M.A., & Gibson, E.J. (1993). Crawling versus walking infants' perception of affordances for locomotion over sloping surfaces. *Child Development, 64*, 1158–1174.

Adolph, Karen E., Vereijken, Beatrix, & Denny, Mark A. (1998). Learning to crawl. *Child Development, 69*, 1299–1312.

Ainsworth, Mary D. Salter. (1967). *Infancy in Uganda: Infant care and the growth of love*. Baltimore: Johns Hopkins Press.

Ainsworth, Mary D. Salter. (1973). The development of infant-mother attachment. In Bettye M. Caldwell & Henry N. Ricciuti (Eds.), *Review of child development research* (Vol. 3). Chicago: University of Chicago Press.

Ainsworth, Mary D. Salter. (1993). Attachment as related to mother-infant interaction. In C. Rovee-Collier & L.P. Lipsitt (Eds.), *Advances in infancy research* (Vol. 8). Norwood, NJ: Ablex.

Akiyama, Hiroko, Elliot, Kathryn, & Antonucci, Toni C. (1996). Same-sex and cross-sex relationships. *Journal of Gerontology, 51B*, 374–382.

Albert, M.S., Jones, K., Savage, C.R., Berkman, L., Seeman, T., Blazer, D., & Rowe, J.W. (1995). Predictors of cognitive change in older persons: MacArthur studies of successful aging. *Psychology and Aging, 10*, 578–589.

Albert, Marilyn S., & Moss, Mark B. (1996). Neuropsychology of aging: Findings in humans and monkeys. In Edward L. Schneider & John W. Rowe (Eds.), *Handbook of the biology of aging*. San Diego: Academic Press.

Aldous, Joan, Mulligan, Gail M., & Bjarnason, Thoroddur. (1998). Fathering over time: What makes the difference? *Journal of Marriage and the Family, 60*, 809–820.

Aldwin, Carolyn M. (1994). *Stress, coping, and development*. New York: Guilford.

Alessandri, Steven M., Bendersky, Margaret, & Lewis, Michael. (1998). Cognitive functioning in 8- to 18-month-old drug-exposed infants. *Developmental Psychology, 34*, 565–573.

Alibali, Martha Wagner. (1999). How children change their minds: Strategy change can be gradual or abrupt. *Developmental Psychology, 35*, 127–145.

Allan, Graham. (1989). *Friendship: Developing a sociological perspective*. Boulder, CO: Westview.

Allen, Stanley E. M., & Crago, Martha B. (1996). Early passive acquisition in Inuktitut. *Journal of Child Language, 23,* 129–155.

Allison, Clara. (1985). Development direction of action programs: Repetitive action to correction loops. In Jane E. Clark & James H. Humphrey (Eds.), *Motor development: Current selected research.* Princeton, NJ: Princeton Book Company.

Als, Heidelise. (1995). The preterm infant: A model for the study of fetal brain expectation. In Jean-Pierre Lecanuet, William P. Fifer, Norman A. Krasnegor, & William A. Smkotherman (Eds.), *Fetal development: A psychobiological perspective.* Erlbaum: Hillsdale, NJ.

Altbach, Philip G. (1998). *Comparative higher education: Knowledge, the university, and development.* Greenwich, CT: Ablex Publishing Corporation.

Alwin, Duane F. (1996). Coresidence beliefs in American society—1973 to 1991. *Journal of Marriage and the Family,* 58, 393–403.

Alwin, D.F. (1997). Aging, social change, and conservatism: The link between historical and biographical time in the study of political identities. In M. Hardy (Ed.), *Studying aging and social change: Conceptual and methodological issues.* Thousand Oaks, CA: Sage.

Aman, Christine J., Roberts, Ralph J., & Pennington, Bruce F. (1998). A neuropsychological examination of the underlying deficit in attention deficit hyperactivity disorder: Frontal lobe versus right parietal lobe theories. *Developmental Psychology, 34,* 956–969.

Amato, Paul R., & Rezac, Sandra J. (1994). Contact with non-resident parents, interparental conflict, and children's behavior. *Journal of Family Issues, 15,* 191–207.

Amato, Paul R. & Rivera, Fernando. (1999). Paternal involvement and children's behavior problems. *Journal of Marriage and the Family, 60,* 375–384.

American Association of University Women Foundation. (1993). *Hostile hallways: The AAUW survey on sexual harassment in America's schools.* Washington DC: AAUW Educational.

American Council on Education. (1999). *The American freshman: National norms for Fall 1999.* Los Angeles, CA: Los Angeles Higher Education Research Institute.

American Psychiatric Association. (1994). *Diagnostic and Statistical Manual of Mental Disorders—DSM-IV.* Washington, DC.

Ammerman, Robert T., Oh, Peggy J., & Tarter, Ralph G. (Eds.). (1999). Prevention and societal impact of drug and alcohol abuse. Mahwah, NJ: Erlbaum.

Anderman, Eric M., Griesinger, Tripp, & Westerfield, Gloria. (1998). Motivation and Cheating During Early Adolescence. *Journal of Educational Psychology, 90,* 84–93.

Anderson, Arnold E. (1998). The self—Bridging the gap between brain and mind. *Contemporary Psychology, 43,* 361–362.

Anderson, Craig A., Lindsay, James J., & Bushman, Brad J. (1999). Research in the psychological laboratory: Truth or triviality? *Current Directions in Psychological Science, 8,* 3–9.

Anderson, D.R., Collins, P.A., Schmitt, K.L., & Jacobvitz, R.S. (1996). Stressful life events and television viewing. *Communication Research, 23,* 243–260.

Anderson, J. (1993). *Rules of the mind.* Hillsdale, NJ: Erlbaum.

Andrews, Melinda, Dowling, W.Jay, Bartlett, James C., & Halpern, Andrea R. (1998). Identification of speeded and slowed familiar melodies by younger, middle-aged, and older musicians and nonmusicians. *Psychology and Aging, 13,* 462–471.

Aneshensel, C.S., Pearlin, L.I., Mullan, J.T., Zarit, S.H., & Whitlatch, C.J. (1995). *Profiles in caregiving: The unexpected career.* San Diego, CA: Academic Press.

Anglin, Jeremy M. (1993). Vocabulary development: A morphological analysis. *Monographs of the Society for Research in Child Development, 58* (Serial No. 238), 10.

Anstey, Kaarin J. & Smith, Glen A. (1999). Interrelations among biological markers of aging, health, actiavity, acculturation, and cognitive performance in late adulthood. *Psychology and Aging, 14,* 605–618.

Ansuini, C.G., Fiddler-Woite, J., & Woite, R.S. (1996). The source, accuracy, and impact of initial sexuality information on lifetime wellness. *Adolescence, 31,* 283–289.

Antonucci, Toni C. (1985). Personal characteristics, social support, and social behavior. In R.H. Binstock & E. Shanas (Eds.), Handbook of aging and the social sciences (2nd ed.). New York: Van Nostrand Reinhold.

Antonucci, Toni C. (1990). Attachment, social support, and coping with negative life events. In E.M. Cummings, A.L. Greene, & K.H. Karraker (Eds.), *Life-span developmental psychology: Vol. 11. Stress and coping across the life-span.* Hillsdale, NJ: Erlbaum.

Apgar, Virginia. (1953). A proposal for a new method of evaluation in the newborn infant. *Current Research in Anesthesia and Analgesia, 32,* 260.

Aquilino, William S. (1991). Family structure and home-leaving: A further specification of the relationship. Journal of Marriage and the Family, 53, 999–1010.

Arbuckle, Tannis Y. (1998). Individual differences in trajectory of intellectual development over 45 years of adulthood. *Psychology and Aging, 13,* 663–675.

Archer, Loran, Grant, Bridget F., & Dawson, Deborah A. (1995). What if American drank less? The potential effect on the prevalence of alcohol abuse and dependence. *American Journal of Public Health, 85,* 61–66.

Archer, Sally. (1994). *Interventions for adolescent identity development.* Thousand Oaks, CA: Sage.

Arden, John Boghosian. (1998). *Science, theology, & consciousness: The search for unity.* Westport, CT: Praeger.

Arendell, Terry. (1995). Fathers and divorce. Newbury Park, CA: Sage.

Arking, R. (1998). *Biology of aging: Observations and principles,* 2nd edition. Sunderland, MA.: Sinauer Associates.

Armstrong, Neil, & Welsman, Joanne. (1997). *Young people and physical activity.* Oxford, England: Oxford University Press.

Arnett, Jeffrey Jensen. (1999) Adolescent storm and stress, reconsidered. *American Psychologist, 54*, 317–326.

Arnett, Jeffrey Jensen. (1999). Learning to stand alone: The contemporary American transition to adulthood in cultural and historical context. *Human Development, 41*, 295–315.

Arnold, Georgianne. (1997). Solvent abuse and developmental toxicity. In Sam Kacew & George H. Lambert (Eds.), *Environmental toxicity and pharmacology of human development*. Washington, DC: Taylor & Francis.

Aron, Arthur, & Westbay, Lori. (1996). Dimensions of the prototype of love. Journal of Personality and Social Relationships, 70, 535–551.

Aron, David C., Gordon, Howard S., Di Guiseppe, David L., Harper, Dwain L., & Rosenthal, Gary E. (2000). Variations in risk-adjusted Cesarean delivery rates according to race and health insurance. *Medical Care, 38*, 35–44.

Aronson, Elliot. (2000). *Nobody left to hate: Teaching compassion after Columbine*. New York: Freeman.

Aronson, Miriam K. (1994). Reshaping dementia care. Thousand Oaks, CA: Sage.

Asch, David A., Hershey, John C., Pauly, Mark V., Patton, James P., Jedriziewski, Kathryn M., & Mennuti, Michael T. (1996). Genetic screening for reproductive planning: Methodological and conceptual issues in policy analysis. *American Journal of Public Health, 86*, 684–690.

Aslin, Richard N. (1987). Visual and auditory development in infancy. In Joy Doniger Osofsky (Ed.), *Handbook of infant development* (2nd ed.). New York: Wiley.

Aslin, Richard N. (1988). Visual perception in early infancy. In Albert Yonas (Ed.), *Perceptual development in infancy*. Hillsdale, NJ: Erlbaum.

Aslin, Richard N., Jusczyk, Peter W., & Pisoni, David B. (1998). Speech and auditory processing during infancy: Constraints on and precursors to language. In William Damon, Deanna Kuhn, & Robert S. Siegler (Eds.), *Handbook of child psychology: Cognition, perception, and language*. New York: Wiley.

Astington, Janet Wilde. (1993). *The child's discovery of the mind*. Cambridge, MA: Harvard University Press.

Astington, Janet Wilde, & Gopnik, A. (1988). Knowing you've changed your mind: Children's understanding of representational change. In J.W. Astington, P.L. Harris, & D.R. Olson (Eds.), *Developing theories of mind*. Cambridge, England: Cambridge University Press.

Atchley, Robert C. (1999). Continuity and adaptation in aging: Creating positive experiences. Baltimore: John Hopkins University Press.

Aureli, Tiziana & Colecchia, Nicola. (1996). Day care experience and free play behavior in preschool children. *Journal of Applied Developmental Psychology, 17*, 1–17.

Avis, Nancy. (1999) Women's health at midlife. In Sherry L. Willis & James D. Reid (Eds.), *Life in the middle*. San Diego: Academic Press

Avolio, Bruce J. & Sosik, John J. (1999). A life-span framework for assessing the impact of work on white collar workers. In Sherry L. Willis & James D. Reid (Eds.), *Life in the middle*. San Diego: Academic Press.

Awooner-Renner, Sheila. (1993). I desperately needed to see my son. In Donna Dickenson & Malcolm Johnson (Eds.), *Death, dying & bereavement*. London: Sage.

Bachman, J.G., & Schulenberg, J. (1993). How part-time work intensity relates to drug use, problem behavior, time use, and satisfaction among high school seniors: Are these consequences or merely correlates? *Developmental Psychology, 29*, 220–235.

Bachu, A. (1999). Trends in premarital childbearing: 1930 to 1994, *Current population reports, 1999*, series P-23, No. 197.

Bagley, Christopher & Thurston, Wilfreda E. (1996). *Understanding and preventing child sexual abuse*. Hants, England: Ashgate.

Bahrick, H.P. (1984). Semantic memory content in permastore: Fifty years of memory for Spanish learned in school. *Journal of Experimental Psychology: General, 113*, 1–35.

Bailey, A., Palferman, S., Heavey, L., & Le Couteur, A. (1998). Autism: The phenotype in relatives. *Journal of Autism & Developmental Disorders, 28*, 369–392.

Bailey, J. Michael, Pillard, Richard C., & Knight, Robert. (1993). At issue: Is sexual orientation biologically determined? *CQ Researcher, 3*, 209.

Baillargeon, R. (1987). Object permanence in 3.5- and 4.5-month-old infants. *Developmental Psychology, 23*, 655–664.

Baillargeon, R. (1995). A model or physical reasoning in infancy. In C. Rovee-Collier & L. Lipsitt (Eds.), *Advances in infancy research*. Norwood, NJ: Ablex.

Baillargeon, R., & DeVos, J. (1992). Object permanence in young infants: Further evidence. *Child Development, 62*, 1227–1246.

Bakan, D. (1966). The duality of human existence: Isolation and communion in Western man. Boston: Beacon.

Baker, Colin. (1993). *Foundation of bilingual education and bilingualism*. Clevedon, England: Multilingual Matters.

Baker, Jeffrey P. (2000). Immunization and the American way: Childhood vaccines. *American Journal of Public Health, 90*, 199–207.

Bakken, B. (1993). Prejudice and danger: The only child in China. *Childhood, 1*, 46–61.

Balaban, Marie T. (1995). Affective influences on startle in five-month-old infants: Reactions to facial expressions of emotion. *Child Development, 66*, 28–36.

Balin, Arthur K. (Ed.). (1994). Practical handbook of human biologic age determination. Boca Raton, FL: CRC Press.

Ball, T.M. & Wright A.L. (1999). Health care costs of formula-feeding in the first year of life. *Pediatrics, 103*, 870–876.

Baltes, M.M., & Horgas, A.L. (1997). Long-term care institutions and the maintenance of competence: A dialectic between compensation and overcompensation. In S.L. Willis, K.W. Schaie, & M. Hayward (Eds.), *Societal mechanisms for maintaining competence in old age*. New York: Springer.

Baltes, Paul B. (1998). Theoretical propositions of life-span developmental psychology: On the dynamics between growth and decline. In M. Powell Lawton & Timothy A. Salthouse (Eds.), *Essential papers on the psychology of aging*. New York: New York University Press.

Baltes, Paul B., Smith, Jacqui, & Staudinger, Ursula. (1992). Wisdom and successful aging. In T. Sonderegger (Ed.), Psychology and aging: Nebraska Symposium on Motivation (Vol. 39). Lincoln: University of Nebraska Press.

Bandura, Albert. (1986). *Social foundations of thought and action: A social cognitive theory*. Englewood Cliffs, NJ: Prentice-Hall.

Bandura, Albert. (1997). The anatomy of stages of change. *American Journal of Health Promotion, 12*, 8–10.

Bandura, Albert. (1999). A sociocognitive analysis of substance abuse: An agentic perspective. *Psychological Science, 10*, 214–217.

Banerji, Madhabi & Dailey, Ronald A. (1995). A study of the effects of the inclusion model on students with specific learning disabilities. *Journal of Learning Disabilities, 28*, 511–522.

Banich, Marie T. (1998). Integration of information between the cerebral hemispheres. *Current Directions in Psychological Science, 7*, 32–36.

Banich, Marie T. & Heller, Wendy. (1998). Evolving perspectives on lateralization of function. *Current Directions in Psychological Science, 7*, 1.

Barber, B.K. (1994). Cultural, family, and personal contexts of parent-adolescent conflict. *Journal of Marriage and the Family, 56*, 375–386.

Barbieri, Robert A. (1999). Infertility. In Samuel S.C. Yen, Robert B. Jaffe, & Robert L. Barbieri (Eds.), *Reproductive endocrinology : physiology, pathophysiology, and clinical management*. Philadelphia: Saunders.

Barinaga, Marcia. (1998). Neurobiology: New leads to brain neuron regeneration. *Science, 282*, 1018–1019.

Barkow, Jerome H., Cosmides, Leda, & Tooby, John. (Eds.). (1992). *The adapted mind: Evolutionary psychology and the generation of culture*. New York: Oxford University Press.

Barnard, Kathryn E. & Martell, Louise K. (1995). Mothering. In Marc H. Bornstein (Ed.), *Handbook of parenting: Status and social conditions of parenting*. New Jersey: Erlbaum.

Barnes, Marcia A., Dennis, Maureen, & Wilkinson, Margaret. (1999). Reading after closed head injury in childhood: Effects on accuracy, fluency, and comprehension. *Developmental Neuropsychology, 15*, 1–24.

Barnett, Ronald. (1994). The limits of competence: Knowledge, higher education, and society. Buckingham, England: Society for Research into Higher Education.

Barnett, Ronald. (2000). *Realizing the university in an age of supercomplexity*. Buckingham: The Society for Research into Higher Education.

Barnett, Rosalind C., & Rivers, Caryl. (1996). The new dad works the "second shift," too. *Radcliff Quarterly, 82*, 9.

Barnett, S. Anthony. (1998). *The science of life*. St Leonards, Australia: Allen & Unwin.

Barr, Rachel, Dowden, Anne, & Hayne, Harlene. (1996). Developmental changes in deferred imitation by 6- to 24-month-old infants. *Infant Behavior & Development, 19*, 159–170.

Barresi, Charles M., & Menon, Geeta. (1990). Diversity in black family caregiving. In Zev Harel, Edward A. McKinney, & Mischel Williams (Eds.), *Black aged*. Newbury Park, CA: Sage.

Barth, R.P., Courtney, M., Berrick, J.D., & Albert, V. (1994). *From child abuse to permanency planning: Child welfare services, pathways, and placements*. New York: Aldine de Gruyter.

Barusch, Amanda Smith. (1994). *Older women in poverty: Private lives and public policies*. New York: Springer.

Basseches, Michael. (1984). *Dialectical thinking and adult development*. Norwood, NJ: Ablex.

Basseches, Michael. (1989). Dialectical thinking as an organized whole: Comments on Irwin and Kramer. In Michael L. Commons, Jan D. Sinnott, Francis A. Richards, & Cheryl Armon (Eds.), *Adult development: Vol. 1. Comparisons and applications of developmental models*. New York: Praeger.

Bassuk, E.L., & Rosenberg, L. (1990). Psychosocial characteristics of homeless children and children with homes. *Pediatrics, 85*, 257–261.

Bates, Betsy. (1995). STD reinfection greatest in teens. *Pediatric News, 29* (12), 8.

Bates, Elizabeth, & Carnevale, George F. (1994). Developmental psychology in the 1990s: Research on language development. *Developmental Review, 13*, 436–470.

Bates, J., Pettit, G., Dodge, K., & Ridge, B. (1998). Interaction of temperamental resistance to control and restrictive parenting in the development of externalizing behavior. *Developmental Psychology, 34*, 982–995.

Bauer, H.H. (1992). *Scientific literacy and the myth of the scientific method*. Urbana: University of Illinois Press.

Bauer, Patricia J., & Mandler, J.M. (1990). Remembering what happened next: Very young children's recall of event sequences. In R. Fivush & J.A. Hudson (Eds.), *Knowing and remembering in young children*. Cambridge, England: Cambridge University Press.

Bauer, Patricia J., & Mandler, J.M. (1992). Putting the horse before the cart: The use of temporal order in recall of events by one-year-old children. *Developmental Psychology, 28*, 441–452.

Bauer, Patricia J., Liebl, Monica, & Stennes, Leif. (1998) PRETTY is to DRESS as BRAVE is to SUITCOAT: Gender-based property-to-property inferences by 4–10-year-old children. *Merrill-Palmer Quarterly, 44*, 355–377.

Baumeister, Roy F. & Boden, Joseph M. (1998). Aggression and the self: High self esteem, low self control, & ego trust. In Russell G. Geen & Edward Donnerstein (Eds.) *Human aggression: Theories research, and implications for social policy*. San Diego: Academic Press.

Baumrind, Diana. (1967). Child-care practices anteceding three patterns of preschool behavior. *Genetic Psychology Monographs, 75*, 43–88.

Baumrind, Diana. (1971). Current patterns of parental authority. *Developmental Psychology, 4* (Monograph 1), 1–103.

Baumrind, Diana. (1991). Effective parenting during the early adolescent transition. In P.A. Cowan & E.M. Hetherington (Eds.), *Advances in family research* (Vol. 2). Hillsdale, NJ: Erlbaum.

Baumwell, Lisa, Tamis-LeMonda, Catherine S. & Bornstein, Marc H. (1997). Maternal verbal sensitivity and child language comprehension. *Infant Behavior & Development, 20,* 247–258.

Bayley, Nancy. (1966). Learning in adulthood: The role of intelligence. In Herbert J. Klausmeier & Chester W. Harris (Eds.), *Analysis of concept learning.* New York: Academic Press.

Bayley, Nancy, & Odin, Melita. (1955). The maintenance of intellectual ability in gifted adults. *Journal of Gerontology, 10,* Section B (1), 91–107.

Baynes, R.D., & Bothwell, T.H. (1990). Iron deficiency. *Annual Review of Nutrition, 10,* (Palo Alto: Annual Reviews), 133.

Beach, Lee Roy, Chi, Michelene, Klein, Gary, Smith, Philip, & Vincente, Kim. (1997). Naturalistic decision making and related research lines. In Caroline E. Zsambok & Gary Klein (Eds.), *Naturalistic decision making.* Mahwah, NJ: Erlbaum.

Beal, Carole R. (1994). *Boys and girls: The development of gender roles.* New York: McGraw-Hill.

Beaudry, Micheline, Dufour, R., & Marcoux, Sylvie. (1995). Relation between infant feeding and infections during the first six months of life. *Journal of Pediatrics, 126,* 191–197.

Bedford, Victoria Hilkevitch. (1995). Sibling relationships in middle and old age. In Rosemary Blieszner & Victoria Hilkevitch Bedford (Eds.), *Handbook of aging and the family.* Westport, CT: Greenwood Press.

Becker, G.S. (1994, March 28). Cut the graybeards a smaller slice of the pie. *Business Week,* p. 20.

Becker, Penny Edgell & Moen, Phyllis. (1999). Scaling back: Dual-earner couples' work-family strategies. *Journal of Marriage and the Family, 61,* 995–1007.

Beckwith, Leila, Cohen, Sarale E., & Hamilton, Claire E. (1999). Maternal sensitivity during infancy and subsequent life events relate to attachment representation at early adulthood. *Developmental Psychology, 35,* 693–700.

Behrman, Richard E. (1992). *Nelson textbook of pediatrics.* Philadelphia: W.B. Saunders.

Beilin, H. (1992). Piaget's enduring contribution to developmental psychology. *Developmental Psychology, 28,* 191–204.

Beizer, Judith L. (1994). Medications and the aging body: Alteration as a function of age. Generations, 18, 13–18.

Bell, Derrick. (1992). *Faces at the bottom of the well: The permanence of racism.* New York: Basic Books.

Bell, M.A., & Fox, N.A. (1992). The relations between frontal brain electrical activity and cognitive development during infancy. *Child Development, 63,* 1142–1163.

Bellantoni, Michele F., & Blackman, Marc R. (1996). Menopause and its consequences. In Edward L. Schneider & John W. Rowe (Eds.), *Handbook of the biology of aging.* San Diego, CA: Academic Press.

Belle, Deborah. (1999). *The after-school lives of children : Alone and with others while parents work.* Mahwah, NJ: Erlbaum.

Beller, A.H., & Graham, J.W. (1993). *Small change: The economics of child support.* New Haven, CT: Yale University Press.

Belsky, Jay. (1990). Infant day care, child development, and family policy. *Society, 27* (5), 10–12.

Belsky, Jay. (1996). Parent, infant, and social-contextual antecedents of father-son attachment security. *Developmental Psychology, 32,* 905–913.

Belsky, Jay, & Cassidy, J. (1995). Attachment theory and evidence. In M. Rutter, D. Hay, & S. Baron-Cohen (Eds.), *Developmental principles and clinical issues in psychology and psychiatry.* Oxford, England: Blackwell.

Bem, Sandra L. (1989). Genital knowledge and gender constancy in preschool children. *Child Development, 60,* 649–662.

Benet, Sula. (1974). *Abkhasians: The long-lived people of the Caucasus.* New York: Holt, Rinehart & Winston.

Bengston, Vern L. (1975). Generation and family effects in value socialization. *American Sociological Review, 40,* 358–371.

Bengston, Vern, Rosenthal, Carolyn, & Burton, Linda. (1996). Paradoxes of families and aging. In Robert H. Binstock & Linda K. George (Eds.), Handbook of aging and the social sciences. San Diego: Academic Press.

Benoit, Diane, & Parker, Kevin C. (1994). Stability and transmission of attachment across three generations. *Child Development, 65,* 1444–1456.

Bensen, Peter L. (1997). *All kids are our kids: What communities must do to raise caring and responsible children and adolescents.* San Francisco: Jossey Bass.

Benson, V., & Marano, M. (1994). Current estimates from the National Health Interview Survey 1993, Vital Health Statistics (Series 10, No. 190). Washington, DC: National Center for Health Statistics.

Bensur, Barbara, & Eliot, John. (1993). Case's developmental model and children's drawings. *Perceptual and Motor Skills, 76,* 371–375.

Berenthal, Bennett I. & Clifton, Rachel K. (1998). Perception and action. In William Damon, Deanna Kuhn, & Robert S. Siegler (Eds.), *Handbook of child psychology: Cognition, perception, and language.* New York: Wiley

Bergeman, Cinty S. (1997). *Aging: Genetic and environmental influences.* Thousand Oaks, CA: Sage.

Berger, Klaus, Ajani, Umed A., Kase, Carlos S., Gaziano, J. Michael, Buring, Julie E., Glynn, Robert J., & Hennekens, Charles H. (1999). Light-to-moderate alcohol consumption and the risk of stroke among U.S. male physicians. *New England Journal of Medicine, 341,* 1557–1564.

Bergman, Abraham B., & Rivara, Fred P. (1991). Sweden's experience in reducing childhood injuries. *Pediatrics, 88,* 69–74.

Bergeman, Cinty S. (1997). *Aging: Genetic and environmental influences.* Thousand Oaks, CA: Sage.

Berkson, Gershon. (1993). *Children with handicaps: A review of behavioral research.* Hillsdale, NJ: Erlbaum.

Bernabel, R., et al. (1998). Management of pain in elderly patients with cancer. *Journal of the American Medical Association, 279,* 1877–1882.

Berndt, Thomas J., & Perry, T.B. (1990). Distinguishing features of early adolescent friendship. In Raymond Montemeyer, Gerald R. Adams, & Thomas P. Gullota (Eds.), *From childhood to adolescence: A transitional period?* Newbury Park, CA: Sage.

Berndt, Thomas J., & Savin-Williams, R.C. (1992). Peer relations and friendships. In P.H. Tolan & B.J. Kohler (Eds.), *Handbook of clinical research and practice with adolescents.* New York: Wiley.

Berrick, Jill Duerr. (1998). When children cannot remain home: Foster family care and kinship care. *The Future of Children: Protecting Children from Abuse and Neglect, 8,* 4–22.

Berzonsky, Michael D. (1989). Identity style: Conceptualization and measurement. *Journal of Adolescent Research, 4,* 268–282.

Besharov, Douglas J. (1998). Commentary 1: How we can better protect children from abuse and neglect. *The Future of Children: Protecting Children from Abuse and Neglect, 8,* 120–123.

Bettes, Barbara A. (1988). Maternal depression and motherese: Temporal and intonational features. *Child Development, 59,* 1089–1096.

Beunen, G.P., Malina, R.M., Van't Hof, M.A., Simons, J., Ostyn, M., Renson, R., & Van Gerven, D. (1988). *Adolescent growth and motor performance: A longitudinal study of Belgian boys.* Champaign, IL: Human Kinetics Books.

Bhopal R, & Donaldson L. (1998). White, European, Western, Caucasian, or what? Inappropriate labeling in research on race, ethnicity, and health. *American Journal of Public Health, 88,* 1303–1307.

Bialystok, Ellen. (1997). Effects of bilingualism and biliteracy on children's emerging concepts of print. *Developmental Psychology, 33,* 429–440.

Beidel, Deborah C., & Turner, Samuel M. (1998). *Shy children, phobic adults: Nature and treatment of social phobia.* Washington DC: American Psychological Association.

Biener, L. & Heaton, A. (1995). Women dieters of normal weight: their motives, goals, and risks. *American Journal of Public Health, 85,* 714–717.

Biernat, Monica, & Kobrynowicz, Diane. (1997). Gender- and race-based standards of competence: Lower minimum standards but higher ability standards for devalued groups. *Journal of Personality and Social Psychology, 72,* 544–557.

Bigsby, Rosemarie, Coster, Wendy, Lester, Barry M., & Peucker, Mark R. (1996). Motor behavioral cues of term and preterm infants at 3 months. *Infant Behavior & Development, 19,* 295–307.

Bijou, S.W., & Baer, D.M. (1978). *Child development: A behavior analysis approach.* Englewood Cliffs, NJ: Prentice-Hall.

Binstock, Robert H., & Day, Christine L. (1996). Aging and politics. In Robert H. Binstock & Linda K. George (Eds.), *Handbook of aging and the social sciences.* San Diego: Academic Press.

Birch, Leann L. (1990). Development of food acceptance patterns. *Developmental Psychology, 26,* 515–519.

Biringen, Zeynep, Emde, Robert N., & Pipp-Siegel, Sandra. (1997). Dyssynchrony, conflict, and resolution: Positive contributions in infant development. *American Journal of Orthopsychiatry, 67,* 4–19.

Birren, James E., & Schroots, Johannes J.F. (1996). History, concepts, and methods in psychology of aging. In James E. Birren & K. Warner Schaie (Eds.), *Handbook of the psychology of aging.* San Diego: Academic Press.

Bishop, Virginia E. (1993). Peter and the watermelon seeds. In P.J. McWilliam & Donald B. Bailey, Jr. (Eds.), *Working together with children & families.* Baltimore: Brookes.

Bjarnason, Thoroddur, Sigurdardottir, Thordis, J., & Thorlindsson, Thorolfur. (1999). Human agency, capable guardians, and structural constraints: A lifestyle approach to the study of violent victimization. *Journal of Youth & Adolescence, 28,* 105–119.

Blaikie, Andrew. (1999). Ageing: Old visions, new times. *The Lancet 2000, 354,* 5103.

Blake, Judith. (1989). *Family size and achievement.* Berkeley: University of California Press.

Blakemore, Ken, & Boneham, Margaret. (1994). *Age, race, and ethnicity: A comparative approach.* Buckingham, England: Open University Press.

Blanchard-Fields, Fredda. (1986). Reasoning on social dilemmas varying the emotional saliency: An adult developmental perspective. *Psychology and Aging, 1,* 325–333.

Blanchard-Fields, Fredda & Hess, Thomas M. (1999). The social cognitive perspective and the study of aging. In Thomas M. Hess & Fredda Blanchard-Fields (Eds.), *Social cognition and aging.* San Diego: Academic Press.

Bloom, Lois. (1991). *Language development from two to three.* New York: Cambridge University Press.

Bloom, Lois. (1993). *The transition from infancy to language: Acquiring the power of expression.* New York: Cambridge University Press.

Bloom, Lois. (1998). Language acquisition in its developmental context. In William Damon, Deanna Kuhn, & Robert S. Siegler (Eds.), *Handbook of child psychology: Cognition, perception, and language.* New York: Wiley

Bloomfield, L. (1933). *Language.* New York: Henry Holt.

Bluck, Susan, Levine, L. J., & Laulhere, T. M. (1999). Autobiographical remembering and hypermnesia: A comparison of older and younger adults. *Psychology and Aging, 14,* 671–682.

Blumberg, Jeffrey B. (1996). Status and functional impact of nutrition in older adults. In Edward L. Schneider & John W. Rowe (Eds.), *Handbook of the biology of aging,* 4th ed. San Diego: Academic Press.

Blythe, Ronald. (1979). *The view in winter: Reflections on old age.* New York: Penguin.

Bogin, Barry. (1995). Plasticity in the growth of Mayan refugee children living in the United States. In C.G.N. Mascie-Taylor & B. Bogin (Eds.), *Human variability and plasticity.* Cambridge: Cambridge University Press.

Bogin, Barry. (1996). Human growth and development from an evolutionary perspective. In C.J.K. Henry & S.J. Uliajaszel (Eds.), *Long-term consequences of early environment: Growth, development and the lifespan developmental perspective.* Cambridge, England: Cambridge University Press.

Bolger, K.E., Patterson, C.J., & Kupersmidt, J.B. (1998). Peer relationships and self-esteem among children who have been maltreated. *Child Development, 69,* 1171–1197.

Borgaonkar, Digamber S. (1997). *Chromosomal variation in man: A catalog of chromosomal variants and anomalies,* 8th Edition. New York, Wiley.

Borland, Moira, Laybourn, Ann, Hill, Malcolm, & Brown, Jane. (1998). *Middle childhood: The perspectives of children and parents.* London: Jessica Kingsley Publishers.

Bornstein, Marc H. (Ed.). (1995). *Handbook of parenting (Vol. 4): Applied and practical parenting.* Mahwah, NJ: Erlbaum.

Bornstein, Marc H. (1995). Parenting infants. In Marc H. Bornstein (Ed.), *Handbook of parenting: Childhood and parenting.* New Jersey: Erlbaum.

Bornstein, Marc H. & Arterberry, Martha E. (1999). Perceptual development. In March H. Bornstein & Michael E. Lamb (Eds.), *Developmental psychology: An advanced textbook* (4th ed.) Mahwah, NJ: Erlbaum.

Bornstein, Marc H., & Lamb, M.E. (1992). *Development in infancy* (3rd ed.). New York: McGraw-Hill.

Bornstein, Marc H., Tamis-LeMonda, C.S., Tal, J., Ludemann, P., Toda, S., Rahn, C.W., Pecheux, M.-G., Azuma, H., & Vardi, D. (1992). Maternal responsiveness to infants in three societies: The United States, France, and Japan. *Child Development, 63,* 808–821.

Borowsky, Iris Wagman, Resnick, Michael, Ireland Marjorie, & Blum, Robert. (1999). Suicide attempts among American Indian and Alaska Native youth. *Archives of Pediatric and Adolescent Medicine.* 153.

Borsting, Eric. (1994). Overview of vision and visual processing development. In Mitchell Scheiman & Michael Rouse (Eds.), *Optimetric management of learning-related vision problems.* St. Louis, MO: Mosby.

Bossé, Raymond. (1998). Retirement and retirement planning in old age. In Inger Hilde Nordhus, Gary R. VandenBos, Stig Berg, & Pia Fromhold (Eds.), *Clinical geropsychology.* Washington, DC: American Psychological Association.

Bossé, Raymond, Spiro A., III, & Kressin, N.R. (1996). The psychology of retirement. In R.T. Woods (Ed.), *Handbook of the clinical psychology of ageing.* London: Wiley.

Bosworth, Kris, Espelage, Dorothy L., & Simon, Thomas R. (1999). Factors associated with bullying behavior in middle school students. *Journal of Early Adolescence, 19,* 341–362.

Bouchard, Claude, & Bray, G.A. (Eds.). (1996). *Regulations of body weight: Biological and behavioral mechanisms.* New York: Wiley.

Bouchard, Geneviève, Lussier, Yvan, & Sabourin, Stéphane. (1999). Personality and marital adjustment: Utility of the five-factor model of personality. *Journal of Marriage and the Family, 61,* 651–660.

Bouchard, Thomas J. (1994). Genes, environment, and personality. *Science, 264,* 1700–1701.

Bouchard, Thomas J. (1997). Twin studies of behavior. In Alain, Schmitt, Klaus, Atzwanger, Karl Grammer, & Schafer, Katrin (Eds.), *New aspects of human ethology.* New York: Plenum.

Boulton, Michael J. (1999). Concurrent and longitudinal relations between children's playground behavior and social preference, victimization, and bullying. *Child Development, 70,* 944–954.

Boulton, Michael, & Smith, Peter K. (1989). Issues in the study of children's rough-and-tumble play. In Marianne N. Bloch & Anthony D. Pellegrini (Eds.), *The ecological context of children's play.* Norwood, NJ: Ablex.

Boulton, M.J. & Underwood, K. (1992). Bully/victim problems among middle school children. *British Journal of Educational Psychology, 62,* 73–87.

Bower, T.G.R. (1989). *The rational infant: Learning in infancy.* New York: Freeman.

Bowers, Bonita F. & Myers, Barbara J. (1999). Grandmothers providing care for grandchildren: Consequences of various levels of caregiving. *Family Relations, 48,* 303–310.

Boyland, Moira, Laybourn, Ann, Hill, Malcolm, & Brown, Jane. (1998). *Middle childhood.* London: Jessica Kingsley.

Boysson-Bardies, B., Halle, P., Sagart, L., & Durand, C. (1989). A crosslinguistic investigation of vowel formants in babbling. *Journal of Child Language, 16,* 1–17.

Braddick, Oliver, & Atkinson, Janette. (1988). Sensory selectivity, attentional control, and cross-channel integration in early visual development. In Albert Yonas (Ed.), *Perceptual development in infancy.* Hillsdale, NJ: Erlbaum.

Bradley, Dana Burr. (1999-2000). A reason to rise each morning: The meaning of volunteering in the lives of older adults. Reasons to grow old: Meaning in later life. *Generations, 23,* 45–50.

Bradley, Robert H. (1995). Environment and parenting. In Marc H. Bornstein (Ed.), *Handbook of parenting (Vol. 2): Biology and ecology of parenting.* Mahwah, NJ: Erlbaum.

Brainerd, C. J., & Reyna, V. F. (1995). Learning rate, learning opportunities, and the development of forgetting. *Developmental Psychology, 31,* 251–262.

Brandtstädter, Jochen. (1998). Action perspectives on human development. In William Damon & Richard M. Lerner (Eds.), *Handbook of child psychology,* fifth edition. Volume 1: Theoretical models of human development. New York: Wiley.

Brandtstädter, Jochen. (1999). Sources of resilience in the aging self: Toward integrating perspectives. In Thomas M. Hess & Fredda Blanchard-Fields (Eds.) *Social cognition and aging.* Orlando, Florida: Academic Press.

Branson, Robert K. (1998). Teaching-centered schooling has reached its upper limit: It doesn't get any better than this. *Current Directions in Psychological Science, 7,* 126–135.

Bray, G.A. (1989). Obesity: Basic considerations and clinical approaches. *Disease a Month, 35,* 449–537.

Brayfield, April A. (1995). Juggling jobs and kids: The impact of employment schedules on fathers' caring for children. *Journal of Marriage and the Family*, 57, 321–332.

Brazelton, T. B., & Cramer, B. (1991). *The earliest relationship*. London: Karnac.

Breakey, G., & Pratt, B. (1991). Healthy growth for Hawaii's "Healthy Start": Toward a systematic statewide approach to the prevention of child abuse and neglect. *Zero to Three* (Bulletin of the National Center for Clinical Infant Programs), *11*, 16–22.

Bremner, J. Gavin. (1988). *Infancy*. Oxford, England: Basil Blackwell.

Brent, David A., Baugher, Marianne, Bridge, Jeffrey, Chen, Tuhao, & Chiappetta, Laurel. (1999). Age- and sex-related risk factors for adolescent suicide. *Journal of the American Academy of Child and Adolescent Psychiatry*, 38, 1497–1505.

Bretherton, Inge. (1992). The origins of attachment theory: John Bowlby and Mary Ainsworth. *Developmental Psychology, 28*, 759–775.

Brett, Doris. (1988). *Annie stories: A special kind of storytelling*. New York: Workman Publishing.

Briggs, Susan D., Raz, Naftali, & Marks, William. (1999). Age-related deficits in generation and manipulation of mental images: I. The role of sensorimoto speed and working memory. *Psychology and Aging, 14*, 427–435.

Bril, B. (1986). Motor development and cultural attitudes. In H.T.A. Whiting & M.G. Wade (Eds.), *Themes in motor development*. Dordrecht, Netherlands: Martinus Nijhoff Publishers.

Brokenleg, Martin, & Middleton, David. (1993). Natifve Americans: Adapting yet retaining. In Donald P. Irish & Middlton (1993). *Ethnic variations in dying, death, and grief : Diversity in universality* (Series in Death Education, Aging, and Health Care). New York: Hemisphere Publishing.

Bromley, Rajput V. (1999). Chronic insomnia: A practical review. *American Family Physician*, 60, 1431–1438.

Brook, Judith S., Richter, Linda, Whiteman, Martin, & Cohen, Patricia. (1999). Consequences of adolescent marijuana use: Incompatibility with the assumption of adult roles. *Genetic, Social, & General Psychology Monographs*, 125, 193–207.

Brooks, G. A., & Fahey, T. D. (1984). *Exercise physiology: Human bioenergetics and its application*. New York, NY: Wiley.

Brooks, Gary R. (1997). The centerfold syndrome. In Ronald F. Levant & Gary R. Brooks (Eds.), *Men and sex: New psychological perspectives*. New York: Wiley.

Brooks-Gunn, Jeanne. (1991). Maturational timing variations in adolescent girls, consequences of. In Richard M. Lerner, Ann C. Petersen, & Jeanne Brooks-Gunn (Eds.), *Encyclopedia of adolescence* (Vol. 2). New York: Garland.

Brooks-Gunn, Jeanne, & Reiter, Edward O. (1990). The role of pubertal processes. In Shirley S. Feldman & Glenn R. Elliott (Eds.), *At the threshold: The developing adolescent*. Cambridge, MA: Harvard University Press.

Brooks-Gunn, Jeanne, Attie, I., Burrow, C., Rosso, J.T., & Warren, M.P. (1989). The impact of puberty on body and eating concerns in athletic and nonathletic contexts. *Journal of Early Adolescence, 9*, 269–290.

Brown, B.B. (1990). Peer groups and peer cultures. In S.S. Feldman & G.R. Elliott (Eds.), *At the threshold: The developing adolescent*. Cambridge, MA: Harvard University Press.

Brown, Bernard. (1999). Optimizing expression of the common human genome for child development. *Current Directions in Psychological Science, 8*, 37–41.

Brown, J.L., & Sherman, L.P. (1995). Policy implications of new scientific knowledge. *Journal of Nutrition*, 2281S–2284S.

Brown, Josephine V., Bakeman, Roger, Coles, Clair D., Sexson, William R., & Demi, Alice S. (1998). Maternal drug use during pregnancy: Are preterm and full-term infants affected differently? *Developmental Psychology, 34*, 540–554.

Brownson, Ross C., Alavanja, Michael C.R., Hock, Edward T., & Loy, Timothy S. (1992). Passive smoking and lung cancer in nonsmoking women. *American Journal of Public Health, 82*, 1525–1530.

Bruck, Maggie, Ceci, Stephen J., & Melnyk, Laura. (1997). External and internal sources of variation in the creation of false reports in children. *Learning and Individual Differences, 9*, 289–319.

Bruer, John T. (1999). *The myth of the first three years: A new understanding of early brain development and lifelong learning*. New York: Free Press.

Bruner, Jerome S. (1982). The organization of action and the nature of adult-infant transaction. In M. von Cranach & R. Harre (Eds.), *The analysis of action*. Cambridge, England: Cambridge University Press.

Brunswick, Ann F., Messerie, Peta A., & Titus, Stephen P. (1992). Predictive factors in adult substance abuse: A prospective study of African-American adolescents. In Meyer Glantz & Roy Pickens (Eds.), *Vulnerability to drug abuse*. Washington, DC: American Psychological Association.

Bryan, Janet, & Luszcx, Mary A. (1996). Speed of information processing as a mediator between age and free-recall performance. *Psychology and Aging, 11*, 3–9.

Byram, Michael. (1998). Cultural Identities in multilingual classrooms. In Jasone Cenoz & Fred Genesee (Eds.), *Beyond bilingualism: Multilingualism and multilingual education*. Clevedon, England: Multilingual Matters.

Bryant, W. Keith, & Zick, Cathleen D. (1996). An examination of parent-child shared time. *Journal of Marriage and the Family, 58*, 227–238.

Buchanan, Ann. (1996). *Cycles of child maltreatment: Facts, fallacies and interventions*. Chichester, England: Wiley.

Buckner, John C., Bassuk, Ellen L., Weinreb, Linda F., & Brooks, Margaret G. (1999). Homelessness and its relation to the mental health and behavior of low-income school-age children. *Developmental Psychology, 35*, 246–257.

Buhrmester, Duane. (1996). Need fulfillment, interpersonal competence, and the developmental contexts of early adolescent friendship. In William M. Bukowski, Andrew F. Newcomb, & Willard W. Hartup (Eds.) *The company they keep: Friendship in childhood and adolescence.* Cambridge, UK: Cambridge University Press.

Bukowski, William M., Newcomb, A.F., & Hartup, W.W. (Eds.). (1996). *The company they keep: Friendship in childhood and adolescence.* New York: Cambridge University Press.

Bukowski, William M., Sippola, Lorrie K., & Newcomb, Andrew F. (2000). Variations in patters of attraction to same- and other-sex peers during early adolescence. *Developmental Psychology, 36,* 147–154.

Bulmahn, Edelgard. (1999). Women in science in Germany. *Science, 286,* 2081.

Bunker, John P., Frazer, Howard S., & Mosteller, Frederick. (1995). The role of medical care in determining health: Creating an inventory of benefits. In Benjamin C. Amick, III, Sol Levine, Alvin R. Tarlov, & Diana Chapman Walsh (Eds.), *Society and health.* New York: Oxford University Press.

Burke, D.M., MacKay, D.G., Worthley, J.S., & Wade, E. (1991). On the tip of the tongue: What causes word finding failures in young and older adults? *Journal of Memory and Language, 30,* 542–579.

Burr, Jeffrey A. & Mutchler, Jan E. (1999). Race and ethnic variation in norms of filial responsibility among older persons. *Journal of Marriage and the Family, 61,* 674–687.

Burton, Linda M. (1995). Intergenerational patterns of providing care in African-American families with teenage childbearers: Emergent patterns in an ethnographic study. In Vern L. Bengtson, K. Warner Schaie, & Linda M. Burton (Eds.), *Adult intergenerational relations: Effects of societal change.* New York: Springer.

Bushnell, E.W., & Boudreau, J.P. (1993). Motor development and the mind: The potential role of motor abilities as a determinant of aspects of perceptual development. *Child Development, 64,* 1005–1021.

Buss, A.H. (1991). The EAS theory of temperament. In J. Strelau & A. Angleitner (Eds.), *Explorations of temperament.* New York: Plenum Press.

Buss, David M. (1994). *The evolution of desire: Strategies of human mating.* New York: Basic Books.

Buss, David M., Haselton, Martie G., Shackelford, Todd K., Bleske, April L., & Wakefield, Jerome C. (1998). Adaptations, exaptations, and spandrels. *American Psychologist, 53,* 533–548.

Busse, Ewald W. (1985). Normal aging: The Duke longitudinal studies. In M. Bergener, Marco Ermini, & H. B. Stahelin (Eds.), *Thresholds in aging.* London: Academic Press.

Bussey, K., & Bandura, A. (1992). Self-regulatory mechanisms governing gender development. *Child Development, 63,* 1236–1250.

Butler, Robert N., Lewis, Myrna, & Sunderland, Trey. (1991). *Aging and mental health: Positive psychosocial and biomedical holdings* (4th ed.). New York: Merrill.

Butler, Ruth. (1998). Age trends in the use of social and temporal comparison for self-evaluation: Examination of a novel developmental hypothesis. *Child Development, 69,* 1054–1073.

Byrd, Raobert S., Neistadt, Allyson, M., Howard, Cynthia R., Brownstein-Evans, Carol, & Weitzman, Michael. (1999). Why screen newborns for cocaine: Service patterns and social outcomes at age one year. *Child Abuse & Neglect, 23,* 523–530.

Cabrera, Natasha J., Tamis-LeMonda, Catherine S., Bradley, Robert H., Hofferth, Sandra, & Lamb, Michael E. (2000). Fatherhood in the twenty-first century. *Child Development, 71,* 127–136.

Cahalan, Don. (1991). *An ounce of prevention: Strategies for solving tobacco, alcohol, and drug problems.* San Francisco: Jossey-Bass.

Cairns, Robert B., & Cairns, Beverly D. (1994). *Lifelines and risks: Pathways of youth in our time.* Cambridge, England: Cambridge University Press.

Calkins, Susan D. (1994). Origins and outcomes of individual differences in emotional regulation. *Monographs of the Society for Research in Child Development, 59* (2–3, Serial No. 240), 53–72.

Calkins, Susan D., Fox, Nathan A., & Marshall, Timothy R. (1996). Behavioral and physiological antecedents of inhibited and uninhibited behavior. *Child Development, 67,* 523–540.

Callahan, Daniel. (1990). Afterword. In Paul Homer & Martha Holstein (Eds.), *A good old age?* New York: Simon & Schuster.

Camp, W. (1990). Participation in student activities and achievement: A covariance structural analysis. *Journal of Educational Research, 83,* 272–278.

Campbell, S.B. (1995). Behavior problems in preschool children: A review of recent research. *Journal of Psychology & Psychiatry & Allied Disciplines, 36,* 113–149.

Campos, Joseph J., Hiatt, Susan, Ramsay, Douglas, Henderson, Charlotte, & Svejda, Marilyn. (1978). The emergence of fear on the visual cliff. In Michael Lewis & Leonard A. Rosenblum (Eds.), *The development of affect.* New York: Plenum.

Canary, Daniel J. & Emmers-Sommer, Tara M. (1997). *Sex and gender differences in personal relationships.* New York: Guilford.

Canetto, Silvia Sara. (1992). Gender and suicide in the elderly. Suicide and Life-Threatening Behavior, 22, 80–96.

Cannon, Tyrone D., Rosso, Isabelle M., Bearden, Carrie E., Sanchez, Laura E., & Hadley, Trevor. (1999). A prospective cohort study of neurodevelopmental processes in the genesis and epigenesis of schizophrenia. *Development and Psychopathology, 11,* 467–485.

Cardon, L.R., Smity, S.D., Fulker, D.W., Kimberling, W.J., Pennington, B.R., & DeFries, J.C. (1994). Quantitative trait locus for reading disability on chromosome 6. *Science, 266,* 276–279.

Carlson, Bruce M. (1994). *Human embryology and developmental biology.* St. Louis, MO: Mosby.

Carlson, Karen J., Eisenstat, Stephanie A., & Ziporyn, Terra. (1996). The Harvard guide to women's health. Cambridge, MA: Harvard University Press.

Child Welfare League of America. (1996). Family Preservation Programs: State agency survey. In Michael R. Petit & Patrick A. Curtis, *Child abuse and neglect: A look at the states: The CWLA stat book*. Washington, DC: Child Welfare League of America.

Chisolm, Kim. (1998). A three year follow-up of attachment and indiscriminate friendliness in children adopted from Romanian orphanages. *Child Development, 69*, 1092–1106.

Chiu, H.F., Leung, T., Lam, L.C., Wing, Y.K., Chung, D.W., Li, S.W., Chi, I., Law, W.T., & Boey, K.W. (1999). Sleep problems in Chinese elderly in Hong Kong. *Sleep, 22*, 717–726.

Chiu, L.H. (1987). Child-rearing attitudes of Chinese, Chinese-American, and Anglo-American mothers. *International Journal of Psychology, 22*, 409–419.

Chmiel, Nik. (1998). *Jobs, technology and people*. London: Routledge.

Chomitz, Virginia Rall, Cheung, Lilian W.Y., & Lieberman, Ellice. (1995). The role of lifestyle in preventing low birth weight. *The Future of Children: Low Birth Weight, 5*, 121–138.

Chomsky, Noam. (1968). *Language and mind*. New York: Harcourt, Brace, World.

Chomsky, Noam. (1980). *Rules and representations*. New York: Columbia University Press.

Chorney, M.J., Chorney, K., Seese, N., Owen, M.J., Daniels, J., McGuffin, P., Thompson, L.A., Detterman, D.K., Benbow, C., Lubinski, D., Eley, T., & Plomin, R. (1998). A quantitative trait locus associated with cognitive ability in children. *Psychological Science, 3*, 159–166.

Christensen, H., Mackinnon, A.J., Korten, A.E., Jorm, A.F., Henderson, A.S., Jacomb, P., & Rodgers, B. (1999). An analysis of diversity in the cognitive performance of elderly community dwellers: Individual differences in change scores as a function of age. *Psychology of Aging, 14*, 365–379.

Cicchetti, Dante & Toth, Sheree L. (1998). Perspectives on research and practice in developmental psychopathology. In William Damon, Irving E. Sigel, & K. Ann Renninger (Eds.), *Handbook of Child Psychology, Volume Four: Child psychology in practice*. New York: Wiley.

Cicchetti, Dante, Toth, S.L., & Hennessy, K. (1993). Child maltreatment and school adaptation: Problems and promises. In Dante Cicchetti & S.L. Toth (Eds.), *Advances in applied developmental psychology series: Vol. 8. Child abuse, child development, and social policy*. Norwood, NJ: Ablex.

Cicirelli, Victor G. (1995). *Sibling relationships across the life span*. New York: Plenum Press.

Clark, Tim, & Rees, John. (1996). *Practical management of asthma*. London: Martin Dunitz.

Clark, William R. (1999). *A means to an end: The biological basis of aging and death*. New York: Oxford University Press.

Clarke-Stewart, K. Alison. (1989). Infant day care: Maligned or malignant? *American Psychologist, 44*, 266–273.

Clayton, R.R., Cattarello, A.M., & Johnstone, B.M.(1996). The effectiveness of Drug Abuse Resistance Education (Project DARE): 5-year follow-up results. *Preventive Medicine, 25*, 307–318.

Clinchy, Blythe McVicker. (1993). Ways of knowing and ways of being: Epistemological and moral development in undergraduate women. In Andrew Garrod (Ed.), *Approaches to moral development: New research and emerging themes*. New York: Teachers College Press.

Cloutier, Richard, & Jacques, Christian. (1997) Evolution of residential custody arrangements in separated families: A longitudinal study. In Craig A. Everett (Ed.), *Child custody: Legal decisions and family outcomes*. New York: Haworth Press.

Cnattingius, Sven, & Haglund, Bengt. (1997). Decreasing smoking prevalence during pregnancy in Sweden: The effect on small-for-gestational-age births. *American Journal of Public Health, 87*, 410–413.

Cobb, Paul, Wood, Terry, & Yackel, Erna. (1993). Discourse, mathematical thinking and classroom practice. In Ellice A. Forman, Norris Minick, & C. Addison Stone (Eds.), *Contexts for learning*. New York: Oxford University Press.

Cochran, Susan D., Mays, Vickie. (2000). Lifetime prevalence of suicide symptoms and affective disorders among men reporting same-sex sexual partners: Results from NHANES III. *American Journal of Public Health, 90*, 573–578.

Coelho, Elizabeth. (1991). Social integration of immigrant and refugee children. In J. Porter (Ed.), *New Canadian voices*. Toronto: Wall & Emerson.

Coffey, C., Wilkinson, W., Paraskos, I., Soady, S., Sullivan, R., Patterson, L., Figiel, W., Webb, M., Spritzer, C., & Djang, W. (1992). Quantitative cerebral anatomy of the aging human brain: A cross-sectional study using magnetic resonance imaging. *Neurology, 42*, 527–536.

Cohen Deborah, Spear, Suzanne, Scribner, Richard, Kissinger, Patty, Mason, Karen, & Wildgen, John. (2000). "Broken windows" and the risk of gonorrhea. *American Journal of Public Health, 90*, 230–236.

Cohen, G. (1993). Memory and aging. In G.M. Davies & R.H. Logie (Eds.) *Memory in everyday life*. Amsterdam, North Holland: Elsevier Science Publishers.

Cohen, G. (1999). Aging and autobiographical memory. In C.P. Thompson, D.J. Herrmann, D. Bruce, J.D. Read, D.G. Payne, & M.P. Toglia (Eds.), *Autobiographical memory: Theoretical and applied perspectives*. Hillsdale, NJ: Erlbaum.

Cohen, L.B., & Oakes, L.M. (1993). How infants perceive a simple causal event. *Developmental Psychology, 29*, 421–433.

Cohen, Leslie B. & Amsel, Geoffrey. (1998). Precursors to infants' perception of the causality of a simple event. *Infant Behavior & Development, 21*, 713–731.

Cohn, Jeffrey F., & Tronick, Edward Z. (1983). Three-month-old infants' reaction to stimulated maternal depression. *Child Development, 54*, 185–193.

Cohn, Lawrence D.S., & Adler, Nancy E. (1992). Female and male perception of ideal body shapes. *Psychology of Women Quarterly, 16*, 69–79.

Coie, John D., & Cillessen, A.H.N. (1993). Peer rejection: Origins and effects on children's development. *Current Directions in Psychological Science, 2*, 89–92.

Coie, J.D., & Dodge, K.A. (1998). Aggression and antisocial behavior. In Damon, William (Ed.), *Handbook of child psychology, Volume 3: Social, emotional, and personality development.* New York: Wiley.

Coker, Ann L., Smith, Paige Hall, McKeown, Robert E., & King, Melissa J. (2000). Frequency and correlates of intimate partner violence by type: Physical, sexual, and psychological battering. *American Journal of Public Health, 90,* 553–559.

Cole, David A., Martin, Joan M. Peeke, Lachlan A., Seroczynski, A.D., & Fier, Jonathan. (1999). Children's over- and underestimation of academic competence: A longitudinal study of gender differences, depression, and anxiety. *Child Development, 70,* 459–473.

Cole, Michael. (1996). *Cultural psychology: A once and future discipline.* Cambridge, MA: Belknap Press.

Cole, M., Gay, J., Glick, J., & Sharp, C.W. (1971). *The cultural context of learning and thinking.* New York: Basic Books.

Cole, Pamela M., Barrett, Karen C., & Zahn-Waxler, Carolyn. (1992). Emotion displays in two-year-olds during mishaps. *Child Development, 63,* 314–324.

Coleman, J.C., & Hendry, L. (1990). *The nature of adolescence* (2nd ed.). London: Routledge.

Coles, Robert. (1990). *The spiritual life of children.* Boston: Houghton Mifflin.

Coles, Robert. (1997). *How to raise a moral child: The moral intelligence of children.* New York: Random House.

Colin, Virginia L. (1996). *Human attachment.* Philadelphia: Temple University Press.

Collinge, John, Sidle, Katie C., Meads, Julie, Ironside, James, & Hill, Andrew F. (1996). Molecular analysis of prion strain variation and the aetiology of "new variant" CJD. Nature (London) 383, 685–690.

Collins, W. Andrew. (1990). Parent-child relationships in the transition to adolescence: Continuity and change in interaction, affect, and cognition. In R. Montemayor, G. Adams, & T. Gullotta (Eds.), *From childhood to adolescence: A transitional period? Advances in adolescent development: Vol. 2. The transition from childhood to adolescence.* Beverly Hills, CA: Sage.

Collins, W. Andrew, Maccoby, Eleanor E., Steinberg, Laurence, Hetherington, E.Mavis, & Bronstein, Marc H. (2000). Contemporary research on parenting: The case for nature and nurture. *American Psychologist, 55,* 218–232.

Collopy, Bart, Boyle, Philip, & Jennings, Bruce. (1991, March–April). New directions in nursing home ethics. *Hastings Center Report, 21,* 1–15 (Special Supplement).

Colonia-Willner, Regina. (1998). Practical intelligence at work: Relationship between aging and cognitive efficiency among managers in a bank environment. *Psychology and Aging, 13,* 45–57.

Commission on the Restructuring of the American High School. (1996). *Breaking ranks: Changing an American institution.* Reston, VA: National Association of Secondary School Principles.

Compas, Bruce E., Banez, Gerard A., Malcarne, Vanessa, & Worsham, Nancy. (1991). Perceived control and coping with stress: A developmental perspective. *Journal of Social Issues, 47,* 23–34.

The Condition of Education (1991). See United States Department of Education.

Coni, Nicholas K., Davison, William, & Webster, Stephen. (1992). *Aging: The facts.* Oxford, England: Oxford University Press.

Connidis, I.A. (1994). Sibling support in older age. *Journal of Gerontology: Social Sciences, 49,* S309–S317.

Conner, David B., Knight, Danica K., & Cross, David R. (1997). Mothers' and fathers' scaffolding of their two-year-olds during problem-solving and literacy interactions. *British Journal of Developmental Psychology, 15,* 323–338.

Conrad, Marilyn, & Hammen, Constance. (1993). Protective and resource factors in high- and low-risk children: A comparison of children with unipolar, bipolar, medically ill, and normal mothers. *Development and Psychopathology, 5,* 593–607.

Constable, Catherine. (1987). Talking with teachers. Increasing our relevance as language interventionists in the schools. *Seminars in Speech & Lanugage, 8,* 345–356.

Constantine, L.L. (1986). *Family paradigms: The practice of theory in family therapy.* New York: Guilford.

Constantine, L.L. (1993). The structure of family paradigms: An analytical model of family variation. *Journal of Marital and Family Therapy, 19,* 39–70.

Cookson, William O.C.M., & Moffatt, Miriam F. (1997). Asthma: An epidemic in the absence of infection? *Science, 275,* 41–42.

Coontz, Stephanie (Ed.) (1998). *American families: A multicultural reader.* New York: Routledge.

Cooper, Richard, Rotime, Charles, Ataman, Susan, McGee, Daniel, Osotimehin, Babatunde, Kadiri, Soloman, Muna, Walinjom, Kingue, Samuel, Fraser, Henry, Forrester, Terrence, Bennett, Franklyn, & Wilks, Rainford. (1997). The prevalence of hypertension in seven populations of West African Origin. *American Journal of Public Health, 87,* 160–168.

Cooper, Ralph L., Goldman, Jerome M., & Harbin, Thomas J. (1991). *Aging and environmental toxicology.* Baltimore: Johns Hopkins University Press.

Cooper, R.O. (1993). The effect of prosody on young infants' speech perception. In C. Rovee-Collier & L.P. Lipsitt (Eds.), *Advances in infancy research* (Vol. 8). Norwood, NJ: Ablex.

Cooper-Hilert, Beth. (1998). *Infertility and involuntary childlessness: Helping couples cope.* New York: W.W. Norton.

Corter, Carl M., & Fleming, Alison S. (1995). Psychobiology of maternal behavior in human beings. In Marc H. Bornstein (Ed.), *Handbook of parenting: Biology and ecology of parenting.* Mahwah, NJ: Erlbaum.

Corti, Maria-Chiara, Guralnik, Jack M., Ferrucci, Luigi, Ismirlian, Grant, Leveille, Suzanne G., Pahor, Marco, Cohen, Harvey J., Pieper, Carl, & Havlik, Richard J. (1999). Evidence for a black-white crossover in all-cause and coronary heart disease mortality in an older population: The North Carolina EPESE. *American Journal of Public Health, 89,* 308–314.

Cosby, Ennis, quoted in Chua-Eoan, Howard. (1997, January 27.) He was my hero. *Time Magazine*, 149.

Costa, P. T., Jr., & McCrae, P. R. (1999). NEO personality inventory. In A. E. Kazdira (Ed.), *Encyclopedia of psychology*. Washington, DC: American Psychological Association.

Cotman, Carl W., & Neeper, Shawne. (1996). Activity-dependent plasticity and the aging brain. In Edward L. Schneider & John W. Rowe (Eds.), *Handbook of the biology of aging* (4th ed.). San Diego: Academic Press.

Cotten, N.U., Resnick, J., Browne, D.C., Martin, S.L., McCarraher, D.R., & Woods, J. (1994). Aggression and fighting behavior among African-American adolescents: Individual and family factors. *American Journal of Public Health, 84*, 618–622.

Council of Economic Advisors. (1999). *Changing America: Indicators of social and economic well-being by race and Hispanic origin*. Washington DC: Council of Economic Advisors.

Courtney, Mark E. (1998) The costs of child protection in the context of welfare reform. *The Future of Children: Protecting Children from Abuse and Neglect, 8*, 88–103.

Cowan, Nelson. (Ed.). (1997). *The development of memory in childhood*. Hove, East Sussex, UK: Psychology Press.

Cowan Philip, Cowan, Carolyn Pope, & Schulz, Marc S. (1996). Thinking about risk and resilience in families. In E. Mavis Hetherington & Elaine A. Blechman (Eds.), *Stress, coping, and resiliency in children and families*. Mahwah, NJ: Erlbaum.

Coward, Raymond T., Horne, Claydell, & Dwyer, Jeffrey W. (1992). Demographic perspectives on gender and family-caregiving. In Jeffrey W. Dwyer & Raymond T. Coward (Eds.), *Gender, families and elder care*. Newbury Park, CA: Sage.

Craik, Fergus I. M. (1999). Memory, aging, and the survey instrument. *Cognition and Aging*.

Cramer, Duncan. (1998). *Close relationships: The study of love and friendship*. London: Arnold.

Creasy, Robert K. (Ed.). (1997). *Management of labor and delivery*. Malden, MA: Blackwell Science.

Crick, N.R., & Grotpeter, J.K. (1996). Children's treatment by peers: Victims of relational and overt aggression. *Development and Psychopathology, 8*, 367–380.

Crick, Nicki R., Casas, Juan F. & Ku, Hyon-Chin. (1999). Relational and physical forms of peer victimization in preschool. *Child Development, 35*, 376–385.

Crimmins, E.M., & Ingegneri, D.G. (1990). Interaction and living arrangements of older parents and their children: Past trends, present determinants, future implications. *Research on Aging, 2*, 3–35.

Cristofalo, Vincent J. (1996). Ten years later: What have we learned about human aging from studies of cell cultures? *Gerontologist, 36*, 737–741.

Crittenden, Patricia McKinsey. (1995). Attachment and psychopathology. In Susan Goldberg, Roy Muir, & John Kerr (Eds.), *Attachment theory: social, developmental, and clinical perspectives*. Hillsdale, NJ: Analytic Press.

Crittenden, Patricia M., Claussen, Angelika H., & Sugarman, David B. (1994). Physical and psychological maltreatment in middle childhood and adolescence. *Development and Psychopathology, 6*, 145–164.

Crockenberg, S., & Litman, C. (1990). Autonomy as competence in 2-year-olds: Maternal correlates of child defiance, compliance, and self-assertion. *Developmental Psychology, 26*, 961–971.

Cross, S., & Markus, H. (1991). Possible selves across the lifespan. *Human Development, 34*, 230–255.

Crouter, Ann C. Bumpus, Matthew F., Maguire, Mary C., & McHale, Susan M. (1999). Linking parents' work pressure and adolescents' well-being: Insights into dynamics in dual-earner families. *Developmental Psychology, 35*, 1453–1461.

Crowell, Judith A., Waters, Everett, Treboux, Dominique, O'Connor, Elizabeth, Colon-Downs, Christina, Feider, Olga, Golby, Barbara, & Posada, German. (1996). Discriminant validity of the adult attachment interview. *Child Development, 67*, 2584–2599.

Crystal, Stephen. (1996). Economic status of the elderly. In Robert H. Binstock & Linda K. George (Eds.), *Handbook of aging and the social sciences*. San Diego: Academic Press.

Csikszentmihalyi, Mihaly. (1996). *Creativity*. New York: HarperCollins.

Csikszentmihalyi, M., Rathunde, K., & Whalen, S. (1993). *Talented teenagers: The roots of success and failure*. Cambridge: Cambridge University Press.

Cummings, E., & Henry, W. (1961). *Growing old: The process of disengagement*. New York: Basic Books.

Curtis, P.A., Boyd, J.D., Liepold, M., et al. (1995). *Child abuse and neglect: A look at the states: The CWLA stat book*. Washington, DC: Child Welfare League of America.

Czech, Christian, Teemp, Günter, & Pradier, Laurent. (2000). Presenilinst Alzheimer's disease: Biological functions and pathogenic mechanism. *Neurobioloby, 60*, 363–384.

Daniluk, Judith C. (1998). *Women's sexuality across the lifespan: Challenging myths, creating meanings*. New York: Guilford.

Darling, N., & Steinberg, L. (1993). Parenting style as context: An integrative model. *Psychological Bulletin, 113*, 487–496.

Dash, L. (1986, January 26). Children's children: The crisis up close. *The Washington Post*, A1, A12.

Datan, Nancy. (1986). Oedipal conflict, platonic love: Centrifugal forces in intergenerational relations. In Nancy Datan, Anita L. Greene, & Hayne W. Reese (Eds.), *Life-span developmental psychology: Intergenerational relations*. Hillsdale, NJ: Erlbaum.

D'Augelli, A.R., & Hershberger, S.L. (1993). Lesbian, gay and bisexual youth in community settings: Personal challenges and mental health problems. *American Journal of Community Psychology, 21*, 421–448.

Davajan, Val, & Israel, Robert. (1991). Diagnosis and medical treatment of infertility. In Annette L. Stanton & Christine Dunkel-Schetter (Eds.), *Infertility*. New York: Plenum Press.

Davidson, Philip W., Cain, Nancy N., Sloane-Reeves, Jean E., & Van Speybroech, Alec. (1994). Characteristics of community-based individuals with mental retardation and aggressive behavioral disorders. *American Journal of Mental Retardation, 98,* 704–716.

Davies, A. Michael. (1991). Function in old age: Measurement, comparability, and service planning. Proceedings of the 1988 International Symposium on Aging (DHHS Publication No. 91–1482) (Series 5, No. 6). Hyattsville, MD: Department of Health and Human Services.

Davis-Floyd, Robbie E. (1992). *Birth as an American rite of passage.* Berkeley: University of California Press.

Day, James M., & Naedts, Myriam H.L. (1999). Moral and religious judgment research. In Ralph L. Mosher, Deborah J. Youngman, & James M. Day (Eds.), *Human development across the life span.* Westport, CN: Praeger.

de Beauvoir, Simone. (1964). *Force of circumstances* (Richard Howard, Trans.). New York: Putnam.

Deeg, Dorly J.H., Kardaun, Jan W.P.F., & Fozard, James L. (1996). Health, behavior, and aging. In James E. Birren & K. Warner Schaie (Eds.), *Handbook of the psychology of aging.* San Diego: Academic Press.

DeFries, John C., Plomin, Robert, & Fulker, David W. (Eds.). (1994). *Nature and nurture during middle childhood.* Cambridge, MA: Blackwell.

DeGarmo, David S., & Kitson, Gay C. (1996). Identity relevance and disruption as predictors of psychological distress for widowed and divorced women. *Journal of Marriage and the Family, 58,* 983–997.

Degirmencioglu, Serdar M., Urberg, Kathryn A., Tolson, Jerry M., & Richard, Protima. (1998). Adolescent friendship networks: Continuity and change over the school year. *Merrill-Palmer Quarterly, 44,* 313–337.

DeKeseredy, Walter S., & Schwartz, Martin D. (1998). *Women abuse on campus: Results from the Canadian National Survey.* Thousand Oaks, CA: Sage.

Delpit, Lisa. (1995). *Other people's children: Cultural conflict in the classroom.* New York: New Press.

DeMan, A.F. (1999). Correlates of suicide ideation in high school students: The importance of depression. *Journal of Genetic Psychology, 160,* 105–116.

Demetriou, Andreas, & Raftopoulos, Athanassios. (1999). Modeling the developing mind: From structure to change. *Developmental Review, 19,* 319–368.

DeMay, Langha, Baartman, Herman E.M., Schulze, Hans-J. (1999). Ethnic variation and the development of moral judgment of youth in Dutch society. *Youth and Society, 31,* 54–75.

Demo, D.H., & Acock, A.C. (1986). Family structure, family process, and adolescent well-being. *Journal of Research on Adolescence, 6,* 457–488.

Dempster, Frank N. (1993). Resistance to interference: Developmental changes in a basic processing mechanism. In M. L. Howe and R. Pasnak (Eds.), *Emerging themes in cognitive development: Vol I. Foundations.* New York: Springer-Verlag.

Dennis, Wayne. (1966). Creative productivity between the ages of 20 and 80 years. *Journal of Gerontology, 21,* 1–8.

Dent-Read, Cathy, & Zukow-Goldring, Patricia. (1997). Introduction: Ecological realism, dynamic systems, and epigenetic systems approaches to development. In Cathy Dent-Read & Patricia Zukow-Goldring (Eds.), *Evolving explanations of development.* Washington, DC: American Psychological Association.

DeRaad, Boele, Perugini, Marco, Hrebickova, Martina, & Szarota, Piotr. (1998). Lingua Franca of personality; taxonomies and structures based on the psychological approach. *Journal of Cross-Cultural Psychology, 29,* 212–232.

Derix, Mayke. (1994). *Neuropsychological differentiation of dementia syndromes.* Berwyn, PAQ: Lisse.

Derochers, Stephen, Ricard, Marcelle, Dexarie, Therese Gouin, & Allard, Louise. (1994). Developmental syncronicity between social referencing and Piagetian sensorimotor causality. *Infant Behavior and Development, 17,* 303–309.

de Róiste, A. & Bushnell, I.W.R. (1996). Tactile stimulation: Short- and long-term benefits for pre-term infants. *British Journal of Developmental Psychology, 14,* 41–53.

Desruisseaux, Paul (1998, December 4) U.S. trails 22 nations in high-school competition. *The Chronicle of Higher Education,* A45.

Detzner, Daniel F. (1996). No place without a home: Southeast Asian grandparents in refugee families. *Generations, 20,* 45–48.

Deutsch, Helene. (1944–1945). *The psychology of women: A psychoanalytic interpretation (Vol. 2).* New York: Grune & Stratton.

Deveraux, Lara L. & Hammerman, Ann Jackoway. (1998). *Infertility and Identity: New strategies for treatment.* San Francisco: Jossey-Bass Publishers.

Dewey, Kathryn G., Heinig, M. Jane, & Nommsen-Rivers, Laurie A. (1995). Differences in morbidity between breast-fed and formula-fed infants. *Journal of Pediatrics, 126,* 696–702.

DeWolff, Marianne S. & van Ijzendoorn, Mariuns H. (1997). Sensitivity and attachment: A meta-analysis on parental antecedents of infant attachment. *Child Development, 68,* 571–591.

de Vries, Brian (Ed.). (1999). *End of life issues: Interdisciplinary and multidimensional perspectives.* New York: Springer.

Diamond, A. (1990). Neuropsychological insights into the meaning of object concept development. In S. Carey & R. Gelman (Eds.), *The epigenesis of mind: Essays on biology and cognition.* Hillsdale, NJ: Erlbaum.

Diamond, Adele, Prevor, Meredith B., Callender, Glenda, & Druin, Donald P. (1997). Prefrontal cortex cognitive deficits in children treated early and continuously for PKU. *Monographs of the Society for Research in Child Development, 62* (Serial No. 252).

Diamond, Marion Cleeves. (1988). *Enriching heredity.* New York: Free Press.

Diaz, Rafael M. (1987). The private speech of young children at risk: A test of three deficit hypotheses. *Early Childhood Research Quarterly, 2,* 181–197.

Dickerson, Leah J., & Nadelson, Carol (Eds.). (1989). *Family violence: Emerging issues of national crisis*. Washington, DC: American Psychiatric Press.

Diekstra, Rene. (1995). Depression and suicidal behaviors in adolescence: Sociocultural and time trends. The positive effects of schooling. In Michael Rutter (Ed.), *Psychosocial disturbances in young people: Challenges for prevention*. Cambridge, England: Cambridge University Press.

Diekstra, Rene F.W., Kienhorst, C.W.M., & Witde, E.J. (1995). Suicide and suicidal behavior among adolescents. In Michael Rutter & David J. Smith (Eds.), *Psychosocial disorders in young people: Time trends and their causes*. New York: Published for Academia Europaea by J. Wiley.

Dietz, T.L. (1998). An examination of violence and gender role portrayals in video games: Implications for gender socialization and aggressive behavior. *Sex Roles, 38,* 425–442.

Dietz, William H. (1995). Childhood obesity. In Lilian W.Y. Cheung & Julius B. Richmond (Eds.), *Child health, nutrition, and physical activity*. Champaign, IL: Human Kinetics.

Dietz, William H. (1999). Barriers to the treatment of childhood obesity: A call to action. *Journal of Pediatrics, 134,* 535–536.

Digman, J.M. (1990). Personality structure: Emergence of the five-factor model. *Annual Review of Psychology, 41,* 417–440.

DiPietro, Janet A., Hodgson, Denice M., Costigan, Kathleen A., & Hilton, Sterling C. (1996). Fetal neurobehavioral development. *Child Development, 67,* 2553–2567.

Dishion, Thomas J., Andrews, David W., & Crosby, Lynn. (1995). Antisocial boys and their friends in early adolescence: Relationship characteristics, quality, and interactional processes. *Child Development, 66,* 139–151.

Dittmann-Kohli, Freya, & Baltes, Paul B. (1990). Toward a neofunctionalist conception of adult intellectual development: Wisdom as a prototypical case of intellectual growth. In Charles N. Alexander & Ellen J. Langer (Eds.), *Higher stages of human development*. New York: Oxford University Press.

Dixon, Roger A. (1992). Contextual approaches to adult intellectual development. In Robert J. Sternberg & Cynthia A. Berg (Eds.), *Intellectual development*. New York: Cambridge University Press.

Dixon, Roger A. (1999). The concept of gains in cognitive aging. In Norbert, Schwarz, Denise C. Park, Knauper, Barbel, & Seymour Sudman (Eds.). *Cognition, aging, and self-reports*. Philadelphia: Psychology Press.

Dixon, Roger A. & Lerner, Richard M. (1999). History and systems in developmental psychology. In Marc H. Bornstein & Michael E. Lamb (Eds.), *Developmental psychology: An advanced textbook*. Mahway, NJ: Erlbaum.

Dixon, Wallace E., Jr., & Shore, Cecilia. (1997). Temperamental predictors of linguistic style during multiword acquisition. *Infant Behavior & Development, 20,* 93–98.

Djerassi, Carl. (1999). Sex in an age of mechanical reproduction. *Science, 285,* 53–54.

Donovan, Patricia. (1997). Can statutory rape laws be effective in preventing adolescent pregnancy? *Family Planning Perspectives, 29,* 30–34, 40.

Dovidio, John F., & Gaertner, Samuel L. (1999). Reducing prejudice: Combating intergroup biases. *Current Directions in Psychological Science, 8,* 101–104.

Downey, Douglas B., Ainsworth-Darnell, James W., & Dufur, Mikaela J. (1998). Sex of parent and children's well-being in single-parent households. *Journal of Marriage and the Family, 60,* 878–893.

Downs, A. Chris. (1990). The social biological constraints of social competency. In Thomas P. Gullotta, Gerald R. Adams, & Raymond R. Montemayor (Eds.), *Developing social competency in adolescence*. Newbury Park, CA: Sage.

Drake, Brett, & Zuravin, Susan. (1998). Bias in child maltreatment reporting: Revisiting the myth of classlessness. *American Journal of Orthopsychiatry, 68,* 295–304.

Dreyer, Philip H. (1994). Designing curricular identity interventions. In Sally L. Archer (Ed.), *Interventions for adolescent identity development*. Thousand Oaks, CA: Sage.

Drobnic, Sonia, Blossfeld, Hans-Peter, & Rohwer, Gotz. (1999). Dynamics of women's employment patterns over the family life course: A comparison of the United States and Germany. *Journal of Marriage and the Family, 61,* 133–146.

DSM IV. See American Psychological Association.

Dubas, Judith Semon, Graber, Julia A., & Petersen, Anne C. (1991). A longitudinal investigation of adolescents' changing perceptions of pubertal timing. *Developmental Psychology, 27,* 580–586.

Dubler, Nancy Neveloff. (1993). Commentary: Balancing life and death—proceed with caution. *American Journal of Public Health, 83,* 23–25.

du Bois-Reymond, Manuela. (1995). The role of parents in the transition period of young people. In Manuel du Bois-Reymond, Rene Diekstra, Klaus Hurrelmann, & Els Peters (Eds.), *Childhood and youth in Germany and the Netherlands: Transitions and coping strategies of adolescents*. Berlin: Mouton de Gruyter.

Dudek, Stephanie Z., Strobel, M.G., & Runco, Mark A. (1994). Cumulative and proximal influences on the social environment and children's creative potential. *Journal of Genetic Psychology, 154,* 487–499.

Duggan, Anne K., McFarlane, Elizabeth C., Windham, Amy M., Rohde, Charles A., Salkever, David S., Fuddy, Loretta, Rosenberg, Leon A., Buchbinder, Sharon B., & Sia, Calvin C.J. (1999). Evaluation of Hawaii's healthy start program. *The Future of Children, 9,* 66–90.

Duncan, Greg J., & Brooks-Gunn, Jeanne. (Eds). (1997). *Consequences of growing up poor*. New York: Russell Sage Foundation.

Duncan, Greg J. & Brooks-Gunn, Jeanne. (2000). Family poverty, welfare reform, and child development. *Child Development, 71,* 188–196.

Dunn, Judy, Bretherton, I., & Munn, P. (1987). Conversations about feeling states between mothers and their young children. *Developmental Psychology, 23,* 132–139.

Dunphy, Dexter C. (1963). The social structure of urban adolescent peer groups. *Sociometry, 26,* 230–246.

Durick, Kyle, Mendekin, John, & Xanthopoulos, Kleanthis C. (1999). Hunting with traps: Genome wide strategies for gene discovery and functional analysis. *9,* 1019–1025.

Durlak, Joseph A. (1997). *Successful programs for children and adolescents.* New York: Plenum Press.

Durlak, Joseph A. (1998). Common risk and protective factors in successful prevention programs. *American Journal of Orthopsychiatry, 68,* 512–520.

Durrant, Joan E. (1996). Public attitudes toward corporal punishment in Canada. In Detlev Frehsee, Wiebke Horn, & Kai-D. Bussmann (Eds.), *Family violence against children: A challenge for society.* Berlin: De Gruyter.

Duster, Troy. (1999). The social consequences of genetic disclosure. In Ronald A. Carson & Mark A. Rothstein (Eds.), *Behavioral genetics: The clash of culture and biology.* Baltimore: Johns Hopkins Press

Duthie, Garry G. & Bellizzi, Mary C. (1999). Effect of antioxidents on vascular health. *British Medical Bulletin, 55,* 568–577.

Dutton, Donald G. (1992). Theoretical and empirical perspectives on the etiology and prevention of wife assault. In Ray D. Peters, Robert J. McMahon, & Vernon L. Quinsey (Eds.), *Aggression and violence throughout the lifespan.* Newbury Park: Sage.

Dweck, Carol S. (1999). *Self-theories: Their role in motivation, personality, and development.* Philadelphia: Psychology Press.

Dykens, Elisabeth M., Hodapp, Robert M., & Leckman, James F. (1994). *Behavior and development in fragile X syndrome.* Thousand Oaks, CA: Sage.

Dykman, Roscoe, & Ackerman, Peggy T. (1993). Behavioral subtypes of attention deficit disorder. *Exceptional Children, 60,* 132–141.

Ebrahim, S. H., Suman, E.T., Floyd, R.L., Murphy, C.C., Bennett, E.M., & Boyle, C.A. (1998). Alcohol consumption by pregnant women in the United States during 1988–1995. *Obstetrics and Gynecology, 92,* 187–192.

Eccles, Jacquelynne S., Lord, Sarah, & Buchanan, Christy Miller. (1996). School transitions in early adolescence: What are we doing to our young people? In Julia A. Graber, Jeanne Brooks-Gunn, & Anne C. Pattersen (Eds.), *Transitions through adolescence: Interpersonal domains and context.* Mahwah, NJ: Erlbaum.

Eckenrode, J., Laird, M., & Doris, J. (1993). School performance and disciplinary problems among abused and neglected children. *Developmental Psychology, 29,* 53–62.

Edwards, Allen Jack. (1993). *Dementia.* New York: Plenum Press.

Edwards, John N. (1969). Familiar behavior as social exchange. *Journal of Marriage and the Family, 31,* 518–526.

Edwards, John R. (1994). *Multilingualism.* London: Routledge.

Egeland, Byron. (1993). A history of abuse is a major risk factor for abusing the next generation. In Richard J. Gelles & Donileen R. Loseke (Eds.), *Current controversies in family violence.* Newbury Park, CA: Sage.

Eimas, Peter D., Sigueland, Einar R., Jusczyk, Peter, & Vigorito, James. (1971). Speech perception in infants. *Science, 171,* 303–306.

Eisenberg, N. (1986). *Altruistic emotion, cognition, and behavior.* Hillsdale, NJ: Erlbaum.

Eisenberg, Nancy, & Fabes, Richard A. (1992). Emotion, self-regulation, and the development of social competence. In M. S. Clark (Ed.), *Emotions and social behavior: Vol. 14, Review of personality and social psychology.* Newbury Park, CA: Sage.

Eisenberg, Nancy & Fabes, Richard A. (1998). Prosocial development. In Damon, William (Ed.), *Handbook of child psychology, Volume 3: Social, emotional, and personality development.* New York: Wiley.

Eisenberg, Nancy, Fabes, Richard A., & Murphy, Bridget C. (1996). Parents' reactions to children's negative emotions: Relations to children's social competence and comforting behavior. *Child Development, 67,* 2227–2247.

Eisenberg, Nancy, Fabes, Richard A., Shepard, Stephanie A., Murphy, Bridget C., Guthrie, Ivanna K., Jones, Sarah, Friedman, Jo, Poulin, Rick, & Maszk, Pat. (1997). Contemporaneous and longitudinal prediction of children's social functioning from regulation and emotionality. *Child Development, 68,* 642–664.

Elder, Glen H., Jr. (1998). Life course theory and human development. *Sociological Analysis, 1* (2), 1–12.

Elder, Glen H., Jr., Rudkin, Laura, & Conger, Rand D. (1995). Intergenerational continuity and change in rural America. In Vern L. Bengtson, K. Warner Schaie, & Linda M. Burton (Eds.), *Adult intergenerational relations: Effects of societal change.* New York: Springer.

Elder Abuse Project. (1991, October/November). Aging today. *American Society on Aging,* pp. 14–15.

Elderhostel. (2000). www.elderhostel.org.

Elias, Gordan, & Broerse, Jack. (1996). Developmental changes in the incidence and likelihood of simultaneous talk during the first two years: A question of function. *Journal of Child Language, 23,* 201–217.

Elkind, David. (1967). Egocentrism in adolescence. *Child Development, 38,* 1025–1034.

Elkind, David. (1984). *All grown up and no place to go.* Reading, MA: Addison-Wesley.

Emde, Robert N., Biringen, Z., Clyman, R.B., & Oppenheim, D. (1991). The moral self of infancy: Affective core and procedural knowledge. *Developmental Review, 11,* 251–270.

Emler, Nicholas. (1998). Sociomoral understanding. In Anne Campbell & Steven Muncer (Eds.), *The social child.* East Sussex, England: Psychology Press.

Emory, Eugene K., Schlackman, Lisa J., & Fiano, Kristin. (1996). Drug-hormone interactions on neurobehavioral responses in human neonates. *Infant Behavior & Development, 19*, 213–220.

Engle-Friedman, M. & Bootzin, R.R. (1991). Insomnia as a problem for the elderly. In P.A. Wisocki (Ed.), *Handbook of clinical behavior therapy with the elderly client*. New York: Plenum.

Engel, Susan. (1999). *Context is everything: The nature of memory*. New York: Freeman.

Enkin, Murray, Keirse, Marc J.N.C., & Chalmers, Iain. (1989). *Effective care in pregnancy and childbirth*. Oxford, England: Oxford University Press.

Ennett, S.T., Tobler, N.S., Ringwalt, C.L., & Flewelling, R.L. (1994). How effective is drug abuse resistance education? A meta-analysis of Project DARE outcome evaluations. *American Journal of Public Health, 84*, 1394–1401.

Epstein, M.A., Shaywitz, S.E., Shaywitz, B.A., & Woolston, J.L. (1991). The boundaries of attention deficit disorder. *Journal of Learning Disabilities, 2*, 78–86.

Erdley, Cynthia A., & Asher, Steven R. (1996). Children's social goals and self-efficacy perceptions as influences on their responses to ambiguous provocation. *Child Development, 67*, 1329–1344.

Ericsson, K. Anders. (1990). Peak performance and age: An examination of peak performance in sports. In Paul B. Baltes & Margret M. Baltes (Eds.), *Successful aging: Perspectives from the behavioral sciences*. Cambridge, England: Cambridge University Press.

Ericsson, K. Anders. (1996). The acquisition of expert performance. In K. Anders Eriksson (Ed.), *The road to excellence: The acquisition of expert performance in the arts and sciences, sports & games*. Mahwah, NJ: Erlbaum.

Erikson, Erik H. (1963). *Childhood and society* (2nd ed.). New York: Norton.

Erikson, Erik H. (1968). *Identity, youth, and crisis*. New York: Norton.

Erikson, Erik H., Erikson, Joan M., & Kivnick, Helen Q. (1986). *Vital involvement in old age*. New York: Norton.

Erwin, Phil. 1998. *Friendship in childhood and adolescence*. London: Routledge.

Eskenazi, Brenda, Prehn, Angela W., & Christianson, Roberta E. (1995). Passive and active maternal smoking as measured by serum cotinine: The effect on birthweight. *American Journal of Public Health, 85*, 395–398.

Espin, Oliva M. (1999). *Women crossing boundaries: A psychology of immigration and transformations of sexuality*. New York: Routledge.

Estes, Carroll L., Linkins, Karen W., & Binney, Elizabeth A. (1996). The political economy of aging. In Robert H. Binstock & Linda K. George (Eds.), *Handbook of aging and the social sciences*. San Diego: Academic Press.

Etaugh, Claire, & Liss, Marsha B. (1992). Home, school, and playroom: Training ground for adult gender roles. *Sex Roles, 26*, 129–147.

Eurostat. (2000). Data from *http://europa.eu.int/comm/eurostat /Public/datashop/print-catalogue/EN?catalogue=Eurostat*

Evans, David W., Leckman, James F., Carter, Alice, Reznick, J. Steven, Henshaw, Desiree, King, Robert A., & Pauls, David. (1997). Ritual, habit, and perfectionism: The prevalence and development of compulsive-like behavior in normal young children. *Child Development, 68*, 58–68.

Evans, Mark I., Belsky, Robin L., Greb, Anne, Clementino, Nancy, & Snyder, Frank N. (1989). Prenatal diagnosis of congenital malformation. In Mark I. Evans, Alan O. Dixler, John C. Fletcher, & Joseph D. Schulman (Eds.), *Fetal diagnosis and therapy: Science, ethics, and the law*. Philadelphia: Lippincott.

Eveleth, Phyllis B., & Tanner, James M. (1976). *Worldwide variation in human growth*. Cambridge, England: Cambridge University Press.

Eveleth, Phyllis B. & Tanner, James M. (1991). *Worldwide variation in human growth* (2nd ed.). Cambridge, England: Cambridge University Press.

Everaerd, Walter, Laan, Ellen T.M., Both, Stephanie, & van deer Velde, Janneke. (2000). Female sexuality. In Lenore T. Szuchman & Frank Muscarella (Eds.), *Psychological perspectives on human sexuality*. New York: Wiley.

Ewing, Charles Patrick. (1990). *Kids who kill*. Lexington, MA: Lexington Books.

Eyberg, Sheila M., Schulmann, Elena M., & Rey, Jannette. (1998). Child and adolescent psychotherapy research: Developmental issues. *Journal of Abnormal Child Psychology, 26*, 71–82.

Eyer, D. (1992). *Maternal-infant bondings: A scientific fiction*. New Haven, CT: Yale University Press.

Faberow, Norman L. (1994). Preparatory and prior suicidal behavior factors. In Edwin S. Schneidman, Norman L. Faberow, & Robert E. Litman (Eds.), *The psychology of suicide* (rev. ed.). Northwale, NJ: Aronson.

Fabes, R.A. (1994). Physiological, emotional, and behavioral correlates of gender segregation. In C. Leaper (Ed.), *Childhood gender segregation: Causes and consequences*. San Francisco: Jossey-Bass.

Fackelmann, Kathy A. (1994). DNA dilemmas: Readers and experts weigh in on biomedical ethics. *Science News, 146*, 408–410.

Fadiman, Ann. (1997). *The spirit catches you and you fall down: A Hmong child, her American doctors, and the collision of two cultures*. New York: Farrar, Straus, and Giroux.

Fagot, Beverly. (1995). Parenting boys and girls. In Marc H. Bronstein (Ed.), *Handbook of parenting (Vol. 1): Children and parenting*. Mahwah, NJ: Erlbaum.

Fagot, Beverly. (1997). Attachment, parenting, and peer interactions of toddler children. *Developmental Psychology, 33*, 489–499.

Fagot, Beverly I., & Leinbach, M.D. (1993). Gender-role development in young children: From discriminating to labeling. *Developmental Review, 13*, 205–224.

Fagot, Beverly I., Leinbach, Mary D., & O'Boyle, C. (1992). Gender labeling, gender stereotyping, and parenting behaviors. *Developmental Psychology, 28*, 225–230.

Fagot, Beverly I., Pears, Katherine C., Capaldi, Deborah M., Crosby, Lynn et al. (1998). Becoming an adolescent father: Precursors and parenting. *Developmental Psychology, 34*, 1209–1219.

Fairburn, Christopher G., & Wilson, G. Terence. (Eds). (1993). *Binge eating: Nature, assessment and treatment.* New York: Guilford.

Falbo, T., & Poston, D.L. (1993). The academic, personality, and physical outcomes of only children in China. *Child Development, 64*, 18–35.

Falk, Ruma & Wilkening, Freidrich. (1998). Children's construction of fair chances: Adjusting probabilities. *Developmental Psychology, 23*, 1340–1357.

Farkas, Janice I., & Hogan, Dennis P. (1995). The demography of changing intergenerational relationships. In Vern L. Bengtson, K. Warner Schaie, & Linda M. Burton (Eds.), *Adult intergenerational relations: Effects of societal change.* New York: Springer.

Farrar, M.J. (1992). Negative evidence and grammatical morpheme acquisition. *Developmental Psychology, 28*, 90–98.

Farrington, David P. (1994). Interactions between individual and contextual factors in the development of offending. In Rainer K. Silbereisen and Eberhard Todt (Eds.), *Adolescence in context: The interplay of family, school, peers, and work in adjustment.* New York: Springer-Verlag.

Farver, Jo Ann M., & Frosch, Dominick L. (1996). L.A. stories: Aggression in preschoolers' spontaneous narratives after the riots of 1992. *Child Development, 67*, 19–32.

Fastenau, Philip S., Denburg, Natalie L., & Abeles, Norman. (1996). Age differences in retrieval: Further support for the resource-reduction hypothesis. *Psychology and Aging, 11*, 140–146.

Fehr, Beverley. (1993). How do I love thee . . . let me consult my prototype. In Steve Duck (Ed.), *Individuals in relationships (Vol. 1).* Newbury Park, CA: Sage.

Fehr, Beverley. (1996). *Friendship processes.* Thousand Oaks, CA: Sage.

Feij, Jan A., Whitely, William T., Diero, Jose M., & Taris, Tom W. (1995). The development of cancer enhancing strategies and content innovation: A longitudinal study of new workers. *Journal of Vocational Behavior, 46*, 231–256.

Feiring, Candice. (1996). Concepts of romance in 15-year-old adolescents. *Journal of Research on Adolescence, 6*, 181–200.

Feiring, Candice, & Lewis, Michael. (1989). The social network of girls and boys from early through middle childhood. In Deborah Belle (Ed.), *Children's social networks and social supports.* New York: Wiley.

Feldman, Ruth, Greenbaum, Charles W., Mayes, Linda C., & Erlich, Samuel H. (1997). Change in mother-infant interactive behavior: Relations to change in the mother, the infant, and the social context. *Infant Behavior & Development, 20*, 151–163.

Feldman, Ruth, Greenbaum, Charles W., & Yirmiya, Nurit. (1999). Mother-infant affect synchrony as an antecedent of the emergence of self-control. *Developmental Psychology, 35*, 3–19.

Felsenthal, G., Garrison, S.J., & Steinberg, F.U. (Eds.). (1994). *Rehabilitation of the aging patient.* Baltimore: Williams & Wilkins.

Fenson, Larry, Dale, Philip S., Resnick, J. Steven, Bates, Elizabeth, Thal, Donna J., & Petchick, Stephen J. (1994). Variability in early communicative development. *Monographs of the Society for Research in Child Development, 59* (Serial No. 242).

Ferguson, Charles A. (1977). Baby talk as a simplified register. In Catherine E. Snow & Charles A. Ferguson (Eds.), *Talking to children: Language input and requisition.* Cambridge, England: Cambridge University Press.

Ferguson, William G. L. (1997). Normal labor and delivery. In Robert K. Creasy (Ed.), *Management of labor and delivery.* Malden, MA: Blackwell Science.

Fergusson, David M., Horwood, L. John, Caspi, Avshalom, Moffitt, Terrie E., et al. (1996). The artefactual remission of reading disability: Psychometric lessons in the study of stability and change in behavioral development. *Developmental Psychology, 32*, 132–140.

Fergusson, David M., & Woodward, Lianne J. (1999). Maternal age and educational psychosocial outcomes in early adulthood. *Journal of Child Psychology & Psychiatry & Allied Disciplines, 40*, 479–489.

Fernald, A., & McRoberts, G. (in press). Prosaic bootstrapping A critical analysis of the argument and the evidence. In J.L. Morgan & K. Demuth (Eds.) *Signal to syntax.* Hillsdale, NJ: Erlbaum.

Fernald, Anne. (1993). Approval and disapproval: Infant responsiveness to vocal affect in familiar and unfamiliar languages. *Child Development, 64*, 657–674.

Fernald, Anne, & Mazzie, Claudia. (1991). Prosody and focus in speech to infants and adults. *Developmental Psychology, 27*, 209–221.

Fernald, Anne, & Morikawa, Hiromi. (1993). Common themes and cultural variations in Japanese and American mothers' speech to infants. *Child Development, 64*, 657–674.

Ferrari, Michel, & Sternberg, Robert J. (1998). The development of mental abilities and styles. In.William Damon, Deanna Kuhn & Robert S. Siegler (Eds.), *Handbook of Child Psychology, Volume Two: Cognition, perception, and language.* New York: Wiley.

Ferron, Christine. (1997). Body image in adolescence: Cross-cultural research. *Adolescence, 32*, 735–745.

Field, Tiffany M. (1987). Affective and interactive disturbances in infants. In Joy Doniger Osofsky (Ed.), *Handbook of infant development* (2nd ed.). New York: Wiley.

Field, Tiffany M. (1995). Infants of depressed mothers. *Infant Behavior and Development, 18*, 1–13.

Fifer, William P. & Moon, Chris M. (1995). The effects of fetal experience with sound. In Jean-Pierre Lecanuet, William P. Fifer, Norman A. Krasnegor, & William P. Smotherman (Eds.), *Fetal development: A psychobiological perspective.* Hillsdale, NJ: Erlbaum

Finch, Caleb E., & Tanzi, Rudolph E. (1997). Genetics of aging. *Science, 278*, 407–424.

Fingerman, Karen L. (1996). Sources of tension in the aging mother and adult daughter relationship. *Psychology and Aging, 11*, 591–606.

Finkel, Deborah, Pedersen, Nancy L., Plomin, Robert, & McClearn, Gerald E. (1998). Longitudinal and cross-sectional twin data on cognitive abilities in adulthood: The Swedish adoption/twin study of aging. *Developmental Psychology, 34*, 1400–1413.

Finkelhor, David. (1993). The main problem is still underreporting, not overreporting. In Richard J. Gelles & Donileen R. Loseke (Eds.), *Current controversies in family violence.* Newbury Park, CA: Sage.

Finkelhor, David. (1994). Current information on the scope and nature of child sexual abuse. *The Future of Children, 4*, 31–53.

Firth, Shirley. (1993). Approaches to death in Hindu and Sikh communities in Britain. In Donna Dickenson & Malcolm Johnson (Eds.), *Death, dying and bereavement.* London: Sage.

Firth, Shirley. (1993). Cross-cultural perspectives on bereavement. In Donna Dickenson & Malcolm Johnson (Eds.), *Death, dying and bereavement.* London: Sage.

Fiscella, K., Kitzman, H.J., Cole, R.E., Sidora, K., & Olds, D. (1998). Delayed first pregnancy among African-American adolescent smokers. *Journal of Adolescent Health, 23*, 232–237.

Fischer, Kurt W., Ayoub, Catherine, Sigh, Ilina, Noam, Gil, Maraganore, Andronicki, & Raya, Pamela. (1998). Psychopathology as adaptive development along distinctive pathways. *Development and Psychopathology, 9*, 749–779.

Fisher, Celia B. (1993). Integrating science and ethics in research with high-risk children and youth. *Society for Research in Child Development: Social Policy Report, 7* (4), 1–26.

Fisher, Celia B. (1999). Preparing successful proposals for institutional review boards: Challenges and prospects for developmental scientist. *Society for Research in Child Development, Newsletter, 42*, 7–9.

Fivush, R., & Hamond, N.R. (1990). Autobiographical memory across the preschool years: Toward reconceptualizing childhood amnesia. In R. Fivush & J.A. Hudson (Eds.), *Knowing and remembering in young children.* Cambridge, England: Cambridge University Press.

Flavell, John H. (1985). *Cognitive development* (2nd ed.). Englewood Cliffs, NJ: Prentice Hall.

Flavell, J.H. (1999). Cognitive development: Children's knowledge about the mind. *Annual Review of Psychology.*

Flavell, John H., Miller, P.H., & Miller, S.A. (1993). *Cognitive development* (3rd ed.). Englewood Cliffs, NJ: Prentice-Hall.

Flavell, John H., Green, Frances L., & Flavell, Eleanor R. (1995). Young children's knowledge about thinking. *Monographs of the Society for Research in Child Development, 60* (Serial no. 243).

Flavell, John H., Green, Frances L., Flavell, Eleanor R., & Grossman, James B. (1997). The development of children's knowledge about inner speech. *Child Development, 68*, 39–47.

Fletcher, Anne C., Darling, Nancy, & Steinberg, Laurence. (1995). Parental monitoring and peer influences on adolescent substance use. In Joan McCord (Ed.), *Coercion and punishment in long-term perspectives.* New York: Cambridge University Press.

Fleming, Alison S., & Corter, Carl M. (1995). Psychobiology of maternal behavior in nonhuman mammals. In Marc H. Bornstein (Ed.), *Handbook of parenting: Biology and ecology of parenting.* Mahwah, NJ: Erlbaum.

Flieller, Andre. (1999). Comparison of the development of formal thought in adolescent cohorts aged 10 to 15 years (1967–1996 and 1972–1993). *Develpomental Psychology, 35*, 1048–1958.

Flisher, Alan J. (1999). Mood disorder in suicidal children and adolescents: Recent developments. *Journal of Child Psychology & Psychiatry & Allied Disciplines, 40*, 315–324.

Flynn, James R. (1998). IQ gains over time toward finding the causes. In Ulric Neisser (Ed.) *The rising curve: Long term gains in IQ and related matters.* Washingdon DC: American Psychological Association.

Foley, D.J., Monjan, A.A., Brown, S.L., Simonsick, E.M., Wallace, R.B., & Blazer, D.G. (1995). Sleep complaints among elderly persons. *Sleep, 18*, 425–432.

Foley, Joseph M. (1992). The experience of being demented. In Robert H. Binstock, Stephen G. Post, & Peter J. Whitehouse (Eds.), *Dementia and aging: Ethics, values, and policy choices.* Baltimore: Johns Hopkins University Press.

Fonagy, Miriam Steele, Steele, Howard, Leigh, Tom, Kennedy, Roger, Mattoon, Gretta, & Target, Mary. (1995). The predictive specificity of the adult attachment interview and pathological emotional development. In Susan Goldberg, Roy Muir, & John Kerr (Eds.), *Attachment theory: Social, developmental, and clinical perspectives.* Hillsdale, NJ: Analytic Press.

Foster, Barbara A., Coffey, Heather A., Morin, Michel J., & Rastinejad, Farzan. (1999). Pharmacological Rescue of Mutant p53 Conformation and Function. *Science, 286*, 2507–2510.

Fowler, James W. (1981). *Stages of faith: The psychology of human development and the quest for meaning.* New York: Harper & Row.

Fowler, James W. (1986). Faith and the structuring of meaning. In Craig Dykstra & Sharon Parks (Eds.), *Faith development and Fowler.* Birmingham, AL: Religious Education Press.

Fox, Nathan A., Sobel, Ana, Calkins, Susan, & Cole, Pamela. (1996). Inhibited children talk about themselves: Self-reflection on personality development and change in 7-year-olds. In Michael Lewis & Margaret Wolan Sullivan (Eds.), *Emotional development in atypical children.* Mahwah, NJ: Erlbaum.

Fox, Nathan A., & Fein, Greta G. (1990). *Infant day care: The current debate.* Norwood, NJ: Ablex.

Fozard, James L. (1990). Vision and hearing in aging. In James E. Birren & K. Warner Schaie (Eds.), *Handbook of the psychology of aging (3rd ed.).* San Diego: Academic Press

Franceschi, Claudio, Monti, Daniela, Barbieri, Daniela et al., (1996). Immunosenescence: Parqadoxes and new perspectives emerging from the study of healthy centenarians. In Suresh I.S. Rattan & Olivier Toussaint (Eds.) *Molecular gerontology: Research status and strategies.* New York & London: Plenum Press.

Franco, N., & Levitt, M.J. (1998). The social ecology of the middle childhood: Family support, friendship quality, and self-esteem. *Family Relations, 47,* 315–321.

Frankenburg, W.K., Frandel, A., Sciarillo, W., & Burgess, D. (1981). The newly abbreviated and revised Denver Developmental Screening Test. *Journal of Pediatrics, 99,* 995–999.

Franklin, Deborah. (1984). Rubella threatens unborn in vaccine gap. *Science News, 125,* 186.

Freedman, Vicki A. & Martin, Linda G. (1998). Understanding trends in functional limitations among older Americans. *American Journal of Public Health, 88,* 1457–1462.

Frehsee, Detlev. (1996). Violence toward children in the family and the role of law. In Detlev Frehsee, Wiebke Horn, & Kai-D. Bussmann (Eds.), *Family violence against children: A challenge for society.* Berlin: de Gruyter.

Frensch, Pater A. & Buchner, Axel. (1999). Domain-generality versus domain-specificty in cognition. In Robert J. Sternberg (Ed.), *The nature of cognition.* Cambridge: The MIT Press.

Freud, Sigmund. (1935). *A general introduction to psychoanalysis* (Joan Riviare, Trans.). New York: Modern Library.

Freud, Sigmund. (1938). *The basic writings of Sigmund Freud.* A.A. Brill (Ed. and Trans.). New York: Modern Library.

Freud, Sigmund. (1963). *Three case histories.* New York: Collier. (Original work published 1918).

Freud, Sigmund. (1964). *An outline of psychoanalysis: Vol. 23. The standard edition of the complete psychological works of Sigmund Freud.* James Strachey (Ed. and Trans.). London: Hogarth Press. (Original work published 1940).

Freud, Sigmund. (1965). *New introductory lectures on psychoanalysis.* James Strachey (Ed. and Trans.). New York: Norton. (Original work published 1933).

Fries, James F. (1994*). Living well: Taking care of your health in the middle and later years.* Reading, MA: Addison-Wesley.

Fries, James F., & Crapo, Lawrence M. (1981). *Vitality and aging.* San Francisco: Freeman.

Fromholt, Pia & Bruhn, Peter. (1998). Cognitive dysfunciton and dementia. In Inger Hilde Nordhus, Gary R. VandenBos, Stig Berg, & Pia Fromhold (Eds.), *Clinical Geropsychology.* Washington, DC: American Psychological Association.

Fry, Prem S. (1999). The sociocultural meaning of dyng with dignity: An exploratory study of the perceptions of a group of Asian Indian elderly persons. In Brian de Vries (Ed.), *End of life issues: Interdisciplinary and multidimensional perspectives.* New York: Springer.

Fuligni, Andrew J. (1997). The academic achievement of adolescents from immigrant families: The roles of family background, attitudes, and behavior. *Child Development, 68,* 351–363.

Fulton, Robert. (1995). The contemporary funeral: Functional or dysfunctional? In Hannelore Wass & Robert A. Neimeyer (Eds.), *Dying: Facing the facts.* Washington, DC: Taylor & Francis.

Furman, W., & Wehner, E.A. (1994). Romantic views: Toward a theory of adolescent romantic relationships. In R. Montemayer, G.M. Adams, & C.T. Fullotta (Eds.), *Personal relationships during adolescence.* Thousand Oaks, CA: Sage.

Fung, Helene H., Carstensen, Laura L. & Lutz, Amy M. (1999). Influence of time on social preferences: Implications for life-span development. *Psychology and Aging, 14,* 595–604.

Furth, Hans G. (1996). *Desire for society: Children's knowledge as social imagination.* New York: Plenum.

Gall, Stanley A. (1996). *Multiple pregnancy and delivery.* St. Louis: Mosby.

Gallagher, James J. (1990). The family as a focus for intervention. In Samuel J. Meisels & Jack P. Shonkoff (Eds.), *Handbook of early childhood intervention.* Cambridge, England: Cambridge University Press.

Gallup, George, Jr. (1996). *The Gallup Poll public opinion 1995.* Wilmington, DE: Scholarly Resources. Copyright © 1996 by the Gallup Organization.

The Gallup Organization. (1995). *Disciplining children in America: A Gallup Poll report.* Princeton, NJ: The Gallup Organization.

Ganong, Lawrence H., & Coleman, Marilyn. (1994). *Remarried family relationships.* Thousand Oaks, CA: Sage

Gantley, M., Davies, D.P., & Murcett, A. (1993). Sudden infant death syndrome: Links with infant care practices. *British Medical Journal, 306,* 16–20.

Garbarino, James. (1988). Preventing childhood injury: Developmental and mental health issues. *American Journal of Orthopsychiatry, 58,* 25–45.

Garbarino, James. (1999). *Lost boys: Why our sons turn violent and how we can save them.* New York: Free Press.

Garbarino, James, Guttmann, Edna, & Seeley, James Wilson. (1986). *The psychologically battered child.* San Francisco: Jossey-Bass.

Garbarino, James, Dubrow, N., Kostelny, K., & Pardo, C. (1992). *Children in danger: Coping with the consequences of community violence.* San Francisco: Jossey-Bass.

Garbarino, James, Kostelny, Kathleen, & Barry, Frank. (1997). Value transmission in an ecological context: The high-risk neighborhood. In Joan E. Grusec & Leon Kuczynski (Eds.), *Parenting and children's internalization of values: A handbook of contemporary theory.* New York: Wiley.

Gardner, Howard. (1980). *Artful scribbles: The significance of children's drawings.* New York: Basic Books.

Gardner, Howard. (1983). *Frames of mind: The theory of multiple intelligences.* New York: Basic Books.

Gardner, Howard (1993). *Multiple intelligences: The theory in practice.* New York: Basic Books.

Garmezy, Norman. (1985). Stress-resistant children: The search for protective factors. In J. E. Stevenson (Ed.), *Recent research in developmental psychopathology*. Oxford, England: Pergamon.

Garmezy, Norman. (1993). Vulnerability and resilience. In David C. Funder, Ross D. Parke, Carol Tomlinson-Keasy, & Keith Widaman (Eds.), *Studying lives through time*. Washington, DC: American Psychological Association.

Garofalo, Robert, Cameron, Wolf, Wissow, Lawrence S., Woods, Elizabeth R., & Goodman, Elizabeth. (1999). Sexual orientation and risk of suicide. *Archives of Pediatric & Adolescent Medicine*, 513, 487.

Garnham, Alan & Oakhill, Jane. (1994). *Thinking and reasoning*. Oxford, England: Blackwell.

Garrity, Carla & Baris, Mitchell A. (1996). Bullies and victims. *Contemporary Pediatrics, 13*, 90–114.

Garrod, Andrew. (Ed.). (1993). *Approaches to moral development: New research and emerging themes*. New York: Teachers College Press.

Garrod, A., & Beal, C.R. (1993). Voices of care and justice in children's responses to fable dilemmas. In A. Garrod (Ed.), *Approaches to moral development: New research and emerging themes*. New York: Teachers College Press.

Garvin, James P. (1994). *Learning how to kiss a frog: Advice for those who work with pre- and early adolescents*. Newburyport, MA: Garvin Consultant Association.

Gatz, Margaret, Kasl-Godley, Julia E., & Karel, Michele J. (1996). Aging and mental disorders. In James E. Birren & K. Warner Schaie (Eds.), *Handbook of the psychology of aging*. San Diego: Academic Press.

Gaulin, S.J.C. (1993). How and why sex differences evolve, with spatial ability as a paradigm example. In Marc Haug, Richard Whalen, Claude Aron, & Kathie Olsen (Eds.), *The development of sex differences and similarities in behavior*. Boston: Kluwer.

Gauvain, Mary. (1990). Review of Kathleen Berger's *The developing person through childhood and adolescence* (3rd ed.). New York.

Geiger, Brenda. (1996). *Fathers as primary caregivers*. Westport, CT: Greenwood Press.

Gelles, Richard J. (1993). Through a sociological lens: Social structure and family violence. In Richard J. Gelles & Donileen R. Loseke (Eds.), *Current controversies on family violence*. Thousand Oaks, CA: Sage.

Genesee, Fred. (1994). *Educating second-language children: The whole child, the whole curriculum, the whole community*. Cambridge, England: Cambridge University Press.

Genesee, Fred. (1998). A case study of multilingual education in Canada. In Jasone Cenoz & Fred Genesee (Eds.), *Beyond bilingualism: Multilingualism and multilingual education*. Clevedon, England: Multillingual Matters.

Gerhardstein, Peter, Liu, Jane, & Rovee-Collier, Carolyn. (1998). Perceptual constraints on infant memory retrieval. *Journal of Experimental Child Psychology, 69*, 109–131.

Gerstein, Dean R., & Green, Lawrence W. (Eds.). (1993). *Preventing drug abuse*. Washington, DC: National Academy of Science.

Geurts, Sabine & Gründemann. (1999). Workplace stress and stress prevention in Europe. In Michiel Kompier & Cary Cooper (Eds.), *Preventing stress, improving productivity: European case studies in the workplace*. London: Routledge.

Giacobini, Ezio. (1995). Alzheimer's disease: Major neurotransmitter deficits. Can they be corrected? In Israel Hanin, Mitsuo Yoshida, & Abraham Fisher (Eds.), *Alzheimer's and Parkinson's diseases: Recent developments*. New York: Plenum Press.

Giacomoni, Paolo U. & D'Alessio, Patrizia. (1996). Skin ageing: The relevance of antioxidants. In Suresh I.S. Rattan & Olivier Toussaint (Eds.) *Molecular gerontology: Research status and strategies*. New York & London: Plenum Press.

Giardino, Angelo P., Christian, Cindy W., & Giardino, Eileen R. (1997). *A practical guide to the evaluation of child physical abuse & neglect*. Thousand Oaks, CA: Sage.

Gibbons, Ann. (1998). Which of our genes makes us human? *Science, 281*, 1432–1434.

Gibson, Eleanor. (1969). *Principles of perceptual learning and development*. New York: Appleton-Century-Crofts.

Gibson, Eleanor. (1988). Levels of description and constraints on perceptual development. In Albert Yonas (Ed.), *Perceptual development in infancy*. Hillsdale, NJ: Erlbaum.

Gibson, Eleanor Jack. (1997). An ecological psychologist's prolegomena for perceptual development: A functional approach. In Cathy Dent-Read & Patricia Zukow-Goldring (Eds.), *Evolving explanations of development: Ecological approaches to organism-environment systems*. Washington, DC: American Psychological Association.

Gibson, Eleanor Jack, & Walk, Richard D. (1960). The visual cliff. *Scientific American, 202*, 64–72.

Gibson, James J. (1979). *The ecological approach to visual perception*. Boston: Houghton Mifflin.

Gilanshah, Farah. (1993). Islamic customs regarding death. In Donald P. Irish, Kathleen F. Lundquist, & Vivian Jenkins Nelsen (Eds), *Ethnic variations in dying, death, and grief*. Washington, DC: Taylor & Francis Ltd.

Gilbert, Enid F., Arya, Sunita, Loxova, Renata, & Opitz, John M. (1987). Pathology of chromosome abnormalities in the fetus: Pathological markers. In Enid F. Gilbert & John M. Opitz (Eds.), *Genetic aspects of developmental pathology*. New York: Liss.

Gilbert, Scott F., & Borish, Steven. (1997). How cells learn, how cells teach: Education in the body. In Eric Amsel & K. Ann Renninger (Eds.), *Change and development: Issues of theory, method, and application*. Mahwah, NJ: Erlbaum.

Giles-Sims, Jean, & Crosbie-Burnett, Margaret. (1989). Adolescent power in stepparent families: A test of normative resource theory. *Journal of Marriage and the Family, 51*, 1065–1078.

Gillberg, Christopher. (1991). Clinical and neurobiological aspects of Asperger syndrome in six family studies. In Uta Frith (Ed.), *Autism and Asperger syndrome.* Cambridge, England: Cambridge University Press.

Gilligan, Carol. (1981). Moral development. In Arthur W. Chickering (Ed.), *The modern American college: Responding to the new realities of diverse students and a changing society.* San Francisco: Jossey-Bass.

Gilligan, Carol. (1982). *In a different voice: Psychological theory and women's development.* Cambridge, MA: Harvard University Press.

Gilligan, Carol, & Murphy, John M. (1979). Development from adolescence to adulthood: The philosopher and the dilemma of the fact. In William Damon (Ed.), *New directions for child development (Vol. 5).* San Francisco: Jossey-Bass.

Gilligan, Carol, Murphy, John M., & Tappan, Mark B. (1990). Moral development beyond adolescence. In Charles N. Alexander & Ellen J. Langer (Eds.), *Higher stages of human development.* New York: Oxford University Press.

Ginn, Jay, & Arber, Sara. (1994). Midlife women's employment and pension entitlement in relation to coresident adult children in Great Britain. *Journal of Marriage and the Family, 4,* 813–819.

Girouard, Pascale C., Baillargeon, Raymond H., Tremblay, Richard E., & Glorieux, Jacquline, et al. (1998). Developmental pathways lending to externalizing behaviors in 5 year olds born before 29 weeks of gestation. *Journal of Developmental & Behavioral Pediatrics, 19,* 244–253.

Gjessing, Hans-Jorgen, & Karlsen, Bjorn. (1989). *A longitudinal study of dyslexia.* New York: Springer-Verlag.

Glasgow, Kristin L., Dornbusch, Sanford M., Troyer, Lisa, Steinberg, Laurence, & Ritter, Philip L. (1997). Parenting styles, adolescents' attributions, and educational outcomes in nine heterogeneous high schools. *Child Development, 68,* 507–529.

Glass, Jennifer. (1998). Gender Liberation, economic squeeze, or fear of strangers: Why fathers provide infant care in dual-earner families. *Journal of Marriage and the Family, 60,* 821–834.

Gleason, Jean Berko. (1967). Do children imitate? *Proceedings of the International Conference on Oral Education of the Deaf, 2,* 1441–1448.

Glei, Dana A. (1999). Measuring contraceptive use patterns among teenage and adult women. *Family Planning Perspectives, 31,* 73–80.

Glenn, Norval D. (1991). The recent trend in marital success in the United States. *Journal of Marriage and the Family, 53* 261–270.

Glenn, Norval D. (1996). Values, attitudes, and the state of American marriage. In David Popenoe, Jean Bethke Elshtain, & David Blankenhorn (Eds.), *Promises to keep: Decline and renewal of marriage in America.* Lanham, MD: Rowman & Littlefield.

Glenn, Norval D. (1999). Further discussion of the effects of no-fault divorce on divorce rates. *Journal of Marriage and the Family, 61,* 800–802.

Glick, J. (1968, February). *Cognitive style among the Kpelle of Liberia.* Paper presented at the meeting on Cross-Cultural Cognitive Studies, American Educational Research Association, Chicago.

Glick, Jennifer E., Bean, Frank D., & Van Hook, Jennifer V.W. (1997). Immigration and changing patterns of extended family household structure in the United States. *Journal of Marriage and the Family, 59,* 177–191.

Going, S.B., Williams, D.P., Lohman, T.G., & Hewitt, M.J. (1994). Age, body composition, and physical activity: A review. *Journal of Aging and Physical Activity, 2,* 38–66.

Goleman, Daniel. (1995) *Emotional Intelligence.* New York: Bantam Books.

Gold, Deborah T. (1996). Continuities and discontinuities in sibling relationships acorss the life span. In Vern L. Bengtson (Ed.), *Adulthood and aging: Research on continuities and discontinuities.* New York: Springer Publishing Company.

Goldberg, Margaret, Lex, Barbara W., Mello, Nancy K., Mendelson, Jack H., & Bower, Tommie A. (1996). Impact of maternal alcoholism on separation of children from their mothers: Findings from a sample of incarcerated women. *American Journal of Orthopsychiatry, 66,* 228–238.

Goldberg, Susan, & Divitto, Barbara. (1995). Parenting children from preterm. In Marc H. Bornstein (Ed.), *Handbook of parenting: Children and parenting.* Mahwah, NJ: Erlbaum.

Goldberg, Susan, Muir, Roy, & Kerr, John. (Eds.) (1995) *Attachment theory: social, developmental, and clinical perspectives.* Hillsdale, NJ: Analytic Press.

Goldberg-Reitman, Jill. (1992). Young girls' conception of their mother's role: A neo-structural analysis. In Robbie Case (Ed.), *The mind's staircase: Exploring the conceptual underpinning of children's thought and knowledge.* Hillsdale, NJ: Erlbaum.

Golden, Michael H.N. (1996). The effect of early nutrition on later growth. In C.J.K. Henry & S.J. Uliajaszel (Eds.), *Long-term consequences of early environment: Growth, development and the lifespan developmental perspective.* Cambridge, England: Cambridge University Press.

Goldenberg, Robert L., Iams, Jay D., Mercer, Brian M., et al. (1998). The preterm prediction study: The value of new vs. standard risk factors in predicting early and all spontaneous preterm births. *American Journal of Public Health, 88,* 233–238.

Goldfield, E. (1995). *Emergent forms: Origins and early development of human action and perception.* New York: Oxford University Press.

Goldman, Connie. (1991). Late bloomers: Growing older or still growing? *Generations, 15,* 41–44.

Goldscheider, Frances K. & Goldscheider, Calvin. (1998). The effects of childhood family struture on leaving and returning home. *Journal of Marriage and the Family, 60,* 745–756.

Goldsmith, H.H., Gottesman, I.I., & Lemery, K.S. (1997). Epigenetic approaches to developmental psychopathology. *Development and Psychopathology, 9,* 365–387.

Goldsmith, Seth B. (1994). *Essentials of long-term care administration.* Gaithersburg, MD: Aspen.

Goleman, Daniel. (1998). *Building emotional intelligence.* APA Convention, San Francisco.

Golinkoff, Roberta Michnick, & Hirsh-Pasek, Kathy. (1990). Let the mute speak: What infants can tell us about language acquisition. *Merrill-Palmer Quarterly, 36,* 67–91.

Golinkoff, Roberta Michnick, Hirsh-Pasek, Kathy, Bailey, Leslie M., & Wenger, Neill R. (1992). Young children and adult use lexical principles to learn new nouns. *Developmental Psychology, 28,* 99–108.

Golombok, Susan, & Tasker, Fiona. (1996). Do parents influence the sexual orientation of their children? Findings from a longitudinal study of lesbian families. *Developmental Psychology, 32,* 3–11.

Golub, S. (1992). *Periods: From menarche to menopause.* Newbury Park, CA: Sage.

Golumb, C., & McLean, L. (1984). Assessing cognitive skills in pre-school children of middle and low income families. *Perceptual and Motor Skills, 58,* 119–125.

Gomby, Deanna S., Culross, Patti L., & Behrman, Richard E. (1999)l Home visiting: Recent program evaluations—analysis and recommendations. *The Future of Children, 9,* 4–26.

Goncu, A. (1993). Development of intersubjectivity in social pretend play. *Human Development, 36,* 185–198.

Goodman, G.S., Rudy, L., Bottoms, B.L., & Aman, C. (1990). Children's concerns and memory: Issues of ecological validity in the study of children's eyewitness testimony. In Robyn Fivush & Judith A. Hudson (Eds.), *Knowing and remembering in young children.* Cambridge, England: Cambridge University Press.

Goodnow, Jacqueline J. (1993). Direction of post-Vygotsky research. In Ellice A. Foreman, Norris Minick, & C. Addison Stone (Eds.), *Contexts for learning: Sociocultural dynamics in children's development.* New York: Oxford Press.

Goodnow, Jacqueline J. (1997). Parenting and the transmission and internalization of values: From social-cultural perspectives to within-family analyses. In Joan E. Grusec & Leon Kuczynski (Eds.), *Parenting and children's internalization of values: A handbook of contemporary theory.* New York: Wiley.

Goodwin, M.H. (1990). *He-said-she-said: Talk as social organization among black children.* Bloomington: Indiana University Press.

Gordon, Debra Ellen. (1990). Formal operational thinking: The role of cognitive-developmental processes in adolescent decision-making about pregnancy and contraception. *American Journal of Orthopsychiatry, 60,* 346–356.

Gordon, George Kenneth, & Stryker, Ruth. (1994). *Creative long-term care administration.* Springfield, IL: Thomas.

Gorman, Elizabeth H. (1999). Bringing home the bacon: Marital allocation of income-earning responsible job shifts, and men's wages. *Journal of Marriage and the Family, 61,* 110–122.

Gould, Stephen J. (1999). *Rocks of ages: Science and religion in the fullness of life* (Library of contemporary thought). New York: Ballantine Books.

Graber, Julia A., Brooks-Gunn, Jeanne, Paikoff, Roberta L., & Warren, Michelle P. (1994). Prediction of eating problems: An 8-year study of adolescent girls. *Developmental Psychology, 30,* 823–834.

Graham, Sandra, & Juvonen, Jaana. (1998). Self-blame and peer victimization in middle school: An attributional analysis. *Developmental Psychology, 34,* 587–599.

Grandin, Temple. (1996). *Thinking in pictures: And other reports from my life with autism.* New York: Vintage.

Gratton, Brian, & Haber, Carole. (1996). Three phases in the history of American grandparents: Authority, burden, companion. *Generations, 20,* 7–12.

Greenberger, E., & Steinberg, L. (1986). *When teenagers work.* New York: Basic Books.

Greenberger, Ellen, & Chen, Chuansheng. (1996). Perceived family relationships and depressed mood in early and late adolescence: A comparison of European and Asian Americans. *Developmental Psychology, 32,* 707–716.

Greene, Sheila. (1997). Child development: Old themes and new directions. In Ray Fuller, Patricia Noonan Walsh, & Patrick McGinley (Eds.), *A century of psychology: Progress, paradigms and prospects for the new millennium.* London: Routledge.

Greenfield, Patricia M. (1997). You can't take it with you: Why ability assessments don't cross cultures. *American Psychologist, 52,* 1115–1124.

Greenfield, Thomas K., Midanik, Lorraine T., & Rogers, John D. (2000). A k10-year national trend study of alcohol consumption, 1984–1995: Is the period of declining drinking over. *American Journal of Public Health, 90,* 47–52.

Greenstein, Theodore N. (1995). Gender ideology, marital disruption, and the employment of married women. *Journal of Marriage and the Family, 57,* 31–42.

Greer, Germaine. (1986, May). Letting go. *Vogue, 176,* 141–143.

Greer, Jane. (1992). *Adult sibling rivalry.* New York: Crown.

Greydanus, Donald Everett. (1997). Neurological disorders. In Adele Dellenbaugh Hofmann & Donald Everett Greydanus (Eds.), *Adolescent medicine* (3rd Ed.). Stamford, CT: Appleton and Lange.

Greydanus, Donald Everett. (1997). Disorders of the skin. In Adele Dellenbaugh Hofmann & Donald Everett Greydanus (Eds.), *Adolescent medicine* (3rd ed.). Stamford, CT: Appleton and Lange.

Griffiths, John, Bood, Alex, & Weyers, Heleen. (1998). *Euthanasia and law in the Netherlands.* Michigan: University of Michigan Press.

Grifo, Jamie A., Tan, Y.X., & Munné, S. (1994). Healthy deliveries from biopsy human embryos. *Human Reproduction, 9,* 912–916.

Grodstein, Francine, Colditz, G.A., & Stampfer, M.J. (1996). Postmenopausal hormone use and tooth loss: A prospective study. *JAMA, Journal of the American Medical Association, 127,* 370–377.

Grolnick, Wendy S., Deci, Edward L., & Ryan, Richard M. (1997). Internalization within the family: The self-determination theory perspective. In Joan E. Grusec & Leon Kuczynski (Eds.), *Parenting and children's internalization of values: A handbook of contemporary theory.* New York: Wiley.

Grossman, Herbert. (1995). *Special education in a diverse society.* Needham, MA: Allyn and Bacon.

Grossman, K., Thane, K., & Grossman, K.E. (1981). Maternal tactile contact of the newborn after various postpartum conditions of mother-infant contact. *Developmental Psychology, 17,* 159–169.

Grotevant, H. & Cooper, C.R. (1998). Individuality and connectedness in adolescent development. In E. Skoe & A. von der Lippe (Eds.), *Personality development in adolescence: A cross-national and life span perspective.* London: Routledge.

Guberman, Steven R. (1996). The development of everyday mathematics in Brazilian children with limited formal education. *Child Development, 67,* 1609–1623.

Guillemard, A.M., & Rein, M. (1993). Comparative patterns of retirement: Recent trends in developed societies. *Annual Review of Sociology, 19,* 469–503.

Guralnik, J.M., Land, K.M., Blazer, D., Fillenbaum, G., Branch, L.G. (1993). Educational status and active life expectancy among older blacks and whites. *New England Journal of Medicine, 329,* 110–116.

Gurnack, A.M. (1996). *Drugs and the elderly: Use and misuse of drugs, medicines, alcohol and tobacco.* New York: Springer.

Guterbock, T.M. & Fries, J.C. (1997). *Maintaining America's social fabric: The AARP survey of civic involvement.* Washington, D.C.: American Association of Retired Persons.

Gutmann, David. (1987). *Reclaimed powers: Toward a new psychology of men and women in later life.* New York: Basic Books.

Gutmann, Daivd. (1994). *Reclaimed powers: Toward a new psychology of man and woman in later life.* Evanston, IL: Northwestern University Press. Evanston, IL: Northwestern University Press.

Gutmann, David. (1996). Psychological immunity and late onset disorders. In Bengston, Vern L. (Ed.), *Adulthood and Aging: Research on continuity and discontinuity.* New York: Springer.

Gutwill, Susan. (1994). The diet: Personal experience, social condition, and industrial empire. In Women's Therapy Centre Institute (Eds.), *Eating problems.* New York: Basic Books.

Haan, Norma. (1985). Common personality dimensions or common organizations across the life span. In Joep M.A. Munnichs, Paul H. Mussen, Erhard Olbrich, & Peter G. Coleman (Eds.), *Life span and change in a gerontological perspective.* Orlando, FL: Academic Press.

Hack, Maureen, Klein, Nancy, & Taylor, H. Gerry. (1995). Long-term developmental outcomes of low birth weight infants. *The Future of Children: Low Birth Weight, 5,* 176–196.

Hagberg, J.M. (1987). Effects of training on the decline of VO_2 max with aging. *Federation Proceedings, 46,* 1830–1833.

Hagerman, Randi J. (1996). Biomedical advances in developmental psychology: The case of Fragile X syndrome. *Developmental Psychology, 32,* 416–424.

Hagino, Nobuyoshi, Ohkura, Takeyoshi, Isse, Kunihiro, Akasuwa, Kenji, & Hamamoto, Makoto. (1995). Estrogen in clinical trials for dementia of Alzheimer type. In Israel Hanin, Mitsuo Yoshida, & Abraham Fisher (Eds.), *Alzheimer's and Parkinson's diseases: Recent developments.* New York: Plenum Press.

Haig, David. (1995). Prenatal power plays. *Natural History, 104,* 39.

Haith, Marshall M. (1990). Perceptual and sensory processes in early infancy. *Merrill-Palmer Quarterly, 36,* 1–26.

Haith, Marshall M. (1993). Preparing for the 21st century: Some goals and challenges for studies of infant sensory and perceptual development. *Developmental Review, 13,* 354–371.

Haith, Marchall M. & Benson, Janette B. (1998). Infant cognition. In William Damon, Deanna Kuhn, & Robert S. Siegler (Eds.), *Handbook of child psychology: Cognition, perception, and language.* New York: Wiley

Haith, Marshall M., Wentworth, N., & Canfield, R.L. (1993). The formation of expectations in early infancy. In C. Rovee-Collier & L.P. Lipsitt (Eds.), *Advances in infancy research, 8.* Norwood, NJ: Ablex.

Hallenbeck, James & Goldstein, Mary K. (1999). Decisions at the end of life: Cultural considerations beyond medical ethics. *Generations: In-depth views of aging, 23,* 24–29.

Halliday, M.A.K. (1979). One child's protolanguage. In Margaret Bullowa (Ed.), *Before speech: The beginning of interpersonal communication.* Cambridge, England: Cambridge University Press.

Halpern, Carolyn Tucker, Udry, J. Richard, Campbell, Benjamin, & Suchindran, Chirayath. (1999). Effects of body fat on weight concerns, dating, and sexual activity: A longitudinal analysis of black and white adolescent girls. *Developmental Psychology, 35,* 721–736.

Hamburg, B. (1991). Developmental factors and stress in risk-taking behavior of early adolescents. In L.P. Lipsitt & L.L. Mitnick (Eds.), *Self-regulatory behavior and risk taking: Causes and consequences.* Norwood, NJ: Ablex.

Hamer, Dean H. (1999). Genetics and male sexual orientation. *Science, 285,* 803.

Hamer, Dean H., Hu, Stella, Magnuson, Victoria L., Hu, Nan, & Pattatucci, Angela M.L. (1993). A linkage between DNA markers on the X chromosome and male sexual orientation. *Science, 261,* 321–327.

Hamil, P. (1991). Triage: An essay. *The Georgia Review, 45,* 463–469.

Hamilton, Stephen A., & Wolfgang, Lempert. (1996). The impact of apprenticeship on youth: A prospective analysis. *Journal of Research on Adolescence, 6,* 427–455.

Hamon, Raeann R., & Blieszner, Rosemary. (1990). Filial responsibility expectations among adult child-older parent pairs. Journal of Gerontology: Psychological Sciences, 45, 110–112.

Hamond, Nina R., & Fivush, Robyn. (1991). Memories of Mickey Mouse: Young children recount their trip to Disneyworld. *Cognitive Development, 6,* 433–448.

Hanninen, T., Reinikainen, K.J., Helkala, E., Kkoivisto, K., Mykkanen, L., Laakso, M., Pyorala, K., & Riekkinen, P.J. (1994). Subjective memory complaints and personality traits in normal elderly subjects. *Journal of the American Geriatrics Society, 42,* 1–4.

Hansen, Karen Kirhofer. (1998). Folk remedies and child abuse: A review with emphasis on caida de mullera and its relationship to shaken baby syndrome. *Child Abuse & Neglect, 22,* 117–127.

Hanson, Sandra L., Myers, David E., & Ginsberg, Alan L. (1987). The role of responsibility and knowledge in reducing teenage out-of-wedlock childbearing. *Journal of Marriage and the Family, 49,* 241–256.

Hardy, Janet B., Astone, Nan M., Brooks-Gunn, Jeanne, Shapiro, Sam, & Miller, Therese L. (1998). Like mother, like child: Intergenerational patterns of age at first birth and associations with childhood and adolescent characteristics and adult outcomes in the second generation . *Developmental Psychology, 34,* 1220–1232.

Harkness, Sara, & Super, Charles, M. (1995). Culture & parenting. In Marc H. Bornstein (Ed.), *Handbook of parenting: Biology and ecology of parenting.* Mahwah, NJ: Lawrence Erlbaum.

Harlow, Clara Mears (Ed.). (1986). *From learning to love: The selected papers of H.F. Harlow.* New York: Praeger.

Harlow, Harry F. (1958). The nature of love. *American Psychology, 13,* 673–685.

Harlow, Robert E., & Cantor, Nancy. (1996). Still participating after all these years: A study of life task participation in later life. *Journal of Personality and Social Psychology, 71,* 1235–1249.

Harrington, Michael. (1962). *The other America: Poverty in the United States.* New York: Macmillan.

Harris, Judith Rich. (1998). *The nurture assumption: Why children turn out the way they do.* New York: Free Press.

Harris, Kathleen Mullan & Furstenberg, Frank F. (1997). *Teen Mothers and the Revolving Welfare Door (Women in the Political Economy Series).* Philadelphia, PA: Temple University Press.

Harris, P.L., & Kavanaugh, R.D. (1993). Young children's understanding of pretense. *Monographs of the Society for Research in Child Development, 58* (Serial No. 231).

Harris, Raymond. (1986). *Clinical geriatric cardiology.* Philadelphia: Lippincott.

Harris, S. B. (1996). For better or for worse: Spouse abuse grown old. *Journal of Elder Abuse and Neglect, 8,* 1–33.

Harrison, Algea O., Wilson, Melvin N., Pine, Charles J., Chan, Samuel Q., & Buriel, Raymond. (1990). Family ecologies of ethnic minority children. *Child Development, 61,* 347–362.

Hart, Carole L., Smith, George Davey, Hole, David J., and Hawthorne, Victor M. (1999). Alcohol consumption and mortality from all causes, coronary heart disease, and stroke: Results from a prospective cohort study of Scottish men with 21 years of follow up. *BMJ, 318,* 1725–1729.

Hart, Sybil, Field, Tiffany, & Nearing, Graciela. (1999). Depressed mothers' neonates improve following the MABI and a Brazelton demonstration. *Journal of Pediatric Psychology, 23,* 351–356.

Harter, Susan. (1993). Visions of self: Beyond the me in the mirror. In J.E. Jacobs (Ed.), *Nebraska symposium on motivation: Vol. 40. Developmental perspectives on motivation.* Lincoln: University of Nebraska Press.

Harter, Susan. (1996). Developmental changes in self-understanding. In Arnold J. Sameroff & Marshall M. Haith (Eds.), *The five to seven year shift: The age of reason and responsibility.* Chicago: The University of Chicago Press.

Harter, Susan. (1999). *The construction of the self: A developmental perspective.* New York: Guilford.

Hartfield, Bernadette W. (1996). Legal recognition of the value of intergenerational nurturance: Grandparent visitation statutes in the nineties. *Generations, 20,* 53–56.

Hartl, Daniel L. & Jones, Elizabeth W. (1999). *Essential genetics,* 2nd Edition. Sudbury, MA: Jones & Bartlett.

Hartman, Donald P. & George, Thomas P. (1999). Design, measurement, and analysis in developmental research. In Mark H. Bornstein & Michael E. Lamb (Eds.), *Developmental psychology: An advanced textbook,* 4th ed. Mahway, NJ: Erlbaum.

Hartup, Willard W. (1996). The company they keep: Friendships and their developmental significance. *Child Development, 67,* 1–13.

Harvey, Elizabeth. (1999). Short-term and long-term effects of early parental employment on children of the National Longitudinal survey of Youth. *Developmental Psychology, 35,* 445–459.

Hashima, Patricia, & Finkelhor, David. (1997). *Violent victimization of youth versus adults in the National Crime Victimization Survey.* Paper accepted for presentation at the Fifth International Family Violence Research Conference, Durham, NH.

Haskins, Ron. (1989). Beyond metaphor: The efficacy of early childhood education. *American Psychologist, 44,* 274–282.

Hatfield, Elaine. (1988). Theories of romantic love. In Robert J. Sternberg & Michael L. Barnes (Eds.), *The psychology of love.* New Haven, CT: Yale University Press.

Hawaii Department of Health. (1992). *Healthy Start: Hawaii's system of family support services.* Honolulu: Hawaii Department of Health.

Hayflick, Leonard (1994). *How and why we age.* New York: Ballantine Books.

Hayflick, Leonard, & Moorhead, Paul S. (1961). The serial cultivation of human diploid cell strains. *Experimental Cell Research, 25,* 585.

Hayslip, Bert, Servaty, Heather L., & Guarnaccia. (1999) Age cohort differences in perceptions of funerals. In Brian de Vries (Eds.) *Kinship Bereavement in Later Life: A Special Issue of Omega-Journal of Death and Dying.* Amityville, NY: Baywood Publishing Co.

Hayne, Harlene, & Rovee-Collier, Carolyn K. (1995). The organization of reactivated memory in infancy. *Child Development, 66,* 893–906.

Heath, A.C., Bucholz, K.K., Madden, PA.F., Dinwiddie, S.H., Slutske, W.S., Bierut, L.J., Statham, D.J., Dunne, M.P., Whitfield, J.B., & Martin, N.G. (1997). Genetic and environmental contributions to alcohol dependence risk in a national twin sample: Consistency of findings in women and men. *Psychological Medicine, 27,* 1381–1396.

Heimann, Mikael, & Meltzoff, Andrew N. (1996). Deferred imitation in 9- and 14-month-old infants: A longitudinal study of a Swedish sample. *British Journal of Developmental Psychology, 14,* 55–64.

Heine, Marilyn K., Ober, Beth A., & Shenaut, Gregory K. (1999). Naturally occurring and experimentally induced tip-of-the-tongue experiences in three adult age groups. *Psychology and Aging, 14,* 445–457.

Held, Richard. (1995). Binocular vision. In P.D. Gluckman and M.A. Heymann (Eds.), *Developmental physiology: A pediatric perspective* (2nd ed.). London: Edward Arnold Publishers.

Hellerstedt, Wendy L., Himes, John H., Story, Mary, Alton, Irene R., & Edwards, Laura E. (1997). The effects of cigarette smoking and gestational weight change on birth outcomes in obese and normal-weight women. *American Journal of Public Health, 87,* 591–596.

Helson, Ravenna, Stewart, Abigail J., & Ostrove, Joan. (1995). Identity in three cohorts of midlife women. *Journal of Personality and Social Psychology, 69,* 554–557.

Helwig, Charles C. (1995). Adolescents' and young adults' conceptions of civil liberties: Freedom of speech and religion. *Child Development, 66,* 152–166.

Hemsrom, Orjan. (1996). Is marriage dissolution linked to differences in mortality risks for men and women? *Journal of Marriage and the Family, 58,* 366–378.

Henggeler, S.W. (1989). *Delinquency in adolescence.* Newbury Park, CA: Sage.

Henke, Robin, Choy, Susan P., Geis, Sonya, & Broughman, Stephen. (1996). *Schools and staffing in the United States.* Washington, DC: U.S. Department of Education, National Center for Education Statistics.

Henry, C.J.K. (1996). Early environmental and later nutritional needs. In C.J.K. Henry & S.J. Uliajaszel (Eds.), *Long-term consequences of early environment: Growth, development and the lifespan developmental perspective.* Cambridge, England: Cambridge University Press.

Herrnstein, Richard J. & Murray, Charles A. (1994). *The Bell Curve: Intelligence and class structure in American life.* New York: Free Press.

Hertzog, Christopher, Lineweaver, Tara T., & McGuire, Christy L. (1999). Beliefs about memory and aging. In Thomas M. Hess & Fredda Blanchard-Fields (Eds.) *Social cognition and aging.* Orlando, Florida: Academic Press.

Herzog, Regula A. (1991). Measurement of vitality in the American's Changing Lives study. *Proceedings of the 1988 International Symposium on Aging. (Series 5, No. 6, DHHS Publication No. 91–1482).* Hyattsville, MD: U.S. Department of Health and Human Services.

Herzog, Regula A., & Morgan, James N. (1992). Age and gender differences in the value of productive activities. *Research on Aging, 14,* 169–198.

Herzog, Regula A., House, James S., & Morgan, James N. (1991). Relation of work and retirement to health and well-being in older age. *Psychology and Aging, 6,* 202–211.

Hesketh, Beth. (1995). Personality and adjustment styles: A theory of work adjustment approach to career enhancing strategies. *Journal of Vocational Behavior, 46,* 274–282.

Hetherington, E. Mavis. (1998). Relevant issues in developmental science. *American Psychologist, 53,* 93–94.

Hetherington, E. Mavis, & Clingempeel, W. Glenn. (1992). Coping with marital transitions. *Monographs of the Society for Research in Child Development, 57* (2–3, Serial No. 227).

Hetherington, E. Mavis, Bridges, Margaret, & Insabella, Glendessa M. (1998). What matters? What does not? Five perspectives on the association between marital transitions and children's adjustment. *American Psychologist, 53,* 167–184.

Hetheringon, E. M., & Stanley-Hagan, M.S. (1999). Divorce and the adjustment of children: A risk and resiliency perspective. *The Journal of Child Psychology and Psychiatry, 40,* 129–140.

Hewitt, M., Simone, J.V., (Eds.). (1999). *Ensuring quality cancer care.* Washington, D.C., National Academy Press.

Higbee, Martin D. (1994). Consumer guidelines for using medications wisely. *Generations, 18,* 43–48.

Higgins, Carol I., Campos, Joseph J., & Kermoian, Rosanne. (1996). Effect of self-produced locomotion on infant postural compensation to optic flow. *Developmental Psychology, 32,* 836–841.

Higginson, Joanna Gregson. (1998). Competitive parenting: The culture of teen mothers. *Journal of Marriage and the Family, 60,* 135–149.

Hill, Hope M., Soriano, Fernando I., Chen, S. Andrew, & LaFromboise, Teresa D. (1994). Sociocultural factors in the etiology and prevention of violence among ethnic minority youth. In Leonard D. Eron, Jacquelyn H. Gentry, & Peggy Schlegel (Eds.), *Reason to hope: A psychosocial perspective on violence and youth.* Washington, DC: American Psychological Association.

Hill, Roslyn, Collis, Glyn M., & Lewis, Vicky A. (1997). Young children's understanding of the cognitive verb forget. *Journal of Child Language, 24,* 57–79.

Hinde, Robert A. (Ed.). (1983). *Primate social relationships.* Oxford, England: Blackwell.

Hinde, Robert A. (1989). Ethological and relationships approaches. In R. Vasta (Ed.), *Annals of Child Development* (Vol. 6). Greenwich, CT: JAI Press.

Hinde, Robert A. (1995). Foreward. In Marc H. Bornstein (Ed.), *Handbook of Parenting (Vol. 4): Applied and practical parenting.* Mahwah, NJ: Erlbaum.

Hinde, R.A., Titmus, G., Easton, D., & Tamplin, A. (1985). Incidence of "friendship" and behavior toward strong associates versus nonassociates in preschoolers. *Child Development, 56,* 234–245.

Hines, Marc. (1993). Hormonal and neural correlates of sex-typed behavioral development in human beings. In Marc Haug, Richard Whalen, Claude Aron, & Kathie Olsen (Eds.), *The development of sex differences and similarities in behavior.* Boston: Kluwer.

Hitchens, Christopher. (1998). Goodbye to all that: Why Americans are not taught history. *Harper's, 297* (1782), 37–47.

Hitt, R., Young-Xu, Y., Silver, M., & Perls, T. (1999). Centenarians: The older you get, thehealthier you have been. *Lancet, 354,* 652.

Hobbs, Frank B., & Damon, Bonnie L. (1996). *65+ in the United States.* Washington, DC: U.S. Government Printing Office.

Hochschild, A. (1975). Disengagement theory: A critique and proposal. *American Sociological Review, 40,* 553–569.

Hochschild, Arlie. (1989). *The second shift: Working parents and the revolution at home.* New York: Viking.

Hochschild, A.R. (1997). *The time bind: When work becomes home, and home becomes work.* New York: Metropolitan Books.

Hodges, Ernest V.E., Boivin, Michel, Vitaro, Frank, & Bukowski, William M. (1999). The power of friendship: Protection against an escalating cycle of peer victimization. *Developmental Psychology, 35,* 258–268.

Hofer, Myron A. (1995) Hidden regulators: Implications for a new understanding of attachment, separation and loss. In Susan Goldberg, Roy Muir, & John Kerr (Eds.), *Attachment theory: Social, developmental and clinical perspectives.* Hillsdale, NJ: The Analytic Press.

Hoff-Ginsberg, E. (1986). Function and structure in maternal speech: Their relation to the child's development of syntax. *Developmental Psychology, 22,* 155–163.

Hoffman, S. D., Foster, E. M., & Furstenberg, F. F (1993). Reevaluating the costs of teenage chldbearing. *Demography, 30,* 1–13.

Hofman, Adele Dellenbaugh. (1997). Adolescent growth and development. In Adele Dellenbaugh Hofman & Donald Everett Greydanus (Eds.), *Adolescent medicine* (3rd ed.). Stamford, CT: Appleton and Lange.

Hokado, R., Saito, T.R., Wakafuji, Y., Takahashi, K.W., & Imanichi, T. (1993). The change with age of the copulatory behavior of the male rats age 67 and 104 weeks. *Experimental Animal, 42,* 75.

Holahan, Carole K., Holahan, Charles J., & Wonacott, Nancy L. (1999). Self-apporaisal, life satisfaction, and retrospective life choices across one and three decades. *Psychology and Aging, 14,* 238–244.

Holliday, Robin. (1995). *Understanding aging.* Cambridge, England: Cambridge University press.

Holliday, Robin. (1999). Ageing in the 21st century. *The Lancet 2000, 354,.*

Hollomon, Holly A. & Scott, Keith G. (1998). Influence of birth weight on educational outcomes at age 9: The Miami site of the infant health and development program. *Journal of Developmental and Behavioral Pediatrics, 19,* 404–410.

Holmbeck, Grayson N., & O'Donnell, K. (1991). Discrepancies between perceptions of decision making and behavioral autonomy. In R.L. Paikoff (Ed.), *New directions for child development: No. 51. Shared views in the family during adolescence.* San Francisco: Jossey-Bass.

Holmbeck, Grayson N., Paikoff, Roberta L., & Brooks-Gunn, Jeanne. (1995). Parenting adolescents. In Marc H. Bornstein (Ed.), *Handbook of parenting: Vol. 1. Children and parenting.* Mahwah, NJ: Erlbaum.

Holmes, Ellen Rhoads, & Holmes, Lowell D. (1995). *Other cultures, elder years.* Thousand Oaks, CA.: Sage.

Holroyd, Sarah, & Baron-Cohen, Simon. (1993). Brief report: How far can people with autism go in developing a theory of mind? *Journal of Autism and Developmental Disorders, 23,* 379–385.

Horn, John L. (1982). The aging of human abilities. In Benjamin B. Wolman (Ed.), *Handbook of developmental psychology.* New York: Wiley.

Horn, John L. (1985). Remodeling old models of intelligence. In Benjamin B. Wolman (Ed.) , *Handbook of intelligence: Theories, measurements, and applications.* New York: Wiley.

Horn, John L., & Cattell, Raymond B. (1967). Age differences in fluid and crystallized intelligence. *Acta Psychologica, 26,* 107–129.

Horn, John L., & Hofer, Scott M. (1992). Major abilities and development in the adult period. In Robert J. Sternberg & Cynthia A. Berg (Eds.), *Intellectual Development.* New York: Cambridge University Press.

Horney, Karen. (1967). *Feminine psychology.* Harold Kelman (Ed.). New York: Norton.

Hornick, Joseph P., McDonald, Lynn, & Robertson, Gerald B. (1992). Elder abuse in Canada and the United States: Prevalence, legal and service issues. In Ray De B. Peters, Robert J. McMahon, & Vernon L. Quinsey (Eds.), *Aggression and violence throughout the life span.* Newbury Park, CA: Sage.

Horwitz, Allan V., & White, Helene Raskin. (1998). The relationship of cohabitation and mental health: A study of a young adult cohort. *Journal of Marriage and the Family, 60,* 505–514.

Horowitz, Frances Degen. (1994). John B. Watson's legacy: Learning and environment. In Ross D. Parke, Peter A. Ornstein, John J. Rieser, & Carolyn Zahn-Waxler (Eds.), *A century of developmental psychology.* Washington, DC: American Psychological Association.

Houts, Renate M., Robins, Elliot, & Huston, Ted L. (1996). Compatibility and the development of premarital relationships. *Journal of Marriage and the Family, 58,* 7–20.

Howard, Darlene V., & Howard, James H., Jr. (1992). Adult age differences in the rate of learning serial patterns: Evidence from direct and indirect tests. *Psychology and Aging, 7,* 232–241.

Howard, Robert W. (1996). Asking nature the right questions. *Genetic, Social & General Psychology Monographs, 122,* 161–178.

Howe, Mark L. (1997). Children's memory for traumatic experiences. *Learning and Individual Differences, 9,* 153–174.

Howe, Neil. (1995). Why the graying of the welfare state threatens to flatten the American Dream—or worse: Age-based benefits as our downfall. *Generations: Quarterly Journal of the American Society on Aging, 19,* 15–19.

Howland, Jonathan, Hingson, Ralph, Mangione, Thomas W., Bell, Nicole, & Bak, Sharon. (1996). Why are most drowning victims men? Sex differences in aquatic skills and behaviors. *American Journal of Public Health, 86,* 93–96.

Hsu, L.K. George. (1990). *Eating disorders.* New York: Guilford.

Hudson, J.A. (1990). The emergence of autobiographical memory in mother-child conversation. In R. Fivush & J.A. Hudson (Eds.), *Knowing and remembering in young children.* Cambridge, England: Cambridge University Press.

Huffman, Lynne C., Bryan, Yvonne E., del Carmen, Rebecca, Pedersen, Frank A., Doussard-Roosevelt, Jane A., & Porges, Stephen W. (1998). Infant temperament and cardiac vagal tone: Assessments at twelve weeks of age. *Child Development, 69,* 624–635.

Hughes, Dana, & Simpson, Lisa. (1995). The role of social change in preventing low birth weight. *The Future of Children: Low Birth Weight, 5,* 87–102.

Hughes, Jan N., Cavell, Timothy A., & Grossman, Pamela B. (1997). A positive view of self: Risk or protection for aggressive children? *Development and Psychopathology, 9,* 75–94.

Hull, Harry F., & Aylward, R. Bruce. (1997). Ending polio immunization. *Science, 277,* 780.

Hunt, Earl. (1993). What do we need to know about aging? In John Cerella, John Rybash, William Hoyer, & Michael L. Commons (Eds.), *Adult information processing: Limits on loss.* San Diego: Academic Press.

Hunter, Ski, & Sundel, Martin. (Eds.). (1989). *Midlife myths: Issues, findings and practice implications.* Newbury Park, CA: Sage.

Hurst, Laurence D. (1997). Evolutionary theories of genomic imprinting. In Wolf Reik & Azim Surani (Eds.), *Genomic imprinting.* Oxford, England: IRL Press.

Hurt, Hallam, Brodsky, Nancy L., Betanourt, Laura, Braitman, Leonard E., et al. (1996). Play behavior in toddler with in utero cocaine exposure: A prospective, masked, controlled study. *Journal of Developmental & Behavioral Pediatrics, 17,* 373–379.

Huston, Aletha C. (1983). Sex-typing. In P.H. Mussen (Ed.), *Handbook of child psychology: Vol. 4. Socialization, personality and social development.* New York: Wiley.

Huston, Aletha C. & Wright, John C. (1998). Mass media and children's development. In.William Damon, Irving E. Sigel, & K. Ann Renninger (Eds.), *Handbook of Child Psychology, Volume Four: Child psychology in practice.* New York: Wiley

Huston, Aletha C., Watkins, Bruce A., & Kunkel, Dale. (1989). Public policy and children's television. *American Psychologist, 44,* 424–433.

Huston, Aletha C., McLoyd, Vonnie C., & Coll, Cynthia Garcia. (1994). Children and poverty: Issues in contemporary research. *Child Development, 65,* 275–282.

Huston, Aletha C., Wright, John C., Marquis, Janet, & Green, Samuel B. (1999). How 2young children spend their time: Television and other activities. *Developmental Psychology, 35,* 912–925.

Huth, Mary Jo. (1997). America's new homeless: Single-parent families. In Mary Jo Huth & Talmadge Wright (Eds.), *International critical perspectives on homelessness.* Westport, CT: Praeger.

Huttenlocher, Janellen, Levine, Susan, & Vevea, Jack. (1998). Environmental input and cognitive growth: A study using time-period comparisons. *Child Development, 69,* 1012–1029.

Huttenlocher, Peter R. (1994). Synaptogenesis, synapse elimination, and neural plasticity in human cerebral cortex. In C.A. Nelson Ed.), *Threats to optimal development. The Minnesota symposia on child psychology, 27,* 35–54. Hillsdale, NJ: Erlbaum.

Huyck, Margaret Hellie. (1995). Marriage and close relationships of the marital kind. In Rosemary Blieszner & Victoria Hilkevitch Bedford (Eds.), *Handbook of aging and the family.* Westport, CT: Greenwood Press.

Huyck, Margaret Hellie. (1999). Gender roles and gender identity in midlife. In Sherry L. Willis, & James D. Reid (Eds.), *Life in the middle: Psychosocial and social development in middle age.* San Diego: Academic Press.

Hwalek, Melanie A., Neale, Anne Victoria, Goodrich, Carolyn Stahl, & Quinn, Kathleen. (1996). The association of elder abuse and substance abuse in the Illinois elder abuse system. *Gerontologist, 36,* 694–700.

Hwang, C. Philip, Lamb, Michael E., & Sigel, Irving E. (Eds.). (1996). *Images of childhood.* Mahwah, NJ: Erlbaum.

Hyde, Kenneth E. (1990). *Religion in childhood and adolescence: A comprehensive review of the research.* Birmingham, AL: Religious Education Press.

Hymel, S., Bowker, A., & Woody, E. (1993). Aggressive versus withdrawn unpopular children: Variations in peer and self-perceptions in multiple domains. *Child Development, 64,* 879–896.

Ilmarinen, Juhani. (1995). A new concept for productive aging at work. In Eino Heikkinen, Jorma Kuusinen, & Isto Ruoppila (Eds.), *Preparation for aging.* New York: Plenum Press.

Ingebretsen, Reidun, & Endestad, Tor. (1995). Lifelong learning experiences from Norway. In Eino Heikkinen, Jorma Kuusinen, & Isto Ruoppila (Eds.), *Preparation for aging.* New York, Plenum Press.

Ingersol-Dayton, Berig, & Starrels, Marjorie E. (1996). Caregiving for parents and parents in law: Is gender important? *Gerontologist, 36,* 438–491.

Inhelder, Bärbel, & Piaget, Jean. (1958). *The growth of logical thinking from childhood to adolescence.* New York: Basic Books.

Institute for Social Research. (1997) *Healthy environments, healthy children.* Child development supplement: Panel study of income dynamics. Ann Arbor, MI: University of Michigan Institute for Social Research.

Irazuzta, José E., McJunkin, James E., Danadian, Kapriel, Arnold, Forest, & Zhang, Jianliang. (1997). Outcome and cost of child abuse. *Child Abuse and Neglect, 21,* 751–757.

Isabella, R.A., & Belsky, J. (1991). Interactional synchrony and the origins of infant-mother attachment: A replication study. *Child Development, 62,* 373–384.

Isolauri, E., Sutas, Y., Salo, M. K., Isosonppi, R., & Kaila, M. (1998). Elimination diet in cow's milk allergy: Risk for impaired growth in young children. *Journal of Pediatrics, 132,* 1004–1009.

Itoigawa, Naosuke, Minami, T., Kondo-Ikemujra, K., Tachibana, H., et al. (1996). Parenting and family support in Japan for 6- to 8-year-old children weighing under 1000 grams at birth. *International Journal of Behavioral Development, 19,* 477–490.

Jaccard, James, Dittus, Patricia J., & Gordon, Vivian V. (1998). Parent-adolescent congruency in reports of adolescent sexual behavior and in communications about sexual behavior. *Child Development, 69,* 247–261.

Jackson, Sharon A., Anderson, Roger T., Johnson, Norman J., & Sorlie, Paul D. (2000). The relation of residential segregation to all-cause mortality: A study in black and white. *American Journal of Public Health, 90,* 615–617.

Jacobs, David R., Meyer, Katie A., Kushi, Larwrence H., & Folsom, Aaron R. (1999). Is whole grain intake associated with reduced total and cause-specific death rates in older women? The Iowa women's health study. *American Journal of Public Health, 89,* 322–329.

Jacobson, Joseph L. & Jacobson, Sandra W. (1996). Methodological considerations in behavioral toxicology in infants and children. *Developmental Psychology, 32,* 390–403.

James, Daivd, Pillai, Mary, & Smoleniec, John. (1995). Neurobehavioral development in the human fetus. In Jean-Pierre Lecanuet, William P. Fifer, Norman A. Krasnegor, & William A. Smotherman (Eds.). *Fetal Development: A psychobiological perspective.* Erlbaum, Hillsdale, NJ.

James, William. (1950). *The principles of psychology* (Vol. 1). New York: Dover. (Original work published 1890.

Janowsky, Jeri S., & Carper, Ruth. (1996). Is there a neural basis for cognitive transitions in school-age children? In Arnold J. Sameroff & Marshall M. Haith, *The five to seven year shift: The age of reason and responsibility.* Chicago & London: The University of Chicago Press.

Jeanneret, Rene. (1995). The role of preparation for retirement in the improvement of the quality of life for elderly people. In Eino Heikkinen, Jorma Kuusinen, & Isto Ruoppila (Eds.), *Preparation for aging.* New York: Plenum Press.

Jencks, Christopher. (1994). *The homeless.* Cambridge, MA: Harvard University Press.

Jendrek, Margaret Platt. (1994). Grandparents who parent their grandchildren: Effects on lifestyle. *Journal of Marriage and the Family, 55,* 609–622.

Jenkins, Jennifer M., & Astington, Janet Wilde. (1996). Cognitive factors and family structure associated with theory of mind development in young children. *Developmental Psychology, 32,* 70–78.

Jenkins, J., & Bell. (1997) Exposure and response to community violence among children and adolescents. In Joy Ofsosky (Ed.), *Children in a violent society,* East Sussex, England: Psychology Press.

Jensen, Peter S., & Hoagwood, Kimberly. (1997). The book of names: DSM-IV in context. *Development and Psychopathology, 9,* 231–249.

Jensen, Peter S., Kettle, Lori, Roper, Margaret T., Sloan, Michael T., Dulcan, Mina K., Hoven, Christina, Bird, Hector R., Bauermeister, Jose J., & Payne, Jennifer D. (1999). Are stimulants overprescribed? Treatment of ADHD in four U.S. communities. *Journal of American Academy of Child and Adolescent Psychiatry, 38,* 797–804

Jessor, Richard, Donovan, John E., & Costa, Frances M. (1991). *Beyond adolescence: Problem behavior and young adult development.* Cambridge, England: Cambridge University Press.

Jo, E. & Berkowitz, L. (1994). A priming effect analysis of media influences: An update. In J. Bryant & D. Zillmann (Eds.L), *Media effects: Advances in theory and research.* Hillsdale, NJ: Erlbaum.

Jockin, Victor, McGue, Matt, & Lykken, David T. (1996). Personality and divorce: A genetic analysis. *Journal of Personality and Social Psychology, 71,* 288–299.

Johnson, C.I., & Baer, B.M. (1993). Coping and a sense of control among the oldest old. *Journal of Aging Studies, 7,* 67–80.

Johnson, Colleen L. (1995). Cultural diversity in the late-life family. In Rosemary Blieszner & Victoria Hilkevitch Bedford (Eds.), *Handbook of aging and the family.* Westport, CT: Greenwood Press.

Johnson, Colleen L., & Fietive, Kin. (1999). Among oldest old: African Americans in the San Francisco Bay area. *Journal of Gerontology, 54B,* S 368-S 375.

Johnson, Mark H. (1997). *Developmental cognitive neuroscience: An introduction.* Cambridge, MA: Blackwell.

Johnson, Mark H. (1998). The neural basis of cognitive development. In William Damon, Deanna Kuhn, & Robert S. Siegler (Eds.), *Handbook of child psychology: Cognition, perception, and language.* New York: Wiley

Johnson, Mark H. (1999). Developoomental neuroscience. In Marc H. Bornstein & Michael E. Lamb (Eds.), *Developmental psychology: An advanced textbook.* Mahwah, NJ: Erlbaum.

Johnson, M.P. (1995). Patriarchal terrorism and common couple violence: Two forms of violence against women. *Journal of Marriage and the Family, 57,* 283–294.

Johnson-Powell, Gloria, & Yamamoto, Joe. (1997). *Transcultural child development: Psychological assessment and treatment.* New York: Wiley.

John-Steiner, Vera. (1986). *Notebooks of the mind: Explorations of thinking.* Albuquerque: University of New Mexico Press.

Johnston, Lloyd D., O'Malley, Patrick M., & Bachman, Jerald G. (1989). *Drug use, drinking, and smoking: National survey results from high school, college, and young adult populations, 1975–1988.* Rockville, MD: National Institute for Drug Abuse.

Johnston, Lloyd D., O'Malley, Patrick M., & Bachman, Jerald G. (1997). *Monitoring the future study: Drug use among American teens shows some signs of leveling after a long rise.* (University of Michigan News and Information Services Press Release, December 18, 1997). Ann Arbor: University of Michigan.

Johnston, Lloyd D., O'Malley, Patrick M., & Bachman, Jerald G. (1998). *Drug use by American young people begins to turn downward.* (University of Michigan News and Information Services Press Release, December, 1998). Ann Arbor: University of Michigan.

Johnston, Lloyd D., O'Malley, Patrick M., & Bachman, Jerald G. (1998). *Monitoring the future study: Drug use among American teens shows some signs of leveling after a long rise.* (University of Michigan News and Information Services Press Release, December, 1998). Ann Arbor: University of Michigan.

Johnston, Lloyd D., O'Malley, Patrick M., & Bachman, Jerald G. (1998). *Smoking among American teens declines some.* (University of Michigan News and Information Services Press Release, December, 1998). Ann Arbor: University of Michigan.

Johnston, Lloyd D., O'Malley, Patrick M., & Bachman, Jerald G. (1999). *The monitoring the future: National results on adolescent drug use.* Overview of key findings, 1999. (NIH Pub. No. 00-4690. Bethesda, Maryland: National Institute on Drug Abuse.

Joiner, Jr., Thomas E. (1999). The clustering and contagion of suicide. *Current Directions in Psychological Science, 8,* 89–92.

Jones, C.J., & Meredith, W. (1996). Patterns of personality change across the life span. *Psychology of Aging, 11,* 57–65.

Jones, Elizabeth, & Reynolds, Gretchen. (1992). *The play's the thing: Teachers' roles in children's play.* New York: Teacher's College Press.

Jones, Harold E., & Conrad, Herbert S. (1933). The growth and decline of intelligence: A study of a homogeneous group between the ages of ten and sixty. *Genetic Psychology Monographs, 13,* 223–298.

Jones, Nancy Aaron, Field, Tiffany, Fox, Nathan A., Lunedy, Brenda, & Davalos, Marisabel. (1997). EEG activation in 1-month-old infants of depressed mothers. *Development and Psychopathology, 9,* 491–505.

Jones, Robin, Schlank, Anita, & Le Guin, Louis. (1999). Assessment of adolescent sex offenders. In Jon A. Shaw (Ed.) *Sexual Aggression.* Washington, DC: America Psychiatric Press.

Jones, Susan S., Smith, Linda B., & Landau, Barbara. (1991). Object properties and knowledge in early lexical learning. *Child Development, 62,* 499–516.

Jorm, A.F., Christensen, H., Henderson, A.S., Korten, A.E., MacKinnon, A.J., & Scott, R. (1994). Complaint of cognitive decline in the elderly: A comparison of reports by subjects and informants in a community survey. *Psychological Medicine, 24,* 365–374.

Jung, C.G. (1961). *Memories, dreams, recollections.* New York: Vintage. (Original work published 1933)

Junger-Tas, J., Terlouw, G. J., & Klein, M. W. (1994). *Delinquent behavior among young people in the Western World.* New York: Kugler.

Jusczyk, Peter W. (1995). Language acquisition: Speech sounds and the beginnings of phonology. In J.L. Miller & P.D. Eimas (Eds.), *Speech, language and communication.* New York: Academic Press.

Jusczyk, Peter W. (1997). *The discovery of spoken language.* Cambridge, Mass.: MIT Press.

Kachur, S. Patrick, Potter, Lloyd B., James, Stephen P., & Powell, Kenneth E. (1995). *Suicide in the United States: 1980–1992* (Violence Surveillance Summary Series No. 1). Atlanta, GA: National Center for Injury Prevention and Control.

Kagen, Jerome. (1994). *Galen's prophecy.* New York: Basic Books.

Kagen, Jerome. (1998). *Three seductive ideas.* Cambridge, MA: Harvard University Press.

Kahn, James G., et al. (1999). Pregnancies averted among U. S. Teenagers by the use of contraceptives. *Family Planning Perspectives, 31,* 29–34.

Kahn, Joan R., & London, Kathryn A. (1991). Premarital sex and the risk of divorce. *Journal of Marriage and the Family, 53,* 845–855.

Kahn, Jeffrey P., Mastroianni, Anna C., & Sugarmen, Jeremy (Eds.). (1998). *Beyond consent: Seeking justice in research.* New York: Oxford University Press.

Kail, R. (1990). *The development of memory in children* (3rd ed.). New York: Freeman.

Kalish, Richard A. (1985). The social context of death and dying. In Robert H. Binstock & Ethel Shanas (Eds.), *Handbook of aging and the social sciences.* New York: Van Nostrand Reinhold.

Kallen, Karin. (1997). Maternal smoking during pregnancy and limb reduction malformations in Sweden. *American Journal of Public Health, 87,* 29–32.

Kamerman, S.B., & Kahn, A.J. (1993). Home health visiting in Europe. *The Future of Children, 3,* 39–52.

Kandel, Denise B., & Davies, Mark. (1996). High school students who use crack and other drugs. *Archives of General Psychiatry, 53,* 71–80.

Kandel, Denise B., Wu, Ping, & Davies, Mark. (1994). Maternal smoking during pregnancy and smoking by adolescent daughters. *American Journal of Public Health, 84,* 1407–1413.

Kanner, Leo. (1943). Autistic disturbances of affective contact. *Nervous Child, 2,* 217–250.

Kanungo, Madhu S. (1994). *Genes & aging.* Cambridge, England: Cambridge University Press.

Kaplan, Elaine Bell. (1997). Adolescent sexual abuse, sexual assault, and rape. *Adolescence, 32,* 713–734.

Kaplan, Peter S., Bachorowski, Jo-Anne, & Zarlengo-Strouse, Patricia. (1999). Child-directed speech produced by mothers with symptoms of depression fails to promote associative learning in 4-month-old infants. *Child Development, 70,* 560–570.

Kaplan, Robert M. (2000). Two pathways to prevention. *American Psychologist, 55*, 382–396.

Kaplowitz, Stan A., Osuch, Janet R., Safron, deborah, & Campo, Shelly. (1999). Physician communication with seriously ill cancer patients: Results of a survey of physicians. In Brian de Vries (Ed.), *End of life issues: Interdisciplinary and multidimensional perspectives.* New York: Springer.

Karpov, Yuriy, & Haywood, H. Carl. (1998). Two ways to elaborate Vygotsky's concept of mediation: Implications for instruction. *American Psychologist, 53*, 27–36.

Kasl-Godley, Julia E., Gatz, Margaret, & Fiske, Amy. (1998). Depression and depressive symptoms in old age. In Inger Hilde Nordhus, Gary R. VandenBos, Stig Berg, & Pia Fromholt (Eds.) *Clinical geropsychology: Contents.* Washington DC: APA Books.

Kastenbaum, Robert J. (1992). *The psychology of death.* New York: Springer-Verlag.

Katchadourian, Herant A. (1987). *Fifty: Midlife in perspective.* New York: Freeman.

Katz, Jeanne Samson. (1993). Jewish perspectives on death, dying and bereavement. In Donna Dickenson & Malcolm Johnson (Eds.), *Death, dying & bereavement.* London: Sage.

Kaufman, A.S. (1990). *Assessing adolescent and adult intelligence.* Boston: Allyn & Bacon.

Kaufman, Joan, & Zigler, Edward. (1989). The intergenerational transmission of child abuse. In Dante Cicchetti & Vicki Carlson (Eds.), *Child maltreatment: Theory and research on the causes and consequences of child abuse and neglect.* Cambridge, England: Cambridge University Press.

Kaufman, Joan, & Zigler, Edward. (1993). The intergenerational hypothesis is overstated. In Richard J. Gelles & Donileen R. Loseke (Eds.), *Current controversies in family violence.* Newbury Park, CA: Sage.

Kaufman, Sharon R. (1986). *The ageless self.* Madison: University of Wisconsin Press.

Kawas, Claudia, Resnick, S., Morrison, A., Brookmeyer, R., Corrada, Maria, Zonderman, A., Bacal, C., Donnell Lingle, D., & Metter, E. Jeffrey. (1997). A prospective study of estrogen replacement therapy and the risk of developing Alzheimer's disease: The Baltimore Longitudinal Study of aging. *Neurology, 48*, 1517–1521.

Keating, D.P. (1990). Adolescent thinking. In S.S. Feldman & G.R. Elliott (Eds.), *At the threshold: The developing adolescent.* Cambridge, MA: Harvard University Press.

Keith, Jennie. (1990). Age in social and cultural context: Anthropological perspectives. In Robert H. Binstock & Linda K. George (Eds.), *Handbook of aging and the social sciences (3rd ed.).* San Diego: Academic Press.

Keith, Jennie, Fry, Christine L., Glascock, Anthony P., Ikels, Charlotte, Dickerson-Putman, Jeannette, Harpending, Henry C., & Draper, Patricia. (1994). *The aging experience: Diversity and commonality across cultures.* Thousand Oaks, CA: Sage.

Kellman, Philip J. & Banks, Martin S. (1998). Infant visual perception. In William Damon, Deanna Kuhn, & Robert S. Siegler (Eds.), *Handbook of child psychology: Cognition, perception, and language.* New York: Wiley

Kelly, Karen. (1998). Working teenagers: Do after-school jobs hurt? *The Harvard Education Letter, 14*, 1–3.

Kemper, Susan & Harden, Tamara. (1999). Experimentally disentangling what's beneficial about elderspeak from what's not. *Psychology and Aging, 14*, 656–670.

Kerr, Margaret, Lambert, William W., & Bem, Daryl J. (1996). Life course sequelae of childhood shyness in Sweden: Comparison with the United States. *Developmental Psychology, 32*, 1100–1105.

Keshet, Jamie. (1988). The remarried couple: Stresses and successes. In William R. Beer (Ed.), *Relative strangers.* Totowa, NJ: Rowman & Littlefield.

Kessen, W. (1990). *The rise and fall of development.* Worcester, MA: Clark University Press.

Keyes, Corey Lee & Ruff, Carol D. (1999). Psychological well-being in mid-life. In Sherry L. Willis & James D. Reid (Eds.) *Life in the middle.* San Diego: Academic Press.

Kiecolt, K.J. (1994). Stress and the decision to change oneself: A theoretical model. *Social Psychology Quarterly, 57*, 49–63.

Kim, Kenneth & Smith, Peter K. (1998. Retrospective survey of parental marital relations and child reproductive development. *International Journal of Behavioral Development, 22*, 729–751.

Kincade, Jean E., Rabiner, Donna J., Bernard, Shulamit L., Woomert, Alison, Konrad, Thomas R., DeFriese, Gordon H., & Ory, Marcia G. (1996). Older adults as a community resource: Results from the national survey of self-care and aging. *Gerontologist, 36*, 474–482.

King, Gary, & Williams, David R. (1995). Race and health: A multi-dimensional approach to African-American health. In Benjamin C. Amick III, Sol Levine, Alvin R. Tarlov, & Diana Chapman Walsh (Eds.), *Society and health.* New York: Oxford University Press.

King, Valerie. (1994). Non-resident father involvement and child well-being: Can dads make a difference? *Journal of Family Issues, 15*, 78–96.

King, P.M. & Kitchener, K.S. (1994). *Developing reflective judgment: Understanding and promoting intellectual growth and critical thinking in adolescents and adults.* San Francisco: Jossey-Bass.

Kisilevsky, B.S., & Low, J.A. (1998). Human fetal behavior: 100 years of study. *Developmental Review, 18*, 1–29.

Kitzinger, Sheila. (1989). *The complete book of pregnancy and childbirth.* New York: Knopf.

Kitzmann, Katherine M. (2000). Effects of marital conflict on subsequent triadic family interactions and parenting. *Developmental Psychology, 36*, 3–13.

Klahr, David. (1989). Information-processing approaches. In R. Vasta (Ed.), *Annals of child development* (Vol. 6). Greenwich, CT: JAI Press.

Klahr, David & Brian MacWhinney. (1998). Information processing. In.William Damon, Deanna Kuhn & Robert S. Siegler (Eds.), *Handbook of Child Psychology, Volume Two: Cognition, perception, and language.* New York: Wiley.

Klaus, Marshall H., & Kennell, John H. (1976). *Maternal-infant bonding: The impact of early separation or loss on family development*. St. Louis: Mosby.

Klee, Linnea, Kronstadt, Diana, & Zlotnic, Cheryl. (1997). Foster care's youngest: A preliminary report. *America Orthopsychiatric Association, Inc., 67*, 290–299.

Kleiber, Douglas A. (1999). *Leisure experience and human development: A dialectical interpretation*. New York: Basic Books.

Klein, Melanie. (1957). *Envy and gratitude*. New York: Basic Books.

Klepinger, Daniel H., Lundberg, Shelly, & Plotnick, Robert D. (1995). Adolescent fertility and the educational attainment of young women. *Family Practice Perspectives, 27*, 23–28.

Klesges, Robert. (1993). Effects of television on metabolic rate: Potential implications for childhood obesity. *Pediatrics, 91*, 281–286.

Kline, Donald W., & Scialfa, Charles T. (1996). Visual and auditory aging. In James E. Birren & K. Warner Schaie (Eds.), *Handbook of the psychology of aging*. San Diego: Academic Press.

Klopfer, P. (1971). Mother love: What turns it on? *American Scientist, 49*, 404–407.

Knäuper, Bärbel. (1999) Age differences in question and response order effects. In Norbert Schwarz, Denise Park, Bärbel Knäuper, & Seymour Sudman (Eds.), *Cognition, aging, and self-reports*. Philadelphia: Psychology Press.

Kochanska, G. (1997). Multiple pathways to conscience for children with different temperaments: From toddlerhood to age 5. *Developmental Psychology, 33*, 228–240.

Kochanska, G., Murray, K., & Coy, K. (1997). Inhibitory control as a contributor to conscience in childhood: From toddler to early school age. *Child Development, 68*, 263–278.

Kochanska, Grazyna, Coy, Katherine C., Tjebkes, Terri L., & Husarek, Susan J. (1998). Individual differences in emotionality in infancy. *Child Development, 64*, 375–390.

Kochanska, Grazyna, Murray, Kathleen T., & Harlan, Elena T. (2000). Effortful control in early childhood: Continuity and change, antecedents, and implications for social development. *Developmental Psychology, 36*, 220–232.

Koepke, Jean E., & Bigelow, Ann E. (1997). Observations of newborn suckling behavior. *Infant Behavior & Development, 20*, 93–98.

Koff, E., & Rierdan, Jill. (1995). Preparing girls for menstruation: Recommendations from adolescent girls. *Adolescence, 30*, 795–811.

Kohlberg, Lawrence. (1963). Development of children's orientation towards a moral order (Part I). Sequencing in the development of moral thought. *Vita Humana, 6*, 11–36.

Kohlberg, Lawrence. (1973). Continuities in childhood and adult moral development revisited. In Paul B. Baltes & K. Warner Schaie (Eds.), *Life-span developmental psychology: Personality and socialization*. New York: Academic Press.

Kohlberg, Lawrence. (1981). *Essays on moral development* (Vol. 1). New York: Harper & Row.

Kohlberg, Lawrence. (1981). *The philosophy of moral development*. New York: Harper & Row.

Kohnstamm, Geldoph A., Halverson, Charles F., Havil, Valeri L., & Mervielde, Ivan. (1996). Parents' free descriptions of child characteristics: A cross cultural search for the developmental antecedents of the big five. In Sara Harkness & Charles M. Super (Eds.), *Parents' cultural belief systems: The origins, expressions, and consequences*. New York: Guilford.

Kolland, F. (1994). Contrasting cultural profiles between generations: Interests and common activities in three intrafamilial generations. *Aging and Society, 14*, 319–340.

Kompier, Michiel & Cooper, Cary (Eds.) (1999). *Preventing stress, improving productivity: European case studies in the workplace*. London: Routledge.

Kools, Susan M. (1997). Adolescent identity development in foster care. *Family Relations, 46*, 263–271.

Koopman, Peter, Gubbay, John, Vivian, Nigel, Goodfellow, Peter, & Lovell-Badge, Robin. (1991). Male development of chromosomally female mice transgenic for Sry. *Nature, 351*, 117–122.

Korbin, Jill E., Coulton, Claudia J., Chard, Sarah, Platt-Houston, Candis & Su, Marilyn. (1998). Impoverishment and child maltreatment in African American and European American neighborhoods. *Development and Psychopathology, 10*, 215–233.

Kosterlitz, J. (1993). Golden silence? *National Journal*, pp. 800–804.

Kotre, John. (1984). *Outliving the self: Generativity and the interpretation of lives*. Baltimore: Johns Hopkins University Press.

Kotre, John. (1995). *White gloves: How we create ourselves through memory*. New York: Free Press.

Kotre, John & Kotre, Kathy B. (1998). Intergenerational buffers: "The damage stops here." In Dan P. McAdams & Ed de St. Aubin (Eds.), *Generativity and adult development: How and why we care for the next generation*. Washington, DC: American Psychological Association.

Kotre, John. (1999–2000). Generativity and the gift of meaning. Reasons to grow old: Meaning in later life. *Generations, 23*, 65–71.

Kovacs, Donna M., Parker, Jeffrey G., & Hoffman, Lois W. (1996). Behavioral affective, and social correlates of involvement in cross-sex friendship in elementary school. *Child Development, 67*, 2269–2286.

Kozol, Jonathan. (1991). *Savage inequalities*. New York: Crown.

Kraft, Joan Creech & Willhite, Calvin C. (1997). Retinoids in abnormal and normal embryonic development. In Sam Kacew & George H. Lambert (Eds.), *Environmental toxicology and human development*. Washington DC: Taylor & Francis.

Krappmann, Lother. (1996). The measurement of friendship perceptions: Conceptual and methodological issues. In William M. Bukowski, Andrew F. Newcomb, & Williard W. Hartup (Eds.), *The company they keep: Friendship in childhood and adolescence*. Cambridge, England: Cambridge University Press.

Krauss, J.B. (1999). Educational innovation and responsibility. *Archives of Psychiatric Nursing, 13*, 225–226

Kroger, Jane. (1989). *Identity in adolescence: The balance between self and other.* London: Routledge.

Kroger, Jane. (1993). Ego identity: an overview. In J. Kroger (Ed.), *Discussions on ego identity.* Hillsdale, NJ: Erlbaum.

Kroger, Jane. (2000). *Identity Development: Adolescence through adulthood.* Thousand Oaks, CA: Sage.

Kromelow, Susan, Harding, Carol, & Touris, Margot. (1990). The role of the father in the development of stranger sociability during the second year. *American Journal of Orthopsychiatry, 6*, 521–530.

Krowchuk, Daniel P., Kreiter, Shelly R., Woods, Charles R., Sinal, Sara H., & DuRant, l. Robert H. (1998) Problem dieting behaviors among young adolescents. *Archives of Pediatric & Adolescent Medicine, 152*, 885–888.

Kübler-Ross, Elisabeth. (1969). *On death and dying.* New York: Macmillan.

Kübler-Ross, Elisabeth. (1975*). Death: The final stage of growth.* Englewood Cliffs, NJ: Prentice Hall.

Kuczynski, L., & Kochanska, G. (1990). Development of children's noncompliance strategies from toddlerhood to age 5. *Developmental Psychology, 26*, 398–408.

Kuhl, P.K., & Meltzoff, A.N. (1988). Speech as an intermodal object of perception. In A. Yonas (Ed.), *Minnesota symposia on child psychology: Vol. 20. Perceptual development in infancy.* Hillsdale, NJ: Erlbaum.

Kuhn, Deanna, Garcia-Mita, Merce, Zohar, Arat, & Anderson, Christopher. (1995). Strategies of knowledge acquisition. *Monographs of the Society for Research in Child Development, 60* (Serial No. 245).

Kulin, H.E. (1993). Editorial: Puberty: When? *Journal of Clinical Endocrinology and Metabolism, 76*, 24–25.

Kurdek, Lawrence A. (1991). The relations between reported well-being and divorce history, availability of a proximate adult, and gender. *Journal of Marriage and the Family, 53*, 71–78.

Kurdek, Lawrence A. (1992). Relationship status and relationship satisfaction in cohabiting gay and lesbian couples. *Journal of Social and Personal Relationships, 9*, 125–142.

Kurdek, Lawrence. (1998). Relationship outcomes and their predictors: Longitudinal evidence from heterosexual married, gay cohabiting, and lesbian cohabiting couples. *Journal of Marriage and the Family, 60*, 553–568.

Labouvie-Vief, Gisela. (1985). Intelligence and cognition. In James E. Birren & K. Warner Schaie (Eds.), *Handbook of the psychology of aging* (2nd ed.). New York: Van Nostrand Reinhold.

Labouvie-Vief, Gisela. (1990). Wisdom as integrated thought: Historical and developmental perspectives. In Robert J. Sternberg (Ed.), *Wisdom: Its nature, origins, and development.* Cambridge, England: Cambridge University Press.

Labouvie-Vief, Gisela. (1992). A neo-Piagetian perspective on adult cognitive development. In Robert J. Sternberg & Cynthia A. Berg (Eds.), *Intellectual development.* New York: Cambridge University Press.

Lagerspetz, Kirsti & Bjorkquist, Kaj. (1994). In L. Rowell Huesmann (Ed.) *Aggressive Behavior.* New York: Plenum.

Lahey, Benjamin B., & Loeber, Rolf. (1994). Framework for a developmental model of oppositional defiant disorder and conduct disorder. In Donald K. Routh (Ed.), *Disruptive behavior disorders in childhood.* New York: Plenum Press.

La Leche League International. (1997). *The womanly art of breastfeeding.* New York: Plume.

Lamb, Michael E. (1982). Maternal employment and child development: A review. In Michael E. Lamb (Ed.), *Nontraditional families: Parenting and child development.* Hillsdale, NJ: Erlbaum.

Lamb, Michael E. (1997). The development of father-infant relationships. In M.E. Lamb (Ed.), *The role of the father in child development.* New York: Wiley.

Lamb, Michael E., & Sternberg, Kathleen J. (1990). Do we really know how day care affects children? *Journal of Applied Developmental Psychology, 11*, 351–379.

Lamb, Wally. (1993). *She's come undone.* New York: Washington Square Press.

Lambert, Wallace E., Genesee, Fred, Holobow, Naomi & Chartrand, Louise. (1993). Bilingual education for majority English-speaking children. *European Journal of Psychology of Education, 8*, 3–22.

Lamy, Peter P. (1994). Drug-nutrient interactions in the aged. In Ronald R. Watson (Ed.), *Handbook of nutrition in the aged.* Boca Raton, Florida: CRC Press.

Lane, Mark A., Tilmont, Edward M., De Angelis, Holly, Handy, April, Ingram, Donald K., Kemnitz, Joseph W., & Roth, Goerge S. (1999). Short term calorie restriction improves disease related markers in older male rhesus monkeys. *Mechanisms of Aging and Development, 112*, 185–196.

Lang, Frieder R., & Carstensen, Laura L. (1994). Close emotional relationships in late life: Further support for proactive aging in the social domain. *Psychology and Aging, 9*, 315–324.

Langkamp, Diane L., Kim, Young, & Pascoe, John M. (1998). Temperament of preterm infants at four months of age: Maternal ratings and perceptions. *Developmental and Behavioral Pediatrics, 19*, 391–396.

Laosa, Luis M. (1996). Intelligence testing and social policy. *Journal of Applied Developmental Psychology, 17*, 155–173.

LaPointe, A.E., Mead, N.A., & Askew, J.M. (1992). *Learning mathematics.* Princeton, NJ: Educational Testing Service.

Larner, M.B., Stevenson, C.S., & Behrman, R.E. (1998). Protecting children from abuse and neglect: Analysis and recommendations. *Future Child, 8*, 4–22.

Larson, David, Swyers, James, & Larson, Susan. (1995). *The costly consequences of divorce: Assessing the clinical, economic, and public health impact of marital disruption in the United States.* Rockville, MD: National Institute for Health-care Research.

Larson, R.W. Almeida D.M. (1999). Emotional transmission in the daily lives of families: A new paradigm for studying family process. *Journal of Marriage and the Family, 61,* 5–20.

Larson, Reed W. & Gillman, Sally. (1999). Transmission of emotions in the daily interactions of single-mother families. *Journal of Marriage and the Family, 61,* 21–37.

Larson, Reed W., & Ham, Mark. (1993). Stress and "storm and stress" in early adolescence: The relationship of negative events with dysphoric affect. *Developmental Psychology, 29,* 130–140.

Larson, Reed, & Richards, Maryse H. (1994*). Divergent realities: The emotional lives of mothers, fathers, and adolescents.* New York: Basic Books.

Larsen, William J. (1998). *Essentials of human embryology.* New York: Churchill Livingstone.

Lattanzi-Licht, Marcia, & Connor, Stephen. (1995). Care of the dying: The hospice approach. In Hannelore Wass & Robert A. Neimeyer (Eds.), *Dying: Facing the facts.* Washington, DC: Taylor & Francis.

Laumann, Edward O., Gagnon, John H., Michael, Robert T., & Michaels, Stuart. (1994). *The social organization of sexuality: Sexual practices in the United States.* Chicago: University of Chicago Press.

Lawrence, Renee H., Tennstedt, Sharon L., & Assmann, Susan F. (1998). Quality of the caregiver-care recipient relationship: Does it offset negative consequences of caregiving for family caregivers? *Psychology and Aging, 13,* 150–158.

Lawrence, Ruth A. (1998). *Breastfeeding: A guide for the medical profession* (5th ed.). St. Louis: Mosby.

Leach, Penelope. (1997). *Your baby & child: From birth to age 5.* New York: Knopf.

Leadbeater, B. (1986). The resolution of relativism in adult thinking: Subjective, objective, or conceptual. *Human Development, 29,* 291–300.

Leaper, Campbell, Anderson, Kristin J., & Sanders, Paul. (1998). Moderators of gender effects on parents' talk to their children: A meta-analysis. *Developmental Psychology, 34,* 3–27.

Lear, Dana. (1997). *Sex and sexuality: Risk and relationships in the age of AIDS.* Thousand Oaks, CA: Sage.

Leavitt, L., & Fox, N. (1993). *The psychological effects of war and violence on children.* Hillsdale, NJ: Erlbaum.

Leekam, Susan R., López, Beatriz, & Moore, Chris. (2000). Attention and joint attention in preschool children with autism. *Developmental Psychology, 36,* 261–273.

Leenaars, Antoon A., & Lester, David. (1995). The changing suicide pattern in Canadian adolescents and youth, compared to their American counterparts. *Adolescence, 30,* 539–547.

Leffert, Nancy, & Petersen, Anne C. (1995). Patterns of development during adolescence. In Michael Rutter & David J. Smith (Eds.), *Psychosocial disorders in young people: Time trends and their causes.* Chichester: Wiley.

Lehman, Darrin R., Wortman, Camille b., Haring, Michelle, Tweed, Roger, G., de Vries, Brian, DeLongis, Anita, Hamphill,

Kenneth J., & Ellard, John H. (1999). Recovery from the perspective of the bereaved: Personal assessments and sources of distress and support. In Brian de Vries (Ed.), *End of life issues: Interdisciplinary and multidimensional perspectives.* New York: Springer.

Leifer, A.D., Leiderman, P.H., Barnett, C.R., & Williams, J.A. (1972). Effects of mother-infant separation on maternal attachment behavior. *Child Development, 43,* 1203–1218.

Lemaitre, Rosenn N., Siscovick, David S., Raghunathan, Trimellore E., Weinmann, Sheila, Arbogast, Patrick, & Lin, Dan-Yu. (1999). Leisure-time physical activity and the risk of primary cardiac arrest. *Archives of Internal Medicine, 159,* 686–690.

Lemery, Kathryn S., Goldsmith, H. Hill, Klinnert, Mary D., & Mrazel, David A. (1999). Developmental models of infant and childhood temperament. *Developmental Psychology, 35,* 189–204.

Lenneberg, Eric H. (1967). *Biological foundations of language.* New York: Wiley.

Leong, Frederick T.L. (Ed.). (1995). *Career development and vocational behavior of racial and ethnic minorities.* Mahwah, NJ: Erlbaum.

Leong, Frederick T.L., & Brown, Michael T. (1995). Theoretical issues in cross-cultural career development: Cultural validity and cultural specificity. In W. Bruce Walsh & Samuel H. Osipow (Eds.), *Handbook of vocational psychology: Theory, research and practice (2nd ed.).* Mahwah, NJ: Erlbaum.

Leonard, K.E. & Blane, H.T. (Eds.). *Psychological theories of drinking and alcoholism.* New York: Guilford Press.

Lerner, H.E. (1978). Adaptive and pathogenic aspects of sex-role stereotypes: Implications for parenting and psychotherapy. *American Journal of Psychiatry, 135,* 48–52.

Leslie, A.M., & Keeble, S. (1987). Do six-month-olds perceive causality? *Cognition, 25,* 265–288.

Lester, Barry M., & Dreher, Melanie. (1989). Effects of marijuana use during pregnancy on newborn cry. *Child Development, 60,* 765–771.

Lester, Barry M., Hoffman, Joel, & Brazelton, T. Berry. (1985). The rhythmic structure of mother-infant interaction in term and preterm infants. *Child Development, 56,* 15–27.

Levenson, Robert W., Carstensen, Laura R., & Gottman, John M. (1993). Long-term marriage: Age, gender, and satisfaction. *Psychology and Aging, 8,* 301–313.

Levin, Jack. (1999, May 7). An effective response to teenage crime is possibleand cities are showing the way. *The Chronicle of Higher Education.*

Levine, Arthur & Cureton, Jeanette S. (1998). *When hope and fear collide: A portrait of today's college student.* San Francisco: Jossey-Bass Publishers.

Levine, Murray, & Doueck, Howard J. (1995). *The impact of mandated reporting on the therapeutic process: Picking up the pieces.* Thousand Oaks: Sage.

LeVine, Robert A., Dixon, Suzanne, LeVine, Sarah, Richman, Ay, Leiderman, P. Herbert, Keeferk Constance H. & Brazelton, Berry. (1994). *Child care and culture: Lessons from Africa.* New York: Cambridge University Press.

Levine, Sarah & Osbourne, Sally. (1989). Living and learning with Sally. *Phi Delta Kappan, 70,* 594–598.

Levinson, Daniel J. (1978). *The seasons of a man's life.* New York: Knopf.

Levinson, D. (1989). Physical punishment of children and wife beating in cross-cultural perspective. *Child Abuse & Neglect, 5,* 193–195.

Levy, Becca. (1996). Improving memory in old age through implicit self-stereotyping. *Journal of Personality and Social Psychology, 71,* 1092–1106.

Levy, B., & Langer, E. (1994). Aging free from negative stereotypes: Successful memory in China and among the American deaf. *Journal of Personality and Social Psychology, 66,* 989–997.

Levy, Gary D. (1994). Aspects of preschoolers' comprehension of indoor and outdoor gender-typed toys. *Sex Roles, 30,* 391–405.

Lewis, Catherine C. (1996). Fostering social and intellectual development: The roots of Japan's educational success. In Thomas P. Rohlen & Gerald K. LeTendre (Eds.), *Teaching and learning in Japan.* Cambridge, England: Cambridge University Press.

Lewis, Lawrence B., Antone, Carol, & Johnson, Jacqueline S. (1999). Effects of prosodic stress and serial position on syllable omission in first words. *Developmental Psychology, 35,* 45–59.

Lewis, M. (1990). Social knowledge and social development. *Merrill-Palmer Quarterly, 36,* 93–116.

Lewis, M., & Brooks, J. (1978). Self-knowledge and emotional development. In M. Lewis & L.A. Rosenblum (Eds.), *The development of affect.* New York: Plenum.

Lewis, M., Sullivan, M.W., Stanger, C., & Weiss, M. (1989). Self development and self-conscious emotions. *Child Development, 60,* 146–156.

Lewis, M., Alessandri, S.M., & Sullivan, M.W. (1992). Differences in shame and pride as a function of children's gender and task difficulty. *Child Development, 63,* 630–638.

Lewit, Eugene M. & Kerrebrock, Nancy. (1998). Child indicators: Dental health. *The Future of Children: Protecting Children from Abuse and Neglect, 8,* 4–22.

Li, De-Kun, Mueller, Beth A., Hickok, Durlin E., Daling, Janet R., Fantel, Alan G., Checkoway, Harvey, & Weiss, Noel S. (1996). Maternal smoking during pregnancy and the risk of congential urinary tract anomalies. *American Journal of Public Health, 86,* 249–253.

Li, Karen Z.H., Hasher, Lynn, Jonas, Deborah, Rahhal, Tamara A., & May Cynthia P. (1998). Distractibility, circadian arousal, and aging: A boundary condition. *Psychology and Aging, 13,* 574–583.

Lieberman, A.F. (1993). *The emotional life of the toddler.* New York: Free Press.

Lieberman, Alicia F., Weston, Donna R., & Pawl, Jeree H. (1991). Preventive intervention and outcome with anxiously attached dyads. *Child Development, 62,* 199–209.

Light, L. (1996). Memory and aging. In E.L. Bjork & R.A. Bjork (Eds.), *Handbook of perception and cognition.* San Diego: Academic Press.

Lightfoot, Cynthia. (1997). *The culture of adolsecent risk-taking.* New York: Guilford Press.

Lillard, A.S. (1993). Pretend play skills and the child's theory of mind. *Child Development, 64,* 348–371.

Lillard, A.S. (1993). Young children's conceptualization of pretense: Action or mental representational state? *Child Development, 64,* 372–386.

Lillard, A.S. (1994). Making sense of pretense. In C. Lewis & P. Mitchell (Eds.), *Children's early understanding of mind.* Hillsdale, NJ: Erlbaum.

Lillard, Angeline. (1999). Developing a cultural theory of mind: The CIAO approach. *Current Directions in Psychological Science, 8,* 57–60.

Lindenberger, Ulman, & Baltes, Paul B. (1994). Sensory functioning and intelligence in old age: A strong connection. *Psychology and Aging, 9,* 339–355.

Lipton, Robert I. (1994). The effect of moderate alcohol use on the relationship between stress and depression. *American Journal of Public Health, 84,* 1913–1917.

Lisak, David. (1997). Male gender socialization and the perpetuation of sexual abuse. In Ronald F. Levant & Gary R. Brooks (Eds.), *Men and sex: New psychological perspectives.* New York: Wiley.

Locke, J.L. (1993). *The child's path to spoken language.* Cambridge, MA: Harvard University Press.

Lockman, J.J., & Thelen, E. (1993). Developmental biodynamics: Brain, body, behavior connections. *Child Development, 64,* 953–959.

Loehlin, John C. (1992). *Genes and environment in personality development.* Newbury Park, CA: Sage.

Loeber, Rolf, Farrington, David P., & Stouthamer-Loeber. (1998). *Antisocial Behavior and Mental Health Problems : Explanatory Factors in Childhood and Adolescence.* Mahwah, NJ:

Loftus, Elizabeth F. (1997, September). Creating false memories. *Scientific American,* 70–75.

Loftus, Elizabeth F. (1997). *Eyewitness testimony: Civil and criminal, 1997.* New York: Lexis Law.

Longfellow, Henry Wadsworth. (1825). *Morituri salutamus: Poem for the fiftieth anniversary of the class of 1825 in Bowdoin College* (Lines (236–271).

Lopata, Helena Znaniecka. (1999). Grief and the self-concept. In Brian de Vries (Ed.), *End of life issues: Interdisciplinary and multidimensional perspectives.* New York: Springer.

Lorenz, John M., Wooliever, Diane E., Jetton, James R., & Paneth, Nigel. (1998). A quantitative review of mortality and developmental disability in extremely premature newborns. *Archives of Pediatric & Adolescent Medicine, 152,* 425–435.

Lowrey, George H. (1986). *Growth and development of children* (8th ed.). Chicago: Year Book Medical Publishers.

Lozoff, Betsy, Klein, Nancy K., Nelson, Edward C., McClish, Donna K., Manuel, Martin & Chacon, Maria Elena. (1998). Behavior of infants with iron-deficiency anemia. *Child Development, 69,* 24–36.

Luke, Barbara. (1993). Nutrition and prematurity. In Frank R. Witter & Louis G. Keith (Eds.), *Textbook of prematurity: Antecedents, treatment, and outcome.* Boston: Little, Brown.

Lund, Dale. (1984–1988). *Longitudinal study on caregivers.* Salt Lake City: University of Utah, Gerontology Center.

Luria, A.R. (1976). *Cognitive development: Its cultural and social foundations.* Cambridge, MA: Harvard University Press.

Luria, A.R. (1979). *The making of mind.* Cambridge, MA: Harvard University Press.

Luthar, Suniya S., & Zigler, Edward. (1991). Vulnerability and competence: A review of research on resilience in childhood. *American Journal of Orthopsychiatry, 61,* 6–22.

Lutz, Donna J. & Sternberg, Robert J. (1999). Cognitive Development. In Marc H. Bornstein & Micheal E. Lamb (Eds.), *Developmental psychology: An advanced textbook, 4th Edition.* Mahwah, NJ: Erlbaum.

Lynam, Donald R., Milich, Richard, Zimmerman, Rick, Novak, Scott P., Logan, T.K., Martin, Catherine, Leukefeld, Carl, & Calyton, Richard. (1999). Project DARE: No effects at 10-year follow up. *Journal of Consulting and Clinical Psychology, 67,* 590–593.

Lynch, Michael, & Cicchetti, Dante. (1998). An ecological-transactional analysis of children and contexts: The longitudinal interplay among child maltreatment, community violence, and children's syptomatology. *Development and Psychopathology, 10,* 235–258.

Lyons, Peter & Rittner, Barbara. (1998). The construction of the crack babies phenomenon as a social problem. *American Journal of Orthopsychiatry, 68.* 313–320.

MacArdle, Paul, O'Brien, Gregory, & Kolvin, Israel. (1995). Hyperactivity: Prevalence and relationship with conduct disorder. *Journal of Child Psychology and Psychiatry and Allied Disciplines, 36,* 279–303.

Maccoby, Eleanor Emmons. (1980). *Social development: Psychological growth and the parent-child relationship.* New York: Harcourt Brace Jovanovich.

Maccoby, Eleanor Emmons. (1992). The role of parents in the socialization of children: An historical overview. *Developmental Psychology, 28,* 1006–1017.

Maccoby, Eleanor E. (1998). *The two sexes: Growing up apart, coming together.* Cambridge, MA: Belknap Press of Harvard University Press.

MacDonald, Kevin, & Parke, Ross D. (1986). Parent-child physical play: The effect of sex and age of children and parents. *Sex Roles, 15,* 367–378.

MacDonald, Shelley, & Hayne, Harlene. (1996). Child-initiated conversations about the past and memory performance by preschoolers. *Cognitive Development, 11,* 421–442.

Mackenbach, Johan P., Looman, Caspar W.N., & van der Meer, Joost B.W. (1996). Differences in the misreporting of chronic conditions by level of education: The effect on inequalities in prevalence rates. *American Journal of Public Health, 86,* 706–711.

MacMillan, Ross & Gartner, Rosemary. (1999). When she brings home th bacon: Labor-force participation and the risk of spousal violence against women. *Journal of Marriage and the Family, 61,* 947–958.

Macpherson, Alison, Roberts, Ian, & Pless, I. Barry. (1998). Children's exposure to traffic and pedestrian injuries. *American Journal of Public Health, 88,* 1840–1845.

Madden-Derdich, Debra A. & Arditti, Joyce A. (1999). The ties that bind: Attachment between former spouses. *Family Relations, 48,* 243–249.

Maddox, John. (1993). Wilful public misunderstanding of genetics. *Nature, 364,* 281.

Maguire, Kathleen, & Pastore, Ann L. (Eds.). (1998). *Sourcebook of criminal justice statistics, 1997.* Washington, DC: U.S. Government Printing Office.

Maguire, Kathleen, & Pastore, Ann L. (Eds.). (1999). *Sourcebook of Criminal Justice Statistics* [Online]. Available: *http://www.albany.edu/sourcebook*

Mahowald, M.B., Verp, M.S., & Anderson, R.R. (1998). Genetic counseling: Clinical and ethical challenges. *Annual Review of Genetics, 32,* 547–559.

Maier, Susan E., Chen, Wei-Jung A., & West, James R. (1996). The effects of timing and duration of alcohol exposure on development of the fetal brain. In Ernest L. Abel (Ed.), *Fetal alcohol syndrome: From mechanism to prevention.* Boca Raton: CRC Press.

Main, Mary. (1995). Recent studies in attachment. In Susan Goldberg, Roy Muir, & John Kerr (Eds.), *Attachment theory: social, developmental, and clinical perspectives.* Hillsdale, NJ: Analytic Press.

Malatesta, C.Z., Culver, C., Tesman, J.R., & Shepard, B. (1989). The development of emotional expression during the first two years of life. *Monographs of the Society for Research in Child Development, 54* (1–2), (Serial No. 219).

Males, Mike A. (1996). *The scapegoat generation: America's war on adolescents.* Monroe, ME: Common Courage Press.

Malina, Robert M. (1990). Physical growth and performance during the transitional years (9–16). In Raymond Montemayor, Gerald R. Adams, & Thomas P. Gullotta (Eds.), *From childhood to adolescence: A transitional period?* Newbury Park, CA: Sage.

Malina, Robert M., & Bouchard, Claude. (1991). *Growth, maturation, and physical activity.* Champaign, IL: Human Kinetics Books.

Malina, Robert M., Bouchard, Claude, & Beunen, G. (1988). Human growth: Selected aspects of current research on well-nourished children. *Annual Review of Anthropology, 17,* 187–219.

Mallory, B.L., & New, R.S. (1994). *Diversity and developmentally appropriate practice: Challenges for early childhood education.* New York: Teachers College Press.

Malmberg, B., & Zarit, S.H. (1993). Group homes for people with dementia: A Swedish example. *The Gerontologist, 33,* 682–686.

Mandler, Jean M. & McDonough, Laraine. (1998). On developing a knowledge base in infancy. *Developmental Psychology, 34,* 1274–1288.

Mange, Elaine Johnson & Mange, Arthur P. (1999). *Basic human genetics.* Sunderland, MA: Sinauer Associates.

Manlove, Jennifer. (1997). Early motherhood in an intergenerational perspective: The experiences of a British cohort. *Journal of Marriage and the Family, 59,* 263–280.

Manning, Wendy D. & Smock, Pamela J. (2000). "Swapping" families: Serial parenting and economic support for children. *Journal of Marriage and the Family, 62,* 111–122.

Mansfield, Christopher J., Wilson, James L., Kobrinski, Edward, & Mitchell, Jim. (1999). Premature mortality in the United States: the roles of geographic area, socioeconomic status, household type, and availability of medical care. *American Journal of Public Health, 89,* 893–898.

Manson J.E., Hu F.B., Rich-Edwards J.W., Colditz G.A., Stampfer M.J., Willett W.C., Speizer F.E., & Hennekens C.H. (1999). A prospective study of walking as compared with vigorous exercise in the prevention of coronary heart disease in women. *New England Journal of Medicine, 341,* 650–658.

Manteuffel, Mary Druse. (1996). Neurotransmitter function: Changes associated with *in utero* alcohol exposure. In Ernest L. Abel (Ed.), *Fetal alcohol syndrome: From mechanism to prevention.* Boca Raton: CRC Press.

Marcia, J.E., Waterman, A.S., Matteson, D.R., Archer, S.L., & Orlofsky, J.L. (Eds.). (1993). *Ego identity: A handbook for psychosocial research.* New York: Springer-Verlag.

Markides, Kyriakos S., & Black, Sandra A. (1996). Race, ethnicity, and aging: The impact of inequality. In Robert H. Binstock & Linda K. George (Eds.), *Handbook of aging and the social sciences.* San Diego: Academic Press.

Marshall, Victor W. (1996). The state of theory in aging and the social sciences. In Robert H. Binstock & Linda K. George (Eds.), *Handbook of aging and the social sciences.* San Diego: Academic Press.

Martin, Carol Lynn, Eisenbud, Lisa, & Rose, Hilary. (1995). Children's gender-based reasoning about toys. *Child Development, 66,* 1453–1471.

Martin, Kelly & Wu, Zheng. (2000). Contraceptive use in Canada: 1984–1995. *Family Planning Perspectives, 32,* 65–73.

Martin, Sandra L., English, Kathleen T., Clark, Kathryn Andersen, Cilenti, Dorothy, & Kupper, Lawrence L. (1996). Violence and substance use among North Carolina pregnant women. *American Journal of Public Health, 86,* 991–998.

Martin, Sandra L., Kim, Haesook, Kupper, Lawrence I., Meyer, Robert E., & Hays, Melissa. (1997). Is incarceration during pregnancy associated with infant birthweight? *American Journal of Public Health, 87,* 1526–1531.

Martire, Lynn M., Stephens, Mary Ann Parris, & Townsend, Alen L. (2000). Centrality of women's multiple roles: Beneficial and detrimental consequences for psychological well-being. *Psychology and Aging, 15,* 148–156.

Marvin, Robert S. (1997). Ethological and general systems perspectives on child-parent attachment during the toddler and preschool years. In Nancy L. Segal, Glenn E. Weisfeld, & Carol C. Weisfeld (Eds.), *Uniting psychology and biology: Integrative perspectives on human development.* Washington, DC: American Psychological Association.

Masataka, Nobuo. (1992). Early ontogeny of vocal behavior of Japanese infants in response to maternal speech. *Child Development, 63,* 1177–1185.

Masataka, Nobuo. (1996). Perception of motherese in a signed language by 6-month-old deaf infants. *Developmental Psychology, 32,* 874–879.

Maslow, Abraham H. (1968). *Toward a psychology of being (2nd ed.).* Princeton, NJ: Van Nostrand.

Maslow, Abraham H. (1970). *Motivation and personality (2nd ed.).* New York: Harper & Row.

Mason, J.A., & Herrmann, K.R. (1998). Universal infant bearing screening by automated auditory brainstem response measurement. *Pediatrics, 101,* 221–228.

Mason, Mary Ann. (1999). *The Custody Wars: Why children are losing the legal battle, and what we can do about it.* New York: Basic Books.

Masoro, Edward J. (1999). *Challenges of biological aging.* New York: Springer.

Masten, Ann S. (1992). Homeless children in the United States: Mark of a nation at risk. *Current Directions in Psychological Science, 1,* 41–43.

Masten, Ann S., & Coatsworth, J. Douglas. (1998). The development of competence in favorable and unfavorable environments: Lessons from research on successful children. *American Psychologist, 53,* 205–220.

Masterpasqua, Frank. (1997). Toward a dynamic developmental understanding of disorder. In Frank Masterpasqua & Phyllis A. Perna (Eds.), *The psychological meaning of chaos: Translating theory into practice.* Washington, DC: American Psychological Association.

Masters, William H., Johnson, Virginia E., & Kolodny, Robert C. (1994). *Heterosexuality.* New York: HarperCollins.

Matricardi, Paolo M., Rosmini, Francesco, Riondino, Silvia, Fortini, Michele, Ferrigno, Luigina, Rapicetta, Maria, & Bonini, Sergio. (2000). Exposure to foodborne and orofecal microbes versus airborne viruses in relation to atopy and allergic asthma. *British Medical Journal, 320,* 412–417.

Maydol, Lynn, Moffitt, Terrie E., Caspi, Avshalom, & Silva, Phil A. (1998). Hitting without a license: Testing explanations for differences in partner abuse between young adult daters and cohabitors. *Journal of Marriage and the Family, 60,* 4–55.

Mayes, L.C., Granger, R.H., Bornstein, M.H., & Zuckerman, B. (1992). The problem of prenatal cocaine exposure: A rush to judgment. *Journal of the American Medical Association, 267,* 406–408.

Mayford, Mark, Bach, Mary Elizabeth, Huand, Yan-You, Wang, Lei, Hawkins, Robert D., & Kandel, Eric R. (1996). Control of memory formation through regulated expression of a CaMKII transgene. *Science, 274,* 1678–1683.

Maylor, Elizabeth A., & Lavie, Nilli. (1998). The influence of perceptual load on age differences in selective attention. *Psychology and Aging, 13,* 563–573.

McAdams, Dan P., & de St. Aubin, Ed. (1998). *Generativity and adult development: How and why we care for the next generation.* Washington, DC: American Psychological Association.

McAdams, Dan P., Hart, Holly M., & Maruna, Shadd. (1998). The anatomy of generativity. In Dan P. McAdams & Ed de St. Aubin (Eds.) *Generativity and adult development: How and why we care for the next generation.* Washington, DC: American Psychological Association.

McAdams, Dan P., de St. Aubin, Ed, & Logan, Regina L. (1993). Generativity among young, midlife, and older adults. *Psychology and Aging, 8,* 221–230.

McCabe, D.L. & Trevino, L.K. (1996). What we know about cheating in college. *Change, 28,* 28–33.

McCarthy, William J., Caskey, Nicholas H., Jarvik, Murray E., Gross, Todd M., Rosenblatt, Martin R., & Carpenter, Catherine. (1995). Menthol vs nonmenthol cigarettes: Effects on smoking behavior. *American Journal of Public Health, 85,* 67–72.

McCarty, Michael E. & Ashmead, Daniel H. (1999). Visual control of reaching and grasping in infants. *Developmental Psychology, 35,* 620–631.

McCrae, Robert R., & Costa, Paul T., Jr. (1990). *Personality in adulthood.* New York: Guilford.

McCrae, Robert R., & Costa, Paul T., Jr. (1994). The stability of personality: Observations and evaluations. *Current Directions in Psychological Science, 3,* 173–175.

McCrae, Robert R., Costa, Paul T. Jr., de Lima, Margarida Pedroso, Simões, António, Ostendorf, Fritz, Angleitner, Alois, Marusic, Iris, Bratko, Denis, Caprara, Gian Vittorio, Barbaranelli, Claudio, Chae, Joon-Ho, & Piedmont, Ralph L. (1999). Age differences in personality across the adult life span: Parallels in five cultures. *Developmental Psychology, 35,* 466–477.

McCourt, Frank. (1996). *Angela's ashes.* New York: Scribner.

McDevitt, Thomas M. (1998). *World population profiles: 1998.* Washington, DC: U. S. Commerce Department.

McElroy, Susan Williams, & Moore, Kristin Anderson. (1997). Trends over time in teenage pregnancy and childbearing: The critical changes. In Rebecca A. Maynard (Ed.), *Kids having kids: Economic costs and social consequences of teen pregnancy.* Urban Institute Press.

McGue, Matthew. (1995). Mediators and moderators of alcoholism inheritance. In J.R. Turner, L.R. Cardon, & J. K. Hewitt (Eds.), *Behavior genetic approaches to behavioral medicine.* New York: Plenum Press.

McGue, Matt. (1999). The behavioral genetics of alcoholism. *Current Directions in Psychological Science, 8,* 109–115.

McGue, M. Hirsch, B., & Lykken, D.T. (1993). Age and the self-perception of ability: A twin analysis. *Psychology and Aging, 8,* 72–80.

McGuire, Judith, & Bundy, Donald. (1996). Nutrition, cognitive development, and economic progress. *Social Policy Report: Society for Research in Child Development, 10,* 26–28.

McKenry, Patrick, Julian, Teresa W., & Gavazzi, Stephen M. (1995). Toward a biosocial model of domestic violence. *Journal of Marriage and the family, 57,* 307–320.

McKenzie, Lisa, & Stephenson, Patricia A. (1993). Variation in Cesarean section rates among hospitals in Washington state. *American Journal of Public Health, 83,* 1109–1112.

McKinlay, John B., & Feldman, Henry A. (1994). Age-related variation and interest in normal men: Results from the Massachusetts male aging study. In Alice S. Rossi (Ed.), *Sexuality across the life course.* Chicago: University of Chicago Press.

McKinley, Nita M. (1999). Women and objectified body consciousness: Mothers' and daughters' body experience in cultural, developmental, and familiar context. *Developmental Psychology, ,* 760–769.

McKusick, Victor A. (1994). *Mendelian inheritance in humans* (10th ed.). Baltimore: Johns Hopkins University.

McLoyd, Vonnie C. (1998). Socioeconomic disadvantage and child development. *American Psychologist, 2,* 185–204.

Meacham, Jack. (1997). Autobiography, voice, and developmental theory. In Eric Amsel & K. Ann Renninger (Eds.), *Change and development: Issues of theory, method, and application.* Mahwah, NJ: Erlbaum.

Meeks, Suzanne, Murrell, Stanley A., Mehl, Rochelle C. (2000). Longitudinal relationships between depressive symptoms and health in normal older and middle-aged adults. *Psychology and Aging, 15,* 100–109.

Mehler, Jacques, & Fox, Robin. (Eds.). (1985). *Neonate cognition: Beyond the blooming buzzing confusion.* Hillsdale, NJ: Erlbaum.

Meis, Paul J., Goldenberg, Brian, Mercer, Brian M., Moawad, Atef, Das, Anita, McNellis, Donald, Johnson, Francee, Iams, Jay D., Thom, Elizabeth, & Andrews, William W. (1995). The preterm prediction study: Significance of vaginal infections. *American Journal of Obstetrics and Gynecology, 173,* 1231–1235.

Meisami, Esmail. (1994). Aging of the sensory system. In Paola S. Timiras (Ed.), *Physiological basis of aging and geriatrics (2nd ed.).* Boca Raton, FL: CRC Press.

Meier, Diane E. & Morrison, R.Sean. (1999). Introduction: Old age and care near the end of life. *Generations, 23,* 6–11.

Melton, Michael A., Hersen, Michel, Van Sickle, Timothy D., & Van Hasselt, Vincent. (1995). Parameters of marriage in older adults: A review of the literature. *Clinical Psychology Review, 15,* 891–904.

Meredith, Howard V. (1978). Research between 1960 and 1970 on the standing height of young chldren in different parts of the world. In Hayne W. Reese & Lewis P. Lipsitt (Eds.), *Advances in child development and behavior* (Vol. 12). New York: Adademic Press.

Merrell, Kenneth W., & Gimpel, Gretchen A. (1998). *Social skills of children and adolescents: Conceptualization, assessment, treatment*. Mahwah, NJ: Erlbaum.

Merrill, Susan S. & Verbrugge, Lois M. (1999). Health and disease in midlife. In Sherry L. Willis & James D. Reid (Eds.), *Life in the middle*. San Diego: Academic Press.

Merriman, W. E. (1998). Competition, attention, and young children's lexical processing. In B. MacWhinney (Ed.), *The emergence of language*. Hillsdale, NJ: Erlbaum.

Messer, David J. (1994). *The development of communication*. New York: Wiley.

Messinger, Daniel S., Fogel, Alan, Dickson, K. Laurie. (1999). What's in a smile? *Developmental Psychology, 35*, 701–708.

Meyer, B.J.F., Russo, C., & Talbot, A. (1995). Discourse comprehension and problem solving: Decisions about the treatment of breast cancer by women across the life span. *Psychology and Aging, 10*, 84–103.

Meyer, Daniel R., & Bartfield, Judi. (1996). Compliance with child support orders in divorce cases. *Journal of Marriage and the Family, 58*, 201–212.

Mezey, Mathy, Miller, Lois L., & Linton-Nelson, Lori. (1999). Caring for caregivers of frail elders at the end of life. *Generations, 23*, 44–51.

Michael, R.T., Wadsworth, J., Feinlab, J., Johnson, A.M., Laumann, E.O., & Wellings, K. (1998). Private sexual behavior public opinion, and public health policy related to sexually transmitted diseases: A US-British Comparison. *American Journal of Public Health, 88*, 749–754.

Michaud, Catherine. (1999). The global burden of disease and injuries in 1990. *International Social Science Journal, 161*, 287–296.

Midanik, Lorraine & Greenfield, Thomas K. (2000). Trends in social consequences and dependence symptoms in the United States: The national alcohol surveys, 1984–1995. *American Journal of Public Health, 90*, 53–56.

Miedzian, Miriam. (1991). *Boys will be boys: Breaking the link between masculinity and violence*. New York: Doubleday.

Mihalic, Sharon Wofford & Elliott, Delbert. (1997). Short- and long-term consequences of adolescent work. *Youth & Society, 28*, 464–498.

Milkie, Melissa A. & Peltola, Pia. (1999). Playing all the roles: Gender and the work-family balancing act. *Journal of Marriage and the Family, 61*, 476–490.

Miller, Patricia H. (1993). *Theories of developmental psychology*. New York: Freeman.

Miller, Richard A. (1996). Aging and the immune response. In Edward L. Schneider & John W. Rowe (Eds.), *Handbook of the biology of aging*. San Diego: Academic Press.

Miller, Ted R., & Spicer, Rebecca S. (1998). How safe are our schools? *American Journal of Public Health, 88*, 413–418.

Mills, James L., McPartlin, Joseph M., Kirke, Peadar N., & Lee, Young J. (1995). Homocysteine metabolism in pregnancies complicated by neural-tube defects. *Lancet, 345*, 149–151.

Mills, Jon K., & Andrianopoulos, Georgia D. (1993). The relationship between childhood onset obesity and psychopathology in adulthood. *Journal of Psychology, 127*, 547–551.

Mindel, C.J., Haberstein, R.W., & Roosevelt, W., Jr. (Eds.). (1988). *Ethnic families in America (3rd ed.)*. New York: Elsevier.

Minkler, Meredith, & Roe, Kathleen M. (1996). Grandparents as surrogate parents. *Generations, 20*, 34–38.

Mintz, Laurie B. & Kashubeck, Susan. (1999). Body image and disordered eating among Asian American and Caucasian college students. *Psychology of Women Quarterly, 23*, 781–796.

Mitchell, D.B. (1993). Implicit and explicit memory for pictures: Multiple views across the lifespan. In P. Graf & M.E.J. Masson (Eds.), *Implicit memory: New directions in cognition, development and neuropsychology*. Hillsdale, NJ: Erlbaum.

MMWR *(Morbidity and Mortality Weekley Report)*. See **Centers for Disease Control and Prevention.**

Mobbs, Charles V. (1996). Neuroendocrinology of aging. In Edward L. Schneider & John W. Rowe (Eds.), *Handbook of the biology of aging*. San Diego: Academic Press.

Moen, Phyllis. (1996). Gender, age, and the life course. In Robert H. Binsock & Linda K. George (Eds.), *Handbook of aging and the social sciences (4th ed.)*. San Diego: Academic Press.

Moen, P. (1998). Reconstructing retirement: Careers, couples, and social capital. *Contemporary Gerontology: A Journal of Reviews and Critical Discussion, 4*, 123–125.

Moen, P. & Yu, Y. (1999). Having it all: Overall work'/life success in two-earner families. In T. Parcel (Ed.), *Research in the sociology of work, Volume 7*. Greenwich, CT: JAI Press.

Moerk, Ernst L. (1996). First language acquisition. In W. Reese Hayne (Ed), *Advances in child development and behavior* (Vol. 26). San Diego: Academic Press.

Moffitt, Terrie E. (1993). The neuropsychology of conduct disorder. *Development and Psychopathology, 5*, 135–151.

Moffitt, Terrie.E. (1993). Adolescence-limited and life-course persistent antisocial behavior: A developmental taxonomy. *Psychological Review, 100*, 674–701.

Moffitt, Terrie E. (1997). Adolescence—Limited and life-course-persistent offending: A complementary pair of developmental theories. In Terence P. Thornberry (Ed.), *Development theories of crime and delinquency*. New Brunswick, NJ: Transaction.

Moffitt, Terrie E. (1997). Helping poor mothers and children. *Journal of the American Medical Association, 278*, 680–682.

Moffitt, Terrie E., Caspi, Avshalom, Belsky, Jay, & Silva, Paul A. (1992). Childhood experience and the onset of menarche. *Child Development, 63*, 47–58.

Molina, Brooke S.G., & Chassin, Laurie. (1996). The parent-adolescent relationship at puberty: Hispanic ethnicity and parent alcoholism as moderators. *Developmental Psychology, 32*, 675–686.

Moller, David Wendell. (1996). *Confronting death: Values, institutions, and human mortality*. New York: Oxford University Press.

Moller, Lora C. & Serbin, Lisa A. (1996). Antecedents of toddler gender segregation: Cognitive consonance, gender-typed toy preferences and behavioral compatibility. *Sex Roles, 35,* 445–460.

Montemayor, Raymond. (1986). Family variation in parent-adolescent storm and stress. *Journal of Adolescent Research, 1,* 15–31.

Monthly Vital Statistics Report. (1998, September 4). *Births and deaths: United States, July 1996–1998.* Atlanta, GA: Centers for Disease Control.

Moon, Christine, Cooper, Robin Panneton, & Fifer, William P. (1993). Two-day olds prefer their native language. *Infant Behavior and Development, 16,* 495–500.

Moore, Keith L., & Persaud, T.V.N. (1998). *The developing human: Clinically oriented embryology.* Philadelphia: W. B. Saunders.

Moore, Chris, Pure, K., & Furrow, D. (1990). Children's understanding of the modal expression of certainty and uncertainty and its relation to the development of a representational theory of mind. *Child Development, 61,* 722–730.

Morgan, Elaine R. (2000). Care of children who are dying of cancer. *The New England Journal of Medicine, 342,* 347–348.

Morin, Charles M. (1993). *Insomnia: Psychological assessment and management.* New York: Guilford Press.

Morin, Charles M., Colecchi, Cheryl, Stone, Jackie, Sood, Rakesh, & Brink Douglas. (1999). Behavior and pharmacological therapies for late-life insomnia. *Journal of the American Medical Association, 281,* 991–999.

Morrison, Donna Ruane & Coiro, Mary Jo. (1999). Parental conflict and marital disruption: Do children benefit when high-conflict marriages are dissolved? *Journal of Marriage and the Family, 61,* 626–637.

Morrongiello, Barbara A., Fenwick, Kimberley D., & Chance, Graham. (1998). Crossmodal learning in newborn infants: Inferences about properties of auditory-visual events. *Infant Behavior & Development, 21,* 543–553.

Mortensen, Preben Bo, Pedersen, Carsten B., Westergaard, Tine, Wohlfahrt, Jan, Ewald, Henrik, Mors, Ole, Andersen, per Kragh, & Melbye, Mads. (1999). Effects of family history and season of birth on the risk of schizophrenia. *New England Journal of Medicine, 340,* 603–608.

Mortimer, David. (1994). *Practical laboratory andrology.* New York: Oxford University Press.

Mortimer, Jeylan T., Finch, Michael D., Dennehy, Katherine, Lee, Chaimun, & Beebe, Timothy. (1994). Work experience in adolescence. *Journal of Vocational Education Research, 19,* 39–70.

Moscovitch, Morris. (1982). Neuropsychology of perception and memory in the elderly. In Fergus I.M. Craik & Sandra Trehub (Eds.), *Aging and cognitive processes.* New York: Plenum Press.

Moshman, David. (1998). Cognitive development beyond childhood. In D. Kuhn & R. Siegler (Eds.), W. Damon (Series Ed.), *Handbook of child psychology* (5th ed.): Vol. 2: Cognition, perception, and language. New York: Wiley.

Mroczek, D.K. & Kolarz, C.M. (1998). The effect of age on positive and negative affect: a developmental perspective on happiness. *Journal of Personality and Social Psychology, 75,* 1333–1349.

Mulrow, C.D., Aguilar, C., Endicott, J.E., Tuley, M.R., Velez, R., Charlip, W.S., Rhodes, M.C., Hill, J.A., & DeNino, L.A. (1990). Quality-of-life changes and hearing impairment: A randomized trial. *Annals of Internal Medicine, 113,* 188–194.

Murphy, J.J., & Boggess, S. (1998). Increased condom use among teenage males, 1988–1995: The role of attitudes. *Family Planning Perspective, 30,* 276–280..

Murray, S.L., Holmes, J.G., & Griffin, D.W. (1996). The benefits of positive illusions: Idealization and the construction of satisfaction in close relationships. *Journal of Personality and Social Psychology, 70,* 79–98.

Musick, Marc A, Herzog, Regula, & House, James C. (1999) Volunteering and mortality among older adults: Finding from a national sample. *Journal of Gerontology, 54B,* S173- S180

Mutchler, Jane E., Burr, Jeffrey, Massagli, Michael P. & Prenta, Ghray. (1999) Work transition and health in alter life. *Journal of Gerontology, 54B,* .

Myers, B.J. (1987). Mother-infant bonding as a critical period. In M.H. Bornstein (Ed.), *Sensitive periods in development: Interdisciplinary perspectives.* Hillsdale, NJ: Erlbaum.

Myers, David G. (1993). *The pursuit of happiness.* New York: Avon Books.

Myers, David G. (2000). The funds, friends, and faith of happy people. *American Psychologist, 55,* 56–67.

Myers, Samuel L., & Chung, Chanjin. (1996). Racial differences in home ownership and home equity among preretirement-aged households. *Gerontologist, 36,* 350–360.

Myers, Scott M. & Booth, Alan. (1999). Marital strains and marital quality: The role of high and low locus control. *Journal of Marriage and the Family, 61,* 423–436.

Nantais, Kristin M. & Schellenberg, E.Glenn. (1999). The mystery of the Mozart effect: Failure to replicate. *Psychological Science, 10,* 366–369.

Narvaez, D., Getz, I., Thoma, S.J. , & Rest, J. (1999). Individual moral judgment and cultural ideology. *Developmental Psychology, 35,* 478–488.

Nasser, Mervat. (1997). *Culture and weight consciousness.* London and New York: Routledge.

Nation, Kate, & Snowling, Margaret J. (1998). Individual differences in contextual facilitation: Evidence from dyslexia and poor reading comprehension. *Child Development, 69,* 996–1011.

National Academy of Sciences. (1994). *Assessing genetic risks: Implications for health and social policy.* Washingtons, DC: National Academy Press.

National Center for Health Statistics. (1995). *Health, United States, 1994.* Hyattsville, MD: Public Health Service.

National Center for Health Statistics. (1997). *Health, United States, 1996.* Hyattsville, MD: Public Health Service.

National Center for Health Statistics. (1997). *National health interview survey, 1997.* Washington DC: U.S. Government Printing Office.

National Center for Health Statistics. (1999). *Health, United States, 1999: With health and aging chartbook.* Hyattsville, Maryland.

National Child Abuse and Neglect Data System. (1997). *U.S. Department of Health and Human Services, Child Maltreatment 1995: Reports from the states to the National Child Abuse and Neglect Data System.* Washington, D.C.: U.S. Government Printing Office.

National Digest of Education Statistics. (1998). *Digest of education statistics, 1997.* Washington DC: National Center for Education Statistics.

National Endowment Goals Panel. (1997). *National endowment goals panel monthly.* Washington DC: National Endowment Goals Panel.

National Heart, Lung, and Blood Institute. *Clinical guidelines on the identification, evaluation, and treatment of overweight and obesity in adults: The evidence report.* National Institutes of Health: *www.nhlbi.nih.gov.*

National Institute of Child Health and Development, Early Child Care Research Network. (1997). The effects of infant child care on infant-mother attachment security: Results of the NICHD study of early child care. *Child Development, 68,* 860–879.

Neilson Media Research. (1997). Neilson Media Research.

Neisser, Ulric, Boodoo, Gwyneth, Bouchard, Thomas J., Boykin, A. Wade, Brody, Nathan, Ceci, Stephen J., Halpern, Diane F., Loehlin, John C., Perloff, Robert, Sternberg, Robert J., & Urbina, Susana. (1996). Intelligence: Knowns and unknowns. *American Psychologist, 51,* 77–101.

Nelson, Charles A., & Bloom, Floyd E. (1997). Child development and neuroscience. *Child Development, 69,* 970–987.

Nelson, Charles A., & Horowitz, Frances Degen. (1987). Visual motion perception in infancy: A review and synthesis. In Philip Salapatek & Leslie Cohen (Eds.), *Handbook of infant perception: Vol. 2. From perception to cognition.* New York: Academic Press.

Nelson, Katherine. (1981). Individual differences in language development: Implications for development and language. *Developmental Psychology, 17,* 171–187.

Nelson, Katherine. (Ed.). (1986). *Event knowledge: Structure and function in development.* Hillsdale, NJ: Erlbaum.

Nelson, Melvin D. (1992). Socioeconomic status and childhood mortality in North Carolina. *American Journal of Public Health, 82,* 1131–1133.

Neugarten, Bernice L., & Neugarten, Dail A. (1986). Changing meanings of age in the aging society. In Alan Pifer & Lynda Bronte (Eds.), Our aging society: Paradox and promise. New York: Norton.

Neumann, C.G. (1983). Obesity in childhood. In M.D. Levine, W.B. Carey, A.C. Crocker, & R.T. Gross (Eds.), *Developmental-behavioral pediatrics.* Philadelphia: Saunders.

Newcomb, A.F. & Bagwell, C.L. (1995). Children's friendship relations: A meta-analytic review. *Psychological Bulletin, 117,* 306–347.

The New York Times. (1997, August 18). Keeping track: Adoptions of foreign children.

Nichols, Francine & Zwelling, Elaine. (1997) *Maternal newborn nursing.* Philadelphia: Saunders.

Nielsen, Geir Høstmark, Nordhus, Inger Hilde, & Kvale, Gerd. (1998). Insomnia in older adults. In Inger Hilde Nordhus, Gary R. VandenBos, Stig Berg, & Pia Fromhold (Eds.). *Clinical Geropsychology.* Washington, DC: American Psychological Association.

Nikiforov, Sergey V. & Mamaev, Valery B. (1998). The development of sex differences in cardiovascular disease mortality: A historical perspective. *American Journal of Public Health, 88,* 1348–1353.

Nilsson, Karina & Strandh, Mattias. (1999). Nest leaving in Sweden: The importance of early educational and labor market careers. *Journal of Marriage and the Family, 61,* 1068–1079.

Nordentoft, Merete, Lou, Hans C., Hanson, Dorthe, Nim, J., Pryds, Ole, Rubin, Pia, & Hemmingsen, Ralf (1996). Intrauterine growth retardation and premature delivery: The influence of maternal smoking and psychosocial factors. *American Journal of Public Health, 86,* 347–354.

Nottelmann, Edith D., Inoff-Germain, Gale, Susman, Elizabeth J., & Chrousos, George P. (1990). Hormones and behavior at puberty. In John Bancroft & June Machover Reinisch (Eds.), *Adolescence in puberty.* New York: Oxford University Press.

Nowak, Rachel. (1995). New push to reduce maternal mortality in poor countries. *Science, 269,* 780–782.

Nowakowski, R.S. (1987). Basic concepts of CNS development. *Child Development, 58,* 598–595.

Nugent, J. Kevin, Lester, Barry M., Greene, Sheila M., Wieczorek-Deering, Dorith, & O'Mahony, Paul. (1996). The effects of maternal alcohol consumption and cigarette smoking during pregnancy on acoustic cry analysis. *Child Development, 67,* 1806–1815.

Nuland, Sherwin B. (1994). *How we die.* New York, Knopf.

Nunan, David & Lam, Agnes. (1998). Teacher education for multilingual contexts: Models and issues. In Jasone Cenoz & Fred Genesee (Eds.), *Beyond bilingualism: Multilingualism and multilingual education.* Clevedon, England: Multillingual Matters.

Nunez, Ralph. (1996). *The new poverty: Homeless families in America.* New York: Plenum Press.

Ochs, Elinor. (1988). *Culture and language development: Language acquisition and language socialization in a Samoan village.* Cambridge: Cambridge University Press

Offenbacher, S., Katz, V., Fertik, G., Connins, J., Boyd, D., Maynor, G., McKaig, R., & Beck, J. (1996). Periodontal infection as a possible risk factor for preterm low birth weight. *Journal of Periodontology, 67,* 1103–1113.

Ogilvy, C.M. (1994). Social skills training with children and adolescents: A review of the evidence of effectiveness. *Educational Psychology, 14,* 73–83.

Ogletree, Shirley M., Williams, Sue W., Raffeld, Paul, Mason, Bradley, & Fricke, Kris. (1990). Female attractiveness and eating disorders: Do children's television commercials play a role? *Sex Roles, 22,* 791–797.

O'Hara, Michael W. (1997). The nature of postpartum depressive disorders. In Lynne Murray & Peter J. Cooper (Eds.), *Postpartum depression and child development.* New York: Guilford.

Ohayon, M.M., Caulet, M., Arbus, L., Bilard, M., Coquerel, A., Guieu, J.D., Kullmann, B., Loffont, F., Lemoine, P., Paty, J., Pechadre, J.C., Vecchierini, M.F., & Vespignani, H. (1999). Are prescribed medications effective in the treatment of insomnia complaints? *Journal of Psychosomatic Research, 47,* 359–368.

Olds, David L., Henderson, Charles R., Kitzman, Harriet J., Eckernrode, John J. Cole, Robert E., & Tatelbaum, Robert C. (1999). Prenatal and infancy home visitation by nurses: Recent Findings. *The Future of Children, 9,* 44–65.

O'Leary, K. Daniel. (1993). Through a psychological lens: Personality traits, personality disorders, and levels of violence. In Richard J. Gelles & Donileen R. Loseke (Eds.), *Current controversies on family violence.* Thousand Oaks, CA: Sage.

Oller, D. Kimbrough, & Eilers, Rebecca. (1988). The role of audition in infant babbling. *Child Development, 59,* 441–449.

Olweus, Dan. (1992). Bullying among schoolchildren: Intervention and prevention. In Peters, R.D., McMahon, R.J. &Quincy, V.L. (Eds.). *Aggression and violence throughout the life span.* Newbury Park, CA: Sage.

Olweus, Dan. (1993). *Bullying at school: What we know and what we can do.* Oxford, England; Blackwell.

Olweus, Dan. (1993). Victimization by peers: Antecedents and long-term outcomes. In K.H. Rubin & J.B. Asendorf (Eds.), *Social withdrawal, inhibition, and shyness in childhood.* Hillsdale, N.J.: Erlbaum.

Olweus, Dan. (1994). Bullying at school: Basic facts and effects of a school based intervention program. *Journal of Child Psychology and Psychiatry, 35,* 1171–1190.

O'Meara, J.J. (1989). Cross-sex friendship: Four basic challenges of an ignored relationship. *Sex Roles, 21,* 525–543.

O'Meara, J.J. (1994). Cross sex friendship's opportunity challenge: Uncharted terrain for exploration. *Personal Relationship Issues, 2,* 4–7.

O'Neill, Molly. (1998, March 14). Feeding the next generation: Food industry caters to teen-age eating habits. *The New York Times,* D1.

Oosterlaan, Jaap, Logan, Gordon D., & Sergeant, Joseph A. (1998). Response inhibition in AD/HD, CD, comorbid AD/HD + CD, anxious, and control children: A meta-analysis of studies with the stop task. *Journal of Child Psychology & Psychiatry & Allied Disciplines, 39,* 411–425.

Opie, I. (1993). *The people in the playground.* Oxford: Oxford University Press.

Opoku, Kofi Asare. (1989). African perspectives on death and dying. In Arthur Berger, Paul Badham, Austin H. Kutscher, Joyce Berger, Ven. Michael Petty, & John Beloff (Eds.), *Perspectives on death and dying: Cross-cultural and multidisciplinary views.* Philadelphia: Charles Press.

O'Rand, Angela M. (1996). The cumulative stratification of the life course. In Robert H. Binstock & Linda K. George (Eds.), *Handbook of aging and the social sciences.* San Diego: Academic Press.

Orbuch, Terri L., & Custer, Lindsay. (1995). The social context of married women's work and its impact on black husbands and white husbands. *Journal of Marriage and the Family, 57,* 333–345.

Osgood, Nancy J. (1992). *Suicide in later life.* Lexington, MA: Lexington Books.

Osofsky, Joy D. (1999). The impact of violence on children. *The Future of Children, 9,* Los Altos, California: The David and Lucile Packard Foundation.

Oster, Gerry, Thompson, David, Edelsberg, John, Bird, Amy P., & Colditz, Graham A. (1999). Lifetime health and economic benefits of weight loss among obese persons. *American Journal of Public Health, 89,* 1536–1542.

Overton, Willis F. (1998). Developmental psychology: Philosophy, concepts, and methodology. In William Damon (Series Ed.), *Handbook of child psychology* (5th ed.): *Vol. 1: Theoretical.* New York: Wiley.

Palmer, Carolyn F. (1989). The discriminating nature of infants' exploratory actions. *Developmental Psychology, 25,* 885–893.

Palmore, Erdman, B. (1977). *The facts on aging quiz.* New York: Springer.

Palmore, Erdman, B. (1998). *The facts on aging quiz.* New York: Springer.

Pampel, F.C. (1994). Population aging, class context, and age inequality in public spending. *American Journal of Sociology, 100,* 153–195.

Panchaud, Christine, Singh, Sushela, Feivelson, Dina, & Darroch, Jacqueline. (2000). Sexually transmitted diseases among adolescents in developed countries. *Family Planning Perspectives, 32,* 24–32.

Panksepp, Jaak. (1998). Attention deficit hyperactivity disorders, psychostimulants, and intolerance of childhood playfulness: A tragedy in the making? *Current Directions in Psychological Science, 7,* 91–98.

Papernow, Patricia L. (1993). *Becoming a stepfamily: Patterns of development in remarried families.* San Francisco: Jossey-Bass.

Park, Denise C. (1999). Cognitive aging, processing resources and self report. In Norbert Schwarz, Denise C. Park, Barbel Knauper & Seymour Sudman (Eds.), *Cognition, aging and self reports.* Philadelphia: Psychology Press.

Park, K.A., Lay, K. L., & Ramsay, L. (1993). Individual differences and developmental changes in preschoolers' friendships. *Developmental Psychology, 29,* 264–270.

Parke, Ross D. (1995). Fathers and families. In Marc H. Bornstein (Ed.) *Handbook of parenting: Status and social conditions of parenting*. New Jersey: Erlbaum.

Parke, Ross D., Ornstein, Peter A., Rieser, John J., & Zahn-Waxler, Carolyn. (1994). The past as prologue: An overview of a century of developmental psychology. In Ross D. Parke, Peter A. Ornstein, John J. Rieser, & Carolyn Zahn-Waxler (Eds.), *A century of developmental psychology*. Washington, DC: American Psychological Association.

Parker, Jeffrey G., & Asher, Steven R. (1993). Friendship and friendship quality in middle childhood: Links with peer group acceptance and feelings of loneliness and social dissatisfaction. *Developmental Psychology, 29,* 611–621.

Parkhurst, J.T., & Asher, S.R. (1992). Peer rejection in middle school: Subgroup differences in behavior, loneliness, and interpersonal concerns. *Developmental Psychology, 28,* 231–241.

Parkin, Alan J. (1993). *Memory: Phenomena, experiment, and theory*. Oxford: Blackwell.

Parrott, Roxanne Louiselle, & Condit, Celeste Michelle. (1996). *Evaluating women's health messages: A resourcebook*. Thousand Oaks, CA: Sage.

Pascarella, Ernest T., & Terenzini, Patrick T. (1991). *How college affects students: Findings and insights from twenty years of research*. San Francisco: Jossey-Bass.

Pasley, Kay, & Ihinger-Tallman, Marilyn. (1987). *Remarriage and stepparenting*. New York: Guilford.

Patel, Vimla L., Kaufman, David R., & Magden, Shelden A. (1996). The acquisition of medical expertise in complex dynamic environments. In K. Anders Eriksson (Ed.), *The road to excellence: The acquisition of expert performance in the arts and sciences, sports & games*. Mahwah, NJ: Erlbaum.

Patterson, Gerald R., DeBaryshe, Barbara D., & Ramsey, Elizabeth. (1989). A developmental perspective on antisocial behavior. *American Psychologist, 44,* 329–335.

Pechmann, Cornelia, Dixon, Philip, & Layne, Neville. (1998). An assessment of US and Canadian smoking reduction objectives for the year 2000. *American Journal of Public Health, 88,* 1362–1367.

Peak, L. (1991). *Learning to go to school in Japan: The transition from home to preschool life*. Berkeley: University of California Press.

Pearlin, Leonard I., Aneshensel, Carol S., Mullan, Joseph T., & Whitlatch, Carol J. (1996). Caregiving and its social support. In Robert H. Binstock & Linda K. George (Eds.), *Handbook of aging and the social sciences*. San Diego: Academic Press.

Pearson, J.D., Morell, C.H., Gordon-Salant, S., Brant, L.J., Metter, E.J., Klein, L., & Fozard, J.L. (1995). Gender differences in a longitudinal study of age-associated hearing loss. *Journal of the Acoustical Society of America, 97,* 1196–1205.

Pecheux, Marie Germaine, & Labrell, Florence. (1994). Parent-infant interactions and early cognitive development. In Andre Vyt, Henriette Bloch, & Marc H. Bornstein (Eds.), *Early child development in the French tradition:* Contributions from current research. Hillsdale, NJ: Erlbaum.

Pedersen, Jørgen Bruun. (1998). Sexuality and aging. In Inger Hilde Nordhus, Gary R. VandenBos, Stig Berg, & Pia Fromholt (Eds.), *Clinical Geropsychology*, Washington, DC: American Psychological Association.

Pelham, William E. Jr., Wheeler, Trilby, & Chronis, Andrea. (1998). Empirically supported psychosocial treatments for attention deficit hyperactivity disorder. *Journal of Clinical Child Psychology, 27,* 190–205.

Pellegrini, A.D. & Smith, Peter K. (1998). Physical activity play: The nature and function of a neglected aspect of play. *Child Development, 69,* 577–598.

Pelton, Leroy H. (1994). The role of material factors in child abuse and neglect. In G.B. Melton & F. Barry (Eds.), *Safe neighborhoods: Foundations for a new national strategy on child abuse and neglect*. New York: Guilford.

Pendergrass, W.R., Li, Y., Jiang, D., Fei, R.G., & Wolf, N.S. (1995). Caloric restriction: Conservation of cellular replicative capacity in vitro accompanies lifespan extension in mice. *Experimental Cell Research, 217,* 309.

Pennisi, Elizabeth. (1999). Bracing p53 for the war on cancer. *Science, 286,* 24–31.

Pennisi, Elizabeth, & Roush, Wade. (1997). Developing a new view of evolution. *Science, 277,* 34–37.

Pepler, Debra, Craig, Wendy M. & O'Connell, Paul. 1999. Understanding bullying from a dynamic systems perspective. *The Blackwell reader in developmental psychology*. Alan Slater and Darwin Muir (Eds.).Oxford, U.K.: Blackwell.

Perez, L. (1994). The household structure of second-generation children: An exploratory study of extended family arrangements. *International Migration Review, 28,* 736–747.

Perlmutter, Marion, Kaplan, Michael, & Nyquist, Linda. (1990). Development of adaptive competence in adulthood. *Human Development, 33,* 185–197.

Perris, Eve Emmanuel, Myers, Nancy Angrist, & Clifton, Rachel Kern. (1990). Long-term memory for a single infancy experience. *Child Development, 61,* 1796–1807.

Perry, David G., Kusel, Sara J., & Perry, Louise C. (1988). Victims of peer aggression. *Developmental Psychology, 24,* 807–814.

Perry, William G., Jr. (1981). Cognitive and ethical growth: The making of meaning. In Arthur W. Chickering (Ed.), *The modern American college: Responding to the new realities of diverse students and a changing society*. San Francisco: Jossey-Bass.

Peters, Arnold & Liefbroer, Aart C. (1997). Beyond marital status: Partner history and well-being in old age. *Journal of Marriage and the Family, 59,* 687–699.

Peterson, Bill E., & Stewart, Abigail J. (1996). Antecedents and contexts of generativity motivation at midlife. *Psychology and Aging, 11,* 21–33.

Peterson, Carole & Rideout, Regina. (1998). Memory for medical emergencies experienced by one- and two-year-olds. *Developmental Psychology, 34,* 1059–1072.

Peterson, Lizette, Ewigman, Bernard, & Kivlahan, Coleen. (1993). Judgments regarding appropriate child supervision to prevent injury: The role of environmental risk and child age. *Child Development, 64,* 934–950.

Petitto, Anne, & Marentette, Paula F. (1991). Babbling in the manual mode: Evidence for the ontogeny of language. *Science, 251,* 1493–1496.

Phinney, J. (1990). Ethnic identity in adolescents and adults: A review of the literature. *Psychological Bulletin, 108,* 499–514.

Piaget, Jean. (1952). *The child's conception of number.* London: Routledge and Kegan Paul.

Piaget, Jean. (1952). *The origins of intelligence in children.* Margaret Cook (Trans.). New York: International Universities Press.

Piaget, Jean. (1970). *The child's conception of movement and speed.* G.E.T. Holloway & M.J. Mackenzie (Trans.). New York: Basic Books.

Piaget, Jean. (1970). *The child's conception of time.* A.J. Pomerans (Trans.). New York: Basic Books.

Pillemer, Karl A., & Finkelhor, David. (1988). The prevalence of elder abuse: A random sample survey. *Gerontologist, 29,* 51–57.

Pinker, S. (1994). *The language instinct.* New York: Morrow.

Pipe, Margaret-Ellen, Gee, Susan, Wilson, J. Clare, & Egerton, Janice M. (1999). *Developmental Psychology, 35,* 781–789.

Priestley, Gina, Roberts, Susan, & Pipe, Margaret-Ellen. (1999). Returning To the scene: Reminders and context reinstatement enhance children's recall. *Developmental Psychology, 35,* 1006–1019.

Pitskhelauri, G.Z. (1982). *The long-living of Soviet Georgia* (Gari Lesnoff–Caravaglia, Trans.). New York: Human Sciences Press.

Pittman, Joe F., & Blanchard, David. (1996). The effects of work history and timing of marriage on the division of household labor: A life-course perspective. *Journal of Marriage and the Family, 58,* 78–90.

Plomin, Robert. (1995). Molecular genetics and psychology. *Current Directions in Psychological Science, 4,* 114–117.

Plomin, Robert, & Rutter, Michael. (1998). Child development, molecular genetics, and what to do with genes once they are found. *Child Development, 69,* 1223–1242.

Plomin, Robert, DeFries, J.C., McClearn, G.E., & Rutter, M. (1997). *Behavioral genetics.* New York: Freeman.

Pogrebin, Letty. (1996). *Getting over getting older: An intimate memoir.* New York: Little Brown & Company.

Pollack, William. (1999). *Real boys: Rescuing Our Sons from the Myths of Boyhood.* New York: Owl Books.

Pollitt, Ernesto, Gorman, Kathleen S., Engle, P., Martorell, R., & Rivera, J. (1993). Early supplementary feeding and cognition: Effects over two decades. *Monographs of the Society for Research in Child Development, 58.*

Pollitt, Ernesto, Golub, Mari, Gorman, Kathleen, Grantham-McGregor, Sally, Levitsky, David, Schurch, Beat, Strupp, Barbara, & Wachs, Theodore. (1996). A reconceptualization of the effects of undernutrition on children's biological, psychosocial, and behavioral development. *Social policy report: Society for Research in Child Development, 10,* 1–21.

Pomerantz, Eva M., Ruble, Diane N., Frey, Karin S., & Greulich, Faith. (1995). Meeting goals and confronting conflicts: Children's changing perceptions of social comparison. *Child Development, 66,* 723–738.

Poon, Leonard W. (1985). Differences in human memory with aging: Nature, causes, and clinical implications. In James E. Birren & K. Warner Schaie (Eds.), *Handbook of the psychology of aging.* New York: Van Nostrand Reinhold.

Poon, Leonard W. (1992). *The Georgia Centenarian Study.* Amityville, NY: Baywood.

Pool, Robert. (1993). Evidence for the homosexuality gene. *Science, 261,* 291–292.

Porter, R.H., Makin, J.W., Davis, L.B., & Christensen, K.M. (1992). Breast-fed infants respond to olfactory cues from their own mother and unfamiliar lactating females. *Infant Behavior and Development, 15,* 85–93.

Porter, Richard, Varendi, H., Christensson, K., Porter, R.H. and Winberg, J. (1998). Soothing effect of amniotic fluid smell in newborn infants. *Early Human Development, 51,* 47–55.

Posner, Richard A. (1995). *Aging and old age.* Chicago: University of Chicago Press.

Poulin, François, & Boivin, Michel. (2000). The role of proactive and reactive aggression in the formation and development of boys' friendships. *Developmental Psychology, 30,* 233–240.

Powell, Douglas H. (1994). *Profiles in cognitive aging.* Cambridge, MA: Harvard University Press.

Power, Rosemary. (1993). Death in Ireland: Death, wakes and funerals in contemporary Irish society. In Donna Dickenson & Malcolm Johnson (Eds.), *Death, dying & bereavement.* London: Sage.

Prado, C.G. & Taylor, S.J. (1999). *Assisted suicide: Theory and practice in elective death.* Amherst, New York: Humanity Books.

Pratt, Michael W. & Norris, Joan E. (1999). Moral development in maturity: Life-span perspectives on the processes of successful aging. In Thomas M. Hess & Fredda Blanchard-Fields (Eds.), *Social cognition and aging.* San Diego: Academic Press.

Pratt, M.W., & Robins, S. (1991). That's the way it was: Age differences in the structure and quality of adults' personal narratives. *Discourse Processes, 14,* 73–85.

Pratt, Michael W., Arnold, Mary Louise, Joan E. Norris, & Rebecca Filyer. (1999). Generativity and moral development as predictors of value-socialization. Narratives for young persons across the adult life span: From lessons learned to stories shared. *Psychology and Aging, 14,* 414–426.

Presser, Harriet B. (2000). Nonstandard work schedules and marital instability. *Journal of Marriage and the Family, 62,* 93–110.

Presley, Cheryl A., Meilman, Philip, & Lyerla, Rob. (1995). Alcohol and drugs on American college campuses. Carbondale: Southern Illinois University Press.

Price, Donald L., Tanzi, Rudolph E., Borchelt, David R., & Sisodia, Sangram S. (1998). Alzheimer's disease: Genetic studies and transgenic models. *Annual Review of Genetics, 32,* 461–493.

Prior, Margot, Eisenmajer, Richard, Leekam, Susan, Wing, Lorna et al. (1998), *Journal of Child Psychology & Psychiatry & Allied Disciplines, 39,* 893–902.

Proos, L. A., Hofvander, Y., & Tuvemo, T. (1991). Menarcheal age and growth pattern of Indian girls adopted in Sweden. *Acta Paediatrica Scandinavica, 80,* 852–858.

Pufall, Peter B. (1997). Framing a developmental psychology of art. *Human Development, 40,* 169–180.

Pyke, Karen. (1999). The micropolitics of care in relationships between aging parents and adult chidlren: Individualism, collectivism, and power. *Journal of Marriage and the Family, 61,* 661–672.

Pyke, Karen D., & Bengtson, Vern L. (1996). Caring more or less: Individualistic and collectivist systems of family eldercare. *Journal of Marriage and the Family, 58,* 379–392

Pynoos, Jon, & Golant, Stephen. (1996). Housing and living arrangements for the elderly. In Robert H. Binstock & Linda K. George (Eds.), *Handbook of aging and the social sciences.* San Diego: Academic Press.

Quadagno, Jill, & Hardy, Melissa. (1996). Work and retirement. In Robert H. Binstock & Linda K. George (Eds.), *Handbook of aging and the social sciences.* San Diego: Academic Press.

Quinn, Paul C., Cummins, Maggie, Kase, Jennifer, Martin, Erin, & Weissman, Sheri. (1996). Development of categorical representations for above and below spatial relations in 3- to 7-month-old infants. *Developmental Psychology, 32,* 942–950.

Rabbitt, Patrick, Donlan, Christopher, McInnes, Lynn, Watson, Peter, & Bent, Nuala. (1995). Unique and interactive effects of depression, age, socioeconomic advantage, and gender on cognitive performance of normal healthy older people. *Psychology and Aging, 10,* 307–313.

Rabow, Michael W., Hardie, Grace E., Fair, Joan M., & McPhee, Stephen J. (2000). End-of-life care content in 50 textbooks from multiple specialties. *Journal of the American Medical Association, 283,* 771–778.

Rahman, Nazheen, & Stratton, Micahel R. (1998). The genetics of breast cancer susceptibility. *Annual Review of Genetics, 32,* 95–121.

Rall, Jaime & Harris, Paul L. (2000). In Cinderella's slippers? Story comprehension from the protagonist's point of view. *Developmental Psychology, 36,* 202–208.

Raloff, Janet. (1996). Vanishing flesh: Muscle loss in the elderly finally gets some respect. *Science News, 150,* 90–91.

Ramey, C.T. & Ramey, S.L. (1998). Early intervention and early experience. *American Psychologist, 53,* 109–120.

Ramey, C.T., Bryant, D.B., Wasik, B.H., Sparling, J.J., Fendt, K.H., & Levange, L.M. (1992). The Infant Health and Development Program for low birth weight, premature infants: Program elements, family participation, and child intelligence. *Pediatrics, 89,* 454–465.

Ramsey, J., Roecker, E.B., Weindruch, R., & Kemnitz, J.W. (1997). Energy expenditure of adult male rhesus monkeys during the first 30 months of dietary restriction. *American Journal of Physiology, 272,* 901.

Rank, Mark R. & Hirschl, Thomas a. (1999). Estimating the proportion of Americans ever experiencing poverty during their elderly years. *Journal of Gerontology, 54B,* 5184–5193.

Ratner, H.H., Smith, B.S., & Padgett, R.J. (1990). Children's organization of events and event memories. In R. Fivush & J.A. Hudson (Eds.), *Knowing and remembering in young children.* Cambridge, England: Cambridge University Press.

Rauscher, F.H., Shaw, G.L., & Ky, K.N. (1993). Music and spatial task performance. *Nature, 365,* 611.

Rauscher, F.H., & Shaw, G.L. (1998). Key components of the Mozart effect. *Perceptual and motor skills, 86,* 835–841.

Ravesloot, Janita. (1995). Courtship and sexuality in the youth phase. In Manuel du Bois-Reymond, Rene Diekstra, Klaus Hurrelmann, & Els Peters (Eds.), *Childhood and youth in Germany and the Netherlands: Transitions and coping strategies of adolescents.* Berlin: Mouton de Gruyter.

Rawlins, William K. (1992). *Friendship matters.* Hawthorne, NY : Aldine de Gruyter.

Ray, Ruth E. (1996). A postmodern perspective on feminist gerontology. *The Gerontologist. 36.*

Reddy, Linda A. & Pfeiffer Steven I. (1997). Effectiveness of treatment of foster care with children and adolescents: A review of outcome studies. *Journal of the American Academy of Child & Adolescent Psychiatry, 36,* 381–588.

Reed, Edward S. (1993). The intention to use a specific affordance: A conceptual framework for psychology. In Robert H. Wozniak & Kurt W. Fischer (Eds.), *Development in context: Acting and thinking in specific environments.* Hillsdale, NJ: Erlbaum.

Register, Cheri. (1991). *Are those kids yours?* New York: Free Press.

Reich, K.H. (1993). Cognitive developmental approaches to religiousness: Which version for which purpose? *International Journal for the Psychology of Religion, 3,* 145–171.

Reiss, David. (1997). Mechanisms linking genetic and social influences in adolescent development: Beginning a collaborative search. *Current Directions in Psychological Science, 6,* 100–105.

Rendell, Peter G., & Thompson, Donald M. (1999). Aging and prospective memory: Differences between naturalistic and laboratory tasks. *Journal of Gerontology: Psychological Sciences, 54B,* 256–269.

Renninger, K. Ann. (1998). Developmental psychology and instruction: Issues from and for practice. In.William Damon, Irving E. Sigel, & K. Ann Renninger (Eds.), *Handbook of Child Psychology, Volume Four: Child psychology in practice.* New York: Wiley.

Renninger, K. Ann, & Amsel, Eric. (1997). Change and development: An introduction. In Eric Amsel & K. Ann Renninger (Eds.), *Change and development: Issues of theory, method, & application.* Mahwah, NJ: Erlbaum.

Rest, James, Narvaez, Darcia, Bebeau, Murel J., & Thoma, Stephen J. (1999). *Postconventional moral thinking: A neo-kohlbergian approach.* Mahwah, NJ: Erlbaum.

Reynolds, Arthur J. & Temple, Judy A. (1998). Extended early childhood intervention and school achievement: Age thirteen findings from the Chicago longitudinal study. *Child Development, 69,* 231–246.

Rhodes, Julia C., Kjerulff, Kristen H., Langenberg, Patricia W., & Guzinski, Gay M. (1999). Hysterectomy and sexual functioning. *Journal of the American Medical Association, 282,* 1934–1941.

Ricciuti, H.N. (1993). Nutrition and mental development. *Current Directions in Psychological Science, 2,* 43–46.

Rice, George, Anderson, Carol, Risch, Neil, & Ebers, George. (1999). Male homosexuality: Absence of linkage to microsatellite markers at Xq28. *Science, 284,* 665–667.

Richards, John E. & Holley, Felecia B. (1999). Infant attention and the development of smooth pursuit tracking. *Developmental Psychology, 35,* 856–867.

Richards, Maryse, Crowe, Paul A., Larson, Reed, & Swarr, Amy. (1998). Developmental patterns and gender differences in the experience of peer companionship during adolescence. *Child Development, 69,* 154–163.

Richards, M.P.M. (1996). The childhood environment and the development of sexuality. In C.J.K. Henry & S.J. Ulijaszek (Eds.), *Long-term consequences of early environment: Growth, development and the lifespan developmental perspective.* Cambridge: Cambridge University Press.

Richardson, Gale A., & Day, Nancy L. (1994). Detrimental effects of prenatal cocaine exposure: Illusion or reality? *Journal of the American Academy of Child and Adolescent Psychiatry, 33,* 28–34.

Riedel, Brant W. & Lichstein, Kenneth L. (1998). Objective sleep measures and subjective sleep satisfaction: How do older adults with insomnia define a good night's sleep? *Psychology and Aging, 13,* 159–163.

Riedel, Brant W., Lichstein, Kenneth L., & Dwyer, William O. (1995). Sleep compression and sleep education for older insomniacs: Self-help versus therapist guidance. *Psychology and Aging, 10,* 54–63.

Riley, Matilida White, & Riley, John W., Jr. (1994). Age integration and the lives of older people. *Gerontologist, 34,* 110–115.

Rind, Bruce, Tromovitch, Philip, & Bauserman, Robert. (1998) A meta-analytical examination of assumed properties of child sexual abuse using college students. *Psychological Bulletin, 124,* 22–53.

Risman, Barbara J. & Johnson-Sumerford, Danette. (1998). Doing it fairly: A study of postgender marriages. *Journal of Marriage and the Family, 60,* 5–22.

Ritchie, K., Kildea, D., & Robine, J. M. (1992). The relationship between age and the prevalence of senile dementia: A meta-analysis of recent data. *International Journal of Epidemiology, 21,* 763–769.

Rivara, Fred P. (1994). Unintentional injuries. In Ivan Barry Pless (Ed.), *The epidemiology of childhood disorders.* New York: Oxford University Press.

Robert, Elizabeth. (1996). Treating depression in pregnancy, editorial. *New England Journal of Medicine, 335,* 1056–1058.

Roberto, K.A. (1993). Family caregivers of aging adults with disabilities: A review of the caregiving literature. In K.A. Roberto (Ed.), *The elderly caregiver: Caring for adults with developmental disabilities.* Newbury Park, CA: Sage.

Roberts, K. (1988). Retrieval of a basic-level category in prelinguistic infants. *Developmental Psychology, 24,* 21–27.

Robin, Daniel J., Berthier, Neil E., & Clifton, Rachel K. (1996). Infants' predictive reaching for moving objects in the dark. *Developmental Psychology, 32,*

Robins, Richard W., Gosling, Samuel D., & Craik, Kenneth H. (1999). An empirical analysis of trends in psychology. *American Psychologist, 54,* 117–128.

Rochat, Philippe, & Bullinger, Andre. (1994). Posture and functional action in infancy. In Andre Vyt, Henriette Bloch, & Marc H. Bornstein (Eds.), *Early child development in the French tradition: Contributions from current research.* Hillsdale, NJ: Erlbaum.

Rochat, Philippe, & Goubet, Nathalie. (1995). Development of sitting and reaching in 5- to 6-month-old infants. *Infant Behavior and Development, 18,* 53–68.

Rogers, Kathleen Boyce. (1999). Parenting processes related to sexual risk-taking behaviors of adolescent males and females. *Journal of Marriage and the Family, 61,* 99–109.

Roggman, Lori A., Langlois, Judith H., Hubbs-Tait, Laura, & Rieser-Danner, Loretta A. (1994). Infant day-care, attachment, and the "filedrawer problem". *Child Development, 65,* 1429–1443.

Rogoff, Barbara. (1990). *Apprenticeship in thinking: Cognitive development in social context.* New York: Oxford University Press.

Rogoff, Barbara. (1997). Evaluating development in the process of participation: Theory, methods, and practice building on each other. In Eric Amsel & K. Ann Renninger (Eds.), *Change and development: Issues of theory, method, & application.* Mahwah, NJ: Erlbaum.

Rogoff, Barbara. (1998). Cognition as a collaborative process. In D. Kuhn & R. Siegler (Eds.), W. Damon (Series Ed.), *Handbook of child psychology (5th ed.): Vol. 2: Cognition, perception, and language.* New York: Wiley.

Rogoff, Barbara, Mistry, Jayanthi, Goncu, Artin, & Mosier, Christine. (1993). Guided participation in cultural activity by toddlers and caregivers. *Monographs of the Society for Research in Child Development, 58* (Serial No. 236).

Rohlen, Thomas P., & LeTendre, Gerald K. (1996). *Teaching and learning in Japan.* Cambridge, England: Cambridge University Press.

Romaine, Suzanne. (1984). *The language of children and adolescents: The acquisition of communication competence.* Oxford, England: Blackwell.

Romaine, Suzanne. (1995). *Bilingualism,* second edition. New York and Oxford: Basil Blackwell.

Romo, Harriett D., & Falbo, Toni. (1996). *Latino high school graduation: Defying the odds.* Austin: University of Texas Press.

Ronca, April E. & Alberts, Jeffrey R. (1995). Maternal contributions to fetal experience and the transition from prenatal to postnatal life. In Jean-Pierre Lecanuet, William P. Fifer, Norman A. Krasnegor, & William P. Smotherman (Eds.), *Fetal development: A psychobiological perspective.* New Jersey: Erlbaum.

Roosa, Mark W., Reinholtz, Cindy, & Angelini, Patti Jo. (1999)The relation of child sexual abuse and depression in young women: Comparisons across four ethnic groups. *Journal of Abnormal Child Psychology, 27,* 65–76.

Rose, Amanda J. & Asher, Steven R. (1999). Children's goals and strategies in response to conflicts within a friendship. *Developmental Psychology, 35,* 69–79.

Rose, Michael R. (1997). Toward an evolutionary demography. In Kenneth W. Wachter & Caleb E. Finch, (Eds.), *Between Zeus and the salmon: The biodemography of longevity.* Washington, DC: National Academy Press.

Rosen, Karen Schneider, & Burke, Patricia B. (1999) Multiple attachment relationships within families: Mothers and fathers with two young children. *Developmental Psychology, 35,* 436–441.

Rosenberg, Elinor B. (1992). *The adoption life cycle.* Lexington, MA: Lexington Books.

Rosenblith, Judy F. (1992). *In the beginning: Development from conception to age two* (2nd ed.). California: Sage Newbury Park.

Rosenblum, Gianine D. & Lewis, Michael. (1999). The relations among body image, physical attractiveness, and body mass in adolescence. *Child Development, 70,* 50–64.

Rosenstein, Diana, & Oster, Harriet. (1988). Differential facial responses to four basic tastes. *Child Development, 59,* 1555–1568.

Rosenthal, M. Sara. (1996). *The fertility sourcebook.* Anodyne: Lowell House.

Rosenthal, Robert. (1996). *Pygmalion in the classroom.* New York: Irvington.

Rosner, Bernard, Prineas, Ronald, Loggie, Jennifer, & Daniels, Stephen R. (1998). Percentiles for body mass index in U.S. children 5 to 17 years of age. *Journal of Pediatrics, 132,* 211–222.

Rosow, Irving. (1985). Status and role change through the life cycle. In Robert H. Binstock & Ethel Shanas (Eds.), *Handbook of aging and the social sciences (2nd ed.).* New York: Van Nostrand.

Ross, J.G., Pate, R.R., Casperson, C.J., Domberg, C.L., & Svilar, M. (1987). Home and community in children's exercise habits. *Journal of Physical Education, Recreation and Dance, 58,* 85–92.

Rosser, Pearl L., & Randolph, Suzanne M. (1989). Black American infants: The Howard University normative study. In J. Kevin Nuegent, Barry M. Lester, & T. Berry Brazelton (Eds.), *The cultural context of infancy: Vol I. Biology, culture, and infant development.* Norwood, NJ: Ablex.

Rossi, Alice S. (1994). *Eros and caritas: A biopsychosocial approach to human sexuality and reproduction.* Chicago: University of Chicago Press.

Rothbart, M.K. & Bates, J.E. (1998). Temperament. In W. Damon (Series Ed.), N. Eisenberg (Volume Ed.), *Handbook of child psychology: Vol. 3. Social, emotional, and personality development* (5th ed.). New York: Wiley.

Rotheram-Borus, Mary Jane, & Wyche, Karen Fraser. (1994). Ethnic differences in identity development in the United States. In Sally L. Archer (Ed.), *Interventions for adolescent identity development.* Thousand Oaks, CA: Sage.

Rovee-Collier, Carolyn K. (1987). Learning and memory in infancy. In J. Doniger Osofsky (Ed.), *Handbook of infant development* (2nd ed.). New York: Wiley.

Rovee-Collier, Carolyn K. (1990). The "memory system" of prelinguistic infants. In A. Diamond (Ed.), *The development and neural bases of higher cognitive functions.* New York: New York Academy of Sciences.

Rovee-Collier, Carolyn. (1999). The development of infant memory. *Current Directions in Psychological Science, 8,* 80–85.

Rovee-Collier, Carolyn K., & Gerhardstein, Peter. (1997). The development of infant memory. In Nelson Cowan & Charles Hulme (Eds.), *The development of memory in childhood: Studies in developmental psychology.* Hove, East Sussex, UK: Psychology Press.

Rovee-Collier, Carolyn K., & Hayne, H. (1987). Reactivation of infant memory: Implications for cognitive development. In H.W. Reese (Ed.), *Advances in child development and behavior* (Vol. 20). New York: Academic Press.

Rowe, David C. (1994). *The limits of family influence: Genes, experience, and behavior.* New York: Guilford Press.

Rowe, David C. & Jacobson, Kristen C. (1999). In the mainstream: Research in behavioral genetics. In Ronald A. Carson & Mark A. Rothstein (Eds.), *Behavioral genetics: The clash of culture and biology.* Baltimore: Johns Hopkins Press.

Rowley, Daniel James, Lujan, Herman D., & Dolence, Michael G. (1998). *Strategic choices for the academy: How demand for lifelong learning will re-create higher education.* San Francisco: Jossey-Bass Publishers.

Rubenstein, Adam J., Kalakanis, Lisa, & Langlois, Judith H. (1999). Infant preferences for attractive faces: A cognitive explanation. *Developmental Psychology, 35,* 848–855.

Rubin, David C. (1999).Autobiographical memory and aging: Distributions of memories across the lifespan and their implications for survey research. In Norbert Schwarz, Denise Park, Bärbel Knäuper, & Seymour Sudman (Eds.), *Cognition, aging, and self-reports.* Philadelphia: Psychology Press.

Rubin, Glenna B., Fagen, Jeffrey W., & Carroll, Marjorie H. (1998). Olfactory context and memory retrieval in 3-month-old infants. *Infant Behavior & Development, 21,* 641–658.

Ruble, D.N. & Martin, C. (1998). Gender development. In W. Damon & N. Eisenberg (Eds.), *Handbook of child psychology, Volume 3: Social, emotional and personality development.* New York: Wiley.

Rutter, Michael. (1980). *Changing youth in a changing society: Patterns of development and disorder.* Cambridge, MA: Harvard University Press.

Rutter, Michael. (1998). Some research considerations on intergenerational continuities and discontinuities: Comment on the special section. *Developmental Psychology, 34,* 1269–1273.

Rutter, Michael & Hagen, John. (1999). Commentary for the behavioral science working group of NIMH. *Society for Research in Child Development, Newsletter, 42,* 1–7.

Rutter, Michael, & Rutter, Marjorie. (1993). *Developing minds: Challenge and continuity across the life span.* New York: Basic Books.

Rutter, Michael, Dunn, Judy, Plomin, Robert, Simonoff, Emily, Pickles, Andrew, Maughan, Barbara, Ormel, Johan, Meyer, Joanne, & Eaves, Lindon. (1997). Integrating nature and nurture: Implications of person-environment correlations and interactions for developmental psychopathology. *Development and Psychopathology, 9,* 335–364.

Rutter, Michael, Giller, Henry, & Hagell, Ann. (1998). *Antisocial behavior by young people.* Cambridge, UK: Cambridge University Press.

Ryan, Sarah. (1998). Management by stress: The reorganization of work hits home in the 1996s. In Stephanie Coontz (Ed.), *American families: A multicultural reader.* New York: Routledge.

Rybash, John M., Hoyer, William J., & Roodin, Paul A. (1986). *Adult cognition and aging: Developmental changes in processing, knowing, and thinking.* New York: Pergamon Press.

Sabatier, Colette. (1994). Parental conceptions of early development and developmental stimulation. In Andre Vyt, Henriette Bloch, & Marc H. Bornstein (Eds.), *Early child development in the French tradition: Contributions from current research.* Hillsdale, NJ: Erlbaum.

Sabin, E.P. (1993). Social relationships and mortality among the elderly. *Journal of Applied Gerontology,* 44–60.

Sacks, Oliver. (1995). *An anthropologist on Mars: Paradoxical tales.* New York: Random House.

Saigal, Saroj, Hoult, Lorraine A., Streiner, David L., Stoskopf, Barbara L., & Rosenbaum, Peter L. (2000). School difficulties at adolescence in a regional cohort of children who were extremely low birth weight. *Pediatrics, 105,* 325-331.

Sallis, J.F., & Owen, N. (1999). *Physical activity and behavioral medicine.* Thousand Oaks, CA: Sage.

Salthouse, Timothy A. (1991). *Theoretical perspectives on cognitive aging.* Hillsdale, NJ: Erlbaum.

Salthouse, Timothy A. (1993). Speed mediation of adult age differences in cognition. *Developmental Psychology, 29,* 722–738.

Salthouse, Timothy. (1999). Pressing issues in cognitive aging. In Norbert Schwarz, Denise C. Park, Barbel Knauper &

Seymour Sudman (Eds.), *Cognition, aging and self reports.* Philadelphia: Psychology Press.

Sampson, P.D., Streissguth, A.P., Bookstein, F.L., Little, R.E., Clarren, S.K., Dehaene, P., Hanson, J.W., & Graham, J.M., Jr. (1997). Incidence of fetal alcohol syndrome and prevalence of alcohol-related neurodevelopmental disorder. *Teratology, 56,* 317–326.

Sampson, Robert J. (1997). Collective regulation of adolescent misbehavior. *Journal of Adolescence Research, 12,* 227–244.

Sampson, Robert J., & Laub, John. (1993). *Crime in the making: Pathways and turning points through life.* Cambridge, MA: Harvard University Press.

Sampson, Robert J., & Laub, John. (1996) Socioeconomic achievement in the life course of disadvantaged men: Military service as a turning point, circa 1945–1965. *American Sociological Review, 61,* 347–367.

Sampson, Robert J., Raudenbush, Stephen W., & Earls, Felton. (1997). Neighborhoods and violent crime: A multilevel study of collective efficacy. *Science, 277,* 918–924.

Sanchez, L. (1994). Gender, labor allocations, and the psychology entitlement within the home. *Social Forces, 73,* 533–553.

Sandelowski, Margarete. (1993). *With child in mind: Studies of the personal encounter with infertility.* Philadelphia: University of Pennsylvania Press.

Sanders, Catherine M. (1989). *Grief: The mourning after.* New York: Wiley.

Sandhofer, Catherine & Smith, Linda B. (1999). Learning color words involves learning a system of mappings. *Developmental Psychology, 35,* 668–679.

Sansavini, Alessandra, Bertoncini, Josiane, & Giovanelli, Fiuliana. (1997). Newborns discriminate the rhythm of multi-syllabic stressed words. *Developmental Psychology, 33,* 3–11.

Santelli, J.S., Brener, N.D., Lowry, R., Bhatt, A., & Zubin, L.S. (1998). Multiple sexual partners among U.S. adolescents and young adults. *Family Planning Perspectives, 30,* 271–275.

Sapolsky, Robert M. (1994). **Why zebras don't get ulcers: A guide to stress, stress-related diseses, and coping.** New York: Freeman.

Sapolsky, Robert M. (1997). The importance of a well-groomed child. *Science, 277,* 1620–1621.

Sargent, James D., Stukel, Therese A., Dalton, Madeline A., Freeman, Jean L., & Brown, Mary Jean. (1996). Iron deficiency in Massachusetts communities: Socioeconomic and demographic risk factors among children. *American Journal of Public Health, 86,* 544–550.

Saudino, Kimberly J., McClearn, G.E., Pedersen, Nancy L., Lichtenstein, Paul, & Plomin, Robert. (1997). Can personality explain genetic influences on life events? *Journal of Personality and Social Psychology, 72,* 196–206.

Saunders, C.M. (1978). *The management of terminal disease.* London: Edward Arnold.

Savin-Williams, Ritch C. (1995). An exploratory study of pubertal maturation timing and self-esteem among gay and bisexual male youths. *Developmental Psychology, 31,* 56–64.

Savin-Williams, Ritch C., & Diamond, Lisa M. (1997). Sexual orientation as a developmental context for lesbians, gays, and bisexuals: Biological perspectives. In Nancy L. Segal, Glenn E. Weisfeld, & Carol C. Weisfeld (Eds.), *Uniting psychology and biology: Integrative perspectives on human development.* Washington, DC: American Psychological Association.

Scarr, Sandra. (1996). Families and day care: Both matter for children. *Contemporary Psychology, 41,* 330–331.

Scarr, Sandra. (1998). American child care today. *American Psychologist, 53,* 95–108.

Schaal, B. (1986). Presumed olfactory exchanges between mother and neonate in humans. In J. Le Camus & J. Cosnier (Eds.), *Ethology and psychology.* Toulouse, France: Private, I.E.C.

Schacter, D.L., & Tulving, E. (Eds.). (1994). *Memory systems.* Cambridge, MA: MIT Press.

Schaffner, Kenneth F. (1999). Complexity and research strategies in behavioral genetics. In Ronald A. Carson & Mark A. Rothstein (Eds*.). Behavioral genetics: The clash of culture and biology.* Baltimore: Johns Hopkins Press.

Schaie, K. Warner. (1989). Perceptual speed in adulthood: Cross-sectional and longitudinal studies. *Psychology and Aging, 4,* 443–453.

Schaie, K. Warner. (1996). *Intellectual development in adulthood: The Seattle Longitudinal Study.* Cambridge, England: Cambridge University Press.

Schaie, K. Warner. (1998). A general model for the study of developmental problems. In M. Powell Lawton & Timothy A. Salthouse (Eds.), *Essential papers on the psychology of aging.* New York: New York University Press.

Schaie, K. Warner, & Willis, Sherry L. (1996). Adult development and aging. New York: HarperCollins.

Schairer, Catherine, Lubin, Jay, Troisi, Rebecca, Sturgeon, Susan, Brinton, Louise, & Hoover, Robert. (2000). Menopausal estrogen and estrogen-progestin replacement therapy and breast cancer risk. *Journal of the American Medical Association, 283,* 485–491.

Schechter, Susan, Beatty, Paul, Willis, Gordon B. (1999). Asking survey respondents about health status: Judgment and response issues. *Cognition and Aging.*

Scheibel, Arnold B. (1996). Structural and functional changes in the aging brain. In James E. Birren &K. Warner Schaie (Eds.) *Handbook of the Psychology of Aging.* San Diego: Academic Press.

Scher, Anat & Mayseless, Ofra. (1997). Changes in negative emotionality in infancy: The role of mother's attachment concerns. *British Journal of Developmental Psychology, 15,* 311–321.

Schilit, Rebecca, & Gomberg, Edith S. Lisansky. (1991). *Drugs and behavior: A sourcebook for the helping professions.* Newbury Park, CA: Sage.

Schiller, R. (1998). The relationship of developmental tasks to life satisfaction, moral reasoning, and occupational attainment at age 28. *Adult Development, 5,* 239–254.

Schlegal, Alice, & Barry, Herbert. (1991). *Adolescence: An anthropological inquiry.* New York: Free Press.

Schlundt, David G., & Johnson, William G. (1990). *Eating disorders: Assessment and treatment.* Boston: Allyn & Bacon.

Schmitt, Alain, Atzwanger, Klaus, Grammer, Karl, & Schäfer Katrin. (1997). *New aspects of human ethology.* New York: Plenum.

Schneider, Jane W., & Hans, Sydney L. (1996). Effects of prenatal exposure to epodes on focused attention in toddlers during free play. *Journal of Developmental & Behavioral Pediatrics, 17,* 240–247.

Schneider, Wolfgang, Bjorklund, David F., & Maier-Bruckner, Wolfgang. (1996). The effects of expertise and IQ on children's memory: When knowledge is, and when it is not enough. *International Journal of Behavioral Development, 19,* 773–796.

Schneider, Wolfgang, & Pressly, Michael. (1997). *Memory development: Between two and twenty.* Mahwah, NJ: Erlbaum.

Schneider, Wolfgang & Bjorklund, David F. (1998). Memory. In William Damon, Deanna Kuhn, & Robert S. Siegler (Eds.), *Handbook of child psychology: Cognition, perception, and language.* New York: Wiley

Schoenbaum, Michael & Waidmann, Timothy. (1997). Race, socioeconomic status, and health: Accounting for race differences in health. *Journals of Gerontology, 52B,* 61–73.

Schooler, Carmi, Mulatu, Mesfin Samuel, & Oates, Gary. (1999). The continuing effects of substantively complex work on the intellectual functioning of older workers. *Psychology and Aging, 14,* 483–506.

Schopler, Eric, Mesibou, Gary B., & Kunce, Linda J. (Eds.). (1999). *Asperger Syndrome or high functioning autism.* New York: Plenum.

Schore, Allan N. (1994). *Affect regulation and the origin of the self: The neurobiology of emotional development.* Hillsdale, NJ: Erlbaum.

Schrijvers, Carola T.M., Stronks, Karien, van de Mheen, H. Dike, & Mackenbach, Johan P. (1999). Explaining educational differences in mortality: The role of behavioral and material factors. *American Journal of Public Health, 89,* 535–540.

Schroots, Johannes J.F. (1996). Theoretical developments in the psychology of aging. *Gerontologist, 36,* 741–748.

Schulman, Kevin A., Berlin, Jesse, William Harless, Kerner, Jon F., Sistrunk, Shyril, Gersh, Bernard J., Dubé, Ross, Taleghani, Christopher K., Burke, Jennifer E., Williams, Sankey, Eisenberg, John M., & Escarce, José. (1999). The effect of race and sex on physician's recommendations for cardiac catherization. *New England Journal of Medicine, 340,* 618–625.

Schulz, Richard, Musa, Donald, Staszewski, James, & Siegler, Robert S. (1994). The relationship between age and major league baseball performance: Implications for development. *Psychology and Aging, 9,* 274–286.

Schweder, R.A., Mahapatra, M., & Miller, J.G. (1990). Culture and moral development. In J.W. Stigler, R.A. Schweder, & G. Herdt (Eds.), *Cultural psychology: Essays on comparative human development*. Cambridge, England: Cambridge University Press.

Scogin, Forrest. (1998). Anxiety in old age. In Inger Hilde Nordhus, Gary r. VandenBos, Stig Berg, & Pia From holt (Eds.) *Clinical geropsychology: Contents*. Washington DC: APA Books.

Scott, Fiona J., & Baron-Cohen, Simon. (1996) Logical, analogical, and psychological reasoning in autism: A test of the Cosmides theory. *Development and Psychopathology, 8,* 235–245.

Scott-Maxwell, Florida. (1968). *The measure of my days*. New York: Knopf.

Scribner, R. (1996). Paradox as paradigm: The health outcomes of Mexican Americans. *American Journal of Public Health, 86,* 303–305.

Seale, Clive, & Cartwright, Ann. (1994). *The year before death*. Aldershot, England: Avebury.

Sedlak, A.J., & Broadhurst, D. D. (1996). *Third national study of child abuse and neglect: Final report*. Washington, DC: U. S. Department of Health and Human Services.

See, Sheree, Kwong, T., & Ryan, Ellen Bouchard. (1999). Intergenerational communication: The survey interview as a social exchange. In Norbert Schwarz, Denise C. Park, Barbel Knauper, & Seymour Sudman (Eds.), *Cognition, aging, and self reports*. Philadelphia: Psychology Press.

Seibel, Machelle M. (1993). Medical evaluation and treatment of the infertile couple. In Machelle M. Seibel, Ann A. Kiessling, Judith Bernstein, & Susan R. Levin (Eds.), *Technology and infertility: Clinical, psychosocial, legal and ethical aspects*. New York: Springer-Verlag.

Seltser, Barry Jay, & Miller, Donald E. (1993). *Homeless families: The struggle for dignity*. Urbana, Illinois: University of Illinois Press.

Seltzer, Marsha M., & Li, Lydia Wailing. (1996). The transitions of caregiving: Subjective and objective definitions. *The Gerontologist, 36.*

Sena, Rhonda, & Smith, Linda B. (1990). New evidence on the development of the word Big. *Child Development, 61,* 1034–1052.

Senior, B. (1997). Team roles and team performance: Is there really a link? *Journal of Occupational and Organisational Psychology, 70,* 241–258.

Serbin, Lisa A. (1997). Research on international adoption: Implications for developmental theory and social policy. *International Journal of Behavioral Development, 20,* 83–92.

Serra-Prat, Mateu, Gallo, Pedro, Jovell, Albert J., Aymerich, Marta, & Estrada, M. Dolors. (1998). Public health policy forum: Trade-offs in prenatal detection of Down syndrome. *American Journal of Public Health, 88,* 551–557.

Settersten, Richard A., & Hagestad, Gunhild. (1996). What's the latest? Cultural deadlines for educational and work transitions. *Gerontologist, 36,* 602–613.

Shanahan, James, & Morgan, Michael. (1999). *Television and its viewers: Cultivation theory and research*. Cambridge, UK: Cambridge University Press.

Shannon, Lyle W. (1988). *Criminal career continuity: Its social context*. New York: Human Sciences Press.

Sharkey, William F. (1993). Who embarrasses whom? Relational and sex differences in the use of intentional embarrassment. In Pamela J. Kalbfleisch (Ed.), *Interpersonal communication: Evolving interpersonal relationships*. Hillsdale, NJ: Erlbaum.

Shatz, Marilyn. (1994). *A toddler's life*. New York: Oxford University Press.

Shaw, Daniel S., Vondra, Joan I., Hommerding, Katherine Dowdell, Keenan, Kate & Dunn, Marija. (1994). Chronic family adversity and early child behavior problems. A longitudinal study of low income families. *Journal of Child Psychology and Psychiatry, 35,* 1109–1122.

Shea, John B., & Powell, Geoffrey. (1996). Capturing expertise in sports. In K. Anders Ericsson (Ed.), *The road to excellence: The acquisition of expert performance in the arts and sciences, sports and games*. Mahwah, NJ: Erlbaum.

Shedler, Jonathan, & Block, Jack. (1990). Adolescent drug use and psychological health: A longitudinal inquiry. *American Psychologist, 45,* 612–630

Sheeran, Pascal, Abraham, Charles, & Orbell, Sheina. (1999). Psychosocial correlates of heterosocial correlates of heterosexual condom use: A meta-analysis. *Psychological Bulletin, 125,* 90–132.

Shephard, Roy J. (1997). *Aging, physical activity, and health*. Champaign, Illinois: Human Kinetics.

Sherman, David S. (1994). Geriatric psychopharmacotherapy: Issues and concerns. *Generations, 18,* 34–39.

Sherman, D.W. (1999). End-of-life care: challenges and opportunities for health care professionals. *Hospital Journal, 14,* 109–21.

Sherman, Stephanie L. & Waldman, Irwin D. (1999). Identifying the molecular genetic basis of behavioral traits. In Ronald A. Carson & Mark A. Rothstein (Eds.), *Behavioral genetics: The clash of culture and biology*. Baltimore: Johns Hopkins Press.

Shiffrin, R.M., & Atkinson, R.C. (1969). Storage and retrieval processes in long-term memory. *Psychological Review, 76,* 179–193.

Shiono, Patricia H., Rauh, Virginia A., Park, Mikyung, Lederman, Sally A., & Zuskar, Deborah. (1997). Ethnic differences in birthweight: The role of lifestyle and other factors. *American Journal of Public Health, 87,* 787–793.

Shneidman, Edwin S., & Mandelkorn, Philip. (1994). Some facts and fables of suicide. In Edwin S. Shneidman, Norman L. Faberow, & Robert E. Litman (Eds.), *The psychology of suicide* (rev. ed.). Northwale, NJ: Aronson.

Shoemaker, Donald J. (1996). *Theories of delinquency: An examination of explanations of delinquent behavior* (3rd ed.). New York: Oxford University Press.

Shore, R. (1997). *Rethinking the brain: New insights into early development*. New York: Families and Work Institute.

Shore, R. Jerald, & Hayslip, Bert, Jr. (1994). Custodial grandparenting: Implications for children's development. In Adele Eskeles Gottfried & Allen W. Gottfried (Eds.), *Redefining families: Implications for children's development*. New York: Plenum Press.

Sickmund, Melissa, Snyder, Howard N., & Poe-Yamagata, Eileen. (1997). *Juvenile offenders and victims: 1997 update on violence*. Washington DC: Office of Juvenile Justice and Delinquency Prevention.

Siegel, Paul. Z., Brackbill, Robert J., & Health, Gregory W. (1995). The epidemiology of walking for exercise: Implications for promoting activity among sedentary groups. American Journal of Public Health, 85, 706–710.

Siegler, Ilene C., Kaplan, Berton H., Von Dras, Dean D., Mark, Daniel B. (1999). Cardiovascular Health: A challenge for midlife. In Sherry L. Willis & James D. Reid (Eds.), *Life in the middle*. San Diego: Academic Press

Siegler, Robert. (1991). *Children's thinking* (2nd ed.). Englewood Cliffs, NJ: Prentice-Hall.

Siegler, Robert. (1996). A grand theory of development. *Monographs of the Society for Research in Child Development, 61*, 266–275.

Siegler, R.S. & Shipley, C. (1995). Variation, selection, and cognitive change. In G. Halford & T. Simon(Eds.), *Developing cognitive competence: New approaches to process modeling*. Hillsdale, NJ: Erlbaum.

Siegler, Robert S., & Thompson, Douglas R. (1998). "Hey, would you like a nice cold cup of lemonade on this hot day?": Children's understanding of economic causation. *Developmental Psychology, 34*, 146–160.

Silbereisen, Rainer K., Robins, Lee, & Rutter, Michael. (1995). Secular trends in substance use. In Michael Rutter & David J. Smith (Eds.), *Psychosocial disorders in young people: Time trends and their causes*. West Sussex, England: Wiley.

Silva, Phil A. (1996). Health and development in the early years. In Phil A. Silva & Warren R. Stanton (Eds.), *From child to adult: The Dunedin multidisciplinary health and development study*. New Zealand: Oxford University Press.

Silver, L.B. (1991). Developmental learning disorders. In M. Lewis (Ed.), *Child and adolescent psychiatry: A comprehensive textbook*. Baltimore: Williams and Wilkins.

Silverman, Sharon L. & Casazza, Martha E. (2000). *Learning and development: Making connections to enhance teaching*. San Francisco: Jossey-Bass Publishers.

Silverstein, Merril & Chen, Xuan. (1999). The impact of acculturation in Mexican American families on the quality of adult grandchild-grandparent relationships. *Journal of Marriage and the Family, 61*, 188–198.

Simmons, Roberta G., & Blyth, Dale A. (1987). *Moving into adolescence: The impact of pubertal change and school context*. New York: Aldine de Gruyter.

Simonoff, Emily, Bolton, Patrick, & Rutter, Michael. (1996). Mental retardation: Genetic findings, clinical implications and research agenda. *Journal of Child Psychology & Psychiatry & Allied Disciplines, 37*, 259–280.

Simons, Ronald L. (1996). *Understanding differences between divorced and intact families*. Thousand Oaks, CA: Sage.

Simpson, Joe Leigh, Grito, Jamie A., Handyside, Alan, & Verlinsky, Yury. (1999). Preimplantation genetic diagnosis: The new frontier. *Contemporary Ob/Gyn, 44*, 55–78.

Sinclair, David. (1989). *Human growth after birth*. New York: Oxford University Press.

Singer, Mark I., Slovak, Karen, Frierson, Tracey, & York, peter. (1999). Viewing preferences, symptoms of psychological trauma, and violent behaviors among children who watch television. *Journal of the American Academy of child and Adolescent Psychiatry, 37*, 1041–1048.

Singh, Gopal K., & Yu, Stella M. (1996). Adverse pregnancy outcomes differences between US- and foreign-born women in major US racial and ethnic groups. *American Journal of Public Health, 86*, 837–843.

Singh, Susheela & Darroch, Jacqueline E. (2000). Adolescent pregnancy and childbearing: levels and trends in industrialized countries. *Family Planning Perspectives, 32*, 14–23.

Sinnott, Jan, & Johnson, Lynn. (1996). *Reinventing the University: A radical proposal for a problem-focused university*. Norwood, NJ: Ablex Publishing.

Sinnott, Jan D. (1998). *The development of logic in adulthood: Postformal thought and its applications*. New York: Plenum Press.

Siperstein, Gary N., Leffert, James S., & Wenz-Gross, Melodie. (1997). The quality of friendships between children with and without learning problems. *American Journal on Mental Retardation, 102*, 111–125.

Skinner, B.F. (1953). *Science and human behavior*. New York: Macmillan.

Skinner, B.F. (1957). *Verbal behavior*. New York: Appleton-Century-Crofts.

Skinner, Ellen A.K, Zimmer-Gembeck, Melanie J., & Connell, James P. (1998). Individual differences and the development of perceived control. *Monographs of the Society for research in Child Development, 63*.

Skinner, John H. (1995). Ethnic racial diversity in long term care use and service. In Zev Havel & Ruth E. Dunkle (Eds.), *Matching people with services in long-term care*. New York: Springer.

Slaby, Ronald J., & Eron, Leonard D. (1994). Afterword. In Leonard D. Eron, Jacquelyn H. Gentry, & Peggy Schlegel (Eds.), *Reason to hope: A psychosocial perspective on violence and youth*. Washington, D.C: American Psychological Association.

Slade, Aarietta, Belsky, Jay, Aber, J.Lawrence, & Phelps, June L. (1999). Mothers' representations of their relationships with their toddlers: Links to adult attachment and observed mothering. *Developmental Psychology, 35*, 611–619.

Sloboda, John A. (1996). The acquisition of musical performance expertise: Deconstructing the talent account of individual differences in musical expressivity. In K. Anders Eriksson (Ed), *The road to excellence: The acquisition of expert performance in the arts and sciences, sports and games*. Mahwah, NJ: Erlbaum.

Smetana, Judith G., & Asquith, P. (1994). Adolescents' and parents' conceptions of parental authority and adolescent autonomy. *Child Development, 65,* 1147–1162.

Smetana, Judith G., Killen, M., & Turiel, E. (1991). Children's reasoning about interpersonal and moral conflicts. *Child Development, 62,* 629–644.

Smith, David J. (1995). Youth crime and conduct disorders: Trends, patterns and causal explanations. In Michael Rutter & David J. Smith (Eds.), *Psychosocial disorders in young people: Time trends and their causes.* New York: Wiley.

Smith, G., Petersen, R., Ivnik, R.J., Malec, J.F., & Tangalos, E.G. (1996). Subjective memory complaints, psychological distress, and longitudinal change in objective memory performance. *Psychology and Aging, 11,* 272–279.

Smith, Jacqui, & Baltes, Paul B. (1990). Wisdom-related knowledge: Age/cohort differences in response to life-planning problems. *Developmental Psychology, 26,* 494–505.

Smith, Jacqui & Goodnow, Jacqueline J. (1999). Unasked-for support and unsolicited advice: Age and the quality of social experience. *Psychology and Aging, 14,* 108–121.

Smith, Jacqui, & Baltes, Paul B. (1999). Trends and profiles of psychological functioning in very old age. In P. B. Baltes & K. U. Mayer (Eds*.), The Berlin aging study: Aging from 70 to 100.* New York: Cambridge University Press.

Smith, L. (1995). Self-organizing process in learning to learn words. In C.A. Nelson (Ed.), *Basic and applied perspectives on learning, cognition, and development* (Minnesota Symposium on Child Psychology, vol. 28). Mahwah, NJ: Erlbaum.

Smith-Hefner, N. J. (1993). Education, gender, and generational conflict among Khmer refugees. *Anthropology and Education Quarterly, 24,* 135–158.

Smith, Peter K. (1997). Play fighting and real fighting. In Alain Schmitt, Klaus Atzwanger, Karl Grammer, & Katrin Schafer (Eds.) *New aspects of human ethology.* New York: Plenum.

Smith, P.K. & Sharp, S. (Eds.). (1994). *School bullying: Insights and perspectives.* London: Routledge.

Smith, Wrynn. (1987). *Cancer: A profile of health and diseases in America.* New York: Facts on File.

Snarey, John R. (1993). *How fathers care for the next generation: A four-decade study.* Cambridge, MA: Harvard University Press.

Snijders, R.J.M., & Nicolaides, K.H. (1996). *Ultrasound markers for fetal chromosomal defects.* New York: Parthenon.

Snow, Catherine E. (1984). Parent-child interaction and the development of communicative ability. In Richard L. Schiefelbusch & Joanne Pickar (Eds.), *The acquisition of communicative competence.* Baltimore: University Park Press.

Snyder, Howard N. (1997). *Serious, violent, and chronic juvenile offenders: An assessment of the extent of and trends in officially-recognized serious criminal behavior in a delinquent population.* Pittsburgh, PA: National Center for Juvenile Justice.

Snyder, Lisa. (1999). *Speaking our minds.* New York: Freeman.

Society for Research in Child Development. (1996). Ethical standards for research with children. *SCRD Directory of Members,* 337–339.

Soken, Nelson H. & Pick, Anne D. (1999). Infants' perception of dynamic affective expressions: Do infants distinguish specific expressions? *Child Development, 70,* 1275–1282.

Solanto, M.V. (1998). Neuropsychopharmacological mechanisms of stimulant drug action in attention-deficit hyperactivity disorder: A review and integration. *Behavioural Brain Research, 94,* 127–152.

Soldo, Beth J. (1996). Cross pressures on middle-aged adults: A broader view. *Journals of Gerontology, 51B,* 271–279.

Solomon, J.C., & Marx, J. (1995). *The psychology of grandparenthood: An international perspective.* London: Routledge.

Solomon, Richard, & Liefeld, Cynthia Pierce. (1998). Effectiveness of a family support center approach to adolescent mothers: Repeat pregnancy and school drop-out rates. *Family Relations, 47,* 139–144.

Sorlie, Paul D., Backlund, Eric, & Keller, Jacob B. (1995). US mortality by economic, demographic and social characteristics: The national longitudinal mortality study. *American Journal of Public Health, 85,* 949–956.

Sourcebook of Criminal Justice Statistics. (1999). See Maguire, Kathleen and Pastore, Ann L.

Spearman, Charles. (1927). *The abilities of man.* New York: Macmillan.

Spieker, Susan J., Larson, Nancy C., Lewis, Steven M., Keller, Thomas E., & Gilchrist, Lewayne. (1999) Developmental trajectories of disruptive behavior problems in preschool children of adolescent mothers. *Child Development, 70,* 443–458.

Sroufe, L. Alan. (1996). *Emotional development: The organization of emotional lie in the early years.* Cambridge: Cambridge University Press.

Sroufe, L.A. (1997). Psychopathology as an outcome of development. *Development and Psychopathology, 7,* 323–336.

Stack, Steven & Eshleman, J. Ross. (1998). Marital status and happiness: A 17-nation study. *Journal of Marriage and the Family, 60,* 527–537.

Staines, Graham L., Pottick, Kathleen J., & Fudge, Deborah A. (1986). Wives' employment and husbands' attitude toward work and life. *Journal of Applied Psychology, 71,* 118–128.

Staples, Robert, & Johnson, Leanor B. (1993). *Black families at the crossroads.* San Francisco: Jossey-Bass.

Starfield, B., Shapiro, S., Weiss, J., Liang, K.Y., Ra, K, Paige, D., & Wang, X.B. (1991). Race, family income and low birthweight. *American Journal of Epidemiology, 134,* 1167–1174.

Starkes, Janet L., Deakin, Janice M., Allard, & Fran, Hodges, Nicola, Hayes, April. (1996). Deliberate practice in sports: What is it, anyway? In K. Anders Eriksson (Ed.), *The road to excellence: The acquisition of expert performance in the arts and sciences, sports & games.* Mahwah, NJ: Erlbaum.

Staudinger, Ursula M. (1999). Social cognition and a psychological approach to an art of life. In Thomas M. Hess & Fredda Blanchard-Fields (Eds.), *Social cognition and aging*. San Diego: Academic Press.

Steele, Kenneth M., Bass, Karen E., & Crook, Melissa D. (1999). The Mozart effect: An artifact of preference. *Psychological Science, 10,* 370–373.

Stein, N.L., & Levine, L.J. (1989). The causal organization of emotional knowledge: A developmental study. *Cognition and Emotion, 3,* 343–378.

Steinberg, Adria. (1993). Adolescents and schools: Improving the fit. *The Harvard Education Letter*.

Steinberg, Lawrence. (1988). Reciprocal relation between parent-child distance and pubertal maturation. *Developmental Psychology, 24,* 122–128.

Steinberg, Lawrence. (1990). Interdependency in the family: Autonomy, conflict, and harmony in the parent-adolescent relationship. In Shirley S. Feldman & G.R. Elliot (Eds.), *At the threshold: The developing adolescent*. Cambridge, MA: Harvard University Press.

Steinberg, Lawrence. (1996). *Beyond the classroom: Why school reform has failed and what parents need to do*. New York: Simon & Schuster.

Steinberg, Lawrence, & Dornbusch, Sanford M. (1991). Negative correlates of part-time employment during adolescence: Replication and elaboration. *Developmental Psychology, 27,* 304–313.

Steinberg, Lawrence, Lamborn, Susie D., Darling, Nancy, Mounts, Nina A., & Dornbusch, Sanford M. (1994). Over-time changes in adjustment and competence among adolescents from authoritative, authoritarian, indulgent, and neglectful families. *Child Development, 65,* 754–770.

Stern, Daniel N. (1977). *The first relationship: Mother and infant*. Cambridge, MA: Harvard University Press.

Stern, Daniel N. (1985). *The interpersonal world of the infant*. New York: Basic Books.

Stern, David. (1997). What difference does it make if school and work are connected? Evidence on cooperative education in the United States. *Economics of Education Review, 16,* 213–229.

Sternberg, Hal. (1994). Aging of the immune system. In Paola S. Timiras (Ed.), *Physiological basis of aging and geriatrics (2nd ed.)*. Boca Raton, FL: CRC Press.

Sternberg, Robert J. (1988). Intellectual development: Psychometric and information-processing approaches. In M.H. Bornstein & M.E. Lamb (Eds.), *Developmental psychology: An advanced textbook (2nd ed.)*. Hillsdale, NJ: Erlbaum.

Sternberg, Robert J. (1988). *The triarchic mind: A new theory of human intelligence*. New York: Viking Press.

Sternberg, Robert J. (1996). *Successful intelligence*. New York: Simon & Schuster.

Sternberg, Robert J. (1999). *When is creativity rewarded and when isn't it?* Paper presented at American Psychological Association convention, Boston MA: August 23, 1999.

Sternberg, Robert J. (1999). A dialectical basis for understanding the study of cognition. In Robert J. Sternberg (Ed.), *The nature of cognition*. Cambridge, MA: The MIT Press.

Sternberg, Robert J., & Barnes, Michael L. (Eds.). (1988). *The psychology of love*. New Haven, CT: Yale University Press.

Sternberg, Robert J., Wagner, Richard K., Williams, Wendy M., & Horvath, Joseph A. (1995). Testing common sense. *American Psychologist, 50,* 912–927.

Stevenson, Harold W., & Stigler, Robert W. (1992). *The learning gap: Why our schools are failing and what we can learn from Japanese and Chinese education*. New York: Summit Books.

Stevenson, Jim. (1999). The treatment of the long-term sequelae of child abuse. *Journal of Child Psychology & Psychiatry & Allied Disciplines, 40,* 89–111.

Stewart, Anita L., & King, Abby C. (1994). Conceptualizing and measuring quality of life in older populations. In Ronald P. Abeles, Helen C. Gift, & Marcia C. Ory (Eds.),. *Aging and quality of life*. New York: Springer.

Sullivan, Amy D., Hedberg, Katrina, & Fleming, David W. (2000). Legalized physician-assisted suicide in Oregon—The second year. *The New England Journal of Medicine* (Special Report), 342.

Stewart, Deborah A. (1997). Adolescent sexual abuse, sexual assault, and rape. In Adele Dellenbaugh Hofmann & Donald Everett Greydanus (Eds.), *Adolescent medicine* (3rd ed.). Stanford, CT: Appleton and Lange.

Stillion, Judith M. (1995). Death in the lives of adults: Responding to the tolling of the bell. In Hannelore Was & Robert A. Neimeyer (Eds*.), Dying: Facing the facts*. Washington, DC: Taylor & Francis.

Stipek, Deborah J., Feiler, Rachell, Daniels, Denise & Milburn, Sharon. (1995). Effects of different instructional approaches on young children's achievement and motivation. *Child Development, 66,* 209–223.

Stipek, Deborah J., Recchia, Susan, & McClintic, Susan. (1992). Self-evaluation in young children. *Monographs of the Society for Research in Child Development, 57* (Serial No. 226), 1–79.

Stones, Michael J. &Kozma, Albert. (1996). Activity, exercise and behavior. In James E. Birren and K. Warner Schaie (Eds.) *Handbook of the psychology of aging*. San Diego: Academic Press.

Stormshak, Elizabeth, Bierman, Karen, & The Conduct Problems Prevention Research Group. (1998). The implications of different developmental patterns of disruptive behavior problems for school adjustment. *Development and Psychopathology, 10,* 451–468.

Stoto, Michael A., Almarino, Donna A., & McCormick, Marie C (Eds.). (1999). *Reducing the odds: Preventing perinatal transmission of HIV in the United States. National Research Council and the Institute of medicine*. Washington DC: National Academy Press.

Strassberg, Zvi, Dodge, Kenneth A., Pettit, Gregory S., & Bates, John E. (1994). Spanking in the home and children's subsequent aggression toward kindergarten peers. *Development and Psychopathology, 6,* 445–462.

Strawbridge, William J., Wallhagen, Margaret I., & Shema, Sarah J. (2000), New NHLBI clinical guidelines for obesity and overweight: Will they promote health? *American Journal of Public Health, 90,* 340–343.

Straus, Murray A. (1994). *Beating the devil out of them: Corporal punishment in American families.* Lexington, MA: Lexington Books.

Straus, Murray A., & Gelles, Richard J. (1990). *Physical violence in American families: Risk factors and adaptation to violence in 8,41 families.* New Brunswick, NJ: Transaction Books.

Straus, Murray A., & Yodanis, Carrie L. (1996). Corporal punishment in adolescence and physical assaults on spouses in later life: What accounts for the link? *Journal of Marriage and the Family, 58,* 825–841.

Strauss, David, & Eyman, Richard K. (1996). Mortality of people with mental retardation in California with and without Down syndrome, 1986–1991. *American Journal on Mental Retardation, 100,* 643–653.

Streissguth, Ann P., Bookstein, Fred L., Sampson, Paul D., & Barr, Helen M. (1993). *The enduring effects of prenatal alcohol exposure on child development: Birth through seven years, a partial least squares solution.* Ann Arbor: University of Michigan Press.

Streitmatter, Janice L. (1988). Ethnicity as a mediating variable of early adolescent identity development. *Journal of Adolescence, 11,* 335–346.

Streitmatter, Janice L. (1989). Identity status development and cognitive prejudice in early adolescents. *Journal of Early Adolescence, 11,* 335–346.

Streri, A. (1987). Tactile discrimination of shape and intermodal transfer in 2- to 3-month-old infants. *British Journal of Developmental Psychology, 5,* 213–220.

Super, Donald E. (1957). *The psychology of careers.* New York: Harper and Row.

Super, Donald E., & Thompson, A. S. (1981) *The adult career concerns inventory.* New York, Teachers College.

Susman, Elizabeth J. (1997). Modeling development complexity in adolescence: Hormones and behavior in context. *Journal of Research on Adolescence, 7,* 283–306.

Sutton-Smith, B. (1997). *The ambiguity of play.* Cambridge, MA: Harvard University Press.

Swain, S.O. (1992). Men's friendships with women: Intimacy, sexual boundaries, and the informant role. In P.M. Nardi (Ed.*),* *Gender in intimate relationships.* Belmont, CA: Wadsworth.

Swann, William B., Stein-Seroussi, Alan, & Giesler, R. Brian. (1992). Why people self-verify. *Journal of Personality and Social Psychology, 62,* 392–401.

Swanson, James M., McBurnett, Keith, Wigal, Tim, & Pfiffner, Linda J. (1993). Effect of stimulant medication on children with attention deficit disorder: "A review of reviews." *Exceptional Children, 60,* 154–161.

Swarns, Rachel. (1998, Feb. 25). Foster agencies called lax, and faulted in a girl's death. *The New York Times.*

Szatmari, Peter. (1992). The validity of autistic spectrum disorders: A literature review. *Journal of Autism and Developmental Disorders, 22,* 583–600.

Szinovacz, Maximiliane E. (2000). Changes in housework after retirement: A panel analysis. *Journal of Marriage and the Family, 62,* 78–92.

Szkrybalo, Joel & Ruble, Diane N. (1999). "God made me a girl": Sex-category constancy judgments and explanations revisited. *Developmental Psychology, 35,* 392–402.

Tangney, J.P., & Fischer, K.W. (1995). *The self-conscious emotions: The psychology of shame, guilt, embarrassment, and pride.* New York: Guilford Press.

Tannen, Deborah. (1990). *You just don't understand.* New York: Morrow.

Tanner, James M. (1991). Growth spurt, adolescent. In Richard M. Lerner, Ann C. Petersen, & Jeanne Brooks-Gunn (Eds.), *Encyclopedia of adolescence* (Vol. 1). New York: Garland.

Tanner, James M. (1991). Menarche, secular trend in age of. In Richard M. Lerner, Ann C. Petersen, & Jeanne Brooks-Gunn (Eds.), *Encyclopedia of adolescence* (Vol. 2). New York: Garland.

Tappenden, Eric C. (1996). Ethical questions in changing funeral and burial practices. In John d. Morgan (Ed.), *Ethical issues in the care of the dying and bereaved aged.* Amityville, NY: Baywood.

Tardif, Twila. (1996). Nouns are not always learned before verbs: Evidence from Mandarin speakers' early vocabularies. *Developmental Psychology, 32,* 492–504.

Tarter, Ralph, Vanyukov, Michael, Giancola, Peter, Dawes, Michael, Blackson, Timothy, Mezzich, Ada, & Clark, Duncan B. (1999). Etiology of early age onset substance use disorder: A maturational perspective. *Development and Psychopathology, 11,* 657–683.

Tatar, Moshe. (1998). Teachers as significant others: Gender differences to secondary school pupils' perceptions. *British Journal of Educational Psychology, 68,* 217–227.

Taylor, Gerry H., Klein, Nancy, Schatschneider, Christopher, & Hack, Maureen. (1998). Predictors of early school age outcomes in very low birth weight children. *Journal of Developmental and Behavioral Pediatrics, 19,* 235–243.

Taylor, J. L., Miller, T.P., & Tinklenberg, J. R. (1992). Coreates of memory decline: A 4-year longitudinal study of older adult with memory complaints. *Psychology and Aging, 7,* 185–193.

Taylor, Jill McLean, Gilligan, Carol, & Sullivan, Amy M. (1995). *Between voice and silence: Women and girls, race and relationship.* Cambridge, MA: Harvard University Press.

Taylor, R.J., Chatters, L.M., Tucker, M.B., & Lewis, E. (1991). Developments in research on black families: A decade review. In A. Booth (Ed.), *Contemporary families: Looking forward, looking back.* Minneapolis, MN: National Council on Family Relations.

Teitelbaum, Philip, Teitelbaum, Osnat, Nye, Jennifer, Fryman, Joshua, & Maurer, Ralph G. (1998). Movement analysis in infancy may be useful for early diagnosis of autism. *Proceedings of the National Academy of Sciences, 23,* 13982–13987.

United States Department of Justice. (1995). *Justice sourcebook, 1995.* Washington DC: Bureau of Justice Statistics.

U.S. Surgeon General's Report. (1996*). Physical activity and health: A report of the Surgeon General.* Atlanta, GA: CDC.

Vaillant, George E. (1977). *Adaptation to life.* Boston: Little, Brown.

Vaillant, George E. (1993). *The wisdom of the ego.* Cambridge, MA: Harvard University Press.

Vaillant, George E. & Davis, J. Timothy. (2000). Social/emotional intelligence and midlife resilience in schoolboys with low tested intelligence. *American Journal of Orthopsychiatry, 70,* 215–222.

Vallee, Bert L. (1998). Alcohol in the western world. *Scientific American, 278,* 80–85.

Valsiner, Jaan. (1997). Constructing the personal through the cultural redundant organization of psychological development. In Eric Amsel & K. Ann Renninger (Eds.), *Change and development: Issues of theory, method, & application.* Mahwah, NJ: Erlbaum

Valsiner, J. (1998). The development of the concept of development: Historical and epistemological perspectives. In R.M. Lerner (Ed.) and W. Damon (Editor in chief), *The handbook of child psychology: Vol. 1. Theoretical models of human development.* New York: Wiley.

Van Biema, David. (1995, December 11). A shameful death. *Time,* 33–36.

Vandell, Deborah Lowe, & Hembree, Sheri E. (1994). Peer social status and friendship: Independent contributors to children's social and academic adjustment. *Merrill Palmer Quarterly, 40,* 461–477.

Van den Boom, Dymphna C. (1995). Do first-year interception effects endure? Follow-up during toddlerhood of a sample of Dutch irritable infants. *Child Development, 66,* 1798–1816.

Van Haeringen, Alison R., Dadds, Mark, & Armstrong, Kenneth L. (1998). The child abuse lottery – Will the doctor suspect and report? Physician attitudes towards and reporting of suspected child abuse. *Child Abuse & Neglect, 22,* 159–169.

Van Ijzendoorn, M.H., & De Wolff, M.S. (1997). In search of the absent father—meta-analyses of infant-father attachment: a rejoinder to our discussants. *Child Development, 68,* 604–609.

Vaupel, James W., & Lundstrom, Hans. (1994). Longer life expectancy? Evidence from Sweden of reductions in mortality rates at advanced ages. In David A. Wise (Ed.), *Studies in the economics of aging.* Chicago: University of Chicago Press.

Veldhuis, Johannes, Yoshida, Kohji, & Iranmanesh, Ali. (1997). The effects of mental and metabolic stress on the female reproductive system and female reproductive hormones. In John R. Hubbard & Edward A. Workman (Eds.). *Handbook of stress medicine: An organ system approach.* Boca Raton, Florida: CRC Press.

Verbrugge, Lois M. (1994). Disability in late life. In Ronald P. Abeles, Helen C. Gift, & Marcia G. Ory (Eds.), *Aging and quality of life.* New York: Springer.

Verhaeghen, Paul, & Marcoen, Alfons. (1996). On the mechanisms of plasticity in young and older adults after instruction in the methods of loci: Evidence for an amplification model. *Psychology and Aging, 11,* 164–178.

Verhaeghen, Paul, Marcoen, Alfons, & Goossens, L. (1992). Improving memory performance in the aged through mnemonic training: A meta-analytic study. *Psychology and Aging, 7,* 242–251.

Vernon-Feagens, Lynne, & Manlove, Elizabeth E. (1996). Otitis media and the social behavior of day-care-attending children. *Child Development, 67,* 1528–1539.

Vickers, James C., Dickson, Tracey C., Adlard, Paul A., Saunders, Helen L., King, Carolyn E., McCormack, Graeme. (2000). The causes of neural degeneration in Alzheimer's disease. *Neurobiology, 60,* 139–165.

Vickery, Florence E. (1978). *Old age and growing.* Springfield, IL: Thomas.

Vinden, Penelope. (1996). Junin Quechua Children's understanding of the mind. *Child Development, 67,* 1707–1716.

Virtual Memorial Garden. (2000). http://catless.ncl.ac.uk/vmg

Vizmanos, B. & Marti-Henneberg, C. (2000). Puberty begins with a characteristic subcutaneous body fat mass in each sex. *European Journal of Clinical Nutrition, 54,* 203–206.

Vitaro, Frank, Tremblay, Richard E., Kerr, Margaret, Pagani, Linda, & Bukowski, William M. (1997). Disruptiveness, friends' characteristics, and delinquency in early adolescence: A test of two competing models of development. *Child Development, 68,* 676–689.

Vogel, Gretchen. (1997). New clues to asthma therapies. *Science, 276,* 1643–1646.

Vondracek, Fred W., & Kawasaki, Tomotsugu. (1995). Toward a comprehensive framework for adult career development theory and intervention. *Handbook of vocational psychology: Theory, research, and practice.* Hillsdale, NJ: Erlbaum.

Vygotsky, Lev S. (1978). *Mind in society: The development of higher psychological processes.* Cambridge, MA: Harvard University Press.

Vygotsky, Lev S. (1986). *Thought and language.* Cambridge, MA: MIT Press. (Original work published 1934)

Vygotsky, Lev S. (1987). *Thinking and speech* (N. Minick, Trans.). New York: Plenum Press.

Wachs, Theodore D. (1995). Relation of mild-to-moderate malnutrition of human development: correlational studies. *Journal of Nutrition Supplement, 125,* 2245S–2254S.

Wachs, T.D. (1999). Celebrating complexity: Conceptualization and assessment of the environment. In S. Freidman & T.D. Wachs (Eds.), *Measureing environment across the lifespan: Emerging methods and concepts.* Washington, DC: American Psychological Association.

Wahlin, Ake, Winblad, Bengt, Hill, Robert D., & Backman, Lars. (1996). Effects of serum vitamin B12 and folate status on episodic memory performance in very old age: A population-based study. *Psychology and Aging, 11,* 487–496.

Wainryb, Cecilia, & Turiel, Elliot. (1995). Diversity in social development: Between or within cultures? In Melanie Killen & Daniel Hart (Eds.), *Morality in everyday life: Developmental perspectives.* Cambridge, England: Cambridge University Press.

Waite, L. J., & Lillard, L. A. (1991). Children and marital disruption. *American Journal of Sociology, 96,* 930–953.

Waldfogel, Jane. (1998). Rethinking the paradigm for child protection. *The Future of Children: Protecting children from abuse and neglect, 8,* 4–22.

Waldron, Nancy L. & McLeskey, James. (1998). The effects of an inclusive school program on students with mild and severe learning disabilities. *Exceptional children, 64,* 395–405.

Walker, Lawrence J. (1988). The development of moral reasoning. *Annals of Child Development, 55,* 677–691.

Walker, Lawrence J., Pitts, Russell C., Hennig, Karl H., & Matsuba, M. Kyle. (1995). Reasoning about morality and real-life moral problems. In Melanie Killen & Daniel Hart (Eds.), *Morality in everyday life: Developmental perspectives.* Cambridge, England: Cambridge University Press.

Wallerstein, Judith S., & Blakeslee, Sandra. (1995). *The good marriage.* Boston: Houghton Mifflin.

Walton, Irene, & Hamilton, Mary. (1998). *Midwives and changing childbirth.* Books for Midwives Press: Cheshire, England.

Wang, Ching-Tung, & Daro, Deborah. (1998). *Current trends in child abuse reporting and fatalities: The results of the 1997 annual fifty-state survey.* Chicago: National Committee to Prevent Child Abuse.

Wannametheen, S. Goya, & Shaper, A. Gerald. (1999). Type of alcoholic drink and risk of major coronary heart disease events and all-cause mortality. *American Journal of Public Health, 89,* 685–690.

Wanner, Eric, & Gleitman, Lila R. (Eds.). (1982). *Language acquisition: The state of the art.* Cambridge, England: Cambridge University Press.

Warash, Bobbie Gibson & Markstrom-Adams, Carol. (1995). Preschool experiences of advantaged children. *Psychological Reports, 77,* 89–90.

Ward, Margaret. (1997). Family paradigms and older-child adoption: A proposal for matching parents' strengths to children's needs. *Family Relations, 46,* 257–262.

Ward, Russell A., & Spitze, Glenna. (1996). Gender differences in parent-child coresidence experiences. *Journal of Marriage and the Family, 58,* 718–725.

Warshofsky, Fred. (1999). *Stealing time: The new science of aging.* New York: TV Books.

Wass, Hannelore. (1995). Death in the lives of children and adolescents. In Hannelore Wass & Robert A. Neimeyer (Eds.), *Dying: Facing the facts.* Washington, DC: Taylor & Francis.

Watson, John B. (1928). *Psychological care of the infant and child.* New York: Norton.

Watson, John B. (1930). *Behaviorism.* New York: Norton.

Watson, John B. (1967). *Behaviorism* (rev. ed.). Chicago: University of Chicago Press. (Original work published 1930).

Weinberg, M. Katherine, Tronick, Edward Z., Cohn, Jeffrey F., & Olson, Karen L. (1999). Gender differences in emotional expressivity and self-regulation during early infancy. *Developmental Psychology, 35,* 175–188.

Weisfeld, Glenn. (1999). *Evolutionary principles of human adolescence.* New York: Basic.

Weiss, Gabrielle. (1991). Attention deficit hyperactivity disorder. In M. Lewis (Ed.), *Child and adolescent psychiatry: A comprehensive textbook.* Baltimore: Williams & Wilkins.

Wellman, H.M., & Gelman, S.A. (1992). Cognitive development: Foundational theories of core domains. *Annual Review of Psychology, 43,* 337–375.

Wendland-Carro, Jaqueline, Piccinini, Cesar A., & Millar, W. Stuart. (1999). The role of an early intervention on enhancing the quality of mother-infant interaction. *Child Development, 70,* 713–721.

Wentzel, Kathryn R. & Caldwell, Kathryn. (1997). Friendships, peer acceptance, and group membership: Relations to academic achievement in middle school. *Child Development, 68,* 1198–1209.

Werker, J.F. (1989). Becoming a native listener. *American Scientist, 77,* 54–59.

Werner, Emmy E., & Smith, Ruth S. (1992). *Overcoming the odds: High risk children from birth to adulthood.* Ithaca, NY: Cornell University Press.

Werner, Lynne A., & Ward, Jeffrey H. (1997). The effect of otitis media with effusion on infants' detection of sound. *Infant Behavior & Development, 20,* 275–279.

Wertsch, J.V. (1985). *Vygotsky and the social formation of mind.* Cambridge, MA: Harvard University Press.

Wertsch, J.V., & Tulviste, P. (1992). L.S. Vygotsky and contemporary developmental psychology. *Developmental Psychology, 28,* 548–557.

West, Elliott. (1996). *Growing up in twentieth-century America: A history and reference guide.* Westport, Conn.: Greenwood Press.

Westendorp, R.G.J., & Kirkwood, Thomas B. L. (1998). Human longevity at the cost of reproductive success. *Nature, 396,* 743–746.

Wharton, Brian. (1996). Nutritional deficiency in the breast-fed infant. In J.G. Bindels, A.C. Goedhart, & H.K.A. Visser (Eds.), *Recent developments in infant nutrition.* Dordrecht: Kluwer Academic Publishers.

Whitaker, Robert C., Wright, Jeffrey A., Pepe, Margaret S., Seidel, Kristy D., & Dietz, William H. (1997). Predicting obesity in young adulthood from childhood and parental obesity. *New England Journal of Medicine, 337,* 869–873.

Whitam, Frederick L., Diamond, Milton, Martin, James. (1993). Homosexual orientation in twins: A report on 61 pairs and three triplet sets. *Archives of Sexual Behavior, 22,* 187–206.

Whitbourne, Susan Krauss. (1996). *The aging individual: Physical and psychological perspectives.* New York: Springer Publishing Company.

White, Charles B., & Janson, Philip. (1986). Helplessness in institutional settings: Adaptation or inotropic disease. In Margaret M. Baltes & Paul B. Baltes (Eds.), *The psychology of control and aging.* Hillsdale, NJ: Erlbaum.

White, Lynn K. (1990). Determinants of divorce: A review of research in the eighties. *Journal of Marriage and the Family, 52,* 904–912.

White, Lynn K. & Rogers, Stacy J. (1997). Strong support but uneasy relationships: Coresidence and adult children's relationships with their parents. *Journal of Marriage and the Family, 59,* 62–76.

Whiting, Beatrice Blyth, & Edwards, Carolyn Pope. (1988). *Children of different worlds: The formation of social behavior.* Cambridge, MA: Harvard University Press.

Wickelgren, Ingrid. (1996). For the cortex, neuron loss may be less than thought. *Science, 273,* 48–50.

Wichstrøm, Lars. (1999). The emergence of gender difference in depressed mood during adolescence: The role of intensified gender socialization. *Developmental Psychology, 35,* 223–231.

Wicker, Allan W., & August, Rachel A. (1995). How far should we generalize? The case of a workload model. *Psychological Science, 6,* 39–44.

Wierson, M., Long, P.J., & Forehand, R. L. (1993). Toward a new understanding of early menarche: The role of environmental stress in pubertal timing. *Adolescence, 28,* 913–924.

Wieseltier, Leon. (2000). *Kaddish.* New York:Vintage Books.

Wilens, Timothy E., Biderman, Joseph, Abrantes, Ana M., & Spencer, Thomas J. (1997). Clinical characteristics of psychiatrically referred adolescent outpatients with substance use disorder. *Journal of the American Academy of Child & Adolescent Psychiatry, 36,* 941–947.

Wilfert, C.M., & McKinney, R.E., Jr. (1998). When children harbor HIV. *Scientific American, 279,* 94–95.

Wilkie, Janme R., Ferree, Mayra M., & Ratcliff, Kathryn S. (1998). Gender and fairness: Marital satisfaction in two-earner couples. *Journal of Marriage and the Family, 60,* 577–594.

Wilkinson, Krista M., Dube, William V., & McIlvane, William J. (1996). A crossdisciplinary perspective on studies of rapid word mapping in psycholinguistics and behavior analysis. *Developmental Review, 16,* 125–148.

Willatts, Peter. (1999). Development of means-end behavior in young infants: Pulling a support to retrieve a distant object. *Developmental Psychology, 35,* 651–667.

Willett, W.C., & Trichopoulos, D. (1996). Nutrition and cancer: A summary of the evidence. *Cancer Causes Control, 7,* 178–180.

Williams, Benjamin R., Ponesse, Jonathan S., Schachar, Russell, J., Logan, Gordon d., & Tannock, Rosemary. (1999). Development of inhibitory control across the life span. *Developmental Psychology, 35,* 205–213.

Williamson, David F., Serdula, Mary K., Anda, Robert F., Levy, Alan, & Byers, Tim. (1992). Weight loss attempts in adults: Goals, duration, and rate of weight loss. *American Journal of Public Health, 82,* 1251–1257.

Williams, Sharon, Denney, Nancy Wadsworth, & Schadler, Margaret. (1983). Elderly adults' perception of their own cognitive development during the adult years. *International Journal of Aging and Human Development, 16,* 47–158.

Willinger, M., Hoffman, H.J., Wu, K.-T., Hou, J.-R., Kessler, R.C., Ward, S.L., Keens, T.G., & Corwin, M.J. (1998). Factors associated with the transition to nonprone sleep positions of infants in the United States: The national infant sleep position study. *Journal of the American Medical Association, 280,* 329–335.

Willis, Sherry L. (1996). Everyday cognitive competence in elderly persons: Conceptual issues and empirical findings. *Gerontologist, 36,* 595–601.

Wilson, Gail. (1995). "I'm the eyes and she's the arms":Changes in gender roles in advanced old age. In Sara Arber & Jay Ginn (Eds.), *Connecting gender and aging.* Buckingham, England: Open University Press.

Wilson, Geraldine S. (1989). Clinical studies of infants and children exposed prenatally to heroin. In Donald Hutchings (Ed.), *Prenatal abuse of licit and illicit drugs.* New York: New York Academy of Sciences.

Wilson, Margo, & Daly, Martin. (1993). Lethal confrontational violence among young men. In Nancy J. Bell & Robert W. Bell (Eds.), *Adolescent risk taking.* Newbury Park, CA: Sage.

Wilson, Robert S., Gilley, David W., Bennett, David A., Beckett, Laurel A., & Evans, Denis A. (2000). Person-specific paths of cognitive decline in Alzheimer's Disease and their relation to age. *Psychology and Aging, 15,* 18–28.

Wing, R.R. (1992). Weight cycling in humans: A review of the literature. *Annals of Behavioral Medicine, 14,* 113–119.

Wingerson, Lois. (1998). *Unnatural selection: The promise and the power of human gene research.* New York: Bantam Doubleday Dell.

Wink, Paul. (1999). Addressing end-of-life issues: Spirituality and inner life. *Generations, 23,* 75–80.

Winner, Ellen. (1996). *Gifted children: Myths and realities.* New York: Basic Books.

Winsler, Adam, Díaz, Rafael, M., Espinosa, Linda, & Rodríguez, James L. (1999). When learning a second language does not mean losing the first: Bilingual language development in low-income, Spanish-speaking children attending bilingual preschool. *Child Development, 70,* 349–362.

Wirth, H.P. (1993). Caring for a chronically demented patient within the family. In W. Meier-Ruge (Ed.), *Dementing brain disease in geriatric medicine.* Switzerland: Karger.

Wishart, Jennifer G. (1999). Learning and development in children with Down's syndrome. In Alan Slater and Darwin Muir (Eds.) *The Blackwell reader in developmental psychology.* Oxford, U.K.: Blackwell.

Wolf, Rosalie S. (1998). Domestic elder abuse and neglect. In Inger Hilde Nordhus, Gary R. VandenBos, Stig Berg, & Diane Fromhold (Eds.), *Clinical feropsychology.* Washington, DC: American Psychological Association.

Wolfe, David A., Wekerle, Christine, Reitzel-Jaffe, Degborah, & Lefebvre, Lorrie. (1998). Factors associated with abusive relationships among maltreated and nonmaltreated youth. *Development and Psychopathology, 10,* 61–85.

Wolfe, Joanne, Grier, Holcombe, E., Klar, Neil, Levin, Sarah B., Ellenbogen, Jeffrey M., Salem-Schatz, Susanne, Emanuel, Ezekiel J., & Weeks, Jane C. (2000). Symptoms and suffering at the end of life in children with cancer. *The New England Journal of Medicine, 342,* 326–333.

Wolfner, Glenn D., & Gelles, Richard J. (1993). A profile of violence toward children: A national study. *Child Abuse and Neglect, 17,* 197–212.

Wolfson, Amy R. & Carskadon, Mary A. (1998). Sleep schedules and daytime functioning in adolescents. *Child Development, 69,* 875–887.

Wolraich, Mark L., Hannah, Jane N., Baumgaertel, Anna, & Feurer, Irene D. (1998). Examination of DSM-IV criteria for attention deficit hyperactivity disorder in a county-side sample. *Journal of Developmental & Behavioral Pediatrics, 19,* 162–168.

Wong, Siu Kwong. (1999). Acculturation, peer relations, and delinquent behavior of Chinese-Canadian youth. *Adolescence, 34,* 108–119.

Wood, Robert, & Bandura, Albert. (1996). Social cognitive theory and organizational management. In Richard M. Steers, Lyman W. Porter, & Gregory A. Bigley (Eds.), *Motivation and leadership at work.* New York: McGraw-Hill.

Woodruff-Pak, Diana S. (1989). Aging and intelligence: Changing perspectives in the twentieth century. *Journal of Aging Studies, 3,* 91–118.

Woodward, Amanda L. & Markman, Ellen M. (1998). Early word learning. In William Damon, Deanna Kuhn, & Rbert S. Siegler (Eds.), *Handbook of child psychology,* fifth edition. Volume two: Cognition, perception, and language. New York: Wiley.

Woodward, Lianne J. & Fergusson, David M. (1999). Childhood peer relationship problems and psychosocial adjustment in late adolescence. *Journal of Abnormal Child Psychology, 27,* 87–104.

Woolley, Jacqueline D., Phelps, Katrina E., Davis, Debra L., & Mandell, Dorothy J. (1999). Where theories of mind meet magic: The development of children's beliefs about wishing. *Child Development, 70,* 571–587.

World Health Organization (WHO). (1994*). World Health Statistics Quarterly, 47,* No. 1.

World Health Organization (WHO). (1995). *World Health Statistics Quarterly, 48,* No. 1.

World Health Organization (WHO). (1998). *World Health Statistics Annual.*

Wren, Christopher S. (1996, February 20). Marijuana use by youths continues to rise. *The New York Times,* A11.

Wright, C.M., & Talbot, E. (1996). Screening for failure to thrive: What are we looking for? *Child: Care, Health & Development, 22,* 223–234.

Wright, William. (1998). *Born that way.* New York: Knopf.

Wrightsman, Lawrence S. (1994). *Adult personality development (Vols. 1 and 2).* Thousands Oaks, CA: Sage.

Wyman, Peter a., Cowen, Emory L., Work, William c., Hoyt-Meyers, Lynne, Magnus, Keith B., & Fagen, Douglas B. (1999) Caregiving and developmental factors differentiating young at-risk urban children showing resilient versus stress-affected outcome: A replication and extension. *Child Development, 70,* 645–659.

Wysong, E., Aniskiewicz, R. & Wright, D. (1994). Turth and DARE: Tracking drug education to graduation and as symbolic politics. *Social Problems, 41,* 448–472.

Yang, Bin, Ollendick, Thomas, Dong, Qi, Xia, Yong, & Lin, Lei. (1995). Only children and children with siblings in the People's Republic of China: Levels of fear, anxiety, and depression. *Child Development, 66,* 1301–1311.

Yerkes, R.M. (1923). Testing and the human mind. *Atlantic Monthly, 131,* 358–370.

Yeung-Courchesne, Rachel & Courchesne, Eric. (1997). From impasse to insight in autism research: From behavioral symptoms to biological explanations. *Development and Psychopathology, 9,* 389–420.

Yglesias, Helen. (1980). Moses, Anna Mary Robertson (Grandma). In Barbara Sicherman & Carol Hurd Green (Eds.). *Notable American women: The modern period.* Cambridge, MA: Belknap Press.

Ying, Yu-Wen & Lee, Peter A. (1999). The development of ethnic identity in Asian-American adolescents: Status and outcome. *American Journal of Orthopsychiatry, 69,* 182–193.

Yllo, Kersti. (1993). Through a feminist lens: Gender, power and violence. In R. Gelles & D. Loseke (Eds), *Controversies in family violence,* Newbury Park, CA: Sage.

Yoder, Kevin A., Hoyt, Dan R., & Whitbeck, Les B. (1998). Suicidal behavior among homeless and runaway adolescents. *Journal of Youth & Adolescence, 27,* 753–771.

Yoon, Keumsil Kim. (1992). New perspective on intrasentential code-switching: A study of Korean-English switching. *Applied Psycholinguistics, 13,* 433–449.

Yoshikawa, H. (1994). Prevention as cumulative protection: Effects of early family support and education on chronic delinquency and its risks. *Psychological Bulletin, 115,* 28–54.

Yoshikawa, Hirokazu. (1999). Welfare dynamics, support services, mothers' earnings, and child cognitive development: Implications for contemporary welfare reform. *Child Development, 70,* 779–801.

You, Roger X., Thrift, Amanda g., McNeil, John J., Davis, Stephen M., & Donnan, Geoffrey A.. (1999). Ischemic stroke risk and passive exposure to spouses' cigarette smoking. *American Journal of Public Health, 89,* 572–575.

Youn, Gahyun. (1999). Differences in familism values and caregiving outcomes among Korean, Korean American, and White American dementia caregivers. *Psychology and Aging, 14,* 355–364.

Younger, B.A. (1990). Infant categorization: Memory for category-level and specific item information. *Journal of Experimental Child Psychology, 50,* 131–155.

Younger, B.A. (1993). Understanding category members as "the same sort of thing": Explicit categorization in ten-month-old infants. *Child Development, 64,* 309–320.

Younoszai, Barara. (1993). Mexican American perspectives related to death. In Donald P. Irish, Kathleen F. Lundquist, & Vivian Jenkins Nelsen (Eds), *Ethnic variations in dying, death, and grief.* Washington, DC: Taylor & Francis Ltd.

Zahn-Waxler, Carolyn, Radke-Yarrow, M., Wagner, E., & Chapman, M. (1992). Development of concern for others. *Child Development, 28,* 126–136.

Zahn-Waxler, Carolyn, Schmitz, Stephanie, Fulker, David, Robinson, Joann, & Emde, Robert. (1996). Behavior problems in 5-year-old monozygotic and dyzygotic twins: Genetic and environmental influences, patterns of regulation, and internalization of control. *Development and Psychopathology, 8,* 103–122.

Zambrana, Ruthe E., Scrimshaw., Susan C.M., Collins, Nancy, & Dunkel-Schetter, Christine. (1997). Prenatal health behaviors and psychosocial risk factors in pregnant women of Mexican origin: The role of acculturation. *American Journal of Public Health, 87,* 1022–1026.

Zarbatany, L., Hartmann, D.P., & Rankin, D.B. (1990). The psychological functions of preadolescent peer activities. *Child Development, 61,* 1067–1080.

Zarit, Steven H. (1996). Continuities and discontinuities in very late life. In Vern L. Bengston (Ed.), *Adulthood & aging: Research on continuities and discontinuities.* New York: Springer.

Zarit, Steven H., Dolan, Melissa M., & Leitsch, Sara A. (1998). Interventions in nursing homes and other alternative living settings. In Inger Hilde Nordhus, Gary R. VandenBos, Stig Berg & Pia Fromholt (Eds.) *Clinical Geropsychology.* Washington, DC: American Psychological Association

Zarit, Steven H., Johansson, Lennarth, & Jarrott, Shannon E. (1998). Family caregiving: Stresses, social programs, and clinical interventions. In Inger Hilde Nordhus, Gary R. VandenBos, Stig Berg, & Pia Fromholt (Eds.), *Clinical geropsychology.* Washington DC: American Psychological Association.

Zavodny, Madeline. (1999). Do men's characteristics affect whether a nonmarital pregnancy results in marriage? *Journal of Marriage and the Family, 61,* 764–773.

Zeanah, C.H., Benoit, D., Barton, M. Regan, C., Hirshberg, L.M., & Lipsitt, L.P. (1993). Representations of attachment in mothers and their one-year-old infants. *Journal of the American Academy of Child and Adolescent Psychiatry, 32,* 278–286.

Zeifman, Debra, Delaney, Sarah, & Blass, Elliott. (1996). Sweet taste, looking, and calm in two- and four-week-old infants: The eyes have it. *Developmental Psychology, 32,* 1090–1099.

Zerbe, Kathryn J. (1993). *The body betrayed: Women, eating disorders, and treatment.* Washington DC: American Psychiatric Association.

Zeskind, Philip Sanford & Barr, Ronald G. (1997) Acoustic characteristics of naturally occurring cries of infants with "Colic." *Child Development, 68,* 394–403.

Ziatas, Kathryn, Durkin, Kevin, & Pratt, Chris. (1998). Belief term development in children with autism, Asperger syndrome, specific language impairment, and normal development: Links to theory of mind development. *Journal of Child Psychology & Psychiatry & Allied Disciplines, 39,* 755–763.

Zigler, Edward. (1998). School should begin at age 3 years for American children. *Journal of Developmental and Behavioral Pediatrics, 19,* 37–38.

Zilberfein, Felice. (1999). Coping with death: Anticipatory grief and bereavement. *Generations: In-depth views of aging, 23,* 69–74.

Zukow-Goldring, Patricia. (1995). Sibling caregiving. In Marc H. Bornstein (Ed.), *Handbook of Parenting: Status and social conditions of parenting.* New Jersey: Erlbaum.

Zwair, M.D. (1999). Cognitive processes and medical decisions. In D.C. Park, R.W. Morrell, & K. Shifren (Eds..), *Processing medical information in aging patients: Cognitive and human factors perspectives.* Mahwah, NJ: Erlbaum.

Zylicz, Zbigniew. (1999). Innovations in end-of-life care. An international journal and on-line forum of leaders in end-of-life care. http://www.edc.org/lastacts/

Illustration Credits

McCoy/Rainbow; **p. 114 (Table 4.4)** From Barbara Luke. (1993). Nutrition and prematurity. In Frank R. Witter & Louis G. Keith (Eds.), *Textbook of prematurity: Antecedents, treatment, and outcome.* Boston: Little, Brown; **p. 115** Andrew Brilliant/The Picture Cube/Index Stock; **p. 115 (Figure 4.5)** From Wendy L. Hellerstedt, John H. Himes, Mary Story, Irene R. Alton, & Laura E. Edwards. (1997). The effects of cigarette smoking and gestational weight change on birth outcomes in obese and normal-weight women. *American Journal of Public Health, 87,* 591–596; **p. 118** Henry Schleichkorn/Custom Medical Stock Photo; **p. 119** *(top)* Laura Dwight; *(bottom left)* William Hubbell/Woodfin Camp & Associates; *(bottom right)* Viviane Moos; **p. 121** J. T. Miller/The Stock Market; **p. 122** ©Mark Richards/PhotoEdit; **p. 123** Jim Pickerell/Stock, Boston; **p. 124** Gregory Dimijian/Photo Researchers, Inc.

CHAPTER 5

Chapter Opener p. 130 Lisl Dennis/The Image Bank; **p. 132** Simon Fraser/Photo Researchers, Inc.; **p. 136** Mark Johnson, Centre for Brain and Cognitive Development, Birkbeck College, London; **p. 139** *(left)* Elizabeth Crews; *(center)* Elizabeth Crews; *(right)* Petit Format/Photo Researchers, Inc.; **p. 141** *(top)* Jose Carrillo/Stock, Boston; *(bottom)* Brady/Monkmeyer; **p. 142** Corbis/Laura Dwight; **p. 143 (Table 5.1)** From W. K. Frankenburg, et al. (1981). The newly abbreviated and revised Denver Developmental Screening Test. *Journal of Pediatrics, 99,* 995–999; **p. 144** Hazel Hankin; **p. 145** Rick Browne/Stock, Boston; **p. 146** From "First Glances" by Davida Y. Teller, *Journal Of Investigative Opthalmology And Visual Science, Vol. 38,* 1997, pp 2183–2203. Photographs copyright of Anthony Young; **p. 147** Peter Menzel; **p. 148** Peter McLeod/Acadia University; **p. 149 (Figure 5.5)** From Lynne Vernon-Feagens & Elizabeth E. Manlove. (1996). Otitis media and the social behavior of day-care-attending children. *Child Development, 67,* 1528–1539; **p. 150** *(all photos)* Laura Dwight; **p. 152** Barbara Alper/Stock, Boston; **p. 153** *(top)* ©Eric Feferberg/Agence France-Presse. **p. 153** *(bottom)* AP/Wide World Photos.

CHAPTER 6

Chapter Opener p. 158 John Eastcott/Yva Momatiuk/Photo Researchers; **p. 160** Catherine Ursillo/Photo Researchers, Inc.; **p. 161** Joe Epstein/Design Conceptions; **p. 162** *(top)* © Innervisions; *(bottom)* Courtesy of Karen Adolph; **p. 163** Ulli Seer/Image Bank; **p. 164** Laura Dwight; **p. 166** Laura Dwight; **p. 167** ©Michael Newman /PhotoEdit; **p. 172** ©Robert Ullman/Monkmeyer; **p. 173** Laura Dwight; **p. 174** Laura Dwight; **p. 176** Corbis/Anthony Bannister; **p. 178** Elliott Varner Smith; **p. 180** Hazel Hankin/Stock, Boston; **p. 181** Betty Press/Woodfin Camp; **p. 185** Renate Hiller/Monkmeyer.

CHAPTER 7

Chapter Opener p. 186 Jenny Hager/The Image Works; **p. 188** Laura Dwight; **p. 189** Susan Lapides/Design Conceptions; **p. 190** Corbis/Michael S. Yamashita; **p. 191** Chromosohm/Sohm/Photo Researchers; **p. 192** Laura Dwight; **p. 193** Peter Southwick/Stock. Boston; **p. 195** Tom McCarthy/The Picture Cube/Index Stock; **p. 197** ©Richard Frieman/Photo Researchers, Inc.; **p. 198** Nancy Sheehan/The Picture Cube/Index Stock; **p. 199** *(top)* Corroon and Company/Monkmeyer; *(bottom)* Leong Ka Tai/Material World; **p. 201** Excerpt from S. Chess & A. Thomas. (1990). Continuities and discontinuities in development. In Lee N. Robbins & Michael Rutter (Eds.), *Straight and devious pathways from childhood to adulthood.*

New York: Cambridge University Press. Reprinted with permission of Cambridge University Press; **p. 202** *(left)* Elizabeth Crews; *(right)* Bruce Plotkin/The Image Works; **p. 203** Betts Anderson/Unicorn Stock; **p. 206** Erik Hesse; **p. 208** *(all photos)* Courtesy of Mary Ainsworth; **p. 211 (Figure 7.1)** From Rosen, Karen Schneider, & Burke, Patricia B. (1999). Multiple attachment relationships within families: Mothers and fathers with two young children. *Developmental Psychology, 35,* 436–441; **p. 212** Corbis/Laura Dwight; **p. 213** James Nachtwey/Magnum Photos, Inc; **p. 213 (Figure 7.2)** From Diane Benoit, & Kevin C. Parker. (1994). Stability and transmission of attachment across three generations. *Child Development, 65,* 1444–1456. Copyright © 1994 Society for Research in Child Development.

CHAPTER 8

Chapter Opener p. 218 Cathy McLaughlin/The Image Works; **p. 220** Laura Dwight; **p. 224** *(top left)* Lew Merrim/Monkmeyer; *(top right)* ©Myrleen Ferguson/PhotoEdit; *(bottom)* Carol Palmer/The Picture Cube/Index Stock; **p. 228** *(top left)* ©Tony Freeman/PhotoEdit; *(top right)* Adam Woolfitt/Woodfin Camp & Associates; *(bottom)* Royce Bair/Monkmeyer; **p. 229** *(top)* Ken Cavanagh/Photo Researchers, Inc.; *(top center)* Ellen Senisi/The Image Works; **p. 229** *(bottom center)* Laura Dwight/PhotoEdit; *(bottom)* ©F.B. Grunzweig/Photo Researchers, Inc.; **p. 230** AP/Wide World Photos; **p. 232** James Nachtwey/Magnum Photos; **p. 234** Margot Granitsas /The Image Works; **p. 236** Michael Grecco/Stock, Boston; **p. 236 (Figure 8.4)** From Ching-Tung Wang, & Deborah Daro. (1998). *Current trends in child abuse reporting and fatalities: The results of the 1997 annual fifty-state survey.* Chicago: National Committee to Prevent Child Abuse; **p. 239** Corbis/Stephane Maze; **p. 241** © Inge King; **p. 257** Corbis/Laura Dwight.

CHAPTER 9

Chapter Opener p. 244 Hinton/Monkmeyer; **p. 247** Hazel Hankin; **p. 249** Dave Bartruff/Stock, Boston; **p. 252** Laura Dwight; **p. 255** James Kamp/LIFE Magazine; **p. 256** Elizabeth Crews; **p. 258** PhotoWorks/Monkmeyer; **p. 260** Laura Dwight; **p. 262** Elizabeth Crews; **p. 267** *(left)* ©Tom Prettyman/PhotoEdit; **p. 267** *(right)* Fujiphotos/The Image Works.

CHAPTER 10

Chapter Opener p. 270 Corbis/Laura Dwight; **p. 272** Laura Dwight; **p. 273** Mel Digiacomo/The Image Bank; **p. 274** © Jerry Cooke/Photo Researchers, Inc.; **p. 276** Margaret Miller/Photo Researchers, Inc.; **p. 278** Laura Dwight; **p. 280** ©Myrleen Ferguson/PhotoEdit; **282** Laura Dwight; **p. 284** David Strickler/Monkmeyer; **p. 285 (Figure 10.1)** From Zvi Strassberg, Kenneth A. Dodge, Gregory S. Pettit, & John E. Bates. (1994). Spanking in the home and childrenís subsequent aggression toward kindergarten peers. *Development and Psychopathology, 6,* 445–462. Used by permission; **p. 287** ©Robert Brenner/PhotoEdit; **p. 288** Brady/Monkmeyer; **p. 289** *(left)* © Erika Stone; *(right)* John Coletti/Stock, Boston; **p. 291** Courtesy of Kathleen Berger; p. 292 Grantpix/Monkmeyer; **p. 294** Sybil Shackman/Monkmeyer.

CHAPTER 11

Chapter Opener p. 300 J. Gerard Smith/Photo Researchers, Inc.; **p. 302** Jeff Greenberg/Photo Researchers, Inc.; **p. 304** Van Bucher/Photo Researchers; **p. 305 (Figure 11.2)** From Robert C. Whitaker, Jeffrey A. Wright, Margaret S. Pepe, Kristy D. Seidel, & William H. Dietz. (1997). Predicting obesity in young adulthood from childhood and parental obesity. *New England Journal of Medicine, 337;* **p. 307** Larry Mulvehill/Photo Researchers; **p. 308** *(right)* Ellen Senisi/The Image Works; *(left)* Bob Daemmrich/Stock, Boston; **p. 309** Bob Daemmrich/Stock, Boston; **p. 311** Lew Merrim/Monkmeyer; **p. 313** © Owen Franken/Stock,Boston; **p. 316** Alan Carey/Image Works; **p. 318** Bob Daemmrich/Stock, Boston; **p. 318 (Figure 11. 6)** From Kate Nation, & Margaret J. Snowling. (1998). Individual differences in contextual facilitation: Evidence from dyslexia and poor reading comprehension. *Child Development, 69,* 996–1011; **p. 319** Nancy Acevedo/Monkmeyer; **p. 320** Ellen Senisi/The Image Works; **p. 323** ©Robin L. Sachs/PhotoEdit; **p. 338** A. Ramey/Stock, Boston.

CHAPTER 12

Chapter Opener p. 326 ©Bachmann/Photo Researchers, Inc.; **p. 329** Will & Deni McIntyre/Photo Researchers, Inc.; **p. 332** ©Bachmann/Photo Researchers, Inc.; **p. 333** *(top)* ©Richard Hutchings/Photo Researchers, Inc.; *(bottom)* Leif Skoogfors/Woodfin Camp & Associates; **p. 335 (Figure 12.2)** From Robert S. Siegler & Douglas R. Thompson. (1998). ìHey, would you like a nice cold cup of lemonade on this hot day?î: Childrenís understanding of economic causation. *Developmental Psychology, 34* 146–160. Used by permission; **p. 338** *(left)* ©Bob Daemmrich/Stock, Boston; *(right)* Joel Gordon; **p. 339** Gary Langley; **p. 341** *(left)* Mike Yamashita/Woodfin Camp & Associates; *(right)* Russell D. Curtis/Photo Researchers, Inc.; **p. 345** ©Jeff Isaac Greenberg/Photo Researchers, Inc.; **p. 346** Hazel Hankin; **p. 349** ©John OÌBrian/Canada in Stock Inc.; **p. 351** George Ancona/International Stock.

CHAPTER 13

Chapter Opener p. 354 ©Rashid/Monkmeyer; **p. 356** ©Lindsay Hebberd/Woodfin Camp & Associates; **p. 357** ©Ellis Herwig/Stock, Boston; **p. 358** Lisa Law/The Image Works; **p. 359** *(left)* Joel Gordon; *(right)* Peter Miller/Photo Researchers, Inc.; **p. 360** ©Jim Weiner/Photo Researchers, Inc.; **p. 362** George White Location Photography; **p. 365** Frank Fournier/Woodfin Camp & Associates; **p. 368** *(top)* James Wilson/Woodfin Camp & Associates; *(bottom)* ©Linda Phillips/Photo Researchers, Inc.; **p. 371** Katherine McGlynn/The Image Works; **p. 373 (Figure 13.2)** From Peter A. Wyman, Emory L. Cowen, William C. Work, Lynne Hoyt-Meyers, Keith B. Magnus, & Douglas B. Fagen, (1999). Caregiving and developmental factors differentiating young at-risk urban children showing resilient versus stress-affected outcome: A replication and extension. *Child Development, 70,* 645–659. Used by permission.

CHAPTER 14

Chapter Opener p. 380 Bob Daemmrich/The Image Works; **p. 383** Richard Hutchings/Photo Researchers, Inc.; **p. 386** *(top)* Bob Daemmrich/Stock, Boston; *(bottom)* Stephen Wilkes/The Image Bank; **p. 388** ©Henley & Savage/The Stock Market; **p. 391** Arlene Collins/Monkmeyer; **p. 392** Bill Gillette/Stock, Boston; **p. 394** *(top)* Fran Heyl & Associates; *(bottom)* ©Michael Newman/PhotoEdit; **p. 395 (Table 14.2)** From Jeanne Brooks-Gunn, I. Attie, C. Burrow, J. t. Rosso, & Warren, M.P. (1989). The impact of puberty on body and eating concerns in athletic and nonathletic contexts. *Journal of Early Adolescence, 9,* 269–290; p. 396 *(top)* AP/Wide World Photos; *(bottom)* Janeart/The Image Bank; **p. 400** Margot Granitsas/The Image Works; **p. 404** Christopher Brown/Stock, Boston.

CHAPTER 15

Chapter Opener p. 406 Mug Shots/The Stock Market; **p. 408** Jim Pickerell/The Image Works; **p. 409** Will McIntyre/Photo Researchers, Inc.; **p. 410** *(left)* Doug Martin/Photo Researchers, Inc.; *(right)* ©Richard Hutchings/Photo Researchers, Inc.; **p. 411 (Figure 15.2)** From Charles C. Helwig. (1995). Adolescentsí and young adultsí conceptions of civil liberties: Freedom of speech and religion. *Child Development, 66,* 152–166; **p. 413** Sybil Shackman/Monkmeyer; **p. 416** Miguel L. Fairbanks; **p. 417 (Figure 15.4)** From Ted R. Miller, & Rebecca S. Spicer. (1998). How safe are our schools? *American Journal of Public Health, 88,* 413–418; **p. 419** Rick Kopstein/Monkmeyer; **p. 420** AP/Wide World Photos; **p. 421** AP/Wide World Photos; **p. 423** Corbis/Michael S. Yamashita; **p. 424** Michelle Agins/NYT Pictures; **p. 425** Rhoda Sidney/Stock, Boston; **p. 428** Richard Hutchin/Photo Researchers, Inc.

CHAPTER 16

Chapter Opener p. 434 Tom & Dee Ann McCarthy/The Stock Market; **p. 436** *(left)* Jeffrey W. Myers/Stock, Boston; *(right)* M. Everton/The Image Works; **p. 437** *(left)* Renato Rotolo/The Gamma Liaison Network; *(right)* Elizabeth Crews; **p. 439** *(top)* Lester Sloan/Woodfin Camp & Associates; *(bottom)* Frozen Images/The Image Works; **p. 441** Rhoda Sidney/Monkmeyer; **p. 442** Paula Lerner/The Picture Cube/Index Stock; **p. 443** Ellen Senisi/The Image Works; **p. 444** *(left)* Joel Gordon; *(right)* Dan Walsh/The Picture Cube/Index Stock; **p. 446** *(top)* ©Lester Sloan/Woodfin Camp & Associates; *(bottom)* Charles Gupton/The Stock Market; **p. 447** Butch Martin/The Image Bank; **p. 448 (Figure 16.1)** From Maryse, Richards, Paul A. Crowe, Reed Larson, & Amy Swarr. (1998). Developmental patterns and gender differences in the experience of peer companionship during adolescence. *Child Development, 69,* 154–163; **p. 455** Joel Gordon; **p. 457** Alon Reininger/Woodfin Camp & Associates.

CHAPTER 17

Chapter Opener p. 464 Carl Schneider/Gamma Liaison; **p. 467 (Figure 17.1)** From Meisami, Esmail. (1994). Aging of the sensory system. In Paola S. Timiras (Ed.), *Physiological basis of aging and geriatrics* (2nd ed.). Copyright © 1994 CRC Press, Boca Raton, Florida; **p. 468** Tom Carroll/International Stock; **p. 471** AP/Wide World Photos; **p. 473** Paul Conklin/Monkmeyer; **p. 475** Hank Morgan/Photo Researchers; **p. 477** AP/Wide World Photos; **p. 479** Paula Scully/Gamma Liaison; **p. 482** ©Tony Freeman/PhotoEdit; **p. 484** AP/Wide World Photos; **p. 485** Greg Riffi/Gamma Liaison.

CHAPTER 18

Chapter Opener p. 488 Terry Wild Studio; **p. 492 (Figure 18.1)** From Fredda Blanchard-Fields. (1986). Reasoning on social dilemmas varying the emotional saliency: An adult developmental perspective. *Psychology and Aging, 1,* 325–333. Copyright © 1986 by American Psychological Association; **p. 493** AP/Wide World Photos; **p. 495** Paul Conklin/Monkmeyer; **p. 497** Margot Granitsas/Photo Researchers, Inc; **p. 499** Howard Dratch/Image Works; **p. 500 (Table 18.1)** From William G. Perry, Jr. (1981). Cognitive and ethical growth: The making of meaning. In Arthur W. Chickering (Ed.), *The modern American college: Responding to the new realities of diverse students and a changing society.* San Francisco: Jossey-Bass. Copyright © 1981 Jossey-Bass Inc., Publishers; **p. 502** Bob Daemmrich/The Image Works; **p. 508** *(left)* Dave Bartruff/Stock, Boston; *(right)* AP/Wide World Photos.

CHAPTER 19

Chapter Opener p. 510 Scott Barrow/International Stock; **p. 514** AP/Wide World Photos; **p. 516** *(left)* Bob Daemmrich/Stock, Boston; *(right)* Tom McCarthy/Folio, Inc.; **p. 521** Greg Baker/AP/Wide World Photos; **p. 523** Blair Seltz/Photo Researchers; **p. 531** *(left)* Terry Wild Studio; *(right)* Cliff Hollenbeck/International Stock; p. 532 Andy Levin/Photo Researchers; **p. 533** Corbis-Bettmann; **p. 536** Spencer Grant/Photo Researchers; **p. 537 (Figure 19.2)** From Presser, Harriet B. (2000). Nonstandard work schedules and marital instability. *Journal of Marriage and the Family, 62,* 93–110; p. 538 Richard Lord/The Image Works.

CHAPTER 20

Chapter Opener p. 544 Bob Daemmrich/Stock, Boston; **p. 546** Robert Ullmann/Monkmeyer; **p. 547** Vaughn Youtz/Liaison; **p. 548** Ann Heisenfelt/AP/Wide World; **p. 551** *(left)* Springer/Corbis-Bettmann; *(right)* Francene Keery/Stock, Boston; **p. 553** Nathan Benn/Stock, Boston; **p. 554** Tom McCarthy/Picture Cube; **p. 559** Mike Yamashita/Woodfin Camp; **p. 560** Cynthia Johnson/Gamma Liaison; **p. 562** Will McIntyre/Photo Researchers; **p. 563** *(all photos)* From: Schulman, et al.: "The Effect of Race and Sex on Physicians' Recommendations for Cardiac Catheterization," *The New England Journal of Medicine,* Copyright (c) 1999 Massachusetts Medical Society. All rights reserved. Photos courtesy of Dr. Kevin A. Schulman; **p. 564** K. Nomachi/Photo Researchers; **p. 567** Steve Starr/Stock, Boston.

CHAPTER 21

Chapter Opener p. 570 Michael Newman/Photo Edit; **p. 573** Laura Dwight/Photo Edit; **p. 575** *(top left)* Cindy Charles/Photo Edit; **p. 575** *(top right)* Nicholas Devore III/Photographers/Apen; **p. 575** *(bottom)* Peter Byron/Monkmeyer; **p. 579** A. Ramey/Photo Edit; **p. 580** National Archives; **pp. 581, 583 (Figures 21.2, 21.4)** K. Warner Schaie. (1996). *Intellectual development in adulthood: The Seattle longitudinal study.* Cambridge, England: Cambridge University Press. Reprinted with permission of Cambridge University Press. Copyright © 1996; **p. 582 (Figure 21.3)** From K Warner Schaie. (1989). Perceptual speed in adulthood: Cross-sectional and longitudinal studies. *Psychology and Aging, 4,* 443–453. Copyright © 1989 by American Psychological Association. Reprinted by permission; **p. 584** Steven Rubin/Image Works; **p. 597** Myrleen Ferguson/Photo Edit.

CHAPTER 22

Chapter Opener p. 590 Jim Pickerell/Folio, Inc.; **p. 592** Robert Ullmann/Monkmeyer; **p. 593** Will Yurman/The Image Works; **p. 595** *(top)* Jim Daniels/Picture Cube; *(bottom)* Ulrike Welsch/Photo Edit; **p. 596 (Figure 22.2)** Robert R. McCrae, Paul T. Costa, Jr., Margarida Pedroso de Lima, AntÛnio Simies, Fritz Ostendorf, Alois Angleitner, Iris Marusic, Denis Bratko, Gian Caprara, Barbaranelli Vittorio, Chae Claudio, Joon-Ho, & Ralph L. Piedmont. (1999). Age differences in personality across the adult life span: Parallels in five cultures. *Developmental Psychology, 35,* 466–477; **p. 598** Mary Kate Denny/Photo Edit; p. 599 Charles Gupton/Stock, Boston; **p. 599 (Figure 22.3)** Jeffrey A. Burr, & Jan E. Mutchler. (1999). Race and ethnic variation in norms of filial responsibility among older persons. *Journal of Marriage and the Family, 61,* 674–687; **p. 601** Tony Freeman/Photo Edit; **p. 604** *(top)* Mark Anderman/Terry Wild Studio; *(bottom)* David Hiser/Photographers/Apsen; **p. 606** Randee St. Nicholas/Archive Photos.

CHAPTER 23

Chapter Opener p. 614 Frederic Reglain/Gamma Liaison; **pp. 615–616 (quiz)** From Erdman B. Palmore. (1998). *The facts on aging quiz.* New York: Springer; **p. 617** Paul Gish/Monkmeyer; **p. 621** Grantpix/Monkmeyer; **p. 624** Bob Strong/The Image Works; **p. 627 (Table 23.1)** From Susan Schechter, Paul Beatty, Gordon B. Willis. (1999). Asking survey respondents about health status: Judgment and response issues. *Cognition and Aging*; **p. 631 (Figure 23.4)** From James F. Fries. (1994). *Living well: Taking care of your health in the middle and later years.* Reading, MA: Addison-Wesley; **p. 633** *(top)* Lawrence Migdale/Photo Researchers; *(bottom)* Catherine Karnow/Woodfin Camp; **p. 635** Meckes/Ottawa/Photo Researchers; **p. 636** Robert Ricci/Gamma Liaison; **p. 638** David Barrit/Gamma Liaison; **p. 641** Jerry Wachter/Photo Researchers; **p. 642** *(all photos)* John Launois/Black Star; **p. 650** Michael Newman/Photo Edit.

CHAPTER 24

Chapter Opener p. 646 Xinhua-Chine Nouvelle/Gamma Liaison; **p. 648** Paul Howell/Gamma Liaison; **p. 649** AP/Wide World Photos; **p. 653** *(left)* Corbis-Bettmann; *(center)* David Redfern/Retna; *(right)* Charles Peterson/Retna; **p. 654 (Figure 24.1)** From G. Smith, R. Petersen, R.J. Ivnik, J. F. Malec, & E. G. Tangalos. (1996). Subjective memory complaints, psychological distress, and longitudinal change in objective memory performance. **Psychology and Aging, 11,** 272–279; **p. 655** Bernard Wolf/Monkmeyer; **p. 659 (Table 24.1)** From Marilyn K. Heine, Beth A. Ober, & Gregory K. Shenaut. (1999). Naturally occurring and experimentally induced tip-of-the-tongue experiences in three adult age groups. *Psychology and Aging, 14,* 445–457; **p. 662** Grantpix/Photo Researchers; **p. 663** Alfred Pasieka/Science Photo Library/Photo Researchers; **p. 665** AP/Wide World Photos; **p. 667 (Figure 24.2)** Adapted with permission of The Free Press, a division of Simon & Schuster from *Brain Failure* by Barry Reisberg. Copyright © 1981 Barry Reisberg; **p. 668** Barbara Alper/Stock, Boston; **p. 669** Richard Sobol/Stock, Boston; **p. 671** Stirling Dickenson/Woodfin Camp; **p. 672** Jim Cartier/Photo Researchers.

CHAPTER 25

Chapter Opener p. 676 Bob Daemmrich/Image Works; **p. 679** Christian Him/Retna; **p. 680** Giboux/Gamma Liaison; **p. 682** Sonda Dawes/Image Works; **p. 683** Cont/Reninger/Woodfin Camp; **p. 686** Jim Harrison/Courtesty of Elderhostel; **p. 687** Susan Greenwood/Gamma Liaison; **p. 688** AP/Wide World Photos; **p. 691** Cynthia Johnson/Gamma Liaison; **p. 692** Bill Weems/Woodfin Camp; p. 693 Paul Conklin/Monkmeyer; **p. 695** Kindra Clineff/Picture Cube; **p. 698** James Schnepf/Gamma Liaison; **p. 699 (Table 25.1)** From Sherry L. Willis. (1996). Everyday cognitive competence in elderly persons: Conceptual issues and empirical findings. *Gerontologist, 36,* 595–601;**p. 702** Eastcott/Momatiuk/Woodfin Camp; **p. 704** Oreganian/Gama Liaison; **p. 705** *(left)* Lester Sloan/Woodfin Camp; *(right)* Charles Gupton/Stock, Boston.

EPILOGUE

Chapter Opener p. 708 Steven M. Stone/Picture Cube; **p. 713** C. Ampanie/Image Works; **p. 716** Steven M. Stone/Picture Cube; **p. 717 (Figure E.1)** From Prem S. Fry. (1999). The sociocultural meaning of dying with dignity: An exploratory study of the perceptions of a group of Asian Indian elderly persons. In Brian de Vries (Ed.), *End of life issues: Interdisciplinary and* *multidimensional perspectives.* New York: Springer; **p. 718** Phyllis Picardi/International Stock; **p. 719** Vanessa Vick/Photo Researchers; **p. 721** A. Ramey/Unicorn Stock Photos.

APPENDIX A

p. A-4 (Figure A-3) From R. J. M. Snijders, & K. H. Nicolaides. (1996). *Ultrasound markers for fetal chromosomal defects.* New York: Parthenon; **p. A-11 (Figure A-12)** From Susan Williams McElroy & Kristin Anderson Moore. (1997). Trends over time in teenage pregnancy and childbearing: The critical changes. In Rebecca A. Maynard (Ed.), *Kids having kids: Economic costs and social consequences of teen pregnancy.* Urban Institute Press.

Name Index

Subject Index